CHINA

THE 50 MOST MEMORABLE TRIPS

中国

The Lunan Stone Forest near Kunming

Aerial view of Hong Kong

Kowloon night market

The First Emperor's terra-cotta warriors in Xi'an

The Li River at Guilin

Sunset in the Li River Valley at Yangshuo

View of the Great Wall

*Palace and moat in Beijing's
Forbidden City*

Statues in the Longmen Buddhist Caves in Luoyang

Workers leaving the rice paddy fields in the evening in Guizhou

Winter palace in Xi'an

The Pamir Mountains on the Silk Road

Frommer's

CHINA

THE 50 MOST MEMORABLE TRIPS

3RD EDITION

by J.D. Brown

中国

WILEY

Wiley Publishing, Inc.

About the Author

J.D. Brown has lived and worked in China and has written about China as a literary traveler, a travel writer, and a guidebook author. His work has appeared in such diverse publications as the *New York Times,* the *Washington Post,* and *National Geographic Traveler.* When he is not traveling in the Far East, he lives in Eugene, Oregon.

Published by:

Wiley Publishing, Inc.

111 River St.
Hoboken, NJ 07030

ISBN 0-7645-2468-2
ISSN 1528-2600

Editor: Kendra L. Falkenstein
Production Editor: Ian Skinnari
Cartographer: Roberta Stockwell
Photo Editor: Richard Fox
Production by Wiley Indianapolis Composition Services

Front cover photo: Rice cultivation along the Yulong River, Baisha, Guangxi
Back cover photo: Wooden opera masks, Guizhou Province

For information on our other products and services or to obtain technical support, please contact our Customer Care Department within the U.S. at 800-762-2974, outside the U.S. at 317-572-3993 or fax 317-572-4002.

Wiley also publishes its books in a variety of electronic formats. Some content that appears in print may not be available in electronic formats.

Manufactured in the United States of America

5   4   3   2

CONTENTS

LIST OF MAPS   V
WHY GO TO CHINA?   XI

Northeast China: Traditions & Treasures   1

Běijīng: The Unforbidden City   3
The Great Wall: Four Views from Běijīng   33
Chéngdé: Summer Home of the Emperors   41
Dàtóng: Hanging Monastery   51
Harbin: Tigers & Ice   63
Qīngdǎo: Beaches & Beer   70
Wéifāng: Kingdom of the Kite   79
Qūfù: Birthplace of Confucius   86

Southeast China: Commerce & Culture   95

Shànghǎi: Back to the Future   97
Sūzhōu: The Garden City   128
Hángzhōu: Tea on West Lake   140
Lake Tài: The Great Lake of China   157
The Grand Canal: The Infinite Waterway   166
Xiàmén: Amoy Mon Amour   172
Guǎngzhōu (Canton): The Gate to China   182
Hong Kong: The Dragon of the South   196

Central China: Antiquities & Adventures   227

Xī'ān: The Ancient Capital   229
The First Emperor's Terra-Cotta Army   248
Kāifēng: The Forgotten Capital   255
Lóngmén Caves: Stone Gate of the Dragon   264
Chóngqìng: Powerhouse of the Yángzǐ   272
Dàzú Caves: The Wheel of Life   283
Chéngdū: Home of the Panda   290
Lèshān: At the Foot of the Great Buddha   304

Southwest China: Searching for Shangri-La   309

Guìlín: The Landscape of Dreams   311
Yángshuò: The Stone Garden   329
Sānjiāng: A Bridge of Wind & Rain   338
Běihǎi: Sandworms & Pearls   347
Kūnmíng: City of Eternal Spring   358
Dàlǐ: The Far Kingdom   379
Lìjiāng: China's Shangri-La   394

Silk Road China: Cities of Sand   409

Jiāyùguān: End of the Great Wall   416
Dūnhuáng: Crescent Moon Lake & the Singing Sands   421
The Caves of Mògāo   428
Turpan: Lost Cities   435
Ürümqi: The Lake of Heaven   444
Kashgar: The Gate to Central Asia   452

Mountain China: Pinnacles & Sacred Peaks   461

Huáng Shān: The Summit of Beauty   465
Wǔlíngyuán: China's Yellowstone   476
Lú Shān: Hill Station of the Rich & Famous   484
Wǔtái Shān: Buddhist Peak of the North   491
Héng Shān Běi Yuè: Sacred Mountain of the North   500
Jiǔhuá Shān: Buddhist Peak of the South   506
Héng Shān Nán Yuè: Sacred Mountain of the South   515
Pǔtuó Shān: Buddhist Peak of the East   525
Tài Shān: Sacred Mountain of the East   534
Éméi Shān: Buddhist Peak of the West   543
Huà Shān: Sacred Mountain of the West   554
Sōng Shān/Shào Lín: Sacred Mountain of the Center   563

Appendices   575

China by River: Up & Down the Yángzǐ   577
Travel in China   594
Customs, Attitudes & Enigmas: The Chinese Way   619
A Quick History   628
Temples, Mosques & Churches   638
The Chinese Language   646

INDEX   669

LIST OF MAPS

China   xii

Northeast China: Traditions and Treasures

Běijīng   4
The Forbidden City   9
Běijīng Metro   21
The Great Wall   35
The Summer Palace at Chéngdé   43
Dàtóng & the Yúngāng Grottoes   52
Dàtóng   57
Harbin   65
Qīngdǎo   71
Wéifāng   81
Qūfù   87

Southeast China: Commerce & Culture

Shànghǎi   98
Hùangpǔ River   107
Sūzhōu   129
The Garden of the Humble Administrator   133
Hángzhōu Vicinity   142
Lake Tài (Tài Hú)   159
The Grand Canal   168
Xiàmén   173
Canton/Guǎngzhōu   184
Hong Kong   198

Central China: Antiquities & Adventures

Xī'ān   230
The Terra-Cotta Warriors   249
Kāifēng   257
Luòyáng Vicinity   265
Chóngqìng   274
Dàzú   285
Chéngdū   292
Lèshān   305

Southwest China: Searching for Shangri-La

Lí River	312
Guìlín	317
Yángshuò	331
Sānjiāng Area	339
Běihǎi	349
Kūnmíng	360
The Stone Forest	371
Old Dàlǐ	381
Ěrhǎi Lake Region	387
Lìjiāng	395
Lìjiāng Area	405

Silk Road China: Cities of Sand

The Silk Road	413
Jiāyùguān Fort	418
Dūnhuáng & the Mògāo Caves	423
Turpan	437
Ürümqi	447
Kashgar	455

Mountain China: Pinnacles & Sacred Peaks

Huáng Shān	467
Wǔlíngyuán	477
Lú Shān	485
Wǔtái Shān	493
Héng Shān Běi Yuè	501
Jiǔhuá Shān	507
Héng Shān Nán Yuè	517
Pǔtuó Shān	527
Tài Shān	535
Éméi Shān	545
Huà Shān	555
Sōng Shān	565

Appendices

Yángzǐ River	579
Qín China	631
Táng China	631
Sòng China	632
Míng China	632

Editor's Acknowledgments

I'd like to thank the **authors,** who worked with a difficult situation; **Bob Cherry** for help on the insert; **Ann Feng** for her quick proofreading; **Lorraine Festa** for signing up the book and providing assistance and knowledge throughout the process; **Brice Gosnell** for allowing us to add extra pages and supporting the project; **Marie Kristine Parial-Leonardo** for not only creating the design for this book, but also for fielding a nonstop barrage of changes, updates, and questions throughout the process; **Kristie Rees,** and everyone else in **Wiley Indianapolis Composition Services,** for working so hard and overcoming numerous challenges to keep this project on time and on track; **Kelly Regan** for all of her guidance, insight, and willingness to discover new solutions or improve on old ones; **Ian Skinnari** for being in the thick of it with me, always knowing what was supposed to be where and when, and never losing his sense of humor; **Roberta Stockwell** and **Nick Trotter** for their hard work on the maps and compliance through a myriad of revisions; **Chris Van Camp** who got us a template and figured out a lot of logistics; **Kathleen Warnock** for editing a chapter for me when I was in a pinch; **Donna Wright** for lending a much-needed hand reviewing the production editorial page proofs; and all of the people who had to hear me talk about this project for 5 months . . . and counting. It's much appreciated!

—Kendra L. Falkenstein

An Invitation to the Reader

In researching this book, we discovered many wonderful places—hotels, restaurants, shops, and more. We're sure you'll find others. Please tell us about them, so we can share the information with your fellow travelers in upcoming editions. If you were disappointed with a recommendation, we'd love to know that, too. Please write to:

Frommer's China: The 50 Most Memorable Trips, 3rd Edition
Wiley Publishing, Inc. • 111 River St. • Hoboken, NJ 07030

An Additional Note

Please be advised that travel information is subject to change at any time— and this is especially true of prices. While we would usually suggest that you write or call ahead for confirmation when making your travel plans, in most cases in China, this will be difficult or ineffective (or both) and, there-fore, probably not worth your time. The authors, editors, and publisher cannot be held responsible for the experiences of readers while traveling. Your safety is important to us, however, so we encourage you to stay alert and be aware of your surroundings. Keep a close eye on cameras, purses, and wallets, all favorite targets of thieves and pickpockets.

While each listing in this book is carefully researched, Frommer's can't guarantee everything in this text will be there in the same condition as it was for our research team: China changes rapidly, often overnight. Hotels and cafes are constantly opening, closing, and reinventing themselves; new competitors are emerging every few months; and prices are shifting. The same rapid changes are happening in matters of China's transport as well: New roads, new rail connections, and new airport routes are opening as cable cars are strung up at remote mountain peaks.

For this third edition, a team of Mandarin-speaking former residents of China, currently working on a new Frommer's guide to the whole of the country, has updated the practical information within the main text, while, in general, leaving the original author's observations and opinions intact. The practical information at the end of each chapter (under separate bylines) has been freshly researched and expanded by this team, while a new language chapter has been provided, and all remaining material revised and updated. In addition, all Mandarin words written out in Romanized form have been tone-marked to help the novice speaker who wants to pro-nounce words the same way the Chinese do.

What the Symbols Mean

The following abbreviations are used for credit cards:

AE	American Express	DISC	Discover	V	Visa
DC	Diners Club	MC	MasterCard		

Frommers.com

Now that you have the guidebook to a great trip, visit our website at **www.frommers.com** for travel information on nearly 3,000 destinations. With features updated regularly, we give you instant access to the most current trip-planning information available. At Frommers.com, you'll also find the best prices on airfares, accommodations, and car rentals—and you can even book travel online through our travel booking partners. At Frommers.com, you'll also find the following:

- Online updates to our most popular guidebooks
- Vacation sweepstakes and contest giveaways
- Newsletter highlighting the hottest travel trends
- Online travel message boards with featured travel discussions

Photo Credits

1. The Stone Forest near Kunming: Kelly/Mooney Photography
2. Aerial view of Hong Kong: Glen Allison/Getty Images
3. The Temple Street Night Market in Hong Kong: Shaun Egan/Getty Images
4. Terra-cotta warriors: Christopher Liu/China Stock
5. The Li River at Guilin: Robert Everts/Getty Images
6. Sunset in the Li River Valley: Catherine Feng/Viesti Associates
7. View of the Great Wall: D.E. Cox/Getty Images
8. Watchtower and moat in Beijing's Forbidden City: Flip Chalfant/The Image Book
9. Statues in the Buddhist Longmen Caves: Glen Allison/Getty Images
10. Workers leaving the rice paddy fields: Yann Layma/Getty Images
11. Winter palace in Xi'an: Suzanne Murphy/Tony Stone Images
12. The Pamir Mountains: David Sanger Photography

WHY GO TO CHINA?

On a recent fall morning in Shànghǎi, where I was sumptuously ensconced in the world's tallest hotel, I switched on the large-screen TV to watch the World Series half a world away. Within minutes after the game, via the Metro, I was whisked into the heart of the city where, in streets lined with the villas of the Westerners who had once made Shànghǎi a notorious colonial capital, I chanced upon a vendor from the countryside hawking tea-boiled eggs from a vat heated by chunks of coal. The vendor's mother rested nearby, her impossibly tiny feet bound in a tradition that winds back through the ages into a land of emperors and implacable dynasties: The great divide between past and present, East and West, had vanished. I was unmistakably in China once again.

For the past twenty years, China has been my destination of choice. No other place on Earth possesses such an intensity of the metaphysical and the earthy, no other nation has a longer or richer historical legacy, and no other country will be more important to the 21st century. My continuing fascination with China past, China present, and China future is embodied in a remark by an early China scholar, Marcel Granet: "By its extent, its duration, its mass, Chinese civilization is one of the most powerful creations of mankind," he wrote. "None other is richer in human experience."

Since 1984, I have repeatedly visited China's ancient capitals, fabled cities, and countryside villages and towns; crossed its rivers, lakes, and seas; admired its ancient stone monuments, from the Great Wall to the Great Buddha; followed the Silk Road across the deserts to the West; and stood on the summits of its nine sacred mountains. Along the way I have been transported by every conceivable conveyance, from bicycle and jet to camel and train; stayed in 5-star international hotels and no-star mountain inns; eaten the most delightful creations of one of the world's great cuisines and swallowed down some less distinguished fare, too. Travel has been hard at times, but it is growing and becoming increasingly easy. Each time I return to the Middle Kingdom, I find large-scale changes as well as opportunities to discover more about China's culture, which remains exotic, despite the rapid modernization and the Western influences that threaten to swallow China whole.

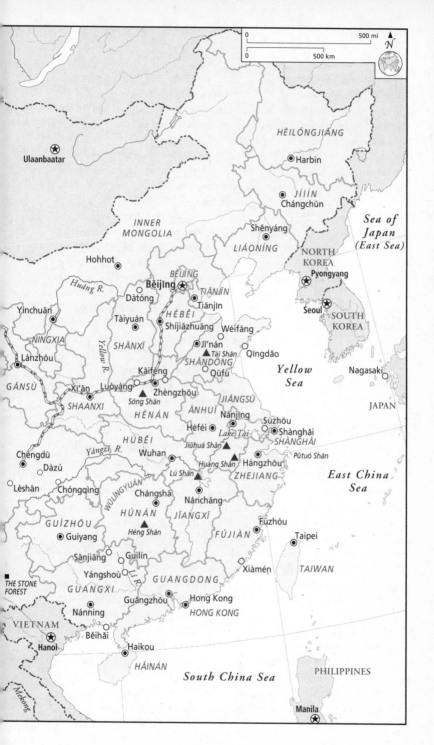

China's past remains visible and striking nevertheless, quite unlike and often at odds with the heritage of the West. The East/West contrasts are palpable in the temples and museums, at city walls and pagodas, and in the enduring social customs, which provide a portal through which I can see my own culture from a larger perspective.

Chinese art and history are continually on display, whether in the vaults where the First Emperor died among his terra-cotta armies or in the Forbidden City, where the last emperor was born. These monuments help to bring the dreamy Middle Kingdom to life.

Modern China (the country that recently entered the World Trade Organization [WTO], will be hosting the 2008 summer Olympics, and the country from which it seems that half of everything one buys these days was made in) is another story, however. The slate of old China is being wiped clean, but this urban metamorphosis casts its own spell. No large country has ever boomed so rapidly and decisively since the Industrial Revolution began its spread across the West two centuries ago. Much of China looks like a construction zone today, but this raw reconstruction actually lends vibrancy to cityscapes: China has its sights locked on the 21st century.

If you want to visit the next superpower as a work in progress, China is your ticket—the new Pacific Century begins in Shànghǎi, Běijīng, and a dozen other boomtowns of the new China. To miss seeing this new China for yourself is to miss what Nicholas Kristof of the *New York Times* recently called "the most important long-term trend in the world—the rise of China." Adds Kristof, "When historians look back on our time, I think they'll focus on the resurgence of China after 500 years of weakness—and the way America was oblivious as this happened."

This new China, which no one in the West should overlook, is not simply an overpopulated carbon copy of the Western world. While there seems to be a Starbucks on every corner in the big cities, China is charting its own course, holding tenaciously to the tattered strands of its own cultural identity. Rapid modernization in a country of ancient monuments makes China one of the most dynamic destinations on any traveler's map—an open gallery of treasures and traditions in vivid transition, where an imperial dragon is transforming itself into a modern phoenix. China is the one Asian country that the world must reckon with in the new century, and traveling through China is the most intimate way to reckon with that power.

It is now possible to travel to most of the interesting places in China in a style not dreamed of a decade ago. Major cities have sufficient Western amenities and foreign tourism facilities in place to make travel on one's own, largely by jet plane, a viable option even for the less adventurous traveler. It's no longer a choice either of hitting the road via ramshackle local buses with backpack and water purification system firmly in hand or spending a small fortune for a grueling seven-day, eight-city, nine-banquet luxury tour. Both these options still exist—they are sometimes the best means to see a place—but China has made touring on one's own a more amenable and comprehensible process, even if one doesn't speak the language. There are plenty of English speakers along the way to make even a remote destination accessible to a novice traveler. And familiar Western tour companies such as Gray Line have set up convenient offices in Běijīng, Shànghǎi, and elsewhere.

In this guide, I've recorded, in frank detail, 50 of my most memorable travels in China. You should be able to follow in my footsteps if you choose, or make your own detours as you go. Whether you choose to see China on your own or book a tour, you should find something useful in the following chapters. As in most guidebooks, you'll find a chapter on Chinese history and culture and a chapter on the practical matters of travel. In both, I explain what I've found most useful to know while traveling in China, from what dynasties really matter to what you absolutely must pack.

At the heart of this guide are my accounts of 50 places worth visiting in China. I steer you to the best sights I know at each stop, both those on everyone's tour and those that aren't, and I warn you about what to avoid, too. I've certainly made my share of poor choices and seen some boring sights, but I have also had the most amazing experiences, sometimes by sheer accident.

These experiences are organized first by region, headlined by the modern capital of Běijīng in the Northeast, by the commercial capitals of Shànghǎi and Hong Kong in the Southeast, by the ancient capital of Xīān and the Yángzǐ River in Central China, and by the scenic capitals of Guìlín and Kūnmíng in the Southwest. These regions are rounded out by sections covering two of China's most exotic itineraries: The Silk Road that once linked East and West; and the sacred mountains that still encircle the Middle Kingdom like a magic compass.

My tastes, responses, and adventures in China may differ from yours, but I've endeavored to give you a full account of my actual experience at each destination rather than a bare recital of facts and statistics. This should help you decide if a place is your cup of tea or simply a bowl of gruel. In each account, I also weave in considerable strands of history and lore, essential to a more meaningful experience.

China is not the place to tour if you're seeking relaxation, pampering, or a week in the mellow tropics. Rather, it's an education—mostly a pleasant and unusual one—but it can require patience and grit. Think of it as a puzzle in which the pieces you're working with are not always what they appear to be and the rules are not always logical. If the picture that emerges is that of a looking-glass world, you're probably on the right track. China is different, but it's no longer alien. Traveling through it has never been easier for an outsider, in part because China—long the self-contained Middle Kingdom mesmerized by its own reflection—is becoming more and more like the world outside, which it has held at arm's length for many centuries.

China is the world's most populous country, but ethnically and culturally, it is not as diverse as North America or Europe. Yet its sights, its landscapes, and its history are quite various. Běijīng is a city quite unlike Kūnmíng. The Great Wall bears little resemblance to the First Emperor's underground realm of terra-cotta soldiers, horses, and chariots. The southern Chinese act and speak differently than the northern Chinese and eat some foods no one else in the world would touch. In fact, each region of China has its own identity, so experiencing Chinese culture, seeing its treasures, and viewing its natural wonders in full requires considerable travel.

That travel can be a movable feast of sights and sensations, new and old. The following pages are a taste of what to expect, culled from one traveler's long, memorable banquet in the Middle Kingdom.

NORTHEAST CHINA:
TRADITIONS & TREASURES

BĚIJĪNG:
THE UNFORBIDDEN CITY
北京

BĚIJĪNG HAS MORE ATTRACTIONS than any other city in China. At one time, these cultural highlights were about all that appealed to travelers. Otherwise, China's capital was a sprawling metropolis of long, flat, monotonous avenues inhabited by uninspired socialist architecture, snarled traffic, and frightful levels of pollution. Běijīng was also subject to shattering dust storms from the Gobi Desert. It was devoid of nightlife and lacking in pleasant neighborhoods for strolling.

This atmosphere has begun to change in the last few years, as Běijīng has blossomed into a city that an international traveler can enjoy. New shops and restaurants have spread across the city: The 13,661 restaurants counted in 1990 had nearly tripled to 39,196 by 1995 and may now have tripled once again. Recently, Běijīng has become one of China's trendiest cities. Pubs and coffeehouses are displacing discos. Teahouses are opening by the score. Bowling, billiards, swimming, and live rock music are increasingly popular. Since July 1, 1997, only unleaded fuel has been sold in Běijīng, the first Chinese city to mandate such a cleanup. And, on a recent annual Tree-Planting Day, over two million "volunteer" Beijingers pitched in to help the capital build its much-needed greenway. The building and beautification programs initiated by the 50th anniversary of the founding of the People's Republic, celebrated on October 1, 1999, have further transformed many of Běijīng's once dismal neighborhoods.

Běijīng is by no means a paradise, and in preparation for the 2008 Olympics, most of its remaining ancient neighborhoods are being flattened, and replaced by new but unimaginative residential and office towers, removing all character from the city. But dreariness no longer defines the cityscape. The first task of visitors, however, is unchanged: to partake of those places for which the Middle Kingdom, and Běijīng, are celebrated. The **Forbidden City,** the **Summer Palace,** the **Temple of Heaven, Tiān'ān Mén Square,** and the **Great Wall** should not be missed. Nor should some of the dozens of lesser historical and cultural draws. At the same time,

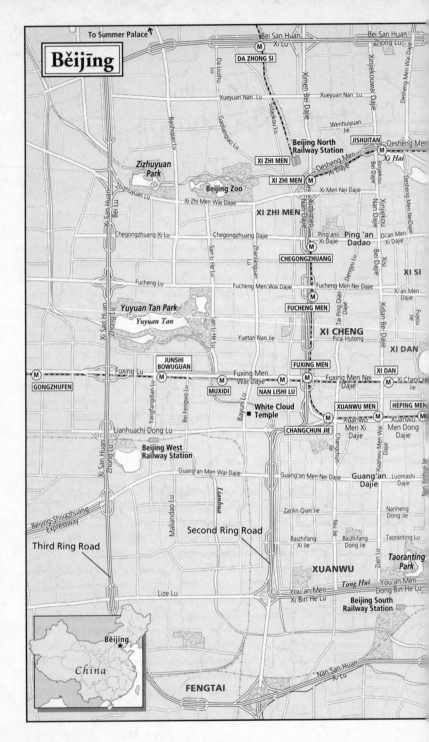

Běijīng

To Summer Palace ↑

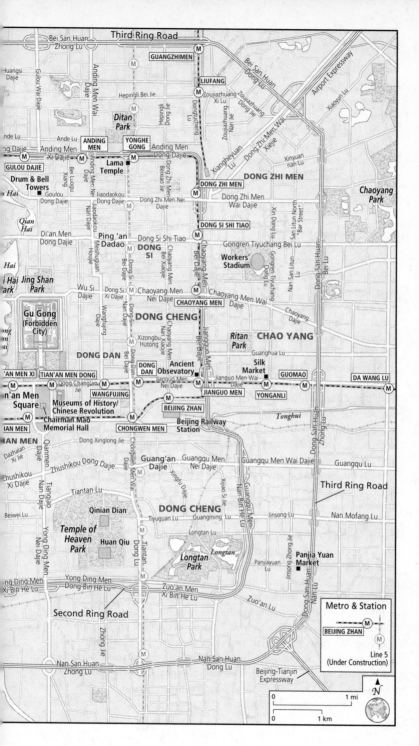

exploring Běijīng's modern delights and side streets has also become a pleasure.

I have been to Běijīng many times under many circumstances, as teacher, tourist, vagabond, and business writer. In this chapter, I'll concentrate on those places most worth exploring, and I'll try to tell you not just what sights to see but how to experience them as deeply as possible. I won't skip the highlights of Běijīng, but I do want to take you on some unexpected detours as well.

Tiān'ān Mén Square

This is the Eye of China, the focus of the nation. In the 20th century, it truly became the middle of the Middle Kingdom. In the 21st century, many believe it will become the symbolic center of the Asia Pacific, perhaps even of the world.

Most foreigners recognize Tiān'ān Mén instantly as the stage for the democratic movement that culminated in the events of June 4, 1989. Tiān'ān Mén Square had been the focal point of earlier movements as well, and officials are no doubt hopeful that its image worldwide has been softened by such recent events as the national celebrations for the return of Hong Kong to Chinese sovereignty on July 1, 1997, and the 50th anniversary of the birth of the People's Republic, held here on October 1, 1999. Tiān'ān Mén Square was renovated in 1999, its cement blocks replaced by .51 million sq. m (1.7 million sq. ft.) of granite and some sections of green lawn, along with 4,535 lamps and a legion of blue trash cans. Chewing gum is now prohibited on the plaza. This is the largest public square in the world, as befits the most populous nation in the world. Every paving block of the square is numbered, partly so that a standing spot can be assigned to each person who attends one of China's great public forums.

Striking out across this wide expanse gives visitors the chance to orient themselves to monuments on every horizon, allowing the immensity of the place to become a microcosm for the immensity of China. On the north side is the **Gate of Heavenly Peace,** a viewing stand where Máo proclaimed, in 1949, that China had stood up on the world stage. His portrait is on the gate, easily visible from the square. Under it is the entrance to the Forbidden City, the palaces of the former emperors.

The avenue between Tiān'ān Mén Square and the Gate of Heavenly Peace is **Cháng'ān Dàjiē,** the capital's main thoroughfare. It was widened, as was the square itself, in a massive public works program initiated by the new ruler, Máo Zédōng, beginning in 1950. The city walls also came down. Opposite Cháng'ān Avenue and the Gate, on the south side of Tiān'ān Mén Square, is a monumental remnant of the city walls, the **Qián Mén** ("front gate"), built in the 15th century as the southern entrance to the imperial city within Běijīng, its two massive stone arches easily visible from inside the square. Straight south from the gate along the old Imperial Way, and just to the east, is the Temple of Heaven, where the Míng and Qīng emperors made annual sacrifices to Heaven.

On the east side, Tiān'ān Mén Square is bordered by the **Museum of Chinese History** and the **Museum of the Revolution,** soon to be merged into a new National Museum. On the west side is the **Great Hall of the People,** China's national hall of Congress, where the world's envoys meet China's leaders. Both these architectural giants are open to visitors, but both are a bit dull.

The **Monument to the People's Heroes** is in the center of the square. This granite obelisk was erected in 1958 to honor soldiers, farmers, and other patriots who became martyrs to the Communist Revolution. Ironically, it became the focal point of the martyrs to the democratic student movement in 1989. Bullet holes and other blemishes from that night have been removed, surveillance cameras remain on surrounding poles, and the marble platform can seem a haunted place even now.

From Tiān'ān Mén Square, all roads radiate out, north to the Forbidden City, south to the Temple of Heaven, northeast to downtown shopping and the diplomatic missions, and northwest to the summer palaces.

Chairman Máo's Mausoleum

In the center of Tiān'ān Mén Square, aligned with the north–south axis that runs through the square and links the Forbidden City to the Temple of Heaven, is the **Chairman Máo Memorial Hall (Máo Zhǔxí Jìniàn Táng).** It was completed in 1977, the year after Máo's death. You can join the long line outside, facing south, for a 60-second look at Máo lying in state in a crystal sarcophagus. He rests on a black granite slab from Mount Tài, recalling one of Máo's favorite quotations from China's Grand Historian: "Although death befalls all men alike, in significance it may be weightier than Mount Tài or lighter than a swan's down." Every evening Máo is lowered into the floor, to be refrigerated underground. At dawn, he rises with the sun in the east. The mausoleum reopened in 1998 after a 6-month cleanup. In its first 20 years, it chalked up 110 million visitors.

This is the quietest, cleanest, and most revered room in China. Cameras and handbags must be checked in at counters in the museums and halls around the square. The Chairman Máo Memorial Hall is open mornings from 8:30 to 11:30am Tuesday through Sunday and 2 to 4pm Tuesday and Thursday. Mornings only in July. Admission is free.

The Forbidden City (Gù Gōng Bówùguǎn)

Home of the Míng and Qīng emperors from 1421 to 1924, the Forbidden City (now usually **Gù Gōng Bówùguǎn** or **Palace Museum**) is said to be the work of 100,000 laborers. The wall that encompasses its 9,000 rooms consists of 12 million bricks. Another 20 million bricks ended up in the walls of pavilions and the surfaces of courtyards. Such is the scale of the Forbidden City, with its gorgeous glazed rooftops, red wooden columns, and uplifted eaves. It is a bewildering complex that defines the very word "imperial." Deep, treeless courtyards are strung between the successive pavilions, with mazes of halls and walls inserted on either side. This is the largest palace enclosure in China, home to 24 emperors, closed off to all but members of the royal court and official delegations for 500 years.

Vastness, beauty, and pleasant confusion are the usual responses once you're inside the compound, and these might be all you take away, too, on the first visit: The Forbidden City is China's Grand Canyon, the nation's most magnificent spectacle, but it's so vast it often numbs the mind. The best way to navigate and make some sense of this collection to get an audio rental of Acoustiguide (¥30/$3.75) as your guide at the entrance. This recorded walk-through hits the high points, identifying the major halls and important museum pieces on display inside, and helps bring sense to the welter of sights within the once-forbidden walls and the grand pavilions— the thrones, the furniture, the porcelains, the costumes.

It's important to hit the stop button often, however, and explore some of the side streets of the palace city. New exhibits open in different halls year-round, offering a chance to actually go inside one of the original buildings (entrances to the main interiors are now blocked off). There are exquisite gardens and lovely courtyards all along the main track, and special exhibits culled from the millions of artifacts owned by the Palace Museum are often placed on temporary display. Making your own detours is also a good way to get away from the newest entrepreneurs to be loosed upon the common visitor: the roving bands of vendors interrupting you, even grabbing your arm, in the hopes you'll buy postcards, souvenir albums, and other bounty.

The basic layout unfolds along a north–south axis (conceived of as beginning and ending at the center of the world, here where the second Míng emperor, Yǒnglè, set to work on the Forbidden City in A.D. 1407). Enter under the **Gate of Heavenly Peace (Tiān'ān Mén)** on Cháng'ān Avenue, doff your worker's cap to Máo, and proceed straight ahead over the moats to the **Meridian Gate (Wǔ Mén)**, where emperors once reviewed their armies. It now houses the ticket booths for entrance into the Forbidden City. Five marble bridges cross the expanse of the first great courtyard, which leads to the final great entryway, the **Gate of Supreme**

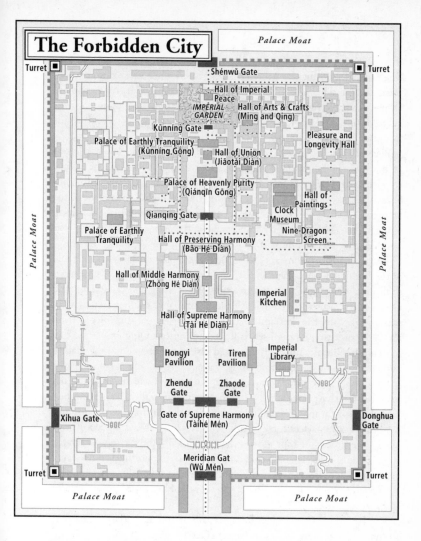

The Forbidden City

Palace Moat

Turret ■ ■ Turret

Shénwǔ Gate

Hall of Imperial Peace

IMPÉRIAL GARDEN

Hall of Arts & Crafts (Ming and Qing)

Kūnníng Gate

Palace of Earthly Tranquility (Kūnníng Gōng)

Hall of Union (Jiāotài Diàn)

Pleasure and Longevity Hall

Palace of Heavenly Purity (Qiánqīn Gōng)

Hall of Paintings

Clock Museum

Qianqing Gate

Nine-Dragon Screen

Palace of Earthly Tranquility

Hall of Preserving Harmony (Bǎo Hé Diàn)

Hall of Middle Harmony (Zhōng Hé Diàn)

Imperial Kitchen

Hall of Supreme Harmony (Tài Hé Diàn)

Hongyi Pavilion

Tiren Pavilion

Imperial Library

Zhendu Gate

Zhaode Gate

Xihua Gate

Gate of Supreme Harmony (Tàihé Mén)

Donghua Gate

Meridian Gat (Wǔ Mén)

Turret ■ ■ Turret

Palace Moat

Palace Moat

Palace Moat

Palace Moat

Harmony (**Tàihé Diàn**), guarded by stone lions. The immense space beyond is where the entire imperial court, 100,000 strong, was once convened, prostrate before the Son of Heaven who lived within. It's not difficult to imagine a crowd that immense these days, as the Forbidden City is one of the most popular attractions in the world. The best time to go is early in the morning, before the crush begins.

The first ceremonial hall, **Hall of Supreme Harmony (Tài Hé Diàn)**, raised upon a triple-tiered terrace and entered via a marble ramp with carved dragons, was the route followed by the emperor's sedan chair. Inside, you can glimpse his golden dragon throne. The massive red columns are covered in a formula of tung oil, clay, hemp, and pig's blood.

The **Hall of Middle Harmony (Zhōng Hé Diàn),** a lesser throne room, is next in line. The third great hall, **Hall of Preserving Harmony (Bǎo Hé Diàn),** was the venue for the state civil service examinations and royal banquets. Inside is a 250-ton marble block carved with dragons and clouds from the Míng Dynasty.

Beyond these three ceremonial halls are the three main living quarters of the rulers, retainers, and thousands of eunuchs. The first, the **Palace of Heavenly Purity (Qiánqīng Gōng),** once contained the emperor's bedroom; the second, the **Hall of Union (Jiāotài Diàn),** the throne of the empress; and the third, the **Palace of Earthly Tranquility (Kūnníng Gōng),** the red wedding chamber where the last emperor, Pǔyí, was wedded as a child groom in 1922.

The emperors spent most of their time in the palaces along the west side of the Forbidden City. On the east side are palaces now serving as galleries to display some of the museum treasures of the Míng and Qīng dynasties. One usually houses the **Clock Museum,** probably the most fascinating small gallery in the Forbidden City, filled with old timepieces from the West and from China itself collected by various Qīng emperors. The museum has been temporarily rehoused just at the east side of the Hall of Supreme Harmony—look for signs.

Near the rear of the complex, the **Kūnníng Gate** opens onto the **Imperial Garden's** ponds, halls, and rockeries. This is the place to rest, buy a drink or snack, and decide if you want to work your way back south into the heart of the palaces for a second look. You can always tag along with one of the dozens of tour groups that continually throng the courtyards and pavilions, their guides chanting facts and recounting lore in every major language. If you're overwhelmed or exhausted by your initial march, head to the exit just north of here, through the **Shénwǔ Mén,** or **Gate of Military Prowess.**

The Forbidden City is open from 8:30am to 5pm daily (last tickets sold at 4pm), half an hour earlier in winter (Oct 15–Mar 31). Full admission, including entrance to special exhibits, is ¥60 ($7.50) or ¥40 ($5) in winter; rental of an audio Acoustiguide is ¥30 ($3.75).

Summer Palace (Yihé Yuán)

In the summer, the emperors pulled up stakes, left the Forbidden City behind, and encamped in the pavilions on the lakeshores of Yíhé Yuán to the northwest. Summer palaces have existed here for at least 8 centuries, but the Qiánlóng Emperor created the present one in the 18th century.

The Summer Palace is the loveliest imperial park in China, landscaped with gardens and graceful pavilions along the shores of **Kūnmíng Lake.** It became the pleasure grounds of Empress Dowager Cíxǐ (1835–1908), who ruled China during the decline of the Manchus. She rebuilt and restored the palace at a time when China needed the funds for its own defense. Particularly shocking was the construction of the infamous **Marble Boat (Shífǎng)** on the northern shore of the Summer Palace grounds. Local guides have dozens of stories describing Cíxǐ's ruinous extravagances and Machiavellian political maneuvers, though it is doubtful that the empress dowager was really such a witch.

The main entrance is the East Gate, site of the new **Cultural Relic Archive,** with 40,000 historic pieces displayed in a two-story Míng/Qīng-style pavilion. The original palaces line **Longevity Hill (Wànshòu Shān).** The empress dowager's throne is in the **Hall of Benevolence and Longevity (Rénshòu Diàn),** now something of a 19th-century furniture museum. Nearby is the **Garden of Virtue and Harmony (Déhé Yuán),** containing a three-level theater where the empress dowager sometimes played the role of Guānyīn, Goddess of Mercy. **Jade Waves Palace (Yùlán Táng)** was the residence of the young Guāngxù Emperor, in whose name Cíxǐ was said to rule for 10 years. In the **Cloud-Dispelling Hall (Páiyún Diàn),** Cíxǐ received birthday greetings from her advisors. If you're curious about what she looked like, you can look at her famous portrait in oil here, painted by Hubert Voss in 1903.

The most delightful construction of the Summer Palace, the **Long Corridor (Cháng Láng),** links these palaces to the Marble Boat. Running about a half mile along the lake, this undulating covered walkway is a gallery of scenes that forms an outdoor encyclopedia of Chinese geography, zoology, botany, and myth. The Qiánlóng Emperor saw to its creation in 1750, the British and French burned it down in 1860, and the empress dowager resurrected it in 1888. The paintings that decorate the ceiling, beams, columns, and the four intersecting pavilions are crude but bright, like century-old cartoons that map the treasures of the Middle Kingdom. Group tours herd visitors the length of the Long Corridor without a break, but if there is anywhere to pause in Běijīng, it is here. The lake scenery is fetching, and the painted arcade is a naive and fascinating window on classic Chinese culture. Unfortunately, the crowds usually spill out of the Long Corridor, making peaceful contemplation impossible. Early mornings and evenings bring the only respites. Beijingers say that the Long Corridor is so long that couples who fall in love after they enter set the wedding date by the time they exit.

Beyond the Marble Boat, looking like a sad cement pavilion in an old amusement park, is a dock where a large ornate ferry takes visitors back to the main gate, for ¥15 ($1.90). The view of the hills and pavilions from the lake is almost as magical as the views from West Lake in Hángzhōu, after which the empress dowager modeled many of the bridges, causeways, and pagodas of the New Summer Palace.

The Summer Palace is open from 6am to 8pm daily, with individual halls open from 8:30am to 5pm. Admission is ¥50 ($6.25) in summer, ¥40 ($5) in winter (Nov 1–Mar 31), including various exhibitions. Entrance only to the park is ¥30 ($3.75) in summer or ¥20 ($2.50) in winter. Starting in late 1999, it became possible to travel to the Summer Palace the way the empress dowager did a century ago, by pleasure boat over the original waterway that led to the Forbidden City. At present, there are two routes to the Summer Palace's South Gate, one leaving 10 times a day from Bāyī Hú in Yùyuán Tán Park, the other leaving 4 times a day from a dock behind the Zoo, the Běizhǎn Hòu Hú Mǎtóu. Both voyages take about 50 minutes, and services run from mid-March to mid-November. Tickets cost ¥40 ($5) one-way, ¥70 ($8.75) round-trip. For exact schedules and bookings, have a Mandarin-speaker call ✆ **010/6852-9428** for departures from Bāyī Hú or ✆ **010/8386-3576** for departures from the Summer Palace.

Old Summer Palace (Yuánmíng Yuán)

Far less crowded is the Old Summer Palace, which was leveled by British and French troops in 1860 to punish the Chinese during the Opium Wars. The ruins, however, are haunting. The Kāngxī Emperor built this original summer palace on an even grander scale than his grandson, Emperor Qiánlóng, built the present Summer Palace. Kāngxī's original contained over 200 pavilions, halls, gazebos, miradors, and man-made lakes stocked with goldfish and lotus. Deer and ducks inhabited the grounds. Curiously, some of the architecture was not Chinese but European; Jesuit missionaries in the Qīng court were pressed into providing blueprints. Foreigners called the Old Summer Palace the Versailles of China, an apt comparison. In its day, it was the largest imperial garden in the world.

Time is running out on these ruins, however. Every year there's a new proposal to restore the Old Summer Palace, a tremendous mistake in my opinion, as these bare ruined choirs give voice to the splendors of the past far more eloquently than any modern copy could. Nevertheless, in 1999, a partial renovation was completed. Now there are pleasure boats for hire in the **Fúhǎi Scenic Area; Qǐ Chūn Yuán Square** has new working fountains; and the **Maze of Myriad Flowers,** originally of boxwood, has been restored in stone.

The Old Summer Palace is just over a mile east of the New Summer Palace, but they are worlds apart. The ruins of the European gardens and Grand Fountains are in the easternmost sector, known as the **Garden of Eternal Spring (Cháng Chūn Yuán).** Built between 1747 and 1759, these European buildings included a concert chamber, an aviary, a maze, and several kiosks, in addition to the fountains where water spouted from 12 stone animals that once constituted an ingenious water clock. The looting of the Old Summer Palace augmented the collections of the British Museum, as well as the private collections of Queen Victoria and Napoleon. The New Summer Palace was also looted, but the empress dowager rehabilitated it in 1888. Yet for all its beauty, it evokes little of the dark romance so palpable in the ruins of the Old Summer Palace.

My own visit there remains vivid in my mind, particularly because of one superb ruin, the **Hall of Tranquility**—the most perfect spot in all of Běijīng for a picnic. The tumbled-down remains of the stone-and-marble arches and Greek columns that once graced the Grand Fountains, decorated in rococo and Qīng patterns, elicit like no other ruins I've seen—even those in Ireland and Greece—the impermanence of man's grandest achievements. The Old Summer Palace is open from 7am to 7pm daily in summer, and to 5:30pm in winter. Admission is ¥10 ($1.25) for park entrance only, ¥25 ($3) for a ticket that includes entrance to the museum.

Temple of Heaven (Tiān Tán Gōngyuán)

Běijīng's grand collection of Míng Dynasty architecture is in the **Temple of Heaven Park (Tiān Tán Gōngyuán)**, about a mile due south of the old Qián Mén Gate on Tiān'ān Mén Square. This was conceived of as the exact meeting point of Heaven and Earth by the Yǒnglè Emperor and his geo-mancers when they completed the round altar on its high square base in 1420. Here, the Son of Heaven was obliged to perform sacrifices after pray-ing for the year's good harvest. The annual procession to the Temple of Heaven was so sacred that the people of Běijīng could not cast their eyes upon it, and the Temple of Heaven complex was itself a forbidden city until China became a republic in 1912.

The main entrance was traditionally from the south. The **Round Altar (Huán Qiū)**, three marble tiers representing Earth, Man, and Heaven, was the Center of the World. It is said that an orator's voice originating from these tiers was magnified and could be heard for miles. Today, the acousti-cally inclined hasten to the next monument, **Echo Wall (Huíyīn Bì)**, another round-walled platform where even a whisper directed into the wall is broadcast around the whole circle. I tested this several times, and it was possible to hear the words whispered from the opposite side. Of course, this phenomenon is transformed into babbling once Echo Wall is engulfed by visitors, all intent on using the wall phone at once.

The primary temple in this heavenly park is the **Hall for Prayer for Good Harvests (Qínián Diàn)**, located to the north. It is one of the most remarkable buildings in China: a round tower capped by a magnificent three-tiered, blue-tiled dome, paneled in the most ornate carvings ever produced in China. The vault, 36m (120 ft.) high, is so perfectly fitted together that not a single nail was used. Fifty thousand glazed tiles coat the conical roof. Four inner columns (the Dragon Well Pillars), representing the four seasons, and two concentric sets of 12 outer pillars, for the months and the 2-hour units of the day, provide the support. The ceiling is a bright, dazzling dragon design. In 1889, a bolt of lightning destroyed the tower, but it has been faithfully reconstructed. These days, visitors can only peer into the grand interior. A decade ago, it was possible to walk inside and feel the full pull of the ancient cosmos.

The park is most heavenly these days in the early morning, before the tour buses pull up. Locals gather for morning exercises: *tàijíquán* (shadow-boxing), sword practice, and strange forms of *qì gōng* (a channeling of internal energies). The retired men stake out benches and display their caged songbirds and crickets or play mahjong and practice their calligraphy on the sidewalks. College students, seeking solitude and space for study, pore over their books on benches under an old cypress grove inside the western gate. There, the main road (Tiān Qiáo Nán Dàjiē) leads straight back to Tiān'ān Mén Square. The park is open from 6am to 8pm, but the various halls inside only from 8am to 6pm in summer and to 5:30pm in winter. Entrance to the park is ¥15 ($1.90) in summer, ¥10 ($1.25) in winter. A ticket which includes entrance to the various halls and exhibitions is ¥35 ($4.40) in summer, ¥30 ($3.75) in winter.

Lama Temple (Yōnghé Gōng)

Běijīng's premier temple, locals agree, is the Lama Temple, northeast of Tiān'ān Mén Square, just inside the Second Ring Road. It first served as the Yōngzhèng Emperor's mansion. The Qiánlóng Emperor, his successor, consecrated it as a lamasery in 1744 and hired 500 lamas from Mongolia to run it. In the early 20th century, it served as the Bureau of Mongolian and Tibetan Affairs, reverting in recent times to its original functions.

Part of its attraction is its grand scale. The **Hall of the Heavenly Kings** contains Maitreya, the Buddha of the Future, smiling broadly on all visitors. Four celestial guardians, one for each cardinal direction, each accompanied by eight of his top generals, protect the Buddha from a horde of demons. Next in line is the **Hall of Harmony (Yōnghé Diàn),** with Buddhas of the past, present, and future. The layout is a lengthy one. In the fourth hall, **Fǎlún Diàn,** the eastern wing contains statuary locked in amorous embraces. They are usually covered in scarves that serve as fig leaves. These and other draped statues in the Lama Temple are regarded as China's Kama Sutra, reputedly serving as an illustrated sex manual for the sons of emperors. As late as the 1930s, the Lama Temple still had an aura of the forbidden about it. "Devil dances," which included rituals imitating human sacrifice, were regularly performed.

The final great hall is the tallest: the **Pavilion of Ten Thousand Fortunes (Wànfú Gé).** Inside is a second rendition of the Buddha of the Future, standing 23m (75 ft.) tall. This sandalwood colossus, a gift to the Qiánlóng Emperor from the seventh Dalai Lama, is considered the world's largest sculpture carved from a single piece of wood. It was here that the Dalai Lama's followers once held sway.

The temple is always busy, not only with local visitors and Chinese worshippers, but with at least 70 monks in brown robes, heads shaven. The Lama Temple has enough diversions and pavilions scattered through its five courtyards to provide hours of quiet diversion. Sometimes you can still hear bronze bells suspended from the yellow-tiled eaves singing in the breeze that rocks the swaying bamboo. If this complex doesn't leave you "templed out," nothing will. My favorite retreat from the crowds is a side tower, the **Pavilion of Perpetual Peace,** which contains a large prayer wheel suspended from its ceiling.

The Lama Temple is open from 9am to 4:30pm with an admission fee of ¥20 ($2.50).

White Cloud Temple (Báiyún Guàn)

Less touristy and more fascinating than the Lama Temple is the White Cloud Temple, in the western Xuānwǔ District. This is Běijīng's most popular Daoist shrine, a favorite of locals, who flock here to burn incense and perform a number of rites in the hopes that the gods will answer their prayers. There are pavilions, halls, and temples that cater to a variety of desires, from passing the college entrance exam to having a healthy baby boy. There's even a hall dedicated to eyes and curing the problems of failing eyesight. The faithful will rub their hands on various golden statues and other images and relics, kowtow before the temple statues, and check on their life expectancy at a hall of the zodiac. This is a very active temple, far more local and vital than many of the other temples in Běijīng; at the rear of the complex is a rock garden where I've often seen novice monks in training. The very best time to drop in on this colorful scene is on a festival day, which occurs on the 1st and 15th of every lunar month. The White Cloud Temple, at Báiyún Guàn Lù 6, is open daily from 8:30am to 4:30pm. Admission is ¥10 ($1.25).

Star Gazing

In 1422, just after the Forbidden City was finished, a celestial observatory was built on a corner of the city wall. The Chinese were keen observers of the heavens (of whom the emperor was the son). The observatory in Běijīng became the most important in the Middle Kingdom. In the early

1600s, Jesuit missionaries in the capital introduced Western methods of astronomy, hoping to attract converts to Christianity through their ability to predict eclipses. Copies of several of the instruments designed by the Jesuits remain on the roof of the **Ancient Observatory (Gǔ Guānxiàngtái)** today. The observatory is located on the south side of Jiànguó Mén Wài Dàjiē—the eastern extension of Cháng'ān Avenue— where it seems like a stranded piece of history, a Míng Dynasty terrace clinging to the last surviving block of the old city wall.

The Ancient Observatory is an incongruity, located as it is in the heart of Běijīng's heaviest traffic and newest office complexes, but it is also a graceful reminder of the imperial past. The eight bronze astronomical instruments on the open roof are visible for better than a mile up and down the busy avenue. Displays inside the two-story museum are usually replicas rather than originals, but the gold foil atlas of the stars, based on Táng Dynasty observations, shows how the Chinese mapped the sky, creating constellations unknown to the West.

This is the ideal place to take a break, both in time and space, if you're walking the seemingly endless street east from Tiān'ān Mén Square. The dragon quadrant, celestial globe, ecliptic armilla, theodolite, sextant, zodiac, and other instruments date from the early Qīng Dynasty. The effect is of an antique world, its eyes fixed on the cosmos and its instruments, mounted on a garden terrace, as beautiful as a starry, unpolluted night. The Ancient Observatory is open from 9am to 5:30pm in summer, to 4:30pm in winter. Admission is ¥10 ($1.25).

Streets & Alleys

Once you gorge yourself on the highlights of old Běijīng, you're ready to wander its streets. There are dozens of other museums, temples, and parks to visit, but time quickly runs out. To miss out on exploring the streets is to miss the experience of China's modern capital.

The essential architecture of Běijīng is not that of the temple or palace but of the courtyard homes and the narrow alleyways, called *hútòng*. A popular tour to join in Běijīng is the **Hútòng Tour,** first organized by a local photographer devoted to urban preservation. Bicycle rickshaws do the heavy work, slicing through the impossible traffic snarls from the back entrance of Běihǎi Park, along the Shíchà Lakes, down to the old **Drum Tower.** The Drum Tower contains an exhibit of hútòng photographs. The tour group finishes up with tea in an elaborate courtyard mansion. The **Běijīng Hútòng Tourist Agency (© 010/6615-9097)** handles two tours daily, starting at 9am and 2pm. They cost ¥240 ($30) and can be booked directly or through hotel travel desks.

The back streets of old Běijīng are fast disappearing and, indeed, they may all have disappeared by the time you arrive, but, for now, the **Qián Mén District** on the south end of Tiān'ān Mén Square is a fine place to wander in search of traditional shops, lanes, and hútòng. Start on the southwest side of the traffic circle, walk southeast through the sidewalk vendors, and turn straight down Jewelry Street (Zhūbǎoshí Jiē). The entrance to Jewelry Street is marked by a large bicycle billboard. This street runs north and south parallel to Qián Mén Dàjiē—the old Imperial Way—and constitutes one of the more crowded outdoor markets in Běijīng. After about 4 blocks, take a right west on Dà Zhàlán Jiē (Dàshílánr St.). Behind the Qīng Dynasty facades lining this old theater street are traditional pharmacies and silk shops. Go about a quarter mile west on Dà zhàlán Lù, past tea shops and herbal medicine stores, and take a turn north and then west along Yángméi Alley, a hútòng of crowded courtyards. The alley soon joins Liúlichǎng Jiē, Běijīng's most famous avenue of antiques. Most of the buildings along here were rebuilt in recent times to resemble an old shopping district. The curio shops, bookstores, musical instrument showrooms, and art galleries here are among the best in China. **Róngbǎozhāi,** at Liúlichǎng Xī Jiē 64, is the most highly regarded art store in the country.

Markets

There's more market shopping east of Tiān'ān Mén Square at the **Xiùshuǐ Silk Market** and the **Friendship Store.** Cháng'ān Avenue turns into Jiànguó Mén Nèi Dàjiē as it heads east toward the Ancient Observatory, then Jiànguó Mén Wài Dàjiē as it passes it. Keep on the north side for the Friendship Store, the largest in China, with its floors of gifts, crafts, foods, and sundries. The Silk Market is located between the Friendship Store and the Jiànguó Hotel. It is a series of stalls pinched into narrow alleyways. You won't find much silk here, but you will find plenty of copies of Western sportswear and other clothing brands, as well as fake watches, cashmere, and pashmina. Get there early to avoid the rush, or shop on a rainy day if you can. Prices on clothing of all sorts, including fake designer labels, can be very low, but be sure to pay no more than a quarter of the vendor's initial asking price.

A far more interesting market is **Pānjiā Yuán,** sometimes known locally as the Ghost Market, or the Dirt Market, at its best on Saturday and Sunday mornings. The market is a ways south of downtown, just inside the Third Ring Road on Pānjiā Yuán Lù; take a cab. The emphasis here is on collectibles, which includes family heirlooms, antique furniture, ceramics, statues, and scrolls. In aisles under canvas canopies, several thousand vendors spread out their wares and upwards of 100,000 browsers take a look.

There are special aisles for jade, teapots, and folk crafts, but almost everything is, of course, fake. Last time I visited on a Sunday morning, there was even an upright piano for sale, as well as treadle sewing machines.

Wángfǔjǐng Shopping Street

My favorite shopping ramble is into the heart of the city on Wángfǔjǐng Street, which runs north off Cháng'ān Avenue a few blocks east of Tiān'ān Mén Square. Begin this jaunt by cutting through the Běijīng Hotel. If you walk through its main corridor from west to east, you'll be walking through an innkeeper's time capsule of grand accommodations in Běijīng. The oldest section, in the middle of the long edifice, dates from 1917. The rooms here are in the French style with brocade wallpapers. The west wing, conjoined in 1954, has a magnificent dining hall up the north stairs. The east wing, added in 1974 and remodeled in 1990, contains 600 modern luxury rooms (but not with service to match). The cathedral ceilings and sweeping staircases run the length of this landmark, which was entirely revamped in 2001. On its east corner is Wángfǔjǐng Street.

Before the communist victory of 1949, Wángfǔjǐng Dàjiē (Avenue of the Prince's Well) was known as Morrison Street to foreign residents. It catered to China's richest Westerners. Nowadays, Wángfǔjǐng caters to China's richest Chinese. The new **Sun Dong An Plaza,** one of China's largest shopping and office complexes, 11 stories of steel and glass and underground parking, intended as a "reconstruction" of the century-old Dōng Ān Market, epitomizes the upscale shopping along Wángfǔjǐng. Actually, the street contains a wide range of **shops and restaurants,** from McDonald's to hole-in-the-wall steamed-dumpling shops, from Louis Vuitton to a local specialty shop selling nothing but stuffed animals. The farther you push up Wángfǔjǐng, the more traditional and varied the stores. The **Chinese department stores** are particularly worth browsing. They feature an increasingly large range of imported commodities, always have an immense uniformed sales staff on the floor, and frequently put on good old-fashioned demonstrations of their goods right in the aisles. I've seen salespeople try out the latest electronic acupressure devices on shoppers, and I've seen both men and women sitting beside counters receiving demonstration hair dyes, their friends and everyone else crowding in for a closer look. Wángfǔjǐng has been undergoing a continuous face-lift since 1999, complete with fresh new granite slabs on its sidewalks, golden placards identifying its most famous stores, bronze statues of Qīng-era shoppers, and special police patrols levying heavy fines for littering and spitting. Asia's largest shopping-residential-office complex, **Oriental Plaza,** now dominates its southern end and runs along Cháng'ān for a whole city block. At night, it is ablaze with neon lights, much like Hong Kong.

Bars & Teahouses

Běijīng's most international neighborhood these days is the **Sānlǐtún District,** northeast of Tiān'ān Mén Square, on the west side of the Third Ring Road, not far from a congregation of foreign-based hotels and businesses (Sheraton Great Wall, Kempinski Hotel/Lufthansa Centre, Hard Rock Cafe). To reach the cafes, bars, and small shops that cater to foreigners and hip Beijingers, walk west from the Kūnlún Hotel to the Huádū Hotel, turn south (left) on Xīn Yuán Jiē, which shortly becomes Sānlǐtún Lù, and follow this tree-lined boulevard past various embassies for a good 6 blocks. Just north of Gōngrén Tǐyùchǎng Běi Lù, Sānlǐtún is occupied by dozens of cafes/bars with outdoor seating, which have now spread south and into various side streets, as well. Clothing stalls, cheese shops, and other private businesses are booming along here, too.

This is one of Běijīng's most popular places to hang out. When the weather is good, hundreds of expatriates and foreign travelers drop by, unwind in one of the cafes, and enjoy life as it passes. The German-style **Kebab Cafe,** with plenty of outdoor seating, a full international menu, and imported beers (all at imported prices), is my favorite. Stacks of pirated CDs, VCDs, and DVDs are hawked from table to table all along Sānlǐtún, priced at about $1 (with no guarantee of quality, of course). New eating and drinking outlets spring up every few weeks, as the demand for international venues continues to outrun supply. Ten years ago, finding an English-language menu, let alone a German beer, outside of the big hotels in Běijīng was something of a fool's errand. Today it's a hot business.

Equally trendy in this surprisingly trendy city are the teahouses, which are more in keeping with the legacies of the capital. Teahouses once drew in Běijīng's literate and wealthy residents, its mandarins, for an evening devoted to the arts and spirited conversation. **Tiān Hǎi Tea House** (located in a hútòng just north of Gōngrén Tǐyùchǎng Běi Lù, off Sānlǐtún; ✆ **010/6416-5676**) is just one attempt to return to that tradition. The interiors of the teahouse, designed by Běijīng artist Song Xiaohong and his daughter, Song Huibin, evoke Qīng Dynasty days with their dark woods, bamboos, and wall paintings. Waiters and waitresses dress up in royal costumes. On weekends, musicians take up traditional instruments, such as the *èrhú* and *pípa,* and Peking opera stars drop in to conduct sing-alongs. The teas of the teahouse are green and jasmine, but fruit flavors have been added, and the menu of northern Chinese steamed snacks and noodles is augmented by salads and ice-cream treats.

Curiously, these new teahouses, based on old traditions, embody the rising spirit of modern Běijīng. In this city, East seems more comfortable with West than ever before, the past keeps finding new ways into the present, and people seem confident of playing a leading role in the future, not just of China, but of the world.

PRACTICAL INFORMATION

by Peter Neville-Hadley

ORIENTATION & WHEN TO GO

Běijīng owes its off-center position in the northeast of China to its founding as a capital by the Mongol invaders from the north who became the Yuán Dynasty. It was later re-established as the capital during the Míng Dynasty so as to co-ordinate resistance to future attacks from the same direction. The best time to visit is from mid-September to mid-November, when the days are warm and dry. Second choice would be mid-March to mid-May, but in early spring, dust storms from the northwest can sometimes make going outdoors uncomfortable for 2 or 3 days at a time, although life continues much as usual. Summers are hot and can be uncomfortably humid and wet. Winter snows greatly improve the look of the city, and the number of visitors and the prices in markets all drop along with the temperature, which can be well below freezing.

GETTING THERE

By Plane Běijīng's **Capital Airport** is served by most of the world's major international airlines, and offers a more comprehensive range of domestic connections than any other airport in China. There are nonstop flights from Chicago, Detroit, Los Angeles, Vancouver, London, and a host of European capitals, as well as one-stop flights from many more destinations, including Melbourne and Sydney. Chinese airlines flying these routes are always slightly cheaper, and it is usually cheaper still to take routes from North America via other Asian destinations (such as Japan or Korea), or via Eastern Europe, Russia, or Pakistan from western Europe.

The airport is about 27km (17 miles) northeast of the city, connected by an expressway, but the point where this reaches the Third Ring Road (called Sān Yuán Qiáo) is jammed all day—consider heading east to the fourth ring, and north from there. Allow an hour to reach the airport, and be thankful when your trip is quicker.

There is a total of four foreign exchange counters at arrivals and departures level, and four ATMs accepting Visa, MasterCard, Cirrus, and PLUS system cards. Rates are the same nationwide, so exchange as much as you need.

If you want to travel into town by taxi, ignore all touts and make for the rank directly in front of the terminal. Taxis costing both ¥1.60 and ¥2 per kilometer are allowed to line up, their rates written clearly on the side window. Make sure the meter is started *after* you get in. The cost in a cheaper cab will be around ¥60 to ¥80 ($7.50–$8), plus ¥10 ($1.25) for the expressway toll. Do not tip.

Drivers waiting at the airport are more likely to be unreliable than those anywhere else, so a better solution is to take one of the frequently departing express buses. Tickets (¥16/$2) are sold both at the left-hand exit as you leave the building, and on the buses themselves. There are three routes, but you should take Line A and get off at the

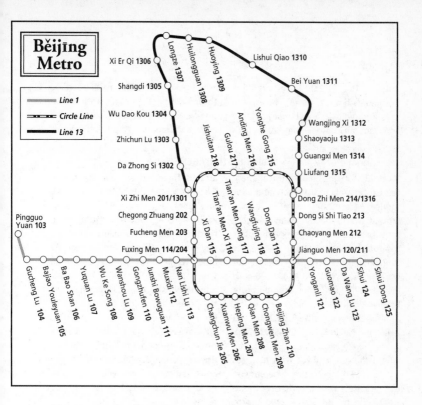

Běijīng Metro

Line 1
Circle Line
Line 13

Xi Er Qi 1306
Longze 1307
Huilongguan 1308
Huoying 1309
Lishui Qiao 1310
Shangdi 1305
Bei Yuan 1311
Wu Dao Kou 1304
Zhichun Lu 1303
Da Zhong Si 1302
Jishuitan 218
Gulou 217
Anding Men 216
Yonghe Gong 215
Wangjing Xi 1312
Shaoyaoju 1313
Guangxi Men 1314
Liufang 1315
Xi Zhi Men 201/1301
Chegong Zhuang 202
Fucheng Men 203
Fuxing Men 114/204
Tian'an Men Xi 116
Tian'an Men Dong 117
Wangfujing 118
Dong Dan 119
Xi Dan 115
Dong Zhi Men 214/1316
Dong Si Shi Tiao 213
Chaoyang Men 212
Jianguo Men 120/211

Pingguo Yuan 103

Gucheng Lu 104
Bajiao Youleyuan 105
Ba Bao Shan 106
Yuquan Lu 107
Wu Ke Song 108
Wanshou Lu 109
Gongzhufen 110
Junshi Bowuguan 111
Muxidi 112
Nan Lishi Lu 113
Changchun jie 205
Xuanwu Men 206
Heping Men 207
Qian Men 208
Chongwen Men 209
Beijing Zhan 210
Yonganli 121
Guomao 122
Da Wang Lu 123
Sihui 124
Sihui Dong 125

first stop, Sān Yuán Qiáo, and flag down a passing cab to complete your journey. (Lines B and C also stop at Sān Yuán Qiáo, but at a different and inconvenient spot.)

By Train Trains from Moscow and Ulaan Baatar arrive at **Běijīng Station (Běijīng Zhàn)**. Trains from Hong Kong and Hanoi arrive at **Běijīng West (Xī Kè Zhàn)**. Between them the two stations provide services to almost every town in China. Běijīng Station is on the metro's circle line, and both stations have cab ranks outside. Again, avoid touts and drivers who approach you, and just join the line.

GETTING AROUND

Běijīng's **metro system** is very limited, though it is easy to use and is undergoing considerable expansion. Traffic congestion at surface level means that it should be your first choice of transport wherever possible. For now, fares are a flat ¥3 (35¢), purchased at clearly marked ticket offices, but will shortly switch to a zoned ticket system whose details have yet to be announced. Platform and train-boarding maps are clearly labeled in Romanized Chinese (pīnyīn), and announcements on board the train are in English and in Mandarin.

Taxi kilometer prices are clearly marked on side windows. The cheapest are ¥1.20 (15¢) per kilometer, an initial charge of ¥10 ($1.25) including 4km (2½ miles). Most comfortable, with better air-conditioning, are those that charge ¥1.60 (20¢) per kilometer, the initial ¥10 ($1.25) including 3km (2 miles). Above 15km (9½ miles), the rate jumps 50%, and between 11pm and 5am, all charges jump 20%. Taxis are largely reliable, but avoid boarding those waiting at popular sites or outside your hotel. Instead, always walk away and flag down a passing vehicle.

TOURS & STRATAGEMS

Tours The major Chinese travel agencies exist merely to scalp you, and their services are unnecessary in a city around which you can easily navigate for yourself. Some bus companies offer comfortable half-day and 1-day city tours—overpriced specially for foreigners at around ¥300 to ¥400 ($38–$50) including lunch. Two examples are **Dragon Bus** (details from a desk in the Jiànguó Hotel, ✆ **010/6500-2233**, ext. 2186) and **Panda Bus** (✆ **010/6803-7045**). Avoid booking cars from your hotel, where charges may reach as much as ¥1,200 ($150) for the day, whereas you can negotiate with taxis for as little as ¥300 ($37) for an out-of-town trip of up to 250km (156 miles). For a day trip around town, simply use the meter. Even in a ¥2-per-km Volkswagen saloon, and going as far out as the Summer Palace and back, you're very unlikely to reach the 184km (115 miles) $37 would buy you. But if you plan to use one driver to go to many places and bring you back, make sure that he merely pulls down the flag and doesn't push the "one-way" button on the front of his meter, which makes the rate jump 50% after 15km (9½ miles). Taxis are often in use 24 hours a day, with two drivers working 12-hour shifts. Keep in mind that around 5pm, your driver may need to disappear to hand over his car to his colleague.

WHERE TO STAY

Běijīng has a large choice of familiar international names among its hotels, as well as representation from Asia-based luxury chains such as Shangri-La, the Peninsula Group (the Palace Hotel), and Marco Polo. If you wish to stay in four- or five-star accommodations, these should be your first choices, along with other hotels mentioned below with foreign senior managers. Chinese-run luxury hotels merely match their Sino-foreign joint-venture counterparts in price, but not in any other way. The hotels below frequently list room rates in U.S. dollars, but they only accept credit cards or Chinese currency as payment, although all offer on-site foreign exchange (forex) services. A wider variety of credit cards can be used when booking via websites or agents overseas. Rates are almost infinitely flexible according to season and demand, and negotiation may also lead to the inclusion of breakfast. High-season rack rates are quoted here; real rates are often drastically lower (frequently half, sometimes a third), and booking in person is almost always cheaper than any other method. Nevertheless, check websites for the latest deals. Add a 15% service charge and ¥6 (70¢) for the "City Development Fund." Avoid, if you can, Chinese New Year, early May, and early October. April, May, and September are also busy periods for foreign tourism.

What follows is an updated version of this book's original selection of the best hotels. Budget travelers can easily find basic but acceptable rooms in

Chinese-run hotels for as little as $30. The **International Youth Hostels federation** has beds in spotless and centrally located premises for under $10 (see www.hostelbooking.com/ibnpub/english/index.asp for more information).

China World Hotel (Zhōngguó Dàfàndiàn) China World, long thought by many to be the city's top business hotel, is now aiming to be the best Běijīng hotel altogether, thanks to a just-completed $30-million renovation. Praised for its comfort and sterling service, the hotel, managed by Shangri-La, has used its most recent face-lift to add up-to-date luxuries, such as an oxygen chamber in the health club. Refurbished standard rooms are somewhat narrow but modern, with glass-topped desks and abstract Asian art as part of the decor. Occasionally, this is the residence not only of CEOs, but of visiting world leaders, too. It also has a range of good restaurants, including The Summer Palace, which serves up-market Cantonese cuisine; Nadaman, one of Běijīng's best Japanese restaurants; Aria, with its good Continental cuisine, which is one of the city's most comfortably elegant restaurants; Henry J. Bean's, an American grill with a patio; and a new fusion restaurant, as yet unnamed, which was scheduled to open after our last visit there.

Jiànguó Mén Wài Dàjiē 1 (at junction with Third Ring Rd.). © *800/942-5050 in the U.S. and Canada, 020/8747-8485 in the U.K., 1800/22-2448 in Australia, 0800/44-2179 in New Zealand, or 010/6505-2266. Fax 010/6505-3167. www.shangri-la.com. 716 units, including 65 suites. $300 standard room. AE, DC, MC, V.* **Amenities:** 5 restaurants; indoor pool (25m/82 ft.); golf simulator; 3 indoor tennis courts; superb health club and separate spa (offers aromatherapy); 24-hr. concierge; business center; shopping plaza; salon; 24-hr. room service; same-day dry cleaning/laundry; valet; nightly turndown service; newspaper delivery; newsstand. *In room:* A/C, TV, minibar.

Crowne Plaza Hotel (Guójì Yìyuàn Huángguān Fàndiàn) The Crowne Plaza, like the Great Wall Sheraton, was one of Běijīng's earlier joint-venture five-stars and has recently become a little tired. It is still one of the finer hotels close to the Forbidden City, however, and plans to renovate its oft-imitated but now outdated central atrium during 2003. A small gallery on the first floor and weekly events in the "art salon" on the mezzanine floor give the hotel a certain credibility with the art world, and added interest for the guest. The Atrium Coffee Shop serves international buffets, the Pearl Garden specializes in Cantonese cuisine, and the Plaza Grill is a respected French restaurant that serves as the backdrop to a popular local TV show on Western table manners.

Wángfǔjǐng Dàjiē 48 (corner of Dēngshìkǒu Dàjiē). © *877/932-4112 in the U.S. and Canada, 0800/917-1587 in the U.K., 1300/363-300 in Australia, 0800/80-1111 in New Zealand, or 010/6513-3388. Fax 010/6513-2513. www.sixcontinentshotels.com. 358 units. $200 standard room. AE, DC, MC, V.* **Amenities:** 3 restaurants; tiny indoor swimming pool; small health club with new equipment; underwhelming Jacuzzi, sauna, and solarium; concierge; Panda Tours desk; business center; souvenir shops; salon; 24-hr. room service; babysitting; same-day dry cleaning/laundry; newsstand. *In room:* A/C, TV, minibar.

Grand Hyatt Běijīng (Běijīng Dōngfāng Jūnyuè) The newest luxury hotel in the city, the Grand Hyatt also has the best position, directly over the Wángfǔjǐng metro station, at the foot of the capital's most famous shopping street, and within walking distance of the Forbidden City. The palatial curved lobby is theatrically lit, and is already a popular meeting place, with live music in the evenings and, at one end, Běijīng's best chocolate shop. Rooms have the signature Grand Hyatt comfortable modernity, with convenient desktop electrical sockets, dataports, and free broadband Internet access. Well-equipped bathrooms have separate shower cubicles. The vast swimming pool is very kitsch and un-Hyatt, buried in mock-tropical decor and a ceiling of electric stars—worth visiting even if you have no plans to swim. Noble Court has some of Běijīng's best Cantonese food. The Grand Café offers the city's most comprehensive buffet breakfast, as well as all-day Italian trattorie, French bistro, and Běijīng sections. Da Giorgio, small and cozy, just off the Grand Café, serves fine Italian food, and Fountain Lounge serves light meals. More restaurants will open during 2003.

Dōng Cháng'ān Jiē 1 (within the Oriental Plaza complex at the foot of Wángfǔjǐng Dàjiē). © 800/633-7313 in the U.S. and Canada, 0845/888-1226 in the U.K., 1800/13-1234 in Australia, 0800/44-1234 in New Zealand, or 010/8515-1234. Fax 010/6512-9050. http:// beijing.grand.hyatt.com. 531 units, including 85 suites. $300 standard room. AE, DC, MC, V. **Amenities:** 4+ restaurants; 50m (165- ft.) resort-style pool; fitness center with latest equipment; Jacuzzi; sauna; solarium; jogging route; children's pool and playroom; airport limousine pickup; business center; shopping arcade; 24-hr. room service; massage; doctor/nurse on call. *In room: A/C, TV, minibar.*

Great Wall Sheraton (Cháng Chéng Fàndiàn) The Great Wall was the first international five-star hotel in Běijīng when it opened in 1984 and remains by far the city's largest. The building is well maintained considering its age, but now seems to have fallen behind some of its competitors in terms of refurbishment. Standard rooms are large but dark with outdated fixtures, although the only slightly more expensive deluxe rooms on the seventh and eighth floors, which were renovated in 2000, are more than comfortable. The Silk Road Trattoria serves solid Italian and mixed Western fare; and the small French Bistro is among the city's better French restaurants. The beautifully refurbished 21st Floor Restaurant now serves up first-class Sìchuān food together with commanding views of eastern Běijīng.

Běi Sān Huán 10. © 800/325-3589 in the U.S. and Canada, 0800/973-119 in the U.K., 1800/81-4812 in Australia, 0800/44-5309 in New Zealand, 1800/597-000 in Ireland, or 010/6590–5566. Fax 010/6590–5938. www.sheratonbeijing. com. 1,007 units, including 56 suites. $240 standard room. AE, DC, MC, V. **Amenities:** 3 restaurants; small indoor pool with sun deck (with snack bar); two outdoor tennis courts; aging health club; Jacuzzi; sauna; concierge; business center; souvenir shops; salon; 24-hr. room service; same-day dry cleaning/laundry; valet; newsstand. *In room: A/C, TV, minibar.*

Kempinski Hotel (Kǎibīnsījī Fàndiàn) The Kempinski's plain but large and very comfortable rooms have recently been refurbished to a high standard, and its position in the vast Lufthansa Centre shopping, office, and apartment complex means every facility imaginable is at hand. These include a specialty wine store, endless airline offices and ticket agents, medical and dental clinics with Western staff and equipment, eight restaurants and cafes, a supermarket, a bookshop, and a complete department store. This is the perfect location for business visitors, and other than for sightseeing, there's scarcely any need to venture out. If you do, large numbers of long-staying expats from the Kempinski's well-fitted apartments help support an assortment of other Western and wannabe-Western enterprises in the neighborhood, including Běijīng's branch of the Hard Rock Cafe. Hotel restaurant choices include Dragon Palace for Cantonese, Salsa Cabana (very lively) for Mexican, Honzen for Japanese, Seasons Café for Western and pan-Asian favorites, Trattoria la Gondola for Italian standards, Paulaner Bräuhaus for top-of-the-range beers brewed on-site and hearty German dishes, the Kempi Deli for an excellent range of baked goods (half price after 8pm), and the relaxing Lobby Lounge, which has light refreshments throughout the day.

Liàngmǎ Qiáo Lù 50 (NE Third Ring Rd., south of the airport expwy. junction). © *800/426-3135 in the U.S. and Canada, 0800/4263-1355 in the U.K., 800/4263-1355 in Australia, or 010/6465-3388. Fax 010/6465-3366. www. kempinski beijing.com. 486 units, including 39 suites. $250 standard room. AE, DC, MC, V.* **Amenities:** 8 restaurants; health club with swimming pool; tennis court; squash court; gym; Jacuzzi; sauna; steam bath; Montessori kindergarten; 24-hr. concierge; free shuttles to airport and city center; fully comprehensive business center run by Regus; 24-hr. room service; massage; valet shop; gardens; flower shop. *In room:* A/C, TV, minibar.

Kerry Centre Hotel (Běijīng Jiālǐ Zhōngxīn Fàndiàn) The latest addition to the Shangri-La-managed properties in the city, the Kerry Centre is also the most trendy, with a clean, stylish, very modern design to its warm, comfortable, and unusually high-ceilinged rooms. Full facilities, such as proper shower cubicles in bathrooms, free in-room broadband Internet access, and particularly attentive staff, have all helped make it quite rightly one of Běijīng's most successful hotels. Executive-floor rooms have unusual extra luxuries for China, such as CD players. The Kerry has three restaurants: a lobby lounge with lighter fare; a 24-hour coffee shop with a variety of popular pan-Asian and Western food; and Horizon, one of the city's best Cantonese restaurants, which also serves Chinese regional dishes prepared by Hong Kong chefs.

Guānghuá Lù 1 (a short walk north of China World/Traders and the Guómào metro station). © *800/942-5050 in the U.S. and Canada, 020/8747-8485 in the U.K., 1800/22-2448 in Australia, 0800/ 44-2179 in New Zealand, or 010/ 8529-6999. Fax 010/8529-6333. www. shangri-la.com. 487 units, including 51 suites. $220 standard room. AE, DC, MC, V.* **Amenities:** 3 restaurants; 25m (82-ft.) lap pool; indoor basketball/tennis/badminton courts; the most comprehensive sport and fitness facilities of any hotel in Běijīng; roof garden encircled by a track for jogging and in-line skating; Jacuzzi; sauna; sun deck; comprehensive supervised children's play area; concierge; tour desk; 24-hr. business center; conference rooms; 24-hr. room service; babysitting; same-day laundry and dry cleaning; valet; nightly turndown; newsstand. *In room:* A/C, satellite TV, free broadband, dataport, minibar, hair dryer, safe.

The Marco Polo (Mǎgē Bóluó Jiǔdiàn) The lobby, although sumptuously decorated with white marble and rippling gold friezes, and with an art-hung stairwell leading to the Café Marco above, is stylish yet of a modest enough scale to give this brand-new 10-story building the atmosphere of a discreet boutique hotel. Rooms are among Běijīng's largest, however, and are fully fitted with broadband Internet and every luxury. Café Marco has dishes from the Mediterranean, Middle East, Southeast Asia, and China in honor of the routes the great traveler took himself (at least according to his book), available either from the buffet or a la carte. Heichinrou is the first branch in China of the highly regarded 110-year-old Cantonese restaurant from Yokohama. The Lobby Lounge serves snacks throughout the day. Although not among the main clusters of foreign hotels, the Marco Polo is as close to the center of things as any of them, yet quieter and better connected than most—just south of the no. 1 line's Xī Dān station, and north of the circle line's Xuānwǔ Mén station, enabling guests to get in and out during even the worst of the rush hour. Highly recommended.

Xuānwǔ Mén Nèi Dàjiē 6 (just south of the Xī Dān shopping area and its metro, a 20-min. walk west of the Tiān'ān Mén). ☏ *800/448-8355 in the U.S. and Canada, 0870/530-0200 in the U.K., 1800/22-1176 in Australia, 0800/93-3123 in New Zealand, or 010/6603-6688. Fax 010/6603-1488. www.marco polohotels.com. 296 units. $170 standard room. AE, DC, MC, V.* **Amenities:** 3 restaurants; indoor swimming pool; fitness center; limousine service; travel service; 24-hr. business center; meeting and conference facilities; valet shop. *In room:* A/C, TV, minibar.

The Palace Hotel (Wángfǔ Fàndiàn) No other hotel in mainland China can offer you a Rolls-Royce to collect you from the airport and whisk you to its very central location. The Palace is run by the same people who run Hong Kong's legendary Peninsula Hotel, and while not quite as charismatic, it does feature many of the same luxuries and the same attentions to guest comfort, such as bedside controls for almost everything in the room and deluxe marble bathrooms with separate faucets containing sterilized drinking water. The hotel sits in the heart of Běijīng's principal shopping district and on top of two basement floors of the capital's most exclusive boutiques, built around a high-tech computerized fountain. Jing has Western food with interesting Asian overtones in one of the best-designed restaurant interiors in the city. Fortune Garden has top-of-the-range Cantonese food in a more traditional setting, and the Lobby Lounge offers all-day refreshments and views of Běijīng's wealthy descending to satisfy their desire for the finest Western playthings.

Jīnyú Hútòng 8 (1 block east of Wángfǔjǐng Dàjié). ☏ *0800/262-9467 or 010/6512-8899 (on the U.S. West Coast* ☏ *310/278-8777, on the U.S. East Coast and in Canada* ☏ *212/903-3073, in the UK* ☏ *020/7823-3111, in Australia* ☏ *02/9252-2888). Fax 010/6512-9050. www. peninsula.com. 530 units, including 52 suites. $320 standard room. AE, DC, MC, V.* **Amenities:** 3 restaurants; indoor swimming pool; fully equipped fitness center; saunas and steam rooms; Clarins Beauty Institute; 24-hr. concierge; travel desk; Rolls-Royce and Mercedes limousine fleet; business center; meeting and conference rooms; bank and ATM within shopping arcade; extensive souvenir shopping; 24-hr. room service; sports massage; babysitting; same-day laundry and dry-cleaning; medical clinic. *In room:* A/C, TV, minibar, safe.

St. Regis Běijīng (Běijīng Guójì Jùlèbù Fàndiàn) Long Běijīng's finest hotel, the St. Regis (formerly the Běijīng International Club Hotel) now faces stiff competition from the Kerry Center and just-renovated China World, whose fresh modernity make the St. Regis's previously untouchable rooms look rather conventional. But its white marble lobby is the still the city's most elegant, and no other hotel offers the same level of personalized service. The St. Regis Spa and Club, open to all guests, is particularly luxurious. Hotel dining is excellent: Danieli's is perhaps Běijīng's best Italian restaurant; the new Astor Grill, a small and stylish American-style steakhouse, boasts well-stocked cigar and wine-tasting rooms; Celestial Court serves Cantonese food; the Shun Sai Japanese Restaurant is popular with Japanese embassy officials; the Garden Court offers a fine international buffet; and the lobby's palm tree–lined Garden Lounge does afternoon tea. The Press Club Bar contains reminders of the days when the neighboring Běijīng International Club was the only entertainment for foreigners. *Jiànguó Mén Wài Dàjiē 21 (entrance a little to the north on the west side of Rì Tán Lù).* C **800/325–3589** *in the U.S. and Canada, 0800/973-119 in the U.K., 0800/814-812 in Australia, 0800/445-309 in New Zealand, or 010/6460–6688. Fax 010/6460-3299. www.stregis.com/ beijing. 273 units, including 137 suites. $340 standard room. AE, DC, MC, V.* **Amenities:** 6 restaurants; gorgeous indoor pool (25m/82 ft.) with bar; outdoor putting green and driving area; squash courts; nicely equipped exercise room; full-service spa; Jacuzzi; sauna; steam room; bowling alley; billiards room; concierge; business center; salon; 24-hr. room service; same-day dry cleaning/laundry; 24-hr. "butler" service; newsstand. *In room:* A/C, TV, minibar.

Shangri-La Běijīng Hotel (Xiānggélǐlā Fàndiàn) Shangri-La is now the biggest player among foreign hotel managements in China (four properties in Běijīng alone), due, perhaps, to its success with staff. Whereas the best elsewhere respond helpfully to guests' requests, here the anticipation of guests' needs marks superior service. The hotel has expanded since its original 1987 opening, and another major refurbishment is on the way. Although off by itself in the northwest, the Shangri-La benefits from having space for a large and lush garden, easy access to the Summer Palaces and the Western Hills, and quick routes around Běijīng via the Third and Fourth Ring roads. The palatial Shang Palace has Cantonese dishes and Běijīng duck. Peppino's serves Italian favorites, Nishimura has Japanese food, and the Coffee Garden has pan-Asian and Western dishes, as well as an excellent breakfast buffet. The Lobby Lounge serves drinks and cakes all day. *Zǐzhú Yuàn Lù 29 (northwest corner of Third Ring Rd.).* C **800/942-5050** *in the U.S. and Canada, 020/8747-8485 in the U.K., 1800/22-2448 in Australia, 0800/ 44-2179 in New Zealand, or 010/6841- 2211. Fax 010/6841-8002. www.shangri la.com. 657 units, including 29 suites and 17 apts. $190 standard room. AE, DC, MC, V.* **Amenities:** 5 restaurants; swimming pool; recreation center with indoor tennis courts; squash courts; billiards; basketball court; recently upgraded health club (in the basement) with exercise machines; sauna;

solariums; concierge; tour desk; 24-hr. business center; conference rooms; shopping arcade; salon; 24-hr. room service; massage; babysitting; same-day laundry and dry cleaning; valet; nightly turndown; florist; newsstand. *In room:* A/C, TV, minibar.

WHERE TO DINE

It sometimes seems as if every other building in Běijīng contains a restaurant (and all the others contain mobile-phone shops). Competition is intense, so of the many new restaurants opening daily, a significant proportion have very short lives, and the continuing destruction of the capital in the name of modernization also means that restaurants recommended below may disappear before you can get to them. During the research for this update, a famous street of 24-hour restaurants, a long-standing Běijīng institution, was reduced to rubble. Most of the finest establishments, and the ones most likely still to be there when you arrive, are in the better hotels, listed above. But these mostly offer foreign food, and the Chinese food offered is mostly Cantonese (albeit extremely good Cantonese). To get a real idea of China's near-infinite gastronomic variety, it's necessary to venture out.

China is the land of copies and "me too" products, so when any new restaurant proves successful, imitators rapidly open up, often right next door. A recent fad for the highly spiced Sìchuān fish dish, *shuǐ zhǔ yú,* has led some restaurants, otherwise offering the subtlest of flavors, to add it to their menus. In the past 10 years, fads have come and gone for the plain, condiment-free foods of Cultural Revolution–era northwest China, for Chairman Máo's favorite spicy Húnán dishes, and for restaurants re-creating the style of late-imperial Běijīng. Now the foods of the Hakka (Kèjiā) minority of the southeast and the tropical dishes of Yúnnán's minorities are in vogue. It will be something else tomorrow.

But a new breed of restaurant has appeared, particularly popular with the employees of joint-venture companies who have a little more disposable income, offering higher standards of hygiene and decor than the average Chinese restaurant, mostly with English as well as Chinese menus, and often with hints of ancient China, or of more rustic lives, although they may be hidden in the most polished of modern towers. To an updated list of some of the most upmarket establishments from previous editions has been added a selection of these newcomers, where a delicious and substantial meal for two is likely to be no more than ¥80 to ¥100 ($10–$13). Expect to see a 15% service charge added inside the big hotels and one or two of the most expensive restaurants outside them, but elsewhere, you pay what you see, and there is no tipping. Prices quoted below do not include service (where applicable) or drinks.

Aria FUSION One of the most thoroughly satisfying dining experiences in Běijīng, from *amuse-bouche* to dessert. The dining room, reached by a spiral wooden staircase from a bustling bar, has a comforting clubby atmosphere, full of woody alcoves and hung with green velvet curtains. All courses come with convenient suggestions for accompanying wines, available by the glass, such as a nicely chilled Moët with the Harbin caviar. Among the specialties are a melt-in-the-mouth braised pig cheek (highly recommended); seared yellowfin tuna with Sìchuān spices, salade Niçoise, and horseradish emulsion; and truffle polenta with Turkish fig jam and sherry vinegar jus. More than one visit may be necessary. *In the China World Hotel (see above). ⓒ 010/6505-2266. Main courses ¥80–¥200 ($10–$25). Set lunches ¥158–¥218 ($20–$27). AE, DC, MC, V. Daily 11am–midnight.*

Běijīng Dà Dǒng Kǎoyā Diàn BĚIJĪNG/ ROAST DUCK If you are on a tour, you'll almost certainly be taken to one of the tired old branches of Quánjùdé, the most famous of Běijīng's duck emporia, but by no means the best. If you are meeting expat friends or relations, you may be taken to the Lìqún Kǎoyādiàn, tucked away in a decrepit courtyard house in the labyrinth of hútòng east of Qián Mén (Běi Xiáng Fēng 11; ⓒ **010/ 6702-5681** for detailed directions).

But if you have any control over matters, try Běijīng Dà Dǒng Kǎoyā Diàn, where the general manager claims to have invented a new method of roasting the duck that reduces the fat by more than half. Whether that's true or not, duck remains a rich meal. It's served in slices, together with pancakes, sliced greens, mashed garlic, and a sour sauce—more choice than at other restaurants. Put sliced duck and your choice of other ingredients on the pancake, roll it up, and you have traditional Běijīng roast duck. The menu, with English and pictures, also offers everything from mustard duck webs to duck tongue in aspic, and an excellent duck soup in a scooped-out orange. There's also a range of excellent *dòufu* (tofu) dishes with thick, tangy sauces. Meals come with a free fruit plate and walnut sago pudding. This is also one of the few restaurants in Běijīng with a

nonsmoking room. *Běi Kǒu 3, on the east Third Ring Rd., east side, north of Tuánjié Hú Park. ⓒ 010/6582-2892. Whole duck ¥98 ($12), half duck ¥49 ($6). No credit cards. 8am–noon and 1:30–5pm.*

The Courtyard FUSION This is perhaps the only restaurant outside a major hotel where you can truly forget you're in China, unless of course you find yourself at the table in an oriel window directly over the Forbidden City's eastern moat. The restaurant is an old courtyard house with a surprisingly modern white and glass interior hung with contemporary Chinese art (whose display continues in a gallery in the basement, open for sales 11am–7pm). Upstairs there's a small and comfortable cigar lounge. The food is broadly Western with pan-Asian overtones, and flavors are generally light and straightforward. The grilled chicken breast (with kailan, sweet potato gratin, and lemon grass curry coconut sauce) must be the most perfectly moist and tender chicken dish in the whole of Běijīng, and worth coming for in its own right. The Alaskan black cod and the cashew-crusted lamb chops are long-term menu favorites. The wine list is far and away the city's most comprehensive— there's nothing to touch it this side of Hong Kong. And there's a surprisingly large range of wines by the glass at very fair prices. *Dōng Huá Mén Lù 95 (north side of the street, next to the moat). ⓒ 010/6526-8883. Reservations recommended for weekends. Main courses ¥160–¥320 ($20–$40); Sun set-menu 3-course lunch ¥150 ($19)— excellent value. AE, MC, V. Mon–Sat 6–10:30pm; Sun 11am–2pm.*

Da Giorgio ITALIAN This small restaurant, with modestly Italianate decor, is in cozy contrast to the general grandeur of the Hyatt. There's a tendency in Běijīng restaurants serving foreign cuisine to tone down the flavors so as not to frighten away still unadventurous and unsophisticated richer Chinese, but if that's been done here, it's only served to let out the honest flavors of the ingredients on a concise but well-executed menu. The beef carpaccio has a liquid freshness, the minestrone (with rosemary and basil pesto) is far more subtle than the hearty stew it can sometimes become, and the roasted Atlantic salmon steak with mushrooms and artichoke basil pesto sauce is meaty and filling. Overall, the tone is rustic, and the portion sizes are correspondingly hearty. *Inside the Grand Hyatt (see above).* ℰ *010/8515-1234. Main courses ¥90–¥195 ($11–$24). AE, MC, V. 10:30am–2:30pm and 5:30–10:30pm.*

Danieli's ITALIAN Danieli's serves some of Běijīng's only truly respectable Italian cuisine in a distinctive if somewhat unimaginative setting. Food is nicely and simply presented and service is professional though slightly over-attentive. The menu combines elements from a number of regions but never ventures too far from established culinary paths. Diners would do well with either the rack of lamb, both tender and flavorful, or the tomato and artichoke risotto with its generous sprinkling of truffle oil. The wine list offers one of the city's best selections of Italian and New World wines, many of them available by the glass. *Inside the St. Regis Hotel, 2nd floor (overlooking the entrance).* ℰ *010/6460-6688, ext. 2441 or 1440. Main courses ¥100–¥250 ($13–$31). AE, DC, MC, V. Mon–Fri 11:30am–2pm and 6–10pm; weekends 6–10pm.*

Hàn Kèjiā Jiǔlóu KÈJIĀ The Hakka, or Kèjiā "guest" people, are Hàn Chinese from central China who migrated southeast generations ago, but who faced (and face) discrimination from locals, and so ended up in the highest and more remote areas, wherever the farming land was poorest. Forced in among themselves, they also kept their own cooking traditions. Try *yánjū sān huáng jī*—moist and tender chicken baked in a mound of rock salt—and perhaps the most popular dish, *mìzhì zhǐ bāo lúyú*—"secretly made" paper-wrapped fish, plump, almost boneless, and in a sweet sauce (actually wrapped in foil) from which clouds of steam erupt when the package is cut open. The restaurants have solid, heavy tables and chairs with a deliberately rustic theme. *In Shíchà Hǎi Dōng Àn on the east bank of the Qián Hǎi north from the north entrance of Běi Hǎi Park.* ℰ *010/6404-2259. 11am–2pm and 5–10pm. Also as* **Lǎo Hànzi Kèjiā Càiguǎn** *at the branch just west of the north end of Sānlǐtún North Bar St.* ℰ *010/6415-3376. Meal for 2 ¥80–¥100 ($10–$12). 11:30am–2pm and 5:30–11pm.*

Horizon CANTONESE With its sumptuous interior, Horizon looks a lot more expensive than it actually is. Cantonese is the subtlest of the Chinese cuisines, and this is the real thing, so don't expect retina-threatening orange sauces or flavors sweet enough to put your teeth on edge. As with all Cantonese restaurants, there's shark's fin, abalone, and bird's nest soup, whose principal purpose is to show off the fatness of your wallet. If, instead, you let your taste buds lead the way, then the stewed beef and dry bean curd with XO (brandy) sauce, and the thick and subtly flavored sweet corn soup with crabmeat should be among your choices, as should the Mandarin fish deep-fried in the lightest of batters, prettily presented with a topping of delicate sweet-and-sour sauce. The restaurant has also responded to the current obsession with Sìchuān food, and the sautéed crab with dried chili should not be missed, nor the sautéed diced chicken with dried chili and pepper, if you're in the mood for more aggressive flavors. *Inside the Kerry Centre Mall, next to the rear entrance of the Kerry Centre Hotel (see above).* ℂ *010/8529-6999. Lunch typically ¥100 ($12), dinner ¥120–¥150 ($15–$18) per person. Set menu ¥88 ($11), express lunch ¥48 ($6). AE, DC, MC, V. 11:30am– 2:30pm and 5:30–10pm.*

Jing FUSION With the most stylish and sophisticated interior of any in Běijīng, Jing has plenty of visual entertainment—a glass staircase, wine stacked in underlit temperature-controlled glass columns, and semi-private rooms whose walls are merely circular curtains of chains. There's a video installation with constant snatches of Běijīng life by a Hong Kong artist, and the hot, cold, and pastry kitchens are all wide open to public view. The food is Continental with pan-Asian influences, such as hot smoked salmon with bonito-crusted green beans and citrus-soy dressing, rack of lamb with a spice crust on dried fig couscous, and Vietnamese king prawns on tandoor salad with spiced nan. There's a proper tandoor oven, too, making the "Jing" sampler of lamb, chicken, and swordfish a must. Flavors are juxtaposed well, and nothing is overwrought. *Inside The Palace Hotel (see above).* ℂ *010/6523-0175. ¥200– ¥300 ($25–$38) per person. An excellent choice of 3-course lunch set menus for ¥160 ($20). AE, DC, MC, V. 5:30am– 11:30pm.*

Lotus in Moonlight Vegetarian Restaurant (Hétáng Yuèsè Sù Cān) VEGETARIAN In Běijīng, when people think of vegetarian food, they often think of food engineered from vegetable matter to be indistinguishable from pork or even lobster. The most famous of these is the long-standing and leaden **Gōngdélín Fànzhuāng,** Qián Mén Dàjiē 158, ℂ **010/ 6511-2542;** and there's a better modern counterpart, the **Tiān Shí restaurant,** at Dēngshìkkǒu Dàjiē 57, just off Wáng-fǔjǐng. Vegetarians who think this all misses the point will head for the Lotus in Moonlight, a little tucked away, but worth the effort. The bright blue-and-yellow interior is sunnily lit by skylights, and while there are imitation dishes on the menu, there are more that bring out the best in their vegetable ingredients, particularly in stews, vegetable hot pots, and *dòufu* dishes. *Building 12, Liǔfāng Nán Lǐ, in the Dōng Zhí Mén area just outside the Second Ring Rd.* ℂ *010/6465-3299. Meal for 2 ¥80–¥100 ($10–$13). No credit cards. 11am–2pm and 5–9pm.*

Noble Court CANTONESE An elegant circular space downstairs from the Hyatt's lobby, the Noble Court's particular strengths are in its Cantonese dim sum and Běijīng-style snacks (which well deserve their "premium" designation), and in a comprehensive range of fish and seafood. Among the snacks, try the shrimp and pork dumplings, the baked seafood in puff pastry and, on the Běijīng side, the particularly piquant sliced goose kidney with preserved vegetable in chili sauce. Steamed garoupa filets with black mushrooms and green vegetables are excellent, the fish hot and firm. Hong Kong influence is visible in popular oddities such as fried coffee-flavored lamb chops, and all your favorite almond, chestnut, and bean deserts are available. Set menus include high-end items such as braised shark's fin and simmered lobster. Service is impeccable. *Inside the Grand Hyatt (see above).* ⓒ *010/8518-1234. Around ¥300–¥500 ($37–$62) for 2. Set lunches of a top-of-the-range Cantonese meal with lobster, shark's fin, abalone, and more are ¥380 ($45) per person. AE, DC, MC, V. 10:30am–2pm and 6–10pm.*

Noodle Loft SHĀNXĪ This is the latest addition to an empire of trendy establishments that includes a spacious restaurant-cum-club in Sānlǐtún called **Loft,** and a rather good, if pricey, Thai restaurant called **Pink Loft** (Sānlǐtún South St.; ⓒ 010/6506-8811). Noodle Loft's specialty is a Shānxī cuisine, almost unheard of outside China, noted for its vinegary flavors and its use of tomatoes, potatoes, flours made from dried beans, and a large variety of interesting noodles. The interior is ultra-modern in orange and gray, with a large open kitchen displaying giant woks, boilers, and steamers. Menus have English translations. Try *yǐ bǎ zhuā* (lightly fried wheat cakes with oil and chives), *qiáo miàn māo ěrduo* (buckwheat pasta in the shape of cats' ears, stir-fried with chopped meat), *suān cài tǔdòu cā* (vinegared potato slices), and *yóu miàn yāo kuài* (oat noodles with kidney pieces). Altogether a range of flavors and ingredients not often seen in Chinese cooking, and which you are highly unlikely to find at home. *Dàwàng Lù 20, in the new Soho district, east of China World, a few min. walk south of Dàwàng metro station.* ⓒ *010/6774-9950. ¥80–¥100 for a 2-person meal. No credit cards. 11am–2:30pm and 5:30–10:30pm.*

Yú Xiāng Rén Jiā SÌCHUĀN This restaurant has bright and bustling interiors with decorative hints of village life. Familiar Sìchuān classics are served here, such as *gōngbǎo jīdīng* (diced chicken with peanuts and peppers); *yú xiāng ròu sī* (shredded pork in a spicy sauce); and several versions of the highly popular *shuǐ zhǔ yú,* a large bowl of sliced fish in water with pepper oil covered in a thick layer of floating chilies, spooned away by the waitress, or the less hot but more numbing variety, *jiāo má yú.* Also try *hé xiāng sān zhēng*— pork ribs in a creamy sauce on a lotus leaf in a steamer. *On the east side of the northeast Third Ring Rd., just north of Xiāoyún Lù.* ⓒ *010/8451-0380. 11am–3pm and 5:30–10pm. A slightly more upmarket branch can be found on the 5th floor of the Liánhé Dàshà, behind the Foreign Ministry building just off the east Second Ring Rd. at Cháowài Dàjiē 20.* ⓒ *010/6588-3841. No credit cards. Meal for 2 ¥80 ($10). 11am–10:30pm.*

THE GREAT WALL:
FOUR VIEWS FROM BĚIJĪNG

万里长城

T HE GREAT WALL IS CHINA'S MOST renowned monument, frequently heralded as the only man-made object visible from space. That is a dubious, if compelling, claim. I have not orbited the Earth, but I do know that the Great Wall, despite its combined 9,982km (6,200-mile) length, is not only slim but is more broken than whole (in fact, it's rife with gaps the size of small countries) and varies in both color and contour. More than half of the Wall has been demolished over the centuries. Much of it lies in ruined, earthen strips that are barely distinguishable from the hills and valleys out of which it was formed. Still, this dragon's spine of Old China, every inch laid by hand, was a massive project, certainly worthy of heavenly praise.

The Chinese call it *Wàn Lǐ Cháng Chéng,* "the long wall of 10,000 lǐ." (A *lǐ* is an ancient unit of measure, roughly equivalent to a third of a mile.) The Wall's origins go back to the 5th century A.D. (and perhaps even earlier), when the rival kingdoms of the Warring States Period (453–221 B.C.) built walls in central China as defensive ramparts against their enemies, including barbarian tribes. The first emperor of unified China, Qín Shǐ Huáng Dì, fortified the barriers in the 3rd century B.C. Over a 10-year period, 300,000 conscripted laborers, many of them slaves, knit the walls into a continuous rampart to protect the northern frontier. New sections extended the Wall east 2,737km (1,700 miles) to the Yellow Sea.

The Great Wall was constantly repositioned and extended along new routes as successive dynasties rose and fell. In the year A.D. 607 alone, more than a million workers toiled on this line of defense, but thereafter the Great Wall was largely abandoned. The conquest by the Mongols from the north and their establishment of the Yuán Dynasty (A.D. 1271–1368) rendered the Wall obsolete. After China reverted to native rule under the Míng Dynasty (1368–1644), however, the rulers became fearful of another barbarian onslaught and set in motion the last great phase of wall building. This was not enough to keep out the Manchurians, who overran the Míng defenses and created China's last dynasty, the Qīng (1644–1911).

Today, the Great Wall can be visited where it meets the sea in the east (at Old Dragon Head near the town of Shānhǎiguān), where it disappears into the desert on the Silk Road to the west (at Jiāyùguān), and at several junctures in between. But by far the most popular approaches are near Běijīng, where there is a choice of four dramatic sections. All four—at Bādálǐng, Mùtiányù, Sīmǎtái, and Jūyōngguān—are within an easy day trip of Běijīng, and all four are appealing. **Bādálǐng** is where most tourists walk on the Great Wall. **Mùtiányù** is a fine alternative, beautifully restored and often less crowded with visitors. **Sīmǎtái** is a wild, nearly unrestored segment, farther from Běijīng and thus far less inundated with tour buses. **Jūyōngguān,** the newest section to open, is near the Míng Tombs on the road to Bādálǐng. All four sections are 300 to 500 years old, dating from the Míng Dynasty, and all four are beautiful stretches of the Great Wall, coiling up and down impossibly steep terrain. Each section is a fitting representative of the greatest wall ever built by man—what one 19th-century traveler called a "fantastic serpent of stone."

The Great Wall at Bādálǐng

Almost everyone who tours China, from heads of state to backpackers, pays a call on the Great Wall at Bādálǐng, 68km (42 miles) northwest of Běijīng. This is a grand section of the Wall, set in a steep, forested mountain range. The Wall, its stairs, and the magnificent watchtowers were carefully restored beginning in 1957. While many a traveler pooh-poohs Bādálǐng as a deplorable tourist trap, crowded beyond all endurance, I have never been disappointed by it. The Great Wall is China's number-one tourist attraction, after all, and China is the world's most populous country. The Great Wall at Bādálǐng, then, is the prime site for immersion into the Chinese world, past and present.

Construction of the Míng Dynasty Great Wall began in 1368 and continued for almost 200 years. Built of stone, it stretched 3,999km (2,484 miles) east to west and averaged 7m (24 ft.) in height, 6m (21 ft.) in width at its base, and 5m (18 ft.) wide on top. The interior was a mixture of tamped earth and rubble. The sides were covered in stone, the top in layers of brick. The brick we associate with the Great Wall wasn't introduced until the Míng builders set to work. Gateway arches and watchtowers run the length of the Wall, which served as a highway through the mountains. Five horses could ride abreast, drawing carriages.

The Wall at Bādálǐng has been restored to reflect its Míng Dynasty grandeur. The main parking lot and squares, filled with vendors these days, reflect China's modern economic boom. A long stairway runs up to the Wall. You can turn left (north) or right (south) and walk a mile or so in either direction. The segment on the left is a bit steeper, but I find it more scenic, so that's the way I usually head.

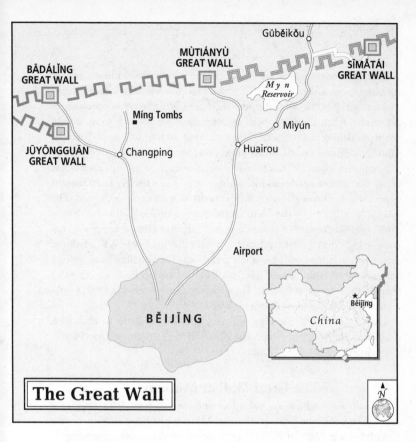

The incredible steepness of the Great Wall and the high rise of its stair treads always astound visitors. Walking up to the highest watchtower is often enough to exhaust a traveler thoroughly, especially on a hot day. There's no reason to hurry. The scenery is splendid. The two-story watchtowers, consisting of a guardroom below and an observation house above, are fine places to recuperate.

The northern section of the Wall rises to the highest watchtower at Bādálǐng, then runs down to the south. If you walk it to the end, about two-thirds of a mile from the entrance, you can head north again on an unrenovated spine of the Wall that has a much more primitive feel. Few tourists venture out this far. The stairs are crumbling and the sides of the wall are broken, exposing the earthen filling.

If you choose to walk Bādálǐng in the other direction, south atop the Wall, the trek is longer, more than a mile. At the far end there's a terminal for the Great Wall cable car. Beyond this point, the Great Wall reverts to its former ruins, which you are free to explore. (Liability laws are weak in China, meaning broken bones and other mishaps suffered in public places are seldom compensated.)

The Qīnglóng Qiáo West train station is near the southern end of Bādálǐng. This is the first railroad to be built entirely with Chinese labor and funds (1909). It tunnels under the Great Wall. Locals tell me that in the winter, when the Great Wall at Bādálǐng is dusted with snow, a train trip from Běijīng is a delight. There are almost no tourists on the Wall, the sun is bright, and the mountain peaks and guard towers are gorgeous.

Since most of us do not visit Běijīng in winter, we must descend the Great Wall in the heat of tourist season—and it is a fiercely steep descent down these high stairs. Some travelers prefer to walk down backward. The modern handrails can also help. At the bottom of the Wall is the "Great Mall" of endless souvenir stands, a movie hall, and cafes. Prices are exceptionally high for trinkets, crafts, and "I Climbed the Great Wall" T-shirts, even when you bargain. I bought a tacky sword at Bādálǐng once, paying half what the vendor asked, which still turned out to be twice the price charged by Běijīng and Hong Kong department stores. Oh well, I told myself, it did come from the Great Wall.

The Great Wall at Bādálǐng is open daily from 6:30am to midnight. Admission March 31 to November 30 is ¥40 ($5), otherwise ¥35 ($4.40). The cable car is ¥100 ($13) round-trip.

The Great Wall at Mùtiányù

The Great Wall at Bādálǐng proved so popular that authorities restored a second section of the Wall, in 1986, at Mùtiányù (89km/55 miles northeast of Běijīng). Mùtiányù was supposed to relieve the overcrowding at Bādálǐng, particularly on weekends. The ploy has not really succeeded, but I'm glad that Mùtiányù is open. Its setting is more rough and rugged than that at Bādálǐng, even if it now has summer traffic jams of its own.

The mile-long segment of the Great Wall of Mùtiányù was among the first built during the Míng Dynasty, beginning well over 500 years ago. As at Bādálǐng, a long stairway leads up to the Wall. The hike can take up to 30 minutes, so you might want to use the nearby cable car. If you turn right at the top of the entrance, you can walk the ramparts for over a half mile. At the end, there is a barrier; visitors are not permitted to venture beyond this point. All you can do is contemplate the Wall in ruins, which gives you an excellent idea of what most of the Great Wall, even those sections built just a few hundred rather than a few thousand years ago, looks like now.

Returning on the Wall in the other direction leads to the cable-car station, which is the kindest way back down (in respect to your knees and thighs).

The Great Wall at Mùtiányù is open daily from 7am until dark. Admission is ¥35 ($4.40). The cable car is ¥100 ($13) round-trip, and a new roller train, which winds up and down the hillsides, is the same price.

The Great Wall at Sīmǎtái

The Great Wall at Sīmǎtái is quiet, remote, and virtually unreconstructed. Fortification aficionados consider Sīmǎtái the most beautiful section of the Great Wall. It is beautiful, but its main aesthetic attraction is its state of ruin. This is how the Great Wall really looks 500 years after the Míng constructed it. Sīmǎtái is also a paradise for hikers and hill walkers, with its dramatic natural scenery. The view of the sharp peaks is heightened by the outline of the Great Wall and its crumbling watchtowers.

I visited Sīmǎtái twice recently, first by hiring a car with driver and guide, then by just hiring a car. This put Sīmǎtái within 2 hours of downtown Bĕijīng. The Jīngchéng Highway to Sīmǎtái is smooth, the countryside green. At Mìyún Reservoir, the terrain steepens. The roadside is clotted with fishing families selling their catch, enormous reservoir trout, many 1m (3 ft.) long, sheathed in plastic and suspended on posts like lanterns. At Gǔbĕikǒu, 113km (70 miles) northeast of Bĕijīng, a country lane winds 10m (6¼ miles) more through the foothills to Sīmǎtái Village and the entrance to the Wall. The town at the base is tiny. The main street leading to the Wall has a few beef noodle cafes, souvenir shops, and vendor shelters stocked with T-shirts and Great Wall tablecloths, but this is a mere minnow pond of sellers compared to the ocean of hawkers flooding the gates to Bādálǐng and Mùtiányù. Towering high over the village is the formidable outline of the Great Wall, slithering like a dragon's back over a series of sharp, clipped peaks.

Beyond the village there is a half-mile walk up to the first stairway and watchtower. The sandy path rises and skirts the small Sīmǎtái Reservoir, where in the heat of summer, tourists from Bĕijīng board pleasure boats for a sail along the Great Wall. But from the water, the Wall remains high and remote. The reservoir lies in a deep crease dividing two sections of the Wall: Sīmǎtái to the east, Jīnshānlǐng to the west. When I first visited Sīmǎtái, in the spring, only four other visitors arrived, and it was only a little busier in the early summer when I returned.

Ascending the stairs to the first watchtower at Sīmǎtái is a matter of pounding a few hundred stone steps, the treads of this staircase often just half as deep as an average foot length. The climb is a struggle, but the view from the first of the ascending towers, taken through open cannon archways, is magnificent: endless mountain chains to the deserted north; watchtowers crowning the ridgelines east and west; and the reservoir, village, and farmlands far below, rolling southward toward Bĕijīng.

This first portion of the Great Wall at Sīmǎtái has been restored, as have virtually all the walkways and towers that tourists see along Bādálǐng and Mùtiányù—but from here on at Sīmǎtái, the Wall has been left to crumble. A sign at the entrance boasts that Sīmǎtái is the most dangerous segment of the Great Wall, and indeed it is: The grand stairways disappear;

the pathway becomes a ledge of rock and sand along the outside of the rising wall, narrowing to sheer drop-offs; sometimes there are no footholds at all; and, at times, the path, grown smooth over the centuries, is as treacherous to scale as a slide of gravel.

The wall bricks, each with its own stamped number, date from the Míng Dynasty. Many of the bricks have fallen away, exposing the original earthen core with which the large work gangs capped the mountain peaks. From the towers on the Wall, signals of fire and smoke once alerted those inside the Wall to impending invasions from without.

At Sīmătái, you can still see the results of the Míng building program. The toll taken by 5 centuries of weather and civilization is substantial, but far from complete. Sīmătái survives as a wild run of ruins, its main outline intact, stretching from peak to chiseled peak on ridges sometimes pitched to 70-degree inclines. Best of all for the traveler, Sīmătái is as peaceful as it is untouched and as beautiful as the mountains it dances across.

Coming down Sīmătái is more daunting than going up. Locals recount stories of visitors who have broken into tears during the descent, unnerved by the steepness, the lack of stairs, the unstable footings. Some come down on the stairless top of the Wall backward, on all fours. The name *Sīmătái* sounds similar in Chinese to the words for dead horse platform, a reference to a horse that fell in a famous battle fought beneath the Wall here. So far, no tourists have added their names to this venerable tradition.

In fact, there is a safer way to scale Sīmătái. East of the entrance is a **gondola.** Visitors can hop a ride partway up and climb a new, safer set of steep stairs to the 787m (2,624-ft.) high eighth tower on the Wall. From here, it is said that on a clear evening you can see the lights of Běijīng.

There are 14 watchtowers at Sīmătái, stationed at quarter-mile intervals and strung across the peaks until the Wall dissolves into scattered bricks, piles of sand, and fragments of bone from the workers who were buried within the Wall. "To think that these walls, built in apparently inaccessible places, as though to balance the Milky Way in the sky, a walled way over the mountaintops, are the work of men," one 19th-century traveler gasped, "makes it seem like a dream." Indeed, Sīmătái is magical, but beauty transcends ordinary reality wherever you walk today along the Great Wall of China.

The Great Wall at Sīmătái is open daily from 8am to 5pm. Admission is ¥30 ($3.75). The gondola is ¥60 ($7.50) round-trip.

The Great Wall at Jūyōngguān

Opened in 1998, the section of the wall at Jūyōngguān is the nearest to Běijīng (58km/36 miles northwest). Here a 3km (2½-mile) section of the old wall was renovated under an extensive 5-year program. An important mountain pass leading directly to the capital and the plain beyond, Jūyōngguān may have been walled as early as the Northern Wèi dynasty of 386–585, before Běijīng was founded, but now boasts impressive reconstructions of the wall and guard towers from the very beginning of the Míng Dynasty in 1368, as well as several temples and a garden. A separate and truly ancient and original stone edifice of 1342, the Yún Tái ("Cloud Platform"), which once supported three stupas, is covered in fine Buddhist figures and text in six languages, including Chinese, Tibetan, and Sanskrit.

Lying just 10km (6 miles) south of the Great Wall at Bādálǐng, Jūyōngguān has become a popular alternative to the more crowded sections of the old wall. CITS arranges some tours here, and the site is also served by tourist bus no. 5 from Qián Mén. Jūyōngguān is open daily from 7:30am to 7 or 8pm depending on demand (to 6pm in winter). Admission from April 1 to October 31 is ¥40 ($8); otherwise it's ¥35 ($4.40).

PRACTICAL INFORMATION

by Peter Neville-Hadley

ORIENTATION & WHEN TO GO

The four sites detailed above are all best visited on weekdays rather than weekends, and certainly outside the peak seasons for Chinese tourism—Chinese New Year (Spring Festival) around the end of January and beginning of February, and the first weeks of May and October. Spring sees many parts of the Great Wall lapped with orchards, which have often been planted right up its slopes. But perhaps the best time to visit is autumn when persimmons glow in the trees, there's a general changing of colors, the air seems relatively clear and crisp, and the afternoon light—warm, yellow, and nearly horizontal—is perfect for photography.

GETTING THERE

To Bādálǐng   Several tourist buses provide highly convenient and economical transport from Qián Mén, Běijīng Station, outside the History Museum, Xuānwǔ Mén (metro northeast exit), and elsewhere. Routes 1 to 4 visit Bādálǐng and the Míng Tombs for ¥40 ($5), and route 5 from the southwest corner of Qián Mén visits Jūyōngguān (see below) for ¥50 ($6.25). Start early: Buses leave between 6 and 9:30am year-round. For those wishing to spend just as long at the Great Wall as you please, the best option is to take the circle line metro to Jīshuǐtán, then walk 10 minutes east to Déshèng Mén, one of the capital's few surviving city gates, or take a taxi directly there. From the gate tower's northeast side, catch modern air-conditioned express bus no. 919 (not its ramshackle stopping counterpart with the same number), which leaves every few minutes and goes nonstop up the expressway to Bādálǐng in just under an hour for ¥10 ($1.25). Catch the same bus back or take its stopping version to Jūyōngguān (20 min., ¥2/25¢) and see two sections of wall in 1 day. Complete the journey back with the stopping bus no. 919, jumping off once inside the Third Ring Road, where taxis become numerous; about 1½ hours to get back.

To Jūyōngguān See above for details of regular buses and tourist buses to this site, which can easily be visited with Bādálǐng in one trip.

To Mùtiányù Tour bus no. 6 leaves from just outside Xuānwǔ Mén metro station (northeast exit) between 7 and 8:30am from April 15 to September 15, reaching the site after about 1½ hours. The tour (¥60/$7.50) goes on to include a visit to the Red Conch Temple and an amusement park, neither of which is very interesting. Public transport also runs from Xī Zhí Mén and Dōng Zhí Mén bus stations to Huáiróu Xiàn, from where there are further buses to Mùtiányù. Also try calling expat Ali Jarrah Pour, who runs an air-conditioned Volvo bus to various Great Wall sites according to demand, picking up outside the Hard Rock Cafe, usually on Tuesdays and Fridays, but more often in high season. Seats, at ¥160 ($20), must be booked in advance: ℂ **0138/0100-4866,** or 010/9089-3026.

To Sīmǎtái Frequent rapid air-conditioned minibus services leave from Xī Zhí Mén bus station for Chéngdé (see separate chapter, beginning on p. 41), and less frequently from Dōng Zhí Mén bus station passing the turning for Sīmǎtái after about 2½ hours (¥40/$5). But a brand-new highway, to be completed in 2003, will perhaps reduce this time by as much as an hour. In busier seasons, farm vehicles and other transportation waits at the turning, eager to take you the remaining 10km (6¼ miles), although this makes for a pleasant hike if you have the time. Returning, simply flag down passing Běijīng-bound minibuses.

TOURS & STRATAGEMS

CITS Tours, even to nearby Bādálǐng, tend to cost at least ¥400 ($50) per person and should be avoided. These are also the tours where the guides will tell you with a straight face that the Great Wall can be seen from the moon. Taxi drivers tend to say the "proper" rate for their services for a half-day trip out there is ¥450 ($56), but even ¥300 ($38), which will be happily accepted, is too much. Either way, it beats the up to ¥1,200 ($150) your hotel transportation desk may think appropriate. The direct no. 919 bus mentioned above is the best choice for most visitors to Bādálǐng. Ali Jarrah Pour's tour bus is good for the other destinations, if it fits in with your schedule, or, again, you should be able to negotiate a taxi for about ¥300 ($38).

WHERE TO STAY

The accommodations at Wall sites tend to be simple guesthouses with beds at around ¥50 ($6.25). Almost all visitors treat the Wall near Běijīng as a day trip from the capital.

WHERE TO DINE

A day out at the Wall is best spent with a picnic lunch, since although all sites have catering of a kind, even including a branch of KFC at Bādálǐng, food tends generally to be poor and overpriced, and to be found only at the main entrance to each site—not convenient if you've spent your morning walking along the Wall away from there.

Chéngdé: Summer Home
of the Emperors

承德

O<small>N</small> S<small>EPTEMBER</small> 14, 1793, <small>THE</small> Qiánlóng Emperor received the first delegation from a Western government ever to set foot in China, a British group headed by Lord Macartney. Matters did not get off to a promising start. The British lord refused to kowtow to the emperor, a ceremony that all visitors to the Middle Kingdom had performed for centuries, bowing deeply and banging their heads upon the ground. The emperor agreed to no treaties with England that day and declared that requests to open up trade were pointless. "We possess all things," he declared. "I set no value on objects strange or ingenious, and have no use for your country's manufactures."

The site of this historic meeting of East and West took place not in the Forbidden City in Běijīng but 250km (155 miles) northeast in a remote imperial retreat built by Qiánlóng's grandfather, the Kāngxī Emperor. This summer palace in the wilderness, located in the country town of Chéngdé (formerly called Jehol in the West), was by no means a primitive outpost. Befitting the station of the Qīng rulers, it was a grand summer palace, larger than Běijīng's summer palace and Forbidden City combined, with numerous halls, pavilions, lakes, and hunting grounds. The retreat has survived, largely intact, and today Chéngdé is a summer resort open to all the people of China as well as sightseers from abroad. City-dwellers seem as anxious as the royal courts of 2 centuries past to escape the heat of Běijīng and partake of the splendors of the countryside.

The stunning temples and the palaces of the Imperial Summer Villa are the last grand expression of the power and wealth wielded by China's final imperial dynasty at its height. The Qīng Dynasty was little over a century away from complete collapse. Largely emptied of monks and worshippers, the pavilions of Chéngdé today serve delegations of tourists.

Mountain Villa for Escaping the Summer Heat
(Bìshǔ Shān Zhuāng)

The road from Běijīng is in excellent condition and the scenery is often spectacular, with sharp wooded peaks and valleys. Chéngdé is surrounded by green mountains—no doubt one reason the emperors favored this place. The town of Chéngdé, which grew up around the parklands, has become a resort center, but it is still no more than a village by Chinese standards, with a population of merely 150,000. Tourism has brought some prosperity, although, in the nearby fields, I saw farmers pulling rounded stones on ropes, used to level the strips between furrows; and I also saw furrows being dug with wooden plows harnessed to the bent backs of peasants, no other beasts of burden being available.

Before the era of automobiles and trains, the journey from the capital to Chéngdé would have been a formidable undertaking. In 1703, the Kāngxī Emperor ordered the construction of the "Mountain Villa for Escaping the Summer Heat." From the first, it was China's court away from court. Even the throne was transported from Běijīng so that the emperor could wield full power while he enjoyed the sports of the privileged. Kāngxī was intensely dedicated to the horsemanship and hunting of his Manchu ancestors, and Chéngdé became his passion. For the next 117 years, this summer retreat was expanded and enriched, the Qīng emperors holding court here 6 months of the year. In 1820, however, the Jiāqìng Emperor died at Chéngdé, reportedly the victim of a lightning bolt, a bad omen. It was decades before the court again began its annual decampment of Běijīng in favor of the lush, cool valley to the north.

What's most striking today is the vast scale of the imperial retreat, which fills much of the great valley of Chéngdé, and its rustic setting. In comparison with the ornate and elaborate pavilions and courtyards of the Forbidden City and summer palaces in Běijīng, Chéngdé's compound is raw and wild. Most of Chéngdé's retreat is given over to water, rock, and grasslands—the grasslands that the once-nomadic Manchus, who had grown civilized as the masters of the Chinese empire, called their spiritual home. One of the first foreigners to see the retreat, a Jesuit missionary living in Běijīng, wrote that the enclosure was so extensive it required an hour to survey on horseback.

Imperial Palace

Today, Bìshǔ Shān Zhuāng (Mountain Retreat for Escaping the Heat) is a park surrounded by a wall 10km (6 miles) in circumference. The **East Entrance Gate (Déhuì Mén)** is at the Wǔliè River, on the northwest edge

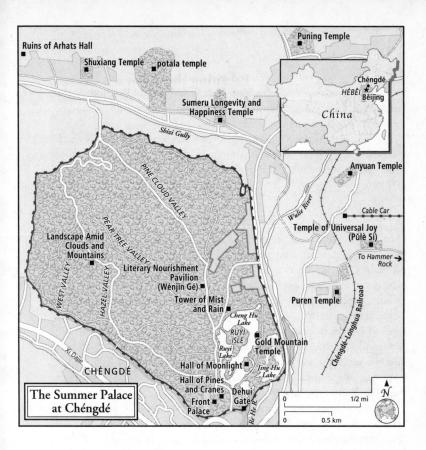

The Summer Palace at Chéngdé

of town, near an intriguing footbridge where locals congregate with long bamboo fishing poles and vendors stock towers of glass aquariums with the fresh catch. No matter that the water under the bridge is turgid and clogged with debris, or that the resort town is noisy and uninviting. The park the emperors built is beautiful and spacious, consisting of enormous fields, lakes, pavilions, and pagodas; this is the largest imperial garden in China.

West of the entrance gate, atop a small rise, is the **Front Palace (Zhèng Gōng),** now the **Bìshǔ Shān Zhuāng Museum.** The Front Palace complex is where diplomatic business was conducted. For several centuries, China in the summertime was ruled from nine courtyard halls, each fashioned from unpainted wood. These are plain, linear buildings, more like imperial lodges than palaces, landscaped in mighty pines, graveled walkways, and convoluted rockeries. The interiors are sparsely decorated with the furniture and armaments of the time, as well as life-sized waxen figures representing emperors, concubines, court advisors, and foreign diplomats. Envoys were once received in the **Hall of Frugality and Sincerity,** constructed of fragrant nánmù wood from southwestern China. The royal bedroom is located in the **Refreshing Mist Veiled Waters Pavilion.** In the **Landscape Amid Clouds and Mountains Hall,** visitors can reach the second floor by climbing the rockery in front.

The Imperial Summer Villa is open from 8:30am to 5pm daily (park gates close at 6:30pm). The park also opens at 8:30am, and is open later than 5pm in summer, but the museums still close at 5pm. Admission is ¥60 ($6).

Royal Garden

Outside the main palace grounds is a set of interlinked lakes, woven with paths, arched bridges, and viewing pavilions, where the Chinese enjoy themselves, rowing boats and splashing each other as they pass. Family picnics and games are popular here. Across the flat grasslands, adults and children together play what looks like Blindman's Bluff and Rover-Red-Rover. Teens circle up for versions of Hacky Sack. The last great private preserve of emperors has become a genuine people's park. Courtyards are commandeered by martial arts demonstrations featuring retired citizens in white uniforms and red sashes. In another courtyard, in front of the emperor's palace, preschool children flash swords in formation, some of them barely old enough to walk.

Many **pavilions** from the days of the emperors have survived. The **Literary Nourishment Pavilion (Wénjīn Gé),** once one of China's four great imperial libraries, is northwest of the lakes on a secluded wooded hill. It resembles the classic gardens of Sūzhōu and Níngbō, with an immense rockery facing a graceful wooden pavilion across a goldfish pool. The rockery has its own caves, paths, and overlooks, and one of its rocks has been shaped and stationed so that from the pavilion those who linger can see the silver image of the moon continuously reflected on the waters.

Along the lakeshores are several dazzling towers and halls, including the **Temple of Eternal Blessing,** a golden birthday gift from the Qiánlóng Emperor to his mother. On **Cānglàng Isle,** Qiánlóng constructed a copy of Sūzhōu's Cānglàng Tíng garden. Even prettier is the **Tower of Mist and Rain (Yānyǔlóu),** perched on a hill and reached by a bridge, favored by emperors for its views of the lake in the fog. On the northeast shore, there is a stunning three-story pavilion, **Gold Mountain Temple (Jīnshān Sì),** bordered by lower halls, which the Kāngxī Emperor, in a poem, likened to a mountain rising from the lake. "To ascend it," he sang, "is like climbing a magical peak."

Lord Macartney rode through the park during his diplomatic mission in 1793 and was charmed by the lake scenes: "The shores of the lake have all the varieties of shape which the fancy of a painter can delineate . . . one marked by a pagoda, or other building, one quite destitute of ornament, some smooth and level, some steep and uneven and others frowning with wood or smiling with culture."

North of the lakes, the grasslands and hills fan out and the walkways become secluded hiking trails stretching beyond the **Garden of Ten Thousand Trees (Wànshù Yuán)** and the **Horse Testing Ground (Shìmǎ Dài),** where emperors once reviewed archers and horsemen. The Imperial Summer Villa at Chéngdé essentially re-creates the wild grasslands of the Manchus north of the Great Wall but softens them with the garden arts and sweeping pavilions of south China.

Little Tibet

The Kāngxī Emperor had a political motive in moving his summer court to Chéngdé. He hoped to impress, to beguile, and to subdue the unruly legions to the north, and to placate restive religious and ethnic factions throughout China. This ploy produced a legacy visible today in the hillsides north and east of the Imperial Summer Villa, a string of Eight Outer Temples built in honor of Tibetans, Kazaks, and other peoples. As fascinating as this Summer Palace of the Wild West is, the array of distant hillside temples is even more striking.

A dozen were built from 1713 to 1779. Eight remain open. Two of the neighboring northern temples, Tibetan in style, are the grandest and most unusual. Built 10 years apart, they are the work of Kāngxī's grandson, the Qiánlóng Emperor.

The **Mount Sumeru Longevity and Happiness Temple (Xūmífúshòu Miào)** was built in 1779 in honor of the sixth Panchen Lama's visit to Chéngdé. The design is based on the lama's residence in Shigatse, Tibet. At the rear of this lavish uphill enclosure is a yellow-and-green pagoda erected to celebrate the Qiánlóng Emperor's 70th birthday. At the entrance are two white stone elephants kneeling on bent legs. In the center is the high red wall of the main temple, decorated with Tibetan windows. The walls enclose a massive squarish four-story hall with a copper-tiled roof gilded in a ton of gold, decorated with eight ridge-running dragons, each weighing 1 ton. The inside of the red walls is lined with tiers of galleries, affording inward views of the square hall and outward views of the valley of Chéngdé. This was the last temple copy built at Chéngdé.

The **Small Potala Temple (Pǔtuózōngchéng Miào),** a mile to the east, was built by the Qiánlóng Emperor 10 years earlier, partly to celebrate his 60th birthday and his mother's 80th. It is the largest temple at Chéngdé, its 60 halls and terraces covering 22 hectares (54 acres).

To reach the main hall requires a long, steep climb up the hillside. Prayer flags and banners drape its golden beams. The great red wall at its rear evokes the wall of the Dalai Lama's Potala Palace in Lhasa. In the front courtyard, a massive four-sided stone tablet inscribed, respectively, in Tibetan, Manchurian, Mongolian, and Chinese, proclaims the temple's links to the Potala. Whitewashed outer buildings, capped with dagobas, are empty shells, built for show rather than worship. Even the richly decorated Tibetan windows on the red wall are blank, serving as pure decorative flourishes to impress the visiting Mongol dignitaries who practiced Lama Buddhism. The stairs up to the red wall are so steep that sedan-chair carriers now do a steady business ferrying visitors to the top.

Within the mammoth red walls is a large square **pavilion,** now empty of its Buddha statue, but capped with an extraordinary tiled roof gilded bright gold. Many of the buildings, such as the **Hall of All Laws Falling into One,** are gradually being filled with religious artifacts and Chinese porcelains. The arcades in the red wall contain hundreds of images of the Buddha. But perhaps the strangest of the displays is in the **East Hall,** situated beneath the red facade, where images of the Red Hat sect perform "esoteric" rituals under cover of their yellow gowns. Such expressions of sexuality, more common in certain holy places in India, are rarely manifested in the temples of China, although at Chéngdé there are other examples.

Temple hours vary slightly but are generally from 8am to 5pm in summer, a little shorter in winter. Admission is typically ¥25 ($3), although some lesser temples charge only ¥10 ($1.25).

A Strange Rock

Standing above the wealth of imperial and religious ruins in Chéngdé's outdoor museum to the glories of the last dynasty is one of the most peculiar natural monuments in China, **Hammer Rock (Qìngchuí Fēng).** It can be seen atop the distant eastern hills from nearly anywhere in Chéngdé, a forlorn stone pinnacle jutting straight up from a flat ridge, its base narrower than its rounded top. Its shape is suggestive of another object altogether—one the modest tourism authorities would never suggest—and I am sure it had a more provocative local nickname.

Hammer Rock is connected to a parking lot on the east side of Chéngdé by hiking trails and a ski lift. I decided to take the ski lift up (¥31/$3.90) and walk back down. The lift is a 20-minute ride over quiet hills and valleys where farmers and horsemen tend the fields. At Hammer Rock, the view down into the valley is wide and peaceful, the arc of the eight temples neatly outlined on the lower hills.

Hammer Rock is at the far end of a terrifyingly narrow ledge with sheer drop-offs on either side. Moreover, when I went, it was teeming with visitors, and no railings or path had been provided. One misstep or shove could be fatal. The 18m (60 ft.) monolith is barely 3m (10 ft.) wide at its base, where everyone gathered for a moment and touched the rock. I inched my way across the flat ledge and touched the rock myself, discovering, later, that to do so ensured I would live to the age of 130.

The trail back to the valley runs south past another formation, **Toad Rock,** then down through desolate country to the **Temple of Universal Joy (Pǔlè Sì),** which is open daily from 8am to 5pm and costs ¥25 ($3) to enter. It was built by the Qiánlóng Emperor in 1766 as a place for yet more Mongol envoys to worship while paying their respects to China's ruler. At the rear of this west-facing temple, more active with monks than the Tibetan-style northern complexes, is a round tower, the **Pavilion of the Rising Sun (Xùguāng Gé),** reminiscent of Běijīng's Temple of Heaven. The altar holds a Tantric mandala in the form of a cross and a copper Buddha of Happiness. What's being portrayed in this theater is cosmic sexual union, a theme typical of Tantric Buddhism. The Temple of Universal Joy is aligned perfectly with Hammer Rock to the east—there's definitely something more pagan than divine afoot on these fringes of Chéngdé.

PRACTICAL INFORMATION

by Peter Neville-Hadley

ORIENTATION & WHEN TO GO

The Qīng emperors came to Chéngdé, set on high ground 235km (146 miles) northeast of Běijīng, to escape the heat, and a summer visit is indeed preferable to a winter one—the weather is best from April to October. May to July is the peak season for Chinese tourism, and, to a lesser extent, August, since the Chinese do not tend to travel much in midsummer; and during the week-long October holiday, they tend to head south. A quick rush round Chéngdé's sights requires at least one overnight stay; two is better, but you may be ready to depart on the morning of the second day. Off season, hotel room prices can be as little as 25% of peak-season prices, since the town's supply of hotels, which can barely cope with May-to-July crowds, is far too great for most of the rest of the year.

The year 2003 has been chosen to mark the 300th anniversary of the mountain retreat, which is partially the impetus behind a massive program of rebuilding in the city center, and renovation within the retreat itself, as well as numerous celebratory events. A railway line that bisects the town carries steam locomotives hauling coal supplies to the power station, and provides a little extra excitement, but this is due to disappear by 2005.

GETTING THERE

Chéngdé is easily visited from Běijīng, by either **train** or **bus.** Minibus departures are more frequent and quicker, but trains are more comfortable.

There are departures from Běijīng's Dōng Zhí Mén long-distance bus station, but there are far more frequent services from the Xī Zhí Mén station, where comfortable Iveco or similar air-conditioned minibuses leave for Chéngdé roughly every 20 minutes from 6am until 5:30pm. (The trip is approximately 233km/146 miles, takes at least 3½ hr., and costs ¥46/$5.75.) Buses from Běijīng usually drop passengers in the square outside the railway station, although this may change when a new long-distance bus terminal is built in Chéngdé in a few years' time.

Locals claim that the new Jīchéng Highway, which might be completed by the time you arrive, will cut the journey time to about 2½ hours, but ticket prices will rise and only the most expensive buses will take that route.

There's a useful all-seater morning train service from Běijīng Station, the K711 at 7:20am, arriving in Chéngdé at 11:18am, returning to Běijīng as the K712 at 2:40pm, and arriving there at 6:38pm. Soft-seat tickets are ¥61 ($8). Staff on board sell useful maps, but you should reject their offers of hotel reservations—you'll do much better for yourself. If you plan to return to Běijīng by train within the next 4 days, book a ticket on arrival in Chéngdé.

TOURS, STRATAGEMS & GETTING AROUND

Even Chéngdé's CITS office says there's little point in using its services. Chéngdé's layout is compact, and all the main sights can easily be reached using ubiquitous local taxis. There's not even any need to use the meter as long as you make things clear (and don't require a receipt)—most trips around town are ¥5, and a one-way trip to the outer temples ¥10. Four of the outer temples are within easy walking distance of each other, and there are plenty of cabs.

WHERE TO STAY

The town center is undergoing massive reconstruction, with several new hotels going up. Since Chéngdé lives on tourism (although there's also a steel works and power station), prices tend to be high, but outside of the first week of May to the first week of October, expect to get an automatic discount of 50% from the prices quoted below, and to bargain down from there, sometimes to as little as a quarter of the published rate. For most of the rest of the year a 20% discount is available when requested.

Hóng Lóu Bīnguǎn This is a smarter-than-average Chinese four-star hotel with fresh interiors (opened in 1998) that has the appearance of an overgrown, white-tile-covered chalet, with the standard shiny marble lobby. It's owned by the Chéngdé Post and Telecom Training Centre, but still has staff who are more willing to be helpful than most government-appointed staff. It mostly serves overseas Chinese tour groups, particularly from Malaysia. *Gāo Xīn Jìshù Chǎnyè Kāifā Qū (a short taxi ride to the south of the center).*

© *0314/212-2288.* Fax *0314/212-2289. 89 units, including 79 standard twins/ doubles. ¥580 ($72) standard room; ¥1,200–¥2,600 ($150–$325) suite. AE, DC, MC, V.* **Amenities:** 3 restaurants (Sichuān, Shāndōng, and local); gym; sauna; bowling; billiards; disco. *In room:* A/C, TV, dataport, fridge.

Huílóng Dàshà This once-glitzy, now-drab 10-floor tower is a short walk from the railway station. Rooms with recently added double beds are in better condition than standard rooms. Steam trains can be seen (and heard) from the rear rooms. Suites have a room with twin beds and a room with a double bed to either side of the sitting room. Proximity to the station and relative economy are the main benefits (pay only 25%–30% off season). *Chēzhàn Lù (just north of railway station).* © *0314/208-5369.* Fax *0314/208-2404. huilong@cd-user.he.cninfo.net. 100 units. ¥480 ($60) standard room; ¥1,280 ($160) 3-bed suite. AE, DC, MC, V.* **Amenities:** Restaurant; lobby bar; gym; billiards; business center; gift shop. *In room:* A/C, TV, fridge.

Mountain Villa Hotel (Shān Zhuāng Bīnguǎn) Once the only hotel in town and still the one with the best location—directly opposite the Mountain Resort—this Chinese three-star, six-building monster has recently given its best rooms a thorough updating and renovation to four-star standard. Usually these long-standing hotels should be your last choice, but here a real effort has been made to stay in competition with the newer hotels, and the broad corridors and high ceilings of these older buildings also make a welcome change. *Xiǎo Nán Mén 127 (opposite the main entrance to the Mountain Resort).* © *0314/202-5588.* Fax *0314/203-4143. 391 units. ¥180*

($22) triple and ¥240 ($30) twin with shared bathroom; ¥480–¥580 ($60–$72) double/twin with private bathroom; ¥880–¥2,000 ($110–$250) suite. AE, DC, MC, V. **Amenities:** 5 restau- rants; garden bar; gym; billiards room; business center; foreign exchange (forex). *In room:* A/C, TV, fridge.

Qǐ Wàng Lóu Bīnguǎ Once good enough for the Qiánlóng Emperor, and these days used by the Héběi provincial government to entertain Party luminaries, most of this hotel occupies early-18th-century courtyard buildings with recently renovated standard hotel interiors, standing inside the Mountain Resort but only accessible from outside. The old buildings have been outlined with fairy lights, but the hotel still has far more charm than most, and while it lacks the full facilities of the town's four-stars, this is a rare opportunity to stay in an ancient Chinese atmosphere (however modernized the fittings). It's popular with expats and some foreign tour groups, and is busy during Western holidays as well as Chinese ones. *Bì Fēng Dōng Lù Běi 1 (through the west wall of the Mountain Resort).* © *0314/202-4385.* Fax *0314/202-1904. 70 units, including 30 in a new building and 9 suites. ¥600 ($75) standard double in new wing; ¥400 ($50) some basement doubles; ¥450 ($56) triple; ¥500 ($62) room in the original buildings; up to ¥4,000 ($500) suite. AE, DC, MC, V.* **Amenities:** Restaurant; bar; gardens. *In room:* A/C, TV, fridge.

Qiányáng Dàjiǔdiàn This hotel consists of four modern buildings, opened in 1998, with standard Chinese four-star fittings pleasantly arranged around pools and gardens and connected by passageways as if they all wish they were something far older and more traditional. *Pǔlè Lù 18 (a few min.*

north up the east side of the Wǔliè River, on the way to Pǔlè Sì). ⓒ *0314/ 205-7188. Fax 0314/205-7777. 96 units, including 10 suites. ¥480–¥680 ($60– $85) standard room; ¥1,480–¥2,000* ($185–$250) suite. AE, DC, MC, V. **Amenities:** 2 restaurants (Chinese and Western); swimming pool; fitness center; sauna; billiards room; forex. In room: A/C, TV, fridge.

WHERE TO DINE

As befits a former hunting ground, Chéngdé's specialty is game. The town is almost like a remote outpost of Guǎngdōng, of whose residents other Chinese say, "They eat anything with legs except a table, and anything with wings except an airplane." This is one of the few times when you might inadvertently order something you really don't want to eat: donkey (actually rather good), dog, and scorpion are on menus. But so are deer, "mountain chicken" (*shān jī*—pheasant), and wild boar—often as unfamiliar ingredients cooked in familiar styles. Venison tends to become a tough chew in response to stir-frying, but wild boar softens up nicely, while retaining its gamy flavor. The best restaurants are in the larger hotels such as the Qiányáng Dàjiǔdiàn: Try *lù ròu chǎo zhēnmó* (venison stir-fried with hazel mushrooms) or *què cháo shān jī piàn* ("sparrow's nest" pheasant slices).

Outside the hotel restaurants, the **Xīn Qiánlóng Dàjiǔdiàn** at Zhōng Xǐng Lù 2, ⓒ **0314/207-6768,** open from 10am to 2:30pm and 4:30 to 9:30pm, has attentive service, good portions, and both rough English translations and pictures in its menu. Plump *jiǎozi* (dumplings) stuffed with game are called *Qiánlóng shuǐjiǎo,* and cost ¥30 ($3.75) a half-kilo, or about ¥3 (40¢) for six. *Cōng shāo yězhū ròu* (wild boar cooked with onions) and *zhēn mó shān jī dǐng* (nuggets of pheasant with local mushrooms) are both good. As long as you don't venture into scorpion or roe deer backbone marrow, a meal is around ¥80 ($10) for two.

DÀTÓNG: HANGING MONASTERY

大同

D ÀTÓNG IS THE COAL FIELD OF China, a northern outpost on the Mongolian frontier that stood for centuries as the Middle Kingdom's barrier against the "barbarians." It is still something of a frontier town, rough-edged and lagging behind China's cities to the south and east, modern cities that Dàtóng still fuels with its coal. The name Dàtóng means "Grand Harmony" and refers to a Confucian concept—a legendary society where all creatures lived in perfect harmony. In modern Chinese, the two characters that make up the name mean "big" and "same." When faced with the vast sameness of this desert plateau scorched with coal pits and riddled with slow-moving coal trucks, the air a black sackcloth of dust, you can't help but think how much better suited the modern meanings are to present-day Dàtóng.

The great tourist attraction here is the **Yúngāng Grottoes,** carved into the nearby cliffs in the 5th century A.D., but Dàtóng has other historic treasures. The gray streets yield some of the largest temples in China, and the **Hanging Monastery** makes the forbidding countryside south of Dàtóng worth crossing. At times, Dàtóng was the supreme city in northern China, capital to dynasties that have all but turned to dust, save for a few monuments—monuments which are nonetheless spectacular.

Yúngāng Grottoes (Yúngāng Shíkū)

Just 16km (10 miles) west of downtown Dàtóng is the most spectacular array of ancient stone carvings, the Yúngāng Grottoes. Here, 40,000 workers and artists set to work on a sandstone cliff, beginning in A.D. 460 (Dàtóng was then capital of the Northern Wèi Dynasty—A.D. 386–534), chiseling out caves and sculpting huge Buddhist statues from stone on a scale not attempted previously. More than 51,000 statues remain at Yúngāng today, most of them completed by the time the rulers moved their capital south to Luòyáng, in A.D. 494, where they set about carving another major Buddhist grotto at Lóngmén, although the work at Yúngāng continued until A.D. 525.

The massive figures carved into the cliffs at Yúngāng are rounded, lively human images. Many have sharp noses and beards, features of Indian and Persian, rather than Chinese, origin. Many of the craftsmen came to Dàtóng from central Asia, crossing the Silk Road into northern China over the same route that Bud-

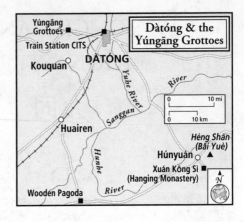

dhism itself traveled. The first caves, however, were finished under the direction of a brilliant local monk, who is credited with creating the most monumental images of Buddha and with initiating the earliest stone-carved caves in China. The Wén Chéng Emperor had appointed this monk, named Tán Yào, China's religious leader, and Tán Yào responded by ordering five statues carved in the cliffs representing the emperor's five predecessors, who had been regarded as living Buddhas. These five monuments are located today in the center of the Yúngāng Grottoes (Caves 16–20), barely changed after 15 centuries.

The Yúngāng Grottoes were built as an illustration of the Northern Wèi Dynasty's power and its dedication to Buddhism as the state religion. Confucians, who dominated the class of scholars and officials for nearly 1,500 years after the Yúngāng Grottoes were completed, sneered at the carvings as the height of folly, dismissing them as if the caves were a big comic book for the superstitious, due in part to the fact that the carvings were created by a non-Chinese dynasty (the "barbarian" Toba tribe from north of the Great Wall) and based on a foreign religion (Buddhism, from India). Thus, the sculptures at Dàtóng were ignored for centuries, not studied seriously until a scholar from Japan, Isoto Chuta, arrived in 1903. Western art dealers followed, crating up several dozen statues and the heads of nearly 700 Buddhas and their religious attendants for shipment to Europe, America, and Japan, where they still remain in various collections. Even so, most of the art is still in place at Yúngāng, which means "Cloud Hill."

While the caves face south, on the bluff above, earthen sections of the Great Wall, plow across the sands like ocean liners stranded in a desert. Centuries of wind-blown sand and dust have eroded the openings of the caves, once protected by wooden pavilions. Therefore, the statues inside are open to the elements and to the eyes of visitors. The 53 major caves cover a half mile of the weathered cliff face.

The Eastern Grottoes   I began my tour of Yúngāng along its eastern cliffs, to the right side of the main entrance. Local guides proved unnecessary: There are plenty of signs in English and even a large signpost with a bilingual map of Yúngāng. The first four caves (**Caves 1–4**), set apart from the rest by a ravine that slashes through the cliff, are not spectacular. **Cave 3,** however, is the largest at the site, 13m (43 ft.) high inside (the cliff looms to a height of 24m/80 ft. at this point). The Monastery of the Enchanted Cliff once stood inside, and Tán Yào himself taught Buddhism here. Three Buddhas remain in Cave 3. The central Buddha, seated, one hand raised to his chest, is 9m (30 ft.) tall. The carving of these statues may have occurred during the Suí Dynasty (A.D. 589–618), as an act of contrition by an emperor who murdered his father.

The Central Grottoes   Caves 5, 6, and 7 are more dramatic than the first four. The **Old Monastery of the Stone Buddhas,** built in 1652, is located here, and **three wooden towers** cover the cliffside, protecting the cave entrances. At one time, many temples fronted the cliff, but only this monastery remains. I wandered through its small courtyards, where monks and vendors had pitched their prayer bead and soda stands, and entered **Cave 5,** where a 17m (55-ft.) tall Buddha with red eyes, blue hair, and a gold face illuminates the shadows. (The image is arresting, even terrifying.) This, Yúngāng's largest Buddha—with ears 3m (10 ft.) long—was probably built to honor one of the Northern Wèi emperors. The bas-relief sculptures that decorate the walls of the cave are delicately carved, and their abundance is typical of the Yúngāng style.

Cave 6 is equally impressive. At the entrance, the Kāngxī Emperor, who visited in 1697, inscribed four characters meaning "the grand unity of all doctrines." Inside, there is a 15m (49-ft.) high square tower carved from rock in the center of the square chamber. The wall and the pillar are densely decorated in ornate carvings with stories from the life of Buddha, vividly rendered in deep relief. **Caves 7 and 8** form a pair that fuses Indian and Chinese art. The Indian gods Shiva, with five faces and six arms, and Vishnu, with three faces and eight arms, ride an eagle and a bull, popular figures from Hàn Dynasty Chinese sculpture. Shiva and Vishnu are also posted at the entrance to **Cave 8;** two carved lions lie contentedly at the foot of Buddha in **Cave 7.**

The remaining caves along the central wall (**Caves 9–15**) are richly adorned in a sea of fine bas-relief and statuary, all carved from stone and often painted in bright colors applied by a 19th-century donor. Hundreds of apsarases (voluptuous nymphs adopted from Hinduism) swirl up the cave walls and across the ceilings. Buddha's followers ride elephants and meditate atop lotus flowers in a universe of plants, animals, and flowing designs. **Cave 12** contains wall carvings of 5th-century palaces and a splendid mural of musicians accompanying Buddha on ancient flutes, drums, and lutes. The large Buddha sitting cross-legged in **Cave 13** has his right arm supported by a four-armed figure standing on his knee, an innovation in Chinese sculpture found first at Yúngāng. **Caves 14 and 15** are heavily eroded, their front walls crumbling over the centuries, but both retain thousands of carved figures in their niches.

The Western Grottoes The most striking caves are on the western side but near the center: **Caves 16 to 20,** the first five caves carved at Yúngāng, have large Buddhas inside commemorating the first five emperors of the Northern Wèi. These caves form a unified cluster. **Cave 16** on the right is filled with a 13m (43-ft.) high standing Buddha, one arm flung outward. The figure, with a heavy appearance, has a round face and deep-set eyes. The lower portions of his body have suffered severe erosion; he seems to be emerging from the dust. **Cave 17** contains an even more massive Buddha, 15m (50 ft.) tall, sitting with legs crossed, with a smaller attendant on either side. In **Cave 18,** the most impressive of the five Buddhas stands on a lotus flower, symbol of beauty flowering out of the muck that constitutes the earthly realm. His legs are short and massive, contributing to his aura of power. The folds of his robe are carved with processions of bodhisattvas (followers who have achieved enlightenment but have chosen to return to Earth to inspire others). The four bodhisattvas who attend the Buddha are the most fully humanized and lively figures at Yúngāng, where the monstrously divine and the merely human seem to meet in this shrine. **Cave 19** consists of three chambers. A 17m (55-ft.) tall Buddha sits in the middle, where surrounding walls, their niches filled with bodhisattvas, resemble the cells of a beehive. The caves to either side are elevated 5m (16 ft.) off the ground and open like enormous second-story windows to reveal the 8m (26-ft.) bodhisattvas inside.

The final cave on the west side of this cluster, **Cave 20,** is scarcely a cavern at all, since an earthquake removed the front of this cave. The Buddha sits exposed in a huge halo-shaped niche, his hands on his legs. This 11m (35-ft.) image has shoulders 6m (20 ft.) wide. He seems set in an immobile eternity, his huge drooping ears a symbol of the worldly decorations he has cast off. A student from Dàtóng, noticing me as I eyed the smiling statue, said this was the Buddha of the Present. On the right, he said, the Buddha of the Past stands against the surviving wall, one hand raised. On the left, there was no figure. The Buddha of the Future, the student said, has been erased. That would be fitting. The carved figures of Yúngāng reflect the glories of the past as resoundingly as any monument in China.

The caves at the far western end of the cliff are small and far less magnificent than those to the east. Many of them are badly eroded inside. **Cave 21** is the most impressive of the group. A tapered five-story pagoda stands in the center, its peak, a lotus flower, touching the ceiling. **Cave 50,** a hike up the end of the sandstone ridge, is worth a peek, too. Its walls are carved with acrobats and its ceiling with angels, birds, and flying elephants, making it a kind of stone Big Top.

Located just 16km (10 miles) west of Dàtóng, Yúngāng is open daily from 9am to 5pm. Admission is ¥25 ($3).

The no. 2 bus, with frequent departures from Dàtóng's northern train station, takes more than 30 minutes to cover this short distance, but costs just ¥8 (95¢). Taxis are quicker and cost about ¥20 ($2.40). CITS offers convenient guided tours. If you are going to be at the caves during lunch, you're best off packing food purchased ahead of time at the Yúngāng Hotel. There are no cafes at the cave sites, although Chinese snacks and drinks are sold at kiosks.

Temple of the Liáo

The remains of Dàtóng's imperial past can be discovered on foot. The streets are those of a city a decade behind the rest of urban China, just beginning to sprout glass-and-steel department stores and international hotel towers. The wide avenues carry bicycles and donkey carts instead of imported automobiles and motorcycles. No lawns, few fountains, no sumptuous greenery under blue skies—this is a hard city of a million workers toiling in the basin of a sea of coal.

It's hard to believe that Dàtóng once housed the royal palaces of the Northern Wèi Dynasty, from A.D. 398 to 493. The Northern Wèi were barbarians, Toba people from the northern plains beyond the nearby Great Wall, thought to be of Turkic origin. They finally abandoned Dàtóng and moved their capital south to Luòyáng, but Dàtóng would become China's capital again. The Kingdom of the Liáo (A.D. 907–1125), consisting of nomadic Khitan people, ruled China until they were overrun here by yet another band of northern invaders, the Jīn, ancestors of the Manchu, who would one day create China's last imperial dynasty. Out of this chaos of invading northern kingdoms, one great temple has survived in Dàtóng: the Huáyán Monastery, ancestral temple of the Liáo kings.

Huáyán Monastery is west of the old drum tower along Dà Xījiē in downtown Dàtóng. Several of its halls date from before A.D. 1100, but the complex was finished under the Jīn Dynasty 40 years later. Every hall and pavilion faces east, not south as in traditional Chinese constructions—a reflection of the sun-worshipping traditions of the Khitan conquerors.

If you walk through the heart of Huáyán's halls, you'll reach the main building, one of the two largest Buddhist temples in China, the **Powerful Treasure Hall (Dà Xióng Bǎo Diàn).** Set on a platform of stone 4m (14 ft.) high, it shatters the horizon. Its walls are 1m (3 ft.) thick. The courtyard contains strange altars on pedestals in the shape of dollhouses. These are used to hold scriptures. Inside, the hall is dark, cool, and spacious. Its centerpiece is the **Five Buddhas of the Five Directions,** some fashioned from wood, some from clay, and all occupying high thrones. They were made during the Míng Dynasty. The ceilings of the great temple are embellished with dragons, flowers, and the Sanskrit alphabet. When I was here, shaven monks in yellow leggings, brown pants, and gray gowns were pacing the courtyards and crossing through the moon gates. Some were old, some very young.

It is a remarkable temple, quiet and unassuming, but it survives on a scale rare in modern China. During the Liáo and Jīn dynasties, Huáyán was the central temple of its own school of Buddhism (later known as Kegon Buddhism in Japan). Huáyán Buddhism, based on the Garland Sutra, upholds the essential sameness of all things. In keeping with this doctrine, the temple in Dàtóng takes austerity to a high level.

After my visit to the temple, I returned to the streets of Dàtóng, where I overtook handcarts of coal pucks on their way to makeshift sidewalk ovens consisting of loose bricks. Lucky toddlers were racing around Post Office Square on electric-powered miniature army jeeps and jet fighters, their grandparents running behind them to catch up. The dust was whipping up, and although the sun was shining hot and hard, I felt as if I were moving through a dirty snowstorm.

I next passed by the wooden gate to the **Nine Dragon Screen (Jiǔ Lóng Bì),** the city's most famous sight—a ceramic mural 45m (150 ft.) long portraying nine dragons rising from the sea in pursuit of the sun. It was created in A.D. 1392 as the spirit wall for the mansion of the provincial viceroy, Zhū Guì, 13th son of the first Míng emperor, but its setting doesn't suit it (it's in a vacant unkempt lot).

I turned east down an odorous back street and came out at the entrance to the old city wall. The **Dàtóng city wall** is as old as the famous city wall of Xī'ān. A general of the early Míng empire oversaw its construction, of stamped yellow earth, in A.D. 1372. Much of the 6km (4-mile) circumference remains, though most of it is neglected, exposed, and subject to erosion. Here, renovation is under way. New stairs lead to the top of a section of the wall that has been freshly bricked in. Sections that haven't been bricked in are often used by locals as storage cellars, earthen caves dug into the walls of the city.

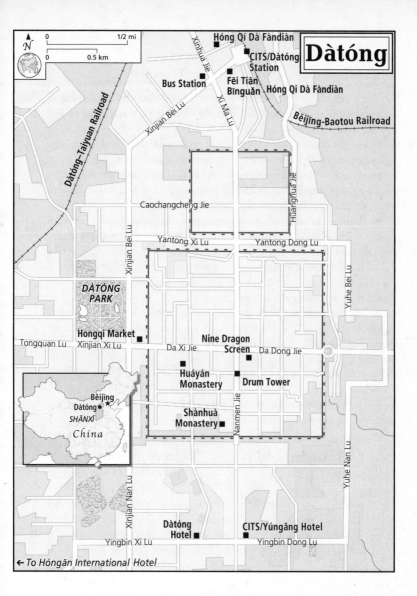

0   1/2 mi

0   0.5 km

N

Hóng Qí Dà Fàndiàn

Xinhua Jie

CITS/Dàtóng Station

Bus Station

Fēi Tiān Bīnguǎn

Hóng Qi Dà Fàndiàn

Xi Ma Lu

Xinjian Bei Lu

Bĕijīng-Baotou Railroad

Dàtóng-Taiyuan Railroad

Caochangcheng Jie

Huanghua Jie

Yantong Xi Lu

Yantong Dong Lu

Xinjian Bei Lu

Yuhe Bei Lu

DÀTÓNG PARK

Hongqi Market

Tongquan Lu

Xinjian Xi Lu

Da Xi Jie

Nine Dragon Screen

Da Dong Jie

Huáyán Monastery

Drum Tower

Bĕijīng

Dàtóng

SHĀNXĪ

China

Shànhuà Monastery

Nanmen Jie

Xinjian Nan Lu

Yuhe Nan Lu

Dàtóng Hotel

Yingbin Xi Lu

CITS/Yúngǎng Hotel

Yingbin Dong Lu

← To Hóngān International Hotel

On the wall is a newly restored eight-sided, seven-story, brown-brick pagoda, **Yán Tower.** Suspended from its eaves are golden bells with velvety clappers. Here I inadvertently flushed out a pair of Chinese lovers in a secret embrace. All of us were embarrassed. We smiled and left in different directions.

The brick soon runs out, and the wall reverts to packed earth. On the southeast corner of old Dàtóng, broken ramparts of a guard tower survive, its archways collapsing. South of the city wall is a uniform housing development a half-mile wide and 15 blocks deep. Each gray-tiled rooftop is punctuated by a half-dozen regularly spaced smokestacks. Touches of life slop over the edges. The rooftops are littered with laundry, logs, sticks of firewood, rolls of sheet metal, tool handles, oil drums, baskets, and a few cats patrolling for rats or scraps.

Back in the hotel, I met a young clerk who spoke excellent English. She had just graduated from Běijīng's top university with a degree in international business, but rather than follow her classmates to the money-cities on the eastern seaboard, she obeyed her parents. They wanted her close to home, in Dàtóng. This is still the traditional way.

She didn't seem to mind. When she spoke of Dàtóng and its future in China, she beamed. She pointed out that uptown there's some new development now: big modern department stores, a Crocodile boutique, a California Beef Noodle outlet. She laughed when I asked her what locals call the tiny, gleaming red, two-cylinder taxis with long snouts that dart hither and yon through the streets. Rats, she said. What do people like to eat in Dàtóng? I asked. Dog meat is extremely popular, she said, but quite expensive at ¥20 ($2.50) per kilogram in the street stalls. She was looking forward to a special graduation dinner of the same at a friend's house. She revealed the secret to cooking dog: Boil it in a pot, she said, but don't forget to throw in one new brick.

She also suggested that I book a tour to the Hanging Monastery and see something of how the people live in the countryside. Many of them, she said, still live in caves.

Hanging Monastery (Xuán Kōng Sì)

The next morning, I met our group: taxi driver, guide, and two Austrian geologists who have been working in Xī'ān. We traveled for 2 hours over the barren rolling hills south of Dàtóng, a plateau of sandstone, coal, and soda ash, a desert shaved down to a stubble. Villages sprout like oases, built of the same dried earth on which they squat. The two vacationing geologists were not impressed with the "Big Sameness" of the landscape.

Sixty twisting, bumpy kilometers (40 miles) later we reached the town of Húnyuán, where concrete and brick replace mud and straw. Ahead is Héng Shān, a high ridge of limestone, parted by the Mouth of the Dragon, the opening in the **Magnet Gorge.** This gorge was bored out in A.D. 397 by a Wèi Dynasty emperor and his 10,000 troops to ease passage through the mountains. On its west wall is **Xuán Kōng Sì,** the Hanging Monastery. It was constructed in the 6th century by a team of Daoist monks known as the Feathered Scholars because to reach the heights of the temple fastened to the immense cliff face must have required wings.

The suspended temple is spectacular from a distance. It consists of 40 cave rooms carved into limestone, fronted with wooden facades, columns, and tiled roofs, all connected by a series of catwalks and bridges perched on jutting beams and posts socketed into solid rock. A mountain gazetteer describes the Hanging Monastery this way: "The Air-Temple is very steep to come up to, without steps. The Temple Tied Up in Emptiness hangs alone in the Gorge of Porcelain and gets scarcely any sunlight. It contains many shrines and is the abode of ox-riding, sword-bearing immortals. Looking over the side, the scene is like a great ocean; only birds can fly over or monkeys climb out."

These days, of course, visitors come to climb up to the temple. There are concrete steps to its entrance, there's a tollbooth, and the way along the river in the gorge is lined with souvenir stands selling polished rocks and charms. The temple retains much the same form it possessed for centuries, and though some of the buildings have been renovated, the wooden catwalks and stairways still appear dilapidated and dangerous. Each small cave hall is festooned with a sacred figure or two, most of them fashioned from plaster and brightly painted. The central altar features a shrine to three religions, with statues of Buddha, Lǎozǐ, and Confucius in a black beard.

The temple has been rebuilt many times over 14 centuries, but the triple-storied main sections of the temple are still pinioned to the rock with simple timbers. Though a new parking lot and suspension bridge have been completed in the last few years, the catwalks of the temple still creak as you walk from shrine to shrine. Above, I could make out evidence of earlier cave altars and footholds. In earlier times, I suspected, the Hanging Monastery sprawled elsewhere, or perhaps hermits pulled up their ladders there as they entered their own cliff-side nests.

Today there was only one monk in attendance, but I did spot the same vendor I saw years ago, wearing a green Máo cap and pacing at the entrance, an eagle perched on his shoulder. The eagle is for hire (¥5/60¢) if you want a snapshot.

The Hanging Monastery is dwarfed by a modern shrine of sorts, a dam and reservoir suspended higher yet at the end of the gorge and hidden from view. But the temple remains as startling as ever, a fairy castle of yellow tiles and red wooden columns pinned impossibly to a face of rock.

Cave Houses & Coal

We headed back on the long winding road to Dàtóng, stopping on the shoulder to visit one of the cave houses dug out of the steep earthen bluffs. The whole family came out to greet us: grandpa, mom and pop, a toddler dressed in a red embroidered suit and plastic orange thongs. The patriarch was burnt black by the sun. His few remaining teeth were sharp and yellowed. He has occupied the house "only 50 years," he said. The inside of the cave consisted of two large curving earthen chambers tamped smooth. The entry room was used for storage. The second room, the family's living quarters, was lighted by a single bare electric bulb and a six-paned glass window and contained a small coal-burning stove in one corner and no running water. Niches had been scraped out of the walls to shelve shoes and clothing and sturdy wicker baskets of empty green bottles awaiting refunds. The walls were decorated with garish posters of pop stars and teen idols; with scrolls, calendars, liquor bottles, and packages of cookies; with bags of rice and bowls of fruit set on a wooden altar under a mirror. Under the window was a kàng, a wide communal bed built of mud and brick, covered by a rattan mat and heated underneath by coal fire.

This cave house was a neat, homey, warm, cheerful abode. Many are 2 centuries old. Outside, even the family dog had a matching mud dog-house, its own semidetached cave. The earthen walls were smooth but flaked at my touch. The toddler was selling tiny cloth horses his mother had stuffed and stitched together. I bought two ornaments for a Christmas tree.

The fields are mean here, their plowed furrows dry. The villages are clusters of hand-shaped earth. Ancient earthen signal towers, left over from the Western Wèi Dynasty, loom like massive shanks. The camel caravans that might have passed this way have been replaced by ranks of 60-ton double-trailered coal trucks, some of them produced by Steyr, an Austrian joint-venture corporation. All these trucks are as slow as dinosaurs after a feast, limping up the hills at no more than 8km per hour (5 mph). The drivers wear leafy branches around their necks. Whenever they have to stop on the road—breakdowns are frequent—they hang branches from the back and front of their trucks as a warning. Our guide told us that recently a truck accident caused a traffic logjam that went on for miles and took 2 days to free up.

As we approached Dàtóng, we saw coal stations, fields with brick shacks where the trucks stop and unload. The coal is sized by hand and restacked. Oxen and donkeys hitched to wooden plows clear rocks from the fields. Nomads on horseback sweep across the valleys between sandstone buttes. The north is a hard region and Dàtóng is a hard city, racked by wind, its air scratchy with coal dust and desert silt, which makes the survival of its imperial temples all the more precious.

PRACTICAL INFORMATION

by Michelle Sans

ORIENTATION

Dàtóng is located between two sections of the Great Wall on a 1,200m (4,000-ft.) plain in northern Shānxī Province, 322km (200 miles) west of Běijīng. Two sights make Dàtóng worth a visit. One is the ancient Buddhist grottoes carved at Yúngāng, 16km (10 miles) west of the city; the other—an hour-and-a-half drive south—is the Hanging Monastery.

Although the city is spread out, it can be toured on foot because the few tourist sights are in a fairly compact area south of Dàxī and Dàdōng Jiē.

Dàtóng is also the gateway to one of the Five Sacred Mountains of China, the northern Daoist peak of Héng Shān, a 2-hour drive south of the city. See the separate chapter on Héng Shān (p. 500) for more information on that mountain.

GETTING THERE

Dàtóng's **airport** is scheduled for completion in 2003, with flights to Shànghǎi, Guǎngzhōu, and Chéngdū. A new expressway between Běijīng and Dàtóng was completed in October 2002, reducing the **bus** trip to 3 or 4 hours. The plan is for Běijīng-bound Volvo and Xīběi large deluxe buses to depart from a new station in the south part of the city. The express **train** to Běijīng is a pleasant 7-hour journey. A convenient way to go from Běijīng to Dàtóng is the overnight train, leaving Běijīng at 10:58pm and arriving in Dàtóng at 7:15am the next morning. Sleepers cost ¥91 to ¥170 ($11–$21). If time is limited, it's possible to take a CITS tour of both Yúngāng and Xuánkōng Monastery during the day and be back in Dàtóng in time for dinner and a quick sweep of the city before taking the overnight train back to Běijīng (leaves Dàtóng at 11:45pm; arrives Běijīng next day at 6:20am).

TOURS & STRATAGEMS

China International Travel Service (CITS) has offices in the Yúngāng Hotel (✆ **0352/502-4176**) and at the train station (✆ 0352/510-1326; fax 0352/510-2046). The train station office, managed by Mr. Gāo Jīnwǔ, is much more helpful and efficient. From there, day tours are easily arranged, train tickets booked, and hotel reservations secured. If a CITS employee does not intercept you at the train station, go into the main entrance and turn left; the office is labeled in English.

For ¥100 ($12) per person, CITS offers a guided tour (with minivan and driver; minimum five people) that includes both the Hanging Monastery and the Yúngāng Grottoes, an excellent value; for ¥210 ($26), lunch and two admissions are included. "Panda Bus Tours" for groups are also available from CITS to the Hanging Monastery and the Wooden Pagoda in Yīngxiàn for the same price. According to CITS's Mr. Gāo, the Dàtóng Locomotive Factory, which used to be open to visitors, has closed, but a showplace is in the works. All tours leave the Yúngāng Hotel at 8:30am, the train station at 9am.

WHERE TO STAY

CITS agents are likely to meet you as you come out of the Dàtóng train station. They can book you a hotel on the spot, but you'll get a better discount if you shop around and do the negotiating yourself. Their economy choices are the 11-story **Fēi Tiān Bīnguǎn** at the south side of the rail station, with doubles costing ¥130 ($16) or, in the same price range, the **Hóng Qí Dà Fàndiàn**, across from the station. This part of town is particularly drab and dingy, and neither of these hotels has charm, but for those who only wish to visit Yúngāng and Xuánkōng, they have the advantage of being near the train station and are relatively inexpensive.

Yíngbīn Lù, south of the city center, has three commendable hotels: the Hóngān Guójì Jiǔdiàn, the Yúngāng Bīnguǎn, and the attractive Dàtóng Bīnguǎn. The Yúngāng used to be the best hotel in town, but the Hóngān and Dàtóng hotels now surpass it.

Dàtóng Hotel (Dàtóng Bīnguǎn) With its manicured gardens and tasteful architecture, this is by far the most attractive of Dàtóng's hotels, which isn't saying much, really, but service is good, rooms are clean and comfortable, and the price is reasonable.

37 Yíngbīn Xī Lù. ✆ *0352/203-2476.* Fax *0352/203-2288. 221 units. ¥456 ($56) double. AE, DC, MC, V.*

Hóngān International Hotel (Hóngān Guójì Jiǔdiàn) Although another uninspired mid-range hotel, this one still offers most of the services expected of an international hotel at a reasonable price.

28 Yíngbīn Hóng'ān. ✆ *0352/210-6655. Fax 0352/210-6665. 98 units. ¥432 ($54) double. AE, DC, MC, V.*

Yúngāng Hotel (Yúngāng Bīnguǎn) This recently renovated three-star hotel has a good location, modest but modern facilities, and a few extra services. It's not a luxury hotel—there's no pool or turndown service—but the rooms and bathrooms are Western style and the TV receives some satellite stations.

21 Yíngbīn Dōng Lù. ✆ *0352/502-1601. Fax 0352/502-4927. 240 units. From ¥400 ($50) double. MC, V.* **Amenities:** 2 restaurants; small lobby bar; business center. *In room:* TV.

WHERE TO DINE

One of the best restaurants near the hotels is **Yúngāng Fēngwèi Miànshí Guǎn**, on the south side of Yíngbīn Xī Lù, across from the Yúngāng Hotel. It's a comfortable little cafe run by a helpful young staff. Main courses cost ¥25 to ¥42 ($3–$5). The big **Hóngqí Restaurant** next door is more formal and twice as expensive, but the food is also quite good.

The **Yúngāng Hotel** and the **Dàtóng Hotel** are the best places to go for a Western breakfast. The Chinese restaurant on the first floor of the Yúngāng Hotel serves delicious *jiǎozi* (dumplings; 12 per serving) for ¥2.50 (30¢). For vegetarian *jiǎozi*, order a half hour ahead.

HARBIN: TIGERS & ICE
哈尔滨

ARBIN, CAPITAL OF HĒILÓNGJIĀNG (Black Dragon River), China's most northerly province, is best known these days for the **Harbin Ice and Snow Festival,** a world-famous ice sculpture display held annually each winter. I visited Harbin (Hā'ěrbīn) in late March, however, after the ice had melted, primarily to see Harbin's newest attraction, its **Siberian Tiger Park,** where 30 of these endangered animals were freely roaming and being trained for eventual release into the wild.

Harbin is a fascinating city even without its tigers and ice. It's located on the endless Manchurian plains, known for vast forests, among the largest left in the Far East. The province borders the former Soviet Union, with the Black Dragon River (better known by its Russian name, the Amur) serving as the northeastern dividing line between China and Siberia. Harbin was built by Czarist Russia, occupied by Japanese forces in 1932, seized by the Soviet Army in 1945, and, finally, taken by the Chinese with the establishment of the People's Republic of China in 1949.

Old Town (Dàolǐ Qū)

The Russian influence is still strong in Harbin, especially in the city's unusual architecture. Onion domes outnumber upturned tile-roofed eaves along Harbin's main street, giving Harbin a cityscape unique among China's major cities. Walking down Zhōngyāng Dàjiē to the Sōnghuā River in the old town, **Dàolǐ District,** a mile's stroll from the Holiday Inn, I passed dozens of these old buildings, with their spires and cupolas, now converted to offices, restaurants, and department stores. The street is made of cobblestones. Several of the side streets were devoted to pedestrian-only outdoor markets at the time of my visit. The largest market was on the street labeled **Xī Shíyī (11) Dàjiē,** unmistakable because of its crowds and the large Russian-style turrets at its entrance.

A number of the Russian facades on Zhōngyāng Dàjiē are being removed, but their modern replacements are tasteful European-style buildings, much in keeping with the old-town atmosphere. One old building worth taking a peek inside is the ironically named **Modern Hotel,** at

Zhōngyāng Dàjiē 89, a Russian-style building opened in 1913 whose lobby had just been colorfully, if a little shabbily, restored at the time of my visit.

On my slow walk down this street in the Chinese city once called "Little Moscow," I also came across a more modern trend: Western commercialization. Amid onion towers, cupolas, and painted plaster columns were a KFC (complete with a white statue of the Colonel), a Playboy logo store, and Bossini and Crocodile boutiques. These signs of Western encroachment are eating into the heart of most Chinese cities, so I was not entirely surprised to find them here—even in this northern outpost.

The leading foreign presence in Harbin remains Russian, however, as it has since Russians began building a train line from Kaidalovo in the Transbaikal through Harbin to Vladivostok in 1897. Later, in 1917, White Russians fleeing the Communist Revolution arrived in Harbin by the thousands, settling in and erecting scores of Russian-style buildings and churches. During the 1930s, half of the 200,000 residents of Harbin were Russian. Although most of them left after China's own Communist Revolution in 1949, Harbin is still a major trading post for consumer goods bound for the north. Most of the Russians come to Harbin on business, not for sightseeing, hoping to pick up items that are scarce enough in Siberia to command high prices. Some Russians trade Siberian goods, such as furs, straight across, with no cash exchanged. Harbin is a center of the fur trade, and there are plenty of coat, hat, and stole outlets along the main street, although these are outnumbered by Western wedding salons featuring photo studios and wedding-gown rentals.

Parks & Temples

Harbin has attractions apart from its old town. **Zhàolín Park (Zhàolín Gōngyuán),** where the ice festival is held, is just a long block east of the main street, on Shàngzhì Dàjiē; and even though the ice sculptures had melted into giant ice cubes by late March, it was worth trooping through the spacious grounds, with their gardens and rock formations.

The splendid, redbrick **Church of Saint Sophia (Shèng Suǒfēiyà Jiàotáng),** at the intersection of Tòulóng Jiē and Zhàolín Jiē (admission ¥20/$2.50), no longer hosts religious services in Russian; it now serves as the Harbin Architecture Arts Center. I found it jammed into an area of new construction, most notably several karaoke entertainment complexes with monumental Roman statuary mounted on their garish facades.

Harbin's **Confucian Temple (Wén Miào),** next to Harbin Engineering University (Hā'ěrbīn Gōngchéng Dàxué) in Nángǎng District, is worth browsing through (admission ¥15/$2). The grounds are large, with a dozen pavilions. Golden dragons emblazon the roofs. Although this complex was not built until 1926, I found stelae (stone tablets) dated A.D. 551 and

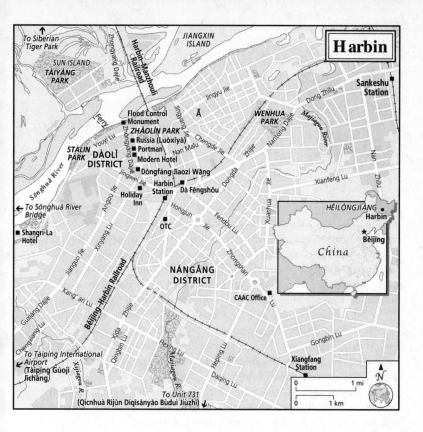

A.D. 587, as well as three ornate triple-footed gates and one yurt (whose purpose I could not determine).

A more interesting complex, the **Temple of Bliss (Jílè Sì),** admission ¥10 ($1.20), is situated at Dōng Dàzhí Jiē. It contains a small statue of the bodhisattva Pǔxián on an elephant, along with the familiar likenesses of Maitreya, Sakyamuni (the present Buddha), and Guānyīn. A fair number of monks inhabit this temple, which is in the shadow of the Qījí Fútú pagoda. Although built recently, in 1924, this is the largest temple in the entire province. The street outside is one of the liveliest in town, filled with stalls selling golden Buddhas and glass shrines to the faithful.

War Crimes

One afternoon, I got up my courage, hired a taxi, and paid a call on the Former site of **Unit 731 (Qīnhuá Rìjūn Qī Sān Yāo Bùduì Jiùzhǐ),** a war crimes exhibit opened in 1982 at the site of a secret germ warfare research center 19km (12 miles) south of Harbin. Here, starting in 1939, the Japanese performed unimaginably horrible experiments on citizens (employing frostbite, bomb explosions, biological agents, and surgical procedures), comparable to those conducted in Nazi Germany's concentration camps. Its existence was covered up until the 1980s.

The exhibit, mercifully, is not so horrifying as the crimes. At the time of my visit, it consisted mainly of a few artifacts from the Manchurian occupation, telltale documents, an incinerator smokestack, and a re-creation of a gruesome operation using life-sized wax figures. The wax figures were removed in a renovation of the facility in 2001.

Sōnghuā River

It was a relief after a detour through the horrors of the past to return to the cobblestone main street of Harbin and resume my pleasant stroll down to the swift-flowing Sōnghuā River. A 42km (26-mile) embankment was constructed along the river after the floods of 1932, and a spacious promenade, now lined with trees and statuary, was developed on the shore. The promenade retains its original name: **Stalin Park (Sīdàlín Gōngyuán).**

The most prominent statue is the **Flood Control Monument,** built the year after one of Harbin's most notable floods, which covered the downtown streets in up to 3m (9 ft.) of water. The monument is now a popular gathering point for visitors and locals. Vendors circle the monument, selling hot pine nuts and kites in the shape of birds.

Like Zhōngyāng Dàjiē, the Stalin Park **promenade** is a prime location for a leisurely stroll, fronting the river for miles. In the summer, scores of tour boats of every possible description take passengers out on the river or across to **Sun Island (Tàiyáng Dǎo).** Fishermen also beach their open boats on the sandy banks, and ice-cream vendors ply their trade along the walkway—it's quite a festive spot when the sun is shining and sailboats are for rent. In the deep of winter, the river freezes solid—often remaining so for half the year—and ice-skating is popular. This is also the place for winter swimmers to take the plunge. Thirty swimmers braved the icy river in 1982, when this ritual began, and, nowadays, as many as 300 brave the water each winter, plunging into a special 18m (60-ft.) long lane carved out of the ice.

Tigers of Siberia

The **Siberian Tiger Park (Dōngběi Hǔ Línyuán)** (daily May–Sept 8am–6pm, Oct–Apr 8:30am–4pm; admission ¥50/$6.25) is located across the Sōnghuā River from Harbin proper on the northeast corner of Sun Island, where a large recreational district has been developed. I hired a car at the Holiday Inn to reach Sun Island via a bridge in the northwest part of town. The Siberian Tiger Park had plans to expand into a large preserve, with areas for deer, bears, and swans, as well as shops, a fishing pond, a restaurant, and a fairy-tale theme village. But when I visited, only a museum and a large fenced tiger reserve had been finished. The museum was a dark, uninspiring cavern of a building with photographic displays (captions were in Chinese), a motley stuffed tiger with its kittens, and an informational film about the tigers projected on a screen through a very dirty lens.

Visitors board a variety of vehicles for an extended drive through the tiger reserve. I was placed on an old bus with sliding windows, filled with Russian teenagers on spring vacation. There was no guide on the bus and no effort was made to keep us from sliding open the unbarred windows during the tour, but there were numerous tigers stalking the grounds. We had plenty of close encounters. At one point, a caged jeep appeared and the gamekeeper placed a live chicken on the roof. A tiger promptly leaped on top and pounced on its prey. All the tigers, including some cubs, looked healthy and seemed at ease on the sandy reserve. The Siberian Tiger Park's mission is to save, study, and breed these great cats in captivity and eventually release them into their native habitat. In order to complete this mission, the tigers must be trained to hunt live prey. I should not have been surprised, therefore, when I learned that a few weeks earlier, the Holiday Inn had donated a live cow to the park. Hotel employees were invited out that day and bussed into the reserve to watch the tigers tackle and devour the poor creature, a spectacle not likely to be offered to visitors at Western zoos!

But then, Harbin is not like most places in the West—indeed, not much like most places in China.

The Far North

Having reached the northern edge of the Middle Kingdom at Harbin, I was struck by the variety of culture and landscape that China encompasses. Returning to the airport, I passed a dozen magazine-cover photo opportunities: a plethora of donkey and horse carts driven by dark-faced peasants in floppy-eared hats, crude vegetable markets on the roadsides, piles of straw heaped high by hand in the flat fields, cold rivers running swiftly through avenues of wiry trees, and, incongruously, clusters of Chinese theme parks awaiting summer visitors with their Disneyesque, Sino-Rococo, Magic Middle-Kingdom turrets and spires.

These were amusements seemingly at odds with the harsh climate and country life of the Black Dragon province—this once distant Manchuria of tigers and ice.

PRACTICAL INFORMATION

by Josh Chin

ORIENTATION & WHEN TO GO

Harbin is the northernmost city of any size in China, roughly 1,385km (860 miles) northwest of Běijīng and 129km (80 miles) south of the Russian border. The city's layout, like its history, revolves around the railroad. Nearly everything of interest falls in one of two old districts—Dàolǐ and Nángǎng—divided by the tracks that run past the main train station. The mighty Sōnghuā Jiāng (Sungari River) forms the city's northern border. The ideal time to visit Harbin is between January and March, when locals take advantage of subzero temperatures to construct impressive sculptures and palaces of frozen water for the **Ice and Snow Festival.** Harbin can be pleasant in summer, too, as milder weather allows for more leisurely investigation of the old Russian architecture. If you decide to travel to Harbin in winter, be sure to bring several layers of clothing, warm gloves, a hat, a scarf, and anything else you can think of to ward off the cold.

GETTING THERE

By Plane Daily flights from both Běijīng (¥830/$104) and Shànghǎi (¥1,520/$190) land at the **Tàipíng International Airport (Tàipíng Guójì Jīchǎng),** 30km (19 miles) south of central Harbin. Airport shuttles to the train station (1 hr.; ¥20/$2.50) leave from the domestic arrivals area every 30 minutes from 6am to 6pm. Taxis (¥60/$7.50) take between 40 minutes and 1 hour, depending on traffic. Make sure your driver uses the meter; otherwise, you risk a severe markup.

By Train Overnight express trains from Běijīng (four per day; ¥290/$36) typically take 13 hours and arrive very early in the morning. It takes only a few minutes to get from the **train station (Hā Zhàn**—short for Hā'ěrbīn Zhàn, which no one can be bothered to say) to the Dàolǐ District by taxi (¥10/$1.25).

TOURS & STRATAGEMS

Tours Harbin's most helpful travel service is the **Hēilóngjiāng Overseas Tourist Company (Hēilóngjiāng Hǎiwài Lǚyóu Gōngsī;** ☎ **0451/366-1159;** fax 0451/362–1088), with offices on the 11th floor of the towering Hùshì Dàshà at Tiělù Jiē 2, on the west side of the square in front of the train station. They offer city tours as well as birdwatching and steam-train treks in other areas of the province. Office staff and guides speak decent English.

WHERE TO STAY

Holiday Inn City Center Harbin (Hāěrbīn Wàndá Jiàrì Fàndiàn) The nicest hotel in Harbin when it opened in 1995, this four-star hotel has started to show signs of age but still offers comfortable rooms, competent service, and a convenient location at the bottom of Zhōngyāng Dàjiē. And even its competitors will admit it still serves the best food of any hotel in the city.
Jīngwěi Jiē 90 (at Zhōngyāng Dàjiē). ☎ *0451/422-6666.* Fax 0451/422-1663.

148 units. ¥880 ($110) double. AE, DC, MC, V. **Amenities:** Health club; sauna; business center; salon; room service (6am–midnight); next-day dry cleaning/laundry. *In room:* A/C, TV, minibar, safe.

Modern Hotel (Mǎdiē'ěr Bīnguǎn) This gorgeous Art Nouveau hotel, built in 1913 in the center of Harbin's Russian district, finally climbed from the ashes of Communist-era neglect with a charming restoration in 2001. Rooms are a bit dark but otherwise pleasant, with large beds and all new furniture. In its heyday, the elegant lobby was a favorite gathering place for pre-1949 luminaries such as Madame Sun Yat-sen (Sòng Qìnglíng) and American journalist Edgar Snow, author of the classic portrait of China's early communists, *Red Star Over China.*

Zhōngyāng Dàjiē 129 (Xī 8 Dàojiē). ℂ *0451/461-5846. Fax 0451/461-4997.*

131 units. ¥584 ($73) twin. AE, MC, V. **Amenities:** Indoor pool; health club (in neighboring building); business center; salon; next-day laundry. *In room:* A/C, TV, minibar.

Shangri-La Hotel Harbin (Hāěrbīn Xīānggélīlā Dàfàndiàn) This five-star hotel is far and away the most luxurious hotel in downtown Harbin. Rooms here are spacious and classy, with spotless carpets and impeccable bathrooms, and service is as good as it gets this far north.

555 Yǒuyì Lù (northwest of downtown, near Sōnghuā River Bridge). ℂ *0451/485-8888. Fax 0451/462-1777. 346 units. ¥1,088 ($136) twin. AE, DC, MC, V.* **Amenities:** Indoor pool; outdoor tennis courts; health club; concierge; business center; salon; 24-hr. room service; massage; same-day dry cleaning/laundry. *In room:* A/C, TV, minibar, safe.

WHERE TO DINE

Sample northeast China's famous and delectable boiled dumplings *(shuǐ jiǎo)* inside **Dōngfáng Jiǎozi Wǎng** (ℂ 0451/465–3920), at Zhōngyāng Dàjiē 39. A steaming plate of pork and cabbage dumplings, enough for two, costs ¥15 ($2); go early or late to avoid the lunch rush. For a taste of other regional dishes, try the mock-countryside **Big Harvest (Dà Fēngshōu;** ℂ 024/6202–2029), at Yīmǎn Jiē 283, north of the traffic circle near the railway bridge. Food here is served in the northeast tradition—simple, delicious, in immense portions—and customers drink beer out of bowls. Try the *jiācháng tǔdòuní,* a successful Chinese take on garlic mashed potatoes. Dinner for two costs ¥30 to ¥60 ($4–$8).

For hearty Western food with a slight Chinese twist, try **Portman**

(ℂ 0451/468–6888), a lively cross between pub and bistro (with an English menu) just north of the Modern Hotel at Xī 7 Dàojiē 63. All dishes, including the restaurant's signature ribs, are nicely presented and go well with a dark draft beer. Main courses cost ¥20 to ¥50 ($2.50–$6.25).

Just up the street at Xītóu Dàjiē 57, **Russia (Luòxīyà;** ℂ 0451/436-3207) is charm incarnate. A quiet cafe set inside one room of an old Russian house, it serves solid coffee and a range of simple Russian dishes—the perfect pause on your way up Zhōnyāng Dàjiē. An old piano stands in the corner, stacked with grainy photos and the scattered belongings of one of Harbin's original Russian families. Main courses cost ¥20 to ¥60 ($2.50–$8). They also have an English menu.

QĪNGDǍO: BEACHES & BEER
青岛

Qīngdǎo, a modern city on the Yellow Sea (Huáng Hǎi) in southeast Shāndōng Province, is China's fourth busiest shipping port, and the site of many foreign joint-ventures, especially factories financed by German and Korean corporations. It's also internationally famous for its Tsingtao beer, one of China's leading exports. Unfortunately, the great brewery, for some reason, is not open for public tours. Instead, Qīngdǎo lures Chinese visitors to its summertime beaches, some of the best in China. For foreign travelers, however, it is Qīngdǎo's legacy as a German concession that makes the city worth seeing. (A "concession" was a district of the city surrendered to foreign colonial control as a result of trade treaties China was compelled to sign following the Opium Wars of the 1840s.) Large sections of Qīngdǎo retain whole neighborhoods of turn-of-the-20th-century Western architecture, adjacent to traditional and modern Chinese development—a mixture that makes this hilly and green city on the coast an invigorating refuge from the noisy, polluted, often ugly modern metropolises. This presence of old Western residences and tree-lined avenues in Qīngdǎo are startling, surprising (there's no equivalent in the West: You don't see large neighborhoods of Chinese temples and tile-roofed shop houses in downtown London or New York), and, ultimately, compelling.

German Town

The greatest concentration of Qīngdǎo's German legacy is in the **Bādàguān District** on Tàipíng Bay near Beach Number 2. A sign in English on Zhèngyángguān Lù directs visitors south into lovely, quiet lanes, each planted with a different tree or flower. There's a maple lane, peach lane, and snow-pine lane, each fronted by Western mansions and landscaped lawns—the area closely resembles an upper-class neighborhood on Lake Geneva. The grand houses, with their spacious yards and gardens, also reminded me of those at Pebble Beach. A number of these old estates have become exclusive summer beach resorts for workers and party bosses of the government agencies and companies that now own them, while many of the houses are rented out as vacation villas. The Bādàguān Hotel, at Shānhǎiguān 19, began as a German hotel in 1903, was expanded by the

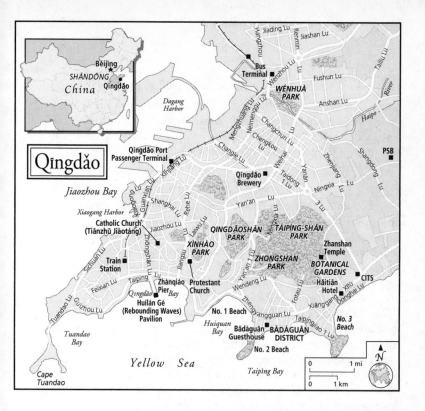

Spanish and Japanese in the 1920s, and became a Chinese hotel in 1953, though its main building dates only from 1988.

The largest structure in Bàdàguān is right on the coastline. This **palace (Huāshí Lóu),** an immense castlelike fortress of stone, was once the German governor's lodge. It's now open to visitors daily from 7am to 5pm (admission ¥5/60¢). Beneath its wall is a rugged beach.

Qīngdǎo's German influence began in 1897, when Kaiser Wilhelm annexed portions of the city and developed them as a railway terminus, deepwater port, and naval station. The brewery went up soon thereafter, in 1903. The Germans controlled Qīngdǎo until 1914, when it fell to the Japanese, and the Japanese occupied Qīngdǎo until 1922, when the Chinese regained it.

The Pier

From Bādàguān it's easy enough to walk down to the **Number 1 Beach,** Qīngdǎo's longest, with its strip of wooden beach houses and changing rooms. From there, I continued west along the white sands through **Lǔ Xùn Park** toward **Beach Number 6** (the beaches are not numbered in geographical order). This is the location of Qīngdǎo's harbor landmark, **Zhàn Qiáo Pier,** which extends 390m (1,300 ft.) into the bay to eight-sided **Returning Waves Pavilion (Huílán Gé).** Dating from 1891 and expanded in 1931, it remains the prime gathering point for locals, visitors, and a tidal wave of vendors hawking ice cream, shells, pearls, and photographs. The beachfront by the pier is rocky, and plenty of people comb those rocks for edible seafood and plants. Overlooking this beach is an esplanade that after dark becomes a lively strolling area for locals. Here, the pace of life is far more relaxed than in most Chinese cities.

Two Churches

Directly north of the pier is **Zhōngshān Lù,** Qīngdǎo's main street, which now rips through a rapidly modernizing downtown of new department stores, small boutiques, and a mixture of old and new shops, some selling designer-name fashions and Swiss watches. I stopped for lunch at one of the many hole-in-the-wall cafes and ordered the local hot pot, as well as clams, bite-sized octopuses, and a 6-inch-wide crab, even though the price was a bit steep; the crab alone was ¥35 ($4.20).

Back on the big avenue, I followed Zhōngshān Lù north until I could see the **Catholic church (Tiānzhǔ Jiàotáng),** located up a steep cobblestone lane, to the east (on Zhéjiāng Lù). This large stone edifice, with its two towering spires, was built by the Germans in the early 1930s. Still quite active with Chinese worshippers, it is also open to foreigners, who can attend mass here. The curious can take a look around Monday through Saturday from 8am to 5pm and on Sunday from 9am to 5pm for ¥5 (65¢). The surrounding streets are lined with German concession buildings, their black iron balconies draped in drying laundry.

East of city center, at Jiāngsū Lù 15, near the entrance to Xìnhào Park (Xìnhào Gōngyuán), is the **Protestant church (Jīdū Jiàotáng),** also built by the German community in the first decade of the 20th century. Look for its high clock tower, which still keeps time. Visitors can tour the interior Monday through Saturday from 8:30 to 11:30am and 1:30 to 4:30pm and on Sunday from 1:30 to 4:30pm (admission ¥3/35¢).

Both the Protestant and Catholic churches underwent extensive interior renovations in 1999. Most of their windows and statues are now new. Both the big churches come into splendid view, along with the red-roofed Western neighborhoods and white-sand harbor beaches, from the top of **Signal Hill Park (Xìnhào Shān Gōngyuán),** a steep trek up from the Protestant church. On the peak there are three domes in the shape of mushrooms, stuffed with vendors and panoramic viewpoints. The park is open daily from dawn to dusk and charges ¥2 (25¢) admission (park only) or ¥12 ($1.25) if you want to visit the mushroom-shaped observatory.

Máo Slept Here

The most curious treasure in Xìnhào Park, however, is down toward the harbor on its grassy flanks, where a magnificent residence was built for the

German governor in 1903. This **mansion,** located at Lóngshàn Lù 26, was converted into a hotel, the **Qīngdǎo Welcome Guest House (Qīngdǎo Yíng Bīnguǎn),** but today it stands primarily as a **museum** (open daily 8:30am–5pm, admission ¥10/$1.25) of the high life enjoyed by colonials during the days of the Qīngdǎo Concession. The stained glass, dark woods, and plush furnishings have survived, perhaps because Chairman Máo and Premier Zhōu Ēn-Lái met here in 1957, and Chairman Máo and his wife occupied one of the suites for a month. Today, it's a little musty, but you can still see Chairman Máo's green felt-top desk, which contains a hidden compartment in the right-hand drawer. The museum's lobby and dining rooms are the original living rooms and dining halls of the mansion, with carved woods, massive chandeliers, and velvet curtains still intact. A German grand piano, built in 1876, occupies one corner of this immense chamber.

A favorite park among locals is **Little Fish Park (Xiǎoyú Shān Gōngyuán),** admission ¥15 ($1.90), a short walk south of the mansion. The **three-story pagoda (Lánchǎo Gé)** on its peak is stocked with souvenir sellers and offers an unfettered view of Bādàguān to the east and the pier (see above for both) to the west. The pavilion, once used as a marine observation post, is a quiet place to survey this seaside city.

Sea Mountain

Next to Qīngdǎo's beaches, which swell with upward of 100,000 vacationers in the summer, the most popular outdoor attraction is **Mount Láo (Láo Shān),** about 40km (25 miles) directly east along the rocky coastline of the Yellow Sea. The highway to Láo Shān runs by one of Qīngdǎo's newest attractions, its **International Beer City,** which is seldom open except for Qīngdǎo's International Beer Festival. The festival runs for 2 weeks in the second half of August, when the grounds host one of the biggest beer gardens outside of Bavaria, supplemented by fireworks, beach volleyball, motorcycle races, sailing and swimming competitions, beer-drinking contests, and whatever else the local promoters can dream up.

The coastal highway is charming any time of year. Stonecutting is a big industry here, where granite dominates the landscape. The Láo mountains (admission ¥50/$6.25) rise abruptly to 900m (3,000 ft.) from the white-boulder shoreline. A trail of stone stairs leads to the peaks (or you can hitch a ride on the chairlift). The path is steep but quite scenic, with increasingly dazzling views down empty abysses to the tiny fishing villages below. Vendors here specialize in strings of **pearls,** the product of those fishing villages, with prices under ¥40 ($5), and you should see the price drop the higher you hike. Another popular trailside commodity is a package of three sea treasures: a dried turtle, a tiny "sea-dragon" eel, and a seahorse. Láo Shān mineral water, the most famous in China and the basic ingredient in Tsingtao beer, originates in the springs of the Láo mountains, where there were once 72 Daoist temples.

There are still a few temples in these mountains. In Daoist legends, this is the home of the Eight Immortals, who could fly with the clouds. Qín Shǐ Huáng, the first emperor of unified China, is reputed to have visited here more than 2,000 years ago in search of the elusive potion of immortality. His visit is commemorated in the sprawling **Tàiqīng Temple (Tàiqīng Gōng)**, a Sòng Dynasty complex spread across the cliffs on the eastern shore of the mountain range.

A Temple by the Sea

If you lack time to make a comprehensive trek of this vast sea mountain park, you can content yourself with a climb up to **Peach Peak** (along the chairlift line) and then a descent to the **Xiàqīnggōng Temple**, located on the southern beachfront. This complex, consisting of three temples and courtyards, was established in 14 B.C. and rebuilt during the Sòng Dynasty 900 years ago. The western temple, **Sānhuáng Hall (Sānhuáng Diàn)**, contains a copy inscribed in stone of Genghis Khan's edict of A.D. 1271 calling for the protection of Daoist culture. The courtyards are home to ancient cypress trees. There's also a statue of the ever-popular Guānyīn, Goddess of Mercy, who the locals tell me has the face of a woman but the body of a man. When I asked why, I was told that the goddess was really a man but took on the face of a woman to show a compassionate face to petitioners.

The seaside temple is surrounded by ancient specimens of elm and cypress trees, a bamboo field, cafes, shops selling sea turtle shells, and a parking lot. A few monks wander about, but I doubt this is a vigorous Daoist temple these days: It is overrun with Chinese visitors in the summer, and moneymaking has become a major religion.

I returned to the city and to the Bādàguān District for a farewell stroll one afternoon in the late spring, finding it the quietest neighborhood I'd ever encountered in China, a green island of parks, beaches, and architecture—if not an elixir of immortality, certainly an ingredient.

PRACTICAL INFORMATION

by Sharon Owyang

ORIENTATION & WHEN TO GO

Located in the southeast of Shāndōng Province on the Yellow Sea (Huáng Hǎi), 318km (197 miles) east of provincial capital Jǐnán, Qīngdǎo is one of China's most famous seaside resorts. It was occupied by the Germans from 1897 to 1914, a fact reflected in much of the city's architecture. With its year-round mild climate and perennial sunshine, Qīngdǎo hosts many fairs and festivals throughout the year, the most famous of which is the Qīngdǎo International Beer Festival, held annually during the last 2 weeks of August. This event now attracts upwards of a million visitors. Summers also see the town packed with

Chinese visitors, making spring and fall better times to visit if you're hoping to avoid the crowds. Tranquility, however, will be even more elusive in the coming years as Qīngdǎo gets ready to host the watersports events of the 2008 Summer Olympics. Check with CITS for other annual events.

GETTING THERE

By Plane Qīngdǎo is well connected by air to many Chinese cities, including Běijīng (1¼ hr.), Guǎngzhōu (2 hr., 45 min.), and Shànghǎi (70 min.). Tickets can be purchased at travel agencies, hotel tour desks, and the **CAAC office (Mínghǎng Dàshà)** at Xiānggǎng Zhōnglù 30 (© **0532/577-5555**). International destinations served include Hong Kong, Seoul, Fukuoka, Tokyo, Pusan, and Bangkok. **Dragonair** (© **0532/577-6110**) has an office at the Hotel Equatorial, Xiānggǎng Zhōnglù 28, as does **Japan Airlines** (© **0532/571-0088**). **Qīngdǎo's Liú Tíng Airport** (© **0532/484-2139**) is located 30km (19 miles) north of the city, a 40-minute taxi ride costing ¥80 to ¥100 ($10–$12). Airport shuttles (¥10/$1.25) depart every hour between 6am and 6pm from the CAAC office, and also meet incoming flights.

By Train Qīngdǎo is connected to Shāndōng's provincial capital Jǐnán and to cities farther afield by rail. There's an express overnight train from Běijīng (T25) that takes 10 hours, and a slow overnight train from Shànghǎi (2106) that takes 18½ hours. There are also many trains during the day that connect to Wéifāng, Tàishān, and Qūfù (see separate chapters). Tickets can be bought at hotel tour desks, at travel agencies, and at the **train station** (© **0532/296-2777**) at Tài'ān Lù 2 in the old city.

By Bus The long-distance bus station is in the northern part of town at Wēnzhōu Lù 7 (© **0532/383-3275**), but the bus station just outside the train station should serve most travelers' needs. Intra-province buses depart from the lot south of the train station for other Shāndōng Province destinations such as Wéifāng (2 hr., 40 min.) and Jǐnán (5 hr.), while long-distance sleeper buses depart from the front of the train station for destinations farther afield such as Shànghǎi (10½ hr., ¥180/$23, departing at 7pm) and Hángzhōu (14 hr., departing at 3:50pm). Daily tour buses to Láo Shān also depart from here.

By Ship There are ferries to Osaka in Japan (twice weekly) and Inch'ǒn in South Korea (four times a week). Tickets can be bought at the Qīngdǎo Port Passenger Terminal (Qīngdǎo Gǎng Kèyùnzhàn) at Xīnjiāng Lù 6 (© **0532/282-5001**).

GETTING AROUND

Downtown and the German Quarter can be toured on foot, but taxis and buses are more convenient for getting to some of the beaches and attractions farther afield. Taxis charge ¥7 (85¢) for the first 3km (2 miles), then ¥1.50 (18¢) per kilometer up to 8km (5 miles), when the price goes to ¥2.15 (26¢) per kilometer. Bus no. 26 runs from the train station along the southern edge of the peninsula toward the commercial district on Xiānggǎng Zhōnglù. Tourist buses to Láoshān (1 hr., ¥12/$1.50) depart from the eastern end of the train station square every half hour from 6:30am to 6pm. Public bus no. 304 also heads to Láoshān from the Ferry Terminal (Lúndù) on Sìchuān Lù.

TOURS & STRATAGEMS

The only way to visit the **Qīngdǎo Brewery** is to book a tour through a travel agency such as CITS, located at Xiānggǎng Xǐlù 73 (© **0532/389-3002** or 0532/389-3062; fax 0532/389-3013) just west of Yánān Sānlù. The cost of touring the brewery with an English-speaking guide is ¥60 ($7.50) per person (not including transportation). CITS can also arrange tours of the city as well as book tickets and accommodations.

WHERE TO STAY

Crowne Plaza Qīngdǎo Located in the heart of the commercial and shopping center of Qīngdǎo on Xiāng Gǎng Zhōng Lù, this latest addition to the five-star hotel scene, recently upgraded from the four-star Holiday Inn, has a certain hip modernity to it, and is popular with Western independent travelers. Rooms are plush and tastefully decorated with all the expected amenities. Views of the sea are especially fine. Facilities are first-rate, and the service is good. Executive business rooms are the largest in town. With six restaurants on the premises, the hotel also has some of the most diversified dining choices.

Xiāng Gǎng Zhōng Lù 76. © *0532/ 571-8888. Fax 0532/571-6666. www.six continentshotels.com. 388 units. ¥996 ($124) double; ¥1,411 ($176) suite. AE, DC, MC, V.* **Amenities:** 6 restaurants; bakery; indoor swimming pool; health club; sauna; bowling alley; concierge; tour desk; free airport shuttle; business center; shopping arcade; salon; 24-hr. room service; same-day dry cleaning and laundry; newsstand. *In room:* A/C, TV, minibar.

Dōngfāng Hotel (Dōngfāng Fàndiàn) This four-star hotel, located near the city center and about a 10-minute walk from the Protestant church, is a popular choice among Western travelers who give it good marks for its comfortable rooms at reasonable prices (after the usual 20%–30% discount). For those who don't require a beach location, this is about the best deal around.

Rooms may not be the height of luxury, but they are clean and very comfortable. There's a full range of facilities here and three restaurants serving Cantonese, Shāndōng, and Western cuisine. The helpful staff speaks some English, and the service is overall quite good.

Dàxúe Lù 2. © *0532/286-5888. Fax 0532/ 286-2741. 146 units. ¥788 ($98) double; from ¥980 ($122) suite. AE, DC, MC, V.* **Amenities:** 3 restaurants; tennis court; health club; sauna; concierge; tour desk; business center; shopping arcade; salon; room service; dry cleaning and laundry. *In room:* A/C, TV.

Gloria Inn Aiming for a four-star rating, this current three-star hotel is a good choice if you want to be closer to the sea and are not too particular about luxurious amenities. Recently renovated rooms are spacious, bright, and comfortable. Seaside rooms have their views somewhat restricted by apartment blocks, but are pleasant enough. Staff is friendly and tries to be helpful at this Hong Kong–managed hotel.

Dōnghǎi Lù 21. © *0532/387-8855. Fax 0532/386-4640. 238 units. ¥1,000 ($125) double. AE, DC, MC, V.* **Amenities:** 2 Restaurants (Chinese, Coffee Shop); bar; lounge; indoor pool; health club; sauna; salon; concierge; business center; forex; shopping arcade; room service; massage; babysitting; same day laundry/dry cleaning; airport shuttle service; executive rooms. *In room:* A/C, Satellite TV, minibar.

Hǎitiān Hotel (Hǎitiān Fàndiàn) Located just east of the Bàdàguān District and overlooking the sea, this 15-story, two-building Goliath of a hotel is a popular choice with Japanese and Korean visitors. Affiliated with the Japanese Nikko group, the hotel has five stars: Its service is good and the facilities are on par with the Shangri-La's. Rooms are comfortable and well equipped with a range of amenities. Best of all, the majority of rooms have sea views. Chinese, Japanese, Korean, and Western restaurants on the premises offer diverse dining choices.

Zhànshān Dàlù 39. © *0532/387-1888. Fax 0532/387-1777. www.sd-trade.com/ hotel/Haitian. 606 units. ¥1,400 ($175) double. AE, DC, MC, V.* **Amenities:** 3 restaurants; indoor pool; tennis courts; health club; sauna; bowling; concierge; tour desk; business center; shopping arcade; salon; 24-hr. room service; dry cleaning and laundry; newsstand. *In room:* A/C, TV, minibar.

Hotel Equatorial Qīngdǎo (Qīngdǎo Guīdū Dàjiǔdiàn) While its service can't quite match the Crowne Plaza's or Shangri-La's, this is a busy and perfectly adequate four-star hotel in the heart of the commercial district. One distinct advantage is that this Malaysian-managed hotel offers good discounts, often up to half off. Rooms are somewhat garishly decorated with chintzy bedspreads, red carpets, and blue chairs, but they are comfortable enough and come equipped with desks, safes, and satellite TV. Bathrooms are spacious and very clean. The Golden Phoenix Restaurant offers a variety of Cantonese and Sìchuān dishes, the Kampachi features Japanese cuisine, and the coffee shop and the Etoile Pastry Shop serve Western foods.

Xiāng Gǎng Zhōng Lù 28. © *0532/ 572-1688. Fax 0532/571-6688. www. equatorial.com. 432 units. ¥1,040 ($130) double. AE, DC, MC, V.* **Amenities:** 5 restaurants; indoor swimming pool; health club; Jacuzzi; sauna; bicycle rental; free shuttle to Huáshān Golf Resort; free airport shuttle; business center; conference rooms; salon; 24-hr. room service; massage center; 24-hr. laundry and dry cleaning; florist. *In room:* A/C, TV, minibar.

Shangri-La Hotel Qīngdǎo (Qīngdǎo Xiānggélǐlā Fàndiàn) Located 15 minutes by car from the east of downtown and the German Quarter, the Shangri-La Qīngdǎo used to be the top choice for many Western visitors, but, lately, it's regarded as a bit stodgy and old, especially when compared with the recently opened five-star Crowne Plaza. Nevertheless, the signature Shangri-La luxury is still very much in evidence here. Business travelers and tour groups from Japan and Southeast Asia especially favor this hotel. All rooms are spacious and well fitted with comfortable beds, desks, sofas, safes, and dataports. The hotel also offers the full range of facilities and fine dining in its three restaurants (Chinese, Western, Japanese). Staff is friendly and helpful.

Xiāng Gǎng Zhōng Lù 9. © *800/942-5050 or 0532/388-3838. Fax 0532/388-6868. www.Shangri-la.com. 502 units, including 25 suites. ¥1,560 ($195) double; from ¥2,560 ($320) suite. AE, DC, MC, V.* **Amenities:** 3 restaurants; indoor swimming pool; 2 outdoor tennis courts; health club; Jacuzzi; sauna; in-house movies; concierge; tour desk; business center; shopping arcade; salon; 24-hr. room service; same-day dry cleaning and laundry; nightly turndown; newsstand. *In room:* A/C, TV, minibar, coffeemaker.

WHERE TO DINE

Qīngdǎo's seafood and its variations of local Shāndōng cuisine *(lǔ cài)* are all worth trying. Venturing outside hotel restaurants, which are good but predictable, is highly recommended. A long-standing institution for Shāndōng cuisine is **Chūnhé Lóu** in an old two-story corner building on Zhōngshān Lù 146 (✆ **0532/282-4346**), in the older part of town. The first floor is for casual fast food while the second floor has large tables and private rooms for more formal dining. The ambience is nothing to write home about, but the food has been gaining devotees throughout the years. House specialties include *yóubào hǎiluó* (fried sea snails), *wēilì xiàoróng quánxiè* (deep-fried stuffed crab claws on a bed of broccoli), *xiāng sū jī* (fragrant chicken), and a great number of seafood dishes. Finish off with some delicious *cōngyóu bǐng* (onion pancakes). There are no menus in English and don't be deceived by the pictures of food on the wall: They serve merely as decoration. Dinner for two averages ¥80 to ¥150 ($10–$18).

Two long blocks east of the Shangri-La Hotel along Xiānggǎng Zhōnglù is **Yúnxiāo Lù,** a lively street of bars and restaurants serving all types of Chinese cuisine into the wee hours. One such restaurant that's foreigner-friendly is **Steven Gao's Restaurant (Gāozi Jiǔdiàn),** at Yúnxiāo Lù 38 (✆ **0532/573-6676**), open 24 hours. Guitars and posters of Jim Morrison and Axl Rose decorate the walls of this three-story restaurant

serving seafood and *jiācháng cài* (home-style cooking). Try the *jīngjiàng ròusī* (shredded pork Běijīng style), *suànxiāng gǔ* (fried pork chop with garlic), or *shāo èrdōng* (sautéed mushrooms with garden asparagus); or choose from the tanks of fresh seafood out front. There are menus in English and they accept Visa credit cards. Prices are ¥60 to ¥120 ($7.50–$15).

For a change of palate, there are many Korean restaurants in town. One inexpensive late-night choice is **Tǔdàlì** at Xiānggǎng Xīlù 52 (✆ **0135/8322-9720**), open from 4pm to 4am. This cozy informal diner has exposed wooden beams and plenty of wall graffiti from happy and appreciative patrons. Barbecued meat and vegetable skewers are the main attractions here, with a set meal of 12 skewers (beef, chicken, fish) costing around ¥20 ($2.50). Also good are other Korean staples like kim chee, fried rice, and chap chae. The menu has pictures but no practical English. Prices are ¥20 to ¥40 ($2.50–$5).

McDonald's and KFC are well represented in Qīngdǎo, and several restaurants serve Western food. **Eden Café** in Parkson's Department Store on Zhōngshān Lù 44–60 (✆ **0532/202-1022**) serves credible pizzas and pastas. However, the most authentic Western fare is still found in hotel restaurants such as **Murano's** (✆ **0532/571-8888**), serving authentic Italian fare at the Crowne Plaza.

WÉIFĀNG: KINGDOM
OF THE KITE

潍坊

A CHINESE ADAGE PROCLAIMS THAT "on the ninth day of the ninth moon, the howl of the wind fills the sky." This is a call to fly kites in the land where kites, according to tradition, were invented over 2,000 years ago. In modern China, kite flying is a common pastime on city squares, in parks, and across country fields whenever the wind rises; but in the city of Wéifāng, in Shāndōng Province, south of Běijīng, it has become an annual rite and passion. Since 1984, Wéifāng has staged an annual international kite festival, an event that has grown by leaps and bounds to become China's premier kiting gala.

Every April 20 and 21, this city of 338,000, otherwise renowned for China's largest reserve of sapphire and a third of the nation's crude salt, doubles its population for a few days of friendly kite flying, open to all nations, drawing both the casual hobbyist and the dedicated aficionado of paper and twine. Venturing across Shāndōng Province in the spring, drawn by the better-known sites there (such as the city of Qīngdǎo, the birthplace of Confucius at Qūfù, and the sacred mountain of Tài Shān), I happened to reach Wéifāng just as the skies were to fill—as perhaps nowhere else in the world—with kites.

Museum & Kite Factory (Fēngzhēng Bówùguǎn)

On the eve of the great kite-flying event, visitors whet their appetites first by paying a morning visit to the **Wéifāng Kite Museum (Fēngzheng Bówùguǎn)**, Xíngzhèng Lù 66 (© **0536/825-1752;** fax 0536/822-7009), located downtown. It's open daily from 8:30am to 6:30pm (to 5:30pm Nov–Mar); admission is ¥20 ($2.50). The museum consists of several exhibition halls that display (without benefit of signs in English) a vast array of Chinese kites of every size and shape imaginable, from miniatures the size of thimbles to stately hand-painted silk box kites to groups of kites strung together, creating a delicate flying centipede of wood, paper, and string as long as a football field. There are also displays here chronicling the history of the kite in China and the West, as well as honoring foreign competitors from around the world who have flown their kites in the Wéifāng festival. The oldest type of kite here is the Lùbān Kite, which is said to have originated in China some 2,400 years ago.

From the museum it's a 20-minute ride by taxi, or 45 minutes by bus, eastward to Wéifāng's most famous kite factory at the printmaking village of **Yángjiābù** (© **0536/796-2581**). The factory consists of workrooms where workers assemble and paint by hand the kites that you may purchase in the salesroom; prices range from ¥40 to ¥240 ($5–$30), including a box. From April to October, it's open daily from 7:30am to 6pm (to 5:30pm Nov–Mar). Admission is ¥20 ($2.50). Yángjiābù is even more famous for its woodblock prints, with scenes from Chinese operas, used to adorn windows and walls during the Chinese New Year. These are printed by hand on presses in the workshop and can also be purchased in the salesroom. The workshops include a museum, which displays historic sets of the New Year prints and the old carved blocks used to print them.

You can wander the grounds of the Yángjiābù workshops, where elaborate gates and historic monuments, such as a model of the Temple of Heaven, are constructed from woodblock prints and kites. On a field above these colorful creations, locals are usually engaged in kite flying, and don't mind if you watch or even join in.

A Village Lunch

Those on a day tour, as I was, can partake of one of the most interesting lunch stops in China, in a farmhouse at **Shíjiā Village (Shíjiā Zhuāng)**, south of Wéifāng, where a family prepares a lavish banquet in their tiny kitchen. Lunch consisted of mounds of *bāozi* (steamed buns filled with vegetables and meats) and big bottles of local beer, served up at the kitchen table by Mr. and Mrs. Shí. Shíjiā Village contains all of 304 households, with a per capita income of about ¥5,000 ($600). The village maintains a dozen different small factories and vegetable farms. I had to sign a temporary resident permit before the meal. The village offers visitors overnight stays with families, arranged by the Wéifāng CITS.

Most day visits include a lively **circle dance** put on by the villagers, who, donning capes and costumes, stilt-walk and ride stick horses around the main square. Foreigners are free to join in, and some try out the stick horses. All in all, this is one of the happier lunchtimes I've spent in China.

Wéifāng International Kite Festival

On the morning of the actual event, buses and taxis converge on the International Kite Flying Arena, a 20-minute journey southwest from downtown Wéifāng. I knew beyond doubt that we were closing in on the

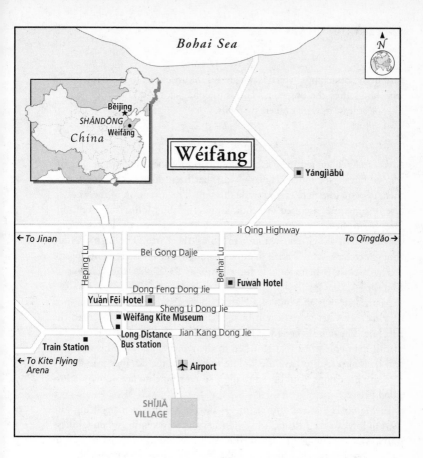

competition grounds when I spotted troupes of schoolchildren flying kites near power lines in the surrounding fields. The festival viewing stands overlook a large, flat, sandy field filled with thousands of kite fliers. Happily enough, visitors are not confined to the stands for this competition; rather, everyone is free to wander for hours among the participants who are engaged in launching kites of every description, seemingly at random.

Teams from several dozen countries unstack immense multiple-kite ensembles and spread out in long lines to launch them; peasants stalk the grounds with simple box kites, schoolchildren with kites in the shapes of butterflies, and businessmen with kites the exact size and color of hawks. One group unfurled scores of linked kites, each kite in this long line the life-size representation of a famous figure from world history. I saw splashy bright kites the size of a basketball court, linked kites with three-dimensional dragonheads as large as telephone booths, and even a kite painted with a laughing Santa Claus. Overhead, the dull blue sky is a slash of kites large and small, with forms from that of a samurai to that of a penguin. The atmosphere is chaotic and festive, warm and spirited. Visitors are invited to take a turn in the launchings, which is not always an easy chore; the field is jammed with kite-lofters and observers. This is the one place of all places to go fly a kite, or at least to watch others fly theirs.

Ancient History

A visit to Wéifāng naturally evokes your curiosity about the origin and history of kites. Not much scholarly work has been done on the topic, and there is more lore than fact to wade through. The invention of the wooden kite is sometimes ascribed to Mòdí, founder of the Mohist School of philosophy in the 4th century B.C. Mòdí is said to have carved wooden kites that could fly for 3 days without touching the Earth. The first kites are thought to have been shaped, naturally enough, like birds, as many are still today. You find them for sale for as little as $3 at the road stands surrounding Wéifāng.

Many a story is also told of a Hàn Dynasty general, Hán Xìn, who tied a string to his hat to retrieve it in the wind and unwittingly invented the first kite. The same general was later credited with using a kite trailing a tail of thin bamboo strips that shrieked in the wind to scare off his enemies, and he is also said to have used a kite to measure the distance into enemy territory his troops would need to dig a secret tunnel to lay siege on a fortified palace.

In Marco Polo's descriptions of his travels, we find a man-lifting kite used to forecast the fortunes of sea journeys undertaken in certain Chinese ports. A sailor, Polo wrote, is lashed to a wicker frame kite and sent aloft in a gale. If he returns alive from his flight, it is a harbinger of a profitable voyage for a merchant ship. In fact, man-lifting kites do seem to have been used to carry spies over enemy territory in ancient China. Their constant use is verified in an anecdote related by Joseph Needham, the West's leading scholar of Chinese science and technology. "About the year 1911," Needham tells us, "an old gentleman taking a stroll in Peking had his attention drawn to an aeroplane flying overhead, but with perfect sang-froid remarked, 'Ah, a man in a kite!'"

I'm not sure that kites are solely the invention of China. The Malaysians may also have invented them about the same time. And the oldest kite festival in the world is not at Wéifāng, but at Ahmedabad in India, where every January a hundred thousand fighting kites tear up the sky at a festival called Makar Sankranti. But the Chinese have as good a claim to kite originality as anyone, and it is probable that some Marco Polo–like explorer or Silk Road merchant did introduce kites to Europe, where they are first mentioned in 1589 and first pictured in a Dutch engraving in 1618. It could be said that without the Chinese invention of the kite, Ben Franklin would never have discovered electricity in the sky.

While the history of the kite is long and mysterious in China, nowhere is its heritage as resplendent at the present time as at Wéifāng, truly the "Kite Capital of the World," as it likes to boast of being. It's the perfect town in which to watch, to fly, and to buy a kite—but don't ever pick up a kite lost by others here. Since the last dynasty, it has been widely believed in China that letting go of a kite means letting go of bad luck or illness, and that is never what you want to pick up on your travels.

PRACTICAL INFORMATION

by Sharon Owyang

ORIENTATION & WHEN TO GO

Wéifāng is located in central Shāndōng Province 196km (121 miles) east of provincial capital Jǐnán. The best time to visit is during the annual Wéifāng International Kite Festival held April 20 to 21. The rest of the year, this is a quiet but interesting place, definitely off the beaten track. Summers are warm and humid and winters cold and gray.

GETTING THERE

By Plane Wéifāng Airport is 10km (6 miles) south of the city center and a 20-minute, ¥20–¥25 ($2.50–$3) taxi ride away. There are several flights a week to Běijīng. Air tickets can be bought at travel agencies, hotel tour desks, and the CAAC office (Mínháng Shòupiàochù) at Wéizhōu Lù 719 (© 0536/827-0000).

By Train Wéifāng sits on the rail line between Qīngdǎo and Jǐnán, the capital of Shāndōng Province, which is in turn on the main Běijīng–Shànghǎi rail line. Trains traveling throughout the day between Jǐnán and Qīngdǎo stop in Wéifāng. It's about a 2½ hour-ride to Jǐnán and a 2-hour ride to Qīngdǎo. From Jǐnán, it's another 5 hours by express train to Běijīng. Tickets can be bought at travel agencies, hotel tour desks, and the **train station** (© 0536/856-4073) itself, located in the southern part of town on Jiànshè Lù.

By Bus From the **long-distance bus station (Chángtú Qìchēzhàn)** (© 0536/856-3433) on Jiànkāng Dōnglù, minibuses and Ivecos head (via the Jǐnán–Qīngdǎo Exprwy.) for Jǐnán (3 hr., ¥32–¥40/$4–$5, every 15 min. 6am–6:30pm) and Qīngdǎo (2½ hr., ¥32/$4, every 15 min. 6:45am–4:30pm). Big air-conditioned buses also go to Jǐnán (3 hr., ¥47/$5.80, once an hour 10am–5pm) and Qīngdǎo (2 hr., ¥30/$3.75, departing at 8:30, 9:30, and 10:30am).

GETTING AROUND

Taxis are the most convenient way of getting to the main sights, which are scattered about town. Flagfall for the smaller Citröen taxis is ¥4.50 (50¢) per 3km (2 miles), then ¥1.40 (15¢) per kilometer. All other taxis charge ¥5 (60¢) per 3km (2 miles), then ¥1.50 (20¢) per kilometer until 8km (5 miles), when the price goes to ¥2.15 (25¢) per kilometer. A taxi out to Yángjiābù will run about ¥35 ($4.50) one-way. **Bus** no. 5 runs from the train station to Yángjiābù (45 min., costing ¥2 (25¢).

TOURS & STRATAGEMS

Tours If you're here during the Kite Festival in April, it is advisable to make all travel arrangements as far in advance as possible. Independent travel is easy enough in Wéifāng, but booking a guided tour would save considerable hassle. Such trips can be booked at CITS branch offices throughout the country, especially if the trips are part of a larger China tour. Locally, the Wéifāng CITS has been replaced by the **Wéifāng Holiday Tour Travel Agency (Wéifāng Jiàrì Lǚyóu Gōngsī)**, currently the main travel agency in town at Dongfeng Dongjie 339 (© **0536/829-8737;** fax 0536/823-3854). They can book organized group tours (including transportation and hotel) or special tours for individual travelers. In Jǐnán, the **China Shāndōng Travel Service (Zhōngguó Shāndōng Lǚxíngshè)** at Lìshān Lù 185 (© **0531/260-8598**) is probably the most experienced in arranging travel around Shāndōng Province.

Recreation The **Fùhuá Amusement Park,** next door to the Fùhuá Hotel on the east end of Dōngfēng Lu (© **0536/ 888-5230;** fax 0536/888-0970), is a Western-style theme park complete with imported rides from America, Europe, and Japan. There are water slides, bumper cars, a merry-go-round, a roller coaster, a Ferris wheel, and other such Disneyland-inspired rides that seem rather out of place in a small Chinese city. Still, this can be an interesting afternoon diversion if you have kids or if you're simply tired of all that kite flying. The park has plenty of restaurants, snack bars, arcades, and shops to further distract you.

WHERE TO STAY

Fuwah Hotel (Fùhuá Fàndiàn) Located about 3km (1¾ miles) east of downtown next to the Fùhuá Amusement Park, this is Wéifāng's only five-star hotel. The hotel seems rather forlorn for much of the year: It's perhaps a case of too much luxury, and not enough guests. Nevertheless, this nine-story, triangular–shaped hotel offers large, comfortable guest rooms well equipped with bathrooms with marble-topped sinks. The hotel's restaurants serve Japanese, Korean, Chinese, and Western food. Service is fairly good but not stellar, though the staff does try to be helpful. Hotel guests are allowed free entry into the neighboring Fùhuá Amusement Park.

Fùshòu Dōngjiē 168 (off Běihǎi Lù). © **0536/888-1988.** *Fax 0536/888-0766. 576 units. ¥1,298 ($162) double. AE, DC, MC, V.* **Amenities:** Restaurant; indoor swimming pool; 2 outdoor tennis courts; health club; aerobics room; Jacuzzi; sauna; billiards; 12-lane bowling alley; concierge; tour desk; business center; conference rooms; shopping arcade; salon; 24-hr. room service; massage; babysitting; next-day dry cleaning and laundry; florist; newsstand. *In room:* A/C, TV, minibar, coffeemaker, hair dryer, safe.

Yuán Fēi Hotel (Yuán Fēi Dàjiǔdiàn) This four-star hotel is located in the heart of downtown, 2 long blocks north of the Kite Museum. Quite popular with business travelers, the hotel has all the trappings of a modern luxury hotel. Rooms are clean and comfortable, if a bit unmemorable. The hotel has a three-star annex where the rooms are predictably more drab but still functional. The hotel offers good dining possibilities, with restaurants serving

Shāndōng, Japanese, Korean, and Western cuisine. The staff is friendly and eager to please, though service is a bit spotty at times.

Sìpíng Lù 31. © 0536/823-6901. Fax 0536/ 823-3840. 368 units. ¥520 ($65) double. MC, V. **Amenities:** 4 restaurants; indoor swimming pool; tennis court; fitness center; billiards; bowling alley; sauna; concierge; tour desk; ticket office; business center; conference rooms; souvenir shops; salon; massage; newsstand. *In room:* A/C, TV, minibar.

WHERE TO DINE

Hotel restaurants offer the best and most reliable fare. The **Yuánfēi and Fùhuá hotels** serve good Shāndōng cuisine and Western buffets.

QŪFǓ: BIRTHPLACE OF CONFUCIUS

曲阜

THE HOMETOWN OF CONFUCIUS (551–479 B.C.), China's great philosopher and social thinker, is a charming spot devoted to honoring its most famous son, although there is no doubt it is equally devoted these days to cultivating the tourist dollar. Despite its legions of hawkers, vendors, and postcard sellers, I found Qūfǔ well worth a stopover. The historic and monumental sites associated, however tenuously, with Confucius are undeniably grand, and you can still come across a degree of small-town innocence and reverence that recalls the Old Cathay that was China for centuries, from the birth of Confucius to the 20th century. The old part of the city is made up of newly constructed shophouses in the Qīng Dynasty style.

The three great sights of Qūfǔ are within walking distance of each other (although the walk can stretch for several miles). The **Temple of Confucius (Kǒng Miào),** the **Confucian Mansion (Kǒng Fǔ),** and the **Cemetery of Confucius (Kǒng Lín)** were all inscribed on the UNESCO World Heritage List in 1994, although that hasn't saved them from damage in the name of mass tourism.

The Socrates of China

As for the Great Sage himself, he is known in China as **Kǒng Fūzǐ,** and scores of his descendants, members of the Kǒng clan, still reside in Qūfǔ. He was the Socrates of China in some ways, a teacher rather than a writer (his followers, led by Mencius, would later put his words to paper in a canon known as the Analects), who received little in the way of acclaim or wealth in his lifetime. His teachings constitute a code of social conduct, rather than a religion, but he was deified nonetheless. Thousands of Temples of Confucius eventually spread throughout China, where the literati, the wealthy, and the bureaucrats worshipped the Great Sage and promoted his rules. The rules are those dear enough to many a bureaucrat, since they established a rigid hierarchy of ruler over subject, society over the individual, boss over employee, man over woman, and father over son.

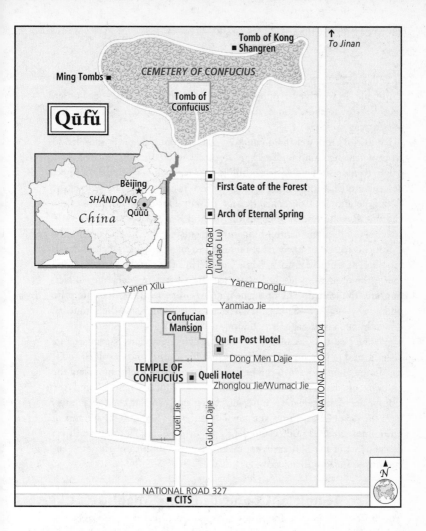

These "harmonious" relationships were considered cosmic—even the emperor was a Son of Heaven and subject to its fateful decrees.

Among the more dramatic developments of Confucian thought, put into practice over the centuries in China, were the rites of **filial piety,** in which children mourned for departed parents to extremes that could last a lifetime; **ancestor worship,** in which respect was extended to all the previous generations of the clan; and the **Imperial Examination system,** which persisted in China for almost 2,000 years and was used to select those who worked for the government at nearly all levels, including the Imperial Court itself. (The basis of the examination was knowledge of the Confucian Analects and one's skill in the traditional arts of China, from calligraphy to poetry.) The teachings of Confucius were conservative even when he formulated them 2,500 years ago. He looked back to a golden age of enlightened emperors, wise and selfless advisors, and strictly regulated family life, in which everyone, depending on his place in the social order, was obedient to those above, respectful of all laws and duties, and selfless in bettering society.

Confucius's followers fell in and out of favor, but they never tumbled so far as when the Communists came to power in 1949 and launched campaigns to root out feudal ways of thinking. That's when a number of direct descendants (including Kǒng Déchéng, the Yánshēng Duke, first son of the 77th generation of Confucius) fled for Táiwān. During the madness of the Cultural Revolution, contingents of youthful Red Guards stormed Qūfù, attacking and often demolishing monuments to the Sage. Fortunately, Confucius has been slowly rehabilitated, like many another fallen leader in more recent Chinese history. While Confucianism is not the party line, neither is the thought of his leading persecutor, Chairman Máo; and, in fact, in Qūfù, the worship of Confucius is quite in line with the free enterprise philosophy of New China, as thousands of money-spending tourists, drawn by the Great Sage, enrich local merchants.

For the past two decades, Qūfù has busily gone about restoring, refurbishing, and re-creating a Confucian Qūfù for tourists and devotees, and it has done a good job. Qūfù can be beautiful, exotic, and refreshing, and the grounds of the Confucian mansion, the Confucian temple, and the Confucian forest cemetery, especially when not overrun by tour groups, have the flavor of a dreamy, antique China. Of the 650,000 inhabitants of Qūfù, more than 125,000 claim the Kǒng surname, but far fewer are direct descendents of the Master, living members of the 69th through 78th generations of the Confucius clan.

Temple of Confucius (Kǒng Miào)

The heart of Qūfù is the Temple of Confucius, a 20-hectare (50-acre) complex said by local boosters to be the largest temple complex in China. Experts regard this as one of China's three greatest architectural complexes (along with Běijīng's Forbidden City and Chéngdé's Summer Retreat). It dates from B.C. 478, but has been rebuilt many times. Some of the pavilions and monuments date from the Míng Dynasty (A.D. 1513), but most are from the more recent Qīng Dynasty. There are nine courtyards running on a south-to-north axis for well over half a mile, so it takes some time to tour. You enter at the **Star Gate (Língxīng Mén).** The many halls, pavilions, and temples are fully restored and grand, with yellow and green tiled roofs and red columns. The courtyards teem with large incense burners, ancient gnarled trees, and over 2,000 historic carved stone tablets. Women were long forbidden to set foot on the temple grounds.

North of the Star Gate are two arches and an inner gate, followed by a long courtyard with stone carvings from the Hàn Dynasty on the left, and the Bì River, crossed by three arched bridges. More gates and a three-tiered wooden **library** come next, followed by 13 small **pavilions** containing commemorative stone tablets, some inscribed over 1,500 years ago. The most important temple, **Dàchéng Hall,** rebuilt in 1724, has its own gate and side halls. In the courtyard on the right is an **ancient cypress tree,** believed by many to have been planted by Confucius himself. It is perhaps the most venerated tree in China, whatever its real age. In front of the grand temple is the **Apricot Terrace (Xìng Tán),** where Confucius is said to have delivered lectures. The temple itself is supported by 28 magnificent columns, carved with twisting dragons and set on white marble; the 10 dragon columns on the front, enhanced with inscribed clouds and pearls, constitute one of the most stunning sets of stone columns in Asia. Dàchéng Hall contains traditional drums, musical stones, and bronze bells once used in Confucian festivals; Confucius was enamored with ancient musical instruments. Here you find the main statue of Confucius and those of 12 of his chief followers. To the east side of Dàchéng Hall is a pavilion honoring the many descendants of Confucius, and at the rear of the complex is a hall displaying 120 **tableaux in stone** illustrating the life of China's number-one sage.

Altogether, this is one of the most magnificent and, at dawn or dusk, one of the most beautiful and peaceful temples in China. It's open from 7:30am to 6pm (from dawn to dusk in summer); admission is ¥50 ($6.50) at the southern gate.

Confucian Mansion (Kǒng Fǔ)

Just northeast of the rear of the Temple of Confucius, along Quèlǐ Lù, which is chockablock these days with souvenir vendors and two-story tile-roofed shophouses, is the historic residence of the Sage's family, the Kǒng clan. The clan claims to have resided here through 77 generations, up until 1948, although the mansion grounds were not constructed on this site until the late 14th century under the Míng Dynasty. The grounds are nearly as large as those of the nearby temple. Its 463 halls are ample testimony to its former status; it is one of the most lavish private estates in Chinese history, surpassing that of many an emperor.

Today, the Confucian Mansion is something of a family museum, with plenty of relics in its halls (which served the family and its servants as offices, libraries, studies, bedrooms, and ancestral shrines). Artifacts range from old furniture and scrolls to personal clothing and ceremonial robes. The first son of the direct descendants of Confucius for each generation, known as the Yánshēng Duke, ruled this mansion and much of Qūfù in the old days; by the time of the last dynasty, this duke had powers and privileges second only to those of the emperor.

The first section of the grounds contains various offices; the second, the family residences; the rear, a rock garden. There were scores of offices and local ministries here, since the mansion served as Qūfù's "Forbidden City." In the first of the three great halls, the duke, seated on a tiger skin, delivered his edicts; in the second hall, he received officials; and in the third, he dealt with family matters and the affairs of his 500 servants.

The inner mansions beyond these halls were the clan's private residences, studies, and ancestral halls, once restricted only to the relatives of Confucius and the duke's concubines. They now contain a fine collection of Qīng Dynasty furniture and ceramics. At the north end of the grounds is the **Iron Mountain Garden (Tiěshān Gōngyuán),** dating from 1503 and decorated with fine rockeries and ancient trees. It makes a serene conclusion to a walk through one of Old China's greatest mansions, through the confines of an aristocratic life that endured even longer than the imperial dynasties. The Confucian Mansion is open daily from 7:30am to 6pm (dawn to dusk in summer). Admission is ¥30 ($3.75).

Cemetery of Confucius (Kǒng Lín)

More properly known as the **Kǒng Forest,** this huge grove—the largest and oldest cemetery park in China—serves as the Confucian burial grounds. The grave of Confucius himself is here. The 200-hectare (500-acre) park is an old man-made forest, a large island of towering trees surrounded by farms and the northern outskirts of the town. It is a 3km (2-mile) walk from downtown, and there are bicycles for rent on the way (about $2 for a morning or afternoon excursion). The road itself is lined with graceful cypress trees, and the great forest of pine and oak that is the cemetery grounds, enclosed within thick, 3m (10-ft.) high stone walls, is dotted with gravestones, small temples, arched bridges, and scores of carved stone animals. In ancient times, admission was barred to all but the Kǒng family and visiting emperors, who came here frequently. Women, except for Confucian wives, were restricted to burial outside the forest walls.

This is a fine place to wander on a sunny afternoon. The main southern gate, **Arch of Eternal Spring (Wàngǔ Chángchūn Fáng),** built in 1594, leads along the Divine Road to the **First Gate of the Forest,** the formal entrance. Turn left at the second gate, and stroll west about 180m (600 ft.) along the **Imperial Carriageway** to the arched bridge over the Zhū River. Then follow the stone path north to the main tomb, that of Confucius. Along the way there are small courtyards and halls, which were once used by participants to cleanse themselves for the Confucian rites of burial and worship.

The **grave of Confucius** is in the last courtyard on the west side. It is a simple mound of green earth, walled off, with an inscribed 15th-century stone tablet as a marker, nearly lost from view in the thick, lush forest. The tomb on the left is that of the grandson of Confucius; on the right is that of Confucius's son; in the center, the final resting place of the Sage. The courtyard that leads to the Great Sage's tomb is lined both with statues and, when I was last there, with a few vendors, including a skilled painter who unrolled his sheets on the cobblestones and turned out colorful, traditional paintings one after the other, all snapped up by the tourists.

Thousands of the descendants of Confucius are buried in this graveyard forest—perhaps as many as 200,000—and the grounds are quite haunting. Many of the graves established here date back over 2,000 years and are but simple mounds among the old trees. If there's time, take an interesting walk that begins back at the Zhū River. There, the western bridge joins a road that follows the river west and north to a haunting collection of Míng tombs and stone statues, seemingly discarded into the forest from the heavens. Follow this road as it circles inside the cemetery walks until you reach another group of stone animals at the grave of Madame Yu, daughter of a Qīng Dynasty emperor who married the head of the 72nd generation of the Confucian clan. Her tomb is followed by that of Kǒng Shāngrén (1648–1718), a celebrated dramatist and 64th-generation descendant, and that of the 76th-generation duke, too. In fact, those in the line of Confucius are still being buried here today, in a forest cemetery that has no equal, in beauty or scale, in China.

The Cemetery of Confucius is open daily from 8am to 6pm (dawn to dusk in summer). Admission is ¥20 ($2.50) to tour.

PRACTICAL INFORMATION

by Sharon Owyang

ORIENTATION & WHEN TO GO

Qūfŭ is located in the southern half of Shāndōng Province, about 150km (93 miles) south of Jǐnán, the provincial capital, and 65km (40 miles) south of Tài'ān, gateway to Tài Shān (see separate chapter, beginning on p. 534). The best times to visit are spring and fall, when temperatures are fairly mild. Summers are hot and dusty, and winters are cold and dry. If you like celebrations

and large crowds, the ideal time for you to visit is on the occasion of Confucius's birthday, September 28, though celebrations are held annually from September 26 through October 10. During this time, there are parades, exhibitions, and musical and dance performances throughout Qūfŭ. Be sure to book well in advance.

GETTING THERE

By Plane The nearest major airport is in Jǐnán (© 0531/694-9400).

By Train The situation is a little confusing as Qūfŭ actually has two train stations serving it. **Qūfù Train Station,** about 5km (3 miles) southeast of the city center, sees little traffic except for trains that stop here between Běijīng and Rìzào or Jǐnán and Rìzào. Train K51 from Běijīng (9 hr.) arrives in Qūfù at 7am, while the return train, K52, departs Qūfù at 9pm. Much more useful is the **train station at Yǎnzhōu** (© 0537/341-5239 or 0537/346-2522), 15km (9 miles) west of Qūfù, which sits on the Běijīng–Shànghǎi rail line. From Yǎnzhōu, there are many daily connections to Tài'ān (1 hr.), Jǐnán (2 hr.), Běijīng (5 hr.), and Shànghǎi (10 hr.). Tickets can be purchased at travel agencies and at the respective train stations, but book as soon as you arrive since allocations are limited.

By Bus   Short of traveling by private car, buses are the most convenient way of reaching Qūfù. The **Qūfù bus station (Qìchēzhàn)** (© 0537/441-1241 or 0537/441-2554) is located 1 long block south of the Temple of Confucius at the corner of Shéndào Lù and Jìngxuān Dōnglù. From here, buses run to Jǐnán (2½–3 hr., ¥21/$2.60, every 20 min. 5:40am–5:30pm), Tài'ān (70 min., ¥13/$1.60, every half hour 6.40am–5.30pm), Wéifāng (4 hr., ¥47/$5.85, 7:40am, 10am, 1:40pm), and Qīngdǎo (7 hr., ¥61/$7.60, every hour 7am–11am and 7–11pm). Minibuses also run to the railway station at Yǎnzhōu (25 min., ¥3/35¢) every 15 minutes between 6:30am and 5:30pm.

TOURS & STRATAGEMS

Tours   There are a number of ways to tour Qūfù: as an excursion from Jǐnán, the capital of Shāndōng Province 150km (93 miles) to the north, or combined with a visit to Tài Shān (see separate chapter, beginning on p. 534) 57km (35 miles) to the north. Because getting to Qūfù is not simple, many Western visitors end up booking day tours from Jǐnán. Travel agencies, such as the **China Shāndōng Travel Service (Zhōngguó Shāndōng Lǚxíngshè)** at Lìshān Lù 185 (© 0531/260-8598), or your hotel desk in Jǐnán can arrange tours that include transportation, an English-speaking guide, lunch, entrance fees, and accommodation if you want to stay overnight in Qūfù. For those who might like to essay Qūfù on your own, it is nevertheless highly recommended that you at least hire an English-speaking guide to take you around the Confucius Temple. This can be done at the temple for ¥100 ($13) or at the **Qūfù CITS office** at the back of the Lǚyóu Bīnguǎn at Dàchéng Lù 1

(© 0537/448-8491), though be sure to give them as much advance notice as possible and don't expect miracles as the office seems to be unattended half the time. Alternatively, try the **Qūfù Tourist Information Centre** at Gǔlóu Běijiē 4 (© 0537/465-5777). Although the office primarily provides information and directs travelers to sights and accommodations, they can be very helpful and resourceful.

It is possible to tour the temple, mansion, and cemetery on foot, though hiring a pedicab or horse-drawn taxi to the cemetery is an inexpensive option. Miàndí taxis cost ¥5 (60¢) per 2km (1¼ miles). Around town, horse-drawn carriages cost ¥2 to ¥4 (25¢–50¢) per person, while a tricycle taxi costs ¥1 to ¥3 (10¢–35¢) per person.

Entertainment   The Quèlǐ Hotel presents **Confucian musical performances** every evening on its second floor. Tickets are for sale in the hotel lobby for ¥50 to ¥100 ($6–$12). From April to

October, there are nightly "Confucius Dream" musical performances at 8pm at the **Xìng Tán Theater (Xìng Tán Jùcǎng;** ℂ **0537/442-4095),** 800m (2,624 ft.) south of the Confucius Temple.

WHERE TO STAY

Quèlǐ Hotel (Quèlǐ Bīnshè) Located in the center of Qūfū, just east of the Confucius Temple, this three-star hotel is the best place to stay in town. The hotel's traditional Chinese buildings, in a courtyard setting, blend well with the surrounding design. Rooms, while not luxurious, are spacious, comfortable, and decorated in a style that combines traditional Chinese design with modern flourishes. Bathrooms are a little tired but acceptably clean. Service is occasionally spotty, but the hotel has a good restaurant that serves Confucian banquets and acceptable Western meals. There are also Confucian musical and dance performances in the evening. Additionally, the hotel provides foreign exchange services.
Quèlǐ Jiē 1. ℂ *0537/486-6818.* Fax 0537/441-2022. 160 units. ¥398 ($49) double; ¥988 ($123) suite. MC, V. **Amenities:** Small fitness center; business center; conference rooms; shopping arcade; salon; next-day laundry and dry cleaning. *In room:* A/C, TV, minibar.

Qūfū Post Hotel (Qūfū Yóuzhèng Bīnguǎn) Centrally located, just to the east of the Kǒng Mansion, this two-star hotel is an acceptable alternative if the Quèlǐ is full. Rooms are clean and comfortable enough and the decor of light wood furniture is inoffensive. Bathrooms are a little tired but otherwise clean. The staff doesn't speak English but tries to be helpful.
Gǔlóu Běijiē 8. ℂ *0537/448-3888.* Fax 0537/442-4340. 66 units. ¥260 ($33) double. **Amenities:** Restaurant; karaoke bar; salon. *In room:* A/C, TV.

WHERE TO DINE

The **Confucius Restaurant** and **Western Dining Room** in the **Quèlǐ Hotel** offer Qūfū's best dining in a relatively clean environment. Right next door, at the intersection of Gǔlóu Jiē and Zhōnglóu Jiē, is **Kǒngfǔ House,** which has an English menu and serves local Confucian specialties like *yángguāng sāndié* (chicken, vegetables, and egg folded together like a fan), *dàizi shàngcǎo* (stewed pork, chicken chestnuts, and ginseng), and *sīlǐ yínxìng* (sweet gingko). Dinner for two averages ¥80 to ¥160 ($10–$20). Farther east along Wǔmǎcí Jiē, a **night market** proffers snacks that include delicious grilled kabobs, roasted nuts, and bean curd.

SOUTHEAST CHINA: COMMERCE & CULTURE

Shànghǎi: Back to the Future

上海

Shànghǎi's journey to the future is underpinned by its colonial and indigenous past, as you can still see in the old architecture of the city and the watery villages on its edges. The dominant thrust today, however, is that indicated by the new area of Pǔdōng. Shànghǎi is clearly one of Asia's most powerful cities, perhaps soon to be its most powerful economically. With 13 million residents, Shànghǎi is China's most populous city, and the United Nations has estimated that by the year 2015, Shànghǎi's population will reach the unimaginable figure of 23.4 million. However, in recent years, it has actually begun to fall, and the city has a surplus of office space. The city government has instituted reforms that are quite remarkable in the Chinese context, allowing graduates of Shànghǎi's universities to obtain instant residence rights, and even permitting foreigners to gain permanent residence without the backing of an employer. One figure Shànghǎi relishes is its visitors' census. Seven of every ten visitors to China now pay a visit here, and the sum of foreign visitors is approaching two million yearly.

Shànghǎi is still something of a construction site over which a blueprint is spread like a dream. But if any city can link China to the outside world on equal terms, it will be Shànghǎi. Aware of its past, but always outward-looking, Shànghǎi is determined to have a preeminent role on the world stage. In few other cities in the world can you feel that future pressing so relentlessly.

The best way to take the pulse of Shànghǎi is to make a long circuit on foot. I always begin uptown on **Nánjīng Road,** China's greatest shopping street, and walk a few miles east to the edge of the **Huángpǔ River,** presided over by the green towering roof of the historic Peace Hotel. There, I turn south down the spacious promenade that runs between the river and that remarkable architectural museum known as the **Bund,** where the neoclassical business offices of Shànghǎi's colonial period form an unforgettable

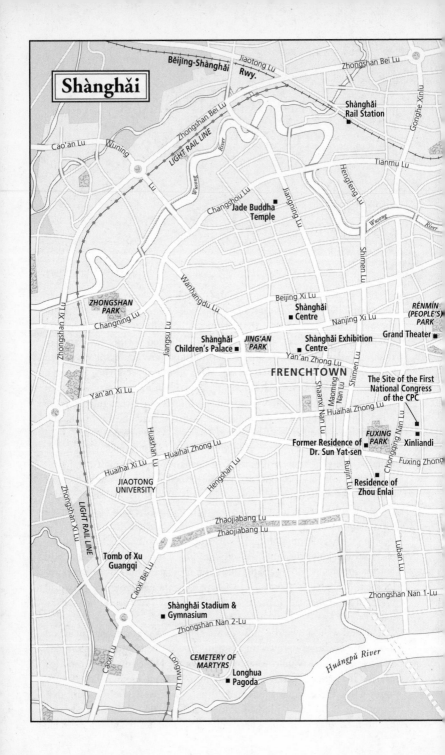

Former Residence
of Lu Xun

Baoshan Lu

Sichuan Bei Lu

Siping

Zhoujiazui Lu

Dalian Lu

Changyang Lu

Haining Lu

Henan Bei Lu

Changzhi Lu

Pingliang

Xizang Bei Lu

Shànghǎi
Mansion

Yangshupu Lu

(Suzhou

Creek)

Sichuan Zhong Lu

Daming Lu

International Passenger
Terminal

Huángpǔ River

Beijing Dong Lu

HUÁNGPǓ
PARK

Xizang Zhong Lu

Shànghǎi No. 1
Department Store

Nanjing Dong Lu

MINZHU
PARK

Convention Center

Pudong Dadao

Pedestrian Mall

Peace
Hotel

THE
BUND

Pearl of the Orient TV Tower

Lujiazui Lu

RÉNMÍN
'PEOPLE'S)
SQUARE

Fuzhou Lu

Henan Zhong Lu

Zhongshan Dong Lu

Jìn Mào Building

PǓDŌNG
NEW DEVELOPMENT
ZONE
(EAST SHANGHAI)

Yan'an Dong Lu

Riverside
Promenade

Pudong Nan Lu

Shànghǎi
Museum

Renmin Lu

Dongchang Lu

HUAIHAI
ARK

Xizang Nan Lu

Henan Nan Lu

Húxīntíng
(Teahouse)

Yù Yuán
Garden

Shiliupu
Wharf

Fuxing Dong

Zhongshan Nan Lu

CHINESE QUARTER
(NÁNSHÌ)

Zhonghua Lu

Lujiabang Lu

Bansongyuan Lu

Pudong Nan Lu

Shànghǎi
Vicinity

Changjiang River

Jiading

Wusong

Wusong
Mouth

Gaoqiao

JIANGSU

Wusong R.

(Suzhou Cr.)

Zhenru
Temple

SHÀNGHǍI

SCENIC AREA OF
DIANSHAN

Dianshan
Lake

Qingpu

Zhōu Zhāng
Water Village

SHÀNGHǍI
MUNICIPALITY

Songjiang

Huangpu River

ZHEJIANG

Jinshan

China

Běijīng ★

SHÀNGHǍI

Shànghǎi

0   1/2 mi
0   0.5 km

N

skyline. Then I head back uptown, dropping by the splendid teahouse and garden in the **old Chinese Quarter.** Continuing west, I pay a visit to the new **Shànghǎi Museum,** then swing through the French Concession back to where I started. It's a long walk with plenty of distractions—sometimes I spend 2 days covering this route—but by the time I finish, Shànghǎi is under my skin and the crowded, hectic, always surprising streets of congested Shànghǎi have swallowed me. These days, there's a detour for any Shànghǎi visitor, too, a new Shànghǎi, called **Pǔdōng,** rising on the east side of the Huángpǔ River, which can no longer be ignored.

Nánjīng Road to the Bund

Of course even the old Shànghǎi, on the west side of the river, has modernized considerably in the past few years, and this is still the place to spend the most time, largely because it has a romantic past that is still accessible. Until 1999, old Shànghǎi was nearly impassable, a patchwork of torn streets and detours, demolitions and new construction sites, but today downtown Shànghǎi no longer resembles a giant erector set dropped from the sky. Ian Buruma, writing for the *New York Times* in the mid-1990s, called Shànghǎi's reconstruction "perhaps the greatest urban transformation since Baron Haussmann rebuilt Paris in the 19th century." Much of the preliminary work, at least, has already been completed.

Shànghǎi is again a city to walk. I begin my explorations at **Shànghǎi Centre,** a complex of offices, apartments, and shops that is still the most prestigious business address in the city. It's located 3km (2 miles) west of the Huángpǔ River up Nánjīng Road, Shànghǎi's main street. Shànghǎi Centre is a city within the city, a joint venture opened in 1990 that has become the emblem of the new international Shànghǎi. Its 472 Western-style apartments house many of the city's high-rolling foreign businesspeople, requiring rents that used to exceed those in Tokyo, London, and New York, although recent competition has lowered prices. Inside you'll find a shopping mall, supermarket, preschool, health club, theater, exhibition hall, and plenty of pricey restaurants, lounges, and even an espresso bar. Some foreign residents scarcely venture out into the city streets, but they are then missing nearly everything the city has to offer.

The length of Nánjīng Road east from Shànghǎi Centre to the **Bund promenade** on the riverfront shows what's happened. I know the road well, having strolled it frequently since 1984, but it now looks like the main route through an entirely different city. There are plenty of new office and shopping complexes, most following the modern Western model inside and out. Within minutes I pass the massive **Westgate Mall** and a sidewalk arcade featuring fast food from McDonald's. A Burberrys of London is followed by a Nautica outlet store and finally a shop that a decade earlier would have been unthinkable anywhere on Nánjīng Road, anywhere in China: a thriving Playboy Store, its bunny logo gracing a variety of upscale merchandise.

I shouldn't be taken aback. This is no longer Máo's fashion show. The younger women in the streets are cavorting in the latest Western styles: high heels, short skirts, black tights, flashy earrings, and curly, red-tinted coiffures. Shànghǎi has long been China's capital of fashion, and it always looks outward with intensity. Young couples flock to Western wedding parlors. A KFC occupies the entrance to People's Park.

The venerable department stores that made Nánjīng Road the most famous shopping street in China have undergone glitzy face-lifts. The **New World Department Store** was one of the first to take the leap into the 21st century, with its bubble-glass walls, curving escalators, and refrigerated photographic film, but now everyone is getting into the act.

The great change on Nánjīng Road is focused on the new **Nánjīng East Pedestrian Mall (Nánjīng Dōnglù Bùxíng Jiē)**, which runs for nearly a mile between Xīzàng Zhōnglù and Hénán Zhōnglù, right through the heart of the great shopping route. Traffic is banished (except at cross streets); red granite walking stones have replaced the pavement; park benches, lamp posts, kiosks, and scores of new shop fronts and department stores have been added; and the mall is as flashy and as easy to walk and as lively as any built in the center of any downtown capital in Europe or North America. The sole difference is perhaps the persistence and outcroppings of Shànghǎi's colonial legacy, the brick and stone towers of its early-20th-century colonial cityscape. From the pedestrian overpasses, you can still glimpse the old in the stranglehold of the new, all the way to the Bund. There's the historic 1934 Park Hotel, once the tallest building in the Far East and Chairman Máo's favorite (now with a nicely restored lobby); the Number One Department Store, also built in 1934 (with the first elevator in China); and the Wing On (1918) and Sincere buildings (1917), former homes of top Chinese clothing stores (now stuffed with new Western-style wares).

All the way along the mall, if you look carefully, there are examples of newborn outlets hunkering down into their 75-year-old shells. The Xīnhuá Bookstore, which has served Chinese cities for decades, has been surpassed here by Shànghǎi's City of Books, a multistoried vendor that has plastered its front windows with its Web address. At the eastern end of the mall there's a commemorative plaque and one of those life-size iron statues of a woman grasping shopping bags in one hand and a young boy in the other, as well as a line forming to board the gaudy little electric trolleys that whisk visitors up and down the mall for ¥2 (25¢).

This giant mall, designed by Arle Jean Marie Carpentier and Associates of France, opened on September 20, 1999, and it has transformed the shopping scene of old Shànghǎi so thoroughly that by the time I finished exploring it, I wondered if I would find the historic Bund on the riverfront intact or repackaged as a Western amusement park. At least the easternmost 2 blocks of Nánjīng Road are largely unremodeled. You return abruptly to the congested, grimy streets; to the narrow, irregularly surfaced, shoulder-pinching sidewalks; to the pockets of earthy odors from no-holds-barred cooking and waste. The new has not entirely erased the old. Not as long as the historic Peace Hotel still stands on the Bund like a sentinel, even if across the river now is Pǔdōng with its 88-story Jīn Mào skyscraper and the Pearl of the Orient TV Tower, a gargantuan Tinkertoy visible over the rooftops of both old and new Shànghǎi.

Peace Hotel (Hépíng Fàndiàn)

Before strolling down the Bund promenade at the east end of Nánjīng Road, I always make a circuit of the lobby of the Peace Hotel. It is Shànghǎi's grand monument to Art Deco, and some of the original design still clings to its walls, columns, furnishings, and carved woodwork.

It was originally the Sassoon House, built in 1929 by one of Shànghǎi's legendary immigrant tycoons, Victor Sassoon, a Jew from Baghdad, who ended up owning thousands of city properties. It included the redoubtable Cathay Hotel, one of the finest in Asia. Sassoon kept his offices in its famous pyramid tower. Noel Coward did some writing in one of its suites. And Steven Spielberg filmed a scene of *Empire of the Sun* here, re-creating the view that a hotel guest would have had of the Japanese bombing of Shànghǎi during World War II.

In the north wing of the hotel, a jazz band plays swing music every evening. One or two of the members started out in the late 1930s, when this was the number-one jazz club in China. Today, it's simply the place for a nostalgic evening of fun. The lobby, a gorgeous reminder of the Jazz Age, is worth gawking at. Sometimes I can find a hotel worker willing to take me on a tour of the hotel rooms; they retain their grand Art Deco form and decor. Otherwise, I just ride the elevator up to the eighth floor, take a look for myself at the old parlor rooms there, each done in a different interna-tional style, then walk upstairs to the roof. The rooftop lounge recently reopened. You can now walk outside, right up to the Peace Hotel's trian-gular dark green tower, and enjoy one of Shànghǎi's most romantic views, south down the Bund into the romantic past and east across the river into China's high-rise future.

East Shànghǎi (Pǔdōng)

In the late 1990s, at any given moment, fully one-fifth of the world's high-lift cranes were at work in the city of Shànghǎi. In one massive convulsion, the urban landscape was being erased and redrawn. As the smoke clears now, China's largest city is slated to assume the position occupied by Hong Kong as the nation's commercial center. The plan has been to make Shànghăi China's first fully modernized metropolis, a Pearl of the Orient for the 21st century, and much of that plan is nearing completion.

Meanwhile, traces of Shànghăi's past—its cultural relics, its quaint architectural monuments to Western colonial days, and its legacy of poverty and pollution—remain at the margins. If Shànghăi is where this new century begins, then the future has been nurtured in the craters of 25,000 construction sites.

When you come to Shànghăi these days, you really find two cities: the romantic Shànghăi of old, still peeking out along Nánjīng Road, and the new Shànghăi that's remaking itself in Pŭdōng. The dividing line is the Huángpŭ River: Along its eastern shore is historic downtown Shànghăi, and along its western shore is the new development zone called Pŭdōng.

Shànghăi's monument to new development is the **Pearl of the Orient TV Tower,** Asia's tallest structure at 461m (1,535 ft.). It's visible for miles, even back across the river in old downtown Shànghăi. Its neighborhood is the Pŭdōng New Development Zone, directly east of the Bund, which is a museum of European customhouses, banks, and taipan clubs that memorializes Shànghăi's business success when foreigners ran the city. Old Shànghăi has certainly modernized itself here, too, but to see the full extent of Shànghăi's economic boom, you need to cross under the river via the new subway line, walk to Pŭdōng via the moving sidewalk in the new underground tunnel, or cross over by taxi or bus via two long bridges or the underground vehicle tunnel. Whatever your choice, all roads now lead east in Shànghăi.

Pŭdōng is the new city's leading edge, its heart of trade, bordered by the river that feeds the interior of China and the ocean that links it to the Western world. It's not what ordinarily attracts visitors to China, but it's the essence of Shànghăi. The TV Tower is a genuine tourist attraction, open daily from 8am to 9:30pm. You buy a ticket outside the gate for ¥50 to ¥100 ($6–$12), depending on how high you want to go. The ¥100 ($12) ticket also allows you access to the **Shànghăi History Museum (Shànghăi Lìshĭ Bówùguăn),** which is on the ground floor of the tower and is open daily from 9am to 9pm; regular admission is ¥35 ($4.50). After checking your handbags and cameras, you enter an elevator that lifts off like a rocket. The uniformed elevator operator recites the TV Tower statistics from memory in Chinese and English as you ascend a quarter of a mile to the observation deck. There, you have a 360-degree view of all of Shànghăi, east and west, new and old, and everything that's being squeezed in between.

From the observation deck in the Pearl of the Orient TV Tower, Pǔdōng looks like a fresh new urban hub of massive skyscrapers. The main developments are concentrated within an easy stroll. The tallest structure is the modern pagoda of Shànghǎi, the 88-story **Jǐn Mào Building,** currently the world's third tallest building, which has its own public observation deck and 79 high-speed elevators (admission ¥50/$6), affording an even higher view of Shànghǎi than the TV Tower, not to mention a high-tech new Grand Hyatt Hotel, starting on floor 54. Nearby is the Shànghǎi Securities and Exchange Building, home to China's most vibrant stock exchange; the new Shànghǎi International Convention Center, with its glass world globes on either side; and the stately new Customs House. At the foot of these and the office towers going up daily are two brand-new parks.

The first is **Lùjiāzuǐ Central Garden,** just east of the TV Tower, with its white magnolias, piped-in outdoor music system, and its own lake with snack stands. The entrance is on the north side. On the southeast side is the Lùjiāzuǐ Development Exhibition Room, actually a large orange and black brick mansion built as a private residence by a foreign tycoon in 1914. This mansion is a museum in its own right, with carved doors, wooden windows, archways, brass door pulls, and green and marble tile floors from the colonial period. Displays of a few artifacts, maps, and photographs record the transformation of Pǔdōng into a 21st-century Manhattan of the East.

The **Riverside Promenade (Bīnjiāng Dàdào)** is on the river side of the TV Tower, running parallel to the Bund for well over a mile. Former site of the Lǐ Xīn Shipbuilding Yard, it affords a view the Bund doesn't, a view of old Shànghǎi on the river. At night, when the Bund is lit up, it's the grandest view in Shànghǎi. By day it is also dramatic, particularly from its northern section, where the "Wave-Viewing Platform" is just a yard above the busy waterline.

This tip of Pǔdōng is developing its own shopping and eating centers, too, although these do not rival those of the Shànghǎi to the west. The **Lùjiāzuǐ Food Square,** located between the TV Tower and the Jǐn Mào Building, contains dozens of restaurants in a "shophouse mall" design encircling a large courtyard fountain. Painted in muted pink, this food mall has sparkling new cafes serving Shanghainese, Korean, and Japanese cuisine. Heading south into the more densely packed streets of downtown Pǔdōng, you'll reach **Times Square,** a shopping complex that boasts the largest department store in Asia, Nextage/Yaohan (second biggest in the world after Macy's). But presiding over it all is the TV Tower, Pǔdōng's chief sightseeing draw, its 11 blue-and-green spheres the pearls in a flashy string of Shànghǎi's sudden wealth, glittering night and day, winking at the streets of the elder city across the river.

Shànghăi's Mississippi

The Huángpǔ River, which divides the two Shànghăis, east and west, past and future, serves as the city's shipping artery both to the East China Sea and the mouth of the Yángzǐ River, which the Huángpǔ joins 29km (18 miles) north of downtown Shànghăi.

The "bunds" of Shànghăi refer to the mud flats on its shores, secured by dikes of stone and earth. The Bund and its promenade are landmarks of Shànghăi's 19th-century struggle to reclaim a waterfront from the bogs of the Huángpǔ.

The Huángpǔ's 58km (36 miles) of wharves are the most fascinating in China. The port handles the cargo coming out of the interior of China, from Nánjīng, Wǔhàn, and other Yángzǐ River ports, including Chóngqìng, the rice bowl of China, 2,415km (1,500 miles) deep into Sìchuān Province. From Shànghăi, which produces plenty of industrial and commercial products in its own right, as much as a third of China's trade with the rest of the world is conducted each year—a substantial part of it flowing up and down the Huángpǔ River. Mile for mile, this is the most important river in China.

Daily tour boats make the 3½-hour voyage up the Huángpǔ to the Yángzǐ River delta. From the river, there are unrivaled views of Shànghăi's port facilities, the ships of the world that dock there, and the junks and Chinese barges that clot the narrow river avenue. Unrivaled, too, are the postcard views of Shànghăi's celebrated European skyline to the west and the booming cityscape of Pǔdōng to the east.

After buying a ticket one Saturday morning on the Bund promenade, I was able to board a tour boat before noon, settling into a soft chair on the upper deck. Surrounded by picture windows, served hot tea and nuts, I leaned back as we pulled away from the Shànghăi waterfront. But I couldn't sit still. I went out on deck as we pulled away. The monumental granite offices, banks, consulates, and hotels of Shànghăi's past colonial masters formed a stately panorama to the west, while the Pearl of the Orient TV Tower and the new skyscrapers commanded the east bank, forming the tallest and most expensive building project in the world. I tried to scan both banks at once, as well as keep my eye on the river traffic itself.

We headed north, passing **Huángpǔ Park** where the Bund begins, across from the **Peace Hotel** and its stunning green pyramid roof, still the loveliest piece of architecture in Shànghăi, east or west. The park borders **Sūzhōu Creek** and is dominated by a new monumental sculpture, soaring ribbons of marble that rise like Shànghăi's economic expectations. Huángpǔ Park was once the British Public Gardens. It is widely reported today that a sign was once posted at its entrance reading DOGS AND CHINESE NOT ALLOWED. In fact, dogs were not allowed in the garden, and according to a separate ordinance, neither were Chinese except by permission of their foreign employers. This insult stung the Shanghainese for a century, until they regained sovereignty over their city in 1949.

Sūzhōu Creek is spanned by **Wàibǎidù Bridge,** which once linked the American and British concessions. The Americans staked out the northern shore; the British claimed the downtown waterfront. Wàibǎidù Bridge was originally a wooden toll bridge built in 1856 by an enterprising Englishman. Steel girders replaced timber in 1906. Eighteen meters (60 ft.) wide, with two 51m (171-ft.) long spans, the bridge was regularly crossed by human-powered rickshaws, introduced to Shànghǎi from Japan by a Frenchman. Trams were soon routed across the bridge, too, as were motorcars, which have been driving the streets of Shànghǎi since 1901.

Less than a mile north of Sūzhōu Creek is the **International Passenger Terminal** where luxurious cruise ships tie up. The Huángpǔ River jogs sharply east at this point on its way to the Shànghǎi shipyards, where cranes and derricks load and unload a logjam of freighters. The freighters are interesting in that they are stamped with the country names of the world's shipping giants: America, Japan, Holland, Russia, Norway. I have seen vessels registered to archenemies unload side by side in Shànghǎi.

Across the river on the eastern shore, vast coal yards crop up, along with petroleum storage facilities. At the **Yángshùpǔ Power Plant,** the stacks are tipped with flames night and day. Here, you begin to sense fully Shànghǎi's industrial might. The river seems endless and its industrial ranks—the dry docks, factories, and power plants—equally unlimited, like an army of millions massed on both shores of a worldwide economic battlefield.

The Bund and the Pearl of the Orient TV Tower rapidly fade from view as the Huángpǔ slowly begins to curve northward again. We crossed under **Yángpǔ Cable Bridge,** and then **Nánpǔ Cable Bridge** to the south, two of the largest such structures in the world, both completed just a few years ago. Shànghǎi's modern boom is accelerating on both sides of the Huángpǔ, which is still its main shipping link to the world and into the rich interior of China.

What overwhelms river passengers even more than the long industrial shoreline is the traffic slinking up and down the waterway. The Huángpǔ is, on the average, just 180m (600 ft.) wide. It's like a superhighway without visible lanes, glutted with gigantic freighters, tugs, tiny sampans, and, above all, the undulating trains of unpainted wooden barges, tied together to save fuel, forming serpentine dragons on the river. Flotillas of these heavily laden barges, their gunwales just above the waterline, usually number a dozen or more. Their open holds are stuffed with coal, lime, brick, produce, scrap metal, and a thousand other commodities in transit. The rear cabins are homes to families who sleep and cook and work and play on the Huángpǔ. The family bicycle is often parked on deck. Potted flowers festoon the cabin

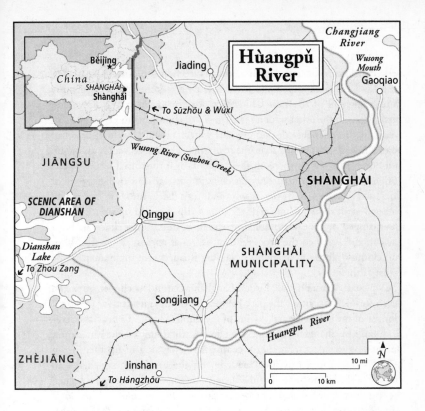

roofs. Noisy outboard engines, often in teams of four or five, propel the
barges from the stern. Laundry lines stretch from cabin roof to prow. Dishes
are washed and meals are cooked with water scooped from the brown river.
More than 2,000 oceangoing ships compete with the 20,000 barges, fishing
junks, and rowboats that stalk the Huángpǔ every year.

There are also navy gunboats and even an occasional submarine
anchored on the shores. A sign in English nailed to the railing of our tour
boat deck sternly warned that photographs of military craft and installa-
tions are strictly forbidden, but there was no one this morning to enforce
the ordinance. A decade ago I spotted a pre–World War II submarine
lounging alongside a pier on the Huángpǔ River. This time, after passing a
dozen gray gunboats, looking less than threatening, I spotted the same
U-boat as before.

I spent most of the cruise outside on the upper deck, leaning over the
rail, absorbed by the continuous parade of barges, ships, and factories. Our
northern destination was **Wúsōng Kǒu,** where the harbormasters wait
beneath a ghostly pale clock tower, its hands frozen. This marks the Yángzǐ
River delta, where the Huángpǔ disappears into the convergence of far
mightier waterways: the Yángzǐ River and the Pacific Ocean. The estuary
seems as vast as an ocean, although it is neither ocean nor river here but a

netherworld of water moving in contrary directions on crisscrossing tides, salted and silted, muddied and fresh. The river currents churn against the implacable wall of the East China Sea. An armada of vessels, large and small, waits in the estuary for a sea change, for shipments to be readied, for a turn at the Shànghǎi docks. On this watery tarmac, the population of boats surpasses that of any man-made marina. The vessels wait and bob up and down, moving nowhere on their anchors as if time itself has stopped.

Our tour boat ventured only far enough out into this twilight zone of tides and currents to pivot slowly and turn back into the narrowing passageway of the Huángpǔ. For the return trip, I pulled up a wicker deck chair; sipped my hot tea; nibbled on the fruit, nuts, and a chocolate bar I packed; and watched the procession of barges as endless as the silk shops and clothing stores on Shànghǎi's Nánjīng Road, where the human traffic is just as thick.

Our boat eventually sailed into Shànghǎi, as countless clipper ships and ocean steamers have over the past 160 years, bearing outsiders for their first glimpse of the great colonial skyline of the Bund. The 1920s neoclassic edifices, built by Shànghǎi's conquering taipans, still dominate the waterfront, but new skyscrapers of the 21st century are crowding in on them from behind now. And across the Huángpǔ, on the eastern shore, there's an entirely fresh skyline mounting the stage, more imposing, soaring far higher, the product of Shànghǎi's modern taipans who are enterprising local Chinese rather than carpetbagging Westerners. Nevertheless, the architecture of East Shànghǎi is also strictly international, a Western import—but now an import rather than an imposition. Our ferry slowly parted this divided architectural curtain of old brick and stone, of new glass and steel, coming to rest at its quay on a river of commerce and industry that has few rivals East or West—a waterway not of China's past but of its future.

Huángpǔ River cruises depart from a wharf on the south end of the Bund promenade. The day-tour tickets can be purchased from a hotel tour desk or from offices on the wharf. I purchased my ticket from the ticket office at 229 Zhōngshān Dōng Lù (on the lower-level sidewalk that runs alongside the promenade, south of the pyramidal Diamond Restaurant looming overhead). The **booking office** (✆ **021/6374-4461;** fax 021/6374-4882) is well marked in English and the clerks can figure out what you want. There is one 3-hour cruise to Wúsōng Kǒu a day, departing at 2pm. Tickets cost ¥70 ($8.75) for first class and ¥50 ($6.25) for second class. There are many 1-hour cruises to Yángpǔ Bridge (Yángpǔ Qiáo) departing during the day (9am, 10:45am, 1pm, 2:30pm, 3:15pm, and 4:30pm), as well as two evening cruises (7 and 8:30pm). Tickets cost ¥25 to ¥70 ($3.10–$8.75), depending on class of service. Cruise schedules vary according to season, so check for times beforehand. The river tour boats are wide two-deckers, about 45m (150 ft.) long, with a kiosk selling snacks; a bar selling tea, coffee, sodas, and beer; and a buffet dining room used for weekend and evening voyages.

The Bund

By the Bund, most everyone means the long promenade along the shores of the Huángpǔ (its proper street name is Zhōngshān Dōng Yī Lù). This is indeed a fine place to stroll, north to south, taking in the views of skyscrapers across the river and the old architecture of Shànghǎi across the street. Despite the city's incredible development, the Bund's stately skyline still defines Shànghǎi, setting it apart from any other city in China. The monumental European architecture here is what interests me most. It is more out of place in Shànghǎi than ever before. These were once the triumphant seats of power of Shànghǎi's Western masters—the banks, private clubs, and grand offices of the taipans who ran Shànghǎi for nearly a hundred years, beginning in the 1840s when Shànghǎi became a treaty port. In the twilight of the colonial period, in the 1930s, there was a popular saying in Shànghǎi that anywhere within a 10-mile radius, you'd see a foreign face.

All of these rock-solid old buildings have new owners and tenants today, mostly financial institutions from inside China. The old occupants included the **British Consulate** and the **Jardine & Matheson trading company,** as well as the stately **Cathay Hotel,** the **Shànghǎi Customhouse,** the **Hong Kong and Shànghǎi Bank** (built in 1921), and the **Dōng Fēng Hotel** (once the site of the Shànghǎi Club and its celebrated Long Bar). Other buildings in this lineup include former consulates; brokerage houses; chambers of commerce; and banks from Japan, India, Denmark, France, Belgium, Britain, and Canada. Several are worth walking into, as they have been restored recently to their original splendor.

From north to south along the west side of the Bund, there are over 20 distinct specimens of colonial architecture. Those with the most dramatic lobbies include the current **Agricultural Bank Building (no. 26),** a 1916 office building; the **Peace Hotel (no. 20)** with the pyramid roof, built by Sassoon in 1929; the **Palace Hotel (no. 19),** built in red-and-white brick in 1906; the current **New China Merchants Bank (no. 16),** which was rebuilt in 1924 in a Western/Japanese style to serve as the Bank of Táiwān; the massive **Customs House (no. 13),** with its stately bell tower, built in 1927; and the current **Pǔdōng Development Bank (no. 12),** which has the Bund's most astounding interior. Some of the old hulks are still unoccupied, awaiting new tenants who must preserve and restore them now by law. Others are of peculiar note: The **China Foreign Exchange Trade System Building (no. 15),** for example, houses the Three Gun Monopoly Shop. This odd name refers to China's largest underwear manufacturer; it comes from Gān Tínghuì, who launched the company in 1937 to alleviate undergarment dependence on archenemy Japan. Gan had previously won renown for his marksmanship, winning three competitions and receiving the prize of a gun each time. The most famous building on the southern Bund, until recently the **Dōngfēng Hotel (no. 2),** was the location of the exclusive Shànghǎi Club when it was built in 1910. It was empty during my last visit (the run-down hotel and even the KFC outlet had been removed), and its Long Bar, once the haunt of every well-to-do business-man and adventurer in Shànghǎi, had disappeared as well.

A word about the Bund's most splendid lobby, at **no. 12:** This great building, with its marble walls and arches, massive wooden revolving doors, and two bronze lions guarding the wide entrance, has a breathtak-ing dome, newly restored, over its lobby. The dome is an eight-sided mural of Greek-styled gods and heroes posing in eight great world capitals: Bangkok, Hong Kong, Tokyo, New York, London, Paris, Calcutta, and, of course, Shànghǎi. The bank and its lobby beyond the dome are also exquis-itely restored in leather and carved wood. The building was opened by the British minister to China on June 23, 1923, to house the Hong Kong and Shànghǎi Bank.

These days, the Bund promenade is filled with far more visitors from inside China than out. This is the place to be for morning exercises, before the working day starts. Hundreds of residents do their morning *tàijíquán* workouts along the riverside, escaping for an hour into their own slow, quiet worlds before entering the maelstrom of work and commerce. Some of that commerce takes place on the promenade. Tour boats depart for Huángpǔ River tours, outdoor cafes sell sodas and snacks, ferries cross the river to the Pearl of the Orient TV Tower, and peddlers push their wagons of ice-cream treats up and down the walkway. Artists also wade through the stream of visitors. One enterprising artist, armed with scissors, struck up a conversation with me as we sauntered along the river. As we walked, he swiftly captured my likeness, cutting out two paper silhouettes, mounting both when we paused, and selling them to me on the spot. A moment later, he vanished, a step ahead of the licensing authorities.

The Best Little Old Teahouse in China

From the Bund it's a short walk southwest to the **old Chinese Quarter.** Throughout Shànghǎi, everyone seems to believe that if you build a mod-ern city, wealth will beat a path to your door. Even **Nán Shì,** Shànghǎi's Old Town, harbors this hope. Yù Yuán, the city's classic garden, and Húxīn Tíng Teahouse, with its zigzag Bridge of Nine Turnings, remain intact in the heart of old Shànghǎi. But these two delightful tourist stops are now surrounded by a new shopping mall. Mo's Burgers and Starbucks rub shoulders with the

Lù Bō Láng restaurant and the Tóng Hán Chūn Traditional Medicine Store. What's surprising is that the commercial remodeling blends in with the old neighborhood of shophouses, pavilions, and the Temple to the Town God. Shànghǎi seems aware of the need to preserve the look and essence of its endangered past, even when redeveloping a tourist zone.

Many feel they already know the garden teahouse, **Húxīn Tíng Teahouse (Húxīn Tíng Chálóu),** at the heart of Old Town the first time they see it; it could well have served as the model for classic Blue Willow tableware. This five-sided, two-story pavilion, with its dramatic upturned eaves and gray-tiled double roof, dates from 1784. It was built by merchants in the cotton trade as a place to broker their products, but became a teahouse a century later. Today, it is the most visited teahouse in China, and a wonderful spot to rest from the surrounding frenzy. It's open from 6am to 9pm, with tea and snacks served all day upstairs.

But even this island of tranquility is responding to the construction mania currently shaking China's greatest metropolis to its foundations. The alleyways surrounding the teahouse, once lined with small shops and stalls, have fallen to the bulldozer of progress, replaced by a modern shopping mall of department stores and fast-food outlets featuring hamburgers as well as dumplings.

This arena of commercial development, officially known as the **Yù Yuán Shopping Centre,** located in the oldest inhabited section of Shànghǎi, reflects the classic Chinese low-rise style. The structures that now hug the shores of the pond where the teahouse floats like a lotus flower are faithful to the architecture of a century past. Sweeping tiled rooflines, ornately carved entryways, and massive wooden columns are the rule. The look of the traditional shophouse is preserved, even when these antique-style facades house outlets for fast food. Another old-fashioned aspect of the Shopping Centre is that it is for pedestrians only. Taxis and tourist buses line up blocks away on the fringes.

Next door to the teahouse, on the south shore, the picturesque **Lù Bō Láng Restaurant** is still serving local Shànghǎi specialties, including spicy hot eel and shrimp dishes. Perhaps the cuisine most often associated with Old Town, however, is snack food. For decades, visitors to the teahouse and garden gorged themselves on a variety of pastries and dumplings, from wheat flour muffins with a variety of fillings to glutinous rice balls (taste better than they sound) with pigeon eggs. This Chinese-style "fast food" (fast to eat but slow to prepare) remains the most popular fare, although hamburgers, milkshakes, fried chicken, and mashed potatoes are catching on.

A few years ago, visitors with a taste for Chinese snacks might have stood in line at the Moslem Restaurant, located on the west shore of the teahouse lake. Crowded and unkempt, this place afforded a splendid view of the bridge and teahouse, but the food was, at best, hearty. Today, the **Nánxiáng Dumpling Restaurant (Nánxiáng Mántou Diàn)** lines the western shore of the teahouse lake. From a picture window outside you can watch the cooks preparing thousands of little pastries in the kitchen. This establishment serves traditional steamed snacks that are delicately fashioned and appealing to the palate.

The entire shopping area, which radiates out several blocks from the teahouse, is far more appealing than in the past. Many of the shops continue to offer the small native commodities that made the old bazaar one of China's most famous marketplaces. Chopsticks fill one specialty store, silk cloth another. The newly expanded **Tóng Hán Chūn Medicine Store** dispenses traditional remedies. Other shops stock bamboo products, fans, and incense sticks, and larger emporiums dispense a full range of regional arts and crafts. Two of old Shànghǎi's best-known products are available at little shops within a block of the teahouse: spiced beans and pear syrup (the latter is Shànghǎi's answer to the cough drop).

There is up-to-date shopping, too. A new department store a few steps from the zigzag bridge does a brisk business in handbags and luggage, including the latest roll-on suitcases embossed with likenesses of Mickey Mouse. The **Yùyuán International Shopping Center (Yùyuán Gāochéng Guójì Gòuwù Zhōngxīn)**, on the mall's southwest corner, carries plenty of Western imports. The largest new structure is an amusement center teeming with the latest electronic and video games. A vending machine invasion has been launched as well. Coca-Cola machines, automatic teller machines, digital height and weight machines, even a brigade of shiny new portable toilets are moving into Old Town Shànghǎi.

Because of the tasteful remodeling of the teahouse shopping area, the old and the new do coexist neatly: Traditional Chinese dining and shopping mix with the latest from the West. One notable beneficiary of redevelopment has been the **Temple to the Town God (Chéng Huáng Miào).** Built on the grounds of a 15th-century temple, its back garden became the southern section of Yù Garden (Yù Yuán) in 1709. During this century, the Temple of the Town God often fell on hard times, once even serving as a warehouse. It is now an active place of worship. In the old days, the temple was the center of seasonal flower shows (plum blossoms in spring, chrysanthemums in autumn), street fairs, and lively markets.

Today, the temple's marketplace atmosphere has returned, particularly on Sunday, when Shànghǎi's largest **antiques market** takes over the temple square. Weekdays are only slightly less crowded. Visitors number up to 200,000 a day. The Húxīn Tíng teahouse is the sole refuge—a fine place to sip tea at your leisure while contemplating the frantic pace of life on every side.

The festive atmosphere of the area recalls the era of the temple bazaar, and the style of the remodeled shops enhances your enjoyment of older pleasures. The newest addition to this quarter of old Shànghǎi Chinese-style is **Shànghǎi Old Street (Shànghǎi Lǎo Jiē),** a half-mile stretch of Fāngbāng Zhōng Lù, which is the east–west street marking the southern border of Old Town. It was remodeled in 1999 as an antiques shopping street. Now lined with charming shophouses and wine shops, colorful antique and jewelry stores, and traditional theaters and teahouses, it is designed to recapture the atmosphere of Shànghǎi shopping under the Qīng Dynasty.

Like the teahouse, **Yù Yuán Garden** is unchanged—a solid, beautiful monument from the past that doesn't require updating. Its undulating dragon walls still shelter its pavilions, pools, rookeries, and winding paths from a changing world outside, making it Shànghǎi's 16th-century retreat in the center of a city readying itself for the 21st century. After my most recent visit to Yù Yuán, I am confident in pronouncing it the single most beautiful classical garden in China, surpassing even those of Sūzhōu. Don't miss it, especially in the morning or late afternoon when the crowds are somewhat less pressing. And don't worry about the name or function of each pavilion. This is a garden to lose yourself in, a maze of delights. It's open daily from 8:30am to 5pm; admission is ¥25 ($3.10).

French Concession

From 1842 on, Europeans carved up Shànghǎi into concessions, large neighborhoods where they built villas and residential blocks in the architectural styles of the West. The French Concession, often called **Frenchtown,** with its Art Deco and Tudor town houses and its neo-Gothic office blocks, survives to this day south of Nánjīng Road and west of the Bund.

To reach Frenchtown from the Chinese Old Town, I walk west along **Huáihǎi Road,** which runs parallel to Nánjīng Road and is also a major shopping street. Locals usually check it out before Nánjīng Road these days, as the trendiest new shops and shopping centers open here.

Frenchtown is over a mile from the Bund, and the walking can be slow owing to the crush of pedestrians—your shoulders may well be sore by the end of the day. But Frenchtown's architecture is worth the trouble. The cityscape is another page from Shànghǎi's colonial days. The best-preserved area is along Màomíng Nán Lù at the **Jǐn Jiāng Hotel,** a massive complex of dark marble. This is where U.S. President Nixon stayed after signing the Shànghǎi Communiqué, the document that reopened China to the West in 1972, and it's also in the heart of the French District. Across the street is the **Garden Hotel,** a modern tower that contains a unique cultural treasure: the original stained glass, carved ceiling, and staircase of the entrance to the Cercle Sportif Français, once the exclusive social center of well-to-do foreigners in Shànghǎi's age of decadence, the 1920s and 1930s.

Many traces of notorious Shànghǎi remain here, even with relentless modernization. The French Quarter still has some avenues lined with the shops and houses of its heyday. Many are being cleaned up and refitted with boutiques for the tourist trade. Several dozen mansions also exist, although few are open to the public. Still, well over 1,400 monumental Western-style buildings have been documented recently in Shànghǎi, and the major European-built hotels, churches, mansions, private residences, garden villas, and public buildings from the past 2 centuries will probably be preserved for the next century—with an eye to capturing the growing tourism dollar, if nothing else, as more and more of these sites are being converted into upscale restaurants. One of the finest examples is the **La Na Thai Restaurant** on the exquisite grounds of the old Ruìjīn Guest House (Ruìjīn Èr Lù 118, just south off Màomíng Lù in Frenchtown).

To see the gentrification of Shànghǎi close up, the combining of old and new at its best, take a stroll down **Héngshān Lù,** just west of Frenchtown. It is the most fashionable area these days among locals, chock-full of upscale eateries, bars, and teahouses. Cafes such as **Sasha's** (in a mansion once owned by the Soong family, at Dōngpíng Lù 9) and teahouses like **Harn Sheh** (at Héngshān Lù 2A) are dazzling.

Shànghǎi Museum (Shànghǎi Bówùguǎn)

There's a great historical legacy in Shànghǎi as well, and it is being preserved, although the chief treasures have moved into modern quarters. The new oval-shaped Shànghǎi Museum, on the south side of **People's Square (Rénmín Guǎngchǎng),** is China's most up-to-date museum. When I visited it on a Sunday morning, the plaza was teeming with skateboarders, in-line skaters, and children flying paper kites purchased from roving vendors.

Inside, the galleries are as modern as any in the world: the floors carpeted, the explanatory signs in English as well as Chinese, the track lighting precise and illuminating. There are four floors of exhibits, each floor looking down on an immense atrium. Stalls on each floor sell gifts and museum reproductions, and there are two larger gift shops on the ground floor. Galleries devoted to bronzes and stone sculpture are on the first floor. Ceramics dominate the second floor. Paintings, calligraphy, and seals (chops) have separate galleries on the third floor; and coins, jade, furniture, and minority displays are on the top floor. The two most impressive galleries are those of sculpture and of jade, featuring artifacts that span all the major dynasties back to the New Stone Age.

Using the audiophone literally throws light on some of the exhibits. The phone is keyed by number to certain exhibits. When you press the number of the selected exhibit, a light beam is activated to highlight that display and an explanatory tape is played on the earphone.

While the museum's 120,000 treasures are not on the scale of those collected in Běijīng, Taipei, or even Xī'ān, Shànghǎi shows that it knows how to display its past to a sophisticated international audience. On the second floor, there's a fine tearoom for refreshment, with traditional Chinese furniture and a choice of cookies, four different teas, mineral water, and even Brazilian coffee. The museum is open daily from 9am to 5pm (until 8pm Sat), but ticket sales stop an hour before closing. Admission is ¥20 ($2.50), and the audio tour costs ¥10 ($1.25) with a ¥100 ($13) deposit.

Newly opened across the street from the Shànghǎi Museum (on the north side) are the **Grand Theater** (admission ¥40/$5), Shànghǎi's premier performance venue; and the **Shànghǎi Urban Planning Exhibition Hall** (admission ¥20/$2.50), which showcases, on five floors, the history of the city's explosive development.

Other Attractions

Shànghǎi has a surprising number of sights for a commercial city. Many of them are included on typical group tours, but most of them are of special interest, of limited interest, or, too often, of no interest at all. Among the best temples to visit are the **Jade Buddha Temple (Yùfó Sì),** with its Buddha of white jade (170 Ānyuán Lù); and the **Lónghuá Temple,** with its wooden pagoda (2853 Lónghuá Lù). The **Jìngān Temple** (1700 Nánjīng Lu) is small but active, and the **Confucian Temple** (Wénmiào Lù) is recently restored.

Among the homes and museums of local luminaries, those that most reward a visit are the former residence of **Sòng Qìnglíng** (at Huáihǎi Zhōng Lù 1843) and the memorial park and museum of writer **Lǔ Xùn** at Jiāngwān Dōng Lù. Shànghǎi 146 is the site of a small Jewish museum, the **Ohel Moshe Synagogue** at Chángyáng Lù 62; the **Shànghǎi Arts and Crafts Research Institute** at Fèngyáng Lù 79; the 19th-century **Xújiāhuì Cathedral** at Pǔxī Lù 158; the extensive **Shànghǎi Botanical Gardens** at Lóngwǔ Lù 1100; and the **Shànghǎi Zoo** at Hóngqiáo Lù 2381, with its pandas. These and other attractions are covered in detail in *Frommer's Shànghǎi.*

Zhōu Zhuāng Water Village

Tour operators offer an array of day trips from Shànghǎi, even to Sūzhōu and Hángzhōu (see separate chapters), but the best 1-day excursion is to the 900-year-old water village of **Zhōu Zhuāng,** a 90-minute bus ride 81km (50 miles) southwest of city center. The tour gives you a good chance to see the flatlands that encircle Shànghǎi, with their mix of farms and factories, and a rare opportunity to see a small village that owes its origins to the Venice-like canals that interlace this vast delta. Tours usually include a stop on **Lake Dǐngshān,** one of China's largest lakes, 60km (37 miles) from Shànghǎi, for a tour of a new theme park, **Grand View Garden,** a reconstruction of the old estate that is the setting of a famous Chinese novel. Few Westerners find this literary amusement park of much interest.

The water village (admission ¥60/$7.50), however, is fascinating, as this canal village resembles an illustration from an antique Blue Willow plate with waterways, Chinese gondolas, arched stone bridges, and tile-roofed wooden houses. Several of the 200- to 400-year-old residences of village leaders are open to tour; there's a village museum, and there are hundreds of quaint shops all along the canal promenade. The two-story traditional wooden courtyard houses, decorated with Qīng Dynasty furniture, consist of a formal meeting room, separate villas for men and women, workshops, bedrooms, and ancestral shrines.

The highlights of a village tour include lunch in one of a dozen canal-side dining rooms (where pork roast and fish are the local specialties), topped off by a gondola ride up the village canal in an eight-person boat. The gondolas are "rowed" by long tillers at the stern, which are expertly maneuvered by the women of Zhōu Zhuāng. This is perhaps as close to the "Venice of the East" as a traveler to China can get these days. Zhōu Zhuāng is extremely crowded on weekends, so aim for a weekday if possible.

PRACTICAL INFORMATION

by Sharon Owyang

ORIENTATION & WHEN TO GO

Shànghǎi, which means "On the Sea," is located on the East China coast about 23km (15 miles) south of the mouth of the Yángzǐ River. It is roughly halfway between Běijīng (1,120km/700 miles) to the northwest, and Hong Kong (1,200km/750miles) to the southwest. Closer to home, it is sandwiched between Jiāngsū Province and Zhèjiāng Province, with Hángzhōu, Sūzhōu, and Lake Tài (each the subject of a separate chapter in this guide) just a few hours away by road or rail. Shànghǎi has four distinct seasons with a tropical marine monsoon climate. Rainfall is abundant throughout the year but especially during the rainy season from mid-June to August. Summers are stiflingly hot and humid, winters can be bone-chillingly cold (even though the temperature seldom falls below freezing), and spring sees intermittent showers, making the balmy months of September and October the best time to visit.

GETTING THERE

By Plane Serviced by two airports, Shànghăi is connected by air to many international destinations and all the main cities in China. The old **Hóngqiáo Airport** (© 021/6268-8899) is 15km (9 miles) west of downtown Shànghăi and is now used primarily for domestic flights, although some of these also land at the new Pŭdōng Airport. There is a **Tourist Service Desk** (© 021/6268-8899, ext. 56750) in the **International Arrival Hall**, which provides maps and information in English (open daily 10am–9:30pm). Taxis (use only official metered taxis waiting in line outside the airport to the right) into town from Hóngqiáo Airport take anywhere from 20 to 40 minutes depending on traffic and should cost between ¥30 and ¥80 ($3.75–$8). Several buses also make the run into town: A CAAC shuttle, Mínháng Zhuānxiàn (Airport Special Line) goes to the Chéngshì Hángzhàn Lóu (City Air-Terminal Building) at Nánjĭng Xĭlù 1600, just west of the Shànghăi Center. Shuttles depart every 20 minutes from 6am to 8:30pm. The Airport Bus Line 1 (Jĭchăng Yĭxiàn) connects Hóngqiáo (buses depart every 20 min. 6am–9pm) with Pŭdōng Airport (every 20 min. from 7:20am to last flight). Public bus no. 941 goes to the railway station from Hóngqiáo Airport while public bus no. 925 runs to People's Square (Rénmín Guăngchăng) from Hóngqiáo Airport. Additionally, many hotels provide free airport shuttles, especially if you fax a request, in advance, with your arrival time.

The new **Pŭdōng International Airport** (© 021/6834-1000), located 45km (28 miles) east of downtown Shànghăi, is the gateway for all international flights (including United Airlines, Northwest, Air Canada, and British Airways) and increasingly more domestic flights. Departure tax is ¥50 ($6.25) for domestic flights and ¥90 ($11) for international flights. Be advised that check-in for international flights officially closes 30 minutes before departure, so allow yourself plenty of time. Taxi transfers on the new highway to hotels in Pŭdōng and downtown Shànghăi run between 45 minutes to 1½ hours (¥160/$20 and up). There are many buses making transfers into town: Airport Bus Line 1 goes to Hóngqiáo Airport (see above); Airport Bus Line 2 (Jĭchăng Èr Xiàn) goes from Pŭdōng (departing every 15–20 min. from 7:20am to last flight) to the City Air-Terminal Building (Chéngshì Hángzhàn Lóu. Buses depart to go back to Pŭdōng Airport every 15–20 min. 6am–7pm) at Nánjĭng Xĭ Lù 1600. Airport Bus Line 3 goes to Zūnyì Lù (with a stop at the Renaissance Yangtze Hotel), and Airport Bus Line 5 goes to the Shànghăi Railway Station. Prices range from ¥17 to ¥25 ($2–$3). Check at the Airport Bus counter in the arrival hall for the number and schedule of the bus that stops at your hotel or at the nearest hotel. When the subway line is completed sometime in 2003, magnetic levitation (maglev) trains will make the 33km (20-mile) run between Pŭdōng Airport and the Lóngyáng Lù Subway Station in 8 minutes. From there, it's an easy connection on the subway Metro Line 2 to destinations in Pŭdōng and the rest of Shànghăi. Hotels also offer shuttle buses but will usually charge a fee for this service.

By Train Shànghăi is well connected by train to many major Chinese destinations, including Bĕijĭng (14 hr. overnight); Guăngzhōu (12 hr.); Hong Kong (12 hr., train no. K99/K100); and the nearby towns of Hángzhōu (2 hr.), Sūzhōu (45 min.), and Wúxī (90 min.). The **train station** (℡ 021/6317-9090) is located in the northern part of town at the intersection of Héngfēng Běi Lù and Tiānmù Xī Lù, and is accessible by taxi or the subway's metro line no. 1. Taxis originating from the train station (¥2/ 25¢ surcharge) can be hailed on the lower level. Train tickets can be purchased at the train station, at CITS (see below), or at any number of train ticket outlets around town, including Xīzàng Nán Lù 121, just north of the YMCA Hotel.

By Ship The once popular Hong Kong—Shànghǎi ferry route is now a thing of the past. Today, Japan's Osaka and Kobe are the only international destinations served by Shànghǎi's International Passengers' Terminal at 1 Tàipíng Lù. Boats leave every 4 days, alternating between the two cities. Domestically, boats to Dàlián (36 hr., once every 4 days) depart from the Gōngpíng Lù Passenger Terminal at Gōngpíng Lù 50, while those bound for Chóngqìng (7 days; departing at 9am daily) and Pǔtuó Shān leave from the **Shíliùpǔ Wharf** (Shíliùpǔ Mǎtóu; ℡ 021/ 6326-1261) south of the Bund. Tickets can be bought at the respective terminals or at travel agencies such as CITS.

GETTING AROUND

Shànghǎi is best toured by a combination of foot, subway, and taxis. Destinations like the Bund, Nánjīng Lù, the French Concession, and the old Chinese city deserve to be toured on **foot,** and can be easily accomplished with the aid of an English-language map (available in most hotels). **Taxis** are plentiful and can be hailed practically anywhere. Flagfall is ¥10 ($1.25) for 3km (1¾ miles), then ¥2 (25¢) per kilometer with a 30¢ surcharge across the board from 11pm to 7am. Most taxi drivers do not speak English, so it's a good idea to have the name of your destination written in Chinese. Be sure also to have the drivers turn on the meter (dǎbiǎo), and ask for the receipt at the end of the trip.

For convenience, the Shànghǎi **subway** (dìtiě) is a good alternative to taxis, which can often get snarled in traffic. In particular, if you're trying to get to Pǔdōng, the subway (via metro line no. 2) is usually more convenient as there are often traffic tie-ups on the bridges and tunnels running to Pǔdōng. Metro line no. 1 runs from the train station in the north to Xīnzhuāng Station in the south, with stops along the way at the major commercial and tourist areas of People's Square (Rénmín Guǎngchǎng, where you can transfer to metro line no. 2), the French Concession (Huángpǔ Nánlù, Shǎnxī Lù, Chángshú Lù), and Xújiāhuì. Metro line no. 2 runs east and west across downtown Shànghǎi, from Zhōngshān Gōngyuán (Zhōngshān Park) in the west through Nánjīng Lù (Hénán Lù stop) to Pǔdōng (Lùjiāzuǐ), ending at the Lóngyáng Lù stop. The subway operates from 5am to 11pm daily and tickets cost between ¥2 and ¥4 (25¢–50¢).

Public **buses** are often crowded and usually require some knowledge of Chinese to get around.

TOURS & STRATAGEMS

Shànghǎi has an official **Tourism Hotline** (© 021/6439-0630), which can be helpful in answering basic questions, but the official travel agencies are more helpful for booking tours and accommodations. **China International Travel Service (CITS)** is headquartered at Běijīng Xīlù 1277, Guólǔ Dàshà, with the **FIT** (Family and Independent Travelers) department located in Room 610 (© 021/6289-2512; fax 021/6289-7838; www.scits.com). CITS can provide maps and information; arrange accommodations; arrange plane, train, and boat tickets; and organize private guided tours of the city and day trips to nearby destinations like Zhōuzhuāng, Sūzhōu, Hángzhōu, and Wúxī, though be sure to give them as much advance notice as possible. CITS also has another outlet at Jīnlíng Dōng Lù (© 021/6321-7200) near the Bund, where you can purchase tickets, but they have not been as helpful as the main office. Another helpful outlet is the **Spring International Travel Service (Chūnqiū Guójì Lǚxíng Shè)** at Dīngxī Lù 155. They have a 24-hour tourist information line (© 021/6252-0000) and can help book tours and arrange tickets and accommodations, as can most hotel tour desks.

The **Jǐnjiāng Optional Tours Center** at Chánglè Lù 191 (© 021/6466-2828; fax 021/6445-9525; sjtopt@online.sh.cn) offers a variety of tours (both group and private) of surrounding areas documented in their brochure. Among the highlights are their 1-day City Tour that takes in the Bund, Yù Yuán, the French Concession, Pǔdōng, the Shànghǎi Museum, and People's Square (Rénmín Guǎngchǎng). The cost is ¥250 ($31) per person, including an English-speaking guide, transportation, lunch, and entrance tickets. They also offer a daily tour of Sūzhōu and Zhōuzhuāng for ¥450 ($56) per person. The English-speaking staff can also help arrange private car rental, English-speaking guides, Pǔjiāng River cruise tickets, and tickets to evening entertainment (acrobatic shows, operas, and drama and musical performances).

A number of **Travel Information and Service Centers** (© 021/6439-8947; www.shanghaitour.net) have popped up around town, but staff, when they can be found in the booths, are not particularly helpful and speak little English. You can pick up maps and brochures and, in a pinch, figure out the quickest way to the nearest travel agency.

The best selection of books on Shànghǎi and China is in the **Foreign Language Bookstore (Wàiwén Shūdiàn)** at Fúzhōu Lù 390. For reading up on Shànghǎi before arrival, try Pan Ling's *In Search of Old Shànghǎi*, Nien Cheng's *Life and Death in Shànghǎi*, Vicki Baum's *Shànghǎi '37*, J. G. Ballard's *Empire of the Sun*, and Sterling Seagrave's *The Soong Dynasty*.

WHERE TO STAY

With practically every major international hotel chain represented in Shànghǎi, visitors have your pick of top four- and five-star hotels. The competition has meant that visitors can often get rates far below those posted here. Travel agents can also help you secure significantly lower rates, so it's worth checking with them before making a reservation yourself. Still, prices here run significantly higher than in the rest of China. While Shànghǎi has some mid-range, economical, three-star accommodations, these tend not to be up to international standards. *Note:* Unless otherwise noted, all rooms are subject to a 15% service charge.

Crowne Plaza Shànghǎi (Yínxīng Huángguān Jiǔdiàn) Tucked away in a comparatively quiet corner of west Shànghǎi, between downtown and the Hóngqiáo District, this four-star hotel is a solid, dependable choice. Delivering consistent service for many years, the hotel is popular with business travelers and attendees of the biannual Shànghǎi Film Festival, which is held next door at the Shànghǎi Film City (Shànghǎi Yīngchéng). Rooms are large, comfortable, and fitted with work desks, safes, dataports, and satellite TV. The marble bathrooms have tub/shower combos. Six executive floors provide more exclusivity. Staff is friendly and helpful.

Pānyú Lù 400 (west Shànghǎi). © *800/ 465-4329* or *021/6280-8888. Fax 021/ 6280-3353. www.sixcontinentshotels. com. 534 units, including 28 suites. ¥1,840 ($230) double, ¥3,120 ($390) and up, suite. AE, DC, MC, V.* **Amenities:** 5 restaurants; several bars and lounges; indoor swimming pool; squash court; fitness club; Jacuzzi; sauna; billiards; concierge; free airport shuttle; business center; conference rooms; shops; salon; 24-hr. room service; babysitting; same-day laundry and dry cleaning; valet; nightly turndown; newspaper delivery; newsstand. *In room:* A/C, TV, dataport, minibar, coffeemaker, hair dryer.

Four Seasons Hotel Shànghǎi (Shànghǎi Sìjì Jiǔdiàn) This newcomer (2002) to the Shànghǎi luxury hotel scene introduces the signature Four Seasons service and pampering to China. Well located right in the thick of Pǔxī (west

Shànghǎi), this modern 37-story tower offers the largest number of suites in the city. Rooms and suites are spacious and warmly decorated in gold and beige with red and blue trim. The furniture is classical and the patented Four Seasons bed alone is worth the stay. In-room safes are large enough for laptop computers. Each room is equipped with three telephones and high-speed Internet access. Marble bathrooms have separate shower and tub. Best of all, this hotel delivers impeccable service, from their 24-hour butler service for each guest to the helpful, friendly, English-speaking staff throughout the hotel.

Wēihǎi Lù 500 (between Nánjīng Xī Lù and Yán'ān Zhōnglù, west Shànghǎi). © *021/6256-8888. Fax 021/6256-5678. www.fourseasons.com. 439 units including 79 suites. ¥2,575–¥2,820 ($310– $340) double; from ¥3,237 ($390) suite. AE, DC, MC, V.* **Amenities:** 4 restaurants; several bars and lounges; indoor pool; state-of-the-art health club and spa; Jacuzzi; sauna; concierge; 24-hr. business center; conference rooms; shops; salon; 24-hr. room service; massage; babysitting; same-day laundry and dry cleaning; valet; 24-hr. butler service; executive level rooms; nightly turndown; newspaper delivery; newsstand. *In room:* A/C, TV, dataport, minibar, hair dryer, safe.

Grand Hyatt Shànghǎi (Jīnmào Kǎiyuè Dàjiǔdiàn) Since its opening in 1999, this much-ballyhooed hotel has gotten a lot of attention for having some of the highest and grandest hotel rooms in the world (from the 54th to the 88th floor of the architecturally fascinating Jīnmào Building), and one of the highest hotel occupancy rates in Shànghǎi. As promised, the rooms are like no other, offering a postmodern mix of

East and West with contemporary furniture against dark wood walls inscribed with Chinese poetry, and stupendous views of Shànghǎi (on the rare smogless day, that is). Bathrooms are brazenly modern with all-glass washbasins and separate tub and shower. All this headiness, however, can also feel a little claustrophobic, and the burden of renown has occasionally made the staff here a mite arrogant. Still, with six international restaurants offering fine dining high above Shànghǎi and a cascading "sky pool" that stretches from window to window, this truly grand Hyatt novelty continues to remain a top choice in town.

Shìjì Dà Dào 2, Jǐn Mào Tower, 54th Floor, Pǔdōng (near Pearl of the Orient TV Tower). © **800/233-1234** *or 021/5049-1234. Fax 021/5049-1111. www.shanghai.hyatt.com. 555 units, including 45 suites. ¥2,655–¥2,780 ($330–$348) double; ¥4,230 ($529) and up for suites. AE, DC, MC, V.* **Amenities:** 6 restaurants; several bars and lounges; indoor lap pool with cascades; highest fitness center in the world; Jacuzzi; sauna; concierge; airport shuttle; business center; conference rooms; shops; salon; 24-hour room service; babysitting; same-day laundry and dry cleaning; valet; nightly turndown; newspaper delivery; newsstand. *In room:* A/C, TV, dataport, minibar.

Hilton Shànghǎi International (Jìnān Dàjiǔdiàn) For a 43-story hotel with the most rooms in town, the Hilton keeps a surprisingly low profile. Maybe it has something to do with the fact that as the first foreign-owned hotel (1987) in a town that likes all things new, the Hilton is seen as a bit fuddy-duddy. But the hotel wears its experience well. Who needs to make waves when the excellent service and first-rate facilities keep guests, mostly business travelers, coming back time and again? Rooms are bright and luxurious. The hotel has three nonsmoking floors and five restaurants offering fine international dining.

Huáshān Lù 250. © **800/445-8667** *or 021/6248-0000. Fax 021/6248-3848. www.hilton.com. 772 units, including 56 suites. ¥1940–¥2,075 ($243–$259) double; ¥3650 ($456) suite. AE, DC, MC, V.* **Amenities:** 5 restaurants; several bars and lounges; indoor pool; tennis court; 2 squash courts; health club; sauna; concierge; tour desk; free airport shuttle; business center; conference rooms; shopping arcade; drugstore; florist; salon; medical clinic; 24-hr. room service; dry cleaning and laundry (24-hr., same day); nightly turndown; newsstand and bookstore; express checkout. *In room:* A/C, TV, dataport, minibar, hair dryer, safe.

Peace Hotel (Hépíng Fàndiàn) Even though its service and amenities do not match those of other local five-star hotels, the Peace's legendary name and history continue to make it a popular choice. The hotel is also ideally located right at the intersection of Nánjǐng Lù and the Bund. The hotel's restored Art Deco decor, fully realized in the lobby, evokes old Shànghǎi at its finest. Rooms are large but a little dark, and some still contain the original woodwork and furnishings. For the full effect, splurge on a suite, each decorated in the style of a particular country: Chinese, British, American, French, and India, to name a few. Unfortunately, service at this classic hotel is inefficient, and the staff is not particularly friendly. *Nánjǐng Dōnglù (on the Bund).* © **021/6321-6888.** *Fax 021/6329-0300. www.shanghaipeacehotel.com. 279 units. ¥1,280 ($160) double. AE, DC, MC, V.*

Amenities: 2 restaurants; several bars and lounges; health club; sauna; billiards; concierge; conference room; shops; salon; 24-hr. room service; next-day laundry and dry cleaning; newsstand. *In room:* A/C, TV, dataport, minibar, hair dryer, safe.

Ritz-Carlton Portman Hotel (Bōtèmàn Dàjiǔdiàn) Despite some heavy competition, this is still Shànghǎi's top choice for business travelers and world leaders (U.S. President Bush stayed here during the APEC Conference in 2001). Fully renovated in 2000, the Portman offers all the luxury and fine service associated with the Ritz-Carlton brand. Rooms are large, plush, and well fitted with writing desks, sofas, three phones, in-room safes, and satellite TV. Service is professional and excellent. The adjacent **Shànghǎi Centre** (ⓒ **021/6279-8009**) provides one-stop shopping with airline offices, a medical clinic, a post office, automatic teller machines, an American Express office, and a Starbucks.

Nánjīng Xīlù 1376 (inside the Shànghǎi Centre). ⓒ **800/241-3333** or **021/6279-8888.** *Fax 021/6279-8800. www.ritzcarlton.com. 564 units. ¥2,400 ($300) double.* AE, DC, MC, V. **Amenities:** 4 restaurants; several bars and lounges; heated indoor-outdoor lap pool; tennis court; 2 squash courts; large health club; Jacuzzi; sauna; concierge; tour desk; free airport shuttle; 24-hr. business center; shopping arcade; salon; World Link medical clinic; 24-hr. room service; dry cleaning and laundry (same day); valet; nightly turndown; newspaper delivery; newsstand; twice-daily maid service; express checkout. *In room:* A/C, TV, dataport, minibar, coffeemaker, hair dryer, safe.

Shangri-La Pǔdōng Hotel (Xiānggé Lǐlā Fàndiàn) Boasting the best location in Pǔdōng, and a gorgeous view of the Bund across the river, the Shangri-La offers top-notch luxury accommodations. Despite its Pǔdōng address, the hotel is within walking distance of the subway and is hence quite convenient to the heart of old Shànghǎi. There is a relaxed elegance to this comparatively older (1998) but still handsome hotel. Guest rooms are very spacious, and while they may not have the latest gadgets, they are more than adequately equipped with large work desks, comfortable furniture, and separate shower and tub. Staff is exceedingly friendly and the service is first rate. Plans are underway to build a new annex.

Fù Chéng Lù 33 (Pǔdōng, east Shànghǎi). ⓒ *800/942-5050* or *021/6882-8888. Fax 021/6882-6688. www.Shangri-la.com. 612 units, including 25 suites. ¥2575–¥2740 ($310–$330) standard room; ¥4315 ($520) suite.* AE, DC, MC, V. **Amenities:** 5 restaurants; several bars and lounges; indoor swimming pool; tennis court; fitness club; Jacuzzi; sauna; free access to Riverside Park; concierge; free airport shuttle; business center; conference rooms; shops; 24-hr. room service; babysitting; same-day laundry and dry cleaning; valet; nightly turndown; newspaper delivery; newsstand. *In room:* A/C, TV, dataport, minibar, coffeemaker, safe.

Sheraton Grand Tài Píng Yáng (Xīláidēng Háodá Tàipíngyáng Dàfàndiàn) The switch from the Westin brand to the Sheraton brand in early 2002 saw the complete renovation of guest rooms, but, otherwise, little is changed at this 27-story five-star hotel that continues to offer good service in a luxurious environment. Rooms are still on the small side but are now decorated in a mix of Chinese and Western styles, with a classical roll-out desktop right under Chinese artwork. Bathrooms are sleek and modern and have shower/tub combos. The hotel has a full range of dining, entertainment, and business-related facilities and can also arrange tee times and transportation to the Shànghǎi International Golf and Country Club.

Zūnyì Nán Lù 5 (Hóngqiáo area, west Shànghǎi). ℂ *800/WESTIN-1 or 021/6275-8888. Fax 021/6275-5420. www. sheratongrand-shanghai.com. 496 units. ¥1,909 ($230) double. AE, DC, MC, V.* **Amenities:** 6 restaurants; several bars and lounges; indoor swimming pool; tennis court; fitness club; Jacuzzi; sauna; billiards; concierge; tour desk; free airport shuttle; business center; conference rooms; shops; salon; 24-hr. room service; babysitting; same-day laundry and dry cleaning; valet; nightly turndown; newspaper delivery; newsstand. *In room:* A/C, TV, dataport, minibar, safe.

St. Regis (Shànghǎi Ruìjí Hóngtǎ Dàjiǔdiàn) As the second St. Regis hotel to open in China in 2001, the Shànghǎi version is a handsome, robust hotel that is quickly garnering a legion of devotees. Were it not for its less convenient location in the still emerging business district of Pǔdōng, it may well be *the* luxury hotel to stay at in town. Rooms are gorgeously furnished with comfortable sofas, large desks, Herman Miller "Aeron" chairs, custom-designed pillow-top mattresses, and Bose CD Wave radios. The marble bathrooms are spacious and fitted with decadent "Rainforest" showers, separate bathtub, and a flurry of amenities by Floris. But the St. Regis truly distinguishes itself with its signature butler service, which it has honed to a fine art. St. Regis butlers will not only make tea and press clothing, they can also help with any computer and Internet hookup problems.

Dōngfāng Lù 889 (Pǔdōng, east Shànghǎi). ℂ *021/5050-4567. Fax 021/6875-6789. www.stregis.com. 318 units, including 48 suites. ¥2,656 ($320) double; from ¥3,071 ($370) suite. AE, DC, MC, V.* **Amenities:** 4 restaurants; several bars and lounges; indoor pool; tennis court; health club and full-service spa; Jacuzzi; sauna; 24-hr. concierge; 24-hr. business center; conference rooms; shops; salon; 24-hr. butler service; 24-hr. room service; massage; babysitting; same-day laundry and dry cleaning; valet; in-room check-in; daily fresh fruit; nightly turndown; newspaper delivery; newsstand; executive-level rooms. *In room:* A/C, TV, dataport, minibar, safe.

YMCA Hotel (Qīngniánhuì Bīnguǎn) With a great location, right in the heart of old Shànghǎi, this is one of the better choices for budget accommodations. This 11-story three-star hotel was Shànghǎi's YMCA when it was built in 1929, and there's a slightly dilapidated air about it. Rooms are fairly drab and nondescript and the beds somewhat lumpy, but the bathrooms are at least fairly clean. Dorm rooms with shared bathroom facilities are also available, though these are basic at best. While the front desk staff is not particularly friendly, they speak a little English and can be helpful when necessary.

Xīzàng Nánlù 123 (2 blocks south of Nánjīng Lù, 1 mile west of the Bund). ℂ *021/6326-1040. Fax 021/6320-1957. www.ymcahotel.com. 150 units. ¥510–¥548 ($64–$68) double. Dorm rooms (4 people) $15/bed. AE, DC, MC, V.* **Amenities:** Restaurant; 24-hr. cafe; small exercise room; free airport shuttle; business center; salon; massage room. *In room:* A/C, TV.

WHERE TO DINE

Shànghǎi easily offers some of the best and most diversified dining in China, with practically every regional cuisine represented here. Shanghainese cuisine, usually subsumed under the umbrella of Huáiyáng Cuisine, one of the four major Chinese cuisines, often features river fish, eel, crabs, and seafood that's braised in red sauce or stir-fried. The main seasonings used are soya sauce, sugar, and oil. Some of the more famous Shànghǎinese dishes include Shīzi Tóu (Lion's Head Meatballs), yóumèn sǔn (braised bamboo shoots), and Zuìjī (Drunken Chicken). On the Western dining scene, many of the international hotels offer excellent, if expensive, fare. More exciting, however, is the increasing number of independent international restaurants that can rival their counterparts in London and New York. Already, there are plans underway for world-renowned chefs like Nobu Matsuhisa and Jean Georges Vongerichten to open their signature restaurants at the toniest address of them all, the Bund. (At the other end of the dining scale, with the proliferation of international fast-food chains like McDonald's, KFC, Pizza Hut, Starbucks, and even the Hard Rock Cafe, visitors can be forgiven for thinking that you've never left home.) With scores of good restaurants to choose from, here's a handful of the best bets:

Cháng Ān Dumpling Restaurant (Cháng'ān Jiǎozi Lóu) DUMPLINGS This local institution recently moved from its Yúnnán Lù address in Pǔxī to Pǔdōng, but not too much else seems to have changed. Certainly, the restaurant's claim to fame—108 varieties of dumplings—is still holding up well. Just don't ask the staff to explain all 108 varieties to you during peak meal hours. Besides the usual pork and leek dumplings, try the pumpkin dumplings and the red-bean dumplings. *Pǔdōng Dàdào 1586 (by Mínshēng Lù, Pǔdōngi).* ☎ *021/5885-8416. Reservations required for sampling all 108 dumpling varieties. Meals ¥15 ($1.90) and up. Daily 6am–9pm.*

Dàjiāng Hú JAPANESE While there are many good Japanese restaurants in town, Dàjiāng Hú has a loyal following for its all-you-can-eat Japanese dinners at a very reasonable ¥200 ($25) per person. From sushi to tempura, noodles to teriyaki, the food is uniformly good, and the ambience is pleasant and relaxed. There's also free-flowing sake and beer, so come early and stay a while. Dàjiāng Hú has another outlet in Xújiāhuì at Xiétǔ Lù 2430 (☎ 021/6468-5177). *Dōnghú Lù 30 (French Concession off Huáihǎi Lù).* ☎ *021/5403-3332. Meals ¥200 ($25) per person. Daily 5:30–11pm (last order 10:15pm).*

Dragon and Phoenix Restaurant SHÀNGHǍI While the food is fine, although certainly not the best in town, diners come here because it is, after all, a part of the Peace Hotel. Furthermore, with green walls, red and gold pillars, and dragons and bats hanging from the ceiling, the kitschy decor has to be seen to be believed. The food here is a mix of Shànghǎi, Cantonese, and Sìchuān dishes. The seafood hotpot, barbecued duck, river eel, and pork chops are all worth trying. Try to get a table by the window, which offers some pretty panoramas of the Bund and Pǔdōng across the river. Service is professional and efficient. *Nánjīng Dōnglù 20 (8th floor, Peace Hotel).* ☎ *021/6321-6888, ext 5201. Reservations recommended for dinner.*

Main courses ¥160–¥280 ($20–$35). AE, DC, MC, V. Daily 11:30am–2pm and 5:30–10pm.

Gōngdélín VEGETARIAN CHINESE Shànghǎi's most well-known vegetarian restaurant has over a half century of experience, and while it may have grown a little stodgy in its old age, it still offers the most reliable and consistent vegetarian fare in town. It's often packed here as diners come to savor the *sùjī* (vegetarian chicken) and *sùyā* (vegetarian duck), all imitations of the real thing made from tofu and soy products. The decor is nothing to write home about but the duck that isn't a duck certainly is. *Nánjīng Xǐlù 445 (west Shànghǎi).* (C) *021/6327-0218. Reser-vations recommended on weekends. Main courses ¥56–¥120 ($7–$15). No credit cards. Daily 6:30–9:30am, 11am–2pm, and 5–9pm.*

Lan Kwai Fong at Park 97 INTERNATIONAL Having undergone a few incarnations through the years, this trendy Art Deco–style restaurant in Fùxīng Park has been remodeled and divided into four different outlets. The Italian-themed Baci, with its sleek black columns and wall of mirrors, serves good homemade pastas and thin-crusted pizzas. Next door, the more subdued Tokio Joe offers sushi rolls, udon, skewers, and weekday Japanese set lunches for ¥95 ($12). Every night after 8pm, the California Club opens up its disco doors right onto Baci, giving patrons a chance to work off their dessert calories. The upstairs section used to be occupied by Indochine, serving Vietnamese food, but it now sits empty as the owners decide what to open in its stead. Regardless of what's to come, however, Park 97 is still the place for the hip set to see and be seen. *Gāolán Lù 2 (inside west entrance of*

Fùxīng Park, central Shànghǎi). (C) *021/ 5383-2328 (Baci/Tokio Joe). Reservations recommended on weekends. Main courses ¥50–¥200 ($6–$25). AE, DC, MC, V. Sun–Thurs 11am–2am; Fri–Sat 11am–4am; kitchen closes nightly at 10:30pm.*

Lan Na Thai THAI Located in a former mansion of the 1930s Morris Estate, this lovely and elegant restaurant serves excellent Thai (mostly Northern) fare. Thai chefs prepare a *tod mun pla* (fish cake) and assorted curries that are especially fine, and service is discreet and professional. Downstairs, there's an Indian restaurant (Hazara) that serves good if expensive Indian food, and a stylish bar and lounge (Faces), designed to make you want to stay awhile. *Ruìjīn Èr Lù 118, Ruìjīn Guest House, Building no. 4, 2nd Floor (French Concession).* (C) *021/6466-4328. Reservations recommended on weekends. Main courses ¥80–¥144 ($10–$18). AE, DC, MC, V. Daily 5:30–11pm.*

Le Garçon Chinois CONTINENTAL/ SHÀNGHǍI Don't let the name fool you. Yes, this lovely little restaurant, hidden in an alley off Héngshān Lù in an old French Concession mansion, serves Continental cuisine, including an excellent osso bucco and a Portugese broiled red snapper with clams, but expatriates flock here for the Shanghainese food served on the third floor. The roast duck breast and the black pepper beef are both popular favorites. The restaurant also has a bakery and cafe on the first floor and a bar that's open until 1am. *Héngshān Lù, Lane 9, no. 3 (west Shànghǎi).* (C) *021/ 6445-7970 or 6445-8217. Reservations recommended. Meals ¥120–¥160 ($15–$20). AE, DC, MC, V. Lunch (Continental only) daily noon–2pm; dinner daily 6–10pm.*

Lǜ Bō Láng SHÀNGHǍI Housed in a three-story traditional Chinese building right next to the Bridge of Nine Turnings, this restaurant is very popular with foreign visitors, some of the more famous of whom have included Queen Elizabeth and Fidel Castro. Specialties here include the seasonal Yáng Chéng Hú freshwater crab, shark's fin, Shanghainese dim sum, and snacks such as *xiǎolóng bāo* (steamed dumplings with crabmeat and pork) and former U.S. President Clinton's favorite, *sānsī méimáo sū* (eyebrow-shaped pastry stuffed with pork, bamboo, and mushrooms). Service is a little brusque, prices are a little inflated, but, by now, you're convinced you really want to see for yourself what all the fuss is about. *Yù Yuán Lù 115–131 (south of Húxīn Tíng Tea House, Old Town Shànghǎi).* © *021/ 6328-0602. Reservations required for dinner. Meals ¥120–¥250 ($14–$30). AE, DC, MC, V. Daily 10am–10pm.*

M on the Bund CONTINENTAL Five years after its opening in 1999, this is still the best and classiest restaurant in town for Western dining, though there are surely upstarts like T8 nipping at M's heels. For now, however, M is pushing ahead with all the confidence of a front-runner, opening an additional Glamour Room for nightly dinners (6–10:30pm) and drinks (5pm–late). In the main dining room, the caviar and lamb are still favorites, and the crème brûlée a must. Another constant throughout the years: Whether you come for Sunday brunch or the weekday set lunches (¥88–¥98/$11–$12), the view of the Bund and Pǔdōng from M's terrace is unparalleled. *Guǎngdōng Lù 20, 7th Floor (entrance on this side street off the Bund).* © *021/6350-9988. Reservations required. Main courses ¥120–¥280 ($15–$35). AE, DC, MC, V.*

Lunch Tues–Fri 11:30am–2:30pm, Sat– Sun 11:30am–3pm; dinner daily 6– 10:30pm.

Méilóngzhèn SHÀNGHǍI/SÌCHUĀN One of the city's oldest (1938) and most famous restaurants, Méilóngzhèn still draws the crowds after all these years. Its cuisine has evolved over time from strictly regional fare to one incorporating the spices, vinegars, and chilies of Sìchuān cooking. Seafood is featured prominently here and popular favorites include the deep-fried eel, lobster in pepper sauce, Mandarin fish with noodles in chili sauce, and twice-cooked pork. The atmosphere is a bit stodgy, with old-fashioned Qīng Dynasty furniture and carved wooden panels. The staff seems harried most of the time, no doubt because of the crowds that throng here. English menus are available. *Nánjīng Xīlù 1081, no. 22 (west Shànghǎi).* © *021/6253-5353 or 6256-6688. Reservations required. Main courses ¥96–¥160 ($12–$20). AE, DC, MC, V. Daily 11am–2pm and 5–10pm.*

T8 CONTINENTAL As a new arrival on the Continental/Mediterranean dining scene, this restaurant is giving M on the Bund a healthy dose of competition, and justifiably so. The decor—a mix of exposed brick, sleek chrome, and muted lighting—is super chic and the food is irresistible, especially with Fusion dishes like the Sìchuān seared king prawns or the slow-cooked lamb and Sìchuān pie. Service is friendly and efficient. *Tàicāng Lù 181, Xīntiāndì, North Block.* © *021/6355-8999. Reservations required. Main courses ¥150– ¥250 ($18–$31). AE, DC, MC, V. Lunch Wed–Mon 11:30am–2:30pm; dinner daily 6:30–11:30pm.*

Tandoor INDIAN This oldest Indian restaurant in Shànghǎi was voted the city's best foreign restaurant in 1998, and it hasn't slipped much since then despite competition from newer restaurants. The chefs are from India, as are the dancers who perform traditional dances every night from 6 to 10:30pm. The food is good all around, from the chicken *chat* starter (barbecue chicken with lemon juice) to the *murgh malai* kabob (tandoori chicken marinated in yogurt) and vegetarian dishes such as the *saag paneer* (spinach with cheese). The staff is courteous and service is professional. *Màomíng Nán Lù 59 (in the New South Building of the Jǐn Jiāng Hotel).* © *021/6258-2582. Reservations required. Main courses ¥120–¥160 ($15–$20). AE, DC, MC, V. Daily 11:30am–2pm and 5:30–10:30pm.*

1221 SHÀNGHǍI Located at the end of an alley between the center of town and the Hóngqiáo district, this classy restaurant has been quietly serving consistently good food at reasonable prices for the last 6 years. With strong devotees in the expatriate and business community, this chic, tastefully decorated restaurant offers Shanghainese cuisine that's neither too greasy nor too sweet. Most things on the menu here are good, but some standouts include the Drunken Chicken, Lion's Head Meatballs, and orange peel beef.

Service is efficient if not particularly friendly. *Yánān Xīlù 1221 (west Shànghǎi).* © *021/6213-6585. Reservations recommended. Meals ¥80–¥200 ($10–$25). No credit cards. Daily 11am–2pm and 5–11pm.*

Va Bene ITALIAN Fresh from his successes with restaurants Gaia and Va Bene in Hong Kong, owner Pino Piano has landed in Shanghai with Va Bene Shànghǎi, luxurious Italian dining at its best. The warm Tuscan decor in this two-story shíkùmén (stone-framed) house is tasteful and elegant with dark wood paneling, striped timber floors, wooden window blinds, and high ceilings. There's a wide range of antipasti, pasta, and gourmet pizzas here, including standouts like the beef carpaccio, the breaded veal loin on the bone with warm tomato basil sauce, and the rosemary roast duck on porcini mushroom risotto. Save some room for the tiramisu and cappuccino with a hint of Grappa. Alfresco dining is available on the patio. *Tàicāng Lù 181, Xīntiāndì, North Block House 7.* © *021/6311-2211. Reservations recommended. Main courses ¥80–¥200 ($10–$25). AE, DC, MC, V. Daily 11am–3pm and 5pm–midnight.*

Sūzhōu: The Garden City

苏州

THERE IS "HEAVEN ABOVE, SŪZHŌU and Hángzhōu below," according to a popular adage. Unlike Hángzhōu (see the next chapter), whose beauty is of a broad, natural nature, Sūzhōu is intimate and artistic. More than 170 bridges arch over the 32km (20 miles) of slim waterways within the moated city. The poetic private gardens number about 70, with a dozen of the finest open to public view. Sūzhōu's interlocking canals, classic gardens, and embroidery and silk studios are the chief surviving elements of a cultural capital that dominated China's artistic scene for long periods during the Míng and Qīng dynasties. Even the women of Sūzhōu, with their rounded faces and pale skin, became the model of traditional beauty in China.

Members of England's first official mission to China (1792–94) summed up Sūzhōu as the home of China's "greatest artists, the most well-known scholars, the richest merchants" and as the ruler of "Chinese taste in matters of fashion and speech." To this day, Sūzhōu retains something of its stylish legacy. Its downtown is a pleasant array of tree-lined lanes, many of them running alongside canals. I must warn you, however, that the city's narrow, soupy canals are not quite those of Venice. Old Sūzhōu certainly contains an element of decay. But in this decay, there is a certain charm and authenticity not found in other old cities that have been remodeled and reconstructed into hygienic picture postcards of their former selves. Even with its darkening patina, Sūzhōu remains one of the most beautiful cities in China.

The focus of the city's beauty is its magnificent collection of private classic **gardens.** These small, exquisite jewels of landscaping art are the finest surviving examples of the tradition. Their enchantment is of a nature both philosophical and sensuous. The closest equivalent in the Western tradition might be Walden Pond, where Henry David Thoreau escaped the confines of city and civilization in order to confront his essential self. For Western romantics, the natural retreat opens ever outward in a widening circle of grass and field—the cosmos of an untamed New World. But for the Chinese mystic, the natural retreat closed ever more inwardly upon itself within the perfect garden—a microcosm of the unchanging ancient Way.

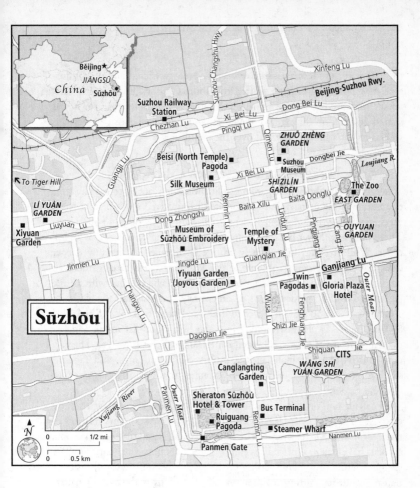

The gardens are often choked with visitors, making a slow, meditative tour difficult, but it is only by taking enough time to lose yourself in them that their power and essence can be discovered. The gardens of Sūzhōu are unlike those we are familiar with in the West—even unlike the Japanese gardens for which they once served as models. When Qí Biǎojiā, a 17th-century scholar, became obsessed with building a garden, he likened himself to both "a master painter at his work, not allowing a single dead stroke" and "a great writer writing essays, not permitting a single inharmonious sentence." A Chinese garden fuses landscape painting and literary composition to create an art of its own in which nature is shaped but not tamed.

Old Sūzhōu, surrounded by remnants of a moat and canals linked to the Grand Canal, has become a protected historical district, 3km by 5km (2 miles by 3 miles) across, in which little tampering and no skyscrapers are allowed. Sūzhōu, in other words, is one of those rare places in China where the ravages of modernization have been severely restricted and new industrial development has been shifted to suburban zones. In Sūzhōu's case, what's preserved is all the more remarkable because the downtown was spared destruction during World War II, and its private classic gardens, as well as its canals, have survived over the centuries.

Forest of Lions Garden (Shīzi Lín)

When I first saw the private gardens of Sūzhōu, they looked to me like large estates consisting of pavilions and open halls, unpaved and irregular pathways, small labyrinths of walls and screens, and heaps of grotesque rocks. There were few flower beds, no manicured lawns, and an absence of logical order. While I could immediately admire their quiet beauty, any deeper design or effects remained obscure. A quick tour of a celebrated garden can be disappointing to an inexperienced visitor from abroad, but with a little patience, a Sūzhōu garden opens up an entirely new vision of the world.

The first Sūzhōu garden I ever toured was **Forest of Lions (Shīzi Lín)** at Yuánlín Lù 23. It was founded in 1336 by a Buddhist monk and last owned by relatives of the renowned American architect I. M. Pei. The garden consists of four small lakes, a multitude of buildings, and random swirls of rockeries. Its elements are strange to those unaccustomed to Chinese gardens.

The principles of garden landscape design in China are often the reverse of those in the West. A classic Chinese garden expresses man's relation to nature, not his control over it. The symmetry and regularity we expect in a garden have been replaced by an organic, spontaneous pattern. The Chinese garden is a manifestation of the essential (even mystical) order of nature, in all its shiftings of vitality and vista. This is the way of nature itself, expressed by the garden at every turn. For this reason, the cult of the lawn never developed in China because the emphasis was always on the spirit of nature, uncultivated and various. As one Chinese critic wrote, the large lawns in an English garden, "while no doubt pleasing to a cow, could hardly engage the intellect of human beings."

Neat flower beds and trimmed hedge borders are likewise eschewed in the traditional Chinese garden, since they are too obviously artificial, too "unnatural." The many human elements in the garden—the halls, verandas, and bridges—are regarded as points of intersection with the natural realm rather than the interventions of a superior human hand. It is ultimately the task of the garden artist to arrange courtyard and screen, lake and path, rock and shadow organically, in obedience to the rhythms and patterns of a purely natural world, heightened in a garden for human contemplation.

While Tài Hú rocks and honeycombed rockeries seem more bizarre than evocative at first, the Chinese landscape artist regards them as an essential component of nature. The Forest of Lions Garden contains the largest rocks and most elaborate rockeries of any garden in Sūzhōu. This garden was designed specifically to emphasize the role of mountains in nature. These miniature monoliths recall the sacred mountains of China's past and the twisted, gouged-out morphology of the quintessential Chinese landscape common to scroll paintings. Mountains are also emblems of the Way (Dào), that process of transformation and transcendence in nature that Daoist monks and hermits achieve in their quests for immortality.

It took repeated visits to Chinese gardens before I developed a feel for these rocks, which I can now contemplate with interest. The Qīng Dynasty Kāngxī Emperor and his grandson the Qiánlóng Emperor were far more knowledgeable in such matters: They valued the rockeries of the Forest of Lions so highly that they used them as models for those in the Old Summer Palace in Běijīng.

The finest of the expressionistic slabs in Sūzhōu's Forest of Lions Garden came from nearby Lake Tài (Tài Hú). Since the Táng Dynasty (A.D. 618–907), connoisseurs have been selecting the best Tài Hú rocks for the gardens of emperors, high officials, and rich estate owners. During the Sòng Dynasty (A.D. 960–1126), rock appreciation reached such extremes that the expense of hauling stones from Lake Tài to the capital is said to have bankrupted the empire.

The Forest of Lions Garden is open daily from 8am to 5pm; admission is ¥15 ($1.80).

Lingering Garden (Lìú Yuán)

The single finest specimen of Tài Hú rock is located in Lìú Yuán, the Lingering Garden, a spacious Míng Dynasty estate at 80 Lìúyuán Lù. Its centerpiece is a 6m (20-ft.) high, 5-ton, contorted castle of rock called Crown of Clouds Peak. Lingering Garden is also notable for its viewing pavilions, particularly the **Mandarin Duck Hall,** which is divided into two sides: an ornate southern chamber for men and a plain northern chamber for women.

Sūzhōu's contemporary painters maintain a sales gallery in this garden, which is planted in osmanthus and willow, varieties that are not known for their brilliant flowerings, in keeping with a traditional prejudice for plain, unshowy vegetation. The Lingering Garden's name is derived from the original owner's family name, which sounds like the character for the word lingering. Subsequent owners continued to use the old name, after they discovered that their own family name for the garden did not catch on with the people of Sūzhōu.

The Lingering Garden is open daily from 8am to 5pm; admission is ¥20 ($2.50).

Humble Administrators & Stupid Officials

While these first two gardens are celebrated for their rockeries, other Sūzhōu gardens emphasize different elements. **Zhuō Zhèng Garden,** at Dōng Běi Jiē 178, one of Sūzhōu's largest and most popular gardens, makes complex use of water. Zhuō Zhèng Yuán is usually translated as "Humble Administrator's Garden," but garden scholar Maggie Keswick points out that the characters in the name have an ambiguous meaning that can be translated either as "Garden of the Unsuccessful Politician" or "Garden of the Stupid Officials." This garden, which dates from the 16th century, is located off Dōng Běi Jiē, just a few blocks northeast of the Lingering Garden.

In Zhuō Zhèng Garden, Tài Hú rocks are not as prominent as the maze of connected pools and islands. This watery maze is in fact an illusion, since there is only a single, long, meandering lake. It's impossible to tell where the water begins or ends; it even seems to flow under waterside pavilions. The creation of multiple vistas and the dividing of spaces into distinct segments are the artist's means of expanding the compressed spaces of the garden. As visitors stroll through the small space, new vistas open up at every turn. Such constant change can be confusing, producing what Maggie Keswick calls "that magical confusion which is the essence of garden architecture." Ideally, you walk through a garden not simply to contemplate nature and learn about its underlying patterns but to feel its disorienting power—to break down logical, social, and human definitions of order and enter a state of direct communion with the natural order.

Zhuō Zhèng Garden is open daily from 7:30am to 5pm; admission is ¥40 ($5).

Master of the Nets Garden (Wǎng Shī Yuán)

While many rich officials and merchants built garden estates simply to entertain, the more scholarly and poetic among the rich wanted to create contemplative retreats. They conceived of the garden as an enclosed series of spaces within spaces, each parcel inviting heightened contact with nature. The human world outside the garden walls was deliberately held at bay. The most perfect of these retreats is Wǎng Shī Yuán, the Master of the Nets Garden, a masterpiece of landscape compression. Hidden at the end of a blind alley off Shíquán Jiē, a busy street of scroll and handicraft shops, the tiny grounds of the Master of the Nets Garden have been cleverly expanded by the placement of innumerable walls, screens, and pavilion halls, producing a seemingly limitless maze. The eastern sector of the garden is a cluster of three interlinked buildings, the residence of the former owner and his family. At the center of the garden is a pond, just 1 square *mǔ* (about 810 sq. m/2,700 sq. ft.), encircled by verandas, pavilions, and

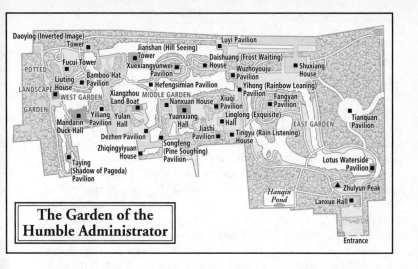

The Garden of the
Humble Administrator

covered corridors, and crossed by two arched stone bridges. Set back from this watery "mirror of heaven," with its proportionate rockeries and bamboo, is a complex of halls and inner courtyards: a garden within a garden. The halls invite rest and meditation. The most lavish hall, **Diǎnchūn Cottage (Diǎnchūn Táng),** furnished in palace lanterns, dark chairs and tables, and hanging scrolls, served as the model for Míngxuán Garden, the Astor Chinese Garden Court and Míng Furniture Room constructed in 1980 in the Metropolitan Museum of Art in New York City. The original, owing to its setting, has a much more open feel than its museum version.

No longer in the hands of a privileged family or restricted to a few upper-class Confucian scholars, officials, and poets, the Master of the Nets Garden has become a favorite retreat of Sūzhōu's own citizenry. Grandparents bring their grandkids here on inaugural outings to pose for ceremonial snapshots. Workers snack on seeds and fresh fruits. Lovers dangle their feet in the motionless pond waters. Children chase each other around the rockeries. Rimmed by galleries of carved stone tablets and poetic inscriptions on wooden plaques, the garden is a relic of Old China. Paths meander like wild geese, pavilions unfold like lotus leaves, rocks rise as sharply as mountain peaks, and the gates open in the shape of a full moon. Here, nature becomes a living poem.

Master of the Nets Garden is open daily from 8am to 5pm; admission is ¥15 ($1.80).

Tiger Hill (Hǔ Qiū Shān)

Even Sūzhōu's best park, **Tiger Hill (Hǔ Qiū Shān),** 3km (2 miles) northwest of the city at Hǔqiū Shān 8, contains classic gardens, although I was stunned on a recent visit to find that large, bright plots of flowers, planted and potted, had become a major feature, as had dozens of robotic figures of the sort you normally see at theme parks or in department store windows at Christmas. These modern additions have jazzed up the park and appeal to young children and their parents, it seems, but they are really just so much garish frosting.

A trail from the entrance passes by a number of the park's historic sights, including several mythic rocks and a **spring** used since A.D. 500, when it cured a monk of blindness. At the very top of Tiger Hill is its remarkable leaning pagoda, **Cloud Rock Pagoda (Yúnyán Tǎ),** a seven-story work dating from A.D. 961, now safely shored up by modern engineering, although it still leans. Under the pagoda is the grave of Sūzhōu's legendary founder, Hé Lǚ, a 6th-century B.C. leader whose arsenal of 3,000 swords is also said to be buried in the park and protected by a white tiger. The artificial hill on which the pagoda stands was once an island. To one side is a stone tablet engraved by the Qīng Qiánlóng Emperor, as well as the plain Great Hall Temple. Down below is a large bonsai garden with over 600 specimens and a big tree said to be over 500 years old.

The most remarkable site at the foot of the Tiger Hill pagoda is a natural ledge, the **Ten Thousand People Rock,** where, according to legend, a rebel delivered an oratory so fiery that the rocks lined up to listen. A deep stone cleavage, the **Pool of Swords (Jiànchí),** runs along one side of it, reputedly the remnants of a pit dug by order of the First Emperor (Qín Shǐ Huáng) 2,000 years ago in a search for the 3,000 swords.

All these legends of Tiger Hill are simply colorful stories, of course; the historic sites of China are decked in many such legends. Sometimes the truth is even more interesting. In the 1950s, excavations of pits at Tiger Hill revealed a three-door passageway with tunnels 9m (30 ft.) into the hill, heading directly under the leaning pagoda. Although unexplored, the tunnels are thought to lead to a major tomb, a hollow creating unstable foundations that might explain why the pagoda tilts.

Tiger Hill is open daily from 7:30am to 6pm; admission is ¥25 ($3).

Water Gates & Canals

Another leading historical site in old Sūzhōu is **Pánmén Gate,** at 2 Dōng Dà Lù, which once operated as a water gate and fortress when the Grand Canal was the most important route linking Sūzhōu to the rest of China. Pánmén, built in A.D. 1351, is the only major piece of the Sūzhōu city wall to survive. Nearby is a large arched bridge, **Wúmén Qiáo,** over the Grand Canal—the finest place to view the ever-changing traffic—and a small arched bridge over a feeder canal that connects to Pánmén. Pánmén also has excellent views of the old city, including a view of Ruìguāng Tǎ, a 37m (122-ft.) pagoda built in A.D. 1119.

When I visited Pánmén, it was teeming with visitors and with an aggressive army of vendors, fortunetellers, and painters. At the top of the bridge to Pánmén, a local street musician was stroking out the refrains of "Oh! Susanna" on his èrhú, a traditional two-stringed instrument. When he spotted me, he grabbed my arm, attempting to shake a few coins into his basket, and he was quite outraged that I, an American, refused to cough up a donation for my traditional song. The Pánmén fortification today charges an admission of ¥15 ($2), which includes entrance to an uninteresting, recently restored royal mansion and an equally uninspiring new amusement park.

The Pánmén district and the southern streets of old Sūzhōu are excellent places to walk at your leisure. Traditional shophouses with galleries predominate; the streets are narrow and shaded by trees; and bridges and lanes provide an excellent vantage from which to watch the canal traffic, an endless stream of barges propelled by hand-held poles as well as motors. Near Pánmén, the old city moat widens and the water traffic thickens.

Uptown, the canals narrow, but the backs of the white houses are still open to the water, and quite a bit of commerce is conducted on the water. The canal scenes are unsanitized. The arched bridges are pocked and mud splattered. The canal houses are coated with a stubble of moss and dirt. Scores of cement barges move from outhouse to outhouse to extract the night soil for use in suburban farms. The gondoliers of Sūzhōu evoke little of the romance of vanished dynasties, but they do reveal the rough-edged world of labor that hundreds of millions of Chinese do each day. And there is something beautiful still in the canal scene of Sūzhōu, when the arched bridges and simple stucco houses and floating barges line up just right. Pánmén is open daily from 8am to 5:30pm; admission is ¥15 ($2).

The Art of Silk

Sūzhōu is known for more than its garden arts. Its silk fabrics have been among the most prized in China for centuries, and the art of silk embroidery is still practiced at the highest levels. Silk is what made Sūzhōu a city of importance in China. The **Museum of Sūzhōu Embroidery (Sūxiù Yánjiū Suǒ)** on Jǐngdé Lù (open 9am–5pm daily; free admission) is both a factory and a sales outlet. It contains the most accomplished silk embroideries I have seen in China. The best work on display there, some of it for sale, are canvases of traditional scenes (landscapes, birds, flowers, bamboos) stitched by one artist over the course of 3 years. A few of the embroidery masters have international reputations, and the prices of their works soar once they retire. The artists working upstairs in this factory stitch with bare hands, depending only on natural light, without magnifying lenses or other aids. They work 2-hour stretches and then take 10-minute tea breaks. The embroidery factory also produces double-sided embroideries on a canvas of thin silk gauze, using a method developed here, in which two different figures, front and reverse, are stitched with two needles simultaneously—the factory guide calls this "a secret technique." The finished embroidery is mounted in a mahogany frame carved in Míng or Qīng Dynasty style.

A less commercial display of Sūzhōu's silk industry is offered by the **Sūzhōu No. 1 Silk Mill (Sūzhōu Dìyī Sīchǎng Yǒuxiàn Gōngsī),** at Nán Mén Lù 94 (open 9am–6pm daily, free admission; ✆ **0512/525-1047**), site of a 60-year-old silk factory where you can still see the old looms in operation. The complete history of silk and the process of its manufacture are explained by English-speaking guides. This factory hasn't changed since I first saw it in the mid-1980s, including its extensive sales rooms of silk clothing and souvenirs.

Temple of Mystery (Xuán Miào Guàn)

One of Sūzhōu's least visited monuments is the **Temple of Mystery,** located in the heart of the old city on Guànqián Jiē, engulfed by Sūzhōu's largest street market. Constructed in the 3rd century A.D., the temple's 31 halls are reduced today to the singular, massive, three-eaved **Hall of the Three Pure Ones (Sān Qīng),** which dates from A.D. 1179. This is the largest early Daoist temple in China, almost 45m (150 ft.) wide. Its courtyard, bordered by a carved stone Sòng Dynasty railing, is a favorite hangout for older citizens. Inside is a golden statue of Guānyīn, Goddess of Mercy, and some 60 Daoist figures in glass cases. South of this is another large building that clearly belonged at one time to the Temple of Mystery. Unchanged on the outside, this runaway hall is now devoted to souvenirs, musical instruments, and other commodities, all displayed in glass-and-metal counters. Meanwhile, the east and west walls of this emporium are still festooned with the massive statues of warriors and gods of the original Daoist hall.

Sūzhōu's Temple of Mystery is emblematic of the state of China's legacies. Hanging on by a thread in the center of a rapidly modernizing city, the temple has been altered, divided, and gutted by time, politics, and economics. Yet something visible remains. The old bazaar has been reincarnated. Small, simple stalls still hug the temple grounds, but the newest sort of shopping bazaar is shouldering its way nearer the Temple of Mystery. A pedestrian mall has sprung up within a block of the old temple, with deluxe department stores, cinemas showing the latest action films from America, KFC emporiums, and boutiques hawking the logos of international fashion chains.

The Temple of Mystery is open daily from 7:30am to 5:15pm; admission is ¥10 ($1.25).

PRACTICAL INFORMATION

by Sharon Owyang

ORIENTATION & WHEN TO GO

Sūzhōu is located in Jiāngsū Province 81km (50 miles) northwest of Shànghǎi. Winters are cold, springs rainy, summers hot and humid, making the more pleasant and balmy months of September to November the best times to visit. Sūzhōu is often visited as a day trip from Shànghǎi, but an overnight stay will allow you to take in its many sights at a more leisurely pace.

GETTING THERE

By Plane The nearest airport to Sūzhōu is Shànghǎi (see the chapter on "Shànghǎi," beginning on p. 97).

By Train There are many trains each day from Shànghǎi. The most popular for day-trippers include train K818, which leaves Shànghǎi at 7:40am and arrives at 8:38am; and train 5068, which departs at 8:28am and arrives at 9:37am. Return trains to Shànghǎi in the afternoon include T731 (departs 5:07pm, arrives 6:30pm) and T715 (departs 5:54pm, arrives 6:42pm). The **Sūzhōu Train Station** (© 0512/6753-2831) is in the northern part of town on Chēzhàn Lù, just west of the Rénmín Lù intersection.

By Bus Sūzhōu is well connected by bus to Shànghǎi, Wúxī, and Hángzhōu (see separate chapters). There are two main bus stations: the **Qìchē Běizhàn**

(© 0512/6753-0686) in the north, and the **Qìchē Nánzhàn** (© 0512/6520-4867) in the south. From the north bus station, buses depart for Shànghǎi (90 min; ¥26–¥30/$3.25–$3.75; every 20 min. 7am–6:20pm), Wúxī (1 hr.; ¥18/$2.25; every 30 min. 7:15am–5:50pm), and Hángzhōu (3–4 hr.; ¥31–¥52/$3.90–$6.50; every hr. 5:30am–6:50pm).

By Ship Sūzhōu is also linked to Hángzhōu to the south by overnight passenger boats on the Grand Canal (see separate chapter, beginning on p. 140). Tickets (¥60–¥130/$7.50–$16 per berth, depending on class of service) can be bought at CITS, at hotel tour desks, and at the dock itself, **Nánmén Passenger Boat Terminal (Nánmén Lúnchuán Kèyùn Mǎtóu)** at Rénmín Lù 8 (© 0512/6520-5720; daily 6:30am–5:30pm) in the southern part of town.

TOURS, STRATAGEMS & GETTING AROUND

Sūzhōu has a tourist hot line (© 0512/6522-3131) that can help answer travelers' questions. **China International Travel Service (CITS),** at Dàjǐng Xiāng off Guānqián Jiē (© 0512/6522-3783), offers a 1-day Panda Bus City Tour (¥280/$35 per person, based on a 2-person tour; cost per person can be reduced according to group size), which takes in Liú Yuán, Tiger Hill, Master of the Nets Garden, Pánmén, and the Silk Embroidery Factory. Lunch, an English-speaking guide, admission tickets, and transportation are included in the cost. Book directly with CITS or through your hotel tour desk.

Alternatively, you can tour the city using a combination of taxis and buses. **Taxis** cost ¥10 ($1.25) per 3km, then ¥2 (25¢) per kilometer, with trips about town averaging between ¥10 and ¥20 ($1.25–$2.50). **Bus no. Y1** ¥1/10¢ runs from Tiger Hill to the train station, stopping along the way at Líuyuán, Xuán Miào Guàn, the Silk Embroidery Factory, Zhuōzhèng Yuán, and Shīzi Lín; while bus no. Y2 runs from Tiger Hill to Pánmén, with a stop along the way at Wǎngshī Yuán (Master of the Nets Garden).

WHERE TO STAY

Gloria Plaza Hotel Sūzhōu (Kǎilái Dàjiǔdiàn) Located a little less conveniently in the eastern part of town, this four-star Hong Kong-managed hotel offers high-end accommodations at reasonable prices (discounts of up to 40% are regularly given). The hotel's decor combines traditional Chinese furniture with modern glass and marble. Rooms are simply but tastefully decorated with large beds and contemporary furniture. The hotel has recently overhauled its restaurants. The Sampan Seafood Restaurant now offers excellent Cantonese cuisine in a luxurious modern setting. Service is friendly and efficient.

Gànjiāng Dōng Lù 535. ✆ *0512/521-8855. Fax 0512/521-8533. www.gph suzhou.com. 294 units. ¥944 ($118) double. AE, DC, MC, V.* **Amenities:** 2 restaurants; fitness club; sauna; tour desk; 24-hr. business center; shopping arcade; salon; 24-hr. room service; next-day dry cleaning and laundry; nightly turndown. *In room:* A/C, TV, minibar, coffeemaker, hair dryer, safe.

Ramada Plaza Bamboo Grove Hotel (Huáměi Dá Zhú Huì Fàndiàn) Located in the southeastern part of town near the Master of the Nets Garden, this hotel has recently come under new management by Ramada Hotels and has received a much-needed face-lift. With its white walls, black-tiled roof, and Chinese garden, this four-star, five-story hotel is a nice place to stay and is very popular with foreign tour groups. Rooms have been tastefully renovated with all new modern furniture and comfortable beds. There are three restaurants here serving Western, Japanese, and local Sūzhōu food. Staff is friendly and helpful.

Zhú Huì Lù 168. ✆ *0512/6520-5601. Fax 0512/6520-8778. www.bg-hotel.com. 356 units. ¥960 ($120) double. AE, DC, MC, V.* **Amenities:** 3 restaurants; indoor swimming pool; outdoor tennis courts; fitness club; sauna; bicycle rental; concierge; tour desk; business center; shopping arcade; salon; medical clinic; 24-hr. room service; next-day dry cleaning and laundry; nightly turndown; newsstand. *In room:* A/C, TV, dataport, minibar.

Sheraton Sūzhōu Hotel & Tower (Sūzhōu Wúgōng Xīláidēng Dàjiǔdiàn) This is easily the top hotel in Sūzhōu, and has itself become a mini-attraction. Located near Pánmén, in the southwest part of town, this five-story traditional Chinese garden–style hotel incorporates the best elements of Sūzhōu—gardens, canals, ponds, city wall—into its own design. Guest rooms are well appointed with plush furniture, comfortable beds, and the full range of amenities. Service is efficient, dining is fine (two restaurants: Chinese and Western), and a stay here is a truly luxurious experience.

Xīn Shì Lù 388 (near Pánmén, southwest Sūzhōu). ✆ *0512/6510-3388. Fax 0512/6510-0888. www.Sheraton.com/ suzhou. 328 units. ¥1,696 ($212) double. AE, DC, MC, V.* **Amenities:** 3 restaurants; bakery; indoor and outdoor swimming pools; tennis court; fitness center; Jacuzzi; sauna; plunge pool and spa; concierge; tour desk; business center; shops; 24-hr. room service; same-day dry cleaning and laundry; newsstand. *In room:* A/C, TV, dataport, minibar, safe.

WHERE TO DINE

Although hotel restaurants offer the most reliable fare and accept credit cards, Sūzhōu has a number of good restaurants that deserve to be tried, many of which are located on Tàijiān Lane (Tàijiān Nòng), also known as Gourmet Street, around the Guànqián Jiē area. Note that Sūzhōu food is in general quite oily. One of the most famous local restaurants is **Pine and Crane Restaurant (Sōng Hè Lóu)**, at Guànqián Jiē 141 (℅ **0512/6727-7006**), which has a history of over 200 years. It's a sprawling place with large dining rooms and ornately decorated private rooms. Sūzhōu specialties include *Sōngshǔ Guìyú* (Squirrel Shaped Mandarin Fish), *Gūsū lǔyā* (Gūsū marinated duck), and *huángmén hémàn* (braised river eel). There's a limited menu in English. Dinner for two ranges from ¥100 to ¥200 ($13–$25). Close by is **Wáng Sì Jiǔjiā**, at Guànqián Tàijiān Nòng 23 (℅ **0512/6523-2967**), which also serves good local fare, including their house specialty, *Jiàohuā Jī* (Mud-baked Chicken); and *sōngzǐ dōngpō ròu* (tender braised pork with pine nuts). ¥120 to ¥250 ($15–$31) for a 2-person dinner. For more informal local dining, the **Sūzhōu Xiǎochīyuán,** a few doors down at Tàijiān Xiāng 21 (℅ **0512/6523-7603**), serves local snacks like *xiāròu xiǎolóng* (steamed shrimp dumplings with zsoup), *sānsī chūnjuǎn* (spring rolls), and *guìhuā tánggǒu* (lotus root pancake). There are no English menus, but there are pictures on the wall to which you can point. ¥15 to ¥25 ($2–$3) for a 2-person dinner.

For Cantonese food, the **Sampan Seafood Restaurant** at the Gloria Plaza Hotel, which has a Hong Kong chef, dishes up classic Cantonese seafood, shark's fin, abalone, steamed fish, and also delicious Yáng Chéng Lake hairy crabs in the fall. Dim sum is available. Dinner for two costs about ¥120 ($15) and up. Reservations are recommended.

HÁNGZHŌU:
TEA ON WEST LAKE
杭州

Reputedly arriving in Hángzhōu 7 centuries ago, Marco Polo pronounced it "the finest, most splendid city in the world . . . where so many pleasures may be found that one fancies oneself to be in Paradise." Today, Hángzhōu's claim to paradise does not lie in its streets, which are ordinary, but in its lake, its shoreline, and the surrounding countryside, where the strolling and biking are the best you'll find in the Middle Kingdom. As many as 20 million visitors throng Hángzhōu yearly, a vast number in a city of little more than one million residents. Yet perhaps because the lake is large enough, the walkways wide, and the causeways long, you do not feel as crowded strolling here as when strutting elbow-to-elbow in the streets of Shànghǎi or upon the Great Wall near Běijīng.

The focus of Hángzhōu's exceptional beauty is **West Lake (Xī Hú).** It's a small lake, about 5km (3 miles) across and 14km (9 miles) around. You can walk the circumference in under 4 hours—longer if you linger at a temple, pavilion, cafe, or park. Two causeways—one running on the north shore, the other on the west shore—vary and shorten the journey. The shallow waters of West Lake are sufficient to fill and beguile the eye's compass but not to overwhelm it. Hángzhōu's West Lake remains to this day what one 12th-century visitor proclaimed it: "a landscape composed by a painter."

I've visited Hángzhōu's West Lake often, finding each time a serenity that I associate with the Middle Kingdom days of mandarins and moonlit courtyards. Strolling the promenades and crisscrossing the causeways of West Lake, I've entered Old China as in a dream. The islets and temples, pavilions and gardens, causeways and arched bridges of this jade-like lake have constituted the supreme example of lakeside beauty in China ever since Hángzhōu served as China's capital during the Southern Sòng Dynasty (A.D. 1127–1279).

Solitary Hill Island (Gū Shān)

I like to begin my early morning rambles at the aptly named Hángzhōu Shangri-La Hotel, situated on the lake's northwest shore, where at dawn the mists wrap the willow-draped shoreline. Crossing **Xī Líng Bridge,** leading to a pavilion dedicated to the courtesan-poet Sū Xiǎoxiǎo, who was entombed near here in A.D. 501, I am quickly transfixed by the lush scenery and old architecture of **Solitary Hill Island,** the largest of the four main islands in West Lake. A roadway sweeps eastward across Solitary Hill Island toward the city skyline, past monumental tile-roofed halls built in the style of Qīng Dynasty palaces.

As a matter of fact, it was on this very island that the two most traveled emperors of the last dynasty, Kāngxī (1662–1723) and Qiánlóng (1736–95), stayed during their own vacations on West Lake. Sailing down the Grand Canal to its terminus at Hángzhōu, these emperors hastened to Solitary Hill Island, staying at pavilions erected solely for their royal excursions. These 18th-century emperors, grandfather and grandson in the Manchu line, came strictly as sightseers. They established a viewing platform on the southeastern tip of the island for a connoisseur's view of sunrise and moonlight. Qiánlóng named the viewing pavilion "Autumn Moon on a Calm Lake," and today there's a fine **teahouse** in its place, perfect for sipping green tea. The view is the same today as that which enthralled generations of emperors.

It's worth returning to Solitary Hill Island later to tour the **Zhèjiāng Provincial Museum,** not only to see the oldest grains of cultivated rice in the world (discovered 7,000 years ago in a nearby Hémǔdù village) but also to survey the skeleton of a whale beached at Hángzhōu centuries ago when it, like West Lake, was connected more spaciously to the East China Sea. West Lake was once a river lagoon, until sedimentation removed it from its source and a series of scholar-administrators designed the causeways and islands that have made West Lake a work of art. The museum is open daily from 8:45am to 4pm. Admission is ¥10 ($1.25); ¥15 ($1.85) if you also wish to visit the separate West Lake Gallery.

Shadowboxing & Ballroom Dancing

Solitary Hill Island is connected to downtown Hángzhōu by Bái Dī, one of the two great man-made causeways that divide West Lake into three parts. These two causeways are the finest stretches to walk on West Lake. Both are scenic and serene. The **Bái Causeway** is named after a Táng Dynasty poet, Bái Jūyì, who served as prefectural governor here in A.D. 822

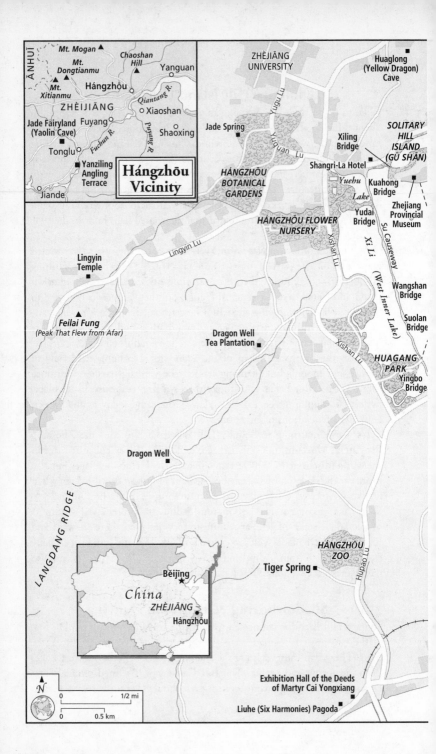

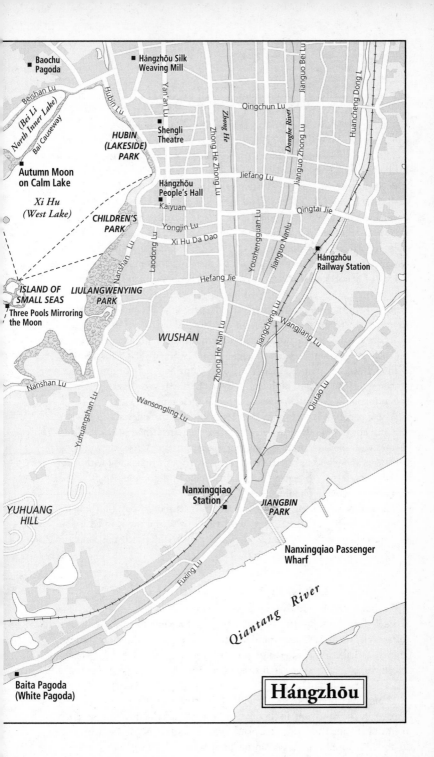

Baochu
Pagoda

Hángzhōu Silk
Weaving Mill

Beishan Lu

(Bei Li)
North Inner Lake

Bai Causeway

Qingchun Lu

Jianguo Bei Lu

Huancheng Dong Lu

Hubin Lu

Yan'an Lu

Zhong He

Donghe River

Jianguo Zhong Lu

HUBIN
(LAKESIDE)
PARK

Shengli
Theatre

Zhong He Zhong Lu

Autumn Moon
on Calm Lake

Jiefang Lu

Xi Hu
(West Lake)

Hángzhōu
People's Hall

Kaiyuan

Qingtai Jie

CHILDREN'S
PARK

Yongjin Lu

Youshengguan Lu

Jianguo Nanlu

Nanshan Lu

Laodong Lu

Xi Hu Da Dao

Hángzhōu
Railway Station

Hefang Jie

ISLAND OF
SMALL SEAS

LIULANGWENYING
PARK

Three Pools Mirroring
the Moon

WUSHAN

Zhong He Nan Lu

Jiangcheng Lu

Wangjiang Lu

Nanshan Lu

Yuhuangshan Lu

Wansongling Lu

Qiutao Lu

YUHUANG
HILL

Nanxingqiao
Station

JIANGBIN
PARK

Nanxingqiao Passenger
Wharf

Fuxing Lu

Qiantang River

Baita Pagoda
(White Pagoda)

Hángzhōu

to 824 and saw to its construction. Composed of silt dredged from the lake, this causeway runs east for half a mile, rejoining the north shore road, Běi Shān Lù, at **Broken Bridge (Duàn Qiáo),** so-named because when winter snows first melt, the bridge appears from a distance to be broken.

The **lakeshore promenade** that encircles West Lake widens at Broken Bridge where it joins the Bái Causeway and runs parallel to the western edge of downtown Hángzhōu. Along the way, I always find the pavilions, with their octagonal tiled roofs and upturned eaves, jammed at dawn with devotees of the latest recreational craze, Western ballroom dancing. At the same time, the walkway teems with a more Eastern, more ancient form of exercise, *tàijíquán* (shadowboxing, "tai chi"). *Tàijíquán* is a formal exercise designed to promote health and spirit by directing and enhancing an inner stream of energy called the *qì*. It has become so popular in China that its basic forms have been systematized by the government, creating an official *tàijíquán* form. But just as there are dialects in the Chinese language, so there are regional differences in exercise. Along West Lake, various *tàijíquán* schools conduct their pre-breakfast classes. Tàijíquán masters tack up their insignia on trees, and their students (women slicing the crisp air with red-tasseled swords, men with bare palm and fist) begin practice, ignoring the pedestrians, bicyclers, baby strollers, street sweepers, and occasional foreign visitors who squeeze through their ranks.

A few paces away, ballroom dancers spill onto the sidewalk in a waltz straight out of Strauss. Partner swings partner until their step-close-step merges with the slow push-and-pull of shadowboxers. Across the widening avenue, at the Children's Palace square, hundreds of workers toil with mass calisthenics. It's worth getting here early to take in the action. All of China seems to be moving its joints.

The ballroom dancing commences about 6:30am every day, finishing up 2 hours later. If you know a few steps, you'll be warmly welcomed if you join in. I did some *tàijíquán* exercises here and found myself the recipient of advice from Hángzhōu's masters.

Lakeside Avenue (Húbīn Lù)

At Húbīn Lù (Lakeside Ave.), the promenade turns south. Along the lake is a delightful encampment of boat launches, souvenir stands, restaurants, Qīng-style mansions, and outdoor cafes. This spacious shore retreat, known as Lakeside Park, is just the spot for tea, snacks, and ice cream. Meanwhile, the city shops across the main street have undergone extensive redevelopment in the last few years. You can edge into the downtown rush at Hángzhōu's branch of TCBY (The Country's Best Yogurt) or Häagen-Dazs. On the lakefront itself there are several cafes, some with English menus. Lakeside Park is also the place for a beer, served at a fashionable pub in an old mansion, the Casablanca Country Bar.

In some ways, Hángzhōu's downtown shoreline is coming to resemble a Western shopping mall, but the lake remains as it has for centuries, a gem best explored by foot, bicycle, or boat. In fact, the true heart of West Lake is only reached by water. There are no sailboats, canoes, or kayaks to rent on West Lake, but you can hire rowboats or paddleboats. There are also sampans propelled by the owner's single oar that will take you out to the islands, as well as an assortment of ferries—flat-bottomed launches seating 20 under an awning to larger vessels and imitation junks—that pick up passengers along the Lakeside Park shore. For the sampans, you have to bargain for the fare, usually under ¥60 ($7.50) for an hour on the water, but ¥80 to ¥100 ($10–$13) in peak season. The passenger ferries usually sell tickets at ¥35 to ¥45 ($4.40–$5.60), including entrance to Xiǎoyáng Zhōu, the Island of Small Seas. The touts will find you if you don't get to a ticket booth first, but tickets for a cruise can be bought back where this morning ramble began, at a dock across the street from the Shangri-La Hotel, as well as at various other lakeshore points. Many a fairly comfortable and sizable motorized launch, its bowsprit the head of a dragon, departs for a 2-hour lake tour, with stops at several of the islands.

Boats on West Lake have a venerable history. Emperors were rowed across these waters in elaborate dragon-headed craft. Even Marco Polo mentions the cruise. "A voyage on this lake," his ghostwriter records him as saying, "offers more refreshment and pleasure than any other experience on earth. On one side it skirts the city so that your barge commands a distant view of all its grandeur and loveliness. . . . On the lake itself is an endless procession of barges thronged with pleasure seekers." Although the downtown skyline has certainly been transformed over the centuries and the boats for hire today are poor relations of the royal barges, West Lake still enthralls pleasure seekers, foreign and Chinese.

Three Pools Mirroring the Moon (Sān TánYìn Yuè)

The island you should not miss is the **Island of Small Seas (Xiǎoyáng Zhōu),** at the center of West Lake. This man-made atoll was formed during a silt-dredging operation in 1607. It is, as another Chinese saying goes, "an island within a lake, lakes within an island." Its form is that of a wheel with four spokes, its bridges and dikes creating four enclosed lotus-laden ponds. The main route into the hub of this wheel is the **Bridge of Nine Turnings,** built in 1727. Occupying the center is the magnificent **Flower and Bird Pavilion,** one of the most graceful structures I have ever visited in China, notable for its intricate wooden railings, lattices, and moon gates. It isn't an ancient work, dating only from 1959, but it's a superb rendition of the best in traditional Chinese architecture. There always seem to be crowds here, although weekday mornings before 10am are the most peaceful times to arrive.

On the southern rim of the Island of Little Oceans is West Lake's defining monument: **Three Pools Mirroring the Moon,** which consists of three water pagodas, each about 2m (6 ft.) tall. They have "floated" like buoys on the surface of West Lake since 1621. Each pagoda has five openings. On evenings when the full moon shines on the lake, candles are placed inside. The effect is of four moons shimmering on the waters. Even by daylight, the three floating pagodas are a startling touch, the grand flourish of ancient engineers and scholar-administrators who shaped the lake into a work as artful as any classical garden. Local legends portray the three pagodas as the feet of an upturned stone tripod plunked into the water to clamp down on a dark monster of the deep.

The floating pagodas were the creation of Hángzhōu's most famous governor, the poet Sū Dōngpō (A.D. 1036–1101), who placed the original trio of pagodas here, at the deepest point in the lake, to stake out an area where water plants were forbidden to grow. Lily, lotus, and a host of other plants had repeatedly strangled West Lake and still pose a threat. Several times I've seen keepers in skiffs weed the island pools as if they were overgrown gardens.

Sū Causeway (Sū Dī)

The best view from land of the Three Pools Mirroring the Moon is from the Sū Causeway, the great dike that connects the north and south shores along the western side of West Lake. This pathway across West Lake has vistas as rewarding as those along the east–west Bái Causeway, but the Sū Causeway is three times as long (nearly 3km/2 miles). Lined with weeping willows, peach trees, and shady nooks, it crosses six arched stone bridges. Locals fish and picnic along its hems. The Sū Causeway is named for the poet Sū Dōngpō, who, as the official in charge, set some 200,000 workers to dredging the lake. Sū also composed a poem comparing West Lake to Xī Zǐ, traditionally the prettiest young girl in ancient China, whose beauty, like that of the lake itself, shone through in laughter or in tears: "Rippling water shimmering on a sunny day/Misty mountains gorgeous in the rain/ Plain or gaily decked out like Xī Zǐ/The West Lake is ever alluring," Sū wrote.

The Sū Causeway begins on the north shore at a small park, **Lotus Stirred by the Breeze,** across from the patriotic monument to Yuè Fēi, a 12th-century general. Favored by the Kāngxī Emperor, this park became the best spot for viewing lotus blossoms. More recently, it has been fronted by a modern shopping center, featuring local crafts and several restaurants specializing in the West Lake carp, considered a great delicacy here.

The carp of West Lake are famous in China. Nine hundred years ago, carp in this province (Zhèjiāng) mutated into the first goldfish, and

Hángzhōu rapidly became the capital of goldfish cultivation, a reputation it enjoys to this day. (It wasn't until 1782 that goldfish were introduced to the West, first reaching London from China.) One of the two best places to observe the giant ornamental carp and goldfish is Jade Spring in the **Hángzhōu Botanical Garden (Hángzhōu Zhíwù Yuán)**, about a mile west of the Shangri-La Hotel; it's open from 6am to 6pm and charges ¥10 ($1.25), sometimes more when there are special displays. The remainder of the garden is open 24 hours. The other is **Flower Harbor Park (Huāgǎng Yuán)**, at the south end of the Sū Causeway, a delightful array of paths and flower gardens; its pavilions and fishponds date back to the Sòng Dynasty. Admission is ¥15 ($2); hours are from 6am to 6pm, from 6:30am to 5:30pm in winter.

Bǎochū Pagoda

Hikes on either of the two great causeways usually take up a morning or an afternoon, depending on your pace. A boat ride and island walk consume another pleasant half day. A shorter but more strenuous ramble is up the green hillside of the lake's north shore to Hángzhōu's most famous landmark, the needlelike Bǎochū Pagoda, which is visible everywhere from West Lake and adds yet another subtle element to the composition. This pagoda dates from A.D. 968, but has exhibited a tendency to collapse, requiring rebuilding most recently in 1933. Young or old, Bǎochū Pagoda is an irresistible symbol of West Lake; one morning I set out to see it close up.

Maps didn't give me clear directions, so I simply set out early, walking toward downtown along Běi Shān Lù from the Shangri-La Hotel. After a 20-minute stroll, I pulled even with the pagoda on the hill and chose a likely looking, rather steep road up. The road petered out into a well-worn trail, which after 10 minutes brought me to the top of the ridge, face-to-face with the solitary 38m (125-ft.) high pinnacle. The vista was worth the climb, even though the pagoda, fashioned from solid stone and brick, was devoid of an inner stairway that might have afforded a still better view.

The real interest here, as is often the case when you wander a bit off the tourist track, was the crowd of ordinary people who had gathered that morning. There was a group of housewives, each in a hand-knit sweater, practicing tàijíquán with a master. Zigzagging through their ranks was a troupe of school kids, dressed like flowers, on a field trip. When they spotted me, they couldn't take their eyes off this unexpected visitor from afar. I rested on a stone wall and watched them play. An old man emerged from the steep path to the pagoda, cane in hand. His mobility was terribly hampered, but he did not pause to rest. He stamped both feet and strode forward, circling the pagoda courtyard in ever-widening circles, determined to keep moving. Then one little girl broke from her school-mates, ran up to me, and opened her hand. In her palm lay a single white Chiclet. I thanked her and placed it in my mouth. She ran back, laughing in delight.

Undertaking such rambles in any Chinese city is a sure way to discover the accidentally strange and beautiful, as well as to gain a feeling for the daily life of China. The visitors' sights you've set out to see are quite often secondary.

Laughing Buddha

China is the land of the **bicycle,** of course. Everyone seems to own one and to use it constantly. Nowadays, automobiles, particularly taxis, are domi-nating the streets, but bicycles often have their own wide lanes. For one not in a hurry, particularly for a visitor, the bicycle is a superb form of move-ment in the city, and in Hángzhōu, out of the city as well. The Shangri-La Hotel rents good multispeed mountain bikes for ¥20 ($2.50) per hour. Their gears are useful for mounting the green hillsides surrounding West Lake on three sides. To the west reside two of Hángzhōu's greatest treasures—the great Buddhist temple Língyǐn Sì and the tea village of Dragon Well—and both lie within an hour's countryside bike ride. From the hotel, the roads are well marked to both locations, and any city map shows the way clearly.

Língyǐn Temple (Temple of the Soul's Retreat) took me just 20 min-utes to reach from the hotel, an easy ride through parklands forested in bamboo and larch, the last 10 minutes on a slight uphill incline. The tem-ple parking lot proved to be extremely crowded, heaped with vendor stalls, buses, visitors, and beggars, but the bicycle parks were clearly marked with pictorial signs. I selected one and paid a small fee, locked up my bike, took my ticket from the vendor, and followed the crowds across a stream to the temple entrance.

Língyǐn Temple has been rebuilt a dozen times since its creation in A.D. 326. The path to the temple complex is lined with attractions, includ-ing a new park to the left (Fēilái Fēng Zàoxiàng), a sculpture garden of statuary, reproductions of famous Buddhist statues from all over China—tacky for the most part and worth skipping.

The real attraction on the road to the temple is the limestone cliff called the **Peak That Flew from Afar (Fēilái Fēng),** so named because it resem-bles a holy mountain in India seemingly transported to China. The peak, nearly 150m (500 ft.) high, contains four caves and about 380 Buddhist **rock carvings,** most of them created over 600 years ago during the Yuán Dynasty. The most famous carving here is of a Laughing Buddha, carved in the year A.D. 1000. This Buddha of the Future is laughing with joy at the ultimate glorious fate of the world and with amusement at the child-ish vanities of the unenlightened. His elongated earlobes symbolize his wisdom. His round bulging belly is a manifestation of his inner powers.

Scholars consider these stone carvings the most important of their kind in southern China. They are more animated, realistic, and gaudy than the Buddhist sculptures done earlier on a more extensive scale in northern China and along the Silk Road, where Buddhism entered the Middle Kingdom from India. Although you will find much grander Buddhist rock carvings in those more remote regions of China, the flying peak is worth a look.

So are the temples. The small **pagoda** at the temple entrance, built in 1590, is the burial marker for a monk who founded Língyǐn 16 centuries ago. The present buildings go back decades rather than centuries, but they are immense—some of the grandest temples in China. The Front Hall and the Great Hall beyond it have the typical Chinese Buddhist layout. The **Front Hall** contains the Four Guardians of the Four Directions, two on either side, protecting a rotund image of Maitreya (the Laughing Buddha). Língyǐn's Maitreya dates from the 18th century, and behind this image is a statue in camphor wood of Skanda, another protector, which dates from the Southern Sòng Dynasty when Hángzhōu was China's capital. The even larger **Great Hall** contains an image of Buddha crafted in 1956 from 24 sections of camphor and gilded with 104 ounces of gold—not a bad modern re-creation. Behind this grand Buddha is a fairyland relief of clay figures, with Guānyīn, the Goddess of Mercy, at its center. Guānyīn, China's most venerated goddess, is still petitioned by those seeking a male child or a miraculous cure. In Língyǐn Temple, she is portrayed as standing on a fish with a bottle of merciful waters in her hand (as she is also a pro-tector of mariners). When I was last in this temple, I saw two old women and one young man kneeling with lighted incense before the goddess.

Língyǐn Temple is always crowded and very popular with Chinese visi-tors, as is all of Hángzhōu. It's open from 7am to 4:30pm, until 5pm in summer; admission is ¥15 ($2).

Dragon Well Tea

A less frantic jaunt by bicycle is toward the village of **Dragon Well (Lóngjǐng),** known for Hángzhōu's famous **Lóngjǐng tea,** grown only on these hillsides and revered throughout China as cool and refreshing—a favorite summertime thirst quencher. Lóngjǐng tea is said to be a supreme vintage with four special characteristics: its green color, smooth appearance, fragrant aroma, and sweet taste. When the Qiánlóng Emperor came to these hills (perhaps after discovering Beggar's Chicken down by the lake), he picked tea at Dragon Well Village and returned to Běijīng with leaves for his mother. Thereafter, yearly tributes of Lóngjǐng tea were shipped via the Grand Canal to the Forbidden City. The best tea at Dragon Well is still picked and processed by hand. The villagers begin picking in late March or early April. The first of the 30 pickings is by far the best of the 16 grades of Lóngjǐng tea now produced. At Dragon Well and in nearby Tiger Spring, where the best spring water for tea brewing was first discovered by a Táng Dynasty monk, you can buy the tea directly from the source.

The bike ride to Dragon Well Village requires nearly an hour and the road is sometimes steep, but the journey is an exceptional one. This is pure countryside, inundated with large tea plantations. On the way, you can stop at the **Chinese Tea Museum (Zhōngguó Chá Yè Bówùguǎn),** open from 8:30am to 5pm, and comb through its extensive displays of Chinese teas, pots, cups, and ceremonial tea implements. The ¥10 ($1.25) admission includes a tea sampling and demonstration of the Chinese tea ceremony in a private tearoom. The first small glass of tea, a sign of friendship, is only served for its aroma; a second, fuller glass is then poured, with tips of the pot, for tasting. The Lóngjǐng tea served here is very clear, and the leaves have the smell of a fresh field. There's a large sales room, too, which seems to be the main purpose of this "museum."

Dragon Well Village, a few miles beyond the Tea Plantation, is where the best tea is grown and processed. Plenty of local grandmas are on hand to kidnap independent travelers, take them into their homes and kitchens, ply them with hand-picked tea, and sell them a few pounds at inflated prices. They can be resisted, but you may not want to. Though three-quarters of China's population lives in the country, few visitors ever get a chance to see their homes. Here you can.

Ten years ago, when I first visited Hángzhōu, I boarded a public bus (no. 27) to Dragon Well Village. A peasant woman latched onto me at once and refused to let go. She couldn't speak a word of English, but she had mastered the jingle, "Lóngjǐng tea, Lóngjǐng tea," and with this mantra she made many a convert. She promised to guide me to the tea hills. When we arrived, she conducted me on a whirlwind tour of the grounds of the village, where to this day there is a stream of rippling waters and an old pool where tossed coins float on its tense surface.

Of course her true objective was to whisk me through the village among clumps of tea bushes and into her house, where she brewed up some Lóngjǐng and launched into her hard sell. An old man sitting out front, drawing on a long, narrow pipe, was exhibited as proof of the amazing benefits of said tea, one of which is said to be longevity. He was 80, the woman said (and I thought at the time, by god, he looks it). Meanwhile, a neighbor lady dropped in hoping to sell me her tea as well. I managed to escape with a pound of Lóngjǐng tea in a plastic bag, but not before my host went so far as to point out her children's badly worn shoes and patched clothing. This Dragon Well tea lady was a terrific operator, a harbinger of the entrepreneurial 1990s, certainly not the last of her kind. Today the village still peddles its wares to visitors as aggressively as ever—but there are few places in China where foreigners are so openly and easily invited into a village home. This village is one place where I didn't mind the vendors. It's impossible to say what you should pay for a bag of loose tea in these circumstances since it depends on the tea's quality (which can vary greatly). Asking prices for a half kilo (1.1 lb.) can reach ¥1,500 ($187), but you should be able to walk away with a 50-gram (9-oz.) sample of what may or may not be real Lóngjǐng for under ¥80 ($10).

Eden of the East

Hángzhōu is a rarity in China: a city in a beautiful setting that's made for strolling and biking. You can do the usual things here, too, and they are pleasant enough fillers: Visit the **museums** (there are new ones devoted to silk, traditional medicines, and pottery, as well as tea), tour the **factories** (the **Hángzhōu Silk and Satin Printing and Dyeing Complex** is China's largest), and patronize the **shops** (tea, silk, and painted fans are nationally famous products). But Hángzhōu's essence is outside, on the lake, on the walkways, and in the folds of the green tea–laden hills. At the end of the Southern Sòng Dynasty, in 1279, just 4 years after Marco Polo may have visited, Hángzhōu was the largest urban center in the world, and probably the most refined. Its Heavenly Avenue was China's main street, lavish and pulsating, a thoroughfare so ripe with splendors it even contained shops for the wealthy featuring fish for pet cats. The imperial glitter has long faded from its more ordinary streets, but the beauty of West Lake endures.

PRACTICAL INFORMATION

by Peter Neville-Hadley

ORIENTATION & WHEN TO GO

Hángzhōu is located in coastal Zhèjiāng Province, a little over 2 hours by the fastest train or bus from Shànghǎi, about 170km (106 miles) away. With its hot and humid summers, Hángzhōu is busiest March to May, and September and October. The modern city wraps itself around the east and north sides of West Lake, with most of the best hotels a short distance from it.

GETTING THERE

By Plane **Dragonair** and **China Eastern** offer between them four flights daily directly from Hong Kong, taking just over 2 hours. Dragonair's office is in the Radisson Plaza Hotel—see below (© **0571/ 8506-8388**; fax 0571/8506-9808), but, as usual, tickets are best bought from agents away from the big hotels. There are direct flights to most major cities across China from Hángzhōu, including at least nine daily to Běijīng with an assortment of airlines, daily flights to Macau, and twice-weekly flights to Bangkok with **Xiàmén Airlines.** The new Hángzhōu airport is a 30-minute drive from downtown; taxi fare is about ¥130 ($16), including highway tolls. There's also a well-signposted air-conditioned bus service (¥20/$2.50) from outside the terminal to the main railway station and on to the Marco Polo hotel (not part of the Hong Kong luxury hotel group, however), which is the nearest stop to Hángzhōu's premier hotel, the Shangri-La. For airport information, call © **0571/ 8666-1234.**

By Train From Shànghǎi, the fastest train is the T701 at 11:43am, which arrives in Hángzhōu at 2pm. Soft-seat train tickets cost about ¥50 ($6) plus typically a ¥20 ($2.50) service charge if purchased from hotel tour desks. The no. 7 bus connects the train station to downtown and to the Shangri-La Hotel for ¥1 (15¢), and its air-conditioned version, the K7, for ¥2 (25¢). For train information, call © **0571/5672-0222.** For ticket bookings, call © **0571/8782-9983** between 8am and 5pm.

By Bus There are regular departures from Hángzhōu's East Bus Station to Shànghǎi until about 7pm.

By Ship Hángzhōu is also served by overnight passenger boats on the Grand Canal from Sūzhōu (see the chapter on the Grand Canal). The return trip to Sūzhōu is also overnight, departing daily from the Wǔlín Mén Kèyùn Mǎtóu, at 5.30pm daily, arriving at 7.30am the next morning. Berths cost ¥65 to ¥95 ($8–$12). For information and bookings, call © **0571/ 8515-3185.**

GETTING AROUND

Bicycle riding can be a pleasure away from the city center, and, at least at the Shangri-La, multispeed bikes are available which enable you to make short work of hills. Rates are ¥20 ($2.50) per hour, ¥80 ($10) per half day (5 hr.), and ¥140 ($17) per full day. At budget accommodations, intermittently functional bikes usually cost ¥10 to ¥15 ($1.25–$2) per day to residents and nonresidents alike. Three-wheeler **pedicabs** (sānlúnchē) should carry you the equivalent of about four bus stops for ¥5 (60¢), but with foreigners, there are almost always problems. Taxis are ¥2 (25¢) per kilometer, with 4km included in the flagfall of ¥10 ($1.25). After 8km (5 miles), the rate jumps to ¥2.40 (30¢) per kilometer. There is no night surcharge. A taxi to the airport will be about ¥130 ($16), including tolls.

TOURS & STRATAGEMS

You can easily get around Hángzhōu yourself by hopping into cabs. China International Travel Service deals principally with groups, and these days has its hands full both with Chinese tours, which vastly outnumber those of foreigners, and with sending Chinese tourists overseas. But all hotels have representatives or agents for individual local guided tours, as does the airport.

The **business center** in the West Building of the Shangri-La Hotel offers escorted half-day and full-day tours of Hángzhōu, conducted by local English-speaking guides, with the price based on the number of participants. Half-day tours cost ¥470 ($57) for a lone individual, ¥300 ($36) per person for groups of 2 to 5 people, ¥200 ($24) per person for groups of 6 to 9, and ¥160 ($19) per person for groups of 10 or more. Full-day tours cost ¥696 ($84) for a lone individual, ¥420 ($51) per person for groups of 2 to 5 people, ¥320 ($38) per person for groups of 6 to 9, and ¥240 ($29) per person for groups of 10 or more.

One-day and more fulsome over-night tours with English-speaking guides, meals, and hotels included are widely available in Shànghǎi, and cost between ¥500 ($62) and ¥1,000 ($125). Far cheaper Mandarin-only tours with lesser facilities are also available. In both cases, however, be sure to discover just how many shopping "opportunities" (visits to factories and souvenir shops with inflated prices) are included.

WHERE TO STAY

Despite Hángzhōu's long history as a leisure travel destination, the city's pre-mier hotels are as much or more the haunt of businesspeople as of tour groups or independent travelers. The busiest season is March to May and September to October when Chinese tourism is at its peak, but even then the best hotels in reality rarely charge more than 50% of the rack rates quoted below. For the remainder of the year, there is an oversupply of rooms at all levels, and discounts can easily reach 60% or even more.

Holiday Inn Hángzhōu (Hángzhōu Guójì Jiàrì Jiǔdiàn) Located a little farther away from the lake than the other hotels discussed here, this is a bustling four-star business hotel, with plain but comfortable rooms, opened in 1999. Multiple restaurants offer everything from Hángzhōu cuisine and *robotayaki* to imported steaks grilled at an open kitchen. The coffee shop overlooking the main lobby serves Western favorites and safe, pan-Asian dishes, while the 25th floor sports bar offers Western snacks and views across the city.

Jiànguó Běi Lù 298, corner of Fēngqǐ Lù (in new central business district, north-east Hángzhōu). ✆ **0571/8527-1188.** *Fax 0571/8527-1199. www.sixcontinents hotels.com. 294 units. ¥880 ($110) stan-dard room; ¥960–¥1,440 ($120–$180) superior and up; ¥2,240–¥6,400 ($280–$800) suite; all plus 15% service charge. AE, DC, MC, V.* **Amenities:** 4 restaurants; deli; indoor swimming pool; health and fitness center; Jacuzzi; sauna; 8-lane bowling alley; billiards; tour desk; free airport shuttle; business center; con-ference rooms; 24-hr. room service; next-day dry cleaning and laundry; news- stand. *In room:* A/C, TV, data-port, minibar, coffeemaker, hair dryer, iron, safe.

International Art Centre Inn (Yìyuàn Bīnguǎn) On the edge of an area of lakeside bars, cafes, teahouses, and gal-leries, this mid-range option (in reality pay no more than 60% of the prices quoted) is an odd four-floor building attached to the China Academy of Art. It opened in 2000 but is still reasonably fresh, and represents good value for money. Staff rarely see foreigners but are helpful and friendly. Facilities are straightforward, but they all work, and surprisingly the TV even has some foreign channels. West Lake is just a minute's walk away, as is nightly entertainment. *Nán Shān Lù 220 (on the eastern shore of West Lake just south of Xī Hú Dàjiē).* © *0571/8707-0100. Fax 0571/8707-0100, ext. 802. 56 units. ¥398–¥430 ($50–$53) twin. No credit cards accepted.* **Amenities:** Restaurant (Hángzhōu). *In room:* A/C, TV.

Radisson Plaza Hotel Hángzhōu (Hángzhōu Guódà Léidísēn Guǎngchǎng Jiǔdiàn) This is an excellently located glass-topped tower right in the center of town, only a few minutes' walk from West Lake. The hotel has a typically Chinese flamboyant luxury, but has foreigners at the top of its management and in the kitchen where it matters. Rooms are well furnished and comfortable, with space for full-size sofas; bathrooms have shower cubicles; and three floors of Plaza Club rooms have extra luxuries such as personal valet service. The hotel has the widest range of bar and restaurant options of any hotel in the city, including Zhèjiāng, Cantonese, Italian (by the swimming pool), Japanese, and Le Rendezvous Café, whose excellent buffet is popular with local families, too. The Sky Bar on the top floor of the hotel has live jazz every evening from 9pm.

Tǐyù Chǎng Lù 333. © *0571/8515-8888. Fax 0571/8515-7777. www.radisson.com/ hangzhoucn. 284 units, including 24 duplex suites on the 24th floor. ¥1,520–¥1,840 ($190–$230) standard room; ¥1,680–¥2,000 ($210–$250) deluxe; ¥2,520–¥3,720 ($315–$465) suite; plus 15% service charge. AE, DC, MC, V.* **Amenities:** 5 restaurants; Splash Club (combined salon, hairdresser, fitness center, swimming pool, Jacuzzi, sauna, and more); bowling alley; snooker;

electronic games; tour desk; airport and railway station shuttle; full-service business center; gift shop; laundry and dry cleaning. *In room:* A/C, TV, dataport, minibar, hair dryer, safe.

Shangri-La Hotel Hángzhōu (Hángzhōu Xiānggélǐlā Fàndiàn) This highly unusual hotel is not only the best in Hángzhōu but one of the best in China. Two separate buildings, originally leadership-only hotels from 1956 and 1962, sit in 16 hectares (40 acres) of leafiness that were once the grounds of a temple, and that include 44 camphor trees thought to be more than 300 years old. The buildings are solid brick with Forbidden City–style trim and toppings, connected by a covered passage (but with golf carts to shuttle you between the two if you need them). The rooms are large and high-ceilinged, and some of the higher ones have fine views over the lake itself. Service is usually as good as it gets in China at Shangri-La hotels, helped here by the particularly visible and genial general manager, Michael Monks. Staff could not be more helpful. Previous guests include Kissinger, Nixon, and Sir Edward Heath. Dining options include first-rate local and Cantonese cuisine at the Shang Palace, plus Italian and Continental restaurants. *Běi Shān Lù 78 (north shore of West Lake).* © *0571/8797-7951. Fax 0571/ 8707- 3545. www.shangri-la.com. 385 units. ¥728 ($91) hill view to ¥2,240 ($280) Horizon Club (business floor) lake-view suite, all plus 15% service charge. AE, DC, MC, V.* **Amenities:** 3 restaurants; heated swimming pool; tennis courts; fitness club; Jacuzzi; sauna; concierge; tour desk; free airport shuttle; business center; conference rooms; shopping arcade; salon; 24-hr. room service; same-day dry cleaning and laundry; nightly turndown; forex.

In room: A/C, satellite TV, in-house movie channels, Internet broadband and dataport, minibar, safe, iron and ironing board (in most rooms).

World Trade Center Grand Hotel Zhèjiāng (Zhèjiāng Shìjiè Màoyì Zhōngxīn Dàfàndiàn) This Chinese-owned and -run luxury hotel is part of a large conference complex that opened in 1998. Its sleek design is matched by smooth service, assisted by the presence of some foreigners in senior management. Popular with Chinese high rollers, its spacious lobby is lined with upmarket retail, including expensive Western brand names. Rooms are spotless, spacious, and practical—Internet access, whether dial-up or broadband, is free. Some rooms have both shower cubicles and bathtubs. Dining options include large Japanese, Chinese, and Western restaurants.

Shǔguāng Lù 15 (a little north of West Lake). ℂ *0571/8799-0088. Fax 0571/8795-0088. WTCghz@mail.hz.zj.cn. 330 units. ¥1,180 ($147) standard room; ¥1,380–¥1,800 ($172–$225) executive room; ¥3,800–¥12,000 ($475–$1,500) suite; all plus 5% service charge. AE, DC, MC, V.* **Amenities:** 3 restaurants; indoor and outdoor swimming pools (in adjacent health club); squash court; fitness center; Jacuzzi; sauna; billiards; mini-golf; concierge; business center; conference rooms; shops; 24-hr. room service; massage; babysitting; same-day dry cleaning and laundry; valet; medical clinic; newsstand. *In room:* A/C, TV.

WHERE TO DINE

Besides West Lake carp, one celebrated local dish is Beggar's Chicken, discovered by the Qiánlóng Emperor during an 18th-century jaunt along West Lake. The emperor, it is said, chanced upon a Hángzhōu peasant who, lacking a proper pan, baked his chicken by coating it in mud and tossing it into a fire. The modern version of Beggar's Chicken *(Hángzhōu jiàohuā jī)* is more refined, of course, being carefully seasoned and slowly cooked in clay. The best place to savor this moist invention is in the Shangri-La Hotel's **Shang Palace Restaurant,** although in deference to strict hygiene standards, clever alternatives to clay have been devised.

Hángzhōu's other famous dishes include *Lóngjǐng xiārén* (shelled shrimp sprinkled with Lóngjǐng tea), *dōngpō ròu* (a soya pork dish named after the poet), and the fish from West Lake. Those visiting on a tour are almost certain to end up at the **Lóu Wài Lóu,** Càiguǎn, on Solitary Hill Island not far from the Zhèjiāng Provincial Museum, at Gū Shān Lù 30 (ℂ *0571/8796-9023*), open from 11:30am to 2:30pm and 4:30 to 8:45pm. The current, rather garishly decorated building only dates from 1980, but the restaurant is something of a Hángzhōu institution, having been around for perhaps 150 years. In China, this is usually an indication that you should look somewhere else, as the restaurant will be resting on its reputation and on tour group business, and be overpriced. The **Shangri-La's Shang Palace** (ℂ *0571/8797-7951*) offers a wide range of Hángzhōu and Cantonese dishes prepared to perfection in sumptuous Qīng-style surroundings. Clay would never be allowed to sully its pristine kitchen and so the restaurant has come up with another way to achieve the same moistness and succulence in the famous Beggar's Chicken. Meals cost ¥200 ($25) and up for two. A far cheaper option, and one packed every night with local people, is the **Zhāngshēngjì Jiǔdiàn,** in Qìngchūn Dōng Lù, not far south and east of the Holiday Inn, open from 11am to 2pm and 5 to 9pm (© **0571/8602-7777**). Meals here cost ¥100 ($13) or less for two. This palatial multistory building has a large and golden Maitreya Buddha in the lobby flanked by lines of young women in pink *qípáo* (cheongsam), one of whom will escort you to a table in the cavernous and brightly lit interior. The menu is partially translated and pictures some of its dishes; at least one staff member speaks a little English. The local favorites are here, but there's more of an emphasis on fish. Try *jǐzhǐ yínxuěyú,*

parcels of fish deep-fried in a light batter and topped with a slightly peppery lemon sauce.

Hángzhōu also boasts the usual range of Western fast food, with KFC currently in the lead in numbers of outlets. Nán Shān Lù sports a number of cafes and teahouses serving distant relations of familiar Western dishes, mostly catering to students and younger people. Browse the menus outside and peer through the windows until you see something you like.

The best Western buffet is at the **Radisson,** and coffee shops at the **Holiday Inn** and **World Trade Center Grand Hotel** have a full range of Western favorites from curry to chowder at reasonable prices.

LAKE TÀI: THE GREAT LAKE OF CHINA

太湖

LAKE TÀI (TÀI HÚ) IS THE MOST fabled body of fresh water in China, a vast natural mirror embracing two ancient kingdoms: the Kingdom of Wú and the Kingdom of Yuè. Tài Hú is often draped in mists, likened by poets to the clouds between water and mountain. On its shores are the ancient garden city of Wúxī and the pottery town of Yíxīng, famous for its caves. In the lake itself are scattered temple islands.

Lake Tài has always had its curiosities, first and foremost the massive limestone boulders that its lathing waters shape and scrape. The Chinese pulled them out of the water for centuries for use in the rockeries of classic gardens. The Huīzōng Emperor, who ruled China from 1101 to 1126, emptied most of the Middle Kingdom's treasury in pursuit of more and more fantastical Tài Hú rocks.

The Gardens of the Grand Canal

The city of **Wúxī,** set on the northeast shore of Lake Tài, has a history of 3,000 years, but it is largely a center of industry today, lacking the natural and cultural beauty of nearby Sūzhōu and Hángzhōu. Nevertheless, Wúxī does retain a few beauty spots apart from Lake Tài. **Xíhuì Park (Xíhuì Gōngyuán),** bordered on the east by the Grand Canal, for instance, is Wúxī's chief downtown attraction (Apr–Nov daily 5am–6pm, Dec–Mar 5:30am–6pm; admission ¥25/$3). The park is topped by the seven-story **Dragon Light Pagoda (Lóng Guāng Tǎ),** first built during the Míng Dynasty. It's attractive enough, but the real treasure within Xíhuì Park's sprawling, well-manicured grounds is **Jìcháng Garden (Jìcháng Yuán).** Open daily from 7am to 10pm (admission after 6pm ¥20/$2.50), it's the most famous of Wúxī's private gardens.

Built on the site of a Buddhist temple, Jìcháng Garden became the retirement villa of an official who finished the original landscaping in 1520. Jìcháng is laid out much like the famous gardens of Sūzhōu, replete with fishponds, halls with slim columns and upturned eaves, old stelae (carved stone tablets), and rockeries consisting of massive Tài Hú stones, whose bizarre shapes and indentations are the result of long dunkings in the great lake. Jìcháng Garden was a favorite of the Qiánlóng Emperor, who in 1750 ordered the construction of a similar garden in Beijïng's Summer Palace. The covered walkways of Jìcháng Garden lead to higher vantage points in which the terrain of the surrounding Xíhuì Park becomes the "borrowed scenery" of this small garden, a fundamental "expansion" technique of Chinese garden design.

Jìcháng Garden also contains a display of Wúxī's most famous handicraft, **Huì Shān clay figures,** which are miniature sculptures of plump little children and rotund characters from operas and plays. They were first fashioned 4 centuries ago by local peasants and now are made at the adjacent **Clay Figurine Factory** at Xíhuì Lù 26 (Mon–Fri 7:30am–11am and 11:30am–4pm). Clay for these figurines, which are produced both by hand and by mold, comes from Huì Shān, a mountain connected to Xíhuì Park by a cable car. I find them a bit hideous, but there's no accounting for taste.

Also in Xíhuì Park is **Tiānxià Dìèrquán,** a Táng Dynasty spring that Lù Yǔ, author of the *Classic of Tea (Chá Jīng),* immortalized as the "Second Spring of the World"—he said that its superb sweetness and viscosity made it perfect for the brewing of tea. During the Sòng Dynasty, Yíxīng clay and Wúxī spring water became the emperor's cup of tea, and both are still found on the shores of Lake Tài. It is also said that the reflection of the moon in Èrquán Pool is exquisite beyond all words. Indeed, when the blind folk musician Ābǐng heard about the moon mirrored in this pool, he was inspired to compose one of China's most enduring and plaintive songs, another echo, faint as mist on a great lake, of the hidden depths of China's history.

Another garden, **Líyuán** (daily 7am–6pm), lies in southern Wúxī on Lí Lake, which is actually a back bay of Lake Tài. Celebrated as the garden of Xī Shī, a legendary beauty of the Spring and Autumn period (403–221 B.C.), Líyuán was rebuilt between 1927 and 1930 and expanded by the government in 1952. It actually consists of two older gardens built along the shore. Noted for its peach blossoms in the spring, this complex of watery gardens features a veranda with 89 windows that frame changing views of fishponds, rockeries, flowering bushes, and the Pavilion of the Four Seasons. A long, covered cement corridor hugs the lakeshore, ending at a floating restaurant. Líyuán is not one of the more beautiful gardens in the region, and I cannot say I was that enthralled when I toured it. I felt it more or less lived up to its name, translated as the "Garden Eaten by the Worms." Admission is ¥30 ($3.75).

Sailing Lake Tài

The best reason to visit Wúxī is Lake Tài. The finest views are at Wúxī's **Turtle Head Isle (Yuántóuzhǔ),** a turtle-shaped peninsula that juts into

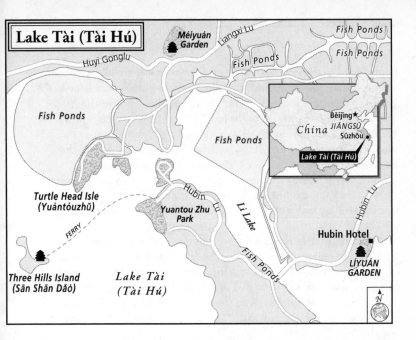

Lake Tài (Tài Hú)

the lake. Turtle Head began as a garden in 1918 and grew into a large park of teahouses, halls, walkways, and vistas. Entrance costs ¥50 ($6), which includes the ferry ride described below. The lake viewpoints along the peninsula's shoreline are equipped with pavilions. The best view of all is from a small modern **lighthouse.**

North of the lighthouse is a large pier with ferries to **Three Hills Island (Sān Shān Dǎo),** a 20-minute boat ride west into Tài Hú. The view back to Turtle Head Isle and the Wúxī lakeshore is splendid. A light fog rose from the shallow, glassy surface where fishermen glided past in their boats. Three Hill Island has been developed recently as a walk-through amusement park with an artificial cave, brand-new pavilions, sedan-chair rides, and groups of wild monkeys. Its local name, **Tài Hú Xiāndǎo,** translates as **Fairy Island,** which befits its new theme-park atmosphere. Views of the lake, its other islands, and distant shores, were once reason enough to cross Lake Tài—reason enough still for me. The center of the island park is a four-story mock temple with the gargantuan, garish plaster statue of an ancient emperor inside its atrium. Again, the views from the top are superb. The return journey on the ferry can be soothing, too. For a moment, skimming the waters, I have a glimpse of the Lake Tài that the old poets celebrated: vast, flat, misty, a contemplative vacuum quietly reflecting the heavens.

The Teapots of Yíxīng

Another aspect of Tài Hú is contained in the area of Yíxīng, the town west of Wúxī, that is one of the most famous centers of teapot production in

China. Though the town itself isn't much of an attraction, the surrounding villages are well worth a visit. Yíxīng teapots are available in any large souvenir shop worth its salt in China. Pottery production began in Yíxīng more than 3,000 years ago. For the last 2,000 years, Yíxīng has turned out the finest glazed china in China, relying on a local clay known as purple sand. Tea sets from Yíxīng are said to impart a taste to brewed tea that is essential for complete enjoyment. The pots are now mass-produced in this region, some in factories employing over 10,000 workers. Even the lakeside freeway from Wúxī is lined with ceramics: with ceramic light poles, with retail yards of glazed roof tiles and garden ornaments, with huge ceramic pots.

The road to Yíxīng is a superhighway through two Chinas: one old, one new. In one respect, the road resembles an old avenue, its median strip decorated in trimmed hedges, its light poles arranged like brown-and-yellow ceramic columns decorated in dragon coils, glass globes suspended on either side like lanterns. Dozens of old canals feed Lake Tài, and slabs of marble and newly raised Tài Hú rocks fill the courtyards of roadside merchants.

In another respect, the road reminds you of China's feverish economic booms. Scores of smokestacks boil over day and night, coughing out black-and-yellow coils of pungent smoke, thick as carpets. This is one of the most visibly polluted areas I have visited in China, sharply at odds with a serene lake and ancient teapots. Officials are aware of environmental problems in the region and they are taking action. Cleaning up Lake Tài was a major priority under the ninth Five-Year Plan (1996–2000); efforts have now been redoubled as we begin the 21st century. Wúxī residents pay a monthly ¥2 to ¥4 (25¢–50¢) sanitation fee for waste treatment, but more is needed. By the year 2010, 90% of city and township sewage discharges will be treated (as will 30% of the rural sewage)—substantial increases over what we see today. So far, though, the venerable waters of Lake Tài are not drinkable.

At Dīngshū, a small town 24km (15 miles) south of Yíxīng, I stopped off at **Purple Sand Village (Zǐshācūn),** a model town of nice new two-story villas with patios, sales rooms, and workshops. Some of China's best-known potters, having made enough to give up their factory jobs, live here. In this model teapotters' village, I met members of some of the most celebrated artisan families and watched them at work, molding the clay by hand on small tables; shaping pots, cups, and saucers; and applying decorative touches with their fingertips. The pots are fired for 24 hours in small kilns, then shipped to galleries or patrons or kept at home on sales shelves. Signed, such sets sometimes command prices above $1,000. Photographs on the walls often show a potter in the embrace of an illustrious visitor such as former Chinese Premier Lǐ Péng. Less refined, far less expensive Yíxīng teapots and cups are for sale at the stalls along Dīngshū's main street. A visit to the town's **Ceramic Exhibition Hall (Táocí Bówùguǎn),** open daily from 7:30am to 5pm (admission ¥10/$1.20), is also worth a half hour, as it features exquisite pots from several dynasties, modern creations by today's artists, and such everyday ceramics as bathroom fittings.

Underground Yíxīng

Yíxīng's reputation for teapots is international, while its reputation for limestone caverns is still confined to China. I visited two of Yíxīng's caverns, both in the countryside east of Lake Tài on roads leading out of Dīngshū. I'm not a devotee of caves, but the caves of China are unusual, almost always fronted by temples and imbued with ancient stories of hermit monks or Romeo-and-Juliet tragedies from feudal times. To me, however, the caves are not brilliant affairs. They are rough-edged and poorly lit, but the roads that lead to them are interesting. Large tea plantations and hulking rock quarries punctuate the flat fields that encircle much of Lake Tài and the lower Yángzǐ River basin. Women in straw hats stuff baskets with tea leaves. The dusty roads are clogged with small tractor-trailers hauling rock from quarry to crusher.

The first cavern I visited, **Shānjuǎn Cave** (open daily 7:30am–5pm; admission ¥38/$4.75), was named for a legendary ancient poet who refused an offer to become king, preferring utter freedom. He lived as a recluse in the cave. Open to the public since 1935, Shānjuǎn contains a large chamber called Lion and Elephant Hall (Shīxiàng Dàchǎng) after its size, the texture of its ceiling, and two large stalagmites that resemble the creatures. In its deepest recesses, an underground river winds for a quarter mile through the Crystal Palace (Shuǐjīng Gōng). There, I boarded a small wooden flat-bottomed boat. The oarsman planted his feet on the deck and pushed off using a long pole, propelling us into the dark. The water chamber is lined with 75 tiny caves, most of them unfathomable, even when our pilot attempted to illuminate them with his flashlight.

Outside Shānjuǎn Cave, a walkway along a stream leads to a temple complex that commemorates China's Romeo and Juliet, two young lovers who met as students 15 centuries ago. Since women were not allowed to attend schools in those days, the girl disguised herself as a lad. At school, she fell in love with another student. By the time this misadventure was disentangled, the boy, learning that the girl was betrothed to another, had taken his life. The girl, about to wed an older man chosen by her parents, threw herself into his grave. They emerged together as butterflies. Their tomb is said to be at this temple, which has dolled itself up with painted wall murals recounting the story. I have heard the same story recounted at two other locations in China, both claiming to be the place of its origin.

The second cavern I visited, **Zhānggōng,** fronted by a sprawling Daoist temple rising up a terraced hillside, proved to be larger and more intricate, with 72 interlinked chambers. Entrance required a local guide with a flashlight and the purchase of a ¥19 ($2.30) ticket. Zhānggōng's bewildering mile of passageways resembles a labyrinth for fairies. The largest room, Hall of the Sea Dragon Kong (Hǎiwáng Tīng), opens through a long funnel of twisting rock to the sky, and the sky in turn is reflected in a pool on the rock floor below. I was glad to emerge into the light, failing to find either of these caves conducive to meditation.

World's Largest Buddha

The newest attraction on Lake Tài is the most massive of all—the largest Buddha in Asia. Erected on Líng Shān, a forested hill 18km (11 miles) west of Wúxī, and unveiled in October 1997, the **Líng Shān Buddha** presides over two new temples and a large wall mural engraved with a pictorial map of the Western Paradise. This is something of a Chinese Land of the Giants. In the shrine's main courtyard, an enormous golden hand sprouts from the Earth, Buddha's hand (11m/38 ft. tall, 5m/18 ft. wide, and weighing in at 13 tons). The Big Buddha is fashioned from bronze—from 1,638 sheets of bronze—each sheet 4.5m (15 ft.) square. Standing atop a hefty 8m (28-ft.) platform, the statue is 86m (288 ft.) tall and tips the scale at 700 tons. By comparison, the Buddha on Hong Kong's Lantau Island, completed by the same company in 1993 and heralded as the largest in its class (seated, outdoor, bronze), is a mere 24m (81-ft.), 250-ton child. Construction of the Big Buddha at Líng Shān was initiated in the fall of 1994. Twenty chanting monks arrived to bless the undertaking. Wúxī and Lake Tài tourism officials are no doubt hoping that a million times that many tourists come to make their own offerings—tickets cost ¥20 ($2.40)—at the feet of the world's biggest standing Buddha.

PRACTICAL INFORMATION

by Sharon Owyang

ORIENTATION

Situated in the southern part of Jiāngsū Province, **Tài Hú (Lake Tài)** is one of China's four largest freshwater lakes. Wúxī, a Grand Canal port, sits at the northern tip of Tài Hú. Shànghǎi is 128km (79 miles) to the east. Yíxīng, the pottery region, is on the west shore of Tài Hú about 60km (37 miles) from Wúxī. This region is characterized by hot and humid summers, cold and gray winters, and windy and wet springs, making autumn (Sept–Oct) the best time to visit.

GETTING THERE

Wúxī has a small airport, but when even local airline officials give it a wide berth due to questionable safety standards, it's best to stick to trains, buses, and cars. Shànghǎi offers the nearest major airline connections.

By Train Sitting on the Běijīng–Shànghǎi rail line, Wúxī is 90 minutes away by train from Shànghǎi, 25 to 35 minutes from Sūzhōu, and 4½ hours away from Hángzhōu (via Shànghǎi), with trains serving all four destinations throughout the day. Train tickets can be purchased at hotel tour desks, at travel agencies, or at the train station ((© 0510/230-1217) in the northern part of town (counters 7–9 sell same-day tickets for Shànghǎi, Sūzhōu, and Hángzhōu).

By Bus From the **Wúxī Bus Station (Wúxī Qìchēzhàn;** © 0510/230-0751), just east of the train station, buses head to Shànghǎi (2 hr.; ¥30–¥43/$3.75–$5.40; leaving every 20 min. 6:30am–7pm), Sūzhōu (45 min.; ¥18/$2.25; every 15 min. 6:50am–6:15pm), Hángzhōu (4 hr.; ¥64–¥78/$8–$9.75; three buses every 2 hr. 7am–5:20pm), and Yíxīng (90 min.; ¥11/$1.40; every 15 min. 6:10am–6pm).

TOURS, STRATAGEMS & GETTING AROUND

The helpful **China Travel Service (CTS)** is located directly across from the train station at Chēzhàn Lù 88 (© 0510/230-0613 or 0510/230-0888, ext.1508; fax 0510/230-4143). They can help with plane, train, and bus tickets as well as arrange customized individual tours around the city and to the pottery shops and caves in Yíxīng County. In high season, a 2-day, one-person tour of Wúxī and Yíxīng with private car, English-speaking guide, and lunch included, will run around ¥1,500 ($188).

Getting around Wúxī on your own is fairly simple. **Taxis** cost ¥8 ($1) per 3km (2 miles), then ¥2.30 (30¢) per kilometer, and ¥2.80 (35¢) per kilometer after 8km (5 miles). Public **bus** no. 1 runs from the train station to Yuántóuzhǔ, with a stop at Líyuán on the way. Bus no. 2 stops at Xíhuì Gōngyuán, between the train station and Méiyuán, while bus no. 88 runs from the train station to Língshān. Public buses cost ¥1 (10¢) per trip. If you're visiting Yíxīng on your own, Tourist Bus no. 1 (¥5/60¢) will take you from the **Yíxīng Bus Station** (© 0510/794-5031) to Zhānggōng Dòng, while Tourist Bus no. 2 heads to Shānjuǎn Dòng.

WHERE TO STAY

Courtyard New World Wúxī (Wúxī Xīnshìjiè Wànyí Jiǔdiàn) Though officially unrated, this hotel is the equivalent of a top four-star hotel catering mostly to business travelers and a smaller number of tour groups. Located in the center of town in the thick of the shopping district, the hotel prides itself on having the largest standard guest rooms in town, and on its highly efficient service drawing repeat customers. Rooms are tastefully decorated and fitted with three phones and a broadband connection. Bathrooms are spacious and have tub/shower combos. The hotel also has three restaurants (Western, Chinese, Japanese) and a full range of facilities. *Zhōngshān Lù 335.* © *0510/276-2888. Fax 0510/276-3388. www.courtyard. com. 266 units. ¥660 ($82) double; ¥1,250 ($156) suite. AE, DC, MC, V.* **Amenities:** 3 restaurants; health and fitness club; sauna; concierge; tour desk; business center; conference rooms;

shopping center; salon; room service; massage; dry cleaning and laundry; valet; newsstand. *In room:* A/C, TV, dataport, minibar, coffeemaker, hair dryer, safe.

CTS Grand Hotel (ZhōngLǚ DàJiǔdiàn) Owned by China Travel Services, this three-star hotel, directly across from the train station, is a solid midrange hotel that offers unremarkable but clean accommodations at reasonable prices, especially after the usual discounts of 30% to 40% are given. Rooms are spacious and fitted with satellite TV (Hong Kong and Japanese channels only) and electric kettle. Bathrooms are very clean and bright and come with tub/shower combos. The hotel has two restaurants (Chinese, Western) and offers foreign exchange services.

Chēzhàn Lù 88. © *0510/230-0888. Fax 0510/230-4561. 131 units. ¥480–¥628 ($60–$78)) double; ¥880 ($110) suite. AE, DC, MC, V.* **Amenities:** 2 restaurants; fitness center; sauna, concierge; tour desk; business center; conference rooms; shopping center; salon; room service; massage; dry cleaning and laundry. *In room:* A/C, TV, fridge.

Sheraton Wúxī Hotel & Towers (Xīláidēng Dàfàndiàn) Located right in the center of town, this five-star hotel offers all the luxuries of a top international hotel. Despite having a slightly worn air about it, this is still the best place to stay for efficient service and first-rate facilities. Rooms are spacious and comfortable, and come equipped with the full range of amenities like robe and slippers, safe and satellite TV (CNN, HBO, BBC). Bathrooms are clean and come with tub/shower combos. The hotel's four restaurants (Chinese, Western, Japanese, pub) offer reliable fine dining. The staff is friendly and very helpful.

Zhōngshān Lù 443. © *0510/272-1888. Fax 0510/275-2781. www.Sheraton.com. 396 units. ¥1,185 ($143) double; from ¥1,869 ($224) suite. AE, DC, MC, V.* **Amenities:** 4 restaurants; indoor/outdoor swimming pool; health and fitness club; Jacuzzi; sauna; concierge; tour desk; business center; conference rooms; shopping center; salon; 24-hr. room service; massage; same-day dry cleaning and laundry; valet; newsstand. *In room:* A/C, TV, dataport, minibar, coffeemaker, hair dryer, iron, safe.

Shuǐxiù Hotel (Húbīn Fàndiàn/Shuǐxiù Fàndiàn) Completely redesigned and rebuilt in 2002 to be a five-star hotel, the Húbīn offers luxury accommodation right on the shores of Lake Tài. Located in the southeastern part of town near Líyuán, this 10-floor, European-style hotel now boasts whitewashed walls, wrought-iron balustrades and balconies, and elegant marble floors. For such an elegant hotel, guest rooms are surprisingly average, although they do have thick carpets, redwood furniture, and some gorgeous views of the lake. Bathrooms, which have shower/tub combos, are somewhat small and even a little old in places. The Húbīn has two Chinese restaurants and a Western restaurant. Located on the same compound and with the same owners and management as the Húbīn, the three-star **Shuǐxiù Hotel (Shuǐxiù Fàndiàn)** is a slightly less pricey (¥418/$52 standard; ¥818/$102 suite) lakeside option. The hotel evokes an English seaside cottage. The lobby and rooms are painted in pastels and are a pleasant change from the average Chinese hotel room. Rooms are spacious and clean.

Húbīn Lù 388. © *0510/510-1888. Fax 0510/510-7274. www.hubinhotel.com. 281 units. Húbīn Hotel ¥850–¥1,000 ($106–$125) double; ¥1,500 ($187) suite.*

AE, DC, MC, V. **Amenities:** 3 restaurants; outdoor swimming pool; tennis court; health and fitness club; sauna; bowling alley; concierge; tour desk; business center; conference rooms; shopping center; salon; room service; massage; dry cleaning and laundry; valet. *In room:* A/C, TV, minibar, hair dryer.

Tàihú Hotel (Tàihú Fàndiàn) Somewhat inconveniently located 10km (6 miles) west of the city center on the northern banks of Lake Tài across from Yuántóuzhǔ, this five-star resort offers a blissful escape from the bustle of the city, but is not very practical for the individual traveler. The hotel's sprawling grounds also contain private villas, huge landscaped gardens, and its own private dock leading to the lake, with plans underway for its own 18-hole golf course. For such a luxurious hotel, the standard rooms are surprisingly small and simply decorated, though all the usual amenities are here. Bathrooms are also on the small side and have shower/tub combos. Deluxe rooms are more spacious and comfortable. The hotel has all the standard five-star facilities and four restaurants (local Huáiyáng, Cantonese, Western, coffee shop).

Huánhú Lù, Méiyuán. ① *0510/551-7888. Fax 0510/551-7784. www.taihuhotel. com.* 57 units. ¥700–¥1,280 ($87–$160) double; from ¥1,500 ($187) suite. *AE, DC, MC, V.* **Amenities:** 4 restaurants; indoor/outdoor swimming pool; tennis court; health and fitness club; Jacuzzi; sauna; bowling alley; concierge; tour desk; business center; conference rooms; shopping center; salon; massage; 24-hr. room service; same-day dry cleaning and laundry; valet; newsstand. *In room:* A/C, TV, minibar, hair dryer, safe.

WHERE TO DINE

The **Wúxī Roast Duck Restaurant (Wúxī Kǎoyāguǎn),** at Zhōngshān Lù 222 (① **0510/270-3210**), is a popular four-story restaurant in the heart of downtown serving excellent local cuisine. Of course, Wúxī roast duck is a must here. It is typically served two ways: with steamed bread, chives, cucumbers, and sweet sauce; and as a soup. Other specialties include *Tàihú yínyú* (deep-fried Lake Tài fish) and the mouthwatering *Wúxī xiǎolóng* (Wúxī dumplings). Service is friendly and there is a menu in English. Dinner for two costs about ¥90 to ¥200 ($11–$25).

Sìchuān Girls Restaurant (Chuān Mèi Zi), at Rénmín Dōnglù 13 (① **0510/282-4148**), serves authentic fiery Sìchuān cuisine in a large dining room complete with fake trees and dark wood furnishings. Specialties here include the delicious *suànxiāng jǐn chǎo xiè* (crab stir-fried with garlic) and *Chuānmèi Hóng Fù Jī* (House Spicy Chicken). Dinner for two runs about ¥80 to ¥160 ($10–$20). *Note:* there's no English menu, and credit cards are not accepted here.

For local snacks, try the popular **Wángxīn Jì,** at Zhōngshān Nánlù 221 (① **0510/272-6484**), where you can sample crabmeat or pork wontons and dumplings at ¥10 ($1.25) for a steamer of 10 dumplings. This no-frills diner also serves a variety of noodles. **Someplace Else** (① **0510/272-1888**, ext. 3291), at the Sheraton Hotel, offers Western comfort food, including burgers, pizzas, pastas, and steaks, for ¥60 to ¥130 ($7.50–$15) a plate. A full bar, checked tablecloths, guitars hanging on the walls, and a foosball table will make it seem like you never left home.

THE GRAND CANAL: THE INFINITE WATERWAY

大运河

CHINA'S GRAND CANAL (DÀ YÙNHÉ), measuring 1,790km (1,112 miles) north to south from Běijīng to Hángzhōu, is the longest canal in the world, and one of the oldest. Its first section was dug in 486 B.C. by the king of Wú in order to dispatch soldiers and grain during a campaign of conquest. In 361 B.C., extensive canals were dug from Kāifēng, connecting it to Běijīng. During the Hàn Dynasty (206 B.C.–A.D. 220) and the Southern and Northern dynasties (A.D. 420–589), weirs and dams were built on the canals that served as locks. Winch systems were also developed, the earliest employment of ship-lifting mechanisms in the world. In 984, the first double-lock was built on the Grand Canal; the first double-lock built in the West, in Italy, was not completed until 1481. During the Sòng Dynasty (1127–1279), the new capital of Hángzhōu hooked itself up to the Grand Canal as far as the Yángzǐ River. And finally, under the Yuán Dynasty (1271–1368), when the capital moved up to Běijīng, the Grand Canal reached its final form, linking Běijīng in the north and Hángzhōu in the south, as it does to this day.

Yángdì, second emperor of the Suí Dynasty (A.D. 589–618), made the longest single contribution to the Grand Canal, conscripting one million workers to construct a shipping channel linking his capital at Luòyáng in central China to the Yángzǐ River basin and to northern China as far as Běijīng. In 611, Yángdì sailed to Běijīng from central China aboard a four-deck, 54m (180-ft.) long royal barge with a carved dragon's head as its mast. A thousand vessels attended the emperor. To haul this procession, 80,000 coolies in harness were employed, and 40 new palaces were built along the way. Yángdì died on the Grand Canal during his third excursion, hanged by rebellious members of his own court.

Like the Great Wall, the Grand Canal has fallen into ruins at many places, although long segments are still in use, particularly in the region of eastern China near Shànghǎi, where many lakes and rivers were realigned and joined over the centuries. The most active segment for modern travelers is now between **Sūzhōu** and **Hángzhōu,** the southern terminus of the Grand Canal for over 13 centuries. It was this stage that I wanted to sail, hoping to trace something of China's long history, where it is still deeply carved into the Earth.

Emperors on the Canal

The motive to build a grand canal on the scale of the Great Wall was chiefly imperial greed. The capitals of successive dynasties always required a water route to the regions that produced not only necessities such as rice but luxuries such as tea and silk. Since the major rivers of China flow from the west to the east, the emperors built an entirely new river over the centuries, as massive as the Yellow River or the Yángzǐ River, in order to create a flow of goods on a north–south axis that bisected their palaces and treasure houses. As they cut the various channels, they encountered an engineering problem. Differences in terrain and water flow led to varying water speeds. To harmonize the Grand Canal, water gates were constructed. The Pánmén Water Gate still stands in Sūzhōu. It was just east of this monument on the city moat that I boarded one of the dozens of passenger ferries that sail the Grand Canal to Hángzhōu.

For the last 6 centuries, the primary function of the Grand Canal has been to transport grain and other articles as tax and tributes north to the capital of Běijīng. There is a saying that it was the Grand Canal that brought the city of Běijīng into existence. The moat surrounding the Forbidden City connects directly to the Grand Canal. The bricks in the Forbidden City, the Temple of Heaven, and the Míng Tombs all came up the Grand Canal. Two hundred thousand tons of rice were required by the rulers in the north, but owing to waste, traveling expenses, and the tenacious middlemen of the Middle Kingdom, twice that much grain had to set out from the south. More than 10,000 rice barges, replaced every 10 years, plied the Grand Canal. Other ships carried cloth, food, salt, porcelain, lacquerware, bricks, bamboo, and timber to Běijīng. Scholars used the canal to reach the capital for the Imperial Examinations. A special bureaucracy evolved to regulate and maintain the canal, repairing the earthen embankments, planting trees, dredging waterways, and arresting pirates. Laborers were stationed every mile, 10 per outpost. In 1902, many of the officials in charge of water management were dismissed and canal transport was officially abandoned. Rail service had come into play.

Smaller boats continued to use segments of the canal for local shipping. In the 1950s, the canal was dredged and enlarged in the south, where it is now open year-round. The section that runs through Sūzhōu down to Hángzhōu contains 20 locks, as well as culverts and water-pumping stations. It is also so thick with ships and barges that I doubt canal travel will ever be a thing of the past in China, the anachronism it has become in America.

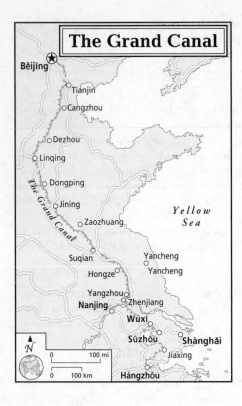

Water City of the East

Sūzhōu is a romantic place to begin a Grand Canal cruise (see the Sūzhōu chapter, beginning on p. 128). Known as the "Venice of the East," Sūzhōu rose to prominence by shipping its silk embroi- dery up the canal to China's imperial courts, establishing a high reputation in the arts that it never relinquished. Square bricks from Sūzhōu's kilns paved the Forbidden City. An inner moat encases this city of interlaced canals; a gated outer waterway connected Sūzhōu to the Grand Canal.

Pánmén, the old water gate in southwest Sūzhōu, consists of two sections: an inner brick gate 4m (12 ft.) wide and an outer granite gate 3m (9 ft.) wide. The walls between were used to entrap and inspect canal ships that called upon the city. The **Pánmén Water Gate** is still in place, as is the nearby **Wúmén Bridge (Wúmén Qiáo),** one of the largest arched stone bridges on the canal and now the entryway to Sūzhōu's wharves. Sūzhōu has everywhere the marks of a Grand Canal city. The whitewashed houses of Sūzhōu still have crimson doors that open on the inner waterways that feed the Grand Canal. You can cross more than a hundred bridges in Sūzhōu: arched stone bridges, ladder-shaped bridges, even house-spanning bridges *(lián jiā qiáo)* that connect two parts of a dwelling.

Three kilometers (2 miles) west of the city, the Grand Canal sweeps by **Cold Mountain Temple (Hánshān Sì),** jogging inland to join Sūzhōu's city moat to the southeast. This is where poet Zhāng Jì, arriving at the temple by canal boat during the Táng Dynasty, wrote this delicate passage:

Moon sets and crows caw in the frosted sky
River maples and the lights of fishing boats break
into my troubled sleep.
Beyond Sūzhōu lies Cold Mountain Temple;
At midnight the clang of the bell reaches the
traveler's boat.

I did not hear the clear bell in the frosted sky clanging in Cold Mountain Temple as I embarked on the canal boat at Sūzhōu. Instead, I heard the horns of two dozen nearly identical canal boats as they backed out from the piers to begin their journeys to Hángzhōu. These are not dainty vessels, outfitted to resemble the elegant dragon boats of the emperors who once sailed the Grand Canal. Nor are they modern ferries, comfortably tailored for the international tourist. They are rusty steel, double-deckered passenger boats that have worked hard and long. Their deluxe staterooms are simple, crude, deteriorating closets with a set of narrow bunk beds, a nightstand, an oil heater, and a spittoon on the floor. They have windows to let in the breeze and glass doors that open directly onto the outside deck. Although the knob was missing from my door, I could still lock it from the inside. But alas, the real drawback is that these ferries cruise by night. We departed in the late afternoon, with only a few hours of daylight on either end. I tried to make the most of the light, clinging to the railing above the bow.

The **city moat** where we pushed off is exceedingly narrow. The ship must pivot neatly and precisely to begin the journey. I was surprised but fascinated when three of these bargelike, flat-bottomed passenger ships undocked together. The vessel on our port side was the only one using its engines. The deck hands, leashing and unleashing the ropes that held the three ships together, maneuvered us into the middle of the canal so that we drifted into a staggered line. Then the crew hooked us together, end to end, using an iron pole on a swivel to lash stern to bow. My canal boat was second in line. The lead boat does all the work. We were gently towed forward, the black smoke of the first canal boat streaming back on us.

Night Passage

The Grand Canal is not beautiful, but it is as fascinating as the work-a-day canal boats, themselves just a step up from the barges that surrounded our small flotilla. These barges, each about 18m (60 ft.) long, with simple cabins on their sterns and open holds running forward to rounded stems, also like to hold hands. They too are often linked end to end in the tow of small tugs. Those barges that choose to go it on their own are powered by outboard engines with long, straight shafts. Often, a single barge will have four or five of these engines mounted in a row across the stern.

We passed scores of fishing junks tied up at docks, white flags fluttering on their sterns, then turned south, passing under a long, blackened bridge. We were on the Grand Canal. Sunset was already coloring the sludge of the sky. The barges were low in the water, crushed by loads of brick, coal, and sand to feed the factories that line the canal. The passage is narrow at times, although once out of Sūzhōu, it widens to 90m (300 ft.) or more. The only scenery on the banks is of flat farmlands and grime-coated factories. The chimneys of coal-powered factories ignite with orange flames. Several discharge effluents into the canal, colored a thoroughly unearthly blue. The Grand Canal is an industrial river, made and run by humans, and it is black with discharges. I could smell from the railing a powerful mixture of diesel oil and diarrhea—it's the smell of an open sewer.

Many waterways cut in and out of the Grand Canal, which is the main artery for farms and factories all across the vast plain of rapeseed and rice that radiates out from Shànghǎi. The Grand Canal cuts straight and true. Scores of low bridges span it. Thousands of vessels run up and down its length, stopping to load or unload at factories and towns and farms on the embankments, or to head down a side canal to towns and businesses that are still served by waterways. There must be hundreds of villages that depend on canal barges, places no tourist ever sees.

The passing barges were also homes. I saw dogs, cats, bicycles, plants, and laundry lines. On deck, a woman cooked the family dinner on a small coal stove. Fourteen barges linked together were the most I saw, and I saw that number often. Perhaps it's the maximum allowed on the Grand Canal.

In the southern outskirts of Sūzhōu, the Grand Canal embankment is straddled by **Precious Belt Bridge,** which consists of 53 stone arches. At over a half mile, it is the longest arched bridge on the canal. It was finished in A.D. 819, after the prefect's governor donated his precious belt to fund its completion. I barely noticed it in passing. I was watching the barges coming at us in the darkness. The running lights I saw turned out to be a son or daughter standing on the bow waving a flashlight.

I lay back on the hard bunk. It was too hot for a quilt. I couldn't sleep long. The oncoming traffic was continuous. Ships passed within a few feet, like apartment buildings hurtling through the night. The engines rattled and screamed, the ship horns blasted away, and the larger vessels such as ours swept the water and canal banks with searchlights. Sometimes I heard shouts.

End of the Grand Canal

After 5am, I didn't sleep another wink. A faint sun crept into overcast skies. I rubbed my eyes, but the panorama of gray factories, coal yards, smokestacks, and cranes did not brighten. The fishermen were up. They were trolling the waters with baskets for shrimp. I wondered how these people can survive on the Grand Canal. It is a severe world. Even this voyage seemed little better than a 13-hour Greyhound bus tour of a sewer.

Yet as we neared Hángzhōu (see the Hángzhōu chapter, beginning on p. 140), last stop on the Grand Canal, the banks became stone, neatly laid by hand, and the promenades were shaded by groves of willow and maple. We docked at Gēnshān Harbor (although now boats continue closer to the center of the city to dock at the Wǔlín dock), near the tripled-arched Gōngchén Bridge, the last ancient stone crossing on the Grand Canal. The lead boat angled in and cut us loose. We drifted into the dock. "Above there is Heaven," goes the popular saying, "Below are Sūzhōu and Hángzhōu." And between these rivers there is still the Grand Canal, reaching across the land like the dark, powerful arm of an ancient warrior, a palpable link with the China of the emperors.

PRACTICAL INFORMATION

by Sharon Owyang

CRUISES

Daylight is longest during the months of June and July, allowing for more time to see the Grand Canal, although these summer months tend to be quite hot and humid.

In Sūzhōu, canal boat passage can be booked through **China International Travel Service (CITS)** at Dàjǐng Xiāng off Guānqián Jiē (✆ **0512/6522-3783,-3593**). Tickets can also be booked at tour desks of hotels, including the **Gloria Plaza Hotel** (Gànjiāng Dōnglù 535; ✆ **0512/521-8855**); the **Bamboo Grove Hotel** (Zhúhuì Lù 168; ✆ **0512/520-5601**); and the **Sheraton Sūzhōu Hotel** (Xīnshì Lù 388; ✆ **0512/510-3388**). Finally, you can buy tickets directly at the dock, **Nánmén Passenger Boat Terminal (Nánmén Lúnchuán Kèyùn Mǎtóu)** at Rénmín Lù 8 (✆ **0512/6520-5720**; daily 6:30am–5:30pm), in the southern part of town just northeast of the bridge that crosses the Nánchéng Hé moat.

There are several different classes of travel, though none of the canal ships are to be confused with luxury cruise lines by any stretch of the imagination.

A berth in the best first-class cabin (two berths) costs ¥130 ($16). It's possible to purchase the entire cabin for more privacy. Second-class cabins (four berths to a room) are cheaper, with tickets between ¥60 and ¥88 ($7.50–$11). All cabins are bare-bones basic without sinks or showers, while toilets are Chinese-style holes-in-the-ground. There is a dining room on board serving relatively expensive and not very appetizing fare without benefit of an English menu, so you might want to think about packing your own meal.

Boats depart the Sūzhōu Nánmén Passenger Boat Terminal daily at 5:30pm, arriving in Hángzhōu at around 7am. The reverse voyage also departs Hángzhōu at 5:30pm and gets into Sūzhōu at around 7am. Tickets cost the same and can be purchased in Hángzhōu at the boat terminal at Wǔlín Mén Kèyùn Mǎtóu (Wǔlín Mén Passenger Boat Terminal). For information and bookings, call ✆ **0571/8515-3185**.

XIÀMÉN:
AMOY MON AMOUR
厦门

FIRST KNOWN TO THE WEST AS AMOY, its name in the local Fújiàn dialect, Xiàmén is among the most charming cities in China, and in the past it has been voted the cleanest as well. An ordinance forbids the honking of horns, mitigating yet another aspect of pollution common to developing cities in China—and Xiàmén is every bit a boomtown. Owing to its location on the East China Sea, directly across from Táiwān, Xiàmén has benefited for years from its connections with overseas Chinese. When I first visited in 1987, Xiàmén showed signs of being the single most developed place in China, if crates of imported appliances, throngs of motorbikes, and jungles of television antennas were any indication. Every other resident of Xiàmén seemed to have relatives abroad and, thus, a ready conduit to the foreign luxury goods, which, until quite recently, few in China had the means to procure.

Xiàmén is still prosperous, but it has had the good sense not to turn its downtown and harbor into a microcosm of Manhattan or Hong Kong. Rather, the old town is still old, and although there's been a fair amount of low-rise building on the island in its harbor, Gǔlàng Yǔ—once the stronghold of foreigners—it remains a resort of mansions, parks, and pedestrian-only streets that is simply China's most charming reliquary of its colorful colonial past.

Old Town Xiàmén

The key intersection in Xiàmén is on the inner harbor at the crossroads of **Lùjiāng Lù** and **Zhōngshān Lù,** near the stately Lùjiāng Hotel, with its sea-view balconies. Until a few years ago, this is where the local buses congregated, the conductors leaning out the windows, shouting their destinations and banging the side of the bus with a wrench. The ferries to **Gǔlàng Yǔ,** the gorgeous island of red-roofed mansions and green hills just west across the waterfront, depart from here. The area around the dock is a lively congregating point for visitors, vendors, and shoppers.

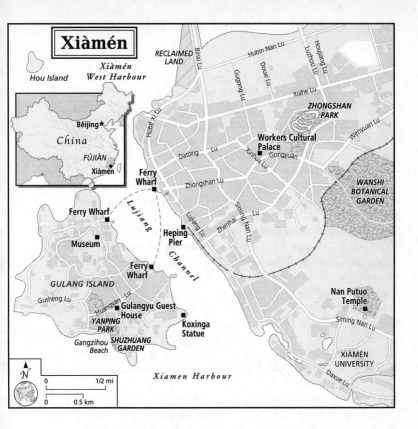

To explore the **old downtown,** just walk east past the curving facade of the Lùjiāng Hotel on Zhōngshān Lù. This is main street, filled these days with shops large and small, old and new. Many of the side streets are as they have been for decades, consisting of row upon row of shophouses, their columns and colonnades covering the sidewalks.

One of the first treks I ever made in Xiàmén was southward from the main ferry dock along **Mínzú Road.** The quays are a feverish sprawl of fishing boats unloading their catches, warehouses shuffling pallets of imported electronics, and factory yards piled with coal and dried fish. One morning I came across two little children frolicking in one factory yard, running and leaping on the other side of the gate, both of them stark naked and laughing.

Temple, School & Disputed Strait

If you're up for a long walk, you can stroll all the way down the east shore of Xiàmén (which is itself an island, not joined to the mainland until a causeway was constructed after 1949). Eventually, Sīmíng Nán Lù leads to **Nán Pǔtuó Temple,** Xiàmén's greatest place of worship (daily 3am– 6:30pm; admission ¥3/35¢). Nán Pǔtuó, built into a rocky hillside, is an active Buddhist complex of grand halls, bell towers, inscribed rocks, and pavilions, striking for its white marble and upswept tiled roofs. The temple dates from the Táng Dynasty, but it has been extensively rebuilt in the thousand years since. This is a fine place to watch locals pray for riches and burn incense (which is collected for reuse by numerous monks). At the highest hall, there is a magnificent red character, meaning Buddha, carved into a massive boulder. The outcroppings beyond this point make for excellent day hikes.

When I visited Xiàmén 10 years ago, much of the Nán Pǔtuó halls and courtyards were undergoing another renovation. A small city of stonecutters was encamped at the temple gates. Today, Nán Pǔtuó has been put back together. It teems with visitors, drawn to this southern "home" of China's most popular divinity, Guānyīn, Goddess of Mercy.

Just south of the temple is one of China's best schools, **Xiàmén University (Xiàmén Dàxué),** founded in 1921 by Tan Kah-kee, a native of the area who moved to Singapore and made his fortune in rubber plantations. If you've never strolled around a campus in China before, this might be your best chance. Ask at the gate if you may enter or wait for helpful students to approach you to practice their English. Lǔ Xùn (1881–1936), China's most famous modern essayist, taught here for a term in 1926 to 1927, and there's a small exhibit in his memory just inside the main gate. One of Xiàmén's students befriended me when I visited here. He gave me a tour of the campus, told me about the inner workings of student dorm life, and took me to lunch at a nearby student cafe.

South of the temple and university is the **Húlǐ Mountain Cannon Platform,** the remnants of German artillery placed here in 1890 (daily 10:30am–4:30pm; admission ¥25/$3). Looking across the Formosa Strait, it's just a few miles to two islands, Jīnmén and Xiǎo Jīnmén, much in dispute between China and Táiwān. For years they taunted each other across this strait with loudspeakers, propaganda balloons, and live explosives. The islands figured in the Kennedy–Nixon presidential debates in 1960, when Jīnmén and Mǎzū, further up the coast (both now open to tourism from the Taiwanese side) were better known to Cold Warriors as Quemoy and Matsu.

Garden Island (Gǔlàng Yǔ)

Xiàmén's most engrossing attraction is **Gǔlàng Yǔ,** the small island in its harbor that is served by innumerable ferries. The main ferry to Gǔlàng Yǔ is across from the Lùjiāng Hotel. Look for the two big entryways to the pier. There's no charge on the way out to Gǔlàng Yǔ, and it's just ¥3 (35¢)

to return. The voyage requires just 10 minutes. These old two-deck ferries have almost nowhere to sit down. With their sliding screen doors, they look rather like cattle cars.

The island fathers have wisely ordered all new buildings to conform in spirit and style to its graceful colonial legacy. Evenings, walking the twisting lanes, I've passed more than one garden villa emitting the soothing sounds of a pianist in rehearsal or a private concert. Many of China's best musicians come from here, and the locals, who number barely 12,000, sometimes call Gǔlàng Yǔ by another name, not on the maps: Piano Island.

Gǔlàng Yǔ is an island for walking. Cars and even bicycles are banned, although electric carts are permitted, giving tours. The island is quite hilly but also quite compact. Straight up from the dock is the town, packed with shops and seafood cafes. The streets are cobbled or paved, and they twist and turn like pretzels. You'll probably get lost, but it's easy to find the way back to the town and ferry dock.

South of the ferry dock is the way to turn: Here, a number of the grand buildings and villas occupy the hillside, survivors of Gǔlàng Yǔ's days as a foreign quarter. Western traders moved onto Gǔlàng Yǔ in 1842. The foreigners built the villas, sanitation system, consulates, schools, churches, hospitals, and roads that remain today. In 1903, Gǔlàng Yǔ became Xiàmén's official foreign concession. The British and Germans had their consulates on the east side of the little island, as did the Amoy Telephone Company. The old **British Embassy building** still stands atop the first hill on your left as you leave the ferry, substantially restored after a fire, and now houses a display of old coins. The towering whitewashed **Roman Catholic church,** on a quiet lane rising above the southeastern shore, is over a century old now (1882) and still used on Sunday, as is the **Sānyī Protestant church,** which the English built in 1904.

Gǔlàng Yǔ seems to be blanketed in hundreds, even thousands, of old villas, many of them now the residences of locals. The original coats of arms in enamel have been removed from the stucco doorways, but the Corinthian columns, two-story porches, plaster curlicues, and immense verandas recall many foreign architectural styles, especially the Portuguese types still prevalent in Macau. Mature banyans, bougainvillea, and bauhinia overhang the winding, walled lanes that enclose luxuriant gardens. Gǔlàng Yǔ seems like a slice of the tropics with only a few Chinese intrusions.

Placed on the southeast cusp of Gǔlàng Yǔ like a beacon is a mesmerizing statue of the robed warrior **Koxinga (Zhèng Chénggōng),** who commanded Xiàmén with his pirate armada said to consist of 8,000 war junks and 250,000 fighting men. Koxinga expelled the Dutch from Táiwān in 1661. He died there the next year, but he has been remembered ever since.

His statue surveys the sea from atop a sea pillar, which visitors reach via a bridge from a lovely seaside garden. This rounded image of Koxinga is as memorable as New York's Statue of Liberty, if less dramatic. Its form also mirrors that of the summit of Gǔlàng Yǔ itself, Sunlight Rock.

Near the Koxinga statue, up Tiān Wěi Lù, is the **Gǔlàng Yǔ Guesthouse compound,** with its 1920s billiard room and seaside terraces, where former U.S. President Nixon stayed in 1972 when opening up relations with the People's Republic.

The island's best **beach** is southwest of Koxinga, on the southern shores. The sands are inviting and a new graceful portico has been built on the shore, but the most interesting areas to explore are along the fringes of the beach, where pathways wind through stone pinnacles that rise from the shore.

Overlooking the beach is one of the island's best-known gardens, **Shūzhuāng,** built in 1913 by a wealthy merchant called Lín, who fled his home in Táiwān when the Japanese occupied it in 1895. It is a small seaside garden that has recently been refurbished with a zigzag bridge, a large goldfish pond, and a massive honeycombed wall of lake rock. Locals seem to like lingering here, and they make a great deal of the pond in a garden on the sea ("A garden in the sea, a sea in the garden," they say). For me it has an artificial, sterile look—an amusement park garden. It's open daily from 8:15am to 5:30pm; admission is ¥20 ($2.50), which includes access to a museum of pianos.

Gǔlàng Yǔ's finest overlook is **Sunlight Rock (Rìguāng Yán),** nearly 90m (300 ft.) above the harbor, the highest of the island's peaks (daily 8:15am–5:30pm; admission ¥60/$7.50). The summit of Sunlight Rock is a short, steep climb along rock paths dotted with flower gardens, old cannons, small cafes, and a number of amusement arcades, yurts, and contemporary metal sculptures. Sunlight Rock has taken on a carnival atmosphere, but at its higher levels, it is simply a beautiful landform of granite boulders and outcroppings rising to a rounded summit of smooth, bare rock. From the top, the outlines of Gǔlàng Yǔ, the harbor, and downtown Xiàmén to the east are in full view. Gǔlàng Yǔ is particularly fetching from this height, an island garden of villas in red brick and tile.

Gǔlàng Yǔ's most prominent building is the **Xiàmén City Museum (Xiàmén Shì Bówùguǎn),** a spacious, colonnaded edifice crowned with a large red dome (8:30am–5pm; ¥10/$1.25). I was determined to see its interior on my most recent visit, so I retraced my steps back into Gǔlàng Yǔ town and at the ferry dock followed the shore northward up Yánpíng Lù. I turned up a nearby street, and after a few blocks and a few false turns, found the museum's gate. It is a curiously hollow, unadorned old hall inside, its four floors divided in the center by a circular atrium. The exhibits are not splashy. The first floor is decorated with photographs of Gǔlàng Yǔ's colonial architecture. Various rooms have different exhibits: relics of recent wars, printing presses, a set of handcuffs. The second floor contains a collection of painted porcelains dating back to the Táng Dynasty; a room devoted to gifts sent by Xiàmén's sister cities from around the world (including Baltimore and Sutter Creek, California); tributes from a number of foreign countries; a hall displaying Iron Age weapons, scrolls, wooden rifles, and pieces from a cart; and a Trophy Room festooned with the prizes of local sports heroes. The top two floors were closed. The staff was drinking tea in the staff rooms, and the doors were swung wide open to the tropical sea breezes.

PRACTICAL INFORMATION

by Peter Neville-Hadley

ORIENTATION & WHEN TO GO

Special economic status has led to rapid growth in Xiàmén, driven by foreign investment, much of it from Táiwān, and the city is now home to more than 1.3 million people. While much of the flatter northernwestern part is covered in the same fairly hideous white-tiled buildings and the gridwork of boulevards found in much of the rest of China, the southwest edge, tucked behind a hilly area, has an unusually well-preserved labyrinth of shophouses.

This downtown area stands opposite the islet called Gǔlàng Yǔ and its collection of decaying foreign mansions.

The climate is subtropical and generally mild, although the local authorities admit to "abundant rainwater." Summers can be scorchingly hot, with nearly 100% humidity, and late spring and early autumn remarkably wet. March, October, and November are the best months to visit.

GETTING THERE

By Plane Xiàmén's **Gāoqí International Airport** (© **0592/602-8940**) is on the north side of the island, only 20 minutes from the downtown area. Airport taxis cost little more than ¥30 ($3.50) to downtown, and there's a shuttle to the railway station from the right of the terminal as you leave for ¥6 (70¢). There are international connections to Bangkok, Kuala Lumpur, Manila, Singapore, and Tokyo, with an assortment of domestic and foreign airlines, as well as flights to Hong Kong, Macau,

and most major Chinese cities. While most airlines maintain offices in the Crowne Plaza or Marco Polo hotels, or elsewhere in the center, you are better off purchasing your tickets from agencies.

By Train On routes to neighboring coastal cities and to Hong Kong, luxury long-distance bus services are quicker and more comfortable, but there are useful trains to Běijǐng and Xī'ān, and the route through mountainous Fújiàn Province is pretty and winding, if slow.

For train enquiries, call ✆ **0592/581-4340**; for booking, call ✆ 0592/398-8662. Ticket windows are open from 8am to 8:30pm.

By Bus Southern China's new highway system is now cruised by air-conditioned buses with frequent services, many of them luxury foreign makes with attendants and lavatories. For all coastal destinations north in Fújiàn and into Zhèjiāng, as well as south and into neighboring Guǎngdōng Province, buses are the quickest way to get there other than by flying. The main long-distance bus station is on Húbīn Nán Lù, just north of downtown, but many of the best services also have agencies conveniently opposite the main ferry terminal to Gǔlàng Yǔ. Try **Lúndù Shòupiàochù** (✆ **0592/213-5051**), where several services pick up passengers, and which has a small waiting room. Sample routes: Guǎngzhōu 770km/481 miles, ¥180 ($22); Shēnzhèn 680km/425 miles, ¥180 ($22); or even directly to Hong Kong 830km/519 miles, ¥350 ($44). One Hong Kong service, the **Eternal East Cross–Border Coach Mgt. Ltd.** (✆ **0592/202-3333**; www.eebus.com), can be booked and boarded at the Crowne Plaza. It departs at 7:30am daily. In Hong Kong, call

✆ **852/ 2723-2923** for details of services from Hong Kong to Xiàmén.

By Ship Although most coastal passenger routes are long gone, the service to Hong Kong survives. There's no better way to approach Hong Kong than by sea, and a relaxing boat trip to relatively clean and civilized Xiàmén makes for a soft landing in mainland China. Service is now provided by the 250-cabin *Wasa Queen* of the **Hong Kong Cruise Ferries** company (www.cruise-ferries.com.hk). The ferry leaves Xiàmén at 6pm on Thursdays, arriving in Hong Kong at 3pm the next day. From Hong Kong, it leaves at noon on Wednesdays, arriving in Xiàmén at 10am the next day. One-way fares for berths in cabins range from HK$320 ($41) to HK$1,120 ($143) per person for individual travelers and couples, and about 20% of those fares for each of the third and fourth persons in any group. Prices payable in Xiàmén are local currency equivalents. Prices rise 50% around the Chinese New Year. Check the website for up-to-date schedule details, or call in Hong Kong (24 hr.), ✆ **852/2957- 8188**; in Xiàmén, ✆ **0592/202-2517**. Xiàmén departures are from the Hépíng Wharf, just south of the Gǔlàng Yǔ ferry terminal.

GETTING AROUND, TOURS & STRATAGEMS

Both the old town and Gǔlàng Yǔ are easily explored on **foot,** and the other sights discussed above are short taxi rides away. Taking a **taxi** out to the Húlǐ cannon, then walking back through the university campus (almost opposite) to the Nán Pǔtuó Temple is the best way to proceed. There's no need of tour companies here, and the many agencies in the streets are the best source of air tickets. **Train** tickets are not hard to obtain at the railway station, or

from agencies and hotel desks. The Nánfāng Lǚxíngshè inside the Hépíng Wharf has a computer on the railway system, and charges a ¥10 ($1.25) service charge per ticket (although it should probably only be ¥5 (65¢). **Bus** companies have convenient offices opposite the ferry to Gǔlàng Yǔ and at the Hépíng Wharf. For a closer look at Taiwanese territory, go to the small dock just beyond and below the Húlǐ cannon. One-hour boat tours take you out to see Jīnmén and Little Jǐnmén for ¥96 ($12). Call ✆ 0592/208-3759 for more information. There are similar services from next to the main ferry terminal on Gǔlàng Yǔ (immediately to the right as you leave the ferry): 12 departures between 8:20am and 3:40pm. For more information on these, call ✆ 0130/5551-9326.

WHERE TO STAY

Xiàmén has a variety of shiny business hotels scattered around the island, but at four-star level, the two to choose are the **Marco Polo** and the **Crowne Plaza.** Both add a 15% service charge, but other hotels do not. There are abundant budget accommodations along the waterfront and on Gǔláng Yǔ itself, which is much quieter, including an unusual opportunity to sleep in a former American consulate. A trade fair makes September a little busier, continuing through the first part of October. Visitor numbers pick up again from March and grow through May, after which Chinese tourism drops to almost nothing, and only the odd foreigner is seen in midsummer. Typically, 40% off rack rates is available; more in lesser accommodations.

Holiday Inn Crowne Plaza Harbourview (Jiàrì Hǎijǐng Dàjiǔdiàn) This is a tapering 22-story tower, visible across the city, with all rooms on higher floors having good views. The building dates from 1992 but a continuous refurbishment program has kept it fresh; all facilities are of a conventional four-star standard, and service is both attentive and efficient. In-room broadband Internet access is ¥50 ($6.25) per day. The hotel is a conveniently short walk from the Hépíng Wharf, 5 minutes from the warren of the old town, and a 15-minute stroll along the harbor front from the main ferry to Gǔláng Yǔ. *Zhènhǎi Lù (downtown) 12–8.* ✆ *0592/202-3333. Fax 0592/203-6666. www.sixcontinentshotels.com. 349 units,* including 6 suites. ¥1,280–¥2,080 ($160–$260) twin/double; ¥2,800–¥6,560 ($350–$820) suite. AE, DC, MC, V. **Amenities:** 4 restaurants (Italian, Chinese, Japanese); 24-hr. coffee shop; cocktail bar; outdoor swimming pool; health club; sauna; concierge; tour desk; free airport shuttle; business center; shopping arcade; salon; medical clinic; 24-hr. room service; babysitting; same-day dry cleaning and laundry; nightly turndown; American Express office; forex; newsstand. *In room:* A/C, TV, dataport, minibar, coffeemaker, hair dryer.

Jǐnquán Bīnguǎn Here, you'll get a chance to sleep in a former U.S. consulate dating from the 1930s (the first consulate burned down). The neoclassical portico (with an oddly Egyptian touch to the tops of its pillars) has been glassed-in and the upper floor extended into that space. What was veranda is now lobby, and upstairs are suites, which have a plate glass wall, excellent light, and good views. Rooms are all wooden floored and in good condition, the building having been refitted and opened as a hotel in 1999. Of the wide variety of room shapes, corners are best, since they provide views of both the sea and the gardens (with tennis courts) below. The entrance is only accessible via a staircase from the garden. There are no luxuries here, but this solid brick building, in a far quieter location than can be found on Xiàmén's main island, deserves its three stars.

Sān Yuè Lù 26 (on Gǔlàng Yǔ, a short walk to the right from the main ferry dock, and served less frequently by ferries to a dock immediately beneath it). © **0592/206-5621.** *Fax 0592/206-4273. 29 units. ¥460 ($57) standard room; ¥660 ($82) suite. Simple doubles in separate newer building ¥280 ($35). No credit cards accepted.* **Amenities:** Restaurant. *In room:* A/C, TV, fridge.

Lùjiāng Bīnguǎn The Lùjiāng is the kind of three-star hotel you should avoid—open too long to have forgotten the bad old days of complete indifference to (if not complete abhorrence of) the existence of guests. However, this six-story building, opened in 1983, refurbished in 1998, had new linen stocked in 2002, and is in good condition for a three-star. It's rarely necessary to pay more than 60% of the overly optimistic rack rates, despite the hotel's excellent location. Service is reasonable, although not enthusiastic. TV service runs to satellite channels from Hong Kong, as well as video-on-demand.

Lùjiāng Dào 54 (opposite main ferry pier for Gǔlàng Yǔ). © **0592/202-2922.** *Fax 0592/202-4644. 153 units. ¥410 ($51) single room; ¥468–¥760 ($58–$95) double/twin; ¥830–¥1,360 ($104–$170) suite. No credit cards accepted.* **Amenities:** 3 restaurants (Chinese and Western; with ocean views); business center; shopping; salon. *In room:* A/C, TV, minibar.

Marco Polo Xiàmén Many of the rooms are arranged on eight floors around a central atrium, but there is a wing off to one side which is a better choice for peace and quiet. The rooms are well appointed to four-star standard, with broadband Internet access and larger than average bathrooms. The concierge desk is particularly well staffed with good English speakers, both eager to help and capable of doing so. The center of town is only a few minutes away by taxi, around the western side of the lake.

Jiànyè Lù 8, Húbīn Běi Lù (on the north shore of Yuándàng Lake). © **0592/ 509-1888.** *Fax 0592/509-2888. www. marcopolohotels.com. 350 units. ¥1,280– ¥2,000 ($160–$250) twin/double; ¥2,000– ¥7,840 ($250–$980) suite. AE, DC, MC, V.* **Amenities:** 3 restaurants (International, Chinese, Japanese); lobby lounge and poolside bar (with views across the lake to the city skyline); outdoor swimming pool; health club; sauna; concierge; tour desk; limousine service; free airport shuttle; business center; shopping arcade; salon; 24-hr. room service; same-day dry cleaning and laundry; nightly turndown; newsstand. *In room:* A/C, satellite TV, minibar.

WHERE TO DINE

Unsurprisingly for a port city, Xiàmén is known for its fresh fish. Those who like to get into the thick of things can find seafood for next to nothing in the back streets of the old center, or more decorous, if more expensive, Chinese eating inside the main hotels. On Gǔlàng Yǔ, small, hole-in-the-wall restaurants just up from the dock await the unwary tourist, although some do have clearly posted prices. Lunch will still be swimming or crawling around plastic tubs set out in the street. Good Western food is only available in the bigger hotels, but there are two McDonald's and a KFC in Zhōngshān Lù alone. A waterfront tower-top Pizza Hut on Tóngwén Lù is visible for miles, and has correspondingly excellent views once you get up there. There's further fast food, both Chinese and Western, close to the ferry dock on Gǔlàng Yǔ, and a currently out-of-place cafe. Perhaps a harbinger of trendiness to come is the Hong Kong–owned coffee shop called **Banana,** with Horlicks, pancakes, and egg sandwiches in a pastel-colored interior hung with Mark Rothko prints (at Lóngtóu Lù 54C; open 10am–10pm).

The rooftop restaurant in the Lùjiāng Bīnguǎn, called **Guān Hǎi Cāntǐng,** ⓒ **0592/202-2922,** ext. 709, open 7:30am to 2pm and 5:30 to 11pm, has excellent seafood dim sum morning and evening, and a good range of well-executed Chinese standards, along with local specials such as *gāli xiàn yóu* (curried squid) and *hǎilì jiā* (pan-fried oysters). Meals cost about ¥100 ($13) for two, including a 10% service charge.

Vegetarians are well served at the **Nán Pǔtuó Temple.** Tickets must first be bought from the "Vegetable Dishes Booking Office." Individual dishes cost from ¥8 ($1), but three-dish set meals from ¥30 ($3.75) per person make life easier. The surroundings are undistinguished and practical, but the food is made with a sensitivity to each ingredient's strengths. Try *xiāng ní cáng zhēn* (vegetables mashed into a paste— much more attractive than it sounds), *luóhàn zhāi* (a stew of pine nuts, cabbage, cucumber, corn, mushrooms, and fresh coriander), *dāng guǐ miànjǐn tāng* (Chinese angelica and gluten soup), or *lú sǔn dòufu tāng* (asparagus and tofu soup). Open noon to 4pm and 5 to 7pm.

Gǔlàng Yǔ has its own specialty snack made on the island, called *wāng jì xiàn bǐng*—small pastries stuffed with a variety of sweet fillings (vegetarian versions available) and usually sold in souvenir boxes. On the way to Xiàmén City Museum, you'll pass a corner pastry shop that specially stocks these (with good prices, too, if you bargain) called **Qín Dǎo Quán Xià Tèchǎn Shāngdiàn,** at Quánzhōu Lù 85.

GUĂNGZHŌU (CANTON):
THE GATE TO CHINA
广州

Guăngzhōu, better known by its
old Western name, Canton, is the center of all things Cantonese—that is
to say, south China's people, language, and cuisine. It is also among my
least favorite Chinese cities. Hardly a stone's throw from Hong Kong,
Guăngzhōu is all business and industry these days, all freeways and skyscrapers and factories—hardly a major tourist stop like Běijīng and
Shànghǎi, eastern seaboard metropolises comparable in size and wealth to
noisy Guăngzhōu. All the same, I discovered, after repeated visits, that old
Canton has its pleasurable treasures, too, several of them unique.

First impressions of Guăngzhōu are seldom promising, unless you are
driven into raptures by construction noise and modern expressways.
Guăngzhōu has some of the most advanced elements anywhere in urban
China, some of the highest salaries and most efficient corporations, and its
network of new roads and elevated freeways is the most impressive in
China. Its traffic is the swiftest and best regulated—or so I thought until
I noticed that the on-ramps to these towering expressways are filled with
cars using them as off-ramps as well. The pace in Guăngzhōu is feverish,
and its drivers have learned to swerve with the flow, even when that flow
instantaneously reverses itself, heedless of head-on collisions, unannounced
U-turns, illegal stops in busy traffic lanes, and other unpredictable detours.
This is Cantonese life in the fast lane, without the impediments imposed
by common sense, courtesy, or police on most other city streets in the
world. The sheer energy, of course, is contagious, and it defines the
Cantonese way as it drives full-throttle into the 21st century. Already, the
Pearl River Delta region accounts for more than half of China's commerce.

Canton's Central Park

At the heart of the city are older, quieter islands of repose and culture. The
city's largest park, **Yuèxiù Gōngyuán,** is its best (daily 6am–10pm; admission ¥5/65¢). Built on a grand scale, the green, hilly, 99-hectare (247-acre)
grounds possess a number of boring features, such as three artificial lakes

and a 40,000-seat stadium. For most foreign visitors, the **Sun Yat-sen Memorial Hall (Zhōngshān Jìniàntáng),** with a separate admission (8am–5:30pm; ¥10/$1.25), located at the southern foot of the mountain that gives the park its name, isn't that exciting, either. Finished in 1931, 6 years after Dr. Sun Yat-sen's death, the hall and its blue-tiled tower host lectures, plays, and other cultural offerings. It's a grand but simple edifice, engineered so that no interior pillars are required for support. Sun Yat-sen is the province's most beloved native son, credited with leading the over-throw of China's last imperial dynasty and the establishment of China's first republic. He founded the Guómíndǎng (Nationalist Party) in 1923 in Canton, the political party that later tried to unite China under Chiang Kai-shek but fell to the victorious Communist revolutionaries under Máo Zédōng. Still, Sun Yat-sen is claimed by both Nationalists (who fled to Táiwān in 1949) and Communists as the founder of modern China, and almost invariably the main street in China's cities today bears Sun Yat-sen's Mandarin given-name (Zhōngshān).

Guǎngzhōu's reputation as a hotbed of revolutionary activity was enhanced not only by Sun Yat-sen's Republican Revolution but by Máo's early Communist movement. From 1924 to 1927, Máo, Zhōu Ēnlái, and other Communist Party founders trained future firebrands at **Canton's Peasant Movement Institute,** located in the former Temple of Confucius. Chairman Máo's spartan bedroom is still on view there, in yet another of Guǎngzhōu's politically correct but touristically dull attractions.

What's interesting in Yuèxiù Park is, of all things, the **Guǎngzhōu Museum** (daily 9am–5pm; admission ¥6/75¢). By the time I actually came to look inside, I'd visited Guǎngzhōu enough times to expect yet another display of photographs and letters tracing the history of the Communist Party or recording one of several massacres of martyrs to China's revolution. Instead, within the graceful **Pavilion Overlooking the Sea (Zhèn Hǎi Lóu),** which European traders called the Five-Story Pagoda, there are fine, well-displayed historical exhibits, arranged chronologically by floor, with signs in English and Chinese. First built during the Míng Dynasty in 1380 and rebuilt as a Pearl River lookout in 1686, this pavilion (Guǎngzhōu's oldest building) is an ideal venue for a historical museum, capped by an elegant teahouse on the fifth floor. My favorite item is a Míng Dynasty water clock, dated A.D. 1316, consisting of three large barrels arranged like stairs that employed a large dipstick to measure the correct time.

The centerpiece of Yuèxiù Park is its **Statue of Five Rams.** The five rams recall the story of Guǎngzhōu's founding, when five fairies from the Celestial Realm rode their rams into town to present the Cantonese with their first grains of rice. I expected this oft-photographed emblem of the city—a modern sculpture always dismissed as of little artistic merit—to be

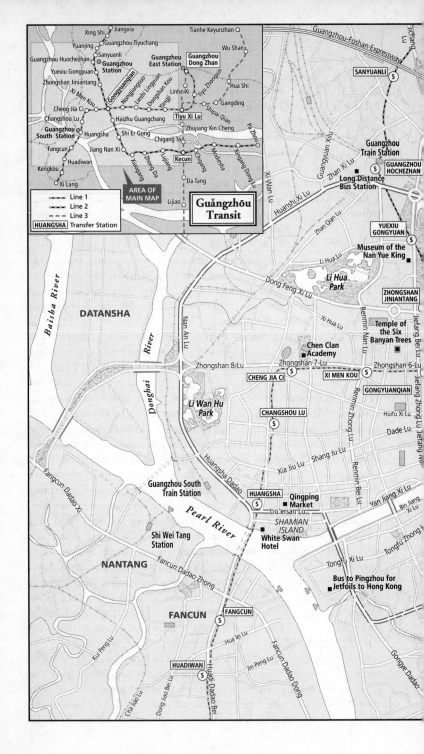

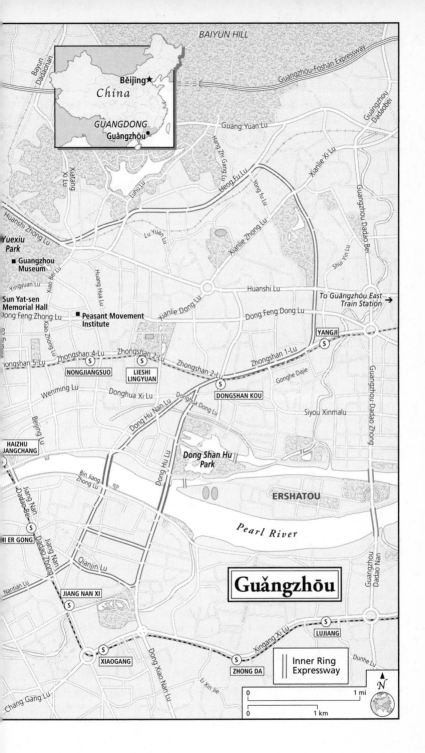

BAIYUN HILL

China
Běijīng★

GUANGDONG
Guǎngzhōu

Guangzhou-Foshan Expressway

Guangzhou Dadaobei

Guangzhou Dadao Bei

Bayun Dadaonan

Xiatang Xi Lu

Luhu Lu

Guang Yuan Lu

Hang Zh Gang Lu

Heng Fu Lu

Yong fu Lu

Xianlie Xi Lu

Huanshi Zhong Lu

Lu Yuan Lu

Xianlie Zhong Lu

Shui Yin Lu

Yuexiu Park

■ **Guangzhou Museum**

Yingyuan Lu

Xiao Bei Lu

Huang Hua Lu

Xianlie Dong Lu

Huanshi Lu

To Guǎngzhōu East Train Station →

Sun Yat-sen Memorial Hall

Dong Feng Zhong Lu

■ **Peasant Movement Institute**

Dong Feng Dong Lu

YANGJI Ⓢ

Dong Feng Xiao Zhong Lu

Zhongshan 4-Lu Ⓢ

Zhongshan 2-Lu Ⓢ

Zhongshan 2-Lu

Zhongshan 1-Lu

Zhongshan 5-Lu

NONGJIANGSUO

LIESHI LINGYUAN

Gonghe Dajie

Wenming Lu

Donghua Xi Lu

Dong Hu Nan Lu

Donghua Dong Lu

Ⓢ **DONGSHAN KOU**

Siyou Xinmalu

Beijing Lu

HAIZHU JANGCHANG

Bin Jiang Zhong Lu

Dong Hu Lu

Dong Shan Hu Park

ERSHATOU

Pearl River

Jiang Nan Dadao Bei

Ⓢ **MI ER GONG**

Jiang Nan Dadao Zhong

Qianjin Lu

Guangzhou Dadao Nan

Nantian Lu

JIANG NAN XI Ⓢ

Guǎngzhōu

Ⓢ **LUJIANG**

Xingang Xi Lu

Dunhe Lu

Ⓢ **XIAOGANG**

Dong Xiao Nan Lu

ZHONG DA Ⓢ

| Inner Ring Expressway

Chang Gang Lu

Li Xin Jie

0 — 1 mi
0 — 1 km

N

hopelessly overrun and tacky to boot, but again I was surprised. Perched on a raised platform, this statue, made of granite chunks fitted together to form the five impish rams with their coiling horns, is actually an intriguing piece from many angles, and the honeycomb of flowery paths that surround it are explored as much by locals and retirees as by visitors.

Temple of the Six Banyan Trees (Liù Róng Sì)

One of the most bizarre halls in any Buddhist temple I ever visited in China was at another of Guǎngzhōu's tourist stops, the Temple of the Six Banyan Trees, open daily from 8am to 5pm (admission ¥1/10¢, ¥10/$1.25 to climb the pagoda). Its main attraction is its nine-story **Flower Pagoda (Huā Tǎ),** first erected in A.D. 537 and situated squarely in the central courtyard. Behind it is a hall with three statues of the Buddha and one of Guānyīn, the Goddess of Mercy, who remains throughout China, as in Canton, one of the most popular deities. Several locals bowed low, with incense sticks extended in prayer to the brass goddess. The most arresting sight, however, is not the pagoda or prayer hall, but the death hall. When I entered this hall, immediately to the left of the pagoda, it took me a while to figure out its function. It's a spare chamber, with one monk in attendance. The walls are coated with strips of paper and pictures of the dead. The cost of getting posted in this prayer hall, where your image and spirit are constantly administered to by a government-approved religious worker, is by no means nominal: a stiff ¥6,000 ($750) per posting.

Qīngpíng Market

A better-known oddity of Guǎngzhōu is fully in keeping with its culinary reputation. **Cantonese cuisine** is China's most complex and varied. The Cantonese tastes are perhaps as wide-ranging and as daring as those of the French. The popular saying in China is that the Cantonese will eat anything on four legs except a table. To see that this is no exaggeration, browse through Guǎngzhōu's most famous street market, **Qīngpíng**—probably China's most notorious open-air market. You can't escape the lurid reports of exotic and domestic skinned animals nonchalantly hung from hooks at vendors' stands: from tigers to kitty cats, from pandas to dogs.

Qīngpíng Market (open 6am until dark) is a large warren of covered stalls, and animals are indeed one of its offerings. I did walk past cages of dogs and cats and even small deer, all still alive and for sale. There were monkeys, snakes, and bats, too, all highly prized and high-priced fare. But this sideshow of animals is a tiny, tiny segment of Qīngpíng Market, as it always has been. Today, you can roam from herb lane to antiques lane to

goldfish lane to mushroom lane to fresh flower lane to songbird lane without coming across a gruesome sight. Of course, the lanes are narrow,
crowded, and pungent, and the walkways are not the world's cleanest—
heaps of atmosphere, in other words.

Island of Sand

Across from the market is Canton's best reason to linger, **Shāmiàn Island,**
a quarter-mile-wide, half-mile-long sandbar that became the chief outpost
of British, French, and other foreign traders who forced the port to open
its doors in 1843. Britain took the lead, backing its merchants in southern
Cathay who hungered to unload opium in Canton and return home with
tea. It eventually won concessions from China in what became known as
the Opium Wars. In 1859, Britain and France were granted territory on
Shāmiàn Island. The foreigners moved right in, shored up the embankments with stone, and maintained two bridges to the quays of Canton,
shutting the iron gates at 10pm every night to keep the Chinese out.
Shāmiàn was soon populated with Western colonial-style administrative
headquarters, banks, Christian churches, a Masonic temple, tennis courts,
and a yacht club on the Pearl River.

By 1911, the population of Shāmiàn had reached 300, including
Americans, Dutch, Germans, and Japanese, as well as the original English
and French residents. On June 23, 1925, Chinese demonstrators, fed up
with these enterprising invaders, massed on the city shore to attack, and 52
were shot to death by Western armies. Shāmiàn continued as a foreign post
until the Communist Revolution in 1949.

The colonial architecture, the lawns and flower gardens, and the great
arching banyan trees have endured, and Guǎngzhōu has seized upon this
rare legacy, sprucing up the broad avenues, planting garden plots, and slap-
ping bright coats of paint on all the Western facades. Meanwhile, a raft of
cafes, craft shops, galleries, and teahouses has moved in. This strange colonial revival has made Shāmiàn into the most pleasant place in Canton and
its chief international gathering point. The old Catholic church, **Our Lady
of Lourdes** (at the intersection of Shāmiàn Yī Jiē and Shāmiàn Dàjiē), has
been reconverted from a printing plant back into a place of worship.

The island is a perfectly shaped oval, great for jogging or strolling, with
a view of colonial architecture and modern enterprise within and the surg-
ing **Pearl River (Zhū Jiāng)** beyond. This river is shorter than the Yángzǐ
or the Yellow River but all the more intense, dumping eight times more
water into the ocean than the Yellow.

I was strolling the riverbanks, watching the women wash their clothes in
the rancid waters on a staircase dipping into the quay, when I was approached

by an artist who offered to sell me antique painted scrolls that he kept rolled up in his Shāmiàn apartment. Whether these were antiques or not, I couldn't tell, but I was intrigued by the scrolls he unrolled on his living room floor, and I parted on happy terms with an ink-wash drawing in hand.

The blossoming of Western-style cafes and foreign boutiques in the old buildings on the island is a recent phenomenon. When I first visited Shāmiàn, the architecture was in languid decay and the main new addition was the stunning **White Swan Hotel** (see "Where to Stay," below), which was very nearly the first modern international hotel to spring up in China, appearing in 1982, and among the first three to receive China's official five-star rating. The White Swan remains hale and hearty as it approaches its 20th birthday, its garden waterfall in the high atrium still flowing like a wild cascade. The hotel is a modern monument of China's opening to the West, still a grand place to poke around among the lavish antiques shops in the basement. Dozens of tour groups throng its lobby and hundreds of overseas businesspeople retire to the Riverside Apartment complex in its spacious banyan garden on the eastern tip of Shāmiàn, where the traffic of Pearl River is always in full swing. Iced tea and a sandwich in the Riverside Garden Coffee Shop with a view of the waterfall within and the river floating by outside at eye level is still a pleasure, a peaceful haven from the commerce of the streets to which the White Swan has been the beacon for 2 decades.

Cantonese Cuisine

Guǎngzhōu has a final appeal: its food. Cantonese, the great cuisine of China, was born here, and you can still find great Cantonese dining experiences in the city. It is often said, however, and not without justice, that the best Cantonese food is served in Hong Kong, Singapore, Táiwān, New York, San Francisco—in nearly any great capital except Guǎngzhōu. Fortunately, there are some brilliant exceptions. Since I am not a true connoisseur of exotic Cantonese dishes, I leave it to others to try the live snake and monkey brain restaurants for which Guǎngzhōu is notorious. My own choices are far more delicate, depending on fresh seafood and the traditional pungent sauces.

My favorite dining in Canton is at **Běi Yuán** (see "Where to Dine," below), the city's most beautiful garden restaurant. Built in the 1930s, Běi Yuán is segmented into over 40 halls, its tearooms and dining pavilions decorated with carved latticework, covered corridors, and etched window glass. Flowers are the decorative motif. Dim sum, the southern Chinese collection of bite-sized steamed dumplings and baked pastries and other small delicacies, is served all day, although it's usually taken on at a leisurely tea-drinking brunch that the Cantonese call *yum cha.* The best dinner dishes are the winter melon with green pepper and the mushrooms stuffed with shrimp; the signature dish is a stew of mixed delights, ranging from abalone and pork to chicken and trout. There's a second, connected, branch specializing in the dishes of Cháozhōu in the northeast of Guăngdōng Province.

A second garden restaurant with an outdoor setting is **Bàn Xĭ,** along the shores of Lì Wān Lake. It, too, is a dragon of dining halls and classic decorations, with black lacquer furniture, gold leaf ceilings, and etched glass from the Qīng Dynasty. Dinners run until midnight, and a lake stroll after dark, after a fine dinner, puts you in the mood to dream of a China that has long passed yet is still accessible in the midst of this supercharged metropolis. The dim sum is superb here, too, but the restaurant is extremely crowded all weekend. The Peony shrimp plate is divine. The menu is in English.

My most memorable Cantonese meal, however, occurred in the restaurant of a third-rate suburban hotel, **Shā Hé** (see "Where to Dine," below), a half-hour taxi ride northeast of Guăngzhōu. The Shā Hé kitchen has been southern China's most famous noodle emporium for 40 years, and nothing would do until I tried it myself. The dining area, on the second floor of the hotel, is dirty on the edges, and the marble tables and stone chairs are a bit cold, but the flat rice noodles *(ho fan)* are hot and succulent. It hardly matters what sauce, vegetable, meat, or sea creature is added. I asked the general manager if I could take a peek at the famous kitchen, where 15 chefs and 30 assistants flail away in utter chaos—or rather, in accordance with a 600-year-old recipe. I was allowed to witness the whole process, from sink to wok, in the confines of the hotel's grease-washed dungeons.

The two chief activities of the Cantonese, it seems to me, are business and eating. Excelling at both, they are making Guăngzhōu the most progressive business city in China and at the same time the tastiest. I know of nothing more divine to do in old Canton than sit down to a Sunday *yum cha* in a decorated hall with the energy cranked high on all sides and the air crackling with conversation like a thousand lightning rods in a thunderstorm. That's when I drift away like an emperor half asleep, my eyes following the rounds of a dumpling cart loaded with its delicate tidbits: prawns sealed in transparent rice envelopes *(har gau),* steamed beef-and-prawn dumplings *(siu mai),* and barbecued pork stuffed inside plump steamed buns *(char siu bao);* red tea arcs into my cup, falling from the long neck of a copper pot, snapping me awake. It seems like morning has just begun in distant China.

PRACTICAL INFORMATION

by Peter Neville-Hadley

ORIENTATION & WHEN TO GO

For most of the time since China's reform and opening got going, Guăngdōng Province's proximity to Hong Kong, and the colony's rapid transfer of almost all its manufacturing to factories across the border, has made Guăngzhōu the capital of China's richest province. It's a sprawling, unattractive city, with enough to see to make it a worthwhile day trip from Hong Kong, but not enjoy to justify a stay of more than 2 days, unless you are attending one of the city's mammoth trade fairs, which fill hotels from here all the way to Hong Kong Island.

Guăngzhōu's climate is similar to Hong Kong's—the most pleasant months are October to March, and for the rest of the year the city can be very hot and humid. In midsummer, there can be heavy rains.

GETTING THERE

By Plane Guăngzhōu's current airport, **Báiyún,** is only 12km (7½ miles) to the north, about 30 minutes from the city center, reached by a new metro line, and served by flights from every major city in China, including Hong Kong (1 hr.—but allowing time for travel to and from airports, check-in, and security, it's faster by train). It's also connected internationally to Amsterdam, Bangkok, Fukuoka, Jakarta, Kuala Lumpur, Los Angeles, Melbourne, Osaka, Phnom Penh, Seoul, Singapore, Sydney, and Tokyo. There's a regular bus service to and from the CAAC office next to the main railway station. As elsewhere, tickets are best bought from agents rather than directly from airlines. CITS (to the right of the main railway station as you face it) is unusually helpful, and air ticket prices can be bargained down (Mon–Fri 8:30am–6:30pm; Sat and Sun 9am–5pm). Some English is spoken.

In July 2004, the New Báiyún International Airport will open, well to the south, at a cost of $2.5 billion on the first phase alone. Its capacity will eventually be several multiples of the old airport's, a threat to the other four airports within 121km (75 miles) of it, including Hong Kong's.

By Train Most trains from elsewhere in China arrive at the **Guăngzhōu Railway Station,** and trains from Hong Kong at **Guăngzhōu East,** which is conveniently at the end of one metro line. There are seven departures a day to Hong Kong between 9:50am and 5:20pm, taking 1½ to 2 hours. There's also a very-high-speed service from the East Station to Shēnzhèn, with departures every few minutes, some of which cover the 139km (87 miles) in under an hour. Shēnzhèn station is right next to the border crossing into Hong Kong at Lo Wu, where there's a rail link to Kowloon. For information on trains to elsewhere in China, call *C* **020/6135-7412** or 020/6135-8952.

By Bus Guăngzhōu has long-distance bus services both just west of the main railway station and opposite it, and a number dotted around the city on the main ring road. All provide services to provincial destinations, most quicker than the train (except Shēnzhèn). Beyond that, except for destinations in southern Fújiàn Province, such as Xiàmén, or in eastern Guăngxī Province, such as Guìlín, it's better to take a train. There's a useful direct bus service to Hong Kong airport, picking up at the China Hotel, White Swan, International Hotel, Holiday Inn, and so on, departing eight times a day from 5:45am to 4:25pm (10:05am–5:15pm from the CTS counter at Hong Kong Airport, ☎ **020/ 8333-6888,** ext. 5384; in Hong Kong, call ☎ 852/2764-9803).

By Ship A twice-daily jetfoil service at 10:30am and 4:30pm takes around 2 hours to reach Hong Kong, for the local equivalents of between HK$189 (US$24) and HK$1,704 (US$218),

depending on the class chosen. A shuttle bus picks up passengers at the Garden and International hotels. See www.turbocat.com and the Hong Kong section below for more details. There's also a catamaran service at 9:15am and 4pm, taking around 2¾ hours, for HK$168 to HK$258 (US$22–US$33) or the equivalent in local currency, with a shuttle bus from the now closed Zhōutóuzuǐ wharf in Hòudé Lù, just across the Rénmín Bridge from Shāmiàn, to the Nánhăi wharf in Píngzhōu. The bus picks up from outside a small shop at the gate of the old wharf, which also sells tickets. Call ☎ **0757/677-2417** (Píngzhōu) for details, or the ticket office in Guăngzhōu at ☎ **020/8441-2267** or 020/8444-8218.

GETTING AROUND

The bedlam around Guăngzhōu's main railway station and long-distance bus stations is intimidating, and will give those newly arrived in Guăngzhōu a poor impression. The **metro** is the most convenient way to get through Guăngzhōu's heavy traffic, and one line (red) usefully passes Shāmiàn Island (Huángshā Station) and two or three other major sights, eventually ending up at Guăngzhōu East railway station. Unfortunately, there are not enough lines, although maps already show two additional lines as if they do indeed exist. The green, which runs north–south and connects the airport to a new exhibition center, opened in early 2003 on the south side of the city. Tickets cost ¥2 to ¥5 (25¢–65¢) according to the

distance to be traveled, as shown on a color-coded sign above ticket machines. Stored-value cards allowing multiple journeys are also available from the metro station ticket desks. The system runs from around 6am until 11pm.

Taxis are among China's most expensive, but still your best choice for getting around. Flagfall is ¥7 (90¢) including 2km (1¼ miles), and ¥2.60 per kilometer (30¢) up to 15km, then 50% more. There are no extra nighttime charges.

Guăngzhōu's **bus** fleet is surprisingly old and battered. Ordinary buses have a flat fare of ¥1 (10¢); newer, air-conditioned versions have a flat fare of ¥2 (25¢).

TOURS & STRATAGEMS

Many visitors will find that the two best sights of Guăngzhōu are the Museum of the Nán Yuè King in Jiěfàng

Běi Lù, just south of the China Hotel, and the Chén Clan Academy (Chén Jiā Cí), next to the metro station of the same name. The museum (9am–5:30pm; ¥12/$1.50) is one of China's better efforts, a modern building encasing a now-excavated burial mound from the Western Hàn Dynasty (206 B.C.–A.D. 9), and which allows both access to the tomb chamber and to the treasures found there, all unusually well lit and displayed. The Chén Clan Academy (8:30am–5pm; ¥10/$1.25) was an ancestral hall constructed by 72 local branches of the Chén family in the last years of the 19th century, and is a fine example of a large southern mansion, with stone screens and wooden beams, all a riot of carved figures. It doubles as a museum of local crafts, with some spectacular pieces on display.

Organized tours in Guǎngzhōu are not really useful, as they tend to include remarkably dull sights glorifying the revolutionary credentials of the city, as well as dull modern monuments, and not necessarily the truly ancient and interesting, or the foreign enclave of Shāmiàn. All of Guǎngzhōu's sights are easily reachable by metro or taxi. All the major hotels have tour desks, and **American Express** has a branch in the office building of the Guǎngdōng International Hotel (see below; Mon–Fri 9am–5pm; ✆ **020/8331- 1311;** fax 020/8331-1616). But most are merely adding a service charge to put you on an already overpriced tour. See www.ctcol.com for an example of a 1-day tour, or call the **Guǎngzhōu Tourism Information Line** at ✆ **020/8666-1275.**

WHERE TO STAY

Until the mid–19th century, Guǎngzhōu was the only place where foreigners were permitted to trade with China, and despite periods of complete closure to outside influences in the 20th century, foreign trade has grown to be the city's raison d'être since the beginning of the "reform and opening" of the Chinese economy. This is one of the last cities where the cavernous hotel with innumerable rooms and endless facilities, once the style of almost all hotels open to foreigners, has survived in any numbers. These are designed to serve the vast numbers of businesspeople attending the trade fairs in the last 2 weeks of October and April, and lesser specialist fairs in between.

The Guǎngzhōu fairs have an effect on room rates as far away as Hong Kong; the major hotels, despite their cavernous size, are likely to be full in that period and offering no discounts. Otherwise, expect to cut 20% to 50% from the prices quoted, although major hotels also add a 10% service charge and a 5% city tax. Lesser hotels conform to normal Chinese standards by not adding service charges and including city tax in the quoted price.

The larger hotels, with the exception of the White Swan, are in the busiest sections of a busy city, and even if you're used to staying at five-star and four-star accommodations, you should consider smaller, quieter hotels on Shāmiàn Island, which is largely pedestrianized, and where a little peace and quiet can be found. Some of those are conversions of old colonial buildings, of considerably more character than the average Chinese hotel, and on a smaller and more human scale.

China Hotel (Zhōngguó Dàjiǔdiàn) This vast, U-shaped hotel has been managed by Marriott since 1999, and its old infrastructure has received a ¥900-million ($113-million) face-lift since

1996. It's a Chinese five-star; the rooms are adequate if unimaginative, rather better on the executive floor, and the cavernous building contains so many different facilities it's unnecessary to leave it. There's broadband Internet in-room (¥100/$13 per day). The location on the (new) metro and close to Yuèxiù Park is convenient. Several consulates have offices here, and it's often the choice of VIP visitors, both Chinese and foreign.

Liúhuā Lù (metro Yuèxiù Gōngyuán, opposite the China Export Commodities Fair). © *020/8666-6888. Fax 020/8667-7014. www.marriotthotels.com. 1,013 units. ¥1,184–¥1,800 ($148–$225) twin/double; ¥1,800–¥12,000 ($225–$1,500) suite (including breakfast, tax, and service). AE, DC, MC, V.* **Amenities:** 12 restaurants and bars (Cantonese, Japanese, sports bar, sake bar, Hard Rock Cafe, and more); outdoor pool; health club (Guǎngzhōu's largest); full spa (nearby); whirlpool; sauna; solarium; travel desk; business center; gift shop; salon; babysitting; laundry and valet. *In room:* A/C, TV, dataport, minibar, coffeemaker, hair dryer, iron, safe.

The Customs Conference and Reception Centre (Hǎiguān Huìyì Jiēdài Zhōngxīn) This place is too new for stars (opened in 1999), but it's a nice little hotel, a solid four-story building of unclear antiquity with a roughly neoclassical exterior, whose interior has had a four-star retrofit. Through the gleaming marble lobby is a five-story atrium, at the base of which, one story down, is a small garden with a stream. Rooms are fresh and bright with wooden floors, and bathrooms have proper shower cubicles as well as bathtubs. Suites are very affordable and come with 1½ bathrooms. Foreign TV access is limited to Hong Kong channels. There's Internet access in a small business center (¥18/$2.25 per hr.).

Shāmiàn Dàjiē 35. © *020/8110-2388. Fax 020/8191-8552. 49 units, including 7 suites. ¥500 ($63) standard room; ¥800 ($100) suite. Rates include service and taxes. No credit cards accepted.* **Amenities:** Restaurant; billiards room; table tennis. *In room:* A/C, minibar, TV.

The Garden Hotel (Huāyuán Jiǔdiàn) The 30-story, Y-shaped Garden Hotel is another Chinese five-star colossus, with every imaginable facility, and it's easily the grandest lobby in Guǎngzhōu (reputedly the largest in Asia). Its level of service is among Guǎngzhōu's best, and its rooms are slightly more imaginative than the China Hotel's. An interior waterfall and garden mimic those of the White Swan Hotel.

Huánshì Dōng Lù 368. © *020/8333-8989. Fax 020/8335-0467. www.garden hotel-guangzhou.com. 1,038 units. ¥1,160–¥2,080 ($145–$260) twin/double; ¥2,740–¥4,980 ($343–$623) suite. AE, DC, MC, V.* **Amenities:** 11 restaurants and bars (including Italian, Japanese, and French, and an extensive international buffet in the revolving restaurant on the 30th floor); swimming pool; tennis and squash courts; gym; sauna; children's playground; tour and ticket desk; limousine service; forex; shopping arcade; salon; babysitting; valet and dry cleaning; post office. *In room:* A/C, satellite TV, broadband (¥100/ $12.50) per day, minibar, hairdryer, safe.

Rosedale Hotel and Suites (Pǒlì Jiǔdiàn) The Hong Kong–managed Rosedale was formerly the Plaza Canton (built in 1988), and it still appears on some maps and in the minds of taxi drivers as that (Jiāng Nán Dàjiǔdiàn). The exterior of the tower looks its age, but the lobby has had a sumptuous retrofit, as have several floors, now in the smart modern style of the sister property in Hong Kong. The as-yet unrefurbished floors are as battered as the refurbished ones are elegant (bathrooms with glass bowls for basins), and generally receive overseas tour groups—pay a little more for a big jump in comfort. On the new metro line, and so giving swift access to the center, this hotel will also be ideally situated for business visitors once a vast new convention center is completed a little to the south. There is now broadband Internet in all rooms.

Jiāng Nán Dà Dào Zhōng 348 (metro Jiāng Nán Xǐ and Xiǎo Gǎng). ✆ *020/8441-8888. Fax 020/8442-9645. www. rosedalegz.com.cn. 406 units. ¥880–¥1,480 ($110–$185) twin/double; ¥1,580–¥8,880 ($198–$1,110) suite. AE, DC, MC, V.* **Amenities:** 3 restaurants (including Cantonese specialties and dim sum at Pak Lai Heen); lobby lounge bar; swimming pool; tennis; badminton; health center (awaiting refurbishment); tour desk; free shuttle to Guǎngzhōu East Station; business center; forex; shopping arcade; valet. *In room:* A/C, satellite TV, dataport, broadband ¥80 ($10) per day, minibar, safe.

White Swan Hotel (Bái Tiān'é Bīnguǎn) This was one of China's first luxury hotels (1982), a labyrinthine monster whose location on Shāmiàn Island and views over the Pearl River make it perennially popular. The more you pay, the higher your room. Refurbishment is a continuous process, and the hotel is unusual among long-standing monsters in keeping up standards and adding facilities. Some rooms come with dataport, some with broadband (¥150/$19 for 24 hr.), and are a little above average in size, with high ceilings and new furniture. The slightly tacky lobby features a waterfall and fish-stocked pools crossed by bridges. Former guests include Queen Elizabeth II and the first U.S. President Bush.

Shāmiàn Nán Jiē 1 (on Shāmiàn Island). ✆ *020/8188-6968. Fax 020/8186-1188. www.whiteswanhotel.com. 843 units. ¥2,320–¥2,800 ($290–$350) twin/double; ¥2,960–¥3,440 ($370–$430) suite. Rack rates are halved outside trade fair periods, and can often be bargained down by a further 30%. AE, DC, MC, V.* **Amenities:** Multiple Chinese and Western restaurants; bakery; night club; 2 swimming pools; golf driving range; 10 tennis courts; squash court; gym; sauna; souvenir shopping arcade; florist; book shop; pharmacy (with infant care products); salon. *In room:* A/C, satellite TV, dataport (some with broadband, ¥150/$19 per day), minibar, hair dryer, safe.

WHERE TO DINE

Unsurprisingly perhaps, Guǎngzhōu (Canton) offers Cantonese food as it should be—much plainer, more subtle, and more delicate than you get at home, with the flavors of the ingredients distinct on the tongue. It's said of the Cantonese that they eat anything with four legs except a table, and anything with wings except an airplane. Exotic items can frequently be seen on menus, but as they tend to be expensive, are unlikely to be ordered by accident, even when no English translation is available. Foreigners often try snake (which tastes like chicken with a tinned tuna texture), and there are a number of restaurants where this is a specialty. Guǎngzhōu has a big enough expat community to support a lively selection of wannabe-Western pubs and bars, and there are plenty of the familiar fast food culprits, too, as well as a branch of the British Hard Rock Cafe (in the China Hotel).

The Cantonese seem to be the most raucous of all Chinese, and two of the main choices for classic Cantonese food, or for dim sum, are bedlam. The famous **Běi Yuán Jiŭjiā**, at Xiăo Běi Lù 202 (© **020/8356-3365**), dates back to the 1920s, although the current two-story courtyarded building dates from 1957, built around a garden and pond. Such long-standing restaurants rarely live up to the quality of their modern competitors, and the presence of tour groups would usually be worrying, but both this and the **Guăngzhōu Restaurant** (below) are exceptions to the rule. The typically garish carpets, screens, and chandeliers are in odd contrast to the central green space. There's trolleyed dim sum here all day (about ¥4/50¢ per steamer), and a generous menu of Cantonese classics, with some English translations. Try *huā zhōu zhù jī* (chicken cooked in yellow wine—although some might argue this is really a Zhèjiāng dish), *táng cù sū ròu* (sweet and sour pork), and *jiŭ huáng ròu sī* (sliced pork with yellow chives). The restaurant is open from 6:50am to 4:30pm and 5:30pm to 12:10am. Meals run about ¥80 ($10) for two. There are twin entrances—the left is for the traditional Cantonese dishes; the right is for a *Cháozhōu* (Chiu Chow) restaurant, with the roast goose dishes typical of that area of northeast Guăngdōng.

The Wén Chāng Nán Lù 2 branch of the **Guăngzhōu Restaurant (Guăngzhōu Jiŭjiā)** (© **020/8138-0388**; www.gzr.com.

cn), which opened in 1939, is one of the city's most celebrated, and is like the Běi Yuán except it has three stories and an even larger assortment of dining rooms and menus. There's canteen-style service on one floor (just go and point), one room specializing in hot pot (more usually associated with Sìchuān and Inner Mongolia); set menus (¥68–¥168/$8.50–$21), and Cantonese set meals for as little as ¥38 ($4.75). The English menu tends to feature the most expensive dishes (shark's fin, abalone, crab, and so forth) for as much as ¥280 ($35), but more straightforward main courses are typically ¥20 ($2.50) to ¥25 ($3). Try baked spare ribs in lemon sauce (*xī níng jú ròu pái*—actually *jú* in this case is a local character meaning "cooked in a pot over a low heat"), stir-fried fresh shrimp with straw mushrooms (*xiān gū xiān xiā wán)*, and some of the restaurant's excellent dim sum, from ¥5 (65¢) or so and shrimp ¥9 ($1.10). Hours are 7am to 10pm.

The White Swan has developed an area of small bars and restaurants aimed at those who dare to venture from the hotel, but not too far. There are a number of similar choices, the most obvious of which is **Lucy's** at Shāmiàn Nán Jiē 3 (© **020/8121-5106**), open 11am to 2am. With a slightly seedy pub-like interior, and tables outdoors on the bank of the river, Lucy's turns out pasta, pizza, fish and chips, burgers, and more—or at least rough impressions of them, for those missing the waist-expanding comforts of home, and the music to go with them (mainly The Eagles).

HONG KONG: THE DRAGON OF THE SOUTH

香港

On July 1, 1997, China resumed sovereignty over its richest, most cosmopolitan city, the former Crown Colony of Hong Kong. Britain had claimed the island of Hong Kong in 1841 after defeating China in the First Opium War and later gained rights over the tip of the Kowloon peninsula, eventually signing a 99-year lease over a much larger area to the north, the New Territories. The expiration of that lease and the refusal of the Chinese authorities to renew it would have left the tiny remainder unsupportable. The Thatcher government had little choice but to agree to return the entire colony to Chinese control, despite lamentations from residents, foreign and Chinese alike. The return was the occasion of carefully orchestrated celebrations on the mainland.

Now known officially as the **Hong Kong Special Administrative Region (SAR),** the territory was assured a high degree of autonomy for 50 years after the handover. Indeed, few changes will be obvious to visitors. Hong Kong is still an international city, vibrant and brash. It is by far the richest, most sophisticated city in China, the one place where East and West meet on confident, familiar footings.

For Westerners, Hong Kong has long been the gateway to China, to its culture as well as to its mainland cities, and it is still the best arrival point for China travelers—a dramatic, fascinating decompression chamber for the journey from the West to the East.

Note that the currency in Hong Kong is still the Hong Kong dollar (HK$), which is pegged to the U.S. dollar. US$1 equals about HK$7.80.

Diving into Hong Kong

Hong Kong is one of the most beautiful big cities in Asia. The harbor, pinched between Hong Kong Island and the southern peninsula (Kowloon), is the focal point of the city. Day or night, the harbor view is dramatic, and the best view is from the **Waterfront Promenade** that skirts the Kowloon shore (immediately east of the Star Ferry concourse). Head there immediately after arrival to immerse yourself in the city. The skyline of Hong Kong Island, scaling the heights of steep hillsides, is among the most magnificent in the world, rivaled only by that of New York City— and at night, no city in the world can match the skyscraping lights of Hong Kong Island for sheer breathtaking beauty.

The green-and-white **Star Ferry fleet** has been crossing the harbor since 1898, and it constitutes one of the cheapest sightseeing thrills in the world. For HK$2.20 (US28¢) you can ride on the upper deck in either direction (daily 6:30am–11:30pm). Take a seat on a hardwood bench as close to the rail as possible. Hong Kong is among the world's busiest ports, and the Star Ferry cuts across a thicket of vessels calling here day and night. The harbor bristles with the container ships and navy gunboats of the world, with the luxury yachts of Asia's tycoons, and with the skiffs and unpainted junks of Hong Kong's fishermen and boat people.

After walking the harbor and riding the Star Ferry, I recommend diving deeper into Hong Kong by walking its 24-hour streets, from Kowloon's **Nathan Road,** the "Golden Mile" of duty-free shopping, to the uphill vendor alleys of the **Central District** on Hong Kong Island. Then hop one of the historic double-decker electric trams (fare HK$2/US25¢) that plow back and forth from Central through the once-notorious **Wan Chai District,** 3km (2 miles) to the east, where the world of Suzie Wong once prevailed. The view of the Wan Chai shophouses and massive neon signs, of the people endlessly shopping and eating in the streets, epitomizes the energy, color, and raw pulse of life that rolls through the concrete mazes of Hong Kong like a dragon that never sleeps.

Victoria Peak

The head of the dragon is Victoria Peak, looming 545m (1,817 ft.) above the harbor on Hong Kong Island. Everyone calls it the Peak, and everyone should take a trip to its summit aboard the historic **Peak Tram.** The panorama unfolds like a vast painted fan at the top. As the extraordinary travel writer Jan Morris once confessed, "For myself there is still no greater pleasure of Hong Kong than the most familiar of all such promenades: the walk around Victoria Peak, crowning massif of Hong Kong Island."

I head up to the Peak whenever I need to escape the crowded, humid, odoriferous streets of the city. From the Peak you can still see Central, Victoria Harbor, Kowloon, and the New Territories beyond, but you see all this from the high, distant remove. The first time I visited the Peak, I had just returned from 6 months of living in a dusty, developing Chinese city, and I was overwhelmed first and foremost by the sweet scent of flowers. The road around the Peak is a botanical paradise, a tropical Eden that soothes the senses that are elsewhere subject to the assault of China's urban environs.

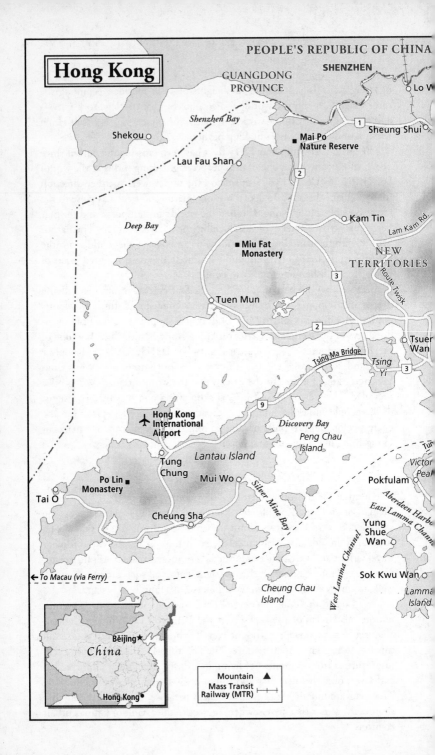

Hong Kong

PEOPLE'S REPUBLIC OF CHINA

SHENZHEN

Lo W

GUANGDONG
PROVINCE

Shenzhen Bay

○ Sheung Shui

Shekou ○

■ Mai Po
Nature Reserve

Lau Fau Shan ○

Deep Bay

○ Kam Tin

Lam Kam Rd.

**NEW
TERRITORIES**

■ Miu Fat
Monastery

Route Twisk

○ Tuen Mun

Tsuen
Wan

Tsing Ma Bridge

*Tsing
Yi*

Hong Kong
International
Airport

Discovery Bay

*Peng Chau
Island*

Lantau Island

Tung
Chung

Mui Wo ○

Tur

Victor
Peal

Pokfulam ○

■ Po Lin
Monastery

Silver Mine Bay

Aberdeen Harbo

Tai O ○

Yung
Shue
Wan ○

East Lamma Chann

Cheung Sha ○

West Lamma Channel

Sok Kwu Wan ○

← *To Macau (via Ferry)*

*Cheung Chau
Island*

*Lamma
Island*

Bĕijīng ★

China

Hong Kong ●

| Mountain | ▲ |
| Mass Transit
Railway (MTR) | ├──┼──┤ |

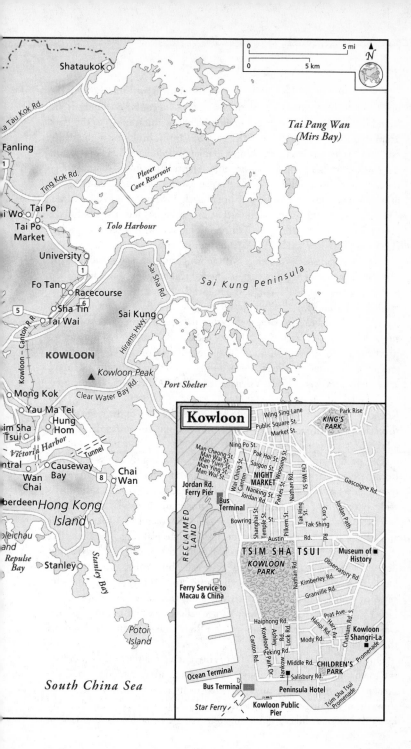

Shataukok

Tai Pang Wan
(Mirs Bay)

Fanling

Plover
Cove Reservoir

Ting Kok Rd.

Tai Po

i Wo

Tai Po
Market

Tolo Harbour

University

Sai Kung Peninsula

Fo Tan

Racecourse

Sai Sha Rd.

Sha Tin

Tai Wai

Sai Kung

KOWLOON

Hirams Hwy.

Kowloon – Canton R.R.

Kowloon Peak

Port Shelter

Clear Water Bay Rd.

Mong Kok

Yau Ma Tei

Hung
Hom

im Sha
Tsui

Victoria Harbor

Tunnel

ntral

Causeway
Bay

Chai
Wan

Wan
Chai

berdeen

Hong Kong
Island

oleichau
land

Repulse
Bay

Stanley

Stanley Bay

Potoi
Island

South China Sea

Kowloon

Wing Sing Lane

Park Rise

KING'S
PARK

Public Square St.

Market St.

Ning Po St.

Pak Hoi St.

Man Cheong St.
Man Wai St.
Man Yuen St.
Man Ying St.
Man Wui St.

Wai Ching St.

Saigon St.

Woosung St.

Chi Wo St.

Canton Rd.

NIGHT
MARKET

Nanking St.

Parkes St.

Nathan Rd.

Gascoigne Rd.

Jordan Rd.
Ferry Pier

Jordan Rd.

Cox's

Tak Hing St.

Jordan Path

Bus
Terminal

Shanghai St.

Temple St.

Pilkem St.

Tak Shing

Bowring St.

Austin

Rd.

RECLAIMED LAND

TSIM SHA TSUI

KOWLOON
PARK

Nathan Rd.

Observatory Rd.

Museum of
History

Ferry Service to
Macau & China

Kimberley Rd.

Granville Rd.

Haiphong Rd.

Ashley Rd.

Kowloon Park Rd.

Hanoi Rd.

Prat Ave.

Har Yau Av.

Chatham Rd. S.

Kowloon
Shangri-La

Canton Rd.

Kowloon Park Dr.

Mody Rd.

Peking Rd.

Hankow Rd.

Middle Rd.

CHILDREN'S
PARK

Promenade

Ocean Terminal

Bus Terminal

Salisbury Rd.

Peninsula Hotel

Tsim Sha Tsui Promenade

Star Ferry

Kowloon Public
Pier

0   5 mi
0   5 km

N

199

The easiest way up the Peak is to catch the **shuttle bus** (the one with the open top deck), located outside the Star Ferry concourse on Hong Kong Island. From 10am to midnight it runs every few minutes up to the Peak Tram station on Garden Road (HK$15/US$1.90). This is one of the steepest "train" rides anywhere, reaching a gradient of 55 degrees. Take a seat in the rear car on the right side, if possible. The ride resembles that of a dignified roller coaster. The scene quickly opens wider, the perspective tilts out of whack, and the city and the harbor fall back downhill as if in a landslide. The tram covers the quarter-mile ascent in 8 minutes, but it seems to take longer. The tram operates from 7am to midnight daily. Tickets are HK$20 (US$2.60) one-way, HK$30 (US$3.80) round-trip.

The lovely polished wooden cars on today's tram are new versions of the cars that began making this curious, neck-breaking climb in 1888, when two gentlemen named Kyrie and Hughes launched the steam-powered High Level Tramway, Asia's first cable railway. The Peak was home to the wealthy and off-limits to others in earlier days. Today there are still mansions on the top of Victoria Peak, but there's also shopping. (You can go nowhere in Hong Kong without the specter of shopping.) The tram loads and unloads inside the **Peak Tower** (1997), which is stuffed with shops, cafes, delis, and even a Ripley's Believe It or Not! Odditorium. On the non-commercial side, there are viewing terraces facing Central, the harbor, and Kowloon to the north. When the fog rolls over the edge of the ridge spines, this classic view of Hong Kong, the favorite of a million postcards, takes on a brooding, primordial face.

The **path** running clockwise around the Peak begins across the street from here, at Harlech Road on the left. Harlech, which is closed to motor traffic, flows into Lugard Road partway around the Peak. The walkway is wide, paved, and flat. I usually walk it in under an hour, even with a dozen stops to admire the views. The broad-leafed woodland that coats the hills and ridges in deep greens is a result of deliberate planting. The Peak, like the whole island, was largely barren rock when the British first arrived, but now it's a garden of blooms, hillside waterfalls, butterflies, and black-eared kites streaking from the heights of nature into the creases of the city canyons below. Circling the Peak yields long views over the other side of Hong Kong Island, down the deep jungle valleys that plunge into the blue-water harbors of Aberdeen, Stanley, and Repulse Bay on the south side of the island.

One day I decided to walk down to **Aberdeen** from the Peak. I could see the town—famous for its seafood, its massive floating restaurants, and the boat people who live on junks sheltered in its harbor—and I had a map showing a walking trail to Aberdeen. I located a signpost on the road by Peak Tower. A hiker's guide suggested that I could reach Aberdeen in

45 minutes. I headed down the path, disappearing into the high bamboo grasses. The walk ended up taking me better than 2 hours, but I did manage to keep from getting lost, always heading southward and downward when the dirt trail split.

The views were lovely, of course, but the human settlements interested me more. I passed through several squatters' villages with shacks pulled together from construction-site discards. I also came across one of the largest Chinese cemeteries I'd ever seen, not far above Aberdeen. The stone chairside graves, to which pictures of the deceased are often attached in bronze frames, were swept clean of leaves here, their urns decorated with fresh flowers. I felt ready for the grave myself, as the humidity was nearing the 100% mark that afternoon, but I managed to walk through the last clearing into Aberdeen. It could have been much more challenging, of course, as I realized when I glanced over my shoulder. A true hill walker would have reversed my course, climbing from Aberdeen back up to the Peak, which from below looked as remote as the summit of a lost world.

Aberdeen

The more conventional way to get to Aberdeen, which lies on the south side of Hong Kong Island, is to catch bus no. 70 at the Exchange Square bus terminal, a few blocks west of the Star Ferry concourse in Central. The HK$4.70 (US60¢) trip takes about 25 minutes. On the piers opposite Aberdeen Centre there are numerous sampan ladies who will practically haul you off the seawall to take you on a motorized tour of Aberdeen's waterborne village. If you decide you want a ride with one of the sampan ladies, bargain them down to a decent fare (less than half of what they're asking).

For a no-hassles tour of the flotilla, look for the **Watertours dock,** where the price is set and the driver speaks some English. A tour gives a close-up look at life on the water and inside the junks, most of which have their own color televisions.

The massive floating restaurants in Aberdeen harbor provide free ferries from their docks. You can poke around the culinary barges and head back without a meal, but if you're hungry, try a few dim sum (steamed pastries). **Jumbo** is the largest and best of the floating restaurants, open Monday through Saturday from 7:30am to 11:30pm and Sunday from 7am to 11pm (© **852/2553-9111**). Its decor includes garish red-and-gold carved dragons and cranes, with several thousand painted paper lanterns thrown up to the ceiling for good measure. Jumbo's food is rather high priced and not Hong Kong's best, but it's all good enough for one happy meal.

Before leaving Jumbo, check out the seafood tanks on the lower deck, where hundreds of specimens are enjoying their last swims. The last time I checked, the tanks were posted with a warning in English that rather mysteriously read PLEASE DON'T DISTURB THE SEAFOOD.

Shop-Walking in Kowloon

The Kowloon side of Hong Kong on the north side of the harbor is where millions go to shop and eat. They all seem to be here at once. **Nathan Road,** 4 blocks east of the Star Ferry concourse, is the main thoroughfare on the peninsula, a Golden Mile of shops that stretches far more than a mile these days. The streets and alleys parallel to and intersecting Nathan Road house still more tiny duty-free outlets. They all hawk the merchandise Hong Kong is famous for: cameras and jade, clothing and computers, luggage and furs, toys and watches. Even if you're not much of a shopper, you can't escape the bug here. Window-shopping spreads to price-comparing and ends in a purchase you didn't know you were going to make. My own weakness is luggage. If I could travel to Hong Kong without a suitcase or pack, I would do so because I could pick up three useful pieces here for the price of one overseas.

An absolute delight in **Tsim Sha Tsui** (pronounced "chim-sha-choy"), the district that covers the southwest Kowloon shopping district, is the landmark **Peninsula Hotel,** one of the grande dames of Asian accommodations, and after 7 decades still one of the top 10 hotels in the world. The lobby, recently refurbished, defines the word "elegance" in the East. I never pass up a quick walk through the Peninsula. The columns are trimmed in gold, high tea looks grand, and the stringed orchestra seems to play from the mezzanine day and night.

The outlets in the shopping arcades to either side and in the basement of the Peninsula are equally elegant—and the prices soar even higher than afternoon tea upstairs. This is the arcade to seek out if your tastes are for the designer names—Gucci, Tiffany, or Armani.

Kowloon also contains the top location for a celebratory drink—not in the stately Peninsula but down on the harbor promenade in its modern competitor, the **Regent Hotel.** The lobby lounge, with its wall of glass at water level, frames the Hong Kong skyline like an immense, glittering, ever-changing mural of neon, saltwater, and steel.

The streets of Kowloon are devoted to little else than shopping. You soon become familiar with the street stores, the Chinese arts-and-crafts stores, the huge arcades that burrow into high-rises like caves. The **New World Shopping Centre** on the Waterfront Promenade and the **Ocean Galleries** due north of the Star Ferry are the most extensive retail malls, good places to go for air-conditioned window-shopping while credit cards heal themselves and revive.

The most sensible way to break this ritual of maniacal "shop-walking" is to make a detour at Kowloon Park.

Kowloon Park

I had been visiting Hong Kong for 10 years before I actually set foot inside this quiet green zone. At 14 hectares (35 acres), Kowloon Park is a fine refuge tucked into the heart of a frantic city. You can enter Kowloon Park at its east gate (on Nathan Rd., just north of the Mosque), at its northwest gate (via the Canton Rd. pedestrian overpass), or at its south gate (on Haiphong Rd., a block west of the Mosque, across from the Kangaroo Pub). The grounds contain waterfalls, bird ponds, a flock of pink flamingos, an outdoor sculpture garden, a Chinese classical garden (not the best I've seen), several sculpted outdoor swimming pools (and an Olympic-sized indoor facility), a totem pole from Canada, and a kiosk from McDonald's.

The **Hong Kong Museum of History,** once housed in the British Army's former Whitfield Barracks here, has now reopened in a splendid new building a 10-minute walk east, at 100 Chatham Rd. S. It's open Monday, and Wednesday through Saturday from 10am to 6pm, Sunday and holidays 10am to 7pm (closed Tues); admission is HK$10 (US$1.30). It presents a visual history of Hong Kong, arranged chronologically. Hands-on, walk-through displays include a sailing junk, a turn-of-the-20th-century downtown street with offices, an opium den, and a Chinese pharmacy with the original cabinets and instruments in place. Luckily, nothing's for sale in this reconstruction of the past. Otherwise, the museum would be as overrun as the streets of Kowloon.

Going Hollywood

Hong Kong Island has its shopping routes, too. The best window-shopping is along **Hollywood Road** and **Cat Street,** where much of China's retail trade in antiques is conducted. From the Star Ferry concourse in Central, walk straight uptown a few blocks and turn right (west) on Des Voeux Road Central. Keep an eye out on your left (uphill) for **Li Yuen streets** east and west (just past D'Aguilar St.). These are Hong Kong's best-known fabric alleys, narrow lanes that are stuffed on both sides with sheds of bargain silks, cottons, and upholsteries. On one pass through here, I noticed that a large number of cats were being kept in the stalls to control the rodents at night. There were many stray cats as well, all of them looking far too thin. I was about to buy some cat food at a corner grocery when I noticed one draper preparing a large communal dinner of fish scraps. She set it down on the sidewalk where the gang of local cats, expecting their daily pay, quickly devoured this pile of leftovers.

If you walk 3 blocks farther west to **Jubilee Street,** you can hook up with the world's longest outdoor escalator and have a free ride uphill. This escalator is worth its own coffee-table book, as it passes over plenty of chaotically compelling intersections while transporting legions of businesspeople and striking characters.

Dismount at **Hollywood Road** and follow it west. Along this twisting street, you'll find junk and antiques shops, the latter with show windows that look like museum displays of dynastic treasures, with prices to match. The furniture stores, with their blackwood and rosewood pieces, are particularly tempting, although free shipping to your home is not included.

Man Mo Temple

Keep on Hollywood Road until you reach Man Mo Temple (open daily 7am–5pm; free admission), at the corner of **Ladder Street** (a stone staircase where the rich were once carried up and down in sedan chairs on the shoulders of coolies). Man, the god of literature, and Mo, the god of war, preside over this temple, one of the most vibrant in China.

Man Mo Temple is run-down inside and out. It's a working temple of the sort that once held sway over China's daily affairs. Inside, the cramped hall is packed with monks, local worshippers, and the thickest clouds of incense I've ever struggled to part. The wooden chairs on display on one side of the hall were once used to carry the statues of the Man Mo Temple gods in street processions. These were probably the most important gods in town at one time, since Man Mo Temple was for many years Hong Kong's civic and cultural center for the Chinese community.

Incense spirals hang heavily from the ceiling like coiled chandeliers. These fragrant dragons can burn for a month, their pungent smoke petitioning heaven for health and wealth. Whenever I've been here a steady stream of worshippers is crowding inside as well, adding their own burning sticks to the blackening flames. Outside, in the tiny courtyard on Hollywood Road, I've seen old beggar women keeping an eye on the sacks containing their worldly possessions. Man Mo Temple has become their street home.

Immediately below Man Mo is **Cat Street (Lascar Row),** once a notorious strip of brothels, gambling dens, and boardinghouses for seamen. Today it's a flea market, stuffed with fascinating bric-a-brac, from Qing Dynasty coins to opium pipes. It was a few blocks from here, in a small cafe at the top of one of the ladderlike vendors' alleys, that I spotted the actor Jeremy Irons, in town to make a film about Hong Kong's return to China, sitting tall and alone at a simple table, his thoughts far afield.

Temple Street Night Market

Hong Kong's chief night market stretches for better than a mile up Temple Street on the Kowloon side. Take the subway to the Jordan Street stop, walk 4 blocks west from Nathan Road (starting at the Yue Hwa Department Store), and turn right up Temple Street. Every day from dusk to midnight and beyond, Temple Street is an open mall of wall-to-wall vendors offering cut-rate designer jeans and shirts, leather handbags, fake "copy" watches, and whatever's hottest in the toy factories and electronics plants of southern China.

The real action is 5 or 6 blocks up Temple Street, where Chinese opera singers come out and perform popular selections in relaxed but highly spirited performances. It's always interesting to watch the men in the audience, sitting on chairs, smoking and eating and gabbing, singing along, clapping fervently, and passing the hat.

A block north of the opera stalls, in the courtyard of a small temple, rows of palm readers and fortunetellers employ birds, cards, turtle shells, old coins, and other props to divine the future of strangers. The tools of their trade are spread out on the sidewalk or placed on card tables under the light of kerosene lamps. Palm readers analyze palms for HK$154 (US$20), discuss a client's fate for HK$231 (US$30), and lay out a whole life's story for HK$308 (US$40). Fortunetellers use songbirds from Vietnam and mainland China to answer whatever question you pose. They telepathically pass on your question to the bird, and the bird in turn pops out of its cage and selects a card from a deck. The fortuneteller then interprets what the card says in answer to your question. The performance can cost HK$77 to HK$231 (US$10–US$30).

My favorite Temple Street character has long been a streetside dentist who treats toothaches on the spot without the benefit of painkillers. I've watched him hunched down for hours over patients sitting on the dark curbside, filling their cavities; attaching stainless steel, ceramic, and gold crowns; and relining false teeth (in 1 hr.). He heats his tools over a flame, but he uses no drill to fill cavities. His prices tend to be 10 times less than those charged in the West, but then Temple Street is a low-overhead operation, small business elevated to the level of performance art.

Stanley

Clear around Hong Kong Island on its southeast side is Stanley, an ancient fishing village once known for its pirates, now known for its designer-clothing market. This is a long-standing tourist stop, so the prices may not be the lowest in Hong Kong, but the selection of name-brand fashions, linens, sports shoes, swimsuits, porcelains, and souvenirs is extensive. Despite its "touristy" reputation, I never fail to enjoy a morning or afternoon in Stanley.

Part of my enjoyment is just getting there. At **Exchange Square bus terminus,** just west of the Star Ferry concourse in Central, I find the no. 6A or 6X air-conditioned double-decker bus, drop my HK$8.40 (US$1.10) fare in the collection box, grab a seat upstairs, and brace myself. This is one of the most thrilling bus rides in China. Everyone drives on the left side, of course, and everyone drives at the fastest speed possible through the narrowest streets imaginable, and there's no bigger vehicle on the road than this tall bus, which seems to hurtle up and down the tight switchbacks like a heat-seeking missile. The steep, cement-sided hillsides whiz by, clearing the bus windows by inches. After 30 minutes of this amusement ride, you become fully accustomed to Hong Kong driving, and as the seaside scenery becomes more and more Mediterranean, you soon arrive at the village of Stanley.

The **Stanley market,** which consists of about 200 covered stalls, is across the street from the bus stop and down the hill toward the beach. At the bottom of the hill, the market splits into two sections, running left and right along the shore. I often explore the left side first, then head back to the end of the western section. Beyond there, a block of trendy bars and grills has recently sprung up, with sidewalk drinking and wonderful Continental lunches and dinners with a view of Stanley beach and the sea.

As for shopping, I usually return from Stanley with a few cheap "designer-label" polo shirts (under HK$77/US$10), a half-dozen "silk" ties (HK$15–HK$23/US$2–US$3 each), sometimes some "hand-embroidered" linen tablecloths, and enough "handmade" souvenirs—that are probably hand-made in mainland China—to stuff a few dozen Christmas stockings. Occasionally, I pick up the Christmas stockings at Stanley market as well.

The squatters' village west of the market, where pigs once were slopped in an ingenious pen fed by a labyrinth of pipes, has been leveled to make way for a massive modern apartment, office, and shopping complex. There are still some brightly painted, hand-built fishing boats on Stanley Beach, but the fishermen have been moved south and east into new low-rise row houses.

The future of Stanley will continue to be shopping, it seems, even after a massive edifice from the past is moved into the village. The historic **Murray House,** built in 1844 in downtown Hong Kong and dismantled brick by brick in 1982 to make way for the Bank of China Tower, has already opened in Stanley—not as a museum, of course, but as a shopping gallery composed of a Chinese department store, souvenir shops, coffee-houses, and delis, and a suitably historic pub.

The Walled City

One of the least visited and most fascinating historic sites in Hong Kong is the **Kowloon Walled City Park.** Governed by neither China nor Great Britain, the old Walled City of Kowloon spent most of this century as a lawless no-man's land within walking distance of Hong Kong's Kai Tak International Airport. In 1898, when the Chinese leased the Kowloon peninsula to the British for 99 years, they retained jurisdiction over this tiny 3-hectare (7-acre) city-fort, whether by design or through a slip of the mapmaker's brush, no one knows. The next year, British soldiers entered the Walled City, ostensibly to quell civil unrest, and evicted the 500 Chinese troops stationed there. But the British never established their authority over the Walled City, nor did the Chinese ever relinquish their claim.

The Walled City became a dark sanctuary, sucking in petty criminals, illegal aliens, opium addicts, prostitutes, fugitives, and the desperately poor. By the time the Japanese occupied Hong Kong in 1941, the Walled City was in shambles. The Japanese pulled down the walls and used them to extend the airstrip along the harbor (at what became Kai Tak Airport).

At the end of World War II, squatters suddenly poured into the remains of the Walled City. By the 1970s, the Walled City consisted of a super-tenement, 12 to 14 stories high. It grew organically. Some 350 buildings went up and each one fused with its neighbor, creating a rabbit warren of interlinked hallways.

Inside this tenement fortress, subject to no building regulations or fire codes, illegal enterprises flourished with impunity. Not all the enterprises were nefarious. Dentists, doctors, and lawyers practiced without licenses, charged rock-bottom rates, and built up a large outside clientele. Well through the 1980s, much of the dim sum prepared in Hong Kong came from basement kitchens inside the Walled City.

I once did a walking tour of the Walled City after it was finally slated for demolition in the early 1990s. Inside was a dark labyrinth. Electricity, water (artesian wells with water pipes connected to rooftop holding tanks), and sewage (trenches) had all been jury-rigged by private developers who charged tenants for their services. The interconnected hallways were a maze for rats and humans alike. Hundreds of rusted crisscrossed pipes and bare copper wires, supporting in their webs an unspeakable mass of wet garbage, paper wrappings, plastic bags, and rotting food scraps, had been strung overhead in the narrow spaces between buildings.

Hong Kong conducted an unannounced census of the Walled City on January 14, 1987, turning up 33,000 residents in 8,300 premises. There were nearly 1,000 businesses, primarily food processors, plastic fabricators, and carpentry shops. On the outside perimeter, 150 unlicensed doctors and dentists maintained busy shop fronts. Residents were for the most part very poor, and many were engaged in or were the victims of crime. The Walled City was home for 20 years to an extraordinary Englishwoman named Jackie Pullinger, who lived among the residents, seeking to rehabilitate the drug addicts. Later, she launched assistance programs for residents suffering from AIDS.

The walls of this 3-hectare (7-acre) tenement started tumbling down on March 23, 1993, when the first bulldozers arrived. The next year construction of a park and classical garden began on the site. Kowloon Walled City Park opened on December 22, 1995, in a ceremony presided over by the last British governor of the colony, the Rt. Hon. Christopher Patten.

This is one of the more interesting, least-visited parks in Hong Kong. Take bus no. 1 (fare HK$4.70/US60¢) from the Star Ferry concourse in Kowloon, a 35-minute ride up Nathan Road and east on Boundary Street. Disembark at the second stop on Tung Street, the northern boundary of the park. The park is surrounded by a wall in the style of an earlier fortification built by the Qīng government in 1843. The eight complementary landscape sectors inside the walls are also derived from Qīng Dynasty models.

The Kowloon Walled City Park should be entered from the old south gate. The foundations of the original south gate and two stone plaques bearing the characters for "South Gate" and "Kowloon Walled City" were discovered here in 1994, in the excavation pit to the right of the entrance. The only historical building still standing is the **Yámen,** a courtyard complex at the center of the park that served as the military command. On exhibit here are old cannons and photographs of the evolution of the old Walled City from fortress to tenement. In one courtyard a stone monument honors Jackie Pullinger for her decades of charitable work.

Frequented by neighborhood Chinese—mostly grandparents and grandchildren spending time together—the Walled City has been transformed yet again, this time into Hong Kong's loveliest classic garden, with graceful pavilions, long covered corridors, garden ponds, and goldfish streams that seem to flow out of an antique century.

The Pink Dolphin

Hong Kong's most beautiful marine animal is also its most endangered—the pink dolphin (*Sousa chinensis*). No more than 150 remain in Hong Kong waters, and their delicate habitat is growing both ever smaller and more polluted. Pink dolphins were first reported in the waters of southern China in the 7th century during the Táng Dynasty, and they were first sighted by Western travelers in 1637. Without a guide, you'd probably never know that there was a single dolphin pod in these busy waters. This is the most beautiful species of dolphins I've ever seen but also the shyest of the dashing sea animals that Melville called "the lads that always live before the winds."

The dolphins feed over a wide area, some of it concentrated in the new **Sha Chau and Lung Kwu Chau Marine Park,** an 8-sq.-km (5-sq.-mile) sector of seawater north of the airport. This "dolphin sanctuary" is subject to the drainage of the Pearl River, which carries much of the sewage and industrial waste of southern China. The new airport has also destroyed portions of the pink dolphin's coastline, and even within the new "sanctuary," gill-netting, dredging, and the off-loading of oil tankers go on unabated. The number of pink dolphins is in steady decline as a result, and Hong Kong's commitment to wildlife conservation and environmental protection is notably and traditionally unenthusiastic. Nonetheless, the pink dolphin continues to swim freely in these dangerous waters.

You can still see these rare creatures by booking passage on a **Dolphinwatch cruise,** the best water tour in Hong Kong. Dolphinwatch sails the waters between massive **Lantau Island** (home of the new Chek Lap Kok Airport) and the New Territories (near the ports of Tuen Mun and Castle Peak), an hour northwest of Hong Kong harbor. The scenery is fascinating enough to justify a day's cruise, but the goal is to spot the elusive, shy pink dolphins, usually swimming in groups of half a dozen, breaking the surface and then diving in search of a meal.

The cruises last for 4 hours. A researcher—often founder Bill Leverett—delivers commentary in English and endeavors to find pods of pink dolphins. The dolphins often surface quite close to the craft, making for spectacular sightings and photos. It's also possible to charter a 7-hour cruise from Dolphinwatch on a much larger two-deck ship. Lunch is taken in a local cafe in the quaint town of Tai O during a stopover on Lantau Island. Since Sunday is such an impossibly crowded day to sightsee anywhere in Hong Kong, a Dolphinwatch cruise (whether the half-day or full-day version) is a weekend adventure hard to match. On my first cruise, after scanning the waters for more than an hour, we spotted a dozen pink dolphins sporting in the waters in front of the Castle Peak Power Station. We spent 2 hours circling the group. Adult dolphins are 1m to 2.4m (3½ ft.–8 ft.) in length. They are a dazzling comic-strip pink, and no one knows why. The infants, who stick close to their parents, are nearly black, the distinctive blush tones emerging only as they mature.

To find out the current schedule, ask at the **Hong Kong Tourism Board (HKTB)** office at the Star Ferry terminal in Kowloon, or, better yet, contact **Dolphinwatch** directly (© **852/2984-1414;** fax 852/2984-7799). Tickets are usually sold in advance at the **Splendid Tours** desk in the lobby of the Sheraton Hotel, 20 Nathan Rd., Kowloon. Tour days and tour lengths vary with the season, but currently 4-hour morning cruises are offered on Wednesday, Friday, and Sunday for HK$320 (US$41) adults, HK$160 (US$21) children under 12. Call to inquire about 7-hour lunch cruises.

Cheung Chau Island

Three of Hong Kong's 230 outlying islands—Lantau, Lamma, and Cheung Chau—are served by frequent passenger ferries from piers in the Central District. The 60-minute cruise is a delight, and so are the islands, which offer a restorative escape from the big city. The best getaway is Cheung Chau Island, 11km (7 miles) west of Hong Kong, an old fishing village without cars, its harbor teeming with sampans and junks.

Cheung Chau is a chapter out of Old China. This 1.6-sq.-km (1-sq.-mile) home to seafarers and pirates has an active waterfront, lively markets, a traditional village, and white-sand beaches where the windsurfing is world-class. The ferry from Hong Kong pulls into the western harbor and docks at the **Praya,** the waterfront promenade lined with vibrant pink and blue buildings, their ornate balconies suggesting a Mediterranean port. You can walk directly through the old village and across the island to the eastern beaches in just 10 minutes, but the scenic route first leads north (to your left) along the Praya.

The Praya is filled with cafes and food stalls selling hot noodles and shrimp dumpling (wonton) soups. The harbor is packed with rows of junks. These are the homes of Cheung Chau's water people, who live and fish from their floating houses. About 3,000 of the island's 23,000 people live year-round on the water.

If you walk north and west to the end of the beach road, you come to the **dry docks** where large junks are still being framed and planked by hand, built in the time-honored manner by craftsmen who keep no blueprints but retain entire designs in their memories. They don't mind if you stop in at their tin-roofed sheds to have a look. Even at its birth, a junk is a gorgeous vessel, its horizontal planks curving in golden stripes from a remarkably high stern to a broad bow, each piece of the puzzle shaped and laid in place perfectly, with room left in the seams for the wood to expand as it cures.

About 5 blocks from the pier, you'll see the **Pak Tai Temple** on your right, just past the community basketball court. Pak Tai is the god of the sea, the great protector of seafarers, and still highly revered on Cheung Chau. The temple was built in 1786. It welcomes visitors. Inside, Pak Tai is wearing a golden crown. His reign over the sea is symbolized by the snake and turtle pinned under his feet. An iron sword from the Sòng Dynasty (A.D. 960–1279) is ensconced beside the temple altar. During the Bun

Festival (held every spring on dates determined at the last minute by village elders), Tai Pak and the sword are carried into the courtyard in a century-old sedan chair to preside over the celebrations. The side halls of the small temple are worth inspecting, too. Carvings of the Green Dragon and the White Tiger are enshrined here.

From the temple, cut through the old-fashioned village. The lanes are narrow. The shops and cafes frequently contain bedrooms and offices upstairs. Family clans and trade guilds have survived intact. There are several street shrines to the Earth god, incense always burning on their stone shelves. Many of the island's elders, dressed in long vests and leaning on wooden canes, stop every day to pray. One of the shrine inscriptions reads "If your heart is warm, you will be blessed in old age."

The east side of the island is another world, designed for leisure and watersports. At **Coral Beach (Kwun Yum Wan)** and **Morning Beach (Tung Wan)**, I saw a local islander, Lee Lai-shan, perfecting her windsurfing skills. She went on to become the first and only Hong Kong citizen to win an Olympic gold medal. Heading down the beach, past the six-story Warwick Hotel, the lower beach road leads out to a **rock carving** from the Bronze Age. These geometric patterns were etched into the sea rocks of Cheung Chau about 3,000 years ago by primitive boat people whose name and fate are lost to history.

If you decide to stay a night or two on Cheung Chau, at either the **Warwick Hotel (© 852/2981-0081;** fax 852/2981-9174) or one of the vacation villas the touts on the Praya recommend, you'll have time to explore the more distant temples, cemeteries, and sea rocks on the large southern half of the island. You'll also have time to climb to the viewpoint at the end of the beach road on the northeastern tip of Cheung Chau.

From the Warwick Hotel, it's a short walk back across the hourglass waist of the island to the Praya. The village of Cheung Chau is densely clogged with old shophouses, fish counters, Chinese pharmacies, bakeries, herbalist stalls, incense shops, bamboo hat stores, mahjong gambling dens, and plenty of curio shops, pubs, and cafes. The fresh shrimp is absolutely superb here. Any cafe will steam up a plateful—you won't even need a sauce.

After staying out on Cheung Chau a few days once, I found it increasingly difficult to return to Hong Kong. The pace of life on this oasis of Old China becomes mesmerizing. As night falls, everyone comes down to the Praya, which is lit by electric lights, lanterns, and candles. The catch of the day sizzles on sidewalk tables. The old women of Cheung Chau, their bare feet up on benches, exchange the day's gossip. Children race by helter-skelter on their bikes. Grandfathers bring out their prized songbirds, hanging the bamboo cages on tree branches or lantern posts. Cats and dogs patrol the streets. Cheung Chau is what Hong Kong must have been generations ago before it became a British colony, an international money-making machine, and finally China's gateway to the future.

Big Buddha

Hong Kong's largest outlying island, **Lantau Island,** is home to the big airport, but its biggest attraction (at least until 2005, when Asia's second Disneyland opens here) is the big bronze statue of Buddha at the Po Lin Monastery. The statue is worth a look, and Lantau Island is worth exploring, too.

Hong Kong claims a population of 800,000 Buddhist followers. About 40 of them are resident monks and nuns at **Precious Lotus Monastery (Po Lin),** which is famous for its vegetarian lunches served from 11:30am to 4:30pm daily, at a cost of HK$60 to HK$100 (US$7.70–US$13). The Tian Tan Buddha towers over the prayer halls and shrines on the hill above; a round altar to heaven leads to the steep 260-stair walkway that tethers this Buddha to Earth. This is the second tallest bronze Buddha in the world (the tallest is the one recently created on the shores of Lake Tài on mainland China). Lantau Island's Buddha was actually constructed on the mainland, beginning in 1986. Five years later the 202 bronze pieces (costing about US$9 million) were shipped to Hong Kong and assembled.

The 30m (100-ft.) tall Big Buddha is now seated in the lotus position on a lotus flower, right palm serenely raised, atop a three-story exhibition hall. Inside the hall are souvenir stands, a mural depicting events in Buddha's life, signs requesting silence (not observed), and an ancestral hall with electric incense burners and wall plaques naming and picturing the deceased (for which families pay a memorial fee of HK$10,000/US$1,300). On the top level of the memorial hall, right under the Buddha, are relics said to be from the real Buddha. Po Lin Monastery claims 18 bone fragments and four teeth of the historical Buddha. In the memorial hall, you can see, if you look very carefully, a tiny fragment of Buddha's bone, like a pearl, on display under a delicate glass cover. The awe-inspiring Buddha statue itself seems to rise above the all-too-human throes of tourism and worship. Buddha's elongated ears, by the way, represent longevity; the swastika-like mark connotes wisdom.

Lantau Island (pop. 30,000) has its more rural pleasures as well. It is twice the size of Hong Kong Island, but its entire population could be placed in a handful of Hong Kong high-rises. Many Lantau Islanders still make a living by fishing or salt processing. Lantau's peaks are high and remote (many accessible only by hiking trails); the name Lantau means "Broken Hat," a term for something wild and remote. The island's beaches are often deserted. **Long Sands (Cheung Sha),** a 3km (2-mile) strand on the south (non-airport) side of the island, does have changing rooms and lifeguards in the summer. Cows often rest on the bluffs here, part of about 300 set free by villagers (who refuse to kill them now, in true Buddhist fashion, because their ancestors worked for the villager's ancestors). The beach is also home to tiger sharks (kept at bay from swimmers by an underwater fence), and the surrounding hills still harbor cobras, green bamboo snakes, and rare barking deer.

The cutest town on Lantau Island is **Tai O,** a 400-year-old port on the west coast that prospered until the 1950s by panning salt. Today its main enterprises are fishing and fish processing. It's a perfect town to stroll. Life is slow, the lanes are narrow, the dogs fall asleep by the steps, fish dry on clotheslines, the shophouses sell medicinal herbs and strange creatures from the sea, and a rope-drawn, flat-bottom ferry, pulled by local Tanka women, crosses the creek that divides the town (although there is now an arched footbridge as well). Tai O is a delight, touristed but somehow undiluted by the modern world.

It's easy to book a **day tour** (see "Tours & Stratagems," below) to see the monastery, Buddha, mountains, and beaches of Lantau Island, with lunch at Tai O, but you can also go on your own, at a considerably more leisurely pace, by taking a ferry to Lantau and using the local buses or taxis for transport. But there aren't many taxis here. The number of private cars is restricted, and by law there are only 50 taxis on the whole island (as opposed to 50 taxis per block in Hong Kong).

PRACTICAL INFORMATION

by Peter Neville-Hadley

ORIENTATION & WHEN TO GO

Whatever residents may say about changes to the city, to the visitor there is no difference between pre-handover Hong Kong and post-handover Hong Kong, although those who haven't visited what is now a Special Administrative Region of the People's Republic of China since before 1997 will note many changes to the city's skyline, and that the land on both sides of Victoria Harbour has flowed out a little further into the sea. But then that always happened every few months in Hong Kong, and so in that way nothing's changed, too. The red post boxes may have been painted green and the royal coats of arms removed from public buildings, but the old English street names remain, traffic still drives on the left, and there are branches of British stores at every corner. Regulations on visitor visas remain as they were.

Despite the presence of a puppet government appointed by Běijīng, Hong Kong remains entirely different in atmosphere from the rest of the PRC, and no one who visits only this former colony can really say he's been to China. The average standard of living is a great deal higher, the standard of education is vastly higher, and the degree of personal freedom is little different from those in most developed nations. Many claim that newspapers have been muzzled, but there's still strident criticism of both the Hong Kong and mainland government in print, something unthinkable only a few miles away across the border. Culturally, the mainland remains decades behind Hong Kong.

The economic roller coaster of the last 5 years has had more impact on ordinary lives than the handover, and tourism has dropped dramatically since 1997, too. Recent rises have been mostly due to ever-relaxing controls on the numbers of visitors from the mainland, who are still treated as foreigners in terms of their paperwork, and as country bumpkins by many Hong Kongers. But money talks, and since many visitors from the mainland come to shop, Mandarin is increasingly heard from staff. However, Cantonese remains the language of the overwhelming majority, and English is spoken everywhere it's likely to be needed. The transportation systems are in some cases better than you have at home, all street signage is in two languages, and getting things done is generally straightforward.

Despite its small size, Hong Kong is still a collection of villages, and there are many residents of the New Territories bordering China who go from one year's end to the next without traveling the few kilometers to Kowloon or Central. So it's worth traveling out to have a look at their way of life. The outlying islands, some only 25 minutes away, are still considered far flung by what remains a clannish society in which family ties, although now weakening a little, are the most important of all. Nevertheless, younger people are gravitating to the densely populated Kowloon peninsula and the north side of Hong Kong Island, and the remaining agrarian activity to the north is dying out—several areas of Hong Kong have wild cows, long abandoned by farmers who've switched to an urban way of living. Hong Kong is full of such surprises, and there's much more to it than the high-speed whirl of the urban areas.

Hong Kong is warm all year-round, and particularly hot and sweaty in midsummer, when the humidity can be high, while building interiors are air-conditioned to cryogenic levels. The best period to visit is October to March.

ENTRY REQUIREMENTS

Citizens of all developed nations with valid passports are given a 3-month visa on arrival (except the British, who get 6 months). This is good only for Hong Kong, and a separate visa must be purchased before entering mainland China. Effectively, the border between the former colony and the mainland is maintained, and PRC citizens without Hong Kong residence rights must also apply for entry permits.

MONEY

The Hong Kong dollar, which is pegged to the U.S. dollar at about HK$7.80 to US$1, was retained after the handover, although there were quick moves to do away with coins and notes featuring the queen. Several different banks issue notes, so there is still a wide variety of designs. As in most countries, exchange rates are poor at the airport. There is, however, a Hong Kong and Shànghǎi Bank ATM at departures level that accepts foreign cards. Neither banks nor hotels give particularly good rates, but street moneychangers do (though, of course, you must be careful).

However, the farther away from the tourist shopping districts you exchange, the better the rate you'll get. If on Nathan Road, Kowloon, walk up the side streets northeast of the Holiday Inn for a block or two to find considerable savings.

GETTING THERE

By Plane   Most of the world's international airlines fly into Hong Kong. When flying from North America, direct flights are more expensive than indirect flights via "intermediate nations" such as Taiwan, Korea, or Japan. When flying from Europe, indirect flights through Eastern European nations, Malaysia, and other neighbors will usually save a good deal of money. From the mainland, several domestic carriers fly into Hong Kong, although because of Hong Kong's odd pseudo-foreign status, it's often considerably cheaper to fly to Shēnzhèn on the mainland border and either take a jetfoil (shuttle bus to the quay included) to Hong Kong or go into the town center and walk over the border.

Flying into and out of Hong Kong's new airport at Chek Lap Kok is very convenient, however. With many airlines, baggage can be checked in at the Kowloon or Hong Kong stations of the airport express rail link several hours in advance (this service is currently suspended on North American routes). Arriving, the airport express platform is directly ahead as you emerge from Customs and takes you straight downtown in 20 minutes. Services run from 5:50am to 12:48am, and stations in Kowloon and on Hong Kong Island have free shuttle buses to major hotels. Single/same-day return tickets cost HK$90 (US$12) to/from Kowloon, and

HK$100 (US$13) to/from Hong Kong. Round-trip tickets cost HK$160 (US$21) and HK$180 (US$23) respectively.

There are multiple Airbus routes, which will take you from the airport to almost every corner of Hong Kong. To Hong Kong Island, the A11 (HK$40/US$5.20) and A12 (HK$45/US$5.80) run every 15 minutes between 6:10am and midnight. To Kowloon, take the A21 (HK$33/US$4.30) or A22 (HK$39/US$5.10). Buses require exact change.

Many hotels operate their own minibus services for guests, or limousine pickup from a signposted VIP section.

Taxis in Hong Kong are color-coded: Take a red taxi to Hong Kong Island or Kowloon (different, well-signposted ranks for Kowloon side and Island side), a green taxi to the New Territories, and a blue taxi to Lantau Island. English comprehension is varied, but all drivers know the names of major sights and hotels, and staff at the airport rank translate if necessary. Meters are used, and a trip to Hong Kong will cost around the equivalent of US$50, to Kowloon US$40. For further taxi tips, see "Getting Around," below.

For the most up-to-date information on the airport, including transport details, see www.hkairport.com. For flight arrival and departure information, call ✆ **852/2181-2400** (English, 24 hr.).

For flights out of Hong Kong, shop around the many agents in the tourist areas, particularly Kowloon, as these will provide far better prices than your hotel's travel desk or the airlines themselves. Many advertise in the *South China Morning Post* or in free weekly what's on–type magazines.

By Train There are five to eight departures hourly between 5:30am and 12:25am from **Hung Hom Station** in Kowloon to and from the border crossing for Shēnzhèn at Lo Wu, costing HK$33 (US$4.30). For a detailed timetable and intermediate stops, see www.kcrc.com and click "Services."

There are also cross-border services to Guǎngzhōu East Station, Běijīng West Station, and Shànghǎi. To Guǎngzhōu, there are seven services a day between 8:25am and 4:45pm, and a similar schedule in the opposite direction, taking just over 1½ hours (HK$230/US$30).

The T97 leaves for Běijīng at 3pm on alternate days (passengers for the Yangtze may alight at Hànkǒu), arriving at 6:05pm the next day. Hard sleepers are of a higher standard than the Chinese norm, and quite comfortable (HK$574–HK$601/US$75–US$78). Soft sleepers are HK$934 (US$121)—a little less for the higher berth—and deluxe soft sleepers, which have only two beds in a compartment usually holding four, are HK$1,191 (US$155).

The K100 for Shànghǎi is similar, leaving at 3pm on alternate days, arriving at 3:54pm the next day, with various stops that include Hángzhōu East. Hard sleepers are HK$508 to HK$530 (US$66–US$69), soft sleepers HK$825 (US$107), and deluxe soft sleepers HK$1,039 (US$135).

Passengers under 10 years old pay about two-thirds of these prices, and for each adult, one accompanying child under five may travel free, providing he or she uses the adult's berth. Tickets can be bought at Hung Hom, at any KCR East station, or through travel agents (with no commission payable). To check the days these trains leave, consult www.kcrc.com and click on "Services" and "Intercity Passenger Services"; or call ☏ **852/2947-7888.**

By Ship Up-to-date timings of jetfoil sailings from Hong Kong to Macau, Shēnzhèn, and Guǎngzhōu can be found at www.turbocat.com/turbo jet_sailing_rev.htm or by calling ☏ **852/ 2859-3333.** Telephone reservations can be made up to 28 days in advance by calling ☏ **852/2921-6688.** In addition to the round-the-clock service to Macau from the Macau Ferry Terminal, and nine daily sailings to Macau from Kowloon, there are seven daily sailings to Shēnzhèn (six from Kowloon and one from Hong Kong, all with a free bus link to Shēnzhèn airport, about 55 min. altogether), and two daily sailings to Guǎngzhōu from Kowloon (with a free bus link to the Garden and China hotels, about 2 hr. altogether). Tickets to Shēnzhèn cost HK$189 to HK$289 (US$25–US$38), and to Guǎngzhōu HK$198 to HK$293 (US$26–US$38). All Hong Kong Island arrivals and departures are at the Macau Ferry Terminal, and Kowloon ones are at the China (HK) Ferry Terminal in Tsim Sha Tsui, just beyond the north end of the Ocean Terminal. Tickets are on sale at ferry terminals. You can also buy them at the Shun Tak Centre 3/F, 200 Connaught Rd. in Central; at the Turbojet Service Counter (Sheung Wan MTR Station, Exit D); and at China Travel Service (CTS) branches. Telephone reservations can be made up to 28 days in advance at ☏ **852/2921-6688.**

There are also catamaran services to Guǎngzhōu twice daily, taking 2¾ hours to Píngzhōu Wharf at Nánhǎi with a free shuttle bus to Zhōutóuzuǐ, just south of Shāmiàn Island. These leave from the China–Hong Kong Ferry Terminal in Kowloon, and tickets are HK$168 to HK$284 (US$22–US$36). See www.cksp.com.hk or call © 852/2859-1584 for full details.

The last remaining coastal ferry service of any significance is a weekly sailing to Xiàmén, a more pleasant and relaxing way to enter mainland China than the alternatives. See the Xiàmén "Getting There" section, visit www.cruise-ferries.com.hk, or call © 852/2957-8188 (24 hr.) for further information. There are also local services to nearby points in Guǎngdōng Province. See www.cksp.com.hk and www.chinatravelone.com for information on these services.

GETTING AROUND

Consider buying a stored-value **Octopus Card** for HK$100 (US$13) from the Airport Express ticket desk or any MTR station, upon your arrival in Hong Kong. When you wave the card at electronic turnstiles on the metro system (MTR), the KCRC railway (to Lo Wu), the Airport Express, the Star Ferry, ferries to outlying islands, and many buses, the cost of the trip is automatically deducted. Value can be added to the card at "Add Value" machines in every MTR station. The card's deposit and any outstanding value can be reclaimed by returning it to any MTR or Airport Express Station upon your departure. These cards can save you a great deal of the time usually spent buying individual tickets and fumbling for exact change.

By Metro The **MTR (Mass Transit Railway)** is one of the world's best underground railway systems. Clean, rapid, and efficient, and with trains every 2 or 3 minutes, it's by far the quickest way to get around, with lines running from the New Territories right across the north side of Hong Kong Island from 6am to 1am.

By Taxi Taxis are metered and generally reliable, although little English is spoken by drivers. When a Kowloon taxi is asked to cross to the Island, or vice versa, double the toll of the tunnel chosen is payable in addition to the metered fare. At major taxi ranks, there are separate lines for Kowloon- and Island-side taxis. Pick a taxi waiting to return to its own side and you'll only pay the regular tunnel toll fee. Most taxi trips are under HK$40 (US$5.20). Tunnel tolls are HK$20 (US$2.60) for the Cross-Harbour, HK$30 (US$3.30) for the Eastern Harbour and Lantau Link, and HK$45 (US$5.80) for the Western Harbour.

By Ferry The century-old **Star Ferry** service remains the cheapest little cruise in the world, wallowing every few minutes across the harbor on two useful routes, from Tsim Sha Tsui to Central, and from Tsim Sha Tsui to Wanchai, from 6:30am to 11:30pm for HK$2.20 (US30¢). There's also a less frequent service from Central to Hung Hom. Fast ferries to outlying islands such as Lantau, Lamma, Cheung Chao, and Peng Chau mostly leave from the Central Ferry Pier next to the Star Ferry terminal in Central. For schedules, see www.nwff.com.hk or call © 852/2131-8181.

By Tram Tram lines lace the north side of Hong Kong Island, with the rattling vehicles still as much a public transport option as tourist attraction. They run from 6am to 1am and cost HK$1.60 (US20¢), which you should deposit in a slot as you alight.

TOURS & STRATAGEMS

Tours/Information Like Macau, but unlike the rest of China, Hong Kong runs a nonprofit organization solely devoted to promoting the city as a tourist destination and to making life easy for visitors. The **Hong Kong Tourism Board (HKTB)** has counters immediately after you clear Customs at the airport (open 7am–11pm), at the Star Ferry concourse on the Kowloon side, and in the basement of The Centre, 99 Queen's Rd. Central (open 8am–6pm), offering a mountain of free maps, guides, magazines, and other literature, as well as detailed answers to individual queries. It runs a multilingual information line from 8am to 6pm (**(** 852/2508-1234), has a comprehensive website (www.discoverhongkong. com), and offers visitors free classes in everything from *tàijíquán* (tai chi chuan) exercises to appreciation of Cantonese opera, antiques, jade, pearls, and tea. It also offers a free ride around the harbor on a junk (the *Duk Ling*).

The HKTB used to run numerous tours, but it has now released these to private enterprises. Nevertheless, it remains the best central source for tours, which it vets and approves, including ones that introduce more aspects of Hong Kong than just the high-tech, fast-paced, shop-at-all-costs one. Heritage tours out to ancient halls in the New Territories are particularly worth considering, as are those to see horse racing, as well as Dolpinwatch tours and other wildlife trips. Hong Kong has vast areas of national parks given its small size, and has some excellent walking trails of varying grades of difficulty, such as the Dragon's Back on Hong Kong Island, and green routes on outlying islands. These you can follow yourself with maps and guidance from the HKTB, or HKTB-sponsored books such as Edward Stokes's *Exploring Hong Kong's Countryside*.

Mainland China Visits A visit to mainland China involves advance purchase of a visa, but these are more easily obtainable in Hong Kong than anywhere else. Numerous agents are eager to get your visa for you, but those within the tourist districts are also eager to charge you 50% to 100% more than you need to pay, so shop around. The Hong Kong operation of **CTS (China Travel Service)** has 36 branches, of which the best known is that at 27–33 Nathan Rd., Kowloon (one floor up in Alpha House, entrance around the corner on Peking Rd.; **(** 852/2315-7188; fax 852/2721-7292; www.chinatravel one.com), open 365 days a year. Come here for commission-free ferry tickets and train tickets to China, as well as advance purchase of tickets for a limited selection of trains from Běijīng, Shànghǎi, Hángzhōu, Guǎngzhōu, Xī'ān, Guìlín, and Shēnzhèn. Visa purchase here, however, is slow and expensive. For air tickets, shop around the many budget travel agents in the area, such as **Shoestring Travel** (next door entrance, same building as CTS, 4th Floor, **(** 852/2723-2306; fax 852/ 2721-2085; www.shoestringtravel.com. hk). Entry visas are cheaper here, too, but agents farther away from the main shopping streets are even cheaper. For the cheapest visas, go to **Grand Profit International Travel Agency** (705AA, 7th Floor New East Ocean Centre, 9 Science Museum Rd., Tsim Sha Tsui, about a 15-min. walk east of Nathan Rd.; ✆ **852/ 2723-3288**). A single-entry tourist visa for HK$150 (US$19) is available the next day if you hand in your passport before noon. That's the same price as the Chinese Ministry of Foreign Affairs Visa Office charges, but 2 days quicker. Same-day service is HK$180 (US$23), which is considerably less than the visa office charges for the same service. Double-entry and multiple-entry 6-month visas are also easily available for low prices.

It is possible to visit Shēnzhèn for 72 hours (but no longer) without purchasing a visa in advance, if you take the option of walking across the border at Lo Wu. Thirty-day visas for the whole of China may be purchased on arrival by through train from Hong Kong at Guǎngzhōu East station. Call the Guǎngzhōu PSB for further information at ✆ **020/6130-0167** (10am–6:30pm). When last heard of, neither of these options was available to British citizens, but check with your consulate for the latest information. Citizens of all developed nations may buy 90-day tourist visas for HK$180 (US$23) at the land crossing between Macau and Zhūhǎi. Go to the **China Travel Service** office immediately on your left as you enter the immigration hall on the mainland side, open from 8am to 10pm; or call for more information (✆ **0756/ 815-6466**).

WHERE TO STAY

Hong Kong has some of the best hotels in the world and is in general well supplied with top-quality accommodations. Room rates tend to reflect the stratospheric land values on which much of the city's wealth is rather precariously based, which means that even rooms costing US$100 per night may be surprisingly small (rooms at the YMCA are more than US$100—but they're as good as any standard hotel room, and the location is unbeatable). More modest pricing means traveling some distance from the center, but as long as the hotel is near an MTR station, this isn't a problem even for those on brief visits. Although rack rates are quoted below, the actual amount you need to pay varies widely according to season and booking method, and may be dramatically less at times. Unlike in mainland China, hotels respond efficiently and publicly to market demands. Room rates are subject to a 10% service charge and a 3% government tax. Below you'll find a small selection of the very best hotels, plus some new, well-located, midrange boutique hotels, as well as a couple of budget choices. High season for Hong Kong is October and November, when rates can be expected to be at their maximum. Otherwise, shop around through agents for often-substantial discounts on the rack rates quoted.

Best Western Rosedale on the Park Handy for some of Hong Kong's best-priced shopping around Times Square, the Rosedale has pleasing modern cream and brown rooms well-equipped with free broadband Internet access, iron and ironing board, and heavyweight cotton sheets and duvet. The hotel describes itself as a "cyber boutique"; the digital phone in each room will conveniently work anywhere in the hotel, and there are Web phones for rent. Soft drinks from the minibar are free. Rooms from the 10th floor upward have views. Rates run at about 50% off season, and there are special discounts for stays of 1 week and longer. Suites with sofa beds in the living room come with small pantries and microwave, convenient and economical for families.

8 Shelter St., Causeway Bay (across the road from Victoria Park, Causeway Bay MTR 5-min. walk). © *852/2127-8888. Fax 852/2127-3333. www.rosedale.com.hk. 274 units, including 45 suites. HK$1,280–HK$1,580 (US$164–US$203) double/twin;   HK$1,980–HK$6,980 (US$254–US$895) suite. AE, DC, MC, V.* **Amenities:** 2 restaurants (international and Cantonese; with halal menu), Sky Zone top-floor wine and cigar lounge; airport shuttle; convention center shuttle during major exhibitions; 24-hr. business center; mobile phone rental. *In room:* A/C, TV, dataport, minibar, coffeemaker, hair dryer, iron, safe.

The Empire Hotel Kowloon The Empire is a sleek, modern tower, only 5 minutes from the nearest Tsim Sha Tsui MTR station exit, and a 20-minute walk from the Star Ferry. Rooms are small but bright, fresh, and modern, with TV-based Internet access. The linen is good quality, and bathrooms have proper shower cubicles. The swimming pool nestles beneath an atrium within the base of the building. Off-season rates November to March can be as little as 40% of rack, making this a very economical choice by Hong Kong standards.

62 Kimberley Rd., Tsim Sha Tsui (Tsim Sha Tsui MTR). © *853/2686-3000. Fax 852/2685-3685. www.asiastandard.com/hotel/kln.html. 315 units. HK$1,400–HK$2,200 (US$179–US$282) double/*

twin; HK$2,800–HK$3,000 (US$359–US$385) suite. AE, DC, MC, V. In room: A/C, satellite TV, video on demand, dataport, internet via TV, minibar, hair dryer.

Grand Hyatt The Grand Hyatt's recently revamped rooms are a combination of the stylish comforts for which the brand is justly famous and marble bathrooms of traditional luxury (fitted with both bathtubs and shower cubicles). In-room amenities include broadband Internet access and dual-voltage electricity via convenient desk-mounted sockets. Seventy percent of the rooms have some of the best shoreline and harbor views available on the Island side. The vast, curved, 1930s-style lobby area overlooked by the Tiffin restaurant, popular for both its afternoon tea and dessert buffet, is one of Hong Kong's most grand.

1 Harbour Rd., Hong Kong Island (next to Convention Centre). © *852/2588-1234. Fax 852/2802-0677. www.hongkong.grand.hyatt.com. 556 units. HK$3,600–HK$4,400 (US$462–US$564) double/twin;   HK$6,400–HK$25,400 (US$821–US$3,256) suite. AE, DC, MC, V.* **Amenities:** Multiple restaurants and bars, including the best Italian restaurant in Hong Kong (Grissini), Cantonese, Japanese, and international cuisine; champagne bar; large swimming pool; golf driving range; floodlit tennis courts; fitness center; 24-hr. concierge; travel bookings; valet car parking; limousine service; "on demand" free shuttle to various points by fleet of London taxis; business center; florist; salon; babysitting; laundry and valet; private yacht. *In room:* A/C, satellite TV, video on demand, broadband, dataport, Internet via TV, fax machine, minibar, hair dryer, safe.

Kowloon Hotel The Kowloon is the ultimate business hotel, although it also welcomes many tour groups and individual travelers. As in most Hong Kong hotels below luxury level, rooms are small, but each features a telecenter— a multi-functional TV-computer with a vast range of functions, including word processing, Web and e-mail access via broadband, facsimile transmission, and satellite TV channels. Personal e-mail addresses are supplied, which regular guests may reactivate on your return. As the last word in high-tech, the lobby has a Presspoint kiosk, which will print out more than 100 different newspapers from 44 countries, on demand. The 12th floor and up have harbor views. Connected pairs of rooms in which the second has a sofa bed suit families of four very well, especially off season when rates are quite reasonable. The Kowloon is managed by The Peninsula Group; in better rooms the bathroom supplies are the same as those enjoyed across the road, and Kowloon guests have signing privileges at Peninsula restaurants.

18–21 Nathan Rd., Kowloon (just behind The Peninsula, Tsim Sha Tsui MTR). © 852/2734-3777. Fax 852/2301-2668. www.peninsula.com. 736 units. HK$1,400–HK$2,650 (US$179–US$340) double/twin, including breakfast at the higher end; HK$3,700–HK$5,100 (US$474–US$654) suite. AE, DC, MC, V. **Amenities:** 4 restaurants and bars; 24-hr. concierge; tour desk; limousine service; airport shuttle bus; business center; currency exchange; shopping arcade; salon; babysitting; laundry and dry cleaning; valet service. *In room:* A/C, TV (with telecenter), minibar, coffeemaker, hair dryer, safe.

Mandarin Oriental The Mandarin's location in the heart of Hong Kong Island's Central District makes its comfortable lobby a popular pre-dinner meeting place for Hong Kong's expats, and its afternoon tea rivals that of The Peninsula in popularity. Opened in 1963, the hotel has a solid, if slightly dated, elegance with a gold and black theme, and sets the standard for gracious and almost telepathic service other hotels strive to match. Almost all rooms have balconies with views over Central and partial views of the harbor. This hotel is regularly voted among the top 10 hotels in the world by major travel magazines.

5 Connaught Rd., Central (a short walk from the Star Ferry terminal, Central MTR). © 852/2522-0111. Fax 852/2810-6190. www.mandarinoriental.com. 541 units, including 55 suites. HK$2,950–HK$4,200 (US$378–US$538) single; HK$5,500–HK$25,000 (US$705–US$3,205) suite. Add HK$250 (US$32) for extra person in room and most suites. AE, DC, MC, V. **Amenities:** 4 restaurants and bars, including the Hong Kong branch of French-Asian Vong; bakery; Roman-style swimming pool; gym; health center; sauna; limousine service; business center; florist; salon and barber; 24-hr. room service; newsstand; direct links by walkway to several major shopping complexes. *In room:* A/C, TV, minibar, hair dryer, safe.

Metro Park Hotel This is a bright, newly opened, 31-story tower with fresh modern rooms featuring plenty of glass and wood and luxurious goose-down duvets, along with high-tech amenities such as broadband Internet access. Seventy percent of the rooms here have excellent harbor views along the north shore, and a spectacular swimming pool occupies most of the hotel's flat rooftop. A regular free shuttle bus links it to shopping in Causeway Bay, a short distance away.

148 Tung Lo Wan Rd., Causeway Bay, Hong Kong Island (Tin Hau MTR). ℂ 852/2600-1000. Fax 852/2600-1111. www. metroparkhotel.com. 261 units, including 57 suites. HK$900 (US$115) single; HK$1,500–HK$1,800 (US$192–US$231) double/twin; HK$2,600–HK$5,500 (US$333–US$705) suite. AE, DC, MC, V. **Amenities:** Restaurant (French/Japanese); drinks and tapas at Vic's with live music; swimming pool; health club; Jacuzzi; sauna; valet parking; limousine service; shuttle bus; business center; foreign exchange; babysitting; same-day laundry; hotel doctor. In room: A/C, TV, broadband (free), minibar.

The Peninsula Hong Kong This is quite simply one of the best hotels in the world. On the one hand, the Peninsula is a grande dame of colonial elegance, just celebrating 75 years in business, its white and gold lobby still looking as if Noël Coward might drop in for tea at any moment; on the other hand, a new tower added in 1994 offers rooms with generous harbor and city views and a high-ceilinged English elegance with Asian overtones. Discreet gadgets galore include CD and DVD players, fax machine, remote-controlled curtains, dual-voltage sockets, free broadband access (local calls are also free), and even a TV in the bathroom, a wilderness of white marble with twin sinks and a separate shower cubicle. The rich fabrics and carpets and the other logo-free high-quality furnishings and amenities help give the impression that you're not renting a hotel room but borrowing a wealthy friend's apartment for a while. To celebrate their 75th anniversary, during 2003, there are special room rates and a variety of entertainments and special packages, climaxing with a gala ball on December 11.

Salisbury Rd., Kowloon (at Tsim Sha Tsui MTR station, a short walk from the Star Ferry in Tsim Sha Tsui). ℂ 852/2920-2888. Fax 852/2722-4170. www. peninsula.com. 300 units, including 54 suites. HK$2,775–HK$2,975 (US$356–US$381) double; HK$4,775–HK$12,275 (US$612–US$1,574) suite. AE, DC, MC, V. **Amenities:** Superb dining at 8 restaurants; luxurious indoor/outdoor swimming pool; health club and spa; Jacuzzi; sauna; concierge; tour desk; helicopter tours; fleet of 14 Rolls-Royces; 24-hr. business center; conference rooms; 24-hr. foreign exchange service; shopping arcade with more than 130 world-famous outlets; florist; salon; 24-hr. room service; babysitting; same-day dry cleaning and laundry; nightly turndown; newspaper delivery; newsstand; twice-daily maid service; valet; butler service; in-house nurse; express checkout. In room: A/C, TV, CD/DVD players, fax machine, minibar, hair dryer, safe.

The Salisbury YMCA Although there's a slightly cafeteria-like feeling to the lobby, forget any notion that you are slumming it if you stay here. Even the seven four-person dormitories are spotless and fully serviced, each with shower. The remaining rooms and suites were renovated in 2000; they are full-featured with broadband Internet and all the usual amenities popular both with business visitors and with families who like the full-scale recreational facilities. Many rooms have superb harbor views and are often booked up a long way in advance. Rates are higher in April and October, but there are reduced rates for weeklong and monthlong stays.

41 Salisbury Rd., Kowloon (next door to the Peninsula Hotel on the Star Ferry side). ℂ 852/2268-7888. Fax 852/

2739-9315. www.ymcahk.org.hk. 363 units, including 62 suites. HK$210 (US$27) dorm bed; HK$600 (US$77) single; HK$700–HK$900 (US$90–US$115) double/twin; HK$1,200–HK$1,400 (US$154–US$179) suite. No tax is payable here. AE, DC, MC, V. **Amenities:** International restaurant (with harbor views) and self-service cafe; large swimming pool; children's pool; squash courts; climbing wall; dance studio; fitness center; Jacuzzi; sauna; children's play area; concierge; tour desk; bookshop; salon; laundry and dry cleaning; self-service launderette; chapel. *In room:* A/C, TV, dataport, minibar, coffeemaker, hair dryer, safe.

WHERE TO DINE

Hong Kong claims to have more restaurants per head than anywhere else in the world. The choice is unlimited, and unlike in most of mainland China, there's a vast range of Western food as well as Chinese—and it's Western food as good if not better than what you'll find at home. There's also plenty of cheap eating in small-scale dim sum, rice-plate, noodle, and congee (rice porridge) houses on almost every street; dozens of branches of excellent local-grown cafes and sandwich bars such as **Pacific Coffee** and **Oliver's;** and many outlets of familiar American fast-food chains. But serious eating, whether Chinese or foreign, isn't cheap. A 10% service charge is often added to the prices below, and a little change should be left for the staff *as well.* Prices given are per person for three courses at dinner, excluding wine. In all cases, judicious menu selections can reduce the price, and lunch menus are often considerably cheaper. For Chinese recommendations, ask the HKTB for the latest edition of their "Best of the Best" booklet, which lists the winning dishes in a recently instituted annual competition for Chinese cooking, and tells you where to find them.

Be sure to try dim sum—snacks mostly in the form of small steamed items in bamboo steamers, many poorly translated as "dumplings" and usually delivered by trolley. At your request, lids are lifted and you can choose the items that appeal to you. You'll probably skip the chicken feet and go for the *siu mai* (small balls of beef and prawn), *har gau* (prawns in a rice-flour wrapping), or *char siu bao* (buns stuffed with barbecued pork).

There's plenty of good eating on outlying small islands such as **Cheung Chow,** where cheap seafood restaurants lining the waterfront serve everything from fresh crab to fish balls as well as simple, serve-yourself dim sum. The chairs are plastic, the chopsticks are best given a rinse with the tea, and the service is basic; but, then, so is the price: perhaps HK$75 (under US$10).

Dim Sum DIM SUM Dim Sum produces the Rolls-Royce versions of these Cantonese tidbits in an interior at once modern and reminiscent of 1930s Shànghǎi, with posters of plump, cheongsam-clad beauties with bee-stung lips. The *leong har gao* contain not merely shrimp but lobster, and the *siu mai* (all delicious) include shark's fin. Try *sheung jee jor* (dumplings with scallops, crab eggs, and shrimp). The menu also offers a variety of delicious Běijīng snacks, allowing a direct comparison between the tastes of north and south.

The Běijīng snacks appear with Cantonese names, such as *kao but lei*—steamed buns with pork and vegetables—slightly sweeter than they would be in the north. *G/F 63 Sing Wo Rd., Wan Chai.* ✆ *852/2834-8893. HK$150 (US$31). AE, DC, MC, V. 11am–4:30pm and 6–11pm.*

Felix FUSION Philippe Starck's entertainingly theatrical interior competes for your attention with sweeping harbor views and Hawaiian chef Dee Ann Tsurumaki's signature sauces, some all day in the making and very intense. "Many fusion dishes involve too many tastes, so they 'fight' with one another," she says, but her layers of sea bass and pickled ginger with a wasabi sauce provide three separate experiences with each mouthful, and all in harmony. Also try the Mongolian grilled barbecued rack of lamb and the misoyaki-marinated Atlantic cod. Images of the faces of Starck's colleagues peer out at you from unoccupied chairs—you never dine alone. Smart casual dress required. *25th floor of The Peninsula (see above—separate elevator from the shopping arcade on the west side).* ✆ *852/2315-3188. www.peninsula.com. Approximately HK$450 (US$58) per person. AE, DC, MC, V. 6pm–2am.*

Gaddi's FRENCH This restaurant has a French menu, with inventive additions from chef Philip Sedgwick's sojourns at various Michelin-starred restaurants around Europe. Try the roast Boston lobster with black Taggiasche olives and fondant potatoes, or the twice-cooked suckling pig with olive oil–braised shallots, baby artichokes, and fondant potatoes in an aged cider vinegar sauce. The smart, chandeliered, blue and gold space is a Hong Kong institution, celebrating its 50th anniversary in 2003. Sedgwick also welcomes four diners to eat at a stainless-steel table in the middle of his enormous kitchen. Advance booking is required, but set meals (Sedgwick's choice—state any aversions in advance) come with a tour of the kitchen and dishes personally introduced by the chef himself. Highly recommended, the three-course lunch is HK$688 (US$88), the five-course dinner HK$1,288 (US$165), and the 10-course dinner HK$1,888 (US$242). *25th floor of The Peninsula (see above).* ✆ *852/2315-3188. www.peninsula.com. HK$800 (US$103) per person. 3-course set lunch HK$340 (US$44) per person, including a glass of house wine. 4- to 6-course dinner menu with wine HK$650–HK$950 (US$83–US$122). AE, DC, MC, V. Noon–3pm and 7–11pm.*

Grissini ITALIAN In a highly competitive field, Grissini comes in first as the best Italian restaurant in Hong Kong, with a chef from Pavia but a menu with Sicilian influences. The cold angel-hair pasta tossed with raw scampi and caviar is complex and lemony, and tempting to order twice. The roasted quail breasts, wrapped in pancetta and filled with goose liver, are memorably rich. The interior has a certain New York black-and-white quality (although Starck gets in again with the chair designs), but eyes, when removed from plates, are mostly turned to panoramic views of Victoria Harbour. *Inside the Grand Hyatt (see above).* ✆ *852/2588-1234, ext. 7313. www.hongkong.grand. hyatt.com. HK$550 ($71). AE, DC, MC, V. Noon–2:30pm and 7–11pm.*

Luk Yu Tea House DIM SUM Start the day with dim sum in the most traditional setting possible—this is the haunt of Central's Chinese businesspeople from 11am, when unfamiliar faces may be turned away until business slows in mid-afternoon. Downstairs is attractive, with its dark carved wood and stained glass, but it would originally have been the haunt of the hoi polloi. Head upstairs to find a woody interior with a low hum of conversation (later a din), heads buried in newspapers, discreet balconies lit through frosted glass, and tasty morsels brought around not on trolleys, but on slender silver trays like those of old-time cinema usherettes. *26 Stanley St., Central.* *(C) 852/ 2523-5464. HK$15–HK$46 (US$2– US$6) per plate. No credit cards. Daily 7am–6pm.*

M at the Fringe INTERNATIONAL The menu consists of Australian expat Michelle Garnaut's favorite dishes— French, European, Turkish, Lebanese, and Italian—and is particularly famous for a salty, melt-in-the-mouth lamb, slowly baked and served with good mashed potatoes, butternut squash, and homemade tomato jam. The technically superb Pavlova is the stuff of legend. The friendly, mutedly arty, and eternally popular interior, all ragworked walls and Portobello Market knickknacks, occupying an extraordinary wedge-shaped building dating from 1913, is still a haunt of Hong Kong celebrities after more than a decade. This place offers essential eating. *2 Lower Albert Rd., Central (above The Fringe Club). (C) 852/2877-4000. www.m-onthebund.com. HK$350 (US$45). Set lunch: 2 courses HK$148 (US$19), 3 courses HK$168 (US$22). AE, DC, MC, V. Lunch Mon–Fri noon– 2:30pm; dinner Sun–Thurs 7–10pm, until 10:30pm Fri and Sat.*

Moon Garden Tea House TEA/SNACKS Furnished with antique screens, lanterns, birdcages, and chairs from an assortment of regions and dynasties, Moon Garden offers 70 different teas, including a number of rare specimens, together with preparation demonstrations and explanations in English. There's no menu, but those who want to eat lightly during the day can sit among elaborate traditional Chinese furniture and sample a variety of northern and southern snacks from whatever's fresh. There's a second location at 149 Hollywood Rd., Mid-levels. *5 Hoi Ping Rd., Causeway Bay. (C) 852/ 2882-6878. HK$150 (US$19). DC, MC, V. Mon–Sat noon–midnight; until 10pm on Sun.*

The Peak Lookout INTERNATIONAL This place is perfect for summer evenings: It's an early-1900s former resting place for sedan-chair carriers near the Peak Tram's upper terminus, now converted into an airy restaurant with a large bamboo-shrouded garden and views out toward Lamma Island. Multiple serving stations supply an eager expat clientele with their favorites from Asia and beyond: excellent fresh oysters, an outdoor barbecue, Indians cooking Indian favorites (tandoori dishes are particularly good), Chinese cooking Chinese favorites, British stodge, American standards, and good pasta, to boot. The interior has an impressive display of early photographs of Hong Kong. *121 Peak Rd., The Peak. (C) 852/ 2849-1000. www.peaklookout.com.hk. HK$220 (US$28). AE, DC, MC, V. 10:30am–11:30pm; Fri, Sat, and eves of public holidays until 1am. Breakfast from 8:30am Sat, Sun, and public holidays.*

Tung Lok Hin CANTONESE This is a new type of Chinese restaurant, with the simple, understated post-modern interior adopted by many Western ones, and with contemporary art on the walls. As is traditional, the seafood is kept alive and visible until needed, but rather than the traditional tanks, here it swims up and down the inside of a glass wall. The menu is of Cantonese classics, with bird's nest and abalone topping a long list of items more interesting to Westerners. Dishes are far plainer than you might expect (as they should be), not smothered by overly syrupy sauces. But there are many new creations, too, which set the restaurant apart from the Cantonese mainstream. An attentive sommelier presides over a startlingly sophisticated wine list. *2/F Oxford House, Taikoo Place, Quarry Bay.* © *852/2250-5022. www. tunglokhin.com. HK$400 (US$51). AE, DC, MC, V. Mon–Sat 11:30am–11pm; Sun and public holidays 10am–11pm.*

Veda INDIAN Hong Kong has plenty of British high-street-style, red-flock-wallpaper Indian restaurants, but this is something quite different: an ultra-modern interior with hammered-silver tabletops, snowy linen, and plenty of glass, including a see-through wall with views of the kitchen—tandoori ovens and all. Chef Rajiv Singh Gulshan's menu is varied and multi-provincial, from Tamil Nadu to Kashmir, with plenty of choices for vegetarians. Familiar dishes have unfamiliar additions and are presented in an unfamiliar style, in the manner of a first-class French restaurant, with an eye for the beauty of the ingredients and their proper arrangement. More surprisingly still, sommelier and manager Franck Crouvezier has a comprehensive international wine list and is willing to demonstrate that diners can and should venture beyond the traditional lager. From samosas filled with tandoor-roasted quails to black cod crusted with homemade lemon pickle on rice vermicelli, this place is a splendid introduction to India's variety for the novice, and an eye-opener for the enthusiast. *8 Arbuthnot Rd., Central.* © *852/ 2868-5885. www.veda.com.hk. HK$400 (US$51). AE, DC, MC, V. Sun–Fri noon– 11pm; Sat 6–11pm. Bar 6pm–2am.*

Yung Kee CANTONESE This restaurant began life in 1942 as a food stall selling roast goose, and by 1968 it was listed by *Fortune* magazine as one of the 15 best restaurants in the world. This is Cantonese food at its plainest, a far cry from the sugary and fatty concoctions fobbed off on us as the real thing on Western main streets. Barbecued goose with plum sauce is still a specialty you should sample. Prawns with mini-crab roe wrapped in tofu skin quite rightly won a "Best of the Best" prize recently. And toad legs with pepper and salt make an interesting change. There are several dining rooms on different floors, richly over-decorated in the usual Chinese way—golden dragons with electric eyes writhe up red pillars, and golden phoenixes dance on screens. *32–40 Wellington St., Central.* © *852/2522-1624. www.yungkee.com. hk. HK$200 (US$26). AE, DC, MC, V. 11am–11:30pm. Dim sum served daily 2–5pm, and Sun and public holidays 11:30am–5:30pm. Closed first 3 days of Chinese New Year.*

CENTRAL CHINA: ANTIQUITIES & ADVENTURES

XĪ'ĀN:
THE ANCIENT CAPITAL
西安

XĪ'ĀN IS CHINA'S CITY OF THE DEAD—
which is to say, China's city of ancient imperial treasures. The First
Emperor, Qín Shǐ Huáng (259–210 B.C.), unified China here. Twenty-two
centuries later, in 1979, the 7,000 life-sized terra-cotta soldiers buried with
him were accidentally unearthed, opening an underground city of the dead
that put Xī'ān on the world map of tourism. But Xī'ān was always China's
leading historical site. It served as China's capital over the course of
11 dynasties, reaching its height in the golden age of the Táng Dynasty
(A.D. 618–907).

As showcases of China's imperial splendors, Běijīng and Xī'ān provide
interesting contrasts. Běijīng was the capital of the last two great dynasties,
the Míng (A.D. 1368–1644) and the Qīng (A.D. 1644–1911); Xī'ān was the
capital of the first two great dynasties, the Hàn (206 B.C.–A.D. 220) and the
Táng (A.D. 618–907). Běijīng reins in tourists with the Great Wall and
the Forbidden City; Xī'ān strikes earlier, with the terra-cotta armies of the
Qín Emperor and the Big Wild Goose Pagoda of the Táng emperors.

Xī'ān's historical monuments and sites are even more extensive than
Běijīng's, stretching from the Bànpō Neolithic Village, occupied 6,000
years ago, to the sole surviving city wall (just the palace wall, in fact) of any
major city in China, built during the Míng Dynasty. If ancient Chinese
history has no attraction for you, then skip Xī'ān altogether. But if you're
like me, its allure runs deep. I have been revisiting Xī'ān ever since I first
lived and worked there in 1984, gauging the changes that China has gone
through during the last 2 decades, always in relation to the broader and
deeper history that is preserved in its streets, walls, and courtyards.

The City Wall

My first glimpse of the massive city wall of Xī'ān transfixed me. This earth
and brick structure stands restored to grandeur, 12m (40 ft.) high, 13km
(8 miles) around, its old archers' towers still intact. The palaces of the
earliest emperors and the temples of the first Buddhists and Daoists have

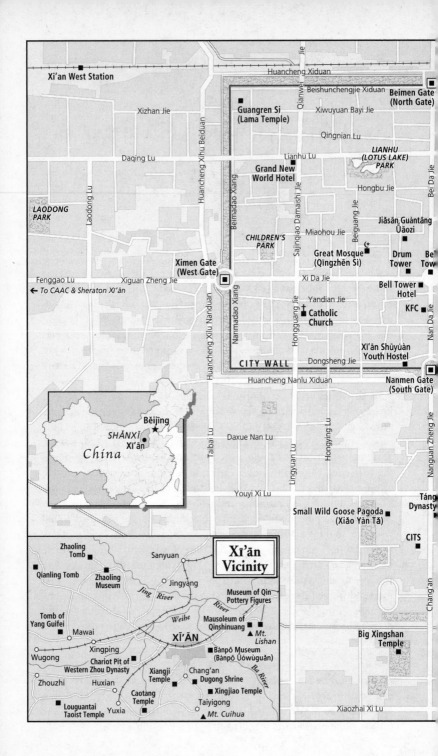

Xi'an West Station

Xizhan Jie

Guangren Si
(Lama Temple)

Daqing Lu

LAODONG
PARK

Laodong Lu

Huancheng Xihu Beiduan

Beimadao Xiang

Lianhu Lu

Grand New
World Hotel

Sajinqiao Damaishi Jie

CHILDREN'S
PARK

Ximen Gate
(West Gate)

Fenggao Lu

Xiguan Zheng Jie

← To CAAC & Sheraton Xi'an

Huancheng Xilu Nanduan

Nanmadao Xiang

Qianwei

Huancheng Xiduan

Beishunchengjie Xiduan

Beimen Gate
(North Gate)

Xiwuyuan Bayi Jie

Qingnian Lu

LIANHU
(LOTUS LAKE)
PARK

Hongbu Jie

Beiguang Jie

Miaohou Jie

Jiǎsǎn Guàntāng
Ûāozi

(*

Great Mosque
(Qīngzhēn Sì)

Drum
Tower

Be
Tow

Xi Da Jie

Bell Tower
Hotel

Yandian Jie

KFC

Hongguang Jie

† Catholic
Church

Xi'ān Shūyùàn
Youth Hostel

CITY WALL

Dongsheng Jie

Huancheng Nanlu Xiduan

Bei Da Jie

Nan Da Jie

Nanmen Gate
(South Gate)

Nanguan Zheng Jie

Taibai Lu

Daxue Nan Lu

Lingyuan Lu

Hongying Lu

Béijīng ★

SHǍNXĪ

Xī'ān

China

Youyi Xi Lu

Small Wild Goose Pagoda
(Xiǎo Yàn Tǎ)

Táng
Dynasty

CITS

Chang'an

**Xī'ān
Vicinity**

Zhaoling
Tomb

Qianling Tomb

Zhaoling
Museum

Sanyuan

Jingyang

Jing River

Museum of Qin
Pottery Figures

Mausoleum of
Qinshinuang

Tomb of
Yang Guifei

Mawai

Weihe

XĪ'ĀN

▲ Mt.
Lishan

Xingping

Bànpō Museum
(Bànpō Ûówùguǎn)

Wugong

Chariot Pit of
Western Zhou Dynasty

Xiangji
Temple

Chang'an ●
● Dugong Shrine

Bā River

Big Xingshan
Temple

Zhouzhi

Huxian

Caotang
Temple

■ Xingjiao Temple

Louguantai
Taoist Temple

Yuxia

Taiyigong

▲ Mt. Cuihua

Xiaozhai Xi Lu

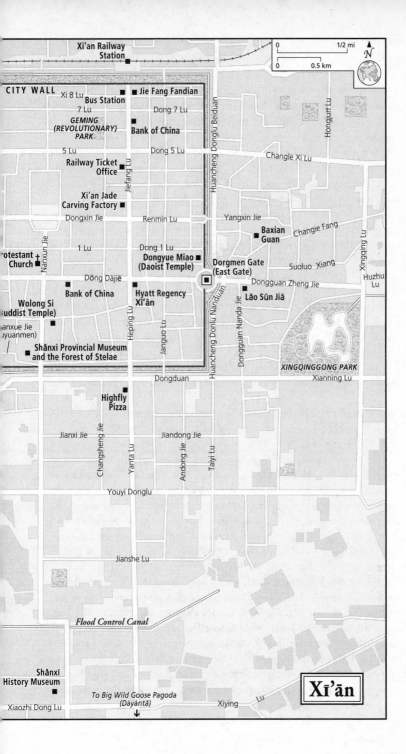

Xi'an Railway Station

CITY WALL

Xi 8 Lu

Bus Station

7 Lu

GEMING (REVOLUTIONARY) PARK

5 Lu

Railway Ticket Office

Xi'an Jade Carving Factory

Dongxin Jie

Nanxun Jie

Protestant Church

1 Lu

Dōng Dàjiē

Bank of China

Wolong Si (Buddist Temple)

Nanxue Jie (Suyuanmen)

Shǎnxi Provincial Museum and the Forest of Stelae

Jie Fang Fandian

Dong 7 Lu

Bank of China

Dong 5 Lu

Jiefang Lu

Renmin Lu

Dong 1 Lu

Dongyue Miao (Daoist Temple)

Heping Lu

Hyatt Regency Xi'ān

Janguo Lu

Dongduan

Huancheng Donglu Beiduan

Changle Xi Lu

Yangxin Jie

Baxian Guan

Changie Fang

Dorgmen Gate (East Gate)

Dongguan Zheng Jie

Suoluo Xiang

Dongguan-Nanda Jie

Lǎo Sūn Jiā

Hongjurt Lu

Xingqing Lu

Huzhu Lu

Huancheng Donlu Nanduan

XINGQINGGONG PARK

Xianning Lu

Highfly Pizza

Jianxi Jie

Changsheng Jie

Yanta Lu

Jiandong Jie

Andong Jie

Taiyi Lu

Youyi Donglu

Jianshe Lu

Flood Control Canal

Shǎnxī History Museum

Xiaozhi Dong Lu

To Big Wild Goose Pagoda (Dàyàntǎ)

Xiying

Lu

Xī'ān

vanished from the old capital, but the last incarnation of the wall (built 500 years ago) remains to mark their birthplace. The moat along the south side is filled with water. A greenbelt of parks, trails, and outdoor amusements is gradually wrapping its way around the outside of the city.

The remnants of old Xī'ān may be viewed from atop the city wall by foot or bike. An admission fee of ¥10 ($1.20) is collected at entrances inside the wall. The best place to begin is on the southeast, across from the old Provincial Museum. There are entry signs in English.

The path is wide and paved in new stepping stones, and the views over the wall, inside and outside, are always fascinating. From late spring to early fall, the wall is lively with souvenir vendors, tourists, and locals out for a stroll. The entire 13km (8-mile) circuit would make a unique annual footrace. There are 18 gates through the wall, the four largest at the north, south, east, and west midpoints, where the traffic now flows in and out. A dozen years ago, much of that traffic was horse and donkey carts, and there wasn't a single taxi. (Much of the old palace wall has been breached to widen old roads and allow new roads to pass through, and a large chunk has been removed from the northeast corner to accommodate the unsightly Railway Square.) What you see now from the wall is a modern city and an old city being shuffled together like two mismatched decks of cards. Solar panels cap the new apartments that rise as high as the wall. At the same time, turn-of-the-20th-century shophouses and old temples hug the foot of the wall for blocks, their roof tiles broken but not destroyed.

From the top of the city wall, the main streets of Xī'ān are laid out like a cosmic chessboard. **Nán Dàjiē** runs straight north, past the big KFC outlet on the left, to the **Bell Tower,** built in 1384. The Bell Tower stands at the center of the city. To its west is the **Muslim quarter,** containing the **Grand Mosque** and the **Míng Dynasty Drum Tower;** to its east is the city's main shopping street, **Dōng Dàjiē.** These areas must be explored on foot, as must the quaint arts-and-crafts lane that stretches from the south gate east along the wall to the museum and its celebrated **Forest of Stelae,** the greatest collection of engraved stone tablets in the world.

Looking south from the south gate down Cháng'ān Lù, it's possible to see the tips of the chief Táng Dynasty structures still standing in Xī'ān's immediate suburbs: the **Big Wild Goose Pagoda,** built in A.D. 652 and, closer to the wall, the **Small Wild Goose Pagoda,** built between A.D. 707 and A.D. 709. For more than 12 centuries, these were the tallest structures in Xī'ān. Today, as skyscrapers begin to surround the old walled city, spotting pagodas becomes increasingly difficult. Just south of the wall there are new hotels, new offices, and, right on the moat, a miniature golf course.

I prefer the old world, even in its restored version, and the restoration of the Xī'ān city wall is not so perfect as to destroy the spell of ruin, decay, and faded grandeur that evokes a royal past. Looking down and into the city, I'm always eager to discover what has changed, what remains, and what is no more.

In a Forest of Stelae

The changed and unchanged, the treasures and the losses, are all to be found in the shadow of the southern city wall. Just east of the big south gate, which has become a flowery, landscaped traffic circle, the sleepy curving lane of **Shūyuànmén Dàjiē** has been transformed into a street out of Old Xī'ān. A brand-new dragon-carved gate arches over its entrance. (The exquisite little pagoda to one side dates from A.D. 706, but it is barely noticed now.) Lined with electrified lanterns, bordered by painted banners, festooned with red-and-yellow paper globes, Shūyuànmén Street has been remade for tourists. Even the wooden-railed balconies are strung with lights. The wooden shop fronts, with their elaborately carved doorways, sell every conceivable souvenir. Several shops sell fine artwork (paintings and scrolls) and the crafts for which Xī'ān and this province are famous: simple folk paintings from the peasant painters of Hùxiàn County, paper cuts, bright folk-art clothing and cloth ornaments, teapots, chopsticks, porcelain, books, and posters. Several of these Qīng Dynasty–style shops sell rubbings made from the priceless stone tablets collected in the city's Forest of Stelae nearby, worth picking up later here or outside the Shǎnxī Provincial Museum if you spot a tablet you like.

The cobblestoned street wanders along the wall for half a mile east to the entrance of the **Shǎnxi Provincial Museum,** Wényì Běi Lù 18 (daily 8:30am–5:30pm; admission ¥30/$3.70). It is located on the spacious garden grounds of the **Temple of Confucius,** built in A.D. 1374. A number of classical pavilions dot the garden pathways to the heart of the exhibit at the back, the **Hall of the Forest of Stelae (Bēi Lín).** This is my favorite Chinese museum. It has not changed since it became the repository of China's engraved stone in 1952, and its collections reach deep into the world's oldest continuous civilization.

The dullest hall of stone tablets is the first. This large grove consists of a complete edition of the Confucian Classics transcribed on 114 stone slabs, front and back, in the year A.D. 837, becoming the centerpiece of the Forest of Stelae collection established in A.D. 1090 under the Sòng Dynasty. The oldest such surviving transcription, the stone classics constitute the literal bedrock of Chinese ethics and social philosophy.

Other carved tablets in the remaining halls are probably more interesting today. There are pictorial stones of Old China, poems written with characters resembling leaves on a bamboo stem, ancient maps, and the

Nestorian Stele (on the left, in Building 2), carved in A.D. 781 to record the arrival of Christianity in China in A.D. 635. Nestorian Christianity, which traveled over the Silk Road from Persia, found roots in the Táng Dynasty capital and flourished for 2 centuries in Xĩ'ān before its complete eradication. The Nestorian Stele typifies the dimensions of many of these tablets: 3m (9 ft.) tall, 1m (3 ft.) wide, .30m (1 ft.) thick—solid limestone weighing in at 2 tons, anchored upright by a turtle-shaped base.

In 1984, I saw several workers making ink rubbings directly from these 1,000 stones, some of them more than 2,000 years old. Each rubbing blackens the stone and takes its toll. A Chinese scholar whom I met on my most recent visit was appalled to see them still making such rubbings. Metallic models of all the stelae have been cast for the creation of commercial rubbings, but as this scholar said, "Money talks," and there are many who will pay for a real rubbing. What I noticed, however, is the damage inflicted by more than ink, cloth, and mallet: Almost all these stones have been broken in half or defaced by vandals, possibly by organized vandals at work as recently as the Red Guard movement. I know from talking to many monks who returned to the remains of the temples in Xĩ'ān after 1976 that the destruction of religious and historical pieces was carried out on an unimaginable scale, and much of the damage will never be undone.

Within the halls, along both sides of the museum grounds, are a number of China's greatest treasures that do survive, few of them protected now from the viewer's touch: unparalleled bronzes and jades from the Zhōu Dynasty (1100–212 B.C.), the world's first seismograph (looking rather like a punch-bowl set) from the Hàn Dynasty, tricolored horses and scraps of silk from the days of the Táng, and massive stone animals fashioned 20 centuries ago. I come back to this place often: It defines what a Chinese museum should be—quiet, old, courteous, Confucian, and infinitely rich within.

Bell Tower & Drum Tower

In the center of Xĩ'ān, visible everywhere from the surrounding walls, are the city's two Míng Dynasty treasures. Bell and drum towers were at one time as much an ordinary fixture of city life in China as city walls. The bell tower housed a massive bronze bell; the drum tower, a massive drum. Every city and town had these towers, but none are now as famous or grand as those at Xĩ'ān.

The two towers are open daily from 9am to 5pm. Both are gorgeous from outside, superb imperial monuments worth viewing and preserving in an increasingly modern city. The Bell Tower is a beacon to all travelers wandering the downtown streets, while the Drum Tower has become the gateway to Xĩ'ān's old Muslim quarter and its historic mosque.

The **Bell Tower (Zhōng Lóu)** is older (1384) and larger than the Drum Tower. It stands, now, in the central traffic circle of the inner city; until 1582, it stood 2 blocks west at the center of the old Táng Dynasty capital, near where the Drum Tower is now. The Bell Tower is a stately edifice, its three tiers of green-glazed roof tiles soaring on eaves flaked in gold. Engulfed in Xī'ān's most congested traffic center, the Bell Tower long ago clanged its last wake-up ding-dong in downtown Xī'ān. The wooden interior feels centuries old, but once inside there's not much to see for the ¥15 ($1.90) admission beyond sets of chimes and, from the balcony, the city traffic and latest construction sites. The Bell Tower's great bell has disappeared, as has the Drum Tower's great drum; reproductions have taken their stations.

The Bell Tower and Drum Tower are tied together now by a sparkling new ultramodern city square, called **Huà Jué Xiàng,** looking like some minimalistic expression of public art transported from the West: a wide, flat, open courtyard with benches and Plexiglas lanterns where smoking is not permitted (perhaps a first in outdoor urban China). Along the north side of Xī'ān's city square are three tiers of a new shopping arcade built in the neo-traditional Chinese style, with bricks and roof tiles. At the west end, on the north side of Xī Dàjiē (Big West St.), stands the venerable Drum Tower, built in 1370.

The **Drum Tower (Gǔ Lóu)** also requires a ¥15 ($1.90) admission fee, and there is probably even less reason to go in it than there is to go into the Bell Tower. The entrance is a stairway on the northwest corner. The upper floor contains Qīng Dynasty furniture and a drum collection. The original drum is gone, though, and the Drum Tower no longer beats out the end of the day for Xī'ān's residents.

The New Museum

Xī'ān's new museum, the **Shǎnxī History Museum (Shǎnxī Lìshǐ Bówùguǎn)** is a state-of-the-art facility on a par with the most modern museums of Běijīng and Shànghǎi. Located 3km (2 miles) south of the city wall at Xiǎozhài Dōng Lù 91 (© **029/525-4727**), it makes an excellent complement to the old Provincial Museum and Forest of Stelae inside the wall. It's open daily from 9am to 5:30pm; admission is ¥35 ($4.40). Signs are in English and Chinese, and the lighting is good for a change. More importantly, the historical artifacts are among the best in the Chinese world.

The major exhibit is on the first floor at the rear: 39 Táng Dynasty (A.D. 618–907) frescoes removed from the walls of underground tombs. These murals provide lifelike snapshots of China's golden past, when traders from the West called upon a capital of camel caravans, hunting dogs, and polo tournaments. These scenes of court musicians, dancers, and eunuchs are rendered in pale oranges, reds, and blues, bringing a distant imperial age to life. Although the museum contains an enormous collection of gold, stone, paper, cloth, and jade relics from all the dynasties, the remains of the Táng naturally stand out here. Xī'ān was the capital of China when the Silk Road routes to the West were at their richest under 18 successive Táng rulers, and the museum is stuffed with silks, tricolored ceramics, and ladies' fashions of the time.

Upstairs, the Qín Dynasty (770–206 B.C.) contributes five of its famous terra-cotta soldiers. While there are thousands of these clay warriors at the vaults of the Qín Emperor's terra-cotta army (see the following chapter), less than 32km (20 miles) away, at this museum you can take a close-up, unhurried look. Separated by an inch of glass, you can make out the bows on a soldier's square-toed shoes. And you can appreciate the art that went into these figures of royal death. The emperor's men look like flesh and blood buried alive inside skins of clay. Two of their steeds are also on display, neither of them protected by glass.

Pagodas

Xī'ān's most monumental relics of the Táng Dynasty are its two pagodas south of the city wall. The **Small Wild Goose Pagoda (Xiǎo Yàn Tǎ)** is the smaller and younger of the sisters but also the prettier. It's missing its upper two stories, and its jagged top looks like an earthquake rattled it. In fact, at least one big one did, reducing the Small Wild Goose Pagoda to a 13-story, gracefully tapered blue-brick tower. What's more, it's said that in 1487, an earth tremor split the pagoda in half, head to toe, but in 1556, a second jolt zipped it back together.

Few Táng Dynasty relics remain in the halls of **Commending Happiness Temple (Jiànfú Sì),** surrounding the pagoda, but the pagoda's dark, winding stairs are worth climbing for the view. The temple, its gardens and courtyards, and the old pagoda were built by order of the Táng Emperor—the temple in A.D. 684 and the pagoda in A.D. 707—as a safe place to store sutras (holy Buddhist manuscripts). At that time there was need for such storage. Increasingly, monks were setting out from Xī'ān and walking west to India, returning after many years with Buddhist texts from the source. The monk Yì Jìng was the first to make the journey to India by sea. He left in A.D. 671, returning 24 years later (after some time in Sumatra) with 400 holy works. He translated these sutras up until his death in A.D. 713 at the new Small Wild Goose Pagoda. The Small Wild Goose Pagoda is open daily from 8am to 6pm; admission is ¥10 ($1.25), and an extra ¥10 to climb the pagoda.

The **Big Wild Goose Pagoda (Dàyàntǎ),** 3km (2 miles) farther south of the city wall, is Xī'ān's most famous Táng Dynasty landmark. This seven-story tower, strong and squarish, with large windows from which devotees toss coins for luck, was erected in A.D. 652, again as a fireproof storage silo for Buddhist sutras. It was the first Chinese pagoda I ever saw and the first I studied at length.

This pagoda was built at the behest of China's most famous Buddhist monk, Xuán Zàng, who returned to Xī'ān in A.D. 652 after 15 years of wandering across the Gobi Desert over the Silk Road to India and Pakistan. Xuán Zàng returned with the requisite sutras, carrying all of them in his enormous backpack. His way was lighted by oil lamps affixed to his pack frame. The Forest of Stelae contains a famous pictorial stone tablet of this monk on the road, my favorite rubbing. Xuán Zàng's journey to the West required 22 years, and the monk's exploits were transcribed into China's most popular epic, usually translated as *The Monkey* or *Journey to the West.* There, Xuán Zàng appears as a clever, heroic, mystically empowered monkey who undergoes a series of fantastic adventures on the distant road.

When Xuán Zàng returned with his 1,500 manuscripts, he set up a bureau at the Great Goodwill Temple (Dàcí'ēn) in the southern precincts to translate them from Sanskrit. The Big Wild Goose Pagoda—its name, I suspect, taken from the geese that once landed on its massive eaves—was built on the temple grounds. The whole complex was immense in those days, with 1,000 rooms and 300 monks. Something of a revival has recently happened. The courtyards have been restored, all the surviving halls cleaned up, and the Big Wild Goose Pagoda is doing big box-office business, second only to the vaults of the terra-cotta warriors. There are vendors galore, a silk carpet factory, a new temple built by local farmers, and, oddly enough (but not so unusual for China), a shooting range with machine guns for hire just south of the pagoda entrance.

As for the Big Wild Goose Pagoda, it still manages to look magnificent, perhaps because it can stretch a full, broad, powerful seven stories (60m/200 ft.) above the tourist frenzy at its feet. One hundred monks service the grounds, along with hundreds of ticket takers, vendors, tour guides, and hustlers. The temple grounds are open daily from 8am to 5:40pm, with an entrance fee of ¥21 ($2.60). The pagoda itself requires another ticket (¥25/$3) just for the privilege of climbing. Both expenses are worth it.

The Big Wild Goose Pagoda was the highest building in central China for over 1,200 years. What's remarkable about ascending the building today is not just that emperors from the Táng Dynasty stood at the same brick portals admiring the view, but that the scale of the ancient capital is revealed by the view from the top. This pagoda and its temples were once a mile inside the walls of the old city, not 5km (3 miles) outside of it. For a thousand years, from the fall of Rome to the Renaissance, this was the greatest city in the East, but it was as remote from the West as Atlantis, and as unreal. The golden age of the Táng Dynasty elevated the city to poetic heights—Xī'ān was seven times larger then, the supreme metropolis of the medieval world.

The Great Mosque (Dà Qīngzhēn Sì) & The Muslim Quarter

The **Great Mosque** of Xī'ān dates back to A.D. 742, barely a century after the founding of Islam. Although it is often claimed that this is the largest and the oldest mosque in China, I'm skeptical about both claims. What I can say is that this is the most active and serene mosque in China. It used to be even more peaceful and idyllic. Over the last 10 years, however, it has been renovated extensively (without disturbing its architectural beauties) and added to virtually every guided tour itinerary. The result is that the narrow alleyway connecting the Great Mosque to Běi Yuàn Mén Lù and the Drum Tower has become clogged with vendors (though they do sell some great walking canes).

The Great Mosque is easy to find. Pass under the Drum Tower and walk north a few blocks. Turn left at the sign to the mosque. Follow the alley (Huàjué Xiàng) of vendors and shophouses as it curves to the right, and look for the entrance on the left. It's open from 8am to 5pm daily; admission is ¥12 ($1.50).

Although the Great Mosque was founded in the Táng Dynasty, its present design is Míng, dating from the same period as the present city wall. In the 1990s, most of the timbers were replaced, fitted, and recarved to mimic exactly the Míng Dynasty model. Some carving and tiling are still going on. The grounds are long and spacious, giving the sense more of a garden than of a temple. Laid out east to west in the Islamic tradition (Chinese temples face south), the four courtyards lead deeper and farther inward to the main prayer hall at the end. Among the treasures of the Great Mosque is a map of the world with a black cube at its center—an Islamic map of the world. Displaced, China lies outside, beyond the western frontier.

In the first courtyard is a 360-year-old carved wooden archway. Side halls off the arch display Míng and Qīng dynasty furniture. The second courtyard contains the wide Five-Room Hall, and through it, carved stone fences and gates, also created during the Míng Dynasty. In the third courtyard is the mosque's most famous and beautiful structure, the triple-eaved

Introspection Tower, the minaret from which Muslims are called to prayer. On either side are halls containing a Míng Dynasty copy of the Koran and a Qīng Dynasty map of Mecca. The One God Pavilion, also called the Phoenix Pavilion, is the final passage to the prayer hall.

The prayer hall is eight bays wide, with a glazed blue tile roof supported by large brackets in the Chinese style. There are stone stairs up to the entrance. Inside, the ceiling is carved in flowery Arabic letters, recounting the scriptures. Pages of the Koran are carved into wooden tablets, half of them in Chinese, half in Arabic. The mihrab (prayer niche) faces Mecca. The floor is covered with prayer rugs. A thousand worshippers can fit inside for a single service. Visitors, after removing your shoes, are often permitted to enter the prayer hall, although when I visited most recently, entrance was barred to non-Muslims.

This is an exceptionally active mosque, as the Muslim quarter of Xī'ān has at least 100,000 resident believers and an Islamic presence that goes back at least 1,200 years. The Muslims who came from the West, even though they put down roots, married, and assimilated, became known as a minority people, the Huí. The Huí of Xī'ān live largely in their own quarter, wear white turbans, and practice circumcision. They reject usury, divination, theater, and pork. They maintain their own schools, slaughterhouses, cemeteries, and mosques (at least a dozen in Xī'ān). Their neighborhoods are now the oldest and their streets the narrowest and most fragrant with cooking in Xī'ān. Their houses are low and conjoined. Some still have packed earth floors and sidewalk water pumps. Vendors tend coal-heated pots in the street, selling lamb on skewers, fried breads, and fresh yogurt—the best yogurt I've ever eaten.

One reason I like to come here is to watch the Muslim Chinese go about their business in the mosque. The other reason is the tranquility. Xī'ān, like all Chinese cities, is constantly making noise. But in this quarter, there is almost a silence. The courtyards are like carved wooden screens. Dozens of Huí men shift quietly from station to station toward the prayer hall, bathed and barefooted, their heads covered in thin white turbans, prostrating themselves before Allah, facing Mecca in prayer.

Temples

During its zenith under the Táng Dynasty, Xī'ān was the home of China's leading Buddhist temples and Daoist shrines. In the 1980s, I explored a number of these sacred sites inside and outside the city walls. Many were just putting themselves back together after coming under destructive attacks during the Red Guard campaigns of the Cultural Revolution (1966–76). Some were destroyed so completely they never reopened.

Today at Xī'ān there is a **Lama Temple (Guǎngrén Sì)** with a library of sutras in the northwest corner of the city, founded in 1705; the Daoist **Eastern Mountain Temple (Dōngyuè Miào)** to the mountain god of Tài Shān near the eastern gate, founded in 1116; the Buddhist **Reclining Dragon Zen Temple (Wòlóng Sì)** where the Chán (Zen) sect was said to have been founded in China in A.D. 520, located just inside the southern city wall; and several other temples with long histories and a recent return to worship.

The temple that has fared the best in this era of reconstruction, however, is the ancient **Daoist Temple of the Eight Immortals (Bāxiān Guān).** Located a mile east of the city wall from Zhōngshān Gate (in a poor, crowded, working-class lane on Dōngxīn Jiē), Bāxiān Guān is the city's most active Daoist sanctuary. Admission is ¥3 (35¢). Scores of monks and nuns in dark robes, heads shaven, circulate through the small restored temples and courtyards, where there are four sites designated for burning incense and several stone tablets engraved with diagrams of a multilayered divine yǐn-and-yáng cosmos. The chief statue is a large image of a many-armed deity remarkably similar to the Buddhist Guānyǐn (Goddess of Mercy) reaching out to comfort her petitioners.

On the steps to the main worship hall, I noticed a young woman alone on her knees. She had spread out a piece of paper and placed a set of keys, a hank of hair, and a small bone upon it. When I asked her the purpose of this, she told me that she was praying for the recovery of her ill father.

The best time to come to the Temple of the Eight Immortals is on the 1st and 15th days of each lunar month, at dusk, when a popular festival is held. I first attended a full moon rite here in 1984, when the halls were in ruins. It was a noisy affair. Worshippers were sending burnt offerings to their ancestors, and one monk stood at the top of the stairs casting down firecrackers to chase away the demons. The rite had no order I could discern. There was singing, the clanging of wooden sticks, the shouting of prayers, and the chanting of rosaries. It was the din of divine chaos, Daoism as it has been in China for more than 20 centuries.

This was the largest Daoist monastery in Xī'ān for a thousand years. New apartments and a machine factory have reduced it to a few blocks of recently restored temples. Across the street, a few other surviving halls have been converted to the city's most interesting flea market, where you can rummage through an odd assortment of old coins, chipped ceramics, and the personal possessions of local families. On Wednesday and Sunday mornings, this temple market expands into a twice-weekly antiques market, selling Cultural Revolution posters, Qīng Dynasty ceramics, snuff bottles, and opium pipes.

Churches

Christianity was first established in China in A.D. 652, according to the stone tablet in Xǐ'ān's Forest of Stelae. The Nestorian version, which traveled out of Persia to the gates of Xǐ'ān in the 7th century, was not quite that of Rome, but the Chinese emperor was satisfied as to the correctness of the "Luminous Religion" (Dà Qín) and encouraged its spread. But in A.D. 845, the edict was reversed, "foreign religions" were banned, and Christianity did not reappear in China until Western missionaries started to arrive almost 700 years later. More recently, Christianity in China suffered persecution throughout the Cultural Revolution. Almost all churches were closed, but in the 1980s, they began, like the temples and mosques, to reopen their doors.

As is common in Chinese cities, Xǐ'ān has two official "patriotic" Christian churches—one Protestant, one Catholic. Foreigners are welcome to attend Sunday services, though they're not publicized.

The **Protestant church (Jīdū Jiàotáng),** which reopened in 1980, is located north off the main shopping street, Dōng Dàjiē. Go 1 block north up Nánxīn Jiē (the Friendship Store is on the right) and turn left on the first lane. The church is on the north side of the lane, tucked within an unmarked gate, smothered by walls and offices. What is visible from the street is the church's curious tower, part traditional Chinese, part northern European. On Sunday mornings, the worshippers overflow the gate yard, pushing back into the street. If they see you, they'll probably let you through.

The services I've attended at the Protestant church have been ordinary enough. The chapel is unadorned, save for a few scrolls and a gold foil crucifix. A trio of ministers addresses the congregation.

A 30-member robed choir leads the singing of hymns, whose melodies may sound familiar to a Western ear. Collection plates are passed. The Lord's Prayer is recited. On your way out, you'll probably be stopped by curious churchgoers, as I have been. Once I was stopped by two old sisters dressed in black, strolling hand in hand. They remembered the Englishmen who had run the church before Liberation (1949). One sister, scrutinizing me matter-of-factly, wondered at last if we were finally coming back.

Xǐ'ān's **Catholic church (Tiānzhǔ Jiàotáng)** is harder to find. Walk due west on Xī Dàjiē from the Bell Tower, past the Drum Tower, on for almost 3km (2 miles) to Hóngguāng Jiē on your left. Turn south and walk 2 long blocks past Yándiàn Jiē, then turn left on Wǔxīng Jiē. The cathedral is tucked back on your left as you turn east. Again, if you go here on Sunday morning, you can follow the crowds. Christianity is quite popular in

Chinese cities these days, among the young as well as the old. After it was closed down in 1966, the Xī'ān cathedral was swallowed up by a candy factory in 1973, which was still running when I first visited in 1984. The priest in those days told me that the cathedral was built about 100 years ago by an Italian mission. The style is Romanesque, the material white marble. Inside, there's room for only a few dozen rows of wooden pews. The stained glass is long gone, as is the original furniture, but there are surviving paintings of the stations of the cross hung in gold frames and of St. Francis, a skull at his feet.

The mass is still said in Latin, the confession conducted without benefit of curtain or door. It is Catholicism much as it came to China a century ago, its rituals, its very language, almost forgotten in the West.

Bànpō

Xī'ān also has an entire chapter from an era of Chinese history that's missing at tourist stops elsewhere: the Stone Age. The **Bànpō Museum (Bànpō Bówùguǎn),** 8km (5 miles) east of the city, isn't exactly a must-see. It's a strange, ugly exhibit, hardly electrifying—yet oddly unforgettable. It's open daily from 9am to 5:40pm; admission is ¥20 ($2.40).

In 1953, a village of what became known as the Yǎngsháo culture (4500–3700 B.C.) was excavated on the bank of the Chǎn River. Much of it is preserved under a large auditorium roof. Inside, visitors snake around the edges of the excavation, peering over the rails at the remains of 46 huts (half underground), fire pits, storage cellars, pottery kilns, and 174 gravesites. The ground has been left here in the middle of the auditorium as it was found.

These ancestors of the Chinese not only fashioned stone weapons, but also created striking pottery painted with sharp geometric shapes and the forms of fish and deer (both pottery and tools are on display in the museum). This artwork has a primitive power as potent as that produced by the early dynasties.

The Yǎngsháo society is believed to have been matrilineal. The skeletons and graves are most haunting. Half a dozen of the skeletons can be seen in a corner of the museum under dusty glass in cement cribs. You can almost make out faces on the skulls. Adults were usually buried alone. Children were buried in jars, 73 of them found on this site. At one excavation near the exit, there are eight burial jars standing next to the foundation of a hut. The pattern of the fish on Stone Age pottery, the funeral urns for children, and the gray of this compressed dust—the gray of brain matter, the color of soil after it has utterly died—can stay with you for years. At the very least, Bànpō taught me how old the human race really is, and how strange and resilient it can be.

A **Stone Age Theme Park** has opened next door to Bànpō, and I haven't found one person who likes it. Even the local tour guides vote thumbs down on this fiberglass village with displays and dancers straight out of a Chinese *Flintstones*.

WHAT TO READ

Digging to China: Down and Out in the Middle Kingdom (Soho Books, 1991, 1994), my own account of living and working in Xī'ān, gives a detailed picture of the ancient capital in 1984 and a means to measure how much the city and China have changed since.

PRACTICAL INFORMATION

by Graeme Smith

ORIENTATION & WHEN TO GO

Xī'ān is 886km (550 miles) west of Běijīng in the north-central province of Shǎnxī. Xī'ān's weather is best in autumn, when it's not as hot and humid as in summer, as cold as in winter, or as dusty as in spring. Xī'ān's most important site is the Museum of Emperor Qín's Terra-Cotta Warriors (see the next chapter). This ranks as China's most important archaeological discovery of the 20th century; nearly all visitors to Xī'ān book a half-day tour to see it.

Xī'ān is 2 hours west of the most beautiful of China's Five Sacred Mountains, Huá Shān (see separate chapter). Recent improvements in transportation to the mountain and the opening of a cable car mean that Huá Shān can be seen as a long day trip from Xī'ān. The city, situated at the terminus of an ancient trade route to the West, also serves as the gateway to the Silk Road (see the "Silk Road China" chapter) and the oases of the Gobi Desert.

GETTING THERE

By Plane   The new **airport** (ⓒ 029/870-8450) is 50km (31 miles) to the northwest at the town of Xiányáng. The **CAAC office** is at Láodòng Lù 296 (ⓒ 029/870-2299). They deliver airline tickets to your hotel free of charge. The airport bus (¥25/$3) stops at the CAAC office on the hour from 5am to 5pm. A taxi from the airport office into town costs about ¥80 ($10). The airport is served from Hong Kong daily by **Dragonair,** whose office is located in the Sheraton Hotel lobby (ⓒ 029/426-2988).

The flight takes 2½ hours. Chinese regional airlines connect Xī'ān to most major cities in China, including Běijīng (1½ hr.), Chéngdū (1 hr., 15 min.), Guìlín (2 hr.), Hángzhōu (1½ hr.), Kūnmíng (2 hr., 15 min.), and Shànghǎi (1 hr., 40 min.).

By Train   The railway station is located just outside the northwest side of the city wall, a 20-minute drive from the main hotel area. The double-decker bus no. 603 connects the two. There's no longer a special ticket counter for foreigners, but the station is open 24 hours, and all windows can be used except nos. 15, 16, and 18. Window no. 17 should have an English speaker. Ticket refunds can be obtained from window no. 2. The station can get crowded, so it's best to book tickets either through your hotel or at a branch of the Industrial and Commercial Bank of China (Gōngshāng Yínháng), which levies a ¥5 (60¢) service charge. Hotel travel agencies will charge between ¥40 ($4.80) and ¥80 ($9.60) to book a ticket. The fastest train to Běijīng is the T42 (13½ hr.) at 5:48pm.

Other useful links are the T140 to Shānghǎi (17 hr.) at 6:26pm; the K84 to Guǎngzhōu (27 hr.) at 9:40am; the K165 at 10:18pm which passes through Chéngdū (14 hr.) and terminates in Kūnmíng (35 hr.); the K762 to Zhèngzhōu (7½ hr.) at 11:06am; the T52/53 to Ürümqi (34 hr.) at 11am; and the monstrously slow 2119 to Chóngqìng (28 hr.) at 2:16pm. Luòyáng, site of the Buddhist caves, is 6 hours east by train; and Kāifēng, another ancient capital, is 12 hours east by train.

TOURS & STRATAGEMS

Tours CITS (Cháng'ān Běi Lù 48; ☏ 029/524-1864; fax 029/526-1454; www.citsxa.com) offers the most expensive tours, charging ¥340 ($43)–¥580 ($72), depending on the tour you choose. They have competent branches in the lobby of the Jiěfàng Fàndiàn (☏ 029/742-2227) and on the second floor of the Bell Tower Hotel (☏ 029/727-9200, ext. 2842). A slightly cheaper option is the **Golden Bridge Travel Service** (Tǐyùguǎn Lù 111; ☏ 029/ 781-5596; fax 029/781-1521; gbtour@ pub.xaonline.com), which charges ¥298 ($36) for the Eastern Route and ¥450 ($57) for the Western Route. Major hotels often offer their own tours, which are also safe bets.

City Layout Since the days of the Táng Dynasty, Xī'ān's streets have been laid out on a north–south, east–west grid. Běi Dàjiē, Nán Dàjiē, Dōng Dàjiē, and Xī Dàjiē—Big North Street, Big South Street, Big East Street, and Big West Street—all converge at the Bell Tower traffic circle in the heart of the city. The walled city is 3km (2 miles) north to south, 2.4km (1½ miles) east to west. Popular walking areas are the city wall, the Old Town street in front of the Provincial Museum, the Muslim quarter (north of the Drum Tower), and Dōng Dàjiē, the main shopping street. Dōng Dàjiē has recently undergone modernization and now features a covered food mall (Tànshì Jiē), a Western fast-food outlet (Bob and Betty's), an enclosed shopping mall, Western-label boutiques (Playboy and Crocodile), and a modern international department store (Parkson). It's possible to tour the sights inside the city wall, and the city wall itself, on foot on your own. Taxis are easy to hail and cost ¥5 to ¥20 (60¢–$2.50) per trip.

WHERE TO STAY

Bell Tower Hotel (Zhōnglóu Fàndiàn) Always the best-situated hotel in town, the Bell Tower Hotel recently underwent some much-needed renovations. Service is competent, but there's an air of state-run indifference that no renovation can fix. There are branches of both CITS and Golden Bridge Travel here.

Nán Dàjiē 110 (southwest corner of Bell Tower; bus no. 603 from the station). © **029/727-9200.** *Fax 029/727-1217. www.belltowerhtl.com. 320 units. ¥748 ($93) twin/double; from ¥1,190 ($149) suite. 10% service charge. AE, DC, MC, V.* **Amenities:** 2 restaurants (Cantonese and Western), cafe; health club; game room; concierge; tour desk; business center; shopping arcade; forex (24 hr.); 24-hr. room service; next-day laundry/dry cleaning. *In room:* A/C, TV, minibar, fridge, hair dryer.

Hyatt Regency Xi'ān (Kǎiyuè Fàndiàn) The Hyatt is the best-situated of the luxury hotels in Xi'ān. The rooms are a little small and, as it opened in 1990, some of the facilities are showing signs of wear. An atrium with flowing streams, dense foliage, and singing birds forms the core of the hotel, and sipping a coffee here is the best way to recover from the heat and the smog. It was Bill Clinton's choice when he was in town and, should your finances allow it, it's the best five-star option.

Dōng Dàjiē 156 (bus no. 611 from the station to Dàchāshì; continue south for 50m/165 ft. and cross over to the southeast side of the street). © **029/723-1234.** *Fax 029/721-6799. www.hyatt.com. 404 units. ¥1,320 ($165) twin; from ¥2,320 ($290) suite. 15% service charge. AE, DC, MC, V.* **Amenities:** 2 restaurants (Cantonese and Western); cafe; bar; tennis courts; health club & spa; bike rental; concierge; airport shuttle; 24-hr. business center; salon; 24-hr. room service; in-room massage; same-day dry cleaning/laundry; executive-level rooms. *In room:* A/C, TV, broadband Internet (¥30/$3.70 per day), minibar, fridge, iron, safe.

Sheraton Xi'ān (Xǐláidēng Dàjiǔdiàn) Located over a mile west of the city wall, the Sheraton has improved

remarkably in recent years. Despite the absence of a formal staff training program, service is the best in Xi'ān. Renovations are ongoing, and the Gate West Restaurant offers fine Western fare. Locals are gradually developing a taste for these luxuries, although they have been spotted adding sugar to fine French red. Rooms are modern and exceptionally well appointed. After a day braving the grimy air of Xi'ān, you can seek refuge in the many toiletries found in the immaculate bathrooms. It's also ideal for families.

Fēnghào Dōng Lù 262 (bus no. 611 from the station and west of the Bell Tower to Fēnghào Dōng Lù). © **029/426-1888.** *Fax 029/426-2188. www.sheraton.com/xian. 438 units. ¥1,370–¥1,743 ($165–$210) twin/double; suites from ¥2,615 ($315) and way up. 15% service charge. AE, DC, MC, V.* **Amenities:** 3 restaurants (Cantonese, Fusion, Shǎnxī), cafe; bar; large indoor swimming pool; health club; spa; game room; concierge; tour desk; airport shuttle; 24-hr. business center; forex (24 hr.); salon; 24-hr. room service; in-room massage; same-day laundry/dry cleaning; executive-level rooms. *In room:* A/C, satellite TV, broadband Internet (¥30/$3.70 per day), minibar, fridge, hair dryer, iron, safe.

Xi'ān Shūyuàn Youth Hostel (Xi'ān Shūyuàn Qīngnián Lǚshè) Long pilloried in the West for their poor locations and nonexistent service, youth hostels are taking over the budget accommodation niche in China. Completed in October 2001, this is the best budget option in town. A magnificent restored three-courtyard residence, it formerly housed the Xiányáng County government. Chinese visitors wonder why foreigners put up with rooms that have concrete and tiled floors and hot water that only runs from 6pm to 12:30am (although you can ask for hot water outside these hours). What you get is a friendly English-speaking staff, an excellent location, impartial information, and ambience. Attention to detail is evident—wooden lanterns, goldfish in huge Míng-replica vases, songbirds in large cages, and mirrors to enhance the fēngshuǐ.

Nán Dàjiē Xǐ Shùn Chéng Xiàng 2A (27m/90 ft. west of the South Gate, just inside the city wall; double-decker bus no. 603 from the railway station to Nán Mén). © **029/728-7720.** *Fax 029/ 728- 7238. 45 units (shower only). ¥160 ($20) double; from ¥20 ($2.50) dorm room. Discounts for YHA members. AE, DC, MC, V.* **Amenities:** *Cafe; bike rental; concierge; tour desk; railway station courtesy car; laundry and kitchen facilities; Internet access. In room: A/C, TV, no phone.*

WHERE TO DINE

Budget choices with English menus include **Bob and Betty's,** Dōng Dàjiē 285, with *jiǎozi* (dumplings) and pizza. **KFC** has a large, clean new outlet on Nán Dàjiē, 3 blocks north of the city wall's south gate. Along Huà Jué Xiàng Square between the Bell and Drum towers are a number of Chinese cafes with English menus; a **Delifrance** which serves good sandwiches and coffee; and an American family-restaurant chain, **Kenny Rogers Roasters.**

Highfly Pizza WESTERN This is the best choice for reasonably priced Western food like real oven-baked penne, tuna sandwiches, chocolate brownies, and even a Texas stew. The pizzas are superb, particularly the four-cheese and pepperoni. Some of the dishes, such as the black pepper spaghetti with beef, are bizarre, but the Swiss breakfast is excellent. There are many vegetarian options, the kitchen is spotless, and the entire restaurant is nonsmoking. It's next to the restaurant of the disastrous Victory Hotel, whose white columns are hard to miss. *Hépíng Mén Wài Shènglì Fàndiàn (bus no. 5 from the station or bus no. 601 from just north of the Bell Tower to Hépíng Mén).* © **029/785-5333.** *AE, DC, MC, V. ¥60–¥100 ($7.50–$12) for a 2-person meal. Daily 9am–11pm.*

Jiǎsān Guàntāng Bāozi MUSLIM It's still the most famous of the Jiǎ Brothers' restaurants; you'll know you're there when you see the monstrous blue arch over the entrance and a wall festooned with photographs of Xī'ān notables— mostly TV hosts, writers, and musicians. One of the better breakfast options, the specialty dish is *Guàntāng Bāozi,* with a choice of beef, lamb, or "three flavors" (lamb, mushroom, and prawn). The filling is cooked with the soup inside, so it's a good idea to let it cool before testing your chopstick skills. This dish is best washed down with *bābǎo tián xǐfàn,* a sweet rice porridge filled with peanuts, sultanas, hawthorn, and medlar berries. *Běi Yuànmén 93 (150m/ 492 ft. north of Drum Tower, on the east side).* © **029/725-7507.** *¥20 ($2.50) for a 2-person meal. No credit cards. Daily 7:30am–midnight.*

Lǎo Sūn Jiā SHĂNXĪ The original restaurant opened in 1898, and this is still the best place to sample Xī'ān's most celebrated dish, *yángròu pàomó.* There are now three branches of this restaurant, two of them on Dōng Dàjiē. You are faced with several dining choices, whose prices rise as you climb the stairs. On the first floor, you can dine with the masses; not recommended unless you want to be the main attraction. The second floor is a point-and-choose *xiǎo chī* (snack) restaurant. Recommended dishes include the lamb dumplings *(suān tāng shuǐjiǎo)*; and a local favorite, *fěnzhēng yángròu*, two steamed buns perched delicately to the side of a pile of mince and flour. Ascending to the third floor, you can enjoy Xī'ān's best *yángròu pàomó*. You will find yourself confronted with an empty bowl and two steamed buns, as well as plates of chili, coriander, and cloves of garlic that have been marinated in vinegar and sugar for several months. Tear the buns into tiny pieces, popping them into the empty bowl. When you've finished, your bowl will be taken away, and topped up with broth and noodles. Stir in the coriander and chili, and when the palate gets too greasy, nibble on a clove of garlic, and encourage your friends to do likewise. If the star dish doesn't fill you up, the stewed oxtail *(hóngshāo niúwěi)* and bok choy with mushrooms *(bǐlǜ zā shuāng gū)* are recommended. *Dōng Guān Zhèngjiē 78 (bus no. 45 from just east of Bell Tower to Dōng Mén, cross the road, walk 27m/90 ft. north, turn right, and walk 45m/150 ft. east).* ✆ **029/ 248-2828.** *Reservations recommended on weekends (2nd floor). ¥60 ($7.50) on 2nd floor, ¥200 ($25) on 3rd floor for a 2-person meal. No credit cards. Daily 11am–9pm.*

Táng Dynasty (Tángyuè Gōng) BANQUET Run by a Hong Kong entrepreneur, this restaurant gives you all your Asian fantasies at once—lavish costumes modeled on the Mògāo cave paintings, a six-course banquet (watch out for the rice wine), hammy acting, and some amazing music and dance. Gāo Míng's performance of the Spring Oriole's Song on a vertical bamboo flute *(pái xiāo)* is almost worth the money itself. If you can get past the slickness and the feeling that it's just for foreigners (the voice-overs are all in English), it makes for a spectacular night out. *Cháng'ān Lù 75 (bus no. 603 from the station or north of the Bell Tower to Cǎo Cháng Pō).* ✆ **029/526-1633.** *www.xiantang dynasty.com. Reservations essential. Dinner and show ¥410 ($51); show and cocktail ¥200 ($25). AE, DC, MC, V. Dinner from 6:30pm; show commences 8:30pm.*

THE FIRST EMPEROR'S
TERRA-COTTA ARMY
兵马俑

ONE OF THE PRIMARY VISITOR DESTI-
nations in China is the tomb and burial site containing the terra-cotta army
of China's First Emperor, Qín Shǐ Huáng (259–210 B.C.). The site lies
29km (18 miles) east of the old imperial city of Xī'ān. The Qín Emperor
spent more years constructing his tomb than he did building the Chinese
capital where he lived and reigned. Capping the tomb is a 38m (125-ft.)
high grassy mound, making it one of the largest tumuli in a region that is
clotted with imperial burial mounds. The mound is the center of a grave
complex the size of a city, its underground walls stretching for miles.

The First Emperor's tomb has not been opened, but a mile to the east,
peasants made an astonishing find while digging for well water in the
drought of 1974: the first of three vaults of life-size terra-cotta soldiers,
horses, and chariots that had stood guard inside the outer wall of the First
Emperor's mausoleum, undisturbed and unremembered for 2,174 years.

The clay army was excavated, painfully reassembled shard by shard, and
opened to public display on National Day, October 10, 1980. As a professor in Xī'ān once remarked to me, only partly in jest, the local people ought
to give Qín Shǐ Huáng the Nobel prize in world tourism. The First
Emperor's terra-cotta armies were a sensation. Hailed as the century's most
important discovery in Chinese archaeology, the buried warriors catapulted
Xī'ān into the forefront of Asian tourism. These excavations rival the Great
Wall as China's most visited sight.

Is the buried army worth such hyperbole and promotion? Yes—even
though increased tourism is doing its best to blunt the full effect and even
though the method of displaying the site has never been satisfactory.
Housed under ugly, massive shed roofs, the vaults must be viewed from distant catwalks, while what you really long for is a close-up look, an intimate
stroll among the infantrymen, archers, generals, and steeds. That's not permitted, unless you're a visiting head of state. Yet the site is still China's
grandest historical spectacle, the field where its first dynasty was buried and
came out of the earth again. Despite the crowds and viewing restrictions,
the site's power and monumental beauty pour through.

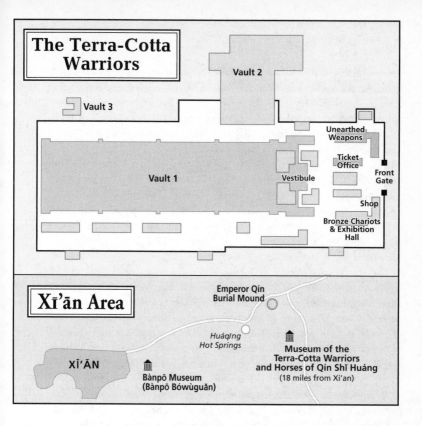

One aspect I've come to appreciate over the years is the workaday manner in which the vaults are displayed. This is still a work in progress. Teams are often gathered in the pits, sifting, cataloging, and assembling more and more figures as tourists file by. The site is expanding. The second and third vaults opened to public view in the 1990s. More excavations will follow. You may not be able to walk up and down the rows where the terra-cotta forces of the First Emperor stand, but you can look over the shoulders of those who have put them back on their feet and opened the vaults after 22 centuries in darkness.

The **Museum of the Terra-Cotta Warriors and Horses of Qín Shǐ Huáng,** as the site is officially designated, has opened three vaults to view. Altogether, they contain about 1,400 items—the soldiers, charioteers, archers, horsemen, and horses of the First Emperor's death guard.

Vault 1

The first vault, the one discovered in 1974, contains 6,000 of the 8,000 horses and soldiers, and this is the place to begin. At first glimpse, this excavated field (61m/203 ft. wide, 227m/755 ft. long) can bewilder. The infantrymen are arranged in columns filling 11 corridors, each furrow 5m (15 ft.) deep. The 38 ranks face east, toward their emperor's tomb. All the soldiers are life-size, standing five-foot-eight to six-foot-one (1.7m–1.8m) in height. All are remarkably lifelike, with individual faces modeled on the faces of actual soldiers in the emperor's army. They carry real weapons—crossbows, spears, swords, and arrowheads steeped in lethal levels of lead. Probably the most astonishing statistic is that just 1,000 of the 6,000 clay soldiers have been reassembled and stationed here.

In this vault lay China's oldest crossbow and its first brick wall. The paint, which has been scorched, eroded, and peeled away from the terracotta figures, once provided a unifying element. The mineral dyes were bright the day they were applied. The gray soldiers we see now were once resplendent—the generals robed in green, the infantry sheathed in black armor—and the ears and nostrils of their horses were painted red as blood, their teeth and hooves white as limestone.

The rear portions of Vault 1 have barely been disturbed, and this is where you'll often get a good view of what the archaeologists are up against: a seemingly hopeless jigsaw puzzle of shattered clay pieces sunken under yet more clay soil, waiting to be put back together. Some workers have been toiling at the pits for more than 20 years. On a typical day, eight people endeavor to solve the puzzle presented by each figure one piece at a time. Fragments can lay in storage for many years before their place is discovered. Computers are beginning to aid in ending this reassembly nightmare.

As impressive as the restored military forces are, I prefer to look into the pits of the unassembled: the disembodied heads, arms, hooves, and raiment still imprisoned by the dust, floating to the surface like the wreckage of an ancient Atlantis.

Vault 2

The second vault, housed in a more pleasing but still gloomy marble hall, opened on October 10, 1994. It displays an excavation in progress as well, but one that has just begun. Few of its pits are opened. It could be decades before before all the pieces are dug up, and reassembly could take longer. A closed-circuit television system was recently installed so that visitors can watch the excavations on monitors.

Vault 2 contains archers, infantrymen, charioteers, and cavalry. Vault 1 is devoted primarily to foot soldiers, while in this vault, the cavalry advances to the fore. One hundred sixteen of the horses are saddled, the earliest evidence in China of such a device. Three hundred fifty-six horses pull 89 war chariots. There are 900 soldiers here, as compared to the 6,000 in Vault 1.

Vault 2 was first detected in 1976 upon the suggestion of a local farmer, test drilled, and covered back up until March 1994, when a formal excavation began. The first step, still under way, was to remove the soil concealing a roof of ancient timbers and mats, and then to remove the roof itself. If you look carefully at the exposed dig, you can see the ancient roof beams used by the original builders. This section of the underground city was built by digging furrows into the ground, paving the floor with bricks, casting the statuary and placing it in precise formation, then covering the furrows with a strong roof that supported a new field of dust, soil, and crops, farmed until the generations forgot what was immediately under their feet.

There is strong evidence that these timbers and ceilings suffered a fire shortly after the death of the First Emperor. Historical accounts indicate that Gen. Xiàng Yǔ looted the royal tomb and torched the underground vaults in 206 B.C. in a failed campaign to succeed to power. (The first emperor of the Hàn Dynasty soon gained the upper hand.)

Several of the figures unearthed in Vault 2 have been put on special display in glass cases on the visitor mezzanine. The kneeling archer is dynamic, the goateed officer is dashing, and the general is commanding, but I prefer the cavalryman and his horse. The stylized steeds of Qín Shǐ Huáng's army, said to be modeled on the desert horses of Gānsù Province, are plump, vivacious, and fluid, just the sort of horse I'd choose for battle—and for beauty.

Vault 3

The third vault is the smallest. It apparently served as the command post. Most of its 68 figures appear to be officers, based on their dress and height. Higher-ranking officers stand taller than those of lower rank. Ordinary soldiers are clad in scaly armor so finely sculpted that the head and stem of each nail are distinct. Generals are clad in war robes, double-tailed caps, and massive square shoes turned up at the toes, like soaring tiled roofs. Their magnificent wooden chariot and its four horses wait in attendance. The figures appear to be in consultation, devising strategies of war, an art that the First Emperor pursued brilliantly and single-mindedly, as he swiftly and often ruthlessly brought all the warlords and kingdoms of China under his rule and molded them into a single Middle Kingdom.

Bronze Chariots

A new two-story **Exhibition Hall** (located to the left of Vault 1 in the entrance courtyard) displays the two bronze chariots found just 18m (20 yd.) west of the base of the First Emperor's burial mound in an 8m (25-ft.) deep pit. Half life-sized, pulled by four bronze horses in gold traces, driven by an intricately rendered driver, each two-wheeled chariot is a decorative piece of extraordinary detail and richness. The windows open, the silver latch on the door of the curved bronze compartment turns, and even the driver's fingerprints are etched in.

These are presumed to be models of the royal chariots of the time. The **High Chariot** is the one with the bronze umbrella and short cart. The **Comfortable Chariot** was designed to carry concealed passengers.

The purpose of these models is no longer known—perhaps merely "to keep a drowsy Emperor awake," as the poet Yeats has written.

On the second floor of the Exhibition Hall there are displays of terracotta warriors and steeds (for close-up inspection), weapons, and other artifacts from the pits. In the center of the hall are bells, helmets, and other recent finds, including a large solid bronze tripod weighing in at 2152kg (468 lb.).

Future Digs

The local authorities have always kept their plans for future excavations around Xī'ān carefully under wraps. Few of the burial mounds of Hàn and Táng emperors have been opened for science or tourism, including the most intriguing tumulus of all, the First Emperor's.

Qín Shǐ Huáng's burial mound is a tourist site, but there's nothing to see there except a view of the plain from the top and a closer view of the vendors, antiques dealers, and folk artists who line the trail. What's inside the tomb—if Qín's successors or later generations of grave robbers haven't already gotten to it—is an ancient city of treasures. China's Grand Historian, Sīmǎ Qiān, the Herodotus of the Middle Kingdom, left a vivid account of what the First Emperor took with him and what his city of endless night looked like. Qín reached the throne at age 13. His buried city consumed the days of 700,000 conscripted laborers over the next 36 years. In life, Qín presided over the unification of China. He regulated the currency, the weights and measures, the span of cart axles, and the writing of the language in his new empire. Qín is also remembered for his pitiless persecution of intellectuals and his burning of ancient books. He is credited with completing the Great Wall. But his greatest surviving artifact is his own tomb and the underground armies that guard it.

The Grand Historian gives this account of the First Emperor's tomb:

> The workers dug through three subterranean streams and poured molten copper for the outer coffin, and the tomb was filled with models of palaces, pavilions, and offices, as well as fine vessels, precious stones, and rarities. Artisans were ordered to fix up crossbows so that any thief breaking in would be shot. The country's rivers, the Yangtze and the Yellow River, were reproduced in quicksilver, and by mechanical means made to flow into a miniature ocean. The heavenly constellations were shown above and the regions of the Earth below. The candles were made of whale oil to ensure their burning for the longest time.

We are also told that the emperor's childless concubines and those who worked on the tomb were buried alive. The mausoleum was planted in trees and grass "to make it seem like a hill," as the burial mound does to this day. There is no mention of the buried city walls, of underground palaces, of a vast terra-cotta army standing a mile to the west.

Yet there are tantalizing hints, thanks to recent digs in the area, of what lies buried between the terra-cotta army and the tomb of the old emperor. We know that the burial mound occupies half the area of Qín's underground inner city. Remains of a palace have been detected within the walls of the inner city. An outer city with its own much longer wall, perhaps 5km (3 miles) around, encompasses the royal mausoleum. Its contents are largely unknown, although the skeletons of horses and the two priceless bronze chariots were found in these precincts. Outside these walls, more skeletons of horses have been found, indicating that it may be the site of the royal stables, and seven human skeletons have turned up as well, which some think are those of the Qín Emperor's own children murdered in a palace intrigue. Ruins of a zoo containing exotic animals and the gravesites of prisoners forced to build the mausoleum have also turned up.

The most recent digs have been centered a few hundred yards east of the Qín Emperor's tomb, where since 1998 some 80 gray suits of armor (made of stone flakes strung together with copper wires) and 30 helmets have been recovered. These are the earliest specimens of stone armor ever found in China. The stone-armor pit is also the largest pit ever opened in the area, and in one chamber a strange discovery was made: life-size terra-cotta figures described by officials as "odd," thought to be Qín Dynasty acrobats.

You can envision the day when the entire buried city of China's first imperial dynasty is revealed, although if mass tourism trends continue, Qín's dead capital could become nothing more than an instant theme park. For me, it has always been a dream city. In dreams, I can strip back all the layers of dust and undress the plains of Xī'ān; I can stroll among the palaces of jade, the streets of blue brick, the garden walls of stamped brick; and I can tarry in the corridors with a motionless army of kneeling archers, wooden chariots, and vigorous horses, their heads straining, necks glistening, manes forever flying over the grasslands beyond the Great Wall.

PRACTICAL INFORMATION

by Graeme Smith

ORIENTATION & WHEN TO GO

The Museum of the Terra-Cotta Warriors and Horses of Emperor Qín Shǐ Huáng (usually called "the Terra-Cotta Warriors," for short) is located 29km (18 miles) east of Xī'ān. The three vaults under excavation cover about 2 hectares (5 acres) and contain 8,000 warriors and horses, as well as 6,000 more artifacts (chariots, bridles, weapons, musical instruments).

There are shops inside all the vault buildings and on the grounds inside the main gate. Outside the gate, where the buses park, a souvenir city flourishes, with everything from postcards to folk-art vests and baby slippers for sale. The stalls now seem calm and well regulated compared to the chaos that used to reign here, though it's still easy to be accosted by a slew of vendors. Stepping off the bus from Xī'ān, visitors used to be rushed by a living terra-cotta army of vendors, all shouting "Yí kuài, yí kuài," which means "One yuan, one yuan" (¥1/10¢). Today's chant is more likely to be "One dollar, one dollar," a good indication of how inflation took off in the more prosperous 1990s.

GETTING THERE

By Bus Independent travelers can take bus no. 306 from the Xī'ān bus station, located to the east of the square in front of the railway station at the northern end of Jiěfàng Lù (¥5/65¢). Look for the larger bus and avoid the minibuses, which take an age to set off and often fail to get you to your destination.

TOURS & STRATEGEMS

Most visitors make the Terra-Cotta Warriors their number-one stop when touring Xī'ān (see previous chapter), the focus of a half-day or full-day guided tour by bus or car. Two hours at the museum is usually enough for a first visit.

Admission & Hours The museum is open daily from 8:30am to 6pm, with admission paid at the main gate now set at ¥65 ($8.10). A separate admission is charged for the hall containing the bronze chariot display (¥12/$1.50).

Tours Tours with English-speaking guides can be booked through hotel tour desks and **China International Travel Service (CITS)** branches in Xī'ān (see previous chapter). Hotel tour desks offer their own day tours. Group tours often include other sites as well, particularly **Huáqīng Hotsprings,** located a few miles from the Terra-Cotta Warriors at **Lí Mountain (Lí Shān).** This used to be an interesting stop, but the old imperial bathhouses are totally remodeled, the massive Nine-Dragon Pool is new, and the surrounding pavilions have received a recent face-lift. Huáqīng no longer possesses the atmosphere it once evoked of an ancient summer retreat for Táng emperors and their favorite concubines. It is open daily from 8am to 6pm; admission is ¥40 ($5).

Photography Photographs inside the vault buildings are strictly forbidden. You can buy sets of slides, photographs, and picture books at concession stands inside and outside the vaults. Official photographers offer to take a group photo with the Terra-Cotta Warriors in the background for ¥150 ($19). Large fines are threatened for photography, but locals snap away, occasionally harassed by bored security guards. If you try the same stunt, a more vigorous response is likely.

WHERE TO STAY & DINE

Since the Terra-Cotta Warriors are just a short trip from Xī'ān, see the listings for hotels and restaurants in the previous chapter.

KĀIFĒNG: THE FORGOTTEN CAPITAL

开封

K̄AIFĒNG IS PERHAPS THE LEAST
visited of China's ancient capitals, a walled city south of the Yellow River
that served as capital of the Middle Kingdom during seven dynasties, culminating in a 168-year reign that spanned the magnificent Northern Sòng
Dynasty (A.D. 960–1127). The splendors of Kāifēng under the Sòng
emperors are immortalized in an ancient 4.5km (15-ft.) long painted scroll
called "Qīngmíng Shànghé Tú (Going Up-river for the Qīngmíng
Festival)" now located in the Forbidden City (Palace Museum) collection
in Běijīng. Here we see Kāifēng at its vibrant zenith, with its wide Imperial
Way, arched stone bridges, gleaming temples, lively merchant districts, and
camel caravans entering its gates. Today, although it remains largely forgotten, Kāifēng is reconstructing itself for visitors as the 12th-century Sòng
Dynasty capital it once was.

I had long dreamed of seeing what treasures remained inside Kāifēng's
city walls. One other attraction, an oddity in China, also appealed to me:
Kāifēng had nourished a Jewish community for many centuries, and remnants, even descendants of that congregation, were said to still exist there.

It was not difficult to book an overnight train from Shànghǎi along the
Yellow River to Kāifēng, but once there I could find no tour desk or roaming tout to guide me through the city's highlights. I grabbed a taxi into the
city, settled into a Chinese hotel, procured a map, and set out to explore
Kāifēng on foot. The distances within the crumbling earthen city walls
proved to be reasonably short. In a matter of hours, I was able to circum-
ambulate the entire city as I searched for two vaunted treasure troves: that
of the Sòng Dynasty capital and that of a Jewish presence in China.

Imperial Way

Striking out from the Dōngjīng Hotel near the southwest corner of the
Kāifēng city walls and walking north along Yíngbīn Lù, I quickly came to
Lord Bāo Lake (Bāogōng Hú) and crossed the bridge that bisects it. I was

immediately impressed by the lack of motorized traffic on the wide thoroughfare. I could easily cross the street almost at will, a feat impossible these days in most Chinese cities. Forty minutes later, I was standing before the massive gates to the **Imperial Way,** Kāifēng's recent reconstruction of the Sòng Dynasty's main avenue. Eight centuries ago, the central passage of the Imperial Way was reserved for China's emperors, and to either side were covered arcades where the leading merchants of the kingdom carried on their trades. The sidewalks for the common folk were once lined with narrow canals planted in flowering lotuses. Today, the tile-roofed shops hawk local snacks, river fish, antiques, calligraphy, and souvenirs. It's a charming, rather sleepy shopping district running 3 blocks north to the entrance of **Dragon Pavilion Park (Lóngtíng Gōngyuán),** once the site of Sòng Dynasty palaces and imperial gardens. The spacious pleasure park with a central causeway dividing Yángjiā and Pānjiā lakes survives today (admission ¥25/$3). The park's centerpiece is the remarkable raised Dragon Pavilion constructed atop a tall pyramid base. Dating from 1378, this pavilion was rebuilt during the Kāngxī Emperor's rule (1662–1723). Joining its massive main hall are eight hallways, one of which contains 63 life-sized imperial figures in wax. In the Dragon Pavilion's courtyard, dozens of sedan chairs, lavishly covered in red silks, were in the hire of Chinese tourists reenacting royal marriage processions. The park is a pleasant place to stroll, teeming with local families, many of whom rent rowboats for the afternoon. There are several floating restaurants in the form of large dragon boats on the two lakes, and the shore is lined with fishermen, many half asleep, their bamboo poles carefully wedged between rocks.

Up the River

Returning to the park entrance, I walked west along the lakeshore for about 30 minutes to the **Stelae Forest of the Imperial Academy,** an outdoor collection, recently opened, of 3,500 stelae (carved stone tablets), many of which date from the Sòng Dynasty. The grounds were unfinished and uninviting, however, and the number of stelae on display was disappointingly few.

Kāifēng's newest grand tourist attraction, adjacent to the stele collection, opened in 1998. Called **Qīngmíng Up the River Park (Qīngmíng Shànghé Yuán),** this theme park, designed to re-create the city pictured in the famous 12th-century scroll of Kāifēng, hugs the Huángxià Hé, a tributary of the Yellow River to the north. Its streets, shops, wharves, ships, gardens, teahouses, and pawnshops are supposed to evoke the ancient capital in all its splendor. There is also live entertainment, including fortune-telling, acrobatics, and stilt-walking. This Sòng Dynasty amusement park,

open daily from 8:30am to 6pm, is located at Lóngtíng Xī Lù 5 (© **0378/566-3928**), and requires a ¥30 ($3.75) admission fee (¥40/$5 during holidays and festivals).

Iron Pagoda (Tiě Tǎ)

Having walked the western side of the walled city, I headed northeastward in the afternoon, walking for over an hour before reaching Kāifēng's landmark, the **Iron Pagoda (Tiě Tǎ),** at Jiěfàng Lù 157. The admission fee is ¥20 ($2.50). Erected in 1049, this slender 13-story octagon, 53m (175 ft.) tall, is actually constructed of brick and covered in glazed tiles that give it a dark metallic sheen. A climb to the top of the pagoda requires a separate fee of ¥10 ($1.25). From its top-story portals, I had a wide view of the walled city, which is almost devoid of high-rises and, from afar, appears as a Chinese city yet to be modernized, a decade out of date or more. There were no towering skyscrapers, no Western fast-food pavilions, and no palaces housing five-star hotels or deluxe department stores.

South of the Iron Pagoda, I discovered a section of the Sòng Dynasty earthen wall that I could mount, but there was little left in the way of archers' towers and watch stations. Weary of walking the dusty back streets, I returned via taxi, dreaming of the Sòng Dynasty wonders barely hinted at today.

The Lost Tribe

Kāifēng is a city of many legacies, the most visible ones from the Sòng Dynasty, but its strangest legacy is that of its **Jewish community,** which written evidence traces back to the late 10th century A.D. The Jews of Kāifēng, thought to have emigrated from Persia over the Silk Road trade routes, have lived in Kāifēng continuously for 1,000 years, establishing their own synagogue here in A.D. 1163. Two pieces of evidence of the Kāifēng Jewish presence can still be seen: the stone tablets recording early Jewish history in China, and the grounds of the great synagogue (destroyed for good in the last century). I set out to see both.

The stone tablets are still kept on the third floor of the **Kāifēng Museum,** located on the south bank of Lord Bāo Lake (although a new facility is rumored to open someday). The museum is a large building graced by upturned eaves but is now falling apart, neglected, its staff openly praying for better days (and more funds). Among its 20,000 relics are some Qīng Dynasty writings by Kāifēng Jews and two stone tablets, inscribed in Chinese, to commemorate the rebuilding of the Kāifēng synagogue. These tablets are dated 1489 (with the reverse side composed in 1512) and 1679. Each assigns a different date to the arrival of Jews in China, but they are consistent concerning the Kāifēng synagogue, which has been restored on at least 10 occasions since the 12th century. The 1679 stele at Kāifēng records the rebuilding of the temple after the Great Flood of 1642, when the Yellow River inundated and destroyed much of the town.

Rumors of a Jewish community in China had been circulating since Marco Polo's time but were only confirmed by Westerners after 1605 when Ai Tan, a Kāifēng Jew, met the preeminent Catholic missionary of China, Matteo Ricci. Ai Tan had come to Běijīng after reading of the European missionaries and their strange new religion. He suspected that the missionaries were Jews. Ricci, for his part, was thrilled at the chance to meet a genuine Chinese Christian, for Ai Tan announced that he was a fellow believer. Ricci soon realized his mistake, but Ai Tan returned to Kāifēng convinced that Ricci was a fellow Jew from Europe though a bit eccentric in his views. Kāifēng's rabbi later wrote to Ricci, begging him to become his successor and pointing out that odd beliefs were less important than the way a man conducted his life. The good Jesuit's reply to the offer of a rabbinical post in Kāifēng is not known.

The Jewish community continued to worship in Kāifēng until the flood of 1852, which again destroyed the synagogue. The temple was never rebuilt and the Jews remaining in Kāifēng gradually ceased to practice the rituals associated with Judaism. Their place of worship, the Hebrew language, and all ethnic and racial distinctions that set them apart disappeared. As several scholars later pointed out, never before had Jews been so thoroughly assimilated as in China.

According to a Chinese scholar's census, there were 166 descendants of Jews in Kāifēng as of 1980. A number of these people continue to regard themselves as Jewish today. In 1985, Rabbi Joshua Stampfer of Portland, Oregon, hosted one of these descendants, Qū Yì-nán, a 25-year-old reporter for the *People's Daily* in Běijīng. She recalled that her family did not eat pork and that her grandfather always wore a blue skullcap. Under the rabbi's tutelage, Ms. Qū quickly became the only Chinese Jew in the world able to read Hebrew and participate in basic Jewish rituals. (She has since married and settled in Los Angeles.)

Curious to see the grounds of Kāifēng's celebrated synagogue, the **Purity and Truth Synagogue (Qīng Zhēn Sì)**, I set out for the intersection of Jiěfàng Lù and Cáizhèngtīng Dōng Jiē. I knew that the site was near the no. 4 People's Hospital, north of both the Catholic church and the Great Eastern Mosque. (In no other city in China, and few in the world, can you find a Catholic church, an Islamic mosque, a Daoist temple, and the site of a Jewish synagogue within a 4-block walk.) I had determined the synagogue's approximate location (west of Cǎo Shì Jiē, east of Jiěfàng Lù, north of Nán Jiāo Jǐng Hútòng, south of Cáizhèngtīng Dōng Jiē, to be precise), but I could not find it in the maze of streets and alleys, shops and shanties. Twice I asked for directions. Ultimately, I stumbled onto a cluttered, nearly vacant, overgrown lot that fit the description. I knew the synagogue had vanished, that pieces of it had been used to build the Great Eastern Daoist Temple; I knew that the Trinity Church had eventually bought the land and rescued some of the relics (including the carved tablets, which until 1912 still stood, in total abandon, in this same yard); and I knew that the no. 4 People's Hospital (at Jiěfàng Lù 59) had taken over the area occupied for 8 centuries by the solitary synagogue. Local sources said the synagogue had stood on the present site of the hospital's boiler. Before its disappearance, the Kāifēng synagogue would have appeared as a typical Chinese temple of gates, pavilions, courtyards, and ancestral halls, except that its entrance faced east and its worshippers faced west, toward Jerusalem, whereas Chinese temples face south. Here, in Kāifēng, I could not even imagine its existence. Nothing was left but a yard. No trace of gate or foundation. Even the stones of the place of worship had been assimilated into the earth of China.

Kāifēng was missing out on a vital, if small, niche in foreign tourism. Clean up the synagogue grounds, build a small memorial and a museum, employ Jewish descendants as guides, and presto: a unique, exotic travel experience, unlike any other on Earth. Perhaps such a project would make things too easy and misleading. Trying to find traces of the Jewish presence in Kāifēng today certainly gives you a more accurate feel for the ravages of history and the sheer force of cultural absorption.

Temple Market

My last morning in Kāifēng, a Sunday, I set out north again. At the bridge over Lord Bāo Lake, a local market was in full swing, its vendors taking over the sidewalks with rather paltry goods. New bras and panties were displayed on clotheslines strung between trees. Belts were custom-cut on the spot from wide sheets of leather.

At the north end of the bridge, I turned east into the heart of the city where the old streets were crowded with Sunday shoppers drawn to the open markets near the **Grand Xiàngguó Monastery (Dà Xiàngguó Sì)** at Zìyóu Lù 54, where admission is ¥15/$1.80. Founded in A.D. 555, Dà Xiàngguó Sì became one of China's most important Buddhist monasteries under the Táng rulers. When Kāifēng became the Sòng capital, Dà Xiàngguó Sì became the number-one temple of the empire, as well as the commercial center of the city. The great floods of 1642 completely erased this monastery, but it was rebuilt under the Qiánlóng Emperor in the 18th century. Within the temple, which is replete with monks hawking trinkets and worshippers burning incense and stroking prayer beads, are assorted small treasures: a 3.6m (12-ft.) tall bronze Frost Bell (cast during the Qīng Dynasty); a Buddhist figure from Sòng days; Míng Dynasty porcelains; an umbrella once owned by the Manchu Empress Dowager Cí Xǐ; and, in its own pavilion, a 1,000-armed statue of Guānyīn, Goddess of Mercy, carved from a single tree. Today, the Dà Xiàngguó Sì area is also Kāifēng's leading open-air market, rife with streetside vendors, creating a pungent, gritty, colorful scene. One enterprising vendor was attracting a large throng with his team of three dancing monkeys.

Modern Kāifēng is a city asleep, a city of possibilities, waiting for its past to awaken. There are hints in its temples, parks, and ruins of an imperial grandeur largely lost elsewhere in China, where modernization has erased much of the earthy grime and street life that came to dominate urban areas when the last of the great dynasties was extinguished early in this century. Kāifēng is a forgotten capital, its old treasures and communities reduced to a few glittering, tantalizing tatters. It still awaits the magic wand of China's economic reforms to spiff up its ancient treasures, but you sense that, with its 42 relics under government protection and 167 places designated as historical sites, Kāifēng will one day recast the rich past within its aging walls and be among China's most visited cities, once it completes its return journey upriver to a festival of clear new brightness.

The Jews of China

Information about Kāifēng's Jewish heritage, sometimes including special-interest tours, is available through the **Sino-Judaic Institute,** 232 Lexington Dr., Menlo Park, CA 94205. In Kāifēng, the best contact is **Zhāng Xīngwàng**, a Chinese Jew who has been working with the Kāifēng Museum to preserve the history of Chinese Jews in Kāifēng. Those interested in finding out more when in town can contact Mr. Zhāng through CITS or the Kāifēng Tourism Bureau (Lǚyóu Jú) (© 0378/398-9388 ext. 6507).

For background on the Jewish community in Kāifēng, read *East Gate of Kāifēng: A Jewish World Inside China,* edited by M. Patricia Needle (University of Minnesota China Center, 1992). For a general portrait of Sòng Dynasty Kāifēng, see Jacques Gernet's *Daily Life in China, On the Eve of the Mongol Invasion, 1250–1276* (Stanford University Press, 1970).

PRACTICAL INFORMATION

by Sharon Owyang

ORIENTATION, WHEN TO GO & GETTING THERE

Kāifēng, population about 700,000, lies in Hénán Province 9km (6 miles) south of the Yellow River and 70km (43 miles) east of provincial capital Zhèngzhōu. As an ancient capital for seven dynasties, the city has a history of over 2,700 years. Winters are cold, spring brings dust storms, and the summers can be stifling hot, making autumn (Sept–Nov) the best time to visit.

Kāifēng is usually visited as a day or overnight trip from Zhèngzhōu. **Buses** run to Zhèngzhōu (1hr. 20 min., ¥11.5/ $1.40, every half hour from 7am–7pm) and from Kāifēng's Kèyùn Xī Zhàn (West Bus Station) on Yíngbīn Lù. Buses also depart for Zhèngzhōu less frequently from the long-distance bus station (Qìchē Zhōngxīn Zhàn), across

from the train station. Private taxi rental between Zhèngzhōu and Kāifēng will run around ¥300 ($37) round-trip.

Kāifēng can also be reached by **train** from Zhèngzhōu (50 min.; many trains throughout the day), Xī'ān (9 hr.; 2 trains daily), and Shànghǎi (13 hr.; 3 trains daily). Kāifēng's train station is in the south of town.

Kāifēng has no airport. The nearest major **airport** is at Zhèngzhōu, from where there are daily flights to Běijīng (1 hr., 10 min.), Guǎngzhōu (2 hr.), Shànghǎi (1 hr., 30 min.) and Xī'ān (45 min.).

Kāifēng's **taxis** cost ¥5 (60¢) for the first 3km (1¾ miles), then ¥1 (10¢) per additional kilometer.

TOURS & STRATEGEMS

The Kāifēng **CITS** has an office just north of the Dōngjīng Hotel at Yíngbīn Lù 98 (© **0378/595-5130** or 0378/595-4370; fax 0378/595-5131) that can help answer questions and arrange accommodations and plane and train tickets. If you're looking to book a local tour with them, try to do so as far in advance as possible.

Note that the fourth-floor display of the Jewish stelae at the Kāifēng Museum (¥10/$1.25) is not ordinarily open to museum visitors. In order to see the stelae, you must first contact the **Kāifēng External Affairs Bureau (Wàishì Bàn)** at Yíngbīn Lù 98 (© **0378/398-9388**, ext. 6507) and pay ¥100 ($13) for a letter of permission.

WHERE TO STAY

Good accommodations in Kāifēng are scarce. The three-star **Yùxiáng Hotel (Yùxiáng Dàjiǔdiàn)**, at Nántǔ Lù 1 (© **0378/599-5588**; fax 0378/599-5566), at least has the benefit of being relatively new (2000) and is also the tallest hotel in town, with 18 floors. Conveniently located in the center of town and steps from Kāifēng's famous night market, the hotel has 140 adequate but unremarkable rooms with central air-conditioning, telephone, and TV. Bathrooms are a little worn but acceptable. A double costs ¥318 ($40), but discounts of 40% are often given. The hotel has a Chinese restaurant and a tour desk that can book tour and travel tickets, but it doesn't have foreign exchange and does not accept credit cards.

Well situated across from the West Bus Station and on the road to Lord Bāo's Lake and Dragon Pavilion, the **Dōngjīng Hotel (Dōngjīng Dàfùndiàn)**, Yíngbīn Lù 99 (© **0378/398-9388**; fax 0378/393-8861), is a large, sprawling hotel owned by the Tourism Bureau and, as such, was once the place where most foreign visitors stayed by default. Today, it still attracts its share of foreigners and, happily, some of the rooms were renovated in 2002, making a stay here a more pleasant experience in general. The newly renovated rooms (¥328/$41, including free breakfast and access to the swimming pool) are clean and comfortable, and come equipped with classical upholstered furniture, air-conditioning, TV, telephone, and fridge. Bathrooms are small but clean and there's 24-hour hot water. Cheaper rooms ¥200 ($25) are available, but they are older and unrenovated, and the bathrooms need a good scrubbing. The hotel has two restaurants (Chinese and fast food), a swimming pool, a salon, karaoke rooms, and a shopping arcade. The staff doesn't speak much English but tries to be helpful.

WHERE TO DINE

Hotels catering to foreigners all have Chinese restaurants that offer decent if unmemorable fare, with dinner for two averaging ¥40 to ¥80 ($5–$10). The **Dōngjīn Hotel** also has a fast-food eatery out front that offers convenient and inexpensive dining (¥4–¥8 or $1 and under per person). Just point to the many buffet dishes that are constantly being replenished. The **Number One Dumpling Restaurant (Dìyīlóu Bāoziguǎn)** at the corner of Zhōngshān Lù and Sìhòu Jiē is a bit of a local institution specializing in dumplings and buns. Their *xiǎolóng bāo*, small dumplings filled with pork and a hint of broth, are a must-try here. A bit farther to the east at Gǔlóu Jiē 66 is another informal diner, the **Xīnshēn Měishíyuán** (© 0378/596-8918), which offers a wide variety of noodles, kabobs, stir-fries, pastries, and snacks to choose from. There is no menu in English, but purchase your meal tickets (¥8/$1 and up) first, then go around to the different stalls and order.

For the more adventurous, the **Drum Tower Night Market (Gǔlóu Yèshì)**, an attraction in itself which starts at around 7pm every night on Sìhòu Jiē and continues into the wee hours of the morning, is a great chance to sample delicious local snacks such as *wǔxiāng shāobǐng* (five-spice roasted bread) and *zhǐma duōwèi tāng* (sesame soup). The shish kabobs, especially the *yángròu chuàn* (spicy lamb kabob), are grilled on the spot over an open fire and are especially tasty. Finally, for those who must have their Western fast food, **Dicos** (the local equivalent of KFC) is at the corner of Nán Shūdiàn Jiē and Gǔlóu Jiē.

LÓNGMÉN CAVES: STONE GATE OF THE DRAGON

龙门

AFTER CREATING THE MASTERPIECE OF Buddhist cave art in Dàtóng, the Northern Wèi Dynasty moved its capital south to Lùoyáng in A.D. 494 and began construction of a second sculptural gallery, the Lóngmén (Dragon's Gate) caves. The project turned out to be even more ambitious. Today, 2,300 caves survive, and 110,000 statues have been catalogued, twice the repository left at the Yúngāng Grottoes in Dàtóng. The larger scale is explained by the longevity of the project: More than half the carvings at Lóngmén date from the much later Táng Dynasty period (A.D. 618–907), when Chinese art and sculpture reached their zenith.

The Northern Wèi artists set to work at a limestone cliff running a half mile north to south along the west bank of the Yī River (known as the Dragon's Gate), 14km (9 miles) south of Lùoyáng. As at the other great Buddhist caves, Lóngmén was raided by Western art collectors in the early 20th century. Thousands of the holy figures were desecrated, their heads sawn off, crated up, and shipped abroad. An entire cave tableau is now on display in New York City at the Metropolitan Museum of Art.

Emperors, generals, rich clans, and devoted Buddhist leaders all took a hand at creating these shrines, for political and social purposes. The carvings cover a history of over 500 years. There are no signposts to help foreign visitors, but the caves are laid out in major clusters, reflecting successive periods of construction. The caves are not deep. Centuries of erosion, flooding, and earthquakes have exposed most of the large figures to the sky, the caves receding to large oval niches. Hundreds of small niches pock the cliff face as well. At dawn, when Lóngmén can be viewed from a distance on the east side of the Dragon's Gate, the rays of the rising sun turn the entire ridge into a golden beehive. The cruder, more rounded figures were carved earliest, in the 5th and 6th centuries. The more complex, ornate, and lively statues date from the 7th and 8th centuries, when Táng art was in flower.

264

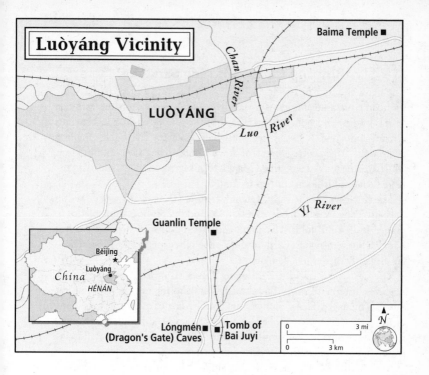

Luòyáng

I reached the ancient capital of Luòyáng by train, traveling east from another old seat of dynastic power, Xī'ān. This is the route that the royal court took in the later days of the Táng Dynasty as its members came to favor Luòyáng over the imperial capital of Xī'ān as their residence. Luòyáng gives almost no impression of its royal past these days. Its landmarks are a tractor factory (China's first), a ball-bearing works, and a mining machinery plant. Little is left of the old capital where Daoist founder Lǎozǐ ran the library 2,500 years ago; where the Hàn Dynasty Imperial College enrolled 30,000 of the nation's finest scholars in the 1st century A.D.; where the Northern Wèi Dynasty opened 1,367 Buddhist temples; where the Suì Emperor connected his palace to the Grand Canal so that officials and merchants could sail from the middle of China northeast to Běijīng and southeast to Hángzhōu in the 6th century; where for 934 years Luòyáng was truly the central point of the Chinese imperial compass. Old Luòyáng has instead made way for a thousand factories. Its million residents are entering the industrial age. The peonies transported from Xī'ān by decree of the Wǔ Empress in the 7th century are famous here still, but the legendary Seven Sages of the Bamboo Grove, who removed themselves from the political turmoil of the Jìn Dynasty (A.D. 265–316) to devote themselves to poetry and music, aren't drinking wine and scribbling in Luòyáng anymore. Their bamboo groves have been bulldozed down.

Bīnyáng Caves (Bīnyáng Sāndòng)

The main entrance to Lóngmén is at the northern end of the cliff, where the road from Luòyáng crosses the river. The bus stops on the east side of the bridge, and you have to walk back to the ticket booth. Spacious cement-and-stone walkways lead southward along the riverbanks. Railings protect the large caves. Dozens of stone figures tower over the walkway, which has the look of a petrified Macy's Thanksgiving Day parade, with the large floats and balloons turned to stone.

The first cave on the right, **Qiánxī Temple (Qiánxī Sì)**, was carved in the early Táng from A.D. 650 to A.D. 683. Buddha sits on a stone platform, draped in graceful folds. His attendants—bodhisattvas who have reached Nirvana but returned to Earth to show others the path to enlightenment—are elegantly carved female figures.

The next three works, the **Bīnyáng Caves (Bīnyáng Sāndòng),** are a massive cluster with many Buddhist figures. Bīnyáng means "Greeting the Sun," as these east-facing monuments do. The first of the three caves is one of the earliest in Lóngmén, begun around A.D. 500, although many of the figures were not finished until 150 years later. The bare-chested Buddha seated in the middle of the first cave measures 7m (24 ft.) tall.

The middle Bīnyáng cave is also among the earliest carved here. An inscription claims that 802,366 craftsmen labored on it for over 20 years. The result is a shrine containing 11 Buddhas. The magnificently robed Buddha seated at the center in the lotus position, one hand raised to Heaven, the other stretched toward the Earth, is 8m (26 ft.) high. His smiling face is surrounded by a halo. Angelic creatures, the Buddhist angels known as apsarases, fly across the half-dome ceiling. In 1935, a large section of this cave with carvings and statues of figures adoring the Buddha was removed and shipped to the United States. Among the missing are the praying figures of the caves' patrons, the Northern Wèi Xuán Wǔ Emperor and his wife. The southern Bīnyáng cave is less richly adorned. It dates from the Northern Wèi as well, but the Buddha at its center seems rather tired and sleepy, more weighed down than buoyant.

The Bīnyáng triptych is followed by the **Veneration of Goodness Temple (Jìngshān Sì)** cave, carved out in the 7th century at the beginning of the Táng Dynasty. Guardians of the Buddhist faith, swords raised, are carved in relief, but they did not have the power to keep out Western art collectors who have beheaded many of the figures in this cave. It is difficult after viewing Lóngmén to innocently enjoy what was taken from it and placed on museum pedestals halfway around the world in the name of preservation.

Cave of Ten Thousand Buddhas (Wànfó Dòng)

Continuing south brings you to one of Lóngmén's greatest treasures, **Wànfó Dòng,** the aptly named Cave of Ten Thousand Buddhas. In fact, there are 15,000 small Buddhas carved into the walls of this profusely decorated cave. The ceiling itself blooms with a single vast lotus flower, inscribed with the date of its carving, A.D. 680. Each of the 54 lotuses on the back wall erupts with a bodhisattva figure in the middle. Buddha sits at the center on a lotus throne, its panels stamped and carved in the "Ten Thousand Buddha" pattern, with seated musicians below and a dancer in swirling silks. At the entrance is a headless statue of Guānyǐn, the Goddess of Mercy, vibrant in her pose, sweeping away the flies of life with a swatter and sprinkling the life-giving dew from a bottle. Her statue was carved in A.D. 681, as a commission of the Wǔ Zétiān Empress.

The Wǔ Empress ruled China at the end of the 7th century, subjugating her Táng Dynasty consort Gāo Zōng and pursuing her devotion to Buddhism by overseeing the construction of thousands of temples and shrines. She is known as a ruthless monarch, the leading figure in many palace intrigues and love affairs. Luòyáng became her second capital (after Xī'ān) and she spent much of China's treasury supporting Buddhism here, initiating many of the splendid caves and sculptures at Lóngmén.

Next door to the Cave of Ten Thousand Buddhas is the **Lotus Flower Cave (Liánhuā Dòng),** which also features a flower on the ceiling. This cave's standing Buddha has been decapitated and the forearms are missing. A fiery halo surrounds the entire body, emphasizing its divine purity. This cave is of earlier origin than its next-door neighbor to the north, having been chiseled out in A.D. 527, when the Northern Wèi still held sway.

The Big Cave

The next major cave to the south is **Honoring Ancestors Cave (Fèngxiān Sì),** by far the largest at Lóngmén. The opening is 30m (100 ft.) wide. The Buddha inside stands 17m (56 ft.) tall. This is the Wǔ Empress's grandest creation at Lóngmén, carved in A.D. 675 and paid for out of her allotment for cosmetics. The celestial guardian who defends the faith, located on the north wall, is a splendid and fierce sculpture. He carries a pagoda in his right hand and tramples a demon under his foot, his left hand defiantly planted on his waist. In her day, the Wǔ Empress entered this shrine through the back of a wooden temple. Never humble, the Wǔ Empress is said to have ordered the sculptor to use her face as the model for that of the colossal Buddha. Art experts consider these figures the best ever sculpted during the Táng Dynasty. They are indeed realistic figures, emanating power, and all are highly decorated, finely detailed, and naturally posed. The large Buddha itself is serene and remote by contrast, elevated by the artist to a higher realm.

Caves of Medicine & Fire

The remaining caves to the south are small. The entrance to the **Medicine Cave (Yào Fáng Dòng)** is engraved with prescriptions for 120 diseases, ranging from diabetes to madness, from the pharmacies of the mid–6th century. The Buddha and his attendants inside date from several dynasties, including the Northern Wèi and the Táng.

The **Gǔyáng Cave (Gǔyáng Dòng)** is the oldest cave at Lóngmén, newly dated at A.D. 478. The Buddha at the center lost his head along the way, but during the last dynasty, the Qīng (1644–1911), it was restored. The new head is said to resemble that of the ancient founder of Daoism, Lǎozǐ, and the cave is locally referred to as Lǎozǐ's Den.

The blackened **Fire-Burnt Cave (Huǒ Shāo Dòng)** next door was also carved early, about A.D. 522. It appears to have been struck by lightning. The **Stone Room Temple Cave (Shí Kù Sì Dòng)** has a fine adoration theme in which a procession of officials in high hats, ladies in long gowns, and court attendants carry umbrellas, fans, and lotus flowers to honor Buddha. In the last cave, **Lùdòng,** which has an inscription from A.D. 539, wall carvings of the halls and pavilions of the time were used to illustrate Buddha's mortal journey through life as Sakyamuni. The cave is also decorated with carvings in the halo flame design, which burns across the walls of the caves of Lóngmén like the morning sun.

Several hours of cave-viewing whetted my appetite. I sat down on a low stool in front of a table where two peasant ladies smiled at me as they scooped up a bowl of cold noodles topped with a hot red paste. They were happy to have me, their only customer at noon, and they didn't even bother to ask where I was from, what I did, or how many children I had, the usual questions asked of lone foreigners. Perhaps they knew nothing of the West. A vendor joined me. A portrait photographer, he tethered his brown horse to a trunk, which contained the imperial costumes in which he decked out his customers. The sun was high and fierce. The golden ridge of Lóngmén turned a dismal yellow-gray, the lifeless color of the surrounding sands. I walked north to the bridge over the Dragon's Gate River. The fire that ignites this ancient gallery of gigantic Buddhas and lotus flowers has been swallowed by the throats of a thousand silent caves, and even the voice of the most powerful empress in China is drowned in the whisper of the wind that pulls the sands across the long cliff like a curtain.

PRACTICAL INFORMATION

by Sharon Owyang

ORIENTATION & WHEN TO GO

The Lóngmén Grottoes (Lóngmén Shíkū) are located in Hénán Province, 13km (9 miles) south of Luòyáng, a former ancient capital. Luòyáng is 322km (200 miles) east of Xī'ān, 150km (93 miles) west of the current provincial capital Zhèngzhōu, and 886km (550 miles) west of Shànghǎi. The Yellow River passes about 80km (50 miles) to the north.

Summers are hot and humid, while spring occasionally brings dust storms, making fall and early winter the best times to visit. A trip to Luòyáng can be combined with a visit to the famous Shào Lín Temple (Shàolín Sì; see p. 568), which is located 87km (54 miles) from Luòyáng.

GETTING THERE

By Plane   Luòyáng has a small airport (© 0379/393-5301, ext. 510) about 11km (7 miles) north of the city center. From here there are daily flights to Běijīng (1½ hr.) and Shànghǎi (1 hr., 40 min.); and weekly flights to Xī'ān (1 hr.), Chéngdū (1 hr., 15 min.), and Chóngqìng (1½ hr). In the summer, there are charter flights to Hong Kong (2 hr., 20 min.). The nearest major airport is at Zhèngzhōu, 150km (93 miles) to the east. Tickets can be purchased at the **CAAC office (Mínháng Shòupiào Chù; © 0379/393-1120)** on Jīchǎng Lù just north of the train station, at CITS, or at hotel tour desks.

By Train   Luòyáng is reasonably well connected by rail to Běijīng (express train 8 hr.), Shànghǎi (15 hr.), Xī'ān (6 hr.), Zhèngzhōu (2 hr.), and Kāifēng (3 hr.). The train station (© 0379/ 395-2673) is located just north of the city center on Dàonán Xī Lù. From the train station, bus no. 81 runs to the Lóngmén Grottoes, bus no. 83 runs to the airport, and bus no. 11 runs to the western part of town via the Friendship Hotel. Around town, taxis cost ¥7 (90¢) per 3km (1¾ miles), then ¥1.60 (20¢) per kilometer.

By Bus   From the long-distance bus station (Chángtú Qìchēzhàn) (© 0379/ 323-9453) opposite the train station on Jīngǔyuán Lù, Iveco buses run to Zhèngzhōu (2 hr.–2½ hr., ¥25/$3, departures every 20 min. 5:40am–7pm), Kāifēng (3 hr., ¥35/$4.50, departures every half hour 6:40am–6pm), and Dengfeng (2 hr., ¥13/$1.60, every hour). **By Car**   Private car rental from Zhèngzhōu will run around ¥300 ($38) one-way and ¥400 ($50) round-trip.

TOURS & STRATAGEMS

There is a Luòyáng Tourist Information hot line, © 0379/431-3824.
Visiting Lóngmén   Morning is the best time to visit the Lóngmén Grottoes (© 0379/598-1650), which face east and catch the light from the rising sun. From April to October, the caves are open daily from 6:30am to 6:30pm; from November to March they are open from 7am to 6pm. Try to arrive before 8am to avoid the tour groups who usually descend on the caves around 9am. Admission is ¥100 ($12).

The Lóngmén Grottoes are easy enough to tour on your own. Public bus nos. 53, 60 (from the western part of town opposite the Friendship Hotel), and 81 (from the train station) run to the caves. (35 min.–45 min.; ¥1/10¢). Taxis make the run for about ¥30 ($3.75). Once inside the main entrance, visitors can hire an English-speaking guide for ¥60 ($7.50). Even for the most

independent of travelers, this is one of those times when having a guide is highly recommended.

Alternatively, **CITS**, located at Jǐudū Xī Lù, Lǚyóu Dàshà (© **0379/433-1337;** fax 0379/432-5200), can provide English-speaking guides for a base rate of ¥100 ($13) with a ¥10 ($1.25) increase for each additional person. Admission and transportation are separate.

WHERE TO STAY

Luòyáng has several four-star rated hotels, but don't expect the facilities, maintenance, or service to match similarly ranked hotels on the international scene or even in China's larger cities. The upside, however, is that prices are considerably more reasonable.

Friendship Hotel (Yǒuyì Bīnguǎn) Dating back to the 1950s, this hotel was the first three-star hotel in town. Last renovated in 1999, it's showing its age with its worn carpets and old furniture. Rooms, however, are large, and bathrooms are dark but spacious and adequate. A better choice would be the more modern **New Friendship Hotel (Xīn Yǒuyì Bīnguǎn),** actuallly a newer annex, next door (© **0379/468-6666;** fax 0379/491-2328). Rooms in the annex cost ¥358 to ¥458 ($45–$57) double. Renovated in 2000, the rooms are slightly nicer than those at the main Friendship Hotel, though they are decorated with the same nondescript furniture. Bathrooms here are small but fairly clean.

Xīyuán Xī Lù 6 (3km/2 miles west of city center). © **0379/468-5555.** *Fax 0379/ 468-5598. www.lfh.com.cn. 258 units. ¥380 ($47) double. AE, MC, V.* **Amenities:** 2 restaurants (Chinese and Western); coffee bar; entertainment center; pool table; shuffleboard. *In room:* A/C, satellite TV (no Western channels); fridge.

Luòyáng Peony Hotel (Luòyáng Mǔdān Dàjiǔdiàn) Located 1.6km (1 mile) west of the city center, this 15-story hotel, newly renovated in 2002, is applying for four-star rating and is recommended. Rooms are a little small but are clean and pleasantly decorated and have comfortable chairs. Bathrooms have tub/shower combos.

Zhōngzhōu Xī Lù 15. © **0379/485-6699.** *Fax 0379/485-6699. 200 units. ¥480–¥550 ($60–$68) double. AE, DC, MC, V.* **Amenities:** 2 restaurants (Chinese and Western); indoor swimming pool; health club; sauna; tour desk; business center; shopping arcade; salon; room service; dry cleaning and laundry. *In room:* A/C, satellite TV, minibar, hair dryer, safe.

Peony Plaza (Mǔdān Chéng Bīnguǎn) Located between the old city center and the new commercial district in the west, this four-star hotel offers some of the flashiest and most modern accommodations in town. A wall of smoked blue glass on the outside, the hotel has a massive three-story atrium lobby and a wide range of facilities inside. Rooms are nice and cozy enough, but the furniture is a little old. Bathrooms are a good size; they have tub/shower combos and a weighing scale but no hair dryer. The hotel has three restaurants, including a revolving restaurant serving a Western buffet breakfast. Service is not quite up to four-star international standards but is adequate.

Náncāng Lù 2. (℃ *0379/493-1111. Fax 0379/493-0303. 163 units. ¥547 ($68) double. AE, DC, MC, V.* **Amenities:** 3 restaurants; indoor swimming pool; health club; sauna; tour desk; business center; shopping arcade; salon; room service; dry cleaning and laundry. *In room:* A/C, TV, minibar.

WHERE TO DINE

One longtime institution still popular with locals is the huge **Zhēn Bù Tóng Restaurant,** housed in a five-story Chinese-style building at Zhōngzhōu DōngLù 369 (℃ **0379/395-2609**). The specialty here is the famous *Luòyáng Shuǐxí* (Water Banquet), consisting of eight cold and 16 hot dishes, all variously cooked in broth, soup, or juice (examples include *zhēnyāncài,* a soup made of ham, radish, imitation crabmeat, mushrooms, and eggs; and the *mìzhī tǔdòu,* sweet-potato fries in syrup). The full complement of dishes costs ¥688 ($86) for 10 people but, happily, the first-floor dining hall offers more reasonably sized four-dish (¥20/ $2.50 per person) or five-dish (¥30/ $3.75 per person) mini-banquets. There are no menus in English, no credit cards are accepted, the staff is a little surly, and service is unexceptional, but the restaurant does offer a unique local dining experience that shouldn't be missed.

The **Friendship Hotel** (℃ **0379/491-2780**) and the **Peony Hotel** (℃ **0379/ 485-6699**) have good Chinese restaurants with English-language menus. Dinner for two averages ¥120 to ¥200 ($15–$25).

For Western food, hotel dining offers the most reliable fare. The **Peony Hotel** (℃ **0379/485-6699**) has a Western dining room serving fish and chips, pizzas, and lamb chops for dinner at ¥20 to ¥40 ($2.50–$5) per entree. **KFC** and **McDonald's** have arrived (in the western part of town at the Shànghǎi Shìchǎng Bùxíng Jiē). There's also **Churrascaria Brazilian Barbecue (Luòyáng Yámǎ Xùn Bāxī Shāokǎo),** at Jīnghuá Lù 278 (℃ **0379/492-2839**), at the northern entrance of the Gōngrén Wénhuà Gōng (Worker's Cultural Palace). The lunch buffet costs ¥38 ($4.75) per person, and dinner is ¥45 ($5.60) per person. **Kè Xiāng Lái,** at Xīyuàn Gōngyuán (℃ **0379/493-2851),** serves both Western and Chinese set meals for ¥20 to ¥50 ($2.50–$6.25).

CHÓNGQÌNG: POWERHOUSE OF THE YÁNGZǏ

重庆

CHÓNGQÌNG, BETTER KNOWN TO Westerners by the earlier Romanization, Chungking, is a city of the future. Located well up the Yángzǐ River, in the steamy southwestern province of Sìchuān, Chóngqìng has not been a favorite of tourists, who have used it mainly as an overnight stop when boarding or disembarking from Yángzǐ River cruises. That was how I first saw Chóngqìng, all in one afternoon after cruising up the Yángzǐ through the Three Gorges, and I did not dream of returning. But return I did, partly to sample some genuine Sìchuān cuisine, partly to see the Buddhist carvings at nearby Dàzú. Finding myself in the city for a few days rather than a few hours, I discovered that there was much more to Chóngqìng than a quick glance revealed.

Chóngqìng is not a romantic city, despite its reputation among Chinese as the "Capital of Mist" and the "City of Mountains." The mist today is liable to be smog; the mountains are simply steep streets winding pell-mell up and down soot-covered hills. Rather, Chóngqìng is a city of the moment, a city of commerce, industry, and development on a scale seen few other places on the planet. It is in every sense a gargantuan city, brimming with raw power and a thirst for the future. Among its many construction sites is that of the Chóngqìng Tower, which will have 114 stories and rise 450m (1,500 ft.)—ending once and for all the debate over whether Chicago's Sears Building or Kuala Lumpur's Patronas Towers is the world's tallest.

Population & Pollution

Chóngqìng has a population that corresponds to its gigantic ambitions. On March 14, 1997, Chóngqìng became a municipality, a designation shared by only three other cities in China (Běijīng, Shànghǎi, and Tiānjīn). No longer part of Sìchuān Province, Chóngqìng is now free to handle its own affairs and finances, answering to no one but Běijīng. The new Chóngqìng Municipality extends over 14 districts, most of them downriver, where 1.3 million people face resettlement before the massive Three Gorges Dam is completed in 2009. The bottom line is that Chóngqìng's municipal population increased rather dramatically on March 14, 1997—to an unimaginable 30-plus million residents.

The downtown population of Chóngqìng, those residing in its "Manhattan," a narrowing peninsula bounded by the confluence of the Yángzǐ and Jiālíng rivers, was unchanged by redistricting. The city of Chóngqìng, as opposed to the municipality of Chóngqìng, numbers a mere 3 million residents, with the close suburbs north and south of the rivers contributing another 11 million.

Chóngqìng is also one of China's most polluted cities. To become a beautiful place, as well as a powerful one, Chóngqìng will need to create environmental cleanup programs on a suitably massive scale. It has already launched a 29-part Green Program designed to reduce acid rain dramatically, and is also committed to building 300 factories to control water pollution, with half these facilities to be placed along the long reservoir created by the Three Gorges Dam. For now, Chóngqìng is an industrial city, a workhorse of commerce and shipping. But mere ugliness does not exclude it from being an interesting place.

Chóngqìng is no tourist town, and that's its attraction. If you want to see a real Chinese metropolis, all its raw edges unconcealed and building for the 21st century, this is the place, 2,415km (1,500 miles) upstream from Shànghǎi. But as much as Chóngqìng is China's gritty city of the future, it is also a product of its past.

Chóngqìng received its present name in A.D. 1190 from the Shào Xī Emperor of the Southern Sòng. He had conquered this city on the Yángzǐ, formerly known as Yúzhōu and later Gōngzhōu, just before he ascended to the dragon throne. Finding himself twice blessed, he named the city that was his stepping-stone to power Chóngqìng, meaning "double celebration" or "twin fortune." That doubling of good fortune is repeating itself today, as this powerhouse of the upper Yángzǐ fuels the expanding economy of China and at the same time opens a new Gate to the Sky.

Industry

While in Chóngqìng in 1945, former premier Zhōu Ēnlái wrote a poem beginning, "We are hoping for brightness, ten thousand miles ahead." Half a century later, this new China has begun to arrive in earnest and Chóngqìng is one of its chief powerhouses. Much of the material that Shànghǎi converts to wealth at the mouth of the Yángzǐ River originates upriver at Chóngqìng. In supplying new China with the basic products of a healthy economy—rice and grain, cotton and silk, coal, iron, and natural gas—Chóngqìng has become a showcase of modernization and economic

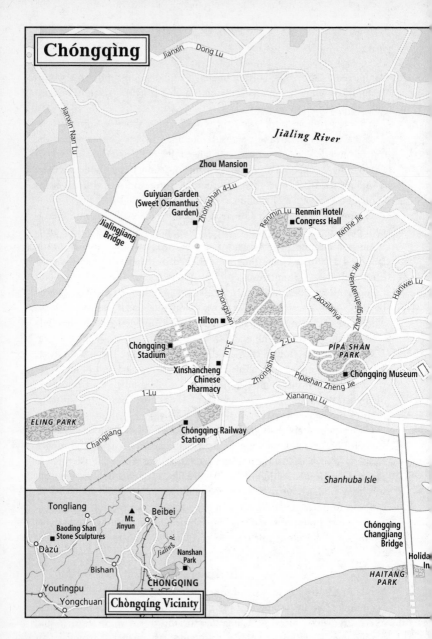

development. Opened to direct foreign trade in 1979, Chóngqìng benefited from early programs that gave its factory managers decision-making power and the freedom to invest in expansion. In the more freewheeling economy of the 1990s, Chóngqìng cashed in on those experiments. Its integrated iron and steel complexes, oil refineries, paper plants, copper smelters, motor vehicle factories, textile mills, and chemical and cement plants have been the

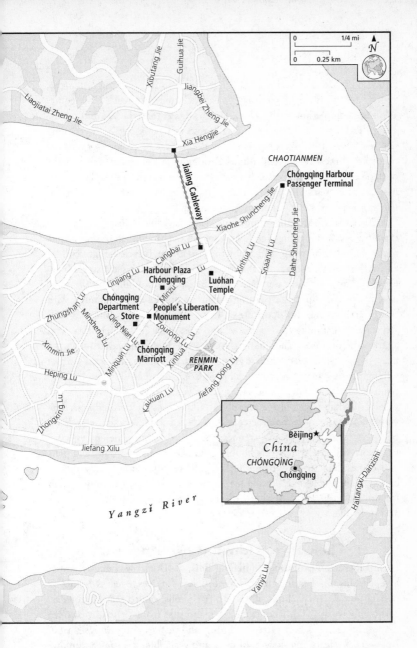

stuff of progress. Chóngqìng is fast becoming the Shànghǎi of western China, the inland colossus of industry and trade.

Chóngqìng's role will inevitably expand over the next 2 decades, as the Yángzǐ River is itself transformed. At present, Chóngqìng's ability to ship its materials and products downstream is limited by the river channel. While shipping is no longer the treacherous business it was in the days of junks and trackers in harness, the Yángzǐ still permits no ships greater than about 3,000 tons (the size of many pleasure cruisers) to reach Chóngqìng. With the completion of the **Three Gorges Dam (Sānxiá Shuǐbà)** on the Yángzǐ early in this century, however, a reservoir 600km (372 miles) long will reach west to Chóngqìng, enabling the passage of cargo ships of more than three times the current tonnage. Along with the anticipated benefits of flood control and increased hydroelectric power in the Yángzǐ basin, this massive project should propel Chóngqìng to even greater prominence as the upper Yángzǐ's chief manufacturer and trader.

Evidence of Chóngqìng's mounting wealth is visible in its rapidly changing cityscape. Chóngqìng is still blanketed in river fog much of the year, its rocky hillsides so steep and numerous that the bicycle—that icon of China—is eerily absent from the streets. In fact, I didn't see a single bicycle during my last visit, not even one being pushed uphill. The alleyways caked with coal dust, the twisting avenues, and the cliffside houses with front doors on the top floors are still part of Chóngqìng's tough-as-nails cityscape, but shining towers of steel and glass—the skyscraper offices and apartments of a new Chóngqìng—are shouldering their way through the heart of the city, displacing these grim reminders of the past. Locals say that Chóngqìng is starting to look like Hong Kong, another hilly city built on manufacture and trade. It's no Hong Kong yet, but it's on its way.

Part of what I find interesting about Chóngqìng is its roughness. The very foundations of its commerce seem exposed to view, like the skeleton of a skyscraper. The curving avenues, the relentless hills, the endless construction sites, the wide rivers bubbling up with boats and ships and piers and cranes, add to its dynamic feel. Chóngqìng has long been a city of energy, a city of furnace-like heat in the summer, a city of shipping and freight and industrial haze. I felt its energy every time I walked its streets and steep alleys.

The Gate to Heaven (Cháotiān Mén)

From **Liberation Monument (Jiěfàng Bēi),** the clock tower at city center, I kept losing my bearings in this metropolis of curves, even as I enjoyed peering into its small shops filled with old scrolls, carved seals, umbrellas, and bambooware, with wool from Tibet and silks from Sìchuān that once made Chóngqìng a port prized by European traders. Along Zhōngshān Lù, I passed cafes featuring skewers of meat and vegetables awaiting a dunking in hot oil—the sidewalk version of Chóngqìng's most celebrated dish, hot pot *(huǒguō),* which is given more elaborate treatment in the city's best restaurants and hotels. Down Shàngqīng Lù, outdoor food markets sell tea-smoked duck and bite-sized *bāozi* (steamed buns) and, after dark, street fairs offer still more food and merchandise.

At the eastern tip of the city, where the Yángzǐ and Jiālíng rivers converge, I explored the number-one urban sight in Chóngqìng: the **Gate to Heaven (Cháotiān Mén),** and its docks, linked to the city by black cliffs that run 300 steps up and down. Here the *bàngbàng jūn,* the porters with cargo strapped to their backs or suspended from bamboo poles across their shoulders, hike the 300 cliffside stairs to and from the mud flats and wharves. During World War II, when Chóngqìng's population swelled as eastern China fell to the Japanese and China's capital moved here, the American general Joseph Stilwell occupied a house high on these flanks above the miserable cantilevered tenements that still survive. Cable cars are strung across both rivers like tourist banners. The northern terminal is a gray cement tower serviced by a wobbly elevator (with an attendant). I rode the dilapidated contraption back and forth (¥1.50/18¢ each way), standing up (there were no seats), a bit terrified but awed by the view. It's a cable car ride over a half-mile-wide wilderness of iron and steel, barges and freighters, oil and fire. In a gritty way, this is the essence of Chóngqìng, the beauty in the marrow of a naked city.

Large bridges connect the downtown peninsula of Chóngqìng with the north and south shores, and rattling steel ferries, without seats or benches, deliver far more workers than the cable cars ever could.

At the turn of this century, Chóngqìng was still a backwater, a walled city enclosing barely 250,000 inhabitants. Between 1937 and 1946, when it served as China's wartime capital, the population tripled and new agencies, industries, and educational institutions poured in from throughout China. Since then, Chóngqìng has never looked back: The Qīng Dynasty city walls came down; an industrial capital took root. Today, a new superhighway runs along the downtown shore, and a subway and light rail are under construction.

Pípá Shān Park (Pípa Shān Gōngyuán)

The full panorama of this increasingly modern industrial megacity unfolds below **Pípa Shān Park** on Loquat Hill, at over 300m (1,000 ft.) the highest point in the city. Weary of more hill walking and doubtful that I could find the way, I hired a taxi to deliver me to the park gate. (I still had to walk up a long hill to the summit.) There, a teahouse pavilion rises from garden terraces, a favorite haunt of retired men intent upon card games. There's also a circular monorail, crude and rusting away; its passengers ride the rail on attached bicycles. But it's the view that consumes your attention. To the north is the Yángzǐ; to the south, the Jiālíng—massive rivers, apparent equals from this perspective, meeting at the Cháotiān Mén docks, the gate to heaven, where the long peninsula of downtown Chóngqìng tapers to a forked point poised to strike like the head of a fire-breathing dragon.

As it was nearly dusk, I waited for the sunset, which got lost in the smudgy horizon. But I was glad that I waited. After dark, the view from Pípa Shān Park is far more dramatic. Ignited by the beacons of office, highway, and factory, Chóngqìng becomes an island winging through the rivers of heaven, an enchanted foundry floating on the arms of two great rivers.

Chóngqìng Museum (Chóngqìng Bówùguǎn)

The next morning I headed back downtown. On the south side of Pípá Shān is the **Chóngqìng Museum** (✆ **023/6385-3533**), an antiquated repository of artifacts. Chóngqìng is supposed to be a city without relics or treasures, without refined Chinese legacies, but the museum offers glints of a deeper, richer past. Human history stretches back 3,000 years in Chóngqìng, to the days of the Bā Kingdom, when nobles were buried in large wooden boats suspended from the river cliffs. Two of these maritime coffins are now suspended in the Chóngqìng Museum, as is a major collection of Hàn Dynasty tomb-bricks, their carvings depicting the courtyards and chariots of 2,000 years ago. There's also a dull display of dinosaur eggs and skeletons, as well as a modern art gallery where artists push their works for sale. The museum is a clunky warehouse, poorly lighted and dilapidated. By the time I left, kids on school field trips were at least adding some high-spirited laughter and chatter to its dark, staid chambers. The museum is open daily from 8:30am to 5pm. The dinosaur museum and the main museum have separate admission fees; each is ¥5 (65¢).

Luóhàn Temple (Luóhàn Sì)

The brightest sight in downtown Chóngqìng is **Luóhàn Sì,** a Buddhist temple that dates from A.D. 1000. It is one of the most active temples in China. At the busy intersection outside its entry gate, the sidewalks are filled with Chinese visitors, local Buddhists, and blind fortunetellers. Inside the gate, a long, narrow entryway is flanked with rock carvings—shrines where dozens of worshippers kneel, burn incense, and pray. Within the pavilions are modern clay statues of the 500 arhats, Buddhist followers who have reached the first state of enlightenment. Behind a large golden likeness of the Buddha is a mural depicting Siddhartha, the living Buddha, as he cuts his hair to renounce the world. The temple looks far older than it is, having been thoroughly reconstructed after the ravages of World War II, but the sheer activity within gives it an unmistakable air of authenticity. This is no tourist trap; it's an island of Old China, bobbing in an ocean of modern commerce and construction. You can visit the temple every day from dawn to dusk; admission is ¥4 (50¢).

PRACTICAL INFORMATION

by Michelle Sans

ORIENTATION

Chóngqìng is located in southeastern Sìchuān Province, far inland on the upper Yángzǐ River. The chief attraction for sightseers is Dàzú, an ancient grotto of Buddhist carvings to the west that makes for an excellent day trip (see the following chapter for more information on Dàzú). Chóngqìng is also the starting point for downriver passage through the Three Gorges and onward cruises to Nánjǐng and Shànghǎi.

GETTING THERE

By Plane   The **Jiāngběi Airport,** serving many cities in China, is 29km (18 miles) from the city center; allow 40 minutes for the taxi ride (about ¥100/$13). The Mínháng (CAAC) airport shuttle bus (¥15/$1.90) leaves every half hour from 6am to 6pm from their office at 161 Zhōgshān Sān Lù (✆ **023/6386-5824**). Domestic and international air tickets can also be bought here; call ✆ **023/ 6386-2970** for the office's ticketing department. Dragonair, serving Hong Kong, has offices in the Holiday Inn (Jiàrì Fàndiàn), Nánpíng Běi Lù 15 (✆ **023/6280-3380**).

By Train   The main rail station and long-distance bus station are next to each other on Nánqū Lù, near the Yángzǐ River. Trains from Shànghǎi and Běijǐng take approximately 44 and 35 hours respectively. Trains to Chéngdū take approximately 10 hours. The overnight leaving at 9:06pm and arriving the next morning at 7:29am is one way to avoid the cost of a hotel for a night. Official reports have it that a new railway line scheduled to open in 2005 will cut the trip between Chóngqìng and Chéngdū to just 3 hours.

By Bus   Luxury buses, quite comfortable and with a bathroom as well as a uniformed attendant on board, now connect Chóngqìng to Chéngdū, Sìchuān's capital, 4 hours and 322km (200 miles) away via the Chéngyú Expressway. The cost is ¥107 ($13).

By Ship   Many visitors arrive at the wharves of Chóngqìng after a Yángzǐ River cruise upriver from Wǔhàn. From there, a taxi to any of the major hotels is less than ¥10 ($1.20). Depending on the type of taxi, the first 3km (1¾ miles) should cost ¥5, ¥6, or ¥7 (65¢, 75¢, or 90¢). Alternatively, the city can be reached by walking upriver to a local ferry and crossing over to the downtown peninsula.

TOURS & STRATAGEMS

If you are arriving or departing by cruise ship, the cruise liner can usually arrange a tour of the city. **China International Travel Service (CITS)** is located near the People's Square (Rénmín Guǎngchǎng) at 120 Zǎozǐ Lányā Zhèngjiē, 2nd Floor (✆ **023/ 6385-0693**; fax 023/6385-0196; citscq@ cta.cq.cn). This branch of CITS is particularly helpful. That said, there's no very compelling reason to pay for a city tour. City maps in English and Chinese can be found in most hotels, bookstores, train and bus stations, and at Cháotiānmén (¥3–¥5/35¢–60¢). Pípá Shān Park and the city museum are within walking distance of the Hilton or a short taxi drive from the Harbour Plaza and Liberation Square area. (*Note:* by 2005, the Chóngqìng Museum will have moved to a new building near Rénmín Dà Lǐtáng.) Luóhàn Sì is within walking distance of the Liberation Square area.

WHERE TO STAY

A number of international-level hotels have opened in the last few years, and more are on the way.

Chóngqìng Marriott (Wànháo Jiǔdiàn) With its high-ceilinged lobby flanked by two sweeping staircases, its steakhouse overlooking the rivers, and a Japanese restaurant with traditional architecture and decor, the Marriott is the most elegant hotel in town. Rooms are large, and many have separate bathtub and shower. The cafe and steakhouse serve arguably the best Western food in Chóngqìng.

Qǐng Nián Lù 77. (**023/6388-8888**. Fax *023/6388-8777. 517 units. ¥1,440 ($180) for a standard room, though a 50% discount is not unusual. AE, DC, MC, V.* **Amenities:** 3 restaurants; indoor swimming pool; tennis courts; fitness club; Jacuzzi; sauna; concierge; tour desk; business center; shopping arcade; salon; 24-hr. room service; same-day dry cleaning and laundry; valet; nightly turndown. *In room:* A/C, satellite TV, high-speed Internet, voice mail, minibar.

Harbour Plaza Chóngqìng (Hǎi Yì Fàndiàn) This five-star luxury hotel (fully renovated in 2001) has a great downtown location (next to deluxe shopping on the city's pedestrian mall) and some of the spiffiest facilities in Chóngqìng. The two-story marble lobby and wood-paneled halls lead to guest rooms done in dark blues and golds. Managed by a Hong Kong firm, this was at one time Chóngqìng's most lavish hotel. Now it has competition.

Wǔyī Lù (downtown, at Zōuróng Lù, 1 block southeast of Liberation Monument). (**023/6370-0888**. Fax *023/ 6370-0778. www.harbourplaza.com/ hpcq. 390 units. ¥1,330–¥1,450 ($160– $175) standard rooms, ¥1,660–¥2,000 ($200–$240) suites. 50%–65% discounts possible year-round; 15% service charge. AE, DC, MC, V. Bus 306, 402, 413, 601 to Jiěfàng Bēi.* **Amenities:** 2 restaurants (Chinese, Western), 4 bars; health club, indoor pool; business center; ticketing; dry cleaning/laundry; 24-hr room service; forex. *In room:* A/C, satellite TV, IDD, dataport, voice mail, minibar, fridge, hair dryer, safe.

Hilton (Xīěrdùn Jiǔdiàn) Opened in 2002, this five-star hotel is one of Chóngqìng's finest. Views are of the rivers and the sports stadium. Rooms are attractively appointed with Art Deco wooden headboards and framed calligraphy on the wall. Plans for a women's floor are in the works. This place is also well located near the business district; less than 3km (2 miles) from the rail station. Highly recommended.

Zhōng Shān Sān Lù 139; near Dàtiánwān Sport Stadium. (**023/6903-9999**; *worldwide 800/820-0600. Fax 023/ 6903-8738. www.hilton.com. 443 units. ¥1440–¥1680 ($180–$210) standard rooms, ¥2160–¥3280 ($270–$410) suites. Hefty discounts possible yearround; 15% service charge. AE, DC, MC, V. Bus: 224, 368, 402, 411, 605 to Liǎng Lùkǒu stop.* **Amenities:** 2 restaurants (Pan Asian/Western, Sìchuān); 2 pools;

indoor swimming pool; fitness club; sauna; concierge; tour desk; business center; shopping arcade; salon; 24-hr. room service; same-day dry cleaning and laundry; valet; nightly turndown; Sunday Kid's Brunch (child-friendly brunch in a private room with a teacher and a clown); forex. *In room:* A/C, satellite TV, IDD, dataport, high-speed Internet, voice mail, minibar, fridge, hair dryer, safe.

Yangtze Chóngqìng Holiday Inn (Yángzǐ Jiāng Jiàrì Jiǔdiàn) Although located well east of downtown, the four-star, 21-story Holiday Inn is the most experienced international-level hotel in town and one of the best managed. The staff speaks English. The spacious, modern rooms offer 30-channel satellite TVs, robes and slippers, and free local calls.

The 16th-floor Executive Club (rooms ¥1,280/$160) has its own lounge. The 12th and 13th floors are nonsmoking. Both the Western and Sìchuān restaurants serve excellent food. This is the hotel where expatriate businesspeople live and relax in Chóngqìng.

Nánpíng Běi Lù 15. © *800/465-4329 or 023/6280-3380. Fax 023/6280-0884. 379 units. ¥1,280 ($135) double (50% discounts possible year-round). AE, DC, MC, V.* **Amenities:** 2 restaurants; deli; outdoor swimming pool; putting green; tennis courts; fitness club; sauna; billiards; concierge; tour desk; business center; ATM in lobby; shopping arcade; salon; 24-hr. room service; babysitting; same-day dry cleaning and laundry; valet; nightly turndown. *In room:* A/C, TV, minibar, coffeemaker.

WHERE TO DINE

Though it may have come from Mongolia, where a milder version is ubiquitous, one of the dishes most identified with Sìchuān cooking is hot pot or *huǒguō* ("fire pot"). It is popular enough in Chóngqìng that a block of Wǔyī Lù (just off Mínzú Lù) is called **Hot Pot Street (Huǒguō Jiē)**. There, street stalls and small restaurants all specializing in this dish line either side of the street. Hot pot restaurants are recognizable by their dining tables, at the center of which is a cooking pot with boiling broth and hot oil. Diners add to it meat, fish, sprouts, scallions, and whatever other ingredients they deem suitable. By tradition in both Sìchuān and Inner Mongolia, locals favor organ meats, intestines, brains, and chicken feet for this poor-man's stew, but these days, in restaurants, the choices abound.

If you're looking for **Western cuisine,** The Holiday Inn has an excellent German bistro, the **Bierstube,** open daily from 6:30 to 11:30pm, with authentic German food and drinks in an intimate setting. The hotel also has Western-style barbecues, seafood, and Italian dishes nightly in the **Sunset Grill** from 6:30pm to midnight. The **Manhattan Steakhouse and View Lounge** in the Marriott Hotel has nearly flawless Western and Continental dishes. The ambience is dictated by a spectacular view of Chóngqìng.

For **inexpensive choices,** check out the inside of the **Luóhàn Temple,** where there's a vegetarian restaurant with inexpensive noodles and *dòufu* (tofu) dishes (open for lunch only, 11:30am–2pm). Also, on the streets surrounding the Holiday Inn, there are several Western-style coffeehouses serving international dishes, such as spaghetti, at reasonable prices. Additionally, a **McDonald's** and a **KFC** are both within a block of Liberation Monument.

Càixiāng Yuán SÌCHUĀN Very popular with locals, this place serves traditional and nouveau Sìchuān dishes. The "strange flavored duck" (*guàiwèi yāzi*, which might more accurately be translated "extraordinarily flavored duck")—with its perfect blending of salty, sweet, tingling, hot, sour, savory, and fragrant flavors—is, for very good reason, a favorite here. *Building C-4, Jiāzhōu Huāyuán (Jiāzhōu Garden in Yúběi District).* ① **023/6762-9325.** *¥20–¥52 ($2.50–$6.50) for a 2-person meal. No credit cards. No English menu. Daily 11:30am–2:30pm and 5:30–10pm.*

Little Swan (Xiǎo Tiāné Huǒguō) HOT POT One of the most popular hot pot restaurants in Sìchuān and beyond is a chain of 126 stores, the first of which opened over 20 years ago in Chóngqìng. Little Swan continues to be one of the best in Chóngqìng. This self-serve restaurant gives patrons a choice of hot or mild broth, and its buffet table of ingredients allows non-Mandarin speakers more control than usual over what goes into their pot. *Jiànxīn Lù 78.* ① **023/6785-5328.** *Dinner for 2 ¥30–¥80 ($3.50–$10). No credit cards. Daily 11am–10pm.*

DÀZÚ CAVES: THE WHEEL OF LIFE

大足

O VER THE CENTURIES, BUDDHIST pilgrims who journeyed to the holiest shrines in western China obeyed a famous dictum: "Go up to Éméi Shān, go down to Bǎodǐng Shān." Éméi Shān is one of Buddhism's four sacred mountains, while **Treasure Peak Mountain (Bǎodǐng Shān)** at Dàzú is one of China's four great centers of Buddhist sculpture. These sacred carvings are located in Chóngqìng Municipality in western China, in the county of Dàzú, about halfway between the cities of Chéngdū and Chóngqìng. Dàzú is not a convenient location for the traveler, but its countryside remoteness is part of its attraction. Moreover, for anyone fascinated by the monumental remnants of Old China, of which so few survive, Dàzú and its Bǎodǐng Shān sculptures are a must.

Bǎodǐng Shān possesses the best of the sacred carvings in Dàzú, containing about 10,000 of the over 50,000 religious sculptures scattered throughout this highland district. Compared with the three other major rock carvings in China (those at Dūnhuáng, Luòyáng, and Dàtóng), the Dàzú specimens are of the most recent composition and are arranged in the most compact arena for viewing. This concentration of thousands of carved images within a natural amphitheater enhances the visual intensity of Dàzú. Dàzú's carvings are also the most realistic of the great holy sculptures, the least abstract and rigid, the most earthy and human, with the broadest social context.

While rock carving began in Dàzú during the Táng Dynasty (618–907) and continued well into the Qīng Dynasty (China's last imperial epoch), the sculptures here reached their artistic zenith during the Southern Sòng (1127–1279), when the sculptors turned their attention to creating the unusually unified, compact, and colorful Buddhist grotto at Dàzú's Bǎodǐng Shān.

Great Buddha Cove (Dà Fó Wān)

A friend and I set out for Dàzú early one morning from Chóngqìng. We hired a local taxi for the 161km (100-mile) journey which, despite the good roads, consumed almost 3 hours in each direction. At Dàzú Xiàn, we parked in the village of **Flower Dragon Bridge (Huā Lóng Qiáo)** and walked to the grotto entrance. The main gate and temple are set on a ridge above a stream. On the other side of the gate, worshippers were burning incense while kneeling before small images in rock alcoves. Below us, the pathway to the Buddhist grottoes wound downward into a lush river valley.

Zhào Zhìfēng, a monk well versed in Tantric (Esoteric) Buddhism, launched this last great venture in outdoor religious sculpture more than 7 centuries ago. The work required 70 years to complete. The setting Zhào Zhìfēng selected is dramatic enough: a horseshoe-shaped gully a third of a mile long with sheer cliffs towering up to 27m (90 ft.) high. Known as the **Great Buddha Cove,** it is a natural grotto, hidden in the folds of misty mountains and terraced slopes below a sleepy village and above a meandering stream.

As we descended into the Great Buddha Cove at Dàzú, we could see several temples towering overhead. The oldest, **Shèng Shòu Sì,** was built by Zhào Zhìfēng himself in 1179 (and last rebuilt in 1684 during the reign of the Kāngxī Emperor of the Qīng). This temple is still active, but most visitors are drawn directly down steep stone stairs into the crescent of cliffs where the carvings were completed in 1249.

The Wheel of Life

The Tantric Buddhism long practiced at Dàzú is noted for its use of incantations, meditations, and mandalas. Mandalas are diagrams of cosmic forces used by the devout to attain instantaneous union with the Buddha, and these mandalas surge through the crescent as a prominent motif, surfacing most strikingly at **The Wheel of Life,** the exquisite figure in **niche no. 3.** This ornate wheel of life and death, carved in relief from solid rock, is supported from beneath by tiny human attendants and gripped in the teeth of a superhuman monster, representative of the forces of death in life. The master artisan Zhào Zhìfēng occupies the center of the wheel; above him is a pavilion of the Western Paradise, the Buddhist heaven beyond the mortal sphere. The outer two rings of the great wheel teem with animals living, dying, and being born, portraying the cycles of birth and death. Ribbons of divine figures ripple outward from the turning wheel. Altogether, it is a dynamic phantasmagoria on the theme of reincarnation, unlike any other figure I've ever encountered in China, and by itself worth the journey to Dàzú.

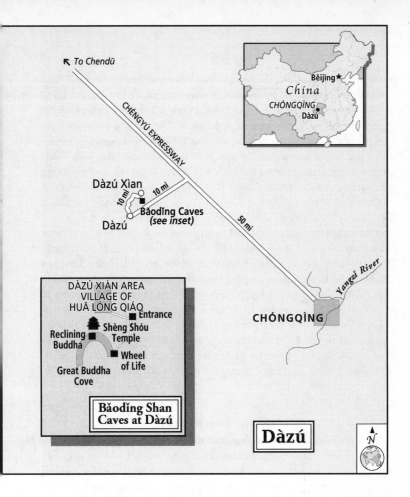

The Wheel of Life is the starting point on one side of this sculpture garden, a section dominated by carvings of the leading deities of Buddhism. In **niche no. 8** (the caves are scrupulously numbered), there is a 1,000-arm **Guānyīn (Goddess of Mercy)**, an all-seeing eye carved into each of her open palms. The many arms represent Guānyīn's almost unlimited capacity to reach out and help others; the many eyes, her ability to see every aspect of life with compassion. Encompassing 88 sq. m (289 sq. ft.) of the recess, this goddess of mercy is the largest representation of its kind in China.

Reclining Buddha (Wòfó)

The central sculpture at Dàzú, however, and one of the most famous in China, is the Reclining Buddha at the midpoint of the crescent. Here, on a grand yet serene scale, the entrance of the historical Buddha, Sakyamuni, into Nirvana is rendered in a dreamscape. The Reclining Buddha unites the formal devotional aspects that characterize older Buddhist grottoes in China with the more down-to-earth, human elements that set Dàzú apart. Here, in the bow of the Great Buddha Cove, Prince Sakyamuni reclines on his right side, his back disappearing into stone. The carving measures 29m (96 ft.) head-to-knees, forming a backdrop for a splendid ensemble of life-sized, lifelike attendants (bodhisattvas and officials in hats) who wade waist-deep through a river of stone in which their prince sleeps the unearthly sleep of the enlightened. The attendants flow gently to and fro before this magnified figure, facing different directions and expressing their individual devotion. They are dwarfed by a divinity so near he can be touched.

The art at Dàzú is dynamic and naturalistic, the figures lively and fluid. The niches alternate between acts of devotion and flourishes of storytelling. Not far from the Reclining Buddha is **niche no. 12, Nine Dragons Bathing the Prince,** depicting the baby Buddha being bathed in a fountain. Water drips into the bathing pool from the mouth of the lowest of nine carved dragons. Farther on are the most populous and lifelike galleries, where thousands of figures adorned in bright colors line tiers on the cliff walls. In **niche no. 15,** the common masses are devoted not to worship but to carrying out the mundane principles of parental care and filial piety. These are among the central themes of native Confucianism. Buddhism, transplanted from India, clearly had to adapt to Chinese ways.

Heaven, Earth & Hell

The scenes of childbirth, nursing, and nurturing carved in relief at Dàzú are unlike any of the representations at the other major Buddhist sculpture shrines in China. At Dàzú, these carvings resemble three-dimensional comic strips complete with engraved captions. A devoted mother washes her infant's clothes. A father offers a peach to the babe nestled in his arms. Century-old parents watch over their 80-year-old child.

In another colossal comic strip devoted to filial piety in **niche no. 17,** Prince Sakyamuni returns to repay the kindness his parents showed him as a child by now offering his own arm as nourishment. This story is an adaptation of an episode from the Confucian canon's "Twenty-four Examples of Filial Piety," in which a daughter-in-law is celebrated for her extreme devotion when during a famine she cuts off a finger to feed her elderly parents-in-law. At Dàzú, in other words, Buddhism and Confucianism merge.

These family scenes are succeeded by two vast tiered niches whose theme is decidedly grimmer: portrayals of the **Final Judgment.** One niche promises elevation from the cycles of death and rebirth to a higher consciousness. **Niche no. 21,** however, illustrates the other side, concentrating on the tortures of the damned. Evildoers are tormented by monsters, hideous machinery, and an unending waterfall of freezing ice in panels reminiscent of the gruesome visions of Hieronymus Bosch or Aw Boon Haw. Numerous transgressions are dramatized. A drunken husband fails to recognize his wife, a drunken father fails to recognize his son, and a drunken elder sister fails to recognize her younger sister. Even a gentle, beatific farmwoman, benignly feeding her chickens, is here consigned to the lower depths, presumably because she will violate Buddhist prohibitions against the slaughter of animals and the eating of meat.

A few of these large stone panels are more formal, peopled with religious figures and worshippers. The tiers of **niche no. 22** and the walls of the **Cave of Full Enlightenment, niche no. 29,** are lined with traditional Buddhist figures, some fierce, some benign. The deep influences of Indian art rise to the surface, reflections of the venerable achievements at the Lóngmén or Mògāo sculpture troves. But it is the new style of the Sòng masters that distinguishes Dàzú. In **niche no. 30,** at the tip of the cove opposite The Wheel of Life (see above), the themes are worldly and entirely indigenous: oxen-raising and cattle-herding. Farmers, displayed in 10 continuous groupings, lovingly tend their beasts and share a genuine comradeship. These scenes of rural life are translated by the devout as symbolic representations of religious obedience and the taming of one's own animal nature, but for the secular tourist, the outstanding elements in these countryside idylls are earthbound and sensuous. In the Sòng, religious sculpture becomes increasingly natural and worldly, more Confucian and more Chinese—hence, the popular saying that at Dàzú's Bǎodǐng Shān, Buddhism becomes "Chinese pure and simple." This type of art— spiritual yet natural, formal yet human—reached its most expansive expression at Bǎodǐng Shān.

Nirvana in Stone

After a few hours of viewing the cliffside gallery, we hiked back up to the village and asked our taxi driver to join us for lunch. She selected one of the unnamed indoor-outdoor shanty cafes. The family that owned the business and lived in its back rooms set to work chopping up the vegetables and preparing the trout that we would soon be dipping fresh and raw into a boiling pot of oil—a rural Sìchuān hot pot that proved to be hearty and nourishing and (because we were presumed to be wealthy foreigners) undoubtedly overpriced at ¥50 ($6) per person, including all the tea and local beer we could consume. We didn't mind the price. We were interested in watching the family prepare our meal in the kitchen at the back of the house, which lacked plumbing, and in the life on the village streets where the children ran up and down the hills rolling metal wheels with long pokers. The wheels were seldom wholly round, but several of the children were quite deft at keeping them rolling despite the bumps, holes, and assorted obstacles on the streets.

After lunch we walked the village and took another look down on the Great Buddha Cove, with its otherworldly art, painted in vibrant reds and blues, and its dreaming Buddha at odds not only with the modern Western world from which we'd come but with the simple, poor village above. Here indeed is the "precious summit" of a monumental Buddhist sculpture that permeated and enriched China for a thousand years and ended at Bǎodǐng Shān, where its receding image now sleeps in a Nirvana of stone.

PRACTICAL INFORMATION

by Michelle Sans

ORIENTATION & WHEN TO GO

The **Bǎodǐng Shān Rock Carvings** are located in Dàzú County, Chóngqìng Municipality, a pleasant 2½-hour drive from Chóngqìng via the Chéngyú Expressway that connects Chéngdū and Chóngqìng. Dàzú is a day trip from Chóngqìng, which is located in southwest China 1,047km (650 miles) from Běijīng, and 2,415km (1,500 miles) upstream on the Yángzǐ River from Shànghǎi.

Summers are extremely hot and humid in the whole region, making spring and autumn the best seasons to travel. Even winters are not too chilly a time to visit the rock carvings, although the days are short and heavy fog is common.

GETTING THERE

By Bus   Buses leave Chóngqìng for Dàzú from both the long-distance bus station (next to the rail station) and from Cháotiān Mén. The earliest bus leaves Chóngqìng at 7am; the last return bus is supposed to leave Dàzú at 5:30pm, but if there aren't enough passengers, it doesn't go. Best to be at the Dàzú bus station by 5pm. The fare is ¥31 to ¥37 ($3.85–$4.60). From the Dàzú bus station, catch a minibus for Bǎodǐng Shān. Buses depart as soon as they fill up. The half-hour ride each way costs ¥2.50 to ¥5 (30¢–60¢).

By Car   A taxi ride from Dàzú city to Bǎodǐng Shān costs about ¥30 ($3.75).

TOURS & STRATAGEMS

Guided trips to Bǎodǐng Shān can be arranged at the travel desk of the **Yangtze Chóngqìng Holiday Inn,** Nánpíng Běi Lù 15 (✆ **023/280-3380**), for ¥500 to ¥1,500 ($62–$185) per person, depending on the number of people in your group (1–6). Prices are roughly the same at the **Chóngqìng CITS,** 120 Zǎozǐ Lányā Zhèngjiē, 2nd Floor (✆ **023/6385-0693;** fax 023/6385-0196; citscq@cta.cq.cn). If you're lucky enough to get a good guide (some—certainly not all—are excellent), you will learn more than you can with a guidebook. But if you'd rather not take a chance, or if you simply like to go at your own pace, the books in English on sale inside the gate are easy to follow and give brief explanations of the more important carvings. (Signs beside the sculptures are in Chinese only.)

You can hire a **taxi** for the day for about ¥350 ($43), negotiating the price yourself on the street. The taxi driver will not speak English and will not serve as a guide.

The admission at Dàzú's Bǎodǐng grottoes is ¥50 ($6) per person. Video cameras used to be forbidden inside the gate; now, you can use them for ¥100 ($13) plus a ¥50 ($6.25) deposit for the permit card you must wear. Plainclothes guards are stationed throughout the grotto area in search of scofflaws, so don't be tempted to tape without a permit. Hours are 8:30am to 5pm.

WHERE TO STAY

Dàzú is a day trip from Chóngqìng. See the Chóngqìng chapter (beginning on p. 272) for lodging choices there. The best place to stay near Dàzú is the **Dàzú Guesthouse (Dàzú Bīnguǎn),** Gōng Lóng Lù 47, in the town of Lónggāng Zhèn, Dàzú County (© **023/4372-1888;** fax 023/4372-2827), which is about 16km (10 miles) south of the Bǎodǐng Shān site. This small hotel is not perfectly kept or furnished, but it has 133 modern three-star rooms, a fitness center, a good Chinese restaurant, and the offices of the **Dàzú CITS (© 023/4372-2245).** This is a good base from which to explore Dàzú's many other Buddhist carving sites, including nearby Běi Shān and Shímén Shān. Doubles cost ¥320 to ¥480 ($40–$60); no credit cards.

WHERE TO DINE

Noodle and *jiǎozi* (Chinese ravioli) restaurants abound in Dàzú and near the Bǎodǐng Shān entrance. Bottled water, soft drinks, and beer are readily available from street vendors in Dàzú.

CHÉNGDŪ: HOME OF THE PANDA

成都

A MASSIVE STATUE OF CHAIRMAN MÁO
Zédōng still presides over downtown Chéngdū, the capital of the southwest
province of Sìchuān. Such monuments were a fixture in all the cities of
China up until the Great Helmsman's death in 1976. With the rise of Dèng
Xiǎopíng and the economic reforms that transformed China from egalitarian communism into a kind of capitalistic socialism, Máo's image lost its
prominence—but not in Chéngdū. In Chéngdū, Máo still gazes southward
to the Jǐn River from his stairway pedestal at Exhibition Hall, where
Rénmín (People's) streets North, South, East, and West converge. He has
become a traffic landmark, a city center beacon for anyone who navigates
the big streets and small lanes of the city, a monument to mapmaking
rather than politics.

Rénmín Nán Lù (People's Street South), a boulevard of shiny modern
hotels, shops, and billboards (one of them, at the bridge, a massive electronic TV screen), runs half a mile from Máo's feet to the Jǐn (Brocade)
River. South of the river on the road to the airport there's an American-style
subdivision of villas where there were dusty fields a decade ago. Today, billboards promote it as a middle-class paradise.

Yet Chéngdū is still crisscrossed by winding streets of century-old shophouses where the merchandise hasn't changed since the age of emperors.
Nor has the fiery Sìchuān cuisine, preserved in Chéngdū as nowhere else.
Chéngdū is one of China's most colorful big cities, always a delight to
explore. And it is the home, too, of China's most famous animal, the giant
panda.

Teahouses & Temples

It's best to begin getting a feel for Chéngdū early, by 8am, with a stop at
one of the outdoor teahouses on the north bank of the Jǐn River. Many of
China's last great teahouses still operate here, recalling the Three Kingdoms
era (A.D. 221–263), when Chéngdū was the capital of the Kingdom of Chǔ

and the scholar-officials gathered for conversation, entertainment, and drink at canteens along the river (though it wasn't until the Táng Dynasty that tea drinking became popular). Perhaps the most famous figure to frequent these canteens of leisure was the Táng poet Dù Fǔ, who composed several hundred poems to the "Brocade City" where he lived in exile.

Dù Fǔ's cottage, his home in Chéngdū, has survived as a park and tourist attraction, but unless you are a scholar of Chinese poetry, there's no reason to visit. I did so some years ago and the visit was not memorable. The park did not come into existence until 3 centuries after Dù Fǔ arrived in Chéngdū (A.D. 759), and there is nothing belonging to him here, certainly not the rather recently constructed thatched hut. The cottage is open daily from 9am to 5pm; admission is ¥30 ($3.75).

Wǔhòu Temple houses the memorial hall of Zhūgě Liàng, China's greatest military strategist and gentleman-scholar, who lived in Chéngdū during the time of the Chǔ rulers 17 centuries ago. However, a visit here is likewise not worth pursuing, unless of course you happen to be imbued with the literature of the Three Kingdoms and the heroic deeds of Zhūgě Liàng. Otherwise, keep to the streets of Chéngdū, its teahouses and temples. The hall is open daily from 9am to 5pm; admission is ¥30 ($3.75).

I prefer to start in Chéngdū by seating myself in a bamboo armchair at one of the **river teahouses,** chosen at random, where you will be quickly served a cup of flower tea. The cup includes a cover to keep the brew hot and an upturned saucer for lifting. To sip tea properly, grip the saucer in thumb and fingers while slipping the lid slightly back with the raised index finger. It takes practice to become a skilled Chéngdū tea drinker. For an investment of 50¢, customers can linger for hours.

Vendors will drift through, hawking trinkets and sticks to clean the ears. Ear cleaning is a passion in Chéngdū. Downriver, *tàijíquán* masters and other early risers were finishing up their exercises on the mist-laden promenade. Tobacco salesmen were also at work on the sidewalks, selling strong, thick sheaves that are meant to be trimmed and stuffed in the tiny bowls of bamboo-stemmed pipes.

Next, you can stop for breakfast at the **Lóng Chāo Shǒu Special Restaurant** a few blocks north of the river, partaking of the "little eats" (*xiǎo chī*—dim sum pastries and dumplings) that make up the traditional morning snacks of Sìchuān.

After a snack, take a cab to the **Wénshū Monastery (Wénshū Yuàn),** a mile north of the Máo statue. It's open daily from 8am to 5:40pm; admission is ¥1 (10¢). Wénshū, the center of Chán (Zen) Buddhism in Chéngdū, was founded 13 centuries ago. Today, it is the city's most popular Buddhist retreat, nearly always crammed with families burning incense and bowing to Wénshū (God of Wisdom), Maitreya (Laughing Buddha

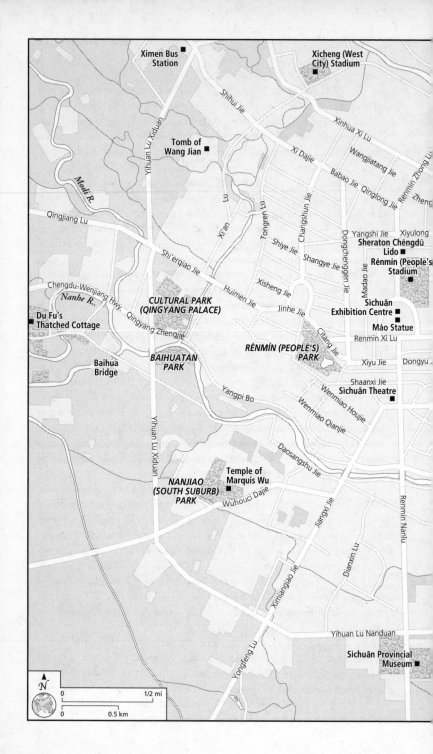

Ximen Bus Station

Xicheng (West City) Stadium

Shihui Jie

Xinhua Xi Lu

Wangjiatang Jie

Xi Dajie

Babao Jie

Qinglong Jie

Rénmín Zhong Lu

Rénmín Zhong

Tomb of Wang Jian

Yihuan Lu Xiduan

Lu

Xi'an

Tongren Lu

Changshun Jie

Dongchengen Jie

Madao Jie

Xiyulong

Modi R.

Qingjiang Lu

Shi'erqiao Jie

Shiye Jie

Shangye Jie

Yangshi Jie

Sheraton Chéngdū Lido

Huimen Jie

Xisheng Jie

Jinhe Jie

Rénmín (People's Stadium

Nanhe R.

Chengdu-Wenjiang Hwy.

CULTURAL PARK (QINGYANG PALACE)

Sìchuān Exhibition Centre

Du Fu's Thatched Cottage

Qingyang Zhengjie

RÉNMÍN (PEOPLE'S) PARK

Máo Statue

Renmin Xi Lu

Citang Jie

BAIHUATAN PARK

Xiyu Jie

Dongyu

Baihua Bridge

Yangpi Bo

Wenmiao Houjie

Shaanxi Jie

Sìchuān Theatre

Wenmiao Qianjie

Daosangshu Jie

Yihuan Lu Xiduan

NANJIAO (SOUTH SUBURB) PARK

Temple of Marquis Wu

Jiangxi Jie

Wuhouci Dajie

Dianxin Lu

Renmin Nanlu

Ximianqiao Jie

Yihuan Lu Nanduan

Yongfeng Lu

Sìchuān Provincial Museum

N

0   1/2 mi

0   0.5 km

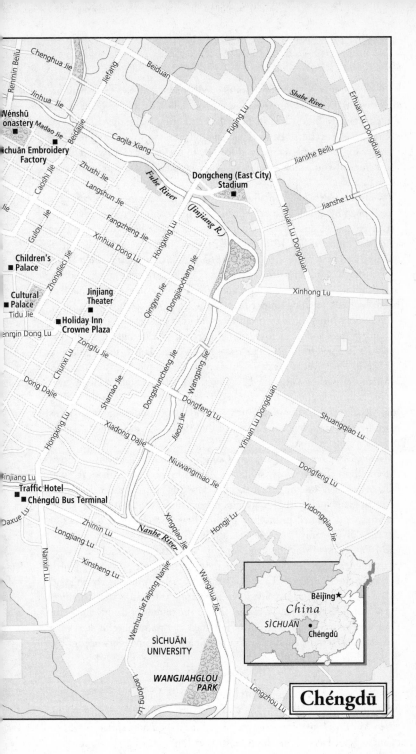

Chéngdū

of the Future), and Guānyīn (Goddess of Mercy). The five great halls are drenched in incense. The carved eaves, doors, columns, and wooden figures are particularly fine work. In fact, the monastery maintains an outdoor courtyard where craftsmen work all day under an awning carving religious statuary for use at the temple and for sale to the public. The woodcarvers don't mind if you watch—many are young apprentices, happy to practice their English.

Wénshū's oldest hall contains images of 17 generations of abbots, duly worshipped by a large number of monks. This is an extremely active temple. Here I met an 86-year-old man named Nán Shèng. He became a Buddhist monk at age 16 in Shǎnxī Province (the next province north). Wénshū had been his residence since 1966. Now extremely frail, Nán Shèng spends much of his time sitting on benches, counseling the younger monks, and napping. A number of temple volunteers, mostly older women, tend to his daily needs, fetching his rice bowl and washing his clothing.

Wénshū maintains its own outdoor teahouse in a garden court shaded by ginkgo trees and its own vegetarian restaurant located inside a hall that is always jammed for lunch. The restaurant is open daily from 10:30am to 10:30pm. The street at the main entrance to the temple, Wénshū Yuàn Jiē, is a **temple market** with a medieval look, clotted with stalls selling prayer beads, holy medallions, incense, and firecrackers, not to mention shoe soles, underwear, and bottled water. After looking through the stalls, cross town by taxi, stopping a mile west of the Máo statue at Chéngdū's most popular Daoist temple.

Green Goat Temple (Qīngyáng Gōng) is as lively a place of worship as the Buddhist shrine. Most Chinese who worship at one of these temples will, in fact, call on the other, thereby doubling their chances that some god will grant their wish. Qīngyáng's main temple, the **Hall of the Three Purities,** is decorated in brightly painted dragons. The bronze statues of the two "divine rams" *(shén yáng)* at the altar have been showered in coins and rubbed smooth by the hands of hopeful worshippers. Golden statues of the Three Purities—the Jade Emperor of Heaven, the god of the North Pole, and the Daoist sage Lǎozǐ—are the focus of continuous bowing and chanting. I walked inside while seven priests and three nuns were conducting a formal service. They were chanting to the sounds of drums and bells. Four very poor peasants in front of me, their clothes turning to rags, were completely prostrate, almost speaking in tongues, echoing every note of the rites fervidly.

Eating Fire

Across the street from Qīngyáng Gōng, try the Sìchuān specialties of the **Chén Má Pó Dòufu Restaurant,** named for the quintessential spicy dish of the region. Fiery *dòufu* (bean curd) is at the heart of Sìchuān cookery.

Mápó dòufu consists of spicy bean curd, ground pork, chopped spring onions, and an intense chili sauce pushed to the limits by aromatic vinegar. This particular restaurant claims to occupy the site where *mápó dòufu* was invented during the Qīng Dynasty reign of the Tóng Zhì Emperor (1862–75). The story goes that a certain Chéngdū chef named Chén was married to a talented *mápó*, which is a woman with a pockmarked face. Her talent was in the kitchen, where she devised a bean curd dish sprinkled with red "pocks" of chili pepper.

The *mápó dòufu* that immortalized this 19th-century "kitchen granny" must be numbingly hot to qualify as authentic; at this namesake restaurant it could not be more authentic or much hotter. Like many restaurants in Chéngdū, this one has communal dining on the ground floor that caters to working-class patrons, while the floor above is reserved for banqueting and more leisurely dining. I savored my meal on the second floor in a room of darkly stained wood and carved columns, its window shutters thrown wide open to the noisy temple street life across the way.

Here, as elsewhere in Chéngdū, I experienced *málà* ("numbing and hot") dining at its best. I alternated between the hot *dòufu* and a milder fish-flavored *dòufu*, its sauce a deft mixture of vinegar, garlic, ginger, spring onions, and a modicum of hot bean paste. I ordered a third bean-curd entree, too, known as drunken *dòufu*, a sweet dish of shredded bean curd in an intoxicating sauce. The hot-and-sour soup *(suānlà tāng)* comple-ments all three strongly flavored, hotly spiced dishes.

"All Sìchuān cooking exists as an excuse to consume hot peppers," a Chéngdū local once told me. Perhaps so, but the chili peppers that now seem to define many Sìchuān dishes are a relatively late addition—and a foreign one to boot. Chili peppers were introduced to China only in the 16th century, by way of Central America.

Pandas

Eighty percent of the world's 1,000 remaining giant pandas reside in Sìchuān Province. In 1978, the **Wòlóng Nature Preserve** was established 138km (86 miles) northwest of Chéngdū to protect this animal from extinction and allow scientists to study it in the wild. While there are tours to Wòlóng from Chéngdū, the trip is usually futile if your goal is to see a free-roaming panda. Dedicated researchers often go months without a sighting. The **Chéngdū Zoo** can also be a disappointment. A half-dozen or more pandas reside here (the most of any zoo in the world), but they are displayed only in cages or on one outdoor cement island with a tree and slide, and most afternoons they are asleep.

The best chance to see a giant panda in the near wild, then, is during an early-morning tour of the **China Research Base of Giant Panda Breeding**

(**Dàxióngmāo Fánzhí Zhōgxīn**), located 11km (7 miles) northeast of city center. The research base hopes to breed both the greater panda and lesser (or red) panda in captivity. But this is not a zoo, at least not an old-fashioned zoo like the Chéngdū Zoo 5km (3 miles) down the road. Although the pandas are caged at times in breeding houses at the research base, they are also let out to roam across 32 hectares (80 acres) of steep hills, forests, and bamboo groves. Visitors follow along on slate walkways, separated by deep moats from a dozen bearlike giant pandas and an equal number of more catlike red pandas who go their own ways, sometimes sitting up a few feet away, other times disappearing into the forest.

I visited in the early morning, starting out at 7am and arriving just after the visitors' gate opened, at 8am. By noon, pandas are usually curled up, out of sight, dead asleep, so morning is the best time to visit. The hills were encased in fog, but before long I spotted a giant panda scratching his back against a stump. He appeared to have just been fed, but he lazily rolled onto all fours, ambled over to a patch of bamboo, sat down, and went to work stripping off shoots. A panda's main occupation is eating bamboo—sometimes it spends up to 18 hours a day this way in the wild (with daily consumption of arrow bamboo averaging over 20 lb. per panda). At the research base, however, the pandas seem to spend more time napping than eating.

The little red pandas are more active. I watched several of them running through the trees, scampering down the steep inner embankments of the moats, and fighting like raccoons over bits of territory.

This was as close to an uncaged panda as I was ever likely to get, so I followed those that I found for about 2 hours. Only a few other tourists were out this early, and the mist still coated the bamboo, blotting out the hilltops. I could pretend for a moment that I was in the unfenced outdoors, that these pandas were free, that I was seeing a sight few humans have ever been allowed to witness.

The research base contains a hospital that is not open for tours and several outdoor panda sculptures. The base hopes to dramatically expand its facilities, acreage, and panda population in the next century, although that depends on finding sources for increased funding. One goal is to release a few captive pandas into the wilds by the year 2005. Recently, two of the base's pandas, Jiūjiū and Huāhuā, were sent halfway around the world to take up a 10-year residence in the Atlanta Zoo (which paid $4 million for the project—and changed their names to Lun-Lun and Yang Yang).

The research base's **Panda Museum,** unheated when I visited in December, is loaded with stuffed pandas. This motley collection of taxidermy, in poorly lit dioramas, belongs in a grim socialist museum of the 1950s, which this display too closely resembles. Some of the exhibits seem overly clinical as well, like the jars preserving specimens of panda sexual organs and the week-old panda baby, 8 inches long. For the most part, the Panda Museum is pathetic. The understocked, uninspired gift counter probably doesn't bolster the funding, and the butterfly museum upstairs wasn't even open when I visited.

The giant panda, which was not known to the Western world until 1869, when French priest Père David purchased a panda skin in Bǎoxīng County, Sìchuān, has become a logo for modern China, particularly its wildlife. Conservation of that wildlife is another matter. With proper management and promotion, the panda base in Chéngdū could easily become southwest China's largest draw for Western tourists, a source of revenue for China's underfunded wildlife conservation efforts. For now, however, the panda research base is a step in the right direction—a small step—and despite its drawbacks, it's still the only site in the world where so many tourists can see so many pandas in one pleasant preserve. The research base is open daily from 8am to 5pm. Admission is ¥10 ($1.25).

Chairman Máo Museum

Mr. Tray Lee is a product of the new, more economically liberal China. He is a freelance tour director who works his way through cafes and hotel lobbies where foreigners gather, dishing out his name card, describing his tours, and opening photo albums of the sights to which he can take you. His business card gives his title as "Mr. Lee, Cultural Interpreter and Ticket Agent" and proclaims, "Mr. Lee—A man understands you in China!!!" He says his tours are "unique personal visits: a reliable and easy chance to know more about China and its people." He lists his phone and mobile phone numbers, fax number, and e-mail address, as well as his home address. Best of all, his tours (to schools, hospitals, factories, kindergartens, and the countryside) are just as Mr. Lee advertises them: fairly priced, efficient, and personal.

Mr. Lee, son of a soccer coach, was born 30-some years ago in Shěnyáng Province, but he grew up in Chéngdū and he knows the older streets well. One afternoon we ended up at Wǔ Fú 23 (Five Blessings St.) in an older neighborhood. The aging wooden shophouse at this address has been converted into the **Chairman Máo Badge Museum and Research Facility.** The mastermind of this collection of Máo memorabilia is Wáng Āntíng. He was sitting back on a bamboo lounge when we entered the front room. Wáng, a former factory worker, is about 60 years old and very hard of hearing. He was born in this house, and his grandson and wife live in the back room, where they have a bed, table, and 27-inch color TV. Wang asked me to sign his large guest book, a register that includes the names of visitors from Germany, France, Japan, Russia, and various cities in China who have come to him to augment their own Máo collections.

The main room and the side room are stuffed—floors, walls, and ceilings—with nothing but Máo: Máo posters, commemorative Máo plates, red flags, ceramic busts, red-and-gold Máo buttons of every size, and Máo's little red book of quotations in its every edition. Corner tables serve as altars to Máo, complete with candles. Coffee tables block the aisles, hundreds of Máo buttons under their sooty glass tops. Red armbands from the Cultural Revolution (1966–76) as well as newspapers from that period of upheaval are pinned to the walls, as are "big character posters" heralding the various social and political movements that tore through the 1950s and 1960s like typhoons.

The nostalgic revival that Chairman Máo has enjoyed since the early 1990s is waning elsewhere, but in Wáng Āntíng's little museum, it's as robust as ever. For a decade, many people felt that an image of Máo, like that of a Buddhist or Daoist god, could bring good fortune. Taxi drivers from Běijīng to Chéngdū had portraits of Máo dangling from their rearview mirrors after a rumor spread about a cab driver with such an emblem whose life was spared in a traffic accident. Although Wang himself told us that the life of the former governor of Sìchuān was recently saved "by the spirit of Máo," the trend these days is a return to Buddhist icons.

Nonetheless, Máo's ghost is certainly visible enough in this cramped pack-rat museum. Wang told us he had "10 big bags" of Máo items in his collection, and I believed it. His own house has been turned upside down by this passion. A few years ago, Wang was desperately looking for a patron to move his museum to larger, classier quarters, but now he seems content to stay here. Meanwhile, he spends each day waiting for the next visitor to drop by while he stamps out his own shiny new Máo buttons on a small press. As I departed, Wáng Āntíng handed me a half-dozen buttons and his bilingual business card on which he is billed as "Head of the Máo Zédōng's Medals Research Society in China (Preparatory)," "Honorable Member of Shànghǎi Researchist Coordination Committee," and "Contemporary Cultural Relic of Chief Editor."

Later, outside the Chéngdū post office, the enterprising Mr. Lee asked me for one of the newly minted Máo buttons, which he proceeded to pawn off on a not-so-wily street vendor as a "Cultural Revolutionary antique."

That evening, when the sky turned copper red, I was walking back to my hotel, past the saluting statue of Máo, clean and white, when I noticed a street musician setting up his act. He was playing an *èrhú,* a traditional Chinese cello with two strings—except that his was an electric *èrhú.* He had wired its sound box to an amp and had strapped a microphone to its neck. As he sawed away with his bow, he stomped out a thunderous rhythm with both feet by beating on metal wash pans flipped upside down. He was the Bob Dylan of a new China. This was where the sidewalks of New York started to merge with those of Chéngdū, where East and West met head-on in the intersections of the next century. This was an *èrhú* unlike any ever strummed before in all the centuries of teahouses and temples, of calligraphers and emperors. It was a tune to the future, a song Máo never heard.

PRACTICAL INFORMATION

by Michelle Sans

ORIENTATION & WHEN TO GO

Chéngdū, a city of over 10 million, including its suburbs, is located in the center of Sìchuān Province, China's subtropical "rice basket," nearly 1,610km (1,000 miles) southwest of Běijīng. Summers are hot and rainy (especially July and Aug), but the average temperature in August is a moderate 78°F (26°C). Winters are cloudy and foggy but also mild, with temperatures rarely dipping below 0°F (–18°C). Tourist season begins in April and ends in November, when the weather is probably at its best.

Chéngdū is a few hours north of one of China's greatest outdoor monuments, the **Great Buddha at Lèshān** (see the following chapter for more information), which can be visited in 1 day. Chéngdū is also the gateway to **Éméi Shān,** the Western Peak of Buddhism (see separate chapter, beginning on p. 543), which requires at least a 2-night stay. Both these sites can be reached from Chéngdū by public bus or with a group tour.

GETTING THERE

By Plane **Shuānglíú Airport** is 18km (11 miles) south of the city. Destinations include Běijīng (many flights daily); Guǎngzhōu (8–9 flights daily); Hong Kong (1–2 flights daily); Kūnmíng (8–10 flights daily); Lhasa (1–4 flights daily); Shànghǎi (6–10 flights daily); and Xī'ān (5 flights daily). Flights can be booked through Tray Lee (© **0139/0803-5353** cellphone; fax 028/8556-4952; lee_tray@ hotmail.com) or any of the several English-speaking travel agents at and near the Traffic Hotel. Many hotels will also book air and train tickets. **Dragon Air** has an office in the Sheraton Lido (© **028/8676-8828;** Rénmín Zhōg Lù 15,

Yì Duàn). The **airport shuttle** from the China Southwest office on Rénmín Nán Lù (next to Mínshān Fàndiàn) takes about 45 minutes and costs ¥10 ($1.25); it departs about every half hour. A less direct **CAAC shuttle (Mínháng Bānchē)**, no. 303, leaves every half hour from 7am to 7pm from the CAAC office at the north rail station. The 23km (14-mile) ride takes 70 minutes and costs ¥6 (75¢). **Taxis** from the city center to the airport cost ¥40 to ¥60 ($5–$7.50), including road fees.

By Train The main **rail station** is at the northern end of Rénmín Běi Lù, about

8km (5 miles) north of the Máo statue in the city center. The ticket office is to the right of the main building. A large sign reading BOOKING OFFICE in orange lettering identifies it. Counters 6 and 7 serve "foreign guests." The office is open 24 hours. Try to purchase tickets at least 2 days in advance. Major destinations are Běijīng (fast trains 28 hr.–31 hr.), Kūnmíng (fast trains 18½ hr.), and Xī'ān (fast train 11 hr.).

By Bus Chéngdū's newly renovated **Xīnnánmén Bus Station (Xīnnánmén Qìchē Zhàn),** at the corner of Xīnnán Lù and Línjiāng Zhōg Lù, and next to the Traffic Hotel, is clean, efficient, and tourist-friendly (has signs in English). Buses leave from here for Lèshān (A/C; ¥37/$4.50; 2½ hr.) and Éméi Shān (A/C; ¥32/$3.90; 2¼ hr.). Daily buses to Chóngqìng leave throughout the day from the equally clean, efficient **Wǔ Guì Qiáo Bus Station (Wǔ Guì Qiáo Qìchē Zhàn),** southeast of the city center on Yínghuì Lù (A/C; ¥107/$13; 4½ hr.).

GETTING AROUND

Chéngdū's flat terrain and numerous bike lanes make walking and biking easy, but blocks are long, and crossing the river can require a trek before you reach a bridge. Rénmín Lù bisects the city on the north-south axis. Its east–west counterpart is less straightforward: At the heart of the city (Tiānfǔ Square), Rénmín Xī Lù runs west from the square and Rénmín Dōng Lù runs east; then, after a block in either direction, the names change every block or so. Unfortunately, most of Chéngdū's avenues have a multitude of names, making a street map essential. Traffic Hotel (Jiāotōng Bīnguǎn), Línjiāng Zhōg Lù 77, rents **bicycles** for ¥10 to ¥15 ($1.25–$1.90) per day. City **buses** (¥1–¥2/10¢–25¢) serve all parts of the city. Routes are on city maps. **Taxis** charge an average of about ¥1.50/15¢ per kilometer (.62 mile).

TOURS & STRATAGEMS

Chéngdū has enough good independent travel agents who speak English that you needn't bother with China International Travel Service (CITS) and its generally higher rates. The best deals can be found inside and in the vicinity of the **Traffic Hotel (Jiāotōng Bīnguǎn). The Traffic Travel Service** (inside the hotel) and **Tiānfǔ International Travel Service** (at the entrance to the hotel) both book air and train tickets and offer a variety of tour packages. Traffic Travel offers round-trip transport and entrance to the Panda Breeding Center for ¥50 ($6.25), which costs slightly more than getting yourself there and back, but is considerably more convenient. Most agents offer a Lèshān/ Éméi Shān combined tour (¥370–¥480/ $46–$60) and a Three Gorges package. For the most personalized tours, talk to **Mr. Tray Lee** who, in addition to offering the usual tours, arranges excellent countryside trips (his favorite); backstage opera trips; and visits to schools, the little Máo Museum, traditional medicine hospitals, factories, and anything else you can dream up. He can also introduce you to local Sìchuān and Tibetan restaurants, and book planes, trains, and buses. His prices are competitive and he is always reachable by mobile phone (✆ **0139/0803-5353** cell phone; 028/8555-4250 voice mail; fax 028/8556-4952; lee_tray@hotmail.com).

WHERE TO STAY

As with many Chinese cities, Chéngdū has an ever-growing selection of high-end hotels, with the result that competition is stiff. The room rates given below are the rack rates, but discounts of 30% to 60% are usually possible—even during high seasons.

Holiday Inn Crowne Plaza (Zǒngfǔ Huáng Guān Jiàrì Jiǔdiàn) This 33-floor tower, opened in 1997, is one of Chéngdū's more luxurious hotels. The lobby, with its Italian marble floors, gold-trimmed columns, and European murals, is opulent and vast. The rooms aren't as attractive as the Sheraton's, but they are larger. Each floor has three suites with bathrooms containing separate showers and bathtubs. There are also two "executive floors."

Zǒngfǔ Jiē 31 (4 blocks east of the Máo statue). © 800/465-4329 or 028/8678-8461. Fax 028/8678-9791. www.crowneplaza.com/hotels/ctuch. 433 units. ¥1,360 ($170) double (40% discounts are standard here). AE, DC, MC, V. **Amenities:** 4 restaurants; indoor swimming pool; tennis courts; health club; sauna; 12-lane bowling alley; concierge; tour desk; 24-hr. business center; conference rooms; shopping arcade (Parkson department store nearby); salon; 24-hr. room service; same-day dry cleaning and laundry; nightly turndown. *In room:* A/C, satellite TV, dataport, minibar, coffeemaker, hair dryer, safe.

Sheraton Chéngdū Lido (Tiānfǔ Lìdū Xīláidēng Fàndiàn) Opened in 2000, the Sheraton may be the most attractive of Chéngdū's luxury hotels. The lobby, with its fountain and large floral arrangement, has a warmer ambience than the standard, and the staff at the front desk is amiable and efficient. Although the standard rooms aren't quite as spacious as those at the Holiday Inn, the decor—including royal blue carpet and a cozy overstuffed chair—is more inviting. Many of the rooms have bathrooms with separate bathtub and shower. Executive rooms occupy five floors.

Rénmín Zhōg Lù, Yī Duàn 15 (10-min. walk from Máo statue). © 028/8676-8999. Fax 028/8676-8888. www.sheraton.com/chengdu. 402 units. ¥1,440 ($180) double. Breakfast included. AE, DC, MC, V. **Amenities:** 4 restaurants; bar; health center with indoor swimming pool; Jacuzzi; sauna; steam bath; 24-hr. room service; massage. *In room:* A/C, satellite TV, dataport, broadband Internet, minibar, hair dryer, iron, safe.

Traffic Hotel (Jiāotōng Fàndiàn) This is among the best-run budget hotels in China, and though it was set up with backpacking foreign travelers in mind, it is suitable for any independent traveler. The front desk staff and the elevator operators are friendly. Standard doubles come with heat and clean private bathrooms that were renovated in 2002. The best rooms are the deluxe doubles (just ¥240/$30), with larger, newer bathrooms. The hotel hallways and lobby are somewhat worn, but there are two gift shops, a kiosk with drinks and snacks, a noticeboard, luggage storage, a computer room, two tour offices, bike rentals, and a new coffee shop in the works.

Línjiāng Zhōg Lù 6 (next to the Xīnnánmén bus station, southeast bank of Jǐn River). © 028/8545-1017. Fax 028/8544-0977. 151 units. ¥200 ($25) standard double; ¥240 ($30) deluxe double. No credit cards. **Amenities:** Snack shop; bike rental. *In room:* TV, 24-hr. hot water.

WHERE TO DINE

If you are coming to China just for the food, Chéngdū can keep you interested for months. Indeed, its Sìchuān dishes alone can do that. In addition to serving up some of the best Sìchuān cuisine, Chéngdū has a broad selection of restaurants that include Cantonese, Korean, Japanese, Indian, Italian, French, and Continental.

Chén Má Pó Dòufu Restaurant SÌCHUĀN Several Chéngdū cafes claim the same name and history as the original site where the Sìchuān masterpiece, *mápó dòufu*, was first served a century ago. This branch serves the best spicy *dòufu* (bean curd) dishes of the bunch. The second-floor tables and carved wooden decor have character and make for a more agreeable setting than the grimy dining hall below. You can look out on the street through wooden shutters while enjoying the complex flavors of Sìchuān and other regional specialties, including a sweetly flavored drunken *dòufu* (*zuì dòufu*). Hot-and-sour soup (*suānlà tāng*) complements any of these meals. *Xī Yīhuán Lù 113 (near Qīngyáng Zhèng Jiē and opposite Qīngyáng Temple and Wénhuà Gōngyuán).* ℂ *028/8776-9737. Reservations suggested for weekends. Main courses ¥16–¥67 ($2–$8). No credit cards. Daily 10:30am–9:30pm.*

Grandma's Kitchen (Zǔmǔ de Chúfáng) AMERICAN HOME COOKING The farm-style chandeliers and wall lamps, straight-back wooden chairs with gingham cushions, and framed photos on the wall give this split-level restaurant, in the south part of town, an appropriately homey atmosphere. While tuna-fish pizza is ill-advised, the rest of the menu, which includes fried chicken, a variety of steaks, pancakes, milkshakes, and great homemade desserts (the peanut butter pie is delectable), is an answer to the prayer of any U.S. resident craving a taste of home. *Kēhuá Běi Lù 75.* ℂ *028/8524-2835. Main courses ¥35–¥50 ($4.35–$6.25). No credit cards. Mon–Fri 8:30am–10:30pm; opens at 8am on weekends.*

Lóng Chāo Shǒu Special Restaurant (Lóngchāoshǒu Cāntīng) SÌCHUĀN Newly renovated, this is Chéngdū's most famous snack restaurant, serving an array of *xiǎochī* ("little eats," or dim sum Sìchuān-style). Dumpling connoisseurs prize these creations for their color, appearance, aroma, and flavor. Order the sampler for ¥25 ($3) at the window and take a place at one of the crowded tables. You'll be served 14 different snacks, including soup, dumplings, preserved meats, pickled vegetables, cabbage flower cakes, wontons, and sweet pastries. During breakfast (8–10am) and lunch (noon–2pm), it can be difficult to find a seat. The snack flavors are strong and varied, underlining an old Sìchuān saying: "A hundred dishes, a hundred flavors" ("Bǎi cài, bǎi wèi"). *Chūnxī Lù, Nán Duàn 6–8 (at Dōng Dàjiē, north of the Jǐn River).* ℂ *028/8666-6947. No reservations. Sampler ¥25 ($3). No credit cards. Daily 8am–9pm.*

Shǔfēng Garden (Shǔfēng Yuán) SÌCHUĀN This is one of Chéngdū's most elegant Sìchuān restaurants. The third floor is a shrine to the hot pot. Buffet tables hold more than 80 ingredients. Weekends are enlivened by musical revues. The decor is Old European, with white plaster walls, gilded moldings, and sculpted cherubs. Chéngdū hot pot begins with a broth made by boiling chicken, beef, or cow bones garnished with hot bean paste from nearby Pí County (renowned for its long-lived population). Peppercorn, spices, and noodles are added. Thin slices of eel, beef, chicken, carp, pig's liver, bean curd, and tender vegetables are boiled to taste at the table. Shǔfēng's hot pot is excellent and only costs ¥40 ($5) per person.

On the second floor, setting and cuisine change. The decor is Qīng Dynasty "southern bridge" style with bright red columns, silken scrolls, and lacquered rosewood furniture. The best dishes are *dāndān* noodles laced with pimentos, dry-fried diced pork with bamboo shoots, boiled beef in hot sauce, cauliflower with Sìchuān-style bacon, chicken-ball soup, sizzling crispy rice with pork and gravy, tea-smoked duck, *gōngbǎo* chicken (known as Kong Pao chicken in much of the West; it's chicken, peanuts, and red chiles in a spicy sweet-and-sour sauce), and chrysanthemum cake for dessert. *Dōng Dàjiē 153 (on corner of Hóngxǐng Lù, southeast of Máo statue).* © **028/8665-7629.** *Reservations advised on weekends. Main courses ¥25–¥125 ($3–$15). No credit cards. Daily 11:30am–2:30pm and 5:30–11pm.*

Tandoor Indian Cuisine NORTHERN INDIAN Of Chéngdū's wide selection of restaurants serving Western and other non-Chinese fare, Tandoor Indian Cuisine is one of the best. Tandoor's Indian chef clearly takes great care in buying and preparing ingredients to make authentic dishes from chiefly the north, but also from southern India. A delicious specialty from Goa is the Portuguese-influenced pork *vindaloo*. This very hot dish is made with Indian spices, vinegar, and chilies. One of the best northern specialties is *murgh malai* kabob, chunks of chicken marinated 6 hours in ginger-garlic paste, then mixed with cheese, cream, coriander, chili, cinnamon, and anisette and cooked in a tandoori oven. The restaurant is airy and handsome; elegant wooden rafters give it flair, and soft Indian music enhances an already pleasing ambience. *Rénmín Nán Lù, Sì Duàn 34, directly behind the Sunjoy Inn (Xīnzú Bīnguǎn).* © **028/8555-1958.** *Reservations recommended. Set meals ¥48–¥110 ($6–$14). A la carte also available. AE, DC, MC, V. Daily 11:30am–2pm and 5:30–10:30pm (with traditional Indian dance 7–9pm).*

LÈSHĀN: AT THE FOOT OF THE GREAT BUDDHA

乐山大佛

AT LÈSHĀN THERE'S A SAYING: "THE mountain is Buddha, Buddha is the mountain." The words may be poetic, but the meaning is quite literal: There is a mountain here, and the mountain is a Buddha.

China has many Great Buddhas, from Lantau Island's giant bronze Buddha to Wúxī's Língshān Buddha, but the gigantic image of the Buddha carved into the cliff face of Língyún Mountain, on the east side of the Mín River at Lèshān, is the greatest. Rising 70m (233 ft.) straight up from the shore, the **Great Buddha of Lèshān (Lè Shān Dàfó)** is one of the few wonders to survive from the Táng Dynasty (A.D. 618–907), and the most monumental.

Building Buddha

The handiwork of a devout, indefatigable monk named Hǎitōng, who set to work with hammer and chisel in A.D. 713, this statue of Maitreya, the Buddha of the Future, is frequently hailed as the largest carved Buddha in the world. Its statistical dimensions befit the superhuman realm. Even seated, hands on knees, the Great Buddha of Lèshān rises to the height of 35 men. Buddha's head is 15m (50 ft.) high. Each eye is 3m (10 ft.) wide. His ears are 6m (20 ft.) long, his shoulders 27m (90 ft.) broad, and his bare feet, which nearly touch the river, 9m (30 ft.) across, wide enough to seat 100 sightseers at a time.

The good monk Hǎitōng did not live to see the completion of his sculpture, which was 90 years in the making. It is said that he plucked out his own eye to impress would-be donors. His mission was to create a guardian presence vast enough to subdue the treacherous waters, to protect the passing boatmen and their cargo, and to suppress the river's floods. Today, the waters still teem with commerce and boatmen, many of whom earn a living by ferrying tourists to this singular shrine.

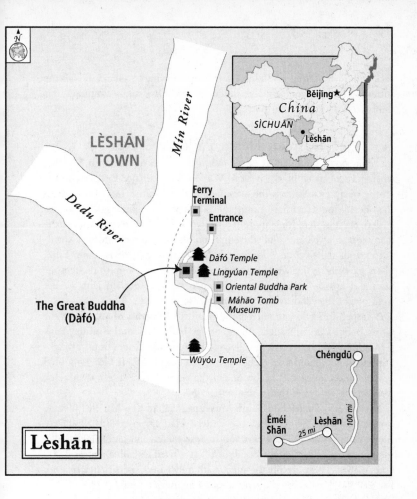

Lèshān

Sailing to Buddha

Although gargantuan, the Great Buddha has a graceful form and benevolent expression. The classic view is straight on from the roiling river Mín, where the statue has survived politics and the ravages of wind and erosion for 13 centuries. Unpainted open tour boats, with standing room only, ply the channel for a full frontal view of the Great Buddha. While these boats are not comfortable, they are sturdy and maneuverable. Smaller speedboats and even a few skiffs rowed by hand also look for passengers at the quay near the main entrance to the Great Buddha. The skiffs look rather fragile. The currents are quite severe.

From the river, Buddha appears to be enthroned in a deep recess—sitting in a closet of red sandstone. You can see tourists and pilgrims streaming up and down the stairs carved into the cliff walls on either side of the great image. They dance across Buddha's toes. The riverboats usually swing back and forth in front of Buddha, sometimes slowing to a standoff with the current so that everyone can get a decent picture. On a sunny afternoon, this can make for a spectacular portrait.

Temples, Theme Parks & Graves

The tour boats tie up at an island mountain south of the Great Buddha, where passengers climb the peak to **Wūyóu Sì,** the major Buddhist shrine on the river. It dates from the same period as the statue, but its four main chambers—the Guardian King, the Maitreya, the Tathagata, and the Mahavira halls—are from more recent dynasties. More recent still are the many kiosks of charms and souvenirs and a teahouse that affords a splendid view of the river and the great holy mountain on the horizon, **Éméi Shān,** gateway to the Western Paradise. It is a steep walk up to the temple, but the river view at the top is worth lingering over, especially with a drink from one of the vendors.

A suspension bridge connects the island to **Língyún Shān,** where the Great Buddha is enthroned. At the bridge is the **Oriental Buddha Park (Dōngfāng Fódū),** a modern collection of Buddhist images from throughout Asia, highlighted by a reclining Buddha 167m (557 ft.) long—touted as the world's longest. It is also one of the world's tackiest, clearly a quick work in plaster rather than a marble carving.

Next door is the **Máhāo Tomb Museum (Máhāo Yán Mù),** with stone coffins and burial relics from the Eastern Hàn Dynasty (A.D. 25–220). Along the river are the tiny **cave tombs** where a few images of the Buddha survive from the days when Buddhism first arrived in China almost 2,000 years earlier. These are off the main path and require persistence to find. Just keep walking along the river, about a quarter of a mile.

Buddha's Feet

Across the bridge, the trail rises again to the heights of Buddha's crown. A series of steps, the **Stairs of Nine Turnings,** descend to the feet of the statue. These narrow stairs are crowded with onlookers who wind down Buddha's left side.

At the base, children usually make a stone stage of Buddha's colossal feet, acting out songs, dances, and kung-fu routines, while parents and grandparents spread out their picnic lunches on the toenails. Recently, however, park authorities have been putting up signs forbidding people to stand on any part of this "Cultural Relic." I doubt this prohibition will last.

The Buddha's recess is honeycombed with cutout shrines where a multitude of holy statues once resided. Almost all have disappeared because of robbery or rain. On the other side of the Great Buddha, nine more turnings of stairs upward bring climbers level with Buddha's ears. Up close, the forehead in profile is a smooth dome, patched with what looks like concrete.

The survival of the statue has had much to do with an ingenious drainage system concealed behind the Great Buddha that empties the rain and hill-side runoff into the river below, but a close inspection of Buddha's head makes me think that the rock has been patched and cleaned up over the centuries, too. Otherwise, this statue seems to be in miraculous condition, impervious to the elements and the passage of time.

Buddha's Crown

Buddha's head was once capped by a seven-story pavilion, but this was dismantled during the warfare that erupted at the end of the Yuán Dynasty. Above and behind the Buddha's head, there's another temple, **Dàfó Sì,** the Great Buddha's own. A short road leads down to the north entrance where the buses and river ferries wait. The temple grounds are an ideal spot to linger and take in the river scenery from the high platforms on Buddha's right side, removed from the world of man below.

On Buddha's south side is another temple, **Língyún,** dating back to the 7th century but renovated in the 17th century, with yet another laughing Buddha of the Future residing inside. From this side of the carving, there are fine views of Buddha in profile and some statues that most tourists don't get to see, images of the sculptor Hǎitōng, and a cave said to have been his monastic retreat.

In Buddha's temple, there is the stone likeness of the Sòng scholar, Sū Shì, who lived near Lèshān. The pond where Sū washed his brushes is still at Buddha's crown. In his most famous poem, Sū relinquishes the desire to become a great figure on the world's stage, preferring to "journey about like a wine-laden cloud" among the rivers and hills of Lèshān.

Through the centuries, through the ebb and flow of empires—even into this age when mass tourism has replaced pilgrimage, and ant-sized gawkers climb from knee to noggin—the Great Buddha maintains its serene countenance, eyes nearly closed, lips in a knowing smile.

PRACTICAL INFORMATION

by Michelle Sans

ORIENTATION & WHEN TO GO

The Great Buddha at Lèshān is 161km (100 miles) south of Chéngdū, the capital of Sìchuān. Lèshān is a small town. Most visitors to the Great Buddha set out from Chéngdū in the early morning, returning in the afternoon. Travelers to the nearby sacred mountain of **Éméi Shān** (see separate chapter, beginning on p. 543) often stop at Lèshān on their way to or from Chéngdū.

Summers are unbearably hot, humid, and rainy here, making early spring and late autumn the most comfortable times to visit.

GETTING THERE

By Bus A/C **buses** depart for Lè Shān from Chéngdū's Xīn Nán Mén Bus Station every half hour from 7am to 7pm. A ticket costs ¥36 ($4.50) and the ride takes 2½ hours. Return buses for Chéngdū leave from the entrance every half hour or so. The last returning bus to Chéngdū from the entrance leaves between 5:30pm and 6pm (whenever it fills up). Buses also leave from Lè Shān's Long-distance Bus Station every 15 minutes, and from the Central Passenger Station every half hour. Buses drive between Éméi Shān and Lè Shān bus stations every few minutes; fare is ¥5.5 (68¢). **Taxi** fare between Éméi and Lè Shān is about ¥60 ($7.50). Buses arrive in one of three places in Lè Shān, the Long-distance Bus Station, Passenger Central Bus Station, or a bus stop on the main road into town. The Long-distance Bus Station is farthest from the Great Buddha site. Taxis from there cost ¥15 ($2). From the Lè Shān

bus stop, take bus 3 to the Great Buddha (¥5/60¢). What should be a 10-minute drive stretches to a half hour as the driver trawls for passengers along a circuitous route. The bus unloads at Lè Shān's north gate. From there, it's a 7-minute walk to the park entrance or you can hitch a motorcycle lift for a few *yuán*. By taxi from the bus stop to Lè Shān scenic area, you can expect to pay ¥12 to ¥15 ($1.50–$1.88).

A round-trip **tour boat** or **motorboat** from the north gate to Wūyóu Temple costs ¥30 ($3.75) and allows time for photos of the Great Buddha. **Ferries** run between the Lè Shān City dock and both Língyún Shān and Wūyóu Sì (¥7/$87¢). The last boat is at 6pm.

At the entrance to Lè Shān scenic area, vendors sell **maps** of the mountain for ¥3 (35¢). They are also sold at the small stands near the head of the Great Buddha. One side of this bilingual map is Lè Shān; the other is Éméi Shān.

TOURS & STRATAGEMS

If you don't wish to travel independently, tour agents in Chéngdū can arrange 1-day tours to Lèshān for around ¥200 ($25), which includes transport, entrance fees, and lunch. Two-day tours combining Lèshān and Éméi Shān are also an option for ¥370 to ¥420 ($46–$52). For agents, see

"Tours & Stratagems" in the preceding chapter on Chéngdū.

Admission & Hours Admission to the Great Buddha Scenic Area is ¥40 ($5) and now includes entrance to all the sights, though a few of the temples still charge a small additional fee of ¥1 to ¥3 (10¢–35¢).

WHERE TO STAY & DINE

At Língyún Temple, the **Jìfēng Bīnguǎn** (© 0833/213-0853) has clean double rooms with private bathrooms for ¥240 ($30). Some, but not all, of the rooms are damp, so be choosy. The most comfortable place to stay in downtown Lèshān is the **Jiā Zhōu Bīnguǎn,** Báitǎ Jiē 19 (© 0833/213-9888; fax 0833/213-3233), a three-star, Chinese-managed

hotel with basic modern rooms and a tour desk. Doubles cost ¥360 ($45). There are a number of good small restaurants in the vicinity of the hotel. A small, inexpensive restaurant, **Yáng's,** with Chinese and Western food and an English menu, is at Báitǎ Jiē 49. The Great Buddha Temple also has a **vegetarian restaurant.**

SOUTHWEST CHINA: SEARCHING FOR SHANGRI-LA

GUÌLÍN: THE LANDSCAPE
OF DREAMS

桂林

THE SCENERY AT GUÌLÍN IS UNLIKE
that of any other city on Earth. Its peaks "rise as suddenly from the Earth
as trees in a forest," writes one Chinese poet, "surrounding the city like
mountains floating in an imaginary sea," claims another. These craggy
peaks and pillars of limestone must have been the models for the traditional
landscapes painted for centuries on silk scrolls. Until I visited Guìlín, I
assumed the impossibly contorted, improbably steep, vibrantly swirling
mountains of these artists simply did not exist. At Guìlín, they do. And
they exist inside the city as well as in the countryside.

Guìlín possesses "five famous virtues": spectacular caverns, exotic rock
promontories, fragrant osmanthus, green hills, and clear waters. It is the hills
that most beguile me. I would return again and again simply for a view of
Guìlín's remarkable hills. There are grander mountain peaks, but none so
peculiar and so numerous, planted thick as a forest. "Only at Guìlín, in a
single sweep of the eye, can you see so many peaks spring from the ground
like shoots of jade bamboo, jostling one another, some as near as a stone's
throw, others faint in the distance," wrote a Sòng Dynasty (A.D. 960–1280)
traveler, Fàn Chéngdà. "For their astonishing strangeness surely the hills of
Guìlín rank first in the world." And so does its Lí River.

The Lí River (Lí Jiāng)

Guìlín's very top attraction is the Lí River (Lí Jiāng), which has posed for
more painters and photographers than any other place in China—and for
good reason. This is "the best scenery under heaven," as an old saying goes,
the best scenery if you like clear rivers, green bamboo, and sheer, twisting
limestone pinnacles. Hán Yù (A.D. 768–824), a Táng Dynasty poet, composed the classic description of the Lí River: "The river is a blue ribbon of
silk, / The hills are hair pins of jade."

Tour boats by the hundreds make the daily 84km (52-mile) journey down the Lí River to Yángshuò. My vessel was typical: a flat-bottomed barge, rounded at each end, with seating and tables inside the long cabin and an open observation deck on top. While waiting to depart, I purchased a pomelo, a thick-skinned gigantic relative of the grape-fruit, from one of the peasant vendors who sailed alongside on a raft of hollow bamboo shafts lashed together like a rural Chinese surfboard.

The first phase of the passage, from Guìlín down to the village of Yángdí, is merely a prelude. **Elephant Trunk Hill (Xiàngbí Shān),** on the west shore, is one of Guìlín's most popular parks and remarkable natural monuments. It clearly resembles an elephant drinking from the Lí River. All the great limestone formations in Guìlín and down the Lí River are said to look like something or someone, but Elephant Hill's resemblance takes little imagination to identify. From the water, I had a perfect view of the hill's trunk, and could see between that trunk and the elephant's legs, **Moon-in-the-Water Cave (Shuǐ Yuè Dòng),** which is said to resemble a silver moon floating on the Lí River. Perhaps if the moon is out, it does. Small boats can enter this cave when the water level permits. Jibei Chushi, a Sòng Dynasty poet, wrote "In Praise of Moonlit Nights" here, a dreamy paradox that reads:

> The silver moon is deep below the river.
> The silver moon floats upon the river.
> The river flows where the moon cannot go.
> Where the moon goes, the river cannot flow.

Elephant Trunk Hill is succeeded on the southeast bank by **Pagoda Hill (Tǎ Shān),** capped by a Míng Dynasty pagoda that is said to imprison a thousand-legged demon. The hill is also renowned for its maple trees and the red leaves that grace it in the fall. **Pierced Hill (Chuān Shān)** stands next to Pagoda Hill; it is noted for the large round opening in its side, aptly named Moon Cave. There follows on the west bank two craggy towers of note: **Fighting Cock Hill (Dòujī Shān),** said to resemble roosters at a showdown, with coxcombs prone and wings spread; and **Clean Vase Lying in the River (Jìngpíng Shān),** both back on the west bank. As I say, this is a mere prelude to the bands of fantastic peaks that lie ahead. At the town of Qífēng (Strange Rock), there's the first hint of the majestic scenery ahead. Here the peaks and hills thicken into a forest.

Three hundred million years ago, this region was swallowed by the sea. Two hundred million years ago it reemerged, and the exposed limestone was sculpted by acidic rain, mist, and wind-blown dust. These karst peaks were then sliced apart and honed into immense pillars over the last two million years. The result is a forest of stone shafts and crags that seems to have grown straight up from the banks of the Lí, topping out at heights of 60m to 90m (200 ft.-300 ft.).

There's a mythic counterpoint to this geological tale of bizarre formations. The story goes that long ago, when the South China Sea threatened to engulf Guìlín, the gods decided enough was enough: They would move the northern hills south as a floodgate. The gods transformed the hills into goats in order to herd them south, but a fierce, blasting wind scattered the goats willy-nilly down the Lí River, where they changed back into the unruly peaks we see today.

None of the strange hills and cliffs that rise directly from the riverbanks are named for goats these days, but there are hills and pillars named for oxen, islands, a ferry, a lonely lady, an emperor's crown, and a panel of natural embroidery, as intricate as stitched silk. Every hill has a story, but I was content to drift unguided. The river is hushed, well beyond the city streets of Guìlín, and the landforms encourage silence. I feasted on each curve of the river, hungering for the next impossible formation. A buffet lunch was served below, a generous one of Chinese dishes, fish, vegetables, and fruits. I saw the foodstuffs cleaned in the river water, but I still decided to eat until I was full. The Lí is one of the clearer rivers in China, cleansed by the reaction of carbonic acids with the limestone rocks.

After lunch, I climbed back up on the observation deck to bathe in the scenery. We passed villages of thatched huts. Fishermen were scooping the river bottom for shrimp with funnel-shaped nets. Children were wading and swimming in the sandy bend of the river. Enormous groves of bamboo reached out from the banks, shooting out like green feathery petals. This is a primeval land of extremes: a tropical valley hemmed in by mountains of cold limestone.

From **Yángdí Village (Yángdí Xiāng),** the midway point of the cruise, it's nearly another hour's float to **Nine-Horse Fresco Hill (Jiǔmǎhuà Shān),** probably the river's most famous cluster of razor-sharp peaks. The shadings and fissures on its many faces are said to resemble a fresco of horses bolting, leaping, neighing, rearing, and running. For centuries, hopeful would-be officials, scholars on their way upriver to attend the Imperial Examinations, scoured Fresco Hill with desperate eyes: The more horses they discerned, the higher their test scores, it was said. To see nine horses engraved on the flanks of Fresco Hill was to secure the highest mark on the exams. I failed to discern a single worthy steed in the hues of this hill, but 800 years ago, the poet Zhōu Háo did better:

> How many thousands of years ago
> Was this screen carved in stone?
> The more it is pelted by rain and winds
> The clearer its image.

South of Mural Hill we passed the village of **Xìngpíng** on the east shore. At this ancient county seat, the scenery is unsurpassed. Xìngpíng is an ink-wash landscape fashioned from water and stone. No artist is required. Scores of myths are stored in the odd karst pillars and peaks that resemble scepters, snails, and carp, as well as the followers and fingers of Buddha. Groves of bamboo and willow wave from the banks, which are here spread 90m (300 ft.) apart as the river's flow becomes almost limpid.

At the end of the river journey, the tour boats pull in at the village of **Yángshuō** (see the following chapter for more information), where the scenery, according to tradition, "exceeds even that of Guìlín." The blue hills stretch forever south, west, and east. We tied up at the wharf under the implacable **Green Lotus Peak (Bì Lián Fēng).** The quay swarms with roving vendors. Fishermen pose with cormorants, the birds they've taught to retrieve fish. The tour buses back to Guìlín are parked nearby. Above the dock, south along the river, is the eight-sided **River Pavilion (Yíngjiāng Gé),** an ideal place for a final view of the river's exquisite landscape.

The buses pull out from the narrow village streets late in the afternoon. The vendors converge on the buses, rapping on the windows, holding up their wares. I first took this road north back to Guìlín 14 years ago. At that time, workers were building a new highway beside the old one. They were building it entirely by hand, hauling rock, splitting it to size with mauls, fitting it stone by stone into the roadbed, and paving it over, shovelful by shovelful. The sole heavy equipment on the site was an old steamroller, like a machine out of a childhood storybook. At night, the road-building brigades lay down in the roadbed and slept under the stars.

No words or pictures precisely express the spell cast by the uncanny scenery of the Lí River. Fàn Chéngdà, who traveled through China during the Sòng Dynasty (A.D. 960–1280), once complained, "I have often sent pictures which I painted to friends, but few believed what they saw. There is no point," Fàn decided, "in arguing with them." Once you've been down the Lí River, you'll know what he meant. The reality of the river surpasses the finest print of the camera, the most fantastic simile of the pen, the most extravagant stroke of the ink brush.

The City of Guìlín

When I first visited Guìlín in 1986, in October, at the peak of tourist season, every hotel authorized to take foreigners was full. I was kicked out of the cavernous Lí River Hotel after a single night, without ceremony or apology. Through sheer determination, luck, and door-to-door begging, I ended up in the older wing of the Rónghú Hotel, where I slept under a torn mosquito net, lulled into dreams by the melodic drip of the toilet.

Almost 2 decades later, at least the hotel situation has changed. International chains like the Sheraton and others have moved into a city that ranks among China's top five tourist attractions. In fact, my complaint about Guìlín these days is that the tourist business is ruining what was once a quiet little city in a sublime setting, driving up prices, knocking down old neighborhoods, and fanning the fires of capitalism's darker side: greed. Nevertheless, I was happy to find a hotel that would accept a reservation and not expel me should a large tour group suddenly appear on the scene.

Solitary Beauty Peak (Dú Xìu Fēng)

Once ensconced in a reliable hotel, I made plans to revisit the places that had made the deepest impression on me. I set out first for Solitary Beauty Peak, one of several limestone pillars in downtown Guìlín that can be climbed. It's open daily during the summer from 7am to 7pm and during the winter from 7:30am to 6:30pm; admission is ¥15 ($1.90). Qīng Dynasty poet Yuán Méi described this peak eloquently:

> No trace of its origins, no clues to parentage,
> Dropped from the sky, a lonely peak.
> Strange are the hills of Guìlín, nine out of ten,
> But Solitary Beauty is the strangest of all.
> Three hundred sixty stairs to the top
> And the whole of Guìlín at its foot.

During the Míng Dynasty (A.D. 1368–1644), the city's ruler, a relative of the emperor, built his mansion at the foot of this peak. Later, it became the regional site for the Imperial Examinations, taken by all those in China who competed for positions in the civil service. Today, Solitary Beauty Peak is enclosed within the walls of **Guǎngxī Provincial Teachers' College.** In fact, as I walked north up Zhōngshān Lù, I was met by an art student from that college, eager to practice his English. We walked together to the college gate, guarded by two stone lions. Inside the walls, I stared up at the 150m (500-ft.) high limestone peak that occupied the center of campus.

At the foot of the stairs to the peak is a chamber called **Book-Reading Cave;** it resembles the reading room of a marble library, an apt site for the old empire's examinations. Like the other famous crags within the city, Solitary Beauty Peak holds the ruins of temples along its flanks and has, at its summit, an unearthly view of the city and the endless chain of peaks. Alone now, I marched up the tall stone-and-concrete steps, a steep and winding trek. The panorama from the top is quite exceptional. To the north, I had a dazzling view of **Whirlpool Hill (Fúbō Shān)** and **Brocade Hill (Diécǎi Shan),** the two other most famous karst towers in town. To the south, I could trace the Lí River as it twisted between **Pierced Hill (Chuān Shān)** and **Elephant Trunk Hill** (**Xiàngbí Shān;** see below).

The city itself was undergoing an extensive rebuilding, as nearly every city in China is. Guìlín's new buildings were not too high: Most seemed to be under eight stories. A campaign of high-rise construction in Guìlín would block its stunning topography, ruining its appeal, but, fortunately, the horizon was still open. The campus spread out below was particularly attractive because it was more traditional, its soaring tiled roofs and courtyards more in keeping with the landscape. Guìlín is not everywhere a beautiful city, but it is enmeshed in a breathtaking natural setting.

Perhaps that's why there are so many art students and art galleries in Guìlín. On top of Solitary Beauty Peak these days, some of the art students have taken to selling postcards and sodas to tourists (they also have a gallery in one of the campus buildings). Guìlín is certainly a city pushing to make a buck off its visitors.

I spent an hour savoring the view from the summit. Solitary Beauty Peak is the most dramatic of Guìlín's vertical hills and its most central. I've climbed the other city hills in the past, but this one was sufficient for my return. A thousand years ago the poet Chang Ku climbed Solitary Beauty Peak and likened it to a stone pillar holding up the southern sky, "standing aloof between Heaven and Earth." Even earlier, in the 5th century, poet Yán Yánzhī had given this peak its name and noted how, "towering, it floats in the middle of the town" like the mast of a stone ship.

At the foot of Solitary Beauty Peak, the student I had met was waiting. We walked down to a local restaurant (named "Local Restaurant") on the

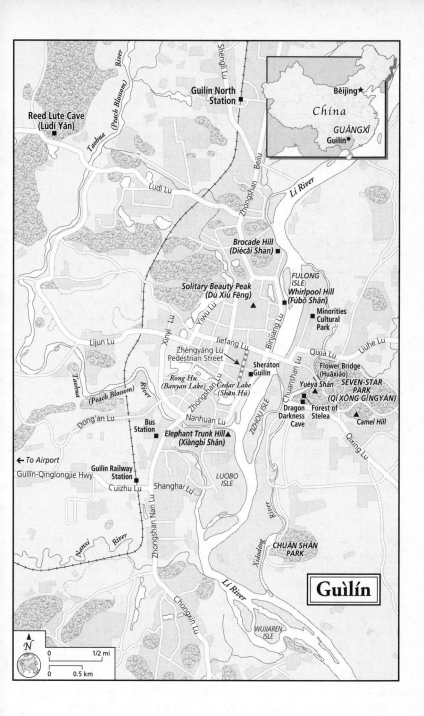

Reed Lute Cave
(Lúdí Yán)

Guìlín North
Station

Shènglì Lu

Li River

Bèijīng★

China

GUĂNGXĪ
Guìlín●

Taohua (Peach Blossom) River

Ludi Lu

Zhongshan

Bellu

Brocade Hill
(Diécǎi Shan)

FULONG
ISLE

Whirlpool Hill
(Fúbō Shān)

Solitary Beauty Peak
(Dú Xiù Fēng)

Minorities
Cultural
Park

Yiwu Lu

Xinyi Lu

Lijun Lu

Jiefang Lu

Qixia Lu

Liuhe Lu

Zhèngyáng Lù
Pedestrian Street

Sheraton
Guìlín

Flower Bridge
(Huāxiǎo)

Binjiang Lu

Rong Hu
(Banyan Lake)

Cedar Lake
(Shān Hú)

Chuanshan Lu

Yuèyá Shān

SEVEN-STAR
PARK
(QĪ XĪNG GŌNGYUÁN)

Zhongshan Lu

Taohua (Peach Blossom) River

Dong'an Lu

Nanhuan Lu

ZIZHOU ISLE

Dragon
Darkness
Cave

Forest of
Stelea

Camel Hill

Bus
Station

Elephant Trunk Hill
(Xiàngbí Shān)

Qixing Lu

← To Airport

Guìlín-Qinglongjie Hwy.

Guìlín Railway
Station

LUOBO
ISLE

Cuizhu Lu

Shanghai Lu

Zhongshan Nan Lu

Nanxi River

Xiadong River

CHUĀN SHĀN
PARK

Li River

Chongxin Lu

WUJIAREN
ISLE

Guìlín

N

0   1/2 mi

0   0.5 km

east end of Cedar Lake (Shān Hú) near the Lí River and feasted on river shrimp. The plates we ordered cost ¥85 ($11) each—my first indication that Guìlín was more than living up to its recent reputation as a tourist rip-off. I had never paid such prices at a street restaurant in China, particularly in a small city where seafood was readily available. At least the seafood was tasty, the owner gregarious, and the lakefront shady.

Elephant Trunk Hill (Xiàngbí Shān)

That afternoon, I visited Elephant Trunk Hill on my own. It's open from 6:30am to 10:30pm daily; admission is ¥15 ($1.90). This park lies on the southeast corner of Guìlín, where the Táohuā River joins the Lí River. I climbed onto the "back of the elephant" where a small pagoda is dedicated to Pǔxián, an immortal servant of the Buddha who is always depicted as riding on the back of a white elephant. From the top of Elephant Trunk Hill, there is a serene view of the Lí River running south through a deep karst valley.

Leaving the park, I took a wrong turn in the streets and ended up walking for several miles through unpleasant, congested city streets before I regained my bearings. While the motorized traffic is much less than in many comparable interior cities, it's still heavy enough in Guìlín to be annoying to pedestrians.

And the city is anticipating even more traffic. A new superhighway connects downtown westward to the new airport. The road is lit. A new economic zone has been staked out along the freeway, its roads paved, utilities laid, apartments and offices completed, and the foreign-venture factories are starting to hum—just out of sight of old Guìlín.

Two Lakes

Guìlín's main north–south thoroughfare, Zhōngshān Lù, divides its two lakes, **Banyan Lake (Róng Hú)** to the west and **Cedar Lake (Shān Hú)** to the east toward the Lí River. These lakes are the remnants of the moat that girded Guìlín during the Táng Dynasty (A.D. 618–907). A section of the city's ancient south gate has been restored on the north shore of Banyan Lake, alongside a banyan tree said to be 8 centuries old.

Banyan Lake is encircled by pathways, roads, and a bridge. It is landscaped in willow and peach trees, as well as the occasional osmanthus (cassia) for which the city is named. Guìlín means "Forest of Osmanthus," a flowering bush whose blossoms exude a sweet aroma each autumn. At dusk, Banyan Lake is fringed in colored lights. Its island pavilions and bridges are lit up, too, making this the ideal place for a romantic stroll. One evening I emerged from the Holiday Inn (now the Guìlín Bravo Hotel) to take a walk around the lake. As soon as I crossed the street, I was intercepted by a pedicab driver claiming to be a moonlighting student. He offered to sell me a trip around the lake. I declined. He then tried to sell me a massage from a young lady and, finally, the young lady herself.

I walked on, remembering a more innocent time, almost 2 decades ago, when I met another young man at Banyan Lake. He was nearly penniless, I'm sure. He spoke enough English to tell me that he was a "bum," a bum in the old sense, I think. He had been wandering China on his own for months, something thoroughly uncommon in the 1980s—or today, for that matter, when resident permits, difficult to obtain without a job, are required to stay in any city. All he had in his possession was a diary. "I am," he said, "a rolling stone." His dream was to get a job as an English-speaking guide for foreign tourists in Guìlín. We rented a rowboat on Banyan Lake and spent the afternoon talking about the world.

Today, the same rowboats with their swan-shaped bows are still for rent on Guìlín's lakes. They appear just as heavy in the water, just as difficult to row. But speed is not the objective on these pavilioned lakes. You really want just to float away. The wanderer I met 10 years ago floated away that afternoon. I'll never know his fate. He despaired of ever landing a government job, since he lacked the right "connections" *(guānxi)*. He told me he enjoyed his unusual freedom to the fullest. He never asked me for money, not even money for food.

But today, more than ever, in this Forest of Osmanthus, amidst these towering stone pillars, it's money that seems to hold everyone in thrall.

Seven Stars & Cormorants

Seven-Star Park (Qīxīng Gōngyuán) is named for its seven peaks, which resemble the stars of the Big Dipper. This constellation fallen to Earth is a lovely park on the east side of the Lí River. I walked to it one morning with my acquaintance from the art school. It's an hour-long walk through the heart of Guìlín's busy downtown, across the Lí River, and onto **Flower Bridge (Huāqiáo),** built of wood in 1456 and rebuilt in stone after the Flood of 1540. Flower Bridge is a graceful arching span encased in a tiled roof gallery over the little Xiǎodōng River, which borders Seven-Star Park.

Seven-Star Park is for walking, and we walked several miles of its pathways, first turning north in search of the park's chief natural attraction, **Seven-Star Cave (Qīxīng Yán).** With its high-season (May–Oct) ¥50 ($6) admission tag (which includes the park and the cave), it's overpriced, but the caves of Guìlín are as famous as its limestone hills, so I won't say you shouldn't take an hour's stroll through this brightly lit cavern, one of Guìlín's most fascinating and biggest—although **Reed Flute Cave (Lúdí**

Yán), west of the city, is more beautiful. Visitors have left messages carved on the walls of Seven-Star Cave for the last 13 centuries.

On the other side of the cave we had a fine view of **Camel Hill (Luòtuo Shān),** which resembles its name. I declined the chance to climb to its summit. The amusement park at its foot was neither inviting nor busy. Its small Ferris wheel, its bumper cars, and even its new water slide seemed to be rusting and cracking into oblivion.

Turning south, we walked downriver along the Xiǎodōng to Seven-Star Park's primary cultural treasure, its **Forest of Stelae (Guìhǎi Bēilín),** an overhanging cliff under which calligraphy, poems, and pictures have been carved on thousands of stone tablets over the past 1,600 years. The peak here is called **Crescent Moon Hill (Yuèyá Shān),** site of **Dragon Darkness Cave (Lóngyǐn Dòng),** renowned for its crinkled, scaly walls that resemble the imprint of a departed dragon.

We decided to follow the path up the side of the hill for a view of the river. It was from here that, 10 years earlier, I'd had my first view of cormorant fishing in China. Fishing with these birds is an old tradition, particularly in Guìlín. A single cormorant, it is said, can catch enough fish to support an entire family. I'd watched an old fisherman below working with five cormorants. He tied each bird's neck with a ribbon to prevent it from swallowing the fish it snatched. To call his cormorants back to the flat bamboo raft where he stood, the fisherman whacked the river surface sharply with his pole while he jumped up and down fiercely in his bare feet. Whenever a bird returned its catch to his hand, he praised it in a voice that carried to the top of Crescent Moon Hill.

It seems that the cormorant fisherman has moved on, too, since then. The only ones I saw in Guìlín this time worked on the river's edge in parks where they charged tourists who wanted their pictures taken with them and their birds.

Minorities, Touts & Discos

The commercialization of Guìlín has reached its newest form with the opening of the **Minorities Cultural Park (Mínsú Fēngqíng Yuán),** which is located on the east side of the Lí River about a 40-minute walk north from Seven-Star Park, one of the ethnic amusement parks so popular in China and throughout Asia. Guìlín's version is open daily from 8am to 11pm, and charges ¥45 ($5.65) by day, ¥60 ($7.50) after dark (perhaps to pay its electric bill). Its grounds are filled with brand-new models of China's minority architecture. The minority people themselves, who perform at each village stop, are authentic enough.

The province in which Guìlín lies, Guǎngxī Zhuàngzú Autonomous Region, consists of over three million members of the Zhuàng minority. Many Zhuàng, as well as Miáo and Dòng people, are thrilled to be spending a summer working in "the big city." While wandering through the village, I witnessed performances by gong-and-drum bands, ethnic dancers, and *qì gōng* experts. The *qì gōng* demonstration consisted of 10 people in colorful ethnic costume standing on two slabs of marble placed across a young girl's stomach for a period of 1 minute. What this had to do with minority culture in China, I could only wonder, but that's show biz. The one display I did enjoy was a lodge devoted to ancient musical instruments of these ethnicities. I was invited to play several of the gongs, and I obliged, even though as I exited the music hall I was charged ¥5 (60¢) for the privilege.

Like most minority villages in China, Guìlín's version is truly set up only for tour groups. There are no explanatory signs in English for independent foreign travelers, who can better spend your time and money by going to the minority regions directly.

We walked back into town and sat down for lunch in what I took to be a real dive, a seafood cafe that advertised itself with tubs of live delicacies outside—fish, eels, crab—and cages of snakes within. There were tree snakes, water snakes, and five-step snakes available (five steps being the farthest you can get after being bitten by one). I skipped the snakes and went straight to regular Chinese fare. First came a plate of fresh greens, then a plate of hacked-up chicken, its head and claws still in view. The third plate was pork slices in bamboo; the fourth, bamboo shoots in vinegar with rubbery slices of pig stomach. The bill came to slightly more than that of yesterday's lunch. It was time to move back into the international hotel restaurants for my dining.

That evening, I succeeded in convincing the art student into taking me uptown to a very local disco for some cheaper entertainment. The venue was an old school gymnasium, so darkened that the waitresses had to locate tables using flashlights. There was no cover charge. I paid only for the sodas. There were flashing lights around the dance floor, where a few young people danced the disco dances of the 1970s, finishing up the evening with what looked like the bunny hop.

Reed Flute Cave (Lúdí Yán)

If you've never ridden a bicycle in China, do so in Guìlín. The hotels rent bikes by the hour or day. Bike riding appears more dangerous than it is. Once you're in the flow with other bicycles, it's a relaxing way to travel—just remember to clang your bike bell like a maniac at every intersection.

Guìlín is compact enough so that you can ride a bicycle into the country-side in a matter of minutes. My favorite destination is Reed Flute Cave (Lúdí Yán), 8km (5 miles) west of downtown, about an hour's ride. You can also reach the cave by public bus, taxi, or organized city tour. From April to November, the cave is open daily from 7am to 5:30pm (last ticket sold at 5:20pm); during other times, hours are shortened by a half hour on both ends. Admission is ¥50 ($6).

Setting out from the Holiday Inn on the southwest tip of Banyan Lake, I cycled north along Xìnyì Lù to Lìjūn Lù, a major intersection. Turning left, I kept on Lìjūn Lù for most of the journey, passing Yínshān Hill, Xīshān Hill, and Báiyán Hill before the road curved north at Lion Crag and hugged the east bank of the Peach Blossom (Táohuā) River. At Lúdí Lù, the road abruptly ended, crossing the river over Fēiluán Bridge and heading northwest another half mile to the entrance of Reed Flute Cave. The countryside was green, the river clear, the scenery increasingly spectacular. At the cave, there were flat rice paddies with some of Guìlín's most dramatic limestone peaks looming in the background. This is the scene that appears on countless travel posters, one of the most beautiful spots for photography in China.

As for Reed Flute Cave, it's worth a half-hour tour. Park your bike in one of the bicycle lots and lock it. This cave once served as an air-raid shelter during World War II, when America's Flying Tiger squadron was based in Guìlín. Today, it is one of China's better-illuminated caves. The quarter-mile-long array of passageways is wet, cool, twisting, and narrow; the stalactites and stalagmites are ornate (lit with colored lights and given names according to what they look like); and there is one grand chamber, the Crystal Palace, where the hero of China's epic novel, *Journey to the West,* is said to have slain the evil Dragon King with a magic needle. The needle, of course, is also in the cave, a garishly lit, harpoon-sized pillar.

I'm not a true spelunker, but it's almost mandatory to take in a cave or two while in Guìlín. There are really two Guìlíns in this karst wonderland. One Guìlín is aboveground. The other is below the surface. Poet Yuán Méi compared the two in a graphic verse:

> Seeing the blue hills from the outside
> Is like touching the exterior of a person.
> Seeing the hills from the caves inside
> Is like plucking the internal organs.

Reed Flute Cave is probably the single most impressive portion of "underground" Guìlín. It's also much too popular. You'll have to shove your way past a hundred vendors and an occasional camel or two towed by aggressive photographers. But for a view of the countryside, its fields and uncanny peaks, it's worth fighting the crowds.

PRACTICAL INFORMATION

by Sharon Owyang

ORIENTATION & WHEN TO GO

Guìlín is located in the northeastern part of the Guǎngxī Zhuàng Autonomous region in southwest China, 1,610km (1,000 miles) from Běijīng, and 362km (225 miles) west of Guǎngzhōu and Hong Kong. Guìlín is one of the top five most visited Chinese cities. The main attraction is cruising the Lí River from Guìlín south to the village of **Yángshuò** (see the following chapter). A visit to Guìlín can also be combined with a trip to the minority villages of Lóngshèng and Sānjiāng (see separate chapter) northwest of Guìlín.

With summer's high heat and humidity and winter's low rainfall affecting water levels in the Lí River, the best months for cruising are April and May, and September and October, when the river is deep enough. April to August also marks the rainy season, however, so be prepared with rain gear. If possible, avoid the first weeks of May and October, when China celebrates national holidays and the Lí River becomes even more congested with tourist boats than usual.

GETTING THERE

By Plane   Guìlín is well connected by air to many of China's major cities, with flights to Guǎngzhōu (1 hr.), Běijīng (2½ hr.), Shànghǎi (2 hr.), Kūnmíng (1½ hr.), Chéngdū (1¼ hr.), and Xī'ān (2 hr.). Air tickets can be purchased at the **CAAC office** at the Mínháng Dàshà on Shànghǎi Lù (© 0773/384-3922), and also at travel agencies or hotel tour desks. There are also international flights from Guìlín to Seoul and to Hong Kong (daily). **Dragonair** has an office at the Guìlín Bravo Hotel, Rónghú Nánlù 14 (© 0773/282-3950, ext. 1150/1160; fax 0773/286-1666). Guìlín's **airport** (© 0773/282-3311) is 29km (18 miles) west of city center. Airport shuttles (¥20 ($2.50) depart every half hour between 6:30am and 8pm from the CAAC office, and also meet incoming flights. Taxis to the airport cost around ¥100 ($13).

By Train   Train travel to and from Guìlín is not very convenient due to the surrounding mountainous topography.

While there are several trains a day to nearby destinations, such as provincial capital Nánníng, trips farther afield often require several days' travel time (24 hr. to Kūnmíng, 26 hr. to Shànghǎi, 29 hr. to Xī'ān, 24 hr.–28 hr. to Běijīng, and 14 hr. to Guǎngzhōu). In addition, sleeper tickets for these destinations are often hard to come by, as few trains originate in Guìlín. Guìlín has two train stations, though the main one used by most travelers is the **Guìlín Huǒchēzhàn** (© 0773/383-3124), in the southern part of town at the intersection of Zhōngshān Lù and Shànghǎi Lù.

By Bus   Guìlín is well connected by bus to other Guǎngxī destinations such as Yángshuò, Lóngshèng, and Běihǎi. From the Guìlín Bus Station (Guìlín Qìchēzhàn) (© 0773/382-2153) on Zhōngshān Lù, just north of the train station, large, air-conditioned direct *(zhídá)* buses go to Běihǎi (7 hr.; ¥150/$19; at 8:30, 9:20, 10:20am), Lóngshèng (2½ hr.; ¥15/$1.90; midsize buses every 40 min. 7am–7pm), and Guǎngzhōu (9 hr.; ¥150/$19; at 9am, 11am, 9pm, 10pm, 11pm). Regular non-air-conditioned buses, minibuses, and sleepers leave for the same destinations throughout the day as well, but these often stop to pick up passengers along the way. The air-conditioned waiting room for direct (zhídá) buses is to the left of the station as you enter.

A new private bus service, the **Guìlín–Hong Kong Express Bus** (© 0773/ **585-7088**; fax 0773/585-7099), now runs between Guìlín and Hong Kong every Friday evening. The luxury air-conditioned bus (¥350/$44 one-way; ¥600/$75 round-trip), with video movies and onboard lavatory, departs from the Guìlín Guìshān Hotel on Chuānshān Lù at 7pm, stops at the Yángshuò Paradise Hotel at 8pm, and arrives in Huánggǎng in Shēnzhèn at 7am. After passengers go through Customs and Immigration, the bus continues on to Shatin, Kowloon Tong, and Tsimshatsui in Hong Kong. For the return, the bus simply retraces the route, departing Hong Kong's Tsimshatsui at 4pm and arriving in Guìlín the next morning around 7am. As of this writing, only one bus a week travels this route, though plans were underway to increase the frequency.

GETTING AROUND

Guìlín is a compact area and is easy to get around by foot or bicycle. Bilingual maps are usually available in hotel gift shops or from street vendors. **Bicycles,** which are useful for reaching Seven-Star Park (a 2.4km/1½-mile ride) and Reed Flute Cave (a 5km/3-mile ride) can be rented at the Bravo Hotel, the Sheraton, and other hotels at rates of ¥25 to ¥50 ($3–$6) per day plus a deposit of ¥300 to ¥400 ($38–$50). **Taxis** cost ¥7 (90¢) for 2km (1¼ miles), then ¥1.60 (20¢) per kilometer, but the fare jumps to ¥2 (25¢) per kilometer after 4km (2½ miles). Getting around town should cost around ¥10 to ¥14 ($1.25–$1.80) per trip. There are also several buses geared towards tourists: Bus no. 58 (free; 8:30am–4:30pm) runs from Nánxī Park in the south to Reed Flute Cave, stopping along the way at Elephant Hill, Seven-Star Park, the Minorities Cultural Park, Fúbō Hill, Diécǎi Hill, and Yùshān Park. A sight-seeing minibus travels a loop around Seven-Star Park, Elephant Hill, Fúbō Hill, Diécǎi Hill, and Reed Flute Cave between 8:40am and 4pm. This bus is also free, but passengers are required to show their entrance tickets to at least one of the five sights upon boarding.

TOURS & STRATAGEMS

There are **Guìlín Tourism Information Service** centers around town, most noticeably outside the train station (© 0773/382-7391) and in the Central Square (Zhōngxīn Guǎngchǎng; © 0773/ 285-4318). They can answer travelers' questions and provide information on hotels and sights.

Local Tours **China International Travel Service (CITS)**, Bīnjiāng Lù 41, near the Sheraton Hotel (© **0773/286-1623;** fax 0773/282-7424), arranges full-day city tours with English-speaking guides for ¥200 ($25) per person. Their CITS Panda Bus picks up daily from the following hotels: Fúbō, Sheraton, Bravo, Royal

Garden, and Guìshān. They can also organize half-day city tours, day trips to Yángshuò (by bus ¥193/$24 per person), and overnight trips to Lóngshèng Minority Village (see chapter on Sānjiāng) and Terrace Fields for ¥450 to ¥550 ($56–$68) per person, including transportation and accommodations. The **Tour Everyday Company (Tiāntiān Yóu Lǚyóu Gōngsī;** ℂ **0773/389-3608)** has outlets all over town, but their day tours are conducted mostly in Chinese. Still, the office in front of Elephant Hill Park has information on hotels and sights, and can arrange in-town accommodations. The concierge desk at the **Sheraton Hotel,** Bīn Jiāng Nánlù (ℂ **0773/282-5588),** also offers a wide variety of local tours, including a Lí River cruise for ¥520 ($65); half-day (¥280/$35) and full-day (¥400/$50) city tours; nighttime cormorant fishing trips for ¥64 ($8); evening cultural performances for ¥96 ($12); and a 1-day tour to Lóngshèng for ¥200 to ¥300 ($25–$38).

Package Tours CITS and the very helpful **China Youth Travel Service (CYTS)** at Yùcái Lù 10 (ℂ **0773/581-2336;** fax 0773/214-9106; gxcyts@163.net) can arrange complete package tours of Guìlín (including a Lí River cruise, a city tour, accommodations, meals, airfare, and an English-speaking guide). Trips can vary to include Yángshuò, Lóngshèng, and Sānjiāng as desired. Many tour operators in Hong Kong offer the same complete package tours for those who are visiting Hong Kong but want to sample the mainland. See the Hong Kong chapter for a description of tour agents and operators.

Lí River Cruise A boat cruise from Guìlín to Yángshuò along the 435m (270-mile) long Lí River is usually sold as the highlight of a Guìlín visit. Currently, river trips for foreigners depart not from Guìlín proper but from Zhújiāng Pier (Zhújiāng Mǎtóu), 24km (15 miles) and a half hour to the south by bus, at around 8:30am. Boats arrive in Yángshuò, 84km (52 miles) south of Guìlín, in the early afternoon after 4 to 5 hours of sailing. There's a stop for shopping in Yángshuò, after which tour buses transport passengers back to Guìlín (1 hr.). Tickets for the cruise (¥460–¥480/$57–$60) can be bought at hotel tour desks, CITS, CYTS, or any travel agency, and include transportation to Zhújiāng Pier, an English-speaking guide, a Chinese lunch, and the return bus trip to Guìlín.

WHERE TO STAY

Given a tourist destination as popular as Guìlín, it's surprising that more international hotel chains are not represented here (the five-star Sheraton is currently the only foreign-managed hotel in town). However, there are two other five-star establishments and many four-star hotels that provide the basic creature comforts. Be sure to book well ahead if you're thinking of visiting during the peak tourist months of May, June, September, and October, as hotels are often heavily booked then. *Note:* Many Guìlín hotels tack on a 5% service charge and a ¥8 ($1) per-person per-night government tax that rises to ¥25 ($3.10) per person per night during the 2nd to the 6th days of the Lunar New Year and also during the May and October national holidays.

Fúbō Hotel (Fúbō Shān Zhuāng) Of the three-star locally managed hotels, this is the best of the lot, close to Fúbō Shān and Dúxiùfēng, and with lovely views of the Lí River. Rooms are a little plain but perfectly comfortable and clean. River-view rooms are quite large, as their balconies have been closed off, while rooms on the fourth floor have been recently renovated and their bathrooms equipped with hair dryers. Best of all, the hotel regularly gives a 30% discount off its rack rate, although the discount rapidly disappears during the first weeks of May and October.

Bīnjiāng Lù 121 (next to Fúbō Hill and the Lí River in northeast Guìlín). © *0773/282-9988. Fax 0773/282-2328. 151 units. ¥640 ($80) double. AE, DC, MC, V.* **Amenities:** 2 restaurants (Chinese and Western); gym; sauna; bike rental ¥8 ($1) per hr.; tour desk; shopping arcade; salon; room service; laundry service. *In room:* A/C, TV, minibar, some rooms with hair dryers.

Guìlín Bravo Hotel As one of the first internationally managed hotels in Guìlín, this former Holiday Inn has earned its stripes and is the best choice of the four-star hotels in town. Located near the city center on the northwestern bank of Banyan Lake (Rónghú), the hotel has comfortable rooms furnished with large twin beds and soft chairs. Rooms on the ninth floor in particular have high ceilings and afford some marvelous views of the lake. Bathrooms are bright and clean and have tub/shower combinations. Service is efficient. The hotel's three restaurants serve good Western, Cantonese, Sìchuán, and local foods.

Rónghú Nán Lù 14 (southwest corner of Banyan Lake). © *800/465-4329 or 0773/ 282-3950. Fax 0773/282-2101. www. glbravohtl.com. 274 units. ¥960 ($120) double. AE, DC, MC, V.* **Amenities:** 3 restaurants; outdoor swimming pool; rooftop tennis courts; health club; Jacuzzi; sauna; bike rental; tour desk;

business center; shopping arcade; salon; room service; next-day dry cleaning and laundry. *In room:* A/C, satellite TV, minibar, safe.

Royal Garden Hotel (Dìyuán Jiǔdiàn) This five-star hotel's chief disadvantage is its location on the east bank of the Líjiāng 10 minutes by car from the city center, making it less conveniently located for the independent traveler. Catering mostly to Japanese and lately also American tour groups, the hotel offers first-rate facilities and all the standard luxuries. Spacious guest rooms are fitted with large twin beds and dark wood furniture, while bathrooms, on the small side, are nevertheless clean and come with tub/shower combos as well as scales. Upon request, business rooms on the sixth and seventh floors can be equipped with computers with broadband connections. The hotel's four restaurants (Western, Chinese, Japanese, coffee shop) offer the city's most diversified choices for hotel dining. *Yánjiāng Lù.* © *0773/581-2411. Fax 0773/581-5051. www.c-b-w.com/hotel/ royalgarden. 335 units. ¥880–¥960 ($110–$120) double. AE, DC, MC, V.* **Amenities:** 4 restaurants; outdoor swimming pool; outdoor tennis courts; health club; sauna; bike rental; tour desk; business center; shopping arcade; salon; 24-hr. room service; same-day dry cleaning and laundry; nightly minority cultural show; 24-hr. medical clinic. *In room:* A/C, satellite TV, minibar, hair dryer, safe.

Sheraton Guìlín (Guìlín Dàyǔ Dàfàndiàn) Although the Sheraton is showing signs of age, it still offers the best and most efficient service in town and is currently still the top choice among foreign tourists. The hotel has an unparalleled location, flanked by the Lí River on one side and the new Zhèngyáng

Pedestrian Street, with its myriad shops and restaurants, on the other. Rooms, arrayed around the modern if somewhat dark atrium lobby, are well appointed and have comfortable beds. The marble bathrooms are clean and have tub/shower combos. The hotel, which has four restaurants (Chinese, Western, Guìlín, coffee shop), offers some of the most reliable Western dining in town, and also boasts a 20m (66-ft.) long swimming pool. Not surprisingly, the staff is professional, friendly, and very helpful.

Bīnjiāng Nánlù (west bank of Lí River). ✆ 0773/282-5588. Fax 0773/282-5598. www.Sheraton.com/Guilin. 430 units. ¥1,245 ($150) double. AE, DC, MC, V. **Amenities:** 4 restaurants; outdoor swimming pool; health club; sauna; bicycle rental; billiards room; concierge; tour desk; airline-ticketing service; airport shuttle; 24-hr. business center; shopping arcade; salon; 24-hr. room service; babysitting; same-day dry cleaning and laundry; nightly turndown. *In room:* A/C, TV, dataport, minibar, coffeemaker, hair dryer.

WHERE TO DINE

A famous and ubiquitous local specialty is Guìlín mǐfěn (Guìlín rice noodles), which is served at practically every street-corner eatery. Order it dry or in broth, then add chives, chili, and pickled sour green beans, according to taste, to the spaghetti-like rice noodles. You can also order the noodles with chicken, beef, and even horse meat (mǎròu). Other local specialties, including snake, dog, seafood, and a variety of wild animals, sometimes too exotic for foreign tastes, are easily available in any number of local restaurants, although many don't have menus in English. Although hotel restaurants offer many of these specialties in a clean if expensive setting, try to venture beyond the hotel for at least a meal or two. Guìlín may not have the most sophisticated dining, but there are now a number of establishments that offer some fine dining at very reasonable prices.

One recommended restaurant is the **Yíyuán Fàndiàn,** located on the north bank of the Táohuājiāng at Nánhuán Lù 106 (✆ 0773/282-0470). The restaurant serves some excellent spicy dishes,

including the tear-inducing diced chicken stir-fried with bushels of chilies and garlic, and the shuǐzhǔ niúròu (tender beef slices and vegetables in a chili sauce). Calm the palate with the tángcù cuìpíyú (crispy sweet-and-sour fish), then accelerate to a spicy finish with the dāndān miàn (Sìchuān dāndān noodles). The pleasant decor is all wood with lattice windows and ceiling fans. Service is friendly and efficient, and there is an English menu. Dinner for two will run you about ¥80 to ¥100 ($10–$13).

Judging by the crowds that throng to the **Guìlinese Good Luck Restaurant (Jùfúlín Měishíyuàn)** during mealtimes and well into the evening, this is one of the more popular restaurants on the new Zhèngyáng Bùxíng Jiē (Zhèngyáng Pedestrian St.) just east of the city center (Zhèngyáng Lù 10; ✆ 0773/280-8748). Housed in a two-story building, this well-lit, clean restaurant offers local food, stir-fries, and dim sum on the first floor and in the outdoor dining area, complete with wrought-iron chairs; the second floor specializes in Cantonese cuisine, focusing on seafood. There is plenty to choose from on the menu, but local favorites include sautéed snails, Lí River shrimp (which can be blanched, sautéed, or deep-fried), steamed Lí River fish, and stewed turtle. Or you can forget the menu and simply order from the food displayed on trays outside the restaurant: Spicy crayfish, skewered meats and gizzards, tofu, and different kinds of vegetables can all be grilled or cooked on the spot as you sit at an outside table, watching all of Guìlín stroll by. Dinner for two is ¥80 to ¥120 ($10–$13). Open daily from 11am to 1:30am; dim sum is not served from 2:30 to 5:30pm.

Vesta Restaurant (Zàowángyé Xiāngwèi Jū) at Nánhuán Lù 96 (© **0773/282-7769**) serves authentic Yáo and Zhuàng minority cuisines. The emphasis here is on spices and fresh ingredients gathered from the countryside. Specialties include *sānchūn tǔjī* (free-range chicken soup), *zháliáng zhútǒng fàn* (bamboo-cooked rice), and *sānchūn làròu zhēngyúpiàn* (steamed taro with smoked meat). Service is friendly. Dinner for two averages ¥80 ($10). The **Guìlín Rén Food Court** at Zhōngshān Zhōnglù 268 (© **0773/283-3068**) offers a variety of fast foods in a large, brightly lit open seating area. After you're seated, the waitress will give you an order form that you take around to the different stalls where attendants will mark it up and deliver the food to your table. There's a good selection of noodles, cold dishes, dim sum, stir-fries, and Chinese desserts to choose from. Meals cost about ¥20 to ¥25 ($2.50–$3).

For Western food, it's best to stick to the international hotel restaurants such as the **Studio Cafe** at the Sheraton or the **Patio Cafe** at the Guìlín Bravo Hotel, where you can get decent pastas, pizzas, burgers, and steaks for ¥40 to ¥100 ($5–$12).

YÁNGSHUÒ: THE STONE GARDEN

阳朔

$\mathbf{G}$UÌLÍN IS REPUTED TO HAVE THE BEST scenery under Heaven, but 81km (50 miles) downriver, the karst landscape at Yángshuò is even more intriguing. Yángshuò, which means "Bright Sun," is a village laid out in a garden of stone towers, haunting and surreal. Here, the swirling, oddly contorted 90m (300-ft.) limestone pinnacles sprout around every corner and in every empty field. The tour boats that ply the Lí River from Guìlín end their trips at Yángshuò, and buses transfer passengers back upstream to Guìlín, but there's reason to linger. Yángshuò is as close to paradise as a traveler gets in southwest China these days. I'd been wanting to explore Yángshuò for a decade, ever since I first set foot in the village, and this time I simply made Yángshuò, rather than Guìlín, my base.

A Traveler's Town

Yángshuò's main street, Xī Jiē, connects the Lí River docks to the Guìlín Highway. The street is an anomaly in China: A cobblestoned pedestrian street, it is dotted with small cafes that cater primarily to independent foreign travelers. After checking in at a hotel, I stopped in for lunch at **Minnie Mao's,** which is decorated rather like a crash pad from the 1960s with guitars and posters on the wall. A few tables and rattan chairs line the side walls, and there's a bar at the back. The menu is in English, and many of the dishes are Western. I ordered a plate of noodles, a soda and, for dessert, a sundae, which consisted of ice cream sprinkled with bits of apple, banana, and mandarin oranges. The bill came to ¥15 ($1.75), about 10 times less than what an international hotel charges.

Minnie Mao's is a complete-service cafe, as are half a dozen others in Yángshuò, meaning it also runs a travel agency—tour prices are posted on the back of the food menu. Other services include cheap faxing, IDD telephones, and even e-mail. It wasn't long before I'd spoken to several backpacking travelers who wandered in. Some of them were staying for weeks.

Yángshuò reminds me of similar towns in Nepal and Thailand, where foreigners can get what they need with ease. Almost none of China's cities have developed along these lines—China started out strictly controlling tourism, favoring well-managed tour groups housed in increasingly expensive and isolated hotels. In Yángshuò, everything is smooth sailing, particularly for outsiders. Prices for tours, hotels, or restaurants are not astronomical. This isn't quite China, perhaps, but it's how China must become if it is ever truly going to be an international crossroads.

My first night in Yángshuò, I ended up eating dinner in another Western cafe run by locals. This one happened to be the first foreign cafe set up in Yángshuò, in 1983, even if it has since moved around the corner and changed its name to **Susannah's.** This is the establishment, at any rate, where former U.S. president Jimmy Carter ate in 1987. The menu is extensive but cheap—nothing over a few bucks. I ordered a plate of mashed potatoes, something I hadn't had for months in China, simple and delicious. The young manager and his "right-hand man" joined me at the table and, by the end of the evening, we had cut a few deals to see some sights together. Yángshuò is the kind of town where it doesn't take long to enter into the daily lives of the people who work with foreigners. Before I left, I would know the people from Susannah's Cafe quite well—again, a rare experience elsewhere in China.

Moon Mountain (Yuèliang Shān)

In the morning, I teamed up with Harold, the manager at Susannah's. We walked down Xī Jiē to a row of bikes for rent on the sidewalk, next to the Paradise Hotel where I was staying. I picked out a mountain bike, paid ¥10 ($1.25), and we headed down the highway, turning south along the Lí River at the bridge. The countryside is, of course, gorgeous, those celebrated rock peaks soaring straight up like enormous pick-up sticks dropped by the gods on both banks of the river. The air was nippy and my hands were completely frozen to the handlebars after the 40-minute, 10km (6-mile) ride to Moon Mountain (Yuèliang Shān).

At the entrance, there's a shack on a dirt road where I bought tickets (¥9/ $1.10) and where the woman in charge watched our bikes. It's another 40-minute hike to the top of Moon Mountain, so named because its peak is an enormous stone arch with an opening the shape of the moon. Stone stairways wind through the thick bamboo and brush to the top. Here I could see the Lí River at its most spectacular, lazily winding through hundreds of stone towers, squares of vegetables and rice checkering the flat ground. Harold knew the way from Moon Hill to nearby caves—Black Water Caves, New Water Caves, Dragon Caves, all with underground

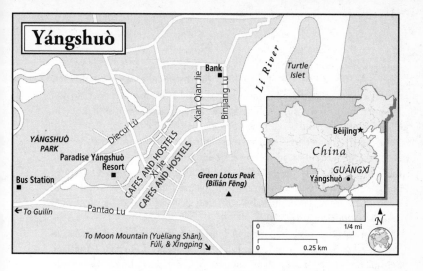

streams, bats, waterfalls, and swimming pools—but I was content to let the morning run its course from the top of this peak. Why go underground when the most monumental stalagmites on Earth are erupting aboveground under a blue sky beside a river? We spent an hour talking about how much money people make in America and how many cars they own. Harold was frantic to make his fortune in China. He'd just turned 24, with no college, but his grasp of English was sharp enough. He was impatient and impulsive.

Later I warmed up in the **Méi Yǒu Cafe,** next door to Minnie Mao's. Méi Yǒu is a play on the Chinese phrase familiar to legions of independent travelers—*méi yǒu,* meaning "don't have," the constant refrain sounded by the staff in hotels, restaurants, stores, and offices when a request is made that is too bothersome at the moment to fulfill. The Méi Yǒu in Yángshuò, however, has just about everything you need—good food, tours, help, and advice. The dining room contains eight tables with tablecloths. The walls are decorated with the flags of many nations, the straw hats of local peasants, farming implements, and hollow gourds called *húlu,* representing longevity. The bar at the back serves imported drinks. The local beer, Líquán, is flat but cheap, just ¥4 (50¢) for a quart bottle.

Breakfast at Méi Yǒu is ¥15 ($1.90) for eggs, toast, coffee, and fresh orange juice. The Méi Yǒu also serves a special snake dinner for gourmets. You get to eat the snake, drink its blood, and keep the skin. At the back of the English-language menu is a breakdown of Yángshuò tours, including a demonstration of cormorant fishing after dark for ¥40 ($4.80). I ordered the trip, not the snake. The woman on duty added some coal pucks to the burner under my table, which warmed me up nicely, then returned to her knitting, a striped wool sweater.

In the afternoon I wandered the cobblestoned street, **Xī Jiē (West Street),** northwest of the Lí River. The street is lined with old wooden buildings, many of them selling scroll paintings, T-shirts, batiks from nearby Guìzhōu Province, and carved stones. The stone of this karst region is famous in China, and these trinkets can be expensive.

At the river, where the tour boats from Guìlín tie up in the afternoon, an extensive outdoor arcade of souvenir and junk dealers is worth combing through. Art students from Guìlín display their latest works. Old coins, probably fakes, as well as Máo buttons, Máo's *Little Red Book,* and other recent artifacts of the Cultural Revolution (1966–76) can be picked up here for a dollar or so.

If you spend a week or longer, Yángshuò is the ideal place to take an introductory course in Chinese culture. The **Buckland Foreign Language School** on Xī Jiē (it also owns Susannah's Cafe) offers quick instruction in the Chinese language, Yángshuò cooking, classical brush painting, kung-fu, and *tàijíquán,* at about ¥25 ($3) per session.

In the evenings, the cafes rock with Western pop music, set up laser video screens, or simply sell big bottles of beer to foreigners who congregate inside. I decided instead to go fishing by moonlight.

Cormorant Fishing

Fishing with cormorants is an ancient tradition in many parts of China. I first saw it done on the Lí River where, to this day, it is an honored enterprise. The birds are outfitted with a noose, tied fairly tightly around their long necks. They then dive in harness for fish, which they capture in their beaks. However, the knotted string prevents them from swallowing the food, so they return to the boat, where their master collects the fish. The boats are flat, narrow rafts consisting of five or six large, round bamboo trunks tied together and upturned at the stem. The fisherman stands on the raft, using a pole to propel the boat. His cormorants perch on his outstretched arms, diving on command. It is said that one good cormorant can feed an entire family.

The **cormorant tours** leave after dark from the Yángshuò docks; they can be booked in many a cafe for ¥30 to ¥40 ($3.75–$5) an hour, usually including dinner afterward. We boarded a large motorized skiff and followed the bamboo rafts as they glided into the river. Lamps on poles illuminated the rafts, their glow luring fish up from the depths. It's a fine adventure for a warm summer's eve, although it was cold as we set out and, after an hour on the waters, I was relieved to return. In Yángshuò, it is said that the fishermen allow their cormorants to swallow every seventh fish they catch. It keeps everyone content.

Fúlì & Xīngpíng

Yángshuò's landscape is stunning enough, but the setting of the nearby villages, such as Fúlì and Xīngpíng, is even more extraordinary. In the summer, boats take passengers downriver to Fúlì or upriver to Xīngpíng. There are even inner-tube rentals for those who prefer less formal passage. The weather was too cool and tour groups too scarce for such ventures when I visited in January, so Harold suggested we take the local bus (¥5/65¢), which, by fits and starts, got us first to Fúlì and then across the Lí River, north to Xīngpíng.

Fúlì is a tiny town that holds an outdoor food and crafts market for locals every 3 days. There isn't much for foreigners to buy here, but the peasants who pour in are fascinating to watch. Many are ethnic minorities, and they come to market in their most colorful clothing. I traipsed back and forth among the rows of produce, pots and pans, hoes and rakes, and harnesses, without my wallet or bag, since teams of pickpockets are known to work these country markets, and foreigners are obvious targets.

Xīngpíng is a river town passed by the tour boats on their way down from Guìlín. It is located in the region's thickest jungle of spiraling karst pinnacles. The streets here are paved in rock, and the houses are made of stone. The port, where dozens of flat-bottomed tour boats dock in the winter, looks like a "Welcome to China" poster, with the sharp peaks standing layer upon layer across the harbor, like a wall of lotus petals. There's a fine, spacious garden for strolling on the far edge of this harbor, where an outdoor banquet was in progress. We almost joined in, until Harold realized it was a wake, the meal following a funeral. Instead, Harold picked out a cafe on the main street of Xīngpíng, run as most of them are by a family, where we ordered up a hot pot and some beer.

Green Lotus Peak (Bìlián Fēng)

Everyone who's ever pulled into Yángshuò on a boat down the magnificent Lí River has been transfixed by Green Lotus Peak, which towers over the harbor. The sheer northern face of its little sister peak is often likened to an ancient bronze mirror, and Green Lotus Peak itself is said to resemble an open bloom reflected in the river. A path leads up from the bank to a two-story pavilion, **Yíngjiāng Gé.** There's a museum nearby with copies of Lí River paintings by Xǔ Bēihóng, the town's most famous artist, who lived in Yángshuò in the mid-1930s.

Green Lotus Peak is the finest spot in Yángshuò to enjoy a snack on a sunny afternoon, while watching the boats come in off the Lí River and snap the harbor market to life. The old fishermen hop down the wharf—pole, baskets, and cormorants in tow—posing for pictures, "10 *yuán*" a shot (¥10/$1.20). The best local snack is the Shātián pomelo, a thick-skinned gigantic relative of the grapefruit renowned for its medicinal properties and loaded with vitamin C. Piled in pyramids on roadside stands, it is sold even at night, the displays lit by fluorescent bulbs.

The river traffic changes minute by minute, the long tour barges giving way to fishing rafts and family junks. There's a legend of the river in which two brothers, Son of the East and Son of the West, compete for the same girl. Her name is Jade. She finally sees both her suitors racing toward her, and in a split second she draws a line across the sand with her hairpin, hoping to separate herself from both of them. The Son of the West is swifter. He crosses the line in the nick of time, before it becomes a wide river, and claims Jade. Her line in the sand becomes the jade hairpin to which poets compare the Lí River, and the Lí River itself carries the meaning of separation.

Yángshuò seems a separate world. Karst castles surround Green Lotus Peak, their names conjuring up a fairy realm of images: Lion Peak and Kitten Hill, Horse Head Ridge and Peach Tower, Dragon Mountain and White Crane Peak. Perhaps this is the landscape the ancients imagined existed elsewhere only on the Moon, a bright garden of limestone parted by a heavenly river with banks of green-waving bamboo. But it is also a place as modern in some ways as the West, a point of international contact as jolting as any in Běijīng or Shànghǎi or Guǎngzhōu.

PRACTICAL INFORMATION

by Sharon Owyang

ORIENTATION & WHEN TO GO

Yángshuò is located 65km (50 miles) south of **Guìlín** in the northeast part of the Guǎngxī Zhuàng Autonomous Region. The climate is subtropical, with high rains and humidity in the summer. Winters are usually mild, although a bit chilly. April, May, September, and October are the best months to visit.

GETTING THERE

The nearest rail and air connections are in **Guìlín**, 65km (30 miles) away by bus. See "Getting There" in the Guìlín chapter, on p. 323, for more information.

By Bus From the Guìlín Bus Station (Guìlín Qìchēzhàn) (✆ **0773/382-2153**) on Zhōngshān Lù, just north of the train station, buses depart for Yángshuò every 15 minutes between 7am and 9pm. From Yángshuò, Guìlín-bound buses (70 min.; ¥7.50/95¢) depart the bus station on Pāntáo Lù every 10 minutes between 7:30am and 5:30pm. Buses also leave for Xīngpíng (1 hr.; ¥3.50/45¢) every 15 minutes between 6am and 7:30pm; and for Fúlì (20 min.; ¥5/60¢) every 20 minutes to ½ hour between 6am and 7pm. There is also once-a-week bus service to Hong Kong. The **Guìlín–Hong Kong Express Bus**

(© **0773/585-7088**; fax 0773/585-7099) runs between Guìlín and Hong Kong every Friday evening and stops in Yángshuò at the Paradise Hotel at 8pm to pick up passengers, but you have to call and book a ticket ahead of time. The luxury air-conditioned bus (¥350/$44 one-way; ¥600/$75 round-trip), with video movies and onboard lavatory, arrives the next morning at Huánggǎng in Shēnzhèn at 7am.

By Taxi Taxis from Guìlín (your hotel in Guìlín can arrange this) will take an hour to get to Yángshuò and will cost around ¥250 to ¥300 ($31–$38).

CITY LAYOUT/GETTING AROUND

The **Guilín Highway** (north to Guìlín, south down the Lí River) cuts an east–west swath through Yángshuò, where it is known as Pāntáo Lù. **Xī Jiē**, also known as Yángrén Jiē (Foreigners' Street), is the main thoroughfare, a cobblestone pedestrian street running from Pāntáo Lù to the Lí River boat docks. Travelers' cafes, shops, and basic guesthouses are clustered along Xī Jiē, with the higher-end hotels toward the southern end of Xī Jiē and spilling onto Pāntáo Lù.

The town itself is so small that it can easily be covered on foot in less than an hour. Bikes are the best means of getting to outlying sights, and are available for rent (¥10/$1.25) at many Xī Jiē cafes and hotels as well as at the southern end of Xī Jiē toward Pāntáo Lù. Covered three-wheel motorcycle taxis will offer to take tourists out to Moon Mountain and nearby caves for ¥30 ($3.75), though be sure to agree on all the desired destinations and costs beforehand, as some drivers have been known to renege after a few destinations.

TOURS & STRATAGEMS

The friendly **Yángshuò Tourism Information Service Center (Yángshuò Lǚyóu Zīxún Fúwù Zhōngxīn)**, just south of the bus station on Pāntáo Lu (© **0773/882-7922**), can answer basic travelers' questions on accommodations, local sights, tours, and bike rental. With three outlets on Xī Jiē, **CITS**, headquartered at Xī Jiē 110 (© **0773/882-7102**; fax 0773/882-7102; citsys@sina.com.cn), is the largest and most effective of the travel agencies in handling plane, train, and long-distance bus tickets. They also offer a plethora of local tours, including 1 or 2-day Lóngshèng Minority Village tours (¥150/$19). For those trips, the bus leaves Yángshuò at 7:30am and returns at 7pm. Day tours can also easily be booked at a number of travelers' cafes, including **Minnie Mao's Cafe** (Xī Jiē 83; © **0773/882-6484**) and **Planet Yángshuò** (Pāntáo Lù 47; © **0135/0783-9231**).

WHERE TO STAY

Lisa's, at Xī Jiē 71 (© **0773/882-0217**), has 24 clean rooms with air-conditioning and TV. Five of these units have private bathrooms with tub/shower combos, while the other doubles have attached showers (but no tubs). Doubles range from ¥80 to ¥120 ($10–$15). Best of all, Lisa is a fount of information and is very friendly to boot.

The **White Lion Hotel (Wèiláién Fàndiàn)** at Xī Jiē 103 (© **0773/882-7778**) is a brand-new (May 2002) mini-hotel with 13 rooms decorated in a combination of Chinese and Western styles. Co-owner American Jeff Powell will give a free night's stay to anyone who donates ¥400 ($50) to support a local child's education for a term. Otherwise, doubles with attached bathrooms are ¥150 to ¥180 ($19–$22), though the prices can go up to ¥400 to ¥450 ($50–$58) during holidays and peak periods. Rooms come with A/C, TV, wooden furniture, and comfortable beds.

Àiyuán Hotel (Àiyuán Bīnguǎn) The newest (Feb 2002) of the hotels on Xī Jiē, this hotel, in a Chinese-style building, offers good-value rooms in a pleasant environment. An enclosed courtyard full of bamboo furnishings adds to the charm. The simply but tastefully decorated rooms have wooden floors, Chinese-style furniture, and average-sized but comfortable beds, while deluxe rooms come with balconies. Bathrooms are clean and come with tub/shower combos.

Xī Jiē 115. © 0773/881-1868. Fax 0773/881-1916. 63 units. ¥360–¥480 ($45–$60) double. AE, DC, MC, V. **Amenities:** 2 restaurants (Chinese and coffee shop); tour desk; business center; shopping arcade; salon; next-day dry cleaning and laundry; Internet service. *In room:* A/C, TV, hair dryer.

Paradise Yángshuò Resort Located in its own compound at the western end of Xī Jiē, this three-star Sino-Malaysian joint venture offers some of the more comfortable and classier accommodations in town. Pictures of visiting foreign dignitaries and heads of state line the lobby walls of this Chinese-courtyard–style, two-story resort. Rooms are furnished with comfortable beds, while bathrooms are clean and have shower/tub combinations.

Xī Jiē 116. © 0773/882-2109. Fax 0773/882-2106. www.paradiseyangshuo.com. 145 units. ¥800 ($100) double; ¥960-¥2,400 ($120–$300) suite. Children under 12 stay free in parent's room. Rooms are subject to an 18% service charge and government tax. **Amenities:** 2 restaurants (Chinese and Western); outdoor swimming pool; health club; sauna; billiards; mahjong; bowling alley; business center; shopping arcade; next-day dry cleaning and laundry. *In room:* A/C, TV, minibar, coffeemaker.

West Street Hotel (Xī Jiē Jiǔdiàn) Located at the western end of Xī Jiē at the corner of Chéngzhōng Lù, this hotel doesn't look like much from the outside, but it is a lovely, friendly, well-run place that makes you feel like you're in someone's home. Rooms have wooden floors, comfortable beds, and rattan furniture, and each is decorated with unique flourishes. Bathrooms are clean and well maintained. A restaurant on the premises serves a Western buffet breakfast and Chinese lunches and dinners. The staff is friendly and speaks some English.

Xī Jiē 108. © 0773/882-8659. Fax 0773/882-8658. 41 units. ¥400 ($50) double; ¥600 ($75) suite. Discounts of 20%–50% may be given. **Amenities:** Restaurant; bike rental; tour information; Internet service. *In room:* A/C, TV.

WHERE TO DINE

There are plenty of cafes on Xī Jiē offering Western, Chinese, and local dishes at very reasonable prices. Although alfresco dining at Xī Jiē cafes is extremely pleasant and allows for interesting people-watching, some tourists have recently complained about being harassed by overeager vendors or would-be English practitioners offering their services as tour guides who think nothing of approaching you in mid-bite. As the first cafe to serve banana pancakes in Yángshuò (1985), **Lisa's** (Xī Jiē 71; *©* **0773/882-0217**) is one of the oldest and most venerable institutions around the cafe scene. Years later, the food is still good and service is friendly. Taught to make pizza by an Italian chef who stayed here for a month, Lisa turns out some of the town's best pizzas as well as all the usual Western and Chinese staples. There's also good local cuisine here, including the *Líjiāng Tiánluó* (river snails stuffed with pork). Main courses cost ¥10 to ¥25 ($1.25–$3.10). Also of note are **Susannah's Cafe,** which opened in 1983 as the Nice Cafe, the first of its kind catering to foreigners (Jimmy

Carter ate here in 1987); **Méiyǒu Cafe,** with its Méiyǒu pancake breakfast for ¥18 ($2.25); and **Minnie Mao's.**

For more elegant dining, delightful **Le Vôtre,** at Xī Jiē 79 (*©* **0773/882-8040**), provides French cuisine in a traditional Chinese setting. Occupying half of the former Míng Dynasty *Jiāngxī Huìguǎn* (meeting place for merchants from Jiāngxī Province; the other half is a hotel), this charming restaurant has exposed brick, antiques, statues, carved wooden panels, and eclectic bric-a-brac. The menu offers everything from T-bone steaks to Chinese dishes, but signature specialties include escargot, *moules chaude* (steamed mussels), and *filet du canard grillé* (grilled duck filet). Finish off with crème brûlée or crêpes suzette. A full bevy of Italian, French, and Chinese wines is available. Main courses cost ¥30 to ¥80 ($3.75–$10).

SĀNJIĀNG: A BRIDGE OF WIND & RAIN

三江

GUÌLÍN, YÁNGSHUÒ, AND THE LÍ River encompass China's most famous scenic landscape, but the province—Guǎngxī Zhuàng Autonomous Region—is elsewhere largely unexplored by tourists. I became curious about some of the villages in the northern region of the province, however, and, teaming up with Klaus, a German I met over dinner in a cafe, I convinced a cafe manager in Yángshuò to act as a guide, something he had done before for other foreign travelers.

I wanted to see the Dòng minority village of **Sānjiāng** and the rice terraces near **Lóngshèng.** Neither Sānjiāng nor Lóngshèng are names that come to the top of the list when you talk about places to visit in China, of course—which made them all the more attractive. I wanted to see villages, sights, and peoples that you ordinarily wouldn't dream exist in the China of Běijīng, Shànghǎi, Xī'ān, and Guìlín.

Across the Dragon's Spine

We set out from Yángshuò at 9am, taking the local bus up to Guìlín, a 70-minute ride. Harold, our guide, was in bad shape. At the Guìlín bus station, he found a Chinese pharmacy and bought pills for his ailing stomach. The 3-hour trip into northern Guǎngxī was rough. The rickety buses were uncomfortable to begin with; the seats were crammed close together, the suspension nearly nonexistent. We rose and fell with every bump in the potholed road. The bus frequently stopped to take on village passengers, many of them loaded down with sacks of produce destined for market. Most of the passengers were men, and they all smoked furiously.

The scenery became more rugged. The northern region of the province is dominated by spectacular mountain ranges. The passes are marked by nearly endless turns and curves in the road, which the driver negotiated at the highest speeds possible. We had glimpses of remote farms, their old terraces climbing steep peaks step-by-step, each green platform formed by hand. Cows and water buffalo frequently blocked the road. Slow-moving

tractors hauled trailers of logs to town. I had never seen this much logging in China. The forests were thick in the mountains. We passed dozens of roadside mills stacked with lumber, bamboo trunks, and sheets of veneer drying in the sun.

At the village of **Lóngjǐ,** 19km (12 miles) south of Lóngshèng, we got off the bus to see the **Dragon's Spine Rice Terraces** (**Lóngjǐ Tītián;** entrance fee ¥30/$3.75). Over the centuries, the Yáo minority people have sculpted 600m (2,000-ft.) peaks here with terraces that are the most astounding in China. Harold was too woozy to make the climb, but Klaus and I were eager to hike, accompanied by several old Yáo ladies who tried to sell us their handicrafts on the way to the top.

The Yáo people are not the only minority in the region. The Dòng, the Miáo, and the Zhuàng also call northern Guǎngxī home. The Zhuàng people are China's largest minority group, numbering more than 15 million, most of them concentrated here in their homeland. Able to assimilate Chinese ways and customs quickly, the Zhuàng are largely indistinguishable today from the Hàn Chinese. Their language, with links to Thai, is distinct, however, and at many of the minority villages, spoken Chinese is as obscure as English.

The town of **Lóngshèng,** where we would spend the night, a busy, ugly urban strip on the Sāng River, is the closest thing to a Zhuàng capital. Harold found a room with three narrow beds at the Xiāntáo Hotel, a six-floor walk-up. Klaus and I decided to do some exploring. We walked into the streets. Along a north-running tributary of the Sāng River, we strolled through the local market, a ripe, odoriferous sidewalk display of bleeding goats freshly slaughtered and dried rats in various sizes ready for frying or boiling.

Mapless, we followed the river west for a mile, crossing a bridge into the terraced farmlands. Cow paths led us through villages of wooden houses and over the boundary walls of dozens of rice plots, fallow in January, but the route was often swallowed up by fields. Farmers greeted us shyly as we made our trek. Fishermen trolling the river sometimes waved to us. By the time we returned to Lóngshèng, crossing another cement bridge, we were ready for dinner.

In the Xiāntáo Hotel's main dining room, we feasted on a variety of local dishes and drank beer and glasses of a sweet wine that was warmed in a hot pot. It was dark when I climbed the outside stairs back up to the sixth floor. On the landing outside the restaurant, I collided with a goat. At first I thought he was stuffed, but he was still alive, tethered to the railing and waiting his turn to visit the kitchens.

Lóngshèng is not a town of delicacy and delight. The dark streets were noisy with the sounds of karaoke bars and cinemas. Our room, a cement shell floor to ceiling, was freezing cold. I slept with all my clothes on under two quilts, and I still shivered. There was a shower nozzle on the wall in our bathroom that belched out hot water in the morning. The toilet had no flushing mechanism beyond the pail that stood like a spittoon to one side. Spittoons were stationed at the foot of each bed as well. I began to dream of a Holiday Inn someday reaching even these mountain towns.

The Bridge at Chéngyáng

We rose early enough to catch the 7am bus to Sānjiāng, the center of a rural region where the Dòng minority still maintains their traditional villages. The bus was a circus. It sounds like a third-world cliché, but part of the way I rode with a bag of live chickens in the aisle wedged against my foot. The engine cover next to the bus driver was piled high with sacks of rice, on which several passengers were seated. The strangest cargo we picked up along the way, however, was 10 large sacks of rocks which, with super-human effort, were loaded by one man, bag by bag, until the aisle was chock-full. Somehow the bus continued under its own power, despite the additional tonnage, completing the trip west to Sānjiāng in under 3 hours.

At Sānjiāng, Harold hired a minivan for the 40-minute drive on country roads to the Dòng village of Chéngyáng. The driver was a young woman with whom Harold flirted. When one of the tires was punctured, she pulled over to change it. None of us gentlemen offered her a hand, nor did she need one. She changed it in a snap.

Klaus and I enjoyed the countryside, particularly when we reached the valley of a small river. The riverbank was lined with a series of wooden water wheels, several of which were still in operation. They are used now as they were in the past, to scoop water from the river to irrigate the fields.

At Chéngyáng (¥10/$1.25 entrance fee to the town) we had our first look at the most famous sight in the region, the **Bridge of Wind and Rain (Fēngyǔ Qiáo),** built by the Dòng villagers in 1916. Construction took 12 years. It is considered the finest and most beautiful of the 100 wind-and-rain bridges still standing in China. These are superbly crafted covered bridges that not only serve as meeting places where people exchange village gossip, protected from rain and wind, but as the locations of religious shrines. Here, five stone piers, one on each bank of the Chéngjiāng and three erected in the shallow riverbed, provide support for the 63m (210-ft.) long, 3.3m (11-ft.) wide span. Each support is crowned with an elaborate three-tiered pavilion with layers of soaring eaves. Matching white-trimmed roofs link the five pavilions. The covered bridge is fashioned from cedar. As with the Temple of Heaven in Běijīng, this pavilion bridge was constructed without a single nail, secured solely by wooden pegs. From a distance, it resembles a bridge transformed into a long imperial corridor and temple complex.

The Dong village of **Chéngyáng** on the other side of the river has occupied the lush green valley for 3 centuries. Dozens of traditional wooden-plank houses the size and shape of barns, built atop mud-brick basements where pigs are penned, surround the village pond and a placid stream called the Píngtán. The upper two stories of a typical house are lined with spacious balconies, supported by peeled timber columns that also support the tiled roofs. A local English-speaking villager invited us inside a house. The living areas are entered by wooden stairs or ladders. Inside are simple, dark, unadorned rooms with bare wooden walls. An open hearth on the floor serves as a stove. We were invited to sample the Dòng tea, made from bricks of tea leaves that steep for 20 minutes. It was a deeply flavorful brew.

The village was electrified, but few cars or trucks traveled the unpaved streets. Hand-pushed wooden carts and bicycles were the principal machines. The women, most of them dressed in gray pants and black coats, with white cotton scarves covering their heads, were washing buckets of laundry in the stream. The hillsides and valley floor were terraced in plots of vegetables, grains, and rice. Lumber, stone, and straw seemed to be the other principal commodities. There didn't seem to be any power tools about, even in the tiny mills. Everything was done by hand.

A small shop selling snacks and village crafts stood by the entrance to the bridge. I bought several carved wooden decorations and a bottle of spring water. As we headed back across the Wind and Rain Bridge, we were intercepted by a gaggle of local women in black and indigo quilted jackets armed with baskets and knit bags of crafts and trinkets. They accompanied us across. All down the river the water wheels turned slowly like ancient bamboo Ferris wheels.

Lóngshèng Hot Spring (Wēn Quán)

The next morning we caught another bus out of Lóngshèng going the other direction, east down the Sāng River. This trip was only an hour but was mostly uphill, past stunning mountain rice terraces and wooden villages. The Yáo minorities dominated the countryside in this direction. Higher up, between forested peaks, we arrived at the local hot spring, **Wēn Quán** (¥10/$1.25 entrance fee).

The hot spring was undergoing a massive hotel and resort development. We walked the road to the pool at the top, about a mile. The road was lined with dozens of restaurants and crude inns. Harold explained that as well as those who came to take the waters, this place was also the haunt of businessmen and officials who came to take pleasures of another order— about 200 prostitutes work the resort. I decided not to indulge in a massage (¥50/$6) and headed instead for the outdoor mineral pool (¥30/$3.75), a large, steaming cement basin surrounded by tiled bathhouses, mountain peaks, and the statue of a goddess. Klaus and I enjoyed a 20-minute soak in the moderately hot spa waters.

A clear stream tumbles out of the mountains by the hot spring. If you cross it via a ragtag suspension bridge, you can hike into the forested hills, where there are wild monkeys, according to the locals. We chose to take lunch instead at one of the sidewalk cafes specializing in two dishes: sticky rice cooked in bamboo, and dried strands of pork.

The road back to Lóngshèng and then south over the winding mountain that passes down into the karst plateau of Guìlín and Yángshuò was like a return from a medieval wilderness to modern Chinese civilization. Harold would find he was without job or girlfriend when he got home, but he seemed unconcerned. He'd made contact with the bus conductress and rode next to her up front on the engine cover.

At the edge of the mountain roads, I kept seeing the villagers, men and women, trekking up and down the terraced slopes. They had machetes holstered to their sashes for slashing tree limbs. The limbs were bundled and driven to town, where they became charcoal sticks for heating stoves. Occasionally we passed hunters, their rifles essentially handguns equipped with long pipes for barrels. From a distance, they looked like blunder-busses. Klaus fell asleep. He didn't seem to know a word of Chinese, or of English either, but he had been on the road in China for 55 days straight, roughing it on buses like this one, alone, visiting villages and waterfalls every bit as remote as the Bridge of Wind and Rain. I began to doze, too, as we came down out of the mountains, descending as if from a lost world where cedar barn houses loom like dinosaurs and bamboo water wheels spin like ancient banners that the passing centuries forgot to tear down.

PRACTICAL INFORMATION

by Sharon Owyang

ORIENTATION & WHEN TO GO

Lóngshèng and Sānjiāng are located on the northern mountainous border of the Guǎngxī Zhuàng Autonomous Region. Lóngshèng is about 90km (55 miles) northwest of Guìlín, and Sānjiāng is another 60km (36 miles) west of Lóngshèng. This remote, hilly area is dominated by minority groups, chiefly the Zhuàng, Dòng, Miáo, and Yáo, who pursue terrace farming, hunting, and logging.

The months of May and August through October are the best times to visit. Winters are quite cold, and spring brings heavy rainfall. Though the rainy season typically lasts from February to May, May is planting season and offers spectacular vistas when the rice fields are submerged in water. In September and October, just before the fall har-vest, the fields are covered in waves of golden yellow. Minority New Years and festivals are also interesting times to visit. One of the biggest Dòng celebra-tions is *Sānyuèsān*, held on the third day of the third lunar month and cele-brated with fireworks, dances, sporting competitions, and abundant feasting. Check with CITS or local travel agencies for exact dates of minority festivals.

GETTING THERE

Lóngshèng From Guìlín's Bus Station (Qìchēzhàn) (© **0773/382-2153**) on Zhōngshān Lù, buses leave for Lóngshèng every 40 minutes between 7am and 7pm. The 3-hour trip costs ¥15 ($1.90). From the Lóngshèng bus sta-tion located at the intersection of Guìlóng Lù and Xīnlóng Xīlù, there are buses back to Guìlín (every 40 min. 6:50am–6:40pm) for the same price, Sānjiāng (2 hr.; ¥8/$1; every half hour 6am–5:50pm), Wēn Quán (1 hr.; ¥4.50/ 60¢; buses depart regularly when full), and Lóngjǐ Tītián (Lóngjǐ Terrace Fields; 45 min.; ¥6.50/80¢; buses depart 7:30am, and every 2 hr. 9am–5pm). Buses depart Lóngjǐ Tītián for Lóngshèng at 7:20am, 8:50am, 11am, 1pm, 3pm, and 4:30pm.

Sānjiāng There are two bus stations in Sānjiāng, but the one with Guìlín- and Lóngshèng-bound buses is on the east side of the Xún Jiāng (Xún River) before the bridge. From here, buses depart for Guìlín (4½ hr.; ¥17/$2.10;

hourly departures 7am–2:30pm) and Lóngshèng (2 hr.; ¥8.50/$1.05; every half hour 6:30am–5pm). From the Qìchē Xīzhàn (West Bus Station), the village of Chéngyáng is another 45 minutes away by bus (¥3/40¢; every half hour 7:10am–5:40pm). The first bus from Chéngyáng to Sānjiāng is at 7:20am and the last at around 6pm.

By Plane & Train The nearest air and rail service is in **Guìlín** (see the Guìlín chapter, beginning on p. 311, for details).

TOURS & STRATAGEMS

Formal and informal guided tours can be arranged in **Guìlín** and **Yángshuò** (see the Guìlín and Yángshuò chapters for more information).

In Lóngshèng, travel information is available at the **Riverside Hotel (Lóngjī Dùjià Shānzhuāng)** at Guìlóng Lù 5 (© 0773/751-1335), which is run by a local English teacher. You can also pick up informational brochures (some in English) on local sights and accommodations at the **Lóngshèng Tourism Company (Lóngshèng Lǚyóu Zǒnggōngsī)** (© 0773/751-7566), located to the left of the waiting room at the bus station. In Sānjiāng, **Chéngyáng Bridge Travel Service (Chéngyáng Qiáo Lǚxíng Shè;** © 0772/)861-6820; fax 0772/861-6820) can provide information on local sights as well as arrange tours and accommodations.

WHERE TO STAY

In Lóngshèng, the best place to stay is not in the town itself but up in the Lóngjī Tītián (Terrace Fields), in the village of Píng'ān. Be advised, however, that accommodations here are in basic traditional wooden homes with few to none of the amenities of a regular hotel. Most of the hostels provide 24-hour hot water, but bathrooms are typically communal. The **Lóngjī Riverside Hotel (Lóngjī Dùjià Shānzhuāng;** © 0773/758-3047)**, close to the Number One Lookout Point, is the best outfitted of the hostels, with 16 doubles (¥70/$9) with private bathrooms. Rooms are clean and comfortable. There is a lovely sitting room and a nice patio where guests can unwind with cool beers after a hard day of trekking. Staff is friendly, speaks some English, and can dish up Western, Chinese, Zhuàng, and Yáo minority food. Plans are underway to provide Internet service. The **Lì Qīng Guesthouse (Lìqīng Lǚshè;** © 0773/758-3048**; Liqing_gh@hotmail.com) has two buildings in different locations and a total of 29 rooms, all with shared toilet and shower. Rooms are spartan but clean, and a bed in one of those shared rooms costs ¥20 ($2.50). While both buildings have good views, the second building, situated higher up the mountain, offers stunning morning vistas. Service is friendly. The hostel serves a combination of Western, Chinese, and Zhuàng meals. Banana pancakes, yogurt, and strong Yúnnán coffee are available for breakfast. If you're looking for unparalleled unobstructed views, then the **View Place Inn (Guānyuè Gé;** © 0773/758-3005; mianbao_cha@ 163.com), just below the Number Two Lookout, is the place to be. One of the highest-situated buildings here, this hostel is especially popular with French travelers, and French appears on welcome signs and menus. Rooms are basic but clean, toilets are communal, and 24-hour hot water for showering and laundry is available.

If you end up having to stay in the town of Lóngshèng, the most modern place is the new two-star **Lóngshèng Hotel (Lóngshèng Dàjiǔdiàn)**, located at the center of town on Zhōngxīn Jiē (© **0773/751-7718**). There are 36 units; doubles with private bathroom range from ¥160 to ¥200 ($20–$25). Rooms are unremarkably decorated but are quite spacious and comfortable. Bathrooms are a little dark and come with shower/tub combos. The hotel has a huge Chinese restaurant on the third floor, which can sometimes be a little noisy for guests on the fourth floor. Affiliated with the Lóngjǐ Riverside Hotel, the **Riverside Hotel (Kǎikǎi Lǚshè**; © 0773/751-1335), at Guilong Lu 5, is favored by backpackers. The basic rooms are rather dingy and there are no private bathrooms, although plans are underway for the rooms to be renovated. A friendly English teacher runs this dormitory/ hostel and she's a great source of information. The price per bed in a shared room is ¥20 to ¥40 ($2.50–$5).

Around Sānjiāng, the best place to stay is at Chéngyáng, at the **Chéngyáng Bridge National Hostel (Chéngyáng Qiáo Zhāodài Suǒ**; © 0772/858-2468), a well-run, 10-year-old hostel favored by foreign travelers. This traditional wooden Dòng-style hotel has 19 inexpensive rooms (¥20/$2.50 per bed or ¥40/$5 double room) fitted with beds and mosquito nets, clean communal showers and toilets, and an upstairs porch that offers some of the best views of the Wind and Rain Bridge. The friendly owners, who speak some English, can organize tours of the surrounding Dòng and Miáo villages, as well as cook excellent traditional Dòng cuisine and Western food. Internet service is available.

In Sānjiāng itself, the best place to stay is the **Guesthouse of the People's Government of the Sānjiāng Dòng Autonomous County (Sānjiāng Dòngzú Zìzhìxiàn Rénmín Zhèngfǔ Zhāodàisuǒ**; © 0772/861-2454), an old standby that was being completely renovated and upgraded to a three-star hotel at the time of this writing. When completed, the hotel will offer several different grades of rooms, including doubles with and without private bathroom and dorm rooms, as well as the restaurants and other facilities of a standard three-star hotel.

WHERE TO DINE

Lóngshèng   In the town of Lóngshèng, the **Green Food Restaurant (Lǜsè Càiguǎn**; © 0773/751-2473), on Xīnglóng Běi Lù across from Zhōngxīn Guǎngchǎng (Central Square), is your best bet for clean, non-hotel Chinese dining. With wooden chairs and green-and-white checkered tablecloths, the restaurant certainly has more ambience than the roadside eateries. The staff effectively speaks no English but is friendly, and there is a basic menu in English. The sautéed chicken with bamboo shoots, beef with green pepper, and homestyle bean curd are all good choices here. Dinner for two averages between ¥40 and ¥60 ($5–$7.50). The **Riverside Hotel** (see above) also has good inexpensive food with an English menu. In the Lóngjǐ Terrace Fields, most of the foreigner-friendly **hostels** offer decent Western, Chinese, Zhuàng, and Yáo food. Be sure to try some Yáo specialties, including *zhútǒng fàn* (fragrant rice cooked in bamboo) or *zhútǒng jī* (chicken cooked in bamboo), as well as *làròu* (smoked pork).

Sānjiāng Just below the West Bus Station (Qìchē Xīzhàn), the relatively clean **Xìngyì Kuàicāntǐng** (open daily 6am–8:30pm) serves a fast-food Chinese buffet with over 15 dishes to choose from. For ¥5 (60¢), you can pick two meat and two vegetable dishes; the most expensive option, at ¥8 ($1), buys four meat and three vegetable dishes.

Purchase your meal ticket before you order. *Guìlín mǐfěn* (Guìlín rice noodles) and a variety of other noodle dishes are available. The best place to eat in Chéngyáng is the **Chéngyáng Bridge National Hostel** (see above), which serves Chinese and Dòng cuisine (¥30–¥60/$4–$7.50), not to mention cold beer, on the upstairs porch.

Běihǎi:
Sandworms & Pearls
北海

Until the 1990s, Běihǎi was an obscure coastal port on Běibù Bay in the South China Sea facing Vietnam. The emperors favored Běihǎi for its pearls, still a thriving industry in this sunny town 443km (275 miles) due south of Guìlín. But the pearl city also has Silver Beach, pronounced the best beach in China; and as the big cities on China's eastern seaboard began to boom, so did Běihǎi, as a tropical resort. The resort boom has already quieted down, though, leaving Běihǎi still largely undiscovered. Few Westerners pass through.

Just 547km (340 miles) west of Hong Kong, a short hop by air, Běihǎi sounded like an ideal getaway. My interest was piqued by stories I heard. Běihǎi had served as a treaty port a century ago, opening to Western traders in 1876, and the European legacy could still be seen in the architecture of its main street. The harbor was said to be crowded with fishing junks, colorful enough to be favored by movie directors filming historical novels about Old China, and the seafood was judged to be exquisite, particularly the shrimp and a local delicacy, the sandworm. And far out in the bay were volcanic islands, virtually untouched by modernization, where Catholic cathedrals were still standing, the islanders predominantly Catholic. I decided I would take a look at this countryside seaport and its silver beaches before it was overrun by yet another resort boom.

Old Town (Zhōngshān Lù Lǎochéngqū)

The four-lane, 14km (9-mile) expressway from the Běihǎi Airport was flat, straight, new, and nearly empty when I arrived. Green fields in red soil stretched toward rolling hills on either side. Water buffalo grazed the median strip, cows crossed the highway, and bicycles rolled along the inside lanes, often heading against traffic. Barefoot peasants in straw hats marched up the off-ramp to the town. They had piled the grain on the pavement to dry. There's plenty of room for country life on the wide expressway.

The entrance to my hotel was lined with massive palm trees. The lobby floors were marble, trimmed in teak. Two-story glass panels framed a picture of the sea. Like most of the resort hotels, this one faced the northern shore of the Běihǎi peninsula. Silver Beach was across town, on the southern shore. I hired a guide at the hotel to show me around Běihǎi. She was from Běijīng. She said she loves the slow, friendly pace of life in Běihǎi, so far from that of the capital.

Běihǎi's fishing industry is concentrated in a protected inlet on the northwest tip of the peninsula. Every morning, the large fishing junks tie up at the pier on Hǎijiǎo Lù and the middlemen meet them. The catch is examined, bartered over, and carted away to markets and cafes in large baskets. The junks and wooden houses along Běihǎi's north shore have barely changed over the centuries. Many of the hundreds of junks anchored here are owned by the families who live in the houses on the shore, but they prospered in the 1990s and no longer man the boats themselves, hiring the captains and crews for the dangerous business at sea. Many of the boats docked here house the more than 10,000 boat people in Běihǎi, ethnic Chinese expelled from Vietnam in the late 1970s.

Much of the day's catch ends up in the fish market on Yúnnán Lù, south of the harbor. A new building has been constructed for the vendors there, but the atmosphere is traditional enough. Under a spacious covered concrete concourse, open on all sides and supported by dozens of square columns, the women of the fishing villages squat or sit on the wet pavement beside their plastic pans filled with live seafood. There are no tables or platforms. The women are mostly minorities, including the Zhuàng who have occupied the southern reaches of Guǎngxī Province for several thousand years, and the Jīng, Vietnamese who have lived on the islands off Běihǎi for the past 4 centuries. They weigh each purchase with the traditional hand-held scale, consisting of a bamboo stick gripped at its midpoint, a weight dangling from one end, the purchase from the other. Dried seafood specialties capture the big prices here.

At the heart of Běihǎi, a mile east of the fishing harbor and market, is **Zhōngshān Lù**, the "Old Street" district of European embassies. The British, French, German, and Dutch all set up consulates here as soon as the Qīng Dynasty signed the Yāntái Trading Agreement of 1876. Foreigners set up their own offices, schools, and churches, and Zhōngshān Lù is still lined with these European-designed edifices, most now occupied by grocery stores, pearl shops, Chinese offices, and apartments.

The buildings the Europeans left behind are not as grand as those on Shànghǎi's Bund, but they are striking. They're built of brick, plaster, and concrete. Their fronts are faced with immense wooden doors, and their upper stories extend into the street, supported by columns and arches, giving

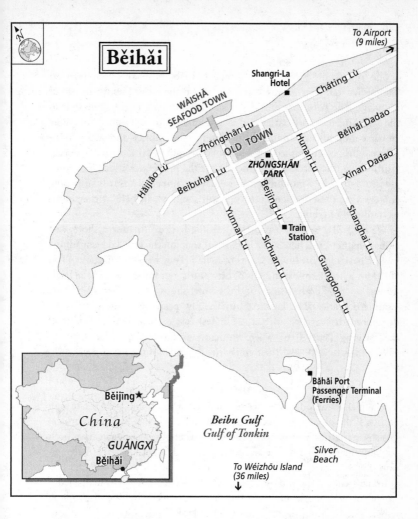

the sidewalk the cool, shady aspect of an arcade. The facades of the taller buildings, usually just three stories, have some decorative flourishes at their peaks, but the overall effect is plain and massive. Pedestrians tunnel through the sidewalk arcades, shopping and running their daily errands.

Walking in those streets, I happened to look up and spot a cross. Below it was a sign, in English: BĚIHǍI CHRIST CHURCH. The windows had arched panes of clear glass, but they could easily have been filled with stained glass a century ago. Since it was Sunday, I suggested we drop in. We were directed upstairs. Inside a large, plain room, a service was under way. A place for us was cleared at once. We sat on a back pew. A psalm was being sung and the church was full. I stayed only a few minutes, feeling like an intruder, no matter how welcome I may have been. They say there are many Christians in Běihǎi, my guide remarked. It was her first look inside a Christian church.

She did know where the former **British Embassy** was, just off Zhōngshān Lù, near Zhōngshān Park, which the locals like for its hill of monkeys. The two-story embassy is a stately building in the same style as the Old Street facades, an arched arcade supporting the upper floor. The embassy grounds, containing a half-dozen colonial brick-and-plaster bungalows, are now occupied by a school. Of course, with so few Western visitors here, the beach and nightclubs are the prime attractions, not some graceful but empty monument of the days of imperialism. It is surprising enough that these foreign embassies still stand at all, here at the southwestern end of China.

We hitched a ride on a pedicab, heading back to the north shore, east along Chátíng Lù. There was a large pearl shop on the way. I'd been admiring the pearls for sale on the streets of Běihǎi. They were cheap, about ¥100 ($12) for a necklace of hundreds of tiny pearls, but my guide said the quality was poor. The pearl stores and the hotel shops sell the best of Běihǎi's "southern pearls." The Japanese buy the raw pearls here; the settings are done abroad. Forty kilometers (25 miles) east of Běihǎi are the ruins of the **Băilóng Pearl City,** where emperors as early as the Hàn Dynasty (206 B.C.–A.D. 220) sent their emissaries in search of the finest pearls.

Sandworms

The **Wàishā** seafood town, located on a flat strip of sand near the fishing harbor, is the place to eat in Běihǎi. Connected to Běihǎi by a small bridge, Wàishā started as a neighborhood village where the fishermen have been cooking their catch at home and serving it on the spot for years. A reputation for freshness, family recipes, and low prices made Wàishā the gourmet's choice for seafood. In 1996, the Běihǎi government opened a "town" of Wàishā restaurants, 72 of them placed side by side in two long wings. The buildings weren't much: They looked like row shacks without fronts. But the seafood inside was superb.

Selecting a **cafe** from the six dozen nearly identical storefronts seemed impossible. They were not numbered or named, but they seemed to all have local followings. Customers window-shopped the tanks and plastic pails until some display of live seafood hooked them. The cafe I selected was superb. It was also the only one with a big fat pussycat out front. Long-haired, white, and reddish yellow, with yellow eyes, she was tethered by a jeweled collar and beaded leash to a folding wooden chair. I knew I'd found the right place.

Four enormous rectangular tiled tanks, the size of bathtubs, each with a pump, were the living menu. The cafe cat's leash couldn't quite reach the tanks. The restaurant had five round tables, each with a cloth, and a floor of beach sand. We ordered seven seafood dishes, including a fresh clam soup for two, accompanied by beer, tea, and a plate of noodles. The clams and the snails were excellent. The shrimp, some enormous in size, were divine. They had to be peeled at the table. A small plate of regional celery refreshed the palate. Snails were next. I dug them out with a toothpick. The last dish was the best: two dozen plump, freshly boiled sandworms, which looked as hideous as their name. Four to six inches long, segmented, wriggling, and pink, they were dug up from these very sands in which my chair sat. They were chopped up and cooked to a divine sweetness.

The cafe cat managed to have her lunch as well. She snapped up fish bones tossed to the sand, took them under a chair, and shredded them over her rice bowl.

If you come here in the evening, my guide confided, you see quite a spectacle, like no other in China. Every night, a procession of luxury cars pulls in and lines up at their owners' favorite restaurants. There are dozens of such exotic cars—we're not talking just the ordinary Cadillac, Lexus, or Mercedes. A Ferrari, for starters. A Rolls-Royce or two. The more expensive and exotic, the better. The real estate boom made a few overnight millionaires in Běihǎi, but their motorized toys arrived illegally via Vietnam and other ports, snatched from the streets of Hong Kong, Tokyo, Los Angeles, and New York, and bought for a song in Běihǎi. The police usually turn a blind eye here. In the rest of China, however, these racing machines remain contraband. Their owners can drive them around and around, back and forth to their heart's content, but only in Běihǎi. They are high-priced adult kiddy cars and, at dusk, they all line up so that their owners can feed on the best fresh seafood in Southeast China.

The Dancing Maidens of Silver Beach

Silver Beach (Yíntān) is 11km (7 miles) south of the fish market and downtown Běihǎi. Ranked as "the first beach in China" by tourism officials, it is a 23km (14-mile) stretch of white sand with gentle waves and a notable absence of sharks. In the summer, the Chinese flock to Silver Beach for sand-castle contests, volleyball, wading, sunbathing and, in the evenings, tent camping on the beach. In the winter when I visited the beach it was nearly deserted, although the sun was out and the temperature mild. A cleanup crew, lying down in the sand, jumped into action when they saw us approach.

One of the oddest things about Silver Beach is the new architecture surrounding it. Dozens of fantasy resorts, white-and-red villas with turrets and towers, vaguely European, now empty, line the highway to Silver Beach, along with Swiss chalets and garish theme parks. During Běihǎi's early 1990s boom, developers and overseas investors moved in, erecting scores of seaside palaces for the expected onslaught of free-spending tourists.

Tourists do come to Silver Beach—which really does look like one of China's finest beaches—but not in the large numbers once dreamt of by landowners and resort operators.

I walked the long, flat beach in January, trying to imagine how it looked in the summer, filled with vacationers like a beach in Thailand or Miami. The wide brick promenade, planted with palms, runs to a horizon punctuated with red turrets. There is almost nothing anywhere that indicates this beach is in China—certainly no temple roofs or tiled pavilions with golden finials. The centerpiece is a curious modern sculpture and **musical fountain:** an immense hollow globe sheathed in writhing copper panels, a massive southern pearl set on a marble pedestal, its equator encircled with eight beautiful maidens. These maidens of the pearl, linked in a circle by garlands held loosely in their hands, are vibrant sculptures twice life-sized. They are also completely unclothed and frightfully well endowed. They are classical nudes borrowed from the Western tradition, as are the other fanciful monuments that populate Silver Beach.

Local boosters hail this musical fountain as the world's largest, its jets spraying more than 66m (220 ft.) into the air every night. On festival days, including the Spring Festival (Chinese New Year), Lantern Festival (Feb or Mar), China Orchid Fair (late Feb), International Sand Sculpture Contest (Aug), and Běihǎi International Pearl Festival (Oct), the fountain square holds exhibits, performances, and nightly fireworks.

A final incongruity is the **camel.** Even before the fantasy resorts encompassed Silver Beach, a local entrepreneur had been trying to drum up business by enticing visitors to take a ride and pose for snapshots on the ocean sands aboard his two-humped business partner, who would probably have been more at home in the deserts of the distant Silk Road. The venture has been successful. Not only is the camel a summer fixture in Silver Beach, he has company: Other camels walk the sands, too.

An Island of Catholics

Due south of Běihǎi, 58km (36 miles) by sea, 145km (90 miles) east of Vietnam, **Wéizhōu Island** is a tropical Eden of lava and coral. It is also where Christians from Běihǎi fled persecution and where a century-old Catholic cathedral stands in the center of a Chinese island village.

I arrived just as the ferry was about to depart. The hotel thought departure from Běihǎi was at 9am, which it was when the fast boat was running, but Monday was a slow-boat day and the departure was at 8:30am. The cab driver knew. When I told him my destination, he began to drive like a maniac, swerving in and out of traffic, nearly driving on the sidewalk. He kept opening the glove compartment to consult his imitation gold Rolex watch, shouting, *"Bà diǎn bàn,"* (8:30) and shifting up another gear. I kept looking through the back window, thinking we were in a movie chase scene. I made it to the ferry landing with 5 minutes to spare, purchased a ticket, and scurried aboard.

The slow boat to Wéizhōu took 3 hours on this particular morning. The seating area reminded me of a bus. There were 50 seats. All faced the TV monitor, which played two complete kung-fu action movies. It was a relief to pull into Wéizhōu harbor. It's a small island, 16m to 19km (10 miles to 12 miles) across in any direction, and a low island—no soaring peaks, just a rolling plateau 30m (100 ft.) above the water. In the port, several dozen large fishing junks were at anchor. Our ferry tied up at the main wharf. There were low, ugly cement buildings along the shoreline, against the banded sandstone cliffs of the plateau; and to the right, a town commercial center with white-tiled walls housing village cafes, shops, and fish markets.

I had no idea what to do on this island—no map, no guidebook. A friendly tout motioned me off the wharf to a bus. I looked inside. There were a few people already seated. I shrugged. There wasn't much option. The bus filled up and departed. The driver gave a tour in Chinese. He drove down the shore, then up to the plateau. Here a dirt road cut across banana plantations. We descended to the beach again, to a much more beautiful stretch, utterly pristine, with dramatic outcroppings of rock.

We took a walk on the beach. What I noticed first were the innumerable shells underfoot, unbroken and brightly colored. Next, I was entranced by the strange sea rocks that rimmed the shore, draped in trees and ferns. They consisted of hundreds of narrow, flat, uniform layers of sand and lava. Several children dressed in red and orange had anticipated our arrival. They were skipping along the sands carrying strings of pearls and baskets of shells for sale. Orange starfish clung to boulders embedded in the beach. Fishing junks were scattered up and down the shore, waiting for the tide to take them out.

Our ultimate destination was the **French cathedral** in a small village in the middle of the island. We followed the red dirt road inward through large sugarcane fields, past a People's Liberation Army outpost, into the village. Many of the houses were built of stone and had dark tiled roofs. Cacti grew beside them, low to the ground. Our bus stopped at the town square. There, like a tropical mirage, rose a three-story, stone-and-brick, century-old cathedral, dwarfing the tiny village of mud streets, stonecutting yards, and ox carts loaded down with cane, rocks, and tree limbs.

The cathedral was built shortly after the Yāntái Trading Agreement of 1876. It seats about 300 under a high arched ceiling. Framed portraits of Christ with Chinese captions are affixed to the walls. To one side of the raised altar is a forest of candles; to the other, a sculptured rock cave. The missionaries to Běihăi seem to have been unusually successful. Hundreds of

Christian converts fled to Wéizhōu Island during times of persecution, finding refuge in this church. Its priest lives in Běihǎi now, and there are services on the island only on important religious occasions, such as Christmas and Easter, despite the fact that at least 80% of Wéizhōu's population is Catholic.

From the village cathedral, this Chinese tour headed over to the island lighthouse, a modern construction. There, on a paved path that leads by a series of switchbacks down the cliff face, we reached a volcanic shoreline, all lava, rife with small sea caves and blowholes. The layered cliffs and volcanic outcroppings were covered in small cactus plants—not at all the kind of beach you associate with China. But this is southern China, nearly as far south as the Middle Kingdom stretches, nearer the equator than Hong Kong or Macao.

The coral island of Wéizhōu, like the pearl city of Běihǎi, is a simple seaside paradise with a curious Western legacy. In a nation teeming with Industrial Age cities and tourist-clogged imperial treasures, both Wéizhōu and Běihǎi are quiet, unhurried, and undiscovered.

PRACTICAL INFORMATION

by Sharon Owyang

ORIENTATION & WHEN TO GO

Běihǎi is a port on the southeastern tip of the Guǎngxī Zhuàng Autonomous Region. Facing the Gulf of Tonkin (Běibù Wān), it's 547km (340 miles) west of Hong Kong and less than 161km (100 miles) east of Vietnam. It lies 443km (275 miles) south of Guìlín, Yángshuō, and the Lí River (see previous chapters). The weather is tropical and warm year-round. High season for Chinese tourists is the humid months of July and August. The spring months of March through May and September through November are all good times to visit.

GETTING THERE

By Plane Běihǎi is connected by air to a number of major Chinese cities, including Běijīng (3 hr.), Shànghǎi (2 hr.), Kūnmíng (1½ hr.), Guìlín (45 min.), and Hong Kong (1 hr.). The nearest city with more extensive and frequent connections is Nánníng, about 240 km (144 miles) to the west. A taxi to the Běihǎi Airport, 20km (11 miles) east of downtown, will run around ¥50 ($6.25). Tickets can be purchased at the **CAAC office** (© **0779/303-3757**) at Běibùwān Xī Lù, on the second floor of the Mínghángá Dàshā. Buses for the airport (¥10/$1.25; 30 min.) leave from here 2 hours before scheduled plane departures and will also meet incoming flights.

By Train Běihǎi is connected to China's rail network via Nánníng. From Nánníng, train lines run northwest to Chéngdū (26 hr.); northeast to Guìlín (10 hr.), Běijīng (41 hr.), and Shànghǎi (46 hr.); east to Guǎngzhōu and Hong Kong

(36 hr.); and southwest to Píngxiáng (4 hr.) on the Vietnamese border. Although frequent buses between Běihăi and Nánníng have made the train a less popular and less convenient option, there are still those who prefer the 3-hour ride on relatively new trains. Tickets can be purchased at the rather forlorn **train station** (☎ **0779/320-9898**) located halfway between downtown and Silver Beach to the south.

By Bus From the long-distance bus station (☎ **0779/202-2094**) on Běibùwān Lù, air-conditioned luxury buses run to Nánníng (2½ hr.–3 hr.; ¥50/$6.25)

every half hour between 6:50am and 9pm. There are also express buses to Guăngzhōu (10 hr.; ¥180/$23; 8:45am, 8:55pm) and Guìlín (¥150/$19; 7½ hr., 8:40am, 9:10pm).

By Ship There is a daily 10-hour ferry to Haikou on Hăinán Island departing at 6pm from the **International Ferry Terminal (Běihăi Guójì Kèyùn Găng; ☎ 0779/388-0711),** located in the south of town approximately 2km (1¼ miles) west of Silver Beach. Tickets range from ¥81 ($10) in a 48-person dorm to ¥211 ($26) for a double (shared bathrooms only).

GETTING AROUND

Běihăi is easy to get around. Xiàlĭ and Citröen **taxis** cost ¥5 (60¢) for 2km (1¼ miles), then ¥1.40 (17¢) per kilometer. Jettas run ¥7 (90¢) for 2km (1¼ miles), then ¥1.60 (20¢) per kilometer. **Motorcycle taxis** are ¥2 (25¢) for in-town destinations. **Bicycles** can be rented at hotels for around ¥15 ($1.90) an hour, but usually require a big deposit of around ¥500 ($62). To get to Silver Beach (Yíntān) from the city center, take a taxi for ¥10 to ¥15 ($1.25–$1.90); or take **bus** no. 3 (¥2/25¢), which runs from Hăibīn Gōngyuán in the northeast to Silver Beach in the south. Bus no. 2 runs from the train station to the ferry docks in the west, passing Wàishā, though you'd still have to get off at the Wàishā Qiáo stop and walk the rest of the way onto Wàishā.

The slow **ferryboats,** known as Fēiyáo vessels, leave for Wéizhōu Island from the International Ferry Terminal in the south of town at 8:30am daily. A sleeper berth costs ¥45 ($5.60), while seats in second and third class cost ¥40 ($5) and ¥35 ($4.40) respectively. The voyage takes about 3 hours. The return trip leaves Wéizhōu at 3pm. The Jìnghăi Hào ferry is a faster alternative (75 min.–90 min.), but it doesn't run every day. Fast ferry tickets cost ¥52 ($6.50) each way. Hotel tour desks and travel agencies can arrange a 1-day guided tour of Wéizhōu for around ¥280 ($35) per person including transportation, entrance fees, lunch, and an English-speaking guide. Alternatively, you can tour the island on your own.

TOURS & STRATAGEMS

China International Travel Service (CITS; ☎ **0779/206-2999;** open daily 9am–6pm) is located in the Shangri-La Hotel at Chátíng Lù 33, and can arrange tours of

Běihăi as well as assist with plane, train and hotel reservations. Hotels can also assist with booking tickets and day tours.

WHERE TO STAY

Beach Hotel (Hǎitān Dàjiǔdiàn) This four-star hotel opened in 2000 and is the best place to stay in the entire Silver Beach tourist area. The W-shaped hotel has many rooms offering stunning sea vistas, especially rooms on the fourth through sixth floors, where views are not blocked by Beach Park (Hǎitān Gōngyuán) across the way. Rooms are large and tastefully furnished with light wood furniture and firm beds. Bathrooms are clean and come with tub/shower combos and anti-fog mirrors. As a bonus, guests are given free daily passes to Beach Park, which hosts a nightly musical fountain performance. Rooms are subject to a 10% surcharge. *Yíntān Dàdào.* ✆ **0779/388-8888.** *Fax 0779/389-8168. www.bh-bh.com. 151 units. ¥580–¥680 ($73–$85) double. AE, DC, MC, V.* **Amenities:** 2 restaurants (Cantonese, Patio Cafe); bar; lounge; nightclub; outdoor pool; health club; sauna; bowling center; concierge; airport shuttle service; business center; shopping arcade; salon; room service; massage; babysitting; laundry/dry cleaning; executive rooms. *In room:* A/C, TV, minibar.

Shangri-La Hotel (Xiānggē-Lǐlà Fàndiàn) As the only five-star hotel in town, this is certainly the best place to stay in Běihǎi, even though it's located less conveniently in the northeastern section of town. This smart 17-story modern hotel has a full range of facilities and offers the usual luxury and quality service associated with the Shangri-La name. Rooms are spacious, comfortable, and pleasantly furnished with large double beds, rattan furniture, and a large writing desk. Bathrooms have tub/shower combos. Other hotel highlights include a large sculptured swimming pool, two restaurants offering fine Chinese and Western dining, and two Horizon Club executive floors. Hotel rates are subject to a 15% service charge. *Cháting Lù 33 (on the north shore).* ✆ **800/942-5050** or *0779/206-2288. Fax 0779/205-0085. www.Shangri-la.com. 364 units. ¥840 ($105) double (30% discount regularly offered). AE, DC, MC, V.* **Amenities:** 2 restaurants; outdoor swimming pool; separate children's pool with water slide; 2 outdoor tennis courts; health club; Jacuzzi; sauna; CITS tour desk; free airport shuttle; business center; conference rooms; shopping arcade; salon; room service (6am–midnight); next-day dry cleaning and laundry; nightly turndown. *In room:* A/C, TV, minibar.

WHERE TO DINE

The best seafood (shrimp, snail, sandworm) is at **Wàishā,** a thin strip of land across a bridge from the town harbor (off Hǎijiǎo Lù in northwest Běihǎi). Where there were once 72 "no-name" cafes, most run by local fishing families, Wàishā today has gone upmarket with bona-fide restaurants housed in large, multi-storied structures that range in architectural styles from modern European to traditional Thai. While much of the informal and fun ambience has been lost in the transition, patrons today can count on a greater degree of cleanliness and order, not to mention higher prices. One such transplanted restaurant is the **Rìrìxiān HǎiXiān Lóu,** Waisha Island, Indonesia Dining District (Wàishā Dǎu, Yìnní Cān Yǐng Qū) (✆ **0779/203-9818**). Popular with locals, this Cantonese/seafood restaurant doesn't have much ambience, with its barren whitewashed walls and large tables, but, happily, patrons can also dine outside on the beachfront in thatched-roof huts. Large glass tanks containing all kinds of fresh seafood greet the arriving guest. Choose your dinner here or consult the extensive menu (Chinese only). Specialties of the house include *jǐnshā yóuyú*, a somewhat spicy cuttlefish dish; and *jiǔwáng chǎo shāchóng* (sandworms stir-fried with leeks). Reservations are recommended. Dinner for two costs ¥120 to ¥180 ($18–$22). Open daily from 11:30am to 1am.

As one of many new seafood restaurants (Cantonese-style) that have cropped up on the new Wàishā dining scene, **Wàishā Fùlóng Chéng Jiǔlóu,** Wàishā Hǎixiān dǎo Xǐqū (✆ **0779/ 203-5588** or 0779/202-0022), gets good marks from locals. Set in a Thai-style building right next to the Rìrìxiān Hǎixiān Lóu, this restaurant has a semi-open kitchen, rattan furniture, and nice Chinese-style flourishes in the dining room. Outdoor seafront dining is also available in thatched-roof huts. While the chefs here can cook your live seafood picks any way you like them, the best dishes in which to fully savor the freshness of the catch include *bái zhuó xiā* (quickly blanched fresh prawns complete with shell) and *qīngzhēng shíbǎn* (steamed garoupa). For meat lovers, there's *tiěbǎn lǐ niúzǐ liáo* (sizzling beefsteak), tender and mouthwatering. Reservations are recommended. Dinner for two costs ¥120 to ¥200 ($18–$25). It's open daily from 11am to 1:30am.

The Cantonese-style **Shang Palace,** Chátíng Lù 33 (2nd Floor, Shangri-La Hotel; ✆ **0779/206-2288**), serves fresh seafood in a clean, elegant environment. Happily, its excellent dining experience is further complemented by magnificent sea views. Chefs from Guǎngdōng Province can prepare the day's live catch in any style (steamed, fried, blanched, stewed, or as sashimi). Favorites include deep-fried stuffed prawn meatballs, steamed garoupa, and braised sea cucumber in abalone sauce. Dim sum is also served from 7 to 11am and 9pm to 1am for ¥3 to ¥9 (35¢–$1.10) per dish. Dinner reservations are recommended. Main courses cost ¥30 to ¥300 ($3.75–$38). American Express, Diners Club, MasterCard, and Visa are accepted. Open daily from 7am to 1am.

The best Western dining in Běihǎi can be found at the Shangri-La Hotel's **Coffee Garden,** Chátíng Lú 33 (✆ **0779/ 206-2288**). Main courses cost ¥40 to ¥120 ($5–$15). Open daily from 6am to midnight, this bright, pleasant restaurant with rattan furniture and floor-to-ceiling windows serves up Western comfort foods like spaghetti, lasagna, steak, and apple pie. There are also Chinese and Asian dishes on the menu, and the restaurant frequently hosts food festivals highlighting different international cuisines. Breakfast and dinner buffets, set lunches, and weekend brunches all help draw the crowds. Service is friendly and efficient. If you prefer to dine alfresco, step outside to the pool area where there is a sumptuous seafood barbecue every night for only ¥98 ($12) per person.

KŪNMÍNG:
CITY OF ETERNAL SPRING
昆明

Situated on a high, lush plateau in Yúnnán Province, bordering Vietnam, Kūnmíng was long regarded by the Chinese as untamed and remote—in fact, as barely civilized. Officials fallen from favor in the imperial capital were routinely banished to these backwaters of the Middle Kingdom, where tribal peoples were constantly in rebellion. Even today, over a quarter of Yúnnán's 35 million people are minorities, members of 24 groups that have retained their non-Chinese customs and dress.

This preponderance of racial minorities imparts a splash of color and diversity to Kūnmíng that is missing in most other cities of China, where the crushingly homogeneous Hàn Chinese, nearly 99% of the population, hold sway. Kūnmíng even maintains an Institute for Nationalities, a university of over 20,000 minority students.

This said, I have found upon several recent returns to Kūnmíng that even here, China's rapid modernization is altering the cityscape. The pace of life in Kūnmíng can no longer be described as that of a village. General Claire Chennault, who stationed the legendary Flying Tigers and the 14th U.S. Air Force here during World War II, described Kūnmíng as a "sleepy backwoods Oriental town" where "water buffalo, cattle, and herds of fat pigs were not uncommon sights." They are uncommon enough now, however. The streets are paved and jammed with new cars, buses, and trucks, like any street in the West, and lined with ever-taller offices and department-store towers. Ten years ago, Kūnmíng bore few outward signs of an American presence. Today, the Americans have returned to Kūnmíng—not in person, for there are few foreign faces in this city, but as models for Kūnmíng's future. The architecture, the automobiles, the department stores, the clothing—it's all in the American mode.

The old Kūnmíng is slipping into the back streets and curling up in a few parks and temples. That's precisely where you have to go these days to find the remains of what has long been one of China's most exotic cities. Fortunately, a search can still turn up strange treasures.

Downtown

The streets of Kūnmíng have lost much of their old exotic flavor since the economic boom of the late 1990s. The original department store at the main downtown intersection of Nánpíng Lù and Zhèngyì Lù, Bǎihuò Dàlóu, has been replaced by a glistening new **super store** (daily 9am–10pm), with an annex. Inside, the marble stairs with spittoons on every landing have been superseded by brand-new escalators. The staff is decked out in clean uniforms. The counters are stocked with heaps of cosmetics and electronic appliances from abroad. There are still enough local commodities to make a quick swing through the aisles worthwhile, but the poorly lit, cavernous emporium of the 1980s is gone.

So too is the Nánchéng Ancient Mosque, for centuries located a few blocks up Zhèngyì Lù (at the corner of Qìngyún Jiē), but replaced recently there by a new **mosque.** The Huí people (Chinese Muslims) have made it into a more formal tourist site, with trinkets and postcards for sale outside. After removing your shoes, you can enter the plain prayer hall upstairs and have a quiet look around. The mosque, even rebuilt, has fared better than a nearby Buddhist temple, which was smashed by the Red Guards during Máo's Great Cultural Revolution (1966–76). Left in a pile of glazed green roof tiles and red bricks, with its stone temple lion toppled onto the sidewalk, this temple has now been replaced by a high-rise office building, four stories of blank concrete and whitewash.

While the back streets in downtown Kūnmíng are beginning to lose their rough appeal, I still saw several **street markets** northwest of the main downtown traffic circle, their stalls stocked with fresh flowers, tropical fruits, and pork bellies. A block west of the mosque on the north side of Jīngxīng Jiē, the **Flower and Bird Market (Huā Niǎo Shìchǎng)** has outgrown its original alley (Tōngdào Jiē), still identifiable by overhanging signs in Chinese and English. Along the side streets you'll find caged songbirds, fish of marvelous shapes and colors, lizards, monkeys, and other creatures from Yúnnán's southern jungles, as well as pets such as small dogs and cats. Continuing north to the next main boulevard, Rénmín Zhōnglù, I crossed through an **open-air market** full of prayer rugs and ethnic handicrafts. This is still an "old" neighborhood, with wooden two-story shophouses looming everywhere, but modernization is closing in.

Some of the street life has been chased eastward from Nánpíng Lù to the huge public square at the **Workers' Cultural Hall.** This is about a half mile from downtown, where Nánpíng Lù turns into Dōngfēng Dōnglù, Kūnmíng's prime east–west boulevard. The square, which occupies both sides of the street, fills up before 8am with Kūnmíng's exercisers—dancers, *tàijíquán* groups, and badminton players. After 8am, it becomes congested with shoppers, idlers, and vendors offering foods I couldn't identify. One entire row of vendors sits behind small tables with hand-painted signs advertising their services. These are the blind masseurs of Kūnmíng who,

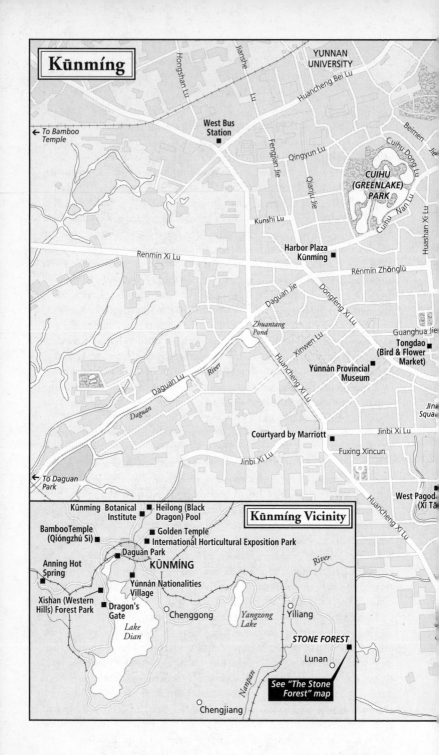

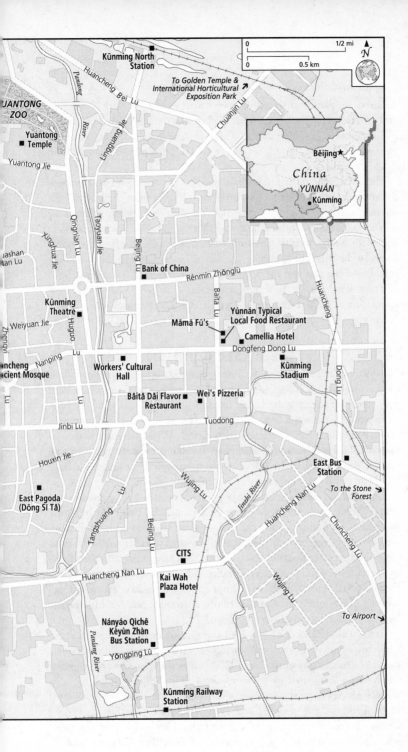

Kūnming North Station

To Golden Temple &
International Horticultural
Exposition Park

YUANTONG
ZOO

Yuantong
Temple

Yuantong Jie

Huancheng Bei Lu

Panlong River

Lingguang Jie

Chuānjīn Lu

Běijīng ★

China
YÚNNÁN
● Kūnmíng

Qingnian Lu

Taoyuan Jie

Beijing Lu

uashan
an Lu

Xinghua Jie

Bank of China

Rénmín Zhōnglù

Baita Lu

Huancheng

Kūnming
Theatre

Weiyuan Jie

Hugup
Lu

Nanping

Zhengyi

uncheng
cient Mosque

Lu

Yúnnán Typical
Local Food Restaurant

Māmǎ Fú's

Camellia Hotel

Dongfeng Dong Lu

Kūnming
Stadium

Dong Lu

Workers' Cultural
Hall

Bǎitǎ Dǎi Flavor
Restaurant

Wei's Pizzeria

Jinbi Lu

Tuodong Lu

Houxin Jie

Tangshuang Lu

East Pagoda
(Dōng Sì Tǎ)

Wujing Lu

Jinbi River

East Bus
Station

To the Stone
Forest

Huancheng Nan Lu

Chuncheng Lu

Beijing Lu

CITS

Huancheng Nan Lu

Kai Wah
Plaza Hotel

Wujing Lu

To Airport

Nányáo Qìchē
Kèyùn Zhàn
Bus Station

Yōngpíng Lù

Panlong River

Kūnmíng Railway
Station

0   1/2 mi
0   0.5 km

N

361

for a pittance ($1.25), will deliver a crushing back massage right on the square or on platforms set up in nearby patches of a city park. Dozens of other masseurs ply their trade from head to foot (reflexology), each dressed like a doctor in a white smock. There are also fortunetellers, ice-cream hawkers, batik vendors and, on any given day, unemployed peasants from the countryside.

These days, the farther you move from the heart of the city, the more country people you see trying to make their way in from the fringes, selling rural crafts, produce, and their skills on the streets. Many of them are dressed in minority clothing, knowing that for today's Chinese visitors, as well as for foreign tourists, an exotic costume gives a sales edge. The longer I wander the streets of Kūnmíng, the clearer becomes the split between the rural life of the past and the urban rush of the present. Mending that split will take decades more. In Kūnmíng, the urbanization of China's vast rural population is at its inception—where it stood in America more than a century ago.

Green Lake (Cuì Hú)

Northwest of city center, a 40-minute stroll up Dōngfēng Xīlù, then a right on Cuì Hú Nán Lù, is Kūnmíng's answer to Central Park, Green Lake (Cuì Hú). Some of the neighborhoods here are still populated with the two-story wooden-shuttered houses that characterized city life in Kūnmíng a century ago, but most are being torn down. At the eastern entrance to **Green Lake Park (Cuì Hú Gōngyuán)**, vendors conduct games of ring toss on the sidewalks: The prizes are cheap ceramic figurines, while stalls sell intricately sliced curlicues of fresh pineapple on sticks.

Lined with willows, Green Lake is gorgeous, crisscrossed by small arched bridges in imitation of Hángzhōu's more famous West Lake. The best time to come is on Sunday, when the pathways are crowded with families on their weekly outings, and the best season is winter, when days are warm and sunny and the large flocks of black-headed "laughing gulls" with their cackling cries arrive from breeding grounds in Siberia, as they have been doing for the last 10 years. The gulls enjoy not only the legendary "eternal spring" weather of Kūnmíng but also the crumbs of steamed bread, sold in plastic bags by vendors, that visitors toss them.

Green Lake Road (Cuì Hú Lù), running south of the park entrance back toward downtown, was developing into a trendy "international" avenue of small cafes in the late 1990s, but as the 21st century begins, it has become dominated by scores of small shops selling everything from mobile phones to souvenirs (batiks, carvings, scrolls, and the traditional clothing of the Bái people), and even real estate. The French Parasol Restaurant and the Cafe De Jack, backpacker bistros, are gone. All that's left here of those easygoing hangouts is the **Blue Bird Cafe,** its open-air wooden porch nudging the crowded sidewalk.

The Best 500 Arhats in China

The temples of Kūnmíng are numerous, and today they can put you more directly in touch with the ancient past. Most tourists bent on seeing a temple at Kūnmíng first head east from Green Lake to **Yuántōng Sì,** a thousand-year-old Buddhist complex with a new statue of Sakyamuni in white marble, a gift from the king of Thailand. A more interesting religious shrine, however, is the **Bamboo Temple (Qióngzhú Sì),** 13km (8 miles) northwest of city center. A taxi is the easiest way to get there; the cost is around ¥30 ($3.80).

The Bamboo Temple dates back to the Táng Dynasty (A.D. 618– 907), but the present halls were rebuilt in the 1880s when the amazing sculptor Lǐ Guǎngxiū arrived on the scene. Molding clay over wooden skeletons, Lǐ composed the most demented congregation in China, perhaps in the world. Had Goya and Dalí collaborated as sculptors, their work would have resembled the 500 arhats of the Bamboo Temple.

The 500 arhats (or 500 *luóhàn*) are a fixture in major Chinese monasteries. They are the 500 followers of Buddha who achieved their own salvation. Concerned only with personal redemption, they practice deliverance from the mortal world in bizarre, often grotesque ways. In Lǐ's version, the 500 figures perch tier upon tier, occupying three halls. Their faces twist and erupt in wild contortions, creating a vivid three-dimensional mural of exaggerated emotions from joy to despair to madness. Devotees ride oceanic crests on the backs of animals, mythic and natural. Eyebrows .6m (2 ft.) long sprout from perplexed foreheads. An arm streaks 3m (10 ft.) across the room, its finger shattering a ceiling of clouds like a thunderbolt. This is the ultimate mixture of surrealism and expressionism, Buddhism and dementia. Lǐ Guǎngxiū is said to have parodied the faces of his contemporaries in Kūnmíng, who criticized his art not for its extreme exoticism and depiction of horrors but for its realism. For sheer inventiveness, these 500 arhats put even modern Western comic book illustrators to shame.

Golden Temple (Jīn Diàn)

Another temple that repays a visit to the outskirts of Kūnmíng is the **Golden Temple,** located atop **Míng Hill (Míngfēng),** 11km (7 miles) to the northeast. At the northern entrance (admission ¥15/$1.90), you must scale a formidable forested hillside via a wide stairway, passing through the First and Second Gates of Heaven (Yì Tiān Mén, Èr Yiān Mén) before making the final push straight up. Near the Third Gate are two rather odd attractions: a camel waiting for tourists to pose with it for portraits, and the **"Golden Temple Alpine Coaster,"** the third longest "tublose-rail" alpine coaster in the world, with two-thirds of a mile of track up and down the sacred slopes.

The main attraction, however, resides still higher, beyond yet another gate (Língxīng Mén), not to mention an upper parking lot favored by tour buses: the Golden Temple itself (also called Tàihé Gōng or Palace of Great Harmony). The Golden Temple is surprisingly small, but exquisite. It was first built in 1602 and moved to this hill in 1637, though the present form was cast in 1671. Weighing in at 250 tons, this is the largest bronze work of architecture in China. Double-tiered, 7.5m (25 ft.) wide, 6m (21 ft.) high, ensconced on two platforms of marble, the Golden Temple has a dark patina and looks its age. Inside, its altar is dominated by the statue of the Zhèngwǔ Emperor, with a Gold Boy and Gold Girl on either side, the altar guarded by images of a fierce tortoise and snake. In the "Chinese Golden Temple Expo Garden" to one side of the temple is the Zhèngwǔ Emperor's own legendary "seven-star" double-edged sword.

The Golden Temple is surrounded by old stelae (engraved stone tablets), including one on the far side of the temple with the image of Laǒzǐ, ancient founder of China's major indigenous religion, Daoism. Chinese visitors here (I was the only foreigner, in fact) often face this engraved image, cover their eyes with one hand, and march forward with an arm outstretched, attempting in a kind of blind-man's-bluff to strike the venerated figure (a successful blow ensures longevity).

Beyond the Golden Temple, in the upper folds of the hills, at the park's true summit (elevation 2,026m/6,752 ft.), is the **Bell Tower.** There are signposts in English and Chinese along the way. This three-story tower with its 36 flying eaves, decorated with singing phoenixes, soars to over 27m (90 ft.), and though it looks old, it was in fact built here in 1984. The ancient treasure hangs inside, a 3m (10-ft.) tall, 14-ton **bronze bell** cast in 1423 that once hung in the south gate of the old city walls of Kūnmíng.

To one side of the Bell Tower is the **Golden Temple Camellia Garden,** particularly glorious in the spring, when its 15,000 flowers (200 varieties) are in bloom. It is billed as the largest camellia garden in China (10 ha/ 25 acres).

Rather than retracing your steps the rather hefty distance back down the hill and searching there for a taxi, you can follow the signs to the **Jīnbó Cable Car,** which connects the Golden Temple park to the International Horticultural Exposition Park below. On my way to the cable car I spotted an old man lying at the side of the road who immediately sprang to life as I neared. He turned out to be an itinerant fortuneteller who could not be dissuaded from reading my palm, my ears, and my head. He cast my fate on the basis of the small metal slats I happened to draw, despite my protests, as I couldn't understand a word of his dialect, nor he of mine. I paid him off and proceeded on. Traveling alone, you are frequently a victim of such colorful inconveniences in China.

The Jīnbó Cable Car, over a half mile in length, opened in January 1999, expressly to connect the Golden Temple with the grounds where the last world exposition of the 20th century was held. Each cable car holds just two persons, and a loudspeaker on each post blasts out Chinese pop music, but the view is spectacular, including a glimpse of the city of Kūnmíng and its skyscrapers in the far distance. The Jǐnbó Cable Car operates from 9am to 6pm daily, and costs ¥15 ($1.90) one-way, ¥25 ($3) round-trip.

International Horticultural Exposition Park

The international horticultural fair (dubbed "Expo 99") is over, but the vast expo grounds (more than a mile across, covering 215 ha/538 acres) are still worth the stroll. The park has kept the **special exhibition gardens** of bamboo, bonsai, herbs, trees, fruits, and teas. Five large **exhibition halls** also remain, foremost the large circular courtyard **Green House.** Its chief display is a miniature Yúnnán alpine landscape of native plants that thrive on the high plateau above 2,700m (9,000 ft). The expo grounds are stuffed with other attractions, too, from a butterfly house and food plazas to viewing towers and an amusement park.

The International Horticultural Exposition Park, about 6km (4 miles) northeast of Kūnmíng (southwest of Golden Temple Park), is open daily from 8:30am to 6pm. Admission is ¥100 ($13). Taxis take 20 to 30 minutes to get there from downtown locations, and charge ¥20 to ¥30 ($2.50–$3.75).

Grand View Park (Dàguān Gōngyuán)

Kūnmíng is a horticultural Shangri-La. The new expo gardens are large, but the city's most famous flower gardens are located at an older site, **Grand View Park,** 3km (2 miles) southwest of city center, a 60-hectare (150-acre) botanical paradise on the shores of expansive **Lake Diān (Diānchí).** The walkways, arched bridges, courtyards, and ponds here are interspersed with luxuriant flower gardens. The queen of England, on the first visit to China by an English monarch in history, planted rose bushes in this park on the afternoon of October 17, 1986. I know because I was caught in Kūnmíng's first major traffic jam that day, the result of streets suddenly closed off in anticipation of the queen's entourage passing by. I visited Dàguān Park the next day but couldn't find the queen's roses.

Returning more than a decade later, I still found no one to direct me to the royal plantings. Dàguān Park has become a playground for Kūnmíng's youth, full of snack stalls and carnival games, but it still has its ancient sites. The **Dàguān Pavilion (Tower of the Magnificent View)** contains poems in fine calligraphy extolling the beauties of the park, including a nostalgic 118-character rhyming couplet, the longest in China, etched upon the gateposts by Sūn Rǎnwēng in the early 18th century (and recarved there in 1888 after Muslim rebels destroyed the original).

Dàguān Pavilion was built over 300 years ago and rebuilt in 1869 after a fire. The Kāngxī Emperor saw to construction of the original tower in 1690. He used it to enhance his view across Lake Diān to the Western Hills. In profile, these hills outline the figure of a woman reclining, her long hair rippling into the lake. Locals call the range **"Sleeping Beauty Hills."** Its steep flanks, connected by ferries from Dàguān Park, are honeycombed with carved stone shrines and temples, capped by Dragon's Gate (Lóng Mén) near the peak.

Dragon's Gate (Lóng Mén)

The **Western Hills (Xī Shān),** a band of sheer cliff faces, rise 600m (2,000 ft.) above the shore of Lake Diān (elevation 1,860m/6,200 ft.) in the flat farmlands 16km (10 miles) southwest of Kūnmíng. A series of paths, stairways, and tunnels—linking a succession of stone temples, seemingly perched in thin air—have been carved into the face of the cliff, spiraling ever upward to Dragon's Gate at the summit. For the fit hiker, the entire 8km (5-mile) journey from the bottom, starting at the town of Gāoyáo, takes nearly 4 hours, particularly if the way is crowded, as it often is, with hordes of fearless Chinese sightseers.

Most of the effect and the best vistas can be had by starting farther up. I hired a taxi from Kūnmíng (¥210/$25 for the afternoon) and was driven most of the way up the Western Hills to the **Pavilion of Three Purities (Sān Qīng Gé),** a Daoist temple complex. Once a 13th-century imperial villa, Sān Qīng Gé is nowadays a parking lot and tourist trap of restaurants and souvenir stands, a 3km (2-mile) walk below Dragon's Gate. Less than a mile from here, the **cliffside grottoes**—originally cut out of the sheer stone walls by Wú Láiqīng and his band of daring monks over a 54-year period starting in 1781—begin in earnest. This is not a walk for those with even a faint touch of vertigo. The caves and niches along the way contain statues trimmed from rock, serving as shrines to Guānyīn (Goddess of Mercy) and other Daoist deities.

Dragon's Gate overlooks Lake Diān straight below. In the far distance eastward, the new high-rises of Kūnmíng are also visible. Lake Diān, 48km (30 miles) across north to south—the sixth largest lake in China—is divided by a causeway. The waters in the northern section were dammed a few years ago to serve as a massive sewage treatment facility.

In fact, the entire lake is so poisoned by pollutants that few fishermen can make a living anymore. Many families have been given permits to pursue a new profession, becoming vendors along the cliff paths and temples of the Western Hills. Their stalls and tables, selling everything from bottled water to polished rock images of the gods, now line the pathway to Dragon's Gate from bottom to top. A new **cable car** stretches from the far side of Lake Diān to Dragon's Gate, too. It is the second cable car built in the Western Hills during the 1990s. Another connects Dragon's Gate to **Tàihuá Temple,** 5km (3 miles) lower down on the Western Hills. The cable car charge is ¥20 ($2.50) one-way, ¥30 ($3.75) round-trip. Dragon's Gate Park is open from dawn to dusk daily and charges ¥15 ($1.90) admission.

The best route remains the 3km (2-mile) walk from Sān Qīng Gé to Dragon's Gate and back. There are fewer vendors, more overlooks, and plenty of recessed shrines here. The cave walls are scorched black with burning incense. At the top, where you can lean out over the stone railings and glimpse the stone path you've just edged up, is one of the grander views in all of China—the view a Daoist immortal might have taken, perhaps, in which all human perspectives dissolve: Cities, farms, lakes, and roads become mere lines on a cosmic map, and the mind floats free of all its past moorings, buoyant as a cloud.

The Big Plaza

A sign of modern Kūnmíng is the new Yúnnán Golden Horse and Green Rooster Tourism and Commercial Plaza, a long-winded title for the shopping and entertainment complex that has just opened on Jīnbì Lù, a block south of the downtown center. **Jīnbì Square,** as it's popularly known, is something of a theme park for shoppers, hearkening back to Yúnnán's traditions. There are three plazas, three main streets, two crossroads, and two open courtyards, all lined by two-story shophouses modeled on the old architecture of Kūnmíng and constructed of blue stone and roof tiles. This is Yúnnán's largest tourism commodities center, built at a cost of US$78 million. There's even an underground plaza, served by many elevators and open-air escalators.

The center contains several craft workshops, two traditional (reconstructed) buildings, a 27,000 sq. m (90,000-sq.-ft.) Jewelry Plaza (the largest in China), and plenty of small cafes featuring local snacks and dishes (from Wēishān long noodles and Dàlǐ fish casserole to Cross-the-Bridge rice noodles). Food fairs and ethnic performances are often staged in the courtyards here.

East & West Pagodas

Oddly enough, you can still walk a few blocks from the city center and the new Jīnbì shopping plaza and find monuments to Kūnmíng's recent and distant past—sacred monuments. At Běijīng Lù 418 (just north of the Tuǒdōng Lù intersection), for example, I came across an active **Catholic church,** a compact two-story structure of cement and marble with a statue of Jesus above its altar. A high-lift crane dangling a wrecking ball on the end of its cable stood ominously close in the rear alleyway. Then, walking west toward Jīnbì Square, I happened upon another church, at Jīnbì Lù 61, this one with new blue-framed windows. An old man sat smoking a small pipe on the steps. I asked if it was all right to go in. He nodded. Inside it was a plain church with brown pews seating a few hundred. There was a balcony and an altar with a gold-colored cross, but very little decoration. It turned out to be a **Protestant church,** again quite active, with YMCA-sponsored meetings.

My destination on this morning ramble, however, was toward a different religious tradition represented by two pagodas, a west pagoda and an east pagoda, mirror images, separated by a few blocks. They stood just south of city center and Jīnbì Square. Once the tallest structures in Kūnmíng— probably the tallest towers for a thousand miles—they were now swamped by the wake of high-rise construction that was sweeping through the city. In fact, I wouldn't have set out to find the two pagodas if I hadn't noticed them from the window of the new hotel tower and been overcome with curiosity.

The **West Pagoda (Xī Tǎ)** is located down a narrow alley off Dōngsì Lù. I could see it as I walked down the street, through an old neighborhood that was fast meeting the wrecking ball; I soon spotted an alley entrance and took it. This pagoda was built between 824 and 895 during the Táng Dynasty, then restored during the Míng Dynasty after an earthquake in 1499. Most recently, it was renovated in 1983. The four-sided pagoda has 13 stories (although I could only count 11), with Buddhist statues in the niches of each story. The pagoda cannot be entered, but there is a pictur- esque, decaying two-story courtyard hall surrounding it, where a few monks live.

The West Pagoda's twin, the **East Pagoda (Dōng Sì Tǎ)** is located on the next major street to the east, at Dōngsì Lù 61. It is newly landscaped and newly opened. Built during those same years (824–895, during the Táng Dynasty) and last thoroughly renovated in 1883, the 13-story East Pagoda stands 40m (132 ft.) tall, has most of its statues in the outer niches, and seems to lean slightly to the west. There's an attached pavilion and garden to the east. Across the street, between the ancient East and West pagodas (largely forgotten, submerged in an armada of modern steel and glass pago- das), I passed by a children's hospital. I could see into the hospital room windows as I passed, and the hospital entrance and courtyard were lined with parents and toy vendors.

Later, as I returned down Běijīng Lù, the remote old China reached out to touch me. An old peasant woman came up to my side as we waited at a busy intersection. She looked up at me, raised her hand, and with one finger lightly stroked the red hairs on my arm. I told her, yes, the hair of the foreign devil is indeed strange, but she didn't understand me. I smiled, but she was transfixed. She raised her hand again, this time to lightly stroke my curling beard with the same extended finger. The light changed, we crossed, and we were separated.

Yúnnán Nationalities Village (Yúnnán Mínzú Cūn)

In 1992, Kūnmíng opened its version of an ethnic theme park, an attraction that is sweeping China and other Asian countries. The Yúnnán Nationalities Village is 11km (7 miles) west of downtown on the shores of Lake Diān. It is linked to Kūnmíng by a wide expressway and to the top of the Western hills by that new cable car.

I've visited several of these parks in China, and Kūnmíng's is the best, or, at least, the most extensive, with two dozen exhibits of ethnic village architecture, crafts, and costumes. There are also regularly scheduled song and dance performances at 10:30am, 1pm, and 3:30pm. A motorized shuttle train links the exhibits. The park is open daily from 8am to 10pm, though it may sometimes close at 6pm if it's raining. Admission is ¥70 ($8.75) between 8am and 6pm. From 6 to 10pm, admission is ¥50 ($6.25).

Some of the minority people, all in village costume, speak enough English to explain a bit about their cultures, and there are snapshot opportunities, but the experience is not one I find worth repeating. Better to see the minorities in their actual villages in Yúnnán (in the Stone Forest, a popular day trip from Kūnmíng), or in the towns of Dàlǐ and Lìjiāng, farther to the west.

Stone Forest (Shí Lín)

Kūnmíng's most celebrated attraction is a geological wonder, the limestone pillars clustered in the Stone Forest, 80km (50 miles) to the east. There's a new highway to the **Sāní minority village,** named Five-Tree, in Lǔnán County at the park entrance. A decade ago, the highway followed a more circuitous route, usually broken by a stop midway at the Nut House, on the shores of Lake Yángzhōng, where the American Air Force partook of R&R during World War II. It constituted a pleasant stop in the 1980s. Tea in a glass and walnuts in the shell were served up in the lobby of the Nut House, which looked like a stately 1940s inn.

As this new century begins, however, the highway to the Stone Forest is becoming overrun with roadside attractions, amusement parks, burgeoning towns, and a raft of gift shops. Many of the Stone Forest tour buses that leave from Kūnmíng's hotels and bus stations every morning stop for shopping along the way. Even placid Lake Yángzhōng has received a face-lift. A large resort village has gone up on its shores, along with a golf course and a factory with a tall, belching smokestack.

Yet the countryside here still ranks among the most beautiful in China. The ride to the Stone Forest can be as interesting as the site itself. Roadside factories are busy carving figures of lions from white stone. Ducks are cooked in small brick furnaces outside cafes, much as lobsters are steamed outdoors in Maine. We passed several horse carts serving as local buses, 10 people standing on each trailer. Trucks haul massive piles of brick and stone; the Yúnnán countryside is a vast quarry. Herds of goats block the side roads. Ponies and water buffalo work the green fields.

At the end of the road, now just a 90-minute ride from Kūnmíng (it used to take nearly 4 hr.), the Stone Forest erupts like a primordial dream. Acres of vertical limestone shafts, exposed 270 million years ago when the ocean receded from southwest China, sprout like an immense grove of bamboo. Wind and rain have drilled creases and fissures into each tall pillar. The Stone Forest is like a cavern raised above the ground, its dome lopped off, open to the blue sky.

Miles of pathways twist through the karst landscape, edging along reflecting pools and rising on stone steps to pavilions perched on the limestone summits. It is a maze of massive stone pick-up sticks, dropped by a playful deity. Sāní women in full ethnic dress stand at every turn, offering to be guides or directing visitors to kiosks.

In the late 1990s, the park painted red signs on the sides of the rocks in English as well as in Chinese. BETTER TO REST HERE FOR A WHILE, one reads. Other signs identify the chief formations: THOUSAND-YEAR-OLD TORTOISE, ELEPHANT ON A PLATFORM. New stones pave the trails and a new section with a broad green lawn has been opened for visitors.

Park admission is ¥80 ($10). I traipsed for several hours through the Stone Forest maze, ending up at **Sword Peak Pond,** where buildings have been erected selling trinkets and fast food. Photographers for hire dress tourists in ethnic outfits for vacation portraits. The Stone Forest doesn't fully emit its grandeur until the tourists disappear in the late afternoon. Then you can take a solitary stroll through this microcosmic version of the uncanny peaks of Guìlín, reduced to a thick grove of 30m (100-ft.) tall stone columns. It resembles a petrified forest left standing in the wake of geologic time, a thicket of gigantic exclamation points, a geologist's field of dreams.

This is why it's best to stay the night at the Stone Forest. There are several guesthouses at the park entrance and in Five-Tree Village across the bridge on the other side of Stone Forest Lake. Just before dusk, you can enjoy the sights and the people at a slower pace, perhaps even make a purchase of Sāní batiks, which are lovely. The people are friendly, once the heat of the sales day wears off. On many nights, there are performances of Sāní dances at the inns or in the park, enthusiastic affairs where the audience is encouraged to join in. And **Stone Forest Lake,** between the park entrance and the bridge to the village, is stunning at sunset, the pillars sprouting from its waters like castle turrets in the fading light. The air is fragrant and the sky is choked with stars.

The ride back across the high Yúnnán plateau is unforgettable. The villages are built of red clay. Long red peppers and yellow ears of corn dangle from gray-tiled roof eaves, curing in the sunlight. The Sāní farmers till

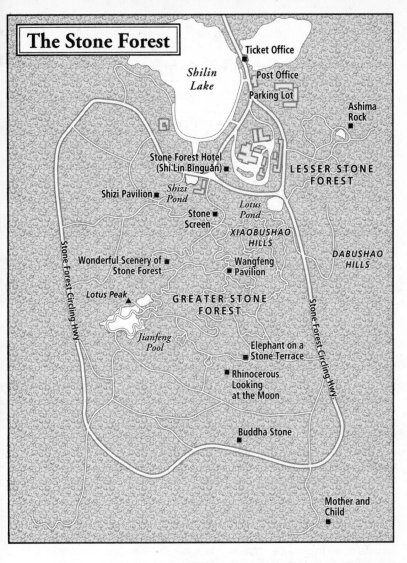

The Stone Forest

Ticket Office

Shilin Lake

Post Office

Parking Lot

Ashima Rock

Stone Forest Hotel
(Shí Lín Bīnguǎn) ▪

LESSER STONE FOREST

Shizi Pavilion ▪

Shizi Pond

Stone ▪
Screen

Lotus Pond

XIAOBUSHAO HILLS

DABUSHAO HILLS

Wonderful Scenery of ▪
Stone Forest

Wangfeng ▪
Pavilion

Lotus Peak ▲

GREATER STONE FOREST

Jianfeng Pool

Elephant on a
▪ Stone Terrace

▪ Rhinocerous
Looking
at the Moon

Stone Forest Circling Hwy

Stone Forest Circling Hwy.

▪ Buddha Stone

Mother and ▪
Child

their fields, dressed in embroidered clothing—bright reds and golds. The shoulders of the road are coated with rice spread out to dry. Along the wide riverbanks, the oval kilns of brickmakers are clustered one after the other like the tents of nomadic tribes. This is the Chinese Connemara, possessed solely by the sharpest elemental colors: the red of the soil, the green of the hillsides, the white of the limestone, the blue of the sky.

But the road from Kūnmíng is turning into one long resort strip, and Kūnmíng is losing its remote and exotic flavors: Unfortunately, the past is nearing obliteration.

Practical Information

by Sharon Owyang

ORIENTATION & WHEN TO GO

Kūnmíng is the capital of Yúnnán Province in southwest China. Situated in the middle of the large province, Kūnmíng is the gateway to many fascinating tourist spots, including the Bái minority village of Dàlǐ, 350km (210 miles) to the west along the old Burma Road; and the Nàxī town of Lìjiāng, 517km (320 miles) to the northwest on the road to Tibet. (See separate chapters on Dàlǐ and Lìjiāng.) Kūnmíng's subtropical location and high elevation (1,864m/6,213 ft.) have given it a mild, temperate climate year-round. Days are filled with sunshine, even in winter, making almost any time good for a visit, though the balmy months of September and October are especially beautiful.

GETTING THERE

By Plane   The **airport** (② 0871/313-3216) is 5km (3 miles) south of city center, a quick ¥15 to ¥30 ($2–$4) taxi ride via city streets or a six-lane expressway if you're headed north to the Cuì Hú area. On the international front, Kūnmíng is served by **Dragonair,** Běijīng Lu 157 (② 0871/356-2828), with a daily flight to Hong Kong (3 hr.). Several Chinese airlines provide connections to and from cities in China, including Běijīng (2½ hr.), Chéngdū (1 hr.), Guìlín (1½ hr.), and Shànghǎi (2½ hr.). There are also daily intra-province flights to Dàlǐ (15 flights a day), Lijiāng, Xiānggélǐlā (Zhōngdiàn), Bǎoshān, Mángshì, and Xīshuāngbǎnnà. You can purchase tickets from the **CAAC/Yúnnán Airlines** office located at Tuódōng Lù 28 (② 0871/316-4270 domestic inquiries; 0871/312-1223 domestic booking; 0871/312-1220 international inquiries); from the Yúnnán Airlines counter at the airport, CITS, and other travel agencies; and from hotel tour desks.

By Train   Kūnmíng is well connected by rail to many major Chinese cities, including Shànghǎi, Běijīng, and Guǎngzhōu, but because of the mountainous geography, these trips can require several days and nights (up to 60 hr.). For these long distances, flying is a more efficient, if costlier, option. There is a long-distance train to Chéngdū (overnight, 24 hr.) that travels through glorious mountain scenery, and overnight trains to the neighboring provincial capitals of Guìyáng and Nánníng. Tickets can be purchased at the **train station** at the southern end of Běijīng Lù (② 0871/612-2492) between 6:30am and 11:30pm, at travel agencies, and at hotel desks. To get to the Stone Forest, see "Tours & Stratagems" below.

By Bus   Kūnmíng has a number of long-distance bus stations, all within 5 minutes of each other and the railway station, but the main one that should serve most travelers' needs is the **Nányáo Qìchē Kèyùn Zhàn** at Běijīng Lù 60 (② 0871/351-0617), at the northwest corner of Běijīng Lu and Yǒngpíng Lù. From here, buses go to Dàlǐ (Xiàguān) (5 hr.; ¥104/$13; 17 buses departing 7:30am–7:30pm), Lìjiāng (9 hr.; ¥152/$19; buses depart at 7:30am, 9:30am, 11:30am, 2pm), Xiānggélǐlā (12 hr.; ¥162/$20; 8:20am), Ruìlì (16 hr.; ¥191/$24; 3:30pm), and Jǐnhóng (16 hr.; ¥150/$19; buses depart 2pm, 4pm, 6pm, 7pm, 8pm). Ticket offices are open daily from 6:30am to 9:30pm. A private bus company, **YNTAC** (© **0872/212-5221**), operates luxury, air-conditioned, non-smoking buses from Kūnmíng to Dàlǐ (Xiàguān) (5 hr.; ¥103/$13; buses depart at 8:30am, 9:30am, 10:30am, 1pm, 2:30pm, 7pm) and Lìjiāng (8 hr.; ¥151/$19; buses depart at 8:30am, 9:30am, 1pm). These buses leave from the Kūnmíng Tǐyùguǎn at Dōngfēng Dōng Lù 99.

GETTING AROUND

Downtown sites can be toured on **foot** or on a **bike.** If your hotel does not offer bike rental, the Camellia Hotel (see "Where to Stay," below) rents bikes for ¥2 (25¢) per hour or ¥15 ($1.90) per day. It takes about 90 minutes to walk across town east to west from the Holiday Inn to Green Lake. Flagfall for Xiàlì and smaller **taxis** is ¥7 (85¢) per 3km (1¾ miles), then ¥1.40 (17¢) per km. For larger taxis, such as Santana's, prices are ¥8 ($1) per 3km (1¾ miles) and ¥1.60 (20¢) per km. Exploring by taxi costs ¥10 to ¥30 ($1.25–$4) per trip. While many of the outlying sights such as the Bamboo Temple and Dragon's Gate can be reached most conveniently by taxi, public buses also travel most of these routes. Local bus no. 52 runs from the airport to Dàguānyuán via the railway station. Bus no. 47 runs from the train station to the International Horticultural Exposition Park, from where you can either take the cable car or bus no. 10 to the Golden Temple (Jīn Diàn). Bus no. 44 goes from a block north of the train station to the Yúnnán Nationalities Village.

TOURS & STRATAGEMS

Visiting Shílín (Stone Forest)   The best way to reach the Stone Forest is via direct train (90 min.; ¥20/$2.50 one-way, ¥30/$3.75 round-trip; departing Kūnmíng daily at 8:10am and returning from the Stone Forest at 4:30pm). A special ticket booth at the southeast corner of the train station next to the gate for the Stone Forest train is open from 7:30 to 8:10am for travelers arriving on overnight trains who may want to head directly to the Stone Forest. During other times, purchase Stone Forest train tickets at counter no. 3 in the main station or from travel agencies or hotel desks. Entrance tickets for the Stone Forest (¥80/$10) can be purchased on the train, where attendants may also try to sell you organized tours taking in additional nearby sights such as the **Nǎigǔ Stone Forest** (additional ¥40/$5, including lunch) or the **Dàdiéshuǐ** Waterfall (additional ¥50/$6.25, including lunch). If you decide to join one of these tours, usually conducted only in Chinese, they will send you to the train station in time for the return train to Kūnmíng at 4:30pm. For the average day visitor to Shílín, even a slow stroll through the forest shouldn't take more than 3½ to 4 hours. If you do not wish to wait around for the 4:30pm return train, you can catch earlier Kūnmíng-bound trains (¥17/$2.10), which pass through the Stone Forest (train no. 1165 leaves Shílín at 1:47pm and arrives in Kūnmíng at 3:30pm), although there are no reserved seats on these earlier trains. In general, avoid anyone who tries to sell you bus trips (¥30/$3.75 round-trip) going to the Stone Forest unless you want to spend all your time shopping along the way and only reach the Stone Forest in the afternoon. For those who wish to overnight at the Stone Forest, the two-star **Stone Forest Hotel (Shí Lín Bīnguǎn),** inside the main gate to the Stone Forest Park entrance (ⓒ **0871/771-1405**), is a decent choice. The rooms (¥280–¥480/$35–$60 double), with private bathrooms, are basic and a little worn, but they are clean and the hotel has a restaurant.

Tours & Travel Agencies Most of the hotels catering to foreigners have tour desks or in-house travel agencies that can arrange day tours of Kūnmíng and the Stone Forest with English-speaking guides. If you're still stymied, check with **CITS** at Huánchéng Nánlù 285 (ⓒ **0871/353-5448;** www.kmcits.com.

cn). Although they're usually swamped catering to large tour groups, the English-speaking staff of the Euro-American Department is exceedingly helpful and friendly, and can help with all kinds of tickets, tours, and accommodations. The **Camellia Travel Service** at the Camellia Hotel, Dōngfēng Dōnglù 96 (ⓒ **0871/316-6388;** Camellia@ynmail. com), can arrange plane, train, and bus tickets, including to the Stone Forest, Dàlǐ, Lìjiāng, and other locations in Yúnnán. They can also arrange tours to Lhasa via plane (¥2,750/$344 per person) or via the overland route (¥5,000/ $625).

WHERE TO STAY

Bank Hotel (Bānkè Fàndiàn) Located in the heart of town on the banks of the Pànglóng River, this luxurious five-star hotel boasts the largest standard rooms in Kūnmíng and they are plushly decorated with classical redwood furniture and large comfortable beds. The spacious bathrooms are clean and come with separate tub/shower. The facilities here are first-rate, and the staff is efficient and professional.

Qīngnián Lù 399. ⓒ *0871/315-8888. Fax 0871/315-8999. www.bankhotel.com. 285 units. ¥1,146 ($138) standard; ¥2,158 ($260) and up, suite. 20%–30% discounts. AE, DC, MC, V.* **Amenities:** 2 Restaurants (Chinese, Western, Japanese), bar, lounge; indoor pool; health club; tennis court; salon; sauna; concierge; business center; forex; shopping arcade; room service; dry cleaning/ laundry; non-smoking rooms; executive rooms. *In room:* A/C, Satellite TV. minibar; hairdryer, safe.

Camellia Hotel (Cháhuā Bīnguǎn) Still the favorite of independent budget travelers, this two-star hotel has three levels of accommodation: recently renovated doubles with private bathroom on the

fourth to seventh floors; older budget doubles, also with private bathroom, but smaller and more run-down; and basic dorms with shared showers that are in high demand. The recently renovated doubles are large, comfortable, and comparable to many three-star hotel rooms. Factoring in the hotel's very reasonable rates and useful facilities—message board, luggage storage, tour desk, foreign exchange counter, bicycle rental (across the street), two restaurants, and an excellent ¥10 ($1.25) Western buffet breakfast—the Camellia is an all-around good choice. The staff speaks some English and can be helpful when pressed.

Dōngfēng Dōng Lù 154 (3km/2 miles east of city center). ⓒ *0871/316-3000. Fax 0871/314-7033. 180 units. ¥200– ¥220 ($25–$28) double; ¥30 ($3.75) dorm. AE, DC, MC, V.* **Amenities:** 2 restaurants; bike rental; game room; tour desk; laundry service; business center; shop; salon; sauna. *In room:* A/C, TV.

Courtyard by Marriott Less conveniently located for the independent traveler in the southwestern part of town, this four-star hotel attracts mostly business travelers and Japanese, American, and European tour groups. While not as luxurious as some five-star hotels, the Courtyard still delivers some first-rate facilities and quality service. Public areas are done in a charming courtyard style complete with wrought-iron furniture, while guest rooms, decorated in a somewhat stuffy style, have classical furniture and large, comfortable beds. The garden-themed bathrooms are large, deliver hot spring water, and have tub/shower combos. Nonsmoking rooms are available. There are three restaurants (Chinese, Western steakhouse, coffee shop) on the premises. *Huánchéng Xīlù 300.* © *0871/415-8888. Fax 0871/415-3282. www.courtyard. com. 263 units. ¥1,024 ($128) double. AE, DC, MC, V.* **Amenities:** 3 restaurants; indoor hot spring swimming pool; tennis court; health club; sauna; tour desk; airport shuttle; business center; conference rooms; shopping arcade; salon; room service; babysitting; same-day dry cleaning and laundry; nightly turndown; in-house doctor. *In room:* A/C, TV, dataport, minibar, coffeemaker, hair dryer, safe.

Harbour Plaza Kūnmíng (Hǎi Yì Fàndiàn) Located along a pleasant street minutes from Green Lake Park (Cuì Hú Gōngyuán), this beautiful 18-story modern hotel offers all the luxuries of a five-star hotel. Hong Kong–managed, the hotel is currently *the* place to stay for higher-end tour groups from Europe and America. Rooms, decorated in earth tones and light woods, are simply but tastefully furnished. Beds are comfortable, the pillows delightfully soft. Bathrooms run a little small but are clean and bright and come with tub/shower combos. There are three executive floors and three restaurants (Western, Japanese, and Cantonese).

Hóng Huá Qiáo 20 (southwest of Green Lake). © *0871/538-6688. Fax 0871/538-1189. www.harbour-plaza.com. 300 units. ¥1,038 ($139) double. AE, DC, MC, V.* **Amenities:** 3 restaurants; outdoor swimming pool; health club; sauna; children's playroom; tour desk; free airport shuttle; business center; conference rooms; shopping arcade; salon; 24-hr. room service; same-day dry cleaning and laundry; nightly turndown. *In room:* A/C, TV, minibar, hair dryer, safe.

Kai Wah Plaza Hotel (Jiā Huá Guǎngchǎng Jiǔdiàn) Located in the heart of town, near the train station and shops, this 37-story modern glass building with a high-tech atrium is as sleek as it gets in Kūnmíng. Formerly managed by Westin Hotels, the Jiā Huá is so large you sometimes feel like you're staying at a convention center (the hotel shares the atrium with an office complex). For all of the hotel's size, rooms here are comparatively small but are well appointed with wooden floors, glass-top work desks, modern furniture, and plush beds. Bathrooms come with separate tub and shower. Service is fine even if the lobby staff can be a little officious at times. Executive floors offer all the usual exclusivity. Facilities are first-rate. There are three restaurants (Chinese, Western, coffee shop) on the premises, as well as a cigar bar.

Běijīng Lù 157. © *0871/356-2828. Fax 0871/356-1818. 555 units, including 134 suites. ¥1,120 ($140) double. AE, DC, MC, V.* **Amenities:** 3 restaurants; bakery; indoor swimming pool; squash court; health club; Jacuzzi; sauna; tour desk; free airport shuttle; 24-hr. business center; conference rooms; 5-story shopping arcade; salon; 24-hr. room service; same-day dry cleaning and laundry; valet; nightly turndown; medical clinic. *In room:* A/C, TV, minibar, safe.

WHERE TO DINE

Yúnnán cuisine has a number of famous dishes. The most famous is **Crossing-the-Bridge Noodles,** a hot pot consisting of steaming chicken broth to which you add rice noodles, vegetables, mushrooms, and meats, seasoned with chili peppers. The oil on top keeps the food swimming below warm. The dish was invented a century ago, according to legend, by the wife of a scholar who carried the pot across the bridge to her husband's study, where he enjoyed the dish hot despite its long trip from the kitchen.

Fried goat cheese and french fries are also local favorites, as are Yúnnán sweet ham and Yúnnán coffee. Yúnnán mushrooms are highly regarded throughout Asia and are considered medicinal by those in the know. Many Yúnnán dishes are laden with an allegedly healthful, fat-reducing pharmacopoeia of herbs and spices. Chicken stewed with medicinal herbs in an earthen dish (qìguōjī) is another ubiquitous specialty that is quite delicious.

Many of the higher-end hotels will have restaurants serving the above-mentioned Yúnnán dishes in a clean, elegant, if more expensive setting. Cheaper versions of the same can just as easily be had just off Dōngfēng Dōng Lù up Báitǎ Lù at the **Yúnnán Typical Local Food Restaurant (Zhǎngxīn Fàndiàn),** Báitǎ Lù 209 (✆ **0871/316-6221**). The decor and service here are unremarkable, but the cafe has low prices (¥18–¥34/$2–$4) and well-prepared local fare, and it's open 24 hours. Also worth trying is the string of franchise restaurants run by the **Brothers Jiāng (Jiāngshì Xiōngdì Qiáo Xiāng Yuán);** they serve some of the best and most consistently reliable Guòqiáo Mǐxiàn (Crossing-the-Bridge Noodles) in town.

The outlet located at Jǐnbì Square (Shūlín Jiē 2; ✆ **0871/364-5275**) is housed in a traditional Chinese building with wooden doors and lattice windows. Inside, bustling waitresses trot out bowl after bowl of steaming noodles as they try to keep up with the usually packed house. The most basic version at ¥10 ($1.25) offers soup, pork, ham, cuttlefish, and chicken. The ¥20 ($2.50) version comes with qìguō jī (steamed chicken in a pot), while the most expensive, at ¥60 ($7.25), has beef liver, duck gizzards, and an assortment of local wild vegetables. There is also a meatless version for ¥10 ($1.25).

For heartier and more formal local fare, **Jǐnbì Chūn,** at Dà Huā Jiāo Xiàng 5, Dōng Sìjiē (✆ **0871/364-1663;** open daily 11am–10pm), provides one of the best dining experiences in town, as it combines the wonderful ambience of a 130-year-old Chinese mansion with delectable local Diān cuisine, freshly prepared in a clean environment. This two-story gray-brick building has private dining rooms arrayed around a once open courtyard that has now been closed off. Red Chinese lanterns, and beautifully carved wooden doors and lattice windows, many of them in the octagonal bāguà shape, help set the right mood. Smartly dressed locals flock here for Diān cuisine specialties such as zhēng lǎo nánguā (steamed pumpkin), jǐnbì cuì huóxiā (prawn sashimi marinated in a salty and spicy sauce), and sùpí guàn gōng jī (chicken soup with puff pastry). The restaurant should have an English menu by the time you read this. Prices are reasonable; dinner for two costs around ¥80 to ¥100 ($10–$12). Reservations are recommended.

For a refreshing change of palate, try the **Báitǎ Dài Flavor Restaurant (Báitǎ Dǎiwèi Tīng)** at Shāngyī Jiē 143, off an alley (© **0871/317-2932;** open daily 11:30am–2:30pm and 5:30–9:30pm). This restaurant's rattan furniture, bamboo booths, and batik prints all give you the feeling that you're in a Southeast Asian country rather than China. Dǎi food (a minority cuisine) spans the taste spectrum with sweet, salty, bitter, sour, and spicy, all well represented on the menu (available in English). Though much of the fare here may be relatively new to foreigners, popular favorites include *yēzi qìguō jī* (coconut chicken), *huǒshāo gānbā* (barbecue dried beef), *zhútōng ròu* (pork cooked in bamboo), and *hùnhé chǎo* (fried mixed vegetables). A variety of local beers and wines is available to complement your meal. Dinner for two averages between ¥50 and ¥70 ($6.25–$8.75).

Primo's Steak House (© **0871/415-8888;** open daily 3pm–1:30am at Courtyard by Marriott) offers succulent chargrilled viands and meats.

Outside of the international hotels, there are several spots where good, inexpensive Western food can be had. **Wei's Pizzeria (Hāhā Cāntīng),** Tuǒdōng Lù 78 (© **0871/316-6189;** megen@public.km.yn.cn; daily 8am–midnight), serves excellent home cooking in an unpretentious, family-friendly environment. Located in a small alley off Tuǒdōng Lù, this casual two-story restaurant also offers practically everything a traveler far from home could want: Internet and book-exchange services, bicycles for rent, a bar with a good collection of beers and wines, and even a playpen for children on the second floor. The restaurant offers dishes from all over the global map and, amazingly, does

everything quite well. Favorites include the Four Seasons Pizza (ham, broccoli, mushrooms, tuna fish, and black olives), vegetable lasagna, enchiladas, and an artery-clogging cheesesteak sandwich. There's also a good selection of basic Chinese dishes like *yúxiāng qiézi* (eggplant with garlic sauce) and *Yúnnán qìguō jī* (Yúnnán steamed chicken). Main courses cost ¥18 to ¥30 ($2.25–$3.75).

Capitalizing on the success of the original Māmā Fū's Restaurant in Lìjiāng, the owner has opened three new outlets in Kūnmíng. **Māmā Fū's 2** at Báitǎi Lù 219 (© **0871/311-1015;** open daily 8:30am–11pm), across from the Kūnmíng Hotel, is a lovely, cozy place with pale yellow walls, wooden furniture, batik tablecloths, plenty of ethnic decorations, and soft Western music playing in the background. The restaurant offers all the Chinese and Western staples you have come to expect from foreigners' cafes in China: fried noodles, fried rice, pancakes, French toast, apple pie, fresh juices, sandwiches, pizzas, and spaghetti. Best of all, the restaurant bakes its own breads, with a delicious whole-wheat bread being the latest addition to the menu. Entrees are very reasonably priced and range from ¥15 to ¥40 ($1.90–$5).

The most vibrant restaurant near Green Lake (Cuì Hú) is the **Blue Bird Cafe (Qīngniǎo),** with two outlets: one at Dōngfēng Xī Lù 69 (© **0871/361-0478**), and another at Cuì Hú Nánlù 150 (© **0871/531-4071**). Both are open daily from 9am to 2am. The one at Dōngfēng Xī Lù is squirreled away in its own alley across from the Yúnnán Yìshù Jùyuàn, with alfresco dining on the lovely patio and plenty of ambience at night. Unfortunately, it also has usually overenthusiastic, not always melodious warbling from karaoke aficionados, which can put a damper on a nice, quiet, candlelight dinner. The cafe on Green Lake South Road (Cuì Hú Nánlù) is quieter and cozier, with wooden floors, wooden furniture, and blue-and-white batik tablecloths. Food at both, however, is consistently decent, and prices are very reasonable, with main courses running between ¥18 and ¥30 ($2.25–$3.75). The whole wheat–crust pizzas are popular here, as are the beefsteaks. Basic Chinese fare familiar to foreigners (kungpao chicken, garlic eggplant, and the like) is also on the menu, as are staples like fried noodles and rice.

DÀLǏ: THE FAR KINGDOM

大理

Dàlǐ IS LOCATED AT THE CROSSROADS to Burma and Tibet, in the western province of Yúnnán. This is a small town with an exquisite setting, pinched in a narrow band between a long lake and a high mountain range. East of Dàlǐ are the shores of Lake Ěrhǎi, 5km (3 miles) across and stretching 40km (25 miles) north; west are the snowcapped Cāng Mountains, whose highest peak is over 4,050m (13,500 ft.). In the past, Dàlǐ was the capital of an indigenous minority kingdom, for centuries independent of Chinese control. Today Dàlǐ is an antique village, home to the Bái minority.

One of the loveliest places in all of China, Dàlǐ is also the friendliest; the Bái people, the warmest. What's more, Dàlǐ's weather is even more pleasant than that of Yúnnán's capital, Kūnmíng, the renowned City of Eternal Spring. If I could choose only one place to spend my days in the Middle Kingdom, it would be here.

Cafe Life

Dàlǐ at the dawn of the 21st century has not been leveled by the tide of modernization that swept the big east coast cities of China leading up to the nation's 50th anniversary party in late 1999. Its main shopping streets and monuments received something of a scouring, but the feel of a remote Shangri-La persists. Some of the familiar faces and places have vanished, but the quaintness of its streets has not been erased. This medieval village is still a place to linger. Cafes and hotels still cater to foreign travelers who have made it to the southwestern edge of China, although there are increasing numbers of domestic visitors in recent years.

There are two main streets catering to travelers: **Hùguó Lù,** also known as **Yángrén Jiē (Foreigner's Street),** running east and west; and **Bó'ài Lù,** running north and south. Parallel to Bó'ài Lù is **Fùxīng Lù,** the main shopping street, which connects the north and south gates of the old city. It won't take you very long to master the layout. The guesthouses along Hùguó Lù have painted wall murals advertising various amenities (usually hot water) in English. Souvenir shops double as full-service tour agencies.

The tiny cafes in wooden buildings, their front walls paneled in glass, provide Western and Chinese foods at rock-bottom prices.

Many of the Bái people heading for work were dressed traditionally, which is to say colorfully, in bright tunics sashed at the waist, dazzling headdresses, and black cotton shoes trimmed in crimson ribbons.

Inside **Cafe de Jack** on Bó'ài Lù, with its down-and-out feel of a coffeehouse in Greenwich Village, circa 1967, I pulled up a rattan chair at a small table under an India bedspread tacked to the ceiling; ordered eggs, toast, and strong coffee for ¥10 ($1.25); and watched the world go by on horsedrawn carts. This is Old China—a remote China as well. Many of the Bái people heading for work were dressed traditionally, which is to say colorfully, in bright tunics sashed at the waist, dazzling headdresses, and black cotton shoes trimmed in crimson ribbons. The Bái, who are a branch of the Yí minority, differ from the Hàn Chinese in at least one fundamental way: They place as high a value on friendship as kinship. Certainly they have made Dàlǐ as friendly a city to outsiders as any in China.

There are still plenty of cafes for those seeking a slow, contemplative pace of life. A block south down Bó'ài Lù, past two bicycle rental shops on the sidewalk, I had coffee at a table outside **Jim's Peace Cafe,** a typical rundown two-story dwelling with a small restaurant just inside and a warren of basic dorms and rooms (all sharing one bathroom) up and down the side stairs. Tibetan medicine and massage are practiced here, as Jim himself is half-Tibetan, and a good storyteller and local guide to boot.

Back past Jack's and around the corner, on Hùguó Lù, there are even more choices. The **Tibetan Cafe** is one of the oldest ("Since 1990"). It has the usual blue-and-white tablecloths, rattan chairs, local tour service, Western breakfasts, sandwiches, steaks, desserts, and coffees (most items $1–$3), as well as a Tibetan menu.

On both these streets, which parallel or cross the main shopping street (Fùxīng Lù), there are new cafes where others stood in previous seasons, with names like Sisters Cafe, the Old Cafe, the Sunshine Cafe, Claire's Cafe, Star Cafe, the Old Wooden House, and the Yak Cafe. They may or may not be here on the next visit, but their immediate descendants will be, expertly run by young Bái folks. The cafe I miss most is Leah's Place, across the street from Cafe de Jack's. Leah, a 22-year-old Bái woman who spoke fluent English and cooked like a dream, had just opened it when I first came to Dàlǐ. I still remember her eggplant stir-fried with ginger, green pepper, and soy sauce, from a recipe she'd acquired from a foreign guest; I remember, too, the smoothies, consisting of banana, yogurt, cinnamon, and ice cream, the dark Yúnnán coffee, and the snow tea brewed from white leaves grown on nearby Cāng Mountain (Cāng Shān).

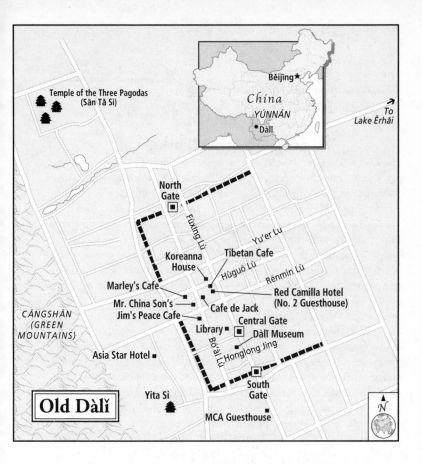

It was at Leah's Place that I met an Englishman named Eric. Dressed in heavy hiking boots and a Guatemalan poncho, carrying a guitar case, and sporting his straight red hair at shoulder length, he'd just arrived from Hong Kong to propose marriage to a local Bái girl. Eric needed the approval of his intended's parents, who lived in a Bái village on the other side of Lake Ěrhǎi. He was 40, she 18. He knew a smidgen of Chinese; she knew almost no English. He was a club musician in Hong Kong; she, a hostel maid. I won't say it was a marriage made in heaven, but several of the women in the village had married Westerners. The Bái people seemed to accept such arrangements. Several of Dàlǐ's cafes are owned by foreigners who have married locals.

By the time we parted, Eric had struck an agreement, brokered by a local cafe owner and author, Uncle Lǐr: Eric was to finance his betrothed's college education starting in the spring, and she was to see no one else in the meantime. Now returning, I found no trace of Leah or her cafe, but Uncle Lǐr was still in town, and I was able to complete the soap opera I'd been a part of: Eric indeed ended up marrying the girl from Dàlǐ, finally taking her back with him to Hong Kong. Meanwhile, Leah herself enrolled in a university in Kūnmíng.

Old Shopping Street (Fùxīng Lù)

The Dàlǐ for sightseers—and there is more each day—is encamped along the 3km (2-mile) pedestrian street of Fùxīng Lù, which runs from the north gate to the south gate of the old city. It turns out that this is where the tourism dollars have been funneled to spiff up the old shop fronts, to open scores of new souvenir and minority craft stores, and to line the pavement with cast-iron lanterns—even to add a brand-new "ancient" central gate. Dàlǐ is still a pretty village of old two-story wooden houses, their double-tiered tiled roofs dividing the upper and lower floors. The fronts are planked and faced with folding doors, carved windowpanes, and wooden railings stained a dark red. A typical Bái house has a courtyard, usually decorated in flowers and shrubs, particularly camellia and bougainvillea. In Dàlǐ, the Bái women are known as "Golden Flowers."

Touches still remain, in the alleys, of Yúnnán's rural life: markets with raw meat, lads manning watch repair booths, a small battalion of young soldiers marching south with straw brooms on their shoulders. But there are plenty of modern touches as well. The old shopping street is dominated now by boutiques and galleries selling slabs of polished marble, by banks with ATMs, and by tiny shops advertising e-mail access.

Between Hùguó Lù, at the heart of downtown, and Rénmín Lù, the next major cross street heading south, is the **Dàlǐ Cultural Center and Library,** a large public courtyard and park with stone tables where the local people gather for mahjong games and *tàijíquán* exercises, and where old men bring their caged birds for an outing. It's a good place to mix with the people of Dàlǐ.

The new **central gate, Wǔhuā Lóu,** farther south on Fùxīng Lù, is built in the ancient style of the original north and south gates. A block farther south, at Fùxīng Lù 111, is the **Dàlǐ Museum** (daily 8:30am–6pm; admission ¥5/65¢). Its halls contain a mishmash of relics from a dozen dynasties: Táng mirrors, a 3rd-century clay vase, a horse with saddle dated at A.D. 289, even some tools from the Stone Age. In a separate museum hall there's a bronze bell under a pavilion, a row of headless men and horses, and two courtyards filled with stelae (engraved stone tablets) bearing dates from the 12th to the 19th centuries. So far, there are no signs in English.

The **south gate** to the old city, **Nánchéng Lóu,** is a two-story pavilion with soaring eaves set on top of a remnant of the 9m (30-ft.) high battlements that once ringed the city. The city wall has very recently been restored and extended, part of the great 1998 project to gentrify old Dàlǐ. From the heights of the south gate tower, there's a complete view of the town, the nearest mountains, and the long lake heading north. South of the lovely, flower-laden courtyard outside the wall, Fùxīng Lù begins to revert to its pre-tourist, pre-modernization days. The shops are rough and plain, the stores carry necessities rather than trinkets, and the shophouses are often workshops where laborers saw and carve wooden furniture by hand and work with the slabs of local marble. The tower over the south gate requires a ¥2 (25¢) admission, but it's a good place for snapshots, and inside there's a Bái teahouse featuring snow tea.

The **north gate** of old Dàlǐ, **Běichéng Lóu,** is a few blocks beyond Hùguó Lù (one of the two main cafe streets). The shops on this segment of Fùxīng Lù haven't been restored recently; older, humbler businesses quickly take over, and the cafes, unscrubbed and undecorated, no longer cater to foreign visitors.

On my way back from the north gate, I once came upon a large funeral in the cobbled streets. It was a simple, happy procession. The mourners of Dàlǐ wield brightly colored banners, and the coffin, carried by hand, is draped in a long, white sheet. As one life ends in Dàlǐ, a new century is set to begin.

The Three Pagodas

On my first visit to Dàlǐ, I became so embroiled in the daily cafe life that I ceased to be a tourist, but you should endeavor to make at least one pilgrimage to the nearest sights. Just a mile north of town on the old main highway is Dàlǐ's most famous historic landmark, the **Temple of the Three Pagodas (Sān Tǎ Sì).** These three towers are situated at the very foot of the 10th peak in the massive Cāng Shān range. Founded in A.D. 825, the temple was later destroyed, but the three pagodas survive. They are the oldest such monuments in the region. The four-sided, 16-story middle pagoda, **Qiánxūn Tǎ,** is the tallest, at 68m (226 ft.); its two eight-sided, 10-story sisters are shorter, at 41m (138 ft.) each. They are a graceful trio from a distance, finely tapered in the style of the Little Wild Goose Pagoda in Xī'ān. The pagoda builders of Dàlǐ, in fact, were said to have come from Xī'ān, which was then the Táng Dynasty capital.

The temple on the grounds is for the worship of Guānyīn, Goddess of Mercy. Locals tell the tale of how a monk was working on a bronze statue of the goddess at this site when he ran out of bronze. Suddenly, bronze balls rained down from the heavens. The people melted down the bronze raindrops and the statue was finished.

There isn't much to do here but admire the beauty of the brick towers and their setting against the snowcapped peaks; the towers are sealed up.

The grounds are ringed by hundreds of vendor's stalls, many of them selling slabs of the local marble, their grains resembling mountain peaks. The temples are open daily from 8am to 5pm (8pm in summer), and charge an admission of ¥50 ($6.25).

A more invigorating excursion is provided free of charge by the slopes of the **Green Mountains (Cāng Shān).** These 19 peaks, 3,000m to 4,050m (10,000 ft.–13,500 ft.) high, form a screen of stone and snow paralleling the city walls of Dàlǐ and the shores of mile-wide Ěrhǎi Lake. Unpaved roads and trails run straight up the mountain from downtown Dàlǐ. With a local map in hand, you can easily walk out of Dàlǐ and into the walls of the stately **Yǐtǎ Temple (Yǐtǎ Sì)** on some nearby slopes. It's easy going, and the 10th-century pagoda within the temple walls is uncanny, silent as the lake below, sealed up and utterly deserted. It looks about a million years old.

Mr. China's Son

The most remarkable person in Dàlǐ, and one of the most remarkable men in China, is **Uncle Lì.** His full name is Hé Lìyì. He was born in a Bái village in 1930. Eventually, he became the first Bái in history to go abroad. He is home now, proprietor of **Mr. China's Son Cultural Exchange Cafe,** on Bó'ài Lù. When I first wandered in 3 years ago, he immediately made me feel at home. His English, Uncle Lì's third language after Chinese and Bái, was marvelous. He had learned it from BBC broadcasts after selling a pig to buy a short-wave radio. Upon my return, it was Uncle Lì who had changed the least, his cafe barely altered by the accelerated stream of time all of China seems to be swept up in.

Uncle Lì's life story is the stuff of 30 novels. In fact, he has published that story in English. *Mr. China's Son: A Villager's Life* appeared in 1993 (Westview Press). His autobiography received excellent reviews in America, but, alas, few copies were sold—a pity, since there are no first-person accounts of 20th-century life in rural China to rival it (but you can still get it; a second edition was printed in July 2002). Uncle Lì has been able to reprint a few copies for sale only in Yúnnán, which he keeps on hand at his cafe. He opened the cafe on June 22, 1995, having reached the age of retirement. I bought a copy of his book. Uncle Lì wrote a long, generous dedication on its title page, puffing away on his long-stemmed pipe.

His story is direct, personal, and extremely frank. In the late 1950s, he spent years in a labor camp. After his release, he made his living by fetching night soil from public toilets for use as fertilizer. He divorced and remarried. He experienced what he calls "years of unspeakable humiliation and suffering," but he is not a bitter man today. After returning from a summer in England in the late 1980s, he settled into village life, opened his cafe, and now hosts foreigners who chance his way.

I signed Uncle Lì's guest book once again, and I asked after his son, Hé Lùjiāng, a teacher in the English section of the Dàlǐ Medical College in nearby Xiàguān. I remembered how I had once helped Uncle Lì with a sign he was writing that announced, in English, that patrons of Dàlǐ's new "plush toilet" were obliged to pay the attendant ¥.50 (about 6¢) per flush. In fact, the sign had needed no correction. The very next day, I saw it posted on the wall when I paid a visit to the ¥200,000 ($25,000) public lavatory at the west end of Hùguó Lù. It was then the only public toilet in all of Dàlǐ that could be described as plush, although there wasn't a piece of tissue paper to be had in the place.

Now, after catching up on the Dàlǐ news, drinking a coffee, having a sandwich for lunch, and reading what was posted from all over the world on the cafe walls, I found that Uncle Lì was spending much of his day behind the small counter typing on a manual typewriter the manuscript of a new book, a memoir of village life that takes up and is intertwined with his own continuing life story. I reviewed an episode and came up with a few suggestions. He is always in search of the pungent phrase, which he savors as though words were truly edible.

By late afternoon, the sunshine had moved across the street and I followed it, basking at an outdoor table at another cafe. After long travels, I was content to let the sun rise and set on Dàlǐ. Leaning back, conversing, eating and drinking, I let the world do the traveling for a change.

Ěrhǎi Lake (Ěrhǎi Hú)

One morning I decided to take a stroll from Dàlǐ to the shore of Ěrhǎi Lake. Dàlǐ is a tiny town, and walking from one end to the other takes only a few minutes. I headed east down Hùguó Lù, south down Fùxīng Lù, then east on Rénmín Lù, the next big street. When Rénmín Lù dead-ended, I jogged south half a block, then continued east toward the lake again on a winding dirt road that starts at a sign in stone reading DA YUANZ.

The dirt road wove through fields to a village named **Cáicūn** along the lakeshore. It was an hour's walk. The wall of mountains behind me took up half the sky. Ahead, Ěrhǎi Lake was a narrow blue band lined with more fierce mountains. The sun shines brightly here almost year-round. Twice I was passed by horse carts ferrying people between the villages, and they stopped for me each time, but I preferred to walk.

The village on the lakefront was a maze of tiny corridors. It's easy to get lost, and I did. Paths branched off to the lake where fishermen dried their nets and cormorants their outstretched wings. Double-ended junks were tied up to stone jetties, and large black-and-white cows wandered the fields. Kids stood in the courtyards of clay and wooden houses setting off firecrackers. Parents were lighting the crackers for the smaller tykes, who were in the throes of exquisite delight.

Eventually I hailed a horse cart and rode back to Dàlǐ, promising myself I would return and sail across the lake to one of the distant village markets on the other side. The next day I did just that.

Wāsè Market

The top day excursion from Dàlǐ is a visit to the market at Wāsè, a tiny village on the other side of Ěrhǎi Lake. Markets are held there every 5 days (on the 5th, 10th, 15th, 20th, 25th, and 30th of the month). I booked a ticket for transportation the day before at Cafe de Jack's for ¥20 ($2.50), which does not include lunch or a guide. Plenty of independent travelers do the same from their guesthouses and at other cafes. The bus left the cafe at 9:30am and rumbled through town to the lakeshore, where a small local ferry was waiting. There was room for about 20 aboard, with benches in the cabin and room to sit on the deck or stand at the rails. It was a superbly peaceful ride of 1 hour and 10 minutes on a sunny, glass-smooth lake rimmed by snowcapped peaks. You can see other local ferries and small fishing boats rowed by hand, the ends of their oars nothing, it appears, but flat squares of wood like crude Ping-Pong paddles.

At Wāsè, we disembarked from the high, pointed bow via a 6-inch-wide plank and walked straight into the market square, which was filled with the rural people of this remote kingdom. The people still keep their own language and colorful dress quite apart from those of the Chinese. Many bring their wares to market on donkeys and horses—and what wares they are, from spices to squash, from chestnuts to rice. I even came upon areas devoted to horse-trading. Several hours slipped by as I strolled through the square and up and down the narrow lanes of the village. There are stalls selling the fantastic woven fabrics of the Bái people; stalls selling basic household goods; stalls selling tea, dried fish, live chickens; stalls selling odds and ends from an attic-cleaning. This is a real market: not an item in sight for a tourist or a foreigner.

Most merchants have no stalls at all, only the woven baskets filled with their wares, and the unpaved lanes are littered with merchandise. The market square has a cluster of large white umbrellas to provide shade. In cement stalls at the rear, the meat sellers hack away, and beyond that is an open yard of live pigs and chickens. Pigs, in fact, are strolling among the buyers and traders and visitors. It's a sweet, unpretentious, rural Chinese market that has not surrendered to the needs of tourists, Chinese or foreign. Here is the serious business of the countryside in full swing.

In the afternoon, at about 2:30pm, I returned to the wharf, and as I waited for our ferry to disembark, I watched a fearless fisherman strip down to his shorts, dive in, and resurface. He held up what turned out to be a television in his arms; but the submerged treasure was broken and he

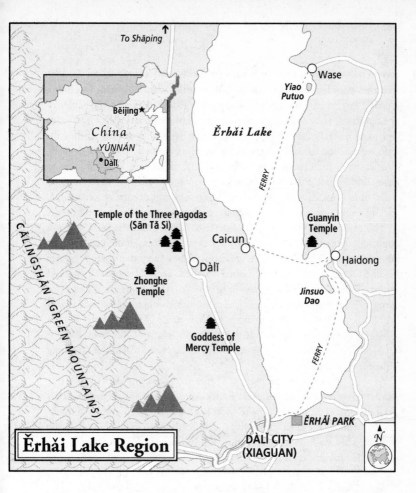

Ěrhǎi Lake Region

tossed it back, swimming out and swimming back, shouting and laughing with his companions on shore.

Shāpíng Market

North of Dàlǐ, the village of **Shāpíng** is also famous for its market, which usually convenes on Mondays. Cafes and tour agencies in Dàlǐ sell bus tickets, costing ¥15 ($1.90), for the round-trip, leaving at 9am and returning about noon. The road edge is planted in mature eucalyptus trees, a legacy of the French influences that once penetrated this part of China from the colonial capitals of Vietnam and Indochina.

The Shāpíng market spreads across a dusty hillside near the highway. When I arrived, the alley into the market was so clogged with vendors on carts and trucks that I had to wait before I could begin to squeeze through. Shāpíng is a marketplace packed with Bái vendors hawking housewares, batiks, vegetables, spices, paintings, silver jewelry, and cut-and-polished stone. Dàlǐ is well known for its marble, and on the road to Shāpíng we'd passed many rock-cutting yards with crude machinery designed to slice the quarried boulders into neat slabs. Dàlǐ marble, with its grains suggesting classical landscapes, has ended up decorating the chairbacks and tables of the Summer Palace at Běijīng and the walls of the private gardens of Sūzhōu.

I spent several hours culling the market stalls. Whole sections of the hill-side are devoted to woven baskets, the vendors pitching umbrellas and sitting down in the dust next to their goods. Yards of dark blue batiks hang from clotheslines. Posters of smiling young women are pinned to a wall of dried mud bricks. Down in a hollow, below a cluster of earthen brick kilns, locals corral dozens of horses, some for trade, most as a means to get home.

The countryside women dress to the nines for the market, many of them topping off their red, white, and blue jackets and long quilted tunics with plumed caps trimmed in bands of sequins. They carry their babies as they do their long fluted baskets, lashed to their backs. I watched two old women in matching red vests and long blue skirts shopping for spices, sampling the wares from open sacks. Farmers rush through the crowded lanes with bright pink piglets squealing in their arms. There's hardly a Hàn Chinese face in the crowd, but there are thousands of Bái faces and the faces of China's other minorities everywhere, sunburnt black, their clothing a dazzling rainbow of dyes.

At one intersection in the market, I came across a young man playing one of the oldest confidence games on Earth. Adroitly shuffling cups over seeds on a newspaper in the dust, he took in loads of cash from gullible onlookers. He worked the shell game with a shill, who sometimes wins, while the innocents always lose. These con men scurry from corner to corner, setting down then folding up their game, always one step ahead of the authorities.

The main road in and out of the Shāpíng market was still jammed when I tried to leave. Vendors and buyers from the countryside were still arriving, standing on the open beds of trailers, their sacks and baskets at their feet. Their smiles were broad. It was market day, the brightest day of the week.

PRACTICAL INFORMATION

by Sharon Owyang

ORIENTATION & WHEN TO GO

Dàlǐ is located 377km (233 miles) north-west of **Kūnmíng,** the capital of Yúnnán Province in southwest China. As the capital of the Dàlǐ Bái Autonomous Prefecture (where over 80% of China's 1.1 million–strong Bái minority live), Dàlǐ is actually made up of the ancient city of Dàlǐ and the new town of Xiàguān, where the local prefecture government is located. Dàlǐ is also a 3-hour minibus ride south of Lìjiāng (see separate chapter), another Yúnnán Shangri-La, via the new expressway that runs along Ěrhǎi Lake.

Dàlǐ is located in a mountain valley at an elevation of 1,949m (6,496 ft.). Its climate is mild and pleasant with many sunny days year-round, although winter mornings and nights can be chilly. Perhaps the most interesting time to visit Dàlǐ is during the annual **Sānyuèjié (3rd Moon Festival)**, which starts on the 15th day of the third lunar month. For 6 days and nights the Bái people of Dàlǐ and minorities from elsewhere in Yúnnán gather in the foothills of the Green Mountains (Cāng Shān) to sing, dance, and attend a large market. Accommodations are extremely scarce then, as they also are in June and July, the months of the high tourist season, so be sure to book your hotel ahead of time.

GETTING THERE

By Plane   The new **Dàlǐ Airport**, at Xiàguān (16km/10 miles south of Dàlǐ), has daily flights (40 min.; ¥340/$43) to and from Kūnmíng, the gateway to Dàlǐ. An airport shuttle bus meets all incoming flights at the Dàlǐ Airport, but don't take it unless you want to go to Xiàguān (16km/10 miles south of old Dàlǐ). If you want to hire a taxi, the transfer takes about an hour and can cost up to ¥100 ($12).

By Train   With the opening of the railway link between Kūnmíng and Xiàguān in 1999, another popular option for getting to Dàlǐ is the overnight sleeper train from Kūnmíng (8 hr.; ¥75–¥95/$9.40–$12 hard sleeper, ¥161/$20 soft sleeper), which leaves Kūnmíng at 10:34pm and arrives in Xiàguān at 6:22am. A later train departs at 11:16pm and arrives at 7:30am. From the train station, a direct bus (no. 8) runs to the West Gate of the Old City (Dàlǐ Gǔchéng Xīmén). Returning to Kūnmíng, trains depart Xiàguān at 9pm and 10:02pm. You can buy train tickets at the train station, at any of the bona-fide travel agencies in town, or at a tourist cafe in Dàlǐ.

By Bus   For a full dose of Yúnnán scenery, passengers have a choice of a number of buses, both sleeper and regular, though all non-air-conditioned, that travel the Burma Road for 414km (257 miles) between Kūnmíng and Dàlǐ. It is a long, not always comfortable, 10-hour trip over a mostly paved, winding road that served as a vital supply link between Rangoon and Kūnmíng during World War II, and few travelers choose this option today. Far quicker (4 hr.–5 hr.) and more comfortable are the many buses that travel a new expressway which is, not surprisingly, less colorful and historic than the Burma Road. Most buses arriving from Kūnmíng stop in Xiàguān (16km/10 miles south of Dàlǐ) at the **Dàlǐ Qìchē Kèyùn Zhàn** (© 0872/218-9330), on Jiànshè Lù between Rénmín Lù and Wénhuà Lù. From here, you have to transfer to a taxi or to bus no. 4 (corner of Rénmín Lù and Jiànshè Lù) to make the final connection to the Old Town. To get from Dàlǐ to Kūnmíng, there are no direct buses except for an Iveco van (¥65) leaving Dàlǐ each day at 8:30am. The rest of the time, you'll have to make your way to Xiàguān by taxi or bus no. 4, and transfer to Kūnmíng-bound buses (5 hr.; ¥104/$13; buses departing every half hour 7:30am–8:30pm), which leave from the Dàlǐ Qìchē Kèyùn Zhàn. You can purchase bus tickets from the **Dàlǐ Passenger Service Ticket Office (Dàlǐ Kèyùnzhàn Shòupiàochù)** on Bó'ài Lù. If you don't wish to navigate the transportation transfers on your own, have a travel agency or tourist cafe in Dàlǐ arrange your Dàlǐ–Kūnmíng bus (¥110/$14), as they will take care of sending you to Xiàguān for the transfer. There is usually a ¥5 (60¢) charge for this service.

Travelers now can choose a private bus company, **YNTAC** (© 0872/212-5221), which operates luxury, air-conditioned, nonsmoking buses between Kūnmíng and Xiàguān. Buses (5 hr.; ¥103/$13) leave from Xiàguān's Cāngshān Hotel (Cāngshān Fàndiàn) daily at 8:30am, 10:30am, 12:30pm, 1pm, 2:30pm, and 7:30pm. They arrive at Kūnmíng's Tǐyùguǎn (Sports Stadium).

From Dàlǐ to Lìjiāng, there is a variety of options, with buses departing every half hour between 7:20am and 7:30pm, but the majority of buses originate in Xiàguān. Regular non-air-conditioned minibuses (*zhōngbā*) cost ¥35 ($4.40), Ivecos and deluxe minibuses cost ¥40 ($5), and large luxury buses (3 hr.; departing Xiàguān at 8:30am, 2pm, 7pm, and 7:30pm) cost ¥50 ($6.30). Again, the most hassle-free option is to have a travel agency or cafe book your ticket.

TOURS & STRATAGEMS

The local CITS, which no longer has an office in Dàlǐ, has pulled up roots and moved to Xiàguān to concentrate on organized tour groups. Happily for the independent traveler, however, the small **storefront travel agencies** on Hùguó Lù, with signboards advertising their prices out front, are all surprisingly efficient and reliable. They provide day tours, taxi rentals, and air and bus tickets, and can direct you to bicycle rental stands. The **Dàlǐ Camellia International Travel Service** (Dàlǐ Cháhuā Guójì Lǚxíngshè), located outside the south gate at Wénxiān Lù 18 (© 0872/266-2368), can organize day tours of surrounding areas as well as arrange plane, train, and bus tickets, though their grasp of English is shaky at best.

Many of the Dàlǐ cafes provide similar services, and, in fact, the cafe managers often serve as guides for foreign travelers and tour groups. A typical cafe travel agency will provide a variety of tours, including a boat trip on Ěrhǎi Lake, which costs ¥20 to ¥40 ($2.50–$5) per person, depending on

group size; horseback riding to a mountain monastery or local Bái village, for about ¥80 ($10) per person; and cormorant fishing on the lake in a fisherman's boat, for about ¥180 ($22) for six people. Local English-speaking guides can be hired through cafes at ¥30 to ¥50 ($3.75–$6) per hour; ¥200 ($25) per day. Michael Yáng of **Dàlǐ Michael Travel Information Consultation** at Bó'ài Lù 68 (© 0872/267-8189) offers all of the above services with the bonus that he will work within your budget and won't hesitate to give you the latest unvarnished lowdown on nearby sights. In addition, he can arrange tai chi, calligraphy, and Chinese-cooking classes. Another fount of information on lesser-known local sights is Marley of **Marley's Cafe**, located at Bó'ài Lù 105 (© 0872/267-6651; marleydali@hotmail. com). In addition to arranging visits to Yí, Bái and Huí markets, Jim (Jǐn Cè) at **Jim's Guesthouse and Jim's Peace Café**, Bó'ài Lù 63 (© 0872/267-1822), can arrange motorcycle trips around Ěrhǎi Lake.

WHERE TO STAY

There are a half-dozen guesthouses in downtown Dàlǐ offering basic dormitory-style accommodations. Favored by

backpacking independent travelers, they offer beds and shared bathrooms and showers for as low as ¥10 ($1.25) per night, with some doubles as well. The **No. 2 Guesthouse** (© **0872/267-00406;** fax 0872/267-0309), also known as the Red Camellia Hotel, located at Hùguó Lù 32, on the western end of Hùguó Lu off Bó'ài Lù, is the old standby, the first guesthouse to open to foreigners in Dàlĭ (in 1984) and lately showing signs of age. The hotel now has 150 rooms of different sizes, with 72 standard rooms; doubles with bathroom cost ¥220 to ¥260 ($28–$33), though they can be had for ¥100 ($13) in the low season. The **Old Dàlĭ Inn (Sìjì Kèzhàn);** © **0872/ 267-0382;** fax 0872/ 267-5360), also known as the No. 5 Guesthouse, at Bó'ài Lù 51 (south of Rénmín Lù), has two wings of two-story wooden Bǎi buildings, a courtyard, and a cafe, and offers basic dorm rooms (¥10/$1.25–¥15/$1.90 per dorm bed), double rooms with shared bathrooms (¥30/$3.75), and a few doubles with private bathrooms (¥125/$16).

The **MCA Guesthouse** (© **0872/267-3666;** fax 0872/267-1999), well south of town at Wénxiāng Lù 7000 (a continuation of Fùxīng Lù), is the pick of the hostels, with beautiful grounds, dorms (¥10/$1.25 per dorm bed), rooms with shared bathrooms, and a few doubles with private bathrooms (¥100/$12.50 double with shower only; ¥120/$15 double with bathtub), laundry service, bicycle rental (¥10/$1.25 per day), a tour desk, a cafe, Internet access, and even a beautiful outdoor swimming pool.

A good newcomer to the hostel scene is the **Koreanna House (Gāolì Tíng),** © **0872/266-5083,** located at Hùguó Lù 115. There are seven standard rooms (doubles and triples) with private bathrooms for ¥200 ($25), which can often be discounted up to 50% in the low season. The rooms, arrayed around a courtyard, are extremely clean and

come with portable heaters and heating pads for the winter months and a mini–water cooler/heater. Bathrooms are clean and there's plenty of hot water to go around. The hostel provides laundry and Internet service, and there is an excellent Korean restaurant up front that also serves Western food. The staff is friendly and helpful.

The **Dàlĭ Hotel (Dàlĭ Fàndiàn),** Fùxīng Lù 245, south of Renmin Lu (© **0872/267-0386;** fax 0872/267-0551), has some newer standard doubles with telephones for about ¥240 ($30), as well as many basic doubles at ¥100 to ¥120 ($13–$15) with private bathrooms that look out on a picturesque courtyard garden, hemmed in by the tiled-roof wings of the hotel. Everything here is in romantic decay: the bed, the shower, the carpets, the courtyard balconies. The Chinese-speaking staff is fairly efficient, and the mute masseur who has an office in one wing is always in the lobby to help guests.

Tour groups seem to favor the two-star **Jĭnhuā Bīnguǎn,** at the corner of Hùguó Lù and Fùxīng Lù (© **0872/267-3343;** fax 0872/267-3846), in the heart of Dàlĭ. It offers double rooms with private bathrooms and showers for ¥180 ($23). Behind the ornate Chinese-style facade is a rather hideous white-tiled building. Guest rooms, cramped and run-down, are furnished with rather uncomfortable Qīng Dynasty furniture and small twin beds. There is a surprising number of in-room amenities, including a hair dryer, slippers, towels, shampoo, a hot water thermos, and teabags. The bathtubs are tarnished and stained, but the water is at least hot. Next-day laundry service is also available.

For those who must have their little luxuries, there is one upscale hotel, 1.6km (1 mile) south of Dàlĭ on the old main highway—not an easy walk from town. The **Asia Star Hotel** (© 0872/267-1699; fax 0872/267-2299), a China–Taiwan joint venture, is a four-star international-class luxury hotel with double rooms starting at ¥900 ($108). Despite the rather ugly furniture and the worn carpets, guest rooms are comfortable and bathrooms are large and come with amenities including a hair dryer and scale. While the hotel surprisingly has no swimming pool, it does offer croquet, bike rental, and shuttle service to Hùguó Lù.

WHERE TO DINE

The traveler's life revolves around the cafe scene in Dàlǐ. The foreigners' cafes are located along Hùguó Lù and Bó'ài Lù. The meals are inexpensive but good, the staff—mostly young Bái—unusually friendly and helpful. Cafes usually open about 7:30am and close around midnight or later.

Cafe de Jack, Bó'ài Lù 82 (© 0872/267-1572), is a popular hangout, renowned for its pizzas and its chocolate cake. It offers outdoor seating, perfect for sunbathing in the late afternoon, and Internet service inside in an annex accessible from the cafe and the street, called **Tim's Internet** (¥6/75¢ per hour). Capitalizing on his successes, Jack is also the owner of **La Stella Pizzeria** (© 0872/266-2881), at Hùguó Lù 58, which serves an excellent pizza Margherita (¥18–¥25/$2.25–$3.10) and a spicy beef pizza very popular with Chinese diners. **Jim's Peace Cafe** (© 0872/267-1822), on the opposite side of Cafe de Jack and south down Bó'ài Lù, serves meals and drinks throughout the day. It's small, but Jim himself is often on hand to tell hair-raising stories of his adventures in China, Korea, and Tibet, and to serve his "famous" grilled steaks, huge slabs laden with fries and vegetables.

Also popular for food and drink is the **Tibetan Cafe** (© 0872/266-2391), at Hùguó Lù 42, just outside the main entrance of the Camellia Hotel. Besides the usual Western and Chinese fare, this cozy cafe offers Tibetan specialties, including stewed lamb, Tibetan omelets, Tibetan pancakes, and Tibetan butter tea. They will organize Tibetan group meals upon request. The owner also runs a tour service and can arrange local day trips.

Another trusty standby is **Marley's Cafe** (© 0872/267-6651), at Bó'ài Lù 105 at the intersection of Bó'ài Lù and Hùguó Lù. Owner Marley, a pleasant and friendly Bái woman, has been on the scene for the last 13 years and is a great source of local information. There's a wonderfully relaxed yet upscale feel to this two-story cafe, which serves consistently good food. Of note are their Bái specialties such as *mùguā jī* (fried chicken Bái style; ¥25/$3.10) and *shāguō yú* (Dàlǐ fish casserole; ¥25/$3.10). Marley also offers a regular Sunday evening "Bái Style" banquet, though you have to sign up for this ahead of time.

For a change of pace, not to mention cultures, **Koreanna House (Gāolì Tíng),** © 0872/266-5083, located at Hùguǒ Lù 115, offers excellent and authentic Korean food. Specialties here include *bulgolgi* (roast beef marinated in a special sauce), *bibimbap* (rice with vegetables, beef, and egg), and a variety of barbecue, noodles, and soups. Entrees average between ¥20 and ¥60 ($2.50–$8).

Contrary to what it must sometimes feel like, there *is* life outside of Hùguó

Lù and Bó'ài Lù. Even walking a block north to Yù'ěr Lù will bring you to a number of traveler-free local restaurants serving authentic Bái food. Many new restaurants have cropped up recently where others stood in previous seasons, so it's a rather futile enterprise to recommend specific restaurants. Simply pick one that looks good to you, pull up a chair, and order like a local: *mùguā jī* (fried chicken Bái style) and *shāguō dòufu* (Dàlĭ tofu casserole).

Stuffed with the local flavor? Try northern Chinese cuisine at the **Zhènzhōng Dōngběi Jiǎozi Guǎn,** at Yù'ěr Lù 6. Since the owner/chef is from Hēilóngjiāng, in northeast China, and many of the restaurant's patrons speak with a distinctive northern twang, you know you're getting the real deal. The restaurant is tiny, with only four mid-size tables and absolutely no atmosphere to speak of, but the food is uniformly good, from the fiery *shuǐzhǔ ròupiàn* (pork cooked in a spicy broth with vegetables) and an excellent kungpao chicken *(gōngbǎo jī dǐng)* to staples like dumplings and wontons. Best of all, the restaurant has an English menu.

By all means, drop in at **Mr. China's Son Cultural Exchange Cafe,** Bó'ài Lù 67–5 (west side, between Hùguó Lù and Rénmín Lù). Although he no longer keeps regular hours at the cafe due to his advancing age and lack of help, when he's there, proprietor Hé Lìyì still sells autographed copies of his riveting autobiography (in English) and does his best to help foreign travelers solve practical problems. He can also make you a nice cup of tea as you surf the Web on his PC.

LÌJIĀNG:
CHINA'S SHANGRI-LA
丽江

Accounts by early travelers all agree: Lìjiāng, located in the remote northwest sector of Yúnnán Province where it touches Tibet, is China's Shangri-La. For centuries Lìjiāng served as the capital of the mountain kingdom of the Nàxī, an indigenous people whose origin is a mystery, whose language and way of life are unique, whose rulers are women rather than men. Untouched by any civilization, East or West, Asian or Caucasian, Lìjiāng was the equivalent on Earth of the Western Paradise evoked in Buddhist scriptures. Its face lies in a veil of snowy peaks beyond the gates to the Middle Kingdom. The 300,000 Nàxī people today live here and in the borderlands of Tibet and Sìchuān to the north.

Lìjiāng was previously the domain of adventurers, explorers, and eccentrics from the West, and then the haunt of hardy backpackers; however, it has recently opened to the world and become the destination of small tour groups and independent travelers from China, Asia, Europe, and North America. A new highway from Dàlǐ and a new airport with 1-hour service to Kūnmíng have put this Shangri-La on the doorstep of modern tourism. The monstrous earthquake of 1996 that leveled much of Lìjiāng but spared the quaint Old Town and its Nàxī architecture ironically prompted a flood of tourists. Lìjiāng joined the UNESCO World Heritage list, development funds poured in, and the legendary village, while still remote and picturesque, surrounded itself with new hotels for visitors and new town sites for residents. I recently joined the rush of visitors to see what was left of China's Shangri-La, following at a considerable distance those earlier explorers who had written Lìjiāng into the world book of romantic travels, from Joseph Rock, who introduced readers of *National Geographic* to the wonders of "the ancient Nakhi Kingdom of Southwest China" in the 1920s, to Bruce Chatwin, the travel writer who ventured here with some of the first foreign backpackers in the 1980s.

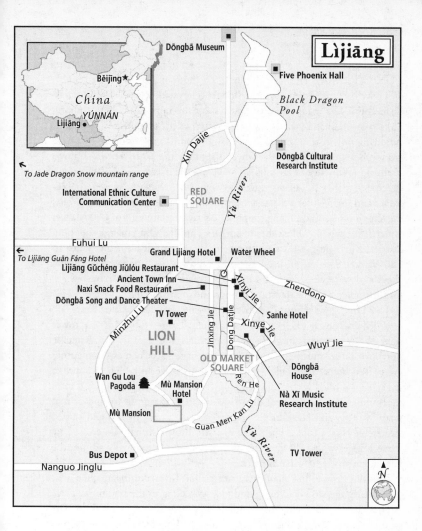

Old Town (Dàyán)

Lìjiāng is situated more than a hundred miles north of Dàlǐ, beyond the Armor Mountains (Tiějià Shān) that divide the Bái Kingdom to the south from the Nàxī Kingdom, itself isolated by even higher ranges to the north. The town is located in a valley sheltered by rugged ridges, right at the foot of the Jade Dragon Snow mountain range (Yùlóng Xuěshān), whose peaks tower well over 5,400m (18,000 ft.). Lìjiāng itself is at 2,340m (7,800 ft.). On the west side of Lion Hill is modern Lìjiāng; on the eastern flanks is Old Lìjiāng, a warren of traditional Nàxī shophouses, market squares, cobbled lanes, canals, and arched bridges.

It is **Old Lìjiāng** that invites the traveler. This antiquated district consists of over 6,000 households, with a history of 800 years. Since it became a UNESCO World Heritage Site in 1997, thousands of its original buildings have been preserved, its stone bridges renovated, its streams and canals cleaned up. The main entrance (located on the north end along Jīnhóng Lù) is now marked by a large wooden water wheel, part of the 1998 renovation of this district and a favorite spot for Chinese tourists snapping group photographs. The water wheel is spun by the Yù River, which flows south along the edge of Lion Hill. Paralleling the river is Old Lìjiāng's main street, Dōng Dà Jiē, newly paved in smooth, irregularly spaced cobblestones and reserved for pedestrians only. Dōng Dà Jiē runs for about a mile, the length of the Old Lìjiāng shopping district, terminating at Old Market Square (Sì Fāng Jiē). The other major lane through Old Lìjiāng's shopping district, Xīnyì Jiē, begins near the water wheel, and it also runs south to Old Market Square, but it does so in a highly serpentine fashion. Several alleys and waterways crisscross these two main north–south passageways, forming a labyrinth of traditional shops and arched bridges.

The **Old Town shopping district** is tiny, but its twisting lanes are crowded and nearly unchartable. Fortunately, Lion's Hill and its TV tower serve as one compass mark (west), the canals and streams run generally north to south, and the meshing lanes do have street names—sometimes even street signs. Old Lìjiāng is a marvelous maze in which to wander. Every lane is filled with shops selling local crafts, Nàxī clothing, and local snacks; and there are several dozen small cafes catering to foreigners that serve Western and Nàxī dishes, coffees, teas, and beer, owned and staffed largely by Nàxī people. The stone-bed streams and canals are crossed by stone bridges where the men sit, swap tales, and occasionally admire the falcons carried by passing hunters.

It is the people of Lìjiāng who make Old Town the dream that it is, particularly the women, young and old, who cling to the traditional dress (smocks with aprons and cross-banded capes in dark blues and whites). The women do most of the business even today, carrying their wares, and sometimes babies, from home to shop on their backs in large wicker baskets. The Nàxī cape is remarkable, its upper back the dark blue of night, its lower back the white of day, this cosmology divided by a sash embroidered with the seven stars of the heavens. Very old women still wear an image of the sun on one shoulder, the moon on the other. The locals are largely oblivious to modern visitors. They go about their tasks, laughing and stopping to chat with their neighbors on the street, or taking the day's wash down to the stream for a beating on the stones and a rinse. Black cats sit or pace at shop entrances, tethered by strings to their jobs: the elimination of mice.

The southern tip of Old Lìjiāng's shopping district is distinguished by the **Old Market Square (Sì Fāng Jiē),** a wide expanse of cobblestones surrounded by shops and bridges. Every day is market day here, with the vendors setting up shop under awnings. Beyond the endless tables of crafts and trinkets are large displays of bright copper pots, plates, and pans, all hammered out by hand. From the Old Market, it's possible to head southwest up Lion Hill or south to Mù Mansion via the narrow Rén Hé Courtyard alley, but to get your bearings, it is wise to stick first with the main shopping district.

Wise, too, to pull off to the side at one of the **cafes** for a drink or a snack. The waitresses are usually willing to converse and answer questions. As in Dàlǐ, there are plenty of street cafes to sample, all of them cozy and inexpensive. **The Blue Page** has an extensive vegetarian menu; the **Well Bistro,** a pleasant coffeehouse atmosphere; the **Dōngbā House,** Tibetan toast and a fascinating corner for people-watching; and **Māmā Fū's,** the best outside dining of all, is located on a curving waterway. There are several strictly **Nàxī restaurants,** too, as well as an assortment of small guesthouses and a growing number of theaters devoted to ethnic music and dance.

It doesn't take long to become swept up in the life of the Old Town. A day or two of wandering unravels the maze of alleys, winding streets, and twisting waterways. It helps to sit still against the flow, to take a seat on the stone ledge at the southeast end of Old Market Square, get your bearings, and watch the people. Chinese visitors outnumber Westerners 13 to 1, according to a waitress with whom I spoke. In the square, Nàxī in bright costume wait to ferry tourists in sedan chairs around town or up Lion Hill; while idle, they joke among themselves and wear their hats upside down. It was while watching the sedan-chair carriers that I got a jolt one early afternoon when a traditional funeral procession came marching down from Lion Hill and along the east side of the square, heading north through Old Town. Every mourner wore white, and the first mourners were littering the path with white confetti. I moved closer to take a picture, but was immediately shamed into proper respect: Many of the marchers were weeping.

From Old Market Square, **Jīnxīng Jiē** runs north, parallel to Dōng Dà Jiē, the big new main street that you usually take down into the market. Jīnxīng Jiē is a bit higher up the slopes of Lion Hill, and it's worth a stroll since the tour groups usually don't have time for it. Its shops, which look decidedly poorer, specialize in Nàxī and Tibetan antiques, wood and stone carvings, and jewelry. It was on Jīnxīng Jiē one morning that I saw a woman shopkeeper knitting in a doorway, her ball of yarn in a basket. As I neared, she suddenly rose from her bench, strode across the lane, her knitting in hand and the yarn ball anchored to the basket, the knitting stretched across the road like a wool umbilical cord; at the riverbank she spit with fervor into the roaring stream and had returned to the bench at her shop by the time I passed.

Nàxī Music

The chief entertainment at night in Old Lìjiāng, apart from coffee and dessert or beer and pizza in the local inns, is traditional music. There are now at least two theaters devoted to nightly performances, both of them quite atmospheric, with wooden stages for the musicians and wooden chairs or benches for the audience. The largest new venue, the **Dōngbā Song and Dance Theater (Dōngbā Gōng)** is on Dōng Dà Jiē (© **0888/ 518-1598**). It has a colorful stage and a dining area, as well as memorabilia and photographs of Austrian-American explorer Joseph Rock, who lived in Lìjiāng for 2 decades beginning in 1922, and who was the first Westerner to document, in detail, Nàxī customs. Performances start at 8pm nightly; tickets are sold at the entrance during the day, for ¥35 or ¥50 ($4.40 or $5.70).

Perhaps the most authentic musical renditions are given at the **Nà Xī Music Research Institute (Nàxī Gǔyuèhuì),** nightly at 8pm. Tickets are available for ¥30, ¥40, or ¥50 ($3.75, $5, or $5.70). This theater is located on Dōng Dà Jiē across from the Dōngbā Song and Dance Theater (Dōngbā Gōng). Under the direction of narrator Xuān Kē, a renowned local expert, the musicians perform many of the two dozen ancient songs that have survived on Nàxī instruments that resemble lutes, banjos, gongs, cymbals, flutes, and drums. Xuān Kē provides information in English. Purchase tickets at the theater as far ahead of time as possible, as the shows often sell out hours before 8pm. Even if you can't attend, drop by during the day to take a (free) look inside the theater, which is intimate and colorful.

Black Dragon Pool (Hēi Lóng Tán)

Directly north of Old Lìjiāng, within walking distance, **Black Dragon Pool Park** rewards a visit. Its vistas, particularly of the nearby Jade Dragon Snow range, are superb. There's a trail along the east bank of the Yù River, which flows into Old Town from Black Dragon Pool, but it doesn't go all the way to the park. The usual stroll is north along busy Xīn Dàjiē. On the west side of this avenue is the new space-age International Ethnic Culture Exchange Center, where conventions and exhibitions are staged. On the east side of the street is **Red Square,** with its monumental white statue of Chairman Máo. Peter's Cafe (with its log-cabin facade) and the Ali Baba Cafe are on the north side of Red Square, and within a block north down an alley is a produce and meat market. If you continue east and north along this alley, it leads to the park entrance; it's a fascinating, winding residential lane, with plenty of courtyard homes. As I was walking it, two kids jumped out, shook my hand, said "Hello," and ran back into their house laughing.

Black Dragon Pool Park is open daily dawn to dusk; admission is ¥20 ($2.50). At the gated entrance, turn right (south) and follow the pathway counterclockwise around the lovely lake. Where the Yù River cascades out of Black Dragon Pool, there's a fine pavilion and arched bridge. Farther up, on Elephant Hill, which forms the eastern boundary of the park, is the **Dōngbā Cultural Research Institute (Dōngbā Wénhuà Yánjìusuǒ),** a collection of halls done in the Nàxī architectural style, as well as a library where local scholars collect and study the ancient Nàxī culture. In this compound, there's a small gift shop next to a fine specimen of a traditional Nàxī log house. *Dōngbā* is the term for the Nàxī shamans, authors of the small booklets in Nàxī language that are studied here. There are currently more than 20 Dōngbās living in Lìjiāng.

Black Dragon Pool is divided into three portions by stone bridges. The longest bridge, Jade Belt Bridge or Five Arch Bridge (Wǔkǒng Qiáo), is capped by **Moon Pavilion (Dé Yuè Lóu),** dating from the Míng Dynasty but reconstructed in 1964 after a local official and his lover, it is said, ignited the old structure in a fiery double-suicide. At the northeast end of the lake is **Five Phoenix Hall (Wu Fēng Lóu),** a 400-year-old Nàxī hall with extravagant eaves that once stood in a major Lama temple complex (Fù Guó Sì), 32km (20 miles) away. It often has displays of varying levels of interest to visitors.

The west side of Black Dragon Pool is highlighted by a long row of Nàxī vendor stalls selling local crafts and souvenirs.

Dōngbā Museum

At the pool's northwest entrance is a new museum that should not be missed. The **Lìjiāng Nàxī Dōngbā Cultural Museum (Lìjiāng Dōngbā Wénhuà Bówùguǎn; ℡ 0888/512-8383),** a 25-minute walk from Old Town Lìjiāng, is open daily from 8:30am to 6pm, and admission costs ¥5 (65¢). This institution holds a remarkable collection of Nàxī relics and cultural displays. The Nàxī people, who have their own Tibeto-Burman language and pictographic writings, were a northern tribe driven southward into remote Lìjiāng a thousand years ago or more. Their creation myth begins with a common ancestor, Tabu, who hatched the tribe from a magic egg. The Dōngbā have recorded the Nàxī history and its elaborate rituals in a series of small booklets, many of which are collected in the new museum. One remarkable characteristic of Nàxī culture is the powerful role of women, who rule the society (and do much of the work). A sort of "walk-in" marriage is still practiced by some Nàxī people today, in which young women choose their partners periodically and invite them into their homes. Partners can change, according to a woman's desire; the children remain with the mother in her home; former husbands return to live with their mothers when a relationship is over.

The museum has interesting displays of Nàxī dress, their wooden homes, their pictographic booklets (5,000 of the 30,000 still in existence), and their rituals, over 80 of which are still practiced in nearby villages (including the sacrifices of pig and sheep). Each of the four buildings in the courtyard-style museum explores a different theme, including one devoted to the Western myth of Shangri-La propagated by 20th-century explorers such as Joseph Rock and Peter Goullart. The artifacts include an inflated sheepskin (used by the Nàxī to ford streams and rivers), and a tombstone from Wutai engraved with the names of eight members of the 20th Bomber Command of the American Air Force killed in World War II, dated July 1944.

Mù Mansion (Mù Fǔ)

Lìjiāng was ruled by the Mù Shì clan from the time of Kublai Khan to the end of the last Chinese dynasty in the early 20th century. The first patriarch was Celestial King Mù (Mù Tiān Wáng), who came to power as a child in 1598, defended China's western borders, and built a series of Tibetan Buddhist temples (Karmapa sect). The **Mù Mansion (Mù Fǔ),** a garden estate from which the clan ruled Lìjiāng for nearly 500 years, has recently been restored on the road south of Old Lìjiāng's shopping district, at the southern foot of Lion Hill.

To reach Mù Mansion, follow Qī Yī Jiē, the lane at the very southeast edge of Old Market Square. It's a 10-minute walk. The route undulates along the river, then takes a right at Guān Mén Kǒu and passes through a traditional archway to a lane crowded with vendors and sedan-chair carriers. Mù Mansion lies in front of you. It's open daily from 9am to 6pm; admission is ¥35 ($4.25).

After the great Lìjiāng earthquake of 1996, a World Bank loan financed a 3-year renovation. The grounds, which stretch for a quarter of a mile, are impressive and expansive, facing east to meet the rising sun. The large halls are separated by white stone courtyards that resemble those of the Forbidden City in Běijīng. In fact, during the Míng Dynasty, Mù Mansion was said to rival in splendor the Imperial Gardens of the distant Chinese capital. Many of the original halls were destroyed during the later Qīng Dynasty and its stone archways by Red Guards during the Cultural Revolution (1966–76). The main gate, consisting of a tripartite stone archway with a tile roof, bears the inscription DÀ YŪ LÍU FÁNG (a homophone in the Nàxī language for "Let Us Read").

There are six main buildings, which ascend Lion Hill a short way. The main meeting hall, where the clan chiefs met, is first, followed by a library (Wàn Juǎn) of Dōngbā writings and paintings and by the Back Hall

(Hù Fǔ), where the family held its own meetings. The fourth building (Guǎng Bì) was dedicated to the gardens, the fifth (Yú Yīn) for singing and dancing, and the last hall (Sān Qīng) for Daoist rites. The halls are rather empty, but there are some treasures, especially in the main building near the entrance, where the Mù throne and a tiger skin are on display.

Mù Mansion gives visitors a sense of the grandeur of the Mù Kingdom of the Nàxī during its semi-autonomous golden days centuries ago. The courtyards sometimes fill with local Nàxī ladies performing circle dances and with musicians, mostly older men, playing traditional instruments. The back gardens and covered corridors are beautifully re-created, and steps at the rear lead steeply up Lion Hill to a hidden back entrance.

Lion Hill (Shīzi Shān)

The formidable hill that forms the western backbone of Old Lìjiāng and the eastern edge of new Lìjiāng, Lion Hill, can be climbed from many points, including the rear of Mù Mansion. I approached it first, however, from Old Market Square, where a cobblestone lane leads up its flanks from the southwest corner. There are signs reading WÀN GǓ LÓU, which is the name of a new pagoda at the summit of Lion Hill built expressly for sight-seeing. I followed the signs as I wound uphill, past tiny shops, local cafes, courtyard dwellings, and two or three estates that had been converted into dorms and cafes, asking the way to Wàn Gǔ Lóu when no more signposts appeared. The slopes of Lion Hill are covered with old Nàxī houses; the neighborhood, known as Huángshān, is one of the region's oldest.

When the lane petered out, I followed a worn trail through the thick woods, finally coming out at a formal stone stairway that seemed to rise forever. I could just make out the square wooden pagoda at the top. Wàn Gǔ Lóu is billed here as the tallest wooden tower in all of China. It was built of old local timbers, which serve as its 16 massive pillars, each 22m (72 ft.) tall. Its 13 upward curving eaves represent the 13 peaks of the Jade Dragon Snow range. Altogether there are over 2,300 Dōngbā designs, such as the moon and stars, carved by Nàxī craftspeople into this structure, and 9,999 motifs, including the grand jade dragon of the snows, etched into its ceiling. The tower was completed in 1998. It stands 33m (108 ft.) tall (each meter meant to represent 1,000 of Lìjiāng's 330,000 people). Surrounded by a wall, Wàn Gǔ Lóu is open from dawn to dusk and costs ¥15 ($1.90) to enter.

The walk up to the observation deck covers five large stories. The deck has windows on all four sides, affording a most exceptional view of Lìjiāng, old and new, and the grand Jade Dragon Snow range to the north. It also has free telescopes turned on the Jade Dragon Snow peaks. This range is extremely steep and sheer, cutting deep gorges into the upper Yángzǐ River.

The highest peak is the glaciated Shànzǐdǒu, at 5,508m (18,360 ft.); its summit remained unconquered until 1963. The tower is the best place to view the mountains, which are about 32km (20 miles) from Lìjiāng, although the range does attract its share of rolling and obscuring cloud banks. This is also the place for a bird's-eye view of Old Lìjiāng, a lava bed of tightly packed, black-tile roofs, and the new town areas that are being built all around it on the high plateau.

The Latest Shangri-La

Old Lìjiāng is beguiling, but it is also surrounded by irresistible wonders. Many travelers spend little time in the village that earlier visitors hailed as Shangri-La and push ever farther into the remoter villages, mountains, and river valleys in search of the "real" Shangri-La.

These excursions, many requiring a day, some a night or more away from Lìjiāng, can be booked in town at the tourist offices or through the hostels and cafes that cater to independent foreign travelers. Popular day trips include the one to **Spruce Meadow (Yún Shān Píng),** 16km (10 miles) north of Lìjiāng on the slopes of the Jade Dragon Snow mountains, where a chairlift travels to an altitude of nearly 4,500m (15,000 ft.); **Bǎishā,** a small Nàxī village 11km (7 miles) north of Lìjiāng, with a temple built during the reign of Kublai Khan and some beautiful frescoes; and **Nguluko (Yùhú),** a small Nàxī village containing the home of anthropologist and adventurer Joseph Rock, who lived here for nearly 30 years, beginning in 1922.

More remote destinations include **Bǎshān Stone City,** a tiny town carved from stone cliffs, perched above the Upper Yángzǐ River; **Shígǔ,** the village at the "First Bend of the Yángzǐ River"; and the celebrated **Tiger Leaping Gorge (Hǔtiào Xiá),** one of the world's deepest (over 3,600m/ 12,000 ft.) gorges, an upper Yángzǐ destination renowned for its rugged hiking and extreme conditions. All these places are within a few hours' drive of Lìjiāng. **Lùgū Lake (Lùgū Hú),** on the Sìchuān border, still plied by native minorities using dugout canoes, requires an overnight stay. Still farther from Lìjiāng (but now a journey of a day rather than of days) is the recently renamed **Xiānggélǐlā** (formerly **Zhōngdiàn**), the gateway to Tibet, an old border town undergoing fierce modernization. There are also other small villages and remote mountains to explore in northwest Yúnnán, where mass tourism has so far feared to tread—these Shangri-Las are still awaiting discovery.

Of course, it is we, the travelers and modern tourists, who have erased one Shangri-La by our very presence and rewritten it into ever more remote mountain valleys. The notion that if a tourist like me can reach Shangri-La, then it can't be Shangri-La anymore, is the catch-22 of modern travel. As for the native residents of this fabled valley, most will tell you without hesitation that Shangri-La is indeed still located in Lìjiäng—not in the Old Town, mind you, with its cisterns and dirt floors; not in the distant villages of stone and poor TV reception, absolutely not; but in the New Town apartment blocks of Lìjiäng, where there's hot running water, central heat, flush toilets, and satellite TV. The real Shangri-La, according to its own residents, is just over the mountain, in Levittown East. This may be, but as a traveler from the already quite modern West, I prefer Old Lìjiäng to a thousand new towns, whether they be in China or Timbuktu.

PRACTICAL INFORMATION

by Sharon Owyang

ORIENTATION & WHEN TO GO

Located in the northwest part of Yúnnán Province, Lìjiäng lies 517 km (320 miles) northwest of the provincial capital Künmíng. Yúnnán Province itself borders Burma, Laos, and Vietnam to the west and south, and Tibet and Sìchuän to the north. Many travelers use Lìjiäng as a gateway to Tibet and Sìchuän. Lìjiäng is also 170km (105 miles) or a 3-hour minibus ride north of Dàlï (see separate chapter, beginning on p. 379), another Yúnnán Shangri-La.

Situated at an elevation of 2,340m (7,800 ft.), Lìjiäng has a pleasant climate year-round, although there are four different altitude ranges and hence four different temperature ranges within a 32km (20-mile) span of the town. Rainy season is from June to October. During the winter months of November through February, early mornings and evenings can be quite cool, although the days are pleasant enough. Average temperatures in spring, summer, and fall are 61°F to 81°F (16°C–27°C). Spring and autumn are the best times to visit, however, as the summer months are often crowded with Chinese tourists.

Many of China's Nàxï minority live in Lìjiäng and the surrounding villages and countryside; the Old Town area of 6,000 households preserves something of the culture of the people, who have their own language, dress, and customs.

GETTING THERE

By Plane **Lijiäng Airport** is 24km (15 miles) southwest of the city, a 30-minute taxi ride away (¥80–¥100/ $10–$13). From the airport there are several flights daily to Künmíng (50 min.; ¥450/$56 one-way) as well as weekly flights to Guǎngzhōu (3 hr.), Shànghǎi (4½ hr.), and Xïshuängbännà (30 min.). Tickets can be bought at the **CAAC/ Yúnnán Airlines** ticket office on the first floor of the Lìjiäng Hotel (Lìjiäng Dàjiǔdiàn) on Xïn Dàjië (© 0888/ 518- 0280; open daily 8:30am–6:30pm). There is another CAAC office at Fúhuì Lù, Mínháng Zhàn (© 0888/516-1289). Travel agencies, hotels, and certain backpacker cafes can also help you purchase airline tickets.

By Bus From Lìjiäng's south (main) long-distance **bus station** on the southwest side of Lion Hill at the southern end of Mínzú Lù (© 0888/512-1106), local buses depart for Dàlï (Xiàguän) every half hour from 7:10am to

6:30pm. Ticket prices range from ¥32 to ¥51 ($4–$6.30) depending on the bus. Three large air-conditioned buses (¥51/ $6.30) leave daily for Dàlǐ at 8:20am, 11:30am, and 2:30pm. Four express buses leave daily for Kūnmíng (8 hr.; ¥152/$19; 8:20am, 9:20am, 11:20am, 3:20pm), and sleeper buses (9 hr.) leave every half hour for Kūnmíng between 5:30pm and 8:30pm. Bus tickets can be purchased from the bus station between 6:30am and 10pm, and from travel agencies, hotels, and cafes in Lìjiāng. A private bus company, **YNTAC** (© **0888/512-5492**), operates luxury air-conditioned buses to Dàlǐ (Xiàguān; 3 hr.; ¥50/$6.25; 8:30am, 9am, 10:30am, 5pm) and to Kūnmíng (8 hr.; ¥151/$19; 8:30am, 9am, 10:30am). YNTAC buses depart from the Nàxī Hotel (Nàxī Dàjiǔdiàn) on Nán Guòjìng Lù just over half a mile west of the bus station.

TOURS & STRATAGEMS

The **Lìjiāng CITS** has a branch in the Yúnlíng Hotel on Xīn Dàjiē (© **0888/ 518-2599** or 0888/512-5991; fax 0888/ 518-5955), just north of Red Square. It caters to independent travelers, offering day trips that include Lìjiāng, Spruce Meadow, and Báishā; overnight trips to Tiger Leaping Gorge; and a 3-day trip to Lúgū Lake. They can also help arrange accommodations and plane and train tickets. In addition, many of the cafes and hostels in Old Lìjiāng have travel agencies that provide day tours, air and bus tickets, and bicycle rentals. The **Dōngbā House**, at Jíshān Xiàng 16, Xīnyì Jiē (© **0888/517-5431**), is a good source of information on backpackers' routes. **Gallery Travel**, diagonally across the way at Xīnyì Jiē, Jíshān Xiàng 39 (© **0888/666-0994**; vision_bh@hotmail.com), has guides who frequently lead trips to Tiger Leaping Gorge. Both can organize ski trips to nearby Hābā Mountain and the Jade Dragon Snow Mountains, as well as overland trips into Tibet. For the less adventurous, Old Lìjiāng has a **Tourist Consultation Service** just inside the northern entrance on Xīnyì Jiē (© **0888/ 511-6666**) that offers more sedate day tours, of surrounding areas. There is an English-language brochure of the available tours but the trips themselves are conducted strictly in Chinese. They can also provide Old Town tour guides (¥50/$6.25 for 2 hr.), some of whom speak a smattering of English.

WHERE TO STAY

Staying in Old Lìjiāng, which has many guesthouses with traditional Nàxī architecture, is highly recommended. Many of these one- and two-star inns offer basic dormitory-style and double-room accommodations (some with private bathroom) and are favored by independent travelers and backpackers. The **Dōngbā House** (formerly called the MCA Guesthouse) at Jíshān Xiàng 16, Xīnyì Jiē (© **0888/517-5431**; fax 0888/ 517-5431), offers small but perfectly adequate Nàxī courtyard rooms for ¥20 to ¥50 ($2.50–$6). It also has a restaurant serving good Western, Chinese, and Tibetan food; a travel desk; Internet access; and bicycle rental (¥15/ $1.90 per day). The clean and popular **First Bend Inn at Xīnyì Jiē** (Míshì Xiàng 43 at Xīnyì Jiē; © **0888/518-1688**) charges ¥80 ($10) for doubles around a Nàxī courtyard. All bathrooms here are shared. One of the newcomers on the scene, the **Tea Horse Family Guest House (Chámǎ Kèzhàn)**, Xīnyì Jiē at Jíshān Xiàng 9, Xīnyì Jiē (© **0888/512-0351**), has six

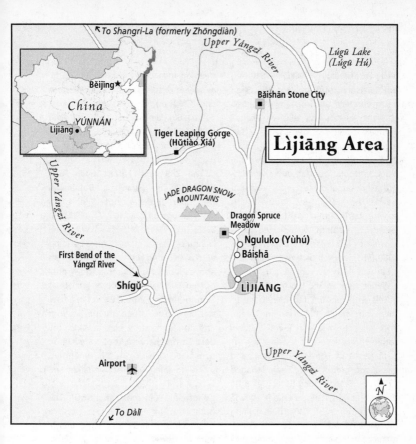

clean doubles with private bathroom (¥200–300/$25–$37 during high season; ¥80–¥100/$10–$12 low season) and eight doubles without bathroom for ¥20/$2.50 during low season. Rooms are clean, with wooden floors, and come with TV. Bathrooms have tub/shower combos and 24-hour hot water. The guesthouse also provides laundry service and a business center that can help you book tickets.

A notch above these guesthouses are several hotels also housed in traditional Nàxī buildings in the Old Town. The **Sēnhé Hotel (Sānhé jiǔdiàn; ☏ 0888/512-0891;** fax 0888/512-0892), at Jíshān Xiāng 4, Xīnyì Jiē, has doubles with air-conditioning (central heating during winter), TV, phone, and private bathroom for ¥280 ($35). Decorated with a pleasing light touch, rooms are comfortable, though the beds are a little soft. Bathrooms are large and bright. Next door, the **Ancient Town Inn (Gǔchéng Kèzhàn; ☏ 0888/515-9000;** fax 0888/515-9018) offers several types of rooms (doubles with and without private bathrooms; luxury rooms with safe, pajamas, and fresh fruit; and large but basic triples) arrayed around lovely courtyards. Rooms vary in size, with the smaller ones quite cramped and dark. During the colder winter months, there is central heating from 7 to 10pm. There is also an informal cafe on the premises with a limited menu. The staff speaks some English and is generally quite helpful. South of Sì Fāng Jiē, right next to Mù's Mansion (Mù Fǔ) on Guāngyì Jiē, is **Mù's Mansion Hotel (Mù**

Wáng Fǔ Kèzhàn; © 0888/510-2810; mu fuhotel@sohu.com), built on the original site where the Mù family used to entertain friends and relatives. There's a lovely courtyard here with rattan rocking chairs, bamboo, and paper lanterns. Rooms retain their original wooden floors, wooden doors, and lattice windows, and are comfortable and clean. The hotel has doubles with private bathroom for ¥180 to ¥580 ($23–$73), doubles with shared bathroom for ¥180 ($23), and two suites for ¥680 ($85), as well as a restaurant and a bar with Internet service.

While New Lìjiāng has more upscale hotels with modern facilities, none of them can match the charming ambience and coziness of their Old Town counterparts.

In terms of comfort, location, and value for money, the Thai-managed 127-room **Grand Lìjiāng Hotel (Gélán Dà Jiǔdiàn)**, at Xǐnyī Jiē, on the Yù River, north entrance of Old Town Lìjiāng (© 0888/512-8888; fax 0888/512-7878), is the best choice of all the hotels outside Old Town. For a three-star establishment, the large rooms are remarkably well-fitted, with a range of amenities including minibar, fridge, robe, hair dryer, scale, safe, A/C, and satellite TV (Hong Kong and Japanese channels, in-house American movies). The marble bathrooms are spacious and have tub/shower combos. The hotel is also ideally located, with Old Town on its southern side and magnificent views of the Jade Dragon Snow range to the north. It has a business center, conference rooms, 24-hour room service, same-day dry cleaning and laundry, a shopping arcade, a bar, and two restaurants (Western and Chinese). Regular doubles cost ¥480 ($60); deluxe doubles cost ¥640 ($80). Children under 12 stay for free in parent's room. The hotel accepts most major credit cards.

The 289-room **Lìjiāng Guān Fáng Hotel (Lìjiāng Guānfáng Dàjiǔdiàn)**, the only five-star hotel in town (at Xiānggélǐlā Dàdào; © 0888/518-8888; fax 0888/518-1999; www.gfhotel Lijiang.com), is a modern glass building with a revolving restaurant that towers above all other buildings as the symbol of New Lìjiāng. Guest rooms are not as luxurious as you would expect in a five-star hotel: The carpets are a little worn and the upholstery clashes with the decor, but, otherwise, rooms are a good size and come with full amenities, including safe, robe, A/C, minibar, and satellite TV (CNN, NHK, National Geographic, Cinemax, and HBO). The hotel also offers an indoor pool, a health club, a sauna, a bowling alley, a business center, room service, dry cleaning and laundry services, a salon, a shopping arcade, and a free airport shuttle. Bathrooms are done in a rather garish tile and have tub/shower combos. Attracting mostly domestic tour groups, the hotel has little personal charm but does offer plenty of dining options with three restaurants (Western, Cantonese, and Sìchuān). Rooms cost ¥960 to ¥1,120 ($120–$140) double and ¥2,000 ($250) suite. Children under 12 stay free in parent's room. The hotel accepts most major credit cards.

WHERE TO DINE

Old Town Lìjiāng offers plenty of good, friendly cafes, and family-operated restaurants catering to foreign travelers with Western, Chinese, and Nàxī food at very reasonable prices. **The Nàxī Snack Food (Nàxī Fēngwèi)**, at Shuāng Shí Duàn 22 (© 0888/518-9591), just inside the northern Old Town entrance on Xīnhuá Jiē, serves some of the best local fare in all Lìjiāng; witness the crowds that throng here every night. The restaurant is so popular it has opened a second outlet two doors down. You can dine outdoors by a running stream or on the significantly less atmospheric second floor. Nàxī favorites here include fried rice with soya bean (jǐdòu chǎo mǐfàn), a local baked pastry that can be either sweet or salty (Lìjiāng baba), and fried goat cheese (zhá rú bǐng). If you're here with a larger group (five persons or more), ask for the Fēngwèi Cān, which consists of 10 to 16 special Nàxī dishes. The food is delicious, the prices inexpensive (dinner for two ¥20–¥40/$2.50–$5); but if you come during peak meal times (6–8pm), service is brusque at best. The **Nàxī Gǔyuè Cāntīng** (© **0888/666-7577**), located right next to the Nàxī Music Research Institute (Nàxī Gǔyuèhuì) on Dōngdà Jiē, serves good Crossing-the-Bridge Noodles for ¥8 to ¥30 ($1–$3.75) as well as Nàxī specialties like barbecued fish (Nàxī kǎoyú) and vegetables in broth (Lìjiāng dàguōcài). The **Lìjiāng Gǔchéng Jiǔlóu** (© **0888/518-1818**), at the Dōngdà Jiē entrance to Old Town, specializes in the Nàxī Sāndiéshuǐ, a 36-course meal divided into cold, steamed, and sweet dishes. Although this banquet, at ¥488 ($61), is designed for six to eight people, smaller groups can order the half portion for about ¥300 ($38). The restaurant also has a more traditional Chinese and Nàxī menu, and serves hot pot and grilled kabobs as well. Meals cost ¥100 to ¥150 ($12–$19).

Of the travelers' cafes, **Māmā Fū's,** (© **0888/512-2285**) located on Xīnyì Jiē just north of the Market Square, is a classic and serves some of the best pizzas around. It's also famous for its homemade breads and apple pie. Sit outside by the running stream and watch Old Lìjiāng go by. The **Blue Page Vegetarian Restaurant** at Xīnyì Jiē, Míshì Xiàng 69 (© **0888/518-5206**), is a quiet, cozy place that offers excellent vegetarian fare at low prices (¥8–¥15/$1–$2 per dish). Standouts include their mushroom and vegetable pie, the veggie burger, and the apple crumble. Fresh flowers on the table add a nice touch. The restaurant also provides Internet access. Across the way, the **Well Bistro** is another popular hangout, this one famous for its pizzas and Dutch coffee. The two-story cafe has wooden tables, wicker chairs, and lots of travel information tacked to the walls. The **Dōngbā House,** at Jíshān Xiàng 16, Xīnyì Jiē (© **0888/517-5431**), serves Tibetan cuisine along with Nàxī, Chinese, and Western food. Staff here is friendly, the people-watching is great, and the cafe offers the fastest and most reliable Internet access around. On the west side of Old Town, the always-crowded **Sakura Café,** at Xīnhuá Jiē, Cuìwén Duàn 123 (© **0888/ 518-7619**), has a truly international menu offering everything from a delicious Korean bibimbap (rice with vegetables, beef, and egg) set meal (¥20/$2.50) to a chicken cutlet Israeli dinner (¥19/$2.40). You know when Che Guevara posters share wall space with "Hello Kitty" paraphernalia that you're someplace truly unusual.

SILK ROAD CHINA:
CITIES OF SAND

E AST AND WEST FIRST MET MORE than 2,000 years ago on the fabled Silk Road, for centuries China's only major connection to the outside world. The Silk Road was a trade route that crossed the Gobi Desert from China into central Asia, where Persian and other merchants transferred fine Chinese silks into the courts of imperial Rome. In return, China received strange new commodities from the West. The most lasting import, however, was cultural, artistic, and religious—the introduction of Buddhism from India.

Buddhism altered the face of China, shaping its temple architecture and religious arts. Buddhist missionaries found a tolerant home in the Chinese capital, Cháng'ān (now Xī'ān) during the Táng Dynasty (A.D. 618–907), when the silk trade reached its zenith and long caravans of up to 1,000 camels routinely arrived at the western gates after crossing the desert frontier. This is the way Marco Polo is said to have reached China from Italy in the 13th century, centuries after the fall of Rome and the disintegration of the mighty Hàn and Táng dynasties.

In the last few years, for the first time in history, a trickle of tourists has entered northwest China, retracing the route of the Silk Road. From Xī'ān, 886km (550 miles) southwest of Běijīng in north central China, modern travelers are now crossing the remote provinces of Gānsù and Xīnjiāng. They are stopping at the legendary oasis towns and rummaging through the medieval marketplaces of Ürümqi and Kashgar. Along the way, they pass the ruins of desert cities, the caves of splendid Buddhist sculptures, the last outposts of the Great Wall, and lakes and mountain passes clinging to the fringes of imagined heavens. The Silk Road spaces through which they move are vast and empty, populated by nomads and wild camels. The towns between are remote, marked by mosques rather than temples, occupied by Uighur Muslims rather than Hàn Chinese. The Silk Road winds through a lost world, an alien landscape of howling sand dunes and silent snowy peaks. It is a China few visitors have seen.

The Explorers

The first official Chinese mission on the Silk Road set out in 138 B.C. from the capital at Xī'ān. The Wūdì Emperor of the Hàn Dynasty (206 B.C.–A.D. 220) charged Gen. Zhāng Qiān and his 100-man caravan to make contact with the desert tribes of the west and to forge an alliance against the Huns (the Xiōngnú), who were raiding China with impunity. The Chinese general made it all the way to Persia. He didn't return from the Silk Road for 13 years. At his death, Zhāng was awarded the imperial title of "Grand Traveler."

Other grand travelers followed, mostly caravans of traders and monks rather than diplomats and soldiers. By the 1st century A.D., silk garments were such a rage in Rome, they were considered a drain on the treasury. Oasis towns sprang up to replenish the Silk Road caravans that sometimes perished in the fierce Taklamakan Desert, whose very name means "enter and do not return."

As trade flourished, Buddhist monks and pilgrims set out from India to China, spreading their art and religion. In the oasis towns of China, wealthy local merchants were soon sponsoring the creation of large shrines in nearby sandstone caves, where Buddhist statues and frescoes were sculpted as divine petitions for the safe passage of the caravans. At Dūnhuáng, where the main north and south routes from the West merged, the greatest repository of Buddhist manuscripts, paintings, and statuary outside of India was fashioned at the Mògāo caves.

Silk Road pilgrimages became a two-way street. The Chinese monk Fǎ Xiǎn (A.D. 337–422) set out from Xī'ān in 399, passed through Dūnhuáng, and crossed over the Himalayas into India. He returned to China by sea 15 years later. China's most renowned religious pilgrim, Xuán Zàng (A.D. 600–664), traveling at night on foot and by horseback, set out on the Silk Road in 629, studied in Indian monasteries for 14 years, and returned to Xī'ān in 645 with over 500 sutras (Buddhist scriptures) and relics. The Big Wild Goose Pagoda, which still stands in Xī'ān, housed his souvenirs, and the 16th-century comic epic, *Journey to the West,* also known as *Monkey,* has immortalized his journey for Chinese readers ever since.

Marco Polo (1254–1324) became the first Western explorer to compose a popular and lasting account of the Silk Road. Many scholars regard his travels as fictional—an account cobbled together from the anecdotes and adventures of many traders—but Marco Polo's observations of the trade route across China often ring true.

In the early 20th century, the Silk Road beckoned to foreign explorers as never before. In a rush to empty the newly rediscovered Buddhist caves and ruined cities of their ancient treasures, Sven Hedin of Sweden, Baron Otani of Japan, Paul Pelliot of France, von le Coq of Germany, Langdon Warner of America, and, above all, Sir Marc Aurel Stein of Britain, made difficult and dangerous forays on behalf of major museums in the West. Thousands

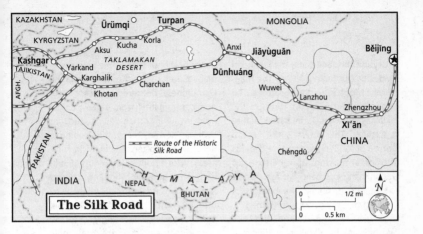

The Silk Road

Route of the Historic Silk Road

KAZAKHSTAN · KYRGYZSTAN · Ürümqi · Turpan · MONGOLIA · Kucha · Korla · Anxi · Jiāyùguān · Běijīng · Kashgar · Aksu · TAKLAMAKAN DESERT · Yarkand · Dūnhuáng · Karghalik · Charchan · Wuwei · Lanzhou · Zhengzhou · Khotan · Xī'ān · CHINA · Chéngdū · INDIA · NEPAL · HIMALAYA · BHUTAN · TAJIKISTAN · AFGH. · PAKISTAN

0   1/2 mi
0   0.5 km

of manuscripts, relics, frescoes, and statues ended up in overseas collections by the time this race was over.

Fortunately, not everything was pilfered in the name of history, scholarship, and nationalism. The Silk Road retains many of its relics and much of its remoteness. Today, for the first time, organized tourism is making inroads, and the Silk Road's exotic treasure house is opening to outsiders.

What to Read

The most complete guide, tailor-made for the China portion of the Silk Road, is Peter Neville-Hadley's *China: The Silk Routes* (Cadogan Books, 1997). Vikram Seth's *From Heaven Lake* (Vintage, 1987) is a fine travel narrative through the region. Peter Hopkirk's *Foreign Devils on the Silk Road* (Oxford University Press, 1986) is a lively history of the gold rush by foreign explorers for the cave treasures of Dūnhuáng and elsewhere earlier in this century. In *Life Along the Silk Road* (J. Murray, 1999), Susan Whitfield has compiled a remarkable series of vivid biographies of early Silk Road residents and travelers based on the original documents obtained from the Mògāo caves.

PRACTICAL INFORMATION

by Graeme Smith

ORIENTATION & WHEN TO GO

Starting from Xī'ān, the Silk Road sweeps northwesterly up through the Héxī Corridor of Gānsù Province. Anyone heading to the west on the road passes through this 1,208km (750-mile) long channel, 201km (125 miles) at its widest, with the Qílián mountains to the south and a series of bone-dry deserts and mountain ranges to the north. The most impressive sight in the Héxī Corridor is Jiāyùguān Pass, where the Silk Road narrows to a bottleneck and the western terminus of the Great Wall served as China's frontier outpost. This area is known as **Yùmén, the Jade Gate,** and to most Chinese minds it was truly the end of the civilized world.

Beyond the Jade Gate, the Silk Road divides at Dūnhuáng, site of the magnificent Mògāo Buddhist grottoes. The north and south routes through the **Taklamakan Desert (Tarim Basin)** reunite at **Kashgar**. The desert is the central feature of Xīnjiāng, a province the size of Alaska making up one-sixth of China. Kashgar is nearly as far west as you can go in China. The borders of Kyrgyzstan, Tajikistan, Afghanistan, and India are close at hand, and so is Pakistan via the Karakoram Highway. From Kashgar, the Silk Road enters the high mountain passes, reemerging at Samarkand in central Asia.

The majority of the 23 million people of Gānsù are Hàn Chinese. Mongols, Tibetans, Kazaks, and Huis (Islamic Chinese) make up a considerable minority population as well. In Xīnjiāng, the distribution changes remarkably. The Turkish-speaking Muslim minority Uighur make up a majority in many places, such as Kashgar, while the Hàn Chinese, bolstered by recent "economic transplants" from eastern China, hold sway in other towns, such as Ürümqi. Kazaks, many still leading a nomadic life, often dominate in rural areas. With a population of just 15 million, the gigantic Xīnjiāng Uighur Autonomous Region feels uninhabited through most of its stretches. The Silk Road becomes increasingly desolate, increasingly Islamic, and increasingly remote as the traveler moves west. By the time you reach the present Chinese border near Kashgar, it again seems as if you are about to step off the edge of the modern inhabited world.

The climate along the long Silk Road varies. For information on the best times to travel, see the individual chapters throughout the "Silk Road" section.

TOURS & STRATAGEMS

Group Tours The most comfortable method of touring the Silk Road is by group. Group tours follow much the same routes and often stay in the same hotels and eat in the same places as independent travelers. Hotel and restaurant conditions are often below international standards, and transport by bus or train can be a hardship, given the large distances and extreme temperatures involved. The Silk Road is an adventure in a remote region of the world, not a luxury cruise.

Many adventure-tour operators offer 16- to 30-day group tours (with usually 12 to 20 people per group) that include sectors of the Silk Road both in and out of China, often with such destinations as Islamabad (Pakistan), Lahore (India), and Hunza (Jammu and Kashmir). Tours of Xī'ān and Běijīng are often included. The cost, including airfare, runs about $5,000 to $12,000 per person. These extended trips on the Silk Road usually depart in May and June and in September and October. Some of the best operators include **Geographic Expeditions** (✆ 800/777-8183; www.geoex.com), **Asian Pacific Adventures** (✆ 800/825-1680; www.asianpacificadventures.com), **Wilderness Travel** (✆ 800/368-2794; www.wildernesstravel.com), and **Mountain Travel/Sobek** (✆ 888/687-6235; www.mtsobek.com).

Local Tours Operators such as CITS and CTS usually offer sub-standard and overpriced services. These agencies can be useful in booking train tickets (although even then commissions can be substantial), but they rarely provide impartial information and are generally best avoided. There are exceptions, such as the **Caravan Cafe** in Kashgar, and **CITS** in Jiāyùguān.

On Your Own While amenities along the Silk Routes (my preferred term, since "Silk Road" gives the impression that there was just one trade route, when, in reality, there were many, which changed with time) are more basic than elsewhere in China, the Silk Routes are one of the most straightforward destinations to visit as an independent traveler. Hotels and tour companies are used to dealing with foreigners, and the major sites are well defined. If you're in Dūnhuáng, you'll want to see the Mògāo caves; in Kashgar, the Old Town; and in Jiāyùguān, the magnificent fort. No need for the disinformation provided by CITS, no need for "guides" who pocket a healthy commission at every turn. Just hail a cab, jump on a bus, or set off on foot.

JIĀYÙGUĀN:
END OF THE GREAT WALL
嘉峪关

Aᴄᴄᴏʀᴅɪɴɢ ᴛᴏ ᴀ ᴘᴏᴘᴜʟᴀʀ ᴍʏᴛʜ, ᴛʜᴇ Great Wall ends at the Jade Pass (Yùmén) near Jiāyùguān, a town far up the Héxī Corridor in the northwestern province of Gānsù. When the First Emperor, Qín Shǐ Huáng (259–210 B.C.), unified ancient sections of the wall in 211 B.C., Jiāyùguān did mark the end of the Great Wall, but during the subsequent Hàn Dynasty (206 B.C.–A.D. 220) the wall was extended farther west, with beacon towers stretching deep into the desert. (These extensions were eventually swallowed up by the desert sands.) When the Great Wall achieved its final form under the Míng Dynasty (1368–1644), including those segments visited today near Běijīng, Jiāyùguān again became the garrison on the final frontier.

In 1372, Gen. Féng Shǎng drove out the Mongols and built a fort at the end of the Great Wall. It became known as "The Greatest Pass Under Heaven," and it remains standing today in Jiāyùguān. West of here, the vast Gobi Desert opens its threatening jaws. Every traveler setting out from Jiāyùguān Pass followed the same custom, hurling a stone at the western wall. If the stone bounced back, it meant the traveler would come back to China. If not, there would be no return.

Wèi-Jìn Tombs (Wèi-Jìn Mù)

On the flight from Xī'ān to Jiāyùguān, which covers a distance of 1,288km (800 miles) and takes nearly 3 hours, I could see an endless pink-and-cream-colored desert below and a few white oasis towns with small fields and blue reservoirs connected by a thin string of roads after only 1 hour. As we set down in Jiāyùguān, I spotted the snowcapped Qílián mountain range to the south, the unbroken wall of the Héxī Corridor.

I was met by a local guide, Martin Yuán, who briefed me on the town: Jiāyùguān has a population of 120,000, of whom 8% work in a single Russian-built steel factory, the largest in northwest China.

We set out first not for the garrison at the end of the Great Wall but for a site less dramatic, although quite ancient: the Wèi-Jìn Tombs. Thirteen tombs were built 19km (12 miles) northeast of town during the Northern

Wèi (A.D. 220–265) and Western Jìn (A.D. 265–316) dynasties. This cluster consists of rounded mounds about 2m (6 ft.) high, heaps of sandy soil scooped up from the desert flatlands—as desolate a graveyard as I have ever seen. Driving out to the Wèi-Jìn Tombs, we passed many fields of such mounds. Some 14,000 tombs of officials have been counted in the area. The 13 Wèi-Jìn Tombs open to visitors were discovered in 1972. They're open between 8:30am and 6:30pm; admission is ¥35 ($4.20). The burial chambers are several stories under the ground—the mounds are merely markers.

We strolled down the stairs into **Tomb 6** which, like many others, has been looted by grave robbers in the past but still retains its chief treasure: the brick paintings depicting daily life. This tomb consists of three burial chambers, representing the three courtyards of the official and his wife who are buried here.

The walls of the first small underground chamber are constructed of 1,700-year-old bricks laid without mortar. The bricks are brightly painted with scenes of animal husbandry—the herding of goats and the tilling of fields by oxen in this oasis, fed by subterranean rivers originating in the distant mountains. In the second chamber, connected by a low archway, the walls depict the journey this official and his wife made to the Chinese capital, Luòyáng, an immense overland trip of more than a thousand miles—the trip of a lifetime. There are scenes of rich banquets, processions, and entertainments enjoyed at the capital. In the final burial chamber, the picture bricks record the official's worldly wealth, his boxes of jewels and shelves of silks, the treasures traded on the Silk Road. These brick paintings are simple renditions outlined in black, with red the most enduring color. The coffins are also here, on the floor against the final wall.

The Fort

Jiāyùguān Fort, the single most stunning sight along the Silk Road, is 6km (4 miles) from town (✆ **0937/639-6218**). It's open from 8am to 8pm; admission is ¥65 ($7.80), including entrance to the recently relocated **Great Wall Museum.** This garrison at Jiāyùguān Pass is magnificent. It rises from the desert sands and is composed of the same earth. The walls are 11m (35 ft.) high, the outer fortifications 1,020m (3,400 ft.) in circumference. The outer wall has turrets for archers and several pavilions at the corners, watchtowers for the troops stationed here during the Míng Dynasty.

It is easy to see why the wall ended here and how the fort could control the traffic of the Silk Road. The Héxī Corridor is pinched between the high Qílián Mountains and the Black Mountains of the Mǎzōng (Horse Mane) range to the north. Across this pass, earthen walls extend like raised arms east and west, forming a long fence.

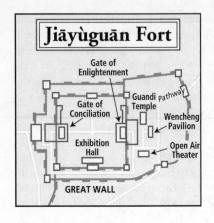

Jiāyùguān Fort

Gate of
Enlightenment

Guandi
Temple

pathway

Gate of
Conciliation

Wencheng
Pavilion

Exhibition
Hall

Open Air
Theater

GREAT WALL

Inside the outer wall is an inner wall surrounding the bar- racks where the general and his troops were stationed. The inner eastern gate, crowned with a 15m (50-ft.) high tower built in 1506, guards a courtyard running to the outer wall where caravans could be held for questioning before continuing into China. The western gate has a similar double-walled courtyard that served as the departure station for those crossing the desert out of China.

Climbing the wall, walking from turret to turret, blockhouse to blockhouse, I looked west from the pass into the desert. China's first official mission over the Silk Road, headed by Gen. Zhāng Qiān, went out through here in 138 B.C. and returned 13 years later with just two survivors. Believers say that even earlier, Lǎozǐ, founder of Daoism, passed through Jiāyùguān and the Jade Gate (Yùmén) on his way to the Western Paradise.

The fort at Jiāyùguān could not be in a more dramatic desert setting, nor could it look at once more imposing and more forlorn. The present fortification is partly reconstructed with brick, with improvements made as recently as 1988, but the original Míng Dynasty earthen walls are fully exposed and the old watchtowers are still in place. Within the inner walls is an ornate, tiled-roof opera theater, built during the Qīng Dynasty (1644–1911) for entertaining the Great Wall troops, its empty open stage sheltered by soaring eaves. A single camel and a saddled horse are tethered in the inner courtyard, their master and his portrait camera waiting for customers.

My guide took me down into the empty yard of the fort and told me some local stories. According to one, the emperor charged a local man with procuring the bricks necessary to build the fort. If his count was off, even by a single brick, he would pay with his life (the ancient answer to cost overruns). The man predicted that 100,000 bricks would be required for the project, and he confidently placed the order. As it turned out, only 99,999 bricks were needed, but he was able to conceal the leftover brick when the royal inspector arrived by placing it unmortared along the inner wall. The unmortared brick is still somewhere on the wall, according to my local guide.

Entering the western courtyard between the inner and outer walls of the fort, he told me another story. Once there were two sparrows, very much in love. One became shut inside the fort; the other escaped into the desert. The trapped bird waited and waited, singing out until it pined away. Today, when you hurl a rock at the inner wall, you can still hear its cry. I picked up a stone, and like thousands of travelers who stood here on the Silk Road, I hurled it against the wall, sanded smooth by the desert winds.

PRACTICAL INFORMATION

by Graeme Smith

ORIENTATION & WHEN TO GO

Jiāyùguān, a trading post and oasis during the Hàn Dynasty, served as the fort protecting the western entrance to China from the Silk Road during the Míng Dynasty. Today it is an industrial town deep in Gānsù Province, 2,093km (1,300 miles) west of Běijīng. Because of its elevation above 1,200m (4,000 ft.), Jiāyùguān is usually not scorching hot in the summer. Early spring and late fall are known for fierce dust storms, however, and winters for extremely cold temperatures.

There are plans to develop Jiāyùguān into a larger tourist attraction, with the re-creation of an ancient marketplace and residence district, a fish and bird garden, an amusement park, horse stables, an archery field, and a complex of "holiday villas."

GETTING THERE

By Plane CAAC can be found at Xīnhuá Zhōng Lù 4-3 (© **0937/622-6237**), 100m (328 ft.) south of the main roundabout, on the west side of Xīnhuá Zhōng Lù. There are direct flights to Dūnhuáng (daily) and to Xī'ān (Mon, Wed, Fri, Sun). All flights leave at 6pm. An airport shuttle (¥9/ $1.10) leaves from outside the CAAC office at 4:30pm.

By Train The train station is about 3km (2 miles) south of the city center. It's served by buses (nos. 1 and 2) and taxis. Jiāyùguān is 21 hours from Xī'ān, 35 hours from Běijīng, and 13 hours from Ürümqi. Tickets can be booked at hotel travel desks.

By Bus The bus station is on the southeast corner of Shènglì Zhōng Lù and Lánxīn Xī Lù. There are daily buses to Dūnhuáng at 9am, 11am, 11:40am, and 1pm (6 hr.; 383km/210 miles; ¥46/ $5.60), with air-conditioned coaches at 2:30pm and 4pm (¥67/$8). After 6pm, the bus station becomes a karaoke bar cum roller disco.

TOURS & STRATAGEMS

Visitor Information A surprisingly competent CITS goes by the name of **Jiāyùguān International Tours,** at Shènglì Běi Lù 2 (© **0937/622-6598;** fax 0937/ 622-6931; www.westtour.cc). The company is run by the friendly Qín Jiǎn, whose office is on the second floor. Rates for booking train tickets and organizing tours are very reasonable. The office is open daily from 8:30am to 12:30pm and 2:30 to 6:30pm.

WHERE TO STAY & DINE

A favorite with tour groups since 1987, **Great Wall Hotel (Chángchéng Bīnguǎn)** is a sprawling, comfortable, 156-room hotel with three stars. Styling itself as a mini-Jiāyùguān fort, it is located at Jiànshè Lù 6, 713500 (© **0937/622-5213;**

fax 0937/622-6016). Take bus no. 2 to Sīfǎ Jú and walk back 50m (164 ft.), and the best-appointed hotel in town is on your right. Service is friendly and efficient—the huge restaurant and the snarling bike-rental service being glaring exceptions. Building nos. 1 and 3 were renovated in 2001; building no. 2 still has lumpy carpets and an aroma of stale cigarettes. The hotel has a restaurant (Chinese homestyle), a large swimming pool, an exercise room, bike rental, a concierge, a tour desk, a business center, same-day laundry/dry cleaning, and 24-hour room service, while rooms have A/C and TVs. Doubles cost ¥280 ($35); suites go for ¥780 ($97). *Note:* This hotel does not accept credit cards.

For the moment, the freshly renovated **Qīngnián Bīnguǎn** hotel (Jiànshè Dōng Lù 3, 735100; *©* **0937/626-7499**) is the best value in town. Take bus no. 2 to Sīfǎ Jú and walk back 50m (164 ft.) to the red building on your left. Built in 1991, the hotel's original target was the backpacker market, but management is now aspiring to the lofty heights of Chinese three stars, so prices will increase in the future. Beyond the absurd exterior—a crimson Disney-inspired castle—the "economy rooms" are of excellent value. Beds in double rooms (likely you'll have a roommate) with cubicle-less shower were being offered for ¥25 ($3) at the time of writing. These rooms do not have air-conditioning (not essential in Jiāyùguān, as it is always cool at night), so it's best to choose a room on the first floor. The hotel has a restaurant (Chinese homestyle), bike rental, a concierge, a tour

desk, a business center, same-day laundry service, and 24-hour room service, while rooms have A/C and TVs. Air-conditioned doubles (not just a bed in a double) here cost ¥188 ($23); dorm beds go for ¥40 ($5). *Note:* This hotel does not accept credit cards.

In a small town like Jiāyùguān, a restaurant with four floors is doing something right. With a Cantonese chef poached from one of Xī'ān's top restaurants, **Lin Yuan Jiǔdiàn** at Xīnhuá Nán Lù 34 (*©* **0937/628-6918**) is where the locals go for a treat, and it makes a welcome break from stodgy noodles. The *fù guì niú ròu* is akin to roast beef on sesame toast. The *jiāngnán qián jiāng ròu*, lightly battered chicken in sweet-and-sour sauce, complements the Cantonese favorite, *xì qíng bǎihé chǎo xiānyóu*, fresh squid on a bed of celery, field mushrooms, and lotus. Main courses cost ¥80 to ¥120 ($10–$15). The restaurant is open daily from 9am to 11pm. Take bus no. 1 to Bǎoxiǎn Gōngsī.

The **Yǎnjìng Kǎoròudiàn (Spectacles) night market** on the north side of Jìng Tiě Shìchǎng is the liveliest in town. Sheep carcasses dangle, beer flows, and vendors make fun of their regular customers. No one knows the name of the night market's greatest showman, who is simply called Yǎnjìng (Spectacles). His shop is easy to spot, under a sign with a caricature of a man with huge glasses and a smock. The caricature is on the mark. Spectacles will serve you tasty lamb skewers (*yángròu chuàn*) or mini-lamb chops (*yángpái*) by the handful (*bǎ*)—about 20 in each serving, give or take a couple.

DŪNHUÁNG: CRESCENT MOON LAKE & THE SINGING SANDS

敦煌

Two thousand years ago, Dūn-huáng (Blazing Beacon) was a vital and flourishing caravan stop, the western-most oasis under Chinese control. Three major trading routes from the West merged here, making Dūnhuáng a major supply center.

The history of this outpost reflects the changing political winds that have swept across the Silk Road over the centuries. Tibetans ruled Dūnhuáng for almost 2 centuries before a Chinese warlord drove them out in A.D. 851. After the Táng Dynasty fell, the Uighur people swept in and established the Kingdom of Shachow in 911. Mongols took over in 1227, as Genghis Khan stormed in from the Gobi. Muslim forces cleared out the region in the 16th century. The Chinese resettled Dūnhuáng once again in 1760.

The most crucial event in Dūnhuáng's history unfolded early on, in the 4th century A.D., when work began on the Buddhist sculptures and murals in the Mògāo caves. As the importance of the Silk Road diminished at the end of the Táng Dynasty (A.D. 618–907), Dūnhuáng languished for centuries; but in the 20th century, these ancient grottoes made Dūnhuáng an important desert town once again and a major stopover for travelers.

Of course, modern travelers no longer arrive on sand dune–marching camels. Tourism has replaced trade as the source of Dūnhuáng's new wealth, and the Mògāo caves are the chief attraction for Chinese, Asian, and the few Western travelers retracing the Silk Road route.

My immediate goal at Dūnhuáng, however, was to get on a camel and cross a few dunes myself. The great Mògāo caves would wait for another chapter of travels (see the next chapter). I wanted to see a still more ancient phenomenon at Dūnhuáng, what Marco Polo called the "rumbling sands" of Crescent Moon Lake.

The Road to Dūnhuáng

The Silk Road across the desert sands from Jiāyùguān northwest up the **Héxī Corridor** to Dūnhuáng used to require 3 weeks by camel caravan. Today there is a 386km (240-mile) blacktop highway connecting the two oases. The **Qílián Mountains** to the south are oil rich. China's first oil field was opened west of Jiāyùguān in the Qílián foothills in 1936. The train cars barreling down the Héxī Corridor are loaded with black oil cars. There's a large nuclear plant as well. Gānsù is a very poor province, but it supplies much of the raw energy for the rest of China.

After a 2-hour drive, the southern mountains fade into the flat horizon. Sand and sand bluffs dominate the severe landscape. Thorn bushes are the only vegetation, except at rare villages where earthen houses are clustered around a green oasis and the domes of small mosques rise toward the clear skies. Goat herders dressed in tatters move across the sandy fields of the Gobi with their small flocks.

Deep into the desert we reached the ruins of **Qiáowān,** the dream city where the Qīng Dynasty Kāngxī Emperor (1654–1722) ordered a palace built. He became obsessed with a dream he had that was set on the Silk Road. In the dream, he saw a palace located on a river with two enormous trees, one shaped like a crown, the other like a sash. He dispatched two officials to locate the place and finance the dream temple. The officials built a humble walled dwelling instead, pocketing most of the construction funds. When Kāngxī discovered their deceit, he had the officials slain, using the skins of the wrongdoers to cover the heads of the palace drums. Only ruins remain at Qiáowān now.

The drive to Dūnhuáng consumes 4½ hours, even on a paved road. Drivers here learn to fight the monotony of interminably straight, flat stretches and the frequent eruption of massive potholes, entire unpaved strips, and barely passable detours that appear unannounced. There are road crews—men and women with nothing but shovels and bicycle carts— patching the roadway every 2 or 3 miles, and traffic must slow to a stop to negotiate what the elements have torn to bits. At noon we reached Dūnhuáng, a long, green oasis lined by trees for many miles where a river, the Dǎng Hé, cuts through the sands, exposing stone bluffs. Here tractors pull carts of crushed stone into town, and hardened, sunburnt men, taking a break from hauling tree limbs to market, nap on their trailers under shade trees.

The Singing Sands

Five kilometers (3 miles) south of downtown Dūnhuáng are enormous white sand dunes, part of the **Singing Sands Mountains (Míngshā Shān).**

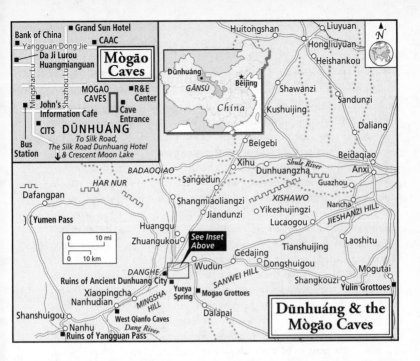

The dunes look like a poster of the Sahara. In their deep folds, they trap underground springs, creating **Crescent Moon Lake (Yuèyá Quán),** a celebrated pool where Silk Road travelers, including Marco Polo, paused to drink.

The afternoon sun was blisteringly hot when Martin Yuán, my local guide from Jiāyùguān, and I set out to cross the fine sands for Crescent Moon Lake. The site is open from dawn to sunset and sometimes after; admission is ¥50 ($6). Donning a straw hat, plastered in sunscreen, I was already sweating after the first few steps. My feet sank several inches into the crunching sands. It was like crossing a beach, a thousand miles from the nearest sea. Under awnings, a hundred camels and their drivers waited for riders. Heated by the sun, slowed by the Gobi sands, I hired us each a camel (¥30/$3.70 each) for the 15-minute trek each way—to avoid the long, hot walk. Obviously, I would have dropped dead in my tracks if I'd been one of the early traders trying to cross these dunes.

The two-humped Bactrian camel has inhabited the Silk Road for 2,000 years. They roam wild over the Gobi to this day. Single-humped camels can carry as heavy a load, but they lack the stamina and speed of their two-humped cousins. These enormous creatures are fairly docile under their masters' watch. My camel knelt on his front legs, then his back legs, and

I climbed aboard between his two humps. The humps, parted by a heavy blanket, proved to be a most comfortable saddle. Tethered to the driver's camel in a caravan of three, we loped across the sands at a steady pace, gently rising and falling with the camels' gait. We skirted a large oval concrete pool on our right, used to store water. On our left was the largest of the sand dunes, towering over a hundred feet above us.

Beyond the pool we turned right and headed for a beautiful three-storied **pavilion** with soaring eaves that had been erected on the edge of Crescent Moon Lake. Martin told me the original pavilion had been savaged by the Red Guards during the Cultural Revolution (1966–76). The restoration was remarkable: The pavilion still had its air of antiquity, and its upper balconies proved marvelous observation points for the dunes and the lake. Our driver halted the little caravan, lowering our camels.

Crescent Moon Lake these days is a narrow slash of water situated between the pavilion and a formidable wall of sand rising 180m (600 ft.) nearly straight up from its northern bank. Dūnhuáng had been experiencing a drought, and the lake was quite low but still pretty, a reed-studded belt of blue in a bowl of white mounds. We ordered cups of tea and sat on a veranda, the remains of a Buddhist temple where incense is still lighted. The lake received its name from its crescent-moon shape. The local people attach a story to the lake. It is a story like many of the Silk Road, of parting and grief. Here in Dūnhuáng a young girl parted with her lover, who set out to cross the desert. The caravan was lost, and he never returned. She died in mourning, with one eye forever opened in the shape of a crescent, watching the desert for the return of her lover.

Returning by camel, we dismounted and climbed the largest mound, **Míngshā Dune,** 246m (820 ft.) high, a veritable mountain of sand that seemed an endless task to scale. Sand sleds and paragliders can be hired here, but I preferred to hike, removing my shoes and soaking in the fine sands. At its summit, the view of the oasis is superb: a long, green island in the midst of a sea of sand and, to the west, whipped-cream dunes that stretch for 130km (80 miles) into the empty horizon. We sat atop the dune until the sun became too fierce, then descended like children, seated, "sand sliding" to the bottom, trying to make the sands sing as they have for eons here, although I could hear only a whisper of their legendary music.

On our way out, Martin told me about a party of 70 foreigners who'd visited the singing sands a few years back and formed a long caravan indeed. The group was led by one of my famous American compatriots, he said, a chap named Bill Gates, founder of Microsoft—one of the richest "traders," I pointed out, who'd ever ridden a camel on the Silk Road.

Then the wind came up, stirring the sands to a fine powder. The sound was a low rumble, often likened to a drum roll by Chinese poets. A

Dūnhuáng legend tells of a Chinese army camped here that was surrounded by the enemy once darkness fell. The Chinese army beat its war drums, and its call to arms was answered by the gods, who dispatched a sandstorm across the desert, burying both armies alive at Crescent Lake. To this day, people claim to hear the buried armies wailing and beating on their drums when the winds roll in.

"Man made the Buddhist caves," according to a local adage, "but the gods made Crescent Moon Lake," and these desert gods, it seems, can unmake caves, lakes, and even whole armies in the wink of an eye.

WHAT TO READ

Cave Temples of Mògāo: Art and History of the Silk Road (Getty Conservation Institute, 2000) by Roderick Whitfield, Neville Agnew, and Susan Whitfield is both scholarly and readable, with superb photography and an interesting section on current preservation techniques. It can be purchased at the caves for around ¥180 ($22) or at bookstores before you leave.

PRACTICAL INFORMATION

by Graeme Smith

ORIENTATION & WHEN TO GO

Dūnhuáng is a desert oasis in northwest Gānsù Province near the border with Xīnjiāng Province, about 2,415km (1,500 miles) west of Běijīng. Summers are very hot; May and October are the mildest months to visit. In July and August, the town fills up with thousands of tourists from China, Japan, and other parts of Asia, with a smattering of Westerners. While the oasis population is over 150,000, the downtown section is small and compact, with about 15,000 urban residents.

The major attractions for visitors to Dūnhuáng are the ancient Buddhist murals and sculptures at the **Mògāo caves** (see separate chapter on the caves, beginning on p. 428). **Crescent Moon Lake (Yuèyá Quán)** and **Singing Sands Mountain (Míngshā Shān)** have the best sand dunes on the Silk Road.

GETTING THERE

By Plane   With the opening of a new airport at Dūnhuáng, flights from Xī'ān (3 hr.), Běijīng (4 hr.), Ürümqi, and other cities in China are becoming more frequent, though there are fewer flights in winter. The airport is 13km (21 miles) east of Dūnhuáng, just past the turnoff to the Mògāo caves. CAAC used to run a bus to the airport, but you are now at the mercy of taxi drivers without meters, who should charge no more than ¥20 ($2.50). The most useful office of **CAAC** is opposite the Tàiyáng Dàjiǔdiàn at Shāzhōu Běi Lù 5 (© **0937/882-2389**). They will deliver tickets to your hotel, so there is no need to book tickets through hotel travel agencies.

By Train The nearest rail link for Dūnhuáng is a 2- to 3-hour bus ride away at Liùyuán. At the station, you will have no trouble finding minibus drivers, who ask ¥30 ($3.70) for the ¥15 ($1.90) trip. Buses for the train station leave the long-distance bus station at 7:30am, 9:30am, 11am, 12pm, 2pm, 4pm, 6pm, and 7:30pm. You can hire a taxi for ¥120 ($15) or a minivan for ¥100 ($12). Heading west, the best train choice is the K889 for Ürümqi (12 hr.) at 8:06pm, which originates in Dūnhuáng. Heading east, you may have to proceed through travel agencies.

The lowest commission is charged by **John's Information Cafe** (¥30/$3.70). If you arrive at the station early, there is a rest area on the second floor that charges ¥5 (60¢) for a cup of tea and a bit of peace and quiet.

By Car & Bus The paved road from Jiāyùguān (386km/240 miles) is served by hired car (4 hr.). The **bus station** is on Míngshān Lù (© 0937/882-2174), close to Fēitiān Bīnguǎn. There are daily buses to Jiāyùguān at 11:30am (383km; 6 hr.; ¥44/$5.40), 1pm (¥56/$6.90), and 2:30pm (¥66/$8.20).

TOURS & STRATAGEMS

Visitor Information The head office of **CITS** is inside the compound of the Dūnhuáng Guójì Dàjiǔdiàn, at Míng Shān Lù 32 (© **0937/882-3312;** fax 0937/882-2173; www.dhcits.com) on the right as you enter. Look for Zhào Wéntíng on the second floor, who speaks excellent English. The CITS office is open daily from 8am to 12:30pm and 3pm to 6:30pm. Booking train tickets and arranging transportation is best done through **John's Information Cafe,** inside the grounds of Fēitiān Bīnguǎn, Míng Shān Lù 22 (© and fax **0937/882-7000** or 0937/883- 7731 in winter; johncafe@hotmail.com). It's open daily from 7:30am to 11pm.

WHERE TO STAY

Grand Sun Hotel (Tàiyáng Dàjiǔdiàn) This is the best hotel situated in Dūnhuáng proper. The immaculate condition of the rooms is a tribute to the hotel's success in attracting guests from Japan. While the new wing hasn't been renovated since 1997, the rooms are spotless. The staff is brilliant, the long off season providing ample time for training. True to the hotel's name, the 24-hour hot water is provided by solar power. There are cheaper rooms in the old building. The Japanese restaurant can safely claim to be the best for miles around.
Shāzhōu Běi Lù 5, 736200. © **0937/882-9998.** Fax 0937/882-2019. dhytn@mail. jq.cninfo.net. 220 units. ¥688 ($86) double; from ¥988 ($123) suite. Rates include full breakfast. AE, DC, MC, V. **Amenities:** 4 restaurants (Japanese, Sichuān, Chinese homestyle); cafe; concierge; tour desk; business center; 24-hr. forex; shopping arcade; 24-hr. room service; same-day laundry/dry cleaning. *In room:* A/C, TV, minibar, fridge.

The Silk Road Dūnhuáng Hotel (Dūnhuáng Shānzhuāng) This is the only hotel in town that rises above the ordinary. The Hong Kong–funded venture, built in 1995, is 4km (2½ miles) south of town, just before the Míng Shān Dunes. The main building is an imposing fortress, surrounded by stylishly renovated courtyard houses. The airy rooms with finely crafted wooden furnishings, cool stone floors, and thick rugs fit in perfectly with the desert surroundings. Apparently Bill Gates was impressed with the villas, which feature a mixture of Táng and Hàn architectural styles. An aptly named "student building" with beds for ¥43 ($5) also houses the staff.

Dūnyuè Lù, 736200. © **0937/888-2088.** *Fax 0937/888-2086. www.the-silk-road.*
com. 300 units, including 21 villas. ¥800 ($100) double; suites from ¥1,200 ($150); villa suites from ¥2,000 ($250). 13% service charge applies. AE, DC, MC, V. **Amenities:** 2 restaurants (Cantonese/Sìchuān and Western); cafe; bar; sauna; bike rental; concierge; tour desk; evening shuttle bus to town; 24-hr. business center; 24-hr. forex counter; salon; 24-hr. room service; massage; same-day laundry/dry cleaning. *In room:* A/C, TV, fridge, hair dryer.

WHERE TO DINE

Near the bus station on Míngshān Lù, there are a number of small **cafes** with cheap Western dishes catering to independent foreign travelers. Their names **(Shirley's, Charley Johng's, John's)** and their menus are in English.

Dá Jì Lǘròu Huángmiànguǎn CHINESE HOMESTYLE Surprisingly, the specialty dish of Dūnhuāng is *lǘròu huángmiàn* (donkey meat yellow noodles). More surprisingly, it's delicious. It is claimed that the method of making the noodles is revealed in Cave 265, but the cave isn't open to the public and the owners of this noodle shop aren't giving away any secrets. A small plate *(xiǎo pán)* is more than enough, the noodles cooked with tomato, tofu, mushrooms, and plenty of garlic. The noodle broth is difficult to stomach, but you can drink as much as you like, and (of course) you are told it is good for your health. To accompany the main dish, order some donkey meat *(lǘròu)*. Half a jīn *(bàn jīn)* is enough for two—the meat is lean and tastes a little like roast beef. You will be presented with a bowl of finely chopped garlic, to which you should add chili sauce and vinegar to taste, before dipping the meat in it. If you want to meet some locals, this market street is a better choice than the tacky main night market *(yèshì)*. An after-dinner stroll through the narrow lanes is also rewarding. *Dà Shìchǎng. ¥10 ($1.25) per person. Daily 10:30am–10:30pm.*

THE CAVES OF MÒGĀO
莫高石窟

Of the top four Buddhist grottoes in China, the Mògāo caves at Dūnhuáng are considered supreme. Nevertheless, visitors are often disappointed. The caves containing the priceless wall paintings and sculptures created at this ancient oasis on the Silk Road, honeycombing a sheer cliff face, are all sealed by locked doors. The guides must constantly search for the person with the key. You must view Mògāo cave by cave, piece by piece: In a morning or afternoon, you can see only a tiny portion of these treasures locked in stone. At the other three major grottoes—the Yúngāng Grottoes at Dàtóng, the Lóngmén caves at Luòyáng, and the Buddha Crescent at Dàzú—visitors can freely wander in front of magnificent sculptures, open to wide and dramatic views.

Nevertheless, the treasures at Dūnhuáng—those not shipped abroad by Western explorers at the turn of the 20th century, that is—are the benchmarks of Buddhist art in China, and I was glad to see them for myself. Several days' viewing here is more rewarding than a few quick hours, and it helps to arrange the caves in rough chronological order in your mind. The styles and themes change over the centuries, and with a little background, the history of Buddhism and the Silk Road itself unfolds at Dūnhuáng like chapters in a stone picture book. For a map of the caves, see p. 423.

The Cave Builders

China's richest treasure house of Buddhist paintings, statues, and manuscripts lies 26km (16 miles) southeast of Dūnhuáng in the Mògāo caves. These magnificent caves were created over a thousand-year period stretching from the 4th century to the 14th century A.D. Nine dynasties rose and fell during this time, and the artists of each period contributed.

The grottoes had as much to do with business and politics as religion. The rich merchant families and the rulers of Dūnhuáng sponsored the carving and painting of many of them. Such acts, no doubt, cast them in a favorable light to Buddhist believers who ran the rich caravan trade. The first cave was hewn in A.D. 366 by Liè Zūn, a Buddhist monk who was inspired by the golden rays of the sun illuminating the cliff face. Liè Zūn commissioned a fellow pilgrim to paint the walls with holy images, decorating a shrine where he could pray for his safe passage over the Silk Road. Thus, the purpose of this desert gallery was set from the first—a divine insurance policy for the caravans of the Silk Road. The grottoes functioned as shrines where traders and pilgrims could pray, but above all as a place where Silk Road travelers and merchants could petition for divine protection of their caravans, which faced daunting obstacles in crossing the deserts that loomed east and west of Dūnhuáng.

Over the centuries, the repute of Dūnhuáng increased. New dynasties often sent their best artists there to construct and decorate new grottoes to commemorate their rules and cement their commitment to the religious community. Over 45,000 murals and 2,000 statues, fashioned from stucco rather than the loose sandstone of the cliff, have survived, housed in almost 500 caves. The desert air has preserved the art for 15 centuries.

The chief dynasties represented are the Northern Wèi (A.D. 386–534), the Western Wèi (A.D. 535–557), the Suí (A.D. 581–618), the Táng (A.D. 618–917), and the Five Dynasties (A.D. 907–960). The styles vary with the dynasties. The themes were all derived from the various schools of Buddhism as they arrived and were adapted in China.

The earlier figures of Buddha and his attendants retain a strong Indian influence, rendered in rigid, geometric poses, but the Chinese gradually added movement and realism to these figures. They reached their zenith with the Táng artists, who created 213 of the 492 caves that survive. The backgrounds painted on the cave walls flow with cloud scrolls, floral patterns, fantastic landscapes, and architecture that almost from the first came from Chinese models. The main themes are derived from the life of Sakyamuni as he journeys to enlightenment and from the holy manuscripts (sutras) that preach the cosmic doctrines of karma and reincarnation and portray the mortal world as one of vanity, illusion, and suffering.

To heighten depictions of these themes, the Dūnhuáng painters plastered the walls and ceilings with mixtures of mud, dung, straw, animal hair, and a smooth coating of clay, to which they applied tempera (water-based) pigments of vivid blues, yellows, greens, reds, cinnabar vermilions, fleshy pinks, and powdered gold leaf. The statues are made either with plaster over wooden frames or with plaster over figures cut from cave rock. The caves are squarish, often with a large figure of Buddha on a dais at the back and attendants on both sides. The large chambers measure about 9m (30 ft.) wide and deep and 5m (16 ft.) high, while the smallest caves are barely the size of a tiny bedroom, with ceilings as low as 54 inches. The ceilings may be sharply pitched, lantern shaped, or domed in a series of tapering, concentric squares.

For the casual observer, the main technical point to note is the evolution of the art from the rigid, narrow, representational figures in the early caves to the rounded, realistically rendered, more human figures portrayed in the later Suì and Táng Dynasty caves, as the gulf between the divine and the earthly all but disappeared.

Guardian Angels & Foreign Devils

The history of Buddhist art in China contained in the gallery of caves at Dūnhuáng is part of the larger political history of the Silk Road. As the Táng Dynasty declined, the Silk Road was subject to invasions from Tibetans and groups spreading a new religion, Islam. The Xī Xià Kingdom (1038–1368) gained the upper hand, chasing Buddhists out of Dūnhuáng. The Mògāo caves were abandoned. Monks sealed their documents and sutras in a single cave and fled the invaders. The Dūnhuáng grottoes remained unused and undiscovered for at least 800 years. Near the beginning of the 20th century, however, a Daoist monk named Abbot Wáng, seeking refuge from the famines in Húběi Province, arrived at Dūnhuáng and, clearing out a cave, discovered a door leading to a dark inner chamber filled with thousands of manuscripts and paintings. The Chinese government, unable to finance the removal of the treasures, ordered Wáng to reseal the inner storehouse, but Wáng, intent on raising funds to restore the Mògāo grottoes, began to sell the treasures to the highest bidders.

It was Westerners who recognized the worth of the newly discovered manuscripts and who came across the Silk Road to snap them up for museums. Sir Aurel Stein arrived first, in 1907. He purchased silk painted banners, 7,000 scrolls, 500 paintings, and other relics, which he crated up and transferred to the British Library, where they still reside. Paul Pelliot came the next year, selecting paintings and 5,000 scrolls for the Bibliothèque Nationale in Paris. Japanese, Russians, and more Western collectors quickly followed, including Langdon Warner, who removed sculptures and wall paintings and shipped them from Dūnhuáng to the Fogg Museum at Harvard in 1924.

In the end, Dūnhuáng was left with virtually no manuscripts. A sutra copied onto paper and dated A.D. 406 and a paper scroll of the Diamond Sutra dated A.D. 868, considered the world's first printed book, are now in England. Fortunately, most of the wall paintings and much of the statuary remains where it was created, in the desert caves of Dūnhuáng, beyond the reach of foreign specialists, who are seen by some as the heroic preservers of a Chinese history that would otherwise have been lost, and by others as modern-day raiders of the Silk Road.

Inside the Grottoes

The **Mògāo caves** (© **0937/886-9060**), 24km (15 miles) southwest of Dūnhuáng, are open daily from 8:30 to 11:30am and 2 to 5pm. The admission of ¥100 ($12) included a local guide. I rented a flashlight at the ticket booth (¥3/35¢, with a deposit of ¥10/$1.25)—the caves are unlighted—and crossed a wooden bridge over the Dǎng Hé to the sandstone cliff.

All the caves are numbered, although not in any discernible order. The oldest are in the central portion of the mile-long cliff. Four tiers of cement walkways with railings, replacing the wooden ladders and catwalks in the 1950s, connect the grottoes.

Roughly 30 of the 492 chambers are usually available to tourists, with the guide deciding which ones to visit. Some caves can be visited only by special advance permission and payment of extra fees; photography inside is forbidden except by special arrangements and fees. Since even the caves open for visitation are often locked and there are no signposts, a guide is useful, although you can crisscross the platforms on your own, dropping in at open doors and latching onto various guided groups. Many interesting caves are off-limits to ordinary visitors, including Caves 462 and 465, containing figures engaged in sexual union. This particular representation of divine enlightenment is a frequent theme of Tantric Buddhism, which was popular during the Yuán Dynasty (1271–1368), when these caves were painted.

The most dramatic sculpture is behind a nine-story wooden pagoda. Decorated with paintings of the zodiac and erected a century ago, the tower of soaring eaves rises to the summit of the sandstone ridge. Inside **Cave 96** is a 34m (113-ft.) tall Buddha, carved from the sandstone cliffs during the High Táng Dynasty (A.D. 705–781). Seated, wearing the robes of an emperor, this **Maitreya Buddha (Happy Buddha of the Future)** is the fourth largest in the world and the largest single clay sculpture at Dūnhuáng. It was repainted in the 19th century and its left hand was repaired a decade ago.

Among the caves I have seen, these are of particular note:

Cave 16 is where Wáng Yuánlù stumbled onto the treasures of Dūnhuáng at the beginning of the 20th century. The nine figures on the platform are a recent addition (Qīng Dynasty, 1644–1911), but the tile floor is probably from the Late Táng (848–906). The west wall is a Five Dynasties (907–960) mural depicting the holy mountain of Wǔtái Shān, its temples labeled, and the east wall contains portraits of a ruling family of the region from the same period, who sponsored the cave art. The ceiling is decorated in the Ten Thousand Buddha motif, the repeated pattern achieved by the use of block stamps or stencils that were painted in. The lotuses decorating the walls date from the 11th century. It was usual for artists of later dynasties to add to or even paint over existing shrines, as space for new caves was eventually exhausted.

Cave 17, linked to the passageway to Cave 16, is where Wáng Yuanlu found the trove of scrolls, sutras, and paintings that Sir Aurel Stein and other Westerners bought and shipped to museums abroad, starting in 1907. Known as the **Cángjīng Kū,** this cave is where the oldest book in the world (A.D. 868), the Diamond Sutra, was discovered.

Caves 61, 62, and **63** date from the Yuán Dynasty (1271–1368), when the Mongols seized control of China. The statues, presumably posed in the sexual positions favored by Tantric Buddhism at the time, were demolished by Moslems. The 12m (40-ft.) long wall mural of the holy mountain of Wǔtái Shān, its scores of temples labeled, is splendid and dates from the Northern Sòng (960–1127), when Dūnhuáng's ruling family opened a painting academy devoted solely to artwork in the Mògāo grottoes.

Cave 98 is from the Five Dynasties (907–960). The ceiling is funnel shaped. The Cáo Yìjìng family, high officials of the period at Dūnhuáng, sponsored this and several other caves, notably Cave 427. The wall portraits are of the ruling family of Khotan, a city on the Silk Road. The king wears a beaded hat. There are also lively scenes of female musicians and a royal hunting party.

Cave 130 contains a magnificent Buddha, 26m (86 ft.) high, carved during the High Táng period (705–781). The platform and statue are original except for the Buddha's right hand, which broke and was replaced during the Northern Sòng (960–1279). The murals on the side walls are also from the Northern Sòng. This is the second tallest statue at Dūnhuáng, and it can be appreciated from the ground or from the two upper galleries. The head measures 7m (22 ft.) high, the ears 2m (6 ft.).

Cave 148 contains the 16m (53-ft.) long, golden-faced Sleeping Buddha of Dūnhuáng. It was carved in 755 to portray Buddha about to enter Nirvana. Seventy-two disciples are in attendance. The east wall contains a painting of the Western Paradise, the Buddhist "heaven."

Cave 152 features a passageway with tiles and ceiling paintings from the Northern Sòng (960–1127), with two Daoist figures in the back chamber.

Cave 237 has a statue of Guānyīn, Goddess of Mercy, in its center; Manjusri, God of War, riding a lion; and the God of Compassion atop the holy mountain of Éméi Shān. These figures were added during the Qīng Dynasty (1644–1911) to a cave whose wall paintings of the Buddha and the Western Paradise were placed here in the Middle Táng Dynasty (781–848).

Cave 257, with a pillar in the center, contains unretouched paintings from the Northern Wèi (A.D. 386–534), some of the oldest art at

Dūnhuáng. The figures are dressed in Indian clothing, and the facial features are not Chinese. The mural on the west wall portrays the story of a drowning man rescued by the Deer King, a representation of Buddha.

Cave 259, said to contain the oldest artwork at Dūnhuáng, holds several statues of Buddha carved during the Northern Wèi (A.D. 386– 534). The figures are stiff, the heads squarish, the noses hooked, the lips curled (into a smile often compared to that of the *Mona Lisa*)—all characteristics of the Buddhist sculpture in India at the time.

Cave 427 was a gift from the Cáo family, high officials at Dūnhuáng during the Northern Sòng (960–1279), who controlled the Silk Road routes for 120 years. Husband, wife, and family are portrayed on the front passage walls. A pillar holds up the gabled roof over the chamber at the back, which contains nine stately, long-bodied statues of Buddha, sculpted during the Suí Dynasty (A.D. 581–618). The three figures in the middle are "Buddhas of the Present"; the three on the left, "Buddhas of the Past"; and the three on the right, "Buddhas of the Future."

Cave 428 has a lotus-and-peacock ceiling and stamped clay figures of the Ten Thousand Buddhas on the walls, but its chief attraction is the picture given of court life in the Northern Zhōu Dynasty (A.D. 557–581), a brief period linking the Wèi and Suí dynasties from which little survives. Over 4,000 royal contributors to the cave art are pictured on the east wall, along with the halls and pavilions of the time. There is also a panel depicting the story of three brothers who hunt a tiger. One brother unselfishly gives his life to the tiger so that she can feed her cubs, and he is reborn as Buddha. My guide told me that in 1922, Russians fleeing the revolution bivouacked in this and other caves (although, in fact, the Chinese local authorities locked them in there), which they blackened with fires, damaged with bullets, and stripped of gold leaf.

Morning or afternoon tours generally take in just a dozen of these and other caves, hardly enough to gain a full appreciation of what exists at Dūnhuáng. Spend a second day, if possible, and by all means visit the museum at the entrance to the site, a joint venture between China and Japan. The **Research and Exhibition Center** (© **0937/882-1981**) is open daily from 9am to 5pm. It contains lighted replicas of seven caves, copies of the missing manuscripts, and relics from the caves. A tour of the center helps put the intricate and complex desert gallery into perspective.

I once covered 17 grottoes in 2 hours with a local guide, but this proved too rapid to enjoy and study the paintings, particularly the details in the murals. At Dūnhuáng, it is the paintings that dominate. At other grottoes, it is the sculpture, much of it on a grander and more prolific scale than at Dūnhuáng. But the painted miniatures of Mògāo, in hundreds of caves, record thousands of stories and scenes from the days of the Silk Road that are otherwise lost. Inspired by the sutras carried across mountains and desert into China on the backs of early pilgrims, artists for 9 centuries painted their best work on the walls of these caves. The holiest shrines of the Silk Road are also its supreme works of art.

PRACTICAL INFORMATION

by Graeme Smith

ORIENTATION & WHEN TO GO

The Mògāo caves (Mògāo Shíkū) are located 24km (15 miles) southeast of Dūnhuáng, a desert oasis in northwest Gānsù Province on the Silk Road, 2,415km (1,500 miles) west of Běijīng. Summers are quite hot, but July and August are high season for tourists, mainly those from China, Japan, and other parts of Asia. May and October are more pleasant and less-crowded months to visit.

GETTING THERE

To reach the caves, minibuses leave from Fēitiān Bīnguǎn at 8am (¥8/$1 one-way, ¥10/$1.20 return), or you can catch one of the local minibuses that line up along Xīn Jiàn Lù for a similar fare. In the busy season, these fill up quickly, but in the off season, you will get a scenic tour of Dūnhuáng before commencing the half-hour journey. If you plan on seeing the Mògāo caves as a half-day trip, get there as early as possible; buses return to Dūnhuáng at noon.

TOURS & STRATAGEMS

Most Westerners reach Dūnhuáng and the Mògāo caves on group tours of the Silk Road.

Tours At the caves, English-speaking guides (¥20/$2.50) are assigned to visitors at the main ticket booth. For information on tour operators in Dūnhuáng, see the previous chapter. Entry to the Research and Exhibition Center is included in the ticket price.

Visitor Information Photography in the caves is strictly prohibited. Cameras and all bags, including purses, must be checked at the ticket booth. A ¥2 (25¢) deposit is required.

WHERE TO STAY & DINE

If you are staying the full day at the Mògāo caves, either pack a lunch or try one of the cafes or stands near the ticket booth. For information on where to stay and dine in Dūnhuáng, see the previous chapter.

Turpan: Lost Cities

吐鲁番

THE FIRST THING THAT STRIKES
outsiders traveling west from Gānsù Province into Xīnjiāng Province is that
you are no longer quite in China. This vast northwestern region—China's
Alaska—is divided into northern grasslands and southern deserts by the
Heavenly Mountains (Tiān Shān). The dramatic, arid landscape is a sharp
break from what's found in the rest of China, but Xīnjiāng's ethnic make-
up is an even more striking departure. Kazakh nomads predominate in the
northern pastures; Uighur farmers are a majority in the southern desert
basin; and most of the Hàn Chinese, a distinct minority, are recent arrivals.

Xīnjiāng is foremost the land of the Uighur, who account for almost half
of the province's 13 million people. They are Turkic-speaking, fiercely
Islamic, and decidedly non-Hàn Chinese. They look and dress like central
Asian people of Turkish descent. Here, the Silk Road passes through a middle ground of history and race like no other land on earth, an Islamic
culture under Chinese rule in a land of irrigated oases and bone-white heat.

An Uighur empire rose up in the Tarim Basin in the 8th century. Uighur
controlled the Silk Road routes through Xīnjiāng. They first adopted
Buddhism, then Islam as their faith. During the Qīng Dynasty, they were
swept up in the 1862 Muslim rebellion led by Yakub Beg. The Chinese did
not regain control over Xīnjiāng, which had become known as Chinese
Turkestan, until 1877. In this century, there has been an uneasy truce
between the Chinese and the Uighur, sometimes broken by protests, even
by violence.

At Turpan, in the heart of Xīnjiāng, the northern route of the Silk Road
steps down into one of the deepest continental basins on Earth. Turpan is
78m (260 ft.) below sea level, while nearby **Moon Lake (Àidīng Hú)** is
152m (505 ft.) below sea level. This low lake is encrusted in salt, freezing
in winter, melting in summer. Two-thousand-year-old beacon towers still
guard the lakeshore, where some of the salt factory workers, sent from
coastal cities to labor here during the Cultural Revolution (1966–76), have
never returned to their homes.

Turpan, just 55km (34 miles) from Moon Lake, is far more hospitable.
In fact, it is a model Silk Road oasis, a sleepy desert town shaded by poplar
trees and grape arbors, peopled by Uighur in traditional dress, and irrigated

by a vast system of hand-dug underground channels that funnel the melting snows of the Heavenly Mountains into Turpan. This 2,000-year-old irrigation system has kept Turpan alive while other desert boomtowns have withered up and died. Two of those ancient cities, empty and returned to the sands with which they were built, still remain on Turpan's doorstep, two of the most impressive imperial ruins anywhere on the Silk Road.

Bezeklik Thousand Buddha Caves (Bózīkèlǐkè Qiānfódòng)

Turpan is China's hottest city, its "Land of Fire," with summer temperatures routinely reaching a roasty 104°F (40°C). I arrived on the first of May and the temperature was already 2 degrees above that. I had been doing nothing but traveling for hours. The day before, I was driven for 3 hours from Dūnhuáng north to Liùyuán, past the earthen ruins of the Hàn Dynasty Great Wall, past a group of five wild camels, and over the Horse Mane Hills, where the sand disappeared and the exposed rock, shattered into bits the size of fingertips, coated everything in lunar gravel. At Liùyuán, I boarded an overnight train and arrived at Turpan at 4am, where my local guide, Christina, and a driver met me in the dark. They suggested I nap a few hours in my room in the Oasis Hotel (a four-floor walk-up) but, of course, I couldn't. I was eager to see the sights of Turpan, its old mosques and graves, its fabulous wells, its ruined cities, the Flaming Mountains, and Bezeklik.

The **Flaming Mountains (Huǒyàn Shān)** line the northern rim of the Turpan Depression. Consisting of barren red limestone, the 100km (60-mile) long bluff resembles a tableau of fiery tongues when ignited by the afternoon sun. It is a sight familiar to Chinese readers of the novel *Journey to the West*, an allegorical version of Buddhist monk Xuán Zàng's historic journey by foot from China to India over the Silk Road in the 7th century. The trip from Dūnhuáng west to Turpan, which took me less than 24 hours by car and train, would have taken Xuán Zàng or any other pilgrim or caravan trader at least 3 weeks—3 terrible weeks in the desert. Xuán Zàng got lost here. Running out of water, he wanted to turn back but instead wandered on, half dead. He made it, of course, to Turpan—or rather, to the city of Gāochāng, now in ruins near the site of the Bezeklik caves—where he taught for several months.

The caves in the heart of these mountains, 56km (35 miles) northeast of Turpan, are a major Buddhist site. Beginning in the Southern and Northern dynasties (A.D. 420–589), caves were hewn into the cliffside, and large murals, like those at Dūnhuáng, were painted on the walls and ceilings. The site is now known as the **Bezeklik Thousand Buddha Caves.** It's

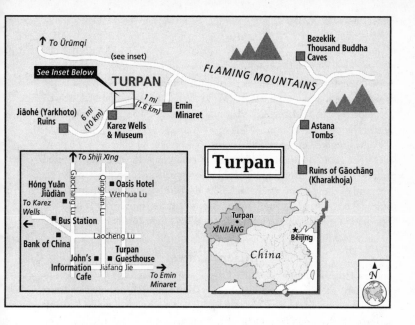

open daily from 9am to 5pm; admission is ¥20 ($2.50). In Uighur, Bezeklik means simply "place of paintings."

Bezeklik is situated in absolutely stunning surroundings, high up a cliff in the Murtuk River gorge. From a distance, the caves cut into the ridge, and the brick temples, as well as the smooth mosque domes, look like a holy city chiseled out of a vertical mountainside. But close up, Bezeklik is nearly empty—worse, it has been looted and defaced. The painted walls of its 83 grottoes, with their arched ceilings, have nearly all been erased or stolen. The Buddhist statuary is also missing. It is a superb Buddhist grotto emptied as if by desert winds or stone-eating monsters.

In fact, Bezeklik has been emptied by men. The Uighur themselves, having converted to Islam in the 10th century, did not look favorably upon the Buddhist images in their midst. They defaced some murals, beheaded statues, sealed the caves in sand, and built domed mosques in place of the brick temples. Much of this took place in the 1870s, when Turpan and most of Xīnjiāng Province broke away from Chinese control and became Chinese Turkestan.

Greater destruction came from the West. The German Albert von Le Coq arrived in Turpan in 1902; he departed with 2 tons of treasures and relics. Two years later, he returned for more. Other expeditions from Europe arrived, crating off whatever remained. At Bezeklik, the German experts found Turpan's treasure house: 1,000-year-old murals in perfect condition with bright portraits of Buddha over the centuries, yellow-robed monks from India, and even a red-haired traveler from the West. The best frescoes were removed and shipped to the Museum for Indian Art in Berlin for safekeeping—beyond the reach of Uighur farmers and Islamic fanatics, it was argued at the time. Later, World War II bombing raids destroyed some of the larger Bezeklik wall murals in Berlin, where only fragments remain on display.

A man with a key opened the doors to several caves. There are 83 grottoes here; about 40 retain frescoes, all in poor condition. The few defaced murals I saw give strong hints of the vibrant reds that dominated the art here and of the glowing greens and blues the painters employed as trim. On one arched ceiling, I could make out a familiar motif, the Thousand Buddhas in meditation, row after identical row, unrestored and crumbling.

Ancient Cities

South of the Thousand Buddha Caves (about 40km/25 miles southeast of Turpan) are the ruins of **Gāochāng (Kharakhoja),** an ancient desert capital founded in the 2nd century B.C. as a garrison on the Silk Road. It served as the capital of Xīnjiāng (the Western Territories) during the Táng Dynasty, starting in A.D. 640. From 840 to 1209, Gāochāng became the Uighur capital. It was destroyed in 1275 and has stood unoccupied ever since.

The dry air and lack of rain have preserved the outlines of Gāochāng's adobe outer walls (5km/3 miles in circumference) and inner buildings—its bell tower and a few of its many Buddhist temples.

At the entrance (¥20/$2.50), we hired a young Uighur driver and hopped aboard his flatbed donkey cart for an hour's ride (an extra ¥15/$1.90) inside the ancient walls. The pace was slow and the donkey driver relaxed—this was the proper speed at which to drive through a ghost town on the Silk Road. At the center of this city of sand, which is nearly a mile across, there is a large temple, its platform and shrine still evident, and close by, a two-story circular pavilion surrounded by a square wall where the pilgrim Xuán Zàng preached in A.D. 630 on his way to India.

The city is empty of human remains, of course, but the royal graveyard, a few miles away, is now receiving visitors. The **Astana Tombs (Ăsītǎnà Mùqún)** are open daily from 9am to 5pm; admission is ¥20 ($2.50). The tombs have been blessed with centuries of dry weather, meaning that the corpses, their silk wrappings, and even the foods buried with them have survived in fine fettle. The earliest of the 500 graves is dated A.D. 273; the latest, A.D. 782. The burial chambers are 5m (16 ft.) beneath the surface. Wall murals depict the pleasures of family life and the beauties of nature, particularly of birds. Among the 10,000 relics excavated at Astana is a pair of woven linen shoes and a fossilized *jiǎozi* (steamed dumpling), both specimens from the Táng Dynasty.

Co-burial of husband and wife was common. Inside the last of the three chambers open to the public, the mummies of a man and a woman lie next to each other, under glass, on a rough mat. Their hair has grown long in death and so have their fingernails. They have barely begun to disintegrate with the passage of 12 centuries, but they look dry, very dry.

On the opposite side of modern Turpan, 10km (6 miles) to the west, is a second ruined city, **Jiǎohé (Yarkhoto),** perched on a leaf-shaped 30m (100-ft.) high plateau between two rivers. A mile long and a quarter mile wide, it's nearly the size of Gāochāng, but in better shape. UNESCO has contributed to its preservation. The outlines of many of its buildings are sharper, and there are some signposts in English. The city is open daily from 9am to 5pm; admission is ¥30 ($3.70).

Jiǎohé, like so many Silk Road towns, began as a garrison during the Hàn Dynasty. It reached its peak under Uighur control in the 9th century during the Táng Dynasty. It has been abandoned for more than 5 centuries, but it has preserved its ancient cityscape in sand and brick. A Buddhist temple stands at city center, with Buddhas (heads now missing) carved into its niches. Streets and the courtyards of houses were dug into the ground. Jiǎohé looks like a life-sized model of a Táng Dynasty city, sculpted from a high sandstone column standing between river gorges, or like an oasis stripped by a miraculous wind of every piece and particle that was not composed of sand or brick.

A Minaret & the Karez Wells

Turpan is roughly 75% Uighur. Christina, my guide, is a local Hàn Chinese, meaning she probably went to a Chinese school and was not taught the Uighur language. Uighur attend their own schools, in which Chinese is studied as a second language. Each side coexists sweetly, it seems. Christina had a dream of visiting America. She wanted to see the West— the Wild West of cowboys that she knew from the movies—and she wanted to listen to jazz in a jazz bar. So pervasive are these media images of America that they penetrate even the remotest oasis on the Silk Road, shaping the images of a generation.

In the morning, we visited **Emin Minaret,** a mile east of the city, the prettiest tower on the Silk Road. It's open daily from 9am to 7pm; admission is ¥20 ($2.50). Also called Sūgōng Tower, the minaret was built of blue brick and completed in 1778. The bricks of the circular, smoothly tapered tower are laid in various patterns: waves, pyramids, and flower petals. The architect was a Uighur named Ibrahim. Attached to the 43m (144-ft.) minaret is a white stone mosque, the largest in the region. Its interior is plain. The roof is of woven mats. The floor is covered in prayer rugs. The Iman's seat is a humble, straw-woven chair.

The Emin Minaret is surrounded by grape arbors. Grape vines came into China on the Silk Road 2,000 years ago, and residents of Turpan planted them immediately. At the western base of the Flaming Mountains, there's an entire valley called **Grape Gorge (Pútao Gōu),** a park of vineyards and fruit groves with trellised walkways and courtyard picnic tables. The grapes are dried in hundreds of ingenious outbuildings ventilated by the open brickwork of their walls, creating the sweet **raisins** for which Turpan is renowned.

The sine qua non for grapes—for all of life along the Silk Road—is water. Turpan's source is locked up in the snows and glaciers of the Heavenly Mountains to the south. For the last 20 centuries, the mountain waters have reached Turpan through a massive underground network of tunnels, an irrigation system known as the **karez.** Karez wells *(kǎn'er jǐng)* are dug to tap the subterranean streams that originate at the foot of the mountain. Tunnels are hollowed out and elevated so that gravity pushes the well water across the desert to the canals of Turpan. More than 1,610km (1,000 miles) of tunnels have been dug under the desert floor at Turpan, some stretching as far as 40km (25 miles). The karez system suffers from continual clogging. To maintain it, a man must frequently be lowered down a shaft into a tunnel. By the use of pulleys, his horse hauls up buckets of mud tethered to a rope until the passage is clear.

One karez well site has opened at an **exhibition center** in Turpan, complete with a museum (admission ¥15/$1.90) offering displays and pictures. Visitors descend into several hand-dug tunnels for a look at the irrigating waters. The tunnels are spacious enough to stand up in, and they are cool, the coolest spots in town. Working in them must be like digging in a mine. The local people regard the karez wells as one of China's three greatest ancient works, the other two being the Great Wall and the Grand Canal.

Falling Down the Well

Turpan is a pleasant town to walk before the sun rises too high or after it sets. The flat roofs of the mud-brick Uighur homes are coated with grains and seeds for drying. Every backyard seems to have its clay bread-baking oven and lattice-roofed patio. In the poplar-lined streets, silk rugs are hung out for sale and donkey-cart taxi drivers cruise the traffic circles looking for riders. Chinese and Westerners are vastly outnumbered here. The sidewalks belong to the Uighur and the white-capped Huí (Islamic Chinese).

Grape trellises are everywhere, sometimes shading entire city blocks. It's a good thing. The summer sun is scorching. This is heat, sucking every ounce of moisture to the surface of the skin like a karez well; heat that makes coffins unnecessary at funerals; an embalming heat that shrivels grapes and turns out mummies guaranteed to last a millennium, no other treatment required. My room's air conditioner was on the fritz and the temperature was pushing 106°F (40°C), but at least I didn't have to fear what foreign travelers reported 60 years ago: scorpions. Neither were there jumping spiders "as large as a pigeon's egg," nor 2-inch-long Turpan cockroaches with hairy feelers and red eyes.

On my last evening in Turpan I walked down to the **Turpan Guesthouse** to enjoy an evening performance of Uighur song and dance. The costumes were flashy and the master of ceremonies was proficient in the three languages Xīnjiāng employs: Uighur, Chinese, and English. A sheepskin tambourine, played with vigor, kept the swirling dancers on track. I walked back through the pitch dark. At the traffic circle, I was in mid-sentence with Christina when I disappeared into an open manhole. Luckily, my momentum tipped me forward when I stepped into open space, so I fell to the pavement on one knee and an elbow, scraping my shin against the manhole rim instead of disappearing. Though I was scraped up and ached in a few places, I could walk, as I had to: I was barely halfway across the Silk Road.

PRACTICAL INFORMATION

by Graeme Smith

ORIENTATION & WHEN TO GO

Turpan (called Tulufan by the Chinese) is a desert oasis on the northern Silk Road in central Xīnjiāng Uighur Autonomous Region, 3,059km (1,900 miles) west of Běijīng. It is located in the Tarim Basin, 78m (260 ft.) below sea level, in the "oven" of China, the hottest city in the country, where summer temperatures routinely soar above 100°F (38°C). The Heavenly Mountains (Tiān Shān) lie to the south; their glaciers and snows feed the underground streams and springs tapped by the karez well system, an ancient engineering feat on a par with construction of the Great Wall and the Grand Canal. Roughly 75% of the 200,000 people in Turpan County are Uighur, a Turkish minority, formerly nomadic, that originated south of Lake Baikal. Here public signs are written in Arabic first, Chinese second. Qīngnián Lù is the main north–south street in town, where the hotels and cafes catering to foreign travelers are located. In late August, there is a vibrant Grape Festival. May and October are the coolest months to visit; winters are freezing.

GETTING THERE

By Plane The nearest airport is at **Ürümqi**, 184km (114 miles) northwest, a 4-hour journey over a paved highway by car or bus from Turpan.

By Train The railway station is located 54km (33 miles) north of Turpan in the unprepossessing town of **Dàhéyàn**. Minibuses for Turpan (¥6/70¢) will probably meet you at the station, along with minivan drivers from **John's Information Cafe** (¥5/60¢), who will pursue you for the rest of your stay. If there are no buses there to meet you, the bus station in Dàhéyàn is reached by heading up the hill in front of the station, taking the first right turn, and continuing along the road for about 200m (656 ft.). The bus station is on your left. To Kashgar (21 hr.), the best train choice is the K887 at 5:40pm. Except in peak season, sleeper tickets are readily purchased in Dàhéyàn. Those heading to Ürümqi are better served by bus. Heading east, sleeper tickets are harder to acquire; proceed through CITS or John's Information Cafe, who both charge a hefty ¥50 ($6) commission.

By Bus The **bus station** is at Lǎochéng Lù 27 (© 0995/852-2325), 90m (300 ft.) west of the central roundabout. Buses for Ürümqi (187km/116 miles; 2½ hr.; ¥25/$3) leave every half hour from 7:30am to 8:30pm.

GETTING AROUND

Turpan is a small town, and nearly everything is within **walking distance** of the center, marked by the intersection of Lǎochéng Lù and Gāochāng Lù. Most sights are outside town and require a **taxi** (¥10/$1.25 within town), **minibus** (¥1/10¢), or **bike** (which can be hired from **John's Information Cafe**).

TOURS & STRATAGEMS

CITS is located on the right as you enter the grounds of the Oasis Hotel at Qīngnián Lù 41 (© 0995/855-3402; fax 0995/852-8688; xjggts@263.net). Staff vary from the competent and friendly to the greedy and mendacious. Open daily from 8am to 9pm.

WHERE TO STAY

Hóng Yuǎn Jiǔdiàn Opened in May 2002, this is one of those rare finds offering three-star facilities at two-star prices. The staff is very helpful; rooms are spotless and well furnished. There are even real potted plants. A lively night market in front of the hotel appears at 7pm, although it resembles a grotty car park during the day. The karaoke-sauna-massage parlor complex is described as "active and full of passion" (read "dodgy"). There is no charming grape garden, but this is the best-value accommodation in town.

Gāochāng Lù, Lǚyóu Wénhuà Guǎngchǎng Xīcè, 838000 © *0995/857-8188. Fax 0995/857-8180. 66 units. From* ¥160 ($20) double; ¥380 ($47) suite. No credit cards. **Amenities:** Restaurant (Muslim); concierge; tour desk; business center; 24-hr. room service; same-day laundry/dry cleaning. In room: A/C, TV.

Oasis Hotel (Lǜzhōu Bīnguǎn) Managed by the same Hong Kong entrepreneur who created the Silk Road Hotel in Dūnhuáng, this expansive three-star hotel is showing signs of age and group-tour syndrome, but it's still the best-run place in town. Uighur-style rooms on the first floor, with low beds and richly colored rugs, are a delight, but are often booked. The dormitory rooms were replaced in 2001 by economy rooms with cubicle-less showers.

Qīngnián Lù 41, 838000. ⓒ *0995/852-2491*. Fax 0995/852-3348. www.the-silk-road.com. 193 units (28 with shower only). ¥140 ($17) economy room; ¥528 ($66) twin; ¥1,088 ($136) suite. AE, DC, MC, V. **Amenities:** 3 restaurants (Western, Chinese homestyle, and Muslim); bike rental; billiards room; concierge; tour desk (CITS); business center; 24-hr. forex; 24-hr. room service; same-day laundry. *In room:* A/C, TV.

WHERE TO DINE

John's Information Cafe WESTERN This cafe offers inexpensive choices (Western and Chinese) and an English menu. It is open all day and well into the night, with Internet hookup available. John's also has branches in Kashgar and Ürümqi, with its own in-house travel agencies catering to independent foreign travelers. *Across the street from the Turpan Guesthouse.* ⓒ *0995/852-4237.*

Shìjì Xǐng UIGHUR Set in grape fields just north of town, with a meltwater stream flowing by, this is the current favorite among the locals for carousing late into the night. Bakri, a tough Uighur entrepreneur from Ürümqi, caters to the fantasies of both locals and foreigners, recruiting handsome waitstaff from Khotan, and dancers from all over Xīnjiāng. Tables are overhung with grape vines; discreet fans keep you cool. Waitstaff shuffle on their knees across the elevated platforms on which many of the tables sit, somehow managing to look elegant. The signature dish, Shìjì Xǐng Yángpái (spicy lamb chops), is worth the expense, and don't miss the chance to cook your own kabobs. For the long-suffering China traveler, this restaurant offers a real treat—dessert! Sweets (tiánshí) are not on the menu, but a platter of shortbread and gingerbread biscuits, many with tart apricot fillings, can be arranged. Try the mulberry wine (sāngshèn jiǔ), which will help if you get hauled onstage. The dance performance (dancers from all over Xīnjiāng) starts at 9:30pm. Xǐnzhàn Dǐngzì Lùkǒu (bus no. 2 or 201 to Xǐnzhàn; walk 150m/ 328 ft. to the northwest side). ⓒ *0995/ 855-1199.* ¥40–¥120 ($5–$15) for a 2-person dinner. No credit cards. Daily 1:30pm and onward.

ÜRÜMQI: THE LAKE
OF HEAVEN

乌鲁木齐

No CITY IN THE WORLD IS MORE distant from the sea than Ürümqi, which lies 2,249km (1,397 miles) away from the nearest ocean. The city's name means "beautiful pastures" in Mongolian, but Ürümqi, capital of the Xīnjiāng Uighur Autonomous Region, is a modern industrial metropolis with a population of 1½ million, and all its beautiful meadows lie well outside the city limits.

Ürümqi is the most Chinese of the Silk Road cities. Nearly 80% of its residents are Hàn Chinese, recent "economic immigrants" who were induced to move west, attracted by the higher wages and better opportunities available on the frontier. However, the Uighur, the nomadic Kazakhs, and other minorities dominate the surrounding lands. Muslim rebels have ruled the city at times, both before and after Ürümqi was declared the capital of China's New Territories (Xīnjiāng) in 1884. At the beginning of the 20th century, the city maintained separate Muslim, Chinese, and Russian quarters. The influence of the three groups remains strong today, but the Hàn Chinese are firmly in control of Ürümqi's administration and factories.

The overriding truth about Ürümqi, however, is that it is an ugly industrial monster set in one of the least appealing spots on the Silk Road—little more than a slag heap on which to heap more slag. On the other hand, the new Chinese workers and investors are planting greenways and replacing slums, making Ürümqi the most modern city on the old Silk Road, a new crossroads for traders from China, Russia, and central Asia. For travelers, the chief attraction of Ürümqi is not trade or industry, of course, but the "beautiful pastures" hinted at in Ürümqi's name, and those places are within reach. In the southern pastures of the Heavenly Mountains and at Heavenly Lake, where the Kazakhs roam on horseback, the alpine beauty of the Silk Road is at its grandest.

The Road to Ürümqi

The highway northwest from Turpan to Ürümqi has no center line and it is under constant repair. The land is flat, bordered on the north by the

Heavenly Mountains (Tiān Shān) and dotted by shrub brush and oil rigs. It took us 4 hours to drive 184km (114 miles). We passed a new wind farm, the propellers still in a light breeze. At the town of **Dàbǎnchéng,** the second largest salt lake in China lies in a basin, its shores ringed by a scum of salt like a dirty bathtub. The road winds up out of the Turpan Depression and crosses a blackened plain into Ürümqi, at an altitude of 900m (3,000 ft.).

Downtown Ürümqi's avenues are tree-lined. Modern construction is underway everywhere. There also are Russian-style buildings left over from the 1950s, their iron roofs painted green and their bright porticoes giving the gray cityscape a splash of color. There are over a hundred mosques, many of them new. Covered Uighur markets throughout the city also break the monotony of modern industrialization.

A touch of Old China is supplied by two parks on the banks of the Ürümqi River, which flows along the western edge of the city. In **Hóng Shān Park** (admission ¥20/$2.50), the nine-story **Pagoda to Suppress Dragons (Zhēnglóng Pagoda)** atop Red Hill (Hóng Shān) towers over Ürümqi. It was erected on the "dragon's head" in 1788 to prevent floods, and the hills became a Buddhist center until war lords burned down the pavilions and temples. The Qīng armies pastured their horses on Red Hill a century ago. Nearby **People's Park (Rénmín Gōngyuán),** on the west bank of the river, has a lake and hall modeled after the Forbidden City in Běijīng, both built in the early 20th century by one of the ruling warlords. This park is popular with locals, particularly on Sunday.

We stopped for lunch at a downtown hotel, the **Liǔguān.** The lobby was chock-full of businesspeople from nearby countries: Russia, Pakistan, India, and Mongolia. Rail links to Kazakhstan have brought a steady stream of traders from central Asia and beyond into Ürümqi since 1992. The Russian presence is strong. Next door to the hotel is a busy Aeroflot office. More than any other city on the Silk Road, Ürümqi has reverted to its glorious past: It is a major crossroads for East–West trade.

Southern Pastures

Every spring and summer, the Kazakhs ride into the **White Poplar Valley** and up into the **Southern Mountains (Nán Shān),** an extension of the Heavenly Mountains. They pack up their families and their tents, called yurts, and make the move on horseback. The attraction is the pastures, where they graze their sheep herds. Farther up the mountain is a 20m (65-ft.) waterfall.

The highway winds up the valley 74km (46 miles) south from Ürümqi. It is a relief to leave the city. The suburbs are filled with shacks and small mosques. Huis (Chinese Muslims), Uighur, and Kazakhs wander through the unpaved lanes, donkey carts in tow. On the southern outskirts of

Ürümqi is the largest chemical factory I have seen in China. Smoke blots the landscape for miles. But the southern meadows are another world entirely. The mountain peaks are steep and green with tall spruces and pines. The river is clear and swift, tumbling by remote mud huts on the hillsides. We slowed for sheep in the road, lovely sheep, black, brown, and white.

At the foot of the waterfall is a **Kazakh village** of huts and yurts, open to tourists. Several of the yurts serve as cafes and souvenir shops. In the late summer, traditional riding games are held on the grassy steppes. Girls court boys in horseback races. Those they catch, they playfully whip.

The **waterfall** is at an elevation of 2,100m (7,000 ft.) in mountains that resemble the Swiss Alps. It plunges through a narrow chute, dropping 27m (90 ft.) into a stony streambed. A rainbow-colored steel arched bridge crosses the stream, but otherwise there is little mark of modernity here. Kazakhs search the mountainsides for ginseng roots.

The Kazakhs descended from the Turkic-speaking Wūsūn nomads who were pushed southward by the Huns into the foothills of the Heavenly Mountains nearly 2,000 years ago. Excellent horsemen, they rode with Genghis Khan and Kublai Khan as the Yuán Dynasty (1271–1368) swept north and east to conquer China. In 1958, the Chinese established pastoral communes in this region of Xīnjiāng, but many Kazakhs continue to follow a nomadic life in the grasslands and mountain valleys surrounding industrial Ürümqi, sustained these days by revenues from tourism and government subsidies. In July, they gather for a 6-day **nadam,** a summer fair with horse racing, wrestling, and competitions involving the sheep and cattle they herd. More than a million Kazakhs live in Xīnjiāng, where they are now outnumbered by Hàn Chinese and Uighur.

By the time we left the southern pastures, a violent downpour was cleansing Ürümqi. The cloudburst had halted hundreds of trucks, buses, and taxis in their tracks, particularly at flooded intersections. The drivers abandoned their vehicles in the middle of the highway. In the darkness, there were no lights to mark the breakdowns. The police passed by, powerless it seems. We ran a dark, wet obstacle course to the hotel in Ürümqi from where even the nearby pagoda on Red Hill had been snuffed out by spring rains.

Heavenly Lake (Tiān Chí)

East of Ürümqi, on the way to Heavenly Lake, two wild camels loitered on the roadside. We pulled off and they scattered. Later, rising into the foothills of the Heavenly Mountains, I saw another camel munching on tree leaves. We entered valleys where sheep and goats blocked the road, where village huts are sometimes made of stone—round huts in the shape

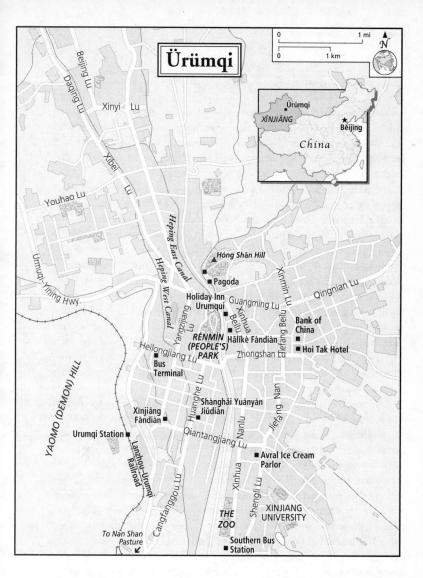

of yurts. Horsemen ride across the hilltops. The countryside belongs to the Kazakh herdsmen.

The road, which did not exist until 1958, winds up the **Stone Gorge (Shí Xiá),** a hillside of white boulders, to a broad, green embankment a quarter of a mile wide. At the end of the embankment, high up under snowy peaks, 121km (75 miles) from Ürümqi and at twice its elevation, **Heavenly Lake** is encased like an alpine jewel. My first glimpse of it was magnificent. No mountain lake is prettier. It reminded me of Canada's Lake Louise, but Heavenly Lake is surrounded by horse trails and yurts. It is 3km (2 miles) long, 1.6km (1 mile) wide, and 90m (300 ft.) deep. Sheep graze on its rocky banks. Tied to a wharf on a green lip of the lake are covered launches and small speedboats for tourists. Several white ponies stand on the shore, their Kazakh masters ready with traditional costumes—red jackets, white lace robes, and gold-trimmed caps—to outfit visitors who want a picture taken on horseback, the divine lake and mountains as a backdrop. In the parking lot, a family was pitching a large yurt, swiftly erecting the wooden accordion that is its skeleton.

According to one legend, 3,000 years ago, the Hàn Wǔdì Emperor was invited by Xī Wáng Mǔ, the immortal Queen Mother of the West, to a banquet at Heavenly Lake. The peach tree of immortality was served. The emperor saved the pits to plant, but Xī Wáng Mǔ told him the soil of China could not sustain them, that fruit appeared but once every 3,000 years.

There are two smaller pools east and west of Heavenly Lake, where Xī Wáng Mǔ washed her feet. She bathed her face in the big lake, which mirrors the solid blue sky and steep mountain peaks that frame it. The two small pools were nearly dry when I visited in the spring. They are located on steep ledges. Christina, my guide, told me that last year one of her colleagues ventured off the path, slipped, and fell to her death beside one pool. Her body had not yet been found. She told me another local legend: Heavenly Lake was created from the tears Xī Wáng Mǔ shed when her lover departed for the East.

It is possible to hike around the lake and into the mountains. **Bogda Peak** is the highest mountain at 5,359m (17,864 ft.), 3,300m (11,000 ft.) above Heavenly Lake. Kazakhs hire out their horses for mountain treks and act as guides; an 8-hour tour costs ¥100 ($13). Higher up, where the snows remain even through summer, there are yurts that take in travelers. I would have loved to make such a trek, but my time was spoken for.

I contented myself with a walk up into a nearby pasture, where a dozen yurts were pitched. A Kazakh woman bid me inside. The inside of her yurt was dazzling. The floor was covered in carpets, woven with wools dyed vibrant blues, reds, and greens. The felt walls were hung with rich embroideries and quilts. A baby was sleeping on a quilt on the floor, mindless of foreign intruders. Children here are named on the second day after birth. The mother leaves the tent and fixes on the first thing that comes into her mind. That becomes her child's name. The mother told me I could stay the night if I wished, but I had to decline. She offered me a chunk of thick baked bread, known as nan, which I saw diligently through, washing it down with Kazakh tea, a brew of mare's milk and the snow lotus that grows in the dragon spruce forests of Heavenly Lake. If I could stay anywhere on the Silk Road it would be here, in the high mountains beside a blue sapphire lake, in the carpeted tents of nomads who roll up their homes as the seasons change and ride across these stream-fed pastures.

PRACTICAL INFORMATION

by Graeme Smith

ORIENTATION & WHEN TO GO

Ürümqi, which the Chinese call Wulumuqi, is the capital of Xīnjiāng Uighur Autonomous Region. It is 3,301km (2,050 miles) from Běijīng, just north of the most northern route of the ancient Silk Road. The city is large and highly industrialized. The majority of the residents are Hàn Chinese who come from other parts of China. Uighur (30%) and Kazakhs (10%) make up the city's largest minorities. Russian businessmen constitute the most noticeable group of visitors. Ürümqi is the largest city in Xīnjiāng and the most modern, although compared to China's other large cities, it is a rugged frontier outpost. Winters are extremely cold. April and October are the most pleasant months to visit, although industrial pollution and dust storms are constant threats.

GETTING THERE

By Plane   Ürümqi's airport, 16km (10 miles) from the city center, has international connections to Moscow, Almaty, Islamabad, Bishkek, Novosibirsk, and Tashkent. Over 30 cities in China are served, including Hong Kong (5 hr.), Shànghǎi (4½ hr.), Běijīng (3½ hr.), Xī'ān (3 hr., 45 min.), and Kashgar (1 hr., 20 min.). Taxis charge about ¥25 ($3) for the 30-minute airport transfer.

By Train   Ürümqi's railway station is located in the southwest corner of town. Nearly all trains heading east and west originate here. Tickets may be purchased at the station from a building to the right and behind the main entrance, but only for the same day. To purchase sleeper tickets, either proceed through your hotel and pay around ¥30 ($3.60) commission, or line up with the masses at the railway ticket office (© **0991/282-8368**) at Jiànshè Lù 3, in the courtyard of the Láiyuǎn Bīnguǎn. There are direct express trains to Běijīng (T70; 43 hr.) at 11:44am, and to Shànghǎi (T54; 51 hr.) at 10:07am, passing through Dūnhuáng, Turfan; and Xī'ān. There is a speedy connection with Dūnhuáng (K890; 12 hr.) at 9:10pm and a sluggish train for Chéngdū (1014; 47 hr.) at 3:38pm.

By Bus   The **Southern Bus Station** (© **0991/286-6635**) has regular buses for Turpan (187km/116 miles; 2½ hr.; ¥25/$3) beginning at 8:20am.

TOURS & STRATAGEMS

Visitor Information   CITS (© **0991/282-6719**; fax 0991/284-6920; www.xinjiang tour.com) has destroyed the fourth and fifth floors of the Holiday Inn, and the physical surroundings point to the level of service you can expect. Unfortunately, other tour operators are equally rapacious, and you are better off organizing everything yourself.

WHERE TO STAY

Hoi Tak Hotel (Hǎidé Jiǔdiàn)
Unquestionably the best-appointed hotel in Ürümqi, the Hoi Tak benefits from aggressive Hong Kong management, rigorous staff training, and plenty of capital from its parent company in Hong Kong for renovations. The 36-story building is the largest in town, and on the rare days when the pollution haze clears, a magnificent view of the Tiān Shān range can be enjoyed. The Uighur concierge, Terry, may be the most effective man in Xīnjiāng—there's nothing he can't arrange! Unfortunately, service can be uneven, and they still have a way to go before they reach the standards set by the Holiday Inn. Discounts of up to 50% can almost always be obtained on the spot.
Dōngfēng Lù 1, 830002. © *0991/232-2828. Fax 0991/232-1818. www.hoitak. com. 318 units. ¥1,400–¥1,600 ($175–$200) twin/double; from ¥2,080 ($260) and way up for suites. 15% service charge. AE, DC, MC, V.* **Amenities:** 3 restaurants (Chinese homestyle, Muslim, Western); cafe; bar; nightclub; large indoor pool; health club; 8-lane bowling alley; billiards and table tennis rooms; concierge; tour desk; courtesy car; business center; 24-hr. forex; salon; 24-hr. room service; in-room massage; same-day dry cleaning/laundry. *In room:* A/C, satellite TV, Internet access (broadband), minibar, fridge, hair dryer, safe.

Holiday Inn Ürümqi (Jiàrì Dàjiǔdiàn)
Despite facing increasing competition from the newer hotels that are popping up all over Ürümqi, the aging Holiday Inn has something no amount of shiny marble or glass can compete with—brilliantly trained staff. Strapped for cash in recent years, they are set to open a new 57-story wing in 2003, add a swimming pool and more restaurants, and fully refurbish rooms in the old wing, which have an undeniably 1980s feel to them.
Xīnhuá Běi Lù 168, 830002. © *0991/281-8788. Fax 0991/281-7422. www. holiday-inn.com/hotels/urcch. 360 units. ¥1,000–¥1,100 ($125–$137) double; ¥1,100–¥1,200 ($137–$150) twin; from ¥1,700 ($212) and way up for suites. 15% service charge. AE, DC, MC, V.* **Amenities:** 3 restaurants (Chinese homestyle, Muslim, Western); bar; nightclub; health club; billiards room; concierge; tour desk (CITS); courtesy car; business center; 24-hr. forex; salon; 24-hr. room service; in-room massage; same-day dry cleaning/laundry. *In room:* A/C, satellite TV, dataport, minibar, fridge, hair dryer, safe.

Xīnjiāng Fàndiàn The concrete corridors and no-frills dormitory rooms of this two-star monolith will be instantly familiar to anyone who has studied in the PRC. However, service is very friendly, and it's close to the railway station. There's also a rare treat for those aching limbs—blind massage (¥40/$5 per hr.). Once one of the most pleasant features of travel in China, blind massage (massages given by blind people) is now hard to find as the more lucrative "keep fit massage" takes over.
Cháng Jiāng Lù 107, 830006. © *0991/585-2511, ext. 2000. Fax 0991/581-1354. 305 units (67 with shower; the rest have a walk down the hall to the communal shower). ¥168 ($21) twin; ¥488–¥888 ($61–$111) suite; ¥20–¥30 ($2.50–$3.70) dorm bed. No credit cards.* **Amenities:** 2 restaurants (Chinese homestyle and Muslim); tour desk; business center; 24-hr. room service; massage; same-day dry cleaning/laundry. *In room:* A/C, TV.

WHERE TO DINE

Avral Ice Cream Parlor (Ā'yóulālī Xiān Niúnǎi Bīngqílíngdiàn) UIGHUR Deep in the heart of what locals jokingly call "the autonomous region" (as the rest of the city is Hàn), is an ice creamery that is exactly like ice creameries once were before God invented the chain store. Rather than hundreds of different flavors with cookies and other nonsense, there's only one (at ¥3/35¢ per bowl). If you don't like pistachio, you're out of luck. If you do, prepare for ecstasy. Grandfathers proudly treat their granddaughters, young lovers slowly and nervously share a bowl, and everyone sits elbow-to-elbow—no waiting around for a table here. Even if you don't like ice cream, this is a magical experience. *Shèng Lù 193. Bus no. 101 to Èrdàoqiáo; continue south under the overpass, keeping to the west side.*

Hālīkè Fàndiàn UIGHHUR Hidden in a small alley behind the Holiday Inn, you'll find simple Uighur fare in simple surroundings, providing a taste of what is to come in Xīnjiāng. The serving of mixed noodles *(bàn miàn)* is big enough to feed two, while the kabobs are more meat than fat, a novelty in Ürümqi. *② 0991/280-2687. Less than ¥30 ($3.70) for a 2-person meal. Daily 8am–11:30pm.*

Shànghǎi Yuányuàn Jiǔdiàn SHÀNGHǍI After the wilds of Xīnjiāng, the subtle flavors and genuinely friendly service of this unlikely restaurant may be just what you need. Astonishingly, there is a well-translated menu, which is a relief, as Shànghǎi cuisine has a weakness for euphemistic and flowery names. Those with few cholesterol concerns should try the *yuányuàn hóngshāo ròu* (stir-fried pork). The vegetarian choices are extensive. The only jarring note is the TV blaring in the corner, which may provide diversion for awkward couples but is annoying to others. *Huánghé Lù 83. ② 0991/ 583-0777. Reservations recommended. ¥60–¥140 ($7.50–$17) for a 2-person meal. No credit cards. Daily 12:30pm– 12.30am.*

KASHGAR: THE GATE
TO CENTRAL ASIA

喀什

THE OASIS OF KASHGAR IS LOCATED
at a great junction in the Silk Road. Heading east, traders swapped horses
and yaks for camels to cross the vast deserts of China. Heading west, they
readied their pack animals to brave the high mountain passes into central
Asia. From Kashgar, the camel caravans trekked eastward from oasis to oasis
to reach the ancient capital of China, while teams of packhorses trudged
westward through India and Persia to Rome. Marco Polo heralded Kashgar
in the 13th century as the "starting point from which many merchants set
out to market their wares to the world."

The westernmost city in China, Kashgar is the place no one traveling the
Silk Road today should miss, if only to see its Sunday market, said by some
to be the largest on Earth. The oasis is overwhelmingly Islamic. More than
90% of its residents are Uighur. The streets are crammed with mud-brick
houses, sidewalk bazaars, and mosques. There are more horse carts than
cars. Chairman Máo's statue presides over People's Park, but Kashgar is a
city from another time and place, a medieval village where women shop the
streets covered in long brown veils.

Kashgar first came under Chinese sovereignty during the Hàn Dynasty
in the 1st century A.D. Under Táng rule, Chinese troops fortified the oasis,
but Tibetans and later Turkish tribes often held sway. Kashgar was just too
remote for China to hold tightly. From the 16th through the 19th centuries, various Islamic leaders ruled the Kashgari kingdom, with the
Chinese mounting periodic assaults to regain control over the region. In
the 1930s, an Islamic movement based in Kashgar declared the formation
of the Republic of Eastern Turkestan, but the city fell again to the Chinese
(assisted by Russian troops from Ürümqi) in 1933. It was not until the
Communists established the People's Republic of China in 1949 that
Kashgar came firmly into Chinese hands. Before that, Kashgar was a pawn
in the "Great Game" played by other major powers in the region, including Britain, which maintained a consulate there, and Russia, whose
embassy, opened in 1882, is now the Sèmǎn Hotel—where I, like many a
modern traveler, began my stay in Kashgar.

Abakh Hoja Tomb (Xiāngfēi Mù)

A dust storm was whipping across the airstrip at Kashgar as my flight from Ürümqi neared it. My plane was an old Russian prop jet, owned by Air Volga, with a small notice on the fuselage stating that it had been rented by Xīnjiāng Air. The cabin was like the inside of a ruined bus. The seats were the most uncomfortable in the sky, but the bag of green raisins handed out for a snack was delicious. The dust thickened as we descended over Kashgar. The plane hit the ground sharply.

I was the first to complete the walk across the tarmac to the waiting lounge. The Japanese tourists lingered, snapping photos of each other disembarking through the blowing dust. Sadik, a local guide, met me. At the **Sèmǎn Hotel,** the century-old former Russian compound, I was also met by dancing girls in Uighur gowns and a band of horns and pipes. The doorman handed me a steaming face towel. It was the most gracious entrance I'd made in China—if this was China. It looked more like eastern Turkey, and I'd yet to see a single Chinese face.

The first place on the tourist route was the holiest site in the entire province of Xīnjiāng, the Abakh Hoja Tomb, in the northeast suburbs of the oasis. This is more than just a tomb: It is a monumental hall, finished in 1640, with a large dome of dazzling glazed green tiles. The **Tomb Hall** reminded me of a small Taj Mahal. Inside, the entire tiled floor is covered in 58 rounded sarcophagi, also beautifully tiled, which contain the remains of five generations of the Islamic prophet and Kashgar ruler Abakh Hoja, who died in 1639. Two of the tombs under the domed ceiling are draped in green: that of Abakh Hoja and the one reputed to contain the remains of his granddaughter, Iparhan, who is known to Chinese history as Xiāng Fēi, the Fragrant Concubine.

Xiāng Fēi was captured by the Qīng army in the mid–18th century and sent from Kashgar all the way across China to the Forbidden City in Běijīng. There she was presented to the Qiánlóng Emperor. For the next 25 years, she lived in the capital, serving the emperor as his "Fragrant Concubine"; it was said that her natural scent was as sweet as the bloom of a flower. She wept for her desert home and rejected the emperor's advances. Obsessed with winning her affections, he built her a Turkish bath and a tower turned toward Kashgar, but she did not give in. Finally, the emperor's mother, fearing that the Fragrant Concubine would murder her son or become the rallying point for a palace coup, ordered Xiāng Fēi to kill herself with her own bare hands in 1761. The coffin of the Fragrant Concubine was wheeled back to Kashgar, in a journey that consumed 3 years.

The story of the Fragrant Concubine is perhaps more fiction than fact, but Chinese and Uighur alike insist on its veracity. The cart that supposedly carried her back over the Silk Road stands near the railing inside the Tomb Hall,

although it is clearly too new and too undamaged to be anything but a reproduction. I have read reports that the Fragrant Concubine's remains are
housed in the Eastern Qīng Tombs in Héběi Province, but, of course, here is
the proper location for her tomb, the perfect ending to her story.

To the right of the Tomb Hall is a large walled graveyard with thousands
more of the coffin-shaped tombs. These are not tiled; they are the color of
sand. Some are pierced so that the soul can escape to travel. A **Teaching
Hall** and a **Prayer Hall** are also open to view at Abakh Hoja.

The grounds of the complex are entered through a magnificent turreted
square gate three stories tall, faced in swirling blue tiles. Abakh Hoja Tomb
is open daily from 8am to 5:30pm; admission is ¥15 ($1.90). There's also
a new ¥2 (25¢) surcharge for those wishing to take pictures. As we explored
the area, my guide just shook his head. He was quite upset. The government was nearing the end of a 3-year project to restore and replace the tile-
work on the main Tomb Hall, and he said they were going about it all
wrong. They should have left it alone, he felt, expressing the common feeling here among the Uighur majority that the Chinese Hàn administrators
don't have the slightest idea how to run things.

Sunday Market

Every cart and camel on the Silk Road seems to pour into Kashgar on
Sunday for one of the largest open-air markets/bazaars in Asia. It's open
daily, but Sundays it is in full swing and the horse traders come into town.
The Uighur call it the **Sunday Bazaar (Yekshenba Bazaar),** and the
Chinese, although not many are in attendance, call it **Western Central
Asia Market (Zhōngxīyà Shìchǎng).** By any name, it has no equal in
China. By dawn, the donkey carts start arriving from the desert and the
mountains, converging on Āzīláitī Lù on the east side of the Tuman River.
The larger carts and trucks carry upward of 20 people standing on their
belongings. Herds of sheep, goats, cows, and horses make their way
through the city to separate trading compounds. The market radiates out
for a dozen blocks and is packed with Muslim farmers, merchants, and
traders, as well as whatever foreign tourists and business travelers happen to
be in town. The crowds are immense. I've seen estimates ranging from
50,000 to 150,000 people, all converging at the Sunday Bazaar.

I entered the market from the east, shouldering my way past the carts
and animals, past large lumberyards and lovely Uighur homes with ornate
columned balconies and shuttered windows lining the upper floors.
Sidewalk merchants line the highway for a half mile down to the river.
There are straw mats unrolled on the dusty shoulder of the street next to
tables of pots and pans pounded out of sheet metal and tin. There are

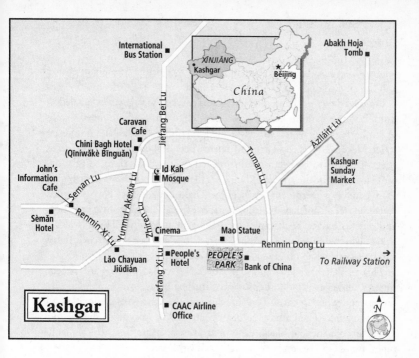

Kashgar

knives and jeweled scimitars, high sheepskin boots and long scarves, and table after table of fresh oasis melons and bagel-shaped breads. There are woven carpets, embroideries, tapestries, and clothing such as the people themselves wear: hats, scarves, veils, jackets, coats, dresses, all dyed in rainbow colors in an endless arabesque of geometric and floral patterns. Several roadside alcoves are filled with hundreds of straw brooms, hand-woven and tied. There are shoemakers stitching without machines, and barbers in belted black tunics and black wool caps trimmed in white fur at work in the shade of white umbrellas, their customers bolt-upright on plain wooden chairs waiting nervously for a close shave.

In the formal market grounds by the river, corrals hold livestock. Sheep, horses, cattle, and donkeys have their own yards. Within each arena, families or clans rope off their animals from those of competitors. Animals and people crowd together, bartering and jostling and braying and neighing, while on the periphery of these delightfully pungent pens, vendors serve up hot noodles, flatbreads, goat soups, milky teas, jars of yogurt, and ice cream. The ice cream is served on sticks or in bowls, kept chilled by enormous blocks of ice wrapped in cloth and delivered by pushcarts to the stands.

Surrounding the animal yards are awnings, tents, and long alleyway arcades. Wooden baby cradles with lathe-turned fences, the knobs painted glossy reds, greens, and blacks, occupy one cobblestoned lane. Down another, red-draped stalls sell bolts of dyed silk and cotton. Another arcade sells nothing but hats—the hats of all the tribes of the Silk Road, cotton and fur, peaked and flat, white and sequined.

On the fringes of the market are streets devoted to vegetables, hauled in from the farms in gunny sacks; streets devoted to debarked, unmilled shanks of lumber, shining white; streets devoted to saddles, bridles, and harnesses; streets devoted to sheepskins and felt carpets draped over donkey carts; streets devoted to baskets woven from red twigs; streets devoted to songbirds in cages. In the shadow of a new gallery of empty shops built by the Hàn Chinese government—which the Uighur merchants have shunned since the day it opened—there is a street of used clothing, of worn shoes and patched coats, of discards that belong in the dump. There is also a square where dog fights were once held and where occasional cock fights still break out when officials are looking the other way.

This market has met in Kashgar for 1,500 years. Walking the streets, squares, and alley arcades, I constantly brushed up against donkeys, sheep, horses, and wooden carts. The sun through the dust gives the market an ancient patina. There are con men squatting low, playing a shell game. There are old men in black, experts in horseflesh, puffing on long, thin pipes. Across the river, above the market swirl, I could see the old town of Kashgar on a hillside, its square huts and houses packed together like crates, a city of unpainted mud and brick, the single color of desert sand, with no hint of the modern world east of the desert or west of the mountain snows.

The Largest Mosque in China

The busiest, and some say the biggest, mosque in China, **Id Kah Mosque (Àití Gǎ'ěr Qīngzhēn Sì)** occupies the central square of Kashgar, where it has stood since 1442. On Friday afternoon, upwards of 20,000 men pack the courtyards and prayer hall inside. My guide, Sadik, took me in on a Sunday. The grounds were filled with worshippers even then, old men and young dressed in long, striped cotton coats *(chapans)* and high leather boots. The prayer hall, holding up to 5,000, is plainly decorated, with 140 carved wooden columns. The carpets on the floor are a gift from Iran. The Iman leads prayers from a simple chair and microphone. Sadik told me there is a mosque for every 20 households in Kashgar, but Id Kah is the grandest. The women and children wait outside the large rectangular yellow-tiled gate with its massive blue doors. Two tall minarets, banded in decorative blue and red tiles, flank the wide facade, shielding the large dome of the prayer hall inside.

The streets running east and west from the mosque constitute a **permanent bazaar** that is in some ways more interesting than the Sunday Market. Shops on Zhīrén Street (to the west) specialize in a variety of goods: skullcaps, fur-trimmed hats, prayer caps, and even the simple Máo caps once favored by Chinese workers; large tin dowry chests, ornately decorated; pots and pans hammered into shape on the street in front of tiny factories. There are even musical instrument shops with miniature two- and five-stringed Uighur guitars (*dutahs* and *rawupus*) hanging above the counters. These small instruments (built of inlaid woods, including apricot) are for decoration, but behind the counter there is often a musician playing the real thing.

Most fascinating are the narrow **jewelry shops.** Gold is the metal of choice in Kashgar. I was told that you can buy an ounce for less than $15 here. I was also surprised to find that many of the jewelers are children. They work at benches inside on raised platforms behind the display counters, shaping gold into pendants, pins, rings, and necklaces.

East of Id Kah Mosque are streets devoted to the sale of **carpets:** felts of rolled wool; rough hand-tied carpets with dyed geometric designs; and sometimes Kashgar kilims, the handiwork of nomads. Many of the carpet outlets are located inside wooden-shuttered shophouses, their front courtyards shaded by second-story balconies supported by finely turned pillars.

South of the mosque, on Jiěfàng Běi Lù, there are larger stores and offices, but even here the street looks more like those of Islamabad than Běijīng. On the corner of Jiěfàng and Rénmín streets, a former cinema, built in 1954, its second-floor shuttered windows and small balconies typical of Uighur architecture, has a Chinese red star emblazoned on its peak. East down Rénmín Dōng Lù is Kashgar's **People's Park (Rénmín Gōngyuán),** a fixture in every Chinese city. An 18m (59-ft.) bone-white statue of Chairman Máo, looking south, faces the park, which is little more than an open, scrubby field. Elsewhere in China, such statues have often come down during the years of economic reform, but I have a feeling Máo is here to stay in Kashgar, where the Uighur feel very much under the thumb of the Hàn Chinese.

I waited for dusk to fall over Kashgar at an outdoor table under a large canvas awning at **John's Information Cafe,** a favorite hangout of foreign backpackers. The cafe is situated a short walk from the compounds of the former British and Russian consulates, now the main hotels of Kashgar. Fierce winds began to shake the awning, and desert sands swept across the city. Uighur women drew their brown veils tight around the necks and hastened home from the bazaars. John's Cafe advertises itself in a sign in English reading A LITTLE BIT OF HOME, but it's difficult to imagine being farther from home than Kashgar, sipping a soda at the end of the Silk Road.

PRACTICAL INFORMATION

by Graeme Smith

ORIENTATION & WHEN TO GO

Kashgar, with a population of 130,000, is an oasis in far western Xīnjiāng Province, more than 3,864km (2,400 miles) inland from Běijīng. The vast Taklamakan Desert stretches eastward into China, and the snowcapped Pamir Mountains form a wall to the west. The Karakoram Highway leads to Pakistan (483km/300 miles), and there are long, difficult overland routes from here to India and Tibet. Ürümqi is over 966km (600 miles) to the northeast. April and October are the most pleasant months to visit, although the middle of summer, when it becomes increasingly hot, is high tourist season.

GETTING THERE

By Plane **CAAC** is located at Jiěfàng Nán Lù 95 (© **0998/282-2113**). In security-conscious Kashgar, there is no ticket delivery service. Do your best not to resemble a separatist, bring your passport, and buy your ticket on the spot. There are two flights daily to Ürümqi (1½ hr.), and onward flights to most parts of China can also be booked. Substantial discounts can be obtained by booking up to 15 days in advance. A taxi to the airport is ¥10 ($1.20), or you can take bus no. 2 from just west of the Peoples' Square.

By Train The railway station is a 15- to 20-minute drive southeast of town. Take a taxi (¥10/$1.20) or bus no. 28 (the People's Square stop) immediately east of the Peoples' Park. Unfortunately, the station only sells tickets for same-day travel and is open from 8:30am to 6pm, so if you want a sleeper ticket, proceed through a travel agency. Tickets can be purchased up to 5 days in advance. The K888 leaves at 5:50pm, bound for Turpan (21 hr.) and Ürümqi (23 hr.).

By Bus Most buses leave from the **International Bus Station (Guójì Qìchēzhàn)** at Jīcháng Lù 29 (© **0998/ 282-2912**, ext. 8003). Sixteen sleeper buses make the 1,470km (911-mile) journey to Ürümqi daily between 10am and 9pm; you can opt for fast, comfortable buses (24 hr.) or cheaper, slow buses (30 hr.).

TOURS & STRATAGEMS

Kashgar, like all the cities of China, is officially on Běijīng time, despite the fact that it should be several time zones west of the capital. Local Kashgar time is 2 hours earlier. Thus, don't expect anything to open until about 10:30am. Breakfast usually begins at about 9:30am, lunch at 1:30pm, and dinner at 7:30pm.

While here, you should dress in a manner appropriate to a Muslim society. That is, cover the body—no shorts, tank tops, and other fashions that might be considered immodest. Arms and legs should be fully covered when entering mosques, with shoes removed when entering prayer halls.

Tours **CITS** is located to the right of the entrance to the Chini Bagh Hotel, on the second floor to the right of the Caravan Cafe. The sales manager, Wú Zuǒjiāng, is effective and speaks excellent English; he can arrange overpriced 1- or 2-day tours for those short on time (© **0998/283-2875**; fax 0998/282-7227; www.caravantours.net). More reliable information may be obtained from the **Caravan Cafe** (©/fax **0998/284-2196**; www.caravancafe.com) or from **John's Information Cafe** (©/fax **0998/255-1186**; johncafe@hotmail.com). The former serves better coffee. **Bīngshān Lǚxíngshè** (© **0998/221-9966**; fax 0998/282-2567; rmfd-ks@mail.xj.cninfo.net), in the foyer of the Peoples' Hotel, is competent and charges the lowest commission for train tickets.

WHERE TO STAY

Chini Bagh Hotel (Qīníwǎkè Bīnguǎn) This two-star hotel is housed on the grounds of the former British consulate. Beds in the new wing are among the most comfortable in town. Currently, only British diplomats are allowed to stay in the old consulate, tucked away at the back of the hotel, but there are plans to redevelop it, hopefully more sympathetically than the rest of the site. Cozy triple rooms in the weathered Jīngyuàn building are excellent value for budget travelers. Discounts of 30% on standard rooms can be easily obtained.

Sèmǎn Lù 144, 844000. © *0998/282-2103. Fax 0998/284-2299. 337 units (shower only). From ¥280 ($35) twin/double; from ¥680 ($85) suite; ¥120 ($15) triple without bathroom. Breakfast included. No credit cards.* **Amenities:** 3 restaurants (Chinese homestyle and Muslim); concierge; tour desk (CTS); 2 business centers; forex counter (8am–midnight); 24-hr. room service; same-day laundry/dry cleaning. *In room:* A/C, TV.

Sèmǎn Hotel (Sèmǎn Bīnguǎn) Set on the grounds of the former Russian Consulate, this huge two-star hotel claims to be "one of the top 10 hotels in the world." Whoever made this statement needs to get out more; in reality, this is a poorly run hotel gradually falling apart from lack of investment. However, standard rooms and suites in the beautifully decorated Russian consulate (with high ceilings and dramatic oil paintings) can be bargained down to ¥300 ($37) and ¥400 ($50) respectively, a steal for soaking up some "Great Game" ambience. The newest building (no. 3) is decorated with sumptuous rugs but was completed in a hurry—the finishing, particularly in the bathrooms, is appalling. The Jīntái "entertainment complex" should be avoided, as should the dorms, which are filthy and overcrowded. The best-value beds are in building no. 3 across the road, which has its own reception. Staff cheerily tell Chinese visitors that the marked prices are just for foreigners. Keep this in mind when bargaining.

Sèmǎn Lù 337, 844000. © *0998/255-2861. Fax 0998/255-2861. 300 units, 284 with bathroom. From ¥200 ($25) twin; ¥15 ($1.90) dorm bed. No credit cards.* **Amenities:** 4 restaurants (Chinese homestyle and Muslim); game room; concierge; tour desk (CYTS); business center; 24-hr. room service; same-day laundry/dry cleaning. *In room:* A/C, TV.

WHERE TO DINE

Caravan Cafe (Kǎiruì Kāfēi) WESTERN After some time in Xīnjiāng, the caffeine-deprived may dream of the smell of freshly ground coffee, of lattes with perfectly formed froth, perhaps accompanied by a cinnamon roll and a bowl of muesli with yogurt, served by handsome and courteous waitstaff. For-tunately, this is no mirage—the coffee, the food, and the service are 100% real and 100% Western. Managed by three Americans with a passion for central Asia, and staffed by friendly English-speaking Uighur, the Caravan Cafe can also arrange top-of-the-line adventure travel to the Taklamakan Desert, Shipton's Arch, and the mighty Mount Mustag. If you want to know what's going on in town, this should be your first point of call. *Sèmǎn Lù 120.* ✆ ***0998/284-2196.*** *¥60–¥100 ($7.50–$12) for a 2-person meal. Daily 9am–11:30pm. Closed Jan to mid April.*

Lǎo Chayuan Jiǔdiàn UIGHUR When the locals treat themselves, they make for this eatery. Service can be frosty and the pseudo-Arabian decor is tacky, but let the food take center stage. All dishes are well presented, often with fancy garnishes, something you don't often see in southern Xīnjiāng. For starters, try *bàn sān sī,* a finely sliced salad of capsicum, onion, carrot, cucumber, and noodles; or the old favorite, roast peanuts. Recommended main courses are a tender beef stir-fry *(chǎokǎoròu);* dry-fried spring chicken *(gānbiān tóngzǐjī);* and field mushrooms steamed with bok choy, ginger, and garlic *(bāchǔ mogu),* although their slippery texture won't be to everyone's taste. *Rénmín Xī Lù 251.* ✆ ***0998/282-4467.*** *¥70–¥150 ($8.70–$19) for a 2-person meal. No credit cards. Daily 10am–1:30am.*

MOUNTAIN CHINA: PINNACLES & SACRED PEAKS

T HE CHINESE, PERHAPS MORE THAN
any other people, have long been enraptured by mountain peaks. For over
2,000 years they conducted pilgrimages to sacred summits, in particular to
the Five Sacred Mountains staked out by the native Daoist priests and to
the Four Famous Peaks established later by the Buddhists. People walked
to the tops of these great mountains by the thousands, even by the hundreds of thousands. Emperors joined them, performing imperial rites in the
temples that lined the slopes. At the summits, pilgrims knelt before the
high altars of the mountain gods and prayed. "Thousands of men and
women who wish for a good harvest, health, heirs, or longevity ascend lofty
mountains," writes an 18th-century man of letters, "climbing like monkeys
and following each other like ants."

China's emperors often ascended the sacred peaks to pray for an end to
a devastating drought. In the past, most Chinese seemed to believe that certain mountains were divine beings with considerable powers. These peaks
were treated as massive stone gods who could be swayed by sacrifice or
prayer. They linked Heaven and Earth and gathered the clouds unto their
heights to deliver timely rains to parched lands.

These nine sacred summits still exist in China, although the great pilgrimages came to a standstill by the early 20th century. The Sacred Five and
the Famous Four once formed the cosmic compasses of Old China. Each
mountain anchored one of the Four Directions—north, south, east, and
west—to which the Daoists added a mountain in the center. Today, despite
decades of neglect and destruction, these peaks retain dozens of venerable
temples, miles of stone stairs for modern pilgrims (mostly Chinese sightseers) to ascend, and summits with the most spectacular views in the
Middle Kingdom.

It is at these nine mountains that Old China still exists within New China.
They have always been, for me, the most fascinating sites in the Middle
Kingdom, combining history, religion, and natural grandeur. On the other
hand, these remote peaks at the four corners of the Middle Kingdom are

modernizing. Most have cable cars in place to take the drudgery (along with the adventure and tradition) out of mountain pilgrimage. A few have decent hotels in nearby villages. Vendors line the mountain stairs, selling snacks and plastic souvenirs. Temples are being renovated rather than razed.

Altogether, the sacred mountains, fusing past and present, present some of the most exhilarating experiences in all of China. But to make your own sightseeing pilgrimage to these peaks is still not an easy undertaking. Some require that you rough it with a long bus or train ride from a major city. The climb to the summit can be arduous, often requiring a 4- or 5-hour ascent on steep stairways and narrow paths. Accommodations and food services are often crude. Yet the undertaking produces unforgettable moments, unlike any others in China.

Mountain (Shān)	Direction	Religion	Elevation	Province
Éméi Shān	West	Buddhist	10,095 ft	Sìchuān
Héng Shān	North	Daoist	6,617 ft	Shānxī
Héng Shān	South	Daoist	4,232 ft	Húnán
Huà Shān	West	Daoist	6,552 ft	Shǎnxī
Jiǔhuá Shān	South	Buddhist	4,340 ft	Ānhuī
Pǔtuó Shān	East	Buddhist	932 ft	Zhèjiali]ng
Sōng Shān	Center	Daoist	4,900 ft	Hénán
Tài Shān	East	Daoist	5,069 ft	Shāndōng
Wǔtái Shān	North	Buddhist	10,003 ft	Shānxī

Huà Shān is the most stunning of the nine, Tài Shān the most interesting and venerated. To these ancient peaks I have added three other spots: **Huáng Shān,** simply the single most beautiful mountain in China; **Wǔlíngyuán,** also known as Zhāngjiā Jiè, the remote Yellowstone Park of China; and **Lú Shān,** a delightful mountain retreat, for centuries a getaway for China's rich and famous.

WHAT TO READ

Edwin Bernbaum. *Sacred Mountains of the World.* San Francisco: Sierra Club Books, 1990.

William Geil. *The Sacred 5 of China.* Boston: Houghton Mifflin, 1926.

Hedda Morrison. *Travels of a Photographer in China, 1933–1946.* Hong Kong: Oxford University Press, 1987.

Mary Augusta Mullikin and Anna M. Hotchkis. *The Nine Sacred Mountains of China: An Illustrated Record of Pilgrimages Made in the Years 1935–1936.* Hong Kong: Vetch and Lee, 1973.

Susan Naquin and Chun-fang Yǔ, editors. *Pilgrims and Sacred Sites in China.* Berkeley: University of California Press, 1992.

HUÁNG SHĀN: THE SUMMIT OF BEAUTY

黄山

Huáng Shān (Yellow Mountain) is the supreme example of Chinese mountain scenery and is a prime model for classic landscape paintings, as the poets and painters of Old China amply testify. From the Táng Dynasty (618–907) to the Qīng (1644–1911), Huáng Shān was celebrated in no fewer than 20,000 poems. Lǐ Bái, the Táng's great poet, compared the cluster of peaks at Huáng Shān to a golden hibiscus. Twelve centuries later, the modern poet Guō Mòruò echoed that sentiment, naming Huáng Shān's vistas "the most spectacular under Heaven."

Skeptical of this high-flown hyperbole, I was eager to see the mountain and to draw my own comparisons. My opportunity came more by chance than design. I was descending a nearby mountain when I was befriended by four young lads from Wǔhàn who were on their way the very next morning for a whirlwind tour of the fabled Yellow Mountain. I couldn't help but tag along. Although I could see the Huáng Shān range from where we set out at dawn, the bus required 6 bone-rattling hours to reach it. On the way, we were stopped cold by a broad placid lake, where the bus had to board a ferry.

It was just after noon by the time we reached the village of Tāngkǒu, at the southern tip of the park. A minibus transported us another hour up the eastern flanks of Huáng Shān to Yúngǔ Temple. From there, a cable car ferried visitors to the peak in 8 minutes (today there are two more cable cars), but my four comrades were not about to waste money on a route they could climb for free. There was plenty of time, they said, to reach the summit via the stone staircase cut into the mountain, a mere 3-hour hike— 8km (5 miles) up, with a mere 20,000 stairs between us and the final peak.

Seeing Is Believing

Huáng Shān, according to tradition, consists of 72 peaks. In fact, there are many more. At least 77 of these stone pillars, formed 100 million years ago, exceed 960m (3,200 ft.) in elevation, the base of the mountain lying at

600m (2,000 ft.). It's a fierce ascent. The highest point, Lotus Flower Peak, rises to 1,835m (6,115 ft.). The network of footpaths, mostly stone steps, makes a circuit exceeding 50km (30 miles). The eastern path to the summit is 8km (5 miles), if no detours up and down individual pinnacles are taken. The western route, by which we descended, is longer and more scenic; it runs for 14km (9 miles), requiring 6 hours to complete.

The cable car is strung parallel to the eastern route, which rises up a deep declivity forested with granite pillars. I was exhausted after the first 20 minutes of the climb, but there was no choice but to keep walking. More than one emperor has ascended Huáng Shān by this same route, albeit in the comfort of a sedan chair propelled on the shoulders of powerful runners. Such chairs are still for hire, at about $100 for the round-trip.

So far, I could see that the peaks of Huáng Shān are towering and exquisite, indeed, granite rivals of the famous limestone karst pillars of Guìlín; but I was like a dead man, hauling my own corpse up an endless flight of stairs. It wasn't until we were almost at the central summit, Běihǎi Peak, that I found a new resource of strength and began to appreciate the grandeur. We struck out on a northern detour to **Seeing Is Believing Peak (Shìxìn Fēng).** This 1,642m (5,472-ft.) promontory has its own wicked set of steep stairs. At the top, I was in a cluster of jagged rock spires. Mist was blowing in and out of the twisted pinnacles. At times, I had glimpses of what's below: pine forests, cascading streams, narrow gorges. There's a legend of an ancient skeptic who denied Huáng Shān's unique beauty until he reached this viewpoint. I seemed to be following in his footsteps. Any doubts I had about the Yellow Mountain's claim to the most dramatic mountain scenery in China were erased here.

Seeing Is Believing Peak is connected by a bridge of stone, **Dùxiān Qiáo,** known as the Bridge to Heaven. By the bridge stands one of Huáng Shān's celebrated pines, **Dùxiān Sōng,** which appears to be bowing to welcome travelers. Many of these bare, swirling granite pinnacles have a pine tree or two sprouting from their joints, pointing like green umbrellas not only vertically but horizontally into misty space. The Huáng Shān pine grows in poor soil and on rocky crags. Its roots secrete an acid that erodes rock, allowing roots to burrow into crevices for nutrients and moisture. The roots are often several times the length of the trunks, enabling the pines to withstand fierce mountain gales. Several of these sturdy mountain pines are believed to be over a thousand years old. Nevertheless, on my most recent visit to Huáng Shān, locals told me that one of the immortal pines capping a crag had been obliterated by a storm; it is said to have been replaced by unknown hands with a plastic stand-in.

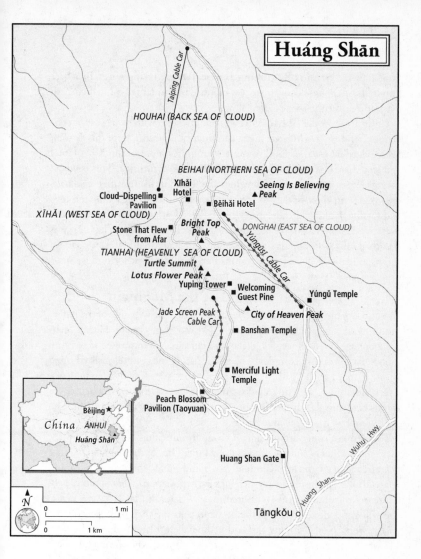

Sea of Clouds

The twin summits, **Běihǎi** and **Xīhǎi**—the Northern Sea of Clouds and the Western Sea of Clouds—are the prime gathering points for watching sunrise and sunset. I was hoping to stay the night at Běihǎi, in a modern hotel, and wake early to join the crowds at sunrise. Běihǎi has some of the mountain's most spectacular scenery. To the east, on the tapered summit of a peak named **Flower Growing Out of a Writing Brush (Chǔbǐ Shēnghuā),** a gnarled pine tree sprouts heavenward like the tip of an artist's brush. To the north is **Refreshing Breeze Terrace (Qīngliángtái),** where hundreds of Chinese congregate just before dawn in rented quilted coats to rhapsodize over the rose-colored sky.

Unfortunately, the Běihǎi Hotel was booked solid with some sort of convention, and the corrugated metal Quonset huts nearby were full as well. We trudged across the cloud summit 30 minutes more to the Xīhǎi Hotel and rested at the **Cloud-Dispelling Pavilion (Páiyúntíng).** This is where young lovers also pause, following the custom of securing padlocks engraved with their initials to the iron fence to pledge their undying love and tossing the keys into the misty gorge. This overlook, which has become overcrowded in recent years, dispelled no clouds today. The sun was absorbed long before it set fire to the horizon. The Xīhǎi Hotel also had no rooms available. My four companions huddled. We decided to move on.

An Inn at the End of the Mountain

The sun was bleeding into dusk. We tacked across the west side of the range, inquiring at several unmarked hostels. No rooms anywhere. Huáng Shān was booked. Full darkness fell like a stage curtain. We encamped in the tiny lobby of a dormitory complex. The two clerks at the counter insisted there wasn't a room to be had, but plenty of other travelers were joining us. Everyone argued with the clerks. An hour passed this way. There were rooms here, people whispered, but the staff was too lazy to open them. The staff withdrew from the counter for dinner.

I waited in a courtyard outside. A group from Běijīng, consisting of three German foreigners and a Chinese, joined me. One of the German women was traveling with her Chinese boyfriend, and she, speaking good Mandarin, went inside to try her luck at negotiations. "She's completely ruthless," the other Germans assured me. "Whatever it takes, even a bribe, she will get it done." One of them, Wolf, told me they had been on the road a week. Nothing quite this bad had befallen them until now, he said. He wondered how I came to be with four Chinese, who meanwhile were talking with some Huáng Shān locals about renting a cottage for the night.

We joked about sleeping on the open trail tonight. About midnight, there was a breakthrough. Places to sleep suddenly materialized. Two bunkhouses up the hill inexplicably opened their doors. We climbed a score of stairs in the pitch dark. Our bunkhouse contained beds for eight. There was nothing more inside, not even a basin of water. The problem was that there were already people sleeping here, and with us joining them, there weren't enough beds. Eventually one of the lads, probably by bribe rather than argument, convinced some of these surplus sleepers to seek other accommodations—this, after we'd already paid twice the going price for the "inconvenience" of needing a place to sleep after dark.

Two of the guys from Wǔhàn slipped out into the dark in search of supper, returning with loaves of bread so heavy I could barely swallow them and with some hideously pale lunch meat processed into finger-shaped wieners.

There was no water to drink or wash up with. I lay down in my bunk. I'd been up since six. Right then I never wanted to see another stone step on another mountain again.

Cloud Ladders

It is twice as far down the west side of Huáng Shān, nearly 14km (9 miles). This is where the great peaks reside, every one of them a stupendous detour by carved stairway. We scaled each and every prong. The climbs are extraordinarily severe, up hundreds of irregular stone steps that end in a singular panorama, followed by a shock-absorber descent, and a few minutes later by another looming precipice.

We began at the **Stone That Flew from Afar (Fēilái Shí),** a 9m (30-ft.) tall rock perched on the top of a stone tower, looking as though it had just sailed in on a cloud. Just to the east is Huáng Shān's second highest peak, **Bright Summit Crest (Guāngmíng Dǐng),** at 1,812m (6,040 ft.). It has its own strange crown: a modern weather station.

Turtle Summit (Àoyú Fēng), slightly lower at 1,752m (5,840 ft.), requires a scramble through a cave whose stairs lead like a ladder to the slim summit. The next stop on this so-called descent was the highest peak in the range, **Lotus Flower (Liánhuā Fēng),** elevation 1,835m (6,115 ft.). It's a climb of 800 steps seemingly straight up—in fact, at an 80-degree incline in some places. Nonetheless, the overlook on the top has become very popular.

The earliest recorded climb of Lotus Flower Peak was in 1268. The party required 3 days to complete the ascent. Of course, there were no cable cars, guesthouses, trails, or stone stairways at Huáng Shān in those days. The first stairways seem to have been cut into the mountain about 1606, when monks began to connect the many temples. During the Yuán Dynasty alone (1271–1368), 64 temples were added to Huáng Shān's slopes. Today, hardly half a dozen remain. It is not a sacred mountain, but it is sublime.

At the foot of Lotus Flower Peak is the site of **Jade Screen Pavilion (Yùpíng Lóu)**—a famous Buddhist temple until it burned down in 1952 and was reconstructed as a guesthouse and restaurant. The Jade Screen Pavilion is the midpoint on the western route, a fine place for a cup of tea. And here, too, is the most photographed panorama of Huáng Shān, featuring a thousand rising peaks and spires and a single, stately pine tree, its boughs outstretched. Known as the **Welcoming Pine of Huáng Shān (Yíng Kè Sōng),** it is believed to be over a thousand years old. Its likeness has been painted on a wall in the Great Hall of the People in Běijīng.

Just south of the Jade Screen Pavilion is Huáng Shān's second-highest granite tower, **City of Heaven Peak (Tiāndū Fēng),** elevation 1,781m (5,938 ft.). It was the last peak I could possibly climb. I was ready to crawl.

City of Heaven Peak is formidable. It's an hour's detour to the top, a 3km (2-mile) long ladder through the clouds ending in an unnerving and narrow 9m (30-ft.) span, lined with a slack chain-link railing and sheer drop-offs on both sides. This lovely single-file passage of terror is called **Carp's Backbone Ridge (Jìyú Bēi).** From it I could see all at once the four elements the Chinese traditionally demand of a perfect mountain landscape: soaring spires, grotesque pines, clear-running mountain streams, and seas of mist and cloud—everything except sanity and safety. At least I had satisfied the ancient dictum: "Without reaching Jade Screen Pavilion, you cannot see the mountain; without climbing the City of Heaven Peak, your trip is in vain."

Peach Blossom Hot Springs (Táoyuán Wēnquán)

After squeezing through a region of boulders and narrow fissures known as the **House of Clouds,** we paused for lunch near Bànshān Temple at a restaurant that, oddly enough, doubled as a brick factory. Porters filed back and forth past our table, bundles of fresh bricks tethered to their poles. The bricks were piled in the back of the cafe, near the mouths of the kilns. The lads from Wǔhàn ordered beer, and feeling euphoric after their successful descent of Huáng Shān, tore off the bottle tops with their teeth. Sheepishly, I fetched a bottle opener from my backpack. Meanwhile, the porters came and went, brickload by brickload, staring at me as I slurped down a bowl of red-peppered noodles.

It was only 2,000 more stone steps down to the bamboo groves and hot springs of **Merciful Light Temple (Cíguāng Gé),** a favorite of the Míng Wànlì Emperor, who visited here about the time the pilgrims landed on Plymouth Rock. All I wanted to land in was a hot tub of water and a comfortable bed.

At **Peach Blossom Hot Springs (Táoyuán Wēnquán),** I parted ways with my four tireless companions from Wǔhàn. They took cheap rooms next to a public bathhouse; I retreated to the slightly more modern Táoyuán Guest House. I'd now felt how the Chinese travel on their holidays—quickly and cheaply—and I must conclude that they are far tougher travelers than I ever was, and in a much madder rush. My tendency is to dwell for hours at a site, for days on a peak, but they chew up entire mountain ranges as if they could hear the tick of each minute on a hand-wound 1-day clock.

One more mountain like this and I was finished. It's important to find your pace and stick with it. I meant to linger in this small village with its hot springs, waterfalls, forested peaks, and pavilions before I moved on. The hot mineral waters of Cinnabar Springs along Peach Blossom Stream are said to heal those who climb the peaks.

Huáng Shān is the most picture-perfect of Chinese mountains, so rife with bizarre rock forms, sword-point peaks, and deep fissures that it resembles a giant's game of pick-up sticks. Surmounting its 77 peaks requires days of climbing the stairs up the steep sides of immense granite pillars and the crossing of stone ladders floating on an everglade of clouds. As the Táng poet Lǐ Bái proclaimed 12 centuries ago, the first ancients to scale these flowery peaks must have been astounded to find that they could look down upon the sky.

PRACTICAL INFORMATION

by Sharon Owyang

ORIENTATION & WHEN TO GO

Inscribed on the UNESCO World Heritage List in 1990, **Huáng Shān (Yellow Mountain),** China's most famous mountain for scenic beauty, is located in southern Ānhuī Province, 310km (192 miles) west of Hángzhōu, 501km (315 miles) southwest of Shànghǎi, and about 65km (40 miles) from Túnxī, which is often called Huáng Shān Shì and is the nearest big town to the mountain. It is from **Túnxī** that many travelers begin their assault on the mountain, since it is the major air and rail link, has better hotels, and provides useful travel agencies for the mountain.

The weather around Huáng Shān is a fickle thing. In general, summers are hot and humid, with rainfall peaking around July. Snow covers the mountain peaks 158 days a year, while fog and mist enshroud the mountain 256 days a year. With the trails usually packed with hikers from May to October, April is often cited as the best time to visit.

Local tourism authorities, however, like to boast that each season highlights a uniquely different aspect of Huáng Shān, and it is true that Huáng Shān in any season is still grand and beautiful. Even winter offers its own delights, and recently, tourism officials have been pushing Huáng Shān winter tours, when at least hotel, restaurant, and ticket prices are all lower. Whenever you decide to visit, one thing is clear: The first weeks in May and October, when China celebrates its national holidays, are times to avoid Huáng Shān, as hotel prices (especially on the mountain) can double at this time. When climbing the mountain, always carry layers of clothing: sweaters and rain jackets as well as T-shirts. Hats and umbrellas are useful, too, as temperatures, even in summer, are subject to sudden changes due to the altitude and winds.

GETTING THERE

By Plane   Huáng Shān's airport (☎ 0559/ 293-4144) is at **Túnxī** (also called Huáng Shān Shì), 65km (40 miles) and a 1½-hour bus ride away. From here, there are daily flights to Shànghǎi (1 hr.), Běijīng (2 hr.), and Guǎngzhōu (1½ hr.); and less frequent flights to Hong Kong (2 hr.), Guìlín (1½ hr.), and Xī'ān (3 hr.). Tickets can be bought at the **CAAC office (Mínháng Shòupiàochù),** Huáshān Lù 23 (☎ 0559/293-4111); at travel agencies; and at hotel tour desks. From the airport to hotels in Túnxī is a ¥20 ($2.50) taxi ride.

By Train   There are two trains a day connecting Túnxī to Shànghǎi (11½ hr.; ¥171/$21 soft sleeper, ¥103/$13 hard sleeper, ¥97/$12 soft seat). Tickets can be bought at the train station (☎ 0559/ 211-6222), at CITS, or at hotel tour desks. **From Túnxī to Huáng Shān**   Túnxī, the main transportation hub for Huáng Shān, is 65km (40 miles) from the town of Tāngkǒu, which in turn is still a few miles south of the mountain entrance. Tāngkǒu-bound buses (¥13/$1.60; 1½ hr.) regularly leave from Túnxī's bus station (Qìchēzhàn) and from the square in front of the railway starting as early as 6:30am to catch arriving train passengers until around 6pm, with buses becoming less frequent in the afternoon and only departing when full. From Tāngkǒu, it is necessary to continue to the east gate at Yúngǔ (1 hr. by minibus or taxi) if you want to use the cable car or the eastern mountain trail (recommended). From the Tāngkǒu bus station, it's a 30-minute walk or a ¥10 to ¥15 ($1.25–$2) taxi ride to the Peach Blossom Hot Springs area and the start of the western mountain trail. If you wish to take the cable car up the western slopes, take a minibus (¥5 to ¥10/ 60¢–$1.25) or taxi (around ¥40/$5, subject to bargaining) from Tāngkǒu to the Mercy Light Temple (Cíguānggé). From Tāngkǒu back to Túnxī, buses leave from the long-distance bus station (Chángtú Qìchēzhàn) just before the main gate to Huáng Shān and from the bridge area in Tāngkǒu. Tickets can be bought at the **bus station** (☎ 0559/ 556-2590) or at the **Lìdū Hotel (Lìdū Jiǔdiàn;** ☎ 0559/556-2289).

TOURS & STRATAGEMS

Visitor Information   Túnxī has a helpful branch of **China International Travel Service (CITS)** at Bǐnjiāng Xīlù 1 (☎ 0559/ 251-5618 or 0559/251-5231; fax 0559/ 251-5255; www.huangshanguide.com). The office can provide English-speaking guides and private car hire as well as arrange accommodations and plane and train tickets.

Exploring the Mountain   From March 10 through November 15, the park entrance fee is ¥130 ($16); at other times it is ¥85 ($11). There are two main trails up the mountain. The 7.5km (4½-mile) eastern trail or Eastern Steps (3 hr.–4 hr.) are compact and steep and are generally considered less strenuous than the 15km (9¼-mile) western trail, which is longer and steeper but which has some of Huáng Shān's most spectacular vistas. For those preferring the path of least resistance, there are two cable cars going up the mountain. The **eastern trail's Yúngǔsì cable car** (Mar 15– Nov 15, 6:30am–4:30pm; otherwise 8am–4pm) has a waiting line for the 6-minute ascent that can take up to 1 to 2 hours. The **western trail's Yùpíng cable**

car (Mar 15–Nov 15, 6:30am–5pm; otherwise 8am–4pm) runs from the Mercy Light Temple (Cíguānggé) to Yùpínglóu, which is just over halfway up the western slope. The one-way cost of both cable cars is ¥66 ($8.25) or ¥56 ($7) November 16 to March 14. Sedan chairs can be hired on both routes and can cost up to ¥500 ($62) for a one-way trip, though there is plenty of room for bargaining. There is a third, less-often used cable car on the north side of the mountain that runs from the **Cloud Dispelling Pavilion (Páiyúntíng)** west of the summit to Sōngguān in Tàipíng Village, from where it's more than an hour's ride back to Tāngkǒu by taxi or infrequent minibuses.

WHERE TO STAY & DINE

Hotels Although Túnxī may be the gateway to Huáng Shān, visitors used to bypass the town (still an hour from Huáng Shān's hiking trails) and head directly for Tāngkǒu and the mountain. Today, however, more travelers are staying in Túnxī and combining their Huáng Shān trip with visits to the surrounding towns of Shèxiàn, Xīdì, and Hóngcūn to view traditional Huīzhōu architecture. As a result, Túnxī now has some nicer hotels, and staying here is not as dreaded as it once was. Nevertheless, spending a night on Huáng Shān's summit is still very popular and highly recommended, even though hotel prices are high and rooms often difficult to come by. Phone ahead for reservations, particularly from May through October.

In Túnxī, there are a number of comfortable hotels to choose from. The four-star **Huáng Shān International Hotel (Huáng Shān Guójì Dàjiǔdiàn)**, at Huáshān Lù (✆ **0559/256-5678;** fax 0559/251-2087), has the most experience with Western guests (since 1995) and is still the most popular choice with foreign visitors, although it's starting to show signs of age. Rooms (¥680 /$80) are spacious, comfortable, and equipped with minibar, safe, robe, in-house movies, hair dryer, and scale.

Service is efficient. The hotel has two restaurants (Western and Chinese) and a wide range of facilities, including a business center, a small gym, tennis courts, a shopping arcade, and a tour desk. Located near the International Hotel on the road to the airport, the newer (2000) **Jiànguó Garden Hotel (Jiànguó Shāngwù Jiǔdiàn)**, at Jīchǎng Dàdào 6 (✆ **0559/256-6688;** fax 0559/235-4580), is a slightly dull, modern hotel that nevertheless has tastefully decorated rooms (¥680–¥780/$85–$97), clean bathrooms, Chinese and Western restaurants, and an outdoor swimming pool. The friendly staff speaks a little English. Situated in the heart of Túnxī near the railway station, the **Huáng Shān Guómài Hotel (Huáng Shān Guómài Dàjiǔdiàn)**, at Qiányuán Nánlù 25 (✆ **0559/235-1188;** fax 0559/235-1199), has the most convenient location of the four-star hotels. Opened in 2000, the modern 11-story hotel caters more to business travelers, and has modern rooms that come with all the standard comforts and amenities. The hotel also has three restaurants (two Chinese, one Western), and its staff is professional.

None of the hotel choices at Tāngkǒu, nearer the Huáng Shān entrance, is particularly attractive, but if you are stuck here for the evening, the two-star

Zhōunán Hotel (Zhōunán Dàjiǔdiàn), on Yánxījiē (☎ 0559/556-3517; fax 0559/556-3519), has basic but clean rooms (¥340–¥380/$42–$47 double). Air-conditioning, a TV, 24-hour hot water, and a hair dryer come with every room. The staff speaks minimal English but tries to be helpful. The hotel has a Chinese restaurant and a tour desk that can help book bus and air tickets. Just down the street, the newer (2001) Hóngdàshì Hotel (Hóngdàshì Jiǔdiàn; ☎ 0559/556-2577; fax 0559/556-1888) has standard-issue Chinese two-star rooms (A/C, TV), but at least they are very clean and the furniture is still new. Bathrooms are basic but clean and have tub/shower combos.

At Hot Springs (Wēnquán), where the western trail begins, the inn of choice is the large three-star Peach Blossom Hotel (Táoyuán Bīnguǎn; ☎ 0559/558-5666; fax 0559/558-5288). Rooms (¥600/$75 double) were renovated in 2002, so the furniture and carpeting are still fairly new. Bathrooms, however, are small, dark, and even a little grotty. The hotel accepts all major credit cards and offers foreign exchange.

About 700m (just under half a mile) down from the Yúngǔsì cable car on the eastern trail is the somewhat remote three-star Cloud Valley Villa Hotel (Yúngǔ Shānzhuāng; ☎ 0559/556-2466; fax 0559/556-2346). Popular with Taiwanese tour groups, this hotel is built in the traditional architectural style of ancient Huīzhōu (Ānhuī, as it was known during the Míng Dynasty), with open courtyards set inside stark white buildings capped by gray tiled roofs. Doubles (¥580/$72) are a little dark and damp but are furnished with the basics like A/C, TV, and telephone. The hotel has a Chinese restaurant, a business center, and a shopping arcade.

On the summit of the mountain, there are several decent but overpriced choices. As the oldest hotel (1958) on the mountain, the three-star Běihǎi Hotel (Běihǎi Bīnguǎn; ☎ 0559/558-2555; fax 0559/558-1996) has at least staked out a good position closest to the sunrise-viewing spot. It also has good views of the Starting To Believe Peak from its front rooms (¥700/$87 double), which are otherwise quite drab. Newer and nicer are rooms in the back wing (¥850/$106). These rooms are clean, fairly comfortable, and fitted with Chinese furniture, central air-conditioning/heating, and jackets for the sunrise viewing. Only bathrooms in the back wing have tub/shower combos. The hotel accepts credit cards but does not provide foreign exchange or laundry service. Service is, at times, uneven. A nicer but pricier option is the Swiss-designed Xīhǎi Hotel (Xīhǎi Fàndiàn; ☎ 0559/558-8987; fax 0559/558-8988), which became a four-star hotel in 2002 and is popular with American, European, and Japanese tour groups. Regular standard rooms (¥960/$120), fitted with comfortable beds, rattan furniture, minibar, TV (HBO), and heater, resemble ship cabins. Some bathrooms are a little run-down. The staff is friendly. There are Western and Chinese restaurants on the premises. The hotel accepts credit cards and can change Japanese and U.S. currency. The newest (1998) of the summit hotels, the four-star Shílín Hotel (Shílín Dàjiǔdiàn; ☎ 0559/558-4040; fax 0559/558-1888; www.shilin.com) has rooms (¥960/$120 double) that are small but cozy and furnished with the usual amenities. Bathrooms are small but clean and come with showers only. There are nonsmoking rooms, and two Chinese restaurants that can serve

Western breakfasts if requested. The hotel accepts all major credit cards and has a foreign-exchange service. Service is adequate if not particularly memorable. **Dining** In Túnxī, hotels like the International Hotel and the Jianguo Hotel all serve Chinese and Western food. For those wanting to venture into town, the clean and popular **Number 1 Restaurant (Lǎojiē Diyīlóu; © 0559/253-9797)**, at the eastern end of Túnxī's Lǎojiē (Old Street), serves a wide range of regional and local dishes in a traditional Huīzhōu-style building. Specialties include *huángshān sùwèiyuán* (a vegetarian dish made of mountain vegetables, tofu, pumpkin, bamboo shoots, mushrooms, and medicinal herbs) and *wǔcǎi shànsī* (eel stir-fried with peppers, mushrooms, and bamboo shoots). The food is good but service is a bit uneven. Meals for two people cost about ¥50 to ¥100 ($6–$12). Right next door, the more informal **Měishí Rénjiā (© 0559/251-2222)** offers dumplings, noodles, dim sum, and Chinese desserts for ¥4 to ¥15 (50¢–$2) per dish.

For dining on the mountain, hotel restaurants provide the most reliable fare. Vendors along the mountain trails sell snacks, drinks, breads, boiled eggs, and instant noodles, but these become increasingly expensive the higher you climb. In Tāngkǒu, **Mr. Chéng's Restaurant (© 0130/8559-2603)**, currently located at Yánxī Jiē but likely to have moved by the time you read this, serves familiar favorites like kung-pao chicken *(gōng bǎo jī dīng)* and fried spare ribs in soya sauce. Meals for two people average ¥40 to ¥80 ($5–$10). There are menus in English. The very friendly, English-speaking Mr. Chéng can help with tour information and in booking accommodations and train tickets.

WǓLÍNGYUÁN: CHINA'S YELLOWSTONE

武陵源

THE CHINA OF VAST, CROWDED cities—and even the China of endless farming communities and terraced fields—occupies but a fraction of the Middle Kingdom's geography. Most of China is rugged and remote, dominated by nearly uninhabitable mountainous terrain. Yet there are few parks devoted strictly to the outdoors, to nature as the supreme destination. The most notable exception I've run across is a park located in western Húnán Province, not near anything at all, known locally as **Zhāngjiā Jiè** but on the World Heritage Site's website as **Wǔlíngyuán Scenic and Historic Interest Area,** a vast nature reserve designated by UNESCO as a World Heritage Site in 1992. Local boosters have proclaimed Wǔlíngyuán "China's first Yellowstone-type national park," but relatively few foreign visitors come here. I used to recommend it only to the hearty, but it has become more accessible in recent years. Improved roads and the opening of a new airport have helped, as have a number of new, upscale hotels that have opened just outside the national park. And an expressway between Chángshā and Zhāngjiā Jiè, slated for completion in 2003, will shorten the drive from the provincial capital from 8 hours to 4 or 5.

For the Chinese, Wǔlíngyuán is synonymous with the remote and the inaccessible. Small mountain villages, some reachable only by ropes, have clung to these slopes since the Míng Dynasty (1368–1644). There are stories of a certain Hàn Dynasty lord named Zhāng Liáng who lived here as a hermit 2,000 years ago. A Táng Dynasty (A.D. 618–906) writer, Liǔ Zōngyuán (773-819), praised its wild scenery, but it wasn't until the Míng Dynasty (1368-1644) that the name crops up more regularly in literature, always as a remote and wild place.

At present, Wǔlíngyuán is a wilderness paradise, an unpolished gem. It already possesses a superb system of paved walkways and stone stairs. But Wǔlíngyuán dreams of placing itself at the forefront of Chinese tourism, improving its facilities in order to pamper as well as delight outdoor vacationers. If the local administrative power moves ahead with its ambitious

476

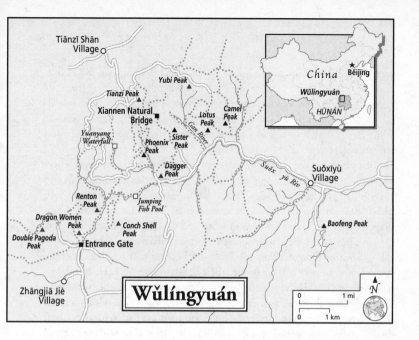

programs of afforestation, conservation, and personnel training, and if the paving of the roads and upgrading of accommodations continue, Wǔlíngyuán could indeed become a Chinese Yellowstone.

On my first visit to the area, I was fortunate. I'd met a local who insisted that Wǔlíngyuán was the most beautiful place in China, and when I challenged him on this point he agreed to take me there. It can sometimes be tough to travel with a local Chinese in the difficult way that Chinese travel. From Chángshā, we took a bouncing overnight bus, equipped with narrow bunk beds and quilts, 403km (250 miles) west to Zhāngjiā Jiè City. The beds weren't long enough, the roads were uniformly unrepaired, and when we arrived 8 hours later at dawn, I'd hardly slept a wink. We ate breakfast on the street, were besieged by touts, and eventually found a minibus that delivered us to the park entrance at Zhāngjiā Jiè Village. Until the expressway opens, I recommend going by overnight train from Chángshā or by air from farther locales.

Dragon Woman's Peak

Wǔlíngyuán has been divided by the local park administration into a 26,083-hectare (65,208-acre) core area and a 12,528-hectare (31,320-acre) buffer zone. The park core is a deep basin of peaks and pillars, streams and limestone caves. A web of hiking trails and steep stone stairways is connected to a road system in the buffer zone. Hillside farms are populated by several of China's national minorities. What makes Wǔlíngyuán distinctive, however, is its array of majestic quartz sandstone pillars, erupting from the valley floor and piercing the constant mist. These strange pinnacles resemble those found at better-known tourist sites such as Guìlín and Yúnnán's Stone Forest, but Wǔlíng's stone columns tower over those in Yúnnán and are more statuesque than those at Guìlín.

I first glimpsed these pillars a few steps beyond the park entrance, where we were surrounded by stone sentinels on a gargantuan scale, as high and as sheer as any I have ever seen. It is as if a thousand steep peaks have been sliced into narrow, vertical shafts hundreds of feet tall, then turned and shaped on nature's lathe by eons of wind and mist, heat and ice.

Consulting the trail maps engraved on stone tablets, we found a path to the summit of Dragon Woman's Peak and beyond that to Huángshízhài. Porters tried to persuade us to hire their bamboo sedan chairs, covered in red awnings, but we were determined to make the climb under our own power. Several times we paused at natural platforms on the winding stone stairway where local vendors, emptying their bamboo packs, hawk tea, soft drinks, and handicrafts. It took us an hour to draw even with the tips of the quartz spires.

Even the sharpest, most inaccessible of these shafts is wreathed in trees and bushes. There are about 3,100 of these strange pillars in the park. Eighty-five have been given fanciful names, such as Double Pagoda, Conch Shell, and Rabbit Watching the Moon which, at 1,245m (4,149 ft.), is one of the highest points in Wǔlíngyuán.

As we enjoyed the scenery, a troupe of minority dancers entertained us. Their children overtook us on our ascent, skipping effortlessly uphill, leaving behind the echoes of their "mountain songs" as we gasped for oxygen. The national minorities add a cultural dimension to Wǔlíngyuán. The Tǔjiā and Bái minorities predominate, with a scattering of Miáo people. The minority farming villages are mostly in the buffer zone. Ten mountain strongholds (shānzhài), built in the Míng and Qīng dynasties and often reachable only by ropes, remain in the park but are no longer occupied. Today, some of the minorities are engaged in performing their songs and dances, selling native crafts, carrying sedan chairs, and running inns and restaurants.

On my first visit, descending the west face of Dragon Woman's Peak, we encountered lines of porters hauling heavy sacks of concrete on shoulder poles for the latest construction project, a cable car to whisk sightseers to the top of nearby 1,031m (3,438-ft.) Huángshí Zhài. It's now in operation; the round-trip costs ¥86 ($11).

A Village on the Rim

When we reached the valley floor, **Zhāngjiā Jiè Village** was clogged with travelers, many dressed in their finest clothes, as if they'd arrived for a wedding reception rather than a backpacking adventure. Wǔlíngyuán receives close to a million visitors yearly, nearly all of them from within China. Some come for a casual stroll, some for a serious trek, some even for a honeymoon.

Having allotted just 2 days to cover the high points of Wǔlíngyuán, we could not tarry. If I ever return here, I'll stay an extra day, to slow the pace if nothing else. We followed the stream running through Zhāngjiā Jiè Village into a valley forest of oak, maple, and Chinese plum, and crossed a flat wooden bridge. There we located another steep stairway rising into the creases of massive stone slivers. Halfway up, a fine mist enveloped us. Wǔlíngyuán is often under clouds, and rain is a constant feature all summer. Farther up, we broke through the clouds.

The trail continued to rise, whipping back and forth a dozen times. Eventually, we headed away from the river valley toward the top of a wide, level ridge, stopping at a hillside village of terraced rice paddies for a simple lunch. An unpaved road runs through the village, and we were able to hail a bus grinding its way east along the northern rim of the basin. An hour later, we stopped at a roadside inn on the ridge and rented a room for the night.

Until a few years ago, a number of inns were located inside the national park, but in the year 2000, then Prime Minister Zhū Róngjī ordered those nearest the main entrance removed. This is a huge improvement. Though the **hotels**—mostly new or renovated—that line the main street outside the park gate charge more for lodging than the spartan inns that were previously inside, they are for the most part reasonably priced and considerably more comfortable.

At dusk, we enjoyed a superb view of the basin below. The canyon walls make a sheer drop. The valley teems with thousands of wrinkled spires that could have served the ink-brush artists of old as the supreme model for their uncanny landscapes. On the horizon are layers of blue-and-gray mountains, softly rounded. I felt as if I were standing atop a roofless cavern where a sea had receded, leaving exposed a chamber of lances and spears, thrust into the earth by a regiment of giants.

The Bridge Across the Sky (Tiānqiáoshēngkōng)

The next morning, we continued on foot along the northern rim of the park toward **Tiānzǐ Shān Village,** pausing at several overlooks to view some of the 239 natural scenic spots identified in the core area. At Tiānzǐ Shān, one vista point has been developed into a wayside commemorating a local military hero. The stone formations below are said to resemble a cavalry division massed for inspection by a general.

Starting at the visitor center in the style of a pagoda, we descended a stone stairway into the heart of the basin, weaving among Wǔlíngyuán's largest columns. The trail branched off, enabling us to climb up and down several sharp peaks before rejoining the main path. At a stone archway known as **The Bridge of the Immortals (Xiānrénqiáo),** we came upon a Chinese tour group decked out in yellow baseball caps. They were being entertained by a vendor with a monkey on a chain, the only specimen of the park's wildlife I'd seen. Wǔlíngyuán is a preserve for nine rare and three vulnerable species of plants, as well as a number of threatened mammals, including the Asiatic black bear, the Chinese water deer, and the clouded leopard. No clouded leopards have actually been seen in the park, but there are signs that a few inhabit the area.

Perhaps the single most spectacular rock formation appeared halfway down the basin trail. **The Bridge Across the Sky (Tiānqiáoshēngkōng)** is an archway joining two massive vertical columns. We eased out to a platform with a metal railing constructed to give a close-up view of the stone bridge, which visitors can also cross if they dare. Under this 39m (130-ft.) long stone span, the canyon walls drop straight into an abyss 351m (1,171 ft.) deep. A survey by UNESCO suggests that it "may be the highest natural bridge in the world." Trees clinging to the arch lend it the appearance of a floating forest spread like a banner between two stone towers.

Yellow Dragon (Huánglóng) Cave

We reached the valley floor at the vacation town of **Suǒxīyù.** Suǒxīyù contains several large, modern hotels, opened a few years ago to capture an anticipated increase in overseas travelers, a boom yet to materialize. This is the place to stay for some luxury and comfort, a good base for day trips whether you come on your own or on a tour. In Suǒxīyù we hired a motorized cart and rode 19km (12 miles) into the countryside to **Yellow Dragon (Huánglóng) Cave**—said to be one of the 10 largest caves in China. About a third of Wǔlíngyuán consists of limestone caves and underground streams. Of the 40 caverns, Yellow Dragon is the most spectacular. About 11km (7 miles) long, it features a chamber with a 45m (150-ft.) waterfall and ferryboat rides on its subterranean river. It's open daily dawn to dusk, and costs ¥62 ($7.75) to enter. The cavern is fully developed for tourists, complete with English-speaking guides, photographers for hire, and an avenue of vendors lining the lane outside its pavilion entrance—a hint of what Wǔlíng Park will become in the future.

Wǔlíngyuán remains somewhat difficult to reach and difficult to travel through—it's still an emblem of the remote and the inaccessible. Whether Wǔlíngyuán is truly the most beautiful place in China, as my friend from the same province insisted, is a matter of taste, but its ranks of stone spears brushing the vaults of heaven in a valley of forests, rivers, and caves form a natural tapestry unsurpassed elsewhere in China.

PRACTICAL INFORMATION

by Michelle Sans

ORIENTATION & WHEN TO GO

Wǔlíngyuán Scenic and Historic Interest Area (usually referred to by the name of its national forest park, Zhāngjiā Jiè) is located in a remote northwest section of Húnán Province, about 1,127km (700 miles) west of Shànghǎi and 150km (500 miles) north of Hong Kong. Wǔlíngyuán became China's first National Forest Park in 1983. In 1992, it was listed as a UNESCO World Heritage Site, and ambitious conservation programs, including limits on tourism, were announced. The nearest major city is Húnán's capital, Chángshā, 269km (167 miles) to the southeast.

With a mean annual temperature of 60°F (16°C) and an annual rainfall of 56 inches, Wǔlíngyuán is humid and has a warm–temperate climate. The rainiest months are April through August, while fog and patchy clouds are common year-round. The best months to visit are March and September through November, months when temperatures are comfortable and rain less likely. Although winters are rarely severely cold, snow is not unheard of. Avoid the park during Spring Festival (a lunar festival in late Jan or early Feb), Labor Day (the 1st week of May), and National Day (the 1st week of Oct), when hundreds of thousands of Chinese visit the park (so much for those limits on tourism) and it becomes nearly impossible to find accommodations.

GETTING THERE

Chángshā, capital of Húnán Province, is the transportation hub of the region. It is 7 to 16 hours' travel by bus or rail to or from Wǔlíngyuán. **Zhāngjiā Jiè City** (formerly called Dàyōng) is about 32km (20 miles) south of the main park entrance. The rail station is 8km (5 miles) southeast of town and 45km (28 miles) southeast of Zhāngjiā Jiè National Park; the airport is 32km (20 miles) south of the national park. At the park entrance, there is a small town called (to confuse matters) Zhāngjiā Jiè Village. A bus from the rail station to Zhāngjiā Jiè Village departs when it's full (an hour-plus wait sometimes). It's better to pay ¥1 (10¢) for a bus into town and from there catch one of the many buses to the village for ¥5 (65¢); trip time is 1 hour. Easier still, take a taxi directly to Zhāngjiā Jiè Cūn (Village) for ¥65 to ¥70 ($8–$8.75).

By Plane   Héhuā Airport, 5km (3 miles) from Zhāngjiā Jiè City and 32km (20 miles) from the village and park entrance, has air routes to 20 cities in

China, including Běijīng (2 hr.), Shànghǎi (3 hr.), and Guǎngzhōu (4 hr.). In 1999, it began air service from Hong Kong. **Chángshā**, a 40-minute flight from Zhāngjiā Jiè, has a major airport with connections to even more Chinese cities.

By Train The **Zhāngjiā Jiè Train Station** is 8km (5 miles) southeast of town. Short of flying, the overnight train from Chángshā is the most comfortable choice. The K525/K528 leaves Chángshā at 7:28pm and arrives the next morning at 9:35am in Zhāngjiā Jiè City; the K526/527 leaves Zhāngjiā Jiè City at 5:05pm, and arrives in Chángshā at 6:49am the next morning. (Sleepers cost ¥150–¥240/$19–$30.) Express train K552/553, leaving Chángshā at 8:20am and arriving in Zhāngjiā Jiè City at 2pm,

is also convenient, though the return train (K554/551), with an evening arrival of 8:31pm, is less so.

By Bus A new expressway is scheduled for completion during 2003, which will make bus travel between Chángshā and Zhāngjiā Jiè fast and comfortable. For now, though, the route, which winds through the mountains, is scenic but slow (7 hr.–11 hr.; ¥50–¥84/$6–$10) and much less comfortable than the train ride. Schedules will change, but for now, buses leave Chángshā daily between 7am and 8am from the station across from the rail station. Returning buses leave Zhāngjiā Jiè at the same time. Sleeper buses aren't recommended because they arrive at either destination between 1am and 3am.

GETTING AROUND

Vehicular and hiking paths provide access to some 240 designated scenic spots within Wǔlíngyuán. Shuttles circle the rim providing transportation between villages. Cable cars (¥48/$6) lead to viewing platforms from Huángshí Zhài in the Zhāngjiā Jiè forest area and from the eastern edge of Tiānzǐ Shān. A local bus connects Suǒxǐyù Village, located at

the southeast entrance to the park, and Zhāngjiā Jiè City. It's a spectacular 3-hour trip over the mountains on the southern edge of the park. Suǒxǐyù Village is also a good base for hiking into the park, viewing the nearby Yellow Dragon Cave, and booking a tame white-water raft trip (summers only) on the Suǒxǐ River.

TOURS & STRATAGEMS

Admission to the park is ¥108 ($14) and is good for 2 days. At the park entrance, your thumbprint is taken and matched with your plastic entrance card so no one else can use your card.

For most of the sightseeing within the park, there is no need for a guide. However, you must join a tour to go river rafting or to visit **Huánglóng Cave (Huánglóng Dòng)** in Suǒxǐyù. These can be organized by **Zhāngjiā Jiè National Forest Park Travel Service,** which is conveniently located and much more customer-oriented than the CITS branches in either Zhāngjiā Jiè City or

Village. Although their storefront has no English signs, they have English guides and materials, and they are happy to answer questions even if you're not booking a tour (not the case with Zhāngjiā Jiè City's CITS office). Their office in Zhāngjiā Jiè Village is located on the main street, on your left as you approach the park. It's next to the Mínsú Mountain Villa (Mínsú Shānzhuāng), easy to recognize by its two-story building constructed of yellow wood and bamboo, on Jǐnbiān Dàdào (© **0744/ 571-2213;** fax 0744/571-2288).

WHERE TO STAY

In Zhāngjiā Jiè City, the only four-star hotel is the **Dragon International Hotel (Xiānglóng Guójì Dàjiǔdiàn),** 46 Jiěfàng Lù (✆ 0744/822-6888; fax 0744/822-2935). Double rooms are ¥600 ($75). Although the Dragon is the best in the town has to offer, it doesn't deserve its four-star rating, nor does it reach international standards in its service or facilities. All that can be said is that the rooms are clean. Hotels in Zhāngjiā Jiè Village are superior in every way. The setting is attractive and close to the park, and room rates are the most reasonable in the area.

One of the best hotels in Zhāngjiā Jiè Village is **Pípáxī Bīnguǎn** (✆ 137/0744-5536; www.pipaxi-hotel.com). From the hotel, it's a 7-minute walk along the main street to the park entrance. The manager, Mr. Táng Míng, speaks English and takes reservations on his mobile phone or by e-mail. Whether you call first, or just turn up, do negotiate for a substantial discount. Rooms (¥400/$50 double; most credit cards accepted) are clean and attractive and most have good views of gardens and/or mountains, not to mention 24-hour hot water. The **Xiāngdiàn Mountain Villa (Xiāngdiàn Shānzhuāng;**

✆ 0744/571-2266; fax 0744/571-2172), renovated in 2002, is slightly nicer and pricier than the Pípáxī. Rooms (¥400/$50 double; most credit cards accepted) are simple but very pleasant and comfortable, and they have 24-hour hot water. Rates will go up as soon as they get the four-star rating they're seeking. There's no street address; approaching the park on the main street, turn left on the small lane just before reaching the park, and walk about 300m (984 ft.).

Hikers inside the park can stay in local inns, which offer no-frills rooms with Chinese-style toilets and showerheads mounted on the bathroom wall (¥80–¥150/$10–$18 per night). Somewhat more upscale hotels are overpriced. The **Wàngxiá Dàjiǔdiàn,** near Hēilóng Zhài, north of Tiānxià Dìyī Qiáo (The First Bridge Under Heaven), is of the latter variety—doubles start at ¥400 ($50), but it's possible to bargain that down to ¥200 ($25), and even lower midweek. In Tiānxià Dìyī Qiáo Village, the **Sì Zhōu Jiǔlóu** is a 5-minute walk from the bridge. Clean doubles with Chinese-style bathrooms are ¥80 ($10). Upstairs rooms have views.

WHERE TO DINE

Zhāngjiā Jiè (both city and village), **Tiānzǐshān,** and **Suǒxīyù** have inexpensive restaurants featuring spicy Húnán dishes, but the food is not outstanding, nor are English-language menus available. Small restaurants serving Tǔjiā dishes can be found all along the main street of Zhāngjiā Jiè. Tǔjiā cuisine specializes in fresh game (such as rabbit and various guinea-pig and weasel-like mammals), reptiles (including poisonous snakes), crawfish, eel, and crab; so if you're adventurous, you can always point to the creature that interests you,

and they'll cook it up. Settle on a price first, though; these dishes can be expensive. The hotels have restaurants that are more accessible to foreign travelers, but again, the food is mediocre. The best I found was inside Xiāngdiàn Shānzhuāng. On the main street, about 150m (500 ft.) before the entrance to the park, across the stream, there's a row of small noodle restaurants where you can sit outside, watch the stream, and eat a bowl of noodles for under a dollar.

LÚ SHĀN: HILL STATION OF THE RICH & FAMOUS

庐山

LÚ SHĀN IS CHINA'S ANSWER TO THE hill stations and highlands of Southeast Asia, notably of Malaysia, complete with tea plantations, villa resorts of the colonial era, misty mountain peaks, and rich green forests. For the Chinese, it is the epitome of nature in its pristine beauty, engraved in tradition by countless landscape artists and classic poets. In recent centuries, Lú Shān became the private retreat first of European traders and missionaries, then of powerful Chinese landowners and political scions, from Chiang Kai-shek to Chairman Máo Zédōng. Today, it is a favorite cool mountain resort for thousands of ordinary Chinese vacationers, affording an ideal combination of outdoor scenery and culture. All summer, it is jam-packed with tour groups, while the rest of the year it can be sacked with cold mists, blowing rains, and freezing snows. By official estimates, at least 190 days of the year Lú Shān is clouded with "vapors," the layers of fog that rise from numerous lakes, rivers, and waterfalls.

Journey to Gǔlǐng

Situated between the mighty Yángzǐ River to the north and the great lake of Póyáng to the southeast, Lú Shān covers an area about 24km (15 miles) long by 10km (6 miles) wide, rising suddenly in a cluster of over 90 peaks with elevations of 1,200m to 1,500m (4,000 ft.–5,000 ft.). The gateway is the city of **Jiǔjiāng (Nine Rivers)** on the south shore of the Yángzǐ River, 32km (20 miles) to the northwest. Jiǔjiāng (Kiukiang in an earlier form of transliteration) became a Treaty Port in 1861, open to foreigners who made the town a major shipping center for tea and porcelain. In the heat of summer, Lú Shān became a hillside retreat for the colonials, who made the steep journey from Jiǔjiāng on the arms, shoulders, and feet of porters— whole families were carried in sedan chairs. Today, the buses from Jiǔjiāng to Lú Shān retrace the old route up a series of switchbacks known locally as the "Four Hundred Turns," reportedly because Chairman Máo Zédōng's driver kept a tally of them using 400 match sticks. However many they

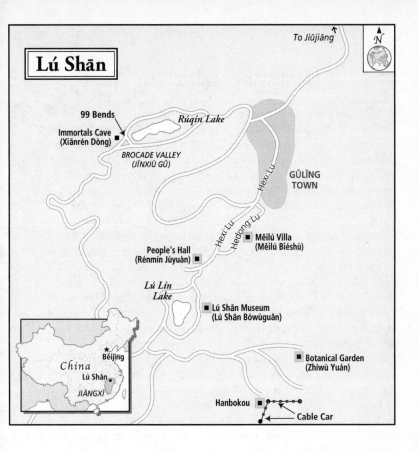

may be, the twists are numerous and sometimes wrenching. Inside Lú Shān Park, there is a charming small tourist town, **Gǔlǐng,** inundated now with shops on its main street—an excellent place to buy pouches or canisters of Lú Shān's most famous product, **Cloud Tea (Yúnwù Chá).**

Gǔlǐng contains scores of European villas and mansions from the colonial days, when wealthy foreign traders and many Christian missionaries sought it out as a cool summer retreat from the intense heat of the lowland Yángzǐ valley. In an earlier form of transliteration, the name was written "Kuling," creating a fortunate pun on the word "cooling," which accurately describes the climatic allure of Lú Shān in the days before air-conditioning. Formally established as a summer resort in 1895 by E. L. Little, an English investor, Gǔlǐng more than a century later retains its original architecture—a residential version of the Bund's commercial row in Shànghǎi. Here are the surviving homes and guesthouses of a foreign summer community that numbered nearly 2,000 by 1917, as well as the villas, training centers, and meeting halls of Chiang Kai-shek's Nationalist government and finally Chairman Máo Zédōng's inner circle of communist bigwigs.

Měilú Villa (Měilú Biéshù)

The most interesting of the colonial mansions to visit these days was built in 1903 and donated by its owner, Mrs. Hallett, wife of a rich Western physician, to the Chinese leader, Chiang Kai-shek, in the 1930s. The house became his personal summer home. Měilú Villa was named for Chiang's wife, Soong Mei-ling. The Soong sisters are legendary in China. One married the founder of the modern Chinese republic, Sun Yat-sen, and stayed active in communist politics after the revolution in 1949; the other, Soong Mei-ling, married China's president, Chiang Kai-shek (Máo Zédōng's foe), and fled with him to Taiwan after the Nationalists' defeat in 1949.

Strangely enough, communist China did not see fit to raze the Lú Shān villa of Máo Zédōng's most bitter enemy; instead, Máo Zédōng himself simply moved in when the mood to escape the summer heat seized him. Today, the crumbling villa and its gardens are the number-one cultural attraction on the mountain. It is not a grand house. Its yellow-walled rooms and stone fireplaces are in disrepair and its overstuffed furniture is worn, but there are plenty of historic relics, such as a large bathroom fitted with Chinese and Western facilities, paintings by Soong Mei-ling herself, Soong's lavish bedroom, photographs of Chiang and Soong, and even an original kerosene-powered Electrolux refrigerator in the kitchen. There's also a photo of Chairman Máo Zédōng in a wicker chair; it was snapped by his wife, Jiāng Qīng, who was later convicted of crimes as the leader of the Cultural Revolution's Gang of Four.

Měilú Villa, which is usually swamped with tourists, is open from 8am to 5pm; admission is ¥15 ($1.90). It's located about a quarter mile southwest of central Gǔlǐng, down the main sightseeing road of Héxī Lù and to the left on Hédōng Lù. Another half mile farther down the main road, at Héxī Lù 504, is **People's Hall (Rénmín Jùyuàn),** which has the same hours and admission charge. This was the conference hall where two major meetings chaired by Máo Zédōng in 1959 and 1970 changed the course of modern communist China; it is now a rather uninteresting museum of the political history of Lú Shān. Still farther down the same road is the more entertaining **Lú Shān Museum (Lú Shān Bówùguǎn),** which has displays of the mountain's political history too, but also exhibits on local religious culture and natural beauty. This museum gives a nice overview of what the park has to offer. A half mile east of the museum is the **Botanical Garden (Zhíwù Yuán),** open daily from 8am to 5pm; admission is ¥10 ($1.25). Famous for its 3,000 native highland plants and its hothouse cacti exhibit, the garden was among the first in China to feature exotic alpine specimens. It dates from the 1930s.

If your time is limited, I would skip all of these sites, except for Měilú Villa, and take a taxi down to **Hán Pó Pass,** south of the Botanical Garden, for the most expansive overlook in Lú Shān. This is where everyone gathers at dawn to see the sun rise over massive Lake Póyáng and the southern Yángzǐ Valley. If you can't make it for sunrise, you should at least take one of the two cable cars here up to lookout points (either ¥60/$7.50 or ¥50/$6.25 round-trip, depending on which one you take) or, if you have time for a leisurely hike into the steep hills for which Lú Shān is celebrated, strike out on the trail to your right.

Immortals Cave (Xiānrén Dòng)

Of the 200 or so officially designated scenic sites at Lú Shān, the one not to miss is Immortals Cave, also called the Fairy Cave. It's located on the mile-long scenic trail in what is known as the Brocade Valley (Jǐnxiù Gǔ) on the southwest shore of Rúqín Lake. The peaks and vistas on this trail are magnificent; you no longer have to wonder what impossible, uncanny mountain landscape inspired China's classic landscape painters. The very best of Lú Shān's mystic scenery is concentrated along this compact but steep path, with its famous "99 Bends." The path was formally laid out in 1980, and its granite bed is just wide enough to allow the hordes of visitors to pass each other in either direction. Its viewing platforms, most without even a cursory railing, are studies in vertigo.

Aside from the overlooks, sheer peaks, ribbons of fog, and deep ravines, you come across several unexpected monuments. The first is a large plaque carved into stone like an ancient stele, except that this is a modern engraving in both English and Chinese. Its carved gold lettering reads exactly as follows:

THE NIGOCIATION PLATFORM

> From July to September, 1946 Five-Star General G.C. Marshall, the special envoy of the president of the United States came to Mt. Lushan eight times to mediate the negociation between the Communist Party of China and the Kuomingtang. This is the place where General Marshall and Chiang Kaishek met.

The Immortals Cave itself is a rock chamber on the edge of a precipice, hollowed out in part by a deep spring inside, which still flows. The altars and carvings of Daoist priests have occupied the chamber for many centuries, creating a remote cave temple. It was here that Lǚ Dòngbīn, one of the Eight Immortals of Daoism, was given a sword by a fire-breathing dragon. With this sorcerer's sword, Lǚ was able to fly through the Middle Kingdom, walking on clouds and slaying all the demons in his path. Lǚ also became the patron saint of China's ink-makers, and the cave of his origin is as inky black and mysterious as ever. It is fronted on the outside by enormous pines, and occupied inside by a large stone shrine and stone railings. Locals say the cave has the shape of Buddha's hand, the five stone fingers held upward like a lotus flower. Monks in white robes, their black hair pinned into buns, preside over the cave temple, selling incense to visitors.

Lú Shān is the lotus flower of Chinese scenery. Over 2,000 years ago, it was mentioned by Sīmǎ Qiān, the Grand Historian to the First Emperor of unified China, Qín Shǐ Huáng Dì (259–210 B.C.). Sīmǎ told the tale of seven brothers who lived in the mountains here, giving the area the name Lú Shān, which means Cottage Mountain. During the Eastern Hàn Dynasty (A.D. 25–220), it became the center of Buddhism in China, with hundreds of temple buildings (Lú Shān is not regarded as a sacred mountain, however). The major surviving temple is the **Temple of the Eastern Grove (Dōng Lín Sì),** where Huì Yuán founded the Pure Land Sect in the 4th century, a form of Buddhism that was to be imported to Japan (where it still flourishes) by Japanese monks who visited Lú Shān.

Lú Shān's two most influential promoters were the Táng Dynasty poets Bái Jūyì (A.D. 772–846) and Lǐ Bái (A.D. 701–762). Bái Jūyì concluded in one of his poems that Lú Shān was unrivaled in its beauty anywhere in China; Lǐ Bái compared the peaks of Lú Shān to "golden lotus sculpted in the transparent sky." Whether you stay a few hours or a few days, you'll see that Lú Shān contains exactly the kind of scenery that strikes at the core of a Chinese sense of beauty—serene yet wild, spiritual yet natural, mystical yet human. In 1996, Lú Shān was designated by UNESCO as a World Heritage Site because of its prominence "as a cultural landscape of outstanding aesthetic value and its powerful associations with Chinese spiritual and cultural life."

PRACTICAL INFORMATION

by Peter Neville-Hadley

ORIENTATION & WHEN TO GO

Lú Shān is usually reached from the Yángzǐ River port of Jiǔjiāng, 40km (25 miles) away by road. Jiǔjiāng is on the main Běijīng-to-Kowloon (Hong Kong) railway line, about 1,300km (813 miles) from the capital, a little less from Hong Kong. Shànghǎi is 728km (455 miles) by road to the east. Established in the 19th century in emulation of the hill stations of British colonial India, Lú Shān is cool in summer, but wet much of the time, and very wet in winter. June to September is peak period, when Lú Shān's hotels, most of which are very modest, charge ridiculous prices and are filled with Chinese tour groups.

GETTING THERE

The airport at Jiǔjiāng is closed, and the nearest well-connected one is on the wrong side of Nánchāng, the provincial capital, well to the south. Rapid and comfortable **buses** connect Nánchāng and Jiǔjiāng, some directly from the airport, and some from the city's main long-distance bus station, from 6am to 7:30pm, every 30 minutes, taking 2 hours. There are also buses directly to Lú Shān from Nánchāng's long-distance bus station in Bāyī Dàdào: 16 per day in peak times, 3 per day in winter, at ¥35 ($4.40).

Major cruise ships do not usually stop at Jiǔjiāng—most ply farther upstream, but there are **local ferries** daily from Wǔhàn and more intermittently downriver to Shànghǎi. For information, call © **0792/812-4998** or 0792/822-2087.

Buses to Lú Shān leave from Jiǔjiāng's main long-distance bus station in Xúnyáng Lù, with eight departures between 6:45am and 5:20pm. The trip takes just over an hour (¥6/75¢). If you want to return between departures, tiny rattletrap yellow vans will do the run back for about the same price, but will first cruise the streets of Lú Shān until full.

GETTING AROUND

Admission to Lú Shān is ¥85 ($11), and individual site entry fees are extra. Maps of the resort are widely on sale for ¥2.80 (35¢). **Taxis** on the mountaintop decline to use their meters and are keen to overcharge foreigners as much as possible, so careful negotiations are necessary. An early start on a clear day is best, tackling the resort on **foot** and taking advantage of paths, which lace the hillsides. These are clearly marked on the map. **Buses** drop you in Gǔlǐng on the eastern side of the resort. Most of the museums, the old colonial villas (many marked with signs to say which leader stayed there), and other buildings of importance to the historian of communism but of little interest to modern visitors, are strung within a 30-minute walk downhill to the southwest—straight through the town and main villa area on Hēxī Lù and Hēdōng Lù. There's now an assortment of **cable cars** and **ropeways** leading to high points all around the resort, as well as a **scenic railway** on the northwest side.

WHERE TO STAY

Lú Shān can easily be visited as a day trip from Jiǔjiāng. The quality of hotels is not high, being in many cases the moldering remains of accommodations from the resort's original foundation (which don't seem to have seen a refit since) or else very modest two-star hotels that have taken a beating from the immense volume of traffic at high season, but still want to charge ¥400 ($50) for a standard room. There are several of these in Gǔlǐng close to the bus station, a minute's walk between them, and they are best inspected to see which is currently in the best condition. Most hotels shut in October and reopen in April, but in 2002, one or two decided to stay open into December, which scared the rest into following suit, although few had heating or were prepared to turn it on if they had it, given off-season occupancy rates of about 1%. Other than in midsummer, bargain to pay no more than 50% of rack rates, which in many cases is still too much.

The threadbare three-star **Lú Shān Hotel (Lú Shān Bīnguǎn),** Hēxī Lù 446 (© **0792/828-2060;** fax 0792/828-2932), has helpful staff and a wide range of room types between ¥540 ($68) and ¥900 ($113). The main building is of solid stone construction, room sizes are large, and there are a number of villas around the hillside behind. A major refurbishment is planned, as well as the construction of a new four-star building next door, which might bring Lú Shān from the 19th into the 21st century.

A similar, very solid building with large rooms but with a quieter location is the **Lú Lín Hotel (Lú Lín Fàndiàn),** on the south side of Lú Lín Lake, past the museum (© **0792/828-2424).** Rooms here are ¥400 to ¥560 ($50–$70).

Most credit cards are accepted at both these hotels, but at few others.

WHERE TO DINE

The best dining is inside the larger hotels, although prices are around ¥150 ($19) to ¥200 ($25) for a 2-person meal. Gŭlĭng's main shopping street, a right turn into a pedestrianized area as you walk into the village, has a number of straightforward restaurants around the post office, producing Chinese standards in surprisingly hearty portions from ¥8 (US$1) a dish.

WǓTÁI SHĀN: BUDDHIST
PEAK OF THE NORTH

五台山

WHEN THE ZEN MASTER XŪ YÚN made his pilgrimage to Wǔtái Shān (Five Platforms Mountain) in 1882, it took him 2 years to walk the 1,500km (900 miles) from Shànghǎi, in part because he insisted on bowing down and bumping his head on the ground every third step of the way. My own 62km (100-mile) journey north from Tàiyuán by car took just 4 hours, but it was bumpy, too. Once we left the main highway and rose into the foothills of Wǔtái Shān, we encountered one of the worst strips of road I've ever traveled: a bed of dirt and rock being dug up and rebuilt by hand. We averaged 8km per hour (5 mph), tops. I counted hundreds of workers with shovels and picks along the way, spread out for miles in small teams. We frequently had to stop for them, and when an oncoming truck asserted its right of way, we had to squeeze over on the shoulder of the lane-and-a-half of plowed furrow that called itself a highway. (By 2002, this stretch of road—finally repaired—was as winding as ever, but considerably less bumpy.)

When we reached the top of the high ridge after 90 minutes of lurching, I could see across the roof of northern China under a bright blue sky. This could have been Tibet, and, in fact, many Tibetans, as well as Mongolians, have congregated at Wǔtái Shān ever since the 13th century, when Lama Buddhism spread to China's borderlands. The founder of the Yellow Hat sect of Lama Buddhism lived here. The exiled Dalai Lama is his divine descendant.

We dropped into a broad crater, encompassed by the Northern, Southern, Eastern, and Western Terraces—peaks in a cluster that make up Wǔtái Shān. In the center of this compass is the Central Terrace, site of a temple village, Táihuái, clotted with more temples than any other city in the Middle Kingdom.

I checked into a new hotel a mile south of the temple village. The desk staff couldn't find me a map of the temples or peaks. They told me it was impossible to walk to the highest peak, the Northern Terrace, because the summit was under snow. Then they issued me a special permit, stamped with a red seal that read "aliens' travel permit."

So branded, I set out on a sunny morning for the temple village and the top of the snowy terrace beyond. On the way to town, horsemen twice passed by. They tried to persuade me to hire their steeds. I was tempted. Such fine horses, the horses of Wŭtái Shān: tall, sleek, brown bodies, black manes and tails, fitted with ornate red saddles and red bridles. But I resisted. I meant to keep walking through the temple village to the top of Wŭtái Shān's Northern Peak, regardless of a scarcity of maps and an abundance of snow.

The Temple Village

The temple village of Táihuái at Wŭtái Shān, in the crater of the terraced valley, is extensive, as beautiful and active as any I've seen in China. That's not to say the temples of Wŭtái Shān are what they once were. A century ago, there were over 300 holy shrines here; 50 years ago, travelers counted 100 monasteries and temples, of which 30 were devoted to Lamaism. Today, the census is down to a few dozen. But the heart of the village is still as it was, a little city of temples crowded one into the next, uphill and downhill, with streets and walls running every direction—enough temples flowing into temples to get lost in, like a maze.

In the center of the village is Wŭtái Shān's landmark, the **Great White Tibetan Pagoda,** often called a *stupa, dagoba,* or *chorten,* meaning a reliquary or monument for a sacred relic *(sarira)* said to have come from the real Buddha—a fingernail or a thigh bone, for instance. The White Pagoda of Wŭtái Shān is shaped like a monumental wine decanter tapering to a golden spire, with an exquisite finial that resembles a folded umbrella. It stands 45m (150 ft.) tall, and was originally constructed 5 centuries ago. Two hundred fifty-two bronze wind-bells dangle like lanterns from the fringes of its finial, chiming in the wind. Devout pilgrims from Mongolia once circled this monument hundreds of times a day, touching the scripture doors around its base with their foreheads. Now, the White Pagoda was deserted, or at least not easily accessible; the closer I got to it, the deeper the maze of walls, courtyards, and shrines surrounding it.

I made my way through temple streets clogged with dozens of vendors offering thousands of trinkets, drinks, snacks, hats, walking sticks, and souvenirs. The stairs and streets between the temples were lined with beggars and cripples, more than you usually see these days in one place in China.

Passing under a large towered gate, I followed a back road along a wall. Six young men squatted along that wall, gambling with cards, all of them dressed in the black sports coats favored by taxi drivers and pickpockets.

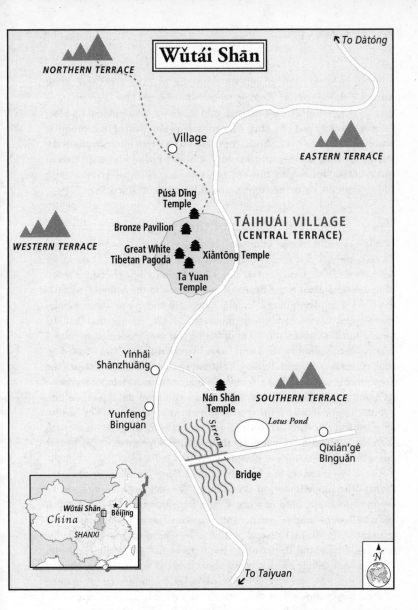

I entered the door of **Xiǎntōng Temple (Xiǎntōng Sì)**, which consists of over 400 buildings. Inside, I walked through several darkened rooms into one that was even darker: a bare brick room with a ceiling high enough to accommodate a slender golden bronze pagoda 13 stories tall, said to house a lock of hair from Wénshū (the Bodhisattva of Pure Wisdom, known in India as Manjusri), who was said to have appeared on Wǔtái Shān.

Surprisingly, this unlit chamber is connected to a shrine of more recent vintage, a shrine to Máo Zédōng, whose white plaster bust is set upon an altar and draped in a bright red-and-gold shawl—a most modern Buddha, the revolutionary god of China. Máo must have slept here. His bedroom is preserved next door to his shrine, complete with a dozen photographs of the chairman pasted above a spacious *kàng,* a heated bed of bricks, covered in wicker mats. Worshippers toss offerings onto his bed: small coins, mostly, and cigarettes. It's a strange shrine, one of hundreds at Wǔtái Shān.

The Mouth of the Dragon

I walked out into another courtyard, heading north for the top of **Central Terrace,** the hill that rises at the far end of the temple village. I could see more stupas and bronze pagodas ahead and dozens of fine glazed-tile roofs. Most splendid of all is the **Bronze Pavilion,** cast in the Míng Dynasty. It resembles a miniature metal temple, barely tall enough to admit human worshippers, coated inside with thousands of tiny bronze Buddhas. Its form is intricate, as if a thin layer of hot bronze were meticulously poured over timbers, columns, tiles, and carved wooden figures and allowed to cool. Ascending Central Terrace, I entered the mouth of the dragon, the dragon being the **Púsà Dǐng Temple,** Wǔtái Shān's most famous lamasery. Its undulating walls and many pavilions are coiled on the top of the hill, 108 stone steps above the many temples and lamaseries below. The faithful once left locks of their hair on each step to the entrance gate, offerings to Wénshū in hopes he would grant them rebirth. One modern-day beggar raised his half leg to me as I passed him on the stairs.

Two Qīng emperors of China made Púsà Dǐng Temple their residence during official pilgrimages to Wǔtái Shān. Wénshū himself is believed to live in this temple. Born of a ray of light from the crown of the Buddha, Wénshū had no earthly parents and was born free of earthly desire. He introduced Buddhism to Nepal and then, by Chinese accounts, made his home on the Central Terrace of the five terraces of Wǔtái Shān. He sits on a lion, a book in one hand, a sword raised in the other.

Wénshū's temple home is encircled today by innumerable vendors. Monks charge admission at his gates. Five thousand lamas lived here a century ago, and some still remain, plodding back and forth in brown robes and caps, yellow sashes, and padded shoes. There are butter lamps, prayer banners, and small brass prayer wheels spinning in the courtyards, and inside one small shrine I spotted some of the old musical instruments from the days when Lamaists gathered here to watch the spirited Devil Dances: two immense demon-mouthed trumpets, as long and heavy as alpenhorns. The yellow roof tiles of Púsà Dǐng Temple, donated by the Qīng Kāngxī Emperor almost 3 centuries ago, gleam in the sun, and the red columns are freshly painted, but the dragon temple seems gutted, barren as the hills that were deforested at the command of that same emperor when he called upon the people to settle the wilds of Wŭtái Shān.

From Púsà Dǐng Temple there is a fine view of the temple village below, as well as the White Pagoda and the river valley. Most of the buildings at Wŭtái Shān are really no older than a century or two, rebuilt countless times after each destructive turn, human or natural. The curious thing is that these days, almost no tourist or pilgrim comes to Wŭtái Shān to climb its peaks. The temples are enough to occupy their curiosity. But to my uninformed mind, these temples are just husks—pretty to look at, a bit strange in form, but nothing much inside for me, whether it be Máo or Wénshū with book, sword, and lion.

The Northern Terrace

It was before noon when I began to climb the highest peak, the Northern Terrace, its summit topping 3,000m (10,000 ft.). I was already at 1,800m (6,000 ft.), and the route to the summit didn't look steep or impossibly far. I skirted the dragon wall of the Central Terrace and found a road up the northern valley. I didn't meet a soul until I came to the end of the pavement and struck up the mountain valley on a dirt road. At the intersection, there was a poor peasant woman, threadbare. She opened both empty hands to me, and I could see that she was the sort of peasant who really has nothing.

The dirt road goes straight up the valley and ends in a farming village. Three children spotted me. They dashed out for a look, but they were afraid to come too close, even though they called out to me. I walked around the village walls, keeping the stream on my left. The houses are fashioned from mud, not brick. There's electricity but no cement.

There's no road, either—only a series of paths that farmers use to tend their plots, walled in with piles of rock. The ground is too rocky for easy agriculture. The peasants work the plots with oxen hitched to plows. I felt like an intruder, wandering among their fields, but they paid me little attention. The hills that fold into the river valley are denuded of trees: hard scrabble up to the peak, a bit of grass and brush for grazing. Black hawks, wings tipped white, sailed across the empty span. I could see the Northern Peak ahead. There were several wide patches of snow near the top, looking like leftover glaciers, but they were too thin to be barriers.

An hour above the village, I could no longer see the temples in the valley. There were snatches of green alpine grasses and tiny wildflowers in the brown stubble. The high slopes were crisscrossed with sheep paths. Shepherds guided their flocks to thin pastures on the flanks.

Near the summit, I found remnants of a stone platform but still no trail. I bushwhacked up the final untracked rise, cutting between snow crusts, crossing a field of buttercups. At the summit, a chilly wind swept over the Northern Terrace southward into China. Here was a forlorn panorama of white stone and soft green meadow grasses with patches of snow and yellow buttercups. I was alone, except for a few hawks, a squirrel by the stream, two golden quail I scared up, and, in the distance, a lone fox sprinting up the slopes.

The bald terraces of Wǔtái Shān are not dramatic, perhaps, but they are severe—the softly colored hills of a broad, high desert. A receptacle for solitude. Other peaks, crowded with temples and tourists, allow no time for meditation, no time for ease. On Wǔtái Shān, the wind is cold and unbroken; it blows without obstacle. As I walked back down the Northern Terrace, the farmers called out to me, resting their arms on the backs of their black oxen.

The Southern Terrace

The sun held court for another day, and I spent it at the Southern Terrace in the **Southern Peak Temple (Nán Shān Sì)** of Wǔtái Shān. At the river, the horsemen tethered their steeds, hoping to sell rides up the steep hillside, but there were no takers. I admired their horses, showy in their imperial outfits. Their owners were the only annoyances pursuing me.

I took a back trail up the Southern Terrace. The Nán Shān temple complex was built during the Yuán Dynasty (1271–1368), when the Mongols ruled China. Rewi Alley, the Australian journalist and traveler, who saw extensive stonework being done on these buildings in 1935, wrote, "This huge temple reminds one of some Norman Castle, for inside are winding stairs through great thick stone walls to towers and pavilions." This morning it was almost deserted. The formal entrance consists of 108 wide cement stairs, fronted by a shadow gate to block the straight lines along which evil beings travel. Its 108 steps are symbolic of the 108 passions, the 108 earthly delusions, and the 108 rosary beads a devout Buddhist clutches. At the top of the stairs, I was stunned to discover a vendor with a pellet rifle, set up for visitors who might want to partake of a bit of target practice before entering the temple.

There are three main temples here; they were joined together for the first time in this century. Although the oldest of the three dates back to the time of the Great Khans, to 1296, all were restored in the Qīng Dynasty and are being redone today. Inside is pretty much whatever you dream of finding in a Chinese temple: 18 *luóhàn* (Buddha's disciples) carved during the Míng Dynasty; a six-armed statue of Guānyīn, Goddess of Mercy; and a fresco called **Journey to the West,** celebrating a Buddhist monk's adventures in the 7th century as he travels to India to bring back Buddhist scriptures. This celebrated fresco, painted on three walls of a pavilion, is crude; worse still, a fourth panel, a modern one, has been added, and it's even more amateurish. Far more striking is a brightly painted version of a **Thousand Buddha Hall,** with its multiple carved images of Buddha. The twisting forms and bold colors give a decidedly fantastical, Lamaist air to their rarefied subjects.

As I climbed from station to station, I was waylaid by monks who begged me to go inside and have a look at what was on display, usually a statue or carving I could barely decipher in the darkness. With one monk, I engaged in a short chat. He was pleased I'm an American and refrained from cajoling me into making a donation.

In the center of one deep courtyard, I found a stupa that seemed to be an exact reproduction of the Great White Pagoda located in the center of the Wǔtái Shān temple village. Here, its proportions no longer seemed monstrous. What relics it housed, I couldn't determine.

After reaching the top of the Southern Terrace, I immediately descended through a maze of marble walls and moon gates, stairways and frescoes, stone courtyards and temples with finely carved wooden doors and porches. I descended in a light breeze and kept moving. The sound of wind cracking stone on the mountain's back drove me down the terrace and up the cold stream into the valley of the temple village.

PRACTICAL INFORMATION

by Michelle Sans

ORIENTATION & WHEN TO GO

The mountain known as **Wǔtái** or "Five Platforms" is actually a cluster of mountains, which long ago collectively became the northernmost sacred peak of Buddhism. Situated in Shānxī Province roughly between Dàtóng and Tàiyuán, Wǔtái Shān is thought to be the earthly residence of the great bodhisattva, Manjusri, who embodies the perfection of wisdom. To this day, though tourists far outnumber them, pilgrims come entreating Manjusri to reveal himself again. The peaks of Wǔtái Shān have an average height of 1,968m (6,561 ft.) above sea level and, from northeast to southwest, they stretch 121km (75 miles). Cradled at their center is the small town of Táihuái, with an elevation of 1,650m (5,500 ft.). Part tourist slum, part sacred site, it is a combination of souvenir shops, restaurants, temples, and shrines. Although its few streets have names, nobody knows them. Directions to anyplace begin with the name of the nearest temple. Summer is the best time to visit—when Wǔtái Shān offers an escape from the heat and humidity of lower climes. In July and August, the average temperature is only about 50°F (10°C), with warm days and cool nights. Even at this most temperate time of year, the mountain itself is rarely over-crowded during the week. Weekends are another story, and national holidays should be avoided at all costs. Winters are severely cold, with temperatures dipping as low as –40°F (–40°C), and, even in June, snow is not unheard of.

GETTING THERE

Wǔtái Shān is located in a remote, mountainous region. The nearest air-port connections are at Tàiyuán to the south and Dàtóng to the north.

To Wǔtái Shān   Most visitors arrive by bus from Tàiyuán to the south or Dàtóng to the north. Wǔtái Shān has no airport.

By Train   The Wǔtái Shān **rail station** is in Shāhé, 48km (30 miles) and a 1-hour-plus drive from Táihuái. There are daily fast trains to and from Běijīng on the Běijīng–Tàiyuán line (K702/701; 6½ hr.; ¥268/$33 for a soft sleeper with A/C); Tàiyuán (4 hr.; ¥50/$6 for an A/C car). Buses between Shāhé rail station and Táihuái Zhōngxīn Tíngchē station leave regularly throughout the day, ¥20 ($2.50). A taxi between Shāhé and Táihuái is at least ¥100 ($12.50). Allow 2 hours if you're catching a train in Shāhé.

By Bus   There are daily **buses** from Tàiyuán (3½–4 hr.) and Dàtóng (about 5 hr.). Buses drive into town and will drop you at your hotel if you know where you're staying. Air-conditioned buses to Tàiyuán (¥40/$5 Jǐnlóng) depart throughout the day beginning at 6am from the Wǔtái Shān station on the main street just south of the Friendship Hotel turnoff. The ticket office opens at 5:30am. Buses to Dàtóng

leave from various small hotels on the main street beginning around 6am and cost ¥45 ($5.60) for an air-conditioned bus. If you'd rather not have to wave one down, ask your hotel or a CITS branch to arrange hotel pickup (no service fee). In summer only, a direct bus to Hohhot leaves daily around 6am from Yíngfāng Street.

The **Wǔtái Shān rail station** is in Shāhé, 48km (30 miles) and a 1-hour-plus drive from Táihuái. There are daily trains to Běijīng (7 hr.; ¥268/$33 A/C soft sleeper) and Tàiyuán (4 hr.; ¥50/$6 A/C car).

Taxis can be hired in Tàiyuán or Dàtóng, but you'll have to bargain for a reasonable price. Most expensive but convenient is to have your hotel arrange a **car.** Expect to pay ¥800 ($100) from Tàiyuán. You can easily pay a frac-tion of that if you shop around and do your own negotiating. Cars can also be hired from CITS offices and hotel desks in Dàtóng (see the chapter on Dàtóng, beginning on p. 51, for more informa-tion). Visitors are required to pay an admission fee of ¥90 ($11) before entering the gate to Wǔtái Shān (all vehicles, including buses, are stopped a few miles outside of town to pay this fee). No other permit is now required.

TOURS & STRATAGEMS

Maps of the mountain with the most important of 58 remaining temples are available in both English and Chinese at hotels and souvenir shops through-out town for ¥3 to ¥5 (35¢–65¢). Many of the temples can be reached on foot, and a **cable car** goes up to Dàilóu Peak, just east of the village. **CITS** has a number of branch offices in Táihuái. The main office is at Míngqīng Jiē 18 (② **0352/654-5909**). They don't have a fleet of vehicles, but they will offer to arrange a car, driver, and English-speaking guide to escort you to the outlying temples of your choice. Guide and car with driver for a full day will cost about ¥380 ($48).

WHERE TO STAY & DINE

Wǔtái Shān has a number of commendable hotels, but none have a foreign-exchange desk or take credit cards. The best take advantage of the scenery by building so that most of the guest rooms have a view. Two that do this well are **Qīxián'gé Hotel (Qīxián'gé Bīnguǎn),** about 5km (3 miles) south of the temple village (② **0350/654-2400;** fax 0350/654-2183); and the **Yínhǎi Mountain Villa (Yínhǎi Shānzhuāng),** 3km (2 miles) south of the village, opposite Nánshān Temple (② **0352/654-2676;** fax 0350/654-2949). To find Qīxián'gé Bīnguǎn, look for a small bridge that spans a stream on the left. After you cross the bridge, the hotel is about 150m (500 ft.) ahead, also on the left. Qīxián'gé has a two-star rating and Yínhǎi has three stars. Both hotels have modern rooms and private bathrooms. Qīxián'gé is off the main road, next to the mountain. As such, it's especially quiet and relaxing, though slightly farther from town. Doubles there cost ¥380 ($48). The Yínhǎi is newer and fancier, and its rooms have equally good mountain views. Room rates are slightly higher: Doubles cost ¥548 ($69), but hefty discounts are standard, so always bargain before settling on a price. Both hotels can arrange travel and transportation.

Few restaurants in town have English menus, but lots have photos of dishes to point to. An excellent Buddhist vegetarian restaurant with an English menu is **Jìngxīn Lián** (which has a sister restaurant in Běijīng). Dinner for two costs about ¥50 to ¥100 ($6.25–$13). The restaurant (② **0350/ 654-5202**) is off the main street, 90m (300 ft.) down on the right side of Yánglín Street. On the main street (Yíngfáng Jiē), **As You Like It Kitchen (Rúyì Shífǔ)** specializes in local dishes. The staff is friendly and the food is good. Dinner for two costs about ¥20 ($2.50).

HÉNG SHĀN BĚI YUÈ: SACRED MOUNTAIN OF THE NORTH

恒山北岳

HÉNG SHĀN (HÉNG SHĀN BĚI YUÈ; often just referred to as Héng Shān) is situated between two sections of the Great Wall of China. For many centuries, it stood as the final barrier against China's ancient enemies, the tribes from the north. The Hàn Dynasty Wǔ Dì Emperor traveled to Héng Shān with China's greatest historian, Sīmǎ Qiān, in 100 B.C.

But despite its symbolism and history, the northern mountain proved to be less than an insurmountable barrier. Eventually the Khans and other outsiders swept down, subdued China, and set up their own dynasties. In response, this sacred mountain of the north was moved to the south. Héng Shān (as it's called locally) was "relocated" for centuries, its title bestowed on another peak, to prevent direct contamination by the invading hordes. Only in the Míng Dynasty, when the Hàn Chinese again ruled the Middle Kingdom, was Héng Shān reestablished on the slopes and peaks where thousands of years earlier it ruled over the mind and spirit of the empire.

Héng Shān is not only Old China's northern defender; it is also the Water Mountain, its god long believed to possess the power to bring rain. As superintendent of rivers and streams, the god of Héng Shān is sought out by farmers seeking his benediction to ensure the health of their livestock and the fertility of their fields. Certain royal ceremonies performed at Héng Shān up until the time of the modern republic (1911) involved the slaughter of an ox in the cold before dawn—the ox's blood offered in a bowl on the altar of the highest temple. The hope was to bring the spring rains to China. As recently as half a century ago, these cliff temples were shining symbols of mountain spirits that both guarded the edges of an empire and delivered the nation from droughts.

When I first saw Héng Shān myself, a massive rampart of stone rising like a natural Great Wall in the midst of a high desert plateau, I understood how the mountain could personify these qualities. Nowhere else in this vast region

Héng Shān Běi Yuè

of dryness did the clouds seem to gather, giving visible shape to the thirst for rains that must have gripped generations of northern Chinese, who repeatedly faced starvation. Times have changed, of course, but this northern mountain of water still holds reminders of its former functions and grandeur, despite a remote, even obscure, site in an isolated part of modern China.

The Road to the Long Mountain

Héng Shān is about 81km (50 miles) southeast of the northern coal city of Dàtóng. The country road from Dàtóng to the mountain is paved most of the way to Húnyuán, the sacred village at the foot of Héng Shān. The terrain is a terraced plateau of sandstone, coal, and soda ash. Between sandy bluffs and pinnacles are cave towns, every dwelling sculpted of dry mud. These villages resemble remote oases. The camel caravans of the past have been replaced by rows of electric power lines and ranks of buses and coal trucks.

Snaking through the crowded streets of **Húnyuán** in a taxi hired in Dàtóng, I could see Héng Shān ahead—more a wall of exposed limestone than a mountain, a high ridge of stone on a plain of gray sand and rock.

From this village—once containing 200 temples and surrounded by an eight-sided city wall—we rose through the Mouth of the Golden Dragon, a valley of exposed limestone that parts to empty a river. This narrow gorge was widened for travel in A.D. 397 by a Wèi Dynasty emperor and his 10,000 men. On the west wall of the gorge is the Hanging Monastery (see the chapter on Dàtóng, beginning on p. 51, for a complete description of this marvel).

At the south end of the gorge, a steel-and-concrete dam (56m/187 ft. high, 101m/338 ft. wide) was completed in 1958, creating the vast Héng Shān Reservoir. The surrounding barren plateau, useful only for its low-grade coal, was long known for its killer droughts. Today, however, it has achieved what incense and pilgrimage failed to secure: a regular supply of water from the mountain, thanks to the gods of science and technology.

The Mountain Gate

We drove up Magnet Gorge in a flurry, through a tunnel on the west wall of Héng Shān, around an edge of the long reservoir, then east and north to the parking lot on the south side of the peak. A traditional three-arched gate with red columns and golden eaves, guarded by two stone lions, marks the entrance to the 30 mountain temples and shrines that rise up the slopes of what the ancients called the "Grand Column of the North."

Héng Shān is a mountain of cliff faces and bluffs. The temples perch on ledges, spread out across terraces, and climb section by section up steep stone walls. A trail from the south entrance saunters up the mountain, threading together the overlooks and shrines, leading to the high peaks and pavilions and finally the summit, **Tiān Líng Fēng** (**Tiān Líng Peak**), at 1,985m (6,617 ft.).

Hall of the Pure Sun (Chūnyáng Gōng)

It took me less than 20 minutes to reach the mountain's first large temple, the **Hall of the Pure Sun.** The inscription at the entrance thanks the mountain god for bountiful harvests. On a clear day, pilgrims can see from here all the way across the barren plains to the sacred mountain of Wǔtái Shān, 81km (50 miles) to the south. Today, the air was filthy with fine particles and I couldn't see the outlines of distant peaks with any precision.

I forged on, pausing only to buy tea from a vendor at the **Traveler's Greeting Pine,** a lonely umbrella of a tree near a pavilion with a famous overlook known as **Gū Sǎo Cliff.** The sheer drop-off is considerable. A local story tells of a widow named Gū who refused to remarry, despite her family's insistence. Gū threw herself from the mountain at this spot. Her brother's wife, Sǎo, understanding her sadness, followed her into the abyss.

Both were transformed by the mountain god into larks who forever chase after each other across the mountain spaces, crying.

Temples of the Míng

After another hour's climb, I reached a cluster of cliff temples and pavilions not far below the summit. The most important shrine here, **Héng Zōng Monastery,** dates from the Míng Dynasty (1368–1644), when Héng Shān reclaimed its importance as a major pilgrimage site for Daoists. The halls have been restored recently, although the red-brick exteriors that rise on stone terraces up a white cliff face look both ancient and Tibetan. Bell and drum towers stand at the bottom. One hundred three stairs lead to the highest hall, in which there is a bearded statue of the supreme mountain god of Héng Shān and an inscription over the shrine entrance written by the Kāngxī Emperor during a 17th-century visit.

Kāngxī, a Manchurian, inherited the Qīng Dynasty his grandfather established. Even if his own ancestors were barbarians from the north, Kāngxī came to Héng Shān as a strictly Chinese monarch, paying homage to China's native religion (Daoism) and legitimizing his rule over the Hàn Chinese nation by honoring its traditional sites.

On terraces below and west of the Héng Zōng Monastery are many halls I barely had time to take in: **Chun Yuan Palace,** which has a statue of Lǚ Dòngbīn, one of the Eight Immortals in the Daoist tradition who has triumphed over death and rides with the clouds; and **Jiǔ Tiān Palace,** where pilgrims pray to the goddess Xié Nǚ for male offspring. The latter is still one of the most active shrines on Héng Shān. These temples are small, humble, gritty abodes, each with a priest or nun in attendance, and they all have an authentic feel that larger, more tourist-laden shrines lack.

The westernmost temple on the mountain is devoted to **Kuí Xīng,** chief star of the Dipper. The statue of this god is portrayed as keeping one foot planted on a sea monster while supporting the Pole Star constellation, which Chinese astronomers picture as a bushel (rather than as a bear or water dipper). Kuí Xīng was also worshipped as god of literature, and hence was once a favorite of China's students, as he was said to light the way to knowledge. Those hoping to pass the national civil service examinations used to troop up the mountain to this shrine by the thousands. Today, the temple to Kuí Xīng is virtually empty.

Other ledge and cliff temples here have their tiny treasures, mainly tablets inscribed by Qīng Dynasty emperors who traced their lineage north to the Mongolian steppes. I stopped at one more shrine, the **Palace of the Immortals,** which has images of 72 minor Daoist immortals, eight cave-dwelling angels, and three other gods—dispensers of wealth, happiness, and long life, gifts even science and technology can't always bestow.

A Summit in Space

Anxious to reach the summit, I climbed above the last of the big temples and wound up the cliff past several pavilions to the **Qínqí Platform (Qínqí Tái)**, a natural stage of solid rock. The backdrop is a smooth cliff face, inscribed with large Chinese characters painted red. As with much of the mountain, this formation refers to another fantastical story in the Daoist tradition, this one concerning two immortals who performed on a cosmic stage before vanishing into the heavens.

The rough trail to the summit brought me to an elevation of 1,985m (6,617 ft.), a rise of 360m (1,200 ft.) gained over a leisurely 2½-hour climb. Southward, the plains on the margins of China simmered with dust, smoking like shaken coal flakes. I looked across an infinity without depth, without exact horizon, with no final line of definition, no known boundary, as if I were standing on the edge of space.

The sacred mountain on the northern frontier is almost forgotten today, but its slopes still hum with some of the temples of old, and the barren vistas are impressive. The summit where I stood is empty but altogether formidable and massive—pure space and dust, as elemental as China gets. This is where the mountain god of the north was worshipped for centuries by commoner and emperor alike as defender against barbarians and herald of rain, as harbinger of good harvests, as protector of farm animals, and as controller of tigers, leopards, reptiles, and worms. His powers may have been usurped by modern science, but his ramparts remain as striking as ever. Even the silence is as vast as any I've experienced, broken only by the song of larks.

PRACTICAL INFORMATION

by Michelle Sans

ORIENTATION & WHEN TO GO

Located in Northern Shānxī Province and Northwest Héběi Province, **Héng Shān,** meaning "Everlasting Mountain," is Daoism's Northern Marchmount, or Sacred Peak of the North. Although its Chinese name is a homophone for the Héng Shān of Húnán Province (the sacred Southern Marchmount), it is neither the same word nor the same character, and should not be confused with it. Stretching 250km (155 miles) in a northeast–southwest direction, the Héng range connects with the Taìháng range in the east. Its highest peak is at 1,985m (6,617 ft.), and it has been regarded since ancient times as the "first mountain beyond the Great Wall." Winters are long and cold, making summer and early fall the best times to visit.

Dàtóng, the gateway to the mountain, is about 81km (50 miles) northwest of Héng Shān and worth visiting for its own attractions, which include the Buddhist grottoes of Yúngāng and the Hanging Monastery (see the Dàtóng chapter, beginning on p. 51). South of

Dàtóng and Héng Shān, in the same province, are the holy Buddhist peaks of Wǔtái Shān (see separate chapter, beginning on p. 491).

GETTING THERE

By Train to Dàtóng The nearest rail terminal is located at Dàtóng. Dàtóng has convenient daily railroad connections with Běijīng (7 hr.) and Xī'ān (20 hr.). In summer and fall, tickets to Xī'ān are often sold out. The alternative is an 18-hour train to Luòyáng, where you can change to a Xī'ān-bound train. If all goes to plan, the Dàtóng airport will open in 2003.

To Héng Shān In fall 2002, public transport from Dàtóng had been stopped for extensive roadwork. Once the road is completed, buses will leave from the Dàtóng rail station and go to Húnyuán. From there, minibuses make the 16km (10-mile) drive to the parking lot at Héng Shān. The fare is ¥15 ($2). Add a few extra yuán to be driven to the entrance another mile up.

TOURS & STRATAGEMS

Check with the **China International Travel Service (CITS)** offices in Dàtóng (© 0352/510-1326) about tours and transportation to Héng Shān. CITS has offices at the Dàtóng train station and in the Yúngāng Hotel, Yíngbīn Dōng Lù 21. You can hire an English-speaking guide and a car for the day, if they are available, but they often aren't. It's difficult to get enough people who want to go to the mountain rather than the Hanging Monastery, which is on the other side of the mountain. However, you may be able to hitch a ride with a CITS tour to Húnyuán or the Hanging Monastery for a reasonable fee, and then take a taxi or bus the rest of the way.

The mountain is a day trip from Dàtóng. Be sure to depart from Dàtóng early. The trail to the summit is about 6.4km (4 miles), and hiking up and back takes 4 to 5 hours. Admission tickets are sold at the entrance gate to Héng Shān (¥14/$1.75) and again at the entrance to the temple area (¥35/$4.35). Now, it's also possible to take a cable car to the top (round-trip ¥35/$4.35).

WHERE TO STAY & DINE

As yet, Héng Shān has no accommodations. The nearby town of Húnyuán has only the most basic inns. The one hotel with official permission to accept foreigners closed in 2001. In any event, the mountain requires no more than 4 or 5 hours, which leaves plenty of time to return to your hotel in Dàtóng in the evening. See the chapter on Dàtóng (beginning on p. 51) for hotel information.

If you go with a CITS tour, you'll be taken to a local restaurant in Húnyuán. Otherwise, if you're on your own, you'll be at the mercy of vendors on the mountain path who sell bottled water and drinks as well as simple dishes such as noodles and hot sauce.

Jiǔhuá Shān: Buddhist Peak of the South

九华山

Jiǔhuá Shān, Nine Glories Mountain, is the supreme dwelling place of Dìzàng, God of the Underworld. Pilgrims used to come to Jiǔhuá Shān to seek this god's intercession in ending the torments their ancestors and family members suffered after being cast into the Buddhist inferno. Getting to this mountain gave me a taste of what the bus system in hell must be like.

I boarded the long-distance bus from Hángzhōu to Jiǔhuá Shān at 6:45am, stuffing my backpack into the corner of the bench seat next to the rear window. Several groups of old women boarded. They were wearing the knit caps and Buddhist rosary beads of Old China's pilgrims. The bus finally lurched out of its slip at 7am. The conductor, sitting across the engine cover from the driver, smoked up a storm; so did many of the passengers.

Our mastodon of a bus, with its petrified suspension, soon struck enough unpatched cracks in the road to make me wish I'd not drunk that second cup of coffee. The seats were spaced so that I barely had room for my lower legs; my knees received a steady pounding. I tried to steel myself against this nasty parody of motion, with little success.

A Chinese bus is not only slow and cramped; it's dangerous. Passing is an adventure. Since a bus is one of the larger vehicles on the narrow open road, whenever it swings out to pass, the rest of the traffic, including those vehicles coming straight at it, shift to the shoulder, scattering bicycles, rototillers, and pedestrians. The bus horn blasts constantly, but most of the way even brute passing is impossible. The highways are just too full. And the villages are so crammed that our bus often had to brake to a complete halt. Top speed between settlements is about 64km per hour (40 mph); average speed, 32km per hour (20 mph).

The fields were full of graves, rock-faced mounds capped with fresh white flags. The farming villages were a swelter of pigs, water buffalo, and pods of ducks and ducklings. Not until midafternoon, 8 hours after departure, did a range of mountains, encrusted in haze, break through the horizon. Our final ascent was via a hairpin road that wound upward between

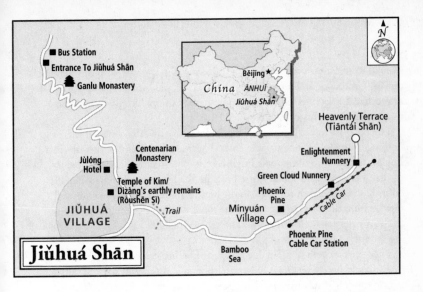

Jiǔhuá Shān

steep green bamboo slopes. The old women slid open every window for a view, but the unpaved road muddied the pure mountain air, lacing it with road dust. We were on the flanks of the holy mountain, and we couldn't see or breathe.

In Buddha's Navel

We corkscrewed halfway up the legendary 99 peaks of Jiǔhuá Shān on a new unpaved road. The old pilgrim route, which the devout walked up until the late 20th century, still exists, but almost no one climbs it anymore. Not far from the top of this spiral highway, I saw the magnificent **Sweet Dew Monastery (Gānlù Sì)**, its white walls five stories high, chiseled into a declivity in 1667. Sweet Dew Monastery was destroyed by the Tàipíng rebels and rebuilt about 1875, but it still looks as ancient as the bamboo rain forest. From the road, I caught only a glimpse of its white walls, enveloped in dust as if in mist. A dozen more turns upward, beyond the Second Gate of Heaven, the bus slumped into Jiǔhuá Terminal and collapsed like a beaten hound.

I had reached what locals call the navel of the potbellied Buddha, the very village of monks and tourists, monasteries and souvenir stands, hotels and cinemas where, 1,700 years ago, after days of hard climbing, solitary monks and nuns pitched their thatched huts in the heart of "Lotus Buddha Land" and meditated upon the mountain void.

The void has been filled in and brought up-to-date, although it's not exactly midtown Manhattan. Hawkers line Jiǔhuá Street, but this is a small, faraway place, and the hurricane of entrepreneurs has not arrived with full force. True, as soon as I got off the bus I was led uphill by a woman to the street's newest hotel, the **Jùlóng,** but she was no pushy vendor on commission. Besides, the Jùlóng Hotel was where I would have stayed had I known it existed. I'd come here with practically no information, except a few historical accounts.

The hotel isn't exactly a palace, but it does have a lobby—even if there's nothing in the lobby, not a single chair. There are no brochures or maps in English, either—no one speaks English here—but the staff is exceptionally cordial: I've dealt with much worse hosts in Shànghǎi and Běijīng. After 11 hours of mechanical chiropractic in the bus, I had just enough flexibility left to walk from the hotel to the end of the road, which is crammed with shops and tiny cafes for 6 blocks. An occasional large temple has been left standing for atmosphere.

Then, at precisely 6:59pm, electricity to the little town blew its central fuse. I could barely see my way back, although a number of stalls were firing up candles and lanterns as I staggered back to the hotel in the dark.

Temples & Mummies

Jiǔhuá Shān was immortalized in Chinese tradition by two contemporaries who met each other on these very slopes. The best known is Lǐ Bái, the magnificent Táng Dynasty poet, who lived in a secluded cottage on Jiǔhuá Shān from A.D. 746 to 747. He penned the lines that not only named the mountain but gave final definition to its castellated crags:

> Looking far beyond this village wall
> I see the peaks of the Southern Mountain
> Emerging from the River of Heaven
> As nine magnificent lotus blossoms.

The other famous resident was Kim Kiao Kak, a monk from Korea, who made a pilgrimage to Jiǔhuá Shān in A.D. 719 and founded a temple to Dìzàng, the God of the Mountain, known in India as Ksitigarbha. As the Earth-Womb bodhisattva, Dìzàng wades into the bowels of Hell to aid the damned. To put it more gently, Dìzàng sets free those who are unhappy—those undergoing the agonies of Hell—and points them to a higher, purer level once they have tasted the pains of the underworld.

Dìzàng is therefore a god of salvation. Like Guānyīn, the Goddess of Mercy, he changed sex during a long translation into Chinese Buddhism. He was taken up in China readily enough, changing to a man and becoming the intercessor before the 10 judges who mete out the 10 punishments for earthly sin.

Prince Kim prayed to Dìzàng for 75 years here, and, upon his death, he became the incarnation of the mountain god. At age 99, he gathered his disciples around him. The Earth split open and into its cleft the monk sank to his death. His disciples buried him on the spot but opened his coffin every 3 years. The corpse refused to age. A pagoda was erected on the tomb, a temple was built around the pagoda, and inside this temple-pagoda resided the undecayed body of the transformed pilgrim-prince, Dìzàng made flesh.

This monk from Korea became the flesh body that has sanctified Jiǔhuá Shān. ("Flesh bodies" are the mummified remains of devout Buddhist monks and patriarchs.) Flesh bodies on the holy mountains of China—and there are scores of them—serve a simple purpose: They sanctify a mountain, demonstrating that it is indeed a place of miracles, of Heaven-infused Earth. When the flesh body was that of a Buddhist, it converted the mountain to Buddhism as well.

Jiǔhuá Street still contains the **Temple of Kim/Dìzàng's Earthly Remains (Ròushēn Sì)** and his indoor seven-story pagoda, reached on a stone stairway of nine-times-nine steps. Branching off Jiǔhuá Street are short paths to a bell tower, an incense hall, and a handful of old monasteries with singularly evocative names: Sandalwood, Illusion City, Centenarian. **Centenarian Monastery (Báisuì Gōng),** consisting of 99½ prayer halls and monks' rooms (to be exact), was first called Star-Plucking Temple but was renamed to honor Wú Xiá, a wandering monk who died here in the 16th century, reportedly at the age of 126. The 350-year-old flesh body of Wú Xiá is now on display in this monastery, his legs crossed in lotus position and arms folded in space—a seated mummy of skull and bones lacquered in gold. Like Prince Kim, Wú Xiá achieved bodhisattva-hood, a complete identity with Dìzàng. His transcription of the *Sutra of the Adornment of Buddha* in 81 volumes, a work over which he labored for 24 years, is also contained in this monastery. What sets this opus of copywork apart is that he brushed each character of it in his own blood after mixing it with gold.

Crossing the Bamboo Sea

Despite all these ancient attractions, the temples and halls of Jiǔhuá Shān, my mind was on the mountaintops. A Chinese guidebook sums it up thus: "Those who have already ascended to Jiǔhuá Street always think of climbing atop Heavenly Terrace Peak to fulfill their wish of reaching the summit and gazing into infinity." Yes: to gaze into infinity—that would do nicely.

Heavenly Terrace (Tiāntái Shān), at 1,302m (4,340 ft.), is the chief peak of the traditional 99 peaks of Jiǔhuá Shān, and the march to its ramparts is 8km (5 miles) of trails and stone stairs. In fact, according to the official census, Jiǔhuá Shān contains 250,000 stone steps, cut and laid by hand.

I set out at 8:30am, following a path of stone slabs east off Jiǔhuá Street. It led me past a stunning public lavatory, a spacious white building with a lofty tiled roof that I would have mistaken for a temple were it not for the characters for man and woman hand-painted on either side. A canal cascaded down from this outhouse, marking the mountain trail.

The old pilgrim women from my bus were not far ahead. Perhaps they'd come with a real purpose: to petition Dìzàng for the release of family members from the prison cells of the afterlife. Most of the people ascending the trail were not so devout. They were sightseers dressed in jeans, V-necked sweaters, blue-jean jackets, and white running shoes. They did not burn joss sticks at every station along the route.

From where I started, I could barely make out Heavenly Terrace, one of the distant jagged peaks in a broad fortress, separated by a deep valley. After surmounting the ridge that rises above Jiǔhuá Street, I descended into that intervening valley.

The stair trail was clean at first, bordered by fields of bamboo, pink blossoms, and tea rows. Vendors had pitched their canvas-topped stalls every so often, and my first stop after an hour's stroll was to buy a bottle of water. Spring water in plastic bottles has flooded the Chinese marketplace. Visitors to Jiǔhuá Shān gulp water and cast the empties into the green margins. At the base of the valley is a village, **Mínyuán,** its buildings washed white. Whitewashed nunneries dot the enfolded hillsides. I don't remember ever seeing so many monasteries and nunneries in one place in China. They face Zhúhǎi, the Bamboo Sea, great repository of those plastic bottles.

The Circles of Hell

Crossing a vibrant stream, I left the valley behind and ascended more stairs to the **Phoenix Pine (Fènghuáng Sōng),** said to have been greeting pilgrims with its wide arms for a thousand years. The pine had been encircled recently with a marble wall. Beside it, visitors gathered to rest and gossip. Some, mounted on brown ponies and costumed in long black robes with matching Stetsons, paid a roving photographer for their portraits. Everyone paused at the pine, including the sedan chair porters. I counted at least 20 carriers. Their chairs are of bamboo and wicker, squarish, straight-backed, with matted headrests. Their long carrying poles are bamboo as well. It's exceedingly tough work for two men: The stairs are steep enough to make me sweat.

The trail beyond the Phoenix Pine meanders from temple to temple, and even right through the heart of a temple, where I brushed past nuns tending open fires of incense. I came across more old women, two of whom were munching on sugarcane, tearing off mouthful after mouthful. They had their sticks of incense, and sheaves of paper money filled their bags. They'd come well stocked with offerings to burn for those in the underworld who are short of cash. These notes from the Bank of Hell, written in monstrous sums, are used by the dead to bribe their way through the Ten Courts of the Underworld, said to be located under this very mountain.

The Chinese Circles of Hell are courts of punishment that grow more severe with depth. The second court, for example, is a great frozen lake for general torture. The third is populated by unfilial sons and disobedient state officials. The fourth is for those who committed fraud and those who let their animals disturb others. Other courts are tailored to the punishment of other sins, and most of the sins are more Confucian than Daoist or Buddhist, concerned with violations of the family hierarchy in all its manifestations. There is a deep court reserved for the most heinous criminals, murderers who must sweat it out until their victims are reincarnated.

Buddha's Bunny

Walking from temple to temple, I came upon a vendor who had vacated his low chair in front of a shop and left tethered to it a fat rabbit—probably more meal than pet or talisman. When Buddha took a stroll in the forest, so one story goes, all the animals showered him with the foodstuffs they had gathered, except for the rabbit, which is not a gatherer. Still, moved to an act of transcendence, the rabbit hurled itself into the flames of the campfire to serve as a meal, and by the time Buddha could rescue it, the rabbit was roasted through. Buddha immortalized the creature by granting it dominion over the lunar orb, and ever after, just as we look for the man in the moon, the Chinese look for the rabbit.

Today, Jiǔhuá Shān is neither lunar nor infernal. If this be hell, it is an absolutely pleasant one. The fires seem confined to incense burners, a few of which, placed in the middle of the road, are towering: 4m (12 ft.) high and tiered like iron pagodas, bells swinging from their pitch-black eaves.

Green Cloud Nunnery

The rock cliffs that make up the summit are perfectly vertical. The stairs coil tediously around and about. I passed through one small temple filled with fire and smoke, its low walls black as a cave. Then came a stretch of yet steeper stairs with a stone railing, called the **Heavenly Staircase (Tiāntī),** which ended high above in the **Green Cloud Nunnery.** Green Cloud is fronted by a narrow gallery affording a splendid view of the valley floor at the bottom of a vast ravine from which I had just climbed. Just below me, on a spur trail, dozens of old women paraded before a small stone incense burner. They collapsed to their knees and elbows to pray. Several were nuns, dressed head to foot in black silk gowns and caps.

Above me, the rock outcroppings tapered into the sky, resembling uplifted sword blades. I inched upward on the steep stairs. Just ahead was **Enlightenment Nunnery (Guānyīn Sì)**, a five-story edifice capping a dramatic drop-off. This nunnery is an impregnable fortress pinioned to a perch under the final peak like a palace for eagles. Here I had reached the sub-realm of Guānyīn, the Goddess of Mercy, and she had endowed the way to the Heavenly Terrace with her own image, transformed into a single slender rock. It is a startling likeness of the goddess, life-sized, with flowing long hair and a meditative posture. Yet it appears to be a natural rock form poised in space, surveying the deep valley I crossed an hour ago. Someone had draped her in a red cape to keep her warm. She's surrounded by other formations, fissured and weathered into suggestive shapes, the candles and censers of a mountain altar. Above this monument to mercy, the mountain belongs to Dìzàng and the Ten Judges of Hell.

Heavenly Terrace (Tiāntái Shān)

The trail twisted up to Heavenly Terrace Peak, Dìzàng's high throne, with its **Temple of Ten Thousand Buddhas (Wànfó Sì)** and the **Sun-Holding Pavilion (Péngrì Tíng)**. I reached this supreme summit with a determined grunt, well before noon. This high platform of Jiǔhuá Shān is nearly bare, paved in large white square blocks. White, not black, is the Chinese color of death, which perhaps explains the white walls of all the nunneries, monasteries, and temples. Pilgrims, even many of the young Chinese tourists, were busy here tossing incense sticks into two round three-legged black pots. A hundred steps below me, vendors did a brisk business in joss and charms.

Beyond this platform, the throng spread out on a narrow spine for views in every direction as far as the Yángzǐ River. For once, the claim of 99 peaks was not a poetic exaggeration: There are hundreds of peaks. I walked along the narrow spine of the summit, sat down in a niche, and took in the view.

The Jiǔhuá Shān I found today may not be the Jiǔhuá Shān of yesteryear. But no matter that there are but half as many temples, nunneries, and monasteries as travelers found a century ago. No matter that the 7,000 pilgrims a day who visited here at the end of the last dynasty have dwindled to a few hundred tourists, a few score believers. I could feel that the old connections were waiting to be seized and plugged in, if only one could recommend how. At the summit of this mountain paradise is the ancient gate to Hell. The line is thin but sublime.

PRACTICAL INFORMATION

by Sharon Owyang

ORIENTATION & WHEN TO GO

Jiŭhuá Shān (Nine Glories Mountain) is located in southern Ānhuī Province, 390km (240 miles) west of Hángzhōu, 450km (279 miles) southwest of Shànghǎi, and 160km (99 miles) northwest of Huáng Shān (Yellow Mountain; a 3½-hr. bus ride on mountain roads).

With wet and cold winters, foggy springs, and hot and humid summers, Jiŭhuá Shān is best visited in September and October. The annual temple fair usually runs from mid-August to mid-September, during which time 100,000 tourists visit.

GETTING THERE

By Train There is no airport or practical rail service near Jiŭhuá Shān. The closest train station is at **Tónglíng**, 1½ hours away by bus, where there are several trains a day to Shànghǎi (6 hr.).
By Bus If you visit Huáng Shān (see separate chapter, beginning on p. 465), there is a daily private bus service (3½ hr.; ¥40/$5; 7am) from Tāngkǒu (at the foot of Huáng Shān) to Jiŭhuá Shān. Have your hotel in Tāngkǒu book you a

seat the night before. In Jiŭhuá Shān, bus tickets can be purchased at the bus station ticket office, which is to your left outside the entrance to Jiŭhuá Village. From here, buses go to Hángzhōu (5 hr.; ¥70/$8.75; 6:30am), Huáng Shān (3½ hr.; ¥35/$4.30; 7am, 2:30pm), and Tónglíng (1 hr.; ¥15/$1.90; 9am, 4:30pm). Renting a private car between Huáng Shān and Jiŭhuá Shān will cost around ¥500 ($62).

TOURS & STRATAGEMS

Visitor Information There is a **China Travel Service (CTS)** office (② **0566/501-1588**; fax 0566/501-1587) in the village on Jiŭhuá Jiē next to the entrance to Precious Hall of the Physical Body (Ròushēn Bǎodiàn). It can provide basic information and maps and tries to be helpful, even if it does not have much experience dealing with Western visitors.
Exploring the Mountain At the entrance to the village, you are required to buy a ticket for the mountain for ¥70 ($8.75) (¥60/$7.50 Dec–Feb), as well as pay another ¥5 (60¢) for the half-hour bus ride up to

Jiŭhuá Village (though you can stay on the same bus you came on). The village, halfway up the mountain range, is where the 8km (5-mile) trek to the 1,302m (4,340-ft.) summit begins. From the village to Phoenix Pine is another 20 minutes by *miàndi* (van) taxi (¥5/60¢). At **Phoenix Pine (Fènghuáng Sōng),** there is a cable car with express service (¥50/$6.25 ascending; ¥36/$4.50 descending) or regular service (Mar–Nov ¥40/$5 ascending, ¥35/$4.30 descending; other times ¥35/$4.30 ascending, ¥30/$3.75 descending) that runs nearly to the summit. Taxis and some minibuses at the village gate go to the cable-car terminal. If you want to see sunrise from the summit, catch the cable car, since its terminal at Phoenix Pine is less than an hour's quick walk from the village.

WHERE TO STAY

There are several two- and three-star hotels to choose from, none of them worth particular recommendation. The most popular choice with foreigners is the three-star **Jùlóng Hotel (Jùlóng Dàjiǔdiàn; ℂ 0566/501-1368;** fax 0566/ 501-1022; www.jiuhuashan.com.cn). Located on the right-hand side of the street a block up from the bus parking lot in Jiǔhuá Village, the Jùlóng has large rooms furnished with the basics: air-conditioning, TV, telephone, and hot water. Bathrooms are small, a bit run-down, but clean enough. Standard doubles cost ¥280 to ¥398 ($35–$49), with a 20% discount given at most times except weekends and holidays. The newer (2000), three-star **Jiǔhuá Hotel (Jiǔhuá Shānzhuāng),** at Dēngtǎ Xīncūn 86 (ℂ **0566/501-1036;** fax 0566/ 501-1032), has nicer rooms than the Jùlóng, but it's located farther away from the center of town on a one-way street leading up from the square in front of the Jùlóng Hotel. Rooms (¥580/$72) in the main building were renovated in 2001. Quite comfortable, they are equipped with fridge, beverages, and hair dryer in addition to the basics. The hotel has a Chinese restaurant, bowling alley, salon, and sauna. The staff speaks almost no English.

WHERE TO DINE

Jiǔhuá Shān has no restaurants of note, certainly none with English-language menus. Stick to the hotels, which all have large Chinese restaurants that serve *jiāchángcài* (home-style cooking) with dinner for two averaging ¥40 to ¥120 ($5–$15). Dozens of small cafes and restaurants along the main street, Jiǔhuá Jiē, serve *jiāchángcài* and noodles, but none of these places have English menus. Along the mountain trail, vendors sell snacks, drinks, boiled eggs, and instant noodles.

HÉNG SHĀN NÁN YUÈ: SACRED MOUNTAIN OF THE SOUTH

衡山南岳

Héng Shān Nán Yuè (simply called Héng Shān or Nán Yuè by local residents) is the southern peak on the Daoist compass of China's Five Sacred Mountains. According to an ancient record, "Héng Mountain rules the Southern Land by the virtue of fire." The fire god lives on the highest of Héng Shān Nán Yuè's peaks, Zhùróng Fēng, elevation 1,270m (4,232 ft.). To see what remained on the highest peak of the sacred mountain of the south, I set out in the morning on a bus from Chángshā, the capital of Húnán Province, to the village of Nán Yuè and the gate to Héng Shān.

Héng Shān is commonly called Nán Yuè, which means "Southern Peak," but knowing its local name didn't help me much. I had no local map, just a rudimentary sense of direction. I walked a mile up an unpaved road to the village at the foot of the mountain. At the end of the village, the road forks up a steep hill, where I found a parked bus aimed up the mountain.

I drew a crowd when I inquired if this was the bus to the *bàn shān tíng,* the station midway up the mountain where I wanted to lodge for the night. People gave me smiling stares and motioned me aboard. The bus was parked in front of the **Temple of the Southern Mountain (Nán Yuè Miào).** This is one of the three most famous Buddhist temples in China. It is also the largest Buddhist complex anywhere on the Five Sacred Mountains. Nán Yuè Miào was built in A.D. 725 but leveled many times, most recently in the 19th century by the Tàipíng Rebels, their leader a rabidly anti-Western Hakka from Húnán who fancied himself the brother of Jesus Christ. The present set of buildings, with their yellow-glazed tiles, dates back only to 1882. When the final emperor of China assumed the throne, an ox was sacrificed at this temple, but aside from its largest hall, supported by 72 pillars, each 22m (72 ft.) high in honor of the 72 peaks of Héng Shān, the temple did not attract me. The mountain did.

The character of the mountain is confusing, or perhaps it is just Daoist. Red is its symbolic color, fire its primordial element, but the mountain has a history shaped by the legendary Yǔ Emperor in his epic struggle against floods 3,000 years ago. Yǔ is credited with subduing the rising waters that besieged the lower Yángzǐ River basin by constructing nine abatement channels. Héng Shān is just south of the Yángzǐ. It has a long history of attracting officials and even emperors to its altars, where they prayed for deliverance from the floods. Perhaps it takes a mountain god of fire to subdue the floods of China's mightiest river.

Mr. Ma Gu

The bus rolled out, and the road up the mountain crisscrossed the stone steps of the old pilgrim path. There has been a paved road to the top for many decades. It was resurfaced in 1933 by order of the governor of Húnán, who maintained his own elaborate summer house partway up the sacred peak, as did many officials and merchants. I could see why they made this their retreat. The scenery is pleasing. In the gentle mist, I had a romantic view of rice terraces along the Nán Yuè Reservoir. Passing a 1942 memorial to those who died when the Japanese invaded here in 1937, we began a steep rise. I disembarked at the midpoint parking lot.

This area was once the site of a Daoist guesthouse, a midway pavilion built in 1878 as a resting place for pilgrims. Today, not a single pilgrim was in sight. In fact, there were no travelers of any description. The rain was pounding down. I opened my umbrella. The road was dotted with a few concession booths, all closed. Not knowing what else to do and where exactly to go, I struck out up the road.

I came to a billboard with a map. An arrow was aimed at a hotel. A boy stopped beside me, staring too at the sign. I asked him if he knew the way to a hotel. He nodded. We came to an intersection. I wanted to go right, since that was the way up the mountain, but he motioned me left. He guided me to a modern guesthouse on a bluff. Inside, the lobby was empty, save for a single clerk fetched by my companion. I was led to the rear and outside, up two flights of stairs to a balcony. I could look over the bright green tiles of the lower roofs and across the valley to a crowded screen of distant peaks.

The accommodations resembled those of an extremely shabby summer resort. The room had a splendid view. In a photograph, my immediate surroundings would resemble a misty mountain paradise, dotted with remote monasteries, temples, and old summer homes. Fifty-some years ago, China's Republican officials were selling housing lots left and right up here for summer homes.

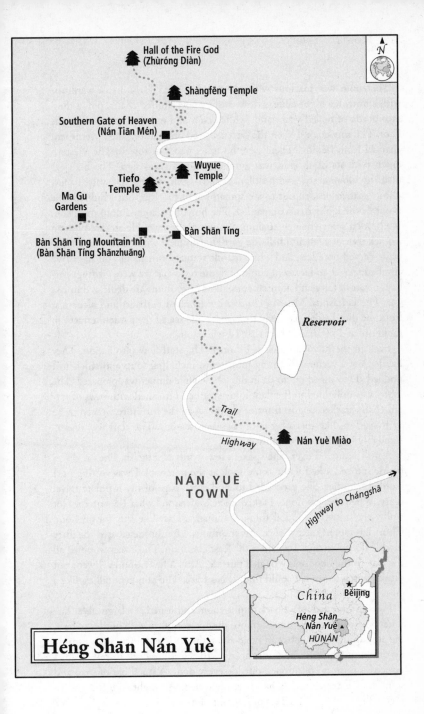

Hall of the Fire God
(Zhùróng Diàn)

Shàngfēng Temple

Southern Gate of Heaven
(Nán Tiān Mén)

Wuyue
Temple

Tiefo
Temple

Ma Gu
Gardens

Bàn Shān Tíng Mountain Inn
(Bàn Shān Tíng Shānzhuāng)

Bàn Shān Tíng

Reservoir

Trail

Highway

Nán Yuè Miào

NÁN YUÈ
TOWN

Highway to Chángshā

China

Běijīng

Héng Shān
Nán Yuè

HÚNÁN

Héng Shān Nán Yuè

The room was spacious with plenty of wooden furniture: a wardrobe with a mirror, a night table, a desk, and two overstuffed chairs, plus a thermos bottle of boiled water and two tea cups and my own spittoon on the floor. The tiny color TV on the desk received one station: the government channel from Běijīng. There were no toilet paper or towels. The Western toilet, with its black seat, was gurgling—not a good sign. The bed was made up Chinese style, with a blanket and a quilt, no sheets. I waited a few minutes, then headed out to see something of the area, but I didn't make it out of the lobby unaccompanied. The hotel boy latched onto me again. We headed somewhere west along a mountain terrace. He escorted me on a quick tour of a fanciful **hillside garden,** complete with pools, stone stairways, carved boulders, and white marble statues of maidens and stags. We climbed terrace to terrace. I couldn't figure out what we were visiting: perhaps a sort of fairyland amusement park. The grounds are dedicated to Ma Gu. The fantastical Mr. Ma Gu was a celebrated herbalist and alchemist from the dim Daoist past. My teenaged guide scaled the garden terraces in rapid order; I persuaded him that I'd had enough.

Back in the hotel, I requested dinner. The staff flew into action. They handed me a menu containing four items, including soup and chicken. I nodded. They asked me to sit in the lobby while dinner was prepared. The lobby was unlighted in the dark rainy weather, furnished with rows of rattan chairs stacked one in front of another—all the furniture seemed to be in transition, like that of a resort between seasons. The staff was understandably idle: I was their only guest.

A girl sauntered over. She spoke a few words of English. She sat down beside me and asked if she could look at the notebook I was writing in. I handed it to her. She proceeded to read every page of my intimate travel diary. When she was done, I asked if she understood what I'd written. Not really, she answered. Good thing, I thought. I sat like this for an hour. China has taught me patience. An enormous water beetle crossed the dirty marble floor. No one else paid it the least attention. The insect wobbled all the way to the door and wriggled outside. After a few minutes, I went out on the porch to see if I could find it. No trace. The rain kept falling like a curse.

I was summoned into a back dining room and seated at a large table. The hotel boy joined me for an enormous dinner, complete with bottles of beer. He ate through every plate in rapid-fire fashion. The dinner cost a fortune by ordinary Chinese standards, nearly $10. Heading back to my room, I noticed a spittoon positioned outside every door. A small bar of soap and some brown paper towels had been delivered. All night, the fire god of Héng Shān delivered buckets of fragrant rain.

Stepping into the Clouds

Forgoing Sunday breakfast at the inn, I sneaked through the lobby and popped out the door before 7am, the hotel boy nowhere in sight. I skipped down the road and inquired of a local the way to **Zhùróng Fēng,** the highest peak of Héng Shān. The morning climb covered about 5km (3 miles) with a 600m (2,000-ft.) rise from my hotel. Once off the highway, I kept to the trail of slab stairs that rises in straight segments, bisecting the curving highway the buses take to the summit.

There was a heavy blanket of fog on the slopes. Nán Yuè is renowned for its storms. I could see only a hundred feet ahead, sometimes half that much. I passed a few inns and cafes, a handful of temples, and several simple tables of souvenirs and foodstuffs. The low visibility, the tea plants, and the bamboo forests baffled the sounds of the outside world. The mountain was silent.

The bamboo forests are impressive, the bamboo stocks as large as water pipes and probably as strong. I saw no wildlife at all—too civilized, given the paved highway to the top. There weren't many other people on the trail, although the slopes were littered with plastic wrappers and containers. Perhaps this weekend's tourists had already ridden a bus to the summit.

I savored the slow pace, the quiet, the solitude. I saw a small herd of black cows, unattended, near a cave temple dedicated to Guānyīn. The Goddess of Mercy seems to be on every mountain, Daoist as well as Buddhist. On this Daoist peak of the south, scores of pilgrims are said to have once leaped from **Guānyīn's Cliff** to their deaths, rapt with divine ecstasy and the hope of breaking through to a better world. That merciful cliff never pierces the fog, which filled in all gaps this morning.

After an hour's walk, a tiny, worn temple parted the fog a hundred stairs above. I could hear chanting within, whispers becoming soft voices as I neared. Cloaked in mist, the temple itself seemed to be speaking. But upon arriving at the door of this enchanted temple, I was hurled back to solid Earth: Two novice monks were manning a card table at the entrance, selling admission tickets to the performance within.

I pushed on, catching up with a peasant boy shouldering a shovel. He kept pace with me. The trail merged with the road and a confusing terrain of buildings. We arrived at a construction site. I could see higher peaks ahead. The boy joined other laborers at an excavation, but he pointed me the right way to the top.

This paved highway certainly robs the mountain of its centuries of romance and remoteness, although in inclement weather, especially in the mist, the intrusion is veiled. Otherwise, Héng Shān would be little short of a Chinese version of Yosemite Park. I scarcely realized that I was passing through more than a construction site, passing through, in fact, the **Southern Gate of Heaven (Nán Tiān Mén)**—a three-legged stone gate (*páilóu*) engraved with this inscription, painted bright red:

> Here is South Heaven.
> Look down at the hills and the five rivers
> One by one etched in the scene.
> Meandering and winding up ascending stairs,
> Step into the clouds.

The Peak of Fire & Rain

I had in fact stepped into the clouds. I was now one slope from the summit, outside the long walls of **Shàngfēng Temple (Shàngfēng Sì),** a large temple. The fog was melting, flying off in long streamers. First I could see the high steel girders of a transmission tower behind the temple, then a garden of radar or microwave dishes—a modern communications center that has nothing to do with Daoism. Before me was the final rise, a newly restored path of granite and concrete, with stone benches for resting along the way. I was not surprised to find a ticket seller charging ¥1 (10¢) for the final hike.

I could see that the path is well worth following, not only for the panorama it affords but for the high altar at the top, the **Hall of the Fire God (Zhùróng Diàn).** Built in the 16th century and restored in the 19th, it was apparently completely rebuilt in the 1930s after a bone-crunching storm. In the near distance, in the banners of fog, it looks much older, like a ravaged remnant of primordial China, an ancient outcropping of mountain worship, the abode of an angry fire god who has not left so much as his own altar unscorched.

I seated myself on the wall of this temple's courtyard, one little stairway below the Fire Temple, waiting for the last wisps of fog to be torn away. The courtyard teemed with sightseers, mostly young people, brightly dressed. Several had donned the yellow robes of high officials and ancient royalty to have their portraits snapped on the summit. Groups of students found me out—as they always do—once I was motionless and visible on a mountain peak. They seated themselves next to me, one by one, while their friends snapped away with their cameras. I was more a sight than any mountaintop or temple. Some practiced a smattering of English, but I was quite surprised when a young woman introduced herself to me in fluent English. She turned out to be one of a half-dozen college students climbing the mountain with their teacher, who was an American, too, I was informed, and more than that, she was a minority. Her students were quite excited about that fact: It made their teacher that much more exotic.

When she arrived with the other students, I learned that she was an anthropologist interested in the struggles of the minority peoples in rural China. She taught English at the university in Xiāngtán, a small city between Héng Shān and Chángshā. As for her minority status, she was Jewish.

I linked up with her entourage. Together we ascended to the Temple of the Fire God. The entrance consists of many folding doors, painted red. A fire extinguisher is posted at one door on the right side, and above it, quite out of place, a huge round clock with a white face, black hands, and Arabic numerals. The walls are square cement blocks; the roof is metal tile. The interior of the shrine is an unlit, humble affair, its dark walls furnished in simple posters. The bust of the Yǔ Emperor—standing in for the fire god—is ensconced in a curtained recess behind the altar. Bedecked in long strands of black beard, hands crossed just below his neck, shoulders draped in a red silk robe, the god of Héng Shān is framed by a wall of frescoes in red paint and gold leaf. Candles and long sticks of incense sputter in iron holders welded to the altar table.

Two long risers before the altar contain several dozen dirty patchwork cushions on which a surprising number of young tourists knelt, clutching lighted incense between their fingers. One of the Xiāngtán students was pushed by her classmates into buying joss sticks from the monks. She took her turn in beseeching the god. As she knelt, she giggled self-consciously; her girlfriends took flash pictures. She bowed her head, whispered, and rose with a smile.

Outside, behind the temple, we had fine views of the many peaks of Héng Shān. Clouds line the deep bowls of the valleys. This is where Hugh Farley, a journalist, spent a night in 1935, a night he wouldn't soon forget, when the Temple of the Fire God was too new, too untempered by the elements to possess any romantic appeal. "It was not a very satisfactory reward for the steep climb," he reported, "as it had been rebuilt last year, and its newness and lack of distinction were rather disappointing. Perhaps I was unduly prejudiced by the masses of ugly stink-bugs that covered its floors, walls, pillars and ceilings with a squirming horde, three or four deep in some places." Farley did not blame the monks for the neglect; they were forbidden by their vows to destroy any form of life, no matter how creepy. "Magnificent, on the other hand, was the view," Farley wrote, "for the temple stands on a pinnacle of rock with unobstructed vision in all directions . . . Never before in China have I so fully appreciated the proximity or contrast of fertility and barrenness, of water and of drought, of living greenness like the sea and stark brownness like the desert."

In the decades since, this vista has endured, although I would not term it spectacular; the Temple of the Fire God has improved with age, however, and is the perfect monument for the highest platform of any holy mountain: decrepit, dark, humble, naked, cold, and forbidding.

The New South

I ate lunch with the five students and their teacher outside the temple, at the rear. The student who first approached me was particularly precocious. She was majoring in linguistics; she had mastered a smooth, slangy English. She asked me about Noam Chomsky, then quizzed me on minute details about the American presidency and international events. She told me that she had just been accepted for graduate studies in Wǔhàn, but she hadn't decided whether to accept. Until recently the great temptation for college students, especially the most brilliant undergraduates, was "to go south" to Shēnzhèn or Guǎngdōng Province, where the Chinese economy was boiling hot and a student who spoke English could get a job on the spot as a company clerk or a hotel receptionist and make a fortune overnight. Such a job paid 10 times what a teacher, even a professor, could expect to pull down. But a few years ago, in an effort to encourage professors to stay put, universities (with the government's nod) raised teachers' salaries and improved housing for many of them.

We descended Nán Yuè in the sun, everyone sweating. I thought of the story of the Daoist pilgrim with a stiff leg of iron who climbed 10km (6 miles) of stairs to this peak and woke to see the sunrise. Looking up, he proclaimed, "The sea of cloud washes my heart clean." I felt cleansed, too, and removed from the world, oddly enough—purged of all particular desires—as I stepped down the mountain, its bamboo forest soaked in the low clouds like a long, ink-brushed scroll.

"What did your schoolmate pray for in the temple?" I asked. I was unable to imagine what people today would pray for at the top of this mountain, where fire and flood once reigned. She prayed for a good job, I was told; for prosperity. Last year, two of her classmates came to the top of Héng Shān and prayed to find high-paying work in the south; their wishes granted, they planned to return this summer, a year later as prescribed, to thank the god of the mountain for his blessing.

So, if the sacred mountains have lost their original powers, they have not lost a certain metaphysical presence. They still act as receivers of personal petitions.

One student draped me in a necklace of brown wooden beads, the pilgrim's rosary. We caught a bus down to the village, where we had lunch in town. Several buses later—nothing according to schedule—we were in Xiāngtán, an hour from Chángshā, just before dark. With the students' help, I flagged down a bus to Chángshā. I sat by an open window. Pure darkness rushed in. Poor workers and peasants jumped on and off at the stops.

I was thinking my own thoughts, unrelated to theirs. I was thinking that a new constellation of gods had risen from the grave of Maoist-Marxism to serve as Dèng Xiǎopíng's divine dispensers of cash; that the sacred compass of China had been realigned, its cardinal points marked with dollar signs; and that today's pilgrims are parading to these mountain altars like contestants in a Wheel of Fortune game show, petitioning the gods of rain and fire for high-paying jobs.

PRACTICAL INFORMATION

by Michelle Sans

ORIENTATION & WHEN TO GO

Located on the southwestern bank of the Xiāng River in the middle of Húnán Province, **Héng Shān**—also known as Nán Yuè, "Southern Marchmount"—is one of the five sacred peaks of Daoism. Its nearest major city is Chángshā, capital of Húnán Province. Springs here bring heavy rainfall, summers are hot and muggy, and winters are cold, making autumn the best time to visit. But even on the best of days, whether due to fog or smog, the sun is rarely without its veil of haze.

GETTING THERE

By Plane There are daily flights to Chángshā from Běijīng (2 hr.), Guǎngzhōu (1 hr.), Shànghǎi (1½ hr.), Xī'ān (1½ hr.), and Hong Kong (1½ hr.). A taxi from the airport costs about ¥100 ($12). An airport shuttle to CAAC's hotel, the Mínháng Dàjiǔdiàn, near the rail station is ¥15 ($2) for the 30- to 40-minute drive. It departs when full, so there may be a wait.

By Train There are overnight trains to Chángshā from Guǎngzhōu (12 hr.), Shànghǎi (15 hr.), and Zhāngjiā Jiè (13½ hr.). A day train to Zhāngjiā Jiè takes only 5¼ hours, but it pulls in at 8:30pm.

By Bus to the Mountain Chángshā is the urban gateway to Héng Shān and the village of Nán Yuè at its base. Morning express/direct buses (Iveco) make the 2¼-hour trip south from Chángshā to the mountain (¥32/$4 each way). Bus tickets can be purchased at Chángshā's south bus station.

TOURS & STRATAGEMS

Visitor Information A branch of **China International Travel Service (CITS)**, in the Fúróng Hotel (✆ 0731/443-3355), dispenses information and books air, bus, and train tickets, as does the main CITS office on the 11th floor of Xiāoyuán Mansion, Wǔyī Dōng Lù (✆ 0731/228-0439). The **Dragonair** office, for tickets to Hong Kong, is at 298 Fúróng Nán Lù in the Grand Sun City Hotel (Shénnóng Dàjiǔdiàn; ✆ 0731/521-8888, ext. 3111).

Exploring the Mountain If you take the first bus that departs Chángshā at 6:30am, it is possible to make this a day trip and still have time to enjoy the mountain, its wonderful trails through the bamboo forests, and the many temples scattered across its slopes.

The mountain park entrance is at **Nán Yuè Temple,** on the north side of the village, along the road leading up the mountain. Admission is ¥40 ($5). Buses to the mid-section of the mountain, which depart often from the park entrance, cost ¥11 ($1.35). A new mile-long cable-car system operates from here. The ride to Nán Tiān Mén at the summit takes 7 minutes (round-trip ¥50/$6.25; one-way up ¥30/$3.75; one-way down ¥25/$3.10). For ¥11 ($1.35), you can take another bus from the midway station to the top. The footpath from bottom to top is 14km (9 miles) long and takes about 5 hours to walk.

WHERE TO STAY

Basic lodging can be found at the summit near Zhùróng Diàn and midway up the mountain just above the bus parking lot and in the vicinity of the cable car. Directly opposite the Xuándū Monastery (Xuándū Guàn) is the 16-unit **Bàn Shān Tíng Mountain Inn (Bàn Shān Tíng Shānzhuāng;** © **0734/567-6239;** mobile 138/7571-4793). Rooms are basic but very clean, and those on the south side have mountain views. A double costs ¥208 ($26); a double in a room with older furniture and fixtures costs ¥148 ($18); 30% discounts are standard. All rooms have TV, bathroom with both bathtub and shower, and 24-hour hot water. The people at the front desk and in the kitchen are friendly and eager to make guests comfortable.

Chángshā has a number of mid- to high-range hotels from which to choose. One of the best for comfort and making guests feel at home is the Hong Kong–managed, 328-unit **Bestride Hotel (Húnán Jiāchéng Jiǔdiàn),** Láo Dòng Xī Lù 386 (© **0731/852-2802;** fax 0731/852-2163; pr@hnbrhotel.com). Management and staff here are professional yet very friendly and eager to please. Guest rooms (¥720/$87 double, though 35%–50% discounts are standard) were renovated in 2001; still look well maintained; and have air-conditioning, TV, dataport, minibar, and safe. The hotel has a fitness room, cold and hot saunas, therapeutic massage, and billiards. There are three executive floors and an executive lounge and study.

WHERE TO DINE

All of the inns on the mountain have small dining rooms and kitchens. Since there are no English menus, you may have to go to the kitchen and point to your order. Settle on a price in advance or you may end up getting the most expensive dish on the menu—or the largest serving. On average, each dish should cost about ¥5 to ¥10 (60¢–$1.25).

Pǔtuó Shān: Buddhist Peak of the East

普陀山

Pǔtuó Shān is an island in the East China Sea, east of Hángzhōu and south of Shànghǎi. In the Chinese tradition, it is the supreme dwelling place of Guānyīn, Goddess of Mercy. For many centuries, pilgrims have worshipped Guānyīn, touched by her compassion. She became the most popular divinity in China. She still is. Pilgrims petition her for the birth of male children and the return of mariners safely to shore. This island mountain remains her home.

I reached Pǔtuó Shān by a circuitous route: a train from Hángzhōu to Níngbō; the wrong ferry from Níngbō, which dumped me at a nearby island; a pedicab across the island to a wharf; and finally a fishing boat to Pǔtuó Shān. The boat was an unpainted motorized skiff. The fisherman placed me down in its hold. A quilt was spread out on the floor. I lay down on it. Beside me was a young monk, head shaven. He was dressed in a golden robe and golden slippers. He sat up, cross-legged; I reclined.

We set out on this final passage to Pǔtuó Shān together, wordless before the roar of the engine. I closed my eyes. The boat rocked like a cradle. The monk sat up straight, eyes cast down, as if in meditation. It was nearly noon, but dark in the hold. Above was the gray sky; on the edges, the spray of rough seas. The diesel cracked like an unoiled clock, its fumes wafting in the wind. The monk seemed to be presiding over me. A patch of faint light swayed overhead. I stared at the monk's white leggings, banded at the calves. I was very nearly rocked to sleep. Then the engine stopped. We drifted.

I peered out from the hold. I could see the huge ornate gate to Pǔtuó Shān, ancient in the fog, resembling a hairy three-legged mammoth turned to stone, mounted on an outcropping of rounded boulders on the southern tip of the island. The romance of its appearance at that moment, at our angle of approach, lent it a rich cloak, one it seems to have worn since the beginning of Chinese time, its three portals capped by soaring tile roofs. Here was the **Southern Gate of Heaven (Nán Tiān Mén),** the pilgrim's entrance to the holy mountain in the sea. For a moment, I felt I had truly crossed into an ancient world, divided from 21st-century China.

Of Incense & Emperors

Pǔtuó Shān has an intense history of worship. In 1638, a gentleman named Chang Tai visited here aboard a pilgrim's boat. Once landed, he accompanied other 17th-century pilgrims through the three great temples on the island to the peak known as Buddha's Head. The devout making this trek had to bow every three steps, shouting the name of the Goddess of Mercy, Guānyīn. Spending the night on Pǔtuó Shān in the Great Hall, clogged with incense smoke as thick as fog, these pilgrims of the past waited for a divine manifestation. Chang Tai set the old scene thus: "Thousands of men and women sit in rows like packed fish . . . not one inch of space is unoccupied. During the night many nuns burn incense on their heads or burn their arms and fingers. Women from good families imitate them. They recite scriptures and try not to show signs of pain."

The pilgrims came then and for centuries more to see Guānyīn float across this seascape of pines and camphors, tea plantations, engraved stones, and "powdered gold" beaches "fine as silk." Guānyīn is still the bodhisattva in residence, one of 33 enlightened ones dedicated to saving the living. Known in Buddhist India as the god Avalokitesvara, Guānyīn changed sex in China, becoming a goddess sought out by those petitioning for the birth of a male child. Over the centuries, her worship spread across China, west to east, culminating at Pǔtuó Shān, the living *Potalaka* (Little White Flower) mentioned in the sutras, the holy mountain wrapped in a sea of water lilies.

In the highest temple on the island, the second emperor of the Qīng Dynasty, Kāngxī (1661–1722), inscribed in stone this homage to Pǔtuó Shān:

> Coming to this island, the moaning of the waves and the chanting of prayers can be heard, the deep purple temples can be seen, and peace can be had as expansive as the wide sea. . . . This renowned island has become a kingdom of the gods. It is like a ship of mercy upon the great sea; hills blue as the fleecy sky, and high as the heavens of Brahma; upon this lucky clean place the waves dash up to bathe the sun. Its reputation stands as a pillar, supporting the sky. From its summit, all places are connected.

High praise and imperial promise—enough to spur me to reach Pǔtuó Shān as quickly as possible, even to the point of boarding a latter-day "pilgrim's" boat. Little had changed: I crossed a sea of iron-pronged water lilies using such conveyances as lay in my path.

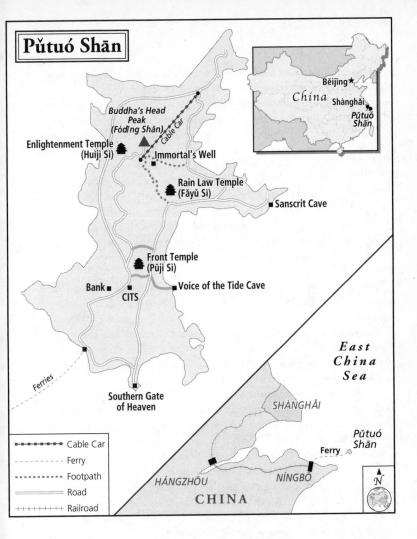

Front Temple (Pǔjì Sì)

I checked in at the Xǐlěi Xiǎo Zhuāng hotel and took a stroll around through the village on the southern tip of the island. Pǔtuó Shān is a sort of summer resort, an island getaway these days, but it has its charms. The old rock formations are trimmed in tea terraces; the large temples are enlivened with bright paint. Near my hotel is a winding cobblestone path with a fine stone wall on either side. And there's the **Pǔjì Sì**—also known as the **Front Temple**—the oldest and most elaborate on the island, its halls and pavilions fronted by an immense lotus pond. It's open from 5:30am to 6pm; admission is ¥5 (65¢).

This pond, rather run-down and devoid of its lotus flowers, is crossed by several arched bridges and presided over by a five-story pagoda, the **Duōbǎo Tǎ,** built in the 14th century. Pǔtuó Shān has been subjected to many cycles of decay and rebirth, fully in keeping with a Buddhist holy place. On one of the imperial tablets stored in this temple, the Kāngxī Emperor recounts how, before the Qīng Dynasty (1644–1911), "the island was overthrown by pirates, and all the temples were destroyed by fire. After the 22nd year of my reign, peace and order were established. Priests returned from the mainland, looked upon the old foundations, cleaned away the weeds and debris, and began to build anew . . . and I myself prayed, saying, 'May the temples forever keep the sea in subjection.'"

The temples are not eternal, however—not in a literal sense. They decay, are soon looted or razed, and are finally rebuilt, often from the ground up. Their lineage may go back 9 centuries and more, but they themselves are more youthful incarnations. Only their natural setting resists the wear and tear of regimes, if not the pummeling of salty waves, cold winds, and hard rains.

Some of the pilgrims here today had resisted politics and erosion. I ran across groups of old women, yellow shan bags slung over their shoulders and tied about their waists. For centuries, pilgrims stopped at each temple on this island, burned incense, and for a small donation had the temple monks affix a red ink seal to their mountain purses. The old women were outnumbered today, however, by young sailors; they were everywhere on the island, giving it the feel of a military base.

On the narrow street rising north of the Front Temple grounds are dozens of hole-in-the-wall cafes with live seafood swarming in plastic pans of water, and plenty of salons, too, mere shacks, doors wide open, hair blowers ablaze, posters of Western pop stars and celebrities pasted to the walls. Farmers in the fields are oblivious to tourism and pilgrimage alike. Tour buses park at the lotus pond, but not a single foreigner had I yet seen. I received a hail of friendly greetings when I walked the southern arc of the island. On my way from the fishing boat to the Xílěi Xiǎo Zhuāng, I passed a dog lying on the centerline of the highway to the village, legs folded under. There were plenty of people walking the shoulder, but no one stopped to examine the dog.

This is no longer an island of mercy—an irony, since as one of the four centers of Buddhism in China and the grand mansion of the Goddess of Mercy herself, you expect all life to be held sacred: horses, dogs, bedbugs. Somewhere on Pǔtuó Shān is a stele engraved with this holy admonition: "All that has life should not intentionally be killed. In the classic it is also said, 'The winter months breed lice; take them and put them into a bamboo joint; keep them warm with cotton, and give them oily food to eat lest they might freeze or starve.' Such is the doctrine of the Goddess of Mercy." But this and other doctrines of its ilk are temporarily out of service in the new, unsuperstitious China.

The View from Buddha's Head

At dawn, when I set out for **Buddha's Head Peak (Fódǐng Shān),** which rises less than a thousand feet above the level sea, I was inspired by one of the many simple inscriptions in the rocks of Pŭtuó Shān: "Ascend and enter the region of formlessness."

From the Front Monastery, I followed the road north, hoping it would dwindle into a forest path long before I reached Buddha's Head Peak. It didn't. The scenery up the western side is fine, and were it not for the asphalt of the curving highway and an occasional Chinese tour bus grinding by, I would have been alone in remote pine forests tumbling steeply down to the sea below. Along the shoulder of the highway, I came across tiny shrines cut into the smooth, moss-covered cliffs. Stone figures of Guānyīn are ensconced inside. I followed the paved road toward Buddha's Head Peak, rising above the saltpans and tea plantations, the nunneries and temples, the beaches and fishing junks.

After a several-mile climb, I reached Pŭtuó Shān's second great temple, the **Enlightenment Temple (Huìjì Sì).** Admission costs ¥5 (65¢), and hours are from 5am to 6:30pm. Buddha's Head Peak looms above. I strolled through a tour-bus parking lot. The halls to one side were stocked with souvenirs, snacks, and drinks. I bought two boiled eggs and a glass of Buddha tea. The summit was immediately above me, connected to the parking lot by stairs. An elderly ticket vendor squatted behind a long table, reading a rented book. He was wrapped in a full-length green army coat, its collar trimmed in brown fur. I bought a ticket from him and started the final ascent. A hundred steps later, I stood on Buddha's Head Peak atop Pŭtuó Shān.

Or almost atop. The summit is actually fenced off. Its gate is locked. A sign on the gate reads NO VISITORS. Inside the fence is a brick building without windows. Perhaps it's a weather station or a communications outpost—certainly a government installation. Near the gate is a coin-operated telescope. Truly, I had reached a state of pure formlessness unique to our century: unimperial and technological. Buddha's Head Peak is closed to modern pilgrims—a military outpost. Pŭtuó Shān is merciless in its emptiness. Yet the view from Buddha's forehead is sweeping. The hills are layered into the hem of the sea, and scores of islands radiate outward all the way to the clouds on the horizon.

Rain & Drought

I descended Buddha's Head Peak by the eastern route: a thousand stone-cut stairs inscribed with lotus petals. This is the path where the faithful were said to touch their heads every third or fifth step. Few such pilgrims were here today, but the grungy Immortal's Well was doing a brisk business hawking incense sticks and magic spring water by the glass in the cleft of a massive rock. Here, a hermit of the Eastern Jìn Dynasty (A.D. 317–420) discovered a source of spring water that never dried up and never turned salty.

This spring was once an emblem to Imperial China of a sacred cure for drought. Emperors petitioned Pǔtuó Shān on several occasions for rain, and, indeed, just a few hundred steep steps below this cave is the third great monastery of the island mountain, **Rain Law Temple (Fǎyǔ Sì).** Rain Law Temple was rebuilt a few years back. It's now open from 5am to 6:30pm; admission is ¥5 (65¢). It rises in tiers up the hillside of Buddha's Head Peak. One of its halls was shipped here from Nánjīng by the Kāngxī Emperor. Its central image is a statue of Guānyīn.

Bridge of Great Being

I paid a visit to the **Voice of the Tide Cave (Cháoyīn Dòng),** along the eastern shore; it's open from 4:30am to 6pm and admission is ¥5 (65¢). Here, for at least 900 years, pilgrims have reported seeing manifestations of Guānyīn, serene, bathed in purplish golden light. In 1209, an abbot ordered the building of the **Bridge of Great Being** from which the faithful could look into the cave for an appearance of Guānyīn as she is described in the Chinese classic *Journey to the West:* in her "white silk robe bathed in holy light." Late in the Míng Dynasty, pilgrims and monks would kneel and kowtow all the way to the tidal cave, arriving blood-soaked. Many threw themselves into the sea at the first appearance of a rainbow in the pinched, sun-struck spray—so many that monks once routinely scoured the waters with baskets, trolling for bones to be cremated.

No such suicidal hopefuls gather here anymore. All that's left to contemplate are a pile of rocks, an old bridge, a pretty jetty, and some dazzling waves. The most hardened devotees of all used to come here to set their fingers afire, to burn them out of existence. A gazetteer for the year 1361 notes that in A.D. 848 "a foreign monk came to the Voice of the Tide Cave. He burned his ten fingers in front of the cave. When the fingers were burned off, he saw the Great Being who preached *dharma* to him and gave him a seven-hued precious stone."

Ten living sticks of incense. . . . I stood on the Bridge of the Great Being looking into the womb of the goddess, trying to imagine how anyone could withstand such pain. From peak to cave, Pǔtuó Shān is exactly as it was in ancient China, but its transfiguration into the island home of the merciful goddess seems to have disappeared from the minds of the people.

Pilgrims & Submarines

On my way to the ferry dock on the southern tip of the island, I met four retired Americans who were teaching in Hángzhōu, accompanied on their tour by a student. With a native guide, everything had gone like clockwork for them. I tagged along, relaxed for the first time on my journey.

We boarded a direct ferry back to **Níngbō** and spread out in the soft-seat lounge up front. The island mountain faded away into the morning mist as it has for centuries. For a moment it was as if nothing had changed. Then I noticed a battered old submarine break the surface, heading for its holy port. Pŭtuó Shān has slipped the reins of emperors, pirates, and abbots, and is now ridden by the Chinese Navy.

I suppose it doesn't matter, this displacement of the spiritual. For the most part, visitors these days are sightseers, more concerned with prices and wages than with visions. But on the rear observation deck, packed shoulder to shoulder with standing passengers, I did come across a handful of true pilgrims: tiny old women with shan bags, rosary beads, and knitted wool watch caps, every one of them smiling. They thought I was quite the strangest sight in the world and they started to giggle. I didn't mind entertaining them.

Is this the same place as the old Pŭtuó Shān where a Sòng Dynasty poet stood a thousand years ago, calling it the mountain that overpowers the sea, the island where "the sun and moon shine before anywhere else"? Everywhere the landscape of this island was once fabulously transfigured, its stones into saints, its ledges into pulpits, its caves into eyes, its springs into elixirs, the very rain into the law of Buddha—and finally the rainbowed sunlight of the sea spray into the halo of the Goddess of Mercy. Today, a familiar disfiguration has assumed control. Vendors offer tapes of chanting monks. Rats dart through the streets. Sailors in blue uniforms stroll in twos and threes. A peasant herds pigs from town to temple. The golden sand beaches are deserted, and so are the long spits of rock where the fishing junks tie up.

Perhaps the Island Mountain retains its ancient power, for those who know how to summon it. Perhaps it is still Guānyīn's home, for those who know how to see it. But for now the tide is out—the tide of ancient empires—and with it the old petals of compassion, carried far and drowned in the wide, wide ocean of China.

PRACTICAL INFORMATION

by Peter Neville-Hadley

ORIENTATION & WHEN TO GO

Pŭtuó Shān is a small island about 6km (4 miles) long, off the coast of northeastern Zhèjiāng Province. It is usually reached by a combination of bus and fast ferry from the mainland port of Níngbō. The island is a summertime weekend holiday resort for urbanites from Shànghǎi trying to escape the heat, who fly into Zhōu Shān airport on the neighboring island of Zhūjiājiān and take boats from there. Summer periods and weekends for most of the year should be avoided, as hotel and food prices are extortionate then. Whatever its traditional devotion to religion, the island is now also devoted to tourism, although three Guānyīn-related ceremonies, in mid-February, June, and September, still attract numerous pilgrims, and more than 500 monks are said to be resident on the island. Year-round, pilgrims can also be found prostrating themselves continuously on the route up to Huìjì Sì.

There's an entrance fee of ¥60 ($7.50), payable as you alight from the boat. Individual temples and other sights have charges in addition to this, between ¥2 and ¥16 (25¢–$2).

GETTING THERE

By Plane Flights arrive at **Zhōushān airport** from major cities that include Běijīng, Shànghǎi, Xī'ān, Xiàmén, and Níngbō. There's a ticket office in the northeast corner of the main square of Pǔtuó Shān, across from Pǔjì Sì, near the exit to the bus station. Flights are typically ¥1,110 ($139) to Shànghǎi and ¥310 ($39) to Běijīng, with 20% to 30% discounts depending on demand. Buses connect the planes and a ferry. The ferry/bus link to the airport costs ¥12 ($1.50). Call ✆ **0580/609-3101** for information and bookings. The peak season for flying is July through September.

By Ship Níngbō is a short rail or bus journey east of Hángzhōu, and there are regular sailings to Pǔtuó Shān from there. Ferries no longer leave from Níngbō's Lúndù Mǎtóu (wharf) as they once did, but tickets are still sold there for ¥58 ($7.25), and buses are boarded for a journey (1 hr., 10 min.) to another dock, where high-speed passenger motorboats complete the journey in a further hour and 10 minutes. There are 11 departures a day between 6am and 4:30pm. The passenger terminal is on Wàimǎ Lù, just north of the Yǒng Jiāng and Xīn Jiāng bridges.

There are daily direct boats to Shànghǎi taking 12 hours for ¥79 ($9.90) to ¥720 ($90) for the best cabin, and a twice-daily combination of 2½ hours by speedboat and 2 hours by bus for ¥180 to ¥220 ($23–$28). Tickets for all sailings can be bought at the pier in Pǔtuó Shān and in Shànghǎi at the main ferry ticket office on the Bund or through agents across the city.

GETTING AROUND

For those who want exercise, the island is easily walked. There are plenty of maps on sale for ¥2 (25¢), and a very limited number of ways in which to get lost. Taxis and pedicabs are tiresome and unreliable, but the **minibus** service is well regulated. Each major stopping point has different lines for different destinations, with signs in English and clearly written prices: ¥2 to ¥6 (25¢–75¢). For those who don't want the penitential trudge up Fódǐng Shān (not a serious climb in holy mountain terms—under an hour), Huìjì Sì is now accessible in 10 minutes by a smart European **cable car** system which runs from 6:30am to 5pm for ¥25 ($3) up, ¥15 ($1.90) down, ¥35 ($4.40) round-trip. It now costs ¥2 (25¢) to walk the last hundred yards to the top. Among a number of attractions not mentioned above is the 33m (109-ft.) giant modern statue of Guānyīn, the Nán Hǎi Guānyīn Lìxiàng, visible for miles (open 6am–6:30pm; ¥16/$2).

WHERE TO STAY

Many hotels in Pǔtuó Shān are not open to foreign visitors, being reserved for employees of banks, the Shànghǎi Post Office, a tobacco company, and so on. The general quality of those that are open to foreigners is above average for Chinese-run hotels, but it's difficult to get a hotel room in Pǔtuó Shān on weekends or during the summer, and prices are disproportionate to the quality of service provided. At other times, discounts of 20% to 50% are available. The three-star, 159-room **Xílěi Xiǎo Zhuāng,** Xiānghuá Jiē 1 (© **0580/609-1505;** fax 0580/609-1812), is one of the better hotels in Pǔtuó Shān, not least because it is less greedy than some others at the more comfortable end of the scale. Built in 1991 and refurbished in 2001, the hotel is a collection of buildings, with block no. 1 being the best, even approaching a Chinese four-star in quality. Staff speaks some English, foreign credit cards are accepted, and rooms are in general small but well appointed. Single rooms are ¥587 ($73), standard rooms ¥493 to ¥792 ($62–$99), and suites ¥2,080 to ¥3,800 ($260–$475). The two-star, 78-room **Bǎotuó Bīnguǎn,** Méicén Lù 118 (© **0580/609-2090;** fax 0580/609-1148), has rooms renovated in 2001 that were still fresh and comfortable at the time of this review, and are worthy of three stars elsewhere. Double and triple rooms cost from ¥400 to ¥560 ($50–$70), and suites are ¥1,080 ($135), but 50% of that off season.

WHERE TO DINE

Fresh seafood is plentiful on menus in Pǔtuó Shān. It's at its cheapest at small, open-fronted restaurants on the two roads leading up from the docks, and in the cluster of store-filled alleys north of Pǔjì Sì. What you eat will be squirming, flopping, or slithering in tubs and bowls at the entrance when you arrive.

Hotel restaurants tend to take advantage of tourists by offering both high prices and small portions, but the restaurant in the **Xílěi Xiǎo Zhuāng** hotel (© **0580/609-1505,** ext. 502) has a wide variety of standard Chinese dishes and a respectable vegetarian menu (many Buddhist guests are not meat eaters). A meal for two costs around ¥100 ($13). Hours are from 6:30 to 9am, 12:50 to 2pm, and 5 to 9pm.

In the square outside Pǔjì Sì, the **Báihuà Cháyì Sù Zhāi Guǎn** (© **0580/609-1208**) has a pleasant interior and a broad vegetarian menu as well as standards, for about ¥80 ($10) for two.

Tài Shān:
Sacred Mountain
of the East

泰山

Tài Shān is said to be the most-climbed mountain in the world, although it is virtually unknown to the West. Situated at the midpoint between Běijīng and Shànghǎi, Tài Shān has been the most celebrated of the Five Sacred Peaks of China for the last 2,000 years, the highest altar in the Middle Kingdom for countless pilgrims and a great many emperors, including China's first. The first recorded temple on the mountain was built in 351 B.C. By the time of the Míng Dynasty (1368–1644), pilgrims numbering over 200,000 annually made the trek to the top of the mountain. Today, the numbers are even more imperial: There are four million visitors annually (including 500,000 foreigners). From this summit, Confucius (Kǒngzǐ) once proclaimed the world small and later Chairman Máo pronounced the East Red. But in post-Máo China, the world view from Tài Shān is altered once again, as I would find when I made my own ascent.

Dài Temple (Dài Miào)

I began my modern sightseer's pilgrimage in the old way, at the temple at the foot of the mountain, in the town of Tài'ān. The Dài Temple is a large walled fortress, a town within a town, of restored halls and pavilions housing ancient relics. Everyone from pickpockets to the imperial family used to set out from this shrine. One visitor described the temple grounds in 1628 as "a motley collection of stalls and stands" inhabited not only by pilgrims but by "cock-fighters, ball players, equestrians, and storytellers." I didn't see anyone kicking a football around this morning, but I did come across scores of vendors encamped within the 9m (30-ft.) walls.

The temple grounds are populated with carved stone tablets, one recording the mountain's appointment as "Emperor of China" by the Sòng Emperor in A.D. 1011. Every city and town in China once had a flourishing Eastern Mountain Temple of its own, part of the massive Tài Shān cult that

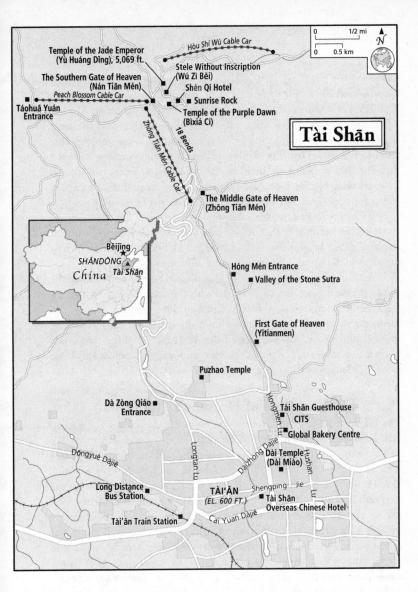

died with the Communist Liberation in 1949. Dài Miào also contains one
of China's oldest stelae, the **Qín Tablet,** thought to have been carved in 209
B.C. when China's First Emperor, Qín Shǐ Huáng Dì, climbed Tài Shān.
This inscribed monument stood on the summit until it was devoured by fire
in 1740. A fragment with nine characters is now preserved, mounted under
a plate of glass, outside the red stone hall where many an emperor once rested before his climb. Sīmǎ Qiān, China's ancient historian, was present when
the Qín Emperor ordered the full inscription "praising his own virtues," and
it was partly Qín's act of hubris on the summit of this Dragon Mountain

that prompted the Confucian intellectuals of the day to censor the First Emperor—which in turn impelled their new ruler to retaliate with the Burning of the Books and the Burying Alive of the 480 Scholars.

The main temple at Dài Miào, called the **Palace of Heavenly Blessing,** is palatial in every sense, including its size: nine bays wide with a double roof of imperial yellow tiles. Within its massive wooden cavity, stained a dark crimson, the **God of the Mountain, Tài Shān Wáng,** is seated on a central altar. His black-bearded face is enameled in gold. Five sacrificial vessels surround him, one for each of the Five Sacred Peaks of Daoism.

This mountain god is the Judge of the Dead, but he maintains no abode on the summit. Rather, it's his daughter, the Jade Woman, who has ascended to the heights. She has usurped her forbidding father and reigns supreme on the supreme summit, a deity of life rather than death.

Since this base temple is where the good pilgrim burns incense before the climb, presenting the god of Tài Shān with the favor nearest his heart, I made my petition, too. I wished to climb to the top of Tài Shān today, spend the night, and see the sunrise from the same spot where everyone from Confucius to Máo has greeted the dawn for the past 2,500 years. From the temple gate, I could see that summit—a jagged, notched cliff face some 6,293 steps away.

The First Gate of Heaven (Yǐ Tiān Mén)

The Pilgrim's Road (Pàn Lù) begins at the north edge of town, at a stone arch known as the **First Gate of Heaven.** Here, I purchased my ticket to Tài Shān (¥60/$7.50). The way up is broad, with spacious ramps and massive granite steps. From the First Gate to the Middle Gate is about 5km (3 miles). From the middle to the top is under 3km (2 miles) but far steeper. There are more than 250 temples and monuments along the way, and every rock and cranny, ravine and stream, wears a poetic name or invokes a romantic tale or two out of China's past. Above all there's the sacred graffiti. Hundreds of flat-faced rocks are etched in calligraphy, some of the finest specimens in the world. There are other signs of the past, too—living signs: beggars, working each rung of the stone stairway; and porters, dozens of them, hoisting their loads on wooden poles, the "bamboo tigers" of New China, as of old.

Many of Tài Shān's holy pavilions have been converted into snack bars and souvenir stands. At one cafe, I found the staff and patrons sitting outside, watching television. At another, there was a computer monitor, a vendor rattling its keyboard like an abacus. The screen radiated a green glow, matching the overarching canopy of trees, a canopy pierced by thick electrical lines running up the mountain. The lower half of the sacred mountain has been modernized, electrified, even computerized, although the stone stairs, tall pines, steep cliffs, and embroidery of carved characters manage to shine through. The gaily dressed, money-spending tourists of

New China are everywhere, far outnumbering a few old pilgrims, wiry porters, and the beggars who cling for life to their single step on the route.

Tiring of the stairs, I made a detour into the **Valley of the Stone Sutra,** where 6th-century Buddhists engraved the 2,500-character Diamond Sutra on the exposed banks of an extinct streambed. The stone banks are wide, flat, and smooth, forming a stone scroll unrolled by nature, but rain and wind have washed over the text, erasing much of it.

The Middle Gate of Heaven (Zhōng Tiān Mén)

After a 3-hour steady march, I reached the **Middle Gate of Heaven.** It was a nightmare, clotted with a thousand vendors and pocked by a gigantic parking lot for tour buses ferrying "climbers" up from the bottom. To top it off, this is where you can catch China's first large-scale **cable car** and thereby reach the holy summit in 8 minutes flat.

Keeping to my regimen, however, I struck out on foot, heading for the **Eighteen Bends,** a gargantuan stone ladder to the Southern Gate of Heaven, still far above. I hoped to leave behind this modern Pilgrim's Way that has been transformed into a high emporium of carnival shooting galleries, cheap charms on chains, shacks serving Coca-Cola, and roving photographers for hire.

The next landmarks belong to China's first emperor: a **pavilion** where Qín Shǐ Huáng took shelter from a storm as he descended in 209 B.C.; a **pine tree** awarded the fifth military rank when it sheltered the Qín Emperor from the rain; a **rock** in the first emperor's calligraphy with characters cut so large it's known as "Stele a Hundred Thousand Feet High." Then there's a **stone arch** named "Rise to Immortality" and, finally, 2,000 ruthless stairs to the top.

I paused on every intervening ramp. So did the porters, resting their bundles and bamboo carrying poles on the stairs. I followed one porter typical of those on Tài Shān, his skin burned auburn, head shaved, blue cotton pants rolled up to his knees, back drenched in sweat, feet shod in black cotton shoes. Dangling from the thick rope on one end of his carrying pole were three heavy gunny sacks; on the other end were two red roosters, suspended by their claws upside down, both still alive. The average porter shoulders 110 pounds on the carrying poles, makes two round-trips a day, and is paid about ¥16 ($2) for a hard day's hauling.

In the middle of one flight of stairs, I stepped around a dilapidated cardboard box, presided over by a tiny plaster figure of Buddha painted gold. It was a beggar's collection box, unattended, but there was a beggar on the next flight, both his legs shorn off at the thigh.

The walls of the ravine closed in on me. This is where the Tài Shān gazetteer mentions that a bully was crushed by a falling rock "so that the fat of his body polished the stairs. Nothing was left. His family could retrieve only one of his fingers." I'm amazed. Here is a mountain where villains are actually punished.

A Milky Way of supplicants still flows up and down this stairway, but now, if indeed people burn incense in the high temples at all, they are probably requesting cash, trunks of it. But even in greed, Tài Shān follows tradition. When the Hàn Dynasty Wǔ Emperor arrived at Tài Shān, the local officials lined both sides of the road on their knees; dispensing with offerings of fruit, they piled cash along the roadside, imploring the imperial blessing.

The Southern Gate of Heaven is a square red tower at the top of this long, long mountain staircase. Its hollow understory dates from 1264. Its upper story is known as **The Pavilion That Touches the Sky**—Heaven was once reckoned to be precisely 17 inches above the roof peak.

The Southern Gate of Heaven (Nán Tiān Mén)

Reaching the Southern Gate of Heaven, I squeezed through the Pavilion That Touches the Sky—and then I realized that I was still not at the summit of Tài Shān. Beyond here was a mile of vendors, coin telescopes, rock carvings, temples, and still more stone stairs. But it was not so steep now. I quickly wound my way to the **Shén Qí Hotel,** where I checked in.

There are plenty of monuments and temples on this broad summit, more than on any of China's other holy peaks. First there are the **Táng Dynasty Rock Inscriptions (Mó Yá Bēi),** the most ostentatious in outdoor China, the ultimate in cliff calligraphy. In A.D. 726, the Xuánzōng Emperor ordered that an account of his own imperial pilgrimage to Tài Shān be carved here—and it was carved large, in huge characters, 996 of them, each measuring a good 7 inches square and gilded in gold foil. The page of rock chosen for the imperial inscription faces south; the golden text is 13m (43 ft.) high and 5m (16 ft.) wide.

Then, on the very tiptop of Tài Shān, there's the Summit of the Celestial Pillar, where the **Temple of the Jade Emperor (Yù Huáng Dǐng)** stands. In its courtyard is a marker stone recording the metric elevation of Tài Shān (1,545m, a mere 5,068 ft.). And in the lower courtyard is the **Stele Without Inscription (Wú Zì Bēi),** one of China's most celebrated tablets, long believed to have been placed here by the First Emperor Qín during his visit in 219 B.C. Everyone who comes this far must touch this wordless stone tablet. The Chinese say it is the most touched stone on Earth, which is perhaps why it is completely blank. Six meters (20 ft.) high, 1.5m (5 ft.) square, the tablet is a true counterweight to the extravagantly wordy cliff carving just down the hill.

Finally, immediately below my hotel is **Bìxiá Cí,** the **Temple of the Purple Dawn/Clouds,** where the **Jade Woman (Bìxiá Yuán Jūn)** resides. She's the pilgrims' favorite, the Daoist equivalent of Guānyīn, Goddess of Mercy. Over the centuries, as more and more sought her out on Tài Shān in preference to her father, Tài Shān Wáng, the Jade Woman assumed two special powers: She could cure blindness, and she could bless a petitioner with children. She became the great midwife of China.

As I wandered across the summit I saw more worship on Tài Shān than I expected, more incense burning at the shrines, more money tossed into the altar boxes, often by parents with young children. And there were forms of worship here I didn't understand at all.

Just below the Temple of the Purple Dawn/Clouds is a large incense burner: It's an entire building, as big as a pavilion, and was well attended this afternoon. There was an offering box in front of its fiery mouth. Alongside were many flowering bushes that had hundreds of stones caught in their limbs and branches—whether by design or nature, I couldn't tell— but dozens of people were down there tying red ribbons to the limbs. I wasn't sure for what they were praying: children, money, health—surely some such universal desire, practical rather than what the West regards as spiritual. You don't climb all this way to engage in abstract reasoning.

While the temples on top of Tài Shān are among the most magical in China, there's also a communications complex with a weather station here rising higher than any temple and piercing the floorboards of Heaven. Pagoda of the Great Transmitter, Stupa of the Satellite Dish, these modern shrines of jade become electric.

Sunrise

At 4am the next morning, there was a knock on my door. Rise and shine for the ultimate ritual of Tài Shān: sunrise. Light is born in the east each day, and Tài Shān, as the Eastern Mountain, presides over all origins, over life itself.

Outside, it was very dark. The winds chewed at my flesh. I joined a stream of sightseers flowing east across the summit. Many had rented full-length padded army coats, green with fur collars. One traveler even carried a large suitcase. A few had flashlights. I was the only Westerner this morning.

At the eastern edge of Old China, we settled into the rock ledges and waited for the sun to rise out of the East China Sea. The stars faded out. At 5:07am, the sun chipped through the cloud bank. The crowd gasped. Everyone pointed toward the sun.

From Confucius to Máo and beyond, we had all gathered here for the dawn of a new day. The sun was a feeble disk of yellow light, barely strong enough to penetrate the gray clouds, the vast haze of industrial progress steamrolling its way through China. Despite Máo, the East is no longer red; it's toxic gray. For the next hour, we watched the rising sun slice through the purple clouds of dawn like pinking shears, trimming away the raiment of the Jade Woman.

Back in Běijīng, Chairman Máo's corpse, that of an emperor out of season, is encased in a slab of black granite from Tài Shān. But the imperial age and the age of the great beliefs—Daoism, Buddhism, Confucianism, and lately even Communism—are passing away. From Tài Shān, you must descend into the modern underworld. At Heaven's highest gate today, a vendor stands. He offers paintings brushed on black velvet: of tigers and dragons, eagles and cute kittens. The colors on these fuzzy, sofa-sized canvases are bright as neon, ideal for tourist and pilgrim alike. They roll up like scrolls. The cable car, and below that, the air-conditioned buses, await. The world no longer seems so small, even if it is fast approaching a commercial uniformity. The world is bigger than a dynasty, bigger than the Middle Kingdom, bigger than the circumference of China's sacred mountains.

PRACTICAL INFORMATION

by Sharon Owyang

ORIENTATION & WHEN TO GO

Inscribed on the UNESCO World Heritage List in 1987, **Tài Shān (Great Mountain),** the most famous sacred peak in China, is located in central Shāndōng Province, midway between Běijīng and Shànghǎi. Its base, in the town of Tài'ān, is 150m (492 ft.) above sea level and its summit is at 1,545m (5,068 ft.). Winters are cold and icy, and summers are rainy, making the best times to visit March to June, and August to October. The annual International **Tài Shān Climbing Festival (Tài Shān Dēngshānjié)** takes place in early September; this can be an interesting time to visit, as hundreds of runners compete in a race up the mountain. Check with CITS or Tài'ān Tourism (see below) for exact dates.

GETTING THERE

By Plane   The nearest major airport to Tài Shān is at **Jǐ'nán,** Shāndōng's provincial capital, 63km (40 miles) to the north. From Jǐ'nán, there are flights to Běijīng (1 hr.), Shànghǎi (1 hr., 40 min.), and Hong Kong (2½ hr.). From Jǐ'nán, travelers must then take the train (1 hr.) or bus (80 min.) to Tài'ān.

By Train   Tài'ān (© **0538/219-6222** or 0538/864-1122), the train station serving Tài Shān, is on the Běijīng–Shànghǎi rail line. Many trains serve Tài'ān daily. From Běijīng, it's a 7-hour train ride, from Jǐ'nán 1 hour, and from Shànghǎi 11 hours. The Tài'ān train station is located just west of the center of town.

By Bus   There are frequent buses to Jǐ'nán (1 hr.; ¥13/$1.50; buses depart every 20 min. 6am–6pm) and Qūfù (70 min.; ¥13/$1.50; buses depart every 30 min. 6am–6:30pm). These buses depart from the square in front of the train station in Tài'ān. For those traveling farther afield, the **Tài'ān Long Distance Bus Station (Chángtú Qìchēzhàn)** (© **0538/833-2656**) is in the western part of town on Dōngyuè Dàjiē Xīshǒu. From here buses run to Běijīng (4½ hr.; 8:30am and 9:10am), Shànghǎi (10 hr.; 7pm and 8pm), and Jǐ'nán (1 hr.; every half hour 6:20am–6:40pm).

TOURS & STRATAGEMS

Visitor Information The **Tài'ān Tourism Bureau** has a branch office located just outside the train station to the right as you exit (☏ **0538/827-2114**). They can answer questions and direct travelers to hotels, sights, and travel agencies. **CITS,** at Hóng Mén Lù 22 (☏ **0538/822-3259**; fax 0538/833-2240), can arrange guided tours of Tài Shān; a private tour for around ¥700 ($88) includes transportation, English-speaking guide, entrance fees, and lunch. They can also arrange accommodations and book tickets.

Exploring the Mountain Like countless predecessors, visitors often start their Tài Shān climb at the Dài Temple (Dài Miào), whose northern gate is at the southern end of Hóng Mén Lù. The temple is open daily from 7:30am to 6pm and charges ¥20 ($2.50) admission. The main entrance to the mountain is north up Hóng Mén Lù, reachable by bus no. 3. Admission to the mountain is ¥60 ($7.50) from February to October and ¥45 ($5.60) from November to January.

There are two trails up to the midway point (Zhōng Tiān Mén): a shorter but less hiked western route that starts at the Dài Temple but detours west before Hóng Mén, and the much more popular eastern route that runs from Dài Temple and up past Hóng Mén for 5.5km (3½ miles). From Zhōng Tiān Mén, it's another 2.6km (1⅔ miles) up some incredibly steep steps to Nán Tiān Mén, and then another 1.5km (1 mile) along flatter, shop-lined **Heavenly Lane (Tiān Jiē)** to the summit. Allow at least 2 hours between major

points. Water and snacks become increasingly expensive the higher you climb, so think about packing enough beforehand. Climbing Tài Shān would not be complete without viewing sunrise from the summit. If you plan to overnight on the summit, be sure to pack warm clothing and a flashlight.

If you wish to reduce your hike, there are now three cable cars that carry visitors up to Nán Tiān Mén. The first and most popular option involves taking bus no. 3 (or a taxi) from the train station to Dà Zòng Qiáo, where you transfer to a minibus (¥16/$2), which, when full, then makes the run to Zhōng Tiān Mén. (There are also direct buses to Zhōng Tiān Mén from the bus station, but these only run in the first half of the morning.) From Zhōng Tiān Mén, it's a 10-minute ride on a six-person cable car to Nán Tiān Mén (¥45/$5.60 one-way). The second cableway runs between the Tiān Jiē Suǒdào Zhàn and **Peach Blossom Ravine (Táohuā Yuán)** on the western flanks of the mountain; it costs ¥20 ($2.50) one-way. The third option connects the summit (Běi Tiān Mén Suǒdào Zhàn) to the more rural but pretty **Rear Rock Basin (Hòu Shí Wù)** and **Tiān Zhú Peak (Tiān Zhú Fēng)** on the northeast side of the mountain for ¥20 ($2.50) one-way. Note that, in an audacious sleight of hand, the entrance fees for the mountain are actually higher at the Táohuā Yuán and the Dà Zòng Qiáo entrances: ¥80 ($10) from February to October and ¥60 ($7.50) from November to January.

WHERE TO STAY

The most luxurious hotel in Tài'ān is the 14-story, 205-unit **Tài Shān Overseas Chinese Hotel (Huáqiáo Dàshà)**, on

Dōngyuè Dàjiē Zhōngduàn (☏ 0538/822-8112; fax 0538/822-8171). Located in the center of town close to the Dài

Temple, this hotel is a rather colorless place, but it offers rooms and facilities that meet the minimum standard for a four-star hotel. Rooms are comfortable enough and are fitted with large twin beds, standard nondescript brown furniture, satellite TV with in-house movies, air-conditioning, and minibar (safes in rooms on higher floors). Bathrooms are a little dark but clean. A double costs (¥480 to ¥680 ($60–$85); American Express, Diners Club, Master-Card, and Visa are accepted. The hotel has a Chinese restaurant that serves a buffet breakfast as well as an indoor swimming pool, health club, sauna, bowling, concierge, tour desk, business center, shopping arcade, salon, room service, and dry cleaning and laundry.

Closer to the mountain is the old standby, the three-star, 110-unit **Tài Shān Guesthouse (Tài Shān Bīnguǎn),** at Hóng Mén Lù 26 (*©* **0538/822-5888;** fax 0538/822-1432). Situated on the road to the main gate to the mountain, this hotel is a comfortable and reasonably priced choice. The large rooms, last renovated in 1999, come with high ceilings, basic furniture, fridge with refreshments, air-conditioning, TV, and hair dryer. Doubles cost ¥300 to ¥420 ($38– $52);

most credit cards are accepted. The hotel also has a small bar and several good Chinese restaurants as well as a health club, sauna, business center, room service, dry cleaning and laundry, tour desk, salon, and shopping arcade. CITS is next door.

The best place to stay at the summit is the three-star, 66-unit **Shén Qí Bīnguǎn,** located about a kilometer from Nán Tiān Mén along Tiān Jiē (*©* **0538/822-3866;** fax 0538/833-7025; www.shenqi hotel.com). Don't expect any luxuries at this rather tired, overpriced hotel, which would likely garner no more than a two-star rating in a bigger city. Rooms are somewhat dark but clean enough and come with air-conditioning, small twin beds, and TVs that seem to receive no stations. Bathrooms are small but clean and have tub/shower combos. A double is ¥680 ($85); most credit cards are accepted. The hotel only has hot water between 8:30pm and 11pm, but they provide thick jackets for the sunrise viewing. The staff speaks Chinese but will make sure you're awake before sunrise. Discounts of up to 20% are often given except on Saturday nights between April and October. The hotel also has a Chinese restaurant.

WHERE TO DINE

No restaurants stand out in Tài'ān or on top of the mountain. In Tài'ān, the **Bǎihuā Restaurant (Bǎihuā Cāntǐng),** in the Tài Shān Bīnguǎn (Tài Shān Hotel; *©* **0538/822-4678,** ext. 666), offers decent Chinese food in a clean environment. There are no menus in English, but you can order simply by pointing to the many ingredients and dishes on display. Dinner for two costs about ¥60 to ¥80 ($7.50–$10). **Global Bakery Centre (Huánqíú Xīshì Miànbāo Fáng),** at Hóng Mén Lù 7, sells pastries, cakes, and snacks for the long hike. Food is

comparatively more expensive along the trail and on the summit. Trailside vendors offer ice cream, bottled drinks, instant noodles, and boiled eggs. At the summit, the Shénqí Bīnguǎn has a Chinese restaurant that serves basic Chinese fare (*jiācháng cài*) as well as delicacies made from local ingredients such as pheasant, wild vegetables, and local medicinal herbs. Dinner for two averages ¥80 to ¥120 ($10–$15). There are also some restaurants along Tiān Jiē, but none have menus in English.

ÉMÉI SHĀN: BUDDHIST PEAK OF THE WEST

峨眉山

"NO SPOT IN THE WORLD COULD BE found more aptly to emphasize and accentuate the lofty ideals and mystic dogmas of Buddhism," Julius Eigner wrote after his visit to Éméi Shān (Eyebrow Mountain) in 1935. "Leopards, even snow leopards, are not infrequent," he claimed. He also spoke of a lost Chinese world:

> Sometimes an old white-haired monk, leaning on a long staff, will slowly descend the steps, looking like an ancient Chinese sage come to life again. Or a water buffalo will peacefully browse along the banks of a rivulet, with a small boy sitting on his back blowing determinedly on a wooden flute. Is it not a picture a Westerner would associate with those pastoral times which reigned in this country in some dim past age, when the gods came down to earth to visit the daughters of man?

Arriving 7 decades later, at a time when the whole country seems to be stretching out toward a technological future, I still harbored the hope of finding such a China of dreams on the slopes of Éméi Shān. If I could take this holy peak at my own pace, lose myself in its folds, and disappear along its lazy trailsides under ink-brushed cliffs; then by the time I stood on its golden summit, perhaps I would be blessed with an ancient vision: a halo in the clouds, framing my shadow for an instant before the sun melted everything down into steel and concrete.

Shrine of Limpid Waters (Jìng Shuǐ)

I boarded a morning bus in Chéngdū, the capital of Sìchuān Province. Éméi Shān is less than 121km (75 miles) to the southwest. I'd joined a Chinese group tour, a no-frills tour to be sure. I was curious to see how the Chinese toured the mountain. By the time we reached the foothills of the mountain, darkness filled the hot sky. I got just one glimpse of Éméi Shān, its massive triple summit rising like a wall over the low plains, the forests, the mountain streams. At 3,050m (10,167 ft.), its summit, **Peak of the Ten Thousand Buddhas (Wànfódǐng),** is the highest of any of the nine sacred mountains of China.

At 8pm, we stopped partway up the mountain at the **Shrine of Limpid Waters (Jìng Shuǐ),** where hotel rooms awaited us. I filled out the registration papers at a counter smack-dab in the middle of a cafeteria and ended up in the one wing that accepts foreigners. My room contained its own bathroom, three beds, and a local tour guide. This guide attached himself to me the moment I entered the hotel and he wouldn't let go. We sat down on bed no. 2 and hammered out tomorrow's itinerary. He spoke not a single word of English. Tomorrow morning we would catch a predawn minibus to see the sunrise from the summit, then come down the mountain on foot. My self-appointed guide would knock at my door at 4:30am.

After he left, I examined my accommodations. The bathroom sink emptied directly onto the floor. I pulled back the quilt on each bed, finding all the bedding, down to the mattresses, equally damp. It would be like sleeping in the tub.

The Bus to Sunrise

I slept a few moist hours before dressing, then greeted my guide at 4:30am. Outside, it was still pitch-black under a crown of stars, but the humidity was high. Éméi Shān was a steam bath. I was eager to see the sunrise from Éméi Shān's **Golden Peak (Jīndǐng).** It's there that worshippers have gathered over the centuries to pay their respects to the mountain god and to look over the edge of a massive precipice. "Éméi is lofty, piercing heaven," writes a Míng Dynasty poet, "a hundred miles of mist, built in the void."

The minibus was late, however—quite late. By the time we drove up the backside of Éméi Shān to the last parking lot under the peak, it was 7am and the sun had been up a good while. So many vehicles were racing to the top this morning that there were several traffic jams. We saved a bit of time by taking the cable car up the last steep slope, although we had to wait another hour in line. Of the 300,000 who visit the summit each year, 200,000 arrive by cable car.

The summit of Éméi Shān is imposing—a vast, nearly vacant plain of rock and sand. To the east, there's a sheer cascade of limestone, a 600m (2,000-ft.) drop; to the west, on a sunny morning like this one, a splendid view of the even more formidable **Kūnlún range (Gòng Gà Shān),** the final horizon of the Middle Kingdom. To the Chinese Buddhist of the past, this chain of eternally snowy peaks was the ever-remote location of the Western Paradise. A Míng Dynasty traveler called them "the Snowy Mountains, running athwart like a long city wall, and looking like festoons of white silk."

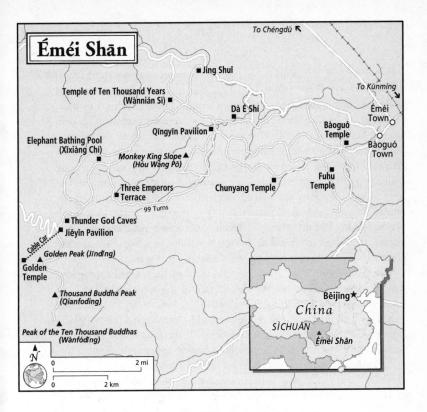

Buddha's Halo

Émei Shān is the final gate to a Nirvana that here assumes physical as well as spiritual definition. To reach the Western Paradise requires the help of the god of Émei Shān, Púxiàn, the bodhisattva of wisdom. He alone can give the faithful pilgrim the final nudge up this last rung on Heaven's ladder.

Púxiàn came from India in the 3rd century on the back of a white elephant. He is the Sun God of Chinese Buddhism, his mountain shrine forever associated with the heat of the southwest and the element of fire. Púxiàn was once the bridge between the ancient worship of nature and the new religion of the Buddha, which arrived in China just 2,000 years ago. Whoever made it to the summit of the Western Peak could then petition Púxiàn to escort them across a river of clouds to the divine shore.

The shortcut to this Western Paradise is Émei Shān's massive cliff. Every holy mountain in China has its legacy of ecstatic suicides, and Émei Shān provides not only the highest but the most inviting platform for the leap. Below this ledge, there is often an ocean of soft and wondrous clouds. There certainly was this morning as I approached the metal railing on **Suicide Precipice,** even though overhead the sky was pure blue and the sun so fierce that those who'd rented Chinese army coats for the morning chill had shed them.

Into the cloudy sea beneath my feet the sun sometimes penetrated so as to create a magnificent halo—the halo of Buddha. These halos are formed as the sun impregnates the water-laden clouds. Framed within this halo, each pilgrim, standing between sun and cloud, sees the shadow of his own head as he bows to Buddha. I was not fortunate enough to see my own head within the mountain halo, but many an earlier traveler had left an account of the phenomenon. In the middle of the 11th century, a Sòng Dynasty traveler reported seeing "an aureole of mixed colors and several layers. Out of the mist was a clearly defined image of a god astride an elephant." In the center of the halo was a "bright space, serenely clear. Each person looking saw the image of himself in the empty place exactly as in a mirror. If I lifted my hand or moved my foot the image followed the motion, but I could not see the person standing by my side."

When Reverend Hart, spreading the word of the Gospel throughout remote western China, reached this terrace in the summer of 1887, he seems to have seen something of Buddha's glory himself, for he found that as he stretched forth his arms, his giant shadow did likewise. He dismissed it all as a natural phenomenon but admitted, "I also found myself when the aureole was brightest making insensible advances toward the image in it."

Autumn afternoons are the best time for halos and suicides—on an April morning I was out of sync with time and the seasons. I contented myself by swaying a moment or two on the terrace, surveying the wide bowl of layered clouds. It was easy to see how a circular rainbow could form here. The air was filled with a million droplets of prismatic water, awaiting the visionary torch of the sun.

Golden Peak Chinese-Tibetan Temple (Jīn Dǐng Huá Zàng Sì)

I can report one phenomenon from Éméi Shān's summit that earlier travelers did not: The wide face of the cliff is coated in tons of trailside garbage—primarily plastic bags and containers—cast from the terrace by a million modern tourists. The eyebrows of Éméi Shān are desperately in need of a divine scouring of wind and rain, snow and lightning.

The summit is flat and empty. Acid rain has devoured entire forests here. To one side, there is a communications tower and a dismal two-story hostel of cement and sheet metal, complete with a medical clinic and restaurant. There are plenty of itinerant vendors, including a few peasants with small monkeys on leashes perched on their shoulders. Éméi Shān is nearly as famous for its bands of robber monkeys as for Buddha's halo. Now the monkeys have become cogs in the moneymaking machine that's bulldozing the mountain into a convenient national park of cable cars and tour buses.

There's still a shrine on top of Éméi Shān, the **Golden Temple**, to house Púxiàn. This was the last stop for the incense-burning pilgrim—once, according to the 19th-century missionary, Reverend Hart, the place "most exalted in the empire," where for "hundreds of years the stream of religious humanity . . . flowed and ebbed without diminution." The Golden Temple has been rebuilt continuously since the Hàn Dynasty. Today's stand-in is but a decade old, rebuilt on the site of a fire that gutted its previous incarnation (a fitting disaster, since Púxiàn is a fire god himself). The new temple is small, set on its own high platform, and while not cast entirely in bronze, the golden tiles of its flying eaves blaze in the sun. Inside, the image of Púxiàn is painted gold.

I took one last glance over the edge of the Golden Peak, hoping to discover my own shadow swaying in the clouds below, but my prayer was unanswered. I witnessed nothing more than a wide cliff drawn closed like a curtain by the clouds, waiting to be parted by the sun on its daily march across the heavens to the snows of Paradise.

Temple of Ten Thousand Years (Wànnián Sì)

Leaving the summit, I persuaded my impatient guide to forgo the cable car. We labored downhill on stone steps for 90 minutes. According to a Chinese gazetteer of Éméi Shān compiled in 1887, there are 5,728 steps down the zigzag slope back to Jiēyǐn Pavilion, where the cable car begins. At this point, we caught a bus to the hotel, ate lunch, and then set out together back up the mountain on foot.

We were climbing the ancient path of the pilgrims at last, no buses nearby, no cable strands. Éméi Shān is a long, intricate mountain of 90,000 stone stairs; trails wind for 81km (50 miles) from the Golden Peak to the base town of Éméi. We began this afternoon above the halfway point, and in 4 or 5 hours, we were able to encircle the main great temples on the body of the mountain. On my own, I could easily spend a week walking this mountain, temple by temple, each concealed within its own green hallowed fold of forest, stream, and terrace. A Chinese tour, however, is measured out in minutes and hours, not days and weeks, and like it or not I had locked myself into mass tourism, Chinese style. My bus back to Chéngdū would leave tomorrow.

Our walk on Éméi Shān began at a monastery converted to an elementary school for children who live on the mountain. There is a resident population of about 2,000 scattered across these slopes. This schoolyard is of packed dirt, a basketball hoop with a tattered net at either end; the yard was empty after lunch except for a half-dozen chickens. Vendors were showing their wares under awnings roofed in galvanized sheet metal. I watched a grandfather and his tiny grandson hire a sedan chair for the climb. The boy sat on his grandfather's lap. Off they dashed together; on either end of the sedan-chair poles, the two porters were stripped down to T-shirts, their pants legs hiked up.

We followed them into the hazy green hills under a bleeding sun, sweating all the way. According to the old book I had in hand, *Omei Illustrated Guide Book* (1891), it is some 1,258 steps up to the first great monastery, **Wànnián Sì**, the **Temple of Ten Thousand Years.** I felt every single stair tread in the heat. Somewhere along here, 4,000 years ago, the legendary Yellow Emperor paused to inquire of a Daoist wanderer the way to the summit, and later the Táng Dynasty poet Lǐ Bái stopped to pen some evocative lines about these temple-infested terraces:

> Bearing the Emerald Tapestry Lute,
> A Sìchuān monk descended the grand western peak.
> With a brush of his hands on the strings
> He made me hear a sound like the rushing
> of pines in deep caverns.
> My heart was cleansed by the flowing waters;
> The lute's quaver mingled with the knell
> of a temple bell in frost.

Uncleansed by any magic lute, we reached Wànnián Sì, founded 17 centuries ago, the oldest temple on the mountain. Although this temple complex is beautiful and in a luxuriant natural setting, most of its great halls, save the one housing Púxiàn and his elephant, burned down in 1946. Wànnián Sì is at an elevation of 900m (3,000 ft.), just above the jungle belt, thick with camphor and banyan, mulberry and banana. I could feel the steam rise and swirl into these highlands, a 24km (15-mile) walk below the Golden Peak where I stood this morning, staring into a mirror of blank fog.

The building that has survived the longest on Éméi Shān, the mountain's holiest shrine, is at Wànnián Sì: a squat hall of brick, 15m (50 ft.) square. Inside, under a beamless vault, is Púxiàn's white elephant, cast in bronze in A.D. 980, now plastered over with painted stucco. Púxiàn, eldest son of Buddha, rides on top, his saddle a golden lotus. Modern pilgrims burn long sticks of incense outside the main doors. I took a gander at elephant and mountain god, then followed my silent guide up and down the 2,436 twisting steps to Qīngyīn Pavilion.

Golden Monkeys

Of the Éméi Shān staircase, an imperial inspector, Shou Pu, once wrote, "When descending the hill, travelers go crab-fashion, with one man's feet on another man's shoulders. When ascending, they go like ants stuck onto each other, with one holding another's foot in his mouth." The trail is everywhere as crowded with trailside vendors as with visitors, the slopes green with bamboo and a few straggly tea plantations. Along this path the Ancient Forest of the Virtuous One once stood, planted by a devout monk in the Míng Dynasty. He is said to have planted 69,777 trees, one for each character of the Lotus Sutra, but not a single one has survived.

At the pavilions of Qīngyīn, we turned west toward the **Monkey King Slope (Hóu Wáng Pō),** pausing to bathe ourselves in the White Dragon stream. I was drenched in sweat, so it felt good to stop for a splash. I was determined to keep going upstream for a glimpse of Éméi Shān's celebrated monkeys. Most of the animals that frequented Éméi Shān in its remoter days, a century or less ago, have fled to more impenetrable Western paradises.

The trail twisted through a narrow river canyon over a series of bridges and planks, with bends so tight only one or two people could pass at a time. The canyon was dark, even on this bright afternoon. The sun must seldom, if ever, sound its depths. The monkeys lay in wait. The Chinese have their own way of dealing with the monkeys. I sighted the first of these golden creatures on the iron railing of a bridge. They were being taunted by the sedan-chair carriers and a crowd of visitors. By the time I reached the railing, the monkeys had scurried up a sandy bank of ferns and bamboo. The crowd tossed them scraps; the monkeys sauntered down to accept the offerings. Several of the Chinese started to tease the monkeys again, luring them down the slope with outstretched palms, then hissing or opening an empty hand and laughing. One monkey suddenly leveled a swipe at the back of a little girl's head. A moment later, another monkey, a mother carrying her baby, bit a woman's extended hand.

This band of monkeys was outnumbered by the hordes of tourists. For the most part, the passing crowds forced them to higher ground. No longer can they block the road like toll collectors. We are making the world a safer place for tourists, if not for the creatures the tourists come to see. On Éméi Shān, the golden monkeys have been subdued. Every temple, every parking lot, now has a handful of portrait photographers bearing monkeys on their shoulders. Many of these captives are dressed in silk; all are chained. For ¥1 (10¢), the handlers allow tourists to pose with a monkey balanced on its hind legs in their hand; pictures are snapped; prints are mailed to purchasers. It's another way to turn a profit in the wilds—rural enterprise, blessed by God and Party, with conservation postponed until the next century.

After watching the crowd taunt a few more monkeys, I turned back. I'd seen enough for today of mountain and temple, bronze elephant and golden monkey.

Pure Sound Pavilion (Qīngyīn Gé)

I rested up at the **Pure Sound Pavilion (Qīngyīn Gé),** so named for the melodious meeting of the White and Black Dragon streams. According to an Éméi Shān gazetteer, "Clear sounds are heard near the lofty pavilion, as if Buddhist spirits were playing musical instruments." I splashed myself with a few wet notes scooped from the chilly stream. With its narrow waterfalls, swift white rapids and cascades, arched bridges, tile-roofed kiosks, and viewing halls perched on ledges and terraces in a rain forest of bamboo, Pure Sound Pavilion is a postcard of the past, before cable cars, buses, and bottled-water vendors lined the 90,000 stone stairs, before the tigers were caged or shot or driven to Tibet, before the golden monkeys were chained.

Below two arched bridges, known as the **Twin Flying Bridges,** the limestone canyon of the river dragon deepens into what a Chinese mountain guide of 1844 describes as the place "with pure sounds of music, where the waters wash the heart of an ox into a Buddha." This is where the White and Black rivers merge—the Ox-Heart Stone beneath the Flying Bridges. I followed my guide downhill. The sun was falling behind the forehead of the mountain.

Thunder Gods

We passed **Dà É Shí,** the **Great Stone** of Éméi, on which a Míng Dynasty minister of education carved a message, "Heaven of the Holy Mystery." I was too beat to entertain more mysteries. We emerged at a small village and waited for bus connections. I bought two boiled eggs from an old woman. She charged me the paltry Chinese price for eggs—a fine, honest woman. Meanwhile, peasant photographers were displaying their leashed monkeys, and a farm girl strolled by, her water buffalo tethered to a rope.

Back in my hotel room at Jìng Shuǐ, I fell into bed before dusk. Éméi Shān was where I had imagined I would spend a week or two wandering from temple inn to temple inn, but now all I could do was sleep. Just past midnight, however, the mountain was socked by an electrical storm, a boisterous one. Crack after crack of lightning woke me. Púxiàn, the mountain god, was speaking. Or perhaps the ancient thunder gods still dwell in the hidden recesses beneath the summit. Less than a century ago, pilgrims and officials gathered on a platform to the thunder gods at the top of Éméi Shān to pray for an end to drought. "First one drops some incense and money down," explained the mountain gazetteer of 1891. "If rain does not come, then one drops in a dead pig and women's clothes. Then the thunder and rain will surely come."

Tonight the thunder and rains had come. I'd hoped to follow in the footsteps of Chung-yo, an artist who a hundred years ago roamed Éméi Shān for months. "So taking my brush along in its bag," he wrote, "I went, combing my hair with the wind and washing my hair with the rain, let down by ropes through dangerous places, and penetrating secluded spots."

I'm no true mountain dweller, I suppose. Sixty years ago, Sheng Chin, abbot of Qīngyīn, described my dream in the simplest manner: "Formerly I constructed a thatched hut in the mountains, and passed several summers and winters there, subduing my passions and destroying desire." I'd built no mountain hut, subdued no passions. I was ready to return to Chéngdū. This was too big a mountain for me.

Éméi Shān's signature is its immensity. Layer after layer of terrace, stream, and pinnacle are peeled back as a traveler rises to the summit. And on the summit, on the wide eyebrows of limestone, the boundary between empire and paradise becomes visible. Halos dance on a sea of clouds. The shrunken cities are a thousand miles to the east and the Western Paradise but one fatal step away.

PRACTICAL INFORMATION

by Michelle Sans

ORIENTATION & WHEN TO GO

Éméi means "Lofty Eyebrows," but it's also a pun of sorts on a poetic expression referring to the delicate brows of a beautiful woman. **Éméi Shān** was named for two of its high adjacent peaks, whose outlines, according to 6th-century commentary on the *Book of Waterways,* did indeed conjure the image of two long, thin, graceful eyebrows. Located in the center of Sìchuān Province, Éméi Shān was inscribed as a World Heritage Site in 1996 along with Lèshān, 47km (29 miles) away. Once richly endowed with both flora and fauna, it is still home to 10% of China's plant species; fauna have fared less well. Threatened animal species include the red panda, Asiatic black bear, Asiatic golden cat, and Tibetan macaque.

Éméi's slopes contain 81km (50 miles) of trails and about 30 active Buddhist temples. Minibuses link major temples along the way with the base and summit, and two cable-car systems also provide conveyance.

The climate ranges from subtropical to cold-alpine, depending on altitude and season. The base of the mountain is at an elevation of about 950m (1,500 ft.), while the summit is just over 3,000m (10,000 ft.). Winters are cold and snowy, making climbing dangerous. Summers are rainy and hot. Early spring and late autumn are the mildest periods to visit.

GETTING THERE

Chéngdū, the gateway to Éméi Shān, can be reached by train or air from all over China. See the Chéngdū chapter (beginning on p. 290) for details.

By Train There are several trains daily serving Éméi Town from Chéngdū. The trip takes 2 to 3 hours. Minibuses and taxis connect the Éméi train station (3km/2 miles east of town) to the mountain entrance at Bàoguó for ¥30 ($3.75); the trip takes 20 minutes.

By Bus The station in Chéngdū with the most buses to Éméi Shān is **Xīn Nánmén** (next to the Jiāotōng Bīnguǎn). The bus from Chéngdū costs ¥32 ($3.90) each way and takes 2 hours. Buses pull in at either the Éméi Shān bus station or Bàoguó Town. Bàoguó is the best terminal since the mountain trails begin there, but fewer buses from Chéngdū go there. The Éméi bus station is connected to Bàoguó Town by minibuses (20 min.; ¥10/$1.20) and by public bus leaving every 5 minutes (¥2/20¢). Buses also travel between Éméi Shān and Lèshān bus stations every few minutes. Buy your ticket inside the terminal (¥5/$60¢; 1 hr.). Buses unload at Lèshān's north gate.

You can also hop on one of the many Lèshān-bound minibuses that wait outside the Éméi gate. They don't depart until every seat is taken, so if you don't want to wait, try to find one that's nearly full (¥4/50¢).

TOURS & STRATAGEMS

Base yourself either in Bàoguó, at the entrance, or 11km (7 miles) by road up the mountain at Jìng Shuǐ. Bàoguó has the best hotels and restaurants, while Jìng Shuǐ puts travelers closer to the major temples and sites. Éméi Shān tickets are sold at the entrance near the Bàoguó Temple and cost ¥80 ($10). The temples on the mountain charge entrance fees, usually ¥6 to ¥10 (75¢–$1.25).

Visitor Information The very modern and helpful **Éméi Shān Tourist Center,** near Bàoguó Temple, opened in 2000. They provide free information and materials about Mount Éméi. Guides can also be hired here, although you're sure to pay less if you hire one of the many freelance guides (whose English may not be as good) outside Bàoguó Temple. For quiet and tranquility, though, there's nothing like going it alone.

Exploring the Mountain Reaching the upper peak at **Golden Peak (Jīndǐng)** for sunrise is a problem. It's too far to hike, especially in darkness. You can stay overnight at Jīndǐng in the temple (see below), or take a predawn bus from Bàoguó (2 hr.) or Jìng Shuǐ (1 hr.). A cable car runs the 500m (1,666-ft.) leg between the last parking lot, at Jiēyǐn Diàn, and the Golden Peak (¥70/$8.65 round-trip), but the lines in early morning are very long for the 5-minute trip.

From the Golden Peak, there are trails to the highest peak (Wàfódǐng), a 30-minute walk. There is also a light

rail between Jīndǐng and Wàfódǐng. The round-trip takes 20 minutes and costs ¥45 ($5.60). It's a 2-hour trek from Jīndǐng back down to Jiēyǐn Diàn. Six to 8 hours later (or more) brings you back to Jìng Shuǐ, halfway down the mountain. A second cableway connects Wànnián Temple to the parking lot just above Jìng Shuǐ. The 8-minute ride costs ¥30 ($3.75) going up and ¥20 ($2.50) descending; round-trip is ¥45 ($5.60).

The mountain has two main trails. The northern and southern trails rise westward to the summit from Bàoguó, coming together at Pure Sound Pavilion (Qīngyīn Gé), and then splitting. The northern trail proceeds through Wànnián Temple, with a branch trail (or cableway line) north to Jìng Shuǐ. The southern trail continues up from Qīngyīn Gé through Monkey Hill (Hóu Shān). The two trails merge again below Elephant Bathing Pool (Xǐxiàng Chí), beyond which there are more packs of monkeys and ultimately the cable car and summit.

Seeing all the temples and fully exploring the trails and vistas takes many days. Weather can change quickly, so layers of clothing are required, as are reliable hiking shoes and rain gear. If you do get caught without enough warm clothing, you can rent a Chinese army jacket for ¥10 ($1.20) at several spots on the mountain, including the Léi Dòngpíng (Léi Dòng parking lot).

WHERE TO STAY & DINE

The monasteries and temples offer basic accommodations (small rooms with dormitory-style beds, quilts, wash basins, and little else) as well as more comfortable lodging (with TV, air-conditioning, and hot showers) for about ¥10 to ¥40 ($1.25–$5) a night up to ¥150 ($20). At **Jiēyǐn Diàn** near the cable-car terminus, at **Jìng Shuǐ**, and in Bàoguó Town, there are also some modest inns and guesthouses that have run-down, moldy doubles with run-down, moldy private bathrooms and not much else. Doubles cost ¥100 to ¥200 ($13–$25). More are under construction, but for now the most comfortable inn on the mountain is **Wòyún Bīnguǎn**, just below Jiēyǐn Diàn and the Jǐndǐng cable car station. The only hotel of note is the **Red Pearl Mountain Hotel (Hóngzhū Shān Bīnguǎn)** in Bàoguó Town, on a side road running south off the highway connecting the town and the temple (© 0833/552-5888; fax 0833/552-5666). Among its dozen wings and buildings (230 units), this villa-style hotel has three- and (since 2002) four-star wings. Numbers 7 and 8 are three-star (¥220–¥500/$28–$63); no. 5 is four-star (¥480–¥580/$60–$72). The hotel offers currency exchange, overnight laundry, and a tour desk where you can get maps of the mountain trails and travel advice. Rooms have air-conditioning, TV, and phone. MasterCard and Visa are accepted.

The major temples all have vegetarian restaurants. The food is cheap—¥16 to ¥25 ($2–$3) a meal—and bland. Trail-side stands serve noodles and soup at even cheaper rates, as well as bottled water and canned sodas. Understandably, food tends to get more expensive the higher you climb.

In Bàoguó Town, the **Teddy Bear Cafe** (on the main road; © 0833/559-0135) has an English-language menu and some inexpensive Western and spicy Chinese dishes. Best of all, this is the place to get practical information on Éméi Shān—where to stay, where to eat, and where to book train or bus tickets. The owner speaks English, and English-speaking local guides often turn up here.

Huà Shān:
Sacred Mountain of the West

华山

The most ancient gods of Chinese civilization once dwelt upon Huà Shān, a mountain strong enough to bend the Yellow River to the sea. The First Emperor and his successors performed the spring and autumn rites here for a thousand years, praying to the mountain god to open Heaven to Earth. Daoist hermits, alchemists, and sorcerers retreated to Huà Shān, where they became the immortals of Chinese tradition. And countless pilgrims, scaling the almost impossible heights, sought a glimpse of Heaven, a taste of immortality in the open hand of Buddha—in the crown of five peaks at the summit of Huà Shān.

I first climbed this mountain in 1984, an altogether remarkable event, and again in 1993. I returned to see if the changes that are transforming China at the dawn of the 21st century have reached all the way to this holy mountain of the West.

At the Gate to the Mountain

At the Xī'ān long-distance bus depot, Eddie Hàn bought us cheap tickets to Huà Shān. Eddie was a young English teacher I'd met a day earlier. When he heard I was returning to the sacred mountain, he offered to accompany me. I knew that with a local Chinese along, the journey would be smoother. The bus depot was infested with beggars, entire families in rags. Eddie said they were lazy, but he gave money to the children.

Every seat on the bus to Huà Shān was taken. Because two passengers refused to pay two extra máo (about 4¢), the bus did not use the new four-lane toll road. After 3 hours of the usual delays and discomforts, a mountain range erupted to the south, dwarfing the mud villages. We reached **Huà Shān Kǒu Village** at the foot of Huà Shān an hour later. Touts hit us like an updraft of gnats.

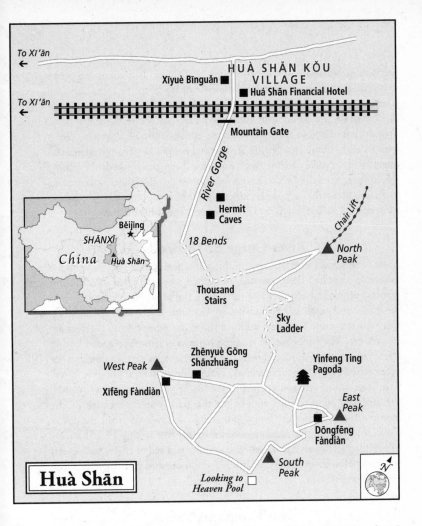

To Xī'ān ←

Xīyuè Bīnguǎn ■

HUÀ SHĀN KǑU VILLAGE

■ Huá Shān Financial Hotel

To Xī'ān ←

Mountain Gate

River Gorge

■ Hermit Caves

18 Bends

Chair Lift

▲ North Peak

Thousand Stairs

Sky Ladder

West Peak ▲

Zhēnyuè Gōng Shānzhuāng ■

Yinfeng Ting Pagoda 🌲

Xīfēng Fàndiàn ■

East Peak ▲

■ Dōngfēng Fàndiàn

South Peak ▲

Looking to Heaven Pool □

Běijīng ★

SHĀNXĪ

China

Huà Shān

Huà Shān

N

This village was a wide spot in the road in the 1980s and 1990s, when I stayed in a one-dollar room, but, today, Huà Shān Kǒu is another tourist trap. The tourists are Chinese; I didn't see a single foreigner. The strip to the mountain gate was glutted with pedestrians, shops, and vendors. A new hotel, half-finished, boasted an amusement arcade in the shape of a fiberglass dragon that swallows families whole. I really didn't recognize the street or the village now, but change in China is always sudden.

Three old women hounded us, selling incense. We were on the grounds of **Jade Spring Temple (Yùquán Sì),** "picturesquely situated at the start of the ascent to the mountain," as Hedda Morrison wrote. The adventurous Mrs. Morrison photographed Huà Shān in the summer of 1935. In her book of photographs, she writes that the "importance of Huà Shān lay partly in its proximity to the early centers of Chinese civilization, and partly in its being a supreme example of the type of landscape so appreciated by Chinese artists." The "spectacular mountain forms" and "solitary, cloud-capped peaks" of Huà Shān captivated her, captivated the great Sòng Dynasty painters, and first captivated me in the 1980s. In 1935, you could spend a night in the Jade Spring Temple and enjoy a hearty vegetarian meal prepared by monks. Today, the temple has been demolished; the meals, served from a hundred stalls, are neither Daoist nor Buddhist. Skirt around to the right of the temple entrance to avoid being charged admission. Altogether, I forked out ¥65 ($8.10) before I could hit the trail.

River Gorge of 18 Bends

It was the same mountain, yet nothing was the same. The trail up the mountain river had been widened, smoothed over, and filled in with solid granite curbstones. A power line runs along the bank. New gates arch over the path, and small vendor-towns, roofed with cloth awnings, crop up every quarter mile. The sheer white cliffs on the other side of the river are altered, too. They once served religious hermits as remote refuges. Carving a few ladder rungs up the cliffside, those ancient ascetics disappeared for months into high, unapproachable caves. Today, several "hermit caves" have been carved out and opened to visitors.

I still saw some Daoist monks on the trail, but the essence of the mountain—wild, distant, fierce, holy—has disappeared from the lower flanks. The dreams that accompanied me on my first trek up Huà Shān dissolved into fresh pavement, souvenir stands, and sedan chairs with green bamboo poles, their carriers for hire. At the mountain gate, there are even tennis shoes for rent.

The Thousand Stairs

The second phase of the journey, however, when we left the river canyon for the stone spires of the peak, was not without its terrors, even in this modern age. People still die on Huà Shān every year, falling from its edges. Even the sedan-chair carriers drop back here, 3km (2 steep miles) from the top. "In places the track led up almost perpendicular rock faces in which steps had been hewn and iron chains of uncertain reliability set in the rock to provide hand-holds," Mrs. Morrison wrote in 1935. "Some of the sheer stretches were for one-way traffic only, and when we reached them we would call out so as to ensure that we did not meet some descending pilgrim half way."

Little had changed here. I knew these stairs well; they are something you never forget. I once saw a porter lose his load on this stone ladder, these "Thousand Stairs." Today, this chimney, which actually consists of two long streamers, has been rehewn and widened, but the chains are still in place. It is just as steep as ever, although there are now separate staircases up and down, and the small temple at the top of the stairs, which once had an iron trapdoor to seal off the mountain from intruders, is long gone.

Other temples along the way have been rebuilt since I visited, but they seemed empty. Those on the North Peak—the thumb of the five-fingered Huà Shān cluster—straddle a narrow spine of stone, dramatic from a distance. Eddie and I reached the North Peak in our third hour of quick climbing. We ordered a roadside dinner, a horrible one, and overpriced. Eddie confided that as soon as vendors see me, the prices double.

Hedda Morrison once tarried for days at the **North Peak Monastery,** where she met five Daoist priests and a boy sent to them for his health by anxious parents in Shànghǎi. Later she would meet a pilgrim who had traveled to the top of Huà Shān by foot, all the way from Běijīng.

The Sky Ladder (Tiān Jǐng)

The North Peak is connected to the other peaks of the compass by "a hair-raising track . . . known as the Sky Ladder," with a sheer drop-off on both sides—the stone web between thumb and fingers. Beyond that lies an even more terrifying traverse, the Azure Dragon's Ledge, which has now been removed from the trail entirely.

A Táng Dynasty poet, Bái Jūyì (A.D. 772–846), described the ledge succinctly: "The chasm beneath me, ten thousand feet; the ground I stood on, only one foot wide."

By the time Eddie and I crossed this final bridge to the peaks of the immortals—where the white fungus of wisdom grows and beans said to satisfy your hunger for 49 days sprout—the sky had darkened, the wind had chilled. We mounted the East Peak, then traversed the hand of the mountain to the West Peak. I was hoping the old monastery where I spent nights on earlier climbs remained, that it had not been redone, that I could say of it, "You're no Holiday Inn."

West Peak Monastery (Xī Fēng Sì)

I was not disappointed: The monastery on West Peak had not been spruced up or made over one iota, save that the outdoor toilet once cantilevered over the cliff edge had been swept away. The rooms were unrepentantly crude. Only the price had kept up with the times: We had to pay ¥25 ($3) apiece (as much as Eddie pays for a modern guesthouse in Xī'ān) plus a ¥15 ($1.80) surcharge for my not being Chinese. Our suite was a cubicle on the top floor with two hard cots, each with a dirty quilt. The foot of Eddie's bed collapsed every time he sat on it.

A bare electric bulb dangled from the ceiling. When it quit, a monk arrived with a kerosene lantern. We secured the door with a brick. There was no bathroom down the hall and no water, neither a thermos nor a basin; we couldn't even wash up. I liked it. The room hadn't improved with the decades. The lattice ceiling was stuffed with bamboo matting and newspaper. A few sections of white butcher paper were tacked up here and there. The wooden floorboards were rotting away. The paper walls and loose windowpanes rattled in the night wind, sounding like a scurrying army of rats.

This monastery would leak and creak all night. I lay back on the hard pillow, zipped up my windbreaker, pulled on my stocking cap, and crawled under the quilt to warm up. I was haunted by a fine photograph that Hedda Morrison composed in 1935 of two Daoist monks in ceremonial combat, one armed with a sword, the other with a fly swatter. "The fly whisk, made from a yak's tail and known as a cloud sweeper," Mrs. Morrison explained, "is thought to impart the ability to ride the clouds."

I felt too heavy in limb and bone to levitate on this edge of the void. There would be no visions of holy peaks and Daoist immortals to sugar-plum my sleep tonight—just hard facts, hard as the pallet upon which I fell to rest.

In Buddha's Palm

We woke on the mountain at dawn, left the monastery, and circled the peaks—the five petals of the stone lotus. We stopped beside an empty crater, the **Looking to Heaven Pool (Yǎngtiān Chí).** In 1932, when the New Zealand maverick, Rewi Alley, accompanied by R. Lapwood, arrived at the summit of Huà Shān after an "ascent that surpassed all our expectations," he discovered the same pool filled with rainwater. "Here farmers still prayed to the Black Dragon for rain," he wrote. Here Alley met a monk who claimed to be 120 years old. He was said to have gone sleepless for 20 years running, tending his herb gardens both by sun and moon.

The mountain was once pregnant with fantastical stories of hermits who became immortals endowed with the power of flight. Ancient kings were said to have paid homage at Huà Shān as early as 1766 B.C. Qín Shǐ Huángdì, the first emperor of unified China, is believed to have reached the summit in his search for the white fungus. The first emperor of the Míng Dynasty dreamed of his ascent up this pillar of Heaven. Lǎozǐ, the ancient founder of Daoism, left his iron plow here, although no one's seen it lately. Guānyĭn, Goddess of Mercy, once had her likeness carved in a valley between peaks at the Holy Stove Temple, where she shared the altar with Lǎozĭ and his cow.

The Jade Maiden of Chinese myth was celebrated on Huà Shān, too— she arrived on the back of an ethereal dragon. The whole mountain is in the shape of a dragon, some say. The true god of this mountain may well be the dragon, once synonymous with China itself. There is a Chinese legend that a dragon coiled itself over these slopes and deposited its skeleton on the outside, forming the dramatic ridges. The steep cliffs are antediluvian.

What struck Eddie about the rock walls of Huà Shān, however, was their color: white, bone white. Indeed, the presiding god of the mountain is the White Spirit. According to Reverend Geil, who left an exhaustive trove of stories about Huà Shān after his visit in the 1920s, the White Spirit resides on the very same West Peak where I spent last night. Wearing white robes and a top hat, the White Spirit could open and close the doorway to Heaven. He rode a white dragon in a procession of 4,100 fairies.

I took a final glance at Huà Shān's **West Peak,** its supreme summit, the edge of the void, with a view of the Yellow River valley, the cradle of Chinese civilization, where Xī'ān stands. You can see why emperors came to this peak to validate their reigns. It is nature at its grandest. Indeed, in 1383, Wáng Lǐ composed his classic album of Chinese travel pictures here, some 40 landscapes that forever defined nature in China. The scenes survive today in the Palace Museum at Běijīng and in the Shànghǎi Museum, but the original persists in nature, little altered by humans. You can still feel how Huà Shān became the ultimate refuge not only for hermits but for exiles of all stripes, politicians out of favor, disinherited children, criminals, and saints. Huà Shān's beauty is wild, belonging more to the clouds than the streams and the earth. It is as if we can see the very mold of nature at the instant it was pulled away into the stars, the rock not quite cooled.

Huà Shān's dome is a summit worthy of the word, composed of bare rounded white granite, with the cleaver mark of a hero of the old myths on its skull, its flanks as sheer and long as any in the Middle Kingdom, seeming to roll straight down to the plains of dust where China was born. This was once the cliff of divine suicides, where pilgrims threw themselves into undifferentiated space, high above all worldly shapes, praying for the heavens to open and swallow them up. But the dragon in stone is today repaved and reinterpreted, its temples transformed into cafes and souvenir sheds, its immortals into faint clouds, its scales into the stuff of a traveler's fantasy.

Back to the Future

We descended Huà Shān rapidly, stopping only once for plastic bottles of mineral water and a repast of boiled eggs, greasy donuts, and millet gruel. There were mothers and fathers coming up the mountain with babies in their arms, but I encountered few of the devout old women, feet bound, who took on Huà Shān the first time I did. There were plenty of couples on outdoor adventures. They purchase padlocks to secure to the chain-link rails near the summit, a way of commemorating their love, and toss the keys into the abyss.

As for China's mythic past, most of that has been looted and dispersed. The essence of the new Huà Shān is a mad rush, a commercial opportunity, a street of touts that runs from Xī'ān to this remote summit once believed to hold up the heavens. Years ago Huà Shān touched and changed me; now, in a harder age, I come and go like a shadow.

PRACTICAL INFORMATION

by Graeme Smith

ORIENTATION & WHEN TO GO

Huà Shān, the most beautiful and steep of the nine sacred mountains, is located 121km (75 miles) east of the historic city of Xī'ān in Shǎnxī Province, 805km (500 miles) southwest of Běijīng in central China near the Yellow River. The village of **Huà Shān Kǒu** is at the foot of the mountain, which reaches an elevation of 1,966m (6,552 ft.). With the area's cold winters and hot summers, spring and autumn are the best seasons to visit. **Xī'ān** serves as the travelers' gateway to the mountain.

GETTING THERE

By Plane & Train   Xī'ān can be reached by air from Hong Kong (2½ hr.), Běijīng (1½ hr.), Shànghǎi (1 hr., 40 min.), and many other Chinese cities. There are also overnight trains from Běijīng (17 hr.), Chéngdū (19 hr.), and Shànghǎi (24 hr.).

Some choose to make the connection between the mountain and Xī'ān by rail, via Huà Shān railway station, which is a bumpy 20-minute bus ride from Huà Shān Kǒu. There is a minibus every half hour (¥3/35¢), or you can hail a red minivan with a cardboard sign that will take you there for the same price (after a little negotiation). Trains back to Xī'ān (2 hr.) cost between ¥10 ($1.25) and ¥20 ($2.50) and run every hour or so.

By Bus   The most reliable way to get to the mountain from Xī'ān is an air-conditioned bus that leaves from the front of the Jiěfàng Hotel at 7:20am (2 hr.; ¥18/$2.20). Ignore the touts who try to drag you away to their minibuses that sit around until they fill up. If you're thinking of a day trip, the last bus leaves for Xī'ān from the cable car at 5:30pm, and minibuses run until 7pm. If you are **walking** up, be sure to ask the bus conductor to drop you at

Huà Shān Kǒu or tell him that you are walking the *lǎo lù* (old road). If you are taking the soft option, continue for a few miles and connect with another bus (¥10/$1.25), which takes a further 25 minutes to reach the cable car. Entry to Huà Shān is ¥60 ($7.50).

TOURS & STRATAGEMS

Visitor Information If you feel that you need a guide, contact **Golden Bridge Travel Service** in Xī'ān, at Tǐyùguǎn Lù 111 ((©) **029/781-5596;** fax 029/781-1521). Simple maps may be obtained from the **Huàshān Tourist Bureau** ((©) **0913-436-3161;** fax 0913-436-3578), inside the grounds of the Huàshān Financial Hotel. Entrance to the mountain is ¥65 ($8.10).

It is now possible to tour Huà Shān as a day trip from Xī'ān, thanks to a new cable car that makes the ascent to the North Peak. It costs ¥100 ($12) round-trip. The cable car's lower terminus is well east of the base village, a ¥10 ($1.25), 30-minute taxi or minibus ride away. Buses return from Huà Shān Kǒu Village to Xī'ān as late as 8pm.

Chinese guidebooks recommend climbing at night with a flashlight to see the sunrise (presumably skipping the entrance fee). The locals say, "You don't fear what you can't see" (*"Bú jiàn bú pà"*), but this is not sensible. Some wealthy locals and Taiwanese get carried up for much the same price as the cable car. The cable car (¥55/$6.90 one-way, ¥100/$12 round-trip) gets you to Běifēng (North Peak) in 10 minutes, about 4 hours quicker than doing it on foot. If you want to save your knees and leave yourself more time on the mountain, take the cable car down.

WHERE TO STAY

Dōngfēng Fàndiàn Location is the main advantage of this hostel, a mere hundred yards from Dōng Fēng (East Peak), where crowds gather to watch the sunrise. The hotel has no charm, and the four freshly renovated twin rooms are the only ones worth considering.
Huà Shān Fēngjǐng Qū Dōngfēng. ((©) *0913/430-0066.* 11 units. ¥320 ($40) twin. **Amenities:** Restaurant; limited room service. *In room:* TV.

Huà Shān Financial Hotel (Huà Shān Jǐnróng Bīnguǎn) This three-star cadre hotel is done in regulation white tile and blue glass. Rooms are overpriced and service can be distant. The best rooms are in Building No. 4, which was renovated in 2001. The hotel is 120m (390 ft.) uphill from the Huà Shān Kǒu intersection, on the left. The **Huà Shān Tourist Bureau** ((©) **0913/436-3161;** fax 0913/436-3578) is located here.

Yùquán Lù Zhōng Duàn. ((©) *0913/436-3120. Fax 0913/436-3124. www.huashanfinancialhotel.com. 180 units. ¥388 ($48) double; from ¥488 ($61) suite. No credit cards.* **Amenities:** Restaurant; bar; concierge; 24-hr. room service; same-day laundry. *In room:* A/C, TV.

Xīyuè Bīnguǎn This hotel is friendlier and much better value than the Financial Hotel. Though the hotel was renovated in 2002, the money clearly ran out at the corridors, which are dark and dank. Located 100m (330 ft.) before the entrance to Yùquán Temple, on the right side, it is easily spotted with its traditional sloping tiled roof.
Yùquán Lù Zhōng Duàn. ((©) *0913/436-3145. Fax 0913/436-4559. 55 units (shower only). ¥190 ($23) double. No credit cards.* **Amenities:** Restaurant; 24-hr. room service. *In room:* A/C, TV.

Zhēnyuè Gōng Shānzhuāng Lying in a valley between the rear peaks, this is the most interesting choice on the mountain. It's based in the north wing of a small Daoist temple; some of the monks here speak English and love a chat. The hostel is a 10-minute walk from Xǐ Fēng (to watch the sunset) and a 30-minute moonlit scamper from Dōng Fēng (to watch the sunrise). The twin rooms upstairs are drier and have the comfiest beds. If Zhēnyuè Gōng is full, look for the Xǐfēng Fàndiàn, 50m (164 ft.) from the West Peak. Also based in a calm Daoist sanctuary, this inn was undergoing refurbishment at the time of writing.

Huà Shān Fēngjǐng Qū Xǐfēng. ⓒ *0913/ 430-0101. 9 units. ¥200 ($25) twin; from ¥50 ($6) dorm bed.* **Amenities:** Restaurant; limited room service.

WHERE TO DINE

If Huà Shān is a day trip, try to carry with you all your food and snacks. Water and drinks can be purchased on the trail. The trailside vendors and village cafes are expensive, and the food is nothing special. The best restaurants are in the hotels and guesthouses, where the dishes are basic Chinese combinations of vegetables, noodles, and meats.

SŌNG SHĀN/SHÀO LÍN: SACRED MOUNTAIN OF THE CENTER

嵩山

SŌNG SHĀN IS THE DAOIST MOUNTAIN at the center of China. According to a Chinese mountain guide, the people "thought that Sōng Shān lay directly under the heart of heaven and on the liver of the Earth," and they called it the "pearl in the cradle of ancient Chinese civilization." Of its many temples, the two most famous still exist: **Zhōngyuè,** China's oldest Daoist temple, and **Shào Lín,** world center of the martial arts and birthplace of Zen Buddhism.

The 72 peaks of Sōng Shān are situated in Hénán Province between two ancient capitals, Luòyáng to the west and Zhèngzhōu to the east. I approached the mythic middle of the Middle Kingdom from Luòyáng, turning east at Shào Lín Monastery for the holy city of Dēngfēng at the southern foot of Sōng Shān.

Dēngfēng is an ugly strip, once glorious. It was the capital of the early Xià civilization, then hometown of the holy Central Mountain. It received its present name in the 7th century when the Wǔ Empress of the Táng Dynasty—one of the most notorious figures in all of Chinese history—built her summer home in the foothills. Dēngfēng means "Ascend to Bestow Honors."

I checked into a modern but already aging and decrepit hotel. The electric lights didn't work, no water ran in the tub, and the door to my room didn't lock. Still, it was spacious and I had a view of the peaks of Sōng Shān to the north. The Central Mountain is a formidable wall of bare white rock peaks, once described by Wáng Wéi, a Táng Dynasty poet, as "towering aloft in the skies and piercing halfway to Heaven."

Imperial Academy

My aim this afternoon was not to climb to the top but to visit a few of the famous sites on the lower flanks of Sōng Shān. I had no map, but I could see the range to the north. I set out in that direction, looking for a likely road out of town. After an hour of bad guesses and detours, I discovered a path into the hills. It quickly led me to **Sòng Yáng Academy.**

When China's capital was at Xī'ān and later Luòyáng, the intelligentsia enjoyed the coolness of summers at Dēngfēng, and there they established this academy, one of China's four great centers of Confucian learning. Sòng Yáng began as a Daoist temple. The Hàn Dynasty Wǔdì Emperor (140–87 B.C.), pausing here on his way to perform the spring rites on Sōng Shān, planted three cypress trees, the **Three Generals,** two of which survive, or so it's believed. They certainly look like antiquities, gnarled and grand, venerable enough to stake a claim to a birthday 2,000 years ago.

The Táng Dynasty Gāozōng Emperor made this site his residence for a short while in A.D. 683. It became an imperial academy as early as A.D. 951 and served as a Confucian college for 9 centuries, reaching its zenith under the Kāngxī Emperor in China's final dynasty. In 1936, Gen. Chiang Kai-shek, who lost the civil war to Máo, celebrated his 50th birthday at the academy and ordered the digging of a well, which still works.

Plenty of history here—but now Sòngyáng Academy is just a few tile-roofed buildings inside a low wall with a ticket taker at a table and some soft drink vendors on the doorstep. The interior is a museum, its 60 rooms all renovated within the last 100 years. The academy's most impressive monument is in the front courtyard, a massive 8th-century stele (carved stone tablet) 9m (30 ft.) tall, crowned with an elaborate sculpture of two lions clasping a ball in their raised paws. Its inscription reports that in A.D. 744, the Xuánzōng Emperor, age 61, took a beautiful young concubine, Yáng Guìfēi, and promptly ordered the Daoist alchemists at the Sòngyáng Academy to hand over the elixir of eternal youth. Apparently, the transaction went awry, as emperor and concubine achieved immortality only in story and myth.

The Oldest Pagoda in China

From the academy, I struck northward through wheat fields, in search of the oldest brick pagoda in China. The land is hard and dry, filled with white stones. There are dirt caves under the green terraces where farmers store seed and cuttings, even machinery. I followed a streambed uphill until I caught sight of a brick pagoda. I cut across a field of brush, scaled a hillside, and forded a rock-terraced stream. Teams of stonecutters, sun-darkened men in black topcoats hauling sizable sledgehammers, were working up and down the streambed.

On the other side of the stream, I found a highway. After walking along it for an hour, I finally reached **Sōngyuè (High Peak) Temple** and the old pagoda. The grounds are in a sorry state. There's some rehabilitation in progress, but the temple walls have caved in. The uncut courtyard grasses,

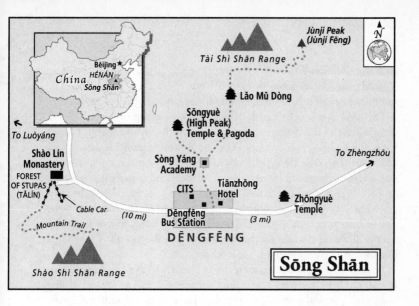

Sōng Shān

green and yellow, nipped at my thighs. Several halls and pavilions are tumbling down. And the complex is deserted. At its heart is China's oldest brick pagoda, 12-sided like the zodiac, 15 stories, and 37m (123 ft.) high, damaged but still solid. It's in the shape of a pine cone growing skyward. The pagoda's tip is carved into an inverted lotus leaf that serves as the platform for the Buddhist Wheel of Life. There are 500 doors and windows in its walls, many fitted with carved figures, including 40 lions.

It's the sole pagoda of this style in China, piled high with small black bricks mortared into a 12-sided cosmic wheel spinning into the heart of Heaven. The Wǔ Zétiān Empress stayed the night here in A.D. 696. The pagoda was already a relic then—nearly 2 centuries old. It dates from A.D. 520. The temple was founded even earlier, in 509, to serve as a portable shrine-away-from-home for the Northern Wèi royals. It still looks as if it were in some kind of catastrophic transit.

I climbed back down the white stone hills. The sky above the distant shafts of Sōng Shān was blue. The riverbed of the mountain was being paved in stone. Work crews were breaking, ferrying, and laying rock. The water that pours down from Sōng Shān has a long tradition of purity and curative powers. Recent reports claim that no one living within 5km (3 miles) of the river has ever suffered a single case of cancer.

First Mountain of the World (Sōng Shān)

The sky was a sharp and even blue when I set out for the central peak of the Central Mountain just after dawn. My destination was **Jùnjí Peak (Jùnjí Fēng),** elevation 1,470m (4,900 ft.). It required 30 minutes to retrace my steps up the river basin to Sòngyáng Academy. I skirted the academy wall and followed the power lines up a steep embankment to a gravel road. A few more twists and I was above the final foothill. The summit of Sōng Shān lay straight ahead, one among a pack of 36 peaks.

The road gave way to a path of stone steps rising up the river basin. A temple hung to the last terrace below the cliffs. In the river basin, I heard the pings of chisels against stone. The temple on the terrace is named **Lǎo Mǔ Cave (Lǎo Mǔ Dòng).** I knew nothing of its heritage, but someone was investing money in its restoration. Vendors had congregated upon its grounds. I purchased two boiled eggs and a can of soda. Behind the temple was a stairway to the summit, fashioned from hewn blocks, each the size and shape of a small stele. I'd spent almost 2 hours just to reach this temple. It would take me another 2 hours to gain the top, all of it by stairs that looked like they would never level out.

I passed through another temple that is on no map I've ever come across. It, too, was being restored. It was already active with monks dressed in long black robes. Several worshippers had black beards, a rare sight in most parts of China.

Against the wall of a massive peak, the trail bent east. I stopped at a shrine, a single building at the back of a ledge. A young man came out on the porch. I couldn't tell if he was monk or merchant. I could tell he was very poor. He also had no hands and no wrists. He smiled at me. He knew one English phrase: "Okay." "Okay," he laughed. "Okay."

Carved into a cliff across the way were characters announcing that Sōng Shān is the First Mountain of the World. Ahead was a staircase of a hundred steps or so, and, beyond that, more staircases switching back and forth up the sheer face of the peak. A steel railing had been installed. I could see a figure or two on the pinnacles above, and I met two or three groups of hikers on the stairs. Otherwise, the trail was deserted. The last vendor I came across had pitched his cart on a narrow ledge between staircases. I bought a can of soda.

This high up, I could survey the entire Dēngfēng Valley to the south, hazy in the dust. To the west, I could see a second mountain range—the western half of Sōng Shān, known as Shào Shì Shān, the junior range, with Shào Lín Monastery at its foot. I was scaling the Tài Shì Shān half of Sōng Shān, the eastern half, the "great" side. These were the same peaks that once attracted emperors and pilgrims, although they now attract almost no one.

Summitry

Each flight of stairs became more tedious. The sun was fierce. It seemed to take me hours to surmount the last ladder of steps. The top of Jùnjí Peak was farther still. Three women gathering plants and herbs motioned for me to sit down beside them on a green patch as they proceeded to eat their lunch. They weren't in the least disturbed that we spoke few words in common. I sat down with them and finished my drink. At noon I reached a construction site marked with red-and-white flags. The summit was a few steps more. And on this summit, this central summit of the Central Kingdom, halfway between the midpoints of Heaven and Earth, what is there? Nothing. No temple, no altar, no marker, no ruin. Not even a vendor. There is only nature: a slope of green grass and white stone.

In December of A.D. 696, the Wǔ Empress stood here, on this summit, paid homage to the earth, and appointed Sōng Shān emperor of Middle Heaven. Wǔ entered royal life as a concubine for one Táng Dynasty emperor, became the consort of his successor, and succeeded them both as supreme ruler and China's first great empress in A.D. 684. Hoping to establish an immortal dynasty of her own, she made Sōng Shān her sacred residence. The mountain was given an imperial title. Her prayer to the god of Sōng Shān, engraved on a tablet of gold weighing 280 grams, was unearthed in 1982 on the summit.

The view on a cloudless day from the top of Sōng Shān was a fine one. For the first time, I saw why the ancients maintained that the sky was round and the earth square.

A Tall, Dark Stranger

An hour passed at the summit. I turned back. As I passed the new buildings, a very dark man with a dark beard, dressed in black patches, stopped me. He raised both hands and touched his fingertips, forming a pyramid at the base of his neck. I mirrored his greeting. He reached out a hand. We shook. He invited me to accompany him inside; I declined. He stood aside; I walked down the mountain.

Máo Qílíng (1623–1716), on his second attempt to scale Sōng Shān, met a stranger, too: one who revealed to him the secrets of true Confucian wisdom, transforming his life. Me, I just keep walking up and down in China. It took me 3 hours to descend, each mile slower than the last, until I was amazed I could move at all. I saw almost no one on the way back. The herb gatherers had disappeared, the stonecutters vanished.

Central Peak Temple (Zhōngyuè Miào)

China's modern travelers do not come to Sōng Shān to climb peaks. They come to visit the temples—either Zhōngyuè, the Daoist temple to the Central Mountain, or Shào Lín, the Buddhist temple to Zen and the martial arts. Zhōngyuè lies 5km (3 miles) to the east of Dēngfēng; Shào Lín, 16km (10 miles) in the opposite direction. Both are on the main highway; neither requires a climb.

Twelve centuries ago, the **Central Peak Temple (Zhōngyuè Miào),** was one of the three greatest Daoist temples in China, consisting of nearly a thousand halls and pavilions. The God of the Central Mountain lived here. Since Hàn times, he had presided over quite an assortment of geographies and beings: rivers and valleys, mountains and fields, sheep and oxen, fruits and food—nearly everything, animate and inanimate.

It is thought that the temple was visited by the Hàn Wǔdì Emperor in 110 B.C. and that it was founded in the time of the 1st Dynasty, the Qín (221–207 B.C.). Today, of course, Zhōngyuè is shrunken—what hasn't of ancient China under the press of the new centuries?—and the buildings aren't old, dating back only a century or two to when the Qīng emperors visited and sacrificed oxen in the spring on the platform of the main hall. Then there were still 11 courtyards and plenty of gnarled trees, as many as 1,000, 300 of them said to have been planted over 1,000 years ago.

A few courtyards deep, I found the famous **Four Iron Guards,** statues 3m (10 ft.) tall, fierce in their armor, modeled after the soldiers of the time and cast in A.D. 1064. Some children swung from their iron fists. Daoist monks sat at tables nearby, dressed in dark blue robes, white leggings, and straw hats, selling incense. The courtyards were full of worldly vendors, too. One photographer posed customers on the back of a stuffed tiger. Another sold shots in a pellet gun aimed at a wall of balloons—strange entertainment at a temple.

The stele I most wanted to find is known as **The True Form of the Five Sacred Peaks (Wǔshān Zhēnxíng Tú).** It was carved in 1604. A magic symbol for each mountain—Héng Shān Nán to the south and Huà Shān to the west, Héng Shān Běi to the north and Tài Shān to the east—is placed on its compass point, with Sōng Shān, where I now stood, in the center. I found the Five Mountains tablet out in the open, exposed to the elements. It's a bit worn these days, its rounded top stone washed smooth, but the five mysterious characters for the Sacred Five are still clear 500 years after they were carved.

Outside the last hall is the path up **Yellow Umbrella Peak (Huánggài Fēng),** where the Wǔdì Emperor noticed a big patch of yellow cloud as he made his ascent of Sōng Shān. An ornate little pavilion stands there now, and those who want a quick holy climb wander up in droves. Admission to the temple complex is ¥15 ($1.90).

The Fighting Wooden Monks of Shào Lín

I returned to the highway and caught a bus back through Dēngfēng and on to **Shào Lín Monastery,** 15km (9 miles) farther west. Shào Lín is a monument to mass tourism, Chinese-style. Open daily from 6:30am to 6:30pm, it's a commercial maze of souvenir vendors inside and outside the temple complex, always crowded. Even the People's Republic of China is doing kung-fu *(gōngfu)* films that glorify the fighting monks of Shào Lín, and they're filming them right here, on the actual site. This is China's Universal City Studios of Flying Fists, the spiritual and commercial world center of the martial arts.

I was here to see history and culture, and I suppose that's what I was seeing. This is the center of the modern Chinese centrifuge—in brute contrast with the quiet old peak I reached yesterday, virtually alone.

Certainly Shào Lín Monastery has plenty of Old China attached to it, too. Shào Lín was founded in A.D. 495 by the Xiào Wéndì Emperor of the Northern Wèi Dynasty and expanded and enriched by the second Táng Dynasty emperor in 625 in gratitude to the monks who helped him wage war against a rival. In between, in 527, Dá Mó, also known as Bodhidharma, the 28th incarnation of the Buddha, arrived from India, crossing the Yángzǐ River on a reed. At Shào Lín, he spent 9 years in solitary meditation staring at the wall of a cave. The cave is still here; even the shadow he left on the cave's wall is still here, or so it's said. When Dá Mó emerged from 9 years of "wall-contemplation," he founded a new sect of Buddhism, known as Chán in China, as Zen in Japan.

Dá Mó also picked up credit for formulating the Chinese style of hand-to-hand combat known as *wǔ shù* or more popularly kung-fu *(gōngfu)*. Unconcerned about shifting from religion to religion, it seems, good Zen Buddhist patriarch Dá Mó is also said to have written Daoist classics on the cultivation of the muscles and the purification of the marrow.

The martial arts, not Zen, are what bring the tourists in these days. In the 15th and 16th centuries, the fighting monks of Shào Lín were taking on the pesky Japanese pirates off China's coast. During the 1920s, when China was in civil turmoil and local warlords held sway, the Shào Lín Temple was a haven for runaway soldiers who terrorized the local population. In 1928, one of the most famous of these warlords, Féng Yùxiáng, the "Christian general," routed the monks and set fire to the monastery. Shào Lín burned for 40 days.

I elbowed my way through the late-morning crowds to see **Thousand Buddha Hall (Qiān Fó Diàn),** built in 1588, with its fading fresco of monks going all out in martial arts battle—it would make a dandy movie poster—and the single most famous temple floor in China, roped off now and unlighted, where the monks practiced their stompings and leaps so diligently that the heavy stone floor became indented. Even cursory inspection suggested to me that the water table was high or the subsoil unstable under this floor, and that here and there it simply sank. I have a concrete driveway that looks about the same, and it was poured long after the 16th century.

To stretch the imagination farther, I lined up for a peek at the **Shadow Stone,** removed from Dá Mó's cave. A Chinese traveler described it this way in 1623: "I saw the shadow stone of Dá Mó. Less than 3 feet high, it was white with the black traces of a vivid standing picture of the foreign patriarch." What I saw was a slab of rock, burned or discolored, with the vaguest outlines of a human figure in meditation.

Shào Lín also contains a magnificent **Forest of Stupas (Tǎlín),** the largest collection in China of these small brick pagodas that hold holy relics and the remains of great monks, abbots, and even their followers. From what were once 500 stupas, 227 of these grave markers remain. They span 1,000 years of burial, from the Táng to the Qīng dynasties. The oldest stupa is that of a Táng Dynasty monk, Fǎ Wán Chánshī, who died in A.D. 791.

More vibrant, and more in keeping with the holy amusement park atmosphere of modern Shào Lín, is a courtyard surrounded on three sides by open-air displays of wooden, life-sized monks in dramatic fighting poses. They look like old carvings, but they may be merely dusty. Some are armed with swords or poles and locked in fierce combat. These mannequins of the martial arts are used as models for monks in training. These days Shào Lín does a hefty business running scores of martial arts schools for everyone from schoolchildren in China to visiting kung-fu clubs from Japan, America, and Europe.

The Far Side of Sōng Shān

Visiting Shào Lín Monastery in 1965, New Zealand journalist Rewi Alley was told about "some temples up on the hills, where in times of trouble the monks had gone." There is now a gondola that ferries visitors up the 36 peaks that make up Sōng Shān's western range—a mirror image of the main cluster of 36 Sōng Shān peaks that make up the Sacred Mountain proper.

I decided to take a look. From the rising gondola, I could see the Shào Lín Monastery and the tourist road that outlined it like a noose. The crowds and tour buses were brushed out of the picture of the tile roofs, brick walls, and green hills rising to the north. I could see Dá Mó's Cave, where he emptied his mind so thoroughly that his shadow stuck to the wall.

At the cable-car terminal on the peak, I followed a trail into the woods. It took me to a world far removed from the Shào Lín circus. Threading my way up towering cliffs, eventually I came out on the southern side of the range. The stone walls that line the back of the western Sōng Shān rise 300m (1,000 ft.) straight up. The trail sliced across the cliff face. Sections of the trail were cantilevered out from the rock, forming catwalks over empty chasms, across which I treaded gingerly.

The far side of Sōng Shān is dazzling. Some parts of the path are wide enough only for single-file passage—hardly a problem, as I met almost no one coming or going. I zigzagged along this natural stonewall for an hour from declivity to declivity. There were a few temples and pavilions in recesses and ledges, but I knew nothing about them, not even their names. They were deserted.

Eventually I came to a house perched on a small rock terrace. An old man and his wife invited me inside. The house had a dirt floor, almost no furnishings, and a shrine in a nook with incense burning. The two didn't seem to want to sell me anything. In fact, they seemed out of touch with the world, or mad. I asked them how to get back to Dēngfēng Town. They pointed straight down, and they were serious.

The long slabs of rock that tumbled down the cliff from their house contained remnants of a railing, enough of it still pinned to the rock to point the way down. After an hour's steady crawl, I reached a long formal stairway of stone that took me down to ground zero. At the bottom of the mountain, I was able to hire a motorcycle-driven cart back to Dēngfēng. The dirt road rolled across the "liver of the Earth" under the shadow of the 72 peaks that once pierced "the heart of Heaven." Silent, nearly forgotten, Sōng Shān, in the middle of the Middle Kingdom, has been reclaimed by nature.

PRACTICAL INFORMATION

by Sharon Owyang

ORIENTATION & WHEN TO GO

Sōng Shān is located south of the Yellow River in northwest Hénán Province, 670km (420 miles) south of Běijīng and 880km (550 miles) west of Shànghǎi. The town at the base of the main Sōng Shān mountain range, Dēngfēng, is midway between the city of Luòyáng (87km/53 miles to the west) and provincial capital Zhèngzhōu (63km/40 miles to the east).

Shào Lín Monastery is 15km (9 miles) west of Dēngfēng, at the base of the western (lesser) range of the Sōng Shān mountains. **Zhōngyuè Temple,** the most important Daoist shrine to the Central Mountain, is about 5km (3 miles) east of Dēngfēng. **Sōngyuè Pagoda,** the oldest brick pagoda in China, is about 5km (3 miles) northwest of Dēngfēng in the eastern or greater (Tàishì Shān) range of Sōng Shān.

Avoid the hot and humid summers and cold winters; the best times to visit are in the spring and fall.

GETTING THERE

There is no airport or train station at Dēngfēng. The nearest airport and rail connections are in **Zhèngzhōu,** from where there are flights to major Chinese cities including Běijīng (1 hr., 20 min.), Guǎngzhōu (2 hr., 20 min.), Hong Kong (2½ hr.), and Shànghǎi (1 hr., 20 min.). Tickets can be bought at

CITS or at hotel tour desks. Trains serve Zhèngzhōu (℡ 0371/697-1920) from Luòyáng (2 hr.), Xī'ān (10 hr.), Běijīng (12 hr.), Shànghǎi (14 hr.), and Guǎngzhōu (36 hr.). From Zhèngzhōu to Dēngfēng, it's necessary to take a bus (1½ hr.; ¥12/$1.50) from the **long-distance bus station (Chángtú Qìchēzhàn)** opposite the train station (℡ 0371/696-2864), or take a taxi (around ¥400/$50, subject to negotiation). When a new highway linking Dēngfēng and Zhèngzhōu is complete around October 2003, the trip should take only a half hour. From Dēngfēng, it's a 20-minute, ¥5 (60¢) minibus ride to Shào Lín Sì (Shào Lín Temple). Minibuses also connect Dēngfēng to Luòyáng (1½ hr.; ¥13/$1.60; departures every 20 min. 6am–5pm). In Dēngfēng, all minibuses depart from the **West Bus Station (Xīkè Chēzhàn)** on Zhōngyuè Dàjiē just west of Sòngyáng Zhōngjiē.

TOURS & STRATAGEMS

Visitor Information The Dēngfēng branch of **China International Travel Service (CITS)** is located in the northwestern part of town in the Guólǚ Dàlóu on Běihuán Lù Xīduàn (℡ 0371/288-3442; fax 0371/287-3137; www.df intertour.com). The staff speaks some English and can provide information on accommodations and help arrange tickets, but they do not organize guided hikes of Sōng Shān.

Martial Arts Training The **Shào Lín Martial Arts Training Center (Wǔ Shù Guǎn)** near the Shào Lín Monastery (℡ 0371/274-9120) is the only public kung-fu training school in Shào Lín. It has a basic hostel for guests and students and an inexpensive restaurant. It is also possible to study at one of the area's many private schools. CITS can arrange such study trips for students staying from a week to 6 months and longer.

Hours of Operation & Entrance Fees As of this writing, no ticket is required to climb the eastern or greater (Tài Shì Shān) range of Sōng Shān (4 hr.–5 hr. round-trip) from the Sòngyáng Academy. However, the situation may well change by the time you read this, as plans are underway to create a **Tài Shì Shān Scenic Area (Fēngjǐng Qū).** Already, a ¥10 ($1.25) entrance fee is required to go up the road to the Sōngyuè Temple Pagoda, which itself requires a ¥4 (50¢) entrance fee. Entrance fees are also charged at Zhōngyuè Temple (¥15/$1.90; open daily 8am–6pm) and the Shào Lín Monastery (¥60/$7.25; open daily 6:30am–6pm). There are two cable cars going up the western range (Shàoshì Shān): a ¥20 ($2.50), 20-minute ride on a chairlift (Sòngyáng Suǒdào) that goes to the Second Ancestor's Nunnery (Èrzhǔ Ān); and a ¥100 ($13), 40-minute cable-car ride (Sōngshān Shào Lín Suǒdào) that goes past Ladder *(Tīzi)* Gully to just below the summit. For the relatively fit, climbing the lesser, western range takes 3 to 4 hours round-trip.

WHERE TO STAY

In Dēngfēng, there are several adequate if uninspiring hotels to choose from. The best option is the palatial **Tiānzhōng Hotel (Tiānzhōng Dàjiǔdiàn)**, located at the eastern end of town at Zhōngyuè Dàjiē 6 (℡ 0371/289-1688; fax 0371/286-1560). This sprawling Chinese-style hotel, complete with grand upturned eaves, is rated four stars, but its rooms and facilities are really closer to those of a three-star hotel. Rooms (¥399/$49) are spacious and decorated with the usual nondescript brown furniture and somewhat lumpy beds. Bathrooms are a little old but clean. This hotel packs in the foreign tour groups, so the staff, which is very friendly, is at least used to dealing with foreigners. The hotel's restaurant can serve Western breakfasts upon request. The three-star **Shào Lín International Hotel (Shào Lín Guóji Dàjiǔdiàn)**, at Shàlín Dàdào 16 (© 0371/286-6188; fax 0371/286-1446), is the oldest of the three hotels and is still popular with independent Western travelers. Rooms are comfortable and have the basic amenities and furnishings, though the carpets are quite old and the bathrooms could use a scrubbing. The hotel offers foreign exchange but will not accept credit cards.

WHERE TO DINE

No restaurants stand out in Dēngfēng, so stick to hotel dining. The **Tiānzhōng Hotel (Tiānzhōng Dàjiǔdiàn; © 0371/289-1688)** offers Western breakfasts (upon request) and Chinese lunch and dinner buffets for ¥30 ($3.75) per person. You can also order from the menu (in Chinese only); dinner for two averages ¥80 to ¥100 ($10–$13). For the adventurous, there is a nightly **food market** at the corner of Zhōngyuè Dàjiē and Càishì Jiē, a block east of Sōng Shān Zhōnglù, where you can eat your fill of spicy kabobs, stir-fries, and the local noodles, *dāoxiāo miàn*.

APPENDICES

CHINA BY RIVER:
UP & DOWN THE YÁNGZĬ
长江

A CRUISE UPON ASIA'S MOST FABLED river, the Yángzĭ (or "Chángjiāng" in China, meaning "Long River"), has been the dream and sometimes the nightmare of millions of merchants and boatmen, farmers and poets, emperors and outlaws, since Chinese civilization began. Barely changed for centuries, the scenery is various, earthy, and spellbinding, particularly at the **Three Gorges,** where the third longest river on Earth is forcibly contained (as a Sòng Dynasty poet wrote) like "a thousand seas poured into one cup." Of pressing concern for travelers is how the upcoming flooding of the Three Gorges all the way upstream to Chóngqìng will affect the area. This dramatic section will eventually be diminished by the world's largest construction project, the Sānxiá Dam, scheduled for completion in 2009. For the time being, the most striking change will occur between June 1 and June 15, 2003, when the Three Gorges reservoir will rise 135m (443 ft.), 40m (131 ft.) short of its projected maximum height of 175m (574 ft.). Though the rush is on to see the Yángzĭ before it changes forever, for the next few years, the high-water mark in the Three Gorges area will only reach 4m (13 ft.) higher than before construction started. By 2009, the water level will rise 40m to 110m (131 ft.–361 ft.). So, yes, the scenery will change, but probably not as dramatically as booking agents would have you believe.

The Yángzĭ is *The Romance of the Three Kingdoms* made visible, each bend in the river a passage from that classic Chinese novel of history, adventure, and lore. Although most Westerners are not familiar with this book, all Chinese (and a good many Japanese) are. The Yángzĭ River has mythic, as well as natural, qualities.

Intrepid independent travelers have been cruising the Yángzĭ for decades, purchasing tickets at river ports and using Chinese cruise ships. Since the early 1990s, however, there have been more luxurious alternatives. I chose **Victoria Cruises,** an American-managed line that has 11 ships on the river. The longest of Victoria's several options is a 10-day, 9-night cruise upriver from Shànghǎi to Chóngqìng, which takes in virtually the entire navigable length of China's greatest river. Unfortunately, the future of this route is uncertain. As of 2003, it had been eliminated, though perhaps only temporarily.

Shànghǎi (Day 1)

I boarded the M.S. *Yangtze Princess* in Shànghǎi at Shíliùpǔ Pier, at the southern end of the Bund, in the early evening. I settled into my stateroom, then had a buffet supper in the dining hall, and came out on deck for a spectacular departure. The Huángpǔ River was lit up on both sides, with the European architecture of colonial days illuminated on the western shore and the new Shànghǎi of Pǔdōng's skyscrapers ablaze on the eastern shore. I was setting out on a voyage into the remote interior of China by passing through a tableau of recent Chinese history, the past on one side, the future on the other.

Yángzhōu/Nánjīng (Day 2)

After an early breakfast the next morning, our ship docked at Yángzhōu for the first of many shore excursions. The Yángzǐ River, between Shànghǎi and Wǔhàn, meanders through vast, flat deltas, its scenery hardly dramatic, but even here the river passes near some of China's greatest sights. Buses on the docks, manned by local English-speaking guides, took us past downtown Yángzhōu for a walk through the grounds of **Tiān Níng Temple,** a 1,500-year-old Buddhist complex where the Qiánlóng Emperor resided during his southern tour of the Grand Canal in the 18th century.

The Yángzhōu guides escorted us along a moat for a brief look at **Slender West Lake (Shòu Xīhú).** There, we strolled the garden shores of the narrow, scenic waterway with its celebrated triple-arched bridge (Wútáng Qiáo), constructed in 1757, about the time the Qiánlóng Emperor came to town to try his luck at fishing. The emperor's fishing platform is still in place here. On our way back to the ship, we passed a funeral procession marching alongside the freeway. The mourners were setting off firecrackers; two of them were pushing their motorcycles.

After lunch aboard the ship and an introductory lecture on the Yángzǐ River, we sailed upriver to Nánjīng, a city with a substantial political history in the 20th century, when it was China's capital under the Nationalist regime. On our city tour, the bus crossed the 3km (2-mile) long **Nánjīng Yángzǐ River Bridge,** China's most famous modern bridge over the Yángzǐ River. Opened in 1968, the bridge created the first rail link between Shànghǎi and Běijīng. The tour concluded with a walk up the 300 wide stairs to the **Sun Yat-sen Mausoleum (Zhōngshān Líng),** an imperial-sized tomb built for the founder of the first Chinese republic. Sun died in

1925; his Nánjīng tomb was begun a year later. Today it is one of the main stops on any Chinese political pilgrimage, as Sun Yat-sen is venerated by both communists and nationalists as the father of modern China.

The evening concluded in high cruise-ship style with a captain's cocktail party (complete with Chinese sparkling wine), dinner in the Dynasty Dining Room, and the Victoria Fashion Show in which members of the 118-person Chinese crew modeled costumes from the major dynasties on the disco floor.

Huáng Shān (Day 3)

During the night, our ship moved upriver another 210km (130 miles) to the tiny port of **Guìchí,** where buses took us another 177km (110 miles) to the foot of China's most beautiful peak, **Huáng Shān (Yellow Mountain).** At the Tàipíng Cable Station, where itinerant beekeepers were encamped, we rode the ropeway 15 minutes to the summit, rising almost 1,200m (3,000 ft.) through the parting mists. There, we received a brief but splendid introduction to the sheer rock formations, gnarled pines, and terrifying overlooks for which the Yellow Mountain is so famous. Armed with wooden walking sticks and cameras, our group enjoyed lunch at the top and spent

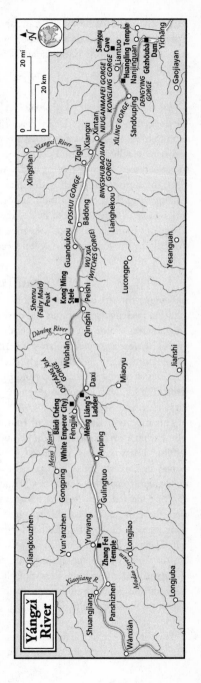

2 leisurely hours exploring the trails and nearby peaks. Descending in the afternoon, we napped on the 3-hour bus trip back to the ship, dined, and then slept soundly as our ship again used the night to traverse another 242km (150 miles).

Lú Shān (Day 4)

We docked in the former Treaty Port of **Jiǔjiāng.** This day's excursion took us to another mountain, **Lú Shān,** the hill station where foreign colonials and later a gallery of China's 20th-century political leaders established a summer resort. Despite the fog and light rain, we were able to tour Měilú Villa, the summer home of both Chiang Kai-shek and his bitter foe, Máo Zédōng, and then hiked a mountain trail in the Brocade Valley (Jǐnxiù) to Lú Cave, a temple carved out of the overhanging rock by nature. The village of Gulǐng at Lú Shān presented excellent afternoon shopping, particularly for the locally grown Cloud Tea.

Wǔhàn (Day 5)

Arriving at the city of Wǔhàn the next morning, we anchored here all day, awaiting passengers joining us the next day for the Wǔhàn-to-Chóngqìng Yángzǐ River Cruise. In the meantime, we explored the waterfront on our own. The streets are well worth wandering; you can view the old European architecture on the shoreline (highlighted by an old clock tower) and stroll the lanes of small Chinese shops and the pedestrian section (Bùxíng Jiē) of Jiāng Hàn Lù, with its boutiques and upscale clothing chains, and its KFC, Pizza Hut, and McDonald's.

The afternoon was devoted to touring two exceptional cultural sights. The **Húběi Provincial Museum (Húběi Shěng Bówùguǎn),** reopened in 1999 in a new building, is one of China's premier exhibition centers, well-signed in English and Chinese. It's the repository of over 15,000 relics unearthed from a Warring States Period (B.C. 475–221) tomb of Duke Yǐ of Zēng located 12m (40 ft.) underground. Among the coffins removed were those of his 21 concubines, ages 13 to 26, who were poisoned upon their master's death, and another for his dog. The duke's own inner and outer lacquer-painted wooden coffins, weighing some 400 pounds each, are displayed in the museum, as are chariot pieces, gold cups, bamboo strips with ancient writing, jade wine glasses, and a large bronze wine cooler. There is also an exquisite bronze drum stand in the shape of a crane with a long neck and deer's antlers (as both the crane and the deer are symbols of longevity).

The centerpiece of the museum is the **Chime Bells of Duke Yǐ of Zēng.** There are 65 bronze bells, suspended in three tiers on a wooden frame. The bells are decorated with 3,755 inscriptions and their collective weight is over 5 tons. These ancient bells, the largest complete set in the world, are tuned to five-, six-, and seven-note scales. Although the original music of the chimes has been lost, scholars have reconstructed songs from other ancient scores. Four times a day in the museum auditorium, a local concert group (which periodically tours the world) plays the songs on a replica of the ancient chimes, accompanied by zithers, drums, flutes, and an English-speaking narrator. Admission to the performances is included in the museum entrance fee of ¥30 ($3.75). The museum is open daily from 8 to 11:30am and 1:30 to 4:30pm.

The second cultural site on our tour drew from modern history, that of Chairman Máo, for whom an elaborate estate was maintained on East Lake in Wǔhàn. Opened to the public in 1993, **Chairman Máo's Villa (Máo Zédōng Biéshù)** is a 1950s Western-style mansion with high ceilings, peeling wallpaper, and stained carpets—strangely enough, it hasn't been renovated since the heyday of Maoist Thought. Máo visited some 25 times, swimming in the Yángzǐ River on several occasions. His large indoor swimming pool is still in place on the estate, as is his huge bed. As recently as 1999, guests who were willing to shell out ¥25,000 ($3,000) per night could have the run of the entire Cold War compound, complete with an air-raid shelter in its basement.

Wǔhàn (Day 6)

After a night at anchor in Wǔhàn, we enjoyed another shore excursion. Wǔhàn is an industrial port that, until Yíchāng took its place, served as the main eastern terminus for most Yángzǐ River cruises. It's usually ignored by tourists, but as we'd seen the day before, it has some cultural treats. The city actually consists of what once were three cities: Wǔchāng, Hànkǒu, and Hànyáng. Hànkǒu, Wǔhàn's city center, where we have anchored, contains the architectural stamp of British, German, French, and Japanese colonials. In Hànyáng, adjacent to Hànkǒu, we toured the 300-year-old **Guīyuán Temple (Guīyuán Sì),** one of the largest along the Yángzǐ, where locals light incense and pray for prosperity and health at shrines to the golden Buddha and Guānyīn, the Goddess of Mercy. The main attraction is a cluster of the 500 arhats (followers of Buddha), molded from clay in the early 1800s by a father and son into lively, sometimes comic poses, painted with gold powder, and placed on benches to face each other.

Across the Yángzǐ in the Wǔchāng district, up a steep hill (known as Snake Mountain), and past the ink stone purported to be that of poet Lǐ Bái, is the **Yellow Crane Tower (Huáng Hè Lóu),** a high pagoda that dates from the 3rd century A.D. Rebuilt countless times (most recently in 1985, in Qīng Dynasty style), it has been renowned through the ages because of its vistas of the Yángzǐ River and because of the many poems in which it is featured. One of the most famed is the one Táng Dynasty master Lǐ Bái wrote on the occasion of saying goodbye to his friend and fellow poet, Mèng Hàorán. Lǐ Bái's poem can be translated as: "At Yellow Crane Tower I bid farewell to my old friend and watch his sail go farther, ever farther, until it vanishes under blue sky; but my heart runs with the Yángzǐ waters, flowing, ever flowing." Our excursion up and down the tower was rewarded with a tea ceremony conducted in a pavilion at the base of Snake Mountain.

For those who boarded at Wǔhàn, as most passengers did, it was the first day of a 6-day, 5-night cruise upriver to Chóngqìng that traverses 1,354km (841 miles) of the Yángzǐ (which is barely a fifth of its east-to-west 6,288km/3,906-mile length). As we pushed out from Wǔhàn, the river darkened. All I could see from the railing were lights, some passing, some receding, and overhead the stars that never seem to move, even over China's longest river.

Yuèyáng (Day 7)

At dawn, after joining the ship's doctor for his daily *taìjíquán* exercise class, I took a look at the Yángzǐ above Wǔhàn. The placid waters were wide, dotted with small whirlpools but devoid of rapids. Long, rusty barges heaped with coal, rice, and other products of the interior chugged downstream toward Shànghǎi, the sailors calling out and whistling as we passed. Sheaves of grain are unloaded along the way and stacked on shore in piles the size and shape of barns. Logs are carried from shore by hand.

Even here, the Yángzǐ is etched with the history of the Three Kingdoms period (A.D. 220–280), when the Wèi, Shǔ, and Wú kingdoms contended for control of China along the Yángzǐ. At **Red Cliff (Chìbì)**—scorched that color, it is said, by the flames that engulfed the Wú and Shǔ armadas in their celebrated battle with the Kingdom of Wèi in A.D. 208—pavilions and a museum of weaponry commemorate this critical confrontation. Zhūgě Liàng, China's most respected military strategist and political advisor, was present at the battle, in which the Wèi army, led by the villainous General Cáo, met defeat at the hands of Zhūgě.

Our ship made a port of call at **Dòngtíng,** China's second largest freshwater lake. Massive accumulations of silt have reduced the size of what was China's largest lake, but its beauty and history are unaffected. On the east side is **Yuèyáng Tower,** where admirals of the Three Kingdoms period once reviewed naval maneuvers. The tower dates from the 8th century. It was most recently rebuilt in Sòng Dynasty style in 1985, complete with the

Thrice Drunken Pavilion where Daoist Immortal Lǚ Dòngbīn engaged in revelries. Unfortunately, this is my least favorite site along the river. There's little to see or do, and the weather is usually miserably wet. I suggest you skip it altogether, stay aboard, and learn to play mahjong (as I did).

From the mouth of Dòngtíng Lake upriver, the land is flat, girded by the 179km (111-mile) long Jīngjiāng Dike originally built 16 centuries ago. This bulwark against flooding ends at Shāshì, 538km (334 miles) from Wǔhàn. Once a separate city, Shāshì is now a district of **Jīngzhōu,** whose city walls—16km (10 miles) long, 9m (30 ft.) high, last rebuilt in A.D. 1646—were fashioned, according to local legend, by Three Kingdoms hero Guān Yǔ, later deified as a Chinese god of war. Jīngzhōu has a **museum** that contains the remains of a Hàn Dynasty county governor, Mr. Suì, who died in 167 B.C. at age 60 of a stomach ailment. Preserved in water and mercury sulfide within a tripartite cedar coffin and buried 9m (30 ft.) deep, the mummy was unearthed in 1975. After 2,142 years, the corpse proved to be perfectly preserved, with arm and leg joints still flexible. Some cruise ships stop to see the walled city of Jīngzhōu, although Victoria Cruises has recently dropped it from the itinerary.

Three Gorges Dam/Yíchāng (Day 8)

The upriver gateway to the Three Gorges is **Yíchāng,** once a foreign treaty port and the great transshipment point for Yángzĭ traffic. Here China's largest dam, Gézhōubà, was completed in 1986. Boats and ships must pass through its hydraulic locks. Gézhōubà has raised the level of the Yángzĭ some 20m (65 ft.) behind its walls. The ship's crew ran an informal lottery with the passengers here. Whoever came closest to predicting the time we passed out of the locks was the winner.

Above Gézhōubà, I spotted the M.S. *Kūnlún* at anchor. It once carried Máo Zédōng through the Three Gorges and served as a luxury cruiser for wealthy tourists. Neglected now, it seems to be quietly rusting away. A new generation of cruisers has usurped its place on the river.

Our next destination was the construction site of **Three Gorges Dam (Sān Xiá),** located at Sāndǒupíng, 43km (27 miles) above the Gézhōubà Dam. When fully operational in 2009, the dam will raise the Yángzĭ to 175m (574 ft.). During the peak of heavy construction between 1998 and 2003, up to 27,000 workers and 650 engineers and technicians were on-site. Situated on a ribbon of granite that crosses the more fragile limestone basin of the Yángzĭ, the Three Gorges Dam span will be 2km (1¼ miles) wide and 182m (607 ft.) high, dwarfing all other dams. The final cost could easily exceed $30 billion.

This cement barrier will create a reservoir 596km (370 miles) long, transforming the wild Yángzǐ into a calm lake that will submerge some 1,400 townships and villages and 30,300 hectares (75,000 acres) of cultivated land, necessitating the relocation of as many as three million people. While the increased water level will no doubt detract somewhat from the scenic splendor of the area, at heights ranging from 800m to 1,100m (2,624 ft.–3,280 ft.), the Three Gorges themselves will still rise a respectable distance out of the water. First proposed by Sun Yat-sen in 1919 and seconded by Chairman Máo in 1958, this project is expected to provide 10% of China's electricity, reduce the severity of flooding, and facilitate passage of considerably larger ships through the Three Gorges to and from Chóngqìng in Sìchuān, China's rice bowl. Our Victoria cruise ship, at 3,000 tons, and others of similar size, were currently the heaviest ships able to navigate the Yángzǐ; after the great dam is completed, ships more than three times that size will make their way from Shànghǎi all the way to Chóngqìng.

We followed a diversion channel (which has since been blocked) on the east side, anchoring at **Máopíng** and boarding buses for a trip to see the dam construction. The sky seemed to be filled—and will be filled for years—with a fine dust. On our way to the Three Gorges Dam Observation Tower, the road through the center of Máopíng Village was jammed. Traffic stopped completely and didn't seem likely to restart. Apparently there were no detours. Our local guide, who had adopted the Western name Hamlet, was at his first day on the job and seemed immobilized. I wasn't. I left the tour bus and walked down the street, finally finding the bottleneck a few blocks around the bend. It was a sign of new times in China: An impromptu strike by local taxi drivers led them to block the thoroughfare with their abandoned taxis. In the course of the next 20 minutes I heard at least five versions of what prompted this strike. The most likely was that a policeman stopped a woman taxi driver, demanded her permit, and struck her when she refused, leading to a sympathetic strike. After an hour, a settlement was negotiated and the traffic rolled.

We traveled through portions of the new town being built for the 100,000 local residents who will lose their old town to the dam, then crossed a new bridge, the 10th over the Yángzǐ, opened in 1997. We could see the sides of the Three Gorges Dam in place on either side of the river now, columns of concrete 180m (600 ft.) high. The Observation Tower lies atop a hill, a round building encircled by a fresco commemorating heroic workers; below it is a hall displaying models of the great project. On one side is the Yángzǐ, soon to be spanned; on the other, parallel to the Yángzǐ, is a new empty river, the cement bed of a massive ship-lock system to raise and lower all vessels.

Returning to the ship, we continued through the first of the three gorges this dam will partially submerge, **Xilíng Gorge.** From here on, the scenery improves rapidly. Mountains rise abruptly from the banks of the Yángzǐ, eventually forming a massive wall on both sides, pinching and speeding the river flow. These gorges were created 70 million years ago as an inland sea withdrew to the east, its waters slicing into the limestone faults and creases where two large mountain systems had been smashed together. This primordial geology is written on the steep cliff sides that threaten to eclipse the sun.

Xilíng, the longest of the three at 76km (47 miles), actually consists of a number of gorges named for legends of the Three Kingdoms or the resemblance of their formations to other objects. **The Sword and the Book of the Art of War** is the gorge where Zhūgě Liàng stored grain for his troops and hid his book of military strategy. Other gorges within Xilíng include the **Ox Liver and Horse Lung Gorge** and the **Gorge of Shadowplay.**

Xilíng Gorge was once one of the most hazardous regions on the Yángzǐ, rife with rapids and whirlpools. A pile of human bones once resided on its banks, heaped in the shape of a white pagoda, as a reminder to navigators of the dangers here. Seventy years ago, a British naval commander described the Three Gorges' "boiling, seething infernos of tumbling, tossing water, whirlpools, eddies, backwaters and sudden vertical 'boils.'" One in 10 junks was stranded in the gorges; 1 in 20, lost forever.

Xilíng Gorge is still not easy to navigate, but more than a hundred shoals and reefs have been dynamited in recent times, and the river is now lined with several thousand navigational buoys with all-weather beacons. These buoys, which resemble small dinghies, must be relocated every 2 weeks, since the channel changes that often as waters rise and fall and silt is carried from bank to bank.

In some places, the gorges are cloven with steep ravines where hillside farms produce wheat, rice, maize, legumes, rapeseed, and tangerines. For some of these isolated farms, junks and small barges provide the main link to the outside world. By 2009, these farms will be underwater.

At **Zǐguǐ,** just past the small Xiāng Stream, home to Hàn Dynasty heroine Wáng Zhāojūn, we passed out of Xilíng Gorge. Cruise ships often spend the night here, entertained on the wharf by local peasant singers and dancers. Zǐguǐ is said to be the home of poet Qū Yuán (ca. 340–278 B.C.), whose Ming Dynasty statue resides at a memorial hall. When his advice went unheeded by the king of Chǔ, Qū Yuán drowned himself in the Mìluó River (in present northeastern Hunan). Ever since, he has been commemorated by China's annual dragon boat races (on the 5th day of the 5th lunar month) and by the eating of *zòngzi,* packets of glutinous rice wrapped in bamboo leaves. It's said that villagers originally tossed tubes of rice-filled bamboo into the river as food for Qū Yuán's spirit. To keep water dragons from eating them, the tubes were tied in bright silk threads, which dragons were thought to fear.

For centuries, the Yángzǐ has served as the graveyard for those too poor to afford a land burial. Even today, you can spot corpses. Our American tour director counted 23 corpses on her 40 trips 2 years ago, including six in a single gruesome day. The ship's captain reported seeing Yángzǐ corpses every day. People fall in and can't swim, he said with a smile. I kept my eyes on the river the whole way, but all I saw were the rowboat channel markers like caskets in a treacherous river.

We tied up at the village of **Bādōng.** The night was black, but warm. I spent a few hours on deck, enthralled by the town's brilliant lights, spilling down the banks like a cascade of Christmas bulbs.

The Three Gorges & the Lesser Gorges (Day 9)

This was the most intense day for sightseeing along the river. We entered the middle gorge, **Witches Gorge (Wū Xiá)** in the morning. Wū Gorge contains the most dramatic mountain peaks on the Yángzǐ, crowned by **Goddess Peak,** which has a likeness in stone of Yáojí, youngest of the 12 daughters of Xīwángmǔ, Queen Mother of the West. These 12 sisters stole away to Earth and met Yǔ the Great, tamer of floods, who was fighting the 12 dragons of the floodwaters. The sisters slayed the dragons and were immortalized as the 12 peaks that assisted mariners in navigating Wū Gorge. In the midst of this gorge is **Gathered Immortals Peak** and the **Kong Ming Tablet,** supposed to have been inscribed by Zhūgě Liàng himself when he served as prime minister of the Shǔ Kingdom. In a Táng Dynasty poem written here, Lǐ Bái (A.D. 701–762) recalled how his boat tried for 3 days to surmount a single set of rapids. "But for all this time the peak remains beside us," he wrote. "I wonder how many of my hairs turned gray."

Wū Gorge ends at the **Golden Helmet and Shining Armor Valley,** where the gray walls of limestone resemble ancient armor and the rounded mountaintop shines like a golden helmet. We docked at the town of Wūshān, home to the legendary emperor Yǔ, who is said to have created the Three Gorges. Wūshān marks the end of the middle gorge and is the gateway to excursions on the **Dàníng River,** site of the **Lesser Three Gorges (Xiǎo Sānxiá).**

We disembarked to get a taste of one of the Yángzǐ's most scenic small tributaries. Trips up and down the **Dàníng River,** first offered to tourists in 1985, are made in motorized boats that seat about 15 people. The day I went, the river was so fierce that, at one point, passengers had to disembark and walk along the bank (lined with local vendors) while the boat struggled to overcome the rapids, the boatmen pushing their bamboo poles into the shallow streambed to gain enough leverage. The 32km (20-mile) trip upriver through the **Three Little Gorges (Xiǎo Sān Xiá)** takes several hours, and many visitors find the scenery more impressive than that along the Yángzǐ, the peaks sharper, the current swifter and more violent. Sights along the way include bands of monkeys and ancient coffins suspended from holes carved into the cliff face—the famous hanging coffins of the Yángzǐ. Lunch is sometimes provided at Twin Dragons Village, where boats turn around for a fast, water-splashed return downstream.

I saw plenty of **monkeys** on my trip, including several youngsters who slipped while running across the cliff faces and plunged into the water. The hanging coffins were still as difficult as ever to pick out, however. A new feature is gangs of roving vendors, some of whom proffer their wares to passengers in fishing nets on the ends of long poles, others who charge the boats as they slow and bark at the windows, and some who even hurl themselves into the boats to make a sale (and are pushed back out into the river by the angry boatmen). Twin Dragon Village, at the upper end of our little voyage, will be submerged when the Three Gorges Dam is completed. So will the city of Wūshān where we were anchored. Residents have already deserted their old homes and moved to Wūshān New Town at the top of the hills.

The Lesser Three Gorges pack the pleasure of mild white-water rafting and the scenery of a deep river valley into one compact package, yet I prefer the bigger gorges, their massive scale emblematic of the great river way dividing north and south China.

In the early afternoon, we reached the westernmost gorge, **Qútáng Gorge (Qútáng Xiá),** the shortest of the Three Gorges (just 8km/5 miles long), but also the grandest and wildest. Here, the Yángzǐ narrows to as little as 100m (300 ft.), and only one ship is allowed to pass at a time; the peaks rise upward of 111m (3,700 ft.); the water deepens, glistens, and charges like molten lava; and the wind itself is flattened and funneled through. As an ancient verse puts it, "Peaks pierce the sky as we course through the deep passage beneath." The mountains appear to have been split apart by the blade of a massive ax. Iron pillars, now submerged, were employed in Táng Dynasty times to string up defensive barriers, and later to tax barge traffic. A stone perched on the top of a black rock far overhead is aptly named **Rhinoceros Looking at the Moon.** At the upstream entrance, there's a series of zigzag square holes cut into the cliffs. Known as **Mèng Liáng's Ladder,** after the exploits of a Sòng Dynasty soldier, it is actually the remains of a stairway to the top of the peak where a city once resided in the 6th century A.D. Wooden coffins suspended on this same cliff have been dated back to 1000 B.C.

At **Báidì Chéng** and **Fèngjié,** cruise ships reach the upriver end of the Three Gorges. It was here that Zhūgě Liàng trained troops during the Three Kingdoms era and here that China's two greatest poets, Lǐ Bái and Dù Fǔ, both of the Táng Dynasty (A.D. 618–907), resided. Dù Fǔ lived for 2 years in Fèngjié, where he composed over 400 poems. At Báidì Chéng, Liú Bèi, ruler of the Shǔ Kingdom, died of despair after failing to avenge his brother, Guān Yǔ. At **Báidì Temple,** these and other heroes of the Three Kingdoms are commemorated today.

Altogether, the Three Gorges occupy only a 201km (125-mile) section of the Yángzǐ, a mere fragment, they form the central scenic gem of the riverway. On an upriver cruise, the gorges become the culmination of a slow battle against the great inland current that crosses China, its power reaching a crescendo as it funnels through the gorges as through an hourglass. Downriver, the gorges appear suddenly, dramatically, and are traversed in a fraction of the time. As Lǐ Bái observed 1,200 years ago: "In the morning leaving Báidì Chéng, it was as if we went on clouds; from there to Jiānglíng is one thousand li, but in one day the racing waters brought us down." (During Lǐ Bái's time, the *li* was an inexact measure of distance equaling about a third of a mile.) Each way, although the sensation is different, the power of the river underlies the experience, its force so compelling that even a modern traveler can taste something of what the Yángzǐ was in centuries past. The paths of the trackers, harnessed by quarter-mile-long ropes of braided bamboo to loaded junks and later steamboats, are still visible where they were carved into the sides of these massive canyons—traces of superhuman labor that will be submerged before long when the river itself is further tamed and modernized.

Fēngdū/Wànxiàn (Day 10)

Our last full day on the river included the chance to stroll through a typical Yángzǐ village, either at Fēngdū or at Wànxiàn, depending on the ship's timetable. On my most recent voyage, **Wànxiàn** was the stop, a hilly, charming town, its wholesale districts near the wharves destined to drown. The shore tour took us up the terraced town in steep zigzags, past the new Government Center, the first building in town with elevators and central air-conditioning.

We stopped downtown twice, first for a stroll through a street market, where hundreds of live ducks were for sale, along with a thousand other fragrant, fresh foodstuffs. Then local acrobats treated us to a performance in the town auditorium. What makes this performance so charming is that the acrobats are children, students in the Wànxiàn Academy devoted to this traditional entertainment. They are not only beautiful and innocent, but also unabashed when they miss a trick or take a fall or drop a spinning plate.

Farther uptown is the **Wànxiàn Three Gorges Museum.** It has a new wing but no signs in English, and its collection of artifacts from the Hàn to Qīng dynasties is nothing special; the museum would not even exist were if not for the mummies and coffin on the second floor. You can see a 2,000-year-old hanging coffin (made from a large tree sliced the long way in half), as well as its contents—the skeletons of a 15-year-old male and a 40-year-old female. They were buried together and suspended in a cave high up the sheer cliffs along the Yángzǐ. The boy died a natural death; the woman did not.

On other cruises, I have stopped instead at **Fēngdū,** China's "Ghost City," where a temple to the God of the Underworld, Yīnwáng, commands the summit of **Míng Shān Peak.** This is the place of final judgment in the Yángzǐ basin, making it an appropriate last stop on the way to Chóngqìng. At Fēngdū, you climb long rows of stairs, 600 steps in all, to meet Yīnwáng. There you must pass through all the stages—from a Míng Dynasty bridge to a Ghost Gate—that the soul is said to travel at the moment of death, as well as perform some feat: Cross a bridge in three steps, run up a flight of a hundred stairs in a single breath, or balance for 3 seconds on a round rock. If you fail, Hell claims you (or so they say). Most visitors do survive this long journey to the top, where Daoist, Buddhist, and Confucian temples mingle; amusement-park statues of the Underworld line the courtyards; and Yīnwáng, the King of Hell, sits in judgment, assisted by four supreme judges. A Swiss-made chairlift whisks the nonbelievers and those in a hurry straight to the top, where the panorama of the Yángzǐ and the surrounding mountains is splendid.

Back in the park at the base of Míng Shān, the locals, along with the blind beggars, gathered in the afternoon. The elders practiced *tàijíquán* at such a slow pace, they seemed to be ghosts themselves. The fog on the water swirled like a weightless cloth, winding and unwinding. The banks of the river grew faint. We resumed our cruise. The last walls of the Three Gorges behind us rose like the sides of a stone crib. When we pulled out from the muddy banks of Fēngdū, even the Mountain of the Underworld was lost in the mists.

Chóngqìng (Day 11)

At Chóngqìng, a city so hilly that bicycles are a rarity, a Yángzǐ cruise can either begin or end. Pulling upriver, you savor the power of the river, as irresistible as the flood of time, silted with the legends and hardships of the past. Speeding downriver, the flow is swifter; the direction is toward the future, when the river's power will be harnessed by the walls of the world's largest hydroelectric plant, at the cost of the drowning of the Yángzǐ's famous towns. The hills are dotted with new billboards now, often placed above old villages, marking the 175m (574-ft.) rim of the coming flood to end all floods.

Sailing downriver, the Three Gorges unroll twice as quickly, rushing by as in a dream. Coal factories drape the steep banks. Fishermen on small trawlers crank in their nets by hand. Women pound the day's laundry on the rocks. The Yángzǐ broadens. The mountains dissolve into fields so level and low you can't see over the border of the river. On one occasion I saw a long, low-laden barge, heaped with black coal, and on top of that coal, a dozen cows huddled together; someone remarked that it was a barbecue waiting to happen.

PRACTICAL INFORMATION

by Michelle Sans

EFFECT OF THREE GORGES DAM ON CRUISES

No one, including cruise directors and travel agents, is entirely certain how the construction of the dam will affect cruise schedules. According to plan, the reservoir was partially filled between June 1 and 15, 2003, which raised the water level in the Three Gorges from 66m (215 ft.) to 135m (443 ft.), where it will stay until September 2006 when the water will rise to 156m (512 ft.). The permanent ship lock was put into operation on June 15, 2003. By the end of 2003, the first set of turbines will generate hydropower, marking the end of phase two of construction. The third and final phase begins in 2004 and will end with the completion of the dam in 2009. At that point, the water level in the Three Gorges will reach 175m (574 ft.) and all 26 generators will be in operation. The question of how this will affect the scenery of the Three Gorges has tour promoters in a quandary. For 10 years they've been saying it's our last chance to see the Three Gorges. By 2009, the cry should be something like, "Be the first to see the greatest dam in the world, and, hey, the Three Gorges are still there, and they don't look that different! Why, they're prettier than ever!"

Following are some of the immediate effects the 135m (443-ft.) water level is expected to have on sights along the Three Gorges route:

- The residents of Fēngdū have already been moved to the new city built across the river on higher ground. The mountain and temple complex, along with most of the "scenes of hell," will remain, but the mountain will be a semi-island.
- The town of Shíbǎo Zhài will be submerged and the water level will reach the base of the fortress. Excursions will still be possible, but the intriguing old town will be gone.
- Báidì Chéng will be half submerged.
- Wànxiàn will be partially submerged.
- The Dàníng and Shénnóng gorges will be somewhat diminished, but not enough to stop tours—naturally.

WHAT TO READ

Your Yángzǐ cruise will be enhanced if you read John Hersey's *A Single Pebble*, a novel about pre-Revolutionary, pre-tourism days on the river; and Richard McKenna's *The Sand Pebbles*, a gunboat epic that was made into a film. Lyman P. Van Slyke's *Yangtze: Nature, History, and the River* is full of intriguing historical and geographical facts, and includes eyewitness accounts of early life along the Yángzǐ. Peter Hessler's insightful *River Town: Two Years on the Yangtze* recounts Hessler's experience as a Peace Corp volunteer in Fúlíng with humor and eloquence. Judy

Bonavia's *The Yángzǐ River,* an Odyssey Illustrated Guide published in Hong Kong and available in many travel bookstores overseas, is a general guide, filled with facts and lore.

The River Dragon Has Come! is a 1998 collection of essays by outspoken Chinese journalist Dài Qíng and other Chinese scholars and journalists who oppose the massive hydroelectric dam project. For *Probe International's* weekly updates on the dam, go to www.threegorgesprobe. org. For the Chinese government's side, see www.china-embassy.org.

WHEN TO GO

The best cruising months are March, April, September, and October. In terms of weather, May, early June, and early November are riskier, but can also be

lovely. Summer is the rainy season, and winter is usually dry, but quite cold; moreover, few ships sail off season, and schedules are less reliable.

LOCAL FERRIES & PASSENGER SHIPS

Yángzǐ River **ferries** depart from Wǔhàn (for upriver trips) and from Chóngqìng (for downriver trips) year-round, but their facilities are foul, and so is the food. They are for transport, not tourism, so they make no effort to go through the gorges in the light of day, and there are no tourist excursions.

Numerous Chinese **passenger boats** operate on the Yángzǐ, some of them with quite comfortable cabins and facilities. Management and staff are not used to foreign travelers and they rarely speak English, but the price, even for first-class, is considerably less than that of a luxury ship. Fourth-class passage from Chóngqìng to Wǔhàn starts at ¥231 ($28) and isn't much better than ferry accommodation. That is, you get a bunk in an eight-person dorm

with a filthy toilet down the hall. Prices for first-class passage (two-bed cabin with private shower/toilet), excluding meals and excursions, start at ¥1,370/ $170 per person. Since you can pay on board or at the site for excursions, make sure they're not included in your ticket price; then, should you decide to forego any, you won't have paid for them. Typically, excursions are to Fēngdū, Shíbǎozhài, and the Three Little Gorges, but these ships do not stop at the Three Gorges Dam construction site. First-class passage from Chóngqìng to Nánjīng starts at ¥1,838 ($230). You can book your passage in Chóngqìng inside the **Navigation Office Building** at Cháotiān Mén near the Cháotiān Mén Hotel (beware of so-called "government-run tour agencies" along the wharf that are likely to charge much higher fees than the actual ticket cost); or through **China International Travel Service (CITS)** in Wŭhàn at Táiběi Yĭ Lù 26, 7th Floor, Xiăo Nánhú Building (✆ **027-8578-4100;** fax 027-8578-4089; citswuh@public.wh.hb.cn) or in Chóngqìng at Zăozĭ Lányā Zhèng Jiē 120 (✆ **023-6385-0693;** fax 023-6385-0196; citscq@cta.cq.cn). There is a booking fee of ¥50/$6.25. The agents in the international divisions of both these offices are knowledgeable and helpful, and speak excellent English. In other words, they are far superior to the average CITS staff.

YÁNGZĬ CRUISES

The following liners have the best English-speaking river guides and the best ships. And, after years of experience with foreign passengers, most have removed from their itineraries excursions that require a thorough familiarity with the characters and events of the Three Kingdoms in order to enjoy them. *Tip:* Take advantage of off-season rates, book and buy in China, compare prices, bargain, and ask what the excursions are. The prices quoted here are rack rates, but 50% discounts are standard even during high season. Prices are expected to drop considerably after June 2003, when the "last chance" hype winds down for a few years—until the next inundation nears.

The cruising high seasons are April, May, September, and October. Shoulder seasons are late March, June, July, August, November, and early December. Some cruise ships offer specials in December, January, February, and March.

Victoria Cruises Based in New York, this is one of the few Western-managed lines. At one time, Victoria had the most luxurious liners on the Yángzĭ. While they still offer first-rate cruises with some of the best English-speaking cruise directors and river guides, other cruise lines equal or surpass their boats' cabins, kitchen, and facilities, and are equally well-staffed. Standard cabins have twin beds and a writing desk, but are slightly smaller than Orient Royal's *East King* and *East Queen*, which have the largest standard cabins on the river. **Routes/Rates:** Between Chóngqìng and Wŭhàn (downriver 4 days; upriver 6 days) $750 to $800 per person, standard cabin; $2,000 per person for the largest suites. Shore excursions cost $85 per person. Between Chóngqìng and Nánjīng (downriver 8 days; upriver 9 days) it costs $1,400 to $1,500 per person, standard cabin. Shore excursions are $225.

57–08 39th Avenue, Woodside, New York 11377. ✆ *800/348-8084 or 212/818-1680. Fax 212/818-9889. www.victoria cruises.com. 74–87 cabins. 50%–60% discounts possible year round. AE, DC, MC, V.* **Amenities**: 1 restaurant (Chinese/Western), bar; fitness room; salon; massage; acupuncture; laundry; forex. *In room: A/C, closed circuit TV, hair dryer on request.*

Orient Royal Cruises Orient Royal's *East King* and *East Queen* are arguably the plushest ships on the Yángzĭ, and they tie with the Yellow Crane for the best food. Their cruise directors, both from the Philippines, do a superior job of attending to passengers' needs and requests, and their Chinese river guides deliver expert commentary in well-spoken English. Standard cabins have twin beds with a handy window ledge and shelf at their head as well as a desk and a small fridge.

Routes/Rates: Between Chóngqìng and Yíchāng (4 days) costs $740 to $800 per person, standard cabin; $2,000 per person for the largest suites. Shore excursions cost $70 per person.

Orient Royal Cruise, Wǔhàn office. Xīn Huá Lù 316, 14th Floor, E Zuò (Block E), Liángyóu Building. ✆ ***027/8576-9988*** *or toll free in the U.S.* ✆ *888/664-4888. Fax 027/8576-6688. www.orientroyal cruise.com. 80 cabins. 50%–60% discounts possible year round. AE, DC, MC, V.* **Amenities:** 2 restaurants (Chinese/Western, cafe), 2 bars; fitness room; salon; massage; laundry; forex. *In room: A/C, closed circuit TV, minibar/fridge, hair dryer on request.*

Presidential Cruises The *Yellow Crane* is built to China's four-star standard. Its cabins aren't as spacious as the *East King/Queen's*, but the ship is attractively appointed and well staffed with an English-speaking crew. While the *Yellow Crane* lacks the slick promotion of Victoria and Orient Royal, the ship itself serves better food, is more luxurious than Victoria's ships, and very nearly meets the five-star standard of the *East King* and *Queen*. Standard rooms are comparable in size and furnishing to those in the Victoria Cruises' fleet.

Routes/Rates: Between Chóngqìng and Wǔhàn (downriver 3 days; upriver 4 days) costs $550–$700 per person, standard cabin. Downstream passage is about $60 more than upstream. (CITS in Wǔhàn and Chóngqìng usually offers these trips for a couple of hundred dollars less. See contact information under "Local Passenger Boats and Tourist Ferries.")

Wǔhàn Empress Travel, 15 Huìjì Lù, 7th Floor Chángháng Dàjiǔdiàn, Wǔhàn. ✆ *027/8286-5977. Fax 027/8286-6351. 77 cabins. 50% discounts possible; AE, DC, MC, V.* **Amenities:** 2 restaurants (Chinese/Western, cafe), bar; fitness room; salon; massage; laundry; forex. *In room: A/C, closed circuit TV, hair dryer on request.*

TRAVEL IN CHINA

While visitors to China can now stay in five-star luxury hotels; dine in excellent restaurants, hire local guides fluent in English; book extravagant tours; board air-conditioned buses; fly aboard state-of-the-art aircraft; and use credit cards, phone, fax, and e-mail, it is worthwhile remembering that China is still a third-world country. As one of the world's oldest continuous civilizations and the most populous modern nation, China also has its own way of doing things. Travel, especially on your own, is not always a smooth, comfortable undertaking. It is best for a foreigner to approach China travel as a journey into a world that is both familiar and alien.

China Today

PEOPLE   China is as spacious as the United States and its geography as various, but its people are overwhelmingly uniform. They belong primarily to one ethnic group, the Hàn Chinese, who constitute 93% of the more than 1.3 billion population.

THE ECONOMY   Despite China's relative poverty, it is becoming the economic powerhouse of Asia. About a third of the workforce is employed by prospering private firms (more than 55 million workers in more than 25 million nongovernmental enterprises). Double-digit economic growth became routine during the 1990s, as did double-digit inflation, although question marks hang over all economic figures produced by the Chinese government. Growth slowed with the dawn of the new century, but continues to be vigorous. The economic improvements have changed the look of China. Taxis, which numbered just 60,000 in 1985, now number more than that in Běijīng alone; and the streets, once filled with bicycles, are now clogged with motorized vehicles, many of them still burning leaded gas (although this is changing in the major cities). Heavy industries are on the upswing: China overtook Japan in 1996 as the world's largest steel producer. China's textile production and clothing exports are also immense. It's quite likely that the clothes you take to China will have been manufactured there. Additionally, 60% of the shoes sold in America are made in China.

China's relatively prosperous cities offer many luxuries unavailable to previous generations. Nearly 90% of urban dwellers watch television daily. The latest pop music, high fashions, and electronic appliances from the West are sold in glitzy shops, boutiques, and department stores. Wal-Mart opened a Super Center and a Sam's Club Warehouse in Shēnzhèn, a Special Economic Zone near Guǎngzhōu (Canton), and then in other wealthy southern coastal cities. Amway, Avon, Mary Kay, and Sara Lee have established sales forces and factories across China. Coca-Cola sells 100 million cases annually.

A 40-hour, 5-day work week was mandated in 1995. Běijīng has instituted a minimum wage ($35 a month) and unemployment benefits ($25–$30 a month). China now has over 120 million telephone subscribers. International credit-card companies predict that soon China's card-carriers will account for one-fifth of the world's total. In response to rapidly rising consumer spending, the number of restaurants in major Chinese cities has been tripling every 5 years.

WAGES   Despite China's recent economic boom, most people do not have wages or standards of living comparable to those in the West. The average income is about $700 per year, although it is about twice that in the big cities on the east coast (from Běijīng down to Hong Kong). Actual wages vary widely, of course. College students in Shāndōng Province, for example, make about $10 a month at work-study jobs, while computer engineers and deputy general managers average over $13,000 per year. Rural residents, who constitute about 65% of the population, usually make less than $50 a month, sometimes far less. The commune system has been disbanded, enabling farmers to cultivate their own plots and sell surplus produce (after meeting state quotas and taxes) in the free market.

The distribution of wealth has become widely disparate since the egalitarian era of Chairman Máo ended almost 30 years ago. There are more than a million millionaires in China today, and nearly everyone dreams of getting rich as quickly as possible. Such dreams run up against the harsh reality of China's overwhelming population. While most Chinese have seen their wages and buying power soar over the last few years, they remain at a level that would be regarded as impoverished in the West. Large segments of the young, particularly in rural areas, are unemployed. Many drift into the overcrowded cities, lured by the chance to get rich. There are currently over a million maids (officially termed "home helpers") employed in China, including nearly 100,000 young women from the countryside in Běijīng alone.

Perhaps the most startling fact is that the gap between the rich and the poor in China is now greater than it was during the feudal days of the 1930s. The current notion that the newly rich will pull up the chronically poor is belied by other statistics, notably that 125 million Chinese people live below the poverty line as defined by the World Bank ($1 per day). China admits that 42 million of its citizens make less than $220 per year. The income gap in China today is greater than in the U.S. or western Europe, greater even than in Indonesia or India.

POLLUTION   With increased production and car traffic, pollution has become a serious problem. You'll notice the poor air quality in the cities, which can make the skies of Los Angeles seem downright pristine. China's cities can handle only 20% of their sewage and less than 50% of the garbage they produce.

CHINA'S PROSPECTS   Whether China can continue to fuel its economic miracle is an open question, and depends upon massive future inward foreign investment. Major challenges looming on the horizon include large underemployment of the workforce, increasing immigration to the cities, unequal spheres of development across the country, pollution, mammoth money-losing state enterprises, and antiquated laws regulating business expansion and investment.

Nevertheless, the future looks rosy to most forecasters. In the 50th commemorative edition (Oct 1996) of the *Far Eastern Economic Review,* David K. P. Li of the Bank of East Asia envisioned the China of the year 2046 as the world's biggest economy (three times the size of the United States), the world's number-one exporter and importer, and the largest consumer nation on Earth. China will then play a dominant role in world affairs, Li suggested, superseding the position held by the United States. Reconsideration of the accuracy of China's economic projections have led subsequent commentators to suggest perhaps China's economy may just about match California's in the same period of time. Some even claim, however, that after English, Mandarin Chinese will rank as the world's most important language—and Běijīng will become the world's leading cultural center.

This expansion affects tourism as well. According to predictions from the nonprofit World Tourism Organization, mainland China will surpass the U.S., Spain, Italy, and Britain and replace France as the world's most popular tourist destination by the year 2020 (and Hong Kong by itself will rise from 18th to 5th during the same period). But the true situation is unclear—figures for inbound international travel to China still include cross-border shopping hops by Hong Kongers, for instance.

Travel Basics

China may be the emerging superpower that will dominate this "Asian Century," but for the traveler, it is not the easiest nation to understand or to visit, although little harder than other non-English-speaking Asian nations. A number of practical facts, tips, and strategies must be kept in mind before and during a journey to the East. What follows is my own list of facts, requirements, and tips for the China traveler.

VISITOR INFORMATION You can procure additional information on Chinese destinations and find answers to your questions by contacting branches of the **China National Tourist Office.** The U.S. offices are at 350 Fifth Ave., Suite 6413, New York, NY 10118 (© **212/760-8218;** fax 212/760-8809; www.cnto.org); and at 600 W. Broadway, Suite 320, Glendale, CA 91204 (© **818/545-7507;** fax 818/545-7506; la@cnto.org). The Canadian office is at 480 University Ave., Suite 806, Toronto, Ontario M5G 1V2 (© **416/599-6636;** fax 416/599-6382; www.tourismchina. org). The U.K. office is at 4 Glentworth St, London NW1 5PG (© **0207/935-9787;** fax 0207/487-5842; london@cnta.gov.cn). The Australian office is at Level 19, 44 Market St., Sydney, NSW 2000 (© **02/9299-4057;** fax 02/9290-1958; sydney@cnta.gov.cn).

VISAS Single-entry tourist visas for China, valid for 1 to 3 months from the date of entry for travel begun within 90 days of the date of issue, can easily be obtained from your nearest consulate. A completed application form (usually downloadable from the website of the embassy in your country) is required, along with a single photograph and a fee of around US$30, depending upon your nationality and/or place of application (Canada C$50, U.K. £30, Australia A$30, New Zealand NZ$60.) Extra fees are payable for applications by mail or courier. If you enter China first at Hong Kong (which I recommend), it is best to purchase your visa there (see below). If you are visiting China on a tour, including a cruise, the operator and your travel agent are responsible for putting you on a group visa. You'll need to provide them with a valid passport and other items they request. Check with them to be absolutely certain you are included on the group visa. Otherwise, you won't be admitted to China. The only drawback to a group visa is that you must stay with the group. Such a visa does not allow personal detours or extensions.

Individual tourist visa applications ("L" visas) usually take 5 working days (1–2 days in Hong Kong), but can be obtained in 3 days or less on payment of express fees. Your passport should have two clear pages, and have at least 6 months' remaining validity. Once in China, a single 30-day extension may be purchased at the Public Security Bureau of major cities a few days before the current visa expires.

In the past, dealing with these bureaucracies could be a nightmare, but their efficiency has improved greatly. In the U.S., determine which consulate to contact by visiting www.china-embassy.org, which has links to all U.S. consular sites, and a downloadable application form. The Chinese embassy's consular section is located at Room 110, 2201 Wisconsin Ave. NW, Washington, DC 20007 (✆ **202/338-6688;** fax 202/588-9760, faxback 202/265-9809; chnvisa@bellatlantic.net). The consulate in Chicago is located at 100 W. Erie St., Chicago, IL 60610 (✆ **312/803-0095;** fax 312/803-0110). The consulate in Houston is located at 3417 Montrose Blvd., Houston, TX 77066 (✆ **713/524-2304;** fax 713/524-8466; automated FAQ 713/524-4311; visa@chinahouston.org), but is temporarily at 3400 Montrose Blvd., 7th Floor. The consulate in Los Angeles is located at 443 Shatto Place, Los Angeles, CA 90020 (✆ **213/807-8006;** fax 213/380-1961). The consulate in New York is located at 520 12th Ave., New York, NY 10036 (✆ **212/330-7409;** fax 212/502-0245). The consulate in San Francisco is located at 1450 Laguna St., San Francisco, CA 94115 (✆ **415/674-2940;** fax 415/563-4861).

In Canada, the Chinese embassy is located at 515 St. Patrick St., Ottawa, Ontario K1N 5H3 (✆ **613/789-9586;** fax 613/789-1414; www.china embassycanada.org). Note that the embassy does not accept mailed applications. These must go to: Golden Mile 2000 Travel Consultant, 203–1390 Prince of Wales Dr., Ottawa, K2C 3K6 (✆ **613/224-6863;** fax 613/224-7863). The consulate in Toronto is located at 240 St. George St., Toronto, Ontario M5R 2P4 (✆ **416/964-7260;** fax 416/324-6468). The consulate in Vancouver is located at 3380 Granville St., Vancouver, British Columbia V6H 3K3 (✆ **604/734-7492;** fax 604/737-0154). The consulate in Calgary is located at 1011 6th Ave. SW, Suite 100, Calgary, AB T2P 0W1 (✆ **403/537-1247;** fax 403/264-6656).

In the United Kingdom, the Chinese consulates are located at 31 Portland Place, London W1B 1QD (✆ **020/7631-1430,** 2–4pm; 24-hr. information at premium rate ✆ 0900/188-0808; www.chinese-embassy. org.uk); at Denison House, 49 Denison Rd., Rusholme, Manchester, M14 5RX (✆ **0161/224-8672**); and at 43 Station Rd., Edinburgh EH12 7AF (✆ **0131/316-4789**).

In Australia, the consulates are located in Canberra at 15 Coronation Dr., Yarralumla, ACT 2600 (✆ **02/6273-4783** or 02/6273-4780, ext. 218 or 258; fax 02/6273-9615; www.chinaembassy.org.au); and in Sydney at 539 Elizabeth St., Surrey Hills, NSW 2010 (✆ **02/9699-2216;** fax 02/9699 8258; www.chinaconsulatesyd.org).

In New Zealand, the consulates are located at 2–6 Glenmore St., P.O. Box 17257, Karori, Wellington (✆ **04/472-1382,** ext. 600; fax 04/4749632; www.chinaembassy.org.nz); and at 588 Great South Rd.,

Greelane, P.O. Box 17123, Greelane, Auckland (© **09/525-1588,** ext. 710 or 707; fax 09/525-0733; www.chinaconsulate.org.nz).

A complete list of all Chinese embassies can be found at the Chinese foreign ministry's website: www.fmprc.gov.cn/eng. Click on "Missions Overseas."

The easiest place to apply for a visa is in Hong Kong. Entry to Hong Kong does not require a visa for citizens of most countries. Once there, you have several China visa options. Single-entry tourist "L" visas valid for 3 months are easily obtainable, as is the double-entry version (although this cannot be extended inside the country). Multiple-entry "F" visas are also easy to obtain via visa agents and without the letter of invitation required to obtain them at home. Single-entry visas bought through Hong Kong agents typically cost HK$120 to HK$150 (US$15–US$19), multiple-entry "F" visas around HK$450 (US$56). China Travel Service (CTS), whose popular office on Peking Road, Kowloon, is a helpful source of commission-free rail and air tickets, significantly overcharges and takes longer than less well-known agents even next door. Those a few minutes' walk away from the main tourist areas charge less still.

TRAVEL AGENTS   In China, cities and towns with tourist attractions all have at least one branch of the official government travel agency originally set up to deal with foreign visitors. It is called **China International Travel Service—CITS** for short, **Zhōngguó Guójì Lǚxíngshè** in Chinese. Any agency offering travel services in China can now help you, but only CITS (or sometimes the equally monolithic CTS and CYTS) is likely to be able to book services other than those in the immediate locale, or to provide English-speaking guides. All vastly overcharge and are dedicated to exploiting your lack of knowledge of what's happening around you to their own maximum financial benefit. They should largely be avoided, although they are occasionally useful for 1-day tours. A CITS branch may ask ¥100 ($13) commission for the purchase of an air ticket, which can be bought from an agent next door for no commission whatsoever (which is where it will be obtained by the CITS employee). Their tours usually include non-optional shopping "opportunities" at which the guides line their pockets with commissions at your expense. Restaurants which refuse to pay kickbacks receive no business from these guides, even if you would like to be taken to them. Even museums must often pay for tour group business. In short, use these organizations, and any others expecting to deal with foreigners (including the travel desks of better hotels), with caution. Commission on rail tickets should usually be no more than ¥20 ($2.50) per ticket, including delivery to your hotel room. Any agency with a terminal on the domestic airline system should be offering you a discount on quoted ticket prices, and should not ask you for any commission at all. Shop around.

Money

CURRENCY China's currency is called Yuán Rénmínbì (¥/RMB), meaning yuán of the people's money (as opposed to Japanese yen, or currency issued under earlier governments), and China is mainly a cash society. Credit-card transactions are only common in major cities, and only for more expensive goods or services. The first personal check in Běijīng was only issued in December 2002, although they've been around a little longer in some cities. Rénmínbì comes in denominations ranging from ¥1 (10¢) to ¥100 ($13), with smaller bills and coins for change. The word "yuán" is rarely spoken, however. Instead, people speak of *kuài qián* or "pieces of money," usually shortened just to *kuài*. *Sān kuài* is how ¥3 is usually spoken. Arabic numerals, familiar to most, are used, as well as Chinese characters.

TRAVELER'S CHECKS, CREDIT CARDS & ATMs While traveler's checks offer security in case of accidental loss or theft, they are increasingly tiresome to use in mainland China. Four- and five-star hotels in larger cities will happily cash them for guests only, but most other hotels, even those offering forex services, will direct you to the nearest branch of the Bank of China, and that branch will direct you to the largest branch, which may well not be open at weekends. Difficulties are sometimes made if signatures do not match to a microscopic degree.

Theft against foreigners is not common in China, and theft against cautious foreigners is very rare. For those visiting larger cities, the best option is to bring an ATM card and a limited amount of money in US$ cash (it's best if the notes are recent and in good condition), which is accepted and exchanged by most branches of most banks and all hotel exchange counters without difficulty. No commission is payable on the exchange of cash, and, as a result, the rate is slightly better than for checks, around ¥8.21 per dollar, whereas the ¥8.24 rate for checks works out lower once a 0.75% commission has been taken off. Exchange rates are set by the Bank of China and are the same everywhere. While the Bank of China runs exchange counters in a few major shopping centers, there are no private street-side exchange offices as there are in Hong Kong.

American Express, Diners Club, MasterCard, Visa, and ATM cards with the Cirrus or PLUS logos can be used at a small proportion of China's innumerable ATMs, principally a limited number of those at the larger branches of the Bank of China, although Běijīng, Shànghǎi, and some larger cities in the south such as Xiàmén and Guǎngzhōu also have branches of the Hong Kong and Shànghǎi Bank, and of America's Citibank, whose machines take just about any card. Consult your card issuer's website for a list of ATMs before leaving home—there are more than enough ATMs if you plan ahead. Some machines have a limit of ¥2,500 ($313) per transaction, but usually accept multiple transactions.

Be sure to restock with cash before leaving major cities. In some provinces, almost all Bank of China ATMs accept foreign cards. In others, not even those in the provincial head office do.

Credit-card signs are frequently seen, but this does not mean that foreign cards are accepted in payment, just as most of the cards carried in China can only be used there. Better hotels, and the shops and restaurants within them, take foreign cards; but, in general, at shops outside hotels, if foreign credit cards are accepted, you are certainly paying too much. In emergencies, you can use American Express, Diners Club, MasterCard, and Visa to draw cash over the counter of larger branches of the Bank of China—the same ones that take traveler's checks. The commission rate is 4%, however, plus whatever your card issuer charges you. The minimum withdrawal is ¥1,200 ($150).

Major branches of the Bank of China will exchange any hard currency currently in circulation, whether as cash or checks, but bringing euros, pounds sterling, Deutschmarks, or Canadian dollars offers a wider choice of exchange locations, and U.S. dollars the widest choice of all.

In Hong Kong, banks, exchange counters, and useful ATMs are legion. As with most other countries, rates are poor at the airport and in major tourist locations. Exchange offices away from the shopping areas offer the best deals, the banks and hotels the worst.

WHAT THINGS COST   The cost of a night in a five-star familiar-name hotel, or a hotel from one of the Asian luxury chains, can cost $150 and up. But very few hotels actually manage to obtain an average room rate of as much as $100, and for most of the year, in most parts of China, $60 to $75 will obtain complete comfort. Rooms in clean three- and four-star Chinese hotels are widely available for ¥200 ($25) or less (although first asking prices may be double that), and in grubby but adequate hotels the choices in the ¥100 to ¥200 ($13–$25) range are legion. Even in central Běijīng, beds in spotless dormitories can be had for as little as $6, and in less spotless hostels on the periphery for $4. A filling bowl of thick noodles with pork or beef taken at a hole-in-the-wall restaurant is only ¥3 to ¥5 (40¢–60¢). In simple restaurants, even in big cities, one meat and one vegetable dish, together with a bowl of rice, can easily be found for around ¥20 ($3.25), and even in upmarket restaurants for around ¥40 ($5). A budget of ¥80 to ¥100 ($10–$13) will provide a major feast for two to four people. Western restaurants in Běijīng and Shànghǎi, both inside major hotels and outside them, can cost as much as the equivalent of $25 to $40 per head, not including wine, but there are also pizza houses and other simpler places at which $10 to $15 will feed two. Set "meals" at McDonald's or KFC cost around $2.50.

Train transport is based on a charge per kilometer, plus surcharges according to the speed and comfort level of the train. But a 14-hour ride overnight in the most expensive bed in the fastest and most comfortable train will be around ¥400 ($50). Air ticket prices are also based on distance but are also responsive to market demands and vary widely according to the season and route chosen, ranging between $75 and $250.

If you have purchased an all-inclusive package tour, take enough money for souvenir shopping, miscellaneous purchases (camera batteries, film, mineral water), and incidentals such as domestic and international airport departure fees (¥50/$6 and ¥90/$11 respectively). You will be able to use your credit card at hotels and in major shopping centers, but if a shop accepts foreign cards, it will certainly charge very high prices—shop else-where. Independent travelers who use modest hotels and public transport, and who eat Chinese food and Western fast food, can still travel around China for $40 per day. Dedicated budget travelers can do it for much less. For $100 to $150 per day, China can be traveled in remarkable comfort, although a trip that only includes major tourism destinations and top-of-the-range hotels will likely cost $200 per day.

China has officially abolished its two-price system, in which visiting for-eigners paid more than residents. Once in a while, visitors find the two-price system in practice, at the admission gate to a remote attraction, for example, but this is no longer legal. Foreigners, always perceived as very rich, are of course often gouged by souvenir salespeople, taxi drivers, and Chinese tourism organizations in general. Never accept a posted price without asking for a discount. Always insist on using the meter. There is no tipping in China. Those over 60 can sometimes receive discounts of up to 50% at historical sites and events; it's worth inquiring about.

Health, Insurance & Packing

HEALTH The most likely source of discomfort for visitors to China is the overall dirtiness of the environment and the general lack of hygiene. Stomach upsets and colds or chest infections are the most common result, and the symptoms of flu may also be experienced as a result of the atmos-pheric pollution. An avoidance of any foods other than those freshly cooked, and the careful and frequent washing of hands, dramatically reduces the chances of picking up an assortment of easily communicable infections, and eye drops and lozenge can help relieve the effects of the pol-lution while the body adjusts. If you have favorite proprietary medicines for cold, sore throat, and so forth, bring those with you.

Those on guided tours concentrating on major cities need to make sure that your standard vaccinations are up-to-date, principally tetanus, diph-theria, and polio. Those traveling into the countryside need to get special advice from a travel clinic or tropical medicine center—family doctors are rarely up-to-date, and you should certainly not depend upon travel website chit-chat for your information: The prevalence of various diseases varies over time and geographical location. An idea of the latest situation can be

gained from The Centers for Disease Control in Atlanta (www.cdc.org or
☏ **888/232-3228**).

You may need coverage for typhoid, meningococcal meningitis, cholera,
hepatitis A (important), and hepatitis B (now often recommended).
Mosquito-borne diseases include malaria (with different prophylactic regimes
recommended for different areas), Japanese B encephalitis, and, recently, in
the very south and southeast, dengue fever (for which there is no protection
other than nets and repellent). Many of these vaccinations are expensive, and
many need to be taken some time apart, so, especially for rural travel, you
should make enquiries no later than 3 months before you leave.

Travel insurance, which includes repatriation in the case of serious accident
or illness, is essential. Although major cities have many Western-trained doctors, Chinese medical facilities are to be avoided whenever possible, and only
the very largest cities have clinics with Western staff. In case of illness, first
approach your hotel reception for assistance—many hotels have doctors and
clinics on-site, and certainly know of the best facilities. In the case of serious
illness, contact your nearest consulate for information on approved medical
services in your area. One reason that hepatitis B immunization is often recommended is because of the risk from inadequately sterile hospital equipment. Therefore, you may wish to consider carrying a small pack of sterile
needles and syringes in case an injection becomes necessary.

As this book went to press, China was experiencing an outbreak of SARS
(Severe Acute Respiratory Syndrome) that was limiting some travel and
activities throughout the country. Officials have taken drastic measures
(closing facilities, quarantining neighborhoods, and more) to prevent the
spread of the disease, but, at press time, it is impossible to know how SARS
may affect your trip to China. For more information on SARS, visit the
Centers for Disease Control's website (www.cdc.gov), which issues frequent
and up-to-date traveler advisories on this and other health problems.

INSURANCE   Insurance is usually either included or presented as an
option by tour operators outside China. You will almost certainly get a
better deal by shopping at an insurance broker, certainly better than at a
bank or travel agent. Cancellation insurance is a good idea, theft insurance
usually has too many exclusions and thresholds to be worthwhile, and medical insurance is absolutely essential. The key issue here is not the sums
to be paid out in the case of serious injury or death (although note that a
simple consultation with one of the international medical services in
Běijīng may cost as much as $150), but that of repatriation in the case of
serious difficulty. Check carefully the clauses that determine under what
circumstances air ambulance or other emergency transport will be provided,
and choose the policy with the most liberal terms. Note that if you do end
up in a Chinese hospital, they'll be happy to rack up the charges for a
foreigner as high as possible, and that you won't be allowed to leave until
you pay in full and in cash.

PACKING   The best advice is this: Pack as little and as light as possible. You never know when or how far you might have to lug your own gear in China, even if you're on a group tour. I never take more than two pieces of luggage, one being a day pack I can strap on my back. In my youth, I traveled with a single bag, a backpack that converted into a hand-held piece of luggage. In my advancing years, I've converted to a small roll-on that also has backpacking straps. Recently, I've been arriving in Hong Kong with old, cheap luggage, which I ditch in favor of a backpack/roll-on combination purchased for a pittance ($25–$35) in one of Hong Kong's luggage shops. Although cheap, such a roll-on holds up for months at a time on the road. One roll-on and one stout day pack or shoulder bag is all you really need in China, where a traveler's wardrobe need not be extensive or formal.

The clothing you take should be simple, durable, and comfortable. Most of what I take are items for health and hygiene, as well as useful gadgets for life on the road. My wife and I have been keeping China packing lists for 2 decades. Here's a peek inside our luggage, with commentary:

Clothing

_____   Pants, two pair (all-cotton, wrinkle-free; a dress or skirt is optional)

_____   Shirts, three (all-cotton, polo-style or basic sports shirts and blouses—it's fairly easy to purchase replacements along the way)

_____   Sweater or sweatshirt, one (to layer over shirts and blouses)

_____   Turtleneck, one (a layer for cold weather)

_____   Underwear, three or four sets (difficult to replace on trip; can be washed and dried overnight in hotel laundry or room sink)

_____   Socks, three or four pair (dark colors, can be laundered overnight)

_____   Raincoat or windbreaker, one (lightweight nylon)

_____   Hat, one (optional; keeps the sun out or head warm)

_____   Shoes, one extra pair (sturdy, comfortable, broken in)

_____   Thongs, one pair (for showers or as slippers)

Accessories & Gadgets

_____   Towel, one

_____   Umbrella

_____   Swiss army knife

_____   Flashlight

_____   Chopsticks, knife, spoon, fork

_____   Clothespins, clothesline, powdered detergent, flat "universal" sink stopper (for doing laundry in room sink)

_____   Clock or watch with alarm

_____   Sewing kit

Cosmetics & Medicines

Take your usual supplies. Be sure to include

_____   Prescriptions

_____   Sterile syringe (in case medical injection is required)

_____   Cold tablets (lots of these—a cold is nearly guaranteed)

_____   Moist towelettes

_____   Glasses (extra pair)

_____   Contact lens supplies

_____   Sunglasses

We also take a passport/money pouch (which is worn almost all the time), a notebook and extra pens, an address book, a camera with film and extra batteries, cups and heating coil with coffee, copies of our passport and traveler's check receipts, and a supply of breakfast bars for use when meals are difficult to procure.

Getting There

AIRLINES   The flight from the United States takes 11 to 16 hours, from the U.K. 10 hours, and from Australia 10 to 12 hours. The best service is almost always supplied by the non-Chinese Asian airlines, although, with the exception of Hong Kong–based Cathay Pacific, using these almost always requires a stopover. Flights with major developed nation carriers come next, then flights with Chinese airlines. Flights with Asia-based carriers such as Korean Airlines or Asiana (also Korea), Japan Airlines or ANA (also Japan), China Airlines or EVA (both Taiwanese, and only connecting to Hong Kong) can be considerably cheaper from North America than nonstop direct flights. From Europe, carriers such as Turkish Airlines, Uzbekistan Airways, Rumania's TAROM, Aeroflot, or Pakistan International Airways can provide significantly cheaper tickets, although at the cost of time and sometimes of comfort. Thai Airways and Singapore Airlines offer both excellent service and relatively cheap connections; even flying with a neighboring western European country's carrier via its capital may be significantly cheaper than flying directly on your own national carrier.

Carriers serving China directly from North America include Air Canada, Air China, Cathay Pacific, China Eastern, China Southern, and United Airlines (Northwest Airlines flies via Tokyo); from Europe, Air France, Austrian, Alitalia, British Airways, Finnair, KLM, Lufthansa, SAS, and Virgin Atlantic all fly directly.

The best-priced tickets are rarely available from the airline directly. Look online for special offers, then scan your local newspaper or weekly magazine for prices from consolidators and discount specialists.

Getting Around

BY PLANE Air travel improvement has been remarkably fast in China. Clean, modern jets put even remote cities just a few hours away. Airline attendants provide basic services, often including a Chinese version of airline food (unfortunately, only on par or below par with that of the West). Planes are often not on time and, when not full, may even leave before scheduled departure times. You must check in early, since check-in windows commonly close 45 minutes before scheduled departures. On the other hand, many planes are delayed, sometimes for hours. The safety record has now reached acceptable international levels (and flying is far safer than braving China's roads).

CAAC (Civil Aviation Administration of China) oversees commercial aviation inside China. Experiments with loosening its control led to vicious price wars and almost all of the 20-odd Chinese airlines plunging into the red. So, in 2001, control was reasserted, prices re-fixed, sales promotions forbidden, and, in 2002, a process of forced mergers began. Airlines still found ways to discount tickets, and control on prices has now been relaxed to let the market play a role. The first or last flight of the day may be cheaper, there are substantial seasonal fluctuations in price or discount, and more popular airlines are less willing to discount.

Tickets should be booked through ticket agents with computers on the national network, commission-free. This is cheaper than booking with the airlines directly. It's best not to use the agents in your hotel (especially if it's four- or five-star), as they are usually more expensive. Agents are numerous in all town centers, usually with plentiful airline logos in their windows, so they're not hard to spot. Whatever first price is quoted, always ask for a discount if one is not immediately offered. Shop around. Different agents have access to different classes of tickets and discounts, and are to different degrees prepared to split part of their commission with you. All airports charge departure taxes, paid for at windows (labeled in English) usually before you go through to check in; prices are currently ¥50 ($6) for domestic flights and ¥90 ($11) for international ones, including flights from mainland China to Hong Kong. These fees are payable in Chinese currency, and only in cash. In Hong Kong, departure fees are included in the ticket price.

BY TRAIN   China is the last great rail-building nation. The current 5-year plan calls for the construction of a further 13,500km (8,437 miles) of track by the end of 2005. The highest railway in the world is under construction across the Qīnghǎi plateau to Lhasa, and the world's first commercial maglev (magnetic levitation) line, which opened at the beginning of 2003, sends passengers at speeds of up to 450km per hour (281 mph) between Shànghǎi and its new airport to the east, making the trip in about 8 minutes.

A typical long-distance train has three classes: soft sleeper, hard sleeper, and hard seat. Most long-distance journeys are overnight. Daytime trains have soft seat and hard seat classes. Most have dining cars and regular trolley services of boxed meals and various snacks and drinks. On-board food is usually appalling, so shop for snacks to take with you. Boiled drinking water is always available from large thermos flasks or from boilers at the end of each carriage, so take a mug and tea or instant coffee (now widely available in China). Cars have washing facilities, and usually a mix of Western and squat toilets. Sleeper berths are provided with sheets, pillows, and quilts or blankets. All but a few trains are now air-conditioned. Smoking is generally confined to the carriage entranceways as long as staff can be bothered to enforce the rules. On slower trains, accommodation is, in general, more primitive, toilets less hygienic, and water for washing may run out. On faster "K" and especially "T" class trains, service may include provision of hotel-style slippers in sealed packages or small wash kits, and spotless washrooms may have hot water, soap, and electric hand-dryers.

Tickets are generally available 4 days in advance, including the day of travel. Computerization means that now almost any ticket window at the station can help you, or agents will get your ticket for you for a fee of around ¥20 ($2.50) or only ¥5 (60¢) if an official railway ticket agent. Hotel ticket services or CITS may attempt to charge as much as five times as much.

Soft sleeper *(ruǎnwò)* is the top class. Each compartment contains four berths in two columns of two, with a small table between. Lower berths are favored by the Chinese, and cost slightly more, but these are where everyone sits in the daytime. There's luggage storage beneath the lower berth and above the compartment entrance.

The other class of berth is called hard sleeper *(yìngwò)*. Hard sleeper class has bunks in columns of three, each pair of columns separated by a partition from the next, but not from the passageway. The higher the berth, the cheaper it is, but the upper berth, although offering much-needed privacy, has little head space. Music and train broadcasts cannot be turned off, and the carriage lights go off at 10pm or so, and on at 6am.

Trains whose journeys begin and end in daylight have comfortable soft seats *(ruǎnzuò),* and some of these are double-decker trains whose upper floors provide good views of the countryside.

The lowest and cheapest class is called hard seat *(yìngzuò).* On modern "K" and "T" class trains, these are much like public buses but with more legroom. For short trips, and where you have a reserved seat, this class is fine if you are on a faster train. If all berths on your train are sold out, you may be offered an unreserved hard seat. Accepting this may subject you to hours of crowded standing misery, although it's often possible to upgrade your seat on the train itself.

Trains are punctual, especially for departures. Train terminals are generally vast and crowded with all sorts of people, including an occasional thief, so watch your luggage. Lines form for the departure of each train by destination. It's useful to know your train number and departure time, usually displayed at the head of the line. If you are traveling soft sleeper or soft seat, you can usually take advantage of a special VIP or *guìbīn* waiting room in the terminal, worth finding. Waylay a train official and show your ticket if you need directions. Once on the train, conductors will assist you. After the train leaves the station, if you are traveling to or from the capital, a conductor may come around to check your passport and register you as if you were checking in to a hotel.

BY BUS   Long-distance buses vary greatly in quality around the country, but China's highway network has been rapidly expanding. In some areas, luxurious Volvo, Mercedes, and Daewoo buses have been introduced, and now journeys on some routes are faster than by train. Some buses have onboard toilets, attendants, and free mineral water. Buses are, in general, better between larger cities in the developed east, but even there, shorter trips to smaller destinations may be served by uncomfortable ancient rattletraps. Always take more powerful and comfortable Iveco minibuses if available, which are usually only a little more expensive. While sleeper buses are also reaching for higher standards on some routes (some are so clean you are even required to remove your shoes when boarding), in general, space is too limited for Western frames. The blare of horns and the inconsiderate behavior of other passengers may mean sleep remains unavailable. Most bus ticketing is now computerized, and any ticket window can help you. Book 1 day in advance to secure a seat at the front of the bus, usually with more legroom and a better view.

City buses usually have a flat fare of ¥1 (10¢) payable into a slot at the front of the bus as you board, with no change given. Others have conductors and fares ranging from ¥.50 (5¢) to ¥3 (40¢), air-conditioned routes sometimes costing more. Hand over ¥2 and see what happens. Bus routes are always shown on city maps. Get your hotel reception to familiarize you with the sound of your destination, and then listen to the announcements. Follow your route carefully on the map, and if there's a conductor, show him or her your destination in Chinese characters. City buses can be very crowded, and the Chinese generally fight their way on like small children scrabbling for treats, running to beat each other to any available seats. In some cities, the pressure has been relieved by minibus services with the same numbers and routes, usually charging double the bus fare.

BY TAXI   Except during rush hours in some major cities (when you should head for the metro, if one exists), taxis are the quickest and most convenient way to get around. Avoid getting in cabs that wait outside your hotel or at major tourist sites. Instead, walk a short distance away and flag down a passing cab. Cabs in lineups outside hotels (even very respectable hotels) have often paid bribes to be there, and may use a variety of methods to bilk you. In general, if the meter is casually obscured by a face cloth, if the supervision card (displaying a picture of the driver with his name and usually a complaint phone number) is absent from the dashboard, of if there's no meter at all, then choose a different vehicle. Cabs waiting outside tourist sights are often targeting the ignorant out-of-towner and will take you for a ride in more than one sense. But better than 9 times in 10, flag down a cab in the street, and you will have no problems.

At airports and railway stations where you can't flag down passing vehicles, always use the rank, and never go with anyone who approaches you. In short, choose your cab and don't let it choose you. Always have the meter freshly started, and if you are by yourself, sit in the front seat, preferably holding a city map to show (whether true or not) you have some idea what you are doing, and so you can show the characters for your destination to the driver. Rates per kilometer are usually posted clearly on the side of the cab, and the initial charge of ¥5 to ¥10 (60¢–$1.25) includes 2km to 4km.

Rates vary from city to city and according to the type of cab chosen, but subsequent kilometers are between ¥1.20 and ¥2.40 (15¢–30¢), usually 20% (sometimes 30%) more between 11pm and 5am. If the "one way" button on the front of the meter is pushed, then the rate goes up 50% after a set number of kilometers. In Běijīng, it's after 15km, but in smaller cities it tends to be after 8km. If you ask the cab to wait and bring you back, then this button should not be pushed. There are also small charges incurred for time spent stopped or traveling very slowly—rush hour travel can add 50% in cost to the same distance traveled in the middle of the day.

BY CAR   Although more and more Chinese own their own private cars (or more commonly motorcycles), driving is largely a profession. Taxi drivers and others must be trained and licensed for the job. It is easy enough to hire a private car with driver through CITS or a hotel, or better still to rent a taxi for the day. However, rental cars that you drive yourself are just at the experimental stage in some large cities and almost always unavailable to foreigners. Once you see how drivers use the streets in the cities and on highways, you probably won't want to try it yourself anyway, unless you're inclined toward car racing and demolition derbies. In a recent case, a thief in Běijīng robbed a woman taxi driver of ¥200 ($25), and then, hoping to use her taxi as a getaway car, forced her to teach him on the spot how to drive it; police apprehended him as he staggered away from the taxi.

ON FOOT   Seeing a city on foot is the best means of getting around. Secure a map at your hotel or from a street vendor. You can use it to ask people directions if you get lost, particularly if the map contains Chinese labels. Blocks tend to be much longer than they look on these maps. Moreover, most Chinese have difficulty making sense of any map in any language, and they often give vague or incorrect directions. It's always a good adventure, however, and it's the best way to get a feel for the city.

Walking does have its share of annoyances and dangers. The sidewalks are often filled with holes or stacked with garbage. Crowds can slow your progress to a standstill. Construction sites, parked cars, vendors, bicycle parks, and a host of other encroachments often make for slow passage or detours. Recently, the sidewalks have become runways for bicycles and even motorcycles in crowded cities, making mere walking a mortal challenge. And street signs aren't always obvious. When you find one, pray that it is written in pīnyīn (the alphabetic rendition of Chinese). Streets are usually called *lù, jiē,* or *dàjiē,* and the four directions are *běi* (north), *nán* (south), *dōng* (east), and *xī* (west). It's easiest to navigate as the Chinese do, by landmarks rather than road signs and numbers—relying on towering buildings, public parks, and other big sites for orientation. If you really get turned around—as I have—flag down a cab.

BY BICYCLE   Many hotels offer bicycle rentals, as do some private enterprises. A typical price is ¥10 ($1.25) per day, but larger hotels may charge 10 times as much. Mountain bikes may be available, but most rental bikes are still the ubiquitous black models with no gears. Check the brakes—you'll need them—and make sure the tires are properly inflated. Bike riding looks difficult and chaotic because it is, and you should proceed with maximum caution. Cars will pull across in front of you as if you don't exist, and many other cyclists will not be paying sufficient attention to what they are doing. Minor collisions are frequent. Bike-only lanes are a standard feature of most downtowns, although cars and pedestrians use them, too, and other cyclists may come at you in the wrong direction. On side streets, you simply have to barrel forward, confident that no cars or trucks will sweep you to one side (usually they don't). Use your bell at intersections.

Be sure you have a bike lock—bikes are often stolen. Try to find a bike parking lot. They usually fill part of a sidewalk. Park and lock next to other bikes. The bike keeper will charge you a small fee and give you a chit.

Tips on Accommodations

When choosing a four- or five-star hotel in China, always choose a familiar name from the West, or one of the Asian luxury chains. These provide as near to Western service levels as it's possible to obtain in China. Unless they have a significant number of foreigners at senior level, hotels owned and managed by Chinese compete with the Sino-foreign joint-venture hotels only insofar as they publish the same prices. Getting a four-star rating is a matter of having a check-list of services and facilities that varies from province to province. In some areas, for instance, it's impossible to obtain a four-star rating unless you have a bowling alley. Five-star ratings work on much the same basis, but are administered directly from Běijīng. Once a hotel gains its stars, it never loses them. It may fail to redecorate for 10 years, and its facilities may become grubby or otherwise unusable, but it will keep its stars. The star system, therefore, has little meaning except in foreign-owned and Sino-foreign joint-ventures, where respectable companies will refuse to renew management contracts unless the building owners spend money on renovations.

The major foreign-managed hotels have centralized booking services, usually reachable toll-free from home (see individual hotel details with each destination in this book). However, booking this way will cost you more than booking directly with the hotel once in China, which will again cost more than simply showing up and bargaining gently for the best price. Some foreign hotel chains now make it a policy to put their lowest published prices on their websites. Avoid hotel booking-agency websites which claim to be able to get you a cheaper room than you can for yourself—this is never true. Many hotels offer special packages that they publicize only within China, typically through expat publications and via English-language "What's On" e-mail newsletters for expats such as *Xiànzài Běijīng* and *Xiànzài Shànghǎi* (see www.xianzai.com for details).

Only the very best hotels in China are likely to remember that you made a reservation anyway and, at others, e-mail and faxes will usually obtain no reply or confirmation. Reservations made by phone may be forgotten, and anyway will not be honored if the hotel fills up and there's someone at reception with money in their hands who wants your room. Credit card numbers are not usually taken, as Chinese hotels are not allowed to charge credit cards "no show" charges (the volume of fraud would be immense). You can always undercut the prices quoted by reservations desks at Chinese airports, who have an unfortunate tendency to charge foreigners more than Chinese.

At all other hotels, regardless of star rating, the best is always the newest. Many brand-new two- and three-star hotels are superior to older Chinese four-star hotels in the same town. Once hotels open, nothing is spent on maintenance, and it's all downhill from there, so youth is everything. Checking in requires a passport and a deposit usually of three times the room rate, although protest may reduce that. At all costs, do not lose your receipt for the deposit or for the room rate. You will need all of these when you check out, and if you cannot produce them, there may be difficulties. You need almost never pay the price printed on the leaflet or listed on the wall—this is just a way for the hotel to tell you how good it thinks it is, and is entirely fictional. A discount of 10% will very often be offered before you can even ask. A discount of 30% is usually obtainable without much difficulty, and, in much of China for much of the year outside peak seasons, discounts of 50% or even more are common. At first, only check in for 1 night. However good the hotel looks, there may be problems the staff hasn't mentioned—crack-of-dawn construction work next door, overly lively karaoke sessions on the floor below, a late-working lathe operator across the road—that may make you move on the next day.

You should also be wary of hotel amenities, which aren't always what they seem. A hotel may boast of a pool, which may be too dirty for a Westerner to go in. Many Jacuzzis have rings round them, and a good number of beauty salons, hairdressers, and massage services can merely be fronts for prostitution. That's not to say that every hotel will be like this, but it is something you should remember and not have expectations about.

Tips on Dining

Chinese food, as served in the West, is adapted for local tastes, rarely resembles the real thing, and is almost never as good as what you will find in China. In terms of variety, cooking methods, ingredients, and flavors, you're in for a treat.

In the past, the best food and service was in hotel restaurants or at a few long-established cafes, but that has changed. Every week new independent cafes and restaurants are opening, offering good food and service at rates lower than in major hotel restaurants. Prices at top hotel restaurants, by the way, may often exceed what you would pay in a fine Chinese restaurant back home.

Surroundings in cheaper restaurants will often be grubby, and it's best not to think about the state of the kitchen. Cooking is usually excellent, portions are often generous, and prices extremely cheap. As long as the food comes freshly cooked and piping hot, you need have few fears. Order by pointing to dishes listed in this book, or at what other diners are eating. Streetside vendors provide the cheapest dishes of all. Xīnjiāng men making tasty *shashlyk* (kabobs; in Mandarin *ròu chuàr*) can be found on street corners in the evenings in almost every city in China.

It's a good idea to practice using chopsticks before your departure. Except in the best hotel restaurants or Western-style cafes, chopsticks are the only utensils. Having compelled restaurants to provide disposable chopsticks in order to improve hygiene, the authorities have been backtracking recently in response to environmentalists' complaints, and some restaurants are now happy to spare their costs by instead giving you a casually rinsed reusable pair instead. Disposable chopsticks, which you can buy for yourself in any supermarket, will usually be produced if requested. Stomach upsets (and hepatitis A) can then be avoided.

China is more difficult for strict vegetarians than might be expected. There are hundreds of possible vegetable dishes—*qīng chǎo* plus vegetable name will get you that vegetable stir-fried, hot and crisp. But it needs to be made absolutely clear to the staff that you eat no meat. Even then, the wok used for making your dish will almost certainly have been used for a meat dish moments earlier, although you almost certainly won't be able to taste it. Steamed and fried fresh and dried tofu *(dòufu)* dishes are another option, but again be careful about the presence of chopped meat. Vegetarian restaurants are not common, although larger cities have one or two, and they can be found at larger Buddhist monasteries.

Good fruit is available from street vendors and at markets, but stick to what you can easily peel, such as bananas and Mandarin oranges. Coke and other canned or bottled soft drinks including mineral water are available on every street corner. Ice-cream treats are safe when purchased from stores, as long as they are packaged in protective wrappers.

More and more small cafes with Western menus and Western dishes are opening across China. Fast-food chains such as KFC and McDonald's have proliferated. They charge about the same as in the West and their products taste about the same, too, although it usually takes considerably longer to fill your order.

Few restaurants, except in large international hotels, accept credit cards or traveler's checks, although this is beginning to change. Always carry plenty of local currency.

Tips on Nightlife

China after dark is mostly about eating, karaoke, and discos, although larger cities, and especially those with a few expats, now have "bar streets" with rows of ersatz Western experiences (German beer hall, British pub, Wild West saloon), bad live music, and beer prices to match. Cities and towns now have night markets in abundance, many within an easy walk of tourist hotels, and these provide fascinating evening strolls. Cinemas are quite popular everywhere, but they usually cater strictly to a local audience. Xī'ān has opened a dinner theater of Táng Dynasty song and dance for foreign guests, Chéngdū has an excellent opera, and Harbin has its ice sculpture park in the heart of winter. You can find out about these and other evening entertainment at your hotel service desk or from your concierge. Special events and performances of interest to foreigners are also presented from time to time.

Three exceptions to these extremely limited nighttime possibilities are in the cities of Hong Kong, Běijīng, and Shànghǎi. Hong Kong is the most startling exception, a neon city that snaps to life when the sun sets. Every conceivable form of nightlife is no more than a taxi ride away. Check the week's entertainment agenda in the English-language newspapers. The Hong Kong Tourist Association (HKTA) and the hotels can recommend a wide range of possibilities, from Chinese opera and Western classical concerts to all-night discos and regional dance performances.

Although the entertainment offerings in Běijīng pale in comparison with those in Hong Kong, there are plenty of bars in the Sānlǐtún bar streets, at the west and south entrances to Cháoyáng Park, and around the Hòu Hǎi (Back Lakes) that cater to foreigners and locals alike; a few cinema clubs featuring English-language films not seen elsewhere in China; and, above all, a number of nightly venues for traditional arts and entertainment. Expat-produced free bi-weekly magazines provide your best sources of listings.

The best bets for the traveler interested in Chinese culture are the **Běijīng Opera** and the **Chinese Acrobats.** There are nightly performances in several theaters—your hotel should be able to book tickets. **The People's Art Theatre of Běijīng** features Western plays. There's also a puppet theater and dance performances. Perhaps the best place to sample a variety of traditional art forms is a teahouse. Běijīng has several teahouses that present evenings of Chinese opera, acrobatics, martial arts, storytelling, and music and dance.

Shànghǎi also hosts an array of concerts and performances, including opera and acrobatics. Many of the top special events take place at the **Shànghǎi Centre** (Nánjīng Xī Lù 1376), which also has its own deluxe cinema, not to mention the **Long Bar,** a favorite of expatriates, visitors, and Chinese yuppies. Entertainment is provided most nights by the **Shànghǎi Acrobatic Troupe** at the Shànghǎi Centre Theatre. The jazz band at the **Peace Hotel** is a nightly favorite. The **Great World Entertainment Centre** (downtown at Xīzàng Zhōng Lù 1) has four stories and two auditoriums of nonstop entertainment, including opera, puppetry, acrobatics, and traditional storytelling.

Other Basics

ELECTRICITY   China uses a 220-volt 50-cycle AC system, and North American devices other than those specifically adapted to twin voltages will be fried. The most common sockets accept both the North American–style twin flat pin, and European-style twin round pin plugs. But newer North American plugs with a third pin, or those with one pin wider than the other, will not fit. Most socket plates also accept the three flat pin plugs common in Australia, with two pins at an angle. More up-market hotels, especially those with some Hong Kong input in their construction (and all hotels in Hong Kong and Macau), may have only the British-style three fat square pin sockets, but adaptors are freely available from housekeeping. All other kinds of adaptors are available for around $1 apiece from super-markets and electrical goods stores. Newer hotels of three stars and up mostly have multi-voltage shaver sockets in the bathrooms.

E-MAIL & INTERNET   Computer communications are beginning to sweep China, and most of China's top hotels now offer state-of-the-art business centers where you can use e-mail or surf the Internet, although often for ridiculously high charges. But there are also plenty of Internet cafes in most towns, only charging ¥2 to ¥3 (25¢–40¢) per hour; double that in larger cities. Many hotels provide in-room hookups and dataports for your laptop, and in all but a very few, the phone line may be unplugged and connected to your computer for going online. Almost all major hotels now have in-room broadband access available to those with Ethernet cards installed. If there are charges, they tend to be around $16 per day, but in many hotels, the service is free. In almost all parts of China, anonymous dial-up is available for a fractional addition to the phone charge, often absorbed by hotels wishing to claim they have free Internet. Common numbers are 163 and 169, although there are variants around the country—your hotel reception will tell you. Simply set the computer to dial 169 (for instance) with account name 169 and password 169.

FAXES　China's main fax centers are the big hotels. You can easily send a fax from their business centers or front desks, although an international fax is rather expensive, rarely less than $6 for a one-page fax overseas. To date, there are few copy shops and business centers independent of the big hotels providing cheaper faxing services, except in Hong Kong.

HOLIDAYS　Many cities and religious sites hold their own holidays and festivals on dates determined by the lunar calendar. Nationwide, the most important lunar festivals are Chinese New Year's (Spring Festival) on January 22 in 2004 and February 11 in 2005 (mass migration around the country—everything except shops shuts down for up a to a week), followed 15 days later by the Lantern Festival; the Qīng Míng Festival (Grave-Sweeping Day), falling April 4, 5, or 6; the Dragon Boat Festival, falling on June 4 in 2003, June 22 in 2004, and June 11 in 2005; and the Moon Festival (Mid-Autumn Festival), falling on September 11 in 2003, September 28 in 2004, and September 18 in 2005. Official state holidays, when many offices close, follow the Western calendar: Western New Year's (Jan. 1), International Working Women's Day (Mar 8—limited impact), Labor Day (May 1, now extended to a full week's holiday), Chinese Youth Day (May 4), International Children's Day (June 1), Founding of the Communist Party Day (July 1), Army Day (Aug 1), and National Day (Oct 1, also now with 1 week off).

METRIC SYSTEM　Like most of the rest of the world, China employs the metric system for measurements. See the inside of this book's back cover for help on metric conversions.

SAFETY　China is a safe country for the foreign traveler, with plenty of very honest people, but pickpockets, thieves, and muggers do target outsiders once in a while (from the big cities to the most remote mountain trails), so you should always be alert—as you should be whenever and wherever you're traveling.

TELEPHONES　Most hotels in China now provide international direct dialing (IDD), meaning you can phone overseas from your room. The charge will appear on your hotel bill, with a service charge added. The telephone system has improved rapidly in the last decade. In nearly all instances, you will have clear connections. By far the cheapest way to call overseas is to use an IP card available from newspaper kiosks, convenience stores, and many other outlets displaying the letters "IP." These have a local access number into which you must dial a password revealed by scratching a panel off the card, and then the number. Instructions and voice prompts are in English. Dial 00, then the country code (1 for the U.S. and Canada), then the number you need, less any leading zero. When phoning or faxing China from overseas, use the China country code (86) and drop the initial zero in the city code. When calling long distance within China, use the complete city code, beginning with the zero. Calling mobile phones registered in a different part of China (mostly numbers beginning 136 to 139) may require a leading zero.

Public phone booths are common, but require the use of an IC card, a stored-value card available from the same outlets as the IP card. Lift the receiver, push in the card, and the screen reveals the remaining value. Smaller shops also often have phones with timers. Local calls are typically ¥.30 (5¢). Unless you speak Chinese, making reservations or seeking information by phone is usually futile. Have the hotel desk make such calls on your behalf.

Caution: As China's telephone system expands, numbers change, often by adding digits. Even area codes are frequently altered.

TIME   Despite spanning what would ordinarily be considered six time zones east to west, China has only one official time zone. Every location is on Běijīng time, from Hong Kong to Kashgar. The time in China is GMT plus 8 hours, which means that wherever you are in China, it is 16 hours earlier in Los Angeles, 15 hours earlier in Denver, 14 hours earlier in Chicago, and 13 hours earlier in New York. China does not use daylight saving time, so during those summer months, it is 15 hours earlier in Los Angeles, 12 hours earlier in New York.

TIPPING   Until recently, hotels often displayed signs forbidding tipping, and some still do. Tipping is not a Chinese custom, and is completely inappropriate in most cases where it would normally be thought necessary in the West. In China, the price listed or the price negotiated for a service is the price to be paid, and that's the end of it. You will not see Chinese tip. If hotel managements hear that staff have hinted they should be given a tip, they will often fire them. Foreign visitors are already routinely overcharged for most services without being aware of it, and unknowingly provide extra benefits to guides and others through kickbacks, whose cost they bear. Taxi drivers and even the humblest bellhop are vastly better off than the average Chinese. Save your charity for those who more obviously need it.

TOILETS   The standard Asian-style toilet is a porcelain bowl in the floor. These are what you usually find in ordinary restaurants, public lavatories, train and bus terminals, sightseeing destinations, and parks. In public lavatories, where you usually purchase an inexpensive ticket of admission, there is little attention to hygiene and no toilet paper. Some Westerners carry their own spray disinfectants into these malodorous chambers. There's also little privacy. In the bigger hotels, the standard Western sit-down toilets, as opposed to squat-toilets, are used. When on foot around town, head for branches of Western fast-food chains, the lobbies of better hotels, or major department stores to find toilets with better standards of hygiene and somewhere to wash your hands afterwards.

WATER   Don't drink the water in China. It is not sanitary. Even the few hotels that now boast purification systems are suspect, in my opinion. Better safe than sorry. Bottled water is widely and cheaply available, even in remote areas. Use it for drinking and for brushing your teeth. The safest of all is distilled water.

Parting Words of Advice

- Always book the best class possible on trains, buses, boats, and other modes of transport.

- Book transportation out of town as soon as you arrive in it.

- Always carry your passport, traveler's checks, and other valuables in a concealed security pouch.

- Carry along an emergency snack, such as a breakfast bar, in case you can't find a suitable cafe, vendor, or grocer.

- If bad air quality is a serious threat, pack a dust mask. Many people in China wear them, particularly during dust storms.

- Take good, comfortable, durable walking shoes. Be sure they're well broken in before you leave home.

- Remember that the best small gifts are books and postcards.

- Camera film and batteries are available in shops and department stores in large cities, but it is best to carry plenty of both. Reduce X-raying at air terminals, train, and bus stations by carrying film in a pouch in your pocket. Put film in clear canisters and bag it in plastic.

- Be patient, flexible, open, and good-natured. China is a learning experience, not an escape; an adventure, not a getaway; a new challenge, not necessarily a holiday.

CUSTOMS, ATTITUDES & ENIGMAS: THE CHINESE WAY

THE CHINESE WAY IS NOT NECESSARILY the Western way. Chinese culture was created in isolation from the West, just as Western culture was created without reference to the Chinese world. Customs, family relationships, and social interactions differ, sometimes only slightly, as modern China adjusts to Western ways. Here's my own list of differences the foreign traveler should expect to encounter while visiting China.

Worldview

CHINA & THE WORLD China has long conceived of itself as the center of the universe. The very name it gives to its nation, Zhōngguó, means "Central Kingdom." At times, China takes an ethnocentric view of itself. All nations and peoples outside its ancient borders—all non–Hàn Chinese—traditionally have been regarded as "barbarians." Outsiders are, if not inferior, at last not real Chinese, and hence are forever at an unfortunate remove from the great motherland. Even today, there are millions of Chinese, even in the cities (though particularly those from the countryside), who have never seen a foreigner up close.

There may be occasions, at restaurants, in department stores, or at train and bus stations, when you will draw stares, openly curious rather than hostile. In Chinese eyes, foreigners have certain remarkable physical characteristics—big noses, curly hair, strange clothes and adornments. In such circumstances, return the stare or ignore it, as you please. Expressions of anger are useless. This is how a rock star or movie hero must feel. On one occasion, I was walking with an American teacher and his 4-year-old daughter in the streets of Chéngdū when a Chinese lady came over and in frank, open curiosity stroked the girl's blond bangs. Having mastered the Sìchuān dialect in 3 short months, the young girl told the admirer in no uncertain terms to desist.

The trick, if stares bother you, is to keep moving. When I first came to China, I used to be able to draw a silent circle of examiners every time I paused in the streets for more than 10 seconds. In large cities, people are more used to foreign businesspeople, students, and tourists in their midst, and staring circles rarely form.

One consequence of the Central Kingdom mentality is that China clings proudly and fiercely to its own way of doing things, particularly when an outsider points out a "better" and more efficient way.

POLITICS You'll run across Chinese who can be surprisingly frank about their political situation. If they bring up these issues first, don't be shy about expressing your opinion. On the other hand, you will really be putting your well-intentioned hosts or acquaintances on the spot if you initiate criticisms of China in respect to its lack of political freedoms. Topics to avoid include freedom of the press, the Tibet situation, the status of Táiwān, the Tiān'ān Mén Square massacre, abortion, prison labor, and the handling of dissidents. Chinese tour guides get such questions all the time, and they have set answers, often quite defensive.

Society

SAVING FACE Fundamental to maintaining harmony in Chinese society is the ancient concept of "face," which on a personal level means your self-respect. Personal status reflects on your family, the paramount institution in China; the family unit, in turn, is related to the greater society. To "lose face" is thus terribly humiliating, and the Chinese will go to great ends to avoid it. "Saving face" often comes through compromise, in which both sides in a disagreement receive a benefit. For the foreign traveler, the concept of "face" seems a matter of common sense, but it takes many unusual forms in China.

There is a reluctance, for example, to deny any request flat out, as this implies that you are not fulfilling your duty as a host. Confronting a Chinese over poor service or demanding something difficult to deliver is often not the best way to reach the desired end. To save face, Chinese, in a position to help, could resort to making a promise they can't keep or to making a firm denial that seems absurd to an outsider. For example, many times in lesser hotels in China, I've asked for a room and been told there were none. In an empty hotel, this seems absurd, but the clerk (aside from perhaps being lazy) may simply be saving face. Rooms may not yet be ready, floor staff may not be in position, or the boss may not have opened a block of rooms. In these cases, I simply retreat and wait in the lobby. Invariably something opens up.

The key in getting things done or corrected is not anger but patience. Patience is the primary virtue for a traveler in China, though it is not a foolproof device. There are many things, often very ordinary things, such as being seated in a restaurant, that sometimes are never resolved. Knowing the reason for a problem seldom helps, but treating the people who can get something done for you with respect and patience is your best bet. If your requests or complaints place a person in the position of embarrassment or of backing down, you have not scored a victory; rather, you've made an enemy, one whose "face" you have erased, whose integrity and worth you have besmirched.

COURTESY   In Old China, especially among the cultured and educated, an elaborate set of social formalities and courtesies evolved. Most of these have disappeared from modern China, though many were adopted and are still practiced elsewhere, particularly in Japan. The Chinese do not bow, for example, nor do they remove their shoes upon entering houses or inns.

The Chinese are courteous and caring hosts. In general, they conduct themselves straightforwardly, frankly, and with openness and good humor. They seldom express their thanks for small favors or transactions, although it is perfectly acceptable for foreigners to do so. When asking favors, however, it is best to be round about rather than direct, giving space for a host to refuse without embarrassment.

The Chinese are generally not overly forward or loud, except in gatherings of family and friends. Compliments are usually best directed to senior citizens, bosses, or children. Bragging about your own accomplishments is not considered good form. Shaking hands has become the acceptable custom when meeting or parting. Kisses on the cheek are not part of Chinese culture, nor for that matter is kissing in public between lovers or partners accepted. On the other hand, the Chinese express their friendship and concern physically, often by placing an arm around the shoulders of the other person. Friends of the same sex sometimes hold hands when strolling.

QUESTIONS FROM STRANGERS   It is perfectly acceptable for a stranger to ask you how much money you make. My response to this "impolite" query is to tell the truth and see the reaction. Wages even in the new, economically booming China are below what's standard in the West. When I taught English in China at a leading medical college, for example, I was paid more than the most skilled Chinese surgeons, more even than the college president, and yet the salary was 10 times less than I could have lived on in the United States.

It is also perfectly acceptable for a Chinese to ask you how many children you have. Since the family has always been the most important entity in China, this is a natural question. If you have no children, the Chinese reaction is likely to be one of bewilderment and concern. It's difficult for them to imagine the curse of a no-child family.

China's number-one problem is its immense population, now at more than 1.3 billion, twice what it was when the Communists took power in 1949. Most Hàn Chinese have been slapped with a policy that allows them only one child. In a nation that puts an absolute value on the family as the primary unit, where traditionally boys are favored over girls, lecturing them on the "immorality" of this policy is rather insensitive. The Chinese feel its harshness and most of them deal with it courageously, patriotically, and sensibly, if not happily. After walking the streets of Shànghǎi or Běijīng for a few days, ask yourself how China would be with two billion people. Even with severe controls on its population growth, China is adding 14 million people a year, more than enough new mouths to feed.

GUĀNXI (CONNECTIONS)   During Chairman Máo's reign, 1949–1976, and for a decade afterward, *guānxi,* the connections you forged with people in positions to get things done, was far more a measure of wealth and power than mere money. Nearly everyone might be paid a pittance and no one could afford a car or a house, but some were more equal than others in Máo's egalitarian society because they knew the person who could get something they wanted. The *guānxi* system worked on the basis of cultivated friendships and favors. This sort of "bribery by barter" permeated most aspects of life, from the political to the economic.

Guānxi is still how much of China operates, only today, as the economy booms, money often replaces favors, or pays for them "under the table." Petty bribery and official corruption have become so rampant at times that many ordinary people, from peasants to professionals, have become deeply upset. At least some of the demands of the Tiān'ān Mén Square protests issued from this widespread repugnance at the spread of corruption, particularly among officials. The government has repeatedly cracked down on corruption, often within its own ranks, and continues to do so.

MEN & WOMEN   By law, there is complete equality between the sexes in the People's Republic of China, a great advance over centuries of feudal practice in which a woman was barely more than a father's or a husband's property. In theory, women today can enter any profession on an equal footing with men. Nevertheless, in daily practice, you will notice that women are still not as highly regarded, at least not as figures of power, in China. When it comes to fieldwork or factory jobs, women are widely employed, but they are less numerous the higher up you go in industry, business, education, and politics. The mandate to bear children and run the household still falls on women's shoulders, although perhaps with no more frequency than in most Western nations. This is a society where men are still in charge, but women are exercising increasing strength and freedom.

Nevertheless, it is still the dream of millions of Chinese to produce a male, rather than a female, heir. In all of pre-20th-century Chinese history, it was the man who carried on the family name, and in rural societies, the man was the head of the clan. Modern education has gone a long way toward changing this perception, but the man is still most often the figure in charge.

WESTERNIZATION   Most Chinese today seem quite enthusiastic about the modernization of their society; few express outrage at the adoption of Western architecture, business management, and popular culture. Yet most Chinese are deeply patriotic. The acceptance of Western ways does not mean an abandonment of Chinese ways and traditions. Westernization has struck so forcefully and suddenly in China that the term "culture shock" seems a bit mild. In many cases, the Chinese seem to be trying to use the best of the West to their own advantage, shaping it with Chinese traditions in mind.

The more negative aspects of Western influences cannot be ignored, however. The crime rate is rising; prostitution and drug addiction have returned from exile; the income gap is widening; the communal, communistic, and Confucian values are being eroded; and even the fabric of family life at the center of the Central Kingdom is feeling the strain. For the first time, retirement homes and senior centers are beginning to displace the extended family. Some couples are choosing not to have children, others are living together, and single-parent families are no longer a complete aberration—although there is still a stigma attached to anything but the conventional two-parent, one-child family with grandparents and other relatives nearby. China's divorce rate has accelerated, from 5% in 1978 to 7% in 1988 to 13% in 1998; it is said to be over 25% in Běijīng and rising.

Family & Social Customs

CHINESE NAMES   The Chinese give their names in a different order than is customary in the West. Fred Allen Smith becomes Smith Fred Allen. The Chinese refer to others by their family names, not their first names. Many educated Chinese also adopt English first names for use with foreigners. Women frequently hold on to their original family names after marriage. Family names in China—which are almost always one syllable in length—are in short supply. There are about 100 million people named Zhāng (or Chan in Cantonese) and nearly as many taking the next most popular names: Wáng (Wong), Lǐ (Lee), Zhào (Chao), and Liú (Liu).

DINING CUSTOMS　There are differences in the way meals are consumed and enjoyed in China. Slurping of soup, noodles, or rice from a small bowl held in one hand is not considered rude. In nicer places, however, Western etiquette is observed.

Large meals and banquets are typically served on round tables, often with lazy Susans at the center. A series of common dishes are presented family style, with diners placing small portions on their plates using chopsticks or, if provided, serving spoons. The host of a banquet will serve you the first portion of each dish. After that, you can serve yourself. It's considered childish to play with your chopsticks; for many foreigners, it's enough of a trial just to be able to use them. There are plenty of dishes served at a big meal or banquet. The first dishes are usually cold appetizers. Don't fill up on them. If you don't like a dish, try to take a taste and leave the rest on your plate. If you're a vegetarian, find out what's in each dish and politely decline those with meat.

A Chinese host will usually propose a number of toasts during the meal. You can follow up with your own toast. The traditional salute is *gānbēi,* which, once spoken, obligates you to try to drain the cup. Many Chinese have limited capacities when it comes to drinking liquor and admire anyone who can drink a great deal. Watch yourself. Group meals are usually boisterous, happy affairs, where everyone is supposed to relax. In fact, eating is the chief Chinese pleasure, and many people spend large portions of their income on food. It is also customary to end a meal soon after the last dish, which is usually fruit, is served. The host will abruptly rise—no more socializing; the meal's at an end.

GIVING GIFTS　Don't give clocks—the Chinese expression *sòng zhōng* ("give clock") sounds too similar to words used in farewell to the dead. And don't wrap a gift in white paper—white is the Chinese color of death. Remember that what we consider rudeness the Chinese consider correct form. Many Chinese won't open a gift in front of you. And don't expect a thank you. Rather than thanking a gift giver and admiring the gift on the spot—thus ending the need to reciprocate in kind—the Chinese often say nothing and wait until they can give a comparable gift in return.

RESPECT FOR AGE　By tradition, people of advanced years are highly respected for their wisdom. This respect, refreshing if you're older and from the youth-oriented West, harkens back to China's Confucian teachings. Just as fathers demand total obedience and respect from children, so anyone of advanced years expects respect from his or her juniors. Moreover, it is the responsibility of the young to care for the elderly. Retirement homes and nursing institutions are relatively new in China, and most families find it a loss of face not to be able to care for their own in their homes. I've found, however, that many young people in China are beginning to resent this burden, and the movement to transfer the care of senior citizens to government programs and institutions is growing. Meanwhile, if you are over 60, you can assume that your younger hosts will treat you with deep respect.

Other Considerations

CLOTHING   A decade or more ago, the Chinese all dressed in dull Máo jackets, matching trousers, and workers' caps. It was as if the whole nation were a vast private school, outfitted in the attire of the great headmaster. However, as the economy heated up and dire restrictions against "spiritual pollution" from the decadent West were eased—a modern version of China's traditional xenophobia and self-absorbing world view—the range of fashions broadened. In the big cities, the young dress in the latest Western fashions available (not so difficult, since much of the world's clothing seems to be made in China). Western attire, including business suits, is commonplace. Máo garb is rarely seen anymore, except in poorer towns and the countryside. Adults still tend to dress conservatively, in drab colors, while outfitting their children in the brightest outfits possible.

As a visitor, I find it best to blend in, selecting darker, duller colors, avoiding revealing clothes, and keeping jewelry to a minimum. Shorts are acceptable for outings, although few Chinese wear them. Bikinis, halter tops, plunging necklines, and short skirts are still too risqué for many Chinese. It's simply more comfortable for foreigners to blend in, avoiding calling attention to themselves as rich visitors willing to overpay for every meal and trinket.

SIESTAS   The afternoon nap, once such a widespread custom in China that it was written into the constitution, is a practice out of fashion in the big bustling cities. Nevertheless, I still find that an extraordinary number of offices and services close their doors for an hour or two starting about noon. In smaller cities, towns, and villages, the noonday snooze is more often observed. Cafes and restaurants are always open, of course, to accommodate those taking "naps." When working in China in the 1980s, I became accustomed to a daily nap and I found it an invigorating custom, making one day seem like two. I still observe this custom when traveling in China, if possible, knowing that the Chinese, who go to bed late and rise early, understand why I need my midday rest.

SMOKING One in three cigarettes smoked today is lit up in China. The majority of men smoke. Few women do so in public. In many restaurants, diners smoke between courses and sometimes during them. For nonsmokers, this can become a gargantuan headache. In some cases, requesting that someone not smoke works wonders; in many cases, it does not. The former supreme leader of China, Dèng Xiǎopíng, always smoked while meeting other heads of state, and he went so far as to claim it was a healthy addiction. As China grows more prosperous, smoking threatens to become even more widespread and continuous.

Nevertheless, health officials in China are aware of the dangers, annoyances, and ultimate price society must pay. Antismoking campaigns have recently been launched and severe restrictions have been placed on smoking in public places. As of May 1, 1997, smoking on public transport—on all trains, buses, planes, ships, and taxis, and in all waiting rooms as well—was banned by the order of six ministries. It had been determined that 60% of the one billion rail passengers in China were smokers. Instant fines of ¥10 to ¥50 ($1.25–$6.25) can now be levied for anyone caught in the act of inhaling on trains, ships, planes, buses, subways, taxis, and terminals, although this is almost never enforced.

SPITTING Hawking and spitting in public used to be an institution, as common as breathing. The same went for clearing your nose. People often spit from passing buses and in packed cafes. The practice was widespread and goes back centuries. Nevertheless, such activities are now illegal in most of China's cities, and public campaigns to improve hygiene and politeness have made large inroads in the last few years, though it's still fairly regular to see such behavior.

TAKING PHOTOS Taking photos of people in the streets of China is permitted, although many Chinese feel much as people in the West do—that it's an unwarranted invasion of privacy. If Chinese don't want their pictures taken, they'll wave their hands or shout. Many don't mind if you take a picture of their children. It's best to ask or motion with your camera. Photos are permitted in most temples and in all public sites except where prohibitions are posted. At some popular sites, there is now a charge for picture taking, paid at the entrance gate.

TRAFFIC China has long been a nation of bicycles, but as motorized vehicles inundate the streets, traffic snarls and unregulated driving patterns have proliferated. You'll quickly notice that cabs, buses, trucks, and everything else on the road moves to a different drummer, that of sheer expediency. In fact, taxis often drive with as little regard for traffic lights and proper lanes as a bicycle might.

Such crazy driving and passing is certainly dangerous, but there's little you can do about it. Drivers, most of whom are still professionally trained, are quite skilled at avoiding collisions. Telling a driver to slow down or not to pass on a curve or hill usually falls on proud and deaf ears.

One lesson is worth mastering: When you cross intersections on foot, be extremely cautious, since vehicles take the right-of-way almost everywhere. Another annoyance you'll just have to get used to is the constant honking of horns. This has become the customary way that drivers communicate their presence and intentions to other drivers. In a few cities, such as Xiàmén, this form of noise pollution has been outlawed.

To Sum Up

It's worth bearing in mind, above all, that Chinese society, despite its apparent chaos, is highly organized and hierarchical, that an individual's power is limited and rigidly defined, and that it is best to make a request or complaint with courtesy rather than in anger, exercising restraint and patience—mountains of patience. The Chinese put great stock in friendship, cultivating long-term personal relationships. Such investments smooth the way and often produce results that uncompromising demands, however rational and obvious they seem to the Western mind, may never yield.

A QUICK HISTORY

CHINA IS THE PRODUCT OF A LENGTHY history conducted in proud isolation. Travelers seldom have time to master the intricacies of Chinese chronologies before stepping off the plane, but a basic briefing is useful. When I travel through China, I always have in mind a simplified time line of China's major dynasties, a rough list of its famous figures, an outline of its major religions, and an acquaintance with its customs and cultural achievements. This background creates a context for much of what I see along the way, a context that is always expanded by direct experience.

The Early History

Bear in mind that Chinese scholars envision the history of their civilization as stretching back 5,000 years. However, it's unlikely that you'll see many sites or relics over 2,300 years old in your travels, with the exception of the Bànpō Neolithic Village in Xī'ān, which amply predates recorded Chinese history and the rise of imperial rule.

The earliest recorded societies in China rose during the **Xià period** (ca. 2100–1500 B.C.), continued through the **Shāng period** (1500–1050 B.C.), and began to become more consolidated during the **Zhōu period** (1050–221 B.C.), when various kingdoms fought to extend their domains. Archaeologists keep finding more relics from these early periods, although relatively little is known about them. Confucius (ca. 551–479 B.C.) lived during the Zhōu period in the Kingdom of Chū, and the shadowy figure of Lǎozǐ, founder of Daoism, also dates from this era.

A Dynasty Primer

China's more recent history is usually—and quite usefully—divided into its successive dynasties. Sometimes it seems there are more dynasties than brain cells in which to store them. I've found, however, that most of the historical sites and treasures on display are the products of six major dynasties spanning the last 23 centuries. When I keep these six periods straight, I can usually come away from a museum display, temple, or

CHINA TIMELINE

Xià Dynasty	
ca. 2100–1600 B.C.	
Shāng Dynasty	1500–1050 B.C.
Zhōu Dynasties	1050–476 B.C.
Western Zhōu Dynasty	1050–771 B.C.
Eastern Zhōu Dynasty	770–221 B.C.
Spring and Autumn Period	770–475 B.C.
Warring States Period	475–221 B.C.
Qín Dynasty	
221–207 B.C.	
Hàn Dynasty	206 B.C.–A.D. 220
Western Hàn	206 B.C.–A.D. 9
Eastern Hàn	A.D. 25–220
Three Kingdoms Period	221–280
Wú Kingdom	220–280
Shǔ Kingdom	220–261
Wèi Kingdom	220–265
Jìn Dynasties	265–420
Western Jìn	265–316
Eastern Jìn	317–420
Northern and Southern States	386–589
Northern Wèi	386–535
Eastern Wèi	534–550
Western Wèi	535–557
Suí Dynasty	589–618
Táng Dynasty	618–906
Five Dynasties and Ten Kingdoms Period	907–960
Liáo Dynasty	907–1125
Sòng Dynasty	960–1279
Northern Sòng	960–1126
Southern Sòng	1127–1279
Western Xià Dynasty	990–1227
Jìn Dynasty	1115–1234
Yuán Dynasty	1279–1368
Míng Dynasty	1368–1644
Qīng Dynasty	1644–1911
Republic of China	1912–1949
People's Republic of China	1949–present
Máo Period	1949–1976
Dèng Period	1977–1997
Jiāng Period	1997–2003
Hú Period	2003–

SIX MAJOR DYNASTIES

Qín	221–207 B.C.
Hàn	206 B.C.–A.D. 220
Táng	A.D. 618–906
Sòng	A.D. 960–1279
Míng	A.D. 1368–1644
Qīng	A.D. 1644–1911

historic monument with an understanding of how it fits into the larger picture.

China's two great imperial showcases, Xī'ān and Běijīng, roughly divide the history of these great dynasties between them. In the ancient capital of Xī'ān, there are fine representatives of the art and monuments created during the Qín, Hàn, and Táng dynasties. In the modern capital of Běijīng, the Míng and Qīng dynasties hold sway. The creations of the earlier dynasties at Xī'ān are simpler but powerful and graceful in style. The later dynasties, based in Běijīng, took art and architecture to more elaborate and ornate extremes.

Viewing Chinese history simply as a succession of dynasties is, however, misleading on many counts. For long periods, centralized control was a dream rather than a reality. The 4 centuries between the Hàn and Táng dynasties, for example, which began with the romantic **Three Kingdoms period** (A.D. 221–280), was an age of division and strife among contending states. The **Northern Wèi** (A.D. 386–535) managed to achieve a brief unification of power, first at Dàtóng, where the Yúngāng Grottoes survive, then at Luòyáng, where the Lóngmén Buddhist caves also remain.

Nor has China always been in the hands of the native Hàn Chinese. The **Yuán Dynasty** (1279–1368), the setting for Marco Polo's travels, was ruled by the Mongols. The Qīng Dynasty (1644–1911), under which Western traders, missionaries, and scholars first entered China in large numbers, was ruled by the Manchus.

Inevitably, the decay and fall of the major dynasties led to massive destruction of relics and monuments. New ruling families often tried to make a clean break with the weighty past, razing the palaces, temples, and capitals of the predecessors they ousted. It's fortunate that anything at all survives today. Dozens of short-lived dynasties rose to power until more lasting central authority was again established. This cycle of creation and destruction seems to be the dynamic force underlying much of Chinese history, and it is repeated in modern Chinese history, too, which is marked by sudden gargantuan shifts in policy and wholesale elimination of the "evils" of the past.

Fortunately for travelers, historic relics, artworks, and monuments have survived in surprising abundance. Keeping straight to which dynasty each belongs is a formidable task, however, as there can be up to 60 or more periods and dynasties to keep in mind, depending on what source you consult. The six major dynasties of my simplified outline cover most of the ground, and they form a practical basis for expanding your knowledge as you see more of historical China.

Qín Dynasty (221–207 B.C.)   The Chinese empire began with the unification of many warring states under the First Emperor, Qín Shǐ Huángdì, in 221 B.C. Qín's rule was brief and his successors could not hold the empire together, but the centralization of power, the bureaucratization of society, and the standardization of writing scripts, weights and measures, and chariot axles set the basis for later dynasties that sometimes ruled for centuries. The chief remains of this 1st Dynasty are the First Emperor's terracotta army, unearthed in Xī'ān.

Hàn Dynasty (206 B.C.–A.D. 220)   After the 1st Dynasty fell apart, a greater one emerged. The Hàn Dynasty extended the borders of the empire and cemented the institutions that would be the basis for Chinese civilization for 2,000 years. Some fine clay crafts and stone sculptures from the Hàn are found in China's museums, particularly in Xī'ān, where the ruins of the Hàn capital are still visible.

Táng Dynasty (A.D. 618–906)   After 4 centuries of warfare and the waxing and waning of many minor dynasties, China's golden age began under a long succession of Táng rulers who lived in the capital of Xī'ān (then known as Chang'an). The Táng traded by the Silk Road, and also by sea. Buddhism had entered China via India and, under the Táng, rulers played a primary role in art and architecture. From this era, we also have woodblock printing and the production of fine silk. Xī'ān contains the richest repository of Táng art and architecture, but temples, pagodas, and artworks all over China date from this prosperous period.

Sòng Dynasty (960–1279) After another period of unrest, the Sòng rulers reunified China and established a dynasty noted for its art and literature. The Sòng had the first paper money, movable type, the compass, gunpowder, and rocket-propelled spears. The Northern Sòng Dynasty (960–1126) made Kāifēng its capital, while the Southern Sòng Dynasty (1127–1279) ruled from Hángzhōu. Both cities have many treasures and temples from the Sòng. Marco Polo found a prosperous empire when he first reached China at the end of the Sòng Dynasty.

Míng Dynasty (1368–1644) The invading Mongols, spearheaded by Genghis Khan and Kublai Khan, established the Yuán Dynasty (1271–1368), but after 2 centuries of Yuán rule, China reverted to a local line of rulers known as the Míng. The Míng capital was Běijīng, and there the Míng emperors built several of China's most famous monuments: the

Forbidden City, the Temple of Heaven, and sections of the Great Wall that millions of tourists visit today. It was also during this period that European ships began to arrive off the coast of China.

Qīng (Manchu) Dynasty (1644–1911)   China's final great dynasty, established by Manchu invaders from the north, brought about the last great flourishes of traditional Chinese art and architecture. The capital, Běijīng, was graced with the Summer Palace. The empire was extended to include Tibet and Mongolia, but the Western powers made intrusions, establishing concessions in Guǎngzhōu (Canton), Shànghǎi, Qīngdǎo, Běijīng, and many other cities. In 1911, the Qīng were overthrown by nationalistic forces. The first Republic of China was then established, ending thousands of years of imperial rule and leading to the slow modernization of the country and the ascendancy of the Communists under Máo Zédōng, who established the present People's Republic of China in 1949.

Modern Politics

In some ways, China underwent more changes in the 20th century than in the previous 20 centuries combined. The Republic of China, which replaced the last dynasty, proved weak and unstable. **Sun Yat-sen** led the powerful Guómíndǎng, the Nationalist People's Party, until his death in 1925. His successor, **Chiang Kai-shek,** became head of China's government, but he was soon involved in violent struggles against two opponents: Japan, which conquered and occupied large areas of China as World War II neared, and the Chinese Communist Party, led by **Máo Zédōng** and **Zhōu Ēnlái.** In 1934, in the face of Chiang Kai-shek's military pressure, Máo's 100,000 supporters retreated to the north of China on the epic **Long March.** The Japanese, who had occupied Manchuria in 1933, went to war with China in 1937, occupying most of the east coast and pushing Chiang Kai-shek's capital all the way inland to Chóngqìng, where his troops were supplied by the legendary Flying Tigers and other American and British units.

With Japan's eventual defeat in 1945, the civil war in China intensified. Máo's People's Liberation Army (PLA) triumphed. Chiang Kai-shek's Guómíndǎng fled to Taiwan. Máo proclaimed China a People's Republic in 1949 and set up his capital in Běijīng. In a few violent decades, China had moved from an imperial dynasty to a modern republic to the largest Communist state on Earth.

Máo ruled Communist China as a new "emperor" until his death in 1976. His regime began on many promising notes. Many of the oppressive institutions of China's feudal past were simply eradicated. Prostitution, drugs, gambling, and other vices disappeared overnight. Peasants—the backbone of Máo's revolution—were given the land to work for the first time in centuries. Women were granted expanded rights. Electricity was spread across the country. Wealth was radically redistributed. For most

Chinese, China had finally stood up to the world and was vigorously setting its own course, without outside interference, for the first time in generations. At the same time, landlords and other members of the "oppressive" classes were imprisoned, expelled, or murdered.

The idealism of the post-Liberation years eventually soured as Máo initiated a number of radical programs, many of which were extreme reversals of Chinese traditions. Intellectuals, highly esteemed in Confucian culture, were denounced and imprisoned in a number of political campaigns, starting with the Anti-Rightist Campaign in 1958. Peasants were forced into massive communes in the same year. Even more disastrous was the abortive **Great Leap Forward** of 1959, an attempt to industrialize the nation overnight that succeeded only in reducing agricultural output to the point where millions of people starved to death. In 1960, the Soviet Union, which had been China's chief supporter, advisor, and aid-giver, withdrew completely, causing China to enter a period of isolation as severe as any during the great dynasties of the past.

The most ruinous campaign of all, the **Great Proletarian Cultural Revolution** (1966–76), turned China upside down and led to 10 years of self-destruction. Máo released millions of young people—who idolized him as a living god and swore by every word in his Little Red Book—to take control of China and cleanse it of all the old evils and ideals. Virtually anyone in power in 1966 would eventually be toppled by this wave of radical reform. Schools closed down and the economy ground to a halt as everyone engaged in political struggles. Unwavering loyalty to the latest politically correct line became the litmus test for keeping a job, a home, a family, life itself. Thousands, mainly the educated, were sent into the countryside where they worked as peasants in long programs of "reform through labor." The Red Guards went on campaigns to erase the past, trashing countless temples and other dynastic treasures of China's feudal days. Tourists still come across the legacies of the Cultural Revolution, not only in ruins (many of which are being restored) but in the minds and hearts of Chinese people who suffered unspeakably and yet survived the ravages of this long nightmare.

The door to China remained closed to the outside world until 1972, when the United States, after a few rounds of "Ping-Pong diplomacy," recognized the People's Republic of China. But it wasn't until the death of Chairman Máo, in 1976, that new leaders emerged to put China back on a rational and practical track. The **Gang of Four,** including Máo's wife, **Jiāng Qīng,** was put on public trial in 1980 for "crimes" perpetrated during the Cultural Revolution. **Dèng Xiǎopíng,** several times removed from office and punished during the Cultural Revolution, assumed power and launched China on an entirely new course, away from radical experiments in egalitarianism and "pure" communism and toward a socialism "with Chinese characteristics" that yielded practical economic results.

China slowly recovered the ground it had lost during Máo's later reign, but a long shadow was again cast over the nation on June 4, 1989, when pro-democracy protesters, who had seized **Tiān'ān Mén Square** in the heart of Běijīng, were evicted by force before the eyes of the world. China was instituting some economic and social reforms by this point, but political freedom was virtually nonexistent. The violent military crackdown on students and others in Tiān'ān Mén Square formed the most dramatic and lasting impression of China for millions of foreign viewers.

When I visited Canton (Guǎngzhōu), Shànghǎi, and Běijīng the following year, I found a nation in shock. I also found almost no Western tourists. An invisible boycott had taken hold.

In 1992, Dèng Xiǎopíng made a historic "southern tour" of China, during which he urged the nation to accelerate its economic liberalization. This set into motion a rapid **Westernization** of China. At times, China seemed the most capitalistic country on the planet, a freewheeling society whose motto echoed Dèng Xiǎopíng's famous epitaph, "To get rich is glorious." Millionaires appeared overnight. Thousands of private enterprises were born in the streets. Greed replaced any lingering hopes for a rebirth of political idealism. The Communist Party, although widely discredited, remained firmly in power, and the people, given economic if not political freedom on a scale never before granted by any of its rulers, concentrated on helping build China into a superpower for the 21st century.

The death of senior leader Dèng Xiǎopíng and the return of Hong Kong to Chinese sovereignty in 1997 marked the beginning of a third era in the history of China since Liberation in 1949. The economy of the 1990s boomed steadily onward. China hurtled through its own Industrial Revolution and beyond in a matter of months and years rather than the decades and centuries experienced by the West. Where this will lead, no one knows. China must initiate far greater, more perilous reforms to keep its economy running, and sooner or later it must liberalize its political system as well. But changes in all spheres do seem possible as a new century begins.

Not only are today's travelers able to feast on the splendors of Old China to a degree never before possible; they can also see this China of the future taking shape minute by minute, emerging from the deep shadows of the recent past into something surely brighter.

Portrait Gallery

China yesterday and today is a stage populated by thousands of actors well known to every Chinese but obscure to the outsider. It helps to have a thumbnail sketch of some of the leading members of the cast, as these names constantly come up as you travel across the country.

Chiang Kai-shek (1887–1975)   Leader of the Guómíndǎng (Nationalist People's Party) and president of China during the war against Japan (1933–45), Chiang fled to Taiwan after his forces were defeated by the Communists in 1949, establishing the Republic of China there in fierce opposition to the People's Republic of China on the mainland.

Empress Dowager Cíxǐ (1835–1908)   The power behind the throne during the last gasps of the Qīng (Manchu) Dynasty and creator of the Summer Palace at Běijīng, she is villainized in the popular imagination as an evil despot and conniving assassin.

Confucius (551–479 B.C.)   This great philosopher, known as Kǒng Fūzǐ to the Chinese, is China's Socrates. His teachings, particularly about the strict relationships of leader to subject, man to woman, and parent to child, underlie the traditional organization of family and society in China.

Dèng Xiǎopíng (1904–1997)   A veteran of the Long March, who later bobbed in and out of Máo's favor, Dèng directed China's economic revolution in the 1980s and 1990s. He is blamed for ordering the military crackdown on Tiān'ān Mén Square in 1989. His most famous saying (applied to competing economic and political proposals) was, "It doesn't matter whether the cat is black or white, as long as it catches mice."

Dù Fǔ (A.D. 712–770)   Considered (along with Lǐ Bái) China's greatest poet, Dù Fǔ wrote powerful, personal lyrics that touch the major chords of Chinese history and human sadness. His "thatched cottage," where he lived in exile from the Táng Dynasty capital, is memorialized in a park in Chéngdū.

Guānyīn   China's most popular Buddhist deity, usually regarded as a woman or a figure combining both sexes, Guānyīn is the Goddess of Mercy, often petitioned to ensure the birth of a male heir. Her temple home in China is the holy island mountain of Pǔtuó Shān.

Jiāng Zémín (b. 1926)   A master politician, Jiāng became paramount leader of China following the death of Dèng Xiǎopíng in 1997, and although replaced as president in 2003, is likely to remain powerful behind the scenes. He is dedicated to economic reforms; all he lacks is charisma.

Kāngxī (1654–1722)   The Kāngxī reign was the second of the Qīng Dynasty, lasting from 1662 to 1722. The Kāngxī Emperor visited most of the important cities and mountains in China, restoring ancient temples and building many new ones. He built the imperial summer palace in Chéngdé (near Běijīng), which still survives.

Lǎozǐ (ca. 570–490 B.C.)   Legendary founder of China's indigenous religion, Daoism, Lǎozǐ emphasized the essential way of nature and the inner, often magical powers of the individual.

Lǐ Bái (A.D. 699–762)   Considered (along with Dù Fǔ) China's greatest poet, Lǐ Bái wrote brilliant lyrics (often while drunk on wine) that celebrated individual power and the realm of the senses.

Máo Zédōng (1893–1976)   Chairman Máo helped create the Chinese Communist Party in 1921 and became the supreme ruler of China in 1949. Venerated as a living god in his lifetime, he led China out of its feudal past and initiated modern reforms, but he also devised campaigns and policies that destroyed the Chinese economy and educational system.

Marco Polo (1254–1324)   In a ghostwritten account, which has become the West's most famous China travel book, Marco Polo claimed to be an emissary of Kublai Khan during a 17-year residence in Old Cathay. Despite recent suggestions that Marco Polo never even set foot in China and merely recycled the accounts of Silk Road merchants who had, his name is synonymous with all that is exotic and mysterious in China.

Qín Shǐ Huángdì (259–210 B.C.)   The First Emperor of unified China, Qín was known as the burner of books and the builder of the Great Wall. The terra-cotta warriors guarding his immense underground mausoleum at Xī'ān are one of China's leading tourist attractions.

Sun Yat-sen (1866–1925)   Patriarch of Chinese reform, democracy, and modernization, known as Sūn Zhōngshān to Mandarin speakers, he headed the Guómíndǎng movement that toppled the last dynasty and propelled China into the 20th century.

Empress Wǔ (A.D. 660–705)   China's most powerful female ruler, Wǔ Zétiān rose to empress of the Táng Dynasty from the position of a concubine and initiated thousands of Buddhist temples and works of art.

Xuánzàng (A.D. 602–664)   China's most famous Buddhist monk, he made a 22-year pilgrimage to India to gather holy manuscripts (sutras), which he translated at temples in Xī'ān that still stand. He is the basis for the fantastical hero of *The Monkey: Or Journey to the West,* one of China's most popular epic novels.

Zhōu Ēnlái (1898–1976)   Confederate of Chairman Máo and one of the founders of the Chinese Communist Party, Zhōu Ēnlái is remembered fondly by many Chinese because, as premier during the nightmare years of the Cultural Revolution (1966–76), he intervened to save many lives as well as temples and historic treasures from the rampaging Red Guards.

Zhūgě Liàng (A.D. 181–234)   During the Three Kingdoms Period (A.D. 220–280), he devised astonishing military strategies. His name is synonymous in China with wisdom and correct conduct. His memorial hall is located in Chéngdū.

TEMPLES, MOSQUES & CHURCHES

AMONG THE MORE INTERESTING BUT often fatiguing sights in China are the temples. There are Daoist temples, Buddhist temples, even Confucian temples. Tourists, particularly on package tours, often get "templed out" after their third or fourth visit (in their 3rd or 4th city) to these ancient shrines. Nevertheless, the religious architecture and art of China are among its most sublime creations, and temples and pagodas reflect much of the essence of Old China. Understanding the history of religion in China can pump some life and individual character into these monuments.

The Five Ways

Daoism (or **Taoism**), the most important indigenous religion, dates back 2,500 years. **Buddhism,** its chief rival among organized religions, is a transplant, introduced from India about 2,000 years ago. **Confucianism—** more a philosophy than a religion, although it does have its own rites and temples—is a way of conceiving of society and family in a series of hierarchical relationships. The Confucian is primarily interested in family, society, and education; the Daoist in nature, the individual, and magic; and the Buddhist in compassion, suffering, and transcendence.

These three ways of perceiving the world spiritually were blended over the centuries. Thus, at first blush, it is not easy to tell, in China, a Daoist temple from a Buddhist shrine from a Confucian pavilion (or even from a royal palace). They share much in common, particularly their architecture. They also share worshippers. As an old adage puts it: "Go to work a Confucian, retire a Daoist, die a Buddhist."

In Old China, Daoism, Buddhism, and Confucianism played a large role in daily life. In modern China, it is quite a different story. Although you'll notice the Chinese thronging the old temples you visit, bowing and burning incense, devoted Buddhists and Daoists make up a tiny portion of the people. Chinese Muslims, actively devoted to **Islam,** also constitute a small minority. These days it is the Chinese **Christians** who are growing in strength, although again they do not constitute more than a small bloc of the Chinese people: Official estimates suggest that 70% of China's people are affiliated with no religion at all, 20% practice ancient folk religions, 6% are Buddhist, 2% are Muslim, and 1% or less are Daoist or Christian.

The temples, when toured with an understanding of China's past, are treasure houses, while China's mosques and churches are vital centers of worship for dedicated segments of the population. Both sorts of religious shrines, old and new, often provide moving experiences.

Daoism & Nature

Daoism is the metaphysical and naturalistic wing of Chinese religion and philosophy. In its pure form, as expounded in the writings of its legendary founder, Lǎozǐ in the 6th century B.C., the *Dào* (or *Tao*) is the way—an absolute way, removed from space, time, society, and tradition, yet one with nature, that can only be discovered by the individual and cannot be described in words, except perhaps through paradox.

Daoism was not intended to be organized as a religion. Its most famous practitioners were usually hermits. The Daoist ideal is to retreat from society and learn from nature: All laws and rules are rejected. Instead, the individual cultivates a life of simplicity and withdrawal. Despite these antisocial ideals, Daoism did achieve an organized form, complete with temples, priests, and its own elaborate cosmology: Daoists became the alchemists of China, seeking the elixir of immortality; consuming gold flakes, cinnabar, and various poisons; practicing extreme methods of control over breathing and other bodily functions. Their history is filled with tales of the superhuman and the magical, and their living gods are the immortals who have achieved everlasting physical life and fly with the clouds. Many Chinese artists, particularly lyrical poets such as Lǐ Bái, have been deeply influenced by Daoism.

There are Daoist temples in nearly all Chinese cities, along with Daoist priests and nuns who have returned in small numbers since their banishment during the Cultural Revolution (1966–76). Some of the more famous Daoist temples can be visited today on the **Five Sacred Mountains of Old China: Sōng Shān, Héng Shān Běi Yuè, Héng Shān Nán Yuè, Huà Shān,** and **Tài Shān.**

Buddhism & Art

Buddhism arrived from India by the same route as goods from the West, by the Silk Road. The new religion took hold in China's desert outposts during the Hàn Dynasty (206 B.C.–A.D. 220). At the oasis of **Dūnhuáng,** devotees created China's greatest storehouse of Buddhist paintings and manuscripts in the caves of Mògāo in the 4th century A.D. By the 9th century, Buddhism was so widely practiced and its temples so rich that the Táng Emperor banished Buddhism altogether as an institution "foreign" to the Chinese way. The temples were reopened or rebuilt shortly after this edict, although Buddhism gradually lost its great power.

Buddhism's most important sites in China include the **Shào Lín Monastery** at Sōng Shān, where the fighting monks developed the martial arts and where Chán Buddhism (known as Zen in Japan) originated; the two great **Táng Dynasty pagodas** and their temples in Xī'ān, the ancient capital, where Buddhism exerted its strongest influence; and the temples on the **Four Famous Peaks of Buddhism: Wǔtái Shān, Jiǔhuá Shān, Pǔtuó Shān,** and **Éméi Shān.**

Buddhism's influence on art and architecture reached its zenith under the Táng and continued through later dynasties. Most of the temples, pagodas, and statues you see all across China today are Buddhist.

Confucianism & Society

Confucius (Kǒng Fūzǐ), rather like Socrates, was a teacher whose ideas were written down by his students. Confucian ideas have had as far-reaching an influence on Chinese philosophy as Socratic ideas did on Western thought.

Confucius laid great stress on education, particularly on the study of ancient classics, since these depicted a more perfect society than what existed in the present, and on traditional rituals and rites, since these also came from an earlier, golden age. He also devised the image of the model gentleman, a highly educated public servant who fulfilled all duties and whose character and integrity were completely unassailable. All these notions became the basis of the Chinese educational system, with its Imperial Examinations, which were the route to a lucrative and influential career as a scholar-official in China's massive civil service system.

Even more profoundly, Confucius formulated the five relationships that all Chinese are traditionally expected to observe. Each relationship is between a superior and an inferior. Those relationships are between ruler and subject, father and son, husband and wife, elder brother and younger brother, and friend and friend. For society—indeed, for Heaven and Earth—to be in harmony, these relationships had to be strictly observed. They extended even beyond the grave: Recently departed family members had to be mourned and ancestors had to be "worshipped" at family shrines.

When the Confucians gained prominent positions in government during the early Hàn Dynasty in the 2nd century B.C., these ideas became state doctrines. The emperor was responsible for running human affairs in a virtuous and just manner or he could lose his "Mandate of Heaven," bringing disastrous consequences to the kingdom. The emperor's royal advisors were required to give their superior the best advice for the welfare of the state, regardless of its effect on an advisor's own career. These officials, in turn, were products of a rigorous state examination system that quizzed its students on the intricacies of Confucian classics. One long-term result still felt in China today is that the rule of law never gained a foothold. Conflicts were settled and policies were determined through negotiations conducted among a few powerful and presumably good and just men. Since they occupied a superior position, and were ideally of unquestionable integrity, their decisions could not properly be questioned by the masses.

In this century, Máo Zédōng turned Confucianism on its head, making the masses superior to the scholar-elites. Ancestor worship, filial piety, respect for the past, deference to elders and the educated, unquestioning obedience of authority, the sanctity of the family—all these Confucian doctrines were for a time denounced as feudal and backward. But while many of these old ideas are not practiced today, they still underlie Chinese responses in subtle but profound ways. The need to "save face," for instance (see p. 620), originally prescribed as a way to protect the family, is still an everyday practice.

While mainly secular in its teachings, Confucianism gradually became China's state religion. The first temples to Confucius were built in the 7th century as shrines where the Great Scholar and his disciples could be worshipped as scholarly ancestors of the nation or at least of its bureaucracy. These Confucian temples can still be found in many cities in China. The Confucian Temple in **Běijīng** is still quite active, and the one in **Xī'ān** now serves as the lovely grounds for the old provincial museum.

Islam & Arabia

China's Muslim population numbers less than 20 million of China's 1.3 billion residents (about 2%), but their struggle to maintain an ethnic as well as religious identity is a major concern of China's leaders, who are wary of any sign of a burgeoning secessionist movement such as that in Tibet. Muslim minorities have therefore been granted many of the special rights enjoyed by China's other minorities, such as exemption from the one-family, one-child rule.

Arab sea traders and Silk Road merchants introduced Islam to the edges of the Chinese empire not long after the faith was born in the 7th century A.D. Today there are historic mosques worth visiting in Guǎngzhōu, Běijīng, Xī'ān, and the Silk Road cities of Gānsù and Xīnjiāng provinces. Most of China's Muslim population resides in the northwest. Cities such as Xī'ān have a Muslim quarter where the people, known as the Huí, are indistinguishable from Hàn Chinese, due to centuries of assimilation, but they strictly maintain many Muslim mandates, running their own schools, butcher shops, and restaurants. There are 6.5 million Huí in China.

In Xīnjiāng Province, the 5.5 million Uighur people, practicing Muslims, dominate the culture of a region that occupies one-sixth of China's territory. The mosques in **Kashgar** and other desert oases, dating from the Míng and Qīng dynasties, are among the most fascinating religious sites in China.

Christianity & the West

Catholic missionaries first arrived in the 16th century in the person of Matteo Ricci of the Society of Jesus, but the Míng emperor was not so interested in Ricci's religious message as he was in the Jesuit's scientific knowledge. Protestant missionaries, making their mark in the mid–19th and early 20th centuries, made few converts while in China. Despite this failure and repeated episodes of persecution in more recent times, Christianity appears to be flourishing now as never before. In the 1990s, an official census put the number of Christians in China at about three million—hardly enough to cause a blip on China's population radar—but in the last few years, and particularly with the addition of Hong Kong, this figure has soared. The government now counts five million Catholics and six million Protestants, and scholars would double these numbers, counting "underground" Christians who attend unofficial home churches. Even state statistics admit that China enrolls 60,000 new Catholic followers a year.

Most Chinese cities now have at least two officially sanctioned Christian churches in operation: one Protestant, one Catholic. The Protestant churches are controlled by the Three-Self Patriotic Movement and are not affiliated with any religious institutions in the West. The Catholic churches are controlled by the Catholic Patriotic Association, which does not recognize the authority of Rome. Catholic mass is still conducted in Latin. In addition, there are numerous illegal "home churches" throughout China that also have a growing membership, despite occasional crackdowns by local police.

I've attended dozens of services in Protestant and Catholic churches in many cities and towns in China. This is often a most interesting experience, even if you're not a Christian. Most of the churches were built in the late 19th or early 20th century in western European styles. Few have any religious decorations left, but most have plenty of bibles and hymnals. Nearly all who attend Christian services today are Chinese. A decade ago, many of the worshippers were elderly, members who had attended churches before their closure either after the communist victory of 1949, or during the

Cultural Revolution (1966–76). Now, more and more young people, perhaps curious about Western institutions of all kinds, are attending.

A traveler recently informed me that when she inquired at a hotel desk about attending Sunday services at a church in Xī'ān, she was told that it didn't accept foreigners. This is nonsense. Foreigners are routinely welcomed with open arms in all the churches in China. Be persistent. The only difficulty in attending church in China is the same difficulty faced almost everywhere: breaking through the crowds and securing a seat inside.

How to Tour a Temple

Monumental Chinese architecture, from temples to cities, was traditionally laid out according to cosmological principles that became known as *fēng shuǐ*—a way of arranging objects to avoid or deflect the invasion of evil forces. In simple terms, this meant that everything from a temple to a city faced south (since evil forces galore swept in from the north), and was surrounded on four sides by a high wall to keep out bad spirits (not to mention ordinary thieves).

The Daoist, Buddhist, and Confucian temples you visit in China today adhere to this geomantically correct scheme. Protected by rectangular walls like a small city, the temple's main entrance faces south. The entrance gate is sealed off by huge wooden doors, near which novice monks collect the modern entrance fees. Immediately inside is a series of pavilions and courtyards lined on both sides by residence and administrative halls. The inner complex can be compact or vast, consisting of hundreds of buildings or a small handful. Usually, the deeper into the courtyards and pavilions you go, the more sacred the shrine.

The temple architecture is virtually identical regardless of the religion practiced within. Variations in style are a product of region and historical period, not the dictates of faith. The main support consists of interlocking wooden beams and enormous columns resting on raised platforms. The curving roof is paved in ceramic tiles. In the early Táng Dynasty, a system of cantilevered brackets enabled the eaves to become a more prominent and showy feature. Carved figures populated the gables. In southern China, ornamentation and increasingly upturned eaves became the fashion. In the north, temple architecture remained more restrained.

While Chinese temples are seldom multistoried, owing to restrictions inherent in their structural elements, the **pagodas** that often rise from temple grounds were deliberately designed to touch the heavens. Derived from religious towers in India, the Chinese versions served two primary purposes: as reliquaries for holy documents and other sacred relics, and as magical monuments to protect monasteries, cities, and the surrounding countryside from natural and man-made disasters. Some pagodas allow visitors to ascend the stairways inside, although many are closed. The Táng Dynasty pagodas in Xī'ān can still be climbed, and they are among the most important to survive in China.

In **Buddhist temples,** the grand entrance often contains two large statues of guardian kings, known as the Èr Wáng, one on either side. The first buildings beyond the entrance are the bell and drum towers, once used to call the faithful to prayer. The first major hall is a holy military complex of sorts with large statues of the four heavenly kings, two on each side. Their tasks are to protect the sacred site, punish evil, and reward the good and just. The yellow Northern King, Duō Wén, carries the banner of sacred truth, which looks for all the world like an umbrella. The white Eastern King, Tè Guó, has a lute to calm the tormented soul with his divine music. The blue Southern King, Zēng Zhǎng, is armed with a demon-defying sword. The red Western King, Guǎng Mù, clutches a snake for power over evil and a pearl for wisdom.

The first Buddha you usually encounter is Maitreya, the Laughing Buddha, with his trademark bulging belly. Maitreya is the Buddha of the Future, technically still a *bodhisattva* (enlightened follower remaining on Earth to help others). His belly is swollen by meditation. His earlobes are elongated by the heavy rings he once wore, signs that he was a respected teacher.

The Great Hall of most Buddhist temples often contains three large golden statues sitting on lotus flowers. These are the Buddhas of the Past, Present, and Future. Maitreya, the Buddha of the Future, you've already met. Sakyamuni, the Buddha of the Present, is the historical figure who attained enlightenment. Dipamkara, the Buddha of the Past, represents all who entered Nirvana before Sakyamuni, the 5th century B.C. northern Indian prince.

The walls of the Great Hall usually contain smaller statues of Buddha's divine followers, the 500 arhats (or *luóhàn*). Immediately behind the Great Buddhas is a statue of the Goddess of Mercy, Guānyīn, who became the most popular Buddhist divinity in China. Guānyīn is often portrayed as having "a thousand arms," representing her great capacity to reach out to others. She is also petitioned to grant a male heir.

The faithful temple-goer purchases prayer beads, amulets, and incense sticks from the temple vendors, placing a burning stick in the incense burners outside each hall and kneeling and praying on the cushions or rugs placed before the altar inside. If the temple has a large and active team of monks, they will often conduct chants inside the fenced-off area in front of the altar.

It's easy enough for a novice visitor to find the main altars in a temple complex: Just keep heading straight north from the entrance through the inner courtyards from hall to hall. Often the back door of a pavilion is open, so that visitors can walk around the altar and statues in the center and exit at the rear into the courtyard of the next pavilion.

In a **Daoist temple,** the layout is much the same, but the gods have changed and the monks are wearing funny leggings. The red columns of a Buddhist temple are painted black, and yĭn-yáng symbols frequently appear on walls. The Three Buddhas are replaced by statues of the Three Immortals riding tiger, deer, and crane. Literary and historical figures, such as the Three Kingdom's Zhūgĕ Liàng, are often memorialized. One figure of adoration and petition that Daoist and Buddhist temples do share, however, is that of Guānyīn, Goddess of Mercy.

Daoist temples tend to be more down-to-earth and eclectic than Buddhist temples. Most of the temples you'll visit in China are Buddhist, but there are plenty of Daoist temples as well. Those at the center of the city often opened their courtyards to Sunday marketplaces, and street markets still often surround Daoist temples. There are fewer **Confucian temples** in China, and they are seldom used by worshippers of the Great Sage these days. The Confucian temples in Bĕijīng and Qūfú, two of the most famous in China, employ the architecture of Buddhist and Daoist temples, but their stately interiors and altars are remarkably bare of the statues that other temples have in numbing abundance, save those of Confucius himself.

THE CHINESE LANGUAGE

by Peter Neville-Hadley

Chinese is not as difficult a language to learn as it may first appear to be—at least not once you've decided what kind of Chinese to learn. There are six major languages called Chinese. Speakers of each are unintelligible to speakers of the others, and there are, in addition, a host of dialects. The Chinese you hear spoken in your local Chinatown, in your local Chinese restaurant, or by your friends of Chinese descent when they speak to their parents is more than likely to be Cantonese, which is the version of Chinese used in Hong Kong and in much of southern China. But the official national language of China is **Mandarin** (*Pǔtōnghuà*—"common speech"), sometimes called Modern Standard Chinese, and viewed in mainland China as the language of administration, of the classics, and of the educated. While throughout much of mainland China, people speak their own local flavor of Chinese for everyday communication, they've all been educated in Mandarin which, in general terms, is the language of Běijīng and the north. Mandarin is less well-known in Hong Kong and Macau, but it is also spoken in Táiwān and Singapore, and among growing communities of recent immigrants to North America.

Chinese grammar is considerably more straightforward than that of English or other European languages, even Spanish or Italian. There are no genders, so there is no need to remember long lists of endings for adjectives and to make them agree, with variations according to case. There are no equivalents for the definite and indefinite articles ('the,' 'a,' 'an'), so there is no need to make those agree either. Singular and plural nouns are the same. Best of all, verbs cannot be declined. The verb "to be" is *shì*. The same sound also covers 'am,' 'are,' 'is,' 'was,' 'will be,' and so on, since there are also no tenses. Instead of past, present, and future, Chinese is more concerned with whether an action is continuing or has been completed, and the order in which events take place. To make matters of time clear, it depends on simple expressions such as "yesterday," "before," "originally," and "next year." "Tomorrow I go New York," is clear enough, as is "Yesterday I go New York." It's a little more complicated than these brief notes can suggest, but not much.

There are a few sounds in Mandarin that are not used in English (see the rough pronunciation guide below), but the main difficulty for foreigners lies in tones. Most sounds in Mandarin begin with a consonant and end in a vowel (or -n, or -ng), which leaves the language with very few distinctive noises compared to English. Originally, one sound equaled one idea and one word. Even now, each of these monosyllables is represented by a single character, but often words have been made by putting two characters together, sometimes both of the same meaning, thus reinforcing one another. The solution to this phonetic poverty is to multiply the available sounds by making them tonal—speaking them at different pitches, thereby giving them different meanings. *Mā* spoken on a high level tone (1st tone) offers a different set of possible meanings from *má* spoken with a rising tone (2nd tone), *mǎ* with a dipping then rising tone (3rd tone), or *mà* with an abruptly falling tone (4th tone). There's also a different meaning for the neutral, toneless *ma*.

In the average sentence, context is your friend (there are not many occasions in which the third-tone *mǎ* "horse" might be mistaken for the fourth-tone *mà* "grasshopper," for instance), but, without tone, there is essentially no meaning. The novice is best off singing his Mandarin very clearly, as Chinese children do—a chanted sing-song can be heard emerging from the windows of primary schools across China. With experience, the student learns to give particular emphasis to the tones on words essential to a sentence's meaning, and to treat the others more lightly. Sadly, most books using modern Romanized Chinese, called *Hànyǔ pīnyīn* ("Hàn language spell-the-sounds"), do not mark the tones, nor do these appear on **pīnyīn** signs in China. But for the latest edition of this book, the updaters, who all speak Mandarin, have added tones to every Mandarin expression, so you can have a go at saying them for yourself. Where tones do not appear, that's usually because the name of a person or place is already familiar to many readers in an older form of Romanized Chinese, such as Wade-Giles, or Post Office (in which Běijīng was written misleadingly as Peking); or because it is better known in Cantonese: Sun Yat-sen, or Canton, for instance.

Cantonese has *eight* tones plus the neutral, but its grammatical structure is largely the same, as is that of all versions of Chinese. Even Chinese people who can barely understand a word each other is saying can at least write to each other, since written forms are similar. Mainland China, with the aim of increasing literacy (or perhaps of distancing the supposedly now thoroughly modern and socialist population from its Confucian heritage), instituted a ham-fisted simplification program in the 1950s; it reduced some characters originally taking 14 strokes of the brush to write, for instance, to as few as three strokes. Hong Kong, separated from the mainland and under British control until 1997, went its own way, kept the original full-form characters, and invented lots of new ones, too. Nevertheless, many characters remain the same, and some of the simplified forms are merely familiar shorthands for the full-form ones. But however many different meanings for each tone of *ma* there may be, for each meaning there's a different character. This makes the written form a far more successful communication medium than the spoken one, which leads to misunderstandings even between native speakers, who can often be seen sketching characters on their palms during conversation to confirm which one they mean.

The thought of learning 3,000 to 5,000 individual characters (at least 2,500 are needed to read a newspaper) also daunts many beginners. But look carefully at the characters below, and you'll notice many common elements. In fact, a rather limited number of smaller shapes are combined in different ways, much as we combine letters to make words. Admittedly, the characters only offer general hints as to their pronunciation, and that's often misleading—the system is not a phonetic one, so each new Mandarin word has to be learned as both a sound and a shape (or group of them). But soon it's the similarities among the characters, not their differences, which begin to bother the student. English, a far more subtle language with a far larger vocabulary, and with so many pointless inconsistencies and exceptions to what are laughingly called its rules, is much more of a struggle for the Chinese than Mandarin should be for us.

But no knowledge of the language is needed to get around China, and it's almost of assistance that Chinese take it for granted that outlandish foreigners (that's you and me unless of Chinese descent) can speak not a word (poor things) and must use whatever other limited means we have to communicate—this book and a phrase book, for instance. For help with navigation to sights, simply point to the characters below. When leaving your hotel, take one of its cards with you, and show it to the taxi driver when you want to return. At the end of this chapter, there's a limited list of useful words and phrases, which is best supplemented with a proper phrase book. If you have a *Mandarin*-speaking friend from the north (Cantonese speakers who know Mandarin as a 2nd language tend to have fairly heavy accents), ask him or her to pronounce the greetings and words of thanks from the list below, so you can repeat after him and practice. While you are as much likely to be laughed *at* as *with* in China, such efforts are always appreciated.

A GUIDE TO PĪNYĪN PRONUNCIATION

Letters in Pīnyīn mostly have the values any English speaker would expect, with the following exceptions:

c *ts* as in bi*ts*

q *ch* as in *ch*in, but much harder

r has no true equivalent in English, but the *r* of *r*eed is close, although the tip of the tongue should be near the top of the mouth, and the teeth together

x also has no true equivalent, but is nearest to the *sh* of *sh*eep, although the tongue should be parallel to the roof of the mouth and the teeth together

zh is a soft j, like the *dge* in ju*dge* and more forward, made with tongue and teeth

The vowels are pronounced roughly as follows:

a as in f**a**ther

e as in **e**rr (*leng* is pronounced as English 'lung')

i is pronounced **ee** after most consonants, but after c, ch, r, s, sh, z, and zh is a buzz at the front of the mouth behind the closed teeth

o as in s**o**ng

u as in t**oo**

ü is the purer, lips-pursed u of French t**u** and German **ü**. Confusingly, u after j, x, q, and y, u is always ü, but in these cases the accent "¨" does not appear.

ou as in t**o**e

ua as in g**ua**va

uo sounds like **or,** but more abrupt

ai sounds like **eye**

ao as in **ou**ch

ei as in h**a**y

ia as in **ya**k

ian sounds like **yen**

iang sounds like **yang**

iu sounds like **you**

ui sounds like **way**

Note that when two or more third-tone "ˇ" sounds follow one another, they should all, except the last, be pronounced as second-tone "´".

English	Pinyin	Chinese
BEIJING	**Běijīng**	北京
Ancient Observatory	Gǔ Guānxiàngtái	古观象台
Chairman Mao Memorial Hall	Máo Zhǔxí Jìniàn Táng	毛主席纪念堂
Forbidden City (Palace Museum)	Gù Gōng Bówùguǎn	故宫博物馆

English	Pinyin	Chinese
Lama Temple	Yōnghé Gōng	雍和宫
Old Summer Palace	Yuánmíng Yuán	圆明园
Summer Palace	Yíhé Yuán	颐和园
Temple of Heaven	Tiān Tán Gōngyuán	天坛公园
Tian'an Men Square	Tiān'ān Mén Guǎngchǎng	天安门广场
White Cloud Temple	Báiyún Guàn	白云观
BEIHAI	**Běihǎi**	**北海**
Old Town	Zhōngshān Lù Lǎochéngqū	中山路老城区
Silver Beach	Yíntān	银滩
	Wàishā	外沙
CANTON	**See Guangzhou**	
CHENGDE	**Chéngdé**	**承德**
Hammer Rock	Qìngchuí Fēng	磬锤峰
Mountain Villa for Escaping the Summer Heat	Bìshǔ Shān Zhuāng	避暑山庄
Mount Sumeru Longevity and Happiness Temple	Xūmífúshòu Miào	须弥福寿庙
Small Potala Temple	Pǔtuózōngchéng Zhī Miào	普陀宗乘之庙
Temple of Universal Joy	Pǔlè Sì	普乐寺
CHENGDU	**Chéngdū**	**成都**
Du Fu's Cottage	Dù Fǔ Cǎotáng	杜甫草堂
Green Goat Temple	Qīngyáng Gōng	青羊宫
Wenshu Monastery	Wénshū Yuàn	文殊院
Wuhou Temple	Wǔhòu Cí	武后祠
Zoo	Dòngwù Yuán	动物园

English	Pinyin	Chinese
CHONGQING	**Chóngqìng**	**重庆**
Chongqing Museum	Chóngqìng Bówùguǎn	重庆博物馆
Gate to Sky	Cháotiān Mén	朝天门
Liberation Monument	Jiěfàng Bēi	解放碑
Luohan Temple	Luóhàn Sì	罗汉寺
Pipa Shan Park	Pípa Shān Gōngyuán	枇杷山公园
DALI	**Dàlǐ**	**大理**
Erhai Lake	Ěrhǎi Hú	洱海
Shaping	Shāpíng	沙坪
Temple of the Three Pagodas	Sān Tǎ Sì	三塔寺
Wase	Wāsè	挖色
DATONG	**Dàtóng**	**大同**
Huayan Monastery	Huáyán Sì	华严寺
Nine Dragon Screen	Jiǔ Lóng Bì	九龙壁
Hanging Monastery	Xuán Kōng Sì	悬空寺
Yungang Grottoes	Yúngāng Shíkū	云岗石窟
DAZU BUDDHIST CAVES	**Dàzú Shíkū**	**大足石窟**
Flower Dragon Bridge	Huā Lóng Qiáo	花龙桥
Treasure Peak Mountain	Bǎodǐng Shān	宝顶山
DUNHUANG	**Dūnhuáng**	**敦煌**
Crescent Moon Lake	Yuèyá Quán	月牙泉
Singing Sand Mountains	Míngshā Shān	鸣沙山
EMEI SHAN	**Éméi Shān**	**峨眉山**
Elephant Bathing Pool	Xǐxiàng Chí	洗象池
Golden Peak	Jīndǐng	金顶

English	Pinyin	Chinese
Jieyin Pavilion	Jiēyǐn Gé	接引阁
Peak of the Ten Thousand Buddhas	Wànfódǐng	万佛
Pure Sound Pavilion	Qīngyǐn Gé	清音阁
Shrine of Limpid Waters	Jìng Shuǐ	净水
Temple of Ten Thousand Years	Wànnián Sì	万年
GRAND CANAL	**Dà Yùnhé**	**大运河**
GREAT WALL	**Wàn Lǐ Cháng Chéng**	**万里长**
Badaling	Bādálǐng	八达岭
Juyongguan	Jūyōngguān	居庸关
Mutianyu	Mùtiányù	慕田峪
Simatai	Sīmǎtāi	司马台
GUANGZHOU	**Guǎngzhōu**	**广州**
Pearl River	Zhū Jiāng	珠江
Qingping Market	Qīngpíng Shìchǎng	清平市场
Shamian Island	Shāmiàn Dǎo	沙面岛
Sun Yat-sen Memorial Hall	Zhōngshān Jìniàntáng	中山纪念堂
Temple of the Six Banyan Trees	Liù Róng Sì	六榕寺
Yuexiu Park	Yuèxiù Gōngyuán	越秀公园
GUILIN	**Guìlín**	**桂林**
Banyan Lake	Róng Hú	榕湖
Brocade Hill	Diécǎi Shān	叠彩山
Cedar Lake	Shān Hú	杉湖
Crescent Moon Hill	Yuèyá Shān	月牙山

English	Pinyin	Chinese
Elephant Trunk Hill	Xiàngbí Shān	象鼻山
Li River	Lí Jiāng	漓江
Minorities Cultural Park	Mínsú Fēngqíng Yuán	民俗风情园
Pierced Hill	Chuān Shān	穿山
Reed Flute Cave	Lúdí Yán	芦笛岩
Seven-Star Park	Qīxīng Gōngyuán	七星公园
Solitary Beauty Peak	Dú Xiù Fēng	独秀峰
Whirlpool Hill	Fúbō Shān	伏波山
HANGZHOU	**Hángzhōu**	**杭州**
Chinese Tea Museum	Zhōngguó Chá Yè Bówùguǎn	中国茶叶博物
Dragon Well	Lóngjǐng	龙井
Hangzhou Botanical Garden	Hángzhōu Zhíwù Yuán	杭州植物园
Flower Harbor Park	Huāgǎng Yuán	花港园
Island of Small Seas	Xiǎoyáng Zhōu	小洋洲
Lingyin Temple	Língyǐn Sì	灵隐寺
Peak That Flew from Afar	Fēilái Fēng	飞来峰
Solitary Hill Island	Gū Shān	孤山
Three Pools Mirroring the Moon	Sān Tán Yìn Yuè	三潭印月
West Lake	Xī Hú	西湖
Zhejiang Provincial Museum	Zhèjiāng Shěng Bówùguǎn	浙江省博物
HARBIN	**Harbin**	**哈尔滨**
Confucian Temple	Wén Miào	文庙
Old Town	Dàolǐ Qū	道理区

English	Pinyin	Chinese
Siberian Tiger Park	Dōngběi Hǔ Línyuán	东北虎林园
Songhua River	Sōnghuā Jiāng	松花江
Stalin Park	Sīdàlín Gōngyuán	斯大林公园
Sun Island	Tàiyáng Dǎo	太阳岛
Unit 731	Qīnhuá Rìjūn Qī Sān Yāo Bùduì Jiùzhǐ	侵华日军七三一部队旧址
Zhaolin Park	Zhàolín Gōngyuán	兆麟公园
HENG SHAN NORTHERN PEAK	**Héng Shān Běi Yuè**	**恒山北岳**
Kui Xing Temple	Kuí Xīng Sì	魁星寺
HENG SHAN SOUTHERN PEAK	**Héng Shān Nán Yuè**	**衡山南岳**
Hall of the Fire God	Zhùróng Diàn	祝融殿
Southern Gate of Heaven	Nán Tiān Mén	南天门
Temple of the Southern Mountain	Nányuè Miào	南岳庙
Zhurong Peak	Zhùróng Fēng	祝融峰
HONG KONG	**Xiāng Gǎng**	**香港**
HUA SHAN	**Huà Shān**	**华山**
River Gorge of 18 Bends	Shíbā Pán	十八盘
Jade Spring Temple	Yùquán Sì	玉泉寺
Looking to Heaven Pool	Yǎngtiān Chí	仰天池
HUANG SHAN	**Huáng Shān**	**黄山**
Jade Screen Pavilion	Yùpíng Lóu	玉屏楼
Lotus Flower Peak	Liánhuā Fēng	莲花峰

English	Pinyin	Chinese
Northern Sea of Clouds	Běihǎi	北海
Peach Blossom Hot Springs	Táoyuán Wēnquán	桃源温泉
Stone That Flew from Afar	Fēilái Shí	飞来石
Turtle Summit	Àoyú Fēng	鳌鱼峰
Western Sea of Clouds	Xīhǎi	西海
HUANGPU RIVER	**Huángpǔ Jiāng**	**黄浦江**
JIAYUGUAN	**Jiāyùguān**	**嘉峪关**
Jiayuguan Fort	Jiāyùguān Chénglóu	嘉峪关城楼
Wei-Jin Tombs	Wèi-Jìn Líng	魏晋陵
JIUHUA SHAN	**Jiǔhuá Shān**	**九华山**
Sweet Dew Monastery	Gānlù Sì	甘露寺
Heavenly Terrace Mountain	Tiāntái Shān	天台山
Phoenix Pine	Fènghuáng Sōng	凤凰松
KAIFENG	**Kāifēng**	**开封**
Dragon Pavilion Park	Lóngtíng Gōngyuán	龙亭公园
Iron Pagoda	Tiě Tǎ	铁塔
Kaifeng Museum	Kāifēng Bówùguǎn	开封博物馆
Lord Bao Lake	Bāogōng Hú	包公湖
Qingming Up the River Park	Qīngmíng Shànghé Yuán	清明上河园
Purity and Truth Synagogue	Qīng Zhēn Sì	清真寺
Grand Xiangguo Monastery	Dà Xiàngguó Sì	大相国寺
KASHGAR	**Kāshí**	**喀什**

English	Pinyin	Chinese
Abakh Hoja Tomb	Xiāngfēi Mù	香妃墓
Id Kah Mosque	Àití Gǎ'ěr Qīngzhēn Sì	艾提噶尔清真寺
People's Park	Rénmín Gōngyuán	人民公园
KUNMING	**Kūnmíng**	**昆明**
Bamboo Temple	Qióngzhú Sì	筇竹寺
Dragon's Gate	Lóng Mén	龙门
Flower and Bird Market	Huā Niǎo Shìchǎng	花鸟市场
Grand View Park	Dàguān Gōngyuán	大观公园
Green Lake	Cuì Hú	翠湖
Lake Dian	Diānchí	滇池
Pavilion of the Three Purities	Sān Qīng Gé	三清阁
Stone Forest	Shí Lín	石林
Yuantong Temple	Yuántōng Sì	圆通寺
Yunnan Nationalities Village	Yúnnán Mínzú Cūn	云南民族村
Le Shan Buddha	Lè Shān Dàfó	乐山大佛
LONGMEN CAVES	**Lóngmén Shíkū**	**龙门石窟**
LIJIANG	**Lìjiāng**	**丽江**
Old Market Square	Sì Fāng Jiē	四方街
Dongba Museum	Dōngbā Bówùguǎn	东巴博物馆
Jade Dragon Snow Mountain	Yùlóng Xuěshān	玉龙雪山
Black Dragon Pool	Hēi Lóng Tán	黑龙潭
Mu Mansion	Mù Fǔ	木府
Lion Hill	Shīzi Shān	狮子山
LU SHAN	**Lú Shān**	**庐山**
Lushan Museum	Lú Shān Bówùguǎn	庐山博物馆

English	Pinyin	Chinese
Meilu Villa	Měilú Biésh	美庐别墅
Immortals Cave	Xiānrén Dòng	仙人洞
LUOYANG	**Luòyáng**	**洛阳**
MOGAO BUDDHIST CAVES	**Mògāo Shíkū**	**莫高石窟**
PUTUO SHAN	**Pǔtuó Shān**	**普陀山**
Front Temple	Pǔjì Sì	普济寺
Buddha's Head Peak	Fódǐng Shān	佛顶山
Enlightenment Temple	Huìjì Sì	蕙济寺
Rain Law Temple	Fǎyǔ Sì	法雨寺
Southern Gate of Heaven	Nán Tiān Mén	南天门
Voice of the Tide Cave	Cháoyǐn Dòng	潮音洞
QINGDAO	**Qīngdǎo**	**青岛**
Badaguan	Bàdàguān	八大关
Catholic Church	Tiānzhǔ Jiàotáng	天主教堂
Returning Waves Pavilion	Húilán Gé	回澜阁
Mount Láo	Láo Shān	崂山
Little Fish Hill Park	Xiǎoyú Shān Gōngyuán	小鱼山公元
Protestant Church	Jīdū Jiàotáng	基督教堂
Qingdao Welcome Guest House	Qīngdǎo Yíng Bīnguǎn	青岛迎宾馆
Signal Hill Park	Xìnhào Shān Gōngyuán	信号山公园
Zhan Bridge	Zhàn Qiáo	栈桥
QU FU	**Qūfù**	**曲阜**
Cemetery of Confucius	Kǒng Lín	孔林

English	Pinyin	Chinese
Confucius Mansion	Kǒng Fǔ	孔府
Temple of Confucius	Kǒng Miào	孔庙
SANJIANG	**Sānjiāng**	**三江**
Bridge of Wind and Rain	Fēngyǔ Qiáo	风雨桥
Dragon's Spine Rice Terraces	Lóngjǐ Tītián	龙脊梯田
Longsheng	Lóngshèng	龙胜
SHANGHAI	**Shànghǎi**	**上海**
The Bund	Wàitān	外滩
French Quarter	Fǎguó Zūjiè	法国租界
Huangpu River	Huángpǔ Jiāng	黄浦江
Huxin Ting Teahouse	Húxīn Tíng Chálóu	湖心亭茶楼
Jade Buddha Temple	Yùfó Sī	玉佛寺
Jin Jiang Hotel	Jǐn Jiāng Fàndiàn	锦江饭店
Nanjing Road	Nánjīng Lù	南京路
Old Town	Nán Shì	南市
Pudong Area	Pǔdōng Xīnqū	浦东新区
Shanghai History Museum	Shànghǎi Lìshǐ Bówùguǎn	上海历史博物馆
Temple to the Town God	Chéng Huáng Miào	城隍庙
Yu Garden	Yù Yuán	豫园
SONG SHAN	**Sōng Shān**	**嵩山**
Central Peak Temple	Zhōngyuè Miào	中岳庙
Shao Lin Monastery	Shào Lín Sì	少林寺
Song Yue Pagoda	Sōngyuè Tǎ	嵩岳塔
SUZHOU	**Sūzhōu**	**苏州**

English	Pinyin	Chinese
Forest of Lions Garden	Shīzi Lín	狮子林
Humble Administrator's Garden	Zhuō Zhèng Yuán	拙政园
Lingering Garden	Liú Yuán	留园
Master of the Nets Garden	Wǎng Shī Yuán	网师园
Museum of Suzhou Embroidery	Sūxiù Yánjiū Suǒ	丝绣研究所
Temple of Mystery	Xuán Miào Guàn	玄妙观
Tiger Hill	Hǔ Qiū Shān	虎丘山
LAKE TAI	**Tài Hú**	**太湖**
Dingshu	Dīngshǔ	丁蜀
Dragon Light Pagoda	Lóng Guāng Tǎ	龙光塔
Jichang Garden	Jìchàng Yuán	寄畅园
Li Garden	Lí Yuán	蠡园
Ling Shan Buddha	Líng Shān Dàfó	灵山大佛
Shanjuan Cave	Shànjuǎn Dòng	善卷洞
Three Hills Island	Sān Shān Dǎo	三山岛
Turtle Head Isle	Yuántóuzhǔ	鼋头渚
Wuxi	Wúxī	无锡
Xihui Park	Xihuì Gōngyuán	锡惠公园
Yixing	Yíxīng	宜兴
Zhanggong Cave	Zhānggōng Dòng	张公洞
TAI SHAN	**Tài Shān**	**泰山**
First Gate	Yī Tiān Mén	一天门
Middle Gate	Zhōng Tiān Mén	中天门
South Gate	Nán Tiān Mén	南天门

English	Pinyin	Chinese
Stele Without Inscription	Wú Zì Bēi	无字碑
Tai'an Town	Tài'ān	泰安
Temple of the Jade Emperor	Yù Huáng Dǐng	玉皇顶
Temple of the Purple Dawn/Clouds	Bìxiá Cí	碧霞祠
TERRA-COTTA WARRIORS	**Bīngmǎyǒng**	**兵马俑**
TURPAN	**Tǔlǔfān**	**吐鲁番**
Astana Tombs	Ā sītǎnà Mùqún	阿斯塔那墓群
Bezeklik Thousand Buddha Caves	Bózīkèlīkè Qiānfódòng	柏孜克里克千佛洞
Emin Minaret	Émǐn Tǎ	额敏塔
Flaming Mountains	Huǒyàn Shān	火焰山
Gaochang Ancient City	Gāochāng	高昌
Jiaohe Ancient City	Jiāohé	交河
Karez Wells	Kǎn'ér Jǐng	坎儿井
Moon Lake	Àidǐng Hú	艾丁湖
ÜRÜMQI	**Wūlǔmùqí**	**乌鲁木齐**
Heavenly Lake	Tiān Chí	天池
Hong Shan Park	Hóng Shān Gōngyuán	红山公园
People's Park	Rénmín Gōngyuán	人民公园
Southern Mountains	Nán Shān	南山
WEIFANG	**Wéifāng**	**潍坊**
Weifang Kite Museum	Wéifāng Fēngzheng Bówùguǎn	潍坊风筝博物馆
Shijia Village	Shíjiā Zhuāng Mínsú Xīn Cūn	石家庄民俗新村

English	Pinyin	Chinese
WULINGYUAN	**Wǔlíngyuán; Zhāngjiā Jiè**	**武陵源; 张家界**
WUTAI SHAN	**Wǔtái Shān**	**五台山**
Pusa Ding Temple	Púsà Dǐng Sì	菩萨顶寺
Southern Peak Temple	Nán Shān Sì	南山寺
Xiantong Temple	Xiǎntōng Sì	显通寺
XIAMEN	**Xiàmén**	**厦门**
Garden Island	Gǔlàng Yǔ	鼓浪屿
Nan Putuo Temple	Nán Pǔtuó Sì	南普陀寺
Shuzhuang Garden	Shūzhuāng Huāyuán	菽庄花园
Sunlight Rock	Rìguāng Yán	日光岩
Xiamen City Museum	Xiàmén Shì Bówùguǎn	厦门市博物馆
Xiamen University	Xiàmén Dàxué	厦门大学
XI'AN	**Xī'ān**	**西安**
Banpo Museum	Bànpō Bówùguǎn	半坡博物馆
Bell Tower	Zhōng Lóu	钟楼
Big Wild Goose Pagoda	Dàyàntǎ	大雁塔
Catholic Church	Tiānzhǔ Jiàotáng	天主教堂
City Walls	Chéng Qiáng	城墙
Daoist Temple of the Eight Immortals	Bāxiān Guàn	八仙观
Drum Tower	Gǔ Lóu	鼓楼
Eastern Mountain Temple	Dōngyuè Miào	东岳庙
Forest of Stelae	Bēi Lín	碑林
Great Mosque	Dà Qīngzhēn Sì	大清真寺
Lama Temple	Guǎngrén Sì	广仁寺
Protestant Church	Jīdū Jiàotáng	基督教堂

English	Pinyin	Chinese
Reclining Dragon Zen Temple	Wòlóng Sì	卧龙寺
Shaanxi History Museum	Shǎnxī Lìshǐ Bówùguǎn	陕西历史博物馆
Small Wild Goose Pagoda	Xiǎo Yàn Tǎ	小雁塔
YANGSHUO	**Yángshuò**	**阳朔**
Fuli	Fúlì	福利
Green Lotus Peak	Bìlián Fēng	碧莲峰
Moon Mountain	Yuèliang Shān	月亮山
Xingping	Xīngpíng	兴坪
YANGZI RIVER	**Cháng Jiāng**	**长江**
Fengdu	Fēngdū	酆都
Red Cliff	Chìbì	赤壁
Three Gorges Dam	Sān Xiá	三峡
Three Little Gorges	Xiǎo Sān Xiá	小三峡
Yueyang Tower	Yuèyáng Tǎ	岳阳塔

Mandarin Bare Essentials

English	Pinyin	Chinese
Greetings & Introductions		
Hello	Nǐ hǎo	你好
How are you?	Nǐ hǎo ma?	你好吗？
Fine. And you?	Wǒ hěn? hǎo. Nǐ ne?	我很好你呢？
I'm not too well/things aren't going well	Bù hǎo	不好
What is your name? (very polite)	Nín guì xìng?	您贵姓？
My (family) name is . . .	Wǒ xìng . . .	我姓 . . .

English	Pinyin	Chinese
I'm known as (family, then given name) . . .	Wǒ jiào . . .	我叫
I'm an [American]	Wǒ shì [Měiguó] rén	我是美国人
I'm from [America]	Wǒ shì cóng [Měiguó] lái de	我是从美国来的
[Australian]	[Àodàlìyà]	澳大利亚
[British]	[Yīngguó]	英国
[Canadian]	[Jiānádà]	加拿大
[Irish]	[Àiěrlán]	爱尔兰
[New Zealander]	[Xīnxīlán]	新西兰
Excuse me/I'm sorry	Duìbùqǐ	对不起
I don't understand	Wǒ tīngbù dǒng	我听不懂
Thank you	Xièxie nǐ	谢谢你
Correct (yes)	Duì	对
Not correct	Bú duì	不对
No, I don't want	Wǒ búyào	我不要
Not acceptable	Bù xíng	不行

Basic Questions & Problems

English	Pinyin	Chinese
Excuse me/I'd like to ask	Qǐng wènyíxià	请问一下
Where is . . . ?	. . . zài nǎr?	. . . 在哪儿?
How much is . . . ?	. . . duōshǎo qián?	. . . 多少钱?
. . . this one?	Zhèi ge . . .	这个 . . .
. . . that one?	Nèi ge . . .	那个 . . .
Do you have . . . ?	Nǐ yǒu méi yǒu . . . ?	你有没有 . . . ?
What time does/ is . . . ?	. . . jǐ diǎn?	. . . 几点?
What time is it now?	Xiànzài jǐ diǎn?	现在几点?
When is . . . ?	. . . shénme shíhou?	. . . 什么时候?

English	Pinyin	Chinese
Why?	Wèishénme?	为什么？
Who?	Shéi?	谁？
Is that OK?	Xíng bù xíng?	行不行？
I'm feeling ill	Wǒ shēng bìng le	我生病了

Numbers

Note that more complicated forms of numbers are often used on official documents and receipts to prevent fraud—see how easily one could be changed to two, three, or even ten. Be particularly careful with *four* and *ten,* which sound very alike in many regions—hold up fingers to make sure. Note, too, that *yī,* meaning "one," tends to change its tone all the time depending on what it precedes. Don't worry about this—once you've started talking about money, almost any kind of squeak for "one" will do. Finally note that "two" alters when being used with expressions of quantity. Thankfully, familiar Arabic numerals also appear on bank notes, most signs, taxi meters, and so on.

zero	líng	零
one	yī	一
two	èr	二
two (of them)	liǎng ge	两个
three	sān	三
four	sì	四
five	wǔ	五
six	liù	六
seven	qī	七
eight	bā	八
nine	jiǔ	九
ten	shí	十
eleven	shí yī	十一
twelve	shí èr	十二
21	èr shí yī	二十一
22	èr shí èr	二十二

English	Pinyin	Chinese
51	wǔ shí yī	五十一
100	yì bǎi	一百
101	yì bǎi líng yī	一百零一
110	yì bǎi yī (shí)	一百一（十）
111	yì bǎi yī shí yī	一百一十一
1,000	yì qiān	一千
1,500	yì qiān wǔ bǎi	一千五百
5,678	wǔ qiān liù bǎi qī shí bā	五千六百七十八
10,000	yí wàn	一万

Money

The word *yuán* (¥) is rarely spoken, nor is *jiǎo,* the written form for one-tenth of a *yuán,* equivalent to 10 *fēn* (there are 100 *fēn* in a *yuán*). Instead, the Chinese speak of "pieces of money," *kuài qián,* usually abbreviated *kuài,* and they speak of *máo* for ¹⁄₁₀ *kuài. Fēn* have been overtaken by inflation, and are almost useless. Often all zeros after the last whole number are simply omitted, along with *kuài qián,* which is taken as read, especially in direct reply to the question *duōshǎo qián*—"How much?"

¥1	yí kuài qián	一块钱
¥2	liǎng kuài qián	两块钱
¥0.30	sān máo qián	三毛钱
¥5.05	wǔ kuài líng wǔ (fēn)	五块零五（分）
¥5.50	wǔ kuài wǔ	五块五
¥550	wǔ bǎi wǔ shí kuài	五百五十块
¥5500	wǔ qiān wǔ bǎi kuài	五千五百块
small change	língqián	零钱

Banking & Shopping

I want to change money (foreign exchange)	Wǒ xiǎng huàn qián	我想换钱
Credit card	Xìnyòng kǎ	信用卡
Traveler's check	lǔxíng zhīpiào	旅行支票

English	Pinyin	Chinese
Department store	bǎihuò shāngdiàn	百货商店
Convenience store	xiǎomàibù	小卖部
Market	shìchǎng	市场
May I have a look?	Wǒ Kànyixia, hǎo ma?	我看一下，好吗？
I want to buy . . .	Wǒ xiǎng mǎi . . .	我想买...
How many do you want?	Nǐ yào jǐ ge?	你要几个？
Two of them	liǎng ge	两个
Three of them	sān ge	三个
One kilo (2.2 lbs.)	yì gōngjǐn	一公斤
Half a kilo	yì jīn; bàn gōngjǐn	一斤；半公斤
One meter (3.28 ft.)	yì mǐ	一米
Too expensive!	Tài guì le!	太贵了！
Do you have change?	Yǒu língqián ma?	有零钱吗？

Time

morning	shàngwǔ	上午
afternoon	xiàwǔ	下午
evening	wǎnshang	晚上
7:00am	shàngwǔ qī diǎn zhōng	上午七点种
8:20am	shàngwǔ bā diǎ èr shí fēn	上午八点二十分
9:30am	shàngwǔ jiǔ diǎn bàn	上午九点半
noon	zhōngwǔ	中午
4:15pm	xiàwǔ sì diǎn yí kè	下午四点一刻
midnight	wǔ yè	午夜
one hour	yí ge xiǎoshí	一个小时
eight hours	bā ge xiǎoshí	八个小时
today	jīntiān	今天

English	Pinyin	Chinese
yesterday	zuótiān	昨天
tomorrow	míngtiān	明天
Monday	Xīngqī yī	星期一
Tuesday	Xīngqī èr	星期二
Wednesday	Xīngqī sān	星期三
Thursday	Xīngqī sì	星期四
Friday	Xīngqī wǔ	星期五
Saturday	Xīngqī liù	星期六
Sunday	Xīngqī tiān	星期天

Transport

English	Pinyin	Chinese
I want to go to . . .	Wǒ xiǎng qù . . .	我想去 . . .
plane	fēijī	飞机
train	huǒchē	火车
bus	gōnggòng qìchē	公共汽车
long distance bus	chángtú qìchē	长途汽车
taxi	chūzū chē	出租车
airport	fēijīchǎng	飞机场
stop or station (bus or train)	zhàn	站
(plane/train/bus) ticket	piào	票

Navigation

English	Pinyin	Chinese
North	Běi	北
South	Nán	南
East	Dōng	东
West	Xī	西
turn left	zuǒ guǎi	左拐
turn right	yòu guǎi	右拐

English	Pinyin	Chinese
go straight on	yìzhí zǒu	一直走
crossroads	shízì lùkǒu	十字路口
10 kilometers	shí gōnglǐ	十公里
I'm lost	Wǒ diū le	我丢了

Hotel

How many days?	Zhù jǐ tiān?	住几天？
standard room (twin or double with private bath)	biāozhǔn jiān	标准间
passport	hùzhào	护照
deposit	yājīn	押金
I want to check out	Wǒ tuì fáng	我退房

Restaurant

How many people?	Jǐ wèi?	几位
waiter/waitress	fúwùyuán	服务员
menu	càidān	菜单
I'm vegetarian	Wǒ shì chīsù de	我是吃素的
Do you have . . . ?	Yǒu méi yǒu . . . ?	有没有 . . . ？
Please bring a portion of . . .	Qǐng lái yí fènr . . .	请来一份儿 . . .
Beer	píjiǔ	啤酒
Mineral water	kuàngquán shuǐ	矿泉水
Bill, please	jiézhàng	结帐

INDEX

A

Abakh Hoja Tomb (Xiāngfēi Mù; Kashgar), 453–454
Aberdeen (Hong Kong), 200–202
Accommodations, tips on, 611–612
Agricultural Bank Building (Shànghǎi), 109
Aidīng Hú (Moon Lake), 435
Airlines, 605–607
Ai Tan, 258
Aití Gǎ'ěr Qīngzhēn Sì (Id Kah Mosque; Kashgar), 456
Ancient Observatory (Gǔ Guānxiàngtái; Běijīng), 16
Antiques, Shànghǎi, 112
Aoyú Fēng (Turtle Summit), 469
Apricot Terrace (Xìng Tán; Qūfù), 89
Arch of Eternal Spring (Wàngǔ Chángchūn Fáng; Qūfù), 90
Astana Tombs (Āsītǎnà Mùqún), 438–439
ATMs (automated teller machines), 600–601

B

Bādàguān District (Qīngdǎo), 70–71
Bādálǐng, Great Wall at, 34–36, 39
Bādōng, 586
Bái Causeway (Hángzhōu), 141
Báidì Chéng, 588
Báidì Temple, 588
Bái Jūyì, 141, 144, 488, 557
Bǎilóng Pearl City, 350
Báishā, 402
Báisuì Gōng (Centenarian Monastery), 509

Báiyún Guàn (White Cloud Temple; Běijīng), 15
Bamboo Temple (Qióngzhú Sì; Kūnmíng), 363
Bànpō Museum (Bànpō Bówùguǎn; Xī'ān), 242
Banyan Lake (Róng Hú; Guìlín), 318–319
Bǎochū Pagoda (Hángzhōu), 147–148
Bǎodǐng Shān (Treasure Peak Mountain; Dàzú), 283–288
Bǎogōng Hú (Lord Bāo Lake), 255–256
Bǎo Hé Diàn (Hall of Preserving Harmony; Běijīng), 10
Bāshān Stone City, 402
Bāxiān Guàn (Daoist Temple of the Eight Immortals; Xī'ān), 240
Beaches
  Gǔlàng Yǔ (Garden Island), 176
  Hong Kong, 211, 212–213
  Qīngdǎo, 71–72
  Silver Beach (Yíntān), 351–352
Beach Number 6 (Qīngdǎo), 71
Běichéng Lóu (Dàlǐ), 383
Běihǎi, 347–357, 467
  practical information, 354
Běijīng, 3–32
  bars and teahouses, 19–20
  markets, 17–18
  practical information, 20
  shopping on Wángfǔjǐng Street, 18–19
  sights and attractions, 3–16
  streets and alleys, 16–17

Běi Lín (Hall of the Forest of Stelae; Xī'ān), 233
Bell Tower (Kūnmíng), 364
Bell Tower (Zhōng Lóu; Xī'ān), 234, 235
Bezeklik Thousand Buddha Caves (Bózīkèlīkè Qiānfódòng; Turpan), 436–438
Bicycling, 611
Big Buddha (Hong Kong), 212
Big Wild Goose Pagoda (Dàyàntǎ; Xī'ān), 232, 237–238
Bìlián Fēng (Green Lotus Peak; Yángshuò), 314, 333–334
Bīnjiāng Dàdào (Riverside Promenade; Shànghǎi), 104
Bīnyáng Caves (Bīnyáng Sāndòng), 266
Bìshǔ Shān Zhuāng (Mountain Villa for Escaping the Summer Heat; Chéngdé), 42–44
Bìxiá Cí (Temple of the Purple Dawn/Clouds), 538
Black Dragon Pool Park (Hēi Lóng Tán; Lìjiāng), 398–399
Boat tours and cruises
  Dolphinwatch cruise (Hong Kong), 209–210
  Grand Canal (Dà Yùnhé), 171
  Great Buddha of Lèshān (Lè Shān Dàfó), 305–306
  Hong Kong, 201
  Huángpǔ River (Shànghǎi), 108–109

Boat tours and cruises (cont.)
Lí River, 312–314, 325
Xiàmén, 178–179
Yángshuò, 332
Yángzǐ River
(Chángjiāng), 577–593
Bogda Peak, 448
Book-Reading Cave (Guìlín),
316
Botanical gardens
Hángzhōu, 147
Lú Shān, 486
Shànghǎi, 115
Bridge Across the Sky
(Tiānqiáoshēngkōng),
479–480
Bridge of Great Being, 530
Bridge of Nine Turnings
(Hángzhōu), 145
The Bridge of the Immortals
(Xiānrénqiáo), 480
Bridge of Wind and Rain
(Fēngyǔ Qiáo; Chéngyáng),
340–341
Bridge to Heaven (Dùxiān
Qiáo), 466
Bright Summit Crest
(Guāngmíng Dǐng), 469
British Embassy (Běihǎi), 350
British Embassy building
(Xiàmén), 175
Brocade Hill (Diécǎi Shān;
Guìlín), 316
Broken Bridge (Duàn Qiáo;
Hángzhōu), 144
Buckland Foreign Language
School (Yángshuò), 332
Buddha's Head Peak (Fódǐng
Shān), 52, 529, 638,
639–640. See also specific
temples
Bezeklik Thousand
Buddha Caves
(Bózīkèlǐkè
Qiānfódòng; Turpan),
436–438
Big Buddha (Hong
Kong), 212
Cave of Ten Thousand
Buddhas (Wànfó
Dòng), 267
Dàzú sacred carvings,
283–288
Five Buddhas of the
Five Directions
(Dàtóng), 56

Great Buddha of Lèshān
(Lè Shān Dàfó),
304–307
Jade Buddha Temple
(Yùfó Sì; Shànghǎi),
115
Líng Shān Buddha, 162
Maitreya Buddha (the
Laughing Buddha),
644
Mògāo caves (near
Dūnhuáng), 428–434
Oriental Buddha Park
(Dōngfāng Fódū), 306
Reclining Buddha (Wòfó;
Dàzú), 285–286
Tantric, 47, 284, 431, 432
temples, 644
The Bund (Shànghǎi),
97, 100, 109–110
Bus travel, 608–609

C

Cafe de Jack (Dàlǐ), 380
Cáicūn, 385
Camel Hill (Luòtuo Shān;
Guìlín), 320
Cángjīng Kū, 432
Cānglàng Isle (Chéngdé), 44
Cāng Shān (Green
Mountains; Dàlǐ), 384
Canton. See Guǎngzhōu
Cantonese cuisine, 186,
188–189
Canton's Peasant Movement
Institute (Guǎngzhōu), 183
Capital Airport (Běijīng), 20
Carp's Backbone Ridge (Jìyú
Bèi), 470
Car travel, 610
Catholic church (Kūnmíng),
367–368
Catholic church (Tiānzhǔ
Jiàotáng)
Qīngdǎo, 72
Xī'ān, 241–242
Cat Street (Lascar Row; Hong
Kong), 203, 204
Cave houses (Dàtóng), 59–60
Cave of Full Enlightenment
(Dàzú), 287
Cave of Ten Thousand
Buddhas (Wànfó Dòng),
267

Caves
Bezeklik Thousand
Buddha Caves
(Bózīkèlǐkè
Qiānfódòng; Turpan),
436–438
Cave of Full
Enlightenment (Dàzú),
287
Dragon Darkness Cave
(Lóngyǐn Dòng;
Guìlín), 320
Immortals Cave (Xiānrén
Dòng; Lú Shān),
487–488
Lóngmén (Dragon's
Gate), 264–269
Bīnyáng (Bīnyáng
Sāndòng), 266
Cave of Ten
Thousand
Buddhas (Wànfó
Dòng), 267
Fire-Burnt Cave
(Huǒ Shāo Dòng),
268
Gǔyáng Cave
(Gǔyáng Dòng),
268
Honoring Ancestors
Cave (Fèngxiān
Sì), 267–268
Lùdòng, 268
Medicine Cave (Yào
Fáng Dòng), 268
Stone Room Temple
Cave (Shí Kù Sì
Dòng), 268
Mògāo (near Dūnhuáng),
428–434
Moon-in-the-Water Cave
(Shuǐ Yuè Dòng;
Guìlín), 312
Reed Flute Cave (Lúdí
Yán; Guìlín), 319–322
Seven-Star Cave (Qīxīng
Yán; Guìlín), 319
Yellow Dragon
(Huánglóng) Cave,
480–481
Cedar Lake (Shān Hú;
Guìlín), 318
Cemetery of Confucius (Kǒng
Lín; Qūfù), 90–91
Centenarian Monastery
(Báisuì Gōng), 509

Central District (Hong Kong), 197

Central Grottoes (Dàtóng), 53

Central Peak Temple (Zhōngyuè Miào), 567–568

Ceramic Exhibition Hall (Táocí Bówùguǎn; Dǐngshū), 161

Chairman Máo Badge Museum and Research Facility (Chéngdū), 297–299

Chairman Máo Memorial Hall (Máo Zhǔxí Jìniàn Táng; Běijīng), 7

Chairman Máo's Villa (Máo Zédōng Biéshù; Wǔhàn), 581

Cháng Chūn Yuán (Garden of Eternal Spring; Běijīng), 13

Cháng Láng (Long Corridor; Běijīng), 11

Chángshā, 481

Cháotiān Mén (Gate to Heaven; Chóngqìng), 276–277

Cháoyīn Dòng (Voice of the Tide Cave), 530

Chariots, at Museum of the Terra-Cotta Warriors and Horses of Qín Shǐ Huáng, 251–252

Chéngdé, 41–50
 practical information, 47
 sights and attractions, 42–47

Chéngdū, 290–303
 practical information, 299
 sights and attractions, 291, 294–299
 teahouses, 290–291

Chéngdū Zoo, 295

Chéng Huáng Miào (Temple to the Town God; Shànghǎi), 112

Chéngyáng, 341–342
 bridge at, 340–341

Chén Má Pó Dòufu Restaurant (Chéngdū), 294–295

Cheung Chau Island (Hong Kong), 210

Cheung Sha (Long Sands; Hong Kong), 212–213

Chiang Kai-shek, 183, 486, 564, 580, 633, 636

Chime Bells of Duke Yǐ of Zōng (Wǔhàn), 580–581

China Foreign Exchange Trade System Building (Shànghǎi), 109–110

China Research Base of Giant Panda Breeding (Dàxióngmāo Fánzhí Zhōgxīn; Chéngdū), 295–296

Chinese language, 646–668

Chinese Tea Museum (Zhōngguó Chá Yè Bówùguǎn; near Dragon Well Village), 150

Chóngqìng, 272–282, 589–590
 industry, 273–276
 population and pollution, 272–273
 practical information, 279
 sights and attractions, 276–278

Chóngqìng Museum (Chóngqìng Bówùguǎn), 278

Christianity, 642–643

Christians, 638–639

Chuān Shān (Pierced Hill; Guìlín), 313, 316

Chǔbǐ Shēnghuā (Flower Growing Out of a Writing Brush), 467–468

Chūnyáng Gōng (Hall of the Pure Sun), 502–503

Chun Yuan Palace (Héng Shān), 503

Churches
 Qīngdǎo, 72
 Xī'ān, 241–242

Church of Saint Sophia (Shèng Suǒfēiyà Jiàotáng; Harbin), 64

Cíguāng Gé (Merciful Light Temple), 470

Circle dance, Shíjiā Village, 80

City of Heaven Peak (Tiāndū Fēng), 470

Cíxǐ, Empress Dowager, 11, 260, 636

Clay Figurine Factory (Wúxī), 158

Clean Vase Lying in the River (Jìngpíng Shān; Guìlín), 313

Clock Museum (Běijīng), 10

Clothing, 625

Cloud-Dispelling Hall (Páiyún Diàn; Běijīng), 11

Cloud-Dispelling Pavilion (Páiyúntíng), 468

Cloud Rock Pagoda (Yúnyán Tǎ; Sūzhōu), 134

Cold Mountain Temple (Hánshān Sì; near Sūzhōu), 168

Commending Happiness Temple (Jiànfú Sì; Xī'ān), 236

Communist Revolution, Monument to the People's Heroes (Běijīng), 7

Confucianism, 638, 640–641

Confucian Mansion (Kǒng Fǔ; Qūfù), 89–90

Confucian Temple (Wén Miào; Harbin), 64

Confucian Temple (Wénmiào Lù; Shànghǎi), 115

Confucius (Kǒng Fūzǐ), 86–91, 636, 640
 Cemetery of (Kǒng Lín; Qūfù), 90–91
 Temple of (Xī'ān), 233

Connections (guānxi), 622

Coral Beach (Kwun Yum Wan; Hong Kong), 211

Cormorant fishing, Yángshuò, 332

Courtesy, 621

Credit cards, 600

Crescent Moon Hill (Yuèyà Shān; Guìlín), 320

Crescent Moon Lake (Yuèyá Quán), 423

Cuì Hú (Green Lake; Kūnmíng), 362

Cuì Hú Lù (Green Lake Road; Kūnmíng), 362

Cuisine, Cantonese, 186, 188–189

Cultural Relic Archive (Běijīng), 11

Cultural Revolution (1966–76), 634

Currency, 600

Customs, etiquette, and attitudes, 619–625

Customs House (Shànghǎi), 109

D

Dàbǎnchéng, 445
Dàchéng Hall (Qūfù), 89
Dàdiéshuǐ Waterfall, 373
Dàfó Sì (Lèshān), 307
Dà Fó Wān (Great Buddha
 Cove; Dàzú), 284
Dàguān Gōngyuán (Grand
 View Park; Kūnmíng),
 365–366
Dàguān Pavilion (Tower of
 the Magnificent View;
 Kūnmíng), 365–366
Dài Temple (Dài Miào; Tài
 Shān), 534–536
Dàlǐ, 379–393
 cafe life, 379–380
 Ěrhǎi Lake (Ěrhǎi Hú),
  385–386
 Old Dàlǐ, 381–382
 Old Shopping Street
  (Fùxīng Lù), 382–383
 pagodas, 383–384
 practical information, 388
Dàlǐ Cultural Center and
 Library, 382
Dàlǐ Museum, 382
Dàníng River, 586
Daoism (Taoism), 638, 639,
 645
Daoist Temple of the Eight
 Immortals (Bāxiān Guān;
 Xī'ān), 240
Dàolǐ Qū (Old Town;
 Harbin), 63–64
Dà Qīngzhēn Sì (Great
 Mosque; Xī'ān), 238–239
Dàtóng, 51–62
 city wall, 56
 practical information, 61
 sights and attractions,
  51–60
Dà Xiàngguó Sì (Grand
 Xiàngguó Monastery;
 Kāifēng), 260
Dà Xióng Bǎo Diàn (Powerful
 Treasure Hall; Dàtóng), 56
Dàxióngmāo Fánzhí Zhōgxīn
 (China Research Base of
 Giant Panda Breeding;
 Chéngdū), 295–296
Dàyàntǎ (Big Wild Goose
 Pagoda; Xī'ān), 237–238
Dà Yùnhé (Grand Canal),
 166–171

Déhé Yuán (Garden of Virtue
 and Harmony; Běijīng), 11
Déhuì Mén (East Entrance
 Gate; Chéngdé), 42–43
Dèng Xiǎopíng, 626, 634,
 636
Dé Yuè Lóu (Moon Pavilion;
 Lìjiāng), 399
Diamond Sutra, 430, 432, 537
Diǎnchūn Cottage (Diǎnchūn
 Táng; Sūzhōu), 133
Diān (Diānchí), Lake, 365,
 366
Diécǎi Shan (Brocade Hill;
 Guìlín), 316
Dǐngshān, Lake, 116
Dǐngshū, 160–161
Dirt Market (Pānjiā Yuán;
 Běijīng), 17–18
Dìzàng (God of the
 Mountain), 506, 508–510,
 512
Dolphins, pink (Hong Kong),
 208–210
Dōngbā Cultural Research
 Institute (Dōngbā Wénhuà
 Yánjiùsuǒ; Lìjiāng), 399
Dōngbā Museum (Lìjiāng),
 399–400
Dōngbā Song and Dance
 Theater (Dōngbā Gōng;
 Lìjiāng), 398
Dōngběi Hǔ Línyuán
 (Siberian Tiger Park;
 Harbin), 66–67
Dōng Dàjiē (Xī'ān), 232, 241
Dōngfāng Fódū (Oriental
 Buddha Park), 306
Dōngfāng Hotel (Shànghǎi),
 110
Dōng Lín Sì (Temple of the
 Eastern Grove; Lú Shān),
 488
Dòng people, 338, 340
Dōng Sì Tǎ (East Pagoda;
 Kūnmíng), 368
Dòngtíng, 582
Dōngyuè Miào (Eastern
 Mountain Temple; Xī'ān),
 240
Dòujī Shān (Fighting Cock
 Hill; Guìlín), 313
Dragon Darkness Cave
 (Lóngyín Dòng; Guìlín),
 320

Dragon Light Pagoda (Lóng
 Guāng Tǎ; Wúxī), 157
Dragon Pavilion Park
 (Lóngtíng Gōngyuán;
 Kāifēng), 256
Dragon's Gate (Lóng Mén;
 Kūnmíng), 366–367
Dragon's Spine Rice Terraces
 (Lóngjǐ Tītián), 339
Dragon Well (Lóngjǐng),
 149–151
Dragon Woman's Peak,
 477–478
Drum Tower (Běijīng), 16–17
Drum Tower (Gǔ Lóu;
 Xī'ān), 234, 235
Drum Tower Night Market
 (Gǔlóu Yèshì; Kāifēng),
 263
Duàn Qiáo (Broken Bridge;
 Hángzhōu), 144
Dù Fǔ, 291, 588, 636
 cottage (Chéngdū), 291
Dūnhuáng, 421–422
 Mògāo caves near,
  428–434
Duōbǎo Tǎ, 527–528
Dùxiān Qiáo (Bridge to
 Heaven), 466
Dùxiān Sòng, 466
Dú Xiù Fēng (Solitary Beauty
 Peak; Guìlín), 315–316,
 318
Dynasties, 628–633

E

East Entrance Gate (Déhuì
 Mén; Chéngdé), 42–43
Eastern Grottoes (Dàtóng), 53
Eastern Hàn Dynasty
 (A.D. 25–220), 306, 488
Eastern Mountain Temple
 (Dōngyuè Miào; Xī'ān),
 240
East Pagoda (Dōng Sì Tǎ;
 Kūnmíng), 368
East Shànghǎi (Pǔdōng),
 102–104
Echo Wall (Huíyīn Bì;
 Běijīng), 13
Economy of China, 594–596
Electricity, 615
Elephant Trunk Hill (Xiàngbí
 Shān; Guìlín), 312, 318
E-mail and Internet access,
 615–616

Éméi Shān (Eyebrow Mountain), 543–553

Éméi Shān (Lèshān), 306

Emin Minaret (near Turpan), 439–440

Enlightenment Nunnery (Guānyǐn Sì), 512

Enlightenment Temple (Huìjì Sì), 529

Ěrhǎi Lake (Ěrhǎi Hú; Dàlǐ), 385–386

Eyebrow Mountain (Éméi Shān), 543–553

F

Fairy Island (Tài Hú Xiāndǎo), 159

Family and social customs, 623–625

Far north, 67

Faxes, 616

Fǎ Xiǎn, 412

Fǎyǔ Sì (Rain Law Temple), 530

Fēilái Fēng (Peak That Flew from Afar), 148

Fēilái Shí (Stone That Flew from Afar), 469

Fēngdū, 588, 589

Fènghuáng Sōng (Phoenix Pine), 510–511

Fèngjié, 588

Fèngxiān Sì (Honoring Ancestors Cave), 267–268

Fēngyǔ Qiáo (Bridge of Wind and Rain; Chéngyáng), 340–341

Fēngzheng Bówùguǎn (Wéifǎng Kite Museum), 79

Fighting Cock Hill (Dòujī Shān; Guìlín), 316

Fire-Burnt Cave (Huǒ Shāo Dòng), 268

The First Gate of Heaven (Yī Tiān Mén), 536–537

First Gate of the Forest (Qūfù), 90

First Mountain of the World (Sōng Shān), 565–566

Fishing, cormorant (Yángshuò), 332

Five Buddhas of the Five Directions (Dàtóng), 56

Five Dynasties (A.D. 907–960), 429, 431, 432

Five Phoenix Hall (Wu Fēng Lóu; Lìjiāng), 399

Five Platforms Mountain (Wǔtái Shān), 431, 432, 491–499

Five Rams, Statue of (Guǎngzhōu), 183, 186

Flaming Mountains (Huǒyàn Shān), 436

Flood Control Monument (Harbin), 66

Flower and Bird Market (Huā Niǎo Shìchǎng; Kūnmíng), 359

Flower and Bird Pavilion (Hángzhōu), 145

Flower Bridge (Huāqiáo; Guìlín), 319

Flower Dragon Bridge (Hu Lóng Qiáo), 284

Flower Growing Out of a Writing Brush (Chǔbǐ Shēnghuā), 467–468

Flower Harbor Park (Huāgǎng Yuán; Hángzhōu), 147

Flower Pagoda (Huā Tǎ; Guǎngzhōu), 186

Fódǐng Shān (Buddha's Head Peak), 529

Forbidden City (Gù Gōng Bówùguǎn; Běijīng), 8–10

Forest of Lions Garden (Shīzi Lín; Sūzhōu), 130

Forest of Stelae (Guìhǎi Bēilín; Guìlín), 320

Forest of Stelae (Xī'ān), 232, 233–234

Forest of Stupas (Tǎlín), 570

Four Iron Guards, 568

French cathedral (Wéizhōu Island), 353–354

French Concession (Frenchtown; Shànghǎi), 113–114

Friendship Store (Běijīng), 17

Front Palace (Zhèng Gōng; Chéngdé), 43

Front Temple (Pǔjì Sì), 527–528

Fúbō Shān (Whirlpool Hill; Guìlín), 316

Fùhuá Amusement Park (Dōngfāng Lu), 84

Fúlì, 333

Fùxīng Lù (Old Shopping Street; Dàlǐ), 382–383

G

Gānlù Sì (Sweet Dew Monastery), 507–508

Gāochāng (Kharakhoja), 438–439

Garden Hotel (Shànghǎi), 113–114

Garden Island (Gǔlàng Yǔ; Xiàmén), 174–177

Garden of Eternal Spring (Cháng Chūn Yuán; Běijīng), 13

Garden of Ten Thousand Trees (Wànshù Yuán; Chéngdé), 45

Garden of Virtue and Harmony (Déhé Yuán; Běijīng), 11

Gardens. See also Botanical gardens

Forest of Lions Garden (Shīzi Lín; Sūzhōu), 130–131

Garden of Eternal Spring (Cháng Chūn Yuán; Běijīng), 13

Garden of Ten Thousand Trees (Wànshù Yuán; Chéngdé), 45

Garden of Virtue and Harmony (Déhé Yuán; Běijīng), 11

Golden Temple Camellia Garden (Kūnmíng), 364

of the Grand Canal, 157–158

Grand View Garden (Lake Dǐngshān), 116

International Horticultural Exposition Park (Kūnmíng), 365

Jìcháng Garden (Jìcháng Yuán; Wúxī), 157–158

Lingering Garden (Liú Yuán; Sūzhōu), 131

Líyuán (Wúxī), 158

Master of the Nets Garden (Wǎng Shī Yuán; Sūzhōu), 132–133

Shūzhuāng (Xiàmén), 176

Sūzhōu, 128–129

Zhuō Zhèng Garden (Sūzhōu), 132

Gate of Heavenly Peace (Tiān'ān Mén), 8

Gate of Supreme Harmony (Tàihé Diàn; Běijīng), 8–9

Gate to Heaven (Cháotiān Mén; Chóngqìng), 276

Gathered Immortals Peak, 586

German Quarter (Qīngdǎo), 70–71

Ghost Market (Pānjiā Yuán; Běijīng), 17–18

Gifts, giving, 624

Goddess of Mercy (Guānyīn), 11, 74, 136, 149, 174, 186, 240, 260, 267, 285, 294, 366, 383, 432, 496, 512, 526, 529–532, 559, 581, 636, 644, 645

Goddess Peak, 586

Golden Helmet and Shining Armor Valley, 586

Golden Peak (Jīndǐng; Éméi Shān), 544

Golden Peak Chinese-Tibetan Temple (Jīn Dǐng Huá Zàng Sì), 546–547

Golden Temple Camellia Garden (Kūnmíng), 364

Golden Temple (Jīn Diàn; Kūnmíng), 363–365

Gold Mountain Temple (Jīnshān Sì; Chéngdé), 44

Gòng Gà Shān (Kūnlún range), 544

Grand Canal (Dà Yùnhé), 166–171
   cruises, 171
   gardens of, 157–158
   history of, 166–167

Grand Mosque (Xī'ān), 232

Grand Theater (Shànghǎi), 115

Grand View Garden (Lake Dīngshān), 116

Grand View Park (Dàguān Gōngyuán; Kūnmíng), 365

Grand Xiàngguó Monastery (Dà Xiàngguó Sì; Kāifēng), 260

Grape Gorge (Pútao Gōu), 440

Great Buddha Cove (Dà Fó Wān; Dàzú), 284

Great Buddha of Lèshān (Lè Shān Dàfó), 304–307

Great Leap Forward (1959), 634

Great Mosque (Dà Qīngzhēn Sì; Xī'ān), 238–239

Great Proletarian Cultural Revolution (1966–76), 634

Great Wall (Wàn Lǐ Cháng Chéng), 33–40
   at Bādálǐng, 34–36, 39
   end of, 416
   history of, 33–34
   at Jūyōngguān, 38–39
   at Mùtiányù, 36, 40
   orientation and when to go, 39
   at Sīmǎtái, 37–38, 40
   tours, 40
   traveling to, 39–40

Great Wall Museum (Jiāyùguān Fort), 417

Great White Tibetan Pagoda (Táihuái Village), 492

Green Cloud Nunnery, 511–512

Green Goat Temple (Qīngyáng Gōng; Chéngdū), 294

Green Lake (Cuì Hú; Kūnmíng), 362

Green Lake Road (Cuì Hú Lù; Kūnmíng), 362

Green Lotus Peak (Bìlián Fēng; Yángshuò), 314, 333–334

Green Mountains (Cāng Shān; Dàlǐ), 384

Guāngmíng Dǐng (Bright Summit Crest), 469

Guǎngrén Sì (Lama Temple; Xī'ān), 240

Guǎngxī Provincial Teachers' College (Guìlín), 316

Guǎngxī Zhuàngzú Autonomous Region, 321

Guǎngzhōu (Canton), 182–195
   practical information, 190

Guǎngzhōu Museum, 183

Guānxi (connections), 622

Guānyīn (Goddess of Mercy), 11, 74, 136, 149, 174, 186, 240, 260, 267, 285, 294, 366, 383, 432, 496, 512, 526, 529–532, 559, 581, 636, 644, 645

Guānyīn's Cliff, 519

Guānyīn Sì (Enlightenment Nunnery), 512

Gù Gōng Bówùguǎn (Forbidden City; Běijīng), 8–10

Gǔ Guānxiàngtái (Ancient Observatory; Běijīng), 16

Guìchí, 579

Guìhǎi Bēilín (Forest of Stelae; Guìlín), 320

Guìlín, 311–328
   Lí River (Lí Jiāng), 311–315
   practical information, 323

Guīyuán Temple (Guīyuán Sì; Wǔhàn), 581

Gǔlàng Yǔ (Garden Island; Xiàmén), 172, 174–177

Gǔlàng Yǔ Guesthouse compound (Xiàmén), 176

Gǔlíng, 484–485

Gǔ Lóu (The Drum Tower; Xī'ān), 234, 235

Gǔlóu Yèshì (Drum Tower Night Market; Kāifēng), 263

Gū Sǎo Cliff, 502

Gū Shān (Solitary Hill Island; Hángzhōu), 141

Gǔyáng Cave (Gǔyáng Dòng), 268

H

Hǎitōng, 304

Hall for Prayer for Good Harvests (Qínián Diàn; Běijīng), 14

Hall of Benevolence and Longevity (Rénshòu Diàn; Běijīng), 11

Hall of Harmony (Yōnghé Diàn; Běijīng), 14

Hall of Preserving Harmony (Bǎo Hé Diàn; Běijīng), 10

Hall of Supreme Harmony (Tài Hé Diàn; Běijīng), 9

Hall of the Fire God (Zhùróng Diàn), 520

Hall of the Forest of Stelae (Bēi Lín; Xī'ān), 233

Hall of the Pure Sun (Chūnyáng Gōng), 502–503

Hall of the Three Pure Ones (Sān Qīng; Sūzhōu), 136

Hall of the Three Purities
(Chéngdū), 294
Hall of Tranquility
(Běijīng), 13
Hall of Union (Jiāotài Diàn;
Běijīng), 10
Hammer Rock (Qīngchuí
Fēng; Chéngdé), 46–47
Hàn Dynasty (206 B.C.–
A.D. 220), 53, 88, 166,
229, 416, 631, 639
Hanging Monastery (Xuán
Kōng Sì; Dàtóng), 58–59
Hángzhōu, 140–156, 166
practical information, 151
sights and attractions,
141, 144–151
Hángzhōu Botanical Garden
(Hángzhōu Zhíwù Yuán),
147
Hángzhōu Silk and Satin
Printing and Dyeing
Complex (Hángzhōu), 151
Hán Yù, 311
Harbin, 63–69
parks and temples, 64–65
practical information, 68
Harbin Ice and Snow
Festival, 63
Health concerns, 602–603
Heavenly Lake (Tiān Chí),
446–448
Heavenly Staircase (Tiāntī),
511
Heavenly Terrace (Tiāntái
Shān), 509–510, 512
Hēi Lóng Tán (Black Dragon
Pool Park; Lìjiāng),
398–399
Héng Shān, 500–505
Héngshān Lù (Shànghǎi), 114
Héng Shān Nán Yuè,
515–524
Héng Zōng Monastery (Héng
Shān), 503
Hépíng Fàndiàn (Peace Hotel;
Shànghǎi), 102, 109
Héxī Corridor, 422
History of China, 628–635
Holidays, 616
Hollywood Road (Hong
Kong), 203, 204
Hong Kong, 196–226
Aberdeen, 201–202
beaches, 211, 212–213

Cheung Chau Island, 210
Kowloon Park, 203
Man Mo Temple, 204
practical information, 213
shopping, 202–204
shop-walking in
Kowloon, 202–203
Stanley, 205–206
Temple Street Night
Market, 205
Victoria Peak, 197,
200–201
Walled City, 207–208
Hong Kong Museum of
History, 203
Hóng Shān Park (Ürümqi),
445
Honoring Ancestors Cave
(Fèngxiān Sì), 267–268
Horse Testing Ground (Shìmǎ
Dài; Chéngdé), 45
Hóu Wáng Pō (Monkey King
Slope), 549
Huāgǎng Yuán (Flower Harbor
Park; Hángzhōu), 147
Huáihǎi Road (Shànghǎi), 113
Huà Jué Xiàng (Xī'ān), 235
Huánggài Fēng (Yellow
Umbrella Peak), 568
Huáng Hè Lóu (Yellow Crane
Tower; Wǔhàn), 581–582
Huánglóng (Yellow Dragon)
Cave, 480–481
Huángpǔ Park (Shànghǎi),
105
Huángpǔ River (Shànghǎi),
97, 105–109
Huáng Shān (Yellow
Mountain), 465–475,
579–580
Huā Niǎo Shìchǎng (Flower
and Bird Market;
Kūnmíng), 359
Huán Qiū (Round Altar;
Běijīng), 13
Huāqiáo (Flower Bridge;
Guìlín), 319
Huà Shān, 554–562
Huà Shān Kǒu Village,
554–555
Huāshí Lóu (Qīngdǎo), 71
Huā Tǎ (Flower Pagoda;
Guǎngzhōu), 186
Huáyán Monastery
(Dàtóng), 55

Húběi Provincial Museum
(Húběi Shěng Bówùguǎn;
Wǔhàn), 580
Húběi Shěng Bówùguǎn
(Húběi Provincial Museum;
Wǔhàn), 580
Húbīn Lù (Lakeside Avenue;
Hángzhōu), 144–145
Huìjì Sì (Enlightenment
Temple), 529
Huílàn Gé (Returning Waves
Pavilion; Qīngdǎo), 71–72
Huì Shān clay figures (Wúxī),
158
Huíyīn Bì (Echo Wall;
Běijīng), 13
Húlǐ Mountain Cannon
Platform (Xiàmén), 174
Hu Lóng Qiáo (Flower
Dragon Bridge), 284
Húnyuán, 58, 501–502
Huǒ Shāo Dòng (Fire-Burnt
Cave), 268
Huǒyàn Shān (Flaming
Mountains), 436
Hǔ Qiū Shān (Tiger Hill;
Sūzhōu), 133–134
Hǔtiào Xiá (Tiger Leaping
Gorge), 402
Hútòng Tour (Běijīng), 16
Húxīn Tíng Teahouse (Húxīn
Tíng Chálóu; Shànghǎi),
111

I

Ice and Snow Festival
(Harbin), 68
Id Kah Mosque (Aití Gǎ'ěr
Qīngzhēn Sì; Kashgar), 456
Immortals Cave (Xiānrén
Dòng; Lú Shān), 487–488
Imperial Carriageway
(Qūfù), 90
Imperial Examination
system, 87
Imperial Way (Kāifēng),
255–256
Insurance, 603
International Beer City
(Qīngdǎo), 73
International Horticultural
Exposition Park
(Kūnmíng), 365
International Passenger
Terminal (Shànghǎi), 106

Internet access, 615–616
Introspection Tower (Xī'ān), 239
Iron Mountain Garden (Tiěshān Gōngyuán; Qūfù), 90
Iron Pagoda (Tiě Tǎ; Kāifēng), 257–258
Islam, 638, 641–642. *See also* Mosques
Island of Small Seas (Xiǎoyáng Zhōu; Hángzhōu), 145

J

Jade Buddha Temple (Yùfó Sì; Shànghǎi), 115
Jade Gate (Yùmén), 413
Jade Screen Pavilion (Yùpíng Lóu), 469
Jade Spring Temple (Yùquán Sì), 555–556
Jade Waves Palace (Yùlán Táng; Běijīng), 11
Jade Woman (Bìxiá Yuán Jūn), 538–539
Jews of Kāifēng, 258–261
Jiànchí (Pool of Swords; Sūzhōu), 134
Jiànfú Sì (Commending Happiness Temple; Xī'ān), 236
Jiāng Zémín, 636
Jiāohé (Yarkhoto), 439
Jiāotài Diàn (Hall of Union; Běijīng), 10
Jiāyùguān, 416
Jiāyùguān Fort, 417–419
Jìcháng Garden (Jìcháng Yuán; Wúxī), 157–158
Jīdū Jiàotáng (Protestant church; Qīngdǎo), 72
Jīdū Jiàotáng (Protestant church; Xī'ān), 241
Jiěfàng Bēi (Liberation Monument; Chóngqìng), 276
Jílè Sì (Temple of Bliss; Harbin), 65
Jim's Peace Cafe (Dàlǐ), 380
Jīnbì Square (Kūnmíng), 367
Jīnbó Cable Car (Kūnmíng), 364–365
Jīn Diàn (Golden Temple; Kūnmíng), 363–365
Jīndǐng (Golden Peak; Éméi Shān), 544

Jīn Dǐng Huá Zàng Sì (Golden Peak Chinese-Tibetan Temple), 546–547
Jìn Dynasty (A.D. 265–316), 265
Jìngān Temple (Shànghǎi), 115
Jìngpíng Shān (Clean Vase Lying in the River; Guìlín), 313
Jìngshān Sì (Veneration of Goodness Temple) cave, 266
Jìng Shuǐ (Shrine of Limpid Waters), 543–544
Jīngzhōu, 583
Jìn Jiāng Hotel (Shànghǎi), 113
Jīn Mào Building (Shànghǎi), 104
Jīnshān Sì (Gold Mountain Temple; Chéngdé), 44
Jīnxīng Jiē (Lìjiāng), 397
Jiǔhuá Shān (Nine Glories Mountain), 506–514
Jiǔjiāng (Nine Rivers), 484, 488, 580
Jiǔ Lóng Bì (Nine Dragon Screen; Dàtóng), 56
Jiǔmǎhuà Shān (Nine-Horse Fresco Hill), 314
Jiǔ Tiān Palace (Héng Shān), 503
Jìyú Bēi (Carp's Backbone Ridge), 470
John's Information Cafe (Kashgar), 457
Jubilee Street (Hong Kong), 204
Jumbo (Hong Kong), 201–202
Jùnjí Peak (Jùnjí Fēng), 565–566
Jūyōngguān, Great Wall at, 38–40

K

Kāifēng, 166, 255–263
Jews of, 258–261
practical information, 261
Kāifēng Museum, 258
Kāngxī, 503
Kāngxī Emperor, 12, 41, 42, 44, 45, 53, 131, 141, 146, 256, 284, 366, 422, 494, 503, 526, 528, 530, 564, 636

Karez wells, 440
Kashgar, 452–464
market, 454–456
shopping, 454–457
Kazakhs, 435, 444–449
Kharakhoja (Gāochāng), 438–439
Kim Kiao Kak, 508–509
Kite factory, Yángjiābù, 80
Kite Festival, Wéifāng International, 80–82
Kite Museum, Wéifāng (Fēngzhēng Bówùguǎn), 79
Kites, origin and history of, 82–83
Kǒng Forest (Qūfù), 90
Kǒng Fǔ (Confucian Mansion; Qūfù), 89–90
Kǒng Fūzǐ (Confucius), 86–91, 636, 640
Cemetery of (Kǒng Lín; Qūfù), 90–91
Temple of (Xī'ān), 233
Kǒng Lín (Cemetery of Confucius; Qūfù), 90–91
Kǒng Miào (Temple of Confucius; Qūfù), 88
Kong Ming Tablet, 586
Kowloon Park (Hong Kong), 203
Kowloon Walled City Park (Hong Kong), 207–208
Koxinga (Zhèng Chénggōng), statue of (Xiàmén), 175–176
Kuí Xīng, 503
Kūnlún range (Gòng Gà Shān), 544
Kūnmíng, 358–378
downtown, 359, 362
Dragon's Gate (Lóng Mén), 366–367
East and West Pagodas, 367–368
parks and gardens, 364–366
practical information, 372
Stone Forest (Shí Lín), 369–371
temples, 363–365
Yúnnán Nationalities Village (Yúnnán Mínzú Cūn), 369
Kūnmíng Lake (Běijīng), 11
Kūnníng Gate (Běijīng), 10

Kūnníng Gōng (Palace of Earthly Tranquility; Běijīng), 10

Kwun Yum Wan (Coral Beach; Hong Kong), 211

L

Ladder Street (Hong Kong), 204

Lakeside Avenue (Húbīn Lù; Hángzhōu), 144–145

Lama Temple (Guǎngrén Sì; Xī'ān), 240

Lama Temple (Yōnghé Gōng; Běijīng), 14–15

Láncháo Gé (Qīngdǎo), 73

Language, Chinese, 646–668

Lantau Island (Hong Kong), 209, 212

Lǎo Mǔ Cave (Lǎo Mǔ Dòng), 566

Láo Shān (Mount Láo; Qīngdǎo), 73

Lǎozǐ, 265, 268, 294, 418, 558, 559, 628, 636, 639

Lascar Row (Cat Street; Hong Kong), 204

Laughing Buddha (Maitreya Buddha), 644

Lèshān, 304–308
  Great Buddha of (Lè Shān Dàfó), 304

Lesser Three Gorges (Xiǎo Sānxiá), 586

Liánhuā Dòng (Lotus Flower Cave), 267

Liánhu Fēng (Lotus Flower), 469

Lǐ Bái, 465, 471, 488, 508, 548, 581, 582, 586, 588, 637

Liberation Monument (Jiěfàng Bēi; Chóngqìng), 276

Liè Zūn, 428–429

Lìjiāng, 394–415
  Black Dragon Pool Park (Hēi Lóng Tán), 398–399
  Dōngbā Museum, 399–400
  Lion Hill (Shīzi Shān), 401–402

Mù Mansion (Mù Fǔ), 400–401

Nàxī music, 398

Old Town (Dàyán), 395–397

practical information, 403

Lìjiāng Nàxī Dōngbā Cultural Museum (Lìjiāng Dōngbā Wénhuà Bówùguǎn), 399–400

Lingering Garden (Lìú Yuán; Sūzhōu), 131

Líng Shān Buddha, 162

Língxīng Mén (Star Gate; Qūfù), 88

Língyǐn Temple (Temple of the Soul's Retreat; Hángzhōu), 148

Língyún (Lèshān), 307

Língyún Shān (Lèshān), 306

Lion Hill (Shīzi Shān; Lìjiāng), 401

Lǐ River (Lí Jiāng; Guìlín), 311–315

Literary Nourishment Pavilion (Wénjīn Gé; Chéngdé), 44

Little Fish Park (Xiǎoyú Shān Gōngyuán; Qīngdǎo), 73

Liù Róng Sì (Temple of the Six Banyan Trees; Guǎngzhōu), 186

Lìú Yuán (Lingering Garden; Sūzhōu), 131

Líyuán (Wúxī), 158

Li Yuen streets (Hong Kong), 203

Long Corridor (Cháng Láng; Běijīng), 11

Lóng Guāng Tǎ (Dragon Light Pagoda; Wúxī), 157

Lónghuá Temple (Shànghǎi), 115

Lóngjǐ, 339

Lóngjǐng (Dragon Well), 149–151

Lóngjǐng tea, 149

Lóngjǐ Tītián (Dragon's Spine Rice Terraces), 339

Lóng Mén (Dragon's Gate; Kūnmíng), 366–367

Lóngmén (Dragon's Gate) caves, 264–269

Long Sands (Cheung Sha; Hong Kong), 212–213

Lóngshèng, 338, 340

Lóngshèng Hot Spring (Wēn Quán), 342–343

Lóngtíng Gōngyuán (Dragon Pavilion Park; Kāifēng), 256

Lóngyǐn Dòng (Dragon Darkness Cave; Guìlín), 320

Looking to Heaven Pool (Yǎngtiān Chí), 558

Lord Bāo Lake (Bāogōng Hú), 255–256

Lotus Flower (Liánhu Fēng), 469

Lotus Flower Cave (Liánhuā Dòng), 267

Lotus Stirred by the Breeze (Hángzhōu), 146

Lù Bō Láng Restaurant (Shànghǎi), 111

Lúdí Yán (Reed Flute Cave; Guìlín), 319–322

Lùdòng, 268

Lùgū Lake (Lùgū Hú), 402

Lùjiāzuǐ Central Garden (Shànghǎi), 104

Lùjiāzuǐ Food Square (Shànghǎi), 104

Luóhàn Temple (Luóhàn Sì; Chóngqìng), 278

Luòtuo Shān (Camel Hill; Guìlín), 320

Luòyáng, 264, 265, 267, 269

Lú Shān, 484–490, 580

Lú Shān Museum (Lú Shān Bówùguǎn), 486

Lǔ Xùn (Shànghǎi), 115

Lǔ Xùn Park (Qīngdǎo), 71

M

Magnet Gorge (Dàtóng), 58

Máhǎo Tomb Museum (Máhǎo Yán Mù; Lèshān), 306

Maitreya Buddha (the Laughing Buddha), 14, 65, 149, 156, 291, 304
  near Hángzhōu, 148–149
  Mògāo caves (near Dūnhuáng), 431

Mandalas, 47, 284

Mandarin Duck Hall (Sūzhōu), 131

Man Mo Temple (Hong Kong), 204

Máopíng, 584
Máo Zédōng, 73, 183, 486, 494, 539, 633, 637
  Biéshù (Chairman Máo's Villa; Wǔhàn), 581
  Chairman Máo Badge Museum and Research Facility (Chéngdū), 297–299
  statue of (Chéngdū), 290
Máo Zhǔxí Jìniàn Táng (Chairman Máo Memorial Hall; Běijīng), 7
Mápó dòufu, 295
Marble Boat (Shífǎng; Běijīng), 11
Marco Polo, 82, 140, 145, 411, 412, 423, 452, 630, 632, 637
Markets
  Běijīng, 17–18
  Chéngdū, 294
  Guǎngzhōu, 186–187
  Kāifēng, 260–261
  Kashgar, 454–456
  Kūnmíng, 359
  Shāpíng Market, 387–388
  Wāsè Market, 386–387
Master of the Nets Garden (Wǎng Shī Yuán; Sūzhōu), 132–133
Medicine Cave (Yào Fáng Dòng), 268
Měilú Villa (Měilú Biéshù; Lú Shān), 486
Mèng Liáng's Ladder, 587
Merciful Light Temple (Cíguāng Gé), 470
Metric system, 616
The Middle Gate of Heaven (Zhōng Tiān Mén), 537–538
Míng Dynasty (1368–1644), 632–633
  Great Wall and, 33, 34, 36–39
Míng Dynasty Drum Tower (Xī'ān), 232
Míngshā Dune, 424
Míng Shān Peak, 589
Míngshā Shān (Singing Sands Mountains), 422–425
Minnie Mao's (Yángshuò), 329

Minorities Cultural Park (Mínsú Fēngqíng Yuán; Guìlín), 320
Mínsú Fēngqíng Yuán (Minorities Cultural Park; Guìlín), 320
Mínyuán, 510
Mògāo caves (near Dūnhuáng), 428–434
Money matters, 600–602
Monkey King Slope (Hóu Wáng Pō), 549
Monument to the People's Heroes (Běijīng), 7
Moon-in-the-Water Cave (Shuǐ Yuè Dòng; Guìlín), 312
Moon Lake (Aidīng Hú), 435
Moon Mountain (Yuèliang Shān), 330–332
Moon Pavilion (Dé Yuè Lóu; Lìjiāng), 399
Morning Beach (Tung Wan; Hong Kong), 211
Mosques
  Grand Mosque (Xī'ān), 232
  Great Mosque (Dà Qīngzhēn Sì; Xī'ān), 238–239
  Kashgar, 456–457
  Kūnmíng, 359
Mountains, 463–464
Mountain Villa for Escaping the Summer Heat (Bìshǔ Shān Zhuāng; Chéngdé), 42–44
Mount Láo (Láo Shān; Qīngdǎo), 73
Mount Sumeru Longevity and Happiness Temple (Xūmífúshòu Miào; Chéngdé), 45
Mó Yá Bēi (Táng Dynasty Rock Inscriptions), 538
Mr. China's Son Cultural Exchange Cafe (Dàlǐ), 384
Mù Mansion (Mù Fǔ; Lìjiāng), 400–401
Murray House (Hong Kong), 206
Museum of Sūzhōu Embroidery (Sūxiù Yánjiū Suǒ; Sūzhōu), 135–136

Museum of the Terra-Cotta Warriors and Horses of Qín Shǐ Huáng, 249–252
Muslim quarter (Xī'ān), 232, 239
Mùtiányù, Great Wall at, 36, 40

N

Nǎigǔ Stone Forest, 373
Nánchéng Lóu (Dàlǐ), 382–383
Nánjīng, 578–579
Nánjīng Dōnglù Bùxíng Jiē (Nánjīng East Pedestrian Mall; Shànghǎi), 101–102
Nánjīng Road (Shànghǎi), 97, 100–102
Nánjīng Yángzǐ River Bridge, 578
Nánpǔ Cable Bridge (Shànghǎi), 106
Nán Pǔtuó Temple (Xiàmén), 174
Nán Shān (Southern Mountains), 445
Nán Shān Sì (Southern Peak Temple; Wǔtái Shān), 496–497
Nán Shì (Shànghǎi), 110–111
Nán Tiān Mén (Southern Gate of Heaven), 520, 525–526, 538–539
Nánxiáng Dumpling Restaurant (Nánxiáng Mántou Diàn; Shànghǎi), 112
Nánxiáng Mántou Diàn (Nánxiáng Dumpling Restaurant; Shànghǎi), 112
Nán Yuè, 515–524
Nán Yuè Miào (Temple of the Southern Mountain), 515
Nathan Road (Hong Kong), 202
Nàxī Gǔyuèhuì (Nà Xī Music Research Institute; Lìjiāng), 398
Nà Xī Music Research Institute (Nàxī Gǔyuèhuì; Lìjiāng), 398
Nàxī people, 396–406
Nestorian Stele (Xī'ān), 234

New China Merchants Bank
(Shànghǎi), 109
New World Department Store
(Shànghǎi), 101
New World Shopping Centre
(Hong Kong), 202
Nguluko (Yùhú), 402
Nightlife, 614–615
Nine Dragon Screen (Jiǔ
Lóng Bì; Dàtóng), 56
Nine Glories Mountain
(Jiǔhuá Shān), 506–514
Nine-Horse Fresco Hill
(Jiǔmǎhuà Shān), 314
Níngbō, 525, 531, 532
Northern Sòng Dynasty
(A.D. 960–1127), 255, 256,
258, 261, 311, 432, 433,
632
Northern Wèi Dynasty
(A.D. 386–534), 51, 52, 55,
264, 265, 429, 432, 433,
630
Northern Zhōu Dynasty
(A.D. 557–581), 433
North Peak Monastery, 557
Number 1 Beach
(Qīngdǎo), 71

O

Observatory, Běijīng, 16
Ocean Galleries (Hong
Kong), 202
Ohel Moshe Synagogue
(Shànghǎi), 115
Old Chinese Quarter
(Shànghǎi), 110–111
Old Dàlǐ, 381–382
Old Market Square (Sì Fāng
Jiē; Lìjiāng), 396–397
Old Monastery of the Stone
Buddhas (Dàtóng), 53
Old Shopping Street (Fùxīng
Lù; Dàlǐ), 382
Old Summer Palace
(Yuánmíng Yuán; Běijīng),
12–13
Old Sūzhōu, 129–130
Old Town (Dàolǐ Qū;
Harbin), 63
Old Town (Dàyán; Lìjiāng),
395–397

Old Town (Zhōngshān Lù
Lǎochéngqū; Běihǎi),
347–350
Old Town Xiàmén, 172–173
Opium Wars, 12, 187
Oriental Buddha Park
(Dōngfāng Fódū), 306
Our Lady of Lourdes
(Guǎngzhōu), 187

P

Packing tips, 604–605
Pagoda Hill (Tǎ Shān;
Guìlín), 312–313
Pagodas, 643–644
    Big Wild Goose Pagoda
    (Dàyàntǎ; Xī'ān),
    232, 237–238
    Cloud Rock Pagoda
    (Yúnyán Tǎ; Sūzhōu),
    134
    Dàlǐ, 383–384
    Dragon Light Pagoda
    (Lóng Guāng Tǎ;
    Wúxī), 157
    Flower Pagoda (Huā Tǎ;
    Guǎngzhōu), 186
    Iron Pagoda (Tiě Tǎ;
    Kāifēng), 257–258
    Small Wild Goose Pagoda
    (Xiǎo Yàn Tǎ; Xī'ān),
    232, 236
Pagoda to Suppress Dragons
    (Zhènlóng Pagoda;
    Ürümqi), 445
Páiyún Diàn (Cloud-Dispelling
    Hall; Běijīng), 11
Páiyúntíng (Cloud-Dispelling
    Pavilion), 468
Pak Tai Temple (Hong Kong),
210–211
Palace Hotel (Shànghǎi), 109
Palace Museum (Forbidden
    City), 8
Palace of Earthly Tranquility
    (Kūnníng Gōng; Běijīng), 10
Palace of Heavenly Blessing
    (Dài Miào), 536
Palace of Heavenly Purity
    (Qiánqīng Gōng;
    Běijīng), 10

Palace of the Immortals
    (Héng Shān), 503
Panda Museum (Chéngdū),
296–297
Pandas, Chéngdū, 295–297
Pānjiā Yuán (Ghost Market or
    Dirt Market; Běijīng),
    17–18
Pánmén Water Gate (Sūzhōu),
    134–135, 167, 168
Pavilion of Ten Thousand
    Fortunes (Wànfú Gé;
    Běijīng), 15
Pavilion of the Rising Sun
    (Xùgāng Gé; Chéngdé), 47
Pavilion of Three Purities
    (Sān Qīng Gé; Kūnmíng),
    366
Pavilion Overlooking the Sea
    (Zhèn Hǎi Lóu;
    Guǎngzhōu), 183
Peace Hotel (Hépíng Fàndiàn;
    Shànghǎi), 102, 109
Peach Blossom Hot Springs
    (Táoyuán Wēnquán),
    470–471
Peach Peak (Qīngdǎo), 74
Peak of the Ten Thousand
    Buddhas (Wànfódǐng), 544
Peak That Flew from Afar
    (Fēilái Fēng), 148
Peak Tower (Hong Kong),
    200
Peak Tram (Hong Kong), 197
Pearl of the Orient TV Tower
    (Shànghǎi), 103
Pearl River (Zhū Jiāng), 187
Pearls, 73
Peasant Movement Institute
    (Guǎngzhōu), 183
Péngrì Tíng (Sun-Holding
    Pavilion), 512
Peninsula Hotel (Hong
    Kong), 202
People's Park (Rénmín
    Gōngyuán; Kashgar), 457
People's Park (Rénmín
    Gōngyuán; Ürümqi), 445
People's Street South (Rénmín
    Nán Lù; Chéngdū), 290
Phoenix Pine (Fènghuáng
    Sōng), 510–511

Photos, taking, 626

Pierced Hill (Chuān Shān; Guìlín), 313, 316

The Pilgrim's Road (Pàn Lù), 536

Pink dolphins (Hong Kong), 208–210

Pípá Shān Park (PíPa Shān Gōngyuán; Chóngqìng), 277–278

Po Lin (Precious Lotus Monastery; Hong Kong), 212

Politics, 620, 633–635

Pollution, 596

Pool of Swords (Jiànchí; Sūzhōu), 134

Powerful Treasure Hall (Dà Xióng Bǎo Diàn; Dàtóng), 56

Praya (Hong Kong), 210

Precious Belt Bridge (Sūzhōu), 170

Precious Lotus Monastery (Po Lin; Hong Kong), 212

Protestant church (Jīdū Jiàotáng; Qīngdǎo), 72

Protestant church (Jīdū Jiàotáng; Xī'ān), 241

Protestant church (Kūnmíng), 368

Pǔdōng, 100

Pǔdōng (East Shànghǎi), 102–104

Pǔdōng Development Bank (Shànghǎi), 109

Pǔjì Sì (Front Temple), 527–528

Pǔlè Sì (Temple of Universal Joy; Chéngdé), 47

Pure Sound Pavilion (Qīngyīn Gé), 549–550

Purity and Truth Synagogue (Qīng Zhēn Sì; Kāifēng), 258, 259

Purple Sand Village (Zǐshācūn), 160

Púsà Dǐng Temple (Wǔtái Shān), 494–495

Pútao Gōu (Grape Gorge), 440

Pǔtuó Shān, 525–533

Pǔtuózōngchéng Miào (Small Potala Temple; Chéngdé), 45–46

Q

Qiān Fó Diàn (Thousand Buddha Hall), 569

Qiánlóng Emperor, 10–12, 14, 15, 41, 44, 45, 47, 49, 50, 131, 134, 141, 149, 155, 158, 453, 578

Qián Mén District (Běijīng), 17

Qiánqīng Gōng (Palace of Heavenly Purity; Běijīng), 10

Qiánxī Temple (Qiánxī Sì), 266

Qiánxūn Tǎ (Dàlǐ), 383

Qiáowān, 422

Qì gōng, 14, 321

Qílián Mountains, 422

Qín Dynasty (770–206 B.C.), 236, 631

Qingchuí Fēng (Hammer Rock; Chéngdé), 46–47

Qīngdǎo, 70–78
　practical information, 74
　sights and attractions, 70–74

Qīngdǎo Yíng Bīnguǎn (Qīngdǎo Welcome Guest House; Qīngdǎo), 73

Qīngliángtái (Refreshing Breeze Terrace), 468

Qīng (Manchu) Dynasty (1644–1911), 12, 16, 17, 19, 33, 41, 42, 47, 432, 503, 633

Qīngmíng Shànghé Yuán (Qīngmíng Up the River Park; Kāifēng), 256–257

Qīngpíng Market (Guǎngzhōu), 186–187

Qīngyáng Gōng (Green Goat Temple; Chéngdū), 294

Qīngyīn Gé (Pure Sound Pavilion), 549–550

Qīng Zhēn Sì (Purity and Truth Synagogue; Kāifēng), 258, 259

Qīnhuá Rìjūn Qī Sān Yāo Bùduì Jiùzhǐ (Unit 731; Harbin), 65–66

Qínián Diàn (Hall for Prayer for Good Harvests; Běijīng), 14

Qínqí Platform (Qínqí Tái), 504

Qín Shǐ Huáng Dì, First Emperor, 33, 74, 134, 229, 416, 488, 535, 537, 558, 631, 637
　terra-cotta army of, 248–254

Qín Tablet, 535

Qióngzhú Sì (Bamboo Temple; Kūnmíng), 363

Qīxīng Gōngyuán (Seven-Star Park; Guìlín), 319

Qīxīng Yán (Seven-Star Cave; Guìlín), 319

Questions from strangers, 621

Qūfù, 86
　practical information, 91

Qútáng Gorge (Qútáng Xiá), 587

Qútáng Xiá (Qútáng Gorge), 587

Qū Yuán, 585, 586

R

Rain Law Temple (Fǎyǔ Sì), 530

Raisins, Turpan, 440

Reclining Buddha (Wòfó; Dàzú), 285

Reclining Dragon Zen Temple (Wòlóng Sì; Xī'ān), 240

Reed Flute Cave (Lúdí Yán; Guìlín), 319–322

Refreshing Breeze Terrace (Qīngliángtái), 468

Regent Hotel (Hong Kong), 202

Rénmín Gōngyuán (People's Park; Kashgar), 457

Rénmín Gōngyuán (People's Park; Ürümqi), 445

Rénmín Nán Lù (People's Street South; Chéngdū), 290

Rénshòu Diàn (Hall of Benevolence and Longevity; Běijīng), 11

Restaurants
　dining customs, 624
　tips on, 613–614

Returning Waves Pavilion (Huílàn Gé; Qīngdǎo), 71–72

Ricci, Matteo, 258

Rìguāng Yán (Sunlight Rock; Xiàmén), 176

River Pavilion (Yíngjiāng Gé), 314

Riverside Promenade (Bīnjiāng Dàdào; Shànghǎi), 104

Rock carvings, Dàzú, 283–288

Roman Catholic church (Xiàmén), 175

Róng Hú (Banyan Lake; Guìlín), 318–319

Round Altar (Huán Qiū; Běijīng), 13

Ròushēn Sì (Temple of Kim/Dìzàng's Earthly Remains), 509

S

Safety, 616

Sailing, Lake Tài, 158–159

Sānhuáng Hall (Sānhuáng Diàn; Qīngdǎo), 74

Sāní minority village, 369

Sānjiāng, 338–346

Sānlǐtún District (Běijīng), 19

Sān Qīng (Hall of the Three Pure Ones; Sūzhōu), 136

Sān Qīng Gé (Pavilion of Three Purities; Kūnmíng), 366

Sān Shān Dǎo (Three Hills Island), 159

Sān Tán Yìn Yuè (Three Pools Mirroring the Moon; Hángzhōu), 145–146

Sān Tǎ Sì (Temple of the Three Pagodas; Dàlǐ), 383

Sānxiá Shuǐbà (Three Gorges Dam), 276, 583–586

Sānyǐ Protestant church (Xiàmén), 175

Saving face, 620–621

Seeing Is Believing Peak (Shíxìn Fēng), 466

Seven-Star Cave (Qīxīng Yán; Guìlín), 319

Seven-Star Park (Qīxīng Gōngyuán; Guìlín), 319

Sha Chau and Lung Kwu Chau Marine Park (Hong Kong), 209

Shadow Stone, 570

Shāmiàn Island (Guǎngzhōu), 187–188

Shàngfēng Temple (Shàngfēng Sì), 520

Shànghǎi, 97–127, 578
    practical information, 116
    sights and attractions, 100–115

Shànghǎi Arts and Crafts Research Institute, 115

Shànghǎi Botanical Gardens, 115

Shànghǎi Bówùguǎn (Shànghǎi Museum), 114–115

Shànghǎi Centre, 100

Shànghǎi History Museum (Shànghǎi Lìshǐ Bówùguǎn), 103

Shànghǎi Lǎo Jiē (Shànghǎi Old Street), 113

Shànghǎi Museum (Shànghǎi Bówùguǎn), 100, 114–115

Shànghǎi Old Street (Shànghǎi Lǎo Jiē), 113

Shànghǎi Urban Planning Exhibition Hall, 115

Shànghǎi Zoo, 115

Shān Hú (Cedar Lake; Guìlín), 318

Shānjuàn Cave (Yíxīng), 161

Shǎnxī Lìshǐ Bówùguǎn (Shǎnxī History Museum; Xī'ān), 235–236

Shǎnxi Provincial Museum (Xī'ān), 233

Shào Lín Monastery, 568–569

Shāpíng Market, 387–388

Shèng Shòu Sì (Dàzú), 284

Shèng Suǒfēiyà Jiàotáng (Church of Saint Sophia; Harbin), 64

Shífǎng (Marble Boat; Běijīng), 11

Shígǔ, 402

Shíjiā Village (Shíjiā Zhuāng), 80

Shí Kù Sì Dòng (Stone Room Temple Cave), 268

Shí Lín (Stone Forest; Kūnmíng), 369–371, 373

Shìmǎ Dài (Horse Testing Ground; Chéngdé), 45

Shí Xiá (Stone Gorge), 447

Shíxìn Fēng (Seeing Is Believing Peak), 466

Shīzi Lín (Forest of Lions Garden; Sūzhōu), 130–131

Shīzi Shān (Lion Hill; Lìjiāng), 401–402

Shòu Xīhú (Slender West Lake), 578

Shrine of Limpid Waters (Jìng Shuǐ), 543–544

Shuǐ Yuè Dòng (Moon-in-the-Water Cave; Guìlín), 312

Shūyuànmén Dàjiē (Xī'ān), 233

Shūzhuāng (Xiàmén), 176

Siberian Tiger Park (Dōngběi Hǔ Línyuán; Harbin), 66–67

Siberian Tiger Park (Harbin), 63

Sīdàlín Gōngyuán (Stalin Park; Harbin), 66

Siestas, 625

Sì Fāng Jiē (Old Market Square; Lìjiāng), 396–397

Signal Hill Park (Xìnhào Shān Gōngyuán; Qīngdǎo), 72

Silk, Sūzhōu, 135–136

Silk Market, the Xiùshuǐ (Běijīng), 17

Silk Road, 411–415, 421–426, 428–430, 432–434, 452

Silver Beach (Yíntān), 351–352

Sīmǎ Qiān, 252–253

Sīmǎtái, Great Wall at, 37–38, 40

Sīmǎtái Reservoir, 37

Singing Sands Mountains (Míngshā Shān), 422–425

Sino-Judaic Institute (Menlo Park, CA), 261

The Sky Ladder (Tiān Jīng), 557

Sleeping Buddha of Dūnhuáng, 432

Slender West Lake (Shòu Xīhú), 578

Small Potala Temple (Pǔtuózōngchéng Miào; Chéngdé), 45–46

Small Wild Goose Pagoda (Xiǎo Yàn Tǎ; Xī'ān), 232, 236

Smoking, 626

Solitary Beauty Peak (Dú Xiu Fēng; Guìlín), 315–316, 318

Solitary Hill Island (Gū Shān; Hángzhōu), 141

Sòng Dynasty (1127–1279), 131, 166

Sōnghuā River, 66

Sòng Qìnglíng (Shànghǎi), 115

Sòng Shān (First Mountain of the World), 563–573

Sòng Yáng Academy, 564

Sōngyuè (High Peak) Temple, 564

Southern Gate of Heaven (Nán Tiān Mén), 520, 525–526

The Southern Gate of Heaven (Nán Tiān Mén), 538–539

Southern Mountains (Nán Shān), 445

Southern Peak Temple (Nán Shān Sì; Wǔtái Shān), 496–497

Spitting, 626

Spruce Meadow (Yún Shān Píng), 402

Stairs of Nine Turnings (Lèshān), 306

Stalin Park (Sǐdàlín Gōngyuán; Harbin), 66

Stanley (Hong Kong), 205–206

Stanley market (Hong Kong), 206

Star Ferry (Hong Kong), 197

Star Gate (Língxīng Mén; Qūfù), 88

Statue of Five Rams (Guǎngzhōu), 183, 186

Stelae Forest of the Imperial Academy (Kāifēng), 256

Stele Without Inscription (Wú Zì Bēi), 538

Stone Age Theme Park (Xī'ān), 243

Stone Forest (Shí Lín; Kūnmíng), 369–371, 373

Stone Forest Lake (Kūnmíng), 370–371

Stone Gorge (Shí Xiá), 447

Stone Room Temple Cave (Shí Kù Sì Dòng), 268

Stone That Flew from Afar (Fēilái Shí), 469

Sū Causeway (Sū Dī; Hángzhōu), 146

Suicide Precipice (Éméi Shān), 545

Suí Dynasty (A.D. 581–618), 429, 433

Summer Palace (Yíhé Yuán; Běijīng), 10–12

Sunday Bazaar (Yekshenba Bazaar; Kashgar), 454–456

Sun-Holding Pavilion (Péngrì Tíng), 512

Sun Island (Tàiyáng Dǎo; Harbin), 66

Sun Yat-sen, 633, 637

Sun Yat-sen Mausoleum (Zhōngshān Líng; Nánjīng), 578–579

Sun Yat-sen Memorial Hall (Zhōngshān Jìniàntáng; Guǎngzhōu), 183

Suǒxīyù, 480

Susannah's (Yángshuò), 330

Sūxiù Yánjiū Suǒ (Museum of Sūzhōu Embroidery; Sūzhōu), 135–136

Sūzhōu, 128–139, 166
  practical information, 137
  sights and attractions, 128–136
  water gates and canals, 134–135, 168–169

Sūzhōu Creek (Shànghǎi), 105–106

Sūzhōu Dìyī Sīchǎng Yǒuxiàn Gōngsī (Sūzhōu No. 1 Silk Mill; Sūzhōu), 136

Sweet Dew Monastery (Gānlù Sì), 507–508

Sword Peak Pond (Kūnmíng), 370

Synagogue, Purity and Truth (Kāifēng), 258, 259

T

Tàihé Diàn (Gate of Supreme Harmony; Běijīng), 8–9

Táihuái Village, 492–494

Tài Hú (Lake Tài), 131, 157–165
  sailing, 158–159

Tàihuá Temple (Kūnmíng), 367

Tài Hú Xiāndǎo (Fairy Island), 159

Tàijíquán (shadowboxing; tai chi), 14, 110, 218, 291, 332

Tai O (Hong Kong), 213

Tàiqīng Temple (Tàiqīng Gōng; Qīngdǎo), 74

Tài Shān, 534–542

Tài Shān Wáng (God of the Mountain), 536, 539

Tàiyáng Dǎo (Sun Island; Harbin), 66

Taklamakan Desert (Tarim Basin), 414, 435, 441

Tǎlín (Forest of Stupas), 570

Táng Dynasty (A.D. 618–917), 229, 235–236, 265, 304, 429, 631–632

Táng Dynasty Rock Inscriptions (Mó Yá Bēi), 538

Tantric Buddhism, 47, 284, 431, 432

Tán Yào, 52, 53

Táocí Bówùguǎn (Ceramic Exhibition Hall; Dìngshù), 161

Táoyuán Wēnquán (Peach Blossom Hot Springs), 470–471

Tarim Basin (Taklamakan Desert), 414, 435, 441

Tǎ Shān (Pagoda Hill; Guìlín), 312–313

Taxis, 609–610

Teahouses
  Běijīng, 19–20
  Chéngdū, 290–291

Teapots, Yíxīng, 159–161

Telephones, 616–617

Temple of Bliss (Jílè Sì; Harbin), 65

Temple of Confucius (Kǒng Miào; Qūfù), 88

Temple of Confucius (Xī'ān), 233

Temple of Eternal Blessing (Chéngdé), 44

Temple of Heaven Park (Tiān Tán Gōngyuán; Běijīng), 13–14

Temple of Kim/Dìzàng's Earthly Remains (Ròushēn Sì), 509

Temple of Mystery (Xuán Miào Guàn; Sūzhōu), 136

Temple of Ten Thousand Buddhas (Wànfó Sì), 512

Temple of Ten Thousand Years (Wànnián Sì), 547–548

Temple of the Eastern Grove (Dōng Lín Sì; Lú Shān), 488

Temple of the Eight Immortals (Bāxiān Guān; Xī'ān), 240

Temple of the Jade Emperor (Yù Huáng Dǐng), 538

Temple of the Liáo (Dàtóng), 55–58

Temple of the Six Banyan Trees (Liù Róng Sì; Guǎngzhōu), 186

Temple of the Soul's Retreat (Língyǐn Temple; Hángzhōu), 148

Temple of the Southern Mountain (Nán Yuè Miào), 515

Temple of the Three Pagodas (Sān Tǎ Sì; Dàlǐ), 383

Temple of Universal Joy (Pǔlè Sì; Chéngdé), 47

Temples. See also specific temples
  how to tour, 643–645
  Kūnmíng, 363–365
  Xī'ān, 239–240

Temple Street Night Market (Hong Kong), 205

Temple to the Town God (Chéng Huáng Miào; Shànghǎi), 112

Ten Thousand People Rock (Sūzhōu), 134

Terra-Cotta Warriors and Horses of Emperor Qín Shǐ Huáng, Museum of the, 248–254

Thousand Buddha Hall (Qiān Fó Diàn), 569

Three Generals, 564

Three Gorges area, 577

Three Gorges Dam (Sān Xiá), 276, 583–586

Three Hills Island (Sān Shān Dǎo), 159

Three Kingdoms period (A.D. 221–263), 290, 291, 582, 585, 588, 630, 637

Three Little Gorges (Xiǎo Sān Xiá), 587

Three Pools Mirroring the Moon (Sān Tán Yìn Yuè; Hángzhōu), 145–146

Tiān'ān Mén Square (Běijīng), 6–7, 635

Tiān Chí (Heavenly Lake), 446–448

Tiāndū Fēng (City of Heaven Peak), 470

Tiān Jìng (The Sky Ladder), 557

Tiān Líng Fēng (Tiān Líng Peak), 502

Tiān Níng Temple (Yángzhōu), 578

Tiānqiáoshēngkōng (Bridge Across the Sky), 479–480

Tiāntái Shān (Heavenly Terrace), 509–510, 512

Tiān Tán Gōngyuán Park (Temple of Heaven; Běijīng), 13–14

Tiāntī (Heavenly Staircase), 511

Tiānxià Dìèrquán (Wúxī), 158

Tiānzhǔ Jiàotáng (Catholic church)
  Qīngdǎo, 72
  Xī'ān, 241–242

Tiānzǐ Shān Village, 479–480

Tibetan Cafe (Dàlǐ), 380

Tiěshān Gōngyuán (Iron Mountain Garden; Qūfù), 90

Tiě Tǎ (Iron Pagoda; Kāifēng), 257–258

Tiger Hill (Hǔ Qiū Shān; Sūzhōu), 133–134

Tiger Leaping Gorge (Hǔtiào Xiá), 402

Times Square (Shànghǎi), 104

Time zones, 617

Tīngkǒu, 465, 472, 473, 475

Tipping, 617

Toad Rock (Chéngdé), 47

Toilets, 618

Tóng Hán Chūn Medicine Store (Shànghǎi), 112

Tóng Zhì Emperor, 295

Tower of Mist and Rain (Yānyǔlóu; Chéngdé), 44

Tower of the Magnificent View (Dàguān Pavilion; Kūnmíng), 365–366

Traffic, 626–627

Train travel, 607–608

Transportation, 606–611

Travel agents, 599

Traveler's checks, 600

Treasure Peak Mountain (Bǎodǐng Shān; Dàzú), 283–288

The True Form of the Five Sacred Peaks (Wǔshān Zhēnxíng Tú), 568

Tsim Sha Tsui (Hong Kong), 202

Tung Wan (Morning Beach; Hong Kong), 211

Turpan, 435–443

Turtle Head Isle (Yuántóuzhǔ), 158–159

Turtle Summit (Aoyú Fēng), 469

Twin Flying Bridges, 550

U

Uighur people, 411, 414, 435, 437–441, 452–454, 456, 457, 642

Uncle Lì, 384–385

Unit 731 (Qīnhuá Rìjūn Qī Sān Yāo Bùduì Jiùzhǐ; Harbin), 65–66

Ürümqi, 444–451

V

Valley of the Stone Sutra (Tài Shān), 537

Veneration of Goodness Temple (Jìngshàn Sì) cave, 266

Victoria Peak (Hong Kong), 197, 200–201

Vineyards, Turpan, 440

Visas, 597–599
Visitor information, 597
Voice of the Tide Cave (Cháoyīn Dòng), 530

W

Wàibǎidù Bridge (Shànghǎi), 106
Wàishā (Běihǎi), 350–351
Walking, 610
Wan Chai District (Hong Kong), 197
Wànfódǐng (Peak of the Ten Thousand Buddhas), 544
Wànfó Dòng (Cave of Ten Thousand Buddhas), 267
Wànfó Sì (Temple of Ten Thousand Buddhas), 512
Wànfú Gé (Pavilion of Ten Thousand Fortunes; Běijīng), 15
Wáng, Abbot, 430
Wángfǔjǐng Street (Běijīng), 18–19
Wǎng Shī Yuán (Master of the Nets Garden; Sūzhōu), 132–133
Wàngǔ Chángchūn Fáng (Arch of Eternal Spring; Qūfù), 90
Wàn Lǐ Cháng Chéng. See Great Wall
Wànnián Sì (Temple of Ten Thousand Years), 547–548
Wànshù Yuán (Garden of Ten Thousand Trees; Chéngdé), 45
Wànxiàn, 588–589
Wànxiàn Three Gorges Museum, 589
Wàsè Market, 386–387
Water, drinking, 618
Waterfront Promenade (Hong Kong), 196
Wéifāng, 79
    practical information, 83
    sights and attractions, 79–82
Wéifāng International Kite Festival, 80–82
Wéifāng Kite Museum (Fēngzheng Bówùguǎn), 79
Wèi-Jìn Tombs (Wèi-Jìn Mù), 416–417

Wéizhōu Island, 352–354
Welcoming Pine of Huáng Shān (Yíng Kè Sōng), 469
Wén Chéng Emperor, 52
Wénjǐn Gé (Literary Nourishment Pavilion; Chéngdé), 44
Wén Miào (Confucian Temple; Harbin), 64
Wénmiào Lù (Confucian Temple; Shànghǎi), 115
Wēn Quán (Lóngshèng Hot Spring), 342–343
Wénshū Monastery (Wénshū Yuàn; Chéngdū), 291, 294
Western Central Asia Market (Zhōngxīyà Shìchǎng; Kashgar), 454–456
Western Grottoes (Dàtóng), 54–55
Western Hills (Xī Shān), 366
Westernization, 623, 635
Western Wèi Dynasty (A.D. 535–557), 429
Westgate Mall (Shànghǎi), 100–101
West Lake (Xī Hú; Hángzhōu), 140, 144–146
West Pagoda (Xī Tǎ; Kūnmíng), 368
West Peak Monastery (Xī Fēng Sì), 557–558
The Wheel of Life (Dàzú), 284–285
Whirlpool Hill (Fúbō Shān; Guìlín), 316
White Cloud Temple (Báiyún Guàn; Běijīng), 15
White Poplar Valley, 445
Witches Gorge (Wū Xiá), 586
Wòfó (Reclining Buddha; Dàzú), 285
Wòlóng Nature Preserve, 295
Wòlóng Sì (Reclining Dragon Zen Temple; Xī'ān), 240
Women, 622–623
Workers' Cultural Hall (Kūnmíng), 359
Worldview, Chinese, 619–620
Wǔ, Empress, 637
Wǔdì Emperor, 412, 500
Wu Fēng Lóu (Five Phoenix Hall; Lìjiāng), 399
Wǔhàn, 580

Wǔhòu Temple (Chéngdū), 291
Wǔhuā Lóu (Dàlǐ), 382
Wǔlíngyuán Scenic and Historic Interest Area (Zhāngjiā Jiè), 476–483
Wulumuqi. See Ürümqi
Wúmén Bridge (Wúmén Qiáo; Sūzhōu), 134, 168
Wǔshān Zhēnxíng Tú (The True Form of the Five Sacred Peaks), 568
Wúsōng Kǒu, 107–108
Wǔtái Shān (Five Platforms Mountain), 431, 432, 491–499
Wúxī, 157–158
    practical information, 162
Wú Xiá, 509
Wū Xiá (Witches Gorge), 586
Wūyóu Sì (Lèshān), 306
Wǔ Zétiān Empress, 267
Wú Zì Bēi (Stele Without Inscription), 538

X

Xiàmén, 172–181
    practical information, 177
    sights and attractions, 172–177
Xiàmén City Museum (Xiàmén Shì Bówùguǎn), 176–177
Xiàmén University (Xiàmén Dàxué), 174
Xī'ān, 229–247, 411
    churches, 241–242
    city wall, 229, 232–233
    Forest of Stelae, 233
    Great Mosque and Muslim Quarter, 238–239
    pagodas, 236–238
    practical information, 243
    temples, 239–240
Xiàngbí Shān (Elephant Trunk Hill; Guìlín), 312, 318
Xiàngfèi Mù (Abakh Hoja Tomb; Kashgar), 453–454
Xiānggélǐlā (Zhōngdiàn), 402
Xiānrén Dòng (Immortals Cave; Lú Shān), 487–488

Xiānrénqiáo (The Bridge of
the Immortals), 480

Xiāntōng Temple (Xiāntōng
Sì), 493–494

Xiǎo Sānxiá (Lesser Three
Gorges), 586

Xiǎo Sān Xiá (Three Little
Gorges), 587

Xiǎoyáng Zhōu (Island of
Small Seas; Hángzhōu), 145

Xiǎo Yàn Tǎ (Small Wild
Goose Pagoda; Xī'ān), 236

Xiǎoyú Shān Gōngyuán
(Little Fish Park;
Qīngdǎo), 73

Xiàqīnggōng Temple
(Qīngdǎo), 74

Xī Fēng Sì (West Peak
Monastery), 557–558

Xīhǎi, 467

Xíhuì Gōngyuán (Xíhuì Park;
Wúxī), 157

Xíhuì Park (Xíhuì Gōngyuán;
Wúxī), 157

Xī Hú (West Lake;
Hángzhōu), 140, 144–146

Xī Líng Bridge (Hángzhōu),
141

Xīlíng Gorge, 585

Xīngpíng, 333

Xìngpíng, 314

Xìng Tán (Apricot Terrace;
Qūfù), 89

Xìnhào Shān Gōngyuán
(Signal Hill Park;
Qīngdǎo), 72

Xīnjiāng, 435

Xī Shān (Western Hills), 366

Xī Tǎ (West Pagoda;
Kūnmíng), 368

Xiùshuǐ Silk Market
(Běijīng), 17

Xī Xià Kingdom, 430

Xuán Kōng Sì (Hanging
Monastery; Dàtóng), 58–59

Xuán Miào Guàn (Temple of
Mystery; Sūzhōu), 136

Xuán Zàng, 237, 412,
436, 438

Xuánzàng, 637

Xuánzōng Emperor, 538, 564

Xùguāng Gé (Pavilion of the
Rising Sun; Chéngdé), 47

Xújiāhuì Cathedral
(Shànghǎi), 115

Xūmífúshòu Miào (Mount
Sumeru Longevity and
Happiness Temple;
Chéngdé), 45

Y

Yámen (Hong Kong), 208

Yángdì, emperor, 166

Yángdí Village (Yángdí
Xiāng), 314

Yángjiābù, 80

Yángpǔ Cable Bridge
(Shànghǎi), 106

Yǎngsháo culture, 242

Yángshuò, 314

Yángshuò, 329–337

Yángshùpǔ Power Plant
(Shànghǎi), 106

Yǎngtiān Chí (Looking to
Heaven Pool), 558

Yángzhōu, 578–579

Yángzǐ River (Chángjiāng),
577–593

Yán Tower (Dàtóng), 57

Yānyǔlóu (Tower of Mist and
Rain; Chéngdé), 44

Yào Fáng Dòng (Medicine
Cave), 268

Yáo people, 339

Yarkhoto (Jiāohé), 439

Yekshenba Bazaar (Sunday
Bazaar; Kashgar), 454–456

Yellow Crane Tower (Huáng
Hè Lóu; Wǔhàn), 581–582

Yellow Dragon (Huánglóng)
Cave, 480–481

Yellow Mountain (Huáng
Shān), 465–475, 579

Yellow Umbrella Peak
(Huánggài Fēng), 568

Yíchāng, 583

Yíhé Yuán (Summer Palace;
Běijīng), 10–12

Yíngjiāng Gé (River Pavilion;
Yángshuò), 314, 333

Yíng Kè Sōng (Welcoming
Pine of Huáng Shān), 469

Yíntān (Silver Beach),
351–352

Yǐtǎ Sì (Yǐtǎ Temple; Dàlǐ),
384

Yǐtǎ Temple (Yǐtǎ Sì; Dàlǐ),
384

Yī Tiān Mén (The First Gate
of Heaven), 536–537

Yíxīng
cavern, 161–162
teapots of, 159–161

Yōnghé Diàn (Hall of
Harmony; Běijīng), 14

Yōnghé Gōng (Lama Temple;
Běijīng), 14–15

Yuán Dynasty (1271–1368),
33, 166, 432, 630, 632

Yuánmíng Yuán (Old Summer
Palace; Běijīng), 12–13

Yuántōng Sì (Kūnmíng), 363

Yuántóuzhǔ (Turtle Head
Isle), 158–159

Yuèliang Shān (Moon
Mountain), 330–332

Yuèxiù Gōngyuán
(Guǎngzhōu), 182–183

Yuèyáng Tower, 582–583

Yuèyá Quán (Crescent Moon
Lake), 423

Yuèyá Shān (Crescent Moon
Hill; Guìlín), 320

Yùfó Sì (Jade Buddha Temple;
Shànghǎi), 115

Yù Huáng Dǐng (Temple of
the Jade Emperor), 538

Yùhú (Nguluko), 402

Yùlán Táng (Jade Waves
Palace; Běijīng), 11

Yùmén (Jade Gate), 413

Yúngāng Grottoes (Yúngāng
Shíkū; Dàtóng), 51–55

Yúnnán Nationalities Village
(Yúnnán Mínzú Cūn;
Kūnmíng), 369

Yún Shān Píng (Spruce
Meadow), 402

Yúnyán Tǎ (Cloud Rock
Pagoda; Sūzhōu), 134

Yùpíng Lóu (Jade Screen
Pavilion), 469

Yùquán Sì (Jade Spring
Temple), 555–556

Yùyuán Gāochéng Guójì
Gòuwù Zhōngxīn (Yùyuán
International Shopping
Center; Shànghǎi), 112

Yù Yuán Garden (Shànghǎi),
113

Yùyuán International
Shopping Center (Yùyuán
Gāochéng Guójì Gòuwù
Zhōngxīn; Shànghǎi),
111, 112

Z

Zhānggōng cavern (Yíxīng), 162

Zhāng Jì, 168–169

Zhāngjiā Jiè Village, 479

Zhāngjiā Jiè (Wǔlíngyuán Scenic and Historic Interest Area), 476–483

Zhāng Qiān, 412

Zhàn Qiáo Pier (Qīngdǎo), 71

Zhàolín Gōngyuán (Zhàolín Park; Harbin), 64

Zhàolín Park (Zhàolín Gōngyuán; Harbin), 64

Zhào Zhìfēng, 284

Zhèjiāng Provincial Museum (Hángzhōu), 141

Zhèng Chénggōng (Koxinga), statue of (Xiàmén), 175–176

Zhèng Gōng (Front Palace; Chéngdé), 43

Zhēnglóng Pagoda (Pagoda to Suppress Dragons; Ürümqi), 445

Zhèn Hǎi Lóu (Pavilion Overlooking the Sea; Guǎngzhōu), 183

Zhōngdiàn (Xiānggélǐlǐ), 402

Zhōngguó Chá Yè Bówùguǎn (Chinese Tea Museum; near Dragon Well Village), 150

Zhōng Lóu (Bell Tower; Xī'ān), 234, 235

Zhōngshān Jìniàntáng (Sun Yat-sen Memorial Hall; Guǎngzhōu), 183

Zhōngshān Líng (Sun Yat-sen Mausoleum; Nánjīng), 578–579

Zhōngshān Lù (Běihǎi), 348–350

Zhōngshān Lù (Qīngdǎo), 72

Zhōngshān Lù Lǎochéngqū (Old Town; Běihǎi), 347–350

Zhōng Tiān Mén (The Middle Gate of Heaven), 537–538

Zhōngxīyà Shìchǎng (Western Central Asia Market; Kashgar), 454–456

Zhōngyuè Miào (Central Peak Temple), 567–568

Zhōu ēnlái, 73, 633, 637

Zhōu Zhuāng, 115–116

Zhuàng people, 321, 339

Zhūgě Liàng, 291, 582, 585, 586, 588, 637

Zhuō Zhèng Garden (Sūzhōu), 132

Zhùróng Diàn (Hall of the Fire God), 520

Zhùróng Fēng, 519

Zǐguī, 585–586

Zǐshācūn (Purple Sand Village), 160

Zoos
Chéngdū, 295
Shànghǎi, 115

FROMMER'S® COMPLETE TRAVEL GUIDES

Alaska
Alaska Cruises & Ports of Call
Amsterdam
Argentina & Chile
Arizona
Atlanta
Australia
Austria
Bahamas
Barcelona, Madrid & Seville
Beijing
Belgium, Holland & Luxembourg
Bermuda
Boston
Brazil
British Columbia & the Canadian Rockies
Budapest & the Best of Hungary
California
Canada
Cancún, Cozumel & the Yucatán
Cape Cod, Nantucket & Martha's Vineyard
Caribbean
Caribbean Cruises & Ports of Call
Caribbean Ports of Call
Carolinas & Georgia
Chicago
China
Colorado
Costa Rica
Denmark
Denver, Boulder & Colorado Springs
England
Europe
European Cruises & Ports of Call
Florida

France
Germany
Great Britain
Greece
Greek Islands
Hawaii
Hong Kong
Honolulu, Waikiki & Oahu
Ireland
Israel
Italy
Jamaica
Japan
Las Vegas
London
Los Angeles
Maryland & Delaware
Maui
Mexico
Montana & Wyoming
Montréal & Québec City
Munich & the Bavarian Alps
Nashville & Memphis
Nepal
New England
New Mexico
New Orleans
New York City
New Zealand
Northern Italy
Nova Scotia, New Brunswick & Prince Edward Island
Oregon
Paris
Philadelphia & the Amish Country
Portugal
Prague & the Best of the Czech Republic

Provence & the Riviera
Puerto Rico
Rome
San Antonio & Austin
San Diego
San Francisco
Santa Fe, Taos & Albuquerque
Scandinavia
Scotland
Seattle & Portland
Shanghai
Singapore & Malaysia
South Africa
South America
South Florida
South Pacific
Southeast Asia
Spain
Sweden
Switzerland
Texas
Thailand
Tokyo
Toronto
Tuscany & Umbria
USA
Utah
Vancouver & Victoria
Vermont, New Hampshire & Maine
Vienna & the Danube Valley
Virgin Islands
Virginia
Walt Disney World® & Orlando
Washington, D.C.
Washington State

FROMMER'S® DOLLAR-A-DAY GUIDES

Australia from $50 a Day
California from $70 a Day
Caribbean from $70 a Day
England from $75 a Day
Europe from $70 a Day

Florida from $70 a Day
Hawaii from $80 a Day
Ireland from $60 a Day
Italy from $70 a Day
London from $85 a Day

New York from $90 a Day
Paris from $80 a Day
San Francisco from $70 a Day
Washington, D.C. from $80 a Day

FROMMER'S® PORTABLE GUIDES

Acapulco, Ixtapa & Zihuatanejo
Amsterdam
Aruba
Australia's Great Barrier Reef
Bahamas
Berlin
Big Island of Hawaii
Boston
California Wine Country
Cancún
Charleston & Savannah
Chicago
Disneyland®
Dublin
Florence

Frankfurt
Hong Kong
Houston
Las Vegas
London
Los Angeles
Los Cabos & Baja
Maine Coast
Maui
Miami
New Orleans
New York City
Paris
Phoenix & Scottsdale

Portland
Puerto Rico
Puerto Vallarta, Manzanillo & Guadalajara
Rio de Janeiro
San Diego
San Francisco
Seattle
Sydney
Tampa & St. Petersburg
Vancouver
Venice
Virgin Islands
Washington, D.C.

FROMMER'S® NATIONAL PARK GUIDES

Banff & Jasper
Family Vacations in the National Parks
Grand Canyon

National Parks of the American West
Rocky Mountain

Yellowstone & Grand Teton
Yosemite & Sequoia/ Kings Canyon
Zion & Bryce Canyon

FROMMER'S® MEMORABLE WALKS

Chicago	New York	San Francisco
London	Paris	Washington, D.C.

FROMMER'S® GREAT OUTDOOR GUIDES

Arizona & New Mexico	Northern California	Vermont & New Hampshire
New England	Southern New England	

SUZY GERSHMAN'S BORN TO SHOP GUIDES

Born to Shop: France	Born to Shop: Italy	Born to Shop: New York
Born to Shop: Hong Kong, Shanghai & Beijing	Born to Shop: London	Born to Shop: Paris

FROMMER'S® IRREVERENT GUIDES

Amsterdam	Los Angeles	San Francisco
Boston	Manhattan	Seattle & Portland
Chicago	New Orleans	Vancouver
Las Vegas	Paris	Walt Disney World®
London	Rome	Washington, D.C.

FROMMER'S® BEST-LOVED DRIVING TOURS

Britain	Germany	Northern Italy
California	Ireland	Scotland
Florida	Italy	Spain
France	New England	Tuscany & Umbria

HANGING OUT™ GUIDES

Hanging Out in England	Hanging Out in France	Hanging Out in Italy
Hanging Out in Europe	Hanging Out in Ireland	Hanging Out in Spain

THE UNOFFICIAL GUIDES®

Bed & Breakfasts and Country Inns in:
California
Great Lakes States
Mid-Atlantic
New England
Northwest
Rockies
Southeast
Southwest
Best RV & Tent Campgrounds in:
California & the West
Florida & the Southeast
Great Lakes States
Mid-Atlantic
Northeast
Northwest & Central Plains

Southwest & South Central Plains
U.S.A.
Beyond Disney
Branson, Missouri
California with Kids
Chicago
Cruises
Disneyland®
Florida with Kids
Golf Vacations in the Eastern U.S.
Great Smoky & Blue Ridge Region
Inside Disney
Hawaii
Las Vegas
London

Mid-Atlantic with Kids
Mini Las Vegas
Mini-Mickey
New England and New York with Kids
New Orleans
New York City
Paris
San Francisco
Skiing in the West
Southeast with Kids
Walt Disney World®
Walt Disney World® for Grown-ups
Walt Disney World® with Kids
Washington, D.C.
World's Best Diving Vacations

SPECIAL-INTEREST TITLES

Frommer's Adventure Guide to Australia & New Zealand
Frommer's Adventure Guide to Central America
Frommer's Adventure Guide to India & Pakistan
Frommer's Adventure Guide to South America
Frommer's Adventure Guide to Southeast Asia
Frommer's Adventure Guide to Southern Africa
Frommer's Britain's Best Bed & Breakfasts and Country Inns
Frommer's Caribbean Hideaways
Frommer's Exploring America by RV
Frommer's Fly Safe, Fly Smart
Frommer's France's Best Bed & Breakfasts and Country Inns
Frommer's Gay & Lesbian Europe

Frommer's Italy's Best Bed & Breakfasts and Country Inns
Frommer's New York City with Kids
Frommer's Ottawa with Kids
Frommer's Road Atlas Britain
Frommer's Road Atlas Europe
Frommer's Road Atlas France
Frommer's Toronto with Kids
Frommer's Vancouver with Kids
Frommer's Washington, D.C., with Kids
Israel Past & Present
The New York Times' Guide to Unforgettable Weekends
Places Rated Almanac
Retirement Places Rated